Mother,
May You Never See
the Sights
I Have Seen

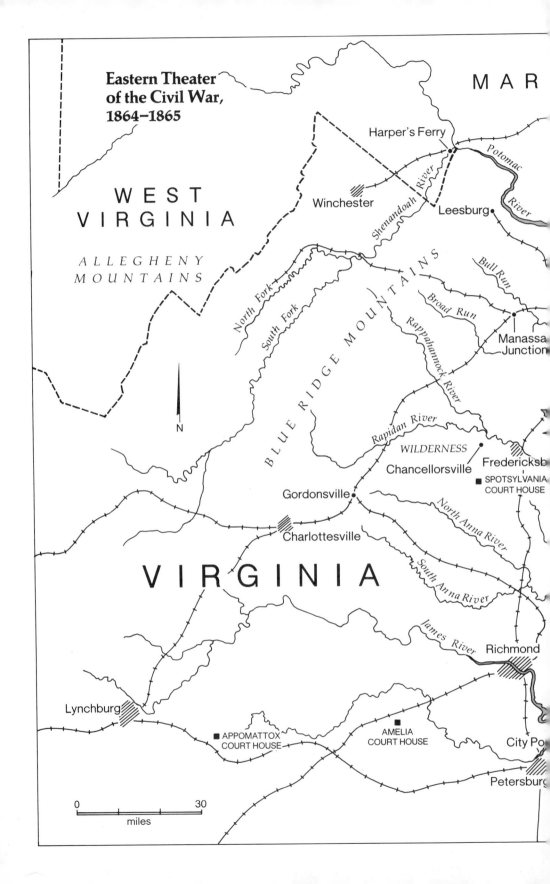

**Eastern Theater
of the Civil War,
1864–1865**

M A R

WEST
VIRGINIA

*ALLEGHENY
MOUNTAINS*

Harper's Ferry

Potomac
River

Winchester

Shenandoah River

Leesburg

North Fork

South Fork

Bull Run

Broad Run

Rappahannock River

B L U E   R I D G E   M O U N T A I N S

Manassa
Junction

N

Rapidan River

WILDERNESS

Chancellorsville

Fredericksb

SPOTSYLVANIA
COURT HOUSE

Gordonsville

North Anna River

Charlottesville

VIRGINIA

South Anna River

James River

Richmond

Lynchburg

APPOMATTOX
COURT HOUSE

AMELIA
COURT HOUSE

City Po

Petersburg

0   30
miles

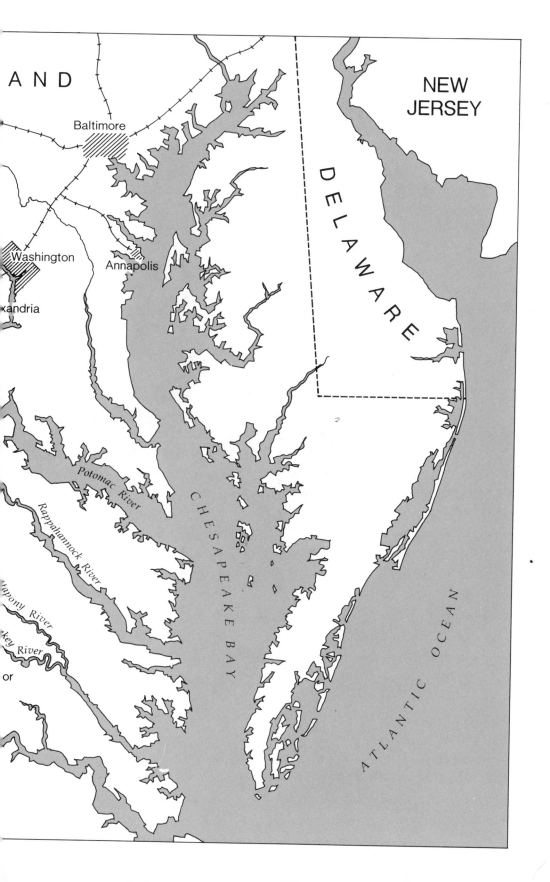

The war-torn battle flags of the 57th Massachusetts, now in the State House in Boston (photo taken at war's end); *left to right:* U.S. colors, IX Corps colors, Massachusetts colors. *(USAMHI, Carlisle Barracks, Pa.)*

Mother, May You Never See the Sights I Have Seen

THE FIFTY-SEVENTH MASSACHUSETTS
VETERAN VOLUNTEERS
IN THE ARMY OF THE POTOMAC
1864–1865

Foreword by
Emory M. Thomas

QUILL
William Morrow
New York

For my wife, Jan
For my son, Renny
For my parents, A. Warren, Sr., and Katherine Wilkinson

The Library of Congress has catalogued the hardcover as follows:

Wilkinson, Warren.
    Mother, may you never see the sights I have seen: the Fifty-seventh
Massachusetts Veteran Volunteers in the Army of the
Potomac, 1864–1865 / Warren Wilkinson.
      p.   cm.
    Includes bibliographical references (p. 643) and index.
    ISBN 0-688-10871-7
    1. United States. Army. Massachusetts Infantry Regiment, 57th
(1864–1865)—History. 2. United States. Army—History—Civil War—,
1861–1865. 3. United States. Army—Military life—History—19th
century. 4. Massachusetts—History—Civil War, 1861–1865
Regimental histories. 5. United States—History—Civil War,
Regimental histories. I. Title.
[E513.5 57th.W5   1991]
973.7'444—dc20
                                                              91-19497
                                                             CIP

Printed in the United States of America

First Quill Edition

2 3 4 5 6 7 8 9 10

Contents

Contents

Maps and Illustrations

Maps and Illustrations

ILLUSTRATIONS

Maps and Illustrations

Foreword

UNIT HISTORIES—most often the stories of individual regiments—were some of the earliest histories of the American Civil War. While generals composed their memoirs and wrangled with each other in print and elsewhere over grand strategies and army strengths, regimental historians, who were usually veterans of the units about which they wrote, attempted to record their memories of the war from the perspective of warriors.

These first unit histories, written in the wake of the conflict by men who believed that their service in the war was likely to be the most consequential thing they would ever do, are some of the best and the worst histories of the conflict. Stephen Z. Starr's three-volume work *The Union Cavalry in the Civil War* is but one example of outstanding recent studies based in large measure on unit histories. Yet for many years the original unit histories from the Civil War gathered considerable dust while writers and readers focused on commanders and campaigns. Scholars, buffs, and general readers seemed to prefer the perspective of army headquarters in their efforts to understand the sweep and scale of this momentous war.

Soldiers certainly never disappeared from discussions of generals and strategy. Bell I. Wiley's two classics, *The Life of Johnny Reb* and *The Life of Billy Yank,* were corporate biographies of the men who actually fought the war. Perhaps because Wiley researched these biographies so thoroughly and wrote them so sensitively and well, most historians believed that he had said all that needed saying about common soldiers in the Civil War.

Recent emphasis by historians and readers on the so-called "new" social history has spread and grown to generate a "new" military history—a military history that attempts to become at once broader and deeper. Military historians are thinking about warfare in the larger contexts of culture, economics, and ideas. At the same time military historians are revising their foci to try to understand sailors and soldiers as well as admirals and generals. Recent contributions to the literature of the Civil War reflect a renewed emphasis on the men in the ranks. Michael Barton, *Goodmen: The Character of Civil War Soldiers;* Gerald F. Linderman, *Embattled Courage;* Reid Mitchell, *Civil War Soldiers;* James I. Robertson, Jr., *Soldiers Blue and Gray;* and Joseph T. Glatthaar, *The March to the Sea and Beyond,* all published within the past decade, offer ample evidence of scholars in search of a perspective of the war from the bottom up—from the mud and blood of combat.

Mother, May You Never See the Sights I Have Seen is a wonderful blend of a unit history and a study of men at war. Warren Wilkinson "wanted to get to know the men—who they were, what they did, good or bad or otherwise." He wanted "to know the day-to-day details of their lives and deaths and suffering in the army—not just as a whole, but individual men by name." He succeeded. Warren Wilkinson knows the men of the 57th Massachusetts Regiment. In some ways he knows them better than they knew themselves. He knows as much as can be known about them, and he knows all of them.

There are other modern unit histories, and some of them are quite good. *The Iron Brigade,* by Alan T. Nolan, and *The Stonewall Brigade,* by James I. Robertson, Jr., are model narratives of legendary brigades. And John J. Pullen's *The Twentieth Maine* has been the standard against which scholars and others have measured regimental histories. *Mother, May You Never See the Sights I Have Seen* establishes a new standard for unit histories. Warren Wilkinson has written the best unit history I have ever read.

The 57th Massachusetts had the misfortune usually to be in the wrong place at the wrong time. Cold Harbor excepted, the regiment was in the thick of the fighting in every major battle on the Eastern Front during 1864 and 1865. Warren Wilkinson has labored indefatigably to get the story right. He has told the story with immense skill and feeling. And he knows what his story means, which is what makes this book history instead of chronicle.

Mother, May You Never See the Sights I Have Seen is about the 57th Massachusetts and the soldiers who composed this regiment. But the book is more than that. It is a story of men and boys in the midst of personal and corporate trauma.

Emory M. Thomas
Athens, Georgia, 1989

Preface

WHILE RESEARCHING my family genealogy some four years ago, I came across my great-great-grandfather, Martin Farrell, an impoverished Irish immigrant who arrived in New York Harbor on March 16, 1846. When I was a child, his granddaughter, my grandmother, had told me about him and how he had been a Civil War soldier, but over the years I had pretty well forgotten him. Martin served as a corporal in Company F of the 57th Massachusetts Regiment of Veteran Volunteer Infantry during the last year of the Rebellion. Upon rediscovering that fact, I felt compelled to read the history of his regiment to learn more of his exploits. Having been an amateur historian of the Civil War for about thirty-five of my forty-four years, I felt that I was in something of a position to understand and interpret what Martin went through as a common soldier—at least, as well as it is possible to understand and interpret such things from this distance in time and experience.

In 1896, E. B. Stillings & Co., of Boston, published *The Fifty-Seventh Regiment of Massachusetts Volunteers in the War of the Rebellion.* Captain John Anderson, a former officer in the regiment, was its principal author, although he was aided by some other former members of the unit. I first read Anderson's work in a reading room at Emory University's library in Atlanta. I read the book slowly, taking copious notes in an old, battered college notebook, and then I reread the book, and, not satisfied, read it yet again. Something nagged. I have, over the years, read many Civil War unit histories, but because this one was of such personal interest to me, I was trying to be objective in the extreme—trying to find enlightenment. In the end, though, it struck me that this regimental history was quite similar to all the other regimental histories that I had ever read. And that was what nagged. Anderson's account, like most others of its kind, is, in short, frustratingly outstanding for what it does not tell you.

In flowery Victorian prose taking up space that would have been served better by facts, Captain Anderson wrote the story of the 57th's participation in the Civil War. Somehow, to me, it seemed to ring of half-truths and things that were to him better left unsaid. I became suspicious. There were no bad soldiers, for instance. All were fearless and gallant men who cheerfully and willingly shed their blood for God and country, particularly the officers. I doubted that. And in another example, the regiment was composed of a substantial number of Irish Catholic immigrants, as well as many first-generation American-born Irishmen and Irishmen born in other countries. It is well known that in mid-nineteenth-century America, the largely Yankee Protestant population of the Northeast was, to put it tactfully, not well disposed to the Irish and their religion and life-style. Yet Anderson, by omission, leads us to believe that no ethnic conflicts occurred in the regiment. I was not so sure. A great many other questions begged answers or explanations, too. The story was just too pat; a sense of the real was missing. It was glaringly free of those controversies and darker events that permeate wars and the experiences of the men who fight them. Nevertheless, a hint of the fact that the 57th did indeed have its shortcomings was betrayed by the captain in his brief roster of the men at the end of his book. This hint was revealed by indicating which soldiers had deserted. But I had to admit, in all fairness to John Anderson and to other regimental historians who were participants in the Civil War, at the time that they wrote their histories, many if not most of the men who survived the war were still living, and certainly those historians did not wish to offend them. That is understandable and speaks volumes for their sensitivity to the feelings of others—after all, to them, the war was over, and what purpose would be served by airing what they undoubtedly considered dirty laundry? But, unfortunately for us, by their actions, a treasure of knowledge was tucked away for eternity. It should also be pointed out that as these men aged in a society that could in no way comprehend what they had been through in the war, and under subtle pressure from that society, they tended to set aside—at least in public—the reality of their service and speak of the ennobling experience to which they had been subjected, as envisioned by those who had never seen a battlefield. And that bow to popular civilian convention can be found in almost any regimental history.

As I continued poking along, I soon found myself abandoning my search for Martin in particular, and began looking for him in the larger sense of the entire regiment. Having always been interested primarily in the common soldier of the Civil War, I wanted to get to know the men—who they were, what they did, good or bad or otherwise. And I wanted to know the day-to-day details of their lives and deaths and suffering in the army—not just as a whole, but individual men by name. It was clear that I would get some of that from John Anderson, but nowhere near enough.

Preface

Emory University's library has a fine collection of Civil War regimental histories and Civil War history books in general. It was the perfect place to start. Over a period of several months I read many books and articles at that library that I thought pertinent to my quest. At first, I concentrated on the histories of other units that either were brigaded with or had served in the same battles as the 57th Massachusetts. Valuable information surfaced almost at once. I took more notes and entered those notes into my word processor each night. This was for my own information. I had no intention of writing a book, let alone having one published. From unit histories, I branched out into official records, specific studies of battles and campaigns, and special studies, on food, clothing, weapons, language, desertion, medicine, and so on. My premise was that the 57th Regiment was a typical regiment raised late in the war, and as it was assimilated into the Army of the Potomac, it became a microcosm of that army in 1864 and 1865. Carrying this reasoning a step further, I felt that the 57th would have experienced pretty much what almost any other regiment in the Federal armies that fought in the Eastern theater of the war at that time would have experienced. In fact, it did. Except in a very few areas common to regiments mustered late in the war, it was a Northern regiment much like any other.

Gradually more pieces of the 57th's puzzle fell into place, and when I felt that the library at Emory could provide me with no further information, I moved on to new vistas. In the Northeast, I checked historical societies, libraries, museums, and archives, and I was helped by some other descendants of the 57th's men whom I was lucky enough to find. The National Archives provided a plethora of material. And for six beautiful autumn days in 1986, I camped out in a tent in a privately owned part of the Wilderness battlefield in northern Virginia, and each day I followed the original routes of the regiment's march and visited a different battlefield upon which the men of the 57th fought, exploring it as thoroughly as I was able.

After about two years, I saw that I had amassed, and was continuing to amass, a staggering amount of primary and secondary source material directly relating to the 57th Massachusetts. And my computer disks were crammed. Fortunately I had entered the information in chronological order, and it was evident that what I printed out was a book—over 1,550 manuscript pages—but it was a book quite unlike John Anderson's, even though I drew much information from his work. Finally, I came to realize that it was actually two books. On the one hand, it was the history of the 57th Regiment, but on the other hand, and in a larger sense, it was the story of the common Union soldier in Grant's Overland Campaign during the last year of the war.

Still, it was a book solely for myself—a book to satisfy my insatiable appetite for obscure facts and minuscule detail—and I had no intention of finding a publisher then. But, as time went on, two eminent scholars and authors of Civil War history read the rough manuscript, approved of it, and recommended that it be published. I took their thoughtful advice, and what follows is the result. I sincerely hope that I have done the men of the 57th Massachusetts Volunteers—as well as the soldiers of the Army of the Potomac and their foes—justice, and I hope, as well, that I have been able to provide a more thorough picture of them as human beings. I have tried. Any historical inaccuracies rest upon my shoulders alone, and I assume full responsibility for them. (In quotations of written material, the original spelling and punctuation have been preserved, without the interpolation of *sic* unless needed for clarity.)

★

Many kind and generous people have given freely of their time and resources in the production of this book, and I would like to acknowledge and thank them. They truly have been wonderful, and I would like to think that I have made many new friends among them.

Without the unwavering and wholehearted support of my wife, Jan, this work would not have been possible, and she can never know how grateful I am for her help with this endeavor and her uncomplaining forbearance with my "living" in the 1860s.

Dr. Emory M. Thomas, Regents Professor of History at the University of Georgia, has taken time from his extremely busy schedule to read every page of my manuscript and offer valuable criticism and suggestions. Over the past three years, as I wrote this story, he always has made himself cheerfully available, regardless of his hectic pace, whenever I needed advice or assistance.

Mr. William C. "Jack" Davis, editor in chief of Historical Times, Inc., likewise was kind enough to read the manuscript and lend his full support to this project. He generously supplied prints for many of the photographs.

Mr. M. S. Wyeth, Jr., vice president and executive editor at Harper & Row, has nursed along the editing of this work patiently and skillfully, culling much confusion, overwriting, and pretension. Any that is left is strictly my own fault. Mr. Nick Allison carefully copyedited the text and did that job beautifully. Grateful thanks are also due to Ms. Florence Goldstein, Ms. Susan H. Llewellyn, Ms. C. Linda Dingler, Ms. Luvon Roberson, and Ms. Debra Ornstein, all of whom helped so much in the production of this book. And I would especially like to thank Mr. Paul Pugliese, who drew the maps.

Dr. James Roark, professor of history at Emory University, gave me the initial direction needed to see this undertaking through to fruition.

Dr. Jon L. Wakelyn, professor of history at the Catholic University of America, read the manuscript and offered much enthusiasm and encouragement.

Preface

Miss Eleanora F. West, director of the Fitchburg Historical Society, from the very first has given untiringly of herself and her resources at the society to help me with primary source material, including many personal narratives of the soldiers who came from Fitchburg and the men's unpublished photographs. Ms. Myrtle Parcher and Dr. Edmund Thomas, professor of history at Fitchburg State College, both affiliated with the society, also contributed their valuable time.

Mr. James E. Fahey, archivist at Military Records, Commonwealth of Massachusetts Military Division, allowed me complete access to his vast storehouse of original papers and records relating to the 57th and other Massachusetts regiments. Mr. John Clarke, then a researcher at Military Records, contributed much time in helping to search out vital information.

Mr. Mark Savolis, curator of manuscripts at the Worcester Historical Museum, liberally supplied information, advice, and some of the unpublished photographs used in this work. Mr. Ron Borjeson, a volunteer researcher at that museum and a member of the Massachusetts Civil War Round Table, by properly locating Camp Wool, helped prevent my making a major blunder.

Ms. Barbara Trippel Simmons, curator of manuscripts at the American Antiquarian Society, graciously allowed me permission to quote from that society's collection of the Barton Family Civil War Letters, which she provided me on microfilm.

Mrs. Fran Doherty, curator of the Northboro Historical Society, after a diligent and intensive search, located Private Francis Harrington's Civil War diary, and with great trust, though she had never met me, sent it to me so that I could transcribe it. Ms. Muriel Ryan, Francis Harrington's grandniece who lives in Northboro, Massachusetts, provided both a copy of the private's photograph and anecdotes about him. Ms. Mary Fran of the *Worcester Transcript* found a letter concerning Frank Harrington's death, which she shared with me.

Mr. Joe Von Deck, Civil War historian at the Ashburnham Historical Society, dug up information on soldiers credited to the town of Ashburnham, Massachusetts, who served with the 57th. He also has given much welcome advice and encouragement over the course of this project.

Mr. Michael J. Winey, curator at the U.S. Army Military History Institute at Carlisle Barracks, offered sound research advice and came up with a number of unpublished photographs of the 57th's men in the enormous photographic collection at his facility.

Mr. Jim Small, lead park ranger and V.I.P. coordinator at Andersonville National Historic Site, provided the use of the William Peabody diary—donated by Mrs. Raymond H. Allard of Dunnellon, Florida—and taught me much about that awful place of incarceration.

Mr. Robert K. Krick, chief historian at the Fredericksburg-Chancellorsville National Military Park, helped me to clear up certain muddled events pertaining to the 57th during the regiment's initial battles. The park also provided the Ralph Happel troop movement maps of those first battles.

The staffs of the different branches of the National Archives provided an almost unbelievable amount of primary source material on the 57th and its soldiers.

The staff of the Technical Information Services, the U.S. Department of the Interior, Denver Service Center, furnished many of the troop movement and historical base maps and technical manuals published by the National Park Service.

Mr. James J. Lewis, curator of the Houghton Library at Harvard University, located a significant letter written by William Francis Bartlett, and Mr. Rodney G. Dennis, curator of manuscripts there, gave me permission to quote it in full.

Mr. Philip L. Budlong, registrar, and Ms. Peggy Tate Smith, photo archivist, Mystic Seaport Museum, furnished the photograph of and information about the *City of Norwich.*

Dr. Christopher Allan, M.D., pathologist at Northside Hospital in Atlanta, gave of his very busy schedule to analyze and interpret original army medical records of the 57th's soldiers and offer a modern diagnosis of given complaints.

Mrs. Landy C. Johnson, reference librarian at the Gale Free Library, gave me copies of the personal narratives of many of the 57th's men credited to Holden, Massachusetts.

Ms. Jean Fuller, of the Athol Public Library, provided interesting newspaper accounts about Captain John Anderson.

Mr. Terrance Ingano, of the Clinton Historical Society, offered information about soldiers credited to Clinton, Massachusetts.

Mrs. Ruth Hopfman, curator of the Sterling Historical Society, found information and personal narratives concerning the men in the regiment credited to Sterling, Massachusetts.

Mrs. Lois S. Greenwood, curator of the Winchendon Historical Society, sent me personal narratives of men credited to Winchendon, Massachusetts.

Mrs. Lynn Lovell, curator of the Milford Historical Society, supplied a wealth of information of the 57th's soldiers credited to Milford, Massachusetts.

Mr. Robert W. Sherwood, of Kingwood, Texas, provided valuable source material on and the photograph of his great-grandfather, Lieutenant Charles Royce.

Mrs. Alice Mainguy, secretary of St. Bernard's Catholic Church in Fitchburg, Massachusetts, sifted through old records to uncover information on some of Fitchburg's Irish soldiers in the 57th.

Ms. Elizabeth Patterson, head of the General Reference Department at the Robert W. Woodruff Library at Emory University, kindly allowed me special permission to do research in the wonderful Civil War stacks located there.

Mrs. Rita Linker, reference librarian at the Bartow County Public Library in Cartersville, Georgia, furnished me with many interlibrary loans of old and rare books needed to complete this work.

Many people other than those previously mentioned helped with the assembly of the photographs that have been used. They are: Mr. Jim Kushlan, of *Civil War Times Illustrated;* Mr. Rex Shattuck, of Acworth, Georgia; Mr. Jim Enos, of Carlisle, Pennsylvania; Mr. A. Warren Wilkinson, Sr., of Cocoa Beach, Florida; Mr. Charles W. Henry, of Fitchburg, Massachusetts; Mr. Henry Deeks, of East Arlington, Massachusetts; and the people at Creative Images in Acworth, Georgia.

Mr. Lee Beitchman, my attorney in Atlanta, helped me to understand the complexities of a publishing contract.

Mr. Chris Killelea, my cousin, generously lent the use of his Wilderness campground in Virginia while Jan and I were researching the battlefields in that beautiful state.

To all the people of Fitchburg not previously mentioned, who provided wonderful hospitality and information while we were researching in Massachusetts, I want to say thanks, and particularly to Mr. Jack O'Donnell, Miss Margaret Kielty, Dr. C. L. John Legere, and especially my boyhood friends Mr. C. J. "Buddy" Anderson, Mr. John Shields, and Mr. Tom Chrost, who put Jan and me up in their homes and furnished lively evenings, cold beers, and good greasy hamburgers at Slattery's. Special thanks also to Mr. Nick Maravell and Mr. Don Lauter.

And lastly I want to acknowledge all those ladies and gentlemen of the many libraries, historical societies, and institutions around the country of whom I inquired for information. Although they found nothing new in their searches, those searches were invaluable in that they told me where unknown primary source material on the 57th Regiment is not located.

If I have forgotten to include anyone, I sincerely apologize.

★

This book was completed in Acworth, Georgia, on Saint Patrick's Day, 1988.

Hi! Ya! See how they drop
'Neath our swift, gleaming steel
We are not human now—
We are raging fiends;
We slash, and seek to kill
While any foeman stays. [1]

1

Camp John E. Wool

ABOUT ONE AND A HALF MILES SOUTH of the city of Worcester, Massachusetts, temporary barracks were constructed in the fall of 1862 on "high, rolling ground where there was ample space for drills and parades, and designated 'Camp John E. Wool.' " It was named after Major General John Ellis Wool, the defender of Fort Monroe on the Virginia Peninsula in 1862 and the antagonist of General George B. McClellan, then commander of the Army of the Potomac. The camp, located on the Brooks farm near Cambridge Street and bordered by the Boston & Albany Railroad on the northwest and on the southeast by the Norwich & Worcester Railroad, was built to be a "camp of instruction"—as Civil War training camps were commonly known.[1]

Several regiments that served the Commonwealth of Massachusetts had been trained in Worcester before departing for the war. The 21st Massachusetts had been the first regiment to be organized there, and it had occupied different grounds in the city during July and August 1861. The 21st was followed by five other Bay State units—the 25th, 34th, 36th, 49th, and finally the 51st. The 49th Regiment had been commanded by an energetic young Boston blue blood and graduate of Harvard College, William Francis Bartlett.[2]

"Frank," as close acquaintances knew him, had been first commissioned as captain of Company I in the 20th Massachusetts during the summer of 1861 and saw his first action at Ball's Bluff, Virginia. There, on October 21, 1861, the Southern forces severely rebuffed the 20th Regiment together with its brother organization the 15th Massachusetts. In the battle of Yorktown during the ill-fated Peninsula campaign, the captain's left leg was seriously wounded on April 24, 1862, and it was amputated at the knee.[3]

Following his recuperation and the fitting of an artificial leg made of cork, Bartlett accepted the colonelcy of the 49th Massachusetts Volunteers in

November of 1862. The 49th Regiment trained in Worcester during the fall of 1862, and on November 29, the unit left the state for service in Louisiana. There, on May 27, 1863, the colonel was wounded again, this time twice in action at Port Hudson, one Minié ball hitting him so severely in the left arm that he was never able to rejoin his regiment.[4]

When President Abraham Lincoln called for an additional three hundred thousand troops on October 17, 1863, the Commonwealth of Massachusetts inaugurated plans to raise four new infantry regiments, to be known as "Veteran Volunteers" as an incentive for former soldiers to reenlist in them. Governor John A. Andrew offered the command of one of these new regiments, the 57th, or 2nd Regiment of Veteran Volunteers, to a now fairly well-recovered Frank Bartlett. The offer was accepted, and Bartlett was commissioned colonel of the 57th Massachusetts Volunteer Infantry, to date from August 17, 1863.[5]

The colonel set to work immediately organizing his new command, calling upon brother officers in the commonwealth whom he knew and offering them opportunities to raise companies for the regiment, in turn for which they would receive commissions as captains of those units. The regiment, he told them, would be trained at Camp John E. Wool.

★

Ten companies made up a Civil War infantry regiment, and all ten companies of the 57th Massachusetts were raised in the same basic manner, mostly in Worcester, Hampden, and Berkshire counties in the fall and winter of 1863–64.[6] Although there were unique circumstances in the raising of each company, the background and recruiting of just one of them is presented here as fairly typical of all.

The town of Fitchburg, Massachusetts, founded in 1764, lay twenty-odd miles north of Worcester in the valley of the Nashua River. Its early settlers had found the plains and gentle hills on the banks of the river agreeable for raising crops and grazing animals on their simple farms, and they had stayed and prospered. Later generations of entrepreneurs had harnessed the power of the Nashua, and a thriving economy from the new mills they built had taken root. Paper, chairs, scythes, cutlery, cloths, shoes, and iron products cast in the local foundries were all produced and distributed to other parts of the thriving United States. But production from the growing demand for the town's goods soon overtook its ability to distribute them—the horse-drawn freight wagons had become incapable of handling the increased requirements imposed on them. In the 1840s all the business and political talk about town focused on railroads, and a priority was placed on a line from Fitchburg to Boston, where rail systems and ships there could move the goods more efficiently. Money seemed to be no obstacle to the developing little community, but labor was. Where to get the men to lay the ties and rails and drive the spikes was the question—the local workingmen wanted no part of such low-paying and backbreaking travail—and Alvah Crocker, one of the town's enterprising citizens, provided the answer.[7]

During the 1840s the great potato famine was raging through Ireland, and the ravaged countryside gave up thousands of its sons and daughters to the New World. Boatloads of those starving immigrants arrived almost daily in the great East Coast ports, and in these squalid square-riggers Crocker found the solution to the labor problem for Fitchburg's new railroad.

In 1843 he began to make frequent trips to the bustling docks of Boston Harbor to offer the penniless Irishmen employment on rail gangs for a dollar a day. With absolutely no idea of how they would survive in their new country, most of them saw Crocker's offer as heaven sent, and willingly they followed him to their waiting futures.

A new problem, however, arose immediately: where to house these indigent souls? Once again Alvah Crocker was the man of the hour, and a tract of land on the Nashua in southeast Fitchburg was designated as the new home for the O'Briens, O'Donnells, Kieltys, Caseys, and their fellow countrymen, who quickly threw up rude shanties with rough board timber provided by the railroad. This parcel of earth was known as Burbank Flats, but soon the neighborhood came to be called, by all in town, "the Patch."

The Patch was a labyrinth of dusty, narrow lanes which seemed to have minds of their own. The dingy little dirt-floor shacks consisted of one or two small rooms, with usually a loft for boarders who paid four dollars a week for the privilege of food and shelter—the extra income was a blessing to the landlord. The rough board walls of the huts were capped with thatched roofs, and through the thatch a stovepipe from a coal-burning cookstove poked skyward. Inside, the walls were whitewashed, and the women took great pains to keep their homes as clean and cozy as circumstances allowed. Camphene lamps and candles provided the only light, and water was carried in wooden buckets. Indoor plumbing was unknown. Next to the neat and attractive homes in other areas of town, the Patch was dreary and wretched.[8]

The men worked on the railroad from sunup to sundown, seven days a week, in nearly inhuman conditions—not the least of which were their Yankee superintendents, who thought them little more than chattel—and the women often hired out as maids to the well-to-do families in town for seventy-five cents a week. The lives of these immigrants were ones of seemingly endless toil and drudgery. They were looked upon as inferiors by the old New Englanders, and their religion, "the Roman menace," was despised by the piously Protestant Yankees. Their Celtic habits of strong drink, brawling, and dancing and singing were roundly condemned. "While one receives the sentence of the law for the violation of the statutes," said Alpheus

Fitchburg, Massachusetts, at war's end: looking north on Main Street
(City Hall in top center). *(Fitchburg Historical Society)*

Williams, the town constable and tax collector, "two others will be selling
[liquor] in his stead to raise money to pay his fine and costs." He called the
Patch "notorious as the stronghold of the rum traffic." But through it all the
Irish generally tried to maintain a cheerful attitude and made every effort to
put out of mind their poverty and misery.[9]

In the late winter of 1845, the forty-nine miles of track connecting
Fitchburg with Boston were completed without an accident, and on March
5, 1845, under gray, rainy skies, a wood-fired steam engine pulled into town
for the dedication of the new spur. Alvah Crocker spoke, and the Fitchburg
band played, and the Irish, for the most part, were looking for new employment. They found it in the factories and mills and on the farms in and around
town. Others hired on to the construction gangs building the new depot near
their neighborhood.[10]

The Irish were not, of course, the only poor in the community by any
means, but those of Yankee Protestant heritage usually were treated in a

much more tolerant fashion. Also, a handful of immigrants from other countries and French Canada were just beginning to appear on the local scene.[11] Their numbers would increase sizably in the next century, but their inroads had started.

By 1861, nearly everyone's lot had improved somewhat, and the town was picturesque, with elm trees and brick-and-white-clapboard two-story buildings lining its gaslighted Main Street. The community was prosperous. When the news of Fort Sumter reached the townspeople in April of 1861, the men of Fitchburg readily and enthusiastically enlisted to quell the Rebellion, and the Irish formed a large part of their numbers as they joined with their New England counterparts to follow the national banner.[12] Alvah Crocker inadvertently had done more than just provide laborers for the railroad; he had provided a ready source of soldiers.

The early war years were hardly productive for the Union cause. Thousands were killed and maimed and few strategic victories gained. Clearly, as the third year of the war approached, more soldiers were needed. Volunteer enlistments dwindled alarmingly—the fires of 1861 had waned in the hearts of a war-weary public—and as a result, a national draft was instituted in the summer of 1863. In Fitchburg, as elsewhere, this conscription was met with intense and bitter hostility, and for those who could not afford the $300 to hire a substitute soldier for themselves, a rush was made to Dr. Alfred Hitchcock's office in town to procure a certificate of exemption for physical disability. The good doctor handed out 181 such certificates, and of the 241 men on the Fitchburg quota, only 4 were actually mustered into service. (The rest found immunity in being over thirty-five and married or heads of fatherless households, or in other reasons.)[13]

This, then, was the situation that Colonel Bartlett and his brother officers faced in Fitchburg. In the other towns and cities throughout the commonwealth the circumstances were much the same.

★

Levi Lawrence, a thirty-eight-year-old carpenter and veteran officer of the 25th Massachusetts Regiment, was chosen by the town selectmen and approved by Bartlett to raise 120 men for Company F of the new 57th and to be the company's captain.[14]

In the late fall of 1863, recruiting advertisements began to appear in local newspapers. Typical of them was: "To the new recruits joining this regiment [57th] the change from civil to military life is gradual and easy. The regiment will go into camp in the barracks at South Worcester. . . ." But despite that promise, the campaign to enlist soldiers in the 57th dragged on at a snail's pace. In late December, several public recruitment meetings followed by a canvass of the community's districts for recruits by a committee of the town's leading citizens produced almost no effect on the enlistment drive. A prime stumbling block seemed to be that many men recently had returned home after the expiration of their one year's service in Companies A and B of the 53rd Regiment, which had seen rough service in the Port Hudson, Louisiana, campaign, and the hardships of those men were plain to all. No one then was keen on the soldier's life, and so it was decided to pay each recruit a town bounty of $100 as an incentive to join up. In addition, much was made to the potential enlistees of the state and federal governments' bounties, $325 and $300 respectively—a handsome sum indeed for 1863.[15] With money such as that, many of the poor, providing that they survived the war, could and would elevate their standards of living by enlisting, even becoming property owners in not a few cases.

From December 26, 1863, through January 9, 1864, recruitment meetings were held every night in the town hall, and all elegible men were urged to attend and sign their enlistment papers. Impassioned, patriotic speeches rang through the auditorium imploring the men to join—and by the way receive their generous town bounty. These orations, spoken by state and local politicians, dignitaries, and businessmen, as well as some veterans who made "eloquent appeals" to the men to follow their examples, finally took effect, with more recruits volunteering nightly.[16]

The *Fitchburg Sentinel* reported,

> The meetings for the purpose of aiding volunteering held in this place [town hall] since our last issue [January 1, 1864], have been well attended, and for the most part a degree of interest worthy of the noble object in view has been maintained. Every motive that could be drawn from patriotic to pecuniary considerations have been eloquently urged upon the attention of the meetings by some of our most able citizens, while not a few of the most effective speeches have been made by those who have enrolled their names as volunteers. The excellent music discoursed by the Fitchburg band contributed much to the enthusiasm of the meetings.
>
> Subscriptions to the amount of between ten and twelve thousand dollars have been made for the purpose of paying a town bounty of one-hundred dollars to each volunteer. We are unable to state the precise number of men who have enlisted since the call, or the number to be credited to the town by re-enlistments, but we are assured that the quota of Fitchburg will be filled without [another] draft. Much credit is due to the gentlemen who have had the matter of raising men and money in hand.[17]

Among the speakers were men such as the industrialist and benefactor of the Irish Alvah Crocker; Hale W. Page; Colonel John W. Kimball, commander of the 15th and 53rd Massachusetts; William H. Vose, superintendent and manager of the Fitchburg Woolen Mill; the Reverend George Trask, pastor of the antislavery Trinitarian Church in Fitchburg, and a leading participant in the antitobacco and prohibitionist movement; the Reverend

Mr. Hamilton; and First Lieutenant Wallace A. Putnam, late of the 10th Massachusetts Volunteers.[18]

William H. Vose was the man credited with signing up most of the company, and each recruit penned his signature or made his mark upon a standard enlistment form that read in part, "I certify, on honor, that I have minutely inspected the Volunteer, (recruit's name) previously to his enlistment, and that he was entirely sober when enlisted; that, to the best of my judgement and belief, he is of lawful age; and that, in accepting him as duly qualified to perform the duties of an able-bodied soldier, I have strictly observed the Regulations which govern the recruiting service." The recruiter then signed the form, and the new soldier pledged that he, in turn, would "bear true faith and alligiance to the United States of America, and . . . serve them honestly and faithfully against all their enemies or opposers whomsoever; and . . . observe and obey the orders of the President of the United States, and the orders of officers appointed over [him], according to the Rules and Articles of War."[19]

On January 20, 1864, the new recruits in Company F were issued their uniforms in Fitchburg. Each man received one greatcoat, one nine-button dress frock coat, one four-button sack coat, one pair of infantry trousers, one forage cap, and one woolen and one rubber blanket.[20] (Most Northern regiments by this stage of the war received their uniforms at camp, and the issuing of clothing to Company F in their hometown appears to have been quite unusual.)

Even though the recruits came slowly, by February 1 enough men had enlisted to muster the company, and they were all notified to prepare to leave for the "camp of instruction." On the cold, clear, and windy morning of Thursday, January 4, 1864, the recruits of Company F were assembled at the Fitchburg railroad station to board a train of the Fitchburg & Worcester Railroad that would take them to Camp John E. Wool to begin their great adventure. Families, well-wishers, some veterans, and a sprinkling of local politicians were on hand in the long, low, covered granite depot to see them off. No bands are known to have played, and the occasion appears to have been subdued. Few of the recruits had many illusions of the romance of war in 1864—although they had no conception whatever of what they were in for—and certainly not the reenlisted veterans. Quiet good-byes were said, and the men, armed with food packages containing all sorts of delicacies from home pressed upon them by doting wives and mothers and fond sweethearts—all had heard of the reputation of army food and a number had experienced it—boarded the cold, wooden cars. There was little sentimentality, as there would be plenty of time for family visits to the camp and soldier furloughs home.[21]

The trip to Worcester took only a short while, and after detraining beyond Norwich Depot, the recruits walked to the camp, thus beginning their long march into history.

★

The 51st Massachusetts had built the barracks at Camp Wool, and those quarters, one for each company and two separate quarters for officers, were now used to house the new 57th Regiment. These temporary structures were long, low, whitewashed affairs framed of rough green pine which had shrunk as it dried, opening large cracks between the vertically hung siding boards, giving "no limit as to ventilation." They were about seventy feet long and twenty feet wide, with shallow pitched roofs. Several windows provided light, and two wooden doors on each gable end allowed access. Only two wood-burning cast-iron stoves had been installed to heat each of the large, open rooms, and they were worse than inadequate, for when the wind blew across the open parade ground—and it blew fiercely during that frigid New England winter of 1864—it often forced the smoke back down the chimneys and into the quarters, choking the men and driving them out into the biting, clear air. As one of the boys put it in a letter home, "[The men] suffer a great deal from the cold and various other causes."[22]

The barracks had been neatly laid out in rows along named company streets. The officers' quarters stood behind the company buildings, and the parade ground was behind them. In addition, cookhouses, a hospital, stables, commissary and quartermaster's warehouses, a transient barrack for recruits, and a guardhouse had been built.[23]

Inside the enlisted men's billets the walls, too, had been whitewashed, but that was the extent of the barracks' luxury. They had lain unused for better than a year and when the recruits first occupied them they smelled musty, but before long the must gave way to the odors of smoke and a hundred men's bodies. And it can be said with certainty that those lax in personal hygiene were dealt with quickly by their superiors and comrades. Sleeping accommodations were virtually nonexistent. No beds had been installed, and "the men slept by twos and threes, or in any other way most convenient for them, upon hard board platforms [built two feet off the floor], which grew harder and harder through the cold winter nights. When aching bones on one side called for a change of position all had to turn together." Some of the more inventive soldiers soon began covering their platforms with straw when they could find any, but it did little to alleviate their suffering.[24]

These sleeping platforms, charitably referred to as "bunks" by the officers, were supposed to be fastidiously maintained, and strict orders were issued as to their arrangement. The heads of the bunks were required to face all in the same direction (presumably towards the long walls), and the beds were covered with the men's rubber blankets, shiny side up. The soldiers' wool blan-

8

kets and uniform clothing were to be folded neatly and placed at the head of the pallet, while rifles and equipment were hung on pegs driven into the walls beside it. Officers and noncommissioned officers were cautioned by the staff that "in inspecting bunks [they] will see that no clothing or articles of any sort are placed *under* the bedsack." This order appears not to have been heeded universally, as company captains were warned on several occasions both orally and in written orders to see that the bunks were arranged according to the regimental directives.[25]

Each day, under the supervision of corporals, two privates from each company were detailed to police in and around their respective barracks and cookhouses, and the corporals were held responsible for the work being accomplished to the rigid standards set by the regimental commanders. Company captains, of course, held the ultimate responsibility for the cleanliness and appearance of the quarters, and they were instructed by staff officers to pay "particular personal attention [to the] health and comfort of the men" and that they "should make every exertion to secure it for them." Throughout the army Sunday morning inspections were held for all soldiers not actively engaged in a campaign, and Camp Wool was no exception to that tradition. Company commanders were compelled to make those barracks and cookhouse inspections held on the Sabbath at nine-thirty "most minute and thorough."[26] Cleanliness was clearly a watchword in the 57th.

Not only were the quarters to be maintained in a neat and orderly fashion, but no less attention was paid to the cleanliness of the men's clothing and their personal appearance. Mondays and Tuesdays were the designated laundry days, and the boys scrubbed their uniforms, underwear, and shirts in tubs filled with water heated over the billets' stoves. Clotheslines were strung on the west side of the quarters six feet above the ground, on which the wet clothing was hung out to dry. In that freezing winter, one can be assured that many a drying uniform froze as rigid as steel. On pleasant days, blankets were ordered hung on these lines to air from ten in the morning until noon, and both wet clothes and blankets were guarded by a sentry, who was stationed opposite the buildings to see that none were pilfered.[27]

As to personal cleanliness and appearance, hair was ordered to be cut short and the men with full beards were shaved upon arrival "leaving only the mustache and imperial [goatee]." They were also to be "thoroughly clensed [*sic*]" before joining their companies. Squad sergeants were directed that they were responsible for looking "out for the personal cleanliness and appearance of [their] men, [and to see that they] wash regularly and thoroughly both person and underclothing."[28]

A problem with the camp's aroma and sanitation arose early. When the first contingents of recruits began arriving at camp in the last month of 1863, they evidently gave little thought to where they would relieve themselves of their bodily wastes. Latrines—or sinks, as they were then called—had been set up, but apparently some of the new soldiers took little notice of them, deciding that they would take care of their business where and how they pleased. But regimental command was having none of that, and those officers issued explicit orders on January 25 that "the men will use the sink intended for their use, and anyone committing any nuisance [a pleasant euphemism of the time] in or around the barracks or campground will be dealt with accordingly."[29] This order seems to have done the job, for no directives of a similar nature were issued ever after.

All in all, Frank Bartlett and his second in command, Lieutenant Colonel Edward P. Hollister, did all in their power to insure a clean, tidy, comfortable, and healthy atmosphere in which to train the new regiment, and they appear to have succeeded in the departments of clean and tidy. Comfortable and healthy were matters of quite a different nature.

★

While Company F had been organizing in Fitchburg, other companies had been coming into camp and settling into their military routines, and by April 6 all ten companies—in order, A, B, H, E, D, C, F, I, G, and K—were accounted for and mustered into United States service. The mustering-in ceremony was a dignified and formal function, and was basically the same for the fledgling 57th Massachusetts as for every Union regiment during the Civil War. After enough men had been assembled at Camp Wool to form the quorum of a company—which at full strength consisted of approximately one hundred soldiers—Colonel Bartlett or Hollister would formally request from the Adjutant General's Office of the Commonwealth of Massachusetts in Boston that a regular army mustering officer be dispatched to swear in the new unit.[30]

The company or companies to be mustered into Federal service typically would be assembled on the parade ground, and after the individual and collective inspection of the men by the mustering officer, they would take the oath of allegiance to the United States prescribed by the tenth Article of War. Next, the mustering officer would read aloud the entire Articles of War. This discourse was a long and tedious process, but because capital punishment was called for in so many cases for infractions of the Articles, the psychology of the procedure was designed to instill fear, subservience, and discipline in the new troops.[31] With many of the boys, this method accomplished its ends, but with many others, as will become evident, the power of its deterrence was nil.

One thousand and thirty-eight officers and enlisted men were mustered into the 57th Massachusetts during its wartime service. With the exception of a handful of recruits sent to the front later in the war, they were all mustered at Camp Wool. They came from 18 states and 13 foreign countries. Fewer than half, 446, were native-born Massachusetts men, while New York and the other five New England states provided almost a quarter of the regiment's strength. Several other soldiers were from some surprising areas of the country, including Virginia, Georgia, Louisiana, Arkansas, Kentucky, and even Utah Territory. Three hundred fifty-eight men were of foreign extraction. Nearly 10 percent of the regiment comprised Canadians from the seven eastern provinces, and half of them were of French descent. Other members of the regiment had been born in nine countries of western Europe, in Turkey, in Hungary, and in New South Wales, Australia. But by far the heaviest concentration of foreigners was the Irish, who were responsible for 197 men, or 18 percent.[32] (The rosters make it apparent that many, many others of American birth or from other foreign countries were of Irish descent as well. The 57th was weighted heavily with Irishmen.)

Two-hundred thirty men gave their occupation as farmer, while 158 gave theirs as laborer. There were 156 boot- and shoemakers and 43 clerks, some of whom were appointed first sergeants and sergeants because of their talents with penmanship and recordkeeping. In all, 121 professions were cited, and they ranged from clergyman to jailer, cigar maker to ax maker, telegraph operator to photographer. There were actors, saloon keepers, firemen, jewelers, teachers and students, barbers and tailors, doctors and druggists and nurses, and watchmakers and gunmakers and candy makers. The trades supplied carpenters, masons, cabinetmakers, and painters, and the factories sent machinists, mechanics, and millwrights.[33] The men reflected the diverse and dynamic America of their time.

And they were men of various cultural backgrounds, too. They were rich and poor, but mostly poor by far. In the ranks were the good and the evil and all the shades between. Most were law-abiding, hard-working Christian family men, but there were also the thieves and pickpockets, the shirkers and malingerers, and those whom their officers called "worthless," "pickpockets," "deadbeats," "scoundrels," and "rascals." And battle would soon bring out the heroes and the foolishly brave, as well as the unfit, the timid, the bummers, and the cowards.[34]

They ranged in age from fifteen to forty-five, but most were in their mid-twenties, and they came in all sizes, from five-foot-one to six-foot-four, with the mean being about five-seven. They came from the picturesque farms nestled in the beautiful Berkshires of western Massachusetts, from the hovels and slums of the country's cities, as well as from the finer side of the tracks. Some were well educated and well read, but most were not, and many were illiterate. They embodied the basic moral values of their time, and viewed the war in ways that today we would find simplistic at best. Some were gentle and loving, some were mean and vile. There were men of temperance, but

11

many still who favored more than an occasional nip.[35] The 57th Massachusetts Veteran Volunteers was typical of the regiments raised in 1864.

★

The Commonwealth of Massachusetts, in authorizing their organization, had mandated that the four new Veteran Volunteer Regiments—the 56th, 57th, 58th, and 59th—be filled with a plurality of former soldiers, but as hard as the recruiters had endeavored, that goal could not be reached, and the 57th enlisted only 245 veterans. Of the number recruited, however, many had seen little combat, serving mostly as garrison troops in New Bern, North Carolina, during 1862 and 1863. A few had fought in the famous battles at Bull Run, on the Virginia Peninsula, at Antietam, Fredericksburg, Chancellorsville, and Gettysburg, but most of the fighting soldiers had been with the western army in its campaign to capture Port Hudson, Louisiana, in 1863. The greater number of previous Bay State regiments were represented by some men formerly in their ranks, but the heaviest concentration—34—came from Colonel Bartlett's old outfit, the 49th Massachusetts. Company D recruited the colonel's former soldiers, and its ranks could boast of being almost half veteran. And with the exception of Companies C, G, and I, made up primarily of rookies, the other companies were populated—by roughly 25 percent each—with seasoned campaigners. Even a smattering of sailors and marines volunteered for the regiment. The 57th's sergeants and corporals and a few commissioned officers were chosen chiefly from the newly enlisted veterans' ranks, and Frank Bartlett looked to those men to help train the raw recruits.[36]

★

Colonel Bartlett appointed First Lieutenant George Priest, a young officer with young, wispy sideburns and mustache, as regimental quartermaster, and he, along with assistants Quartermaster Sergeant James Robbins, Commissary Sergeant David Lawry, and a small number of privates temporarily detailed as helpers, worked long hours to ensure that the recruits were supplied adequately and in regulation fashion.[37]

Upon arrival in camp, and after a cursory medical check by the regimental surgeon, Dr. Whitman White,[38] the boys lined up at the quartermaster's supply house and were issued their gear. Their civilian clothes, they were told, were to be sent home.

The uniforms worn by the regiment were those prescribed by U.S. Army regulations. The wearing of fancy Zouave and militia uniforms was, in 1864, almost a thing of the past, except for a few diehard units still in the field that had enlisted in the heady and romantic early days of the war and still clung to their nonregulation clothing out of unit pride.[39]

Civil War regulation uniforms for enlisted men were issued in four sizes only, and no allowance was made for the unusually built individual, who was generally out of luck in the fit department unless he happened to be handy with a needle and thread—which was highly unlikely. An option was to employ the seamstress talents of the many women who constantly flowed in and out of the camp. Of course, the veterans in the ranks had learned long ago how to deal with such problems, and there was a smattering of tailors in the ranks, as well.[40]

The men were issued the same clothing as that drawn by Company F, mentioned previously. In addition, however, they were allowed two gray or blue flannel shirts and two sets of long underwear made from the same material. They were supposed to have been issued socks, or as they were then known, stockings, but George Priest's logistical system had snagged with regard to that item of clothing, and as late as March 23, 1864, "a blustering cold day," Private Edward M. Schneider of Company K was writing home that they still had not been distributed. Most of the men solved the problem by having socks sent from families,[41] but there were those few who did not have that resource, and how they must have suffered in the blowing snows and bitter temperatures of that hard winter.

The uniforms themselves, however, along with the flannel underwear, were perfectly adequate to meet the test of the season's numbing chill. Lined, dark blue coats and hats and sky-blue trousers and greatcoats of heavy flannel and kersey, augmented with scarfs, mittens, and heavy woolen socks from home, kept the men more or less comfortable while drilling in the New England elements. The heavy, rough leather brogans, or "bootees," with their sturdy rawhide laces, also served the men well—at least after they were broken in thoroughly.[42]

A holdover from early days—even though still called for in the regulations—issued to the soldiers was the Hardee hat, a high-crowned, wide-brimmed, black felt hat with one side of the brim pinned up by a brass eagle badge. It sported a light blue cord, designating infantry, around its base and the brass hunting-horn insignia of the foot soldier on the front, along with the regiment's numbers and the company's letter made of the same metal. On one side was fixed a huge, black ostrich plume. It was a silly and pretentious piece of gear, and most of the men despised it, only donning it when so ordered. They much preferred the comfortable and practical forage cap, and some of them appear to have taken pride in the brass hunting horn denoting their branch of the service when it was pinned to the top of their cap. Private William T. Peabody of Company F noted in his diary on March 14, 1864, "[Sergeant John M.] Hastings put the bugle upon my cap and I responded by a speech." Brass regimental numbers (the numerals 5 and 7, ¾ inch high) and company letters (one inch long) were required to be worn on the cap also, the letter below the horn and the numbers above it.[43]

One further item of clothing favored over another seems to have been the dress jacket—a nine-button frock coat with a stand-up collar that was, along with the front button edge and the cuffs, trimmed with a thin sky-blue welt. That garment apparently was more popular with many of the recruits than the loose-fitting, far more comfortable four-button fatigue "sack coat" with its floppy collar. It can only be assumed that the men enjoyed the martial appearance of the impractical frock over the inelegant but pragmatic sack. In any event, the wearing of the formal coat while in camp was prohibited quickly by Lieutenant Colonel Hollister under Regimental General Orders No. 4, issued on February 3, in which he also forbade the wearing of any nonregulation clothing among the enlisted men.[44]

The officers' uniforms were similar in appearance to those worn by the common soldiers, but that was the end of the similarity. The commissioned officers were required to furnish their own clothing, and they frequented the tailor shops in their hometowns to have that clothing custom made. Their uniforms were constructed with superior material both in quality and comfort, and they fit well. Many of the commanders and junior officers—no doubt to create an image cultivated during those days as to what the mien of the noble warrior should be, as well as to boost individual vanities—had the chests of their frock coats padded with quilted material, thus giving them the appearance of physical attributes not in fact possessed. Another major departure from the livery worn in the line was, of course, the badge of rank sewn on the shoulders, commonly known as "shoulder straps."[45] This term, from early on in the war, had taken on the air of a double entendre, often used sarcastically among the enlisted men for officers who were not in the men's good graces.

As with uniforms, the arms and equipment drawn by the enlisted personnel of the 57th were mostly of the standard patterns. The regulation model 1863 Springfield .58 caliber rifled musket, issued to the regiment on Saturday, March 5, 1864, and distributed to the men on the following Monday, was the firearm used by Companies A through I. "The boys are much pleased with the weapons," reported the *Massachusetts Spy* on March 9. The leather accoutrements—waist belt with brass U.S. buckle, cap box, cartridge box with a brass U.S. box plate and shoulder strap adorned with a brass eagle breastplate, and triangular bayonet and leather scabbard—were also of the regulation patterns. Painted black canvas knapsacks with 57 MVM (57th Massachusetts Volunteer Militia) stenciled in two-inch white letters across the front, haversacks made from similar material, and wool-covered tin canteens were also standard issue. To protect against the theft of these items, each man in the various companies was numbered in alphabetical order, and the number assigned each individual was marked on his rifle and all pieces of clothing and equipment. It was also common practice for soldiers to print or stencil their names or initials on their gear.[46]

The exception to standard issue lay with Company K, which was organized as a sharpshooter company, and was to be armed with Spencer repeating rifles. Those firearms could not be procured while the regiment was at Camp Wool, however, so that company had to borrow rifles in order to practice the manual of arms.[47]

Apparently not a few of the men sought to enhance the government weapons issue by providing themselves with personally purchased revolvers and pistols. This was against army regulations, and arming with handguns among the enlisted men appears to have gotten out of hand. On February 12, Frank Bartlett decided to take steps to remedy the situation, and in paragraph 1 of Regimental General Orders No. 6 he directed that "commanders of companies will cause all pistols in possession of their men to be disposed of immediately or given into their charge."[48]

2

Forming the Line

A S IN ALL ARMIES since the beginning of military organization, food was a paramount consideration with the officers and enlisted men of the 57th. At Camp Wool, cookhouses were provided where meals were prepared and consumed. Those cookhouses, located in the vicinity of the barracks, were constructed and whitewashed in the same way. Benches were provided upon which meals could be made ready, and large cast-iron stoves were used for the cooking. A sergeant was detailed in charge of each kitchen, and every morning at eight o'clock, he drew the daily rations for his domain from the quartermaster.[1]

And as in the barracks, the staff officers took great pains to see that the cookhouses were maintained in a neat and orderly manner. Wood for the stoves was stacked squarely in two piles on one side of each building, and "the sawing and splitting done between these piles." Fresh coats of whitewash were applied, both inside and out, at intervals.[2]

Two men from each company were appointed as cooks. Upon what merits they were chosen is unknown, but judging from their civilian occupations, those jobs certainly played no part. Captain John Anderson, the regiment's original chronicler, tells us, "Men were detailed as cooks, often without any previous knowledge of this art, and no one seemed to know how to economize the government ration. . . ."[3] Not only did they not know how to economize the ration, but it may be assumed safely that many a meal was a culinary disaster in the hands of those neophyte chefs.

The food served was plain, but generally filling and nourishing and resembled nothing in the way of what the troops would face once in the field. Boiled salt beef or ham, cold or boiled potatoes or rice, dry white bread, and coffee was standard camp fare. William Peabody, who had been assigned duty in the kitchens, mentions that his company, F, was issued on March 18 "73 loaves of bread today." The *Fitchburg Sentinel* published the following assessment of the regiment's food supplies on March 19: "We visited the quartermaster's department on the same day [March 13], and found everything there in perfect keeping with other sections of the encampment. Quartermaster Priest seems at home and fully understands his business by anticipating the wants of those for whom it is his duty to provide. His stores, consisting of ham, beef, rice, sugar, coffee, & c., each of excellent quality, were ample, and systematically arranged, yet not overabundant for want of room, thereby making frequent requisitions necessary."[4]

By the men in the ranks who came from poverty, most notably the Irish and other immigrants, meals of this nature were received well, but for others of more substantial means, used to better fare, army food was anathema, and those men quickly found ways to improve their diets. Food was liberally requested and sent to them from the home front, and the proliferation of local Worcester ladies and visiting wives and female relations, who often stayed in local hotels and boardinghouses, added greatly to the quality of the regiment's nutrition and culinary enjoyment. The women provided a variety of special treats, or "goodies" as the boys called them, to the officers and enlisted men alike, such as roast chickens and turkeys, baked hams, fresh butter, cakes, preserves, jellies, pickles, and the like. In addition, the patriotic local citizenry frequently invited some of the soldiers to their homes for meals. John Anderson wrote that the enlisted men seemed to have benefited more from this generosity than did the officers, but it is certain that the brass did not suffer. Overall, the regiment ate well.[5]

The ladies also helped with the cooking and cleaning in the cookhouses. Private Peabody relates how, on the eve of a visit from Governor Andrew, "Hannah [his wife] and I scrubbed all the tins" in the kitchen.[6]

★

The duty roster—or daily schedule—was not overly strenuous, at least according to officers like John Anderson. Reveille was sounded by the drummers and fifers soon after daylight, and the men were turned out, shivering and stomping in the snow with chattering teeth, and dressed into line in front of their barracks for roll call by the first sergeants. Roll calls were strictly adhered to in the 57th in a not very effective attempt to stem desertions, and they were taken every three hours during the day. At least one commissioned officer also was required to be present when any of these rolls was taken. In fact, Lieutenant Colonel Hollister had ordered that at least one officer be with his company at all times. Failure of an enlisted man to be present at roll call without adequate reason usually brought some form of mild punishment, and there were always those laggards in every company who consistently earned extra duty or time in the guardhouse for this offense. After roll call, while the first sergeants were preparing their morning reports, the men returned to their quarters to make up their sleeping areas, wash and shave, use the sinks, light their pipes, and, for some, catch a little more sleep.[7]

★

Breakfast call or "peas on a trencher" came next, and, following breakfast, sick call. Those men reporting illness were marched by the first sergeants to Camp Wool's hospital for examination by Dr. White, who held the rank of major and surgeon, and Assistant Surgeon and First Lieutenant Charles Heath. Most of the men reporting truly were sick, but as in any Civil War regiment, the 57th had its quota of chronic malingerers and goldbricks, whom the doctors usually diagnosed as such without much effort. Their usual complaints included stiff joints, bad backs, and stomach pains. But the veteran army surgeon White had pretty much seen and heard it all before, and those men were lectured and returned to duty. Often these individuals, dismissed by the doctor as shirkers trying to get out of drill and other duties, would appeal to the sympathies of their company commanders, and for a time some of them were able to beat the system. But Lieutenant Colonel Hollister had no intention of allowing that practice to continue, and on January 17 he forbade company commanders from excusing any man from drill, "the surgeon being the only officer having that authority." For a while the habit ceased, but it soon picked up again, angering Frank Bartlett. On March 17, he reiterated Hollister's original order strongly and clearly, directing that "captains of companies will not excuse any man from any drill except by the recommendation of the surgeon," but he added, "Men coming off guard duty are excused from drill until the afternoon." The genuinely sick were admitted to the hospital, where they were treated with the mostly inadequate methods of that time. Those men judged ailing seriously were normally transferred to the U.S. Army general hospital at Camp Meigs in Readville, Massachusetts, or recommended for a discharge from the service for physical disability, which they usually received.[8]

Diseases contracted by the men ranged from simple colds and fevers to, among others, measles, diarrhea, and pneumonia. The only man to die in the regiment while it was at Camp Wool was Private Nelson Burroughs of Company D, who succumbed to pneumonia on April 3, 1864. In an article published in the *Fitchburg Sentinel* on March 25, the reporter wrote of the 57th's medical facilities:

On Sunday afternoon [March 19, 1864], by invitation of Surgeon W. V. White, we visited the hospital, where we found Assistant Surgeon C. E. Heath in attendance, and while a sudden sadness came over us in sympathy for the inmates who were laboring there with disease, we were gratified with the general arrangement, comfortable accommodations, kind and attentive treatment, and consequent good and wholesome air throughout. There were less than twenty inmates, most of whom were convalescent from the measles, and no one whose disease was not apparently under the control of the physicians in attendance.

Although the quantity of patients in the hospital fluctuated from day to day, company morning reports indicate that the number of cases under treatment reported by the *Sentinel* was about the daily average for the regiment.[9]

★

Policing of the camp and chopping of the day's firewood followed sick call on the duty roster. Snow was shoveled as well, when required. The fatigue parties for those chores were, to a great extent, formed by men being punished. One particularly nasty job, no doubt destined for special cases, came about on Friday, March 4, when Colonel Bartlett instructed, "Captains of companies will have their barracks whitewashed on the inside, also the cookhouses. They will purchase the lime necessary and a brush out of the company fund. The white washing [*sic*] must be *finished* before the Sunday morning inspection." Groans certainly must have been forthcoming at the prospect of having to perform this unappealing task, but the work was finished on time, and the *Fitchburg Sentinel* of March 11, 1864, reported, "During the past week [ending March 5, 1864] the barracks have been thoroughly cleansed and whitewashed, rendering them much more pleasant and healthy."[10]

At the same time as the fatigue parties began working, the "mounting of the guard" took place. Personnel for the twenty-four-hour guard mounts for Camp Wool were selected by the regimental sergeant major, Albert Murdock, and the companies fell into line to the calls of the 57th's drummers and fifers. Murdock chose the three reliefs of the guard mount, "from each company in proportion to the number [of men] reported for duty [that day]," each usually led by a corporal, and the whole under the command of a lieutenant. The detachment formed on the drill field, and the sergeant major would report to the regimental adjutant, First Lieutenant George Barton, who "verified the number of men and assigned the different non-commissioned officers to their places." Before the guard was posted, Frank Bartlett required the regimental Officer of the Day—usually a captain—to read aloud to the men the army regulations "on the subject of guards, and duties of sentinels." The three reliefs were then marched off to their posts at the guardhouse, headquarters, quartermaster's department, and the camp's entrances. The lieutenant in command of the guard remained with his detail, and along with the Officer of the Day would inspect his sentries from time to time throughout their period of duty.

The three-man details were arranged so that each soldier stood guard two out of every six hours.[11] Two hours may not seem very hard duty, and no

19

doubt was not in favorable weather, but two hours standing or pacing his beat in a raging and freezing New England "nor'easter" certainly must have taxed the most hearty soul's patience. And trying to sleep at intervals of four hours in soaking wet woolen clothing would not have been exactly the men's idea of amusement either.

★

As soon as the guard details had been marched off, the companies were reassembled and the entire regiment "enjoyed" drill instruction on Camp Wool's spacious parade ground. The order for the morning drill was that the companies "be divided into squads and drilled by the officers and non-commissioned officers at open ranks under the immediate supervision of the captain" and that "each captain will see that his company is drilled in the 'school of the soldier' [squad drills] one hour and a half every morning and in the 'school of the company' two hours every afternoon." The "school of the soldier" consisted of teaching the fundamentals of military drill, marching, weapons instruction, and tactics according to the official U.S. Army three-volume manual, *System of Infantry Tactics*, written by Lieutenant Colonel Silas Casey, U.S.A., in 1862. This manual was informative especially for its treatise on brigade- and division-level tactics, which had not been contained in earlier instruction texts. The regiment also was fortunate to have a veteran officer corps, as well as a significant number of seasoned campaigners in the ranks, but although those fellows knew pretty much what they were doing on the parade ground, much of their example did not rub off on the green recruits.[12]

The rookie soldiers were taught to stand erect and dress their lines, face left or right, salute, march forward, march to the rear, and march by the flank and by the oblique, and they were drilled endlessly in the manual of arms. They learned to shift their rifles to the various positions necessary for the battle line, to load "in nine times" (the nine formal steps specified in the regulations to load a rifled musket properly), "in four times" (a quicker version of the nine steps), and "at will" (to load and fire individually as fast as possible with no formal commands); to fire from standing, kneeling, or prone positions; and to "thrust and parry" with the bayonet. Colonel Bartlett was present often at these exercises, and he occasionally removed his artificial limb and, standing only on his sound leg, performed the entire manual of arms in front of the regiment, flawlessly, astonishing the men who had never before served with him and earning their devotion and respect.[13]

This training was all contingent on the "weather permitting," which was not often. One of Frank Bartlett's chief complaints about the 57th was that it was sorely lacking in the ability to execute the correct tactical movements and procedures as a unit because the inclement and fickle Northeastern winter so often brought drill practice to a stop. (For example, the *Massachu-*

setts Spy for March 9 reported that "the recent rains have rendered pedestrian exercises in the vicinity of the camp almost impossible. . . .")[14]

The cookhouses served the regiment dinner, also known to the men as "roastbeef," at precisely twelve noon, and then it was back to the drill field, and part of the afternoon, again weather permitting, was spent in continuing instruction in the practical and theoretical military maneuvers needed to be mastered by the regiment.[15]

After the individual and squad tactics of the morning came company tactics and then skirmish drill. On paper, the training paid off with ramrod-straight soldiers marching in precise files to the clear commands of their officers, but unfortunately, this ideal never was realized to its full potential in the 57th. Aside from weather problems, some men simply could not—or would not—grasp this training, and Colonel Bartlett was frustrated by those individuals. Being a meticulous soldier, but not an overly patient commander, he issued the following order on March 17, 1864: "Every commanding officer of a company will institute an 'awkward squad.' Men who are backward in drill, slow to learn, careless or inattentive to orders, will be placed in this squad and drilled carefully by a good non-commissioned officer in addition to the regular drill hours of the company." This effort apparently produced few positive results, as the regiment was known throughout its service by others in the army as being undisciplined in the art of drill.[16]

A further clue to Colonel Bartlett's protracted disappointment with his regiment's inability to come to terms with the parade ground is found in Regimental General Orders No. 10, dated March 16, 1864, in which he directs, "Non-commissioned officers will be drilled and examined in their duties not only in the manual of arms in the ranks but in quarters and on guard one hour each evening by the comdg. officers of the company. Officers and non-commissioned officers in drilling the men will follow the rules and observe the directions prescribed by the 'tactics' [i.e., the manual of arms cited above] with the modification of the comdg. officer of the Regt and will *use no other method.*"[17]

★

A new ritual was added on March 17—dress parade. For the first time, on that chilly Thursday, Bartlett formed the line of the entire regiment. Uniforms had been brushed, leather blackened, brass and steel polished, and the approximately nine hundred soldiers then at camp presented an impressive sight to civilian onlookers, who "much frequented" the event. "Judging from our stand point [*sic*]," wrote the *Fitchburg Sentinel*'s correspondent, "the line was nearly perfect and the movements well executed, but the Colonel noticed 'some imperfections' which if we mistake not, will not be repeated many times."[18]

Every pleasant afternoon thereafter, the formal parade was held on the green at four-thirty, and even though socks still had not been issued to them, the colonel required his men to purchase at their own expense, and wear at that function, white cotton gloves.[19]

★

Sunday was the only day on which the duty roster varied. After breakfast, the barracks and grounds were tidied as usual, but at nine-thirty, the regiment was formed in full equipment for inspection, or as some of the men called it, "knapsack drill." Traditionally, Company A took the right of the line and Company B the left, with the other companies positioned in alphabetical order between them. The adjutant, Lieutenant Barton, took this opportunity to read pertinent orders to the troops, and staff officers generally had something to add. Then the men, by companies, would stack their arms and unsling their knapsacks, place them on the ground in front of them, and open their packs for the scrutiny of Colonel Bartlett, or, in his absence, the staff officer in charge that day, either Hollister or Major James W. Cushing, third in command of the 57th. The officer would then proceed down the line checking the contents of each pack to see that nothing but regulation material was in them, and that the arms, equipment, uniform, and appearance of the soldier were in order. Any man found not to be in compliance with Colonel Bartlett's strict requirements was noted and the company commander, trailing the inspecting staff officer, was reproved.[20] Once back at the barracks, the enraged captain was certain to have shared his displeasure with the man or men responsible for his embarrassment.

After the barracks were inspected, cookhouses, grounds, and other facilities were checked, and then the men not on guard or hospital duty were dismissed from military operations for the rest of the day.[21]

The Reverend Alfred Dashiell, a Protestant minister, was the regimental chaplain,[22] and although no record of his theological administrations at Camp Wool has been found, it pretty much can be taken for granted, given the religious temper of the times, that he held services for the men of like faith in one of the post's buildings on Sunday afternoons.

But much of the regiment was Roman Catholic, including at least two officers, Captain James Doherty of Company G and Second Lieutenant John Reade of Company K,[23] and, because of their religion's rigid stance against attending Protestant worship, they were prohibited from taking part in any of the chaplain's assemblies of prayer. That Frank Bartlett never tried to force them to participate in the Protestant rites is beyond question. Though he probably held the same attitude toward the Church of Rome as did his fellow Protestant New Englanders, he had been in the army long enough to know that by trying to coerce the men of the Catholic faith into committing what they held to be heresy as well as a mortal sin, he would gain their enmity, and would appear to endorse, and thereby possibly let surface, the Protestant soldiers' hatred of "Papists," with results unpredictable on both sides. Such a decision might well have ripped his command in half, and under no circumstances would a man of his intelligence and experience have allowed such a conflict to arise. He very likely allowed a visiting priest to say Mass in a discreetly designated area of camp on Sundays, or issued men of that faith passes to attend a Catholic church in Worcester, under the supervision of Doherty or Reade.

Apart from the Catholics, there was at least one man in the regiment, Color Sergeant Leopold Karpeles of Company E, who was a Jew.[24] In the company rosters several names appear that are commonly Jewish, and so he may not have been alone. How his and any Jewish comrades' spiritual needs were met is likewise a mystery, but here again Frank Bartlett is likely to have been tolerant.

★

On all other days of the week supper was served directly following afternoon parade, and the soldiers were free from duty after that meal if they were not on guard. At nine o'clock, the drummers beat tattoo for the day's final roll call, and a half-hour later they signaled lights out with taps. Taps finished, the boys were supposed to "cease all noises, and every man be inside his quarters." But more often than not, this rule was not followed to the letter— to say the least. John Anderson remembered that "very many of 'the boys' went on little escapades [into Worcester] after nightfall, crossing the guard line without permission, and report, which was generally believed, had it, that they went to see some friends, or, perhaps, sweethearts. It was even rumored that some of the young officers indulged in such pranks, but, as none of them were caught, there seemed to be a lack of evidence sufficient to make history." The facts clearly affirm Captain Anderson's contention, at least with respect to the enlisted men, but those same facts also clearly show that these "pranks" were not taken lightly.[25]

If a man left camp without a pass and did not return before morning roll call, he was routinely listed as a deserter. The terms "desertion" and "absent without leave" were in use by the military during the Civil War, and the former held much graver implications and penalties than the latter. Yet the term "absent without leave" is rarely found in the 57th's company morning reports. That it is found at all, however, indicates that its different meaning was known and understood by the officers and first sergeants writing those reports.[26]

While it is true that many of the men who were listed as deserters in the morning reports returned to camp voluntarily and usually within twenty-four hours, many others did not. Those who were caught but not deemed to be actual deserters (that is, whose intentions were only to have a bit of fun) were given light sentences. Private Peabody gives us an example in his diary: "Sunday Apl 3 Night. Micel Cory [Private Michael Carey, Company F] ran guard to the city and was caught and put on guard [duty] Monday." On the other hand, actual desertion was rampant in the 57th Massachusetts. But it was rampant in nearly all regiments recruited at that time. There were three basic patterns of desertion in the regiments raised in 1864: desertion from the training camps, desertion from the field, and desertion from hospitals; and while none of these patterns can be delineated clearly, each seems to follow a trend.[27]

Money was the principal, but certainly not the only, motive for running. As we have seen, the men were promised what was for the time a fabulous sum of cash for signing the enlistment papers. To a man making a dollar or two a day, there was almost no other way that he would ever have a chance to have that amount of money all at once. Most were willing to risk their lives for the proffered bounties. But not all. The key words are *promised* and *proffered*. The men did not receive a penny of this money upon enlistment—they only received a pledge of its payment on some unspecified date. When the town bounties were paid to the regiment's recruits is not known, but the disbursement dates for state and federal monies are partially available from records. Installments on the $300 Federal government bounties of 25 dollars each were made on March 19 and April 15, 1864. In addition the private soldiers—who were paid at that time 13 dollars a month—received about two and a half months' pay on April 15: $32.75. So by that date the men had been paid a total of $82.75, plus some advanced monthly pay they had received upon being mustered, the amount of which is unknown.[28]

On Friday, April 16, "the payment of bounties to [most of] the men of the 57th regiment was commenced . . . and . . . continued on Saturday," reported the *Massachusetts Spy* on April 20. That payment was the Massachusetts bounty of $325, and for those that hoarded their money, or were lucky with cards, they now had in excess of $440.[29]

That was too tempting for the "bounty jumpers." The "high number bounty regiments"—as they were, and are still, known—recruited in late 1863 and 1864 contained numbers of men who joined a regiment, usually under an alias, solely to receive the offered dollars, and once the money was in hand, they deserted at the earliest opportunity. Many of them made a career of it—and a lot of money, if they were not caught. And many were not.[30] In a world sparsely settled and lacking high-speed communications and the distribution of accurate images of the culprit's face to law enforcement agencies, odds favored, and often won, success.

The 57th, of course, had its share of these shady characters, and a great wave of desertions of this sort took place between April 16 and April 18, 1864, the day that the regiment left Camp Wool. A very few were eventually caught, and at least one of them sentenced to be shot.[31]

The other sort of financially motivated deserters were the men who had expected the bounty money to be paid to them upon muster-in or who did not receive their bounties at all (because of red tape or misplaced enlistment papers, something that happened not infrequently).[32] These were the soldiers who had been perfectly willing to fight for their rewards, but it is easy to imagine the emotional trauma—the guilt and anxiety—of some of those men during that depressing winter, agonizing over the fact that their families were enduring unspeakable poverty and misery at home, the more so now that they were away, and both they and their families living off government promises to pay them money that seemed never to be forthcoming. But there was a reason for that. Government officials had learned from experience with other bounty regiments the hard lesson imparted by bounty jumpers, and the bureaucrats tried to time major disbursements of funds to coincide with the regiments' dates of departure for the front, thereby reducing the opportunities for those criminals to make good their escapes. But the average soldier did not know—or care—about those government strategies. His thoughts centered only on the well-being of his family, and, in frustration, he sometimes left the army to be where he felt he was needed most. (It should be noted, however, that the Commonwealth of Massachusetts paid its soldiers an extra twelve dollars a month in the form of a relief fund, ostensibly to aid families.[33] How well the fund was administered is unknown, but if it was managed like other bureaucracies of that era, there can be little doubt that the money was poorly disbursed to individual households, if in fact it was disbursed at all. Even if families did receive it, though, it was precious little to live on in those days.)

There were also many cases of fraud on the part of the various town selectmen and the unscrupulous recruiting brokers who enlisted some of the men. One man cheated of his bounty was Corporal Alonzo Place of Company C. (Place did not desert, but his story surely is typical of those who did.) In his behalf, Place's company commander, Captain Charles D. Hollis, wrote a letter to Adjutant General William Schouler complaining in mid-April 1864 that the corporal had been defrauded of a portion of his state bounty.[34] The outcome of the captain's efforts is, unfortunately, unknown, but Hollis's actions point out that cheating the men out of their bounty money was a problem in the 57th.

Remunerative motivations were far from the only reasons that men deserted the regiment. There are many cases of men quitting on the day they were mustered, perhaps frightened out of their wits by the reading of the Articles of War. Others left because they did not get along with their comrades, or could not abide the army life, the food, the bleakness of winter at Camp Wool, or their sometimes overbearing, pompous and pretentious officers, or for a myriad of other causes. One young recruit, Private Robert Clark, of Company B, held the regimental record for attempts—four times.[35]

Private Clark, a lad of seventeen, had been arrested for desertion and returned to the regiment for the third time when Dr. White happened upon him. He wrote,

> During a Sunday morning inspection . . . in the guardhouse, I found a young boy with a log of wood chained to his ankle. He had been a prisoner for several days, and had been obliged to do police duty about camp, sweeping and sawing wood, such as is done by the prisoners. From his appearance, I thought that his punishment was too severe, and so I turned to the officer of the day, and said, "I want this log of wood taken off and the boy sent to his quarters under guard." I was told that he had been very bad and deserved his punishment, as he had, on one or two occasions [actually three], attempted to desert. My suggestion in regard to the boy was carried out. On the next Sunday inspection of the guardhouse, I was told by the officer of the day that the prisoner I had ordered released had deserted [on April 1]. The captain of the company [Joseph W. Gird] said that he would bring him back to camp, if it cost him a thousand dollars.

(Fees of twenty or thirty dollars were commonly paid for the arrest and return of the 57th's deserters.)

Two weeks later White again found Clark handcuffed and shackled in the guardhouse:

> He was not allowed to leave the place, and was obliged to sleep on the floor, with nothing but a blanket under him and a single blanket over him. I immediately ordered him to the hospital. In the absence of Colonel Bartlett, Major Cushing was in command. He sent for me to report to him, and when I arrived said, "I learn that you have ordered this boy Clark to the hospital, but I shall not send him unless you will be responsible for his safe keeping." "You *will* send him," I replied, "and as I do not keep this camp, you cannot hold me responsible, but if he is not sent immediately, I will prefer charges against you."

White found Clark in the hospital under guard that afternoon.

> I then sat down beside him, and taking his hand said, "James [Dr. White's memory seems to have faded about Clark's first name, or he was trying to protect the soldier's anonymity], you have had a hard time." I learned that his father and mother had thought him incorrigible, and therefore placed him in a reformatory at Westborough [Massachusetts], from where he had enlisted. The superintendent of the reform school said he was glad to get rid of the worst boy he had. I sent for a bowl of mutton broth, and sitting beside him while he ate it, said, "I know that you have had a hard time, and have been neglected and punished and often imposed upon, but I am going to be your friend if you will only do right, and if you have any

complaints to make, come to me and I will help you." As he looked up at me with a pleasant, trusting expression, I felt sure that my efforts had not been in vain, and that I had made an impression upon this little villain.

And apparently he had, as Clark never deserted again.[36]

Exactly 100 men, nearly 10 percent of the regiment, were listed on the morning reports as having deserted from Camp Wool, and of those desertions 61 were successful. Company D had the most total desertions with 24, about 22 percent of the company, and Company H the fewest, with none.[37]

★

Captain John Anderson wrote of the men, "There was very little friction; every one took hold with zeal to learn the duties of a soldier."[38] With due respect to the captain, that was not true. When he published the regiment's history in 1896, many of the 57th's veterans were still living, and he, no doubt, did not want to open any old emotional wounds. Perhaps he was guided by the Duke of Wellington's thought that "I should like to speak the truth, but if I do I shall be torn to pieces."[39] The turn of the century was a time for forgetting as well as remembering.

There was, in fact, a significant amount of friction, primarily among the enlisted men, because of the large number of Irish soldiers in the regiment. The Irish, to most Northerners, were, as we have seen, but little above what the blacks were to most Southerners. The feelings of the native-born Americans towards the Irish had moderated a bit since the 1840s, but not much. The war, out of the necessity for manpower, had brought a more tolerant attitude towards the "Paddys," and sometimes even open admiration for their fighting spirit. But this forbearance was shallow. The old prejudices, such as were explored briefly in the raising of Company F, still were held strongly by the Protestant Yankees, and it did not take much to set tempers flying—on either side.

"A fight in the evening and 3 sent to the Guard House," noted William T. Peabody in his diary on March 15, 1864. This incident occurred in Company G, which had been mustered into service just five days before. Irish-born acting Corporal Daniel Monahan apparently had tried to give an order to Vermont-born Private Carlos Parker and another unidentified American-born member of the company, the result of which was a bare-knuckled brawl, two against one. It was broken up quickly, but as Private Peabody tells us, Major Cushing was "cross as hell" and had them all thrown into the guardhouse and "put in irons and a gag in their mouths" for two days. Monahan was stripped of his temporary corporal's rank also. The blue-eyed Irishman somehow managed to escape later that same night and tried to desert the regiment, but was caught and returned to camp. (He attempted desertion twice more, and his third attempt was successful. He never was seen again.) Parker, on the other hand, soon was transferred at his own request to Company K. He was promoted later to corporal and earned an impressive war record, serving in most of the regiment's battles until wounded.[40]

Fist fighting, although uncommon in the regiment, is not the only evidence available of this antagonism between the Americans and the Irish.

Company K, the sharpshooter company, was to be the elite organization of the regiment, and as one of its members, Private Edward M. Schneider, born in Bronza, Turkey, of American missionary parents, related in a letter, "Every effort is being made to have all Americans, and no Irishmen." It was to be the crack company, he reported, with a strong "brotherhood among the sharpshooters." There was only one enlisted man in the company who was Irish, Private Daniel Boyce, but he deserted, and Schneider and his American comrades nearly realized their wish. But a sense of gloom and betrayal must have overcome them on April 6, however, when Colonel Bartlett appointed John Reade their new second lieutenant—in effect, their commander, as no captain or first lieutenant had been assigned to the company. Privately, Lieutenant Reade surely ought to have thought his position ironic, possibly a sign that justice had been served. He came from Kilkenny.[41]

Out of the necessity for survival, the tension between these two groups would mellow with their experiences in the field, but would never end, and even when the war was over, and they aged into old men, the native-born Americans would find ways to blackball many of the Irish from their veterans' organizations.[42]

The Irish were the largest minority in the regiment, but not the only one.[43] No evidence has been uncovered as to how, for example, the nearly fifty French Canadians were treated. But a good guess would be that they were held in little better favor, as they were Roman Catholics, too, and their limited English was spoken with a thick accent that probably was offensive to the intolerant natives.

It would be unfair to say that all American-born members of the regiment felt this way about the foreign-born soldiers—or soldiers born of immigrant parents—in their ranks. Captain Anderson, for example, in mentioning the death of Sergeant John Cooley of Company A, born in Galway, Ireland, and killed in battle, referred to him as "a good soldier, a gallant man, and a genial comrade."[44]

As for everyone taking "hold with a zeal to learn the duties of a soldier," in Captain Anderson's words, it must be added that while this was generally the case, the facts tell us it was not universally so; witness, for instance, the one hundred deserters, the "awkward squads," and the sink issue. The morning reports show that as many as two dozen men on any given day were spending time in the guardhouse. The regimental general orders suggest some of the reasons for those incarcerations. Orders No. 3 directs, "The men will be instructed as to the respect due to the officers . . .," and No. 5 orders, "No gambling will be allowed in this camp. Commanders of companies will see that this order is strictly enforced." Soldiers were commonly punished for "disobedience of orders." Noncommissioned officers were often broken to the ranks for "unsoldierly conduct" or "incompetency" throughout the regiment's existence, and at least one officer, Captain Joseph Gird of Company B, was placed under arrest on February 6, 1864, although it is not known why.[45]

Major James W. Cushing was made the regiment's judge and jury in Colonel Bartlett's Regimental General Orders No. 12 of March 24, and he performed that duty with a heavy hand. The morning reports show a marked rise in the daily inmate population of the guardhouse after his appointment. Cushing was a shadowy figure, thoroughly disliked by officers and enlisted men alike, who would later resign in the field under mysterious circumstances. In a thinly veiled reference to his behavior, Anderson tells us, in discussing the problem of men slipping out of camp at night, of the "veteran 'Blue Beard' [it is hoped this is not to be taken literally] who was usually left in command when the day's exercises were over. To ask permission of him to visit the city was like 'bearding the lion in his den.' Leaving his presence with the invariable refusal, one's disappointment found some comfort in the thought that he would make quick work with the rebel hosts if he should ever be turned loose in their midst while in such a savage disposition. It was also," the captain goes on to say, "an assurance that he would do all the fighting for the whole regiment." (Although Cushing was a veteran of the 31st Massachusetts, he had served in that regiment as its quartermaster and had never been in action.)[46]

The *Fitchburg Sentinel* told its subscribers on March 4 that "good order . . . [and] healthy military discipline pervad[ed] the entire encampment."[47]

It would be incorrect to leave the impression that, in comparison with other regiments raised during that period of the war, the 57th had unique disciplinary problems overall. It did not. But neither was it composed of choirboys.

★

The regiment made its first public appearance on February 1, when five companies—A, B, D, E, and H—under Lieutenant Colonel Hollister marched into Worcester and formed part of an escort for the reenlisted members of the 21st Massachusetts home on furlough as part of their reward for having signed on for a second hitch in the army. Their train had arrived at eight o'clock the previous evening, and thousands had been at the station to welcome them home amid great shouting and cheering. At ten o'clock that

February morning, the 57th and five additional companies of the 25th Massachusetts formed their lines in front of city hall, and the returning veterans were escorted to their reception at Mechanics Hall under the command of Colonel Josiah Pickett of the 25th. Down Main Street through Lincoln Square, along Summer and Front streets, and finally back to Main they marched with local bands, cadets, fire companies, and government officials and distinguished citizens accompanying them. All along their parade route, cheering crowds lined the sidewalks, and the buildings were decorated with bunting and the national colors.

One man, marching in the van of the 21st Regiment, drew particular attention from the onlookers. He was twenty-one-year-old Sergeant Thomas Plunkett, winner of the Medal of Honor. At the battle of Fredericksburg, on December 13, 1862, he had "seized the colors of his regiment, the color bearer having been shot down, and bore them to the front, where both his arms were carried off by a shell."[48] His armless sleeves were a great curiosity to the townspeople watching him pass by.

Looking at the veterans, "all thought that their faces looked noble and stalwart,"[49] and a good deal of civilian pride was displayed for their stained and battle-worn colors. (The men of the 57th, with the possible exception of some of the regiment's own veterans, must have presented a stark contrast to these combat-hardened troops.)

At Mechanics Hall, food was served liberally to all the soldiers and civilians, after which Worcester's Mayor D. Waldo Lincoln gave a speech cordially and formally welcoming the veterans home. Colonel Clark, Governor Andrew's representative, spoke next, followed by the 21st's own Lieutenant Colonel George P. Hawkes, who described the hardships endured by his men without complaint, and boasted that 251 of them had reenlisted to see the war through. At the mention of that number, a tumultuous and spontaneous cheer from the gathering filled the hall.

The Honorable A. H. Bullock spoke following Colonel Hawkes, and his theme, accompanied by much cheering also, focused on the 21st Regiment's shredded battle flag. Using all the clichés and platitudes common to politicians of that era, he exhorted the men of the 57th to do their duty, while at the same time heaping lavish praise on the returned and reenlisted veterans and their dead comrades. "Look upon it [the flag] ye men of the Fifty-seventh . . .," he concluded, "and behold what exalted honor is in store for those who go forth for Union and Liberty and Humanity." Three cheers were given him, and the ceremonies finished.[50] The 57th would fight alongside the 21st soon in the coming campaign, but just then, neither regiment had any hint of that destiny.

On February 22, the regiment, now strengthened to seven companies with the addition of companies C and F, participated in a similar event for the returned and reenlisted men of the 25th Massachusetts. And this time, at least one member of the 57th was paying no mind to the political harangues. Sergeant James O. Halloran, of Company E, slipped away and deserted while the regiment was on parade in the city. But he soon was arrested, stripped of his rank, and thrown into the guardhouse.[51]

★

Winter let go a blast on March 30. Snow, hail, and fierce winds swept across the parade ground. The camp looked desolate, and the weather-depressed soldiers stayed in their barracks.[52]

But two days later, on April 1, 1864, it was obvious to all that winter was coming to a close. Camp Wool was turning comfortable—the snow was melting fast, and the mud drying. On the previous Monday, March 28, 898 men were listed on the regiment's rolls with only 55 of them reported unfit for duty. With the changes for the better in the weather and the now nearly full ranks, everyone knew that the day of departure was drawing near. The *Fitchburg Sentinel* speculated that "they will probably go at once to the rendezvous of Gen. Burnside's corps at Annapolis."[53] However, there were several details that had to be taken care of first.

Thursday, April 7, was a balmy, bright, sunny day, and the green of spring was beginning to make its appearance. Frank Bartlett thought it the perfect weather to parade the 57th through the streets of Worcester, and so, in full dress uniforms, the men "arrived in town at 3 P.M., and, preceded by their drum corps and a detachment of police, marched down Main street, and through Highland, Harvard, Chestnut and Pleasant streets, to the City Hall. Although their visit was unexpected, they had a crowd of spectators and admirers, for the streets were already filled with promenadors, and the sound of music attracted others to the line of march. After drilling in front of the Old South church, the regiment marched on the Common, and halted again preparatory to a dress parade."

After the dress parade, in an unexpected ceremony, the regiment was presented the national colors on behalf of the ladies of Worcester by Miss Frances M. Lincoln, a tall, slender spinster and daughter of the mayor. A large crowd had gathered spontaneously, including Miss Lincoln's father and local dignitaries. Colonel Bartlett, unsteady on his leg, accepted the flag for the regiment, and a few impromptu remarks were exchanged between him and Frances Lincoln. As she handed it to the commander, who entrusted it to the color sergeant, "the flag gently unfolded and gracefully floated out upon the evening breeze and was received by the regiment with hearty cheers." The order "rest" was given to the troops, and "immediately a veteran near the center of the line, cried out, 'How are you, colors?' which called out a general shout of laughter. The line of march was resumed, and the regiment returned to camp, with drums beating and the newly acquired colors flying as if in triumph."[54]

On Saturday, April 9, "this crack regiment [which was] getting to be a city institution . . . visited Mechanics Hall . . . to witness the exhibition of the stereoscopticon, and had a fine time."[55]

A flurry of snow fell on April 10, but the day was not cold, so the ground dried quickly, and the men were marched in full dress to Sunday services at the Old South Church in Worcester. There they were assailed with a sermon by the Reverend E. A. Walker, who took his text from Judges 5:23, that John Anderson described as "interesting and patriotic," by which Anderson, considering his penchant for the dramatic turn of phrase to describe that which did not impress him, may have meant "boring." And that afternoon, Captain Albert Prescott treated his men of Company I, in their barracks, to "a clam chowder of unexceptionable quality. The boys did the subject justice. . . ."[56]

On April 12, the Worcester State Guards and their ladies paid a social call upon Company K, and while there presented First Sergeant Samuel Souther of Company B, a graduate of Dartmouth College and Bangor Theological Seminary and a Congregationalist minister, with a sword belt and sash. After several speeches the ladies spread out a feast, which was invaded quickly by men from other companies who could not resist the delicious aromas.[57]

Governor John A. Andrew, a short, corpulent professional politician with blue eyes, came to camp for his second visit to the 57th Regiment on April 14. The colonel formed the line at eleven that morning and put the troops through their drills for the pleasure of the commonwealth's chief executive and his accompanying staff. The men then passed in review with the fife and drum corps playing rousing martial music and the new flag flying in the blue April sky. Finally, Bartlett formed the soldiers into the traditional infantry hollow square, and the governor formally presented the regiment with the state and national colors. The state flag had a white field with the blue and gold shield of the Commonwealth of Massachusetts and the regiment's number and title on it. Andrew then orated to the boys—the usual political rhetoric and hyperbole—and Frank Bartlett responded in kind. Nevertheless, the men, for the most part, were impressed to be in the presence of such distinguished company, and after the speeches cheers went up, and "hearty applause" was rendered. William Peabody's son, Frank, was visiting him at the time, and the elder Peabody wrote in his diary that "Frank shook hands with the governor. Complimented very highly."[58]

During the festivities, Colonel Wetherell of the governor's staff presented Captain Joseph Gird of Company B with an expensive field glass.[59] Why he was singled out for that presentation is not known. (He was the only officer in the regiment to be arrested at Camp Wool, it will be remembered.)

The night of April 15 was a gloomy time for the men, as they watched a late spring blizzard cover all the green that they were just beginning to enjoy, and in the morning details were organized to shovel and clear some of the parade ground. When that had been done, the regimental line was formed, and as a man's name was called, he stepped forward, signed the payroll, and was paid his state bounty by the commonwealth's paymaster. Colonel Bartlett had some things to say to his soldiers also. He announced, in his "deep bass voice," that Lieutenant Colonel Hollister had resigned that morning, but he did not tell them why. It seems that Mrs. Hollister had had enough of her husband's soldiering, and had convinced him to quit the army. In his journal entry of March 31, 1864, Bartlett wrote, "[Hollister] came back last night. He is going to resign, I am sorry to say. His wife has persuaded him. It is the weakest thing I ever saw in him. I lose faith in man's firmness and woman's fortitude."[60]

The second bit of news he had for them was far more important. The regiment would leave for the "seat of the war" in two days, on Monday, April 18, 1864.

3

The Girl I Left Behind Me

F OR THE REST OF THE DAY on Saturday and all of the next day, Sunday,
April 17, the regiment was busy preparing to depart for the war. Some
of the men were able to wrangle last-minute passes home, such as Private
Francis Harrington of Company K, who noted in his diary that he received
"a pass tonight until 11 O'clock P.M. tomorrow," while others, like William
Peabody, had their families with them at camp right up to the last moment;
he wrote in his journal on the 18th that "Hannah and Ellen [his daughter]
were at Camp Wool until I left. . . ."[1]

On Sunday, the camp "was thronged with visitors who wished to see and
bid farewell to the men of the 57th regiment," recorded the *Massachusetts
Spy* on April 20. The article continued, "It was a cold, windy and dusty day,
but that did not prevent a crowd at camp. While most of the visitors [were]
those who were willing to aid the departing soldiers in any way possible, there
were a few depraved villans who took occasion to steal from two or three
soldiers their bounty money, and late in the afternoon, citizens were ordered
over the lines. There was the usual dress parade, Major Cushing commanding, and at which the captains of companies were ordered to get ready two
days cooked rations for their men."[2]

The boys checked their gear and packed their belongings in their knapsacks. "These articles when packed upon a man's back," wrote John Anderson, ". . . made considerable of a load. A small man looked all knapsack, with
his legs hanging outside to steer by."[3]

★

Monday was beautiful, the weather balmy and clear. It was April 18, 1864.
Shortly after the noon meal, the 57th Massachusetts Volunteers formed on
the camp's parade ground for the last time, and the men were given their final
instructions. The regiment then marched a short distance east across their

campground to board a special train of the Norwich & Worcester Railroad that was waiting for them on the tracks that ran through the edge of Camp Wool.[4]

Nine hundred and sixteen officers and enlisted men of the regiment, with the fifers and drummers playing "The Girl I Left Behind Me," and with the colors softly fluttering in the gentle spring breeze, left Camp Wool that day, and the grounds were filled with civilians who watched with pride as Colonel Bartlett led the nearly quarter-mile-long column of blue-uniformed soldiers past them. It was a grand sight, and the people cheered the new regiment.[5]

Most of the boys were in "excellent spirits" as they started their journey, but Frank Bartlett had taken precautions against desertion on the trip. A number of the men who had been confined in the guardhouse for trying to run from camp had been released that morning to join their comrades in the ranks, and that fact, coupled with the wave of desertions that had occurred in the past two days since bounties had been paid, induced the colonel to place trusted guards strategically, but discreetly, in the formation. The company officers alternated heading up this detail, and First Lieutenant George Barton of Company C wrote his mother on April 26 that he "had command of the guard on Sunday and Monday [April 24 and 25]." (The 57th's brother regiment, the 56th Massachusetts, traveled all the way to the front completely under guard.)[6]

After final good-byes with families, sweethearts, and friends, the men loaded the regimental baggage and horses, clambered aboard the cars, stowed their rifles and knapsacks, and found their seats. They hung out of the open windows for farewell kisses and handshakes and grabbed last-minute food packages that, in not a few cases, contained carefully hidden whiskey bottles. All this activity was zealously, but quietly, watched by the guards, officers, and noncommissioned officers, who carefully checked for men trying to escape in the commotion. But one did anyway. Private Franklin Card, of Company D, managed to elude the watch. But Card, possibly because of his conspicuous height—he was over six feet tall—was arrested later that day and sent back to the regiment on Tuesday.[7]

When all the soldiers were finally on and counted by the first sergeants, the conductor, at Colonel Bartlett's instruction, gave his signal, and the train pulled out of the Worcester station at two o'clock that afternoon for the sixty-mile trip to Norwich, Connecticut, on the first leg of the regiment's journey. It was a lovely, warm ride through the little villages of Auburn, Oxford, and Webster, Massachusetts, and then, after entering Connecticut, due south through Wilsonville, North Grosvenor Dale, Mechanics Ville, Putnam, Killingly, Wauregan, Plainfield, Jewett City, and finally, the regiment's port of embarkation, Norwich. The trip took but a few hours.[8]

Some of the men came from the towns through which they passed on that bright April afternoon,[9] and there were sure to have been long, last looks at their villages by those boys. Meanwhile, for most of the regiment's soldiers, there was the general relief of being on the move at last. They were finally heading for the great unknown adventure and leaving behind the monotony and routine of Camp Wool and winter. Exhilaration certainly must have bounded through the cars, helped along by the fine spring weather, the beautiful green countryside, the pleasant New England hamlets passing them by, and, probably for some, a few drops of whiskey.

★

The regiment arrived on the siding at the run-down First Ferry Street Station in Norwich later that afternoon, and the men climbed off the train and formed in columns of companies for roll call. When Frank Bartlett was satisfied that all was in order, the command formed in line of march, and the men tramped off to the gaily painted and beflagged Norwich Line terminal at Pier 40 along the river. After loading the regimental baggage and the staff officers' horses, the boys climbed over the gunwales, and crowded onto the decks and into the passenger cabin of the leased government steam transport *City of Norwich,* for departure on the next leg of their journey.[10]

The *City of Norwich* was a relatively new vessel, and she was probably in not as bad condition as most military transports of the time, which were usually filthy and infested with rats and vermin. She was a low-slung, long, shallow-draft wooden boat with enormous paddle wheels on either side of the hull and two slender, black smokestacks towering high above the white-painted cabin on her weather deck. Rectangular open windows measuring one and a half by two feet were provided every few yards around the cabin for passengers to enjoy the ocean views. The steamer was packed with soldiers and equipment, and barely an inch of deck space was left unclaimed.[11] Sentries probably were posted on the bow and fantail and on top of the wheelhouse to see that no one slipped over the side and swam to the safety of the riverbanks. No one did.

At eight o'clock that evening the captain shouted orders to the ship's crew to get under way.[12] When everything was ready, the bow and stern lines were cast off, and, laboriously, the vessel slipped her moorings and maneuvered out into the stream. The clumsy transport plodded down the Thames River trailed by flocks of hungry sea gulls catching fish churned up by the giant wheels.

Looking through the windows of the cabin or leaning against the railings in the salty breeze on the deck over the passenger cabin, the soldiers chatted and enjoyed the twilight scenery along the riverbanks as they steamed past Allyn's Point, Gales Ferry, and the port city of New London, Connecticut, on their fifteen-mile excursion to the mouth of the Thames and Block Island

The *City of Norwich* at the docks in Norwich, Connecticut.
(Mystic Seaport Museum, Mystic, Conn.)

Sound.[13] After dark, most of the men searched out places to lie down for the night—likely a few simply passed out from too much drink and slept where they fell.

Steering south-southeast and passing between Montauk Point and Block Island that night, the *City of Norwich* came around Long Island, and the captain reckoned a westerly course past Brighton Beach. Going through the Narrows at dawn, the ship entered New York Harbor, passing Brooklyn and the Battery at lower Manhattan on the starboard side, and then docked at six o'clock the following morning, April 19, at the bustling, international port of Jersey City.[14]

New York Harbor must have been a thrilling sight for most of these provincial New Englanders, and, in their perfect innocence, it seemed all part of the grand adventure of soldiering. Francis Harrington noted that he had had "a pleasant trip," but William Peabody, not exactly an excited tourist, wrote nonchalantly that "nothing of importance occurred on the passage." The officers seemed to have enjoyed themselves well enough, though. First Lieutenant George E. Barton of Company C commented in a letter sent home to his mother, "We had a very pleasant trip," and he added, "The regiment behaved splendidly everything goes well."[15]

However, not everyone in the regiment behaved as splendidly as Lieutenant Barton would have liked his mother to believe. The men disembarked at eight that morning, and while waiting on the docks, which were bristling with activity, former Sergeant Charles Abbott of Company E saw his chance and took off in the bedlam of the busy wharves. He was never heard from again. It was hardly difficult for a man to go unnoticed on those clamorous piers. Soldiers, sailors, and civilians mingled everywhere, and army and commercial goods were piled high all along the quays. Keeping track of everyone was impossible.[16]

The 57th waited on the Jersey City landings until twelve-thirty that afternoon, when the men were loaded on cars for Philadelphia, and the train pulled out of the Jersey City station at two o'clock. The trip was a pleasant one of seventy-five miles, and the regiment arrived at Baltimore Station in Philadelphia early that evening. The boys had passed fat, prosperous farms and lovely, green forests along the way, and their spirits, for the most part, remained high.[17]

Following another roll call in the station, which showed three more desertions, the regiment marched into the city, and there the soldiers were feasted and entertained at the Cooper Refreshment Rooms on Otsego Street, near Washington Avenue. Those rooms were located in a privately funded complex of buildings staffed and maintained by patriotic and sympathetic locals for the purpose of providing refreshment to the troops as they passed through the city on their way to the front. Hundreds of Union regiments en route to battle had been cared for at Cooper's during the war, and it was an extremely popular place with the troops.[18]

After passing several hospitable hours gorging themselves in the brightly lighted rooms containing row upon row of long tables heaped with delicious food, and washing off the grime of the journey with washbasins and clean towels provided them by the volunteers at Cooper's, the men of the 57th Massachusetts formed the line for yet another roll call. The regiment then marched back across the city to the depot and at ten o'clock took cars of "all descriptions" to Baltimore, Maryland.[19]

The hastily assembled train of passenger cars of the Philadelphia, Wilmington, & Baltimore Railroad, along with boxcars that had uncomfortable, rough wooden seats crudely nailed to the inside walls and no ventilation or windows except cracks between the siding boards and partially opened side doors, took them an additional eighty-five miles through Pennsylvania, Delaware, and Maryland. At Havre de Grace, Maryland, the entire train was loaded onto a huge ferry to cross the Susquehanna River. The men marveled at this modern triumph of engineering.[20]

From Havre de Grace to Baltimore, the railroad—especially its bridges and crossings—was guarded by strong picket details.[21] The army was taking no chances of sabotage in that region of vacillating loyalties, and for many in the regiment this was their first observation of military operations in the field.

In Baltimore, where the train arrived at six o'clock the next morning, April 20, 1864, the regiment "marched part way through the city stacked arms and about 11 O'clock took dinner," and the new men were introduced to field army rations—hardtack and salt pork. The realities of soldiering were being revealed rapidly, and the recruits did not like some of those realities at all. Army food was nothing new to the veterans, and they had cautioned the new men about military fare. Nevertheless, the food was a shock to the soldiers who were used to the "uneatable rations" of Camp Wool, and they moaned and groaned about it. "Very tired and no appetite for this grub," commented William Peabody, but he added, "I think I shall stand the press if I take care of myself and that I intend to do." But the recruits' complaining fell on deaf ears, and their officers and the veteran soldiers told them to get used to it.[22]

After the stop in Baltimore, the regiment loaded up again at noon, and the train—which did not get under way until 3:00 P.M.—clattered and swayed over the rickety tracks of the Annapolis & Elkridge Railroad to Annapolis, Maryland, forty miles further. Most all of the men's conversations were focused on events to come, and, except for the disappointment over the quality of military food, their enthusiasm had not dwindled much as they passed over the rolling, green countryside.[23]

The 57th arrived in Annapolis at nine o'clock that night, April 20, at the huge IX Army Corps encampment beside the blue waters of Chesapeake Bay, and after detraining and roll call, all of the companies except K were directed by an army guide to a plowed field two miles from the center of the city, where the men set up camp. This was the first time that most of the soldiers had had the pleasure of sleeping on the hard ground, and few of the novices spent a comfortable night.[24] But to the veterans, of course, bivouacking in the field was old hat.

Company K was detailed to unload the quartermaster's and commissary stores and regimental baggage from the train, and those men did not reach camp until two o'clock the next morning.[25]

★

For miles and miles, as far as the eye could see, the camps of the IX Corps' regiments stretched in all directions in and around the buildings and property of the United States Naval Academy—the school's administration and classes had been moved to Newport, Rhode Island, in May of 1861 for the duration of the war. The bivouacs were laid out perfectly, with almost mathematical precision, to military regulations. New white "A" tents (so named for their shape), gaily decorated with wreaths and boughs of pine and holly, lined wide, clean company streets with the colorful individual regimental flags floating above each of their brilliant headquarters tents. However, the situation was not completely idyllic, and flies known as bluebottles infested the camp.[26]

There were some exceptions to the cleanliness and order. The men of the 35th Massachusetts Volunteer Infantry, newly arrived from Tennessee after long and hard service with the corps, still had their mildewed and smoke-stained tents—along with their campaign-worn uniforms and equipment. (Some of the veteran regiments, with the exception of the 35th and several others, had drawn new clothing and supplies from the quartermaster's department after arriving in Annapolis.)[27]

One of the new cavalry regiments clinging to the spirit of 1861, the 3rd New Jersey Hussars, had shown up wearing European-style uniforms with so much gold braid on their jackets that the veterans, in their plain blue clothes, ridiculed the dandies at every opportunity, derisively dubbing them "The Butterflies."[28] But this regiment was an exception in the sea of standard 1864 army blue.

The activities in the camps were never ending. Regiments of infantry and cavalry and batteries of artillery drilled and paraded constantly, and bands played day and night. The veteran outfits were not nearly as prone to participating in these activities as the new regiments, and they took extraordinary measures to avoid any but the most vital duties, to the disdain of the new men, who thought them sloppy and insubordinate. In turn, the tried campaigners took pleasure in needling the rookie soldiers and playing practical jokes on them whenever possible, even though they thought that their discipline was too harsh. Soldiering had become an ordinary way of life to the old-timers.[29]

★

Soon after the 57th's arrival in Annapolis, Lieutenant Colonel Charles Lyon Chandler, a twenty-four-year-old civil engineer and veteran combat officer of three Massachusetts regiments (1st, 34th, and 40th), reported to the regiment and took over the resigned Lieutenant Colonel Hollister's duties as second in command.[30]

★

Thursday, the 21st of April, was pleasant, but a stiff breeze was blowing in off the bay. Twenty men were detailed to police the 57th's new camp that morning, the commander wishing to make a good impression on the other regiments and the general staff of the IX Corps. The enlisted men dutifully set about their job, and picked up the area. When they had finished, the lieutenant in charge of the work party reported the assignment completed to the regimental Officer of the Day. The Officer of the Day, whose identity, unfortunately, is unknown, then made an inspection, and not finding the work done to his apparently meticulous standards, "disapproved the report in a very positive manner," ordering the lieutenant to have the men do the job again. But this time he told him to have the whole campground swept with brooms. The boys, probably guessing what was going to happen (and very likely seeing a good chance to embarrass the foolish martinet, as well), swept the field as ordered, creating large dust clouds that the strong breezes carried throughout the bivouac and into neighboring camps. Howls of protest undoubtedly sprang from the affected camps, and John Anderson noted sardonically, "The sanitary improvements that were thereby made have not been discovered to this day."[31]

While the camp was being policed by some men, others were assigned different tasks. Private Harrington wrote in his diary on April 21 that he "worked all day fixing Co[mpany] stores," and Private Peabody complained, "Here at Camp Annapolis cooking and working hard for U.[ncle] Sam. Most tired out. Work too the hardest I ever done in my life or ever wish to Hannah."[32]

★

Major General Ambrose E. Burnside's IX Army Corps, after arriving from rough duty in eastern Tennessee, was being reorganized at Annapolis for the spring campaign. Among the new additions to the corps were five regiments of cavalry and twelve of infantry (one being the 57th), and five batteries of light artillery. This brought the corps' effective strength up to about twenty-five thousand men, including the newly added 4th Division, which was made up entirely of black troops commanded by white officers. There were some six thousand men in the 4th Division.[33]

The 57th was assigned to the 1st Brigade, 1st Division, of the IX Corps under Brigadier General Thomas G. Stevenson, and the brigade was commanded by Colonel Sumner Carruth of the 35th Massachusetts.[34]

The 1st Brigade was composed of the 35th Massachusetts and the 4th and 10th United States Regular Infantry Regiments (the latter two had not yet arrived), all of which were tried and true veteran combat outfits with a good deal of iron-hard fighting service tucked under their belts. The new boys on the brigade's block were the 56th, 57th, and 59th Massachusetts Volunteers, and part of the reason the green regiments were assigned to this brigade was for the veteran organizations to keep them in line and set them a good example. The battle-hardened infantrymen of the old regiments were tough, no-nonsense fighters, and, aside from the mutual respect they shared with the reenlisted soldiers of the three rookie regiments, they thought little of these new outfits of Johnny-come-lately bounty men—nor did they trust them.[35] Moreover, the high number of Irish immigrants in their ranks—whom, for the most part, those veterans cared little for—probably only fueled the fires of their disdain.

The regiment remained in camp at Annapolis for a little over two days getting organized, and the men familiarized themselves, as best they could, with the massive army corps to which they now belonged. The activity, noise, and power surrounding them was dynamic and tremendous, and the new soldiers were overwhelmed and fascinated by the great energy of that military body.

Fortunately for Colonel Bartlett, the 57th had arrived late at the IX Corps rendezvous. The city of Annapolis was seething with cheap saloons and with whores, thieves, murderers, gamblers, and other unsavory types ready to prey on the soldiers whenever the chance presented itself. Other regiments which had been in the camp for several weeks, such as the 56th Massachusetts, had serious problems maintaining discipline with its soldiers, who sneaked into town whenever they could to get drunk and visit the bawdy houses. Desertions were just as high with most of those new regiments as with the 57th, which lost six more soldiers while at that encampment—some of the shrewd men very likely buying civilian clothes, which made escape quite easy. Other soldiers carelessly fell in with the wrong elements, and several cases of murder and robbery were reported at the camp (but not in the 57th). It was not uncommon to find soldiers in the woods with their throats slashed and their pockets turned out. Courts-martial were held every day, and many of the new regiments had had guardhouses built in their bivouacs, which were generally full of prisoners.[36]

★

The men spent all day Thursday, the 21st, packing their dress, nine-button frock coats and Hardee hats and donning their standard, four-button fatigue blouses and forage caps. The fancy uniforms were boxed and left with the quartermaster's department in Annapolis to be forwarded to the regiment at an unspecified future date. The boys also drew shelter tent halves and other camp equipment.[37]

Company K's men, who had been without firearms—as they had been promised the Spencer repeaters which could not be procured while they were at Camp Wool—finally were issued rifled muskets from the IX Corps' ordnance depot on April 22, but unlike the other companies of the 57th, which all had Springfields, the sharpshooter company's boys drew English-made Enfields. This no doubt pleased them somewhat, because unlike the Springfields, which had all bright surfaces on the steel parts and rusted easily, the Enfields' steel barrels were blued and many of the fittings were made from brass, and keeping them clean was much easier. Their disadvantage, however, was that they weighed somewhat more than Springfields, and on a march, that weight difference made the men a little less comfortable.[38]

Also on the 22nd, parties of men from each company were detailed to go into Annapolis to draw rations for the regiment. Those parties returned to camp around three that afternoon, and the company cooks immediately got busy preparing five days' rations to be distributed to the men on Saturday morning. Other preparations for departure also continued all day Friday along with last-minute drills.[39]

When they arrived on the 20th, the men had been told at evening roll call that they would start for the front at 4:00 A.M., Saturday, April 23, and the groups around the campfires on Friday night were abuzz with chatter. The soldiers talked over the rumors and speculations that had been circulating among the veteran regiments of the IX Corps that they would set off soon for the Carolinas, where the corps had achieved a very respectable record before being transferred to eastern Tennessee—no one was especially longing for a fight in 1864, and the Carolinas were considered easy duty. But nobody, except the highest officers, knew where they really were going. Ever since the corps had arrived at Annapolis, the men had stared off into Chesapeake Bay looking in vain for transport ships that would ferry them back to the North Carolina coast. The veterans of the IX Corps could see no other logic in their being sent to a port for reorganization, and their reasoning made sense to the new soldiers.[40]

★

The drummers beat reveille at four o'clock on the morning of April 23, and after a hasty breakfast, the men struck their tents and loaded the 57th's baggage wagons. Then they stood in line to draw their rations from the company cooks. The boys also were told that they were heading to Virginia, and thoughts of going to North Carolina were generally abandoned.[41]

At six o'clock the 57th was formed in a column of companies with ranks open and knapsacks unslung for a thorough inspection by company commanders, with Colonels Bartlett and Chandler supervising. The purpose of that inspection was to see that the men carried nothing not authorized by regulations. The plan of the day was "heavy marching order," and extra weight would slow the men down.[42]

In their knapsacks they had their underwear, extra clothing and shoes, stationery, photographs, toothbrushes, razors, soap, books, letters, playing cards, and their "housewives," which were carried rolled up and tied. (When unrolled, they revealed scissors, sponges, combs, brushes, and pockets for needles and thread and other items. The housewife was not an issued item, but it was a very necessary piece of personal equipment, and many of the men bought theirs or were given them by friends or relatives while at Camp Wool.) Their fully loaded knapsacks weighed about twenty pounds, with six different straps to attach them to the men's bodies, and the soldiers frequently complained of their discomfort. (Veterans often discarded them in favor of putting their personal items in their blankets, which they rolled up and wore slung over one shoulder and tied at the opposite hip.)[43]

The 57th's soldiers were permitted only their arms and equipment, five days' rations in their haversacks, and one each of a change of underwear, a blanket, a greatcoat, an extra pair of shoes in their knapsacks, a tin cup, a tin plate, and a fork, knife and spoon. During the inspection, however, the officers found a considerable surplus of material in the men's packs, and they ordered them to throw away all their unauthorized personal items and mementos, which they did—very reluctantly. But, just as soon as the officers' backs were turned, the boys "slyly" retrieved their little treasures and slipped them back into their knapsacks. "It seemed like such a sacrilege to leave such things scattered upon the ground."[44]

Inspection over, nothing seemed to happen. Private Harrington wrote that at "7 A.M. The Regt is resting in front of camp." Forming twenty-five thousand men and masses of horse-drawn equipment into marching order was no small task, but at about eight-fifteen the mighty IX Corps began to move. The 57th fell in with the corps' ranks at nine o'clock.[45]

In a fanfare of regimental bands and singing soldiers, Ambrose Burnside's men were off for the spring campaign. The 35th Massachusetts led the 1st Brigade of the 1st Division as it followed in its place in the command. The land over which the soldiers marched following the line of the Annapolis & Elkridge Railroad was fairly level, so the boys had few hills to climb, and at first the journey seemed little more than a pleasant outing. But the temperature rose quickly as the morning wore on, and soon the fifty pounds or so of gear that each man carried and their hot woolen uniforms became unbearable in the steaming Maryland sun. So the recruits did what thousands of inexperienced soldiers had done before them—they started throwing their equipment away.[46]

Most of the novice Federals' parochial attitudes about climate and geography told them that the first item of discomfort to go was the gray, woolen army blanket. After all, they reasoned, wasn't this the South where it never got cold? That train of logic then extended to the bulky, kersey greatcoats, and that garment became the next item to litter the dusty road. Why would anyone in his right mind need something as useless as this in the hot Southern summer? In a short while some of the men were down to their rifles, the necessities with which to fire them, and the clothes on their backs.[47]

The majority of the new men were told by the veterans—most of whom threw little if anything away—to keep their gear because they would need it very soon. The nights got cold sometimes, they warned. However, human nature being what it is, the rookies paid no attention, never realizing that their amateur weather predictions were to prove drastically miscalculated.

The Bladensburg road on which the men were marching rather quietly— the bands and singing had died out early in the heat—presently became utterly littered for miles and miles with every conceivable item of military issue and hundreds of stragglers. Twenty-five thousand soldiers could dispose of a lot of material, and some of the men took note of the "number of Jewish traders from Annapolis" who were following the corps in their wagons that day, reaping a very profitable harvest of tossed-off army property.[48]

The IX Corps made fourteen hard miles that Saturday, and in the evening the men went into bivouac on some rolling meadows near a clear, winding brook a mile east of the Patuxent River. William Peabody noted that for "3 hours the [other] troops have been passing a given point," meaning a point in the 57th's camp. Company assignments were made, tents were set up on company streets, and coffee and supper cooked. The veteran outfits, who had done away with most military formalities long ago, had their camps in order quickly, but the new regiments, including the 57th, did everything according to regulations, taking time to stack arms formally and march off in formation, by companies, to draw water from the creek. The well-seasoned campaigners of the old fighting units thought all this by-the-book nonsense hilarious, and they taunted the new soldiers without mercy.[49]

The boys were now on a steady diet of hardtack and salt pork, and they detested it. A few were getting sick from it, but they had no choice but to eat the awful stuff and grumble. And grumble they did—ceaselessly throughout their military service.[50]

They also complained that they were being marched too hard, and when the soldiers in the veteran regiments got wind of that, their amusement turned to unease. If these new men could not take a simple march, what good would they be in battle? they asked one another. Those men who had marched and fought so long and so hard were genuinely concerned for the safety of the army and a Northern victory in the war, and to them these greenhorn regiments seriously jeopardized their welfare and that victory. However, Lieutenant Barton took a different view of his regiment's performance: "the boys stood it well and deserve just praise our men behaved like old veterans all the way through."[51]

Pickets were thrown out around the camp, and the men of the 57th, who were bivouacked near the center of the corps—possibly to intimidate would-be deserters—could see the thousands of twinkling and flickering campfires up and down the creek banks, some being eclipsed from time to time by a passing sentry as he paced his beat. As the evening slipped into night, the temperature dipped sharply, and the fair-weather forecasters spent a miserable night with no protection from the cold. And few took pity on them either. John Anderson reported that the boys were "no doubt, reflecting upon the fast fading glamour of soldier life as the stern realities were appearing. How changed everything seemed."[52]

Fifes and drums and bugles sounded reveille throughout the massive IX Corps camp at dawn the next morning, and the soldiers assembled for morning roll call with aching legs, swollen feet, and limitless complaints. No deserters were noted in the 57th, and Doctors White and Heath saw to the men's disorders. After the soldiers were dismissed, they set to work fanning the embers of the previous night's fires to boil their coffee and cook their breakfasts. When they were finished eating, they struck their tents at 5:00 A.M. and loaded them into the regimental baggage wagons. At six o'clock the men hefted on their equipment and shouldered their rifles, and the companies, regiments, brigades, and divisions of the corps were mysteriously formed into marching order by the shrill commands of officers, sergeants, and corporals amid the clanking of gear, floury dust, coughing, chattering, cursing, and confusion, the latter prevalent mostly in the new, poorly drilled regiments like the 57th—and very much to the frustration of their embarrassed officers.[53]

The orders of march were relayed from top to bottom, and at eight o'clock the long, blue files set off on the next leg of their southwestern trek towards Washington, with Carruth's 1st Brigade taking up the van of the corps.[54] The miles-long column of blue-clad soldiers, with their endless wagons and thousands of horses and mules, with their richly embroidered and colorful flags flying, and drummer boys beating cadence for the men to keep step, and the regimental bands playing lively marching tunes, was a remarkable spectacle. And the talking, shouted commands, tramping feet, banging equipment, braying mules, snorting horses, and creaking wagons and artillery sounded a cacophonous low roar. The sweet scents of spring were overpowered by the chalky dust, human sweat, and animal odors and droppings. The thousands and thousands of brightly polished Springfields on the shoulders of the men gave off dazzling reflections in the bright sun, and the corps, balanced against the lush green landscape, presented a masterpiece of ambling and swaying color.

The day started comfortably, with the dew of the early morning covering the land, but as the sun rose towards meridian passage, the temperature soared once again, and the inhuman conditions of the previous day prevailed among the men. George Barton wrote that "Sunday [April 24] was not a day of rest by any means we spent long morning very *warm*, little water only a few men fell out." The morning's march was also especially irritating because the column had to halt every few minutes to close up its ranks. Every time the soldiers got started, it seemed, some officer was stopping them, and that annoyance, combined with the heat, quickly rubbed nerves raw.[55]

When they had arrived at the Patuxent, the crossing was made laboriously at a knee-deep ford of the river.[56] Those who had not removed their shoes were miserable as the cheap leather dried on their feet in the hot sun, causing painful chafing and blisters.

Once more, as the temperature rose, the road became covered with army gear thrown away by the green soldiers, but this time, in the 1st Division, the 35th Massachusetts was marching at the rear of its brigade, and the men of that regiment had a wonderful time picking up the tossed-off goods. They had not been resupplied at Annapolis, and their uniforms and equipment were in rough shape, so, as they followed the new 56th, 57th, and 59th Massachusetts regiments, they felt like they had been turned loose in the quartermaster's stores. They picked up everything of value to them: books, stationery, toilet articles, new uniforms, and shoes thrown out of knapsacks, plus blankets, overcoats, and other gear.[57] It was Christmas. Those men, from hard-learned experience, knew very well the necessity of being properly supplied in the field, and they wasted no time taking advantage of their rearguard situation.

Stragglers and exhausted and overheated men also lined the road and wandered in nearby woods and pastures looking for creeks. The soldiers' canteens had run dry, and water was paramount to them—the thirst of the men was brutal. And as the day slowly wore on—as days of suffering seem to do—relief appeared to be coming as the troops looking at the sky off to the southwest saw big, black thunderheads forming. The boys were marching directly into them, and presently the weary corps was enjoying the welcome raindrops, that then turned to heavy showers, and finally to a drenching, driving downpour. At last the men made camp at ten o'clock that night along the Bladensburg road on Folly Branch River after a soaking and muddy march. They had tramped twenty more miles that day, and they were "tired, hungry and wet."[58] The corps was now seventeen miles by road from Washington.

Following a miserable night's sleep on the mucky campground, the troops were up and through their early morning routines and on the march toward Washington by seven o'clock the next morning, April 25. At three o'clock that afternoon the dinner halt was made at Camp Barry, four miles from Washington, and after fording several more creeks and branches, they were on the outskirts of the capital, and they could see the unfinished capitol dome in the distance. "Took a survey of the city," commented Private Peabody. "It is rather a nice place [and] . . . a splendid sight."[59]

With dinner finished, the officers had their men clean their equipment and brush their uniforms. Then the soldiers were formed by platoons into neat columns of march behind their colors, bands, and field and staff officers, and with all the pomp and protocol of a great army, the IX Corps began the march into Washington. The rain of the previous day and night had settled the dust, and the weather was cool and clear—not a cloud in the sky. The men of the 57th were eager and expectant as they paced off down New York Avenue at the head of the column in their best marching order—they were anxious for the president to see what a proud new regiment they were.

Thousands of cheering spectators, the poet Walt Whitman among them, lined the streets, and the men in the veteran regiments were amused by the comments and finger-pointing from the citizenry about themselves and their worn battle flags. Bunting and the national colors were displayed on buildings everywhere, and the military brass bands struck up their liveliest airs. The atmosphere was electric with color and sound, a feast of pageantry for the senses. At Fourteenth Street the column halted briefly to close ranks in preparation for passing in review.

The grand parade began with the drummers beating cadence, and the men got into step and marched past Willard's Hotel, where, on a balcony over the entrance, President Lincoln, head uncovered, General Burnside, and dignitaries and staff officers watched them pass. Both houses of Congress had adjourned for the occasion, and the senators and congressmen were on hand for the festivities. "Every man was enabled to get a good look at [the president]," and when the six new regiments of the recently joined all-black 4th Division passed him, the former slaves went wild with jubilation and cheers for Lincoln, while the white soldiers and the crowds giggled and laughed at their rhythmic antics, which they thought hilarious.

When the 57th had completed its part in the parade, "the Colonel [Bartlett] complimented the regiment very highly for their marching when passing in review after such a hard march as we had today."[60]

The 57th Regiment, along with the rest of the 1st Division, continued south straight across the Long Bridge over the Potomac River and "encamped at the base of Alexandria hights [sic] under the guns of Fort Scott . . . just before dark near good water." A portion of the regiment, including Company F, did not arrive in the camp until midnight, however, because "3 baggage wagons turned over made us late." And those men were reported as "very tired."[61]

4

Storm Across the Rapidan

THEY WERE NOW in Virginia—"on the blood-stained soil." But, even so, some of the IX Corps' rank and file were still of the opinion that they were in Alexandria solely for the purpose of securing water transportation to the Carolinas.[1]

Near some old whitewashed barracks in the fort, the regiment's camp was laid out quickly, tents erected, firewood and water foraged, fires lighted, and supper eaten. The men were exhausted from their hard marching, and Colonel Carruth, commander of the brigade, ordered the 56th Massachusetts' band to play for the soldiers' pleasure. It was an excellent band, and the musicians serenaded the boys with "The Soldiers' Chorus" by Faust and other "melodies of home and love." Following the performance of the 56th's band, the band of the 10th United States Regulars—which was with the Corps despite the fact that the regiment's infantrymen had still not rejoined the ranks—played, and it, too, was well received by the soldiers. The music was soothing, and it lifted the men's spirits.[2]

★

The 57th spent Tuesday, April 26, in regular camp routines and drilling. The 1st Division's bivouacs were visited and inspected by General Stevenson—especially those of the new men. This was his first chance to take a close, hard look at his brand-new regiments in the field. The veterans were very pleased to see him, and the recruits were proud to be in his command. He was extremely popular with the soldiers. Stevenson was the only general officer present with the IX Corps at that time, and several junior officers were concerned about the absence of the other generals. The impression of those subalterns was that the IX Corps was "loosely conducted."[3]

General Burnside, famous for his enormous side whiskers, had not officially rejoined his corps, and Brigadier General Orlando B. Willcox, formerly colonel of the 1st Michigan Volunteer Infantry and now commander of the

3rd Division, was temporarily in charge of the IX Corps. He too, however, was away at that time.[4]

Mail was delivered to the regiment that day, and during their free hours, the men wrote letters home and gossiped with their messmates.[5] The pass in review before the president had been thrilling, and they all agreed that it had been an event they would remember to their dying day—which for many would not be long. They spoke their minds about the hardships of army life, and the excitement of finally being on Southern soil. They pondered the battles sure to come, and they talked tenderly of the families certain to miss them if the worst should happen.

Lieutenant Barton wrote to his mother, "We are now in camp enjoying a *short* rest, for the 9th Corps never rests a great while at a time. I presume we are to join the *Army* of the *Potomac* but do not know certain at all events we mean *business.*"[6]

William T. Peabody noted in his diary that he "rested in camp. Many sick with sore feet and tired."[7]

★

Two failed to answer roll call in the 57th on the morning of April 26. Privates Charles St. Onge of Company E and Alfred Taft of Company G had deserted the regiment in Washington. Nineteen days later, Taft, known to his officers as a "thief," joined Company B, 11th Connecticut Volunteer Infantry. He soon deserted that outfit for bounty, too. He surrendered to the authorities the following March, and was pardoned under a presidential proclamation of amnesty. St. Onge was never seen again. Men of their character would have been small use in battle; still, they were depleting the regiment's ranks at an alarming rate. There were also a substantial number of men who would be left in army hospitals in the Washington area when the 57th moved on. The march had been too much for them, and they were unfit for further travel. Private William Rice of Company A, a veteran of the 13th Massachusetts Volunteers, had become so disabled during the journey that the surgeons felt he would never again be fit to be a soldier, and he was discharged for disability from an army hospital in Alexandria on April 24. The regiment now stood at just a little under three-quarter strength.[8]

★

Reveille sounded at four o'clock, and at five on Wednesday morning, the 27th of April, camp was broken. The men of the 57th Massachusetts, as well as the soldiers of the other regiments in the corps, had been issued four days' rations and forty rounds of ammunition each the previous evening. And the top brass was beginning to make an appearance. "Genl Burnside is here riding around," wrote Francis Harrington in his diary that day.[9]

The IX Corps moved out, heading west-northwest on the Leesburg Turnpike at eight o'clock with its destination the Rappahannock River and its purpose to link up with the Army of the Potomac, which was still camped in winter quarters along that river's banks and in neighboring areas.[10] The veterans knew instinctively that they were in for some hard campaigning under the brand-new lieutenant general commanding all the Union armies, who had made his headquarters with the Army of the Potomac—Ulysses Simpson "Sam" Grant, the diminutive, cigar-addicted Federal chief. Unlike most past Union army commanders, Grant never seemed to quit until he had victory, and Abraham Lincoln had appointed him to his new position for that very reason. In the Western campaigns, he had been virtually unstoppable. Nevertheless, the men of the Army of the Potomac were skeptical; from hard experience, they knew that Robert E. Lee was not just some frontier Confederate general.[11]

The day was hot and dusty as the IX Corps took up its march across the rolling, green, unfenced fields, dotted here and there with woods near the streams. The men were on their way towards Fairfax Court House, Virginia, and as the hours went by and the sun climbed to its zenith, the day grew hotter, and the boys choked on the powdery dust raised by the massive marching corps. Canteens soon ran dry, sweat streamed down their dusty faces, and the soldiers cooked in their hot, woolen uniforms and heavy equipment. The veterans, too, began casting off some of their gear. "I threw away my Overcoat this morn," noted Private Harrington, a veteran of the Port Hudson, Louisiana, campaign with the 53rd Massachusetts.[12]

The agony of their parched throats and dust-caked nostrils was almost as bad as their newly and painfully sunburned necks, faces, and hands. Their feet were in terrible condition and developed agonizing blisters that broke and bled and oozed in their rough, black army brogans. "Many of the men were footsore," recorded Captain Anderson, "and the march seemed to drag heavier than any previous one."[13] In vain, the new soldiers tried to remain cheerful, but the excruciating circumstances would not allow it. The veterans laid into them without pity, offering little sympathy.

By midafternoon, after they had branched off on the Columbia Turnpike, the sweltering sun became unholy, and the consensus in the 57th Massachusetts was that this was, hands down, the most trying march that had been endured. Horace Clark, of Company H, could take no more, and he collapsed alongside the road. Dr. White pronounced him dead from severe sunstroke. The regiment was ordered out of line and halted in a grassy meadow nearby while a few men were detailed to dig a shallow grave. Reverend Alfred Dashiell, the regimental chaplain, said a few words for Private Clark, who was buried with full military honors. He was the first to die in the regiment since it had left Camp Wool and the only man to receive a formal military burial in the field. His death was probably the first ever witnessed by many of the new soldiers, and surely most of them must have whispered respectfully about their dead comrade as they fell back into marching order. Others were more callous, though, and Private Peabody wrote that evening, "Nothing of importance occurred [during the march]. one man died in Co. H." And the veteran Francis Harrington was more interested in recording the loss of his greatcoat than the death of a comrade.[14]

In the evening, at six o'clock, the regiment made camp near the battle-scarred town of Fairfax Court House after a grueling fifteen-mile tramp.[15] The men slept deeply that night, except for the unlucky pickets.

Private Charles Burno of Company C, another of the regiment's French Canadian soldiers, had somehow been discovered to be a bounty jumper from the 1st West Virginia Cavalry, and Frank Bartlett ordered him turned over to the army provost marshall at Fairfax Court House to be returned to his original regiment. But Burno managed to elude the military police, deserting once more, never to be seen again.[16]

Reveille brought to roll call the following morning, April 28, weary men who wondered, more and more, how they had been foolish enough to be cajoled by the politicians and recruiting officers into volunteering for this misery. The significance of the bounty money was beginning to pale beside the truth of soldiering. After they drank their coffee and ate their hardtack and their salt beef, the men formed their columns to resume the Corps' odyssey at seven that morning. As they passed through Centreville, Virginia, on that cool and pleasant day, they noted the deserted little village that had nearly been destroyed from the battles and occupations that had taken place around it since the war began. "But few buildings were standing," wrote John Anderson, adding, "and those were badly battered." Off in the distance, some of the boys caught a glimpse of several Confederate scouts near the town, who were observing the corps' movements. For the new men, the sight of the Rebels was somewhat unnerving, but it brought home hard the realization that they were indeed on enemy ground.[17]

Leaving Centreville, the column crossed Bull Run Creek at Blackburn's Ford and swung south towards Manassas Junction. There General Burnside permanently rejoined his corps, and the soldiers felt relieved having their commander with them.[18]

At Bull Run, the 57th halted for dinner with the IX Corps near the southern part of the old battlefield where the men "cooked meat at 12 o'clock." No doubt many expressed wonder and revulsion at the rotting wreckage and whitened bones that still littered the fields all around them. A few of the regiment's veterans had fought at either the first or second battle of Bull Run, and they remembered the fighting they had done in those famous contests. Some of the soldiers searched for a relic or two small and light enough to carry as a memento of their visit, which they could send home later. At three that afternoon the column continued on its route south, and some of the men later recalled the miles and miles of road lined with hundreds of dead and rotting horses and mules that had succumbed from exhaustion and had simply been cut from their traces where they fell. The boys observed that they "stank." Also along the roads there were plenty of wild blackberry bushes, and some of the men broke ranks to pick a few handfuls to augment their dreary army rations.[19]

Although that Thursday was not as hot as the previous days had been, Sergeant Daniel Simons of Company B fell out suffering from severe sunstroke, and, as a result, the veteran of the 10th United States Regular Infantry was diagnosed permanently affected. He was discharged from the service for disability on May 9, 1864, from an army hospital in Alexandria.[20]

"An hour or two before dark," the regiment went into bivouac at Bristow Station, Virginia, along the Orange & Alexandria Railroad, which the entire IX Corps had been detailed to patrol against Rebel raiders. The railroad was the main supply line for the Union forces, and under no circumstances could it be compromised, or the umbilical cord of the Army of the Potomac would be cut off.[21]

John Singleton Mosby, the notorious Confederate guerrilla, was operating in that area of Virginia, and the corps was ordered to watch vigilantly for him and his partisan troopers. When the enlisted men of the veteran regiments were told their assignment, they were pleased. They felt sure that they had drawn easy duty, and even though the Rebel raiders were ruthless, in the opinion of the seasoned soldiers, they were far easier to handle than Robert E. Lee and his seemingly invincible Army of Northern Virginia.[22]

Nevertheless, straggling in the corps grew less frequent then, because the Federal troops were terrified of being captured and tortured by Mosby and his men. The stories of his atrocities circulating among the rank and file were gruesome, so everyone stuck close together, and the new soldiers assigned as pickets and flankers were wary and nervous. The boys were getting deeper and deeper into Confederate territory, and everyone was edgy. But, at about dark when the IX Corps camped, the bone-weary men were soon in a dreamless sleep, in spite of their fears. Some things simply had priority after a twenty-mile march.[23]

At 7:15 the next morning, April 29, the regiment, along with the corps, continued on south "with occasional halts" through Warrenton Junction via Catlett's Station. After an all-day march during which thirteen more miles were logged, the men bivouacked for the night at Licking Run, about three miles beyond Catlett's, ever more alert.[24]

At roll call that night, First Sergeant George Whitney of Company G discovered that one of his men, Private John Towner, had deserted on the march. Towner was later found to be a bounty jumper from the 1st Illinois Volunteer Infantry, and one of his company officers in the 57th referred to him as a "scoundrel."[25]

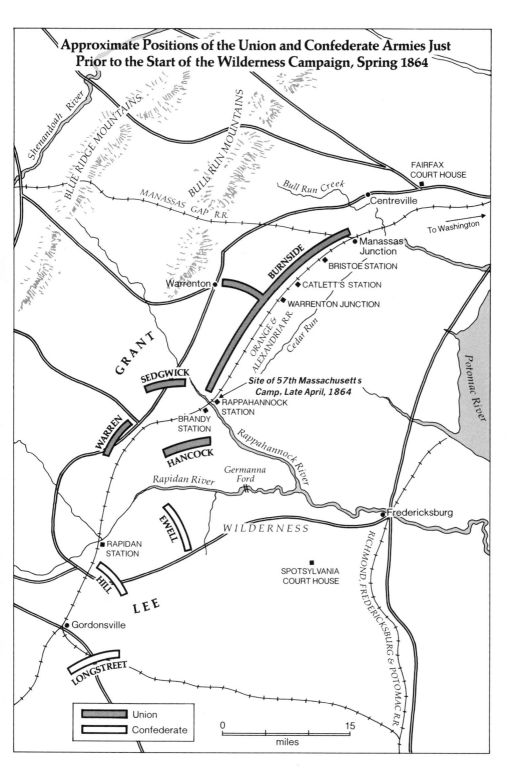

Approximate Positions of the Union and Confederate Armies Just Prior to the Start of the Wilderness Campaign, Spring 1864

Shenandoah River

BLUE RIDGE MOUNTAINS

BULL RUN MOUNTAINS

MANASSAS GAP R.R.

Bull Run Creek

FAIRFAX COURT HOUSE

Centreville

To Washington

Manassas Junction

BRISTOE STATION

BURNSIDE

Warrenton

CATLETT'S STATION

WARRENTON JUNCTION

ORANGE & ALEXANDRIA R.R.

Cedar Run

GRANT

Potomac River

SEDGWICK

Site of 57th Massachusetts Camp, Late April, 1864

RAPPAHANNOCK STATION

WARREN

BRANDY STATION

Rappahannock River

HANCOCK

Rapidan River

Germanna Ford

Fredericksburg

EWELL

WILDERNESS

RAPIDAN STATION

SPOTSYLVANIA COURT HOUSE

RICHMOND, FREDERICKSBURG & POTOMAC R.R.

HILL

LEE

Gordonsville

LONGSTREET

Union
Confederate

0   15
miles

★

In the new 57th, the men's sunburns were beginning to peel and tan a little now, and their bodies were just starting to show the lean toughness that would characterize them later. A good number of the soldiers were aching with pain from the torturing marches they had suffered, and Private Peabody noted that "many [were] lame and sore," and that he himself was "tired and jaded." But he was far from alone. Many of his comrades were tired and jaded, and homesickness was prevalent in the regiment. Nevertheless, most were adapting gradually to military life. The army food was more despised with each passing day, but not much could be done about it on the march unless the men foraged about the countryside. However, this part of Virginia was just about picked clean after two and a half years of war, and, besides, Mosby could be anywhere.[26]

The next day, Saturday, April 30, at 9:15 in the morning, the IX Corps swung southeastward and, after an eight-mile hike which took them nearly until dark to complete, finally linked with the Army of the Potomac. The 57th made camp on that cloudy and damp night near Bealton Station, just south of the Orange & Alexandria Railroad and about four miles north of the Rappahannock River. The men's first long march was over, and they could enjoy a short period of rest. "We have had some very hard marching," Lieutenant Barton wrote his mother. The boys had marveled, as they marched into camp at sundown, at the magnificence of the great Army of the Potomac, which was spread out in all directions before them with all its soldiers and equipment and activities.[27]

★

On the 1st of May, the regiment "releived [*sic*] the 20th Maine [Volunteer Infantry] from Guard Duty at this [Rappahannock] station this morning (for them to go [to] the front) about 9 O'clock we took possession of their [winter quarters] camp on a hill the north side of the R. R. near the Bridge." That famous Maine regiment, which had so distinguished itself on Little Round Top at Gettysburg the previous year, actually moved to Brandy Station, a few miles away.[28] Most of the Army of the Potomac's veteran regiments that had camped for the winter in this part of Virginia had been ordered out of their vermin-infested huts for sanitary reasons, and they were directed to bivouac in the open air in shelter tents to improve their health.

★

The whole army was astir with anticipation and gossip of the campaign that the excited soldiers knew was at hand. Rumors spread around every campfire, and all the men were certain that the spring march to Richmond would begin at any time. Winter was over, and the mud was gone. The weather was turning warmer, and spring was just beginning to bud over the beautiful Virginia landscape.

Activity was intense all through the colossal Army of the Potomac. Wagon trains hauling new supplies of uniforms, equipment, rations, ordnance, and ammunition were on the roll day and night from the depots along the Orange & Alexandria Railroad. Sutlers, camp followers, and others not necessary to the fighting had been ordered to the rear on April 16, and trains carrying excess regimental baggage were speeding daily from the camps back to Washington.[29]

The 20th Maine's camp was located on the heights of the east bank of the Rappahannock River by a railroad bridge of the Orange & Alexandria. Captain Anderson wrote that the camp was "pretty" and "quite comfortable," and he went on to describe it:

Temporary shelter was made of logs, the interstices between being filled with small stones and mud, a fireplace in each, with a chimney built of stone and mud, or two barrels, one fitted on top of the other. The roofs were made of shelter tents. Pieces of packing boxes were laid upon the ground for flooring; in some cases covered with an old rug or piece of carpeting. Temporary bunks had been constructed of pieces of packing boxes or barrel staves and pliable poles. These huts seemed palatial compared to sleeping under shelter tents on the ground and spoke well for the good taste and enterprise of the 20th Maine. Much time and labor had been expended in the construction of this camp and everything showed neatness and order. The huts of the enlisted men were equally as good as those of the officers. Each company formed a street, the huts in two lines facing each other, the officers' huts on another line and at right angles with the line of company streets; at the farther end of the streets were the company kitchens. The situation was delightful, overlooking an extensive landscape stretching for miles away into Culpepper [*sic*] County

where the boys could see Confederate pickets on the other side of the Rappahannock.[30] Not everyone agreed with the captain's assessment, however.

"Worked the rest of the day cleaning up [the camp]," recorded Francis Harrington in his diary on May 1, and on the 2nd he continued, "Worked all the forenoon cleaning up the Huts and streets which were pretty filthy." William T. Peabody agreed with his comrade and noted on May 1 that he, too, "cleaned up the camp" and "cooked and worked hard all day" on May 2.[31]

The night of May 2 turned sinister, with pitch-black skies that poured torrential rains. The temperature dropped dramatically, and the wind gusted through the company streets, howling around the huts and occasionally tearing off a tent-covered roof. The men felt themselves quite lucky that they did not have to spend another night on the ground. The guard mount that night did not fare as well, though, as the rain stirred up acres of thick, sticky mud, and on top of being cold and wet, the pickets could barely walk in the muck.[32]

The deluge continued all the next day, May 3, but it afforded the men no opportunity to remain warm and dry in their huts. Colonel Bartlett ordered them out for "drill in the principles of Target Practice . . . [and] drill in loading and firing." And the company cooks got no sleep that night, as Private Peabody tells us: "just as I got ready to go to bed Orders came to cook 3 days rations. Ready at 9 in the morning. . . ." "Camp rumors afloat that we march tomorrow [May 4]," noted Private Harrington.[33]

The enlisted men might have been drilling and cleaning and cooking army grub, but at least one officer had his mind on more delicate matters with regard to his stomach. "I should like a box sent to me filled with good things," wrote George Barton to his mother at about that time, *"Condensed Milk* in Cans and various other things in cans, minse [sic] pies. I await this in a great hurry." And the hungry lieutenant of Company C added a postscript just in case: "P.S. don't forget that box."[34]

There were some changes made in the 57th that stormy day. Second Lieutenant Alfred O. Hitchcock of the Fitchburg Company was detailed to take charge of a detachment of Company F, which had been detailed as part of the guard for the IX Corps' huge cattle herd.[35]

Hitchcock was a twenty-three-year-old medical student from Fitchburg and a veteran of Company A of the 53rd Massachusetts Volunteers. On June 14, 1863, during the assault on Port Hudson, Louisiana, he had been wounded in the right eye while serving as a private soldier. A comrade who was there relates his story: "In the midst of the fight Col[onel] [John W.] Kimball's [commander of the 53rd] orderly, Priv[ate] A. O. Hitchcock received a buckshot in his right eye. He sat on a stump while a comrade produced a large pin. Col. Kimball went to work with the pin and his jacknife. While artillery fire crashed around them he successfully dislodged the bullet." The young private's sight in that eye, however, was permanently lost.[36]

Twenty-nine enlisted men from Company F were detailed to serve under the popular lieutenant's command, and First Sergeant Charles Barnard and Corporal Martin Farrell were chosen as the noncommissioned officers.[37] It is quite likely, given the nature of this lowly and unromantic duty, that those detached men took some good-natured kidding about their new assignment from the other soldiers in the regiment. Be that as it may, their new jobs would save most of their lives.

★

On that third of May, the situation changed rapidly for the Army of the Potomac. At four that afternoon, orders dated May 2, 1864, filtered down to its many regiments from Lieutenant General Grant for the command of nearly one hundred thousand to prepare to march that night. Apprehension, speculation, and expectation filled the camps as the men got ready for the move, and shortly after midnight, on the starry morning of the 4th, the largest army America had ever known got under way for the grand march south across the Rapidan River and the start of the spring offensive toward Richmond.

The IX Corps was independent of the Army of the Potomac at that time, and, for the present, General Grant assigned most of it to remain in the rear at Warrenton Junction and continue its task of keeping a sharp eye out for Confederate raiders or other rear-guard action along the Orange & Alexandria Railroad. The one thing that Sam Grant could not afford was to have his supply lines cut—especially now—and his great army, therefore, stranded and helpless for want of bullets and food. Nevertheless, General Burnside was directed by the lieutenant general to advance as soon as he received word from the high command that the Army of the Potomac had crossed the Rapidan River successfully. While the three white divisions of the corps guarded the railroad, the black 4th division was given the responsibility of watching over the Army of the Potomac's massive wagon trains, which if lined up, would have stretched sixty-five miles.

★

At 4:35 on the morning of May 4, the rattle of drums sounded reveille in the 57th's camp, and the boys climbed out of their blankets and gobbled their breakfasts. The quartermaster, Lieutenant Priest, issued each man forty rounds of ammunition and three days' rations, and thirty minutes later the regiment was formed into column with the 1st Brigade to make the six-mile march to the wide, treeless expanse of Brandy Station. There, it was to stand by for further orders and wait for the teamsters to catch up. The infantrymen reached the station at "a little after sunrise" that morning, but apparently there was little for them to do there, and Francis Harrington tells how he "loafed untill 5 P.M."[38]

★

Emotions certainly must have run the gamut among the soldiers of the 57th, from the fever-pitch excitement of some of the new boys to the more realistic outlook of the veterans.[39] Even though no one in the ranks had any conception whatever of the grand schemes of Mr. Grant, the men were aware instinctively that their first fight was not far off. All knew that Lee's hard-fighting legions were nearby.

Bustling activity surrounded them, and nerves were tense, stomachs in knots, in anticipation of battle. Everyone was aware of Grant's order to

Burnside that the IX Corps would not remain detached from the campaign for long. (One soldier in the II Corps thought that the men of Burnside's organization were reluctant to join the Army of the Potomac, as its record of victories had been poor, and that the troops of the Army of the Potomac were demoralized. He prophesied defeat based on that record.) And, too, the men in the 57th's ranks, like all soldiers, worried about death, about living out a life crippled by disfiguring wounds, and about their performance in battle, both as individuals and as a unit. There was naive boasting by several of the new men, but most of the recruits felt genuine terror and regret for having joined the army. They were determined to behave themselves honorably, though, because almost no one wanted the stigma of a wound in the back or the scandal of cowardice attached to his name or to that of the regiment.

One fellow who seemed to care little about stigmas or scandals, but who did retain a fondness for health and well-being, was First Sergeant Oscar Davis of Company F, and the confidence shown in him by Captain Lawrence through Davis's promotion to the highest grade attainable as a noncommissioned officer of a company—in effect, fourth in command—had been a mistake. He deserted on the march from Brandy Station to the Rapidan River that night. The shock and embarrassment of such a senior noncommissioned officer running away surely must have been felt throughout the company. He was arrested in Baltimore later by the provost marshal, but he slipped his guard and deserted once more from the giant supply depot at White House Landing, Virginia, on June 12, 1864. No one heard from him again; no one wanted to. To the company, he was a "coward."[40]

★

With the certain knowledge soldiers seem to feel of a coming fight, the men were unusually quiet and introspective. Frivolity ceased; the business of death was lurking close by. The few words spoken were generally with messmates and friends, and those conversations dealt with the mysteries of the unknown and unknowable. Requests of comrades to take proper care of their burials and grave markings and to write to their families, if necessary, were made by almost all the soldiers in the 57th. All "works of the Devil" such as playing cards, dice, and the very soft pornography of that era were discarded assiduously by those devout Protestant, Catholic, and in at least one case Jewish boys. "It would be a trifle singular," wrote a private in the 17th Maine Volunteer Infantry, "if, surrounded as we are by soul harrowing memories, we were not apprehensive. We comfort ourselves with the rumor that Lee has only about one-third of our force."[41] That soldier could have been speaking for many in the 57th.

The officers and enlisted veterans tried once more to explain to the novice soldiers how to behave and what to expect on the battlefield, but there was simply no way that those new men could visualize the horror that awaited them. However, with nearly a quarter of their ranks made up of veterans and an almost one-hundred-percent-veteran officer corps, the recruits considered themselves fortunate.[42]

★

After they waited in the hot sun all day, the inevitable order to proceed to the front finally reached the 1st Brigade—and the 57th—at Brandy Station at quarter past four that afternoon, and at five o'clock the IX Corps resumed its forced march southeast across Mountain Run toward the Rapidan. A driving rain, combined with the sticky, brown Virginia mud and their wringing wet uniforms, exhausted the men and made them thoroughly miserable. During the black, rain-soaked night, the right wing of the regiment took the wrong road and became hopelessly separated from the left. The mistake was not discovered until around midnight, and the rest of the night was spent in a bone-wearying countermarch until the two halves were reunited at daybreak on May 5, almost exactly where they had started. The entire exercise had been a bungling and futile bit of incompetence, and the worn-out ranks were furious with their officers and stupid with exhaustion. (But not all of them made it to the rendezvous. Several fell out on the trek, including two veterans, Private Harrington and Sergeant William Oakes of Company F, who left the column at 2:00 A.M., too weary to continue.)[43]

A halt was called, and the men soon had their coffee boiling on their fires that they built in the road. The rain had stopped, and a huge blood-red sun was climbing into the eastern sky—the day would be a scorcher. Their uniforms were beginning to dry, and they wiped down their Springfields and Enfields with anything handy. While they were halted, the 35th Massachusetts was detached from the brigade to cross the Rapidan at Ely's ford with the 1st Division's wagons.[44] There were now no veteran regiments with Sumner Carruth's brigade.

Frank Bartlett had had a difficult time on the march. He was riding his horse, Billy, which he described as "wild, fractious, and stubborn . . . of great strength, endurance, and mettle," but which was his only method of traveling any distance with his artificial leg. The animal threw him twice, since keeping a tight grip on his horse's sides was difficult for the handicapped colonel. After the second time he was bucked off, he found a briar caught in Billy's skin. He removed it, and the unpleasant problem was solved.[45]

★

The men badly needed rest that morning of Thursday, May 5, but that luxury was not in the cards, for the corps was formed soon again, and it proceeded on to the Rapidan and the crossing at Germanna ford.[46] The countryside was alive with the awakening spring as the soldiers marched over its rolling hills. Green buds tipped the ends of tree branches, wildflowers of all colors were sprouting all around, and dogwood was beginning to bloom throughout the forests and meadows. There was a soft and fragrant breeze that morning that smelled of honeysuckle, wild roses, and pine, and all variety of birds were chirping their melodic notes. It was a beautiful day interrupted only by the steady, low rumbling of the passing army, punctuated here and there by brassy military bands playing lively marching tunes with choruses of blue soldiers singing patriotic songs as they tramped along.

As always on a great march, the road was littered with tossed-off military gear, stragglers, cavalry provost and scouting detachments, light artillery batteries with their brass-and-iron field pieces and olive-drab-painted limbers and caissons, and countless white-topped supply wagons hitched to horses and recalcitrant mules that were whipped to a frothing frenzy by screaming, cursing teamsters. There was very little dust because of the previous night's rain, and except for the exhaustion of some of the men and the anxiety of all, the march might have been a pleasant walk through the countryside.

★

Stevenson's 1st Division of the IX Corps, with the 57th in its columns, marched down the long, gently sloping trail along the north bank of the Rapidan and swiftly crossed the hundred or so yards of current on one of the two swaying, wooden pontoon bridges that had been constructed recently by the army engineers. Quickly climbing south on the narrow, dusty Germanna Plank road—crowded with troops, wagons, and artillery—to the high, wooded ground on the other side of the river, the division halted to cover the crossing of the rest of the IX Corps, minus the black division, which had remained behind with most of the army's wagons. Then, after a two-mile march, the men filed off to the right at dusk and bivouacked in the meadows of Mrs. J. R. Spotswood's farm on the west side of the Germanna Plank road, close to a field hospital belonging to the VI Corps that had been set up earlier that day. Arms were stacked and fires kindled immediately; the men were hungry.[47] They were now just a few miles from the fighting that had been raging since early that morning.

★

After the three infantry corps making up the Army of the Potomac, the II, V, and VI, had crossed the Rapidan the night before, they began early the next morning to pass through a tangle of forest, about fifteen miles long and ten miles wide, known as the Wilderness. The II Corps, under Major General Winfield Scott Hancock, had succeeded in reaching the far side of the woods

The Army of the Potomac crossing the Rapidan River at Germanna Ford, May 4, 1864. (USAMHI, Carlisle Barracks, Pa.)

by traveling on a route east of the Germanna Plank road, but as the V Corps under Major General Gouverneur Kemble Warren marched south on the Germanna road, it encountered the Confederate veterans of General Richard S. Ewell's corps rushing from the west on the east-west Orange Turnpike towards the intersection of the north-south Germanna road, attempting to smash that Federal corps in its right flank. The V Corps faced west and engaged these advance elements of the Army of Northern Virginia, and the first battle of Grant's Virginia campaign—which would continue almost nonstop for nearly a year—was on.

Warren soon was reinforced by elements of Major General John Sedgewick's VI Corps, and army headquarters dispatched orders to Hancock for him to return immediately with his II Corps to join the fight. The II Corps reached the vicinity of the intersection of the Orange Plank and Brock roads, about two miles south of the Germanna Plank road and Orange Turnpike crossing, later that morning and engaged the Confederate troops of General Ambrose Powell Hill's corps that afternoon. Grant had hoped that he could get his army through the Wilderness to more favorable fighting ground, but Lee was not about to let Grant gain the upper hand, and the 5th of May, 1864, was a day of intense fighting between the Army of the Potomac and the Army of Northern Virginia, minus General James Longstreet's corps, which had not yet arrived on the field.

The battle was in fact two battles, with Warren and Sedgewick fighting Ewell in the northern part of the woods, and Hancock slugging it out with Hill in the southern section.

★

Meanwhile, Stevenson's 1st division of the IX Corps remained in its position on the south side of the river until two o'clock the following morning, and during that time his soldiers were able to get some much-needed rest.[48]

All day long on May 5, the men heard the sounds of the battle storming in the Wilderness off to the south. It came to them as a steady roar sprinkled with intermittent lulls. "It spoke in no tremulous or uncertain voice," remembered John Anderson, "but in one steady roar like Niagara, with occasional brief lulls like moaning wind gathering strength for a heavier blast." No one had any doubt that he would see action soon, and the troops grew increasingly nervous and apprehensive, yet they went to great lengths to keep that nervousness and apprehension to themselves—to reveal any sign of a lack of courage was unthinkable. Fear was weakness, and weakness was not tolerated by Civil War soldiers. Nevertheless, they were human, and talk around the campfires could not help but be strained as each of the boys lost himself in his thoughts and dwelled inwardly on his own well-being and loved ones at home. This would be life's last day for many of them, and they all knew it.

Hasty, sentimental letters were written, and prayers silently said. The Irish and others of the Roman Catholic faith in the regiment sought out chaplain priests in the division for confession and absolution, and Reverend Dashiell ministered to the Protestants. "All thought of the coming morrow," wrote the 57th's historian. "As night came on and twilight deepened into darkness, the distant sounds gradually died away. All felt it was not yet over, only the calm which precedes the storm."[49] How prophetic was that sentiment.

The officers and noncommissioned officers ordered the men to check their rifles and gear—to make sure that everything was in good order. Advice from the veteran soldiers was sought out and carefully listened to now.

★

Private George Damon of Company G, a professional bounty jumper of three regiments—the 1st New York Light Artillery, the 53rd Massachusetts, and the 15th Massachusetts Volunteers, using the alias George W. Clarke—ran away during the march. His officers described him as a "villain: dyed in the wool." In all, twenty-one men had deserted since the 57th left Camp Wool, but three were caught and returned to the regiment in time to fight in the Wilderness. One of those three, Private John White, also of Company G and described as a "thief & pickpocket," would be taken prisoner of war and held by the Confederates until the following March. A soldier who did make good his escape was Private Albert Warren of Company A. He deserted on May 4, and his offense would be unremarkable except for the fact that his father, Hosea, was a member of the same company. Perhaps to compensate for his son's treachery, Hosea was to prove a brave soldier, fighting in most of the regiment's battles until captured by the Rebels in July, and imprisoned at Danville, Virginia, where he was destined to die from disease.[50]

★

The 4th and 10th Regulars had finally caught up with the brigade that day, and many of the officers and men were quietly relieved to have those veterans by their sides.[51]

After dark, when the firing to the south tapered off, besides military bands playing far in the rear and shouting teamsters bringing up fresh supplies for the next day's fight, the men heard only the whippoorwills and the owls and the other noises of the forest, and those not on picket duty settled down under the starry sky to get what sleep they could under the circumstances. In their anxiety, many of the boys stayed awake lost in anticipation and wonder—tomorrow would be their day.[52]

5

Hellfire . . .

T HE REGIMENT was awakened just before two o'clock that morning. Shrug-
ging off sleep, the men boiled their coffee while some of their comrades
poked off to Flat Run, a sluggish, brown creek a half-mile in the rear, and
filled the unit's canteens for the day. At 3:00 A.M., under a star-filled sky, the
57th Massachusetts moved quietly off to the left across the Spotswood clearings into the road. The boys formed into column with their brigade, and after
joining with the 2nd Brigade, the five thousand soldiers of Stevenson's division advanced two miles south on a forced march along the Germanna Plank
road, past woods still burning from the previous day's fighting, toward the
battlefield.[1] The men knew now that it was at hand—the great trial.

In the tramping columns the Irish and others of the Roman Catholic
faith—to the distaste of their Protestant comrades—fingered their rosary
beads, their Hail Marys and Our Fathers murmured quietly and repeated
mechanically as they moved along.

New sensations of dread accompanied the rookies on this first march into
battle. Accounts of survivors of Civil War battles report fluttering hearts, a
sour taste that water could not help, cold sweats, heavy chests, rubbery legs,
and labored breathing. The certainty of death preoccupied them, and, inside,
they were terrified, but only the pallor of their faces, their compressed lips
and clenched hands, and the anxiety in their eyes would have given away that
terror had the dark predawn not hidden it. And suffering their fear wordlessly
only intensified it. The officers and most of the veteran enlisted soldiers in
the regiment tried to act confident, helping a little, but only a little, to bolster
morale among the spring-green recruits. The new soldiers were about to "see
the elephant," as the old-time campaigners described going into action. Only
the men's fierce pride, complete unwillingness to be branded as cowards, and
enforced discipline kept them from falling to pieces as their time approached.

The predominant sounds that black morning were the clanking, banging, and tramping of the long, long files on the march, with the soft noises of the forest and the crackling of the burning woods in gentle counterpoint. Except for an occasional command to "close up," hoarsely bellowed by a company sergeant, or a feeble attempt at a joke by a regimental clown, there was little talk. Occasional shots were fired by the column's nervous flankers at imaginary Rebels lying in ambush behind the trees along the lane.

About half a mile from the Orange Turnpike, Stevenson's 1st Division turned off to the left, skirting the left flank of Colonel Benjamin Christ's brigade of the 3rd Division, IX Corps, which was halted in and across the road. The 1st crossed some pastures owned by a farmer named Sutherland and then turned right, back into the Germanna Plank road, to move around the twenty-two guns of C. M. Tompkin's four batteries of light artillery parked in reserve in the adjoining Childress meadow.[2]

"The sun rose" on that second morning of the great battle of the Wilder-

Intersection of the Orange Turnpike and the Germanna Plank road on the Wilderness battlefield. *(USAMHI, Carlisle Barracks, Pa.)*

ness, ". . . at two minutes of five," remembered one of the 57th's men, and an hour later, at six o'clock, with the sun well above the horizon, the regiment, along with the 1st Division, reached Wilderness Run, another slow-moving, muddy little branch. It flowed just northeast of the intersection of the Orange Turnpike and the Germanna Plank road, close to the Wilderness Tavern, a run-down, two-story, wood-frame structure, not far from where Generals Grant and George Gordon Meade, commander of the Army of the Potomac, made their headquarters during the engagement. There, a halt was called for a hasty breakfast in Childress's large, green pasture behind another of the VI Corps' field hospitals, and a few of the boys may have caught a glimpse of the famous commanders. Fires were kindled in a hurry, and those who could keep food in their stomachs downed their coffee, salt meat, and hardtack quickly. Rifles were loaded and equipment and ammunition were checked and rechecked, and Stevenson's men spent their seemingly endless time in reserve resting with their muskets at their sides.[3]

The high command had issued orders for the day's attack to begin promptly at 5:00 A.M., and the renewed battle was well under way now all through the forest—the roar of musketry unbroken and steady. The boys watched, awestruck, as the wounded came stumbling, running, and crawling out of the woods to the field hospital, many of them hideously shot up, broken, and covered in blood. Some were stoic—biting their lips to mask their anguish—but some screamed and sobbed with their terrible pain as they were helped along by comrades. Others, more severely injured, were carried out in blankets, each corner of which was held by an assisting soldier, or on stretchers frequently manned by musicians and those rating noncombatant status.

Pandemonium prevailed. The clamor was deafening. The smoke from brush fires and discharging rifles hung in the trees. Staff officers and couriers galloped back and forth on lathered, wild-eyed horses with orders and messages, creating dusty clouds. Ambulances and ammunition wagons and cavalry provosts choked the roads with harried teamsters and troopers screaming at each other to get the hell out of the goddamn way. No one on either side of the battle, including Grant, Meade, and Lee, had any real idea of what was actually going on. It was bedlam—a soldiers' fight, over which the generals had almost no control.

Many of the officers were drunk on commissary whiskey, too, and there was an epidemic of "Dutch courage" going around the army that day. Even though those officers tried to hide the drink, they could not fool the enlisted men, a few of whom also managed to forage a little taste for themselves to help strengthen waning resolve.

The neophyte warriors of the 57th looked on all these comings and goings with open-mouthed amazement, and they sat mesmerized by the carnage, the turmoil, and the earsplitting clamor.

While they were being held in reserve—with the interminable waiting grinding their nerves raw—Company K, temporarily under Captain Albert Prescott, was detached to help the 35th Massachusetts guard the division baggage wagon train. There were fifty-five men of that company on hand that morning who were detailed on the guard. Fifteen others who had fallen out on the march, such as Harrington and Oakes, however, would arrive late, yet in time to go into battle, and three of that number would die. Private Harrington wrote in his diary on the night of May 5 that he had "worked hard all day trying to find the Regt but did not make out to do so."[4] However, feelings of relief must have welled through the fortunate sentries as they realized that their death sentences were suspended—for the time being, anyway.

As those left behind watched the happy detachment march away to its new guard duty, they probably called out unpleasant, offhand remarks at those men, some playfully, some not so playfully. The unlucky soldiers were simply envious, and many of them would have instantly exchanged places with the detailed guards or the other detached men if the chance had come their way. On the other hand, there were a few who looked forward to glorifying themselves on the field of battle, and, to be sure, there were several who were skulking, straggling, or feigning illness to ward off danger. One such was Duty Sergeant Augustus Trussell of Company A. Trussell, known in his company as a "regular deadbeat," would somehow manage to avoid fighting in the battle of the Wilderness, as well as every other engagement in which the regiment fought, until he was finally shot in the leg under mysterious circumstances while in the rear during the 57th's sixth combat.[5]

The bloody and filthy wounded continued to stream by the regiment searching out the field dressing stations, and the 57th's soldiers appeared in total disharmony with them in their relatively unsoiled uniforms and polished equipment. However, some of the men were on their second pair of shoes from all their marching since leaving Annapolis, and those who had thrown away their knapsacks that held their backup brogans were close to being barefoot.

★

At a little after seven o'clock that morning, a staff officer galloped up to General Stevenson's headquarters with orders for the 1st Division to proceed to the battle lines at once. In no time the orders filtered down to the regimental commanders, who rapidly formed their columns. It was customary for regimental commanders to address their men with final orders and other last-minute instructions. Precisely what the battle-hardened Frank Bartlett said to his new outfit has not been discovered, but, based on the accounts of other commanding officers' prebattle speeches, he undoubtedly spoke to his men in an encouraging manner, telling them to do their duty, wait for commands, and aim low and deliberately. In his diary entry that morning before the battle he wrote, "It will be a bloody day. . . . I believe I am prepared to die." Not many days earlier, he had shown grave concern in his journal when he noted, "My regiment is in no condition to take into action, but I must do the best that I can. It will be a long and hard fight. God, I hope, will give us the victory. The chances I think are even. . . . Give me twenty days and I could make a splendid regiment of this, but man proposes and Grant disposes."[6]

He was disturbed because of the regiment's lack of drill in battalion and regimental tactics, which had been curtailed by the severe weather at Camp Wool, and he was quite worried that the companies would not act in concert during the confusion of battle.[7] But that was all academic now, the matter was out of his hands—and he knew it.

★

The 57th, at about half strength—548 officers and enlisted men—assembled with the rest of Sumner Carruth's 1st Brigade, and the whole took off "at the double-quick" down the rolling Germanna Plank road deeper into the forbidding forest. Color Company H took the regiment's lead with Color Sergeant Leopold Karpeles of Company E and his seven color corporals marching in front of the colonel and the drummers and fifers. Lieutenant Colonel Chandler brought up the rear.

Soon, the long blue lines of Stevenson's 1st Division turned off the Germanna Plank road to the right and headed almost due south along a narrow byway known as the Brock road. Continuing along that country lane through the vast woodland, the 1st Brigade filed off to the right near the intersection of the Brock road and the Orange Plank road and into a small clearing, to re-form its lines.[8]

★

The Orange Plank road was beginning to fill with crowds of uncontrolled and uncontrollable blue-uniformed soldiers, who were blocking the way, or calmly trying to find respite in the rear or at dressing stations along the Brock road. Although there was an unusual serenity about these infantrymen as they ambled along in the opposite direction, the situation was chaotic, with soldiers separated from their companies and companies separated from their regiments. These were mostly troops from General Hancock's II Army Corps, easily identified by their three-leaf-clover corps badges stitched onto their caps and hats. And mixed in with that blue mob were hundreds of Confederate prisoners, disarmed by their Yankee captors and told to hustle off to the Union rear.

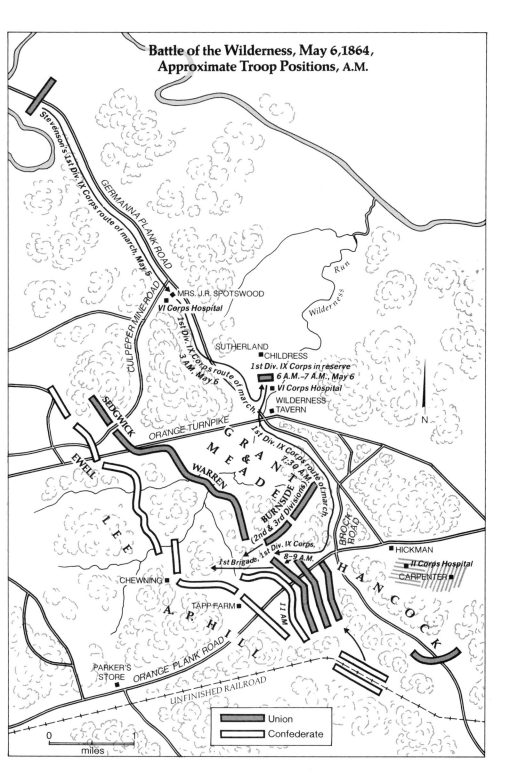

Battle of the Wilderness, May 6, 1864,
Approximate Troop Positions, A.M.

Stevenson's 1st Div. IX Corps route of march, May 5

GERMANNA PLANK ROAD

CULPEPER MINE ROAD

1st Div. IX Corps route of march, 3 A.M., May 6

Wilderness Run

MRS. J.R. SPOTSWOOD

VI Corps Hospital

SUTHERLAND

CHILDRESS

1st Div. IX Corps in reserve
6 A.M.–7 A.M., May 6

VI Corps Hospital

WILDERNESS
TAVERN

N

SEDGWICK

ORANGE TURNPIKE

G R A N T
&
M E A D E

1st Div. IX Corps route of march, 7:30 A.M.

EWELL

WARREN

BURNSIDE
(2nd & 3rd Divisions)

BROCK ROAD

HICKMAN

II Corps Hospital

L E E

1st Brigade, 1st Div. IX Corps, 8–9 A.M.

CARPENTER

CHEWNING

A. P. HILL

TAPP FARM

11 AM

H A N C O C K

PARKER'S
STORE

ORANGE PLANK ROAD

UNFINISHED RAILROAD

| | Union |
| | Confederate |

0   1
miles

71

These II Corps soldiers belonged to stalwart veteran regiments who had seen it all, and they had been fighting in the Wilderness since the previous afternoon, with little or no sleep that Thursday night, and they had had enough. Many of them had been in the war since the first shots of 1861, and their enlistments were soon to expire. They had come through all of the Army of the Potomac's campaigns safely, and they had no intention of dying here when they knew that home was just a matter of days away. Officers were yelling themselves hoarse, desperately trying to rally the re-treating foot soldiers, with no result whatsoever. Nothing in heaven or on earth could get these men back into the lines. They had done all that they were going to do, they said, and that was final, and it was time to get the hell out of those goddamned woods. Coolly, they turned deaf ears to the pleading and threatening staff officers and cavalry provost who cried, "Show blood!" a method used by the army to determine if a man moving to the rear had actually been wounded or was faking. If blood could not be exhib-ited, the soldier was either prodded back into line or arrested. But the system was not working well that day, and the situation would worsen as the morning wore on.[9]

In contrast to the flow of those weary fighters resolutely coming off the firing line was the flow of the fresh and agitated IX Corps troops going into the woods. Warnings from the rear-moving II Corps men to the effect of "Don't go in there, boys, the Rebs'll eat you for dinner!" or "Go on boys, take a turn at 'em, we done all's we're goin' to do!" and such were no doubt heard by the new soldiers, and the words surely added to their trepidation.

The 57th, along with the rest of the brigade, proceeded down the Orange Plank road pushing through the throngs of Hancock's soldiers and Southern prisoners as best it could, following the terrible clatter of the fight in front of them, until the men came to an old cart road in the woods on the right, where they halted briefly to remove and stack their knapsacks on the ground with a few lucky soldiers detailed to guard them.[10]

After the men capped their rifled muskets, already loaded, and fixed their bayonets, commands were screamed above the rolling wickedness of the gunfire and accompanying din, and the 548 frightened and nervous men of the 57th and their officers, obedient to their orders, double-quicked it down the cart path with the brigade through the brambles, briars, and scrub pines in rear of the II Corps lines. They took a position on that corps' extreme right next to the 1st Massachusetts (4th Division, II Corps) and 19th Maine (2nd Division, II Corps) Volunteer Infantry regiments.[11]

To the rattle of the long roll of drums, the brigade formed in lines of regiments with the 4th and 10th Regulars in the first rank and the 56th Massachusetts behind them. The 59th Massachusetts was third, and the 57th was in the rear. (The 35th Massachusetts, it will be remembered, was detached with the wagons and was not present for the battle.) In the 57th, as well as in the other new regiments in the brigade, the veterans and noncommissioned officers were used as file closers, and they did their duty earnestly, making certain that no one fled to the rear. While waiting for orders to advance—which were not long in coming—the 1st Brigade, facing west with its left flank resting on the Orange Plank road, was instructed by its officers to lie down for safety, and the musicians were ordered to the rear.[12]

The distance covered to the field from their reserve position had been a sweat-breaking three miles on the run with full equipment, and the men were winded and tired. They welcomed the opportunity to get off their feet for a few minutes.

Following what seemed an eternity of waiting, but was really only a few minutes, the brigade at last dressed its battle lines—as well as it could in the tangle of scrub cedar, oak, underbrush, second-growth pine, holly, stubbed chaparral, swamps, creeks, and ravines—near the right flank of what was left of Brigadier General Alexander S. Webb's 1st Brigade of the 2nd Division, II Corps. The 57th faced the sinewed, veteran scrappers of General Ambrose Powell Hill's Third Corps of the Army of Northern Virginia, and more formidable, ruthless, battle-blackened fanatics they could not have drawn as midwives to their birth as combat soldiers.[13]

After Carruth's brigade had advanced about a half-mile west with sparse opposition, the regulars in the front line fired their first volley at the Confederate lines in front of them, which they could not see for all the smoke and tangled forest. The fierce Southern reply came immediately.[14]

Mounted on little black Billy, Colonel Bartlett, unsteady in the saddle with his cork leg, was ordered by General Hancock to have the 57th advance past a regiment that was frozen by fear in position and would not move one way or the other no matter how many times the men were ordered to do so. (It is known that these were veteran troops, but not which regiment. Given the battle lineup, it could very well have been one of the U.S. Regulars.)

The 57th proceeded over them in good order—("We did it in perfect line," noted Frank Bartlett)—stepping soundly on their bodies and heads as they went and listening to their curses and warnings to "Get down, you goddamned silly fools!" and such. To the veterans hugging the earth the new regiment looked utterly foolish, as its men attacked standing straight up, exposing themselves fully in parade-ground ranks.

Company H, the color company, with its seven color corporals flanking the color sergeant, in place just to the left of right center in the line with the regimental banners proudly unfurled, led the charge with Bartlett in the van. General Hancock later, in great praise of the 57th Massachusetts, called the regiment's advance "glorious."[15]

★

The 1st Brigade's attack was directed at Confederate Generals Perry and Perrin's brigades of Anderson's division of Hill's corps. Brigadier General Abner Perrin's troops were made up of the 8th, 9th, 10th, and 14th Alabama Volunteer Infantry regiments, while the 2nd, 5th, and 8th Florida composed Brigadier General E. A. Perry's Southern boys. These Confederates were occupying ground near the Chewning Plateau, slightly to the northeast of the Widow Tapp's meager little farm further west along the Brock road, which provided one of the few clearings on the Wilderness battlefield and which was occupied, in part, by Confederate Lieutenant Colonel William Poague's four batteries of artillery. Poague's guns were some of the very few pieces of heavy ordnance on the battlefield, and his gunners were doing their level best to smash apart the blue ranks with double-shotted grapeshot and canister.[16]

There, also on the Tapp farm, the commander of the Army of Northern Virginia, General Robert E. Lee, made his headquarters.

Company H burst to within ten feet of the Rebel breastworks, a conglomeration of fence rails, trees, brush, and any other battlefield trash that could be scavenged, looming deadly in the battle smoke in front of the regiment. Many of the men had to crawl the last fifty yards of the advance on their hands and knees in the nearly impenetrable thickets. The 57th kept good formation for a while in the battle lines that ebbed and flowed continuously, but the soldiers simply could not maintain their ranks in the ghastly tangle and killing gunfire on that field of murder. Many could not see their own colors in the blinding smoke, and became totally disoriented, not knowing where they were or where the rest of the regiment, let alone their company, was. The charge disintegrated into spontaneous, miniature battles, and each man fought with chaotic ferocity for himself. The firing was so profligate that some of the boys drove into it head down and back bent, as if they were in the middle of an intense New England blizzard.[17]

For many of the Massachusetts soldiers, however, after the first pull of the trigger their earlier apprehension was greatly, almost magically, relieved, and they seemed to take on new personalities. Most of them refused to lie down or take cover, for they reasoned, in the innocence of the first day of their fighting career, that such behavior was shameful, disgraceful, unmanly, and, more importantly, cowardly. And many, but not all, of the pragmatists in their ranks did not dare to dissent and seek shelter for fear of their comrades' reprisals, not to mention official censure. So the men of the 57th continued their debut in combat as if they were participating in a grand parade-ground pageant.[18]

Some of them climbed to a plateau of exhilaration with the violence and destruction and were transformed into tough, mean, deadly fighters. And for their senseless bravery, they were slaughtered. They fought like savage, wild animals with all of their primal instincts surfacing in a blind, possessed rage of frustration and anger, and in most cases the regard for personal safety was completely repressed. Some were filled with plain blood lust; when a comrade was hit, his friends sometimes exploded in a fury of barbarism, screaming like banshees and shooting like wildmen. And many reacted with cries of insane glee and satisfaction at each shot they fired.

Others were strangely calm. Lieutenant Barton described to his mother how his cousin, Color Corporal Ira Bullard, when his musket had become so fouled that he was unable to discharge it, *"quietly* took his *wrench* from his Cartridge box, unscrewed the Cone on which the *Caps* are placed, took his *primer* And Cleaned out the cone, then screwed it on again and *blazed away* all this under a heavy fire of *musketry* from the 'Johnnies.' "[19]

Soon the boys' mouths and faces were blackened with powder from furiously tearing open the paper cartridges with their teeth. Ears rang from the seething tumult, and many men were partially, though temporarily, deaf. Eyes were reddened and irritated, and they watered from the rotten-egg-smelling, sulfurous gun smoke and the piny wood smoke from the innumerable brush and forest fires which were raging all around, ignited by sparks from the musket fire falling on dry leaves and timber. The helpless injured and the corpses of the dead smoldered and burned outright when those fires reached them, and the stench was nauseating. Wounded men who were stranded often loaded their rifles so that they could shoot themselves in the event they caught fire.

The men swore in a manner that many would never have under any other conceivable conditions. They swore at the Rebels, they swore at each other, they swore at themselves, at shirkers, incompetent officers, and the governments, both North and South. They cursed their rifles, the miserable woods in which they were forced to fight, their ammunition and lack of it, and anything which came to mind, in order to vent their boiling rage and incomprehensible mania.

For they truly were maniacs at that moment, and some of them felt a black, exquisite ecstasy at the surrounding havoc, an emotion that none of the rookies had ever dreamed, in his wildest fantasy of war back in peaceful New England, that he would ever feel. They became indifferent to the mindless orders and prattle of their equally confused officers, noncoms, and file closers. The horribly mangled, bloody dead and wounded became abstractions in the misty smoke of the battlefield unless they were friends or messmates, and, even then, too much time could not be wasted on them, unless there was a chance of getting them to the safety of the rear or of giving them a drink of water. A few, however, did take advantage of those unfortunate, hurt men to help them off the field to the dressing stations, thus insuring their own well-being.

From every point on the battlefield the screaming, screeching, begging, and pleading thousands of maimed and mutilated soldiers was heard amid the gunfire as they lay everywhere, saturated in their own spurting and dripping blood, with wounds at every conceivable location on their bodies. The slain and wounded had every imaginable part of their bodies shot off, and heads, arms, legs, hands, feet, fingers, toes, ears, noses, genitals, entrails, and brains were scattered and splattered everywhere, and in some places the sticky, slippery blood was so thick that a man occasionally slipped in it and fell down.

The Minié balls whizzed, whistled, whined, hummed, and buzzed on their trajectories, and when they struck, they slapped, thumped, twanged, pinged, and clopped into bodies, trees, and the ground. They spun, echoed, keyholed, and ricocheted, and their deadly sounds spanned several octaves of the chromatic scale.[20] Artillery could not be used with much effect in the dense forest, so little of it was employed, and the sounds of the big guns played only a minor role in the murderous symphony.

The regiment exposed itself in such a suicidal manner to such murderous, devastating fire that in this, its very first combat, 262 of its 548 officers and men were killed, wounded, missing, or taken prisoner, nearly all of them before nine o'clock that morning.[21]

★

The confusion of that part of the Union army became all-encompassing, and disorder prevailed. The only battle flags that could be seen on the right of this area of the forest were the now shot-up rags of the 57th, far in the advance. Color Sergeant Karpeles had mounted a stump with his banner, waving it back and forth so that all could rally to it. Brigadier General James S. Wadsworth, commander of the 4th Division of the V Corps, who had just taken field command of Stevenson's division and Webb's brigade because of his seniority, tried, in desperation and without success, to rally the disoriented mobs of retreating men of other regiments to the 57th's colors.[22] (Just after noon that day, Wadsworth was shot down, mortally wounded in the back of his head with a bullet in his brain. He died in a Confederate field hospital on May 8.)

The miles of woods, with all the smoke from the guns and fires, became darker, as the battle haze hung low through the trees with no breeze to blow it away. The atmosphere was suffocating with the heat of the intense sun and the fires, and the men were soaked in sweat. Those who were not wounded outright were cut, bruised, and contused from the tangle and from falling branches shot off the trees and bark and chips that splintered in their faces and eyes when bullets slammed into the timber. Many were singed from the fires and covered in soot, and they were spattered with blood, brains, and pieces of flesh and bone from comrades who had been shot near them. But they fought on, oblivious to all.

They lost caps and pieces of their uniforms and equipment. The pernicious Confederate rifle fire shot away belts and straps and left bullet holes in their clothes from near misses. They were filthy and tattered. Their fingernails and hands were caked with black powder, which had become viscous as it mixed with their sweat. Their salty perspiration dripped through their eyebrows, stinging their eyes, and their mouths were full of sulfurous, dirty powder grit and smoke.

Some had black-and-blue shoulders from the constant recoil of their discharging rifles. Their hair was greasy, matted, and dirty, and a few had teeth knocked out from the constant pushing, shoving, and hitting. A number of them were injured from tripping over the impossible underbrush, bodies, or even an untied leather shoelace.

Ramrods were occasionally lost or fired off in the confusion, mainsprings sometimes snapped in the locks of the usually reliable Springfields and Enfields, and some muskets were so hot and fouled from constant firing that they could not be loaded or touched until they were swabbed out and cooled with water, a practically impossible task under the circumstances. In such cases, the soldiers simply threw away their useless guns and picked up new ones from the dead and wounded. (Many of the veterans of older regiments, who had rifles worn out from three years of fighting, were able to reequip themselves in this way with nearly brand-new weapons from the dead of the fresh regiments.)[23] And then there were the few terrified, green men who loaded their pieces over and over again, but never capped them. Not being experienced enough to notice the absence of recoil when the trigger was pulled, the soldier would eventually remember to put on a fulminate ignition cap, and when he squeezed the trigger this time there were so many charges down the barrel that the gun blew up in his face, often tearing his head to ribbons.

The battlefield was a bloody slaughterhouse of sheer frenzy, and wild rabbits became so terrified they were tamed in their fright and sought refuge snuggling against prone soldiers and corpses. Alarmed birds circled and fluttered vigorously above the smoke and squawked in mad protest. Deer bounded wildly in all directions, in sheer panic, seeking safety, and raccoons, squirrels, possums, quail, and other creatures of the usually sleepy forest scampered about in dread looking for someplace to escape this human outrage.

★

The 57th was suffering horrendously in casualties, even though it was responsible for a good deal of pain and misery inflicted on the other side, as well.

Later that morning, at about eleven o'clock, Colonel Bartlett was struck directly above the right temple by a Rebel Minié ball just after he took a drink of water from Sergeant Edwin McFarland's canteen. It was only a glancing blow, but the colonel was dispatched to the rear, with his arms around Billy's neck for balance, exhausted and bleeding, in the company of several very lucky men as escorts. While moving out of the battle lines, he had barely avoided capture in the confusion. Lieutenant Colonel Chandler then assumed command of the regiment. However, he was soon lost from the majority of the men as he remained in the very front with the colors, and Major Cushing, next in line, was put out of action shortly afterward, with sunstroke. Command of the regiment changed so rapidly that no one could say, at any given time, just who was in charge.[24]

A Minié ball drilled through young Captain Joseph Gird's head early in the fight, killing him instantly. He had just finished instructing the men of his company how to behave during the first charge. As he turned around, the Rebel bullet hit, and he threw up his hands as he fell to the ground.[25]

Sergeant Charles Knox of Company C was shot dead square between the eyes.[26]

Charles Everett, Company D's young drummer boy and quartermaster's clerk, did not survive, either. Despite Frank Bartlett's firm order to him to remain in the safety of the rear, he had grabbed a musket and a pocket full of ammunition and had gone to the front lines, where he was soon mortally wounded in the right hip. Captain Warren B. Galucia, commander of Company E of the 56th Massachusetts, as well as a family friend of the Everetts, asked Color Sergeant Robert C. Horrigan of the 56th, as the sergeant made his way to the front, to check on the boy's well-being. Later the color sergeant reported back to the captain that he had found Everett severely wounded, and that he "had left him lying at the foot of a tree." The young drummer's body was never found.[27]

Private David H. Tolman's career as a Civil War combat soldier was remarkably short—probably only a few minutes. Tolman, of Company A, tells his story: "At the Battle of the Wilderness we went into the fight in the middle of the forenoon formed lines and I had fired twice and as I was reloading, a spent shell struck me in the left thigh. I was carried to the rear and taken to the field hospital, until the next morning when we were taken to Fredericksburg [Virginia] where we stayed two nites in the basement of the Methodist church." Private Tolman never returned to the regiment and was discharged from the service for disability.[28]

Surely there were few greater tragedies during the Civil War than that suffered by the Maynard family of Sterling, Massachusetts. Both Maynard brothers, George, seventeen, and William, nineteen, were killed that bloody day. A third brother, Charles, eighteen and a member of Company C of the 34th Massachusetts, had died from disease just three weeks before at Harper's Ferry, West Virginia.[29] How their parents must have suffered.

First Lieutenant Edward Dewey, a former corporal in the 10th Massachusetts Volunteer Infantry who had fought in all the battles of the Peninsula campaign, at Fredericksburg, Chancellorsville, Gettysburg, and Mine Run, without a scratch, finally had his luck run out when he went down with a Minié ball in his leg. He would recover and return to duty—for a while.[30]

Corporal George Hodge, a veteran of Frank Bartlett's old 49th Regiment, had his arm mangled by a Confederate bullet. Later in the month Acting Assistant Surgeon F. G. H. Bradford found it necessary to remove the arm at the elbow, but the surgery was too much for the young corporal, and he succumbed from exhaustion on June 4. Meanwhile his younger brother, James, was lost during the battle and listed as missing in action and presumed killed.[31]

The men were being mowed down all along the line, and the 57th was losing its men on the average of one every fifteen seconds.

While trying to rally the left wing of Company H, Lieutenant Charles Barker, of the Fitchburg Company, had his thigh blown apart and then was hit in the arm, suffering indescribable agony. Captain Lawrence immediately went to his aid, but while he was bandaging Barker's leg the captain was critically wounded with a load of buckshot in the neck. Barker tried to improvise a crutch out of a musket, but he could not stand the strain, and so Lawrence, who was not yet feeling the full effects of his shotgun wound, helped him from the field with the aid of one of Company F's men.

Later, while being transferred in an ambulance to the field hospitals in Fredericksburg, Lawrence, Barker, and several other officers were set upon by some of Colonel John Mosby's guerillas—but more on their adventures later.[32]

Corporal Aaron Wilkins and his son, Henry, went down together, the father severely wounded in the right arm and the boy shot in the back and the left thigh.[33]

Private Horace Danyon had deserted Company G at Annapolis, but he had been caught and returned to the regiment. Thrown into the 57th's battle line, he took a Rebel ball and lingered until July 18, when he died in a Washington army hospital.[34]

Corporal John Fleming, whom Company G's officers thought "worthless," fell wounded in the head.[35]

Private Frank Smith, of Company G, deserted during the battle, the only man of the 57th to do so.[36]

"A good soldier, cheerful companion, a true patriot, and an unflinching hero" is how the *Massachusetts Spy* eulogized twenty-two-year-old Private Charles H. Leonard of Company H. Shot through the head, the bullet fracturing his skull, Private Leonard lasted until May 17, when he expired from cerebritis at Columbian U.S. Army General Hospital in Washington.[37]

The regiment was torn to shreds in that morning's bloodbath. Company

G put 58 men on the line and lost 39 of them—over 67 percent—and Company F followed a close second with 25 out of 42, or nearly 60 percent, down or prisoners of war.[38]

★

Around ten o'clock, there was a lull in the fighting, followed not long after by a furious and frantic Confederate assault at eleven. Brigadier General Gershom Mott's 4th Division of the II Corps, holding the left and unprotected tip of the miles-long Federal battle line that extended out across the Orange Plank road, was flanked and broken in following a headlong surprise attack by the men of General James Longstreet's corps of ragged, frenzied Confederate infantry led by Lieutenant Colonel G. Moxley Sorrel. The Union ranks were rolled up "like a wet blanket," as General Hancock later—and aptly—portrayed the Northern disaster.

The decimated 57th was soon caught by that turn of events on the left of the Federal line, as the destruction swept along the Yankee front like the fires raging through the woodland, infecting the troops with terror. Private Harrington had finally found the regiment and breathlessly described the scene on the spot at that time: "Our men are falling back on our left 15 min later our regt has fallen back it could not be got into line and is broken."[39] At last, with no other choices left, the men were ordered by Frank Bartlett, just before his wounding, to fall back with the other regiments to the rifle pits along the Brock road, as the Union lines continued to buckle and snap under the pressure from Longstreet's flanking movement and as the rest of the IX Corps' 1st Division disintegrated from a front-end smash by Hill's men on the Federal right. Many of the Union soldiers began to panic, and the retreat turned into a rout, with feet flying through the snarled and tangled forest.

★

Further east on the Brock road, however, the scene, augmented by thousands of additional men, was greatly expanded from what it had been when the 57th went into battle earlier that morning. Still more II Corps men had left the front lines and the soldiers were walking for the most part calmly, but determinedly, rearward in huge clogging masses for safety as if they were "returning disatisfied from a muster." As before, the rallying cries and begging and threatening of their officers fell on deaf ears, and the multitudes ignored everything but the sanctuary of the army's rear. It was not that they were cowards or shirkers—far from it; they were, like the other soldiers who had been retiring down the road earlier that morning, just played out, finished. And that was that.[40]

★

There were no clear lines or identifiable landmarks on the Wilderness battle-field, and, out of sight of roads, everyone was bewildered. Men ran in the wrong direction, and many were captured in that way, with the 57th losing its fair share of prisoners of war, thirty-two in all that May 6.[41] Regiments and companies were disoriented, and inextricably mixed with others. Brigades were in the same shape. No one could tell where anyone else was in the incredible disorder, with visibility generally only a few yards in any direction.

As the withdrawal swiftly disintegrated into an unholy stampede through the forest, the men of the 57th ran as fast as they could for the haven of the trench lines on the Brock road, praying aloud to sweet Jesus that they would not get shot in the back, but many—like eighteen-year-old Henry Wilkins, as noted earlier—were.

A soldier in the 13th Massachusetts Volunteers remembered seeing the boys of the 57th that day, "coming to the rear like frightened sheep."[42] Their reckless bravado of just several hours ago had evaporated.

Some of the soldiers smashed their rifles to smithereens against trees along the way so that they would not fall into Confederate hands. Nothing could stop those terrified, sprinting young men until they reached comparative safety in the vicinity of the Brock and Orange Plank road intersection. There, Colonel Daniel Leasure, formerly of the veteran 100th Pennsylvania Regi-ment and now commander of the 2nd Brigade of Stevenson's division, mounted a brass twelve-pounder field piece that was on station in the dusty road, and he bellowed orders at the top of his lungs until a semblance of ranks was re-formed out of the remnants of several regiments, including a few of the men of the 57th. He was helped by commissioned and noncommissioned officers alike, who had finally come to their military senses, and the ever-present—in the rear at least—and ever-despised provost guards, formed in three lines that day and derisively called by the men "turkey drivers," who were prodding soldiers into line with their bayonets and sabers.

Leasure then cried, "Advance first line," and after the artillerymen fired a round of grapeshot into the oncoming Rebels, the reorganized infantry soldiers let go a volley and drove the Confederates back to a point just about where they had had their lines originally. However, the Northerners could not hold the position. They were beaten back quickly, and the Union rout rear-ward to the Brock road trenches continued.[43]

★

In the meantime, Reverend Dashiell and the 57th's musicians were minister-ing to the wounded who could be reached and doing their best to help them to safety, either at the II Corps field hospital at Carpenter's farm one and a half miles east of the Federal lines along the Orange Plank road, or at the 1st Division's dressing station near the II Corps' hospital, where Dr. White and other IX Corps surgeons and their staffs were working feverishly, bandaging wounds and amputating hundreds of mutilated limbs. The 57th had not as yet organized a stretcher corps, and all not on combat duty who could be rounded up helped the afflicted as best they could.[44]

★

During the mad retreat, the regiment's colors became tangled in the underbrush close to the front lines, and when Colonel Chandler saw what was happening, he shouted to Leopold Karpeles, "Color Sergeant, what's the trouble?" "Colonel, the rebs are around us," the color sergeant yelled back to Chandler. Chandler then pointed to Karpeles, who had again mounted a stump waving the regimental banner, and hollered above the racket to the fleeing soldiers, "For God's sake boys, don't forsake your colors!" Thirty-four of the 57th's men halted and rallied around the color sergeant. First Lieutenant Henry Ward, of Company G, ordered those soldiers to lie down and hide the flags. "I directed him [the color sergeant] to conceal the colors, as we were surrounded by the enemy, front, flank, and rear," remembered Ward years later in a letter to John Anderson. The soldiers released the banners from the brush and quickly furled them. Chandler, Ward, and thirty-five men, including Sergeant Karpeles and Company I's Sergeant Edwin McFarland, and one other officer, Second Lieutenant Charles H. Royce, of Company C, remained behind to protect the regimental standards.

Francis Harrington was one of the group, and he scrawled hastily in his diary during the fight that "there is about 20 [actually thirty-four] of us and Lt. Col. [Chandler] have rallied around the flag and going [through] heated times." Heated times indeed.

The pathetic little band of soldiers remained surrounded by Hill's men, who advanced and retreated over them several times, and they only escaped capture because they went unnoticed in the utter confusion of the great battle. "While we were lying on the ground we could see the rebels going up the plank road," wrote Edwin McFarland. "One came into the brush where we were. Colonel Chandler pointed his revolver at him and told him to surrender. He threw down his gun, and lay down beside us and we brought him in a prisoner."

The men remained in this precarious position, along with some soldiers from the veteran 45th Pennsylvania Volunteer Infantry, throughout most of the day and were only able to find refuge in the regiment's lines at sunset. "We crawled on our hands and knees a long distance, I don't know how far," recalled McFarland, "but it was a number of hours before we reached our lines. I remember at last of finding ourselves near the [Brock] road we went over in the morning and came back up that road. . . . I remember seeing the sun almost down when we reached our regiment."

For his part in that action and for rallying the troops to the colors under intense fire to check an earlier Confederate advance, Sergeant Karpeles received the Medal of Honor, and Private Harvey Gould, one of the men who had stayed with the flags and a member of McFarland's Company I, received his corporal's chevrons that evening for "good conduct in action."[45]

★

Meanwhile, most of the rest of the men, with the Rebels in pursuit close on their heels, shooting at them and trying to needle them with their bayonets, had finally made it back to the Brock road. The used-up survivors of the 57th, except for the thirty-seven men still on the field and a number of others temporarily lost in the confusion, leaped into the safety of the shallow, hastily dug rifle pits in the area and quickly returned a pounding volley into the pursuing Southerners. The battle, on the left of the Army of the Potomac's position, continued like this until about noon that Friday, when the gunfire gradually subsided due to the sheer exhaustion of the troops on both sides. Sporadic shooting was kept up throughout the day, but the worst fighting was essentially over for now in that southern part of the line. Both of the contesting armies were nearly fought out.

The men of the 57th were in a stupor, their catharsis of battle all but complete now. After catching gasping breaths and swallowing hurried mouthfuls of welcome, if tepid, canteen water, they immediately began to improve their entrenchments by digging feverishly and determinedly with bayonets, tin cups and plates, or anything they could improvise.

At about four o'clock that afternoon, one last attempt was made by General Lee's men to carry the breastworks on the Brock road. On came the Rebel troops furiously, but the dry logs on top of the trenches caught fire from the guns' muzzle flashes, and the flames and smoke kept the two sides from dangerous contact. A breeze was moving just enough from the west, and the Union soldiers faltered for a short while as the smoke and flames drove them back and allowed the Rebels to plant a few of their colors on the earthworks. The Yankee lines quickly re-formed, however, and the Confederates were driven off with heavy casualties.

And that part of the battle of the Wilderness was over.

6

. . . And the Fires of Hell

B Y SIX O'CLOCK that afternoon, the lines were relatively quiet in the
southern part of the four-and-a-half-mile Union front, but the men could
still hear heavy gunfire off to the north. There the VI Corps, aided by
elements of the V Corps, was engaged yet in a desperate struggle with
General Richard S. Ewell's butternuts, who were making a last-ditch effort
to turn and smash the Federal right flank. The attack was not successful,
however, and presently the Confederates were beaten back.

As the sun went down that day, some of the men who had become
separated during the confusion of the battle began to return to the 57th
Regiment, and Private Harrington related that by "nearly night the Regt
[was] together." (There were actually about two hundred men in the 57th's
lines that night; the remaining survivors returned the following day.) A few
of the wounded who had been lying on the battlefield all day also were able
to be rescued. One such was Corporal Daniel Sullivan of Company G, who
had been born in Ireland in July 1837. Sullivan had been conscripted in the
1864 draft, but, being a farmer of some means—rare for an Irish immigrant—
he hired a substitute for the substantial going rate of $300, to take his place
in the ranks. Some unknown process, however, had acted upon him—perhaps
a surge of patriotic guilt for not defending his newly adopted country—and
on February 29, 1864, he signed the regiment's enlistment rolls as a private.
During the fight, he had been wounded and left behind on the field. The
Southerners had taken him prisoner, but soon forgot about him in the disorder of the battle, and when the firing ceased, he had been able to find his
way into friendly lines. He was later sent home to recuperate, but he never
became well enough to rejoin the regiment.[1]

The 57th's soldiers, along with their comrades in the other regiments of
Stevenson's division, continued working to better their fortifications in their
second line of trenches on the Brock road. In his diary entry for May 7,

Francis Harrington reported that the men had "worked some last night building earthworks with our bayonets and tin plates," and while so doing, he explained, they had "laid upon our arms Half the troops at a time" while the other half worked.[2]

The conversations that night focused mainly on the events of that bloody day and the probabilities for the next. The regiment's remaining men were drained of strength and energy; nonetheless, they lit fires and cooked their rations. They were hungry from the labors of battle.

Before the sun set that evening at ten minutes to seven, letters were written home by many of the survivors anxious to inform their families of their own good fortune in still being alive, and to describe, in their limited way, the day's happenings. Most of the men played down the gruesome aspects of the battle, lest the home folks become overly concerned about them. The soldiers were insular in their knowledge of the great combat and perplexed concerning the realities of what had actually happened as a whole, because this battle often had been a fight between small groups and individuals. Formal battle lines had been out of the question in many sections of the dense and smoke-filled hollows and ravines of the impenetrable forest, where it had been nearly impossible to see the enemy. Their letters could only encompass vignettes of the day, and they had to struggle to describe even those.

Regardless of how they viewed the events in the Wilderness on that terrible sixth of May, almost all of them had gained in self-assurance and self-respect, and the new boys felt now that they had what it took to be soldiers. And the men had learned a great many lessons of combat, too, lessons that no training camp could teach them. There just were not words enough to really explain the things that they had witnessed and endured.

And, too, the recruits who had performed well achieved a new kinship and favored status with the veterans in the regiment and the brigade.

The men felt sorrow for their dead comrades and were hopeful for those in the field hospitals or on their way to Fredericksburg, but mostly they felt helpless for those wounded who still cluttered the battleground.[3]

As the 57th lay in earthworks in the northeast corner of the Brock and Orange Plank road intersection,[4] they could hear those torn-up men throughout the night screaming, cursing, moaning, crying, and begging for help, for water, or to be shot to end their insufferable agony. Thousands upon thousands of wounded Federal and Confederate soldiers were heaped and strewn about the battlefield together with thousands and thousands of multilated corpses. The din raised by these men was horrifying and sickening, and even though it was night, hardly anyone dared risk a Confederate volley to go out and rescue any of them. Any noise of movement outside the trenches was reason enough for the nervous infantrymen of both sides to start shooting—

everyone was certain that another attack was imminent. After dark a stiff little breeze came up, fanning and spreading the blazes rapidly through the timber. The fires reached some of those unfortunate wounded from time to time, and the insane, gut-wrenching screaming and shrieking that came from those helpless soldiers being burned alive was unendurable. About two hundred living men were incinerated in the Wilderness.

Frequent picket shots and taunts from one side to the other occurred throughout the evening, with the appropriate replies made in return by angry comrades of the suffering wounded lying between the lines.

The forest fires crackled and snapped across the landscape all night long, fueled by the dry wood of the timberland, and their all-pervasive smoke continued to hang in the trees and trenches. The temperature began to drop, and the men inched closer to their campfires. The air was fetid and foul with the smell of the rapidly decomposing and burning bodies of the dead. The panorama was horrifying, almost supernatural, even haunting—but it was real. Nothing could have ever prepared those young soldiers, including many of the veterans, for a situation such as the Wilderness, and they would find it difficult to ever articulate those scenes and events to anyone. But they would never, for the rest of their lives, forget the impact those scenes and events had upon them.

Because the soldiers saw the tragedy only from their own isolated points of view, and remembered only their own, and closely shared, triumphs and calamities, they had no idea who had won—if indeed either side had—the colossal battle, and when they queried their officers, the officers replied that they did not know either; that they all would have to wait to read the stories in the *New York Herald.* (But when they did get copies a couple of days later, the newspaper did not settle the issue.)[5] In fact the battle of the Wilderness had been pretty much a draw, with the Southerners favored better than two to one in their killing abilities. Still, each side held roughly the same position it had occupied at the beginning of the day's fighting. Even though the Rebels had the edge on the carnage inflicted, the casualties of both sides were appalling; nearly 18,000 Union and 8,000 Confederates had been killed, wounded, captured, or listed as missing.

As the night grew cooler and the campfires died down, the exhausted fighters called it a day. Since they had not been able to recover their knapsacks and blankets, they snuggled against one another, spoon fashion, to stay warm, keeping their loaded rifles close at hand. Sleep was deep and trancelike for some, while others hovered nervously on its threshold in fear of another reprisal. Still others could not sleep with the awful racket coming from the wounded on the battlefield. Some of the men actually had to sleep among the corpses, but they were so tired, they paid little attention to them.[6]

"Every man felt a just pride in the brave deeds of his own regiment and loved to feel he had a share in them," wrote John Anderson years afterward.

And the captain went on to describe the setting in the 57th's earthworks that evening of May 6, 1864:

The dark shadows of night at last fell upon the awful scene of carnage and the turmoil of battle gradually died away, leaving only the watchful, warning shots along the confronting lines of pickets. Both sides were well nigh exhausted, but still defiantly confronting each other upon nearly the same ground as when the battle had commenced two days before. The tired men dropped upon the ground for rest and sleep, the living and dead lying side by side. It was a long, gloomy night. Even the partial unconsciousness of sleep could not dispel the surrounding scenes of horror. With momentary wakefulness came the wondering thought of what the morrow would bring forth; if the light of coming day would witness a renewal of the struggle.

It seemed that nothing more of horror could be added. The mind could not comprehend the hundredth part of what had already transpired, simply what each had seen personally became [a] matter of contemplation. A feeling of thankfulness came to those who had been spared, yet the thoughts could not but dwell with lingering sorrow upon the less fortunate comrades of those who had marched side by side over many a weary mile and stood shoulder to shoulder in the shock of battle; who had often shared their blankets of a chilly night and talked of the loved friends, the distant home and the dearly anticipated return when the war would be over. Solacing thoughts that came in the phantasm of dreams never to be realized by many.

The glories of war were lost in its sickening sights. The gay parade, with the old-time flag gracefully floating in the evening breeze, the nodding plumes, gaudy uniforms with brightly polished buttons, which were the admiration of the fair sex, the inspiring notes of the military band and all the pomp and glamor of war that shone so beautifully as the regiment marched out from their home camp for embarkation, had lost their charms for him, although his aching heart still clung tenderly to the pathetic notes of "The girl I left behind me." Now it had become a life of real danger, hardships, deprivation and suffering. He looked for the bright side which he knew could only come with returning peace. He tried in vain to understand why all this misery and human suffering should be. As the night grows more chill, he snuggles nearer his sleeping comrade and pulls the blanket [as noted previously, the blankets actually had not been recovered at that time] around him, occasionally opening his eyes to look for the old familiar stars which are hidden by the thick smoke of battle that still hangs over the dense forest, then, closing them again, he tries to sleep as he listens to the random shots and hears the whiz of the bullet on its mission of death as it goes cracking through the slender branches of the trees. These messengers tell him that the enemy is still there "on mischief bent," but he feels secure in the answering fire of our own sentinels who keep vigil while others sleep. Such is night upon a battlefield.[7]

It is certain that not all felt quite as secure as Captain Anderson would have liked to have us believe.

★

Of the 262 casualties sustained by the 57th Massachusetts Volunteers during the battle of the Wilderness, 54 had been killed outright, 29 had been mortally wounded, and 10 were listed as missing in action and presumed killed, making a total of 93 deaths directly attributable to that fight. One hundred and fifty-six had been wounded, and of those wounded 20 had been captured and confined as prisoners of war by the Confederates. Twelve other men also had been seized by the Rebels. Many of those captured would languish for months in the barbaric conditions of Southern prisons only to die from starvation or a host of diseases—and in one case, violence. And one man, Private Frank Smith of Company G, it will be remembered, had deserted in action.[8]

Because the 57th's regimental baggage, retained rolls, and official records were sunk in the James River when the unseaworthy barge *General McClellan* went down while transporting them from White House Landing to City Point, Virginia, later that summer, the precise number of men present for duty during the battle of the Wilderness was impossible for John Anderson to determine when he published the regiment's original history in 1896. However, records other than those lost did—and still do—exist, and those numbers now can be set down with reasonable confidence. Of the Massachusetts infantry regiments engaged with the 1st Brigade, 1st Division, IX Corps, during the battle of the Wilderness, the 57th sustained the highest losses.[9]

The 57th's firing line was extremely fluid during the battle, with men like Harrington and Oakes of Company K coming into the fracas late, for example, while others were going to the rear wounded, to procure a fresh supply of ammunition, to fill canteens, or to convey messages. After the regiment's formation broke during its first charge, the unit's cohesiveness was never regained again that day. There could be found in the 57th's actions later that morning not the slightest resemblance to the paintings and drawings of orderly battle lines fashionable during the time. We know who went into the battle, and, overall, we know what happened to all of them, but except for a very few cases, we do not know their individual stories.

All contemporary accounts indicate that the fledgling Massachusetts regiment acquitted itself as well as could be expected on that awful day. And Colonel Bartlett was pleased and surprised with its performance under fire. "The loss in my regiment is great," he wrote from his ambulance on May 8, "[but] I am satisfied with their conduct."[10]

Most of the officers and men felt a deep loss with Frank Bartlett's wounding, and George Barton remembered how many of the wounded enlisted men had "asked about the Colonel inquiring if he was badly wounded and when I told them slightly wounded they seemed very well satisfied."[11] That this was a sentiment shared by all, however, was probably not the case. Frank Bartlett had been a strict disciplinarian with his troops, and his heavy-handedness, coupled with his lordly, Brahmin bearing, no doubt won him varying degrees of animosity with a few in the rank and file.

Another casualty of the day was the 1st Brigade's commander, Colonel Sumner Carruth, who was carried from the field suffering from severe sunstroke. He was subsequently replaced by Colonel Jacob Parker Gould of the 57th's brother regiment, the 59th Massachusetts, but Gould, a veteran of the 13th Massachusetts, was soon beset by sunstroke as well. In his absence, command of the brigade was then assumed by twenty-two-year-old Lieutenant Colonel Stephen Minot Weld, Jr., of the 56th Massachusetts, who had been made commander of his regiment on the battlefield of the Wilderness after its colonel, Charles E. Griswold, was shot in the jugular and killed.[12]

★

The regiment was awakened with the first streaks of dawn the next morning, Saturday, May 7, and, surrounded by an eerie daybreak fog, the men got up with their loaded muskets in hand. They shook and stretched themselves awake, and prepared for the early morning renewal of the battle they were sure was to come. But it was not to be—not on that day, at least—as both armies were so thoroughly worn out that it was impossible to continue the contest.[13]

The men of the 57th stood or kneeled at their posts in the breastworks and rifle pits on the Brock road, keeping a sharp vigil on the ground in their front and surveying the awful human carnage and battlefield junk slowly being illuminated by the rising sun. Some of the smoke had lifted during the night, and the men had a little better view of the woods, yet it was still impossible to draw a breath of fresh air. Whole trees and thousands of saplings had been shot down and ripped to kindling. The forest was a dump of wrecked bodies shot through and through with repeated hits as they had lain in death. Guns, knapsacks, canteens, cartridge boxes, caps, shoes, bayonets, and other items of warfare were scattered helter-skelter everywhere, and scraps of torn uniforms hung all over the bushes. And to augment the scene of destruction, bleached bones of soldiers and horses killed just a year ago in that jungle during the battle of Chancellorsville were mixed with the fresh ruins.

The stench of the putrefying dead grew worse and worse as the rising sun slowly warmed the cadavers, which were turning black and bloated and distorted beyond recognition from unexpelled bodily gases. Their eyes bulged almost out of their sockets, their blackened tongues swelled, filling their mouths, uniform buttons popped from the strain, and their arms reached for the sky in rigor. Flies buzzed around the rotting flesh, landing and depositing maggot eggs in mouths, ears, nostrils, and wounds. Some soldiers with weak stomachs were so nauseated that they had the dry heaves.

Many of the wounded had died during the night, but many others had not, and there was still a great deal of screaming and moaning heard all through the forest. The most pressing need of those suffering men was water, for that is an utter necessity to a man in shock, and some of the boys in the earthworks threw out their canteens hoping that the injured soldiers of both sides would be able to reach them.

While most of the men stood at their posts with nervous trigger fingers and ever-alert eyes, some of the others got the fires going and boiled the coffee.[14] The regiment had breakfast on its feet that morning, and the men kept one hand on their Springfields while eating with the other.

From time to time, someone in the brigade, as in other parts of the lines, would be taken out with a sharpshooter's round, and if the boys could see where the rifleman was—by watching for the puff of smoke or flash from his gun's muzzle—they would blaze away in that direction until they heard the crashing thud of the marksman as he tumbled from his perch in a tree and fell through the branches to the ground. Because the forest fires were still flickering throughout the thick timberland, it was not easy to see the telltale rifle smoke, but the men remained vigilant for it anyway. In the dense Wilderness, those snipers had to get fairly close to the Union lines because of the limited visibility, and many of them paid the price for their proximity. The Federal army, too, had plenty of its own sharpshooters, and those skilled gunmen labored with the same diligence as their Southern confreres.

After the early breakfast, light musket fire started all along the lines, and it was kept up by each side all day. "There has been some firing on the left during the day," wrote Francis Harrington, adding, "Fell in several times but nothing serious occurred."[15]

Later in the morning the men of both armies finally began retrieving those wounded whom it was safe enough to reach, although many of the rescuers were picked off while on their errands of mercy.[16]

And up and down the lines, sporadic cheering could be heard from time to time during the day, while Federal bands played[17]—some in the army evidently thought the battle of the Wilderness a Union victory.

The sun on the seventh of May was scorchingly hot once again, but all day long, stragglers and lost and detached men searched out and rejoined their companies, so that by nightfall, nearly everyone in the 57th was accounted for in one way or another.

★

All that Saturday the Yankee soldiers continually made preparations for a renewal of battle by reinforcing their earthworks, but the expected fight never materialized and, after dark, the four stung corps of the Federal army began to leave their works and move out. They left behind their thousands of unburied dead to the elements and the scavengers.

(Some time later, men were assigned to return to the battleground and

Eastern section of the Wilderness battlefield from in front of Downdall's Tavern:
the Wilderness Church is on the left, Hawkins' Farm is on the right, and the Orange
Plank road is in the foreground. *(USAMHI, Carlisle Barracks, Pa.)*

inter the corpses in trench graves on the field. Remains that could be identified were sent home at their relatives' expense if they wished to bury them
in their local cemeteries.)

As the soldiers of Stevenson's 1st Division shouldered arms and filed out
east along the Orange Plank road with the IX Corps, they delighted in
breathing fresh air. The night was chilly and starry and black as the men
passed the old, insignificant, wood-framed Wilderness Church and the dilapi-
dated Dowdall's Tavern on their way to Chancellorsville. In the long, dark
columns, illuminated intermittently by burning trees set on fire to mark the
way, there was a considerable amount of chattering among the men as to what
lay in store for them next on this so-far deadly adventure. Many of the
old-time campaigners thought that Grant was going the way of so many of
the Army of the Potomac's previous commanders, and that when they
reached Chancellorsville, the army would turn north at the four-way road
junction and reford the Rapidan or continue east to Fredericksburg and cross
the Rappahannock there—either way in ignominious defeat—and they were
heavy-hearted at the idea of another such humiliation.

At the intersection of the Orange Plank road and the Orange Turnpike,
the IX Corps fell in behind John Sedgewick's VI Corps, the men of which

were equally downcast at the prospects of another retreat, but as the miles of soldiers came to the crossroads, they made the turn, not to the left as supposed, but to the right, towards Richmond. The gloom of the earlier hours was dispelled quickly and spirits soared—soldiers broke out in song, cheered, and tossed their caps, to the consternation of the army commanders, who had ordered that the withdrawal be made silently so as not to alert the Southerners of the Federal intentions. Especially cheerful were the old veterans, who noted with satisfaction the familiar stars and constellations—like Polaris and the Big Dipper to the north and Arcturus to the east—which told them that they were definitely on a southerly course and not headed back across the Rapidan or the Rappahannock via Fredericksburg. This was a new experience for the men of the Army of the Potomac, who had retreated so many times in the past that it seemed to them a way of life, and they were jubilant. At last, they felt they just might have their general, and U. S. Grant was held in a little higher esteem in the ranks.

7

My Soul to Keep

B Y SUNDAY MORNING, May 8, with the rising yellow sun sparkling off of the dewy green forests and fields, the entire Army of the Potomac, along with the IX Corps, was well out of the dark hollows and jungles of the Wilderness. After the 57th passed through the crossroads of Chancellorsville village, one and a half miles beyond the Wilderness Church, the tired soldiers of the 1st Division, IX Corps, halted close to noon that morning for rest and coffee and remained there for much of the day, waiting for the ambulances and wagons carrying the wounded to the field hospitals in Fredericksburg to pass. The corps' 4th Division was still detached on guard duty, and the black soldiers were protecting those wagons ferrying the injured to safety. Later in the day, the men turned south and marched on close to where the Alrich family's house stood beside the intersection of the Orange Plank and the Cartharpin roads, and camped there for the night.[1]

★

Twenty-two-year-old First Lieutenant George Edward Barton of Company C was a pleasant-looking young aristocrat from Worcester and first cousin to Clara Barton, the famous Civil War hospital administrator and nurse and the renowned founder of the Red Cross. He had been detached from the regiment and detailed as commander of the ambulance train of the 1st Division, IX Corps, on April 26—much to his satisfaction. "I am now mounted being *Chief* of the 1st Division of Ambulances. . . . I like it very much and find it much easier *than walking* I am also as you must know on a *Division Gens.* [Stevenson's] Staff all of which is very gay," he wrote his mother enthusiastically from Bealton Station, Virginia, on April 30.

Barton had been assigned two second lieutenants, one of whom was Homer Foote of the 14th New York Heavy Artillery, plus 106 enlisted men chosen from the division's assorted regiments, including 7 from the 57th. He

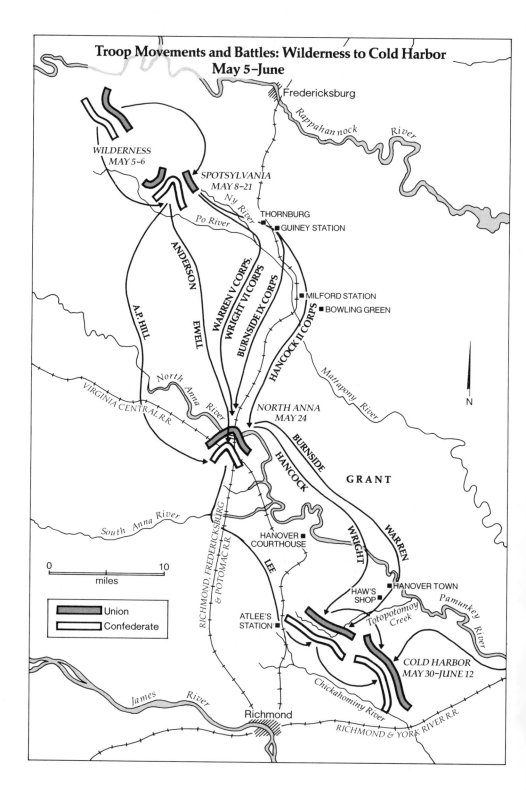

Troop Movements and Battles: Wilderness to Cold Harbor
May 5–June

Fredericksburg

Rappahannock River

WILDERNESS
MAY 5–6

SPOTSYLVANIA
MAY 8–21

Ny River

THORNBURG

Po River

GUINEY STATION

ANDERSON

A.P. HILL

EWELL

WARREN V CORPS

WRIGHT VI CORPS

BURNSIDE IX CORPS

HANCOCK II CORPS

MILFORD STATION

BOWLING GREEN

Mattapony River

N

North Anna River

VIRGINIA CENTRAL R.R.

NORTH ANNA
MAY 24

BURNSIDE

HANCOCK

GRANT

South Anna River

RICHMOND, FREDERICKSBURG & POTOMAC R.R.

HANOVER
COURTHOUSE

WRIGHT

WARREN

LEE

0   10
miles

HANOVER TOWN

HAW'S
SHOP

Pamunkey River

Totopotomoy Creek

ATLEE'S
STATION

Union
Confederate

COLD HARBOR
MAY 30–JUNE 12

James River

Chickahominy River

Richmond

RICHMOND & YORK RIVER R.R.

was also supplied with 50 ambulances, 2 army transport wagons, over 100 horses, and all the equipment necessary to operate his new command—from handsaws to halters, monkey wrenches to mess kits, axes to augers, and a liberal supply of hay and oats.

The 51st Massachusetts Volunteers, of which Lieutenant Barton had been sergeant major on the noncommissioned officer's staff, had seen very limited combat in North Carolina during late 1862 and early 1863, losing to disease rather than to Rebel bullets the great majority of its men who had died in service. George Barton, as a result of his light duty in the 51st, was hardly prepared to face the carnage with which he would be expected to deal during the Wilderness campaign, yet he would somehow manage until being relieved and sent back to the regiment in June.

When the IX Corps advanced to the battle of the Wilderness on May 4, Lieutenant Barton and his ambulance train still had been at Bealton Station, but as the fighting raged in the forest, he brought up his command, and with untiring devotion he and his men had been conveying the 1st Division's wounded—as well as injured men from other commands, including Confederate soldiers—to the temporary hospitals that had been set up in every house, commercial building, and church in Fredericksburg by people

Burial of Federal soldiers who died in Fredericksburg military hospitals, May 1864, from wounds received during the battles of the Wilderness and Spotsylvania. (*USAMHI, Carlisle Barracks, Pa.*)

like his cousin Clara Barton. The round trips had been arduous and seemingly never-ending—the field hospitals on the battlefield had been overflowing with bloody, shot-up soldiers, and he and his men never seemed to dent their numbers as they continued to transport them to Fredericksburg for eventual water transport to U.S. Army general hospitals in and around Washington.[2]

Captain Anderson described the grisly scene at Fredericksburg:

Here every church in the city was a hospital and every one was full, while all around outside lay wounded men ready to take the places of those who were dying within or being removed to Washington, Alexandria and Baltimore, via Belle Plain. Every public building was full, while in the smaller houses were wounded men who had personal friends or relatives in the Christian or Sanitary Commission, or friends who had been passed from Washington for that purpose, and were being kindly cared for. The large agricultural warehouses were also full of soldiers, placed in rows, upon muddy and bloody blankets, while nurses were going up and down between the rows with pails of ice water.[3]

Another of the 57th's soldiers, who was there, continues the narrative:

For the first few days at Fredericksburg it was almost impossible to obtain bandages. The women, with a few exceptions, were bitter rebels and would do all they could to prevent us from finding or buying a single piece of cloth. The bandage with which my own wound was bound up was part of the white skirt belonging to an elderly lady who brought roses into the Southern Methodist Episcopal Church where I was lying, a Mrs. McCabe. Seeing the need of a bandage, she loosed her skirt, cut it into strips, and handed it to my father, who proceeded to dress my own and other soldiers' wounds.[4]

But it was not only the Southern women who hampered the wounded men's comfort when they first began arriving. The Federal provost marshal at Fredericksburg refused to force the citizens of the town to admit "dirty common soldiers" into their homes. However, that officer's dictum was reversed rapidly by senior commanders.[5]

★

All of the highways leading out of the Wilderness and into Fredericksburg on May 8 were jammed for miles and miles with government vehicles, and the lanes and roads were in pitiful condition from the constant traffic of these military carriers moving the afflicted to the hospitals in the historic village. Those trundling army wagons and skinny-wheeled ambulances, which were poorly sprung, if sprung at all, were unbearable to the wounded, as they pitched and banged around on the rutty roads, and the screaming and swearing from those men, some of whom had wounds that were now three days old, was unearthly as it echoed over the otherwise quiet countryside.[6]

By midday, with the sun at maximum intensity, the heat was insufferable to those torn, shattered soldiers. As in other regiments, details from each of the 57th's companies were pulled from the ranks and assigned to help their bleeding comrades in any way to ease their terrible suffering. As George Barton's ambulances, blood dripping through the floorboards and buzzing with flies, made their agonizingly slow way along, halting every few moments from the incessant traffic jams, the boys did everything in their power for the wounded soldiers. Some put cool water to the injured men's dry lips with the pewter spouts of their canteens, holding the weakened heads of the broken men up tenderly by their necks so they could swallow, while others gently bathed their wounds in the refreshing liquid. Those of the regiment who had extra underwear in their recently recovered knapsacks generously tore them into strips for bandages and wrapped the wounded soldiers' festering injuries as best they knew how. Dr. White, Dr. Heath, and hospital steward Henry G. Prout, one of the 57th's Southerners from Fairfax, Virginia, did all known to medicine to comfort the maimed, and they were as sympathetic as it was possible to be to their needs.

There were many Confederate wounded that were being treated by the Union army, too, and, usually they received the same compassionate attention as their brothers in blue.[7] Most of the 57th's infantrymen, like the great majority of Civil War soldiers both North and South, were men who had been raised with strong Christian morals and values, and, with a hiatus in the fighting, they felt no compromise of principals in treating the helpless from either side equally. That there were, however, atrocities committed on the wounded in some cases is on the historical record.

Many of the thousands of the more seriously wounded soon died. Medical science then was poor at best, and the destructive power of a soft-lead conical Minié ball, more than half an inch in diameter, was awesome when it shattered bone and tissue. The sole treatment that the doctors had for such mutilation, if the bullet only hit an extremity—a direct body shot generally was fatal—was amputation. Chloroform and ether were the only anesthetics available during the Civil War, and they were often in short supply. When neither was at hand, the surgeons cut and sawed anyway, with maybe a little commissary whiskey to stun the patient—or themselves—and two or three assistants to hold the unfortunate man down. The pain was, of course, indescribable.

Complicating surgery was the want of knowledge of antiseptics. If the soldier lived through the operation, which was performed by doctors who never sterilized their instruments and infrequently washed their hands, he was very likely to become infected and linger in agony for days—and even weeks and months in not a few cases—until he died from gangrene or other complications. Compounding all of this was the lack of a satisfactory transportation system to get the wounded from the battlefield to the field hospitals quickly—horse-drawn ambulances on inadequate roads were hardly the answer. The soldiers received the best medical care possible for the time, but in almost every way, it was woefully insufficient.[8]

★

Captain Levi Lawrence and First Lieutenant Charles Barker of Company F had made it safely to the field hospital after their woundings during the battle of the Wilderness, and there they remained until, as Lieutenant Barker related,

> the surgeon gave orders to move all who could be moved as quickly and quietly as possible, as [to all appearances] the 'rebs' were preparing to shell the hospital; so we started [in an ambulance] and traveled until morning, until we came to a plantation where we were cared for and rested part of the day, when we were again started for Rappahannock Station [on the Orange & Alexandria Railroad], but were met by a band of 'loyal farmers.' We fell back in rear of the army. In the afternoon [of May 7] we started with a long [wagon] train for Fredericksburg, where we arrived on the 9th, remaining until eleven that night; we started for Belle Plain en route for Washington. About one A.M. of the 12th, we were stopped by the Mosby gang who fired into us, overhauled and ordered us out of the wagons in terms more impressive than elegant or refined. I did not obey. I was sitting on the bottom of the wagon between Captain [Charles D.] Hollis [of Company C, badly wounded in the genitals] and a lieutenant of the 51st New York, who were lying down when they, the guerillas, presented pistols and demanded watches and money. I hid mine in the straw and told them I had nothing for them. Someone gave them a watch, which partially pacified them, and, as they were in a great hurry, they took the horses and left us in the mud where we remained until the supply [wagon] train returned from Fredericksburg, which we had met as it was going there the day before. They took us to Belle Plain where we took the boat for Washington and arrived about midnight of the 12th, being six days from the day I was wounded.[9]

Corporal J. Brainard Hall of Company B, who had been stationed on the left of the regiment's line and had been shot through the body early in the battle on May 6, related in a letter to Captain Anderson that "I was wounded, went back nearly to the Brock road, loaded into an ambulance, taken half way to Chancellorsville house, captured and recaptured twice and taken to the Fifth Corps Hospital near the Wilderness Run, all before nine o'clock A.M." Anderson then picks up the story: "The night after the battle [May 6] the hospital had to be abandoned by reason of the near approach of the enemy.

All the wounded that were able to be moved in army wagons were carried to the rear." Corporal Hall then goes on:

About fifty of us were so badly wounded that it was believed it would be safer to remain than to be transported with the conveniences at hand. The shells from the rebel batteries fell all around us that night. The assistant surgeon of the 59th [Massachusetts] Regiment [First Lieutenant Thomas Gilfillan] and [Private] Antonio Phillips [of Company B] volunteered to remain with us. Early the next morning lieutenant . . . George E. Barton, . . . knowing of our perilous condition, came to the rescue with a small squad of cavalry. He arrived just in time and all were taken off in time to avoid capture by the rebel advance with two exceptions, Doctor [Private Austin K.] Gould [of Company F] and Antonio Phillips, who stopped to pick up something that had been left by a wounded comrade and were gobbled up.[10]

Dr. Austin K. Gould had signed on as a private soldier with the 57th, refusing for the second time an officer's commission. He had had prior service as a private during the Port Hudson, Louisiana, campaign with the 53rd Massachusetts in 1863, where he was placed in charge of one of the XIX Corps' field hospitals. Immediately upon his enlistment with the 57th, Gould had been detached from Company F to serve on the regimental hospital staff, and throughout the contest at the Wilderness, he had braved the storm of battle treating the wounded in the thick of the fight, miraculously receiving no injury. Now he was a prisoner of war, but when taken, he had refused to tell his Confederate captors his profession.[11]

One of two native-born Italians in the regiment, Private Antonio Phillips, a professional nurse, had been detailed to regimental hospital duty as well. Phillips was a veteran of two Massachusetts regiments, George Barton's old 51st and the famous 15th, which had been cut to ribbons early in the war at Ball's Bluff.[12]

"Arose, washed, shaved and shirted for the first time and started for the Regimental Hospital," wrote Private William T. Peabody in his diary on May 8, and he went on to add, "walked into the Enemy's lines and taken prisoner." The following day, Monday, May 9, Peabody penned, "Marched [under guard] I don't know how far—15 miles I should think. Camped in a hollow with [Dr.] Gould and Antonio [Phillips]. Had one cake of Indian meal & it was odd. Fighting today. The boys are in good spirits, may as well be so as anyway."[13] So the three men, Gould, Phillips, and Peabody, were together; their odyssey would reach the depths of human suffering, and only one would ever see home again.

Private Edward Sansoucy and Private Gilbert Sandy, both from Company C and both French Canadians from Quebec, had each been wounded in the Wilderness. While on the way to Fredericksburg for treatment on May 8, they were captured and sent to a Confederate prison. They survived their wounds and their captivity of almost a year, a development that was little short of miraculous.[14]

★

There had been some mean little skirmishes on the march, but no serious incidents occurred in the 57th, and the men welcomed a rest from the killing and bloodshed. The regiment had "halted about Daylight (to let another Corps [no doubt the VI Corps] pass [as well as the ambulances]) and made coffee," and was later bivouacked on part of the old Chancellorsville battlefield,[15] where almost a year ago to the day, General Lee had ingloriously routed Mr. Lincoln's Army of the Potomac, then commanded by Major General Joseph Hooker, back across the Rappahannock River. But the great Southern commander also had sustained a serious loss there with the wounding and subsequent death of his enigmatic and intrepid general, Thomas Jonathan "Stonewall" Jackson.

Some of the men took time to wander the historic battleground, and they found the fields and woods still cluttered with chalky skulls, decaying equipment, and other gruesome relics of the disastrous Union defeat. They discovered scores of shallow trench graves where the earth had been washed away by the rain and snow, and in them they saw the whitened bones of hundreds of soldiers of both armies, identifiable only by fragments of rotten uniforms still clinging to their broken remains.[16]

★

The situation on this sultry Virginia day was one of steady fighting for some parts of the two great armies. Major General Richard H. Anderson, who had succeeded in command of Longstreet's First Corps of the Army of Northern Virginia when that awesome general had been accidentally wounded in the Wilderness by his own men, had moved his fighters on a nearly parallel southeasterly course with that of the Federal V Corps, following a trail just cut by Southern work parties through the woods from the right flank of the Army of Northern Virginia to Shady Grove Church. The path, known as "Pendleton's Trace," was named for the officer who oversaw its construction, Brigadier General William Pendleton. The V Corps had been on a forced march south along the Brock road toward the village of Spotsylvania Court House, and all along its route, Warren's men had been menaced by Rebel cavalry patrols harrassing and bushwhacking them, and by trees that had been chopped down across the road by Rebel sappers to impede their progress, not to mention the Federal cavalry units, which blocked the way for a while.

It had been impossible for the Confederates to bivouac in the burning forest along the trace, as they were supposed to have done, so they raced on through the woods to Spotsylvania, a sleepy hamlet situated on a very strategic crossroads, about twelve miles distant. They promptly entrenched themselves behind rail breastworks, which had been thrown together in short order by leading elements of Confederate cavalry, in order to cut off Sam Grant's grand flanking movement designed to skirt Lee's right, and therefore move the Union forces deeper into Southern territory in the direction of Richmond.

Anderson had arrived in the area at about eight o'clock that morning, and not a moment too soon. The winded Northern troops were right behind him—the leading elements not but sixty yards—racing in a mad dash for possession of the vital road crossing. Both sides dug in hard, and the battle of Spotsylvania Court House began immediately as Major General Gouverneur K. Warren's salty V Corps boys faced off with Anderson's equally tough veterans of Lee's army. Later that afternoon, Anderson was reinforced by Major General Jubal Anderson Early's 1st Division of the Confederate Second Corps, and, partially as a result, what had been a shaky Southern hold in the morning became a formidable grasp for the Confederates late in the day.

★

The fighting down toward the southeast was intense all that Sunday, and the men of the 57th, held in their reserve position near the Alrich house with the IX and II Corps, guarding against a Rebel attack from the rear, could hear the gunfire from morning until night. Their combat labors were far from over, and they knew it, and none of them was looking forward to the next pounding sure to come. Men, like those of Company K and others, who had been sick or detached and who had not had their chance to "see the elephant" in the Wilderness, would soon earn their place in the veteran ranks— or in the ground.[17]

Around the campfires that night, the men talked about the new battle and the old one, and they contrasted the realities of war with their previously held notions of the glories of bloodless battles portrayed in the paintings and books of the day. The fantasies of the contemporary Victorian writers and artists, as well as writers and artists of old, had perpetrated an awful lie in the minds of many of those new soldiers, and had they known the truth—or believed the terrible stories told by the discharged veterans on the streets of their hometowns—most of them never would have allowed themselves to have been dragged into this madness.[18]

★

Early the next morning, May 9, Brigadier General Orlando Bolivar Willcox's 3rd Division of the IX Corps moved southeastward to the crossing of the Ny

101

River, an inconsequential little stream with heavily wooded banks, on the Fredericksburg road north of Spotsylvania. While about a mile from the bridge, the division ran into sharp Rebel resistance, but Willcox's men drove it in and seized the span over the river. Colonel Benjamin C. Christ's 2nd Brigade, 3rd Division, with Captain Jacob Roemer's 34th New York Light Battery of three-inch ordnance rifles and Captain Adelbert Twitchel's 7th Maine Battery of the division's artillery, raced over the bridge and forward for about a quarter-mile to a small hill where the infantry formed and the artillery unlimbered and wheeled its guns around, and the whole attacked in force. But the ground was strongly held by the stalwart Southerners, who were backing down not one foot, and the Yankees were reversed on the run. The Federal infantry staged a rapid counterattack and by noon had repulsed the Confederates.

Meanwhile, orders came down from General Burnside for Stevenson to get his 1st Division on the move as quickly as he possibly could and be ready to reinforce Willcox if he needed help. The 57th clanged and banged itself into line early that morning, drew forty rounds and rations, and formed up with the brigade. Taking off on the double-quick along the dark and dusty back-country lanes and roads of Spotsylvania County with the eastern sky just beginning to lighten, the division rolled southeast in the direction of the shooting, "but got on to [the] wrong road and went about 8 miles out of [its] way." Finally, after getting back on track and enduring numerous frustrating halts, the 1st Division infantrymen came to within three miles of the little town. Ordered on a forced march from there at noon, the division reached the Ny River "at about 2 O'clock." General Stevenson's men hustled off to the left into the woods. The 1st Brigade, with the 57th, was ordered held in reserve on the north side of the river "and took position in the rear of a battery." From their vantage point, the men had an excellent view of the enemy trenches and the Confederate troops with their wagon trains moving near the town of Spotsylvania about a mile away to the south. Orders from division headquarters dispatched the 57th, along with the 56th Massachusetts, to a new position on the northern bank of the stream, where the two regiments remained for some time.[19]

The IX Corps moved as far as it could down the Fredericksburg road that day, pushing the Confederates back toward the courthouse in town as it advanced in force. Thomas Stevenson, as sweaty and dirty as any of his men, moved his division across the river and off to the left of the road again and into the dark pine, oak, and hazel forest, where the 1st Brigade took up station at "Sunset," near Whig Hill, behind Christ's brigade, the six rifled guns of Roemer's battery, and the 14th Massachusetts and 2nd Maine batteries. The men dug in quickly, improving their crude breastworks, and they kept a nervous watch with light skirmish fire flashing up and down the trench line under the black evening sky. The 4th and 10th U.S. Regulars of the 1st Brigade were detailed as pickets that night, and with the guard mounts from the other brigades of the division, the soldiers were cordoned off by those sentries.[20]

The boys were in position on the left of the Federal lines, about a mile to the northeast of the old, red brick Spotsylvania courthouse building, and their nerves, on that strangely quiet night, like those of all the soldiers in both armies, were raw. "Fighting severely in front," wrote Private Francis Harrington in his diary late that afternoon.[21]

This had been a reconnaissance action, and the fighting had been relatively mild—nothing akin to the Wilderness. Nevertheless, dead and wounded lay all around from the vicious little fight.

Ambrose Burnside had thought that Rebel resistance this far away from the new battle taking shape southwest of his line indicated that Lee had split his forces and sent part of them off to Fredericksburg to capture the huge Union stores stockpiled in that town. He was quite mistaken, as was too often his problem, for in fact the Confederates that the IX Corps encountered in the action at the Ny River that day were mostly some of General J. E. B. Stuart's cavalrymen, who were fighting dismounted. Stuart's troopers were tough little scrappers, on or off horseback, and they gave the IX Corps Federals a good going-over that hot Monday.

★

Tuesday, May 10, was a pleasant day. Francis Harrington recorded in his diary that in the late afternoon there began "considerable (art[illery]) firing on the right" side of the Federal lines as elements of the VI and II Corps attacked the Confederate trenches from the west. At five o'clock an attack along the whole line was launched, and at sunset Private Harrington tells us that there was "heavy firing all along the line we [Company K] are helping work (the guns [of the 7th Maine Battery])".[22]

In the meantime, from their position guarding the approaches to the village, the 1st Division of the IX Corps made a reconnaissance in force to test the strength of the Southern fortifications in front of the courthouse. As the 57th regiment scampered out of its trenches late that sunny Tuesday afternoon, with Company E spread out in front as skirmishers, and moved forward across the spring-green meadows along the east side of the Fredericksburg road, the men soon engaged the Rebel picket lines, which fell back in order maintaining a steady, sustained fire.

In full view of the Confederates, the boys advanced towards them, in solid ranks, across an open field south of the Beverly house that descended toward a glade in the dense woods in front of them. As the brigade had been entrenched close to the Fredericksburg road and only a short distance from the enemy, the men did not have far to go to get into trouble with the Southerners, and both sides soon tore into one another with murderous volleys of musket fire.

The 57th finally got as far as an old weatherworn fence, at the foot of which were wild hedgerows of snarled brush and briars. There, in the tangle of thorns, a quarter-mile in front of the courthouse near the road, they made their stand. From this new position, the men had an excellent view of the seemingly impregnable Rebel defenses dug in on a ridge in front of them, and they kept a nasty little firefight going for quite some time.[23]

The men of 57th once again were fortunate on that day, and took only two losses in wounded, but Brigadier General Stevenson had not fared as well. That morning, the general had been lying under a terrace on the left side of the Fredericksburg road thinking he was pretty well protected, when a sniper, high in a tree, blew part of his brains out at 8:30. He died a half-hour later and was succeeded, temporarily, by Major General Thomas Leonidas Critten-den, the son of the famous Kentucky politician John J. Crittenden, who would soon assume official command of the division. Crittenden, a man whose career had been blighted at Chickamauga the previous September when his XXI Corps was overrun by Southern forces, felt the command of a mere division beneath his military status, and, in a swirl of egomania, he would resign on June 9.[24]

Sporadic fire was kept up until late that night, when it finally died down and the soldiers were able to get some rest. With the Rebels so close the pickets were uneasy and highly excitable, and many a shot was squeezed off on both sides of the lines by the apprehensive soldiers. A good sleep was hardly possible, but the men dozed a little with their loaded Springfields close at hand. "Laid by the stack of arms all night had some rest did some Fatigue duty," commented Francis Harrington.[25]

★

The next day, May 11, Burnside ordered his men to withdraw back across the Ny River. This they did, taking up a position on the right of an old road located a quarter of a mile east of the creek. The 1st Brigade was spread out in line over one and a half miles of rolling, generally open ground, from northwest to southeast, and its order of battle was, starting at the southeast, the 57th, the 2nd Michigan Volunteer Infantry (temporarily in position with the brigade), the 56th Massachusetts, the 10th Regulars, the 59th Massachu-setts, and the 4th Regulars. The 57th, on the extreme left of the brigade, was the only unit of the 1st Brigade remaining on the east side of the Fredericks-burg road now, and Charles Chandler, still in command of the regiment, had his men in a fairly secure position to the rear and left of Roemer's battery.[26]

The terrain on the east side of the IX Corps' position was not really very much different from the Wilderness, and once again, a gloomy and forbidding forest of pine, hardwood, and undergrowth surrounded the 57th's soldiers. Wood ticks, garter snakes, and beetles abounded. There were old grown-over cow paths, dusty, snaky lanes, and wandering wagon roads that arrived at no particular destinations throughout these woodlands filled with thickets, oaks and cedars, marshes, dirty streams, and stagnant, slimy pools that bred the relentless mosquito. The days had been stifling, and the boys had suffered from heat and thirst. Although they were very near the Ny River, getting close enough to draw water was quite another matter because of Confederate sharpshooters and patrols roaming all through the area, so the filthy creeks and pools were their only source of water, and they had no choice but to drink it.

During the day of May 11, the men occupied themselves with improving their defenses and preparing for a renewal of the battle. As the unseasonably warm, oppressive heat continued, they felled trees and scavenged dead logs from the woods and fence rails from the local farmer's pastures to strengthen their breastworks. And they resisted, as well as they could, the annoying sniping and bushwhacking of the Rebel sharpshooters. Skirmishing and reconnoitering otherwise occupied their time, and the men of the 57th, as well as the soldiers of the other regiments, remained edgy and on their toes.

"About noon," Harrington reported, his company, K, "moved [with the 7th Maine Battery] about ½ mile to a hill in the rear, not much firing."[27]

The drizzle started in the afternoon, and at first the men welcomed the cooling relief it brought, but the light rain soon turned into a driving downpour that soaked everyone clean through. The ground rapidly turned into a quagmire with sticky, brown mud everywhere. From the agony of the blistering heat, the soldiers now had to deal with the misery of ankle-deep bogs and drenching showers. Work slowed to a crawl as they trudged and slipped through the morass carrying their loads of logs and rails.

The night was pitch black as the low storm clouds hid the starry heavens, and because their precious knapsacks had once more been left in the rear in the regimental baggage wagon near Burnside's headquarters, the men of the 57th had no shelter of any kind, and they were, as they would have put it, "as mad as a stumped tail bull at flytime." Sleep was impossible in the scud, and their uniforms were soaked and filthy. Some simply stood or sat in the mud all night, while others, who could not bear that proposition, lay in the muck with no cover. All were wretched. Private Harrington, who rarely complained of anything, noted, with characteristic understatement, that "it is rainy and uncomfortable tonight."[28]

★

When the Massachusetts men were turned out early on the the 12th, a layer of cold fog, so thick that it delayed first light until after four-thirty that morning, slithered around the entrenchments and woods. The temperature had dropped abruptly during the night, and the exhausted soldiers shivered with chattering teeth, trying to keep warm. Chilling little gusts whined through the dripping trees, adding to their distress, as they listened attentively for noises from the Confederate trenches and to owls hooting in the branches of nearby pines. The rain came down in sheets, the men were not able to start fires to boil their coffee or fry their salt pork or keep warm, and they were thoroughly disgusted and entirely sick of the whole business of soldiering.

After roll call, they were issued their forty rounds of ammunition and put on alert for action at a moment's notice.

★

All the previous day, General Grant had been putting into effect a plan for a grand assault on the Confederate works. His idea came as result of an action on a lesser scale on Tuesday by Colonel Emory Upton, a brigade commander in the VI Corps, who successfully advanced on the left of the long wedge-shaped Rebel lines. Had not darkness interfered—the colonel began his charge late in the day—and had he been supported as he was supposed to have been, his attack could very well have resulted in a stunning Union victory. At any rate, Grant had thought the young colonel's tactic deserving of much merit, and the Federal army commander had moved the II Corps from the far right to the center of the concave Federal lines, instructing its leader, Winfield Hancock, to hit the Rebels hard at first light on the 12th. The V and VI Corps would simultaneously attack the Confederate left, while the IX Corps would assault the right. All over the northern part of the battlefield that night and into the early hours of Thursday men in both armies could hear the eerie, low-pitched roar of thousands of shuffling II Corps soldiers as they took up station in the pouring rains for their battle assignments. The V, VI, and IX Corps remained pretty much where they were, as they were already in the positions desired by U. S. Grant and George Meade.

★

Before dawn that morning, the spread-out regiments of the 1st Brigade re-formed, crossed the river, and advanced along with the IX Corps, occupying a position behind earthworks on the west side of the Fredericksburg road. From there, at about 4:30 A.M., the 1st Division, with the 1st Brigade in the van, gradually moved forward through the woods and fields. The 1st Division followed the 2nd on the right side of the road facing the Confederate salient, which was about a mile to the southwest. Colonel Simon G. Griffin's brigade of the 2nd Division, which linked to the left of the II Corps, led the IX Corps' advance. Soon, Crittenden's men would link up with Willcox's 3rd Division, which would come up in echelon on their left. For the present, though, the 3rd Division was being held in reserve.[29]

The men in these heavily fortified Southern works were the tough and stringy veterans of General Richard S. Ewell's Second Corps and Ambrose Powell Hill's Third Corps (Hill's corps was being commanded temporarily by General Jubal Anderson Early) of the Army of Northern Virginia. As the men of the IX and II Corps formed lines of battle in the black and rainy morning, they stumbled and banged around so much in the darkness and mud that the nearby Confederates could hear them clearly, and the Southerners knew something was in the wind.

Roman Catholic chaplains moved through the Federal formations absolving the Irish and other soldiers of that faith. The self-righteous Methodists, Episcopalians, and Baptists thought the scene contemptible and vile, and they sneered at the "popery."

At four-thirty that morning, Brigadier General Francis Channing Barlow's 1st Division of the II Corps led off the attack against the apex of the Rebel salient known as the "Mule Shoe," because of its curved shape, and shortly after that, the IX Corps advanced its formations against the east face of that jutting peninsula of earthworks. General Crittenden caught up with his new command and relieved the courageous and daring Pennsylvanian, Colonel Daniel Leasure, who had been temporarily in charge of the 1st Division these last two days pending the general's arrival. The colonel returned to his brigade.

With the tumult of the II Corps' assault growing in intensity on the right, and the eastern sky just beginning to lighten behind it, the men of the IX Corps moved forward over the dark, slippery landscape with skirmishers out in front peppering the Rebels. They had difficulty seeing the Confederates against the dark western horizon through the sheets of falling rain, and they made significantly better targets for the Southerners. Unbroken volleys of musketry rattled the air as the corps struggled to overrun the Confederate trenches. Robert Potter's 2nd Division broke through clouds of gun smoke and fog in a frenetic charge, taking a number of prisoners and two field pieces. But those men could not maintain their grip on their newly won position against a murderous enfilading fire from the Rebels and eventually were driven back, seriously smashed up. Desperate for safe haven, they were forced to give up their captured artillery.

The 1st Division, to the left of the 2nd, and the 3rd Division, now moved up to the left of the 1st, then repeatedly attacked the strong Confederate positions in suicidal charges, only to be forced back each time with monstrous losses. The 3rd Division got within yards of the enemy trenches at one point, but it was soon routed by killing musket fire and double-shotted charges of canister and grape from the Rebel cannon of William Poague's artillery in

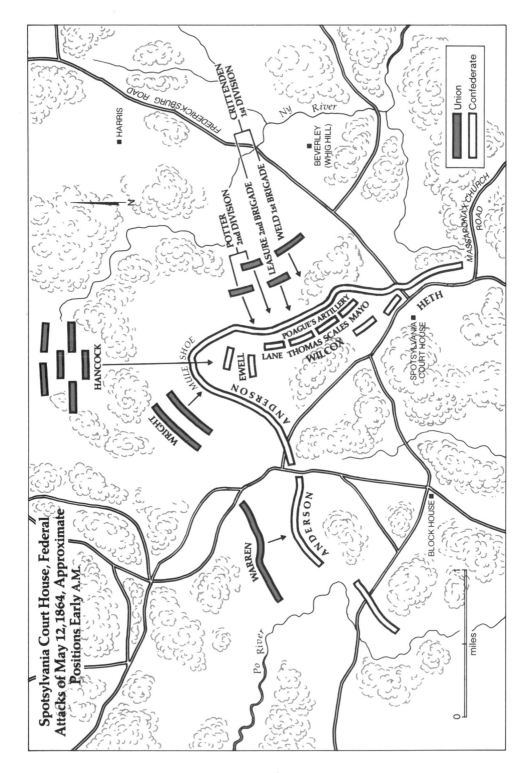

Spotsylvania Court House, Federal Attacks of May 12, 1864, Approximate Positions Early A.M.

battery behind the works. At about nine o'clock, the Rebels counterattacked, but after a severe battle, they could not force Burnside's men back. However, the Southerners did prevent them from gaining any further ground. Undaunted, the IX Corps continued the attacks, eventually gaining and holding an advanced position, but failing in its objective of crushing the Confederate lines. Under a storm of bullets, cannon fire, and pounding rain, the men dug in fast and erected makeshift breastworks in the mire.

The 57th had been in the IX Corps' action all morning, but had been detached by Colonel Weld to fight along with Colonel Leasure's 2nd Brigade that battled alongside the 1st Brigade. After a brief lull in the fighting around noon, the 57th Massachusetts, in concert with the corps, again moved forward towards the southwest through the gnarled underbrush and unrelenting downpour. This time the men drove the Southerners back a little further, then were halted quite close to the Rebel lines and ordered to lie down in the mud and shoot from prone positions. The fire from both sides continued nonstop.[30]

As the boys lay in their muddy positions, the Confederates began to re-form their lines for a counterthrust, and the men of the 57th could hear distinctly above the gunfire the Southern officers ordering, "Move forward! Sustain an unbroken line! Fire low!" But at the instant the next command of "Forward!" was given, Colonel Chandler stood up tall, taking the Confederates by surprise, and shouted, "Attention 57th! Fix bayonets! Forward at the double-quick! Charge!"[31]

The regiment attacked with a rush and a deep-throated cheer and the Rebel plans for a countercharge were turned on end. Utterly befuddled, the soldiers in the butternut uniforms of the Confederacy fell back with the 57th screaming down on their heels, shooting them to the ground and running them through with their bayonets, yelling and laughing with glee as Lee's veterans tumbled in the mud.

The problem was, though—and the 57th never ceased to find more than its share of that commodity—that in their enthusiasm, the men had advanced much too far, and they were now in deep trouble with both flanks hanging in the air lacking adequate support, if any at all. Colonel Chandler, thinking quickly, ordered the men to lie down as fast as they could just as Poague's Rebel batteries opened on them with everything they had. Concentrated artillery fire was a new and frightening experience for most of the young Massachusetts soldiers, and they hugged the ground as flat as they could. But, after what seemed an eternity, a portion of the IX Corps artillery—the eight cannons belonging to the 19th and 34th New York Light Batteries—started to answer the Southern guns with ruinous fire, and the relieved infantrymen cheered their Yankee cannoneer comrades.

The Rebel cannon fire was, nevertheless, nerve shattering. Shells swished and whirred through tree branches and smacked into the muddy ground. Each time the men heard a round whooshing and screaming toward them, they flattened out and clenched their teeth and shut their eyes in abject fright. Often a shell would not explode on contact, and the frustration and tension of waiting for it to go off were agonizing. Occasionally the artillery rounds failed completely, but when they did explode, they blew deep pits in the earth and threw mud and debris all over the prone men, who clutched and covered their heads with their hands and arms and prayed faster and harder.

Quite a few of these holes were large enough to give shelter, and resourceful soldiers breathlessly rolled and jumped into them for better cover. Others, who were lying near unexploded shells, were paralyzed in terror and would not move, nor could they be ordered to move for any reason. But after a continuous shelling for some time that actually inflicted almost no physical damage to the regiment, most of the men began to get the notion that this particular Southern battery had no idea what it was doing, as the random firing was so uneven that it harmed no one seriously. They also came to the conclusion that the Confederate gunpowder was hardly of the highest quality, and they began to relax a little.[32]

During the battle, Captain James Doherty of Company G, known among the troops for his rash Irish behavior, spotted a Rebel infantryman in front of the regiment's position crying for help. He was lying in the quarter-mile no man's land between the opposing lines, and he had been severely wounded in the thigh and was bleeding badly. The captain called for volunteers to go out and bring him into the regiment's trenches as he was sure that the man would drown in the deep puddles of rainwater or suffocate in the mud. But there were no takers. The supply of foolhardy bravery apparently had waned somewhat in the 57th. "Who will go and rescue that man?" yelled Doherty, as all around Confederate sharpshooters were now picking off anything that showed so much as a square inch of blue. When none of the boys responded to his request, he announced, self-righteously, "Well, I never asked any man to do what I would not do myself," and up and over the breastworks leaped the dauntless captain as the men followed him with their cynical eyes. Unbelievably, amid a hail of snipers' bullets, Doherty reached and dragged back the wounded Confederate, who, unfortunately, died later in the 1st Division's field hospital. The men were awe-struck at the unscathed captain's luck.[33]

Shortly after this incident, the IX Corps' commanders decided that the Confederates, who were trying desperately to turn the Federal left flank, were close to success, and they ordered the wounded who could be moved to be taken to the rear, while the front line soldiers retreated. In the 1st Division's hospital, however, about sixty men were too seriously injured to be taken anywhere, so volunteers were requested to stay with them. Dr. White, Reverend Dashiell, and several male army nurses, with one day's rations and one case of surgical instruments, remained behind as the ambulatory wounded and the combat troops fell back. Not long after they had been left in their tenuous position, a company of Rebel troopers rode up to the hospital to investigate the situation. Since they found nothing but a doctor, a minister, and a few nurses, plus a number of their own wounded being cared for among the mutilated, the Southern cavalrymen disturbed no one and soon galloped off. In a short time, the cheering Union troops from the IX Corps successfully moved back to their original position, restoring their newly won lines and protecting the hospital, to the great relief of the Union men in it.[34]

8

Mother, May You Never See the Sights I Have Seen

A FTER NEARLY twenty hours of nonstop fighting, a macabre silence settled over the battlefield around midnight. From time to time crickets chirped, owls hooted, and whippoorwills sang. The weather alternated between periods of drizzle and torrential showers, and rainwater dripped from the trees and the brims of the men's caps. In a stupor from exhaustion, they lay soaking in the mud in their trenches in the woods, staring with blank, unseeing eyes. With no opportunity to bathe or change clothes for the past nine days, they were filthy and smelled foul. Their equipment was battle-scarred and their Springfields were rusty, but their bodies were toughening. While each man was aware of and uncomfortable with his own appearance, he frequently found the distressing sight of his comrades hysterically funny. They could still laugh heartily, but they were miserably discontent.

Three-hundred and thirty-three of the 57th's officers and men had been engaged in the fighting of May 12, and of that number, 12 had been killed, 5 mortally wounded, and 56 wounded, with 1 missing and 4 more captured for a total loss of 78.[1] The once-mighty numbers of the regiment were being pared down to small change in very short order, and the little band of torpid combat soldiers in the trenches was just about used up.

Company A had been on the skirmish line in advance of the regiment on the 12th, and it had lost the most heavily—18 of its 41 men, nearly 44 percent of its combat strength. Feisty little Billy Martin, a twenty-three-year-old private in that company from Waterford, Ireland, who had been employed as a bootmaker in Milford, Massachusetts, and had served previously with the 1st Massachusetts Volunteer Cavalry until wounded at Aldie, Virginia, in June of 1863, finally had gone down after taking four wounds in succession, "two balls through left hand, piece of shell in right side, and . . . a ball in right side of breast all during same day." Clearly one tough customer was Billy. But his wounds were serious, and after his recuperation, the War Department discharged him for disability in July.[2]

Another boy on the skirmish line that day had been Corporal John Mills from Providence, Rhode Island. The corporal, too, had taken a piece of shrapnel in the side from an exploding shell, but unlike Billy Martin, Mills would return to duty only to reach a tragic end.[3]

Private Henry Black of Company B took a fatal bullet in the head, but it took until February 22 of the following year for him to die of an "inflamed brain." He had been only eighteen.[4]

A native of Massachusetts from Norton, Company B's Corporal Benjamin Dayton, also eighteen, took a vicious wound in his left leg, and Dr. O. A. Judson sawed the mangled limb off. But the surgery was not successful, and the leg had to be reamputated higher up in August.[5]

One of the regiment's older men, forty-three-year-old Private Oliver Fosgate from Winchester, New Hampshire, had his right index finger mutilated. The lower third of his right forearm went to the scalpel, but he recovered and served out his enlistment with the Veteran Reserve Corps after the doctors diagnosed him as having a "sound stump."[6]

Over in Company H, yet another eighteen-year-old, Private Charles Fitts from Manchester, New Hampshire, was mortally wounded in both legs, and died five days later.[7]

Private Rodney Loomis of the same company, a glassy-eyed, slow-witted-looking carpenter from St. Albans, Vermont, had his left leg removed on May 13, as a result of a crippling gunshot wound.[8]

Severely wounded in the right thigh, Private James Stetson of Company H had his leg cut off in the 1st Division field hospital the day after the battle, but he died, nevertheless, from pyemia on the last day of May.[9]

One of the boys who had drawn baggage wagon-train guard duty with Company K during the battle of the Wilderness, Private William Andrews, "accidentally" wounded himself with his own rifle just before the regiment engaged the enemy. After he had sufficiently recuperated in an army hospital, he was given a furlough home later in the summer and deserted.[10]

A "brave soldier," young Private Lowell Daniels, from upstate New York and also a member of Company K, was fatally wounded that day fighting side by side with his older brother by a year, Charles. Lowell died later that afternoon in the 1st Division, IX Corps, field hospital.[11]

Company K had been lucky again. It had supported the 7th Maine Battery in the fight, and the boys of that company had not taken much abuse, losing but four men, and with some of the regiment's companies now only numbering combat soldiers in the teens, K stood strong, mustering sixty-one effectives on the line.[12]

But there were some brighter sides to the battle. Newton B. Pepoon, an eighteen-year-old blacksmith from Stockbridge, Massachusetts, and one of the regiment's cocky, colorful characters, was promoted corporal for "gallant conduct" on the field that May 12.[13]

And the "little villain" Robert Clark in Company B, of whom we heard earlier at Camp Wool, had become a "good soldier" and was one of those wounded on the 12th. Dr. White wrote to John Anderson, concerning his behavior on the battlefield, that Clark had

> marched from Annapolis to the battle of the Wilderness, where he was in the thickest of the fight. On the 12th of May, at the battle of Spotsylvania, our army was devastated, and among the wounded was this boy. He came to me, and I found that the ball had passed through the top of his shoulder, carrying away the middle of his collarbone, and making its exit at the top of the shoulder blade. With his eye bright with satisfaction he said to me, "Doctor, I have stood all the marches, and the battle of the Wilderness, and this is the first time I have been to the rear." I said, "I knew there was something good in you, and you have shown it, for you have acted nobly. You have your wound, but it is not a serious one. It is a wound that you will be proud to go home and show to those who thought you were worthless, and you will carry it as a mark of heroism and patriotism through your whole life."

Young Clark would return to duty in November and serve to the last, being mustered out of service with the regiment after the war ended.[14]

★

This had been a day of the most brutal combat that the Army of the Potomac had ever seen—worse in its barbarity than Antietam, Fredericksburg, or the Wilderness—especially as the men of the II and VI Corps tried to take the salient from the northwest side where the fighting was at close quarters and hand-to-hand for more than nineteen hours. Twelve thousand bloody, broken casualties, strewn around and upon each other, lay in an area not much larger than a square mile. Twenty-four Union brigades had battled savagely to the death with the Army of Northern Virginia until the Southerners finally retired to their inner defensive works, fighting for every miserable inch of dirt along the way, and this spot in the Confederate defenses became known to history as "The Bloody Angle." It was aptly named, and its nightmare never was to be forgotten by the men of either side who had been locked in combat there.

Although the IX Corps had fought mostly on the other side and slightly south of the "Mule Shoe," the men of that corps did not have it much easier with the rugged Confederate soldiers they had faced. As in the Wilderness, the dead and dying were everywhere, and in some cases they were piled three and four deep around the areas where the fighting had been the heaviest.

Corpses often covered wounded soldiers who, in their helplessness, frequently suffocated under the weight of the cadavers. Men had drowned in the water and smothered in the muck, and many a downed soldier had been trampled to bloody pulp in the frenzied charges and countercharges.

It had been hell—described by many of the participants as indescribable, an event that they themselves would never have believed possible had they been told by someone else that it had happened. The battlefield was a ghastly and gruesome tangle of butchered flesh and splintered bone and broken and torn army accoutrements. Whole copses of large trees—one hardwood two feet in diameter—had been shot down by small arms fire alone, but unlike in the Wilderness the rain had kept forest fires from springing to life. And also in contrast to the Wilderness, the mud and rain made the fighting fiercely hard work. Blood literally stood in pools until it finally diluted in the rainwater. The Army of the Potomac's surgeons, working with only lanterns to light their grisly production, hacked and sawed all night in vain efforts to keep up with the wounded streaming into the dressing stations and field hospitals.

Meanwhile, the survivors of the 57th passed out in the mire from mind-bending exhaustion.

★

The 13th of May was fairly quiet, and the IX Corps maintained its position just west of the Fredericksburg road. The 1st Division was manning low, hastily constructed trenches on the near slope of a slight elevation close to a small, swift brook, in which some of the men took the opportunity to bathe. The ground in front of the works was open for about fifty feet, and then a pine woods with thick underbrush rose abruptly beyond. On the right of the 1st Division, another green growth of timber concealed troops of the 2nd Division, IX Corps, who connected to the left of the II Corps. On the left of Crittenden's command was more grassy, open ground in which the 3rd Division was entrenched. Supporting Burnside's lines, behind stoutly built redoubts, were twenty-eight guns of the IX Corps' artillery on duty in batteries.[15]

During the dark and stormy night of May 13, the boys had been directed to move to a new position in order to prepare for an attack scheduled for the 14th. It was tough going as the frazzled men slogged their way through the treacherous mud in the blackness. They were so tired that they could not reason when they finally clanked into battle lines and dressed ranks. But at the last moment, the attack was canceled by General Grant when the V and VI Corps were late in coming up into position. So, back they trudged, madder than hornets, to their miserable rifle pits to get what sleep they could.[16]

"Had a good nights rest," wrote Francis Harrington upon awakening, having fallen asleep after the regiment's return to its trenches that early Saturday morning. He continued, "There has been troops moving by here all this morning towards the left flank we expect to move about noon." Later in the day he penciled in his diary, with filthy hands that left reddish-brown finger and palm prints all over some of the pages, "moved back to our position of Thursday and bivouacked in the edge of (the pine) woods the hill in front of us is covered with rifle pits."[17]

★

On May 14, Brigadier General James Hewett Ledlie, a thirty-two-year-old New Yorker and civil engineer in private life, relieved Colonel Weld and assumed command of the 1st Brigade. Ledlie previously had been a colonel in the 19th New York Volunteer Infantry, which later was redesignated the 3rd New York Heavy Artillery. He had secured his promotion to general officer through political maneuvering in Washington, and he was destined to become the bane of his men's existence.[18]

★

From May 14 until May 18, little except skirmishing and sniping occurred. The rain hardly ever let up until the 17th, making the roads totally impassable, and active operations of both armies temporarily ground to a halt.

The trench lines of the opposing forces were so close together that each side could hear the other clearly, and the sharpshooters of both armies were always on the prowl with their long-range, telescope-equipped rifles. They stayed deep in the rear, often lashing themselves with rope to the trunks and branches high up in the oaks and pines, and they caused considerable mayhem with their dead-on marksmanship.[19] (Private Charles Brown, of Company G, had been slightly wounded in the battle of the 12th and sent to the hospitals in Fredericksburg to be patched up. On the 14th he was discharged as fit for duty, and as he was leisurely walking down the Fredericksburg road searching for the regiment, a Confederate sharpshooter drew a bead on him and ended his luck forever.)[20] By taking advantage of lessons learned in the Wilderness, such as moving often so they would not be detected by their rifle smoke, the snipers proved very effective, and not many of them were eliminated.

During this lull in the long battle, the dead that could be brought in safely were buried hastily in shallow trench graves, and if the remains could be identified, their names and regiments were scrawled or scratched on a piece of scrap wood from a hardtack or ammunition box and stuck in the ground as a temporary marker. The wounded were backed up at the field hospitals, and the doctors, working themselves to exhaustion, tried to get caught up. They knew perfectly well that when the rain stopped, there would be thousands of fresh cases for them to treat. The men used this natural truce to try to wash themselves and their clothes in the swollen creek nearby, but fighting the dirt and filth was one battle they could not win; the rain would not quit, and the mud would not go away.

★

On the 17th, the showers finally stopped, and the sun shone with the intensity of summertime, rapidly drying the roads and surrounding countryside, bringing the misery of humidity and heat to the hapless soldiers.

Orders filtered down to the army's regiments that afternoon from the lieutenant general, Grant, and the commander of the Army of the Potomac, George Meade, for a resumption of Federal offensive operations by all the four corps to begin early on the following day.

After dark, the 57th, along with the rest of the IX Corps, began to take up positions for the next attempt to take Spotsylvania. Following a short, unsatisfying rest, the men were roused at three-thirty on the morning of May 18. Under a clear sky with a crescent moon setting in the west, the veteran 35th Massachusetts came marching into the lines to rejoin the brigade for active duty in the field. This was the first time since before crossing the Rapidan that the men of the 35th had seen the previously green and untested new regiments, and they were "shocked" by the change in their appearance, at how beaten and worn out they were.[21] Never again would those veterans of the 35th doubt the fighting spirit of their new comrades; the latecomers had become part of the brotherhood—and rightfully so.

With a sliver of first light creeping over the eastern horizon, the 57th Massachusetts was supplied with rations and ammunition, formed into the front rank of the double line of the brigade, and moved "into rifle pits." The regiment numbered about 250 effectives present for combat duty now, and the men knew that they would be cut down even more before nightfall. They were just as afraid as they had ever been, but they hid that fear better now. The 57th's soldiers took pride in their withered status and hard-won battle honors.[22]

At four o'clock that morning the 56th Massachusetts, with the 35th as support in a second battle line, moved forward up the slope to within about one hundred yards of the thick Rebel abatis—sharpened stakes and trees planted close together facing the oncoming troops in order to thwart, or at least delay, the enemy attack. The Rebel works were heavily constructed and staunchly manned with the steely veterans of both Brigadier General Edward L. Thomas's brigade of the 14th, 35th, 45th, and 49th Georgia Infantry regiments, and Brigadier General Alfred M. Scales's brigade, consisting of the 13th, 16th, 22nd, 34th, and 38th North Carolina Volunteers of Willcox's division, Third Corps, Army of Northern Virginia.[23]

The 56th Massachusetts charged and reached the formidable defenses, but the Confederates unleashed a killing cross fire of musketry, caseshot, and canister, forcing the Federal attackers to lie flat in order to survive. The supporting men of the 35th Massachusetts were ordered to double-time it up to the forward lines to come to the aid of the 56th, but the veteran campaigners of the 35th refused, and instead ran the other way, back down the hill to safety. The 56th was ordered to withdraw with them, and the frantic men of that regiment moved to the rear as quickly as they could, taking up station a little in front of their rifle pits. Once more the 56th and 35th were ordered forward, but this time when they reached the abatis they were instructed to lie down where they were until the rest of the 1st Brigade came to their assistance.

At 5:00 A.M., along with the 59th Massachusetts and the 4th and 10th U.S. Regulars as support in the second line, and flanked by Griffin's 2nd Brigade of Potter's 2nd Division on the right, the 57th tried its hand at storming the Rebel position, advancing up the slope and over the open ground, covered by the IX Corps' twenty-eight field pieces firing low over the boys' heads. Making it across the cleared terrain, the men advanced rapidly through the woods, and came out in the fields on the other side that were still littered with the putrid, unburied dead from the fighting on May 12 and the fallen of the 56th and 35th Massachusetts from earlier that day.

Even though the sharpened trees were serving as abatis in the Southern front to discourage charges, the men got to the edge of those formidable obstructions—about thirty yards from the enemy trenches near the Harrison house—and exposed themselves to a scathing barrage of musket fire and artillery canister. The second wave of the 1st Brigade was culled, and the torn survivors limped, crawled, and ran to the safety of their lines, leaving many dead and wounded behind. "About Sunrise [the 57th] left the rifle pits and advanced to the abbattis of a rebel battery [Poague's] but were forced back and laid in the woods till about 10 A.M." is how Private Harrington coolly summarized the regiment's activities that morning.[24]

★

At that time of day the conflict was raging ferociously all over the battlefield. All the corps were fighting desperately for possession of the Confederate entrenchments, and the Southerners were staving them off with equal tenacity. The roar of the gunfire was thunderous and unwavering throughout the armies. Thick battle smoke spread over everyone and everything, and the men choked and gagged on it, barely able to see. The dead and wounded lay all around in pools of their own blood, and the injured screamed and moaned for mother, death, and water. Officers bellowed orders, often unheard or unheeded, and the soldiers cheered, yelled, and cursed with almost psychopathic vehemence as they zealously tried to hold every square foot of ground won. It was another day of savage and bloody butchery on Virginia's lovely, green landscape.

★

After several unsuccessful attempts to take the Rebel works, Ledlie's brigade once again formed to the long, rattling roll for yet another try. As the regiments advanced up the rise to a ridge, the first line commenced firing into the Rebel trenches. The Southerners quickly opened with a volley of their own, and as soon as they did, an unidentified man in the front line, who was later accused of being a bounty jumper, yelled, "Retreat!" Panic spread like wildfire through the ranks, and even though the officers desperately tried to assure the men that it was a false alarm, they turned and fled to the rear, anyway, in terror. Falling back into the second line, the men spread panic among those soldiers, and they, too, hightailed it for dear life back into their own trenches. After a frightening race down the slope and through the woods to the swale in front of their works, the men of the 1st Brigade realized that they were not being chased, and their distraught officers re-formed the lines for yet another go at the Georgians and North Carolinians.

It was at this time that a dark-eyed, pudgy little man with a huge black mustache walked among the soldiers repeating over and over, "Steady, boys, steady." None of the men recognized him, and they ignored his orders and ridiculed him in whispers. Fortunately the man they all took to be a brand-new second lieutenant did not overhear the wisecracks. This was the enlisted men's first look at their new commander, James H. Ledlie.

The brigade stepped off again for the Confederate position with the 57th advancing in good order on the left flank. The 35th Massachusetts was on its right in the line, and the 4th and 10th Regulars on the right of the 35th. The regiments moved forward through the woods and were ordered to lie down for cover in front of the Rebel lines. There they remained for three hours under a heinous storm of Southern lead which, miraculously, caused comparatively little damage.

But, during a lull in the Southern target practice, a very strange, even bizarre incident occurred in the brigade. A man, recognized by no one and dressed as a Union staff officer, carrying a cannonball in his hand and asking for the location of a particular battery, to the astonishment of all the prone men who witnessed it—no soldier had ever seen anything quite like this before—calmly and proudly sauntered through the 1st Brigade troops. He then turned to the front and, never uttering another word, continued his leisurely stroll across the lines until he took out a white handkerchief and "sprang lightly" into the Confederate earthworks. No one ever learned his identity or purpose, and for months afterward, the men told the curious story, over and over again around the campfires, of the "Mysterious Stranger," as they called him.[25] "I thought I'd seen everything," they would recount.

Another incident involved Private Waldo Sherwin, of Company C. Sherwin had moved to an advanced position in front of the regiment to cause some mischief to Lee's men, and, taking cover behind a tree, he began to methodically pick off William Poague's artillerymen in one of the Rebel batteries across from the 57th's position. He concentrated his fire on one particular gun crew, driving them off several times. Finally, however, a Confederate sharpshooter flanked him and wounded him severely in the right arm. Sherwin retired back to the regiment where he was aided to a field dressing station by some of his comrades. He was soon moved to a hospital in Washington, where his wound proved fatal, and the courageous but foolhardy soldier died on June 2, mourned by many of his fellow soldiers for his bravery.[26]

Orders finally came for the soldiers to abandon their position and fall back to their trench lines. Under the covering fire of the 56th and 59th Massachusetts, now in the front line, the 57th's men retired by the right flank as if they were on the parade ground—so perfectly was their maneuver executed that all who saw it remembered. The regiment lost 3 killed, 6 mortally wounded, 13 wounded, and 1 prisoner of war on the battlefield that day. This had been a relatively short action for the soldiers, but once more they had suffered significant losses.[27]

The companies were becoming so decimated from death, wounds, sickness, straggling, desertion, prisoners of war, and men on detached duty that, except for Company K, the total number of men present in each of them for battle was small and getting smaller. Twenty-three men lost was a substantial toll considering the regiment's total combat strength at that time, and the 57th had gained nothing for its bloody investment.

That night, the boys from the 35th Massachusetts moved about the campfires of the other regiments in the brigade, socializing and getting to know their new comrades.[28] It was an honor for the men of the 57th to be recognized as brothers in arms by such an old-time fighting regiment as the 35th, and they took the friendly overtures of those men deeply to heart. (It is not known whether the 35th Regiment was ever censured for its refusal to support the 56th Massachusetts, but no record of such a censure has been found.)

★

Before first light on the morning of May 19, the IX Corps was forced-marched four miles around and to the left of General Horatio Wright's VI Corps. Wright had taken command of that corps when its former chief,

General John Sedgewick, had been killed by a sniper's round on May 9. Private Harrington recorded in his diary: "Started early on the march halted about seven nearly an hour and a half for breakfast when we marched about a mile [farther] the army halted & formed in line of battle three lines [deep] we are now on the left of line probably on a flank movement the troops laying still in line of Battle." The men had taken up station on the extreme left and southern flank of the Army of the Potomac east of the Quisenberry house. "Twilight the troops are throwing up earthworks no firing except some skirmishing," wrote Company K's diarist.[29] Without delay, the men soon had put together a very strong position in which they felt reasonably safe.

While on the march to this new position, the IX Corps soldiers had stopped in some clearings at General Burnside's headquarters to boil their coffee and fry some salt meat, and they had chuckled about the Rebels that they had heard furiously chopping wood for defenses while they were quietly pulling out of their now abandoned works. Slapping their knees and laughing, they had a high time at Confederate expense.[30]

★

"Dear Mother & Sister," wrote George Barton from the 1st Division Ambulance Corps Headquarters in Fredericksburg on May 19,

I am very glad to hear that you are all well. There is so much suffering here that it is good to know that there are some dear ones at home safe and free from pain. We have had some *fearful* fighting have lost a great many men in killed wounded and missing The 57th is *used* up We only muster 270 [actually 237] fighting men in line of battle this does not include the men on detached Service—I am on Genl. Crittenden's Staff A son of Senator Crittenden Ohio [actually Kentucky] has a brother [Major General George Bibb Crittenden] in Lees Army. Our Corps, the 9th has moved this morning *Where* to, I do not know but shall be with them tonight. My ambulance train has been Conveying Wounded Men of our division (1st) to Fredericksburg for the last three days All the houses there are used for Hospitals The Amount of Suffering endured there is incalculable and I pity the *Noble fellows* for they bear their wounds without a grumble

On our first days fight at the "Wilderness" when I asked the "boys" about their wounds they all seemed cheerful. . . . Our Lt. Col. Chandler has won for himself the respect and love of the whole Regiment by his Cool and daring behavior in the various fights in which we have already been engaged he seems to bear a Charmed life.

The 57th stands very high and will do so till not a man is left.

. . . Our Corps advanced yesterday and took two lines of Rebel brestworks. They dispute the Rebs every inch of *ground* and will continue to do so all the way to Richmond, but they *Must Come down* though our losses will be *fearful.* God "Grant" us a speedy *issue* to this Contest ending of *course* in victory

. . . We intend to *Celebrate* the "Fourth of July" in *Richmond.*

. . . God bless you all May you never see the sights I have seen for the last week[31]

Confederate dead at the Alsop House, Spotsylvania, May 19, 1864;
burial detail from the 1st Massachusetts Heavy Artillery in right background.
(*USAMHI, Carlisle Barracks, Pa.*)

Dead Confederate soldier
at Spotsylvania, May 19, 1864.
(*USAMHI, Carlisle Barracks, Pa.*)

Confederates captured at Spotsylvania, May 1864.
(Western Reserve Historical Society, Cleveland, Ohio)

★

Later that Thursday, May 19, General Ewell attempted a sortie in force trying to find a soft spot over on the right flank of the Union forces in the vicinity of the II Corps' position. The 57th took no part in this action, but the men could hear the fighting clearly. Ewell was later forced back by several Federal cavalry squadrons and some brand-new heavy artillery regiments fresh from the Washington defenses—who had been severely verbally abused by the veterans for the soft life that up to that time they had been enjoying in the capital. But the rookie combat soldiers with the scarlet trim on their uniforms performed remarkably well and ended the action victoriously—as well as the taunts of the old soldiers.

The battle of Spotsylvania Court House effectively was finished for the 57th Regiment on the 18th, and for the whole army on the 19th. The fight had gained little, and killed and maimed thousands—over 18,000 Union and around 10,000 Confederates. Unfazed, Ulysses S. Grant would merely shift to the left again in his bid to flank Robert E. Lee and continue the Northern drive towards Richmond and the ultimate destruction of the Army of Northern Virginia.

9

To Go to Your Cupboard, Hannah

ONE HUNDRED AND THIRTY-SEVEN MEN of the 57th Massachusetts were taken prisoner of war during the regiment's term of service. Forty-nine of those prisoners of war died in captivity or soon after release, either from disease, neglect, exposure, or as the result of wounds received in battle prior to their capture. One of them was murdered. Many of the survivors of the Confederate prisons were incapacitated for the rest of their lives as a result of their incarceration. Except for forty-eight men who were taken prisoner during the regiment's last battle and who were all released within a matter of days, the majority of the prisoners were captured in the battles north of the James River and in the first two major engagements south of it.[1]

Until Grant took command of all the Union armies, there had been a general system of paroles and exchanges between the opposing forces. This meant that a soldier could give his word—his parole—that if released he would not rejoin his army until properly exchanged by his government. His exchange usually came when a sufficient number of men from the opposite side were paroled also. In other words, there had to be a balance, of sorts, of parolees exchanged. And this is precisely why Grant and Secretary of War Edwin M. Stanton ended the system.

Stanton and Grant knew very well that the South had almost no manpower reserves left to draw upon by 1864. Putting a stop to paroles and exchanges was one of the strategies they employed to strangle the Confederate armies through attrition in their ranks caused by wounds, death, sickness, imprisonment, detached duty, and desertion. The South was not able to replace the soldiers lost to those causes, but the North was. The supply of manpower was very respectable above the Mason-Dixon line, and it remained so throughout the war, as Stanton and Grant surmised it would.

So, for the men of the 57th who were captured in the early battles of the Overland Campaign, there was little or no hope of repatriation until the fall of 1864, when a few exchanges again began to be made mainly for humanitarian reasons. Most of the prisoner soldiers of the regiment were unaffected by these late exchanges; indeed, by that time many of them had died. Only those with the strongest constitutions, wills, and instincts made it though their captivity. In every sense, it was the survival of the fittest while in Confederate captivity.[2]

All the names of the 57th's men who were prisoners of war are known. And the outcomes of their incarcerations are known also. They were sent to Confederate prisons throughout the South, including Richmond's Libby Prison; Danville, Gordonsville, and Lynchburg, in Virginia; Salisbury, North Carolina; Florence, South Carolina; and Millen, Georgia.[3] All those prison were wretched places, but by far the prison with the worst reputation was the stockade camp in Andersonville, Georgia, officially known as Camp Sumter, where the great majority of those captured early on were sent. Andersonville Prison, as it was commonly called, was an abominable place. It was overcrowded for most of its existence and filled with disease and human suffering almost impossible to imagine or describe. There was never enough food and what there was was unfit to eat. Men suffered severely from diarrhea, dysentery, and starvation, as well as a myriad of other ailments. Sanitation was unknown and the medical facilities were, for all intents and purposes, nonexistent. Neither decent shelter nor clothing was provided, and, as a result of all of those deficiencies, scores of prisoners died there daily. Of the approximately 35,000 men imprisoned at Andersonville while it was in use during 1864 and 1865, approximately 13,000 died as a result of their incarceration.

While Andersonville nearly always is credited with being the most vile, the other Southern prisons were little better. And to be fair, Confederates confined in Northern facilities fared little better than their Federal counterparts.

★

As mentioned earlier, the names and fates of the 57th's prisoners of war are known, but as to their personal day-to-day existence, very little is known of most of them except for a few oblique references. Fortunately, however, two of the men kept diaries of their experiences and a third wrote a short essay of his ordeal immediately after the war ended. The diarists were William T. Peabody of Company F and Francis Harrington of Company K. Austin K. Gould, also of Company F, was the essayist. All these men have been introduced in preceding chapters. Harrington was sent to Danville, Virginia. Peabody and Gould were taken at the Wilderness and shipped to Andersonville. Peabody left a particularly fascinating psychological account of his trials, and there is every reason to believe that Gould wrote objectively of his imprisonment. (Austin Gould was a medical doctor, and although his knowledge of medicine was in no way comparable to that of today's physicians, he was a trained scientist and an educated observer—an individual not given to flights of fancy. Also, his account was written while the events he described were relatively fresh in his mind—although it is difficult to imagine any former prisoner of Andersonville forgetting the horrors of that place.) These accounts, of course, are the experiences of only three of the regiment's captured soldiers, but it is certain that the adversity to which these men were subjected is fairly typical of what all the 57th's as well as the vast majority of Federal prisoners suffered. Beginning with Peabody's diary, we are able to trace the men's journey from the battlefield to prison.

★

After William Peabody was captured at the Wilderness, he wrote in his journal on May 10 that he had "marched 15 miles, destination Richmond at least [we] expect so." However, he and his fellow prisoners were actually being held behind the Confederate lines at Spotsylvania.

For the next five days, Peabody and "1117 [Federal] prisoners" lay uneasily in their muddy camp with no shelter from the rains as they heard the battle of Spotsylvania raging around them. Each day new prisoners taken in the battle joined their ranks. Little other than one cup of flour and one or two slices of rancid ham were issued daily to the prisoners for rations, and Peabody lamented this lack of food so much that he commented, as if writing to his wife, "Like to go to your cupboard, Hannah, or [even your] swill pail. Very tired."

On Sunday, May 15, the Rebels issued the prisoners some meager rations, and at two o'clock that afternoon fourteen hundred Northern soldiers began their odyssey under guard for an unknown destination. After marching about ten miles and fording a waist-deep river, the men bivouacked in some wet fields with no shelter. With no breakfast issued, the Federals continued their trek the next morning for another twenty miles. Although exhausted and hungry, Peabody, with the sharp eye of a rural New Englander, took time to remark that they had marched "through splendid country" with the "Corn up ready to hoe."

"Devilish tired," the prisoners reached Gordonsville, Virginia, on the 17th, following an eighteen-mile march, and after an examination by Confederate authorities, they were locked up in hog pens with nothing to eat that night. There many of them remained for almost two days. Peabody reported that the men got no sleep—undoubtedly because of their overcrowded and offensive surroundings.

The following day, May 18, about half of the prisoners were singled out and purportedly sent to Vicksburg, Mississippi. Those who remained behind, including Peabody and his comrades, were issued twenty ounces of pork which pleased them mightily. They soon got word that a train was being readied to ferry them to another destination in the Confederacy, and the Northerners waited anxiously all day for that to happen. The men hoped to depart Gordonsville and the filthy hog pens as soon as they could. At ten that night the train was ready, the prisoners were loaded aboard, and the doors locked. At noon on May 19, they arrived in Lynchburg, Virginia, and, Peabody, still in good spirits, apparently was thinking of little except his surroundings. He described Lynchburg as "rather a pleasant place. Corn 4 inches high; gardens looking well flowers in full bloom look splendid. [The James] River runs through this place."

After spending over a day in Lynchburg, the men were loaded onto some dirty cattle cars the next afternoon. Provided no rations, they rode all night and arrived in Danville, Virginia, the next morning at nine o'clock. The trip to Danville, located on the North Carolina border, was 166 miles, according to William Peabody. It had been a rough trip, and the prisoners had not been able to sleep. Still, spirits remained relatively good, and they "passed through several pleasant places for this country."

When they had detrained, the Federals were marched through town for about a mile and locked into a brick storehouse. There they were issued "Indian bread and poor ham," which Peabody thought was "better than nothing." Tensions, however, were building between the prisoners and their guards, and during the day one of the captives was shot for "looking out a window."

On Sunday, May 22, Peabody noted that "this day has been spent in a Danville rebel prison with 500 others [Union prisoners], and a rougher crew I never saw. I can't associate with them at all, but I have a friend Doc Gould, we are friends. Corn bread is our food."

At two the next morning, the men were again put aboard freight cars, and, after traveling nonstop, they passed through Greensboro, North Carolina, later that morning where they halted for a short time. The prisoners were given "2½ pies" to eat of which Peabody remarked that they were "very poor, could not eat them at home." He wrote that he "was very hungry" but there was "not much grub to eat." And again as if writing to his wife, he mentioned, "I would give ten dollars [nearly a month's pay for a soldier] to eat with the family tonight, Hannah this is so."

Later in the morning the train started south again, and some of the men, including Peabody, were forced to ride on the tops of the cars in the rain. The journey continued all day and into the night until they reached Charlotte, North Carolina. There the prisoners were unloaded and made to sleep in the open "in the mud and raining all night; wet through and nothing to sleep in or on; just stood up and walked until morning."

Cold and wet, the men continued their journey the following morning,

May 25, headed for Columbus, Georgia. That night the soldiers were allowed to sleep in the cars, but the cold and rain to which the men had been exposed began to show its effects. Peabody wrote that he was "very sick with a severe cold; the sickest I ever was but one time. Pleurisy in the side, headache. . . ."

Early the following morning the trip started again and continued through that night. "Slept all day and rode all night, the hardest night I ever saw in my life," noted the private.

On the morning of the 27th, the train reached Augusta, Georgia, where the men spent the day. Even though still sick, Peabody seemed impressed with his surroundings once again. "[Augusta] is a pleasant place and large. We just crossed the Savannah River; it is a large stream. The town is pleasantly situated, or rather city. I like it better today. We have food here the best of any place and I like the people. First, Frank [his son], there are smart boys here I tell you, I wish you were here with me."

Leaving Augusta at three o'clock in the afternoon of May 28, the men traveled all night, and "at noon arrived at our place of destination which is called Camp Anderson Georgia [Camp Sumter in Andersonville] and there is a crowd of prisoners here. I would just like to have you see this place and still I would not, it is horrid to see."[4]

Austin Gould, Peabody's comrade and fellow prisoner from Company F, related his initial experiences and impressions of the prison camp:

Well do I remember when I first arrived in sight of this terrible place, on the 29th day of May, 1864, and of my first interview with the rebel officer in charge of it, Capt. Henry Wirtz, [actually Wirz] a most savage looking man, and who was as brutal as his looks would seem to indicate. He offered us all the abuse he was capable of, and then marched us into prison. It was no uncommon thing for this brute to strip the prisoners of their clothing, and everything of value about them, before sending them inside the stockade. The stockade in which we were confined was made by setting logs upright in the ground, as closely as they could be driven, standing above the ground about fourteen feet, and enclosing about nineteen acres of land, about half as wide as it was long. Running through or across this lot, was a brook about four feet wide, and generally, two or three inches in depth, thus giving us water to use, but of the filthiest character, on account of there being just above us, a camp of three thousand rebels, and as many more negroes, (serving as guard over us) [blacks did not serve as guards—Gould simply put this phrase in parentheses in the wrong place] all of whose filth [human waste] and refuse was emptied into the brook and swept down to us. In addition to this, the land on either side of the brook, to the extent of six acres, was a complete swamp. A portion of this was used by the thirty thousand prisoners, more or less, for "sink" [latrine] purposes, and its effects upon the water, can better be imagined than described.

It may be interesting to know how we lived. We dug holes or burrows, in the ground, thus forming a little shelter for us. Once a day we had brought in to us our rations, which consisted of one-half pint of cob corn meal, coarsely ground, or its equivalant of beans or rice, or sometimes bacon, and all of these of the poorest quality. One of the most dreadful things in this dreadful place was the "dead line." This was a furrow turned up, about twenty feet [inside] the stockade all around, and was called the "dead line," and if a man dared to step over this line, or cross it by mistake, he was at once shot by the guard, without a word being said. It was sickening to see the dead as they lay in prison. It was the custom to carry them out every morning, the prisoners being hired to do this, their pay being an extra ration and a chance to bring in an armful of [fire]wood when they returned; and these inducements were so great, that sometimes one squad would steal a dead body from another, in order to get a chance to go out and get wood and more to eat. Others were detailed for that purpose, how eager the men were to get a chance to go, and how savagely they were treated when refused. So many of those barbarities crowd themselves upon my mind, that I hardly know where to stop.[5]

So began the fearful incarceration of some of the regiment's soldiers.

10

The Brave Amongst the Bravest

R ETURNING TO VIRGINIA by early morning on May 20, the new veterans of
the 57th had their rifle pits completed and their abatis in place near the
Quisenberry house. Heavy fogs had allowed them to work all night undis-
turbed by Confederate interference, and the men were exhausted. Now they
were given a chance for a short rest, and, without delay, they took it. "All
still this morning and remained so during the day. Drew rations again today
O[ur] Troops are strongly intrenched here now," wrote Francis Harrington
later on that Friday afternoon.[1]

Towards evening, after the brigade had reconnoitered in a two-mile loop-
ing movement to the west probing Rebel strength, the 57th made another
small reconnaissance for the same purpose to the east in the direction of
Smith's and Stannard's mills on the Ny and Po rivers, respectively.[2] The men
ran into no Confederate troops, and the day was relatively peaceful. Most of
them took this opportunity for a quick bath in the Ny River, by turn, while
their comrades stood lookout on its banks.

The regiment now mustered 237 officers and enlisted men present for
combat duty. It was badly bled down, nearly worn out. George Barton and
his men had managed to transport most of the 57th's wounded to the field
hospitals in Fredericksburg by nightfall, and those who had sustained serious
injury—and that was most of them—were then transferred from there by
water transport to the huge medical institutions in Alexandria and Washington. From those overcrowded hospitals, a few were sent to facilities in Philadelphia, Baltimore, New York, Boston, Worcester, and Readville, Massachusetts.[3]

Many of the wounded had incurred severe trauma from the fighting on
May 18, one of whom was Company H's Corporal Michael Bowen. Bowen
had received a bloody wound in his left foot, and acting Assistant Surgeon
F. G. H. Bradford had to remove it ten days later.[4]

James Brooks, of Company K, a veteran of the 6th New Hampshire Volunteers, who had been promoted sergeant for bravery in action on May 12, had taken a Minié ball in his left leg on May 18, but the injury was not considered serious at that time. Nevertheless, his wound festered and his leg finally had to be amputated by regular army surgeon C. Page on June 5. Brooks's prognosis was good following the operation and after sufficient recovery he was sent to Depot field hospital at City Point near Petersburg. However, complications set in and the young sergeant died from typhoid fever on July 14. His officers described him as a "good soldier."[5]

Some of the wounded men were discharged from the service as soon as their treatment was complete, and only a handful returned to duty with the regiment after recuperation. Yet others—although only a small number— took advantage of the lax security offered by the hospitals, or the kindness of the medical administration in granting furloughs, to desert.[6] These deserters were not bounty jumpers; quite the contrary. For the most part they had behaved well in battle, but they had simply taken all they could of the miseries and horrors of the war and the hospitals, and they wanted out. Most just went home to try to pick up their lives where they had left them back in the winter of 1864 before they had enlisted, and the majority of them never were caught or prosecuted for their conduct. However, many of them were shunned by their communities and their former comrades at war's end—a disgrace that would haunt generations of their families for years to come.

There was another type of trauma suffered by at least one of the regiment's men that May 18, and that was psychological trauma—battle fatigue, shell shock. A young man in Company K, who had been on the wagon-train guard detail during the engagement at the Wilderness, Private Erastus Pond, got his first taste of severe combat on May 12, and he had found that he could not reconcile himself to the terror of battle, and had shirked the fight on May 18. His officers, however, had viewed his state of mind with rare understanding, and rather than punish him, they transferred him to brigade headquarters as a hostler. Later in the war, Pond was relegated to the duties of brigade headquarters orderly, and although he never again saw action, he remained with the regiment until it was mustered out of service.[7]

★

Until May 20, the 57th Regiment had had no organized mail delivery service within its ranks, that task usually falling to the chaplain. But with the depletion of the unit's soldiers, Reverend Dashiell had his hands full writing letters of condolence to bereaved families and forwarding the deceased men's effects to their homes. Visiting and consoling the wounded taxed his time also, and his normal duties had to be accomplished as well, so a regimental postmaster was appointed on May 20. One of the thirty-four enlisted men who had remained with Lieutenant Colonel Chandler and the colors at the Wilderness was Private Frank H. Lowell, from Portland, Maine. Lowell, a member of Company K, had fought courageously during the battles at Spotsylvania, taking a bullet in the shoulder on the 18th. But Frank Lowell was not one to take advantage of his condition and stay in the rear. He had his wound dressed and returned to the lines for duty with the regiment. As a reward, Charles Chandler awarded him the position of postmaster. But that duty, which would have given the young man the opportunity to remain safely out of service at the front, would not deter the private from joining his comrades on the line in combat, and by war's end he would amass a distinguished fighting career, taking a further and more serious wound and becoming a prisoner of war. However, he would return to the regiment for muster-out, earning on his service record the infrequently used sobriquet—at least in the 57th Massachusetts—"Brave Soldier."[8]

★

During the quiet, black night the Army of the Potomac, for the second time, began a flanking expedition to the left of the Army of Northern Virginia, in a southeasterly direction. The II Corps took the lead, Grant hoping that Lee could be baited into exposing himself on open ground, in order that the Army of the Potomac could deliver him the death blow, at last, on a battlefield favorable to the Union forces, by attacking Hancock's men before his Confederates had time to entrench strongly. But Lee was having none of that. His men were just too worn out for an offensive action at that time. Instead, he would take his army down to the south bank of the North Anna River near Hanover Junction—a much shorter march for his army, as that organization held the interior lines, so that while Grant had to move his troops in a long, swinging arc to the east, Lee could travel its chord—and dig in hard in a nearly impregnable V-shaped trench system with its apex resting on the North Anna near Ox Ford. Hoping to stay between Grant's Union forces and Richmond, twenty-five miles distant, the Rebels would man their earthworks and wait patiently for the Federals to appear in their front. Because they would arrive so much faster then the Northerners, the butternuts also would gain the advantage of almost a full day's rest, rest of vital importance to the men of both armies at that point in the wearying campaign.

★

On May 21, the 57th still remained in its trenches at Spotsylvania opposite A. P. Hill's corps for most of the day except for a sortie during the morning by Ledlie's 1st Brigade as a covering movement for other departing Federal troops.[9] There was activity everywhere as the Union soldiers prepared to abandon for good their positions on the battlefield, and by nightfall much of the Army of the Potomac was on the move, its seemingly endless blue columns groping their way over the terrible, newly cut military roads in the forbidding, dark forests.

At five o'clock that afternoon, relieved in its earthworks by Wright's VI Corps, the 1st Division fell in behind Potter's 2nd of the IX Corps, which followed for a short while directly behind Warren's V Corps. The route took Burnside's troops south of the Massaponax Church road, with the corps' tired men marching in a heavy shower through the unfamiliar territory, stumbling in ditches and entangling themselves in brush. A few even fell asleep as they marched.[10]

Tramping along, the boys could hear the Rebel attack on the men of the VI Corps who were occupying their former position in the trenches. It was a short fight which started and ended abruptly, but all were relieved they were not involved.[11]

At the little brick Massaponax Church, the men turned south on the narrow Telegraph road, crossed the Ny at Smith's Mill and the Po at Stannard's Mill, and continued south along the north bank of the Po through the dark pine alleys via Thornburg, covering a distance of about eight miles during the very early hours of May 22.

The march had continued all night under a full moon, the column's right guarded by nervous and apprehensive flankers. At Thornburg, the 1st Division turned east, continuing on to Guiney Station on the Richmond, Fredericksburg & Petersburg Railroad, and crossed the tracks there just after sunup. At about that time the division caught up with the rear of the rest of the IX Corps, from which it had become separated during the night.

A halt was called at eight o'clock that morning for breakfast near some old wood-framed houses in a plowed field along the road beyond the station, and the men quickly kindled fires and had their coffee boiling. During the march onto the field, a window suddenly was thrown open in one of the nearby dwellings on the left. An ancient, wizened head appeared, its mouth spewing vile curses at the Yankee soldiers. The boys found the tirade so funny that some of them were doubled up on the ground, holding their sides, laughing with tears rolling down their cheeks. Everyone thought the situation hilarious except the wizened old head, who, upon seeing the effect he was having on the Federals, withdrew with a huff into his house, slamming the window shut with a glass-rattling bang. That, of course, only added to the comedy, and the men howled in delight.[12]

After the refreshing stop near Guiney Station, the 57th Massachusetts carried on south at ten that morning, marching along the east side of the Richmond, Fredericksburg & Petersburg Railroad tracks with the IX Corps. The country through which the troops were traveling was rich and fertile, and the rolling earth, frequented with clear, cool brooks, was full of cornfields and wheat fields, bounded by good rail fences and leafy, green trees. And the homes along the way, too, were well kept with "comfort and plenty." But the roads on which the men were marching were choked with supply wagons and artillery batteries, and the marching was not easy.[13]

Early in the afternoon, the boys passed the Tyler house, which sat on high ground overlooking the lush Mattaponi Valley. In that house, General Grant and his staff were resting. General Burnside was also there, conferring with the lieutenant general, and as the men filed passed the makeshift headquarters, Ambrose E. Burnside stepped outside onto the lawn and reviewed his battle-torn corps. His soldiers raised their caps and cheered him enthusiastically.[14]

The soldiers plodded along lethargically all day in clouds of choking, powdery dust. That evening at five o'clock along the Mattaponi River just west of Bowling Green, Virginia, they camped for the night with the other regiments of the 1st Division.[15]

★

Early the next morning, May 23, at about five o'clock, the division formed its ranks with the corps and, after a delay of nearly two hours, the forced march south over the old plantation roads in the lovely, open country got under way. It was another day of slow progress with frequent and annoying starts and stops. Most of the IX Corps troops were out of rations by now, and hundreds straggled along the way to rest from the heat and to forage blackberries in the meadowlands and water from the creeks and farmers' wells. At noon a short halt was called for dinner, and those with any provisions left ate their meals. Another short halt was made to rest the troops at four that afternoon.

Toward twilight, at about six, the men heard heavy cannonading in the distance ahead—the regiment was three miles north of the North Anna and had stopped for another break near the IX Corps' wagon train. Clearly, something important was happening in front, and the men knew that they would be in the thick again soon. The new veterans of the 57th Massachusetts had learned to read the grim signposts of war quickly, and the anticipation and excitement of yet another battle flowed through them once more. The march south continued.

For the second night, the 1st Brigade bivouacked in a cornfield at half-past seven, about a mile upcountry from the high-banked North Anna River. When their arms had been stacked under the moonlit skies, the boys lined up at the division commissary wagons that had arrived in the meantime and "drew two days rations to last three days." Following supper, roll call, and guard mounting for picket duty, most every one of the exhausted soldiers quickly fell into a deep sleep.[16]

Federal Military Bridge at Quarles Mill on the North Anna River, near where the 57th Massachusetts crossed, May 24, 1864. *(USAMHI, Carlisle Barracks, Pa.)*

★

On the morning of May 24, after a two-mile march over a lane that wound through pine woods covered with the dust churned up by the passing army, the soldiers of the 57th reached the northern banks of the North Anna River at Quarles Mills around noon.[17] It was intended for the IX Corps to cross the river there and then move swiftly south to reinforce the II Corps at Ox Ford, about a mile and a quarter downstream.

The North Anna was a cold and rapidly eddying river and difficult to ford. Its bottom was rocky, and its banks were heavily wooded and precipitous, and the men, especially those who could not swim, were not at all eager to test its strong current, especially weighed down with their heavy gear.

With the 1st Brigade leading the crossing, the division spent the afternoon fording the river near the mill's picturesque waterfall. In some places the water was quite deep and the men held their cartridge boxes over their shoulders with one hand and their rifles high in the air with the other, while trying to keep their balance in the swift, brown water. (They also carried their heavy knapsacks strapped to their backs—they were taking no more chances by leaving them behind again.) It was tough going, but they could not afford to let their muskets or ammunition get wet. Lee's army was nearby, and the men knew they had to be ready for anything from their stealthy foes.

The slow and dangerous fording continued, and the soldiers floundered on the slime-covered rocks in the whirling currents, but the operation went unchallenged by the Rebels. A skirmish line was established immediately on the south bank of the river as cover for the rest of the men of the division crossing behind the leading elements.[18]

Lieutenant Colonel Chandler rode his horse across the ford with Reverend Dashiell. "We had some pleasantry about the passage and I was pleased to find him [Chandler] in such a fine flow of spirits," wrote the chaplain later. The lieutenant colonel was given a gun belt with a revolver and bayonet in it by Private George Robinson, of Company H, in whose feet it had become entangled while he was crossing the river, and, keeping the sidearm for himself, jokingly offered the bayonet to the men of the 57th as they reached the south bank.[19] It is not recorded that anyone accepted the proffered souvenir.

After all were across, the officers halted the brigade for five minutes to allow the men to empty the water out of their shoes, wring out their socks, and rearrange themselves. All were soaked up to their armpits, but the day was hot, as usual, and their clothes soon dried.[20]

At about three o'clock that afternoon, the 1st Brigade formed its lines, with the 35th Massachusetts in front deployed as skirmishers, and, not waiting for the other brigade of the division to finish its crossing, advanced southeastward through the heavy forest, the lines of men swaying from side to side over the rough, tangled ground. The ranks of advance had the 56th Massachusetts following the skirmishers, with the 57th second, backed up by the 59th Massachusetts, and followed by the 4th and 10th Regulars.

After moving forward for about three-quarters of a mile, Companies H and I of the 35th's skirmishers encountered a Rebel picket line which they quickly drove in, and a short distance further, the brigade emerged from the woods into a clearing. Eight hundred yards beyond lay a high, semicircular ridge of hills, and on it the men could see a Confederate battery well protected by earthworks and heavily supported by the bristling guns of the Rebel infantry.[21]

★

James Hewett Ledlie was a general only because of high political connections in Washington, and he was anxious to advance his reputation by extraordinary feats of military derring-do. The problem was, however, that he was totally incapable of accomplishing those feats, and to compound his military incompetence, he was not overly concerned with who got hurt in the process of his battlefield experiments. The 57th and the other regiments of the brigade had the great misfortune of having this man as their commander, and the 24th of May would prove only a taste of dark days to come for the soldiers as a result of Ledlie's ineptitude.

General Ledlie was an impetuous man, and he was hot to charge the enemy on this spring day. He was also drunk. His intention was to attack the Rebels before the other of the 1st Division's brigades, the 2nd, came up—to secure the glory for himself. "He therefore called upon an officer of the Fifty-Seventh, who was the only officer at the time with his company," to find division commander Thomas Crittenden and deliver an oral request: "Give my compliments to General Crittenden, and tell him there is a Rebel battery in my front; ask him to please send me three regiments immediately, one on my right, one on my left, and the other in rear for support, and I will charge and capture it," he commanded the officer. That officer was Second Lieutenant John Anderson of Company E.

Lieutenant Anderson continues the story:

The bearer of the message [Anderson] was not a staff officer, was wholly unknown to General Crittenden and knew not where to find him, yet he followed the direction as near as he could back to the ford, and by good fortune, went directly to him and delivered the message. The General looked somewhat surprised that this singular request had not come through one of the brigade staff, and at first seemed a little suspicious; but after a few questions and becoming satisfied with the identity of the officer, he directed him to return immediately with this verbal reply, which, in substance, is correct, and in words as near as can be remembered: "Go back to General Ledlie immediately. Give him my compliments, and tell him I have not the regiments to spare. The division is not across the river yet. Tell him my orders are not to charge."

Anderson saluted, turned around, and began to return to the brigade on the run, but before he got but a few yards, General Crittenden called him back and modified his orders slightly: "Tell General Ledlie not to charge unless he sees a sure thing where he can capture a battery not well supported; to use the utmost caution. Tell him that I have information that seems reliable, that the enemy is posted in force in his front, and if he charges I am afraid it will be a failure and result in bringing on a serious engagement which we are in no condition to meet now, as a large part of my division is still on the other side of the river with the rest of the corps; tell him to use the utmost caution."

On his return, the courier Anderson observed Ledlie beginning to form the brigade for an attack without having waited for him to return with word from Crittenden. Because he had emerged from the woods on high ground to the right of the brigade, Lieutenant Anderson had a good look at the Southern position, and he found it strongly held by "other batteries in position, with a strong line of infantry intrenchments, while over and beyond could be seen clouds of dust which indicated that a large force was hastening toward the threatened point of attack." Running up to the massing troops, he reported to the brigade commander, giving him Crittenden's message and his own observations, but the general, in a state of drunken excitement, ignored him. "It is doubtful if he heard [Anderson's report], or if he did, that he understood one word or cared a 'continental.' "[22]

★

Off to the west, the men of the 1st Brigade could see black storm clouds rapidly approaching them as they removed and stacked their knapsacks in preparation for the charge. The boys then formed into battle lines, with the 57th drawn up on the left of Colonel Leasure's 100th Pennsylvania, which had just arrived and was temporarily attached to the brigade.[23]

★

In the 57th Regiment, the "bluebeard," Major James W. Cushing, suddenly began to develop acute cold feet at the time that John Anderson was returning from his mission to General Crittenden's field headquarters, and very quickly the major came down with a timely case of "chronic sunstroke." He was carried off the field by a couple of soldiers. Because of the overcast, he was putting nothing over on the men, and they thought him a fool for trying. "His frantic gesticulations disclosed his eagerness to grapple with the Confederate army single handed, but the unfortunate sunstroke had prostrated him; only for this the war would have been closed that very day," remembered Anderson in his regimental history.[24]

★

Meanwhile, General Ledlie's drunken conduct was evidently somewhat infectious, and the men saw one of his small-framed staff officers, similarly full of "tanglefoot," as the soldiers sometimes referred to ethyl alcohol, out in front of the lines, but way beyond the range of the Southern rifles, menacingly firing his small-caliber Smith & Wesson revolver in the direction of a Rebel battery. "It has never been learned what damage he did; at all events, the battery did not surrender," wrote Anderson.[25] The men in the ranks, no doubt, were openly embarrassed.

As the sky grew darker, the general led his brigade "in person," arrayed in two battle lines, across the open fields towards the formidable Confederate defenses.[26]

After a short distance, the 35th's skirmishers began to fire in volleys, but the brigade's lines quickly disintegrated. A "wild tumultuous rush" for the Southern earthworks ensued with the soldiers cheering loudly. The brave and reckless men were far in the advance, some ahead of the colors, while the more cautious, quite happy to let them take the lead, hung back.[27]

All the while, a number of the Rebel soldiers stood on their breastworks gesturing with their arms and taunting the Union soldiers with cries of "Come on, Yanks, come on to Richmond!"[28]

As soon as the brigade came within one hundred yards of the Confederate works, manned by some of the same troops that the 57th had engaged at the Wilderness—Brigadier General Edward A. Perry's brigade of Florida soldiers—both sides opened a killing barrage of musketry. But the charging Federals, once again in their completely exposed ranks, were chopped like cotton by the well-protected Southerners. Color Sergeant Karpeles was badly wounded and dropped the regimental flag. As he retrieved it and rejoined the fight, Colonel Chandler attempted to grab it away from him, ordering the sergeant to the rear. But Karpeles would not give up his banner until he was so weakened by loss of blood that he no longer had a choice. He finally retired to find a dressing station, helped along by one of his men.[29]

The 57th and the 1st Brigade had almost reached the Rebel trenches when the Southern gunners opened their battery on them, mowing the Federals down with case and canister that "shook the very ground and swept everything in front."[30] Those soldiers in the front were blown to bits, showering the men behind them with blood, flesh, and pieces of bone.

Broken, bloody human wreckage littered the ground, and the thick, gray battle smoke hung low over the fields beneath the clouds. The Confederate infantry, aiming their rifles low into the assaulting men's knees, continued to pour their lethal volleys into the decimated ranks, and the boys, who took whatever cover they could find, remained in this position, pinned down hard, for several hours, while the Rebel sharpshooters calmly went to work on them, plying their deadly trade with awful efficiency.[31]

At quarter to seven that evening, the heavens began to bang around with violent thunderstorms, and presently sheets of rain were falling, drenching everything. Just as the skies broke, the men looked and saw a line of Southern infantry advancing through the foggy, sulfurous gun smoke on the left, right, and center of the brigade's position. The left of the Union line, which was closest to the Confederates and poorly protected by its own skirmishers, was overpowered soon and crumbled quickly. Officers hollered commands above the gunfire and thunder for the Federal troops to retreat, which they started to do in fairly good order, but the withdrawal quickly became a wild and panicked rout with men falling at every step. The chasing Southerners, sprinting after their enemy and screaming their ear-piercing Rebel yells, were giving no quarter as they fired without mercy into the backs of the stampeding Northern soldiers.[32]

After the brigade had fallen back to the haven of some trees on the edge

of the fields, Colonel Chandler stopped Colonel Weld of the 56th Massachusetts.

"Weld, what are you going to do?" he asked.

"I don't know," Weld replied.

"I am going to rally my men and try to make a stand," said Chandler.

"I will join you," said Weld.

The two colonels found about fifty men apiece, and as they were forming
them for a countercharge, General William Mahone's rangy Confederates
came out from seemingly nowhere and got within forty yards of the Yankee
boys, giving them a volley that tore them to shreds. Colonel Chandler fell
from his horse, mortally wounded, and Colonel Weld was scratched on his
side by a glancing Minié ball.[33]

Captain Albert Prescott of the 57th, who had arrived recently on the
battlefield, and Sergeant Ed McFarland of Company I, along with some of
the other men, tried to pick Chandler up and get him off the killing ground
to a dressing station, but the colonel realized that his wound was mortal, and
he told them, "You can do nothing for me, save yourselves if you can." So
the captain, the sergeant, and the others made him as comfortable as possible
and then "ran for their lives."[34]

While Chandler and Weld were attempting their maneuver, the rest of
the men raced on to relative safety deeper into the timberlands, ducking
behind trees and logs and jumping in muddy ditches trying to dodge the
whining, singing Confederate bullets and shrapnel. The whole brigade was
wildly out of control and scattered in the dark and confusion, but the soldiers
continued on, out of breath and in utter chaos, back to the North Anna to
a point just below where they had crossed the river earlier that day.[35]

The night was black, and the rain continued in torrents, and the river's
dark waters had risen so high and were running so swiftly that no retreat could
be made to the opposite bank. The gloomy and disconcerting situation of
deep, fast water in the rear and desperate Rebels in the front was saved only
by the opaque night when the fighting lessened somewhat, and most of the
Confederates retired at their unhurried and unthreatened leisure back to their
works, swearing violently at the IX Corps Federals whom they had whipped
so soundly.[36]

★

The day had been completely confusing and utterly demoralizing. No attempt to rally the 1st Brigade's troops had been made by the drunken
commanding general, and the attack had resulted in a humiliating defeat.
The men's patience was sorely tried with their new commander, for they
knew that he had led them in a suicidal attack over open ground against
impregnable works packed with murderous artillery, and when they had run

into trouble, as they had known that they would, the alcohol-soaked general had been nowhere to be seen to rally the troops and re-form the battle lines. "General Ledlie made a botch of it. Had too much [liquor] on board, I think . . . ," noted Stephen Weld.[37]

Some of the other officers had tried to regroup the men on the battlefield that day, but they had gotten nowhere. None of them was the brigade commander, after all. General Crittenden, that evening, put Colonel Weld in temporary command of the brigade until General Ledlie sobered up: "General Crittenden placed me in charge of the brigade as General L. was sleepy and tired."[38]

Soon after Weld's interim appointment the boys were all back hugging the muddy riverbanks. The firing had died down and Ledlie reappeared and managed to lead the survivors, with Weld doing the navigating, back upriver to reunite with the division, where the worn-out soldiers quickly took cover behind some breastworks hastily thrown up by the 2nd Brigade of the 1st Division. Patchy shooting continued on into the forbidding night while the men worked feverishly in the mud fortifying their trenches.[39]

★

Colonel Chandler died from his wounds two hours after he was shot. During the night, under a flag of truce, Brigadier General Nathaniel H. Harris, commander of a brigade of Anderson's division, Third Corps, Army of Northern Virginia, against which the regiment had also fought that day, returned Chandler's personal effects, which included a daguerreotype of a young woman, to the 57th so that they could be sent home to his mother. Most all of the men of the regiment had greatly admired the colonel, and they were truly sorry for his loss. "Our *Noble & Brave* Lt. Col." is how Private Harrington expressed his feelings toward his dead commander, and George Barton commented in a letter home, *"His place* cannot be filled by *any* officer now in the Regiment." He had treated his soldiers fairly, and he had been with them always in the thick of battle, never using his rank to seek safety. He was the type of officer the men admired, and they missed him greatly.[40]

"Our Regt is in poor shape laying in rear," Francis Harrington wrote. It had been cut up badly again—9 killed, including Chandler, 4 mortally wounded, 13 wounded, including Lieutenant Royce of Company C, 2 missing, and 10 captured. Surprisingly, Company F lost not one of the 16 men it had taken into battle, but Company H took 8 casualties of its force of 26 soldiers, losing nearly 31 percent of its strength. Thirty-eight more were gone from the regiment, a 16-percent loss. One-hundred and ninety-nine combat soldiers remained in the 57th's ranks.[41]

Two of the regiment's Irish soldiers, Private William Mooher, from County Limerick, and Private Michael Morris, from County Tyrone, both members of Company A, had been among the prisoners of war taken by the Confederates that day. Mooher would live and be paroled later that fall, but Morris would succumb from chronic diarrhea at Andersonville in October.[42]

Private Oliver Gosler, of Company E, who had fought in all of the regiment's battles, deserted during the fight at the North Anna. But his choice of direction was poor, and the Confederates took him prisoner also. He, too, would die from disease later in the Southern prison at Salisbury, North Carolina.[43]

The wounded color sergeant, Leopold Karpeles, heard "a rumor that night in the hospital that" Colonel Chandler had been killed because he had tried to save the colors. "There was no ground for the rumor," claimed Reverend Dashiell, "but the poor fellow [Karpeles] was inconsolable. All night long he charged himself with the death of his 'dear colonel' because he had left the field." Sergeant Karpeles would rejoin the regiment briefly in the fall, but his wounds, insufficiently healed, would prevent him from further service, causing his discharge for disability.[44]

Color Corporal Ira Bullard had taken a nasty wound in the upper left forearm and a somewhat less serious one in his leg. His cousin, Lieutenant George Barton, wrote his own father that he had taken Ira "from the field in one of my Ambulances *going* with the Ambulance *Myself* in order to pick out the *best road* possible, and to Make *sure* that he should be 'handled Carefully' when he arrived at the 'field Hospital.' " George Barton took the corporal to the 1st Division field hospital, where Bullard's arm was amputated "at the upper left radius" that night, but his wound—or the surgery—was fatal. Transported to Mount Pleasant U.S. Army General Hospital in Washington via Port Royal, the young veteran of the 51st Massachusetts Volunteers expired on May 30. Captain Julius M. Tucker, Bullard's commanding officer in Company H and later lieutenant colonel of the regiment, told Barton that "Ira proved himself to be an *excellent* soldier both *Cool* and plucky when in a *fight* and always *faithful* when on duty." And Color Sergeant Karpeles, upon his return to the regiment in October, stated to Lieutenant Barton, "He was the *best Corporal* I had on the 'Color Guard' always in his place *Close* to the 'Colors.' "[45]

★

The 1st Brigade of the 1st Division, IX Corps, had been in ruins before the battle of North Anna River from the continuous fighting since May 6, and now it was just a fragment of its former self. Nothing whatever had been accomplished in the day's attack except the horrible loss of life and a shameful defeat, and the men were bitter that they had made such sacrifices for such a blind-drunk fool of a leader. They lost all confidence in General Ledlie as a result of his performance that May 24, and it would never be regained.[46] In their eyes, he was a coward, a poltroon.

★

The men worked all night building fortifications and lashing logs together into rafts. The river was raging, and the only way of getting the wounded who were with them to the field hospitals on the north side was to ferry them over on those homemade floats. It was backbreaking labor as the young soldiers slipped and clogged on the muddy banks in the coal-black night and soaking downpour. They were on the verge of dropping with their overpowering fatigue, and they were filthy and drenched.

It was impossible for them to get their fires going to cook supper that night, and they were famished. Nothing had changed, they complained to no one in particular; it was fight, march, and dig, with little sleep and little food.[47]

The 57th had been earning a good reputation in the IX Corps for its fierce fighting qualities, and Colonel Leasure remarked of the regiment's soldiers that day that "they fought like lions."[48] When the men later got wind of that fine praise, they swelled with boyish pride.

★

One other significant event occurred on May 24, and that was the incorporation of the IX Corps into the Army of the Potomac. Although it had been an autonomous unit until now and only attached to the mighty army, General Burnside agreed that it be permanently integrated with the other three corps under the command of Major General Meade. For Ambrose Burnside, this was a giant step in humility, as he was not only senior in rank to Meade, but he had commanded, at one time, the Army of the Potomac himself—albeit disastrously.

★

At dawn on the 25th, as the thunderstorms continued, the lines of the two armies were face to face, and trigger fingers were itchy on both sides. "Musketry is heavy in front this morning," noted Francis Harrington. The 57th, with its brigade, was lying in rain-soaked rifle pits opposite General Hill's corps and General George Pickett's division. No firing of consequence occurred between these two particular forces except from the anxious picket lines in front of the earthworks. During the afternoon, Crittenden's 1st Division joined a reconnaissance in force by Warren's V Corps to reconnoiter the enemy's strength and location. The men got within a few hundred yards of the Southern positions when they found the Confederates solidly dug in on high ground with large forces, and the Union commander wisely decided to retire—a pitched battle against those formidable defenses would have cost the Army of the Potomac dearly. The soldiers returned to their works and spent the rest of the day maintaining an uneasy watch in the direction of the Rebel lines, while some of their comrades buried the dead on the field.[49] The battle for the North Anna River had been a useless slaughter, gaining nothing for the Federal army except shame.

★

Major Cushing resigned from the regiment on May 26. "The regiment at this time lost the services of their fighting major," wrote John Anderson, and added caustically, "not by death, but by resignation." First Sergeant William Shaftoe of Company K was one of the 57th's seasoned veterans, formerly a member of both the 10th and the 31st Massachusetts Volunteers, Cushing's former regiment—he no doubt knew him well for what he was. In a letter written to William Schouler, the adjutant general of the Commonwealth of Massachusetts, while convalescing at home from a wound received nine days later at Cold Harbor, Shaftoe related of Cushing, ". . . but one coward was amongst us, but [Major Cushing] was my superior officer at the North Anna River were [sic] our Brave & Lamented Lt-Col Chandler Fell, the Brave amongst the Bravest. . . ."[50]

11

Shelter Without Fire

DURING THE LANGUID DAY of May 26, Captain Julius M. Tucker became the temporary commander of the 57th Massachusetts because of his seniority of commission. Captain Tucker was a genial and sensitive young man with dandified cropped brown hair and muttonchop side whiskers that stuck far out on his cheeks. He had achieved a very respectable record of leadership as head of Company H, and most of the men of the regiment thought well of him.[1]

That Thursday, the 26th, was a day of rest for the regiment. At five o'clock in the afternoon, however, the men were issued five days' rations and told to pack up and be ready to march.[2]

After dark the IX Corps was ordered out of its pits. The officers whispered as loudly as they dared to the men to keep quiet and not let their equipment bang together, lest the Rebels discover the Federal withdrawal plan. The corps retreated, along with the rest of the Army of the Potomac, to the northern bank of the North Anna River. Thunderstorms had started again early in the evening, and the rain pelted the soldiers all night.[3]

Unopposed by the Southerners, the IX Corps crossed the river on the bobbing pontoon bridges that had been camouflaged with brush and floored with grass and moss to keep the men hidden and their march quiet, and as soon as the crossing was made, the nervous, scarcely protected army engineers immediately disassembled the bridges to secure the ford from any rear-guard action.[4]

The 1st Brigade of the IX Corps moved to Jericho Ford, one and a half miles upstream, and held that position until morning.[5]

★

For the third time, a flanking movement to Lee's left was Grant's strategy, and the IX Corps, following the V Corps and a small part of the VI Corps, stepped off on a forced march by way of Shady Grove toward the Pamunkey River and the Hanovertown crossing, which lay just a few miles north of Richmond.

Those units of the Army of the Potomac were headed by two divisions of Major General Philip Sheridan's Cavalry Corps. The troopers served as guides and scouts, reconnoitering the countryside and local roads to maintain a clear passage for the infantry and the accompanying artillery batteries, wagons, baggage, and cattle herds. The IX and V Corps were moving to the north and east of, and on a parallel course with, the II and the main body of the VI Corps, and their marching distance was longer than those two outfits—about thirty-two miles altogether—even though the Union army's destination was only a little under twenty miles in a straight line down river from its rifle pits along the North Anna. The march was arduous, and it was kept up day and night until the footsore men thought they would drop from exhaustion.[6]

And many of them did. There were also hundreds of stragglers and malingerers who filled the woods and fields all about the march. The only halts made were for meals, and those pauses were very short. The men were weary and bleary-eyed, but, obediently, on they went, once again certain that the next fight was not far off. Most of them felt they were walking dead men, and they were resigned, through fatigue and intimidation and despair, to that fateful destiny.

★

The 57th, with the 1st Brigade, had been given an opportunity to relax a bit early on the morning of May 27, and at 6:00 A.M. Private Harrington wrote that the men were "now resting in the road near the stacks" of arms, and at 8:00, he noted that the regiment had marched a little further on from Jericho Ford and was then halted for breakfast.[7]

After being relieved by a detachment of Federal cavalry at 8:30 that morning, the 1st Brigade left Jericho Ford and proceeded towards Bethel Church. Julius Tucker led his small band of Massachusetts soldiers along the march with the IX Corps, which had been deployed as rear guard behind the wagon trains. Because the men had to halt every few minutes for one reason or another, the 1st Division made only eleven miles that day, and the men camped that night at about 11:00 just after meeting the Bowling Green road. Many of them claimed that it had been one of the most fatiguing marches that they had yet had. Still exhausted from the action on the North Anna, they were frustrated at the slow progress of the army, and there were many stragglers in the 57th on that wearying trek that day.[8]

Concentrated in the vicinity of Mt. Carmel Church, the men took up their march again at about 9:20 the following morning as the rear brigade in the division. The morning hike was easy, but "quite steady," and the soldiers stopped for dinner at noon at a plantation that one soldier described as a "princely establishment with slave cabins all around." After an hour's rest, they continued on through "fine, open country, level and well cultivated," until 6:00, making fifteen more miles. The afternoon march had been severe, with many stragglers. The wagon trains and artillery choked the roads, and the troops had to march around them over bottomlands and fields. Some men who had gotten too close to the road and fallen asleep from exhaustion had had to be awakened quickly by their comrades so they would not be run over by the artillery. For the next two hours, the advance was held up by the wagon trains that jammed the road in front. After clearing the traffic snarl, they carried on their journey all night along roads "ablaze with burning rails and tall pines" to light the way, which "presented a most picturesque and brilliant scene." The 57th reached the narrow and sluggish Pamunkey River with the 1st Division late on May 28, and crossed it on two pontoon bridges at Hanover Ferry around midnight.[9]

★

The Pamunkey ran toward the southeast and was formed by the confluence of the North Anna and South Anna rivers and several other, smaller creeks. The terrain in the area was heavily wooded, and the riverbanks were low and swampy, with marshy little streams snaking out in all directions. It was a dark and haunting landscape full of eerie sounds and tall pines and hardwoods that cast sinister shadows on the forest floor.

The many roads in the territory wound around in all directions through the copses and glades, seeming to have no destination, and none except the Richmond Stage road—and that only in comparison—was of any practical value to the huge army on its grand expedition. At any other time the area could well be called picturesque and serene, but the highways were muddy and wet then, and they were badly rutted from the late rains and the traffic of the Army of the Potomac. The soldiers slogged and stumbled through the sucking mire up to their ankles and often their knees.

Some of those roads were worn down well below ground level,[10] and it was not uncommon to see artillery limber and caisson drivers screaming, cursing, coaxing, and yanking their belly-deep, wild-eyed horses by their reins and traces out of the chowdery slop, themselves spattered with mud from head to toe as result of their ordeal.

The soldiers then began passing through terribly destroyed landscape— wholly different from what they had seen during the march to the North Anna River and beyond. They now were gazing upon abandoned and ruined houses, barns, mills, and fields. The early years of the war—the Peninsula campaign, particularly—had caused awesome suffering in that part of Virginia, and forlorn women, dirty little orphans, homeless slaves, and defiant old men were passed by more and more as the soldiers progressed on their route. It was a pitiful sight, but not many of the men felt pity.

★

The soldiers kept on through the mosquito-ridden swamps, across the creeks, and over the foul lanes until they reached the vicinity of Haw's Shop about three miles southwest of Hanovertown, Virginia, at six o'clock on the morning of May 29, when a halt was called for breakfast. They had made an additional thirteen miles. At eight, the march continued until the soldiers were "halted about 2 P.M. and got dinner," after which they "commenced to build intrenchments but had orders to stop and laid idle all the Aft[ernoon]." The IX Corps established camp there and was ordered held in reserve. The camp—located between the II and V Corps—was "in a pine grove, through which flowed a stream of water in close proximity to the wagon train." The soldiers pitched tents taken off of regimental baggage wagons and then wandered down to the creek to wash their clothes and themselves. They also spent their time cleaning their equipment and making preparations for movements on the following day. The men got what rest they could, curling up under their tents on damp ground and closing their red, crusted eyes, and after a short sleep, they replenished their cartridge and cap boxes, wrote letters home, and caught up on their eating. That evening was "bright and beautiful," and the headquarters band played "patriotic and sacred music and songs of home."[11]

★

On May 27, Lee realized that Grant had begun a flanking movement again, and he pulled his Southern troops out of their trenches on the North Anna and began a forced march of eighteen miles to Atlee's Station on the Virginia Central Railroad, which his leading elements reached that afternoon. East of the station, Lee positioned his three corps in such a fashion as to put his Army of Northern Virginia between the Army of the Potomac and Richmond, by sealing off the approaches from the Pamunkey. Continuing to hold the interior lines, the Confederate general and his soldiers were able to travel much faster than the Federal forces, and the Rebels were digging in at a place called Cold Harbor to await the arrival of the Northern army.

★

On the 30th, the IX Corps was directed to form its battle lines on the left of the II Corps and on the right of the V Corps. The men were again moving to the southwest around noon when they waded dirty little Totopototomy Creek, a mile north of Pole Green Church, after a four-mile hike, and ran into brisk Rebel skirmishing, which they beat back in short order. Francis Harrington wrote at the time that the regiment then "Started on the march towards night this afternoon and marched to the front and took our position just in front of pine woods just about dark [nine o'clock] and we are to throw up breastworks before morning." (Some soldiers thought those pine woods all too reminiscent of the Wilderness.) He later reported that the 57th "worked until after midnight building intrenchments." The men remained in their fortifications through the night.[12]

The next morning the regiment's men "got up early and Drew A Days rations and meat and worked about ½ the forenoon on intrenchments."[13]

At noon on the 31st, Ledlie's brigade was ordered to take possession of some abandoned Rebel rifle pits in its front, and the soldiers advanced about half a mile and occupied them. But the occupiers did not stay in the old Southern works long, as they found the Confederates strongly manning the surrounding area, and after a half-hour they returned to their own rifle pits. Some men of the brigade's other regiments were picked off by Southern snipers as the Federal troops withdrew to their former position. At two o'clock in the afternoon, the brigade moved out again, with the 56th Massachusetts in front as skirmishers. The troops, ordered not to "speak above a whisper" or to "break twigs," continued forward and recaptured the pits that they had given up earlier. At sundown, they were withdrawn again, however, and the 1st Brigade finally took up station three and three-quarter miles northwest of Old Cold Harbor in a clearing just northeast of the Butler family's home. The position occupied by the men was annoying, as a road ran directly behind their works, and moving troops on that road created large dust clouds during the night—from the now dried-out countryside—that covered the men of the brigade with powdery dirt.[14]

★

Late on June 1, General Crittenden's 1st Division advanced again toward the southwest for about a half-mile. Ledlie's 1st Brigade took the right flank, Colonel Joseph M. Sudsburg's 2nd Brigade, the center, and Colonel Elisha G. Marshall's Provisional 3rd Brigade, the left. (The division had recently been reorganized. Sudsburg had replaced Colonel Daniel Leasure as commander of the 2nd Brigade, and a provisional brigade had been added under Colonel Marshall. The 35th Massachusetts also had been designated the division's acting engineers and were detached from the 1st Brigade on May 26.) Ledlie's brigade, in two lines of earthworks, now occupied ground to the northwest of the Butler house. The 57th lay in the second line in reserve.[15]

At about seven that night, a strong Confederate column composed of General Early's troops attacked the IX Corps on the left, and the men fell back under heavy fire. But one of the V Corps' brigades fighting near Crittenden's 1st Division, Joseph J. Bartlett's, held its own, and seeing those men tenaciously fighting for their position, the other Federals rallied, and the Rebels were driven back to their lines. It was a sharp little engagement, and after dark, strong pickets were posted, and the men got what sleep they could. Private John Gaskell, of Company G, who was described as a "brave soldier," was the only man killed in the regiment that June 1. He had been hit by a sharpshooter while the 57th was held in reserve earlier that morning.[16]

But another soldier in the 57th, Hubbard Carleton, also lost his life that day. The thirty-four-year-old farmer dropped dead from "disease" (likely a stroke or a heart attack) while on the march.[17]

★

That same Wednesday, about ten at night, Grant and Meade issued orders for an offensive to begin with a general attack by the Federal army all along the Confederate lines on the morning of the 2nd of June. However, the order was countermanded when the II Corps could not get into position on time, and the assault was postponed until four-thirty on the morning of June 3.[18]

★

Early in the afternoon of June 2, with the 2nd Michigan Volunteer Infantry covering the rear, the IX Corps withdrew one and a half miles southeastward through fierce, tangled country on a forced march and took up a new position near Bethesda Church on the extreme right (north) of the Union forces connecting to the V Corps on their left, in order to guard the Army of the Potomac's flank. The day had been relatively quiet, otherwise. But at about two o'clock, the corps's skirmish line that was covering the right was vigorously attacked and pushed in by Generals Henry Heth's and Robert Rodes's divisions, supported by other units of Hill's corps and General John Gordon's division, which moved in on the road from Hundley's corner off to the west in a driving rain. Marshall's and Sudsburg's brigades were then forced to retire from their breastworks on the right of the line as the Confederates rolled on. The whole IX Corps, General Burnside commanding in person, then rallied and formed on open ground in three long lines of battle by division fronts, with the 1st Division in the first line supported by the 2nd and 3rd. "It was a review under fire," remembered one soldier in Crittenden's division. Two Northern batteries, the 7th Maine and the 34th New York, opened and the Rebels replied in kind, and in the ranks on both sides "the firing commenced heavy." As the result of heavy Federal resistance and the coming of darkness, the corps finally repulsed the Southern attack, but a great many of the 1st Division's skirmishers were captured and a number of men were killed and wounded.[19]

150

The men then set to work digging trenches and fortifying them with logs, and it was sheer drudgery in the rain and mud with the Rebels sniping at them. When night came, the firing died down, and the men relaxed as best they could and ate supper. They were in dreadful shape. Their uniforms were not much more than rags and getting worse daily. And many of them were barefoot. Rations were being issued very irregularly at that time, and the Massachusetts infantrymen were constantly suffering from hunger. They were filthy and lousy and exhausted, and they saw no end to their anguish in sight. That night they had no shelter and most could not sleep.[20]

Ledlie's brigade was now in position on the Old Church road, near the Burnett house, a half-mile northeast of Bethesda Church. Sudsburg's brigade was in front of it, and Christ's brigade of the 3rd Division, IX Corps, was on its left. The 57th was lying in rifle pits along with its brigade, and, for the moment, the regiment's soldiers were assigned as guards and reserves.[21]

★

The Union battle lines ran from north to south facing the Army of Northern Virginia to the west. The Federal corps' positions along the six-mile front were—from the north—IX, refused, or bent backwards, towards the northeast and facing Early to the northwest; V; XVIII, which had arrived recently from General Ben Butler's Army of the James at Bermuda Hundred; VI; and II, with Hancock's veterans squaring off against Lee's tough campaigners as far south as the Grapevine Bridge on the Chickahominy River. Heavy skirmishing occurred up and down the line all during the day on June 2, and the sharpshooters on both sides bushwhacked with alacrity at every chance.

★

The army was stretched over such a distance and the lines were so thin that in some places it looked like a skirmish line, and this was the case in the 57th's area. The men could scarcely expect much success charging the enemy's breastworks, spread out as they were. This was going to be the apocalypse all over again, and every one of them was well aware of it, but although Cold Harbor was one of the bloodiest battles of the Civil War—during the charge against the center of the Confederate lines on the morning of June 3, about 8,000 Federals were lost in 8 minutes, an average of 16 per second—the 57th was to get off lightly with only 1 killed, 2 deaths from disease, 7 wounded, and 4 taken prisoner of war during the entire Cold Harbor campaign. But at that time, the Massachusetts men had no way of knowing their fate, and they were as frightened as ever. They were breathing hard, and their pulses pounded. They said their prayers, and they wrote what many believed were their last letters home. Most pinned pieces of paper to their coats—as did thousands of others in the Army of the Potomac that day—that had their names and regiments written on them, so that their bodies could be identified when they were killed, as they were sure that they would be.[22]

At first light, June 3, the entire Northern army was on its feet, and the men were jostling noisily for position in the miles-long battle lines. The soldiers' spirits were at their nadir, and they were worried and anxious as they drove fresh charges home with clanking ramrods and twisted steel bayonets onto steel rifle barrels. Their trepidation kept them obedient, even though they were certain their chances of living were less than marginal, and looking out at the rugged Rebel works fortified by deadly Southern cannon across the open ground, and glancing left and right at their own thin ranks, the stoic but shifty-eyed men of the Union army figured that they were about to be massacred. They knew that the generals were insane to send them on such a reckless and irresponsible mission. They were men of reason, if not sophistication, and they did not need genius to peer across the lines in the early morning light to see what was waiting for them. The recent past was vivid in their memories.

★

There were two Cold Harbors—Old and New—and this battle was to take place between the hamlets, near the site of the old battlefield of Gaines Mill where Major General George Brinton McClellan was mauled by Robert E. Lee in that futile battle that had been part of the Peninsula campaign in 1862. It was a land full of swamps, thickets, fields, hills, and meandering creeks, and it was as miserable a battlefield as any on which the armies had ever fought—the Wilderness notwithstanding. New Cold Harbor was a mere speck on the landscape, and Old Cold Harbor, while an insignificant hamlet, was a strategic crossroads that hosted several run-down, clapboard buildings. It took its name, as one theory has it, from way stations along highways in England and signified a "shelter without fire," an appellation that would have been of great irony to the survivors of the battle had they known its meaning.

★

At precisely 4:30 A.M. on June 3, the several corps of the Army of the Potomac, stretched along their immense battlefront, rushed against the nearly impregnable Confederate earthworks, cheering and yelling and firing wildly away. The Southerners, waiting patiently in their solid defenses until the Federals were in easy range, then opened fire on the charging Northerners. The volleys poured from their rifle barrels in killing sheets of yellow and red flame in the semidarkness of dawn, and the unprotected aggressors in blue were blasted to scrap all along the line by the well-entrenched Rebels.

The IX Corps' charge on the northern front of the Cold Harbor battle-field was kicked in swiftly by the Southern artillery, which slashed the leading regiments of the corps to bloody splinters with demolishing double charges of canister and grapeshot. Potter's 2nd Division and Willcox's 3rd Division, along with elements of Crittenden's 1st, supported by the several batteries of the Corps' artillery, rallied and countercharged in a terrifying frenzy, capturing the rifle pits of Jubal Anderson Early's men and shoving those Confederates back to breastworks along the Shady Grove Church road. The corps' charge had taken Burnside's men almost a mile to the northwest near the positions that they had occupied two days earlier,[23] and at 5:00 A.M., the morning's battle was all but over for the IX Corps as well as the rest of the Union line. It had been an unmitigated disaster for the Federal army, which was torn to shreds. Grant had not learned from Burnside's terrible failure at Marye's Heights during the battle of Fredericksburg in December 1862, or Lee's on the third day at Gettysburg, where similar tactics were tried with similar results.

The 2nd and 3rd Brigades of the 1st Division had been on the right in the front lines of the advance, but Ledlie's 1st Brigade had been in the rear behind General Christ's troops and they had been fairly well protected. James Ledlie's men, including those of the 57th, had been fortunate, and they suffered only minor casualties in the ghastly fracas.[24]

Orders came down later that morning for the entire IX Corps to charge Early's Confederates again at one o'clock in the afternoon, but when the supporting batteries were late taking position, the order was rescinded. The notoriously Yankee-hating Early made an attempt to take advantage of the Federal dilemma and he viciously charged Burnside's corps, but the black-ened Federals blew his troops apart and then countercharged and ran him and his men back—beyond the Shady Grove Church road this time—pinning the Rebels down in their dusty earthworks and ending the action in that part of the battle for the day.[25]

Although the IX Corps had not been as heavily engaged as the other corps of the Army of the Potomac that day, its casualties amounted to over eight hundred killed, wounded, and missing.[26]

★

The 57th Massachusetts was present for the entire battle of Cold Harbor on June 3, and it took part in most all of the IX Corps' movements. In the morning it had been detailed to support Captain Edward J. Jones's 11th Massachusetts Battery, attached to the 2nd Division, IX Corps, that was posted in a strong position 250 yards west of the Old Church road in the Burnett family's backyard, and the artillerymen were providing supporting fire for the charging infantry. When some Southerners broke through the Union forward lines and threatened to overrun the battery's four field pieces, the 57th spurned the enemy sharply for the gunners.[27]

While the regiment was on station with the battery, one of the boys, irrationally daring from getting through too many battles unharmed, decided that he wanted a better view of the goings-on. Captain Anderson related the story in his history of the regiment.

One reckless young fellow of the 57th was curious to watch the artillery fire which was going on between this battery [11th Massachusetts] and one of the enemy's [probably William Poague's guns again], which was posted in the woods about half a mile distant. For the purpose of better observation he seated himself upon a rotten stump and was evidently greatly interested in the artillery duel. He was several times cautioned that he was in a dangerous place and advised not to expose himself needlessly, but to lie down with the others. He boastingly remarked that the shot had not been made that could hit him. Just that instant a solid shot struck the stump, smashing it in pieces and letting the fellow to the ground so suddenly that for some seconds he thought he had actually been hit.[28]

(Unfortunately that soldier has not been identified, but it is certain that he took plenty of ribbing from his comrades.)

Another incident occurred just after that which was not humorous in the least. While they were lying in their breastworks, one of the men in Captain Doherty's Company G was very slightly wounded—so slightly that no wound was recorded for anyone in that company that day—and as he started for the rear to find an aid station, another soldier got up to assist him to safety. Doherty, catching sight of this second soldier's activity—wanton cowardice in his opinion—became furious and called the shirker back into the trenches. The man, head down in shame, reported to the captain and after he was given a ruthless and embarrassing tongue-lashing in front of all of his comrades, Captain Doherty marched him forward to the top of the breastworks and proceeded to drill him in the manual of arms in full view of the Rebel soldiers eight hundred yards away. The Southerners were loving every minute of it, and the riflemen did their best to pick the two men off. The 57th's men looked on as the captain presented himself and the miscreant private to almost certain death. Once again, though, Doherty miraculously beat the odds with only two or three bullet holes in his uniform coat. And luck held up for the unidentified soldier, too, who must have been trembling in terror as he reached the safety of the earth and log fortifications.[29]

Sporadic gunfire snapped along the line all day under the now broiling sun, and when the boys sighted over their breastworks, they could see heavily fortified Rebel entrenchments. They saw no advantage in another suicidal charge against those well-built Southern barricades. The battlefield between the trenches was a butchery, with thousands of dead lying in every possible grotesque and convoluted position, hideously ripped to pieces from the small arms and cannon fire. As usual, the wounded were sending up a fearsome racket, but the men were unable to help them until after dark, when rescue parties went out and brought some of them back. And many who went to the aid of their wounded comrades were shot and killed for their acts of compassion.

During the night when the firing slacked off, the 57th was assigned to picket duty far out in front of its trenches on wide-open ground. It was a dreadful duty, but the men slipped quietly out of their works and obediently crawled along the ground until they reached their position, where they took cover behind any tree, log, rock, dead body, or battlefield trash that could be found, and countered shots with the Southern sentries all night without a break. The picket lines were only fifty yards apart, and for any of the men to change position was extremely hazardous, so the panicky soldiers stayed where they were, tearing at the ground with their fingers, digging makeshift rifle pits and improvising shelters—a task they had learned with great proficiency.

"One Confederate posted behind a tree directly in front seemed to feel particularly ugly and annoying," recalled John Anderson.

[He] kept busy all the time loading and firing from behind it. Finally, as he reached around to fire, the crack of a rifle was heard a few feet from our [meaning his own—the captain was very fond of speaking of himself in the first person plural] left and he fell to the ground never to rise again. Some evidently thought he was "playing possum" in order to get a better shot at a new victim; hence, he became a target for a score or more of Federal muskets. When our line advanced the next morning he was found riddled with more than a hundred bullets. After the first shot it little recked to him, poor fellow, whether it were a hundred or a million. He had passed beyond being an enemy, and one could not help thinking that he, too, had loved ones in some Southern home, who were anxiously hoping and praying for his safe return,—perhaps little ones saying "God bless papa" in their evening prayers.[30]

★

The 57th's casualties were not very great in that battle because the regiment simply had so few men to lose by then, and those available to fight had not been heavily engaged. The boys had been under fire twice that day, and in the words of one of the privates who was with the regiment during the fighting at Cold Harbor, Private Edward Schneider of Company K, "the 57th stood like a rock" each time. The line of the regiment was growing shorter with each passing day, and now it could muster for combat duty barely enough men to form two complete companies—about two hundred soldiers. (On May 30 and June 1, a number of men were sent sick to hospitals, while a nearly equal number who had been absent for various reasons since before the Wilderness reported to the regiment for duty.) The actual companies were little more than squads, and the men constantly contrasted their diminishing number of scraggly veterans to the 916 healthy, handsome soldiers who had marched proudly off to war from Worcester less than two months previously. Men were being lost every day, killed, wounded, captured, deserting, or sick. There were still a number of the regiment on detached duty, and others, it will be remembered, such as the musicians, teamsters, and medical, commissary, and quartermaster staff normally did not fight.[31]

The men of the 57th, for the greater part, had had enough; they wanted an end of it, and they wanted to go home. One of the regiment's soldiers wrote his sister at about that time telling her that he "was entirely worn out. . . ." They questioned the gains of their sacrifices, and they came up with no satisfactory answers. They certainly knew what had been lost, and they saw only stalemate in the campaign, with no clear victories and several glowing defeats. The only fact they knew for certain was that their regiment was fading a whole lot faster than it had been recruited.[32]

One brave fellow wounded that day was one of the two Private Patrick Flynns in the 57th. Born in Limerick, young Flynn of Company A had fought faithfully in all the regiment's skirmishes and battles and endured every march. He was sent to Fort Schuyler U.S. Army General Hospital in New York Harbor to recuperate, but apparently the hardships of the battlefield were easier for him to deal with than the conditions of an army medical facility, and he deserted in September.[33]

Another Irishman, from County Galway, was Private John Gahagen, of Company A, who was taken prisoner of war on June 2. Like Pat Flynn, John Gahagen had fought beside the 57th from the beginning, but his fate now would be to rot to death from chronic disease in the Confederate prison in Millen, Georgia.[34]

Private Charles S. Morse, of Company K, an artist from Readville, Maine, was one of the men who joined the regiment in the field for the first time on May 30. That unlucky soldier was captured on June 2, after just two days of combat service in the war. Sent to Florence, South Carolina, he, too, would waste away from disease until he succumbed on November 13.[35]

Struck over the right eye by a shell fragment, Sergeant William Shaftoe, of Company K, would never fully recover from the effects of his wounds, and after the war, in 1869, a pension examiner would report that as a result, "he was incapable of enduring labor. He had lost his hearing in his right ear, and he suffered from headache, giddiness, and fainting fits, and his disability was undoubtedly permanent."[36]

General Grant had changed his base of supply from Fredericksburg to White House Landing on the Pamunkey River, and food and ammunition were beginning to reach the front a bit more efficiently. A large shipment of fresh vegetables had arrived recently, and they were distributed to the men whenever possible. The soldiers were greatly pleased to have this welcome supplement to their unspeakable diets.

The wounded were evacuated to field hospitals that had been set up at the landing on the river, with the worst cases being put on steam transports and ferried down the York River and up the Potomac to the army medical facilities in and around Washington.

★

Full-scale operations were not resumed on June 4, and when the men of the 57th Massachusetts returned from the picket lines, answered roll call, and had their breakfasts, they began to work, in utter exhaustion, fortifying their defenses. All this labor was done very, very carefully, for skirmish and sharpshooter fire was incessant, and any human figure that appeared in the Rebel gunsights was fair game.[37] It was dangerous, hot work with the unmerciful Virginia sun beating down on the wretched soldiers, who could find no relief from the misery it wrought.

The regiment was still stationed with the 1st Brigade directly in the rear of Sudsburg's brigade, and during the early morning hours, General Burnside ordered several patrols on a forced reconnaissance to move forward and feel out the Southern positions. They reported back that the Confederates had retired and abandoned their works. That afternoon, the IX Corps was ordered to move a little over two miles south to a new position at Beaulah Church near the Woody house, on the right flank of General William F. Smith's XVIII Corps. With Crittenden's 1st Division occupying their trenches as covering fire, Potter and Willcox's divisions took up the march to their new assignment.[38]

As soon as those two divisions were safely under way, General Crittenden got his division on the road at four o'clock, and the men marched along the meandering country lanes through the dark woods until they arrived at their new post at nightfall. They dug in rapidly just north of Burnside's headquarters, and the 1st Division was ordered held in reserve. The soldiers soon had their campfires going, and they settled down in relative quiet to boil their coffee and smoke their pipes. But Francis Harrington reported that they had "no supper tonight."[39]

On the 5th, after drawing four days' rations in the morning, Crittenden's men were ordered to take up a new post fourteen hundred yards north of their trenches at the Martin house behind three batteries of light artillery and

Colonel Nathan T. Dushane's brigade of the V Corps, and they moved to occupy their new area at 6:00 P.M., arriving at about 8:00. They were well protected in their position behind the front lines by some high ground ahead of them, and they felt fairly secure. Nevertheless, they maintained a tight watch for any funny business in the direction of the Confederate lines, and they kept a sharp eye on their unprotected rear, as well. During the early morning hours of the 6th, the 57th's soldiers languished in their entrenchments with neither side showing much inclination to bring about a major attack.[40]

After daylight on June 6, the Confederates made a couple of feeble assaults to determine the strength of the Federal works, but most of their sorties collapsed quickly under Union fire. However, the Southerners did manage to drive in Robert Potter's skirmishers in the IX Corps lines.[41]

The 1st Division of the IX Corps, meanwhile, had pulled back to a new position in breastworks a half-mile west of their June 4 location, in the rear of the Union lines, and the men spent their time strengthening their trenches and constructing traverses—never-ending work. Later in the day, the V Corps was ordered to move on an arc to the east to protect the northern flank of the Army of the Potomac. As that corps moved to its new position in the open fields between the Leary and Burnett houses, Crittenden's division moved on a nearly parallel course slightly to the south of that of the V Corps to protect the right flank of the IX Corps. The division spread out, with Ledlie's 1st Brigade moving the farthest. Ledlie's troops marched one and a half miles to the east of the main Union lines and entrenched on the northeast side of Allen's Mill Pond close to the mill, just north of Warren's V Corps, at 10:00 A.M. on June 6. Later in the day the 37th Massachusetts took up position on the 1st Brigade's left flank.[42]

The men took one look at the inviting little lake (Private Harrington referred to it as a "swamp"), shaped like a half-mile-long, jumping northbound whale, and the first thought of many on that steamy June day was to jump into the water for a bath, and their second thought was to catch some fish. But the situation was too explosive for personal needs just then, and they burrowed in strongly, keeping a steady eye northward towards the Rebels in the woods. At midnight, the Southerners made a strong charge on the IX Corps' lines, but after a savage little firefight that inflicted heavy losses on the Rebels, the Confederates retreated back to their earthworks with nothing gained but more destruction. The men in the 57th also drew three days' rations that night.[43]

★

The battlefield at that time was revolting. Hundreds of the wounded had died from exposure and lack of care, but the men did not dare risk their lives trying to drag them to safety. The maimed soldiers' pleas for help over the past few days had been nerve wrenching, but there was nothing that anyone in the trenches had been willing or able to do for them then.[44]

On the evening of June 7, a truce was called between six and eight o'clock in order to bury the dead and relieve the suffering of the injured, most of whom had been lying between the lines since the attack of June 3. When the men went out on the field, they found very few of the wounded still alive, and they were furious at the Southerners, who had shot many of the helpless just for target practice, while Lee procrastinated for several days at Grant's attempts to negotiate a cease-fire. The men buried their comrades where they fell, and marked their graves—when it was possible to identify the bodies from something in their pockets. Burial detail was a loathsome job on that battlefield, as the dead had lain for so long that they were black, bloated, and decayed beyond recognition. Many of the soldiers were sick from their nauseating stench, and they returned to their lines unintimidated by the threats of officers and noncoms to punish them if they did not continue their work. Over on the right side of the IX Corps trenches, however, where the 57th was in position near the pond, the truce was largely ignored, and intermittent skirmishes were kept up all during the two-hour truce period that evening, making it impractical to venture out in burial parties except for brief intervals. The Rebels were "hungry and mad"—as their own commander later described them—and they acted brutally, and the Federal soldiers reacted in kind whenever the opportunity presented itself.[45]

On June 8, General Crittenden requested to be relieved of command of the 1st Division, and General Ledlie, to the misfortune of the 1st Division, assumed his position and passed the brigade on to Colonel Jacob Parker Gould of the 59th Massachusetts, who now was recuperated sufficiently from the effects of his earlier sunstroke to assume his new duties.[46]

Over at the mill pond, the morning of the 8th was quiet enough for everyone in the brigade to strip down and take a bath.[47] The men, of course, jumped in the lake by turns while the rest of their comrades kept watch, and the feeling of the cool water and soap on their bodies, which had not been washed or out of their filthy rags for over a month, must have been magnificent. And when they saw each other naked, they no doubt howled with laughter. From their necks to the tops of their heads, and from their wrists to the tips of their fingers, they were the color of oiled mahogany, but every other part of their bodies was snow white, and the contrast surely was hilarious to them. After bathing, they did their best to scrub their rotten uniforms, underwear, and socks. Anything they did, they reasoned, would be an improvement. And it was. After their wash morale improved substantially. Some of the resourceful soldiers improvised fishing poles and hooks baited with bits of army salt meat, and several of the messes that night fried fresh fish in their blackened frying pans. Though short-lived, it was a delightful change in their dreary routine—clean bodies and fresh food.

At eleven that morning, the regiment "moved to rear on to the brow of the hill not but a few rods and threw up more earthworks [and] finished about 4 O'clock P.M." The men remained in this position for the next four days.[48]

★

For the 57th Massachusetts and the 1st Brigade the situation remained about the same until June 12, with the men skirmishing from their foul trenches every day, but engaging in no major combat. The ground between the lines was an awful sight, strewn thickly with the putrid dead that could not be buried during the truce and that continued to rot in the hot sun. Dead horses and mules also littered the woods and swamps and added their own ugly aroma to the air. The odors were unendurable, and they continued to make many of the men sick to their stomachs.

On Saturday, June 11, the brigade received its mail, and the men that got letters or packages from home were ecstatic. (Those that did not were down-hearted. Private Harrington wrote dejectedly, "I got nothing.") Communication with family and friends was vital to them—they had to know that their sacrifices were appreciated. Sometimes, though, the letters were painful. Many families suffered terrible financial burdens with the heads of their households in the service, and when wives and mothers wrote of the problems that they were facing, it added to the soldiers' depression. The men were not paid regularly—sometimes going for months with no money—and they could not send home what they did not have. The meager stipend of aid from the Commonwealth of Massachusetts did not stretch far, either, and knowing that their families were suffering as a result of the military's red tape incensed them. The Irish and the other poor suffered terribly from this problem. Worse, however, as in Francis Harrington's case, was getting no letter at all.[49]

The weather remained hot and oppressive, and some of the men in the Union army developed malaria from mosquito bites. The stagnant, stinking swamps at Cold Harbor were rich breeding grounds for those pests, and the insects were everywhere. Medical science had no idea of the true nature of malaria then, and the army surgeons were baffled by the high incidence of it on that particular battleground. They knew that the sickness came from the wet bottomlands, but they misidentified its cause as the swamp gases in the atmosphere.

Pestilence of all kinds proliferated in the squalid trenches, and the men had to deal with rats, mice, insects, and poisonous snakes. Their food was inhabited with wormy maggots, and they themselves were infested with lice, which were so annoying that the Yankee soldiers had dubbed them "graybacks" in honor of their Southern opponents. The boys were forever itching and scratching, and their bodies were covered with bites and welts. Chiggers and wood ticks also did their best—succeeding magnificently—to add to the men's wretchedness.

On Sunday, June 12, the 57th Regiment drew new uniforms for the first time since leaving Camp Wool, and the men also drew two days' rations that were to last them until June 15. Expecting orders to move later in the day, the soldiers were packed and ready to take up their new line of march by six o'clock that evening.[50]

The last casualty sustained by the 57th at Cold Harbor was Private Danforth Glazier, from Duane, New York, who died from disease there on the 12th.[51]

★

That day, General Grant, after accepting unqualified defeat for the regrettable battle of Cold Harbor, decided for the fourth time to flank Robert E. Lee on the left, and the high command issued orders to all the corps to begin moving that night.

The IX Corps, with the men instructed to keep silent, withdrew from its works at eight o'clock that evening and got under way towards the southeast with the VI Corps following and Union cavalry covering the rear. The soldiers tried to move quietly, but they nevertheless stumbled and banged around somewhat along the lanes leading through the forest as they left Allen's Mill on the pond. The night was black and starry with a waxing moon, and the roads were covered with a powdery dust that rose as the men tramped along, covering them with the fine stuff and making breathing difficult and visibility poor. The column changed direction and traveled north of the south fork of the Matadequin River to Burstin's farm, past Turner's store, and arrived at Tunstall's Station on the Richmond & York River Railroad at 2:00 A.M. on June 13, where the men halted in the road. After allowing the XVIII Corps to pass them by, and taking a needed bivouac in some grassy green fields close by, Burnside's troops continued on at daylight, marching until six o'clock that morning when some of the IX Corps regiments, including the 57th, stopped near White House Landing for three hours to get breakfast.

The men then continued their line of march until about noon, when they again halted for dinner. At 2:00 they carried on to Baltimore Crossroads, where another halt was called for an hour at 3:00 to rest. At 4:00 P.M. they "marched rapid in a group" until 5:30, when they took a further break for supper until 8:00 that evening. Taking up the last leg of their journey that day, the boys finally reached Olive Church at midnight, where they camped for the night, three miles from the Chickahominy River. The trip had taken them twenty miles on a long swing (and on the outside of the arc traced by the other corps of the Army of the Potomac) to the east and then south, and the soldiers were footsore and exhausted.[52]

There were only three divisions of the corps on that march, as the black 4th Division had been dispatched to the depots at White House Landing and Cumberland Landing to guard the army's huge supply centers, which they did well—some of them getting into their first skirmishes with their former masters.

12

The Cockade City

WITH THEIR BLANKETS ROLLED and strapped to their knapsacks, the men of the 57th Massachusetts were ready to go at 4:30 the following morning, June 14. After the inevitable delays inherent to a large army, they began marching south with the IX Corps at 7:15 following General Horatio Wright's VI Corps. Wading a creek at Pollock's Mill, they halted for a short time three-quarters of a mile above the Chickahominy River to allow the VI Corps to clear the crossings, then crossed that swampy creek at 8:30 A.M. on canvas-covered pontoon bridges laid by the VI Corps' engineers. At that point, known as Jones' Bridge, the Chickahominy, with its thicket-riddled banks, was divided by an island in the middle, and the two branches were not more than twenty-five feet wide each, which made the crossing easy.[1]

However, because the VI Corps' wagon trains were blocking the road beyond the stream, Burnside's entire corps was halted after reaching the south bank, and the men waited around the grounds of the Jordan family's home, a simple dwelling close by the route of march, until twelve o'clock, when the traffic became unsnarled.[2]

Continuing nearly due south after noon, in the heat and dust, the corps traveled along roads shaded by cherry and mulberry trees that were too much for some of the hungry men to resist. Soldiers broke rank by the score to pick and eat the delicious berries. The country south of the Chickahominy again changed dramatically from that which they had been through around Cold Harbor. It was open and cultivated, with elegant mansions and well-tilled fields. "The blight and devastation of war was nowhere visible," wrote one veteran.[3]

The regiment halted again at around four o'clock—after making about ten miles—for an hour opposite former President John Tyler's "splendid" house at Tyler's Mills.[4] The 57th was now several miles northeast of the point

Confederates captured during Grant's Virginia campaign. *(Rinhart Galleries, Colebrook, Conn.)*

on the James River chosen for the Army of the Potomac to cross it—the last river of any importance that army would cross as a body during the war.

Following this short, welcome rest, the men continued another three miles through the shady village of Charles City Court House, Virginia, on the south side of which they halted again at eight-thirty a half-mile north of the James. There they immediately began to dig defensive works to cover the crossing of the Army of the Potomac presently to be made over the great river. The IX Corps had moved to a "position on the right of the Sixth Corps, [the IX Corps'] right resting near the Jones' house, on an arm of the James River, the line extending in a northwesterly direction until it joined the line of the Sixth Corps. This position was fortified."[5]

Burnside's men camped in their newly built works and stacked their arms in anticipation of battle. The soldiers had been without food for twenty-four hours, but they were supplied with rations that evening. A soldier in the 1st Division left a description of the camp that night. "Men were gathered in groups," he remembered, "around piles of blazing [fence] rails, busily cooking their evening meals; the bands were discoursing patriotic music, and the whole scene was one of the most striking and magnificent of war."[6]

Exhausted from the demanding forced marches of twenty-five to thirty-five miles a day, however, the troops soon turned in and slept the sleep of the dead that night. For six weeks now, the army had been fighting, marching, and fortifying in very trying weather and in extremely difficult country, with almost no time for adequate sleep and sometimes going for days without food.[7]

Although the 57th's enlisted men had been issued new clothing at Cold Harbor, the officers had not been able to change uniforms because orders were that there would be no delay in the corps' movements to allow the regimental wagons to come up and resupply them. "They [the officers and surely the enlisted men, as well, after their hard march] were so covered and begrimed with dust and dirt that they would have been ashamed of themselves in any other place or position," remembered John Anderson, "yet they wore this evidence of hard service, as a distinctive mark of honor earned in the field in defense of their country."[8]

The 1st Division of the IX Corps remained in its rifle pits most of the torrid day of June 15 with muskets ready, and the men suffered from the relentless sun beating down on their heads. But at five minutes after six that afternoon, chief of staff Major General Andrew A. Humphreys sent orders from Grant's headquarters for the IX Corps' boys to get on the march as soon as possible toward the James to make the crossing, and then to move in the direction of Harrison's Creek near Petersburg, Virginia, to join the II Corps. At 11:15 that morning Burnside had been ordered to see that his men were supplied with food, but that task was not accomplished until 6:00 in the evening, when the teamsters finally brought up large quantities of rations and each man in the corps drew four days' supply of hardtack and ham, and two of coffee and sugar. At last, the columns began to form at about 6:30, and, by 8:00, the IX Corps commenced its march to the bridge, keeping to the fields so as not to interfere with the flow of the huge supply wagon trains using the roads.[9]

Passing General Meade's headquarters along the way, some of the men no doubt caught a glimpse of the Army of the Potomac's acerbic commander and wondered what Grant and he had in store for them this time.

★

Lieutenant Barton had rejoined the regiment for duty on June 13. On the 7th of the month, he had written his mother from his camp near Gaines Mill,

Since writing you my last letter I have been relieved from duty on the Ambulance Corps and shall report to my regiment in a few days I need not tell you that I am entirely satisfied with the change for I have felt for the last two weeks as though I ought to be with my company to share in their dangers rejoice when they rejoice and weep with them when they weep *That* is my place as I have *always* said and I am glad to be able to go back to them. It may seem strange to you that I should prefer to go back to the regiment to risk my life and limbs but so it is. When such men as Col. Bartlett and Lt. Col. Chandler with many others are willing to stand at the *front* it is time *I* was there.

And from the regiment's camp near the James on the 15th, he again wrote his mother,

I am once more with my regiment and it seems like *Home* to me. I reported to my regt just in time to participate in a long hard march from Coal [*sic*] Harbor to this point. Where we shall go to from this place I am not able to state, but no doubt to meet the Rebs. Thats what we want—give us *good action* and we can whip them every time but it takes lives to do it as it has already done but the tug has not come yet—I have yet to learn what has been accomplished this far. We have tried Genl Grants route to Richmond and have been obliged to give it up. We are now about to try another which I hope will be more successful than the first—

My *health* continues good so of course I have no reason to complain though we sometimes get very short of *rations* We have not had any *hard* bread for two days and are not able to get sugar and coffee as the Commissary is so *far back* [Obviously this letter was written prior to the supply wagons reaching the 57th that evening.]

Our regiment numbers about 190 guns for duty in line of battle *They are veterans* Those that are left will fight to the death. They can be depended on in any emergency. . . .[10]

★

166

The majestic James River was 700 yards wide at the crossing, and on June 14, 450-odd army engineers, split into two groups, had begun working simultaneously, half from a point near Fort Powhaten on the south bank and the remaining half from Weyanoke Point five miles south of Charles City Court House on the north shore, to fix into place the 101 pontoons needed for the bridge across the river's 15-fathom-deep, blue-brown waters. The castle soldiers, under the direction of Captain George H. Mendell, had started the backbreaking job at four o'clock that afternoon, and they had the traverse ready for traffic at eleven that night. It had been a tremendous undertaking, but the engineers, under Mendell's expert guidance, spanned the swift, deep current of the river, which had a tide in excess of four feet, in record time. U.S. Navy vessels, lying in the water above and below the structure, were anchored in midstream, and stout steel cables from those ships had been attached firmly to the pontoons to steady the long waterborne bridge.[11]

The army began to move across the bridge almost at once. The moon was full and high in the heavens that morning at one o'clock on June 15, as the IX Corps' artillery, ambulances, and supply wagons led the advance of the foot soldiers. The IX Corps vehicles, protected by one brigade of infantry, began crossing at 3:00 A.M. on the 15th and were all over and parked on the south side by 8:00 in the morning.

That night the IX Corps' soldiers started their march across the mighty stream at the head of the Army of the Potomac. (The II Corps had made the journey the night before on ferries that had been operating north of the bridge at Wilcox's Landing, and the V Corps later followed Hancock's men on the afternoon of the 16th. The XVIII Corps of the Army of the James previously had proceeded by river transports from White House Landing to Bermuda Hundred, where it crossed the Appomattox River, a tributary of the James, at Broadway Landing.) One division of the VI Corps followed Burnside's men during the evening of June 16. Tens of thousands of soldiers were crossing all during the night of June 15 and the early morning of June 16, and the approaches to the bridge were jammed with thousands more waiting their turn to pass over to the south bank. "On shore," a 1st Brigade veteran recalled, "the masses of troops, with bright gun barrels and brilliant flags, covered the hills, waiting to cross."[12]

Bandmasters conducted their military bands with flair, and the musicians played lively quickstep marches. The drummer boys beat out steady cadence, and torches were lit at intervals to guide the combat soldiers' passage over the river, their flickering lights playing on the moving troops and black water, creating an eerie, shimmering glow. The marching was hazardous on the fragile wood-and-canvas pontoons, and the bridge dipped and swayed as the men, singing and cheering, staggered over the plank walkway, unable to keep

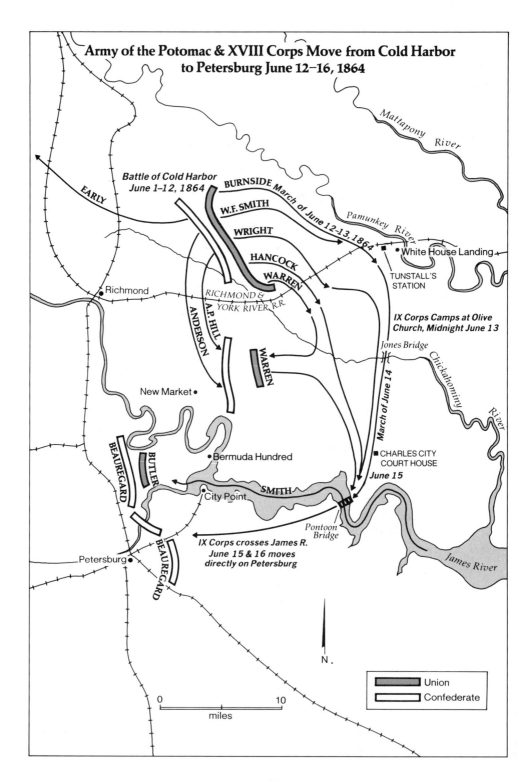

Army of the Potomac & XVIII Corps Move from Cold Harbor
to Petersburg June 12–16, 1864

Mattapony River

EARLY

Battle of Cold Harbor
June 1–12, 1864

BURNSIDE March of June 12–13, 1864

W.F. SMITH

WRIGHT

Pamunkey River

White House Landing

HANCOCK

WARREN

TUNSTALL'S
STATION

Richmond

RICHMOND &
YORK RIVER R.R.

IX Corps Camps at Olive
Church, Midnight June 13

Jones Bridge

Chickahominy

A.P. HILL

ANDERSON

WARREN

New Market

March of June 14

River

BEAUREGARD

BUTLER

Bermuda Hundred

CHARLES CITY
COURT HOUSE
June 15

City Point

SMITH

Pontoon
Bridge

IX Corps crosses James R.
June 15 & 16 moves
directly on Petersburg

James River

BEAUREGARD

Petersburg

N.

0   10
miles

Union
Confederate

168

pace with the bands' martial rhythms. Federal river gunboats floated upstream covering the enterprise, and transports lay downstream laden with supplies. The whole undertaking and all the accompanying activity was a colossal spectacle. Heavy wheels ground, steam whistles blew, weary soldiers tramped and yelled, and brass music drifted across the starry sky.[13]

By June 17, the Army of the Potomac and all of its complex impedimenta were safely across the river, and many of its regiments were encamped near Fort Powhatan, Virginia, not far from Coggin's Point on the southern bank of the James. But the 57th Regiment, along with the rest of the IX Corps, immediately upon reaching the south side of the James, had taken up the march along the pine-shrouded forest road for Petersburg to the west—a twenty-two-mile hike—following the sounds of the artillery in front of them that began again early on the morning of the 16th of June.[14]

★

The 15,000 men belonging to Major General William F. "Baldy" Smith's XVIII Corps had arrived at Petersburg the previous day, and that evening at seven o'clock, those troops had engaged the 4,000 home-guard, defending Rebels, commanded by General P. G. T. Beauregard, battering the well-intentioned but amateur fighters out of their positions and capturing about 1,800 yards of trenches 2 miles east of the city. The renewed battle was well in progress as the IX Corps marched toward the dark western horizon.

The XVIII Corps was reinforced by the II Corps, which had arrived seemingly too late on the evening of the 15th to be of any help. The Confederates, too, were being buttressed, although very slowly. Lee, at that time, was not certain what Grant's intentions were or exactly where the Army of the Potomac was, and he was reluctant to commit too many of his troops to Beauregard. The Northern general had stolen a march on him.

The shamrock soldiers of the II Corps, however, were in a dark disposition that 16th of June because they were convinced that a chance for an easy victory—and possibly the end of the war—had been lost the evening before when they had felt, regardless of the hour, that they could have attacked successfully the Rebel entrenchments which had not yet been strengthened by Lee's old campaigners of the Army of Northern Virginia. The greater part of those Rebel troops still were north of the James River, and the works, up until then, were manned by mostly inexperienced men, no match for the Army of the Potomac—and in particular, the no-nonsense warriors of the II Corps. But Smith had vacillated and Hancock had been given no orders to attack, and the II Corps' troops had been sent into bivouac, steaming with frustration and cursing their lost opportunity. History would favor the common soldier's common sense this time.

★

The young men of Petersburg had responded to war's challenge fifty-two years before, forming a regiment that had gone off to defend the United States against the British in 1812. On the sides of their hats they had worn red, white, and blue cockades, and ever after, the city of Petersburg, astride the southern banks of the Appomattox River, was known to all as the cockade city.

In June of 1864, it was probably the most strategically important city in North America. Peter Jones had founded a trading post there in 1645, and the town had been called Peter's Point at first. In 1748, the city was incorporated, and its name changed to Petersburg. General the Marquis de Lafayette had driven out the British, who had occupied it briefly during the American Revolution, and the local citizenry had rebuilt it after it was nearly destroyed by fire in 1815.

The town, peaceful and serene, populated by a little more than 18,000 souls, was rather progressive, and quite wealthy, in the largely agricultural South, and it was a major hub of a rail, water, and highway system of paramount importance to the Confederacy. Railroads such as the Weldon & Petersburg that ran to Wilmington, North Carolina, 225 miles distant, helped to funnel goods to other important parts of the deep South, as well as to carry the products and troops from those areas to the upper Confederacy when needed.

The city's white population operated a variety of businesses vital to the Southern cause, among them cotton and tobacco warehousing, shipping, and foundries. Forty-seven hundred slaves and 2,600 free blacks also lived in town, and the free Negroes were proprietors of livery stables, and barber and blacksmith shops. Others of African descent plied their skills as carpenters, bricklayers, and shoemakers.

Petersburg's shadowy, cool streets ran straight and true and were lined with handsome, sturdy red-brick commercial buildings and fine wood-framed homes with grassy lawns and picket fences. There were several beautiful churches in town, too, whose spires rose high above the other structures. The Tabb Street Presbyterian Church was one such, and its lofty steeple stood 120 feet above the ground, making it a perfect point at which to aim, and the Yankee artillerymen manning long-range rifled guns in the Federal lines would never tire of using it as a target, striking and denting its copper sheathing often.[15]

Here at Petersburg Ulysses S. Grant hoped to cut off the five vital and strategic railroad arteries that passed through the area and intersected in the city, and thus strangle the supply lines to Lee's army and the Confederate capital at Richmond, twenty-three miles in a straight line to the north. If he could accomplish his objective, he might literally starve the Army of Northern Virginia out of existence, guaranteeing Union supremacy and final victory.

Petersburg at the time of the siege. *(National Archives, Washington, D.C.)*

★

With each passing mile as the IX Corps moved west, the fighting at Petersburg could be heard more distinctly, and the soldiers of the 57th Massachusetts kept in step by singing along with the other troops the popular Union marching song "We'll Hang Jeff Davis to a Sour Apple Tree," which they intoned with gusto—and meant literally. In the van of the corps was the 3rd Division, with the 1st between it and the 2nd, which brought up the rear, and all the men understood that more suffering and death were in the cards. Nevertheless they continued to belt out their choruses, confident that they would demolish the Confederacy—sooner or later, anyway.[16]

The march to Petersburg, however, was not an easy march, and many soldiers straggled. General Ledlie complained in strong language of those "coffee boilers," as the men called them. Nevertheless, the general's complaints apparently did little good; men continued to fall out of the column. Soon after daylight, the weary troops of the IX Corps were given a one-hour halt near Old Court House, and then they continued their journey toward the sound of the guns.[17]

As they neared the new battleground, the men passed the thousands of black troops of Maine-born Brigadier General Edward Winslow Hinck's division lining the way, who had been attached recently to the XVIII Corps. The black soldiers were having a grand time, singing and dancing and carousing over six pieces of Rebel field artillery that they had captured the day before, and the whites were amused at their "peculiar," remarkable antics, calling out condescendingly encouraging remarks to the ex-slaves. Those battle-blooded Negro regiments had been among the first Federals to arrive at Petersburg, and they were sorely proud of their accomplishments over their former masters.

The 3rd Division's advance elements of the IX Corps reached the outer defense lines on the east side of Petersburg at about ten in the morning on June 16 with the 1st Division in close support, and at nearly one in the afternoon the men of the IX Corps were all up and in position on the left of the II Corps.[18]

Soon after arriving, Ledlie's 1st Division was ordered to move a short distance down the Prince George Court House road—which ran northwest to southeast from Petersburg to Prince George County Court House—turn south through the countryside for about a mile, and take up station in some former Confederate redan batteries behind Potter's 2nd Division of the IX Corps. General Ledlie positioned his troops "at right angles to the Petersburg road and the Suffolk State road [more commonly known as the Baxter road], covering a wood road running through a piece of timber in front of the main line of the enemy's work." The men arrived in their new location around six o'clock and bivouacked there for the night, constructing breastworks until long after dark.[19]

The blue lines ran north to south on the battlefield, and the men could see clearly the city's suburbs and church belfries. The Confederates had cut the trees down for about a half-mile in front of their earthworks and redoubts in order to open an unobstructed area for cannon and rifle fire.

Those Rebel fortifications were originally known as the Dimmock Line after Confederate Captain Charles H. Dimmock, a Northerner by birth, who had overseen their construction. The captain had begun building them in the summer of 1862 under the direction of the Confederate Engineer Bureau, and the breastworks and artillery redoubts originally had stretched around the city in a great arc beginning along the eastern side of the Appomattox River and terminating on its banks just west of town. In the defenses there were 55 artillery batteries consecutively numbered from the eastern end, and although the works were stoutly built, their weakness was in their extraordinary length. To defend 10 miles of trenches required a vast complement of troops, and therein would lay part of Grant's eventual strategy for the destruction of Lee's army. (The 1,800 yards of trenches captured by the XVIII Corps earlier had been the eastern section of the Dimmock Line. The beaten Confederate home guards had pulled back towards the city, and with the help of the experienced men of the Army of Northern Virginia who were beginning to move in to replace them all day on June 16—Lee now knew where his enemy was—the Rebels had thrown up new works just as formidable as the old.)

★

That evening at around six o'clock, the II Corps along with two brigades of the IX Corps and two brigades of the XVIII Corps made an attack on the Southern position in their front, battling furiously for almost three hours with little result. A small amount of ground was captured by General David Bell Birney's division of the II Corps, and the Confederates in that area retreated a short distance to construct new defenses during the night. Darkness called a halt to the contest, and the worn-out men slumped down in their barricades and rifle pits.

The 57th Massachusetts, as well as most of the IX Corps, were held in reserve during that action, but the men were close enough to observe it, and they were quite content that they were not involved. Burnside's troops were exhausted from the long, hot, and dusty forced march, and they badly needed rest.

Later that night, headquarters of the Army of the Potomac circulated orders that soon filtered down through the corps, division, brigade, and regimental levels of the army for the men to be prepared to attack the Confederate defenses at first light the following morning.[20]

Before dawn on June 17, the long, blue ranks assembled into battle lines, and the assault on Confederate General Beauregard's entrenchments was gotten under way. The 1st Division of the IX Corps was now posted due east of the city of Petersburg towards the left of the Union lines and on the immediate left of the II Corps and the right of General Warren's V Corps, which had arrived during the early morning hours.

The 57th had occupied ground about one half mile east of Batteries 15 and 16 of the Dimmock Line just southeast of the Shands house when they were held in reserve on the 16th, but now the men were up in the 1st Division's battle formation and were to act as support for Robert Potter's division in the attack. In the darkness of the early morning, the 2nd Division was ordered to advance quietly across the cleared field without firing a shot, and surprise and capture the sleeping Rebels at the point of the bayonet. This it did in superb order, capturing 4 cannon, 5 stands of colors, 600 prisoners, 1,500 stands of small arms, and a line of trenches on a strategic ridge.

Potter's veterans kept on going until they came up against a line of Southerners that they just could not dislodge despite a sharp and bloody fight, but they fought on, impatiently awaiting the 1st Division to get up on the line and reinforce them.[21] But Ledlie's troops were having troubles of their own. As the 1st Division followed over the fields on that dark morning, someone made a navigational error, and the men stumbled into a deep ravine that the Rebels had filled with dangerous slashed and broken timber, and they were having a time getting themselves free of the mess and reorganized. They would be of no use to the pinned down 2nd Division just then, and Potter's assault failed as a consequence.[22]

The 57th Massachusetts, being assigned to the 1st Division, was part of this foul-up, and none of the boys had yet been engaged in battle that day. Several hours later, the division's men finally extricated themselves from the tangle in the ravine and sorted out their lines.

At 4:00 P.M., the 1st Division was ordered to move to support General Orlando Willcox's 3rd Division, which was getting ready to launch an assault against the Confederate works in its front. In compliance with instructions, Ledlie's division continued on until it reached another ravine in front of and to the right of the Shands house and occupied it about three hundred yards from the Rebel entrenchments. In the meantime, Willcox's ranks formed and charged, but they were driven back to the Union lines by overwhelming Southern firepower, leaving hundreds of dead and wounded on the field.[23]

The men of the 1st Brigade of the IX Corps' 1st Division remained in their supporting position until four o'clock that afternoon, when finally they were directed to assault the Rebel trenches towards sundown. At five-thirty, the division was formed for a charge to be made due west from the ravine over the three hundred yards of intervening ground. The 1st Division, along with General Christ's brigade of the 3rd Division, was ordered to capture the earthworks in front of them, where both the 2nd and 3rd Divisions had been hurled back earlier in the day.[24]

Ledlie's men closed battle ranks on the western side of the ravine below the crest of a hill with the 1st and 2nd Brigades in the front line, and the Provisional 3rd Brigade in the second. In the 1st Brigade were the 56th, 57th, and 59th Massachusetts (the 4th and 10th Regulars had been reassigned on June 10, to the 1st Brigade, 2nd Division of the V Corps), and in the 2nd Brigade, the 21st and 29th Massachusetts, and the 179th New York and 100th Pennsylvania Volunteers. The 21st Massachusetts was placed on the right of the line at about forty-five degrees to act as flankers, and the veterans of the 100th Pennsylvania were detailed as skirmishers for the whole formation.[25]

In the 3rd Brigade, formed about one hundred paces behind the first two, were two new regiments recently pulled from the defenses around Washington, the 14th New York Heavy Artillery and the 2nd Pennsylvania Heavy Artillery,[26] both of which stood in stark contrast to the other decimated regiments of the division, with their swollen ranks of over a thousand men each. Those two units had been compelled to surrender their big guns and soft lives in the comfortable forts around the capital, and take on the duties of line infantrymen, even though they still wore their scarlet-trimmed uniforms and crossed cannon insignia on their caps and hats.

Colonel Jacob Parker Gould of the 59th Massachusetts was in overall command of the two brigades in the front line, and he turned over direct control of the 1st Brigade to Colonel Stephen Weld, who ordered his men to remove the percussion caps from their loaded rifles. Weld was certain from previous experience that they would reach the Rebel lines, fire a volley, and turn and run for safety, and as a result the assault would fail. He knew that the only chance for success was a steady rush upon the Southern works, storming them with the bayonet. Once inside, according to his theory—a common theory among field officers at that time—the men would be trapped in combat with little opportunity for retreat, and then they could concern themselves with shooting.[27]

The 2nd Brigade Gould entrusted to Lieutenant Colonel Joseph H. Barnes of the 29th Massachusetts.[28] While waiting—in vain, as it would turn out—for the commander, Ledlie, to make an appearance, Colonel Gould had to assume command of the whole 1st Division. General Ledlie was running true to form.

13

You Leg It Like the Devil

STEPHEN WELD explained to the 57th and the other regiments of the brigade what he expected of them. "When you get the order to charge," said the young colonel firmly, "you leg it like the devil. Don't stop for anything, just run as tight as you can."[1]

Around four o'clock, the men quietly crept to the edge of the ravine, where they lay prone until their five-thirty formation, waiting for the final order to move forward. The time seemed an eternity, as they nervously surveyed the deadly open ground in front of them, knowing there was almost no chance for a successful assault. In the intervening space was a golden-green field of young, ten-inch-high corn, and across that field, menacing Rebel fortifications.[2]

At 6:00 P.M., orders came for the 57th Massachusetts to move forward with the brigade to the level ground in front of it and lie down and wait for the order "Forward." Watches, wallets, keepsakes, and other personal items of value were given to Lieutenant John Cook, who was not going into action that day—as well as to other noncombatants in the regiment—for safekeeping, along with instructions of where to forward them in the event the owner did not return.[3]

Meanwhile, the Confederate gunners adjusted a slight angle of elevation on their field pieces and put a small amount of coarse black powder down the barrels and began firing solid round shot that, because of the guns' elevations and the amount of powder used, skipped and bounced wildly among the prone Federal soldiers.[4]

The men were jumping and rolling, trying to dodge the heavy iron balls, which could carry away instantly a leg or an arm or a head, when one of those curious and comical ironies of war occurred: the mail was delivered. Private Lowell, the regimental postmaster, was not one to let a mere Confederate artillery barrage interfere with his duties, and he brought his mail sack to the front to have its contents distributed to the regiment's men. The soldiers were amused at the delivery under fire, but pleased to see the brave mailman dropping off his bundle with the regimental adjutant, Lieutenant Edwin Coe, who passed the mail around by companies to the first sergeants, who, in turn, called out the names and handed the boys their letters while the cannons boomed and the killing artillery shells dropped all around. "The men who had received letters took the risk of reading them, while those who received none kept watch for ricochet shots," remembered John Anderson. Unfortunately for some of them, they would never be able to send an answer after that day. His postal responsibilities complete, Frank Lowell fell in beside his comrades on the battle line.[5]

★

The commander of the 1st Division never materialized that evening to lead his troops in the fight, and the officers and men were about fed up with him—even though they had no recourse short of mutiny to alter their plight. Ledlie did, however, send word by one of his staff officers that he was depending on his old brigade to win the day. Poor consolation, that, for the fighting man. The men knew they were being robbed of divisional leadership on the battlefield and being sacrificed for his venal political ambitions, and they were disgusted and discouraged with his selfishness, drunkenness, and cowardice. First Brigade leader Gould remained in charge as temporary division commander, and the soldiers later learned that General Ledlie had stayed behind in the ravine, raving like a lunatic in an alcoholic frenzy about how he was going to topple the Confederacy single-handedly and the like.[6]

After the interminable wait, at about eight o'clock that evening, under a cloudless sky with a nearly full moon that lit up the gently rolling landscape, the order of "Attention! Forward, double-quick!" was given throughout the 1st Division. The men leaped swiftly to their feet, and with their officers leading, raced the three hundred yards for the Rebel stronghold with a mighty cheer for the Union. The wall of rifle and cannon fire that they ran into was staggering, and the front ranks were mowed down. Undaunted, the adrenalin-charged survivors ran on, cresting the earthworks like an ocean wave over the beach, and leaping over the parapets they grabbed some of the Southerners by their collars and violently yanked them out of their rifle pits, prodding them off to the Union rear as prisoners of war. Many other Confederate soldiers rushed into the Federal lines to surrender, simply to get something to eat and quit their miserable existence. After some brutal hand-to-hand fights, the IX Corps' men captured the Rebels' trenches at the point of the bayonet, just as Stephen Weld had surmised. But their initial success was short-lived, as the Confederates quickly regrouped.[7]

Although the men had possession of that section of the Confederate lines, those trenches formed an angle on the left with another section of ditches, and close by this angle there was a strongly built redoubt containing a battery from which the Southerners maintained a killing, dead-on fire of double-shotted grapeshot that tore the Federals into bloody shreds. While the Confederate gunners were reloading, some of the 57th's boys saw a chance to put an end to the artillerymen's work, and the men charged and took the battery. Although quite a number of the Rebels managed to escape capture during that part of the battle, the 1st Division's soldiers took over one hundred prisoners—whom they quickly dispatched to the Federal lines—a stand of colors, and the several field pieces from the battery.[8]

Meanwhile, the Confederates who had fallen back to another section of close-by breastworks were being reorganized. Confederate General Pierre Beauregard was attempting to rally his troops, when Brigadier General Archibald Gracie, Jr., a New Yorker by birth, arrived on the field from Chapin's Bluff just in time with his Alabama butternuts—the 41st, 43rd, 59th, and 60th regiments.[9] Gracie's men were ordered to counterattack the Union soldiers, and the Southerners returned an iniquitous, enfilading storm of lead, subsequently bringing more field guns into position and raking the Federals with canister, grapeshot, rocks, railroad iron, bags of Minié balls, and any scraps of junk that would fit down the hot cannon barrels' muzzles. The boys were being cut to ribbons, and they furiously threw up earth and log traverses to protect their flanks, using anything at hand to dig with and any material they could find to build protection. It was frantic, wild work as the men desperately tried to erect walls under the unstoppable Rebel fire. They labored and stumbled over downed, wounded comrades who were piling up rapidly in the trench and getting their sticky blood on everything.

The scene was an uproar as some men worked while others fought back. The gunfire was deafening, and the soldiers were screaming and swearing and choking on the dust and gunsmoke that hung in the limpid night air. It was nearly impossible to see anything through the battle haze and darkness except the man on either side, and shots were fired wildly in the general direction of the enemy, with precision aiming virtually out of the question.

Men were wounded and killed at intervals of seconds or less, and the injured lay broken and begging for help everywhere, but nobody could take the time just then to help anyone. It was a wicked fight to the death, and neither side gave quarter.

Julius Tucker, commander of the 57th, had just been promoted to major on June 14, and as he was giving instructions to his men about how to shore up the traverses, he was shot in the left side of his face, the bullet passing through his head. Lieutenant Anderson was standing beside him, and he and everyone else were convinced the major was dead, or at least mortally wounded. Anderson had his body sent to the rear at once. The shot that hit Tucker took out eleven upper back teeth, a portion of his palatal bone, and the sight of his left eye.[10]

The Rebel fire increased with unmerciful vengeance as the 57th's—as well as the rest of the division's—decreased. The men were running out of ammunition, and in desperation, "cartridge boxes were cut from the dead who were lying upon the field and their ammunition used until that, too, was expended." Colonel Weld repeatedly sent runners to the rear requesting more bullets, but none ever arrived. The Confederates took advantage of their opportunity quickly and stormed into the Northern troops, screeching like banshees, driving the Massachusetts soldiers back on the run to their original position in the ravine, where they could only maintain sporadic fire until their ammunition was replenished. Just in time, fortunately, enough rounds were delivered to compel the Rebels to return to their own lines. It had been a close call for the 57th as it was almost captured as a unit for want of cartridges, but most of the boys who were still alive made it, and now they hugged the dirt in the trench and tried to quell the trauma of the fracas. There they remained for the night, closely guarding their precarious position and regrouping.[11]

As soon as he could, young Colonel Weld, in an absolute rage at his commander's betrayal, sought out General Ledlie to report the disaster and vent his spleen. He found him passed out on the ground near his field headquarters in the rear of the ravine. Ledlie's own adjutant, equally furious, went over to the general and kicked him until he woke up, and then poked the drunk commander and said, "Colonel Weld wishes to report." Weld, barely able to control himself, then said, "General, we have been driven back and our men are all scattered, and I don't know what to do." In an alcoholic fog, Ledlie clumsily sat up and replied, "Why Colonel Weld, there are thousands of men all around here," and he passed out again. Later in life, Weld, evidently still angry, wrote, "If I had been older or had more sense, I should have preferred charges against him."[12]

★

Just prior to the charge, seventeen-year-old Private Edward Schneider of Company K boasted to his comrades, whose favor he was desperately trying to win back, "I intend to be the first one to enter their works." As the assaulting blue lines approached the Southern position on the run, good to his word, he broke ranks, dashed ahead of the regiment "a rod or two," and was the first man of the 57th to stand on the Rebel parapet. Instantly, he was shot in the left arm, the right arm, the right hand, the left leg, and through the stomach. Schneider had felt he had a score to settle. During the battle at the North Anna River, he had been slightly wounded in the foot—not even seriously enough to qualify for the casualty lists—and, after lying in the woods that night and all day following the battle, he had gone to the rear seeking medical attention. Some of the other boys in the regiment had harrassed him severely, calling him a coward and a shirker. The truth was, however, that although his wound had not been serious, it had been painful. When he reported to the hospital at White House Landing for transportation to the medical facilities in Washington, the surgeons had denied him passage and put him down as a malingerer.

The Reverend Addison P. Foster of Lowell, Massachusetts, and several other prominent men from the commonwealth were visiting the Army of the Potomac at that time, observing the condition of the Massachusetts soldiers within its ranks, when they happened upon young Schneider sitting under a tree, crying. When pressed as to the reason why, the boy soldier explained his predicament, and two of the delegates, moved by his situation, went to see the army surgeons on his behalf. The doctors were persuaded to reverse their earlier diagnosis, and Schneider was allowed to join the wounded at Port Royal to wait for transportation by boat to Washington. But while waiting there, his conscience got the better of him, and he decided to rejoin the regiment and accept the consequences, as well as his pain. Upon returning to his company at Cold Harbor, his comrades ridiculed and shunned him, as he had expected.

Schneider was the son of American missionary parents, and he had been born in Bronza, Turkey, and brought up in Aintab, Turkey. When he was old enough for school, he had returned to the United States and attended the seminary at Phillips Academy, in Andover, Massachusetts. He was a devout Christian—probably too devout for some of his comrades—and no coward, and their harsh treatment of him only reinforced his will to prove his worth during the charge that day. He had "entered the battle burning with a desire to show himself no shirker."

The next morning, Charles Newcomb, a member of the Christian Commission from Boston, found him "lying under a tree, torn and bleeding. . . ." He was carried from the field to the V Corps field dressing station, where Dr. White pronounced his abdominal wound mortal—the fatal bullet had torn up his intestines and lodged in his spine. He died at 3:00 A.M. on June 19 with Sanborn Howe, also of Company K, by his side. His last words were reported to have been, "Tell my brother to stand by the dear old flag, and cling to the cross of Christ." Reverend Dashiell refused to bury him in a common grave, and later that morning, he laid his body to rest, with a cloth covering his face, under a tall pine, near the V Corps hospital, fifteen feet from the Prince George Court House road and one mile east of the Dunn house. A wooden railing was erected around the grave and a crude inscription was nailed to the tree: "Edward M., son of Rev. Dr. Schneider, of Aintab, Turkey, of Co. K., 57th Mass. Reg't Inf." He had dispelled his image as a coward with his combat-hardened comrades in the 57th, and on his army record his officers listed him as a "Brave Soldier."[13]

One man most of the men were inclined to feel for, as well, was Sergeant John Cooley of Company A, from County Galway, Ireland, and a veteran of the originally all-Irish Massachusetts 28th Regiment. The men discovered his body in the cornfield the next day. His friends dug a shallow grave and buried him on the spot, and Lieutenant Anderson remembered that Cooley had done the same for some of the others of the brigade who had died at Cold Harbor just a few days before, saying, "I wonder who will do this for me?" His comrades admired him for his tender-heartedness and coolness under fire, and they felt his loss deeply.[14]

Second Lieutenant Edwin Coe was the regimental adjutant. The nineteen-year-old lieutenant, who looked sixteen, had a bizarre premonition before the battle. At Spotsylvania, during the regiment's charge on May 12, Coe, then serving with his company, Company A, was seen by the men throwing up his hands and falling, and all believed him killed or severely wounded, but there had been no time to stop just then to aid him. A short while later, however, he returned to his company and reported that the bullet had struck only a glancing blow on his head, and that except for a bruise, he was all right. The night before the June 17 assault, Edwin Coe had a vivid dream in which he saw himself killed in the coming battle, and he reported it to some of the other officers, who shrugged his story off, telling him not to worry. Unsatisfied with his fellow officers' attitudes, the baby-faced lieutenant told them that not only was he certain that he was going to die, but that the bullet that would kill him would strike the same place as the one that had slightly wounded him at Spotsylvania. The other officers were still unconvinced, and they tried to reassure him that it was only a dream, an aberration. But, following the battle, they found Lieutenant Coe, the only officer of the 57th killed that day, shot through the head exactly as he had predicted. It was uncanny, and the other officers were shaken and impressed. Coe's brother, an officer in the 11th United States Regular Infantry, came later that day and took his body away for embalming and burial on the battlefield.[15]

Captain Doherty, ever the showboat, had been severely injured by canister in the hand, one of his fingers having been blown away. Running up to some of the other officers of the regiment, prominently displaying his bloody wound, he exclaimed, "Now, see what the damned Rebels have done!" His brother officers told him to leave the field immediately for an aid station, but he replied, loud enough for everyone nearby, including the enlisted men, to hear, "Do you think I am going to desert the boys now? No sir! Not until we get that battery!"[16]

Major Tucker, whom all had thought at least mortally wounded, was to survive with some of his tongue and jaw cut away. His wound was extremely painful, and for some time afterward, Julius Tucker could neither talk nor eat. He would return to the regiment as lieutenant colonel after his recuperation.[17]

Two brothers in Company A, Privates Adolphus and Alfred Porter, young men who had been with the regiment in every fight and on every march, were both wounded that Friday—Adolphus in the leg and Alfred in the foot. Sent to Dale U.S. Army General Hospital in their home town of Worcester, Adolphus would survive and be discharged from the army, but Alfred was destined to succumb to chronic diarrhea.[18]

Private John Bradley of Company B, born on Christmas day of 1823 in County Donegal, was another of the 57th's men to have been in all its actions, but his luck ran out on June 17. The courageous soldier took gunshot wounds first to his right hip and then in his right side, but he stayed on and only left the field when finally he was shot through the chest. A chest wound was considered almost always fatal in those days, but the tough Irishman would recover and return to the regiment in time to be honorably mustered out with his comrades after the war ended.[19]

Canadian Charles Brigham received a fatal wound in his genitals and his comrade, Albert Gerry, took a nonlethal round in the face. Both men were also privates in Company B.[20]

Joseph Farnsworth of the Fitchburg Company, a veteran of the 3rd Rhode Island Cavalry, took a mangling round in his left leg during the battle, and Dr. T. Fletcher Oakes of the 56th Massachusetts amputated it by the flap method the following day. But complications set in, and the limb had to be reamputated higher up in March of 1865. Discharged on a Surgeons Certificate of Disability, the former horse soldier would survive his ordeal.[21]

A "Splendid Soldier" is how thirty-five-year-old English-born Private David Charlesworth was characterized by his officers. Charlesworth was another of the regiment's men who had been through it all, but he was wounded during the assault and eventually wound up in an army hospital in Philadelphia. Like many of his other wounded comrades, the hospital was a place that he could not abide, and he fled the following January. He later surrendered and was exonerated and discharged from the army while absent wounded.[22]

Corporal John B. Rogers of Company K, from Newton, Massachusetts, was wounded severely in his left hand by a Minié ball and Surgeon M. K. Hogan removed several of his fingers at the 1st Division, IX Corps field hospital that night. The surgery did not remedy the corporal's injuries. After he was admitted to Emory U.S. Army General Hospital in Washington on June 24, acting Assistant Surgeon E. B. Harris found it necessary to amputate at the middle third of Rogers' left arm. Infection set in and the doctors reported. "Death resulted on the morning of July 26, 1864." The stump of his amputated arm was sent to the army medical museum.[23]

Private Fred Stevens from Marlboro, Massachusetts, and also a member of the sharpshooter company, had decided that he had had enough of war after the fighting at Spotsylvania. Remaining absent in the rear during the North Anna action, and all during the Cold Harbor campaign, he again shirked the assault at Petersburg; "cause; 'SORE FEET,'" wrote one of his exasperated officers on Stevens's military record.[24]

★

The 57th Massachusetts had taken into battle that day 186 officers and enlisted men, and the regiment lost 11 killed, 8 mortally wounded, 30 wounded (one of whom was taken prisoner of war), 1 missing in action and presumed killed, and 2 more captured, for a total loss of 52 men, nearly 28 percent. The regiment mustered only 134 combat soldiers after the battle on June 17.[25]

★

Much of the fighting on that June day was done by the IX Corps. The 1st Division had been supported on the left by Christ's brigade of the 3rd Division and General Samuel W. Crawford's division of the V Corps, and the hill at the Shands house, just three hundred yards west of Confederate Battery 14 in the original Dimmock Line, had been captured for good. Two thousand yards to the northwest, Hare House Hill had been taken as well, and the Union soldiers would later transform it into Fort Stedman, a place that would figure prominently in the history of the 57th Massachusetts.[26] But the day had not been a good one for the men of the Army of the Potomac— let alone successful (the ground taken amounted to no strategic victory)— because of a lack of coordination among the corps and divisions and poor leadership on the part of the commanding officers. The Federal soldiers had done their best, but without those other elements of leadership in play, the men simply could not accomplish any more than they did. They were demoralized and disheartened with the army brass, and many of them almost certainly made no secret of their disaffections. Undoubtedly, they were warned by their company officers to watch what they said, but most probably paid no attention and spoke their minds anyway, the Irish especially.

★

George Barton wrote his account of the 57th's activities that June 17. This letter first appeared in John Anderson's history of the regiment, but the captain evidently felt it necessary to edit the original and add to it. The following is Barton's original text.

In Line of Battle
Near Petersburg
June 20th 1864

Dear Mother

I know you must feel anxious about me for in my last letter of the 17th I told you that we were going in to make a *charge* The order came about four o'clock in the afternoon that the 1st Division of the 9th Corps was to charge upon the enemy's brestworks at sundown The 2d Division had already made one charge and were *driven back* with a *heavy* loss and now the 1st Div had got to try it Their chances were very *dubious* Genl Ledly [Ledlie] who now commands our division sent word by one of his Staff officers that he *depended* upon his old 1st Brigade—our Brigade—we lay upon our arms in a ravine for nearly two hours so that we had plenty of time to *think* upon our *chances* for coming out all right about six o'clock the order came to advance to the level ground beyond the ravine and there to lay down and wait for the order *forward,* it was a trying moment *Watches* and other valuables were handed to one of our Lieuts who was not *going in* Lt. John H. Cook I handed him my watch scarcely expecting to see it again. The shot and shell were flying around in good style for the Rebs. had a good range upon us but as [we] were lying down but few were wounded. Now comes a little *personal* matter. I lay with my company in line just in a hollow exposed to a raking fire of artillery and musketry, as I was looking out for my men cautioning them to lay low I happened to glance to the left of me [at ten minutes before eight] when I saw a *solid* shot coming directly towards me I had just time enough to whirl over on to my left side when it struck just in the place where I sat, *grazing* my right arm and tearing my coat sleeve almost entirely off smashed a musket into [*sic*] and covering my 1st Sergt [Charles L. Defose] with sand.

(The rifle, a Springfield, belonged to Sergeant Edwin McFarland of Company I, who was furious with the Rebel gunners for destroying his weapon. He had carried that particular gun since Camp Wool, fighting in every one of the 57th's actions with it, and he had become sentimentally attached to his firearm. He had no choice but to go into battle unarmed until he could forage another from a dead soldier.)

Two or three of our officers came running up to me thinking I was either killed or badly wounded I was advised by the comdg officer, Capt Tucker to get to the rear which of *course* I *declined* when I found that it was only a slight contusion. [None of the 57th's men was killed during the bombardment, but several were wounded, and thirty-two men from other regiments in the division were killed before the advance began.] In about ten minutes the order attention came then *forward* double quick and through such a fire of grape *and* canister *solid shot* railroad iron minnies and I don't know what not with a regular *Yankee yell* we went through it and up on to the rebel outer entrenchments and then it was *blaze away* The Rebs were *Staggard* The movement was too rapid and impetuous it was amazing to see some of our boys grab a Reb and hustle him over the rifle pits and take him to the rear as a prisoner They did not seem at all bothered [by this] but many of them rushed into our lines of their own free will

We had the works until our ammunition gave out—and then we were obliged to fall back we lost in that one charge 10 killed 30 wounded & 32 missing [see above for correct casualty figures] Among the officers [Lieutenant Coe, acting] adjutant was killed shot straight [through] the head Capt Tucker who was Comdg the Regt was shot through the face and his case is a very doubtful one He cannot eat or speak Capt. Lawrence [of Company F] who had just recovered from a wound in the neck [received at the Wilderness] was again wounded in the leg. I helped him off the field he was acting as Major [after Tucker's wounding]. Lieut Ward wounded in the leg. Capt Doherty finger shot off We are to have an Inspection Thrs. morning so I cannot stop to write more I have had a touch of the Chronic diaria hope to get over it soon Otherwise I am *all right* love to all Hoping this war will soon be over for if it is not we all know our fate I am very truely and sincerely your soldier boy. by the way I must

Captured Confederate trenches at Petersburg
near the ground assaulted by the 57th Massachusetts, June 17–18, 1864.
(*MOLLUS—Penna., War Library and Museum, Philadelphia*)

tell you that Genl Burnside gave our Brigade & Division a very high compliment & he said that he expected we should be repulsed for he thought the position too strong for infantry to take well adieux love to all from Geo. E. Barton 1st Lt 57th Mass Comdg C Company.[27]

On the morning of June 18, at 2:00 A.M., the II, V, and IX corps were moved forward into position to renew the battle, scheduled to resume at four o'clock. The baggy-eyed, battle-weary boys of the Army of the Potomac drew fresh supplies of ammunition and fell into their assigned formations, and at first light the assault began promptly, under heavy enemy volley fire and cannonading, with the II Corps, on the right of Burnside's men, leading the attack.[28]

General Burnside was not pleased with the plan for the morning's assault, and he had sent a message by army telegraph to General Meade at 3:15 A.M. indicating that Ledlie's division was used up and that "scarcely anything" was left of it. He also warned Meade that of his other three divisions, Potter's 2nd and Willcox's 3rd were "very much wearied as we made three assaults yesterday." Ambrose Burnside agreed to attack the Southerners if the commanding general so desired, but the IX Corps commander was not "confident of doing much." "Shall I attack them?" Burnside inquired. George Gordon Meade promptly replied that yes, he should commit all of his available troops and attack as scheduled.[29]

So, the wasted regiments of the IX Corps advanced at four-thirty that June Saturday morning, the thinned, blue ranks firing first in volley and then at will and then charging the Petersburg defenders with fixed bayonets. (Whether Stephen Weld had his particular command repeat his attack plan of the day before is not known.) The 1st Division, moving behind Willcox's 3rd Division, which was leading the IX Corps' assault, recaptured the Confederate trenches that the men had abandoned the day before. The Rebels had left their dead and wounded, and at the angle where the Confederate battery had been placed to enfilade the Northerners, bloody Southern dead were heaped like cordwood, and the surrounding ground was thick with their mutilated, putrid corpses. The delightful little green cornfield had been trampled and shot to bits, and it was littered with bloated Yankee cadavers— several of them from the 57th—whose black blood dried on the brown earth and the shredded green stalks.[30]

The Rebels fell back under a hammering Union fire to new lines in and around a deep cut on the Norfolk & Petersburg Railroad near the remains of the Taylor house and quickly threw up makeshift rifle pits to protect themselves from another Federal assault. These were Lee's men, not the local garrison troops, and the men of the Army of the Potomac were mighty wary of assaulting those well-dug-in veterans who had been slaughtering them

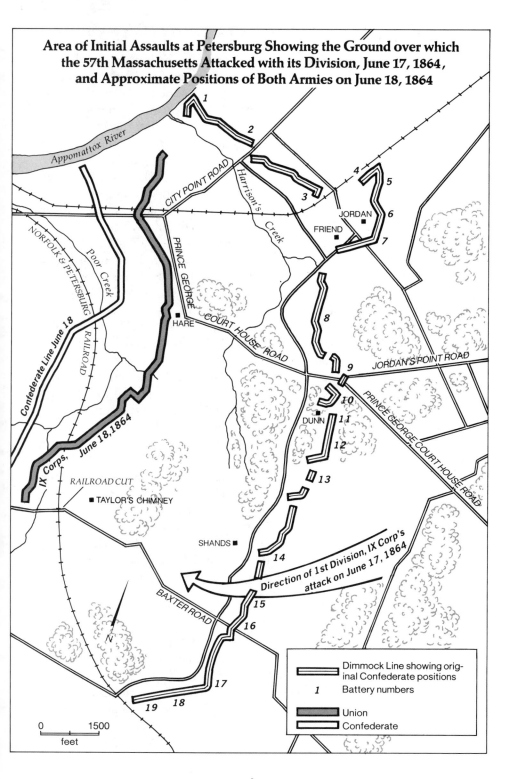

Area of Initial Assaults at Petersburg Showing the Ground over which the 57th Massachusetts Attacked with its Division, June 17, 1864, and Approximate Positions of Both Armies on June 18, 1864

Appomattox River

1

2

CITY POINT ROAD

Harrison's Creek

3

4

5

JORDAN

6

FRIEND

7

NORFOLK & PETERSBURG RAILROAD

Poor Creek

PRINCE GEORGE

HARE

COURT HOUSE ROAD

8

JORDAN'S POINT ROAD

9

10

DUNN

11

PRINCE GEORGE COURT HOUSE ROAD

12

13

Confederate Line June 18

IX Corps, June 18, 1864

RAILROAD CUT

TAYLOR'S CHIMNEY

SHANDS

14

Direction of 1st Division, IX Corp's attack on June 17, 1864

BAXTER ROAD

15

16

N

17

19 18

0   1500

feet

Dimmock Line showing original Confederate positions

1   Battery numbers

Union

Confederate

187

those past six weeks under similar conditions. The Federal soldiers knew a charge over open ground against these wiry, tough Southerners would be nothing short of near-annihilation, and they were scared to death of another fight like that of the previous day. Regardless, a new attack time was fixed by the Army of the Potomac's commanders for noon, and the army's corps moved forward to their new positions to begin a battle to drive the Confederates out of their current defenses around Poor Creek.[31]

In another disastrously orchestrated onslaught, the II Corps started out first, with the IX Corps trailing later on its left flank, and the V Corps moving up in the rear. The IX and V Corps had moved forward nearly a mile through snarling, thorny brush, dead fallen timber, and deep, dark ravines, all of which delayed their progress, to get into their starting positions. The II Corps had arrived on station on time, but the other two corps were late, and at twelve o'clock, Hancock's men, now led by General David Bell Birney (who had been assigned temporary command of the corps when an old Gettysburg wound of General Hancock's flared up, incapacitating him), made two assaults on their own near Hare House Hill, both of which were repelled violently with heavy Federal losses. Meanwhile, the IX and V Corps, now engaged in battle to the south of the II Corps, were trying to clear the railroad cut of the Norfolk & Petersburg, which was filled with Southerners trying to force the Yankees back. Clearing the cut took some time, and the II Corps was deprived of the support of these two corps during its assault.[32]

Passing into open fields in their attempt to take the cut and get up in support of the II Corps, the Union troops of Burnside and Warren's corps were opened up on immediately by Confederate batteries that had wheeled into position west of the railroad cut, and the effect of those guns was devastating. The Federals remained there taking what cover they could until late in the afternoon, when another attack was ordered. At five-thirty, the 3rd Division of the IX Corps led the way in that assault with the 2nd behind it and the depleted 1st as support. The men charged wildly at the Confederate works, driving the Rebels out of the natural defenses made by the steep embankments of the cut and routing them through the woods. The IX Corps took over and occupied the railroad ditch and kept up a steady fire at the Rebels in their works a short distance beyond to the west, where the batteries were located. The lines were closer here than on any other part of the battlefield.[33]

The 57th's men remained in this new position that night, fortunate that they had taken not a single loss on that day of bitter fighting. After the firing had died down, the boys helped bury the dead, both Union and Confederate, which had been collected during the advances of the past four days. Aside from the usual stench of the corpses, the air was reported balmy and soft that spring evening, and the sweet fragrance of magnolia drifted through the woods. Nature seemed beautiful and peaceful as the men laid the dead soldiers into the ground without ceremony or coffin in common graves on the awful battleground, with the only salute being the artillery in the background making sure that not a moment was lost in the killing business.[34]

Around the 57th's campfires that night, the blazes flickered shadows on the pensive, brown faces of the Massachusetts men, and the young soldiers sang sad songs as they remembered their killed and mutilated friends.

> *Soon with angels I'll be marching,*
> *With bright laurels on my brow.*
> *I have for my country fallen,*
> *Who will care for mother now?*[35]

A few of them surely must have questioned just how much more they could take. The regiment was nearly destroyed, and the men felt whipped. Their weariness was indescribable, and they could not say exactly what it was that kept them going.

★

The last four days' activities had been an utter failure for the Northern army, despite the fact that some ground had been won. Had the attacks on the Confederate entrenchments been better organized and coordinated among the Union commanders, the Southerners may very well have been rolled up and Petersburg taken. Lee had not gotten all of his soldiers in place even when the Union troops began the last day's battle, and the Federal forces missed several golden opportunities for shortening the war by almost a year. General Meade's famous temper was very much in evidence over his corps commanders' behavior, but there was nothing left to do now, according to Lieutenant General Grant, but to rest the men and dig in for a long, hard siege.

14

Black Interlude

B ETWEEN June 19 and July 30, 1864, little fighting of significance occurred at Petersburg. The men of the Army of the Potomac and the Army of Northern Virginia were engaged in the deadly activity of grinding siege warfare and the tedium of life in the trenches.

★

When the 57th Regiment crossed the James River, Private Francis Harrington had been detailed to remain behind and look after a sick comrade, Private Elijah B. Hayward, and Harrington did not return to the front until noon on June 18. From his diary entry for that day we learn that the men received four days' rations after sunset to last them through the 24th and were ordered to pack up and be ready to move out at any time.[1]

On Sunday, June 19, Private Harrington noted that the lines had been "All quiet last night," and that "just before noon," the regiment "moved out a little way in [rear] of the Earthworks stacked arms and pitched tents and laid idle not much firing today."[2]

The 57th remained in the 1st Division's second line of works of the Federal trenches near the Norfolk & Petersburg Railroad cut, and on June 20, the 1st Brigade's soldiers spruced themselves up for a review and inspection. It was held at nine o'clock that morning by Colonel Gould and General Ledlie and his staff, behind the main lines and out of range of Confederate mischief. The men cared little for those bothersome affairs, feeling that they were being asked to "play soldier," as they called marching in the formal parades, but they were pleased to have the chance to get clean after all their hard campaigning.[3]

The review over, the regiment "rec'd orders to pack up and be ready to move at a moments notice," but it was not until dark—and after drawing more rations—that the 57th, as well as the entire 1st Division of the IX

Corps, headed out and relieved General Francis Barlow's division of the II Corps and elements of the V Corps in the front-line trenches. James Ledlie's men took their positions in the forward works with division skirmishers posted in the deadly, mostly open ground toward the Southern fortifications beyond. The soldiers and their company officers were ignorant of either side's tactical plans, and they were nervous and anxious, expecting a Confederate attack, or to make an assault of their own, at any time. But neither situation developed, and the men spent the next several weeks shuffling back and forth between picket stations, front trenches, and rear trenches along the Union army's main line of works every three or four days, manning the earthworks, picking off careless Southerners or being themselves picked off, and, most importantly, keeping low. The skirmish fire was heavy and constant day and night, and each man tried not to show his head over the parapets—it was almost certain death to do so.[4]

The IX Corps occupied two lines of trenches a half-mile long on the left of the II Corps from what would later be Fort Haskell on the south side to Hare House Hill on the north, two miles due east from the center of the city of Petersburg. The front lines in the IX Corps' position were separated from the Southern emplacements by only a few hundred yards or less in some places, making that area one of the most dangerous along the whole string of Union fortifications. The Rebels had the advantage of being on higher ground, and the Union soldiers built bulletproof walls of logs on the exposed sides of their tents, which were pitched in the safer rear lines. To guard themselves from the fiery sun, they used pine boughs to make shady arbors, but in the forward trenches there was little shade, and there were no tents or pine boughs, and the only protection available to the enlisted men was their blankets or shelter tent halves, which they often stretched over the ditches to provide at least some covering. The officers lived in dug-out holes in the ground 4 to 5 feet deep and about 10 feet long by 6 feet wide that were covered with logs and dirt for shelter from the weather and gunfire—all of which the enlisted soldiers, naturally, had to build for them.[5]

When the lines were first occupied, drinking water was readily available from the myriad creeks and springs in the area, but the demand for it by the thousands of thirsty, sun-baked soldiers soon overtaxed the supply, and the creeks and springs dried up. To alleviate the problem, the men dug wells, sinking as many as four empty wooden barrels, with their tops and bottoms removed, into the ground as liners. The water drawn was sweet and cool, and there was enough for an occasional light wash, the officers, of course, enjoying that privilege far more often than the enlisted men.[6]

The Virginia climate varied little that June and July, remaining hot and suffocating, and the men suffered abysmally from the fierce weather conditions. Most of the dead from the initial assaults had been buried carelessly in shallow trench graves, and the smell of the decomposing corpses easily seeped into the still air, nauseating many of the soldiers on station near the burial sites. On June 27, though, some welcome light showers began falling in the afternoon, and the next several days were cooler and more pleasant—a thoroughly delightful change for the men.[7]

The trenches in the front lines daily became a more dreadful place in which to be as they began to fill with garbage and human waste, attracting all sorts of vermin. The intensity and accuracy of the picket, artillery, and sniper fire increased as the men of both armies became accustomed to the tricks of trench warfare, and that fire was sustained twenty-four hours a day, every day, by both sides, with deadly effect.[8]

When not in the forward trenches, the 57th Massachusetts, along with the rest of Gould's brigade, was held in the reserve line just north of its original position in the captured Petersburg & Norfolk Railroad cut at that time in late June. Other than nonstop skirmish fire, numerous artillery duels, and constant sharpshooting along the main line of works, the trenches remained reasonably quiet—at least in comparison to what the young veterans had been experiencing since crossing the Rapidan—and free from any major battle activity, and, when not on picket duty, the boys usually engaged themselves in fortifying and improving their entrenchments. They made abatis out of sharpened tree trunks that they stuck into the ground close together and at a slight elevation in front of their works—a dangerous job that was done at night and very quietly under the protection of the pickets—to discourage enemy charges, and built chevaux-de-frise from four- or five-foot-long pointed stakes driven at intervals of every few inches through longer, thicker logs at right angles to each other. These were positioned in front of the trenches for the same purpose as abatis. (Regardless of how the chevaux-de-frise were placed, rolled, or moved, they were a nasty impediment to an assaulting force.) Gabions were fashioned, too. Those were large, cylindrical, open-ended basketlike devices made of woven saplings and twigs that were packed with dirt. When placed on end and in rows they offered formidable protection from enemy fire.[9]

The men also took as much opportunity as they could to relax, rest, and eat.

The trenches at Petersburg, constructed in long, irregular, and broken lines, were dug about 3 feet deep and 6 to 8 feet wide. As the dirt was excavated it was thrown on top of the trench's front wall and supported from collapsing inwardly with horizontally placed timbers held together by stout vertical poles to a height of six feet or more. Usually, on top of the logs sandbags were located and arranged so that small, exposed places between them, called loops by the soldiers, would allow the sharpshooters in the very forward lines a somewhat protected opening through which they could fire. The officers also could use the loops to observe activity in the Confederate trenches, while they themselves remained relatively free from danger. (Very little small-arms firing was allowed from the rear main line because it was too hazardous to the men in the works and picket lines in front of them and was generally considered a waste of ammunition.) At about 4½ feet below the top log a 3-foot-wide step 2 feet high above the trench floor, known as a banquette, often was constructed to provide the men a platform upon which to stand while shooting. When reloading or not on duty, they could step down and stand upright with little fear of being hit. If a banquette was not available, the soldiers would improvise their platforms by standing on hard-tack or ammunition boxes.

Approximately every twenty feet, the officers had the soldiers build thick traverses perpendicular to the pits' walls to cover the men from enemy rifle or artillery fire on their flank. Those defenses, too, were constructed from logs and dirt, and because they completely sealed off one section of the trench from another, a deep, narrow ditch was dug parallel to the forward earthworks with other thin channels emanating from it to the various segments. That

Typical trench system at Petersburg.
(*MOLLUS—Penna., War Library and Museum, Philadelphia*)

system allowed the officers and men a degree of safe access to any area in the lines.[10] Life in the Petersburg trenches was the life of rats in a maze.

★

The IX Corps extended its lines on June 21 (that extension did not affect the 57th's position), relieving the II and VI Corps for a planned action against the Weldon Railroad several miles to the south. Burnside's men now connected to the left of Smith's XVIII Corps, which stretched to Harrison's Creek and the Appomattox River on the northern end of the front.

★

On that Tuesday, June 21, Private Harrington recorded from the front lines that the men had "laid still in the works all day (a pretty good place too, good shade) There has been a good many shots exchanged on our skirmish line which lays behind [that is, on the far side of] the R. [ail] R. [oad] embankment about 30 yards from our front."[11]

The next day beginning before eight in the morning, the firing along the regiment's section of trenches was brisk both from artillery and small arms on the right and left on the 57th's front. But the men got a pleasant surprise that Wednesday. "Blouses [unlined four-button sack coats], Drawers, Shoes, Haversacks & Rubber Blankets" were issued to the enlisted soldiers, as Private Harrington happily noted. The men also drew infantry trousers, socks, shirts, shelter tents, forage caps, knapsacks, and canteens that day.[12]

George Barton left a captivating account of what life was like at the front in a letter that he wrote on June 23.

—On Front line—
Near Petersburg Va
June 23d 1864

Dear Mother

Having another opportunity to write I embrace it forthwith Our regiment and Brigade are now posted on the *front line* towards the city our skirmishers being about 200 [There seems to have been quite a difference in estimation between Barton and Harrington.] yards in front of us and about 20 yards from the rebel pickets quite *near on* ofensive. On the night of the 21st I was detailed as officer of the Picket relieved our Picket about 9 o'c that night. We remained on the skirmish line all the next day 22nd in the broiling sun without anything to shelter us from the sun in little pits about the size of a *common* grave though not half so well *furnished*. There we lay and everytime a man Show his head Zip would come a minnie The bullets would just skin the top of the pit that I occupied warning me to keep close to my mother earth which I did you may be sure I thought of you while lying there as to what you would say could you have looked in upon me It was a beautiful moon light night everything looked so calm and peaceful overhead It did not seem right that we should be making so much noise and I thought to myself that the same beautiful moon was looking down upon my peaceful home in old Worcester and I must confess I had a strange longing to be there (just now one of the detail was reported to me by the sergeant as shot through the head—killed a member of Co.K Chapin Rice a son of the Deputy Sherif of Marlboro He raised his head to take a look at the Rebs when Zip goes a minnie through his temple

(Private Edwin Chapin Rice, eighteen, from Marlboro, Massachusetts, was killed on the morning of July 22. This letter was probably written over a period of two days, but dated the 23rd. Rice left a twin brother, Lucien B., also a member of Company K. Those boys had been the only set of twins in the regiment.)

Well after a hard days work we were relieved and it was a relief to me and my feelings as well as to the men I had the body of Rice taken off the field he was buried this morning A member of G Company [Private Abner Leland, forty-four, from Milford, Massachusetts] was just sitting down behind the brestworks and had taken out his portfolio to write a letter home when a ball came from the enemy glanced on a limb of a tree and went through his neck he died in five minutes So it is in the midst of life we are in death *We* can realize these things much better than our brave home guards I am now commanding two *companies* or rather *squads* C & I. . . .13

At midnight on the 23rd, the regiment, along with the 56th and 59th Massachusetts, retired from the forward trenches and returned to the second lines, and the 2nd Brigade of the 1st Division took their place at the front for a few days.14

The 1st Brigade returned and relieved the 2nd Brigade in the advanced earthworks about midnight on June 28, amid rumors of impending charges along the entire line to be made by the Army of the Potomac. Those unfounded speculations were circulating constantly among the soldiers, but as each day passed with no major activity, the talk died down, and the men resigned themselves more and more to long siege operations, digging, building, and strengthening their positions without letup and forever dodging enemy bullets.15

But the sniping and bushwhacking were hardly all one-sided, and the Yankee sharpshooters and pickets caused their share of mayhem in the Rebel trenches. Many men on both sides were killed, wounded, or unaccounted for each day.

As the weeks passed with little tactical activity other than an occasional raiding party, the problem of boredom became more acute in the ranks, and General Ledlie ordered the superb band of the 56th Massachusetts, alternating with those of the other brigades of the division, to play for the men at his headquarters in the rear, morning, noon, and night. The twenty musicians of the 56th were anything but the spit-and-polish performers they had been in training camp so long ago, now wearing their ordinary fatigue coats and floppy, wide-brimmed black felt hats, but they were a first-class band, and in the beginning, their playing soothed and cheered the tattered and depressed combat soldiers. But, as usual, the general made a poor decision, this time in allowing too much of a good thing. The continual music began to have the opposite effect on the soldiers' morale, and the men soon became exasperated hearing the same repertoire over and over and over, until they could not stand to listen to one more note. Even the Confederates, who could hear the music clearly in their close-by trenches, had had enough, and they countered with threats and insults and tried to drown out the repetitious Northern songs with patriotic Southern airs played by their own bandsmen.[16] The outcome of that situation was not recorded, but it is easy to imagine the effect on the ears and nerves that the cacophonous combat had on those soldiers of both sides who were trapped between the warring bands.

Every night the artillery of both armies provided spectacular displays of pyrotechnics as they tried to blow each other off the face of the earth. The exploding shells with their magnificent yellow and red bursts showed brilliantly against the black night sky, and the men watched the sparkling fuses on the mortar shells, as they were lobbed high in the air, to see which direction they would take so their detonations could be avoided. Those displays were mesmerizing, the noise of the explosions earsplitting, and occasionally a soldier watched in hypnotic fascination as a shell came right at him until it burst, fragmenting him into eternity. But, while the arching shells were easily seen at night—and great fun for the men to watch, at least at first—the opposite was true during the day. The bright sun obscured the fuses, and the men depended on the whistling sounds of shells' flights to gauge their landing zones.[17]

When those mortar shells blew up in the densely packed trenches, the jagged iron shrapnel from the fragmented casings, as well as the blast itself, was devastating, creating havoc and tearing to bits men, equipment, and excavations and showering all nearby with dirt and debris. The regular field artillery did little damage to life because the long guns' trajectories were essentially flat, and the men could duck easily behind their barricades to avoid harm, but the mortars were an entirely different matter, with their high, arching tracks and nearly vertical landing paths, and the soldiers were, quite rightly, deathly afraid of them. The artillery redoubts along the lines on both sides, which protruded at angles to provide enfilading fire upon assaulting troops, were bristling with cannons and mortars of all descriptions, and the gunners dueled constantly, trying to obliterate each other's batteries and fortifications.[18]

Lieutenant Barton had some thoughts about the artillery at Petersburg, as well as a few other items, which he relayed to his mother and family in a letter dated July 3.

. . . I sometimes think of a short method of closing this fearful struggle, if some three or four of the Rebel leaders including Jeff. Davis would ride down their lines some fine night. And the fact being known we could open on them with our *Mortars* for we have quite a number of them Now let one of our bombs drop *providentially* amongst that party and sweep them out of the world and the Cause of the Rebels would "go up" but this is too good to be true I suppose we must "fight it out on this line if it does take all summer" i.e. if we have the *men* to do it with for we must keep throwing them in in order to keep the Mill going and satisfy the public No doubt the Cry will soon be why dont the Army move Those that wish to ascertain [that answer] would do well to Come down here and see They would return home *perfectly satisfied*

The Rebs are very strongly entrenched in front of us. The fighting must be done chiefly with artillery it would be more than useless to throw men against such works as they have Genl Grant may pursue the same course that he did at Vicksburg. *Under mine* them and blow them up. I understand that something of that kind is realy under way *good if true*

We lose more or less men on this line every day from *Rebel sharpshooters* so that the utmost care is necessary to keep the men under the cover of our works. Men are very apt to become careless as they become used to this constant popping and singing of ye *Minnes* We frequently compare them to pretty birds, but they have a very sharp sting. . . . No. of guns in the regiment for duty [that day] 181. This does not look like the regiment that left Massachusetts on that fine April afternoon with 900 strong. Rather a sad picture is it not. . . .[19]

And every day Francis Harrington would remark on the artillery. June 28: "some shelling done the enemy throwing a few shell over near us towards night." June 29: "some shelling all day by both sides. strengthened the Breastworks some this afternoon." June 30: "Musketry on our right on the picket line this afternoon Fell into line behind the Breastworks and laid two or three hours considerable shelling going on tonight on both sides." July 1: "Co[mpany] worked most all the forenoon on breastworks The rebels threw a few shells among us today, but did no damage I believe. Considerable firing on our left on picket line just about dark." July 2: "some shelling during the day. Heavy Cannonading covering on our right in front of 18th Army Corps." July 3: "(twilight) Picket firing now with lively Mortars throwing shell every few minutes." But on the Fourth of July, strangely, he noted that it had been "quiet all day except for an occasional (shot) from Sharpshooters and the Artillery." On and on, day after day, in the young private's diary, the shelling is sustained.[20]

★

But if the shelling was bad, and the sniping worse, duty on the skirmish line was a loaded deck. The Federal picket posts were out in front of the main lines anywhere from fifty to three hundred yards and, in most cases, within easy hailing distance of those belonging to the Confederates, and these extremely forward areas consisted of hundreds of shallow depressions dug by the men. Each of those holes held two or three soldiers, and the pits were stifling hot during the day, cold at night, and literally small ponds during the rains—thoroughly miserable places. The firing up and down the picket lines was perpetual and precarious, and many were slain every day while they were on duty in them.[21]

Every one of the combat soldiers in the 57th, as well as the other regiments' men in Gould's brigade, took his turn manning the picket lines on a four- to five-day rotation, with each new detachment having a twenty-four hour tour in those outposts. Once again we turn to our prolific letter writer, Lieutenant George Barton, who aptly described that duty. The following excerpt also was included in Captain Anderson's regimental history, and it, like the manuscript previously cited, was heavily edited and amended. This is Barton's original text.

The process of relieving "Picket" is this The new Picket are ordered to report to the Brigade Officer of the Day at the right & rear of the Brigade line about 8 o'clock in the evening The Picket consists of two 2nd Lieuts & 100 men from our Brigade After having reported to the O. of D. and he seeing that they are properly divided into two divisions of fifty men each and placed a lieut in Charge of each division then gives his instructions

The old Officer of the Day having arrived about the time we start for the *Picket line*

By this time it is almost pitch dark and as we go stumbling through the woods, Much emphasis is oftentimes placed upon various expressions to numerous to mention. We reach the outer edge of the woods An open field must now be Crossed in order to reach our "old Picket" who are waiting no doubt anxiously to be relieved for they have been on all day in the broiling sun say nothing of the night before A heavy fog has settled on the field which renders it almost impossible for the Johnnies to see us distinctly. Nevertheless the "Minnies" sing round our heads very unpleasantly. having crossed the field we find ourselves fast under the brow of a hill here we are as safe as "Camp Wool" barracks. They form into line by file after which the officer of the Picket gives the men their orders. The line must be held at all *hazards* there being no retreat. That no man shall discharge his rifle unless he sees something to fire *at* and that only when the rebel pickets attempts to *advance* The picket then deploy from the right & left—take possession of the *pits* which are just large enough to hold two men, about as large as a dog like old "Hero" [presumably the Barton family pet] could scratch out in half an hour. The old Picket Creep slowly out of their pits but when fairly out take the double quick down the hill each man for himself 'Zip Zip' go the Minnies after them, but what in the day time would be for sure death at night is very uncertain. The Picket having been relieved and the Officer of the Day "done his rounds" he just retires to his quarters and gives himself up to the influence of ye god of sleep. Rise at 6 o.c. AM and report at Brigade Hd. Qrs. to the a.a.I.G. [acting assistant inspector general] of the Brigade Then another report must be made at six o.clock P.M.

About nine o.c. in the evening the relief Picket goes on Having turned over his instructions to the new Officer of the Day after conducting him to the Picket line he considers himself relieved and retires feeling no doubt oftentimes that through his vigilance the slumbers of his comrades in arms have not been disturbed *Picket duty in front of Petersburg* means "business."[22]

The killing was brutally in earnest by the Confederates on the IX Corps picket lines and trenches for one reason alone. On June 21, the Negro 4th Division had been relieved of duty guarding the army's wagons and supply bases, and the black soldiers were ordered into the corps's works. When the Confederates became aware of their presence, they fired on Burnside's pickets and trench lines with unleashed vengeance. Never a day passed without substantial casualties, and although in other parts of the picket line, which eventually grew to a length of thirty-five miles, soldiers of both sides often mingled freely and traded coffee, sugar, and Northern newspapers for tobacco and Southern journals, and frequently even warned each other of impending gunfire, absolutely no such socializing or swapping, let alone warnings, took place in the IX Corps' stations.[23]

The Southerners were incensed beyond all reason at the North's use of black soldiers against them. It was simply beyond comprehension to those men that the Federal government would stoop to the mustering of their former property as soldiers. It was insulting, mortifying, and outrageous to each and every officer and enlisted man in the Army of Northern Virginia, be he in civilian life an aristocratic slaveholding Virginia planter, a poor Georgia dirt farmer, or a West Texas plainsman. In fact, a few of the Texans quite probably never had even seen a black man until they came east to the war. To be shot by a former slave, a human of an inferior race in their eyes, would be the acme of humiliation, and the Rebels, to a man, vented their unabashed hatred of the black soldiers with ferocity at every opportunity. The white soldiers of the IX Corps who, more often than not, had no great admiration for their black comrades either, suffered equally the unbridled Southern wrath. A man in that section of the Federal lines dared not expose any part of his body for even an instant to Lee's marksmen, and short work was made of those who did. Mercy was unknown in Confederate hearts opposite Burnside's lines, and no quarter was given.

Francis Harrington noted the intensity of the firing on the IX Corps' works.

July 6, 1864 Wednesday In the front line of works where we came last night about 11 O clock P.M. Pickets rather quiet today, but the enemy's sharpshooters fire into our works quite lively have to keep close to the works but the casualties are 1 wounded [Private Darby O'Brien of Company F, mortally wounded] in 57th M[ass]

July 7, 1864 Thursday The enemy's sharpshooters kept up the game of yesterday, firing at us whenever we showed our heads or left our works.

July 8, 1864 Friday Pickets quiet untill late this afternoon when there was heavy firing on the right where our pickets fired quite a number of shots.

And as with the many references to constant artillery fire mentioned in his diary, daily he wrote that the sharpshooting continued ceaselessly.[24]
George Barton, too, had much to say on the subject.

> Hd Qrs. Company C 57 Mass Vols
> 'In the Trenches' July 11, 1864

Dear Mother
. . . we hold a rather more exposed position in the line. The regiment having been changed round. [The previous night about 10:00 P.M., the 57th had moved to the second line of works "a little to the left of our old position."] We now hold posish. [position] that renders it unsafe for a man to *leave* the trenches at *all* for fear of *sharpshooters.* Nevertheless we are obliged to sometimes. The men must have water. So one or two men are detailed by the 1st Sergeant [Defose] who gives them a pass to go to the *rear* for no man can go without [a pass] They take the canteens of the company (16 [present] for duty) and start on the double quick Zip Zip go a dozen bullets after them but they *cant wait* for *them* The boys in the trenches meanwhile laugh & shout after them to see them "sail" dodging to and from from one tree to another till they are out of danger Then they have the same gauntlet to run when they return crouching *low* for they have *learned how,* being "Veterans". They get within ten or fifteen rods of the trenches give a yell and in they go On the whole it is very *amusing* but oftentimes proves to be an expensive pleasure. . . . The 1st Brigade 1st Division [IX Corps] holds the most exposed position on the line, but we can stand it. . . . This *Campaign* is taking off our men by the scores & hundreds what bullets do not remove sickness will men cannot lay in their trenches day after day and not get used up. For myself I cannot Complain as long as *health* is continued to me, but my men *suffer* more or less everyday. . . .[25]

And in Barton's next three letters to his mother he continues to give us fascinating firsthand glimpses of the 57th's dangers and hardships in the Petersburg trenches. (How Mrs. Barton maintained her sanity after reading her son's graphic descriptions of his experiences mailed home almost daily is beyond comprehension.)

Black Interlude

Letter of July 14, 1864:

We are still at the front and right under the artilery fire of the Rebs day and night Our Artilery in the Meantime is not idle we *tender* our Compliments to the "Johnnies" every few minutes with Considerable effect. We can see the sand fly from their works at every discharge of our rifled guns & "morters" I do not write this letter with the intention of telling you every news for there is none, it is the same old story of lay low and Keep as cool as possible. The shell explode all round *us* but have not yet *Killed* any of our boys [that day]. While I am writing a shell explodes *near* my quarters wounding one of our boys taking his thumb off [Private Daniel O'Keefe of Company D, eighteen, from County Kerry, Ireland], one of the boys upon hearing him *groan* & take on about it Made the remark that he "ought to kneel down and thank God that it didn't take your *head off* instead of making a fuss about a *small* matter." So it is as we become *accustomed* to these things we think a man *lucky* if he is *only* wounded slightly. . . .

Letter of July 19, 1864:

. . . Our regiment is now on the "2d line" where we shall remain for a *few* days only. We are more exposed to the shells of the enemy here than on the *front* line as their morters throw over [into the second line of trenches]. We have had some very narrow escapes since we took this line, and at the moment their shells are bursting all round us, so you must excuse the *appearance* of this epistle written under such trying Circumstances

Last night one of their "morter" shells "10 inch," burst right in our *Trenches,* striking the ground between five of our men who were laying down upon their rubber blankets. it tore the blanket all to pieces but *Killed* no one, slightly bruising one of the boys and tearing the pants of another. I can assure you it is a very "dangerous thing being *safe*" [the second line of trenches was thought to be safer than the front lines] when such Compliments are sent over to us. . . .

While I am writing word was brought in to me by one of my brother Lieuts that *one more* of our gallant *band* has gone to his long home

Lieut. E. Dexter Cheney 1st Lieut Comdg B Co. 57th Mass while looking at one of our Morters was *shot* through the head, it is supposed by a sharpshooter, from the Rebel works, he was killed instantly. . . . We shall try to send his body *home* to Worcester if we can get it *Embalmed.*

Letter of July 20, 1864:

. . . We are having narrow escapes *here this morning,* the "Johnnies" are dropping their Morter Shells right Among us 4 of our regiment have been wounded this morning within half an hour. Two of *my own Company.* My 1st Sergeant Chas L. Defose & Corporal [Samuel] Allman The latter was wounded by a piece of shell the size of my hand. It tore open his face & nearly took his left arm off. it was a hard looking wound Sergt Defose was hit with a minnie the ball just passing under the skin back of his shoulder. . . .

Mother, May You Never See the Sights I Have Seen

As my "Chum" Lieut John H Cook said to me last night as we lay under our "shelter", who will go next? And it is a *solemn thought,* that no one can *answer the question* we can only wait.

Not five minutes ago a shell exploded, "8 inch," just in our trenches covering the men with dirt but injuring no one. it Struck about two yards back of my quarters "Whiz" how the pieces did fly. . . .[26]

It can only be imagined—as well as it is possible to imagine—the terror that the 57th's men, like all front-line soldiers North and South, endured at Petersburg. And the soldiers' necessarily acquired callousness and cynicism, as in the attitude towards young Private O'Keefe when he had his thumb blown off, can be justified and explained in light of that terror. Nevertheless, there were some humorous incidents that occurred as a result of those trying times, too—humorous in retrospect, anyway.

Two of the boys were hugging the earth, as the Minié balls whined and whizzed about them and as cannon and mortar fire shook the ground and sprayed dirt and shrapnel in unpredictable directions, when they thought of a solution to their predicament. They wrote the following letter.

Before Petersburg
July 11, 1864

Brig Gen James B. Fry
Honored Sir

We the undersigned being very desirous of getting transferred into the Navy, We take this opportunity of addressing you these lines hoping they will receive favor at your hands. We wish to know how the transfer is to be made and by whom; if it rests with you, we desire you to forward the necessary papers for a transfer Yours Respectfully. William C. Park Co. H, 57 Mass. Vols. Andrew Murray Co. H, 57 Mass. Vols.[27]

Their story would be truly amusing if those two young men had not met tragic ends. They never received a reply to their homely plea, and twenty-one-year-old Private Andrew Murray was to live only nineteen days longer, while eighteen-year-old Sergeant William Park was wounded and taken prisoner of war in as many days, finally dying as a result of his wounds in Confederate hands the following January.[28]

15

To Just Endure

THE SUFFERING sustained by the soldiers of the Army of the Potomac at Petersburg was awesome, and duty in the trenches and rifle pits in Virginia's torrid heat and chilly, soaking rains took a fearful toll on their health. Diseases of all sorts spread throughout the Union forces, and the men of the 57th contracted their quota of them. But many of the regiment who discovered symptoms of sickness were too proud—or too afraid of the ridicule of their comrades and the horrible conditions encountered in the army hospitals—to report to the medical authorities for what they considered minor and inconsequential problems. In many of their minds, nothing short of a bullet or piece of shrapnel warranted a trip to the surgeon, and except for the chronic malingerers, the majority of the sick stayed behind in the earthworks until they became so weak that they were ordered to the rear by their officers.

The relentless sun was a prime source of irritation to those who had to stand under it in the trenches all day, and many soldiers suffered heat prostration. The only relief from the stifling temperatures was to stretch a blanket or shelter tent half over the parapets to capture some shade.[1]

But if the sun was bad, the rain—when it came that summer—was worse. The excavations dug into the Virginia clay held water like sinks, and sometimes the men were knee deep and more in the swamps that the trenches became, with no place to sit or lie down to sleep. Culverts and slit trenches were cut to help drain the earthworks, but they were often ineffective. The boys tried to bail the water out with cans and tin drinking cups, but in a storm it was impossible to keep up with the pouring rain. Insects, rats, snakes, and all varieties of vermin and parasites abounded in those noxious pits, and all of the men's efforts to keep them clean and dry were ineffective.

Every one of the soldiers was infested with lice, from the generals on down to the privates, and an unwavering but losing battle was waged upon those ubiquitous and iniquitous pests. In the cool of the early mornings the men were seen sitting in the trenches with some part of their uniforms removed and turned inside out, intently hunting along the stitching and concentrating ardently on the destruction of the six-legged enemy that, when found, was squeezed to death diligently between dirty, brown fingertips. While one soldier was reconnoitering the seams of his uniform, a comrade would often preen his scalp and beard, and, with every bit as much concentration, push apart tufts and strands of hair in search of the insatiable little bloodsuckers.

The men kept their hair cut fairly short, especially during the latter part of the Civil War, in order—at least in part—to keep this menace at bay, and almost every company could boast of at least one barber. (It was the vain, high-ranking officers that sometimes sported dandified, curly long locks, but even most of them by 1864 had abandoned those elaborate hair styles.) When a soldier's hair was fairly clean of the scourge, he reciprocated the process on his partner. Those sights were often the source of laughter and jokes. The men found each other's tenacity and acuity in the hunt for lice hilarious, and for the most part, they took their situation good-naturedly and tried to keep the grumbling to a minimum. After all, they reasoned, it did no good to complain and only irritated someone else. But if a man insisted on airing his grievances, he was likely either to be told plainly to shut up, or sometimes asked by a relatively cheerful comrade how he would like to trade his current condition for a free one-way ticket to the resort at Andersonville, Georgia. Enough horror stories were in circulation among the soldiers in the Union army that just the mention of that hellish place usually would silence the most ardent complainer.[2]

★

The men still endured the unspeakable army food, and although they were given plenty of it by the army's Commissary Department while their counterparts starved over across the way, it was appalling in quality. The Army of the Potomac tried to issue fresh vegetables two or three times a week, but the Commissary Department's system of distribution was poor and not always dependable. Even when it was, the greens usually were not fresh. The companies were supposed to be allowed to draw thirty pounds of potatoes three times a week and generally did, but the staples remained hardtack, salt meat, coffee, sugar, and salt. The soldiers found the meat so tough they joked that they had to eat it four or five times before they got it into their stomachs.

The men fried nearly everything, fashioning frying pans by melting the welds on a discarded canteen and attaching one of its halves to a stout forked stick or a scrap of junk steel that they had foraged. Those messmates who had a little cash sometimes pooled their money and took a trip to the sutler's store to buy a manufactured iron model, which made them the envy of their neighbors.

When the soldiers did get vegetables, some of the more creative trench chefs roasted them on a stick or merely threw them on the fire's coals until they were done, but mostly the men fried them in pork fat along with everything else. They soaked their hardtack in water until soft and fried it in fat, too, and often heaped it with underdone beans or burned rice when those commodities were available, and these affairs, though popular and reasonably edible, were a sloppy, slimy mess.

The Army of the Potomac also issued dehydrated food which came in solid form, roughly one inch thick by one foot square, known as "dessicated vegetables." When the men threw one of those whole "bricks," as they called them, into a small cook pot full of boiling water, they often learned the hard way that dehydrated vegetables would absorb a tremendous amount of water and expand hugely, welling up in the pot and overflowing into the fire, causing a fiasco.

The larger camp kettles were very effective sources of dysentery, diarrhea, and other digestive ailments, although the soldiers did not realize it at the time. The big, black iron pots frequently doubled as laundry tubs when they were not being used for cooking, and, as a result, they often were coated with a barely noticable film of soap suds and dead lice which the company cook overlooked when he began his culinary preparations. Abetting this problem was the almost total lack of hygiene on the part of the cooks because of their ignorance and living conditions.

The designated company cooks of the 57th, like their counterparts in other regiments, rarely washed their hands and nearly always performed their duties in their filthy service uniforms. (As a rule, company cooks could be used only when the boys were off the firing line and in camp at the rear. In the front-line trenches, it was every man for himself.) The high incidence of intestinal disorders among the soldiers reflected that lack of sanitation—twice as many men in the Civil War died from disease as from battle wounds. The problem was further augmented by maggots, rats, weevils, and other pests infesting the food, where they either left their droppings or were themselves eaten by the men. Worms got into the dried fruit that the army issued, and mold frequently covered it.

Most of the men neglected to wash their dishes, or found it impossible to do so under the circumstances, and some simply mopped them up with a piece of bread which they then popped into their mouths, joking to their comrades that they were "eating the dishrag." Others poured hot coffee over their untensils and dried them with grass. The tin plates were black from use over the fires, and knives and forks were often jabbed carelessly into the ground a few times to remove food particles.

Water was never boiled for drinking except for coffee, and almost every man suffered from the effects of stagnant, foul water at one time or another while he was a soldier. Pasteurization was still in the future, and the army hospitals were overflowing with sick soldiers complaining of spastic, uncontrollable bowels and cramping stomachs.

The trenches were rife with garbage that attracted rats and insects, and nearby latrines drew swarms of flies that in turn infected food supplies. Men under fire had no choice but to urinate or defecate where they were standing, further compounding the sanitation dilemma. The sum of all of those odors, from the rotting flesh of death to the stench of human waste, from the odious decomposing garbage to the sulfurous tang of black powder, made the earthworks at Petersburg smell to a degree impossible to put into words, particularly during the summer months when the heat of the sun made the stink increase.

Since the battle of the Wilderness, another disease had developed in the Army of the Potomac—scurvy. Some of the men's teeth had loosened from bleeding and receding gums, and occasionally their legs had turned black, but that condition, fortunately, was understood by the military doctors, and, at that time, the army began issuing dessicated vegetables to the soldiers as an "anti-scourbatic." But the men hated that ration, dubbing it "baled hay," "sanitary fodder," and "desecrated vegetables," and they threw it away.

In July, at Petersburg, General Meade's commissary chief, Colonel Thomas Wilson, informed Washington that the men would not eat the dehydrated fare. What they wanted, and desperately needed, were fresh vegetables, he told the authorities. So the Commissary Department and the Sanitary Commission in Washington got together and sent to the front train-car loads of fresh vegetables, barrels of kraut and pickles, and raw potatoes in vinegar, and the scurvy soon was under control.

There was a tremendous amount of waste in the Union army at Petersburg by men who threw away food they did not like and refused to eat. They could not stand canned vegetables because they tasted so bad compared to fresh, or "refrigerated" meat for essentially the same reason. (Most meat was preserved by soaking it in brine—hence "salt meat"—but some was shipped on blocks of ice in the railroad cars, and it was tagged "refrigerated" by the soldiers.)

The army had a large cattle herd near its supply base at City Point that still was being guarded, in part, by some of the men of the 57th, but most of those steers, even though the herd was constantly replenished, were never much more than bones on the hoof, and the men remarked that "it would take a dozen cows to make a decent shadow" on any one soldier. Fresh beef was hardly a mainstay of the Federal army.

Even though the surgeons had no understanding of bacteria and their deadly effects, they realized that all of the fried food the troops were eating was hard on their digestive systems, and they incorrectly concluded that that method of preparing rations was responsible for many of the intestinal disorders contracted by the men. For a time, they mounted a campaign to teach them alternatives to frying, but their efforts went for naught as the soldiers continued with their favorite recipes. It was quite often said throughout the army that burned beans killed more men than bullets, and while this assessment was not very close to the truth, it was generally believed at the time.

Now that they were holed up in the trenches of Petersburg, the delivery of packages from home was more efficient, and quite regularly relatives and friends sent food for their loved ones on the line, who often shared it with their messmates. Those packages usually contained sausages, preserves, hams, cheeses, and cakes, and the men were joyous when they received these welcome goodies. Most of the parcels were shipped through the Adams Express Company, a private forwarding firm which had a virtual monopoly on goods sent to the soldiers at the front. But the company's distribution system was not very efficient, and many of the boxes from home took a long time to reach their destinations. They often arrived with their contents damaged, pilfered, or spoiled, and not a few were stolen outright by unscrupulous people in the delivery process who gave little thought to the needs of the suffering men in the earthworks.

Besides packages sent from concerned family and friends, the soldiers often received needed supplies from the United States Sanitary Commission, which provided—apart from food such as lemons, oranges, other fruits, and vegetables—medicine, clothing, bedding, and tobacco, without charge. Those gifts were delivered sporadically, but when they did arrive, they were accepted gratefully.

Far less appreciated were the donations from the Christian Commission, which sent almost exclusively religious literature that many of the hard-core veterans considered worthless except for lighting campfires. Bibles, too, were distributed in large quantities throughout the army by this organization, but even though almost all of the soldiers held a deep respect for the Holy Book, they were much more in need of refreshments of the flesh.

The army had set up huge bakeries at City Point, and thousands of loaves of soft white bread were made daily, but the system of distributing them over the growing lines of trenches—with every flanking move to the left made by the Army of the Potomac during its ten-month occupation, large stretches of new Petersburg real estate were occupied—was not very effective at the outset of the siege, and the bread sat in the sun at the depots, turning stale and sour. Many of the men refused to eat the soft bread when finally it was distributed, until they discovered that if sliced and toasted over the fire on a piece of scrap wire, it was not too bad. But the soldiers were so used to their hard bread—hardtack—that they generally favored it, and towards the end of the war, many of them bragged that they knew at least fifteen ways to prepare the hardy crackers.

A sampling of their inventive recipes showed their resourcefulness. Sometimes they would take hardtack and drape raw bacon over it and then cover this sumptuous dish with sugar, washing it down with sooty, green coffee. Others prepared the delicacy known as "Scouse," a concoction of salt pork, hardtack, and potatoes boiled to perfection in a cook pot. Yet others thought their evening repast incomplete without the venerable "Skillygalee." That culinary treasure was prepared the day before by delicately pulverizing some hardtack in a haversack with a musket butt, soaking the fragments overnight in water, and then frying them in pork grease. A variation of that recipe was to form the mixture into thin cakes and bake them when an oven was available or could be fashioned from rocks and mud. Those little cakes were called "Washington Pies." More often, though, the soldiers would simply soak a whole piece of the bread in cold water until it was fairly soft and fry it in pork fat, producing "Burnside Stew," after their famous commander. And then there was the ever-popular "Hellfire Stew," a curious blend of everything available at any given moment boiled in a pot and seasoned with dirt, soot, and dried soap, sometimes known by its other name, "Son of a Seadog."

When on the march or in the forward lines the men frequently nibbled on the oversized soda cracker, and a few seriously debated whether their hardtack could have been left over from the War of 1812 because it was so rock-hard and rotten. (Some claimed to have seen dates for that war and the Mexican War stamped onto some of the wooden boxes in which it was delivered.) Others joked that it could follow the army on its own, so infested was it with maggots and weevils. Many of the boys often toasted the crackers to drive out the pests, but others simply ignored them, claiming that the insects had no flavor, and when hardtack was eaten at night, there was no way of knowing that the pests were even there.

But, hardtack, or "pilot bread," or just plain "cracker," was a principle staple of the army, and, unless they wanted to starve, the soldiers had no choice but to eat it, even though some unscrupulous government contractors, in order to increase their profits, substituted ingredients such as pipe clay and ground white soapstone when manufacturing the bread.

Coffee, referred to by many of the men as "subtle poison," was, nevertheless, all-important to them, and the opportunity was never lost to boil a pot whenever circumstances allowed. The soldiers carried the uncooked beverage loose in their haversacks mixed with sugar. At Petersburg, coffee was issued ready-ground, so the soldiers did not have the problem of atomizing beans with a rock or rifle butt. Their unique coffee pots were often made from large tomato cans or similar items which they scrounged from the rubbish of the officers' trash heaps. They attached a handle made of scrap wire and, putting a stick through it, they were able to hold the can safely over the flames.

The men liked their bacon, but they detested the grease that often seeped out through worn seams on their canvas haversacks and onto their uniforms—everyone seemed to have a greasy left hip. Some tried wrapping it in newspaper or carrying it in a can. The bacon was another of the staples of their diet, but it frequently arrived rancid from the heat, wormy, or spoiled because the brine had leaked out of the wooden barrel in which it had been stored. But, of course, it was eaten anyway by the always-hungry soldiers.

One of the most common complaints, apart from the fattiness of the pork, was directed at the beef ration, and it was ridiculed because it had no fat at all. The salted beef was so bad and smelled so awful that mock funerals were known to have been held for it in the rear lines. The men would pile the stinking meat on a board, raise it to their shoulders, and solemnly march off to the latrine trenches while one or two of the regimental bandsmen played the funeral dirge. A eulogy was reverently spoken, and the unfortunate beef dumped ceremoniously into the excrement pile. (Whether a scene of that nature occurred in the 57th is not known.)

Occasionally the men were issued corn, which they had no use for, and they would raise an awful fuss. To them corn was animal fodder, and they were insulted by its distribution as food for human consumption. But if they were really hungry, they ate it anyway, preparing it by grating the kernels over tin plates and cartridge-box tins that they had punched with holes, and mixing the results with water and sugar to make hoecakes and corn bread.

In August 1864, the Commissary Department was ordered by Brigadier General Amos B. Eaton, its head, to economize on salt pork because speculators had driven up its price from twenty-five to forty-three dollars a barrel, and the department was told to issue more beef and salt fish. Most of the fish found its way to the Army of the Potomac, but the New England boys, for the most part, were the only ones who would eat it. The men were used to living on the blue and sticky beef and pork four or five days a week, and the Yankee soldiers from other parts of the country wanted no part of the fish. But for the New Englanders, some of whom came from coastal towns, and the Irish and other immigrants, the fish was a great treat, and they welcomed it to their diets.[3]

★

Several miles to the east of the sprawling Petersburg battlefield lay a promontory of land on a high bluff at the confluence of the James and Appomattox rivers known as City Point. There, less than a month after arriving at the new fighting area, the Union army established its great base of operations to care for its nearly 100,000 soldiers. From 150 to 200 ships, river transports, and barges arrived at all hours each day unloading cargo and troops along the seven teeming wharves, nearly 3600 feet long, built along the James on the northeastern bank of that peninsula.

Day and night—after the tracks of the captured City Point Railroad had been repaired and put back into operation by July 7—trains of the U. S. Military Railroad, trailing smoke and cinders, moved vital supplies from off-loading vessels and warehouses, in their boxcars and on their flatcars, along the southbound rails to the troops at the northern front of the battlefield. From there, wagon trains guarded by cavalry detachments hauled the tons and tons of rations, ammunition, forage, and other indispensable material of war over the rutty, narrow country lanes to the men beyond the railroad's reach. Meanwhile, soldiers and civilian laborers, the majority of them liberated slaves and free blacks, were continuously at work during the early weeks of the siege constructing the undulating tracks of the new City Point & Army Line Railroad that soon would swing around the rear of the whole Army of the Potomac, supplying the miles of lines occupied by the Federal soldiers in front of Petersburg with vastly improved efficiency.

The massive, bustling environs of the military complex at City Point included, among other things, the huge Depot Field Hospital that opened on June 20, soldiers' cemeteries, army repair shops of all descriptions, giant commissary, ordnance and quartermaster warehouses, provost guard operations, and the notorious prison stockade known as "The Bullpen." Enormous stables, campgrounds, bakeries, slaughterhouses, blacksmith, carpenter, and coffin shops, embalming and photography parlors, and churches covered the landscape. General Grant's headquarters was located there also. The area was one of unimaginable dusty and smoky confusion, with constant, grinding activity.

Construction of new buildings and facilities seemed to be unending, and the army sawmills turned out tens of thousands of board feet of lumber to raise the slightly less than three hundred military installations that stood there during the siege. Tents were pitched in disorder everywhere, housing personnel assigned to duty at City Point, and, except for the several civilian homes of the local citizens, the whole place was one of rough pine planks and mildewed gray canvas.

City Point and all its bustling activity were well known to the men in the 57th Massachusetts, and they all, at one time or another, frequented the huge supply center for various reasons. For those that were very sick or wounded, it was the first stop along the way to Northern hospitals and home—if they survived.[4]

★

Now that the Union army seemed to be settling in for a long siege, the sutlers who had been sent to the rear by Grant and Meade long ago, before the battle of the Wilderness, were returning to the army and setting up shop in relative safety at City Point and other secure areas. With very few exceptions, those men were motivated only by profits, and they had no desire to get any nearer

Wharves at City Point, July 1864. (USAMHI, Carlisle Barracks, Pa.)

the shooting than necessary. The men in the front lines rarely, if ever, saw them there.

Several hundred feet across the railroad tracks from Wharf No. 2 on the James, in the area of the Christian Commission buildings, were located some of the sutlers' canvas-covered log stores and wood-framed shops standing in rows. They were built on two levels of ground, with plank stairs running to the higher area between a restaurant and the military post office. The civilian merchants who operated from those buildings provided the soldiers with goods unobtainable from the government—and at greatly inflated prices— and although the men considered the sutlers thieves and robbers, they readily spent their money at those establishments.

The alternative to eating army rations was to buy food from the sutlers. Just as most of the other outfits in the Army of the Potomac did, the 57th Massachusetts had its own official sutlers who served the regiment. They were Charles Colis and A. B. Long. It is not known whether they represented two different operations at different periods in the regiment's existence—only one sutler was allowed each regiment at a time—or whether they were partners. Which one served the 57th at Petersburg, if they were not partners, is likewise unknown. At any event, one of them would have been commissioned by the Commonwealth of Massachusetts to serve the men in Virginia.

Regiments were permitted to trade with their own sutlers only, and the merchants used their monopolies to take scandalous financial advantage of the soldiers. The men retaliated by raiding the villains from time to time and stealing their goods, while their sympathetic officers frequently looked the other way. To guard against those attacks and to keep from granting credit— payment of which was more often than not ignored by the indigent soldiers— the sutlers sometimes did not open their doors until payday.

As was the case with most regiments, the 57th's men received their pay on a very irregular schedule—going for months without compensation was the rule rather than the exception. But when they finally did see the army paymaster, which was generally during an inspection in the rear, most of them could be found later at their sutler's shop trying to relieve the boredom of army food and buying personal necessities.

Some of the more popular items with the men were salmon, sardines, and green peas that had been canned in France—as opposed to those canned in America, which they despised—and were usually in good condition when opened. Borden's canned milk, Hecker's farina, butter (often rancid), ginger ale, hard candy, cookies, and pastry also were important items to the soldiers.

The official vendors were forbidden to sell beer, wine, or hard liquor to the enlisted men, but they kept it on hand for the officers—many of whom consumed alcohol in rivers—and whenever they could, the men in the ranks would manage to get their hands on it one way or another. Other products were available for them to buy that seemed innocent enough, but that, in reality, contained a heavy dose of whiskey, gin, brandy, or rum, such as canned milk drinks with names like "Lediard's Army Tonic" and "Soldier's Friend." There were always ways for the private soldier to skirt the rules.

The men bought other things from those unprincipled entrepreneurs which now and again made them sick. Cat- and dog-meat pies and other shoddy and inferior products were pressed upon naive young soldiers, usually making them quite ill with diarrhea. The surgeons were always busy with those cases of stomach disorders, and they generally treated them with Epsom salts. The Sanitary Commission, on the other hand, prescribed lager beer to clear up the same problems, a treatment to which many soldiers were quite pleased to submit. And the sutlers themselves were far from immune from making a profit dispensing medicine, and Hostetter's Bitters—which was 32 percent ethyl alcohol—and Dover's Powders, among others, were sold by the carload for rheumatism, measles, typhoid fever, mumps, and "the itch." Ayer's "Extract of Sarsaparilla" was pawned off on the unsuspecting men to "eliminate poisons from the blood and tissue."

Nothing was more popular with the soldiers than tobacco. They smoked or chewed it voraciously, and they craved it when it could not be had. Its absence lowered the men's spirits, making marches seem longer and picket duty more tedious and monotonous. It was used almost universally by the troops, and even the doctors thought at the time its effects were beneficial, considering it a natural antidote for malaria. The army surgeons also believed that it reduced deaths from diarrhea and "camp fever." When it was unavailable the resourceful soldiers smoked tea leaves, crushed coffee grains, white oak bark, and even moss. The brown leaf came in all varieties of cigars, loose cigarette and pipe tobacco, and twists and plugs, commonly called "cut" and "rope," and it was labled with numerous trade names such as "Lone Jack" and "Kinnikinnick."

Nearly everything that a soldier could want that was not provided by the army was carried by those profiteers, the sutlers, but their prices were outrageous, and considering that the private soldier's pay was sixteen dollars a month, and was often not paid when due, it was hardly surprising that the plundered enlisted men seized the sutlers' supplies when they felt they had been pushed too far. Typically, a dozen eggs would cost 50¢, a pound of cheese 40¢, a deck of playing cards $2.00, a frying pan $1.25, a pencil 15¢, a package of envelopes 30¢, a bottle of pickles $1.00, a can of oysters $1.00, a cake of soap 30¢, a rubber comb $2.50, a pair of boots $15.00, a pound of raisins 75¢, a bottle of hair oil 50¢, a tin of lobster 75¢, a pair of gloves $5.00, and two plugs of tobacco 25¢. After sending most of his money home—or losing it in a poker game—there was little difficulty for a soldier to fall quickly into debt at the sutler's store.[5]

★

Music played a big part in the men's lives, and around the campfires at night they often sang the popular and patriotic songs of the day. The Irish, great lovers of music, frequently reminisced of their homeland with native ballads and folk songs. Sometimes the music lifted the soldiers' spirits, and sometimes it depressed them, but either way, it helped to maintain their camaraderie and cohesiveness. The bands, for the most part, were used to good effect on the men's morale, entertaining them with martial as well as well-known civilian tunes. Some of the soldiers played instruments themselves, usually the guitar, violin, or harmonica, and those who had that talent were always in demand around the evening fires.

Some of the best-known and probably the best-liked songs among the soldiers were "Tenting Tonight," "Just Before the Battle Mother," "John Brown's Body," "The Battle Hymn of the Republic," "The Girl I Left Behind Me," and "The Battle Cry of Freedom."[6]

Games, when they could be played in the safety of the rear, were a popular way to pass the time. Among the most common were a crude form of baseball, leapfrog, and tag. Cards, checkers, chess, dice, and whittling and carving were engaged in also to help the boring, hot days go by. Letter writing was prolific, and many men faithfully recounted their experiences and feelings in journals and diaries. Books were read by some, and newspapers were always in high demand. Cockfights, horse racing, and prodigious drinking bouts were enjoyed occasionally by the officers.[7]

★

Most of the men stayed within the boundaries of the army's rules and regulations. However, not all did, and from time to time, crimes including desertion, robbery, rape, and murder were committed (although the last two are never known to have occurred in the 57th). At times a man would be sentenced to be executed by firing squad, and on such occasions, the whole brigade or division to which he belonged was required to be present to witness the carrying out of the court-martial decision. (The 57th was ordered to witness one such execution at Petersburg in the fall of 1864.) Now and then the firing squad would only wound the condemned soldier, who was made to sit on his coffin, hands and feet bound and eyes blindfolded, facing his executioners. The firing squad party, as well as the troops in attendance, were often nervous and upset about killing one of their own, no matter what he had done, and they frequently aimed poorly—no one wanted to feel that he was responsible for the doomed man's death. After the wounded prisoner was propped back up on his wooden casket, the whole business was carried out again until he was killed. It was usually a gruesome, sloppy affair, and when finally he was pronounced dead by the surgeons, every man observing was directed to file past and look at his body, ostensibly as a warning to any men contemplating a capital offense. The corpse was then buried face down in an unmarked grave. Soldiers of all ranks felt utter revulsion at these executions, and they detested them bitterly.

Other forms of punishment ranged from time in the guardhouse on bread and water to being drummed out of the service to walking around all day with a knapsack full of bricks strapped on the back, plus various other types of painful humiliations. The form of penalty often depended on the whim of the officer responsible for the soldier, and sentences were not always passed out equitably.[8]

The 57th had its share of miscreants. There was a general court-martial for Private William Parks of Company A in August 1864. Born in County Leitrim, Ireland, Parks had deserted the regiment on January 5, one day after being mustered at Camp Wool, and was unlucky enough to be apprehended and arrested on July 6 and sent back to the regiment. He was tried and sentenced in July to lose all pay and allowances for an unknown period and to be held in confinement. After his release in the fall, though, he served honorably and was discharged with the other men of his company after the war. Parks, however, was hardly the lone court-martialed member of the regiment.[9]

★

After nearly three months of being in the field, mingling with other veteran regiments, the men of the 57th gradually picked up something particular to military life in war—army slang. The soldiers of both Civil War armies had a colloquial and humorous way of expressing themselves, and except by the few purists who maintained a strict and proper use of the English language, homespun jargon was used commonly throughout the Army of the Potomac, and the men always got a good laugh when they learned another funny phrase.

"Sardine boxes" were shoulder straps and "shoulder straps" were officers. A blanket roll was called a "horse collar," an army mule termed a "brevet horse," a "beehive" or "patent bureau" was a knapsack, "layouts" and "coffee coolers" were skulkers, and hardtack was known variously as "sinkers," "weevil fodder," or "death bells." "Chin music" was conversation, "slapjacks" were pancakes, a "shin plaster" was paper money, "bumblebees" or "swifts" were bullets, and "camp kettles," "cook stoves," "lampposts," "iron foundries," "tubs," and "bootlegs" were artillery shells. ("The Rebs is throwin' camp kettles at us!" was an everyday way of describing an artillery bombardment.) "Old Scratch" was the Devil, "little coots" was a name given the Yankees by the Confederates, "showing the white feather" was cowardice, "forty dead men" was forty rounds of ammunition in the cartridge box, a haversack was a "breadbag," a "fast trick" or a "pretty rapid little case" was a lady with a loose reputation, and "fire and fall back" meant to throw up.

Stealing was "cabbaging," "sowbelly" was bacon, to "rag out" was to dress well, and "the opening of the ball" the start of a battle. To "peddle lead" was to shoot fast and a "discharge" was a serious but not dangerous wound leading to the permanent parting of company with the army. "Trappings" or "traps" were a soldier's possessions, "gunboats" were army shoes, "tenements" were winter quarters, and to "make a cathole" meant to shoot someone. To "grab a root" was to eat, a comrade was a "pardner," whiskey was "bug juice" or "tanglefoot," and bad whiskey was "forty-rod," which meant that "it was so strong that it would kill at forty rods and around a corner!"

A retreating Rebel was said to be "going in search of his rights," a fearless soldier on the battle line was talked of as being "so cool that water froze in his canteen," and of a panicky soldier in battle the men remarked that he "jumped up and down like a bobtailed dog in high oats." A man asking another if he wanted a drink of liquor might inquire if the other wanted to "change his breath," and a soldier with a serious hangover might claim to have been "squashmolished." A sharp operator was said to be able to "sell shit to a stable," and a "dogrobber" was a cook. "Paddy," "Mick," "Hibernian," "cottier," "son of Erin," "spalpeen," and "Fenian" were used by both native-born Americans and Irishmen to describe the male Irish immigrant, and "Bridget" was any of his womenfolk. Soldiers of German ancestry, on the other hand, were "Dutchmen."

The ragged Southerners often taunted their well-dressed adversaries, yelling across the trenches that "we'uns don't put on our best suits when we go out to kill hogs," and a Northerner confronted by one of his officers about illegally stealing Southern civilian livestock might answer that he never killed a chicken or hog unless "it refused to take the oath of allegiance" (to the United States Government) or "give the proper countersign."[10]

★

And so the oppressing days of boredom, skirmishing, and dying passed on in the trenches and rear-guard areas for the 57th Massachusetts, in the same manner as for any other outfit in the Federal army. The few remaining men of the regiment suffered constantly, but, still, the depleted ranks held together. Those intent on bounty jumping had pretty well done so long ago, and the desertions that occurred now were committed mainly by men recovering in hospitals or convalescing at home. A few of the wounded who had been recuperating had returned, strengthening the regiment a little, but the 57th's numbers of men present for duty at roll call were always fluid with men out sick or injured.[11]

16

A Continual Rattle of Musketry

ON THE FIELDS of Petersburg, during the month of July, the men of the 57th continued to give and take in the unceasing fire, and endure the unrelenting heat and the never-ending boredom. In their filthy trenches they played games to try to make the time pass. Sometimes they placed bets to see if their own sharpshooters would find their marks, or, just for the fun of it, stuck one of their caps on the end of a ramrod, raised it above the parapet, and wagered on how many Confederate bullet holes would be put in it in a given amount of time. Other pastimes were rat or lice racing, tossing dice, and playing cards. Still, monotony and death and wounds and sickness plagued them as they plagued every soldier in both armies.

On July 5, Private Darby O'Brien of Company F, wounded in the June 17 assault and just recently returned to duty, was shot and killed at his station on picket duty. He had married just before enlisting in the regiment, and he had survived all of the 57th's battles only to be picked off in a filthy ditch.[1]

Private Patrick McCarthy, who also had been wounded in the assault of June 17, died that 5th of July as well, in his hospital bed in Harewood U.S. Army General Hospital in Washington. He had served honorably with Company F and the regiment in most of the 57th's engagements until taking his mortal wound, and his officers had thought his "military character good." McCarthy, too, left a young widow.[2]

The regiment's only Australian member, Private Michael Dwyer of Company I, from New South Wales, was wounded seriously in the trenches while on duty, July 12. He was a veteran of the regiment's entire campaign, and he would return in the spring for muster-out.[3]

Not all of the 57th's casualties were victims of Confederate lead, however. For Private Henry Patterson of Company D, a native of Mansfield, New Jersey, who also had fought in all of the regiment's battles, the strain of soldiering finally took its toll on his forty-four-year-old constitution, and the

Sandisfield, Massachusetts, farmer suddenly dropped dead in the trenches on July 14. At first his friends thought that he had been shot, but when they found no evidence of wounds, they took his body to the rear to be examined by the surgeons. No cause of death was ever determined by the doctors, but the men knew what killed him; he was simply too old for soldiering.[4]

Company K's Private John Woodruff had been detailed as Lieutenant Priest's hostler with the regimental quartermaster's department from the start. Having never been in the front lines and with the probability of never having to go, he was caught by the misfortunes of war anyway. On the Fourth of July, he was shot accidentally in the leg while at the rear, the wound serious enough to require amputation. A Surgeon's Certificate of Disability removed him from any of the war's further dangers.[5]

Private Henry Savage of Company H was wounded by the accidental explosion of gunpowder while on duty as a clerk in the rear at 1st Brigade headquarters in July. He, too, had never been a combat soldier, and after recuperating at Camp Meigs hospital in Readville, Massachusetts, he would be transferred to the Veteran Reserve Corps.[6]

There were other reasons that the regiment lost men, as well. Never in combat, Private George Alexander, a veteran of Frank Bartlett's old 49th Regiment, and Private Edward Hawes were both court-martialed and dishonorably discharged with loss of all pay and allowances on June 29. Both were members of Company D, and neither had ever been in battle with the 57th.[7] Their offense has not been determined, but shirking is certainly possible.

Sergeant William Richards of Company H had no love for the battlefield. He had been slightly wounded in May, and upon his return to the regiment he accepted a position as a clerk at the IX Corps' 4th Division headquarters, for which he was broken to the ranks. But his plan for safe duty may have been his undoing. On March 16 of the following year, young Richards died from chronic diarrhea contracted in the service.[8]

★

The men drew new clothing and equipment on July 16, and at ten o'clock that night the regiment was relieved of front-line duty and withdrawn to the ravine in the rear. The following day, Sunday, the boys "had Divine services in camp. . . ."[9]

On Monday, July 18, the 57th moved further to the rear in the morning and in the afternoon the men fell in to be inspected with the 56th Massachusetts and the 100th Pennsylvania. Their new uniforms notwithstanding, no two of them, it seemed to the inspecting officers, were dressed or equipped exactly alike, and the short regimental lines looked sad and pathetic. But the inspectors saw tough, veteran combat soldiers with mahogany-colored faces and hard eyes, troops to be depended on.[10]

In the evening, after the formalites, the men took up position on the left of the 1st Brigade's earthworks, with the 56th Regiment on the right, in the second line of defense about one hundred yards behind the front trenches. There they remained for two days.[11]

As George Barton had mentioned in one of his letters, First Lieutenant E. Dexter Cheney of Company B was killed on the 19th of July. He had been on his way to observe some of the mortars firing from the Union batteries early that morning. He was supposed to have been accompanied by several other officers of the regiment, but at the last moment, they all begged off for one reason or another. So Eben Dexter Cheney left on his own to have some fun watching the artillerymen pound the Rebels. But ten minutes after he had gone, one of the enlisted men ran up to Major Albert Prescott's hut, breathlessly announcing that the lieutenant had just been shot through the head by a Southern sharpshooter. The major and some of his brother officers took off on the run down through the zigzagging trenches, sprinting to the lieutenant's aid, but when they arrived they found a mortally wounded Cheney with blood and brains oozing from his wound onto the ground, and they knew that they were helpless. The twenty-one-year-old clerk and veteran of the 51st Massachusetts died shortly afterward, and his body was embalmed and sent home to Worcester for burial.[12]

Later that morning, dark storm clouds appeared over the trenches, and the heavens soon opened up, pouring a vigorous summer rainstorm onto the men. At first the cooling relief was welcome, but the showers kept a steady pace, soaking the soldiers and filling the trenches with ankle-deep water. The dusty earth quickly turned to sticky mud, and officers and men alike had a miserable sleep as the showers continued all through the night and into the next day along with a thick fog that reduced forward visibility, making them anxious and wary that the Confederates might take advantage of the conditions and stage an attack on their lines. But nothing unusual happened. After noon on July 20, the rain let up, and the clouds gave way to the hot Virginia sun. The deluge had been a mixed blessing. It was the first precipitation of any consequence that had fallen in six weeks, so the creeks and springs were replenished somewhat and the dust settled, but the oppressive humidity that lingered in its wake made everybody feel sticky and miserable, and the mosquitoes and flies swarmed around in droves everywhere, biting the men viciously and unmercifully. The mud, too, was hardly welcome and the men were covered with it. It was past argument that there was any joy or comfort to be found in trench warfare.[13]

The intrepid first sergeant of Company I, Edwin McFarland, who had fought in all of the regiment's engagements without serious injury, was wounded on that 20th of July while on duty in the rifle pits. A Confederate bullet slammed through both of his wrists, putting him out of active duty for the rest of the war. When he had recovered sufficiently for light duty, however, he was transferred—as were many of the soldiers in the 57th, as well as those in other regiments in the army, who had nondebilitating wounds—to the army's Veteran Reserve Corps, a unit organized for men permanently unfit for front-line duty but capable of serving as prison camp guards, hospital and provost guards, and in other similar duties in the rear and in different parts of the country.[14]

The Veteran Reserve Corps, or V.R.C., had begun as the Invalid Corps under General Orders No. 105 issued by the War Department on April 28, 1863. But the name was changed to the Veteran Reserve Corps by the War Department's General Orders No. 111, dated March 18, 1864, because the men who served in its ranks, veterans to a man injured in the line of duty, and proud of that distinction, were disatisfied with the Invalid Corps' initials, which they were required to wear prominently on the left breast of their sky-blue uniform shell jackets. *I.C.* were the initials stamped by military inspectors on government goods of inferior and unusable quality, and they stood for "inspected and condemned." The men in the ranks had often taunted the Invalid Corps' soldiers with humiliating references to the initials, and those wounded veterans had had enough, finally succeeding in having their unit's name changed.

Two battalions comprised the V.R.C. The 1st Battalion was composed of men whose injuries were relatively light, and who, therefore, were still capable of performing many of the duties of a healthy soldier, such as marching and using a weapon. Often, those men were posted to guard duties. The guard detachments at prisoner of war camps at Point Lookout, Maryland, Elmira, New York, Johnson's Island, Ohio, and others were made up of 1st Battalion men. They were employed as provost marshals, engaged in arresting bounty jumpers and other deserters, quelling riots and civil disturbances, and enforcing the draft laws. Unwilling recruits, untrustworthy substitutes, and prisoners, Union and Confederate, were guarded by them to and from the front. Railroads were picketed by those men, and many of the sentries in Washington were 1st Battalion soldiers. The 2nd Battalion, on the other hand, mustered men with more serious wounds, even in some instances amputees. Cooks, nurses, and orderlies were generally the assignments for those troops. During the war there were only a third to half as many men in the 2nd Battalion as there were in the 1st.

There were twenty-four regiments in the V.R.C., and, as originally organized, the 1st Battalion's regiments each contained six companies while the 2nd Battalion's had four. The V.R.C. was credited with rendering excellent service throughout its existence, freeing many hundreds of healthy men for front-line duty who would have otherwise had to perform the tasks undertaken by the Veteran Reserve Corps.[15]

★

Since 1863, when the Army of the Potomac was commanded by Major General Joseph Hooker, patches of cloth cut in various shapes had been worn officially by the soldiers in all the Union armies to identify them as belonging to a corps and a particular division within it. The IX Corps had never adopted a badge until April 10, 1864, when General Burnside ordered one to be used, under General Orders No. 6 from his headquarters. General Orders No. 10, issued shortly thereafter, defined its design. The IX Corps' badge was elaborate compared with those of the other organizations, and it consisted of an anchor crossed with a cannon barrel and a fouled rope line meandering through them that was partially shaped in the form of the numeral 9. All of that was placed on a device in the pattern of a shield—a complex little affair. Its configuration symbolized the amphibious operations in which the corps had engaged during its campaign in North Carolina earlier in the war. The enlisted men were instructed to cut out the outline of the shield only and sew or pin it onto their hats, caps, or tunics. Each division had a different color: red for the first, white for the second, sky blue for the third, and green for the fourth. The men were allowed to substitute custom-made emblems. "Those who desire can also wear a medal of the same design, made of gold or gilt, silver or white metal, bronze or copper, to be attached to the left breast of the coat as a pin suspended by a red, white, and blue [and presumably green] ribbon. The designs for this badge are now in the hands of Messrs. Tiffany & Co., New York, and samples will be at headquarters about the 27th [of April]."[16]

The badge had been worn laxly in the IX Corps ranks, and on July 20, corps headquarters issued orders requiring all the men to affix it to their uniforms at once.

In the 57th, the men cut out their two-inch-square badges from scrap red flannel and attached them to the crowns of their caps by pinning their brass regimental numbers, 5 and 7, in their centers positioned above the hunting-horn insignia of the infantry. Many of them, particularly the officers, purchased the commercially available metal devices from sutlers and stores, and, as time went on, the regiment's men, as well as most all IX Corps soldiers, took the same great pride in their symbol as did the other army corps in theirs, and many of the war's survivors wore them proudly for the rest of their lives.[17]

★

Lieutenant Colonel Napoleon Bonaparte McLaughlen, a forty-one-year-old regular army veteran from Chelsea, Vermont, was assigned command of the 57th Massachusetts Regiment on July 21, but he did not actually assume his duties until September 14. McLaughlen had begun his military career in

1850, when he enlisted as a private soldier in the 2nd United States Dragoons. Having risen to the rank of sergeant, at the outbreak of the war he was commissioned second lieutenant in the 1st United States Cavalry and finally promoted to captain in the 4th United States Cavalry in August 1862. In the fall of that year he accepted a commission from the commonwealth in the 1st Massachusetts Volunteer Infantry. He was breveted major at the battle of Chancellorsville in early May 1863, for "gallant and meritorious service," and lieutenant colonel at the battle of Gettysburg, two months later, for the same reason, but he was not finished with his rise in rank for "gallant and meritorious service" by any means.

N. B. McLaughlen wore his hair short on top of his stern, angular face with its square chin and dark, deep-set eyes, and although he grew no beard, half his face seemed hidden behind his huge walrus mustache. He was a strict and formal regular army disciplinarian who expected rigid obedience to his orders, and he had little use for volunteer troops. When he finally joined the regiment that fall, the soldiers of the 57th would think him an outsider, an interloper, and a martinet as he strutted around with his chest puffed out and shoulders thrown back. A Frank Bartlett he was not.[18]

Cool breezes and fair skies prevailed on the 21st, and the trenches were drying out, making them more habitable and improving the mood of the soldiers.

★

The breechloading Spencer repeating rifles, thirty-four of them, with their tubular seven-shot magazines running through the buttstocks, finally had arrived for sharpshooter Company K on the evening of July 19, and the men were thrilled with their up-to-date firearms. "Have tried our rifles some this forenoon and like them first rate," wrote Francis Harrington in his diary several days later. Harrington, as a member of Company K, had, of course, been issued one of the Spencers. (The other companies were equally admiring—and quite envious.) First Lieutenant John H. Cook recently had been given command of that company, and on the morning of July 21, he ordered it on a foray to test the new weapons. The Company K men felt they could lick the entire Army of Northern Virginia with their lever-action rifles as Cook led them over the top of the parapet and into a patch of woods between the lines to hunt some Southern army game. When the soldiers of Company K were concealed behind some pines, they sighted in on the Confederate pickets across the open ground in front and fired away at them with their new .52 caliber, rimfire copper-cartridge guns. They soon grew overconfident with their superior firepower, though, and Lieutenant Cook, thinking himself invincible, stepped completely around from behind the cover of his tree to fire at a Rebel picket, but the Confederate beat that foolishly exposed officer to the punch, squeezing the trigger first and blowing a gaping, messy hole in the lieutenant's side with his muzzleloading Enfield. Cook's comrades swiftly drove off the enemy with their hammering Spencer repeaters, and, picking up their wounded officer, they beat a hasty path back to the 57th's trenches. Cook was taken to the division field hospital where Doctor White removed the bullet, which had come to rest in the injured man's spine. The lieutenant remained on the verge of death for some time, but because he was basically in very good physical condition, he eventually recovered enough to receive a medical discharge from the service and go home. He lived for many years, finally succumbing to complications of his wound at his home in Roxbury, Massachusetts, in August of 1893.[19]

Lieutenant Barton described the events of July 21 to his mother:

> *"On Picket"*
> *near Petersburg*
> *Va*
> July 21, 1864

Dear Mother

There I am on Picket again, let me attempt to give you some idea of my situation just at this present moment

Reclining in a "pit" or more like a half made grave only wider with the dirt thrown up on either side just high enough to protect me from the minnies. A rubber blanket under and a piece of shelter tent over me stretched upon four ramrods to protect me from the sun—no small item by the way—for a writing desk I have half the cover of an ammunition box, with a pencil about an inch and a half long—Shot & Shell from both sides pass and repass my *rat hole* frequently—then shells bursting short of their *intended* destination make your humble subscriber decidedly nervous, to say the *least.* What a *fearful noise* they do make—There *goes* one *now*—I cant describe it in writing, but if I ever get *home,* and *do* not forget the *sound,* which I *could* not if I *would*—I will give you an imitation of it. Oh! Well, never mind—the saying here is that a *"Miss* is as good as a *mile of old women"* 12 o ck M. I have just sent my orderly after my grub, and told him to enquire at the Hd. Qrs. of the regiment if there were any letters for me, for I always make it a rule to expect a letter *every* mail— though I oftentimes get "specks in my eyes" as the boys say

How the flies do bite! What were they made for, unless to vex soldiers in warm weather, or hazy [sic] in the kitchen?

We expect music [battle] here before long—Hope Lee will not be able to draw Gen. Grant away from here, by that raid toward Washington—

The sixth Corps has already gone from here, & more may go

Tonight our *Regmt* and some portion of the *Brigade* will go to the *rear,* for a couple of days to wash up—inspect &c. We need it *bad*—

Well mother this is pretty hard for an *old man* of my age! *Guess* we shall be *able* to *stand it* I dont allow myself to *think* a great deal about peaseful homes &c. but bone right down to sterne every day war & blood letting! Here I stop the flies plague me so that I cant write. . . . —George[20]

First Lieutenant John Goodwin returned to duty with Company H at that time after recuperating from a thigh wound he had received in the Wilderness. Within two days, while on duty in the trenches on July 22, the unlucky Goodwin was shot severely in the top of his right foot by a Rebel sharpshooter, the bullet fracturing several bones and requiring the partial amputation of the extremity. His army days were ended, and he was discharged later for his disability. But Goodwin, a veteran of the 25th Massachusetts, had seen too much hard service, and its effects caught up with him quickly. In 1867, just twenty-five years old, he passed away from consumption, contracted while in uniform during the war.[21]

★

Shortly after sending packages of hometown newspapers to the soldiers of the 1st Brigade announcing his arrival and giving notice of his kind intentions toward his men, William Francis Bartlett returned to duty on July 23 with a brand-new star in the center of his shoulder straps. He had been promoted to the rank of brevet brigadier general while he was absent wounded and assigned permanent command of the 1st Brigade, and he was there to relieve Colonel Gould of his temporary position.

More suited to regimental command, the colonel objected not in the slightest to his reassignment to the 59th Massachusetts. Although the men of the 57th liked him well enough because he was the type of officer that was always out in front of his troops and never shirked his duties, they never felt that Jacob Parker Gould would stay on as permanant brigade chief, and they welcomed Bartlett eagerly because they trusted his judgment and courage, and were acquainted with him personally. Even though not all of the men of the regiment liked him, they all respected him as a good officer and leader, and his return to duty and new assignment brought a sense of security to the soldiers of the 57th Regiment.[22]

As the new general took charge that hot day the brigade could count but 1300 men present for duty on its muster rolls. The regiments of Bartlett's new command, all but one from Massachusetts (the brigade had been reorganized again), averaged only just over 200 men each—about enough soldiers to make up slightly more than one full-strength regiment. All of those outfits had been luckier than the 57th, and their ranks contained many more than its 100-odd remaining combat soldiers.[23]

Brigadier General Bartlett set up brigade headquarters some two hundred and fifty yards in the rear of his regiments' lines and immediately put some of his men to work felling trees and surrounding his quarters with a four-foot-high stockade. He kept the brigade bandsmen, also protected by a stockade, playing at intervals twenty-four hours a day for his pleasure and amusement and the enjoyment of his command. Unlike Ledlie, however, Bartlett doled out the music to the brigade in measured amounts, and this time, the men did not complain. One day soon after arriving at Petersburg, as he was writing a letter attempting to describe conditions along the lines, he counted the number of shots that he could hear per minute from his concealed position and concluded that one or two rounds were fired from small arms each second in his area of command alone, without cease, day and night. "The bullets patter like rain at times," he wrote, "against the outside of this stockade. . . . It is a continual rattle of musketry, sometimes swelling into a roar along the line, varied with the artillery and mortars. . . ." And in another letter the general described the firing: " 'Zip, prrr' goes another bullet. . . . Bullets flying very lively tonight." And "the bullets are singing around my tent as usual. 'Spat'—there goes one into a tree, making the bark fly."24

Even though the men respected him and were glad to see him, their feelings towards Frank Bartlett, in many cases, would have been similar to those of the peasant for the lord of the manor, for Bartlett was an aristocrat, a Harvard man, and he surely held little truck with fraternizing with his low-born, plebian soldiers except for the rare enlisted man on his social and intellectual level who was in the ranks by choice. To the new brigadier, the common soldiers were just that—common.

★

July 24 began as a fair summer day. The regiment had moved to the front-line trenches the night before and some of the enlisted men were engaged in rebuilding and repairing damaged officers' bombproof quarters with logs and dirt. After church services, several of the 57th's officers and Captain Warren B. Galucia of the 56th Massachusetts, who was the 1st Brigade's Officer of the Day that Sunday, had gathered outside one of the 57th's hot, six-foot-square, bombproof officers' huts, which were dug into the ground twenty feet behind the regiment's lines. The men were telling stories and jokes, smoking their pipes, and just having a generally pleasant time chatting the warm afternoon away under an arbor of green pine boughs and old canvas that provided some shade from the beating sun. The bombproof was located to the left of and fairly near a Union battery that was dueling with its Confederate counterpart across the lines, and both sides were lobbing ten-inch mortar shells at each other. Lieutenant John Anderson, of Company E, was sitting on an empty hardtack box underneath the arbor, and Second Lieutenant Charles Royce, of Company C, was lying on a blanket reading newspapers that had been received recently, while the others in the group carried on with their conversations. Company A's First Lieutenant Samuel Bowman soon joined the little assembly of officers after he returned from the 1st Division hospital, where he had been visiting his friend, Lieutenant Cook, whom no one at that time expected to live. Bowman mentioned to John Anderson that

Cook wanted to see him very much, and Anderson, thinking he had little time to lose in doing all he could for his wounded comrade, got up right away and began walking to the hospital in the rear. Meanwhile, Lieutenant Bowman took over the hardtack box vacated by John Anderson and began writing a letter to his fiancée.

Anderson had not gotten very far when he heard a loud explosion in the vicinity of the bombproof, and quickly he turned around to see smoke and dust in the air above it. Returning on the run, he found the quarters partially destroyed, and all of the officers lying wounded in the wreckage, including newly commissioned First Lieutenant Albert Doty, in command of Company K since July 22 but still retaining his duties as acting regimental sergeant major, who had been part of the gathering also. A stray Confederate mortar shell intended for the Federal battery had, with no warning, plowed into the arbor, exploding, and had blown it and part of the hut to fragments.

Most of the dazed, bewildered officers, three of whom were seriously injured, stood up and beat their arms in the air to clear the smoke and dust so they could assess the damage done, and when they were able to see again, they found the bleeding, mangled Bowman lying mortally wounded in the debris. Aside from other injuries, one of his legs had been shattered, the thigh mangled. He died several hours later from his terribly painful wounds, his last letter to his sweetheart only just begun and never to be finished. Lieutenant Royce had been sliced up the back by a sharp fragment of the shell as if he had been slit open with a skinning knife, and his left leg had been severely burned and peppered by flying granules of unburned black powder and sand kicked up in the explosion. Captain Galucia had the toes of both feet blown back and impacted by the concussion of the blast. George Barton, another member of the group that day, and Doty received only minor cuts and abrasions. Men from the regiment came running to the aid of their officers, some of whom they liked and respected, and helped them to the field hospital in the rear.[25]

Once again we turn to Barton for an eyewitness account of the event and subsequent happenings on that July 24, which he wrote about in a letter home later that day.

I am now acting as Adjutant, and am driven all most "up a tree" there being so few Officers with the Regiment and the "Johnnies" are reducing us more & still more every day. Within the last six days we have lost, six Officers, one *Killed instantly,* and *two* more that *may die* of their wounds. The remainder have *bad wounds.* My quarters Hd. Qrs. are in a hole in the ground about six feet square Covered over with *logs* and *dirt.* There is a little space in front of the *pit* that is *not covered.* Just before I began to write A *bomb shell* Struck in this open space where sat *three* Officers while *I* was sitting *inside,* with the *Acting Sergeant Major* [Doty]—one of the Officers of the three was a Capt. [Galucia] 'Brigade Officer of the Day' from the 56th Mass. and two Officers of the 57th Lieut S. M. Bowman 1st Lieut of A Co. and Charles H. Royce 2d Lieut *C Co.* The shell exploded scattering the pieces in every direction didnt I *hug Mother* earth Oh: no "perhaps not." In an instant the pit was *full* of *smoke.* The *concussion alone sent me over* to the corner of the pit. I knew "Nothing Much" for about 2 minutes. My *first step* was to learn the *fate* of my comrades. There lay poor *Bowman* his *leg and thigh* badly mutilated his wounds I fear will prove *mortal* Lieut Royce 2d lieut of my Company C was badly burnt with *powder* do not know the extent of his injuries but think they are not serious. Oh! it was *tough!* And *is* hard to see one after *Another* taken off until you stand all most alone. I *count* this as another very narrow escape for *me,* a piece of shell just cleaning the top of my head, struck a log and bounded back into the pit. . . .

There! A shell struck this *very minute,* not one rod from this Hd. Qrs. The "Major" [Albert Prescott] jumped and tiped my *ink bottle over.* But as I said to the Acting Sm [sergeant major] this letter must be finished, and sent off tonight Shells or no Shells. We shall move from this position tonight I tell you this to comfort you a little for I think you must need it I am sure I do. . . . *Another man: Shot dead* Geo. R. Hubbard [known to his comrades as "Query"] Private Co. B shot by a sharp-shooter. If we lose *one man* for *every day* how many days will it take to use up *one regiment?*[26]

It had been a tragedy, the enlisted men felt—they were almost out of leaders. The rain poured down again that night, and many of the boys must have found it symbolic in light of the afternoon's catastrophe.[27]

★

During the storm that night of July 24, the brigade was ordered out of its trenches and moved to the rear for dress parade in preparation for another inspection and review on the 26th. Clean yourselves up as best you can, the first sergeants told their men, and make sure your guns and gear are in good shape.[28]

The following day, the regiments of the 1st Brigade formed their pitiful little lines at nine-thirty in the morning, and they marched lethargically in review past their division and brigade commanders, Ledlie and Bartlett, and their staffs. The inspections were completed at one-thirty that afternoon. Mr. Ledlie, ever so careful of his personal safety, had chosen an area well to the rear and out of range of Rebel artillery, and as the scruffy veterans marched by him, they felt nothing but contempt and disgust for their reprehensible commander and for this silly, time-wasting parading when they had a real war to fight. General Bartlett was embarrassingly disappointed with his regiments, and he later remarked that they "did not make a very good appearance," and that the "officers, even of the old regiments," like the 35th Massachusetts, were "ignorant." This referred to their lack of knowledge and proficiency in drilling their men, and some of the officers were in turn embarrassed by his comments, but the enlisted men, for the most part, could not have cared less. They had more important things to worry them than fancy parade marching, and the vast majority of them seldom gave a second thought to what anybody in shoulder straps said or felt about their abilities to drill properly.[29]

★

During that six-week period in the Petersburg trenches, the 57th lost two officers and 8 enlisted men killed or mortally wounded, 1 dead from a probable coronary, and 23 wounded, for a total loss of 34 soldiers. And there was a constant exodus of men moving to the hospitals to be treated for disease, largely bowel complaints. Some of the men wounded in earlier battles or who had been sick were beginning to return to the regiment, but their numbers could not make up for those men being taken out almost daily from death, wounds, and illness. The regiment was getting progressively smaller and smaller—just withering away from war's attrition. There were fewer than 100 men on the regimental line at the end of the month of July.[30]

The only combat officers remaining on duty by July 29 were Albert Prescott from Charlestown, Massachusetts, formerly captain of Company I, who had been promoted to major and given temporary command of the regiment on June 17, after Major Tucker had been wounded in the assault; Second Lieutenant John Reade; First Lieutenant George Barton; Second Lieutenant John Anderson; and the recently promoted First Lieutenant Albert Doty, mostly recovered from his slight wounds of five days earlier, who was appointed the new regimental adjutant.[31]

The 57th's commander, Major Prescott, was a roly-poly little man with a goatee, whom the men liked for his easygoing personality. But he fretted constantly about the fate of his family should he be killed, and his melancholy was perceived clearly by the boys, who knew that the quality of their leadership was deteriorating steadily, and that they were certain to pay the price for it.[32]

★

"July 29, 1864 Friday," noted Francis Harrington. "In our original position in front line where we came just after dark last night. Orders just rec'd. pack up and be ready to move."[33]

And move they would.

17

Rumors

A LL THROUGH the Army of the Potomac during the month of July rumors abounded, scarcely believable tales partly started by the appearance of some Pennsylvania soldiers, covered in yellow dirt and clay, who had been seen from time to time since the closing days of June at the sutlers' stores in the rear. The story circulating among the men was that a group of their fellow soldiers had been digging a mine shaft through a small hill, the entrance located just in the rear of Burnside's trenches, clear across to the Confederate works. And, the rumors continued, within a matter of days, the Southerners, scarcely one hundred yards distant from the IX Corps front lines, were going to be blown to kingdom come. The gossip was so pervasive and persuasive that even the Rebels had gotten wind of it—perhaps picking up the tales initially from a Yankee braggart during the nightly trading parties that occurred between the Union and Confederate sentries in the less hostile portions of the miles-long Petersburg picket lines.

But the Confederate officers were skeptical when they learned the intelligence, most feeling such a project to be impossible. They reasoned that to dig a tunnel more than four hundred feet long without fresh air ventilation was an engineering impossibility, and to install vents would give its location away immediately. Since no such structures had been observed anywhere along the lines, ergo the Yankee project was a product of someone's lively imagination. Although the Rebel commanders did not believe the shaft was being constructed, they had their men dig vertical holes in the earth to probe for it anyway, just to be on the safe side. But, despite their efforts, the Southerners found nothing, just as their officers had presumed.[1]

Nevertheless, the stories persisted on both sides of the lines. The Federal soldiers took the rumors of the mine as gospel, but as to the date and time of its detonation and the strategy to be associated with that detonation, they had no clue. The prognostications continued without cease in the Yankee camps, and the sages in the Union ranks finally realized an affair of major proportions was afoot during the early morning hours of Wednesday, July 27, when the shamrock corps, the II, was ordered to the north side of the James River at Deep Bottom near Chapin's Bluff as a diversionary force. Part of the II Corps' mission was to attempt to lure Robert E. Lee into removing a large portion of the Army of Northern Virginia from the Petersburg trenches and send it in pursuit, thus clearing the defensive lines at the front for the planned Union onslaught. (This, however, was not immediately known to those who remained at Petersburg.) At the same time, two divisions of the Army of the Potomac's cavalry were to accompany the II Corps, and with the infantrymen protecting the rear, the troopers were to destroy the bridges of the Virginia Central Railroad over the North and South Anna rivers, as well as the span on the Little River. The movement of the II Corps was a sign of something big happening—at long last—in the dormant Union army, but how its actions would tie into the explosion of the mine completely eluded the soldiers. That somehow it would, however, was doubted by almost no one.

All through the dark hours that morning of July 27 the men of the 57th Massachusetts, like the rest of the Northerners, could hear the rumble made by the marching Union troops as the II Corps, preceded by General David Gregg's and General A. T. A. Torbett's divisions of Federal cavalry, slipped around behind and to the right of the Federal army. The noise created by those moving columns was loud and conspicuous, and well it was intended to be, for the commotion was choreographed to impress upon General Lee that Ulysses Simpson Grant had something rather large in mind.

The Confederates, just as planned, could hear clearly the II Corps' men and the accompanying horse soldiers, and the ruse worked. Lee sent most of his hard-bitten veterans—four divisions of infantry and two of cavalry—double-quicking it up to the south bank of the James to dig in hard and fast and put the brakes on any new flanking movement planned by the Union commander-in-chief. Only about eighteen thousand Southern fighters were left to man the trenches at Petersburg—a better situation than what the fox, Sam Grant, had hoped for.[2]

Major General Winfield Scott Hancock, the II Corps' commander, had orders from the lieutenant general commanding that, if he, Hancock, found the Rebels too strongly fortified when he reached his new position on the James, he was to return his command to the main lines at Petersburg immediately and fall in as support for an upcoming offensive. Besides reinforcing the cavalry, his primary infantry objective at Deep Bottom was a feint, Grant told him; his secondary goal was to pound Lee to pieces if conditions proved favorable.[3]

★

230

Meanwhile, the IX Corps remained in its position in the lines in front of the fourteen-gun battery known as Fort Morton, which was about eight hundred yards east of the Confederate post at Elliott's Salient. The Rebel works there contained a four-gun redan battery and Brigadier General Stephen Elliott's brigade, composed of the 18th and part of the 23rd South Carolina Volunteer Infantry regiments. The rough and wiry campaigners of those regiments and others in the Confederate trenches in the vicinity continued to maintain a brutal and intense fire at all times on the 57th and the rest of the IX Corps because of the 4th Division black troops. In the rear of Elliott's South Carolina brigade was a ridge of small hills west of the Jerusalem Plank road, where very active and annoying Confederate marksmen and several other Southern batteries were entrenched, trying to shoot anything wearing blue that moved. Everyone was constantly on the alert, and relaxation was virtually unknown in that part of the Federal forward lines.[4]

★

In General Robert B. Potter's 2nd Division of the IX Corps was a regiment of its 1st Brigade made up mostly of anthracite coal miners from eastern Pennsylvania. This outfit was the 48th Pennsylvania Volunteer Infantry, commanded by a mining engineer named Henry Pleasants, who held the rank of lieutenant colonel. Pleasants had been born in Buenos Aires, Argentina, to a gunrunning father and a Spanish mother and later educated in the United States, and he and his men were some very tough customers who had been in the war almost since the first shots of 1861.[5]

As he was milling among his troops one day in late June, Colonel Pleasants chanced to overhear one of the enlisted men of the 48th's Company C discussing with some of his messmates the possibility that the fort at Elliot's Salient could be blown up if only a mine shaft could be dug under the Confederate works and a powder charge detonated in it. The private's idea lingered in the colonel's mind, and after seriously weighing the pros and cons of the notion and receiving favorable reactions to it from two friends, Captain George Gowan of the 48th and Captain Frank Farquhar, chief engineer of the XVIII Corps, he concluded that such a project was quite feasible. Enthusiastically, Pleasants then approached his commanding officer, Robert Potter, and laid the scheme before him, and that general, in turn, saw the merit of the plan. Together the two officers traveled over to IX Corps headquarters to pay a visit to Ambrose Burnside, their venerated chief.[6]

Major General Burnside also liked what he heard and immediately went to the commander of the Army of the Potomac, George Gordon Meade. Meade, however, was not sold on the probability of the success of such a bold plan, and he was reinforced hastily by his West Point–trained professionals of the army's Engineer Corps, particularly Major James C. Duane, who ridiculed the plan as a pipe dream. To a man, the engineers held that a tunnel as long as Pleasants was proposing could not be ventilated without giving away its position and that the colonel's men would either be suffocated from lack of air or buried by a cave-in. Colonel Pleasants dismissed their opinions as "all clap-trap and nonsense." Even so, it was not until it came to the attention of the lieutenant general that Henry Pleasants made any progress with his idea.[7]

When U. S. Grant was apprised of the project, he saw some credence in the scheme and thought it just might work, and he overruled Meade and the engineers and gave the go-ahead to the young Pennsylvania colonel. If nothing else, the project might bolster the troops' sagging morale—give them something to hang onto, he reasoned. The mining engineer turned soldier also was promised full cooperation from the army's Engineer Corps, in addition to all the material that he would require to see the construction through.

So, on June 25, Henry Pleasants set the four hundred men of his 48th Pennsylvania to work digging around the clock, while he and his officers supervised. The promised help from the engineers never materialized, and the colonel had to improvise everything. He dismantled a bridge for lumber, and when that supply was exhausted, he operated an old sawmill in the rear for shoring timber, hauled dirt away in used hardtack boxes, hiding it in brush behind the lines to keep it out of Confederate view, and shortened and straightened the tines of standard army picks at the division's blacksmith's shops in order to turn them into the variety used in mining operations.[8]

But the most imaginative product of his engineering skills lay in his solution to the ventilation question. This problem he ingeniously overcame by building a twenty-seven-foot-long, two-foot-square vertical shaft at the mouth of the tunnel and lighting a fire under it. He then fitted an airtight canvas cover over the entranceway and ran a square wooden box pipe up as far as the shaft had been excavated, adding new sections as the work progressed. Because hot air rises, the fire, which was kept burning continuously, day and night, drew the foul air up the chimney, while the wooden pipe, in turn, sucked fresh air from the outside into the void. It worked perfectly, and the Union army's skeptics were silenced and the Confederates deceived. More important, of course, the miner-soldiers were able to continue their labors without fear of suffocation.[9]

By July 17, the main gallery of the mine—511.8 feet long and 4 feet high by 5 feet wide—was finished, stopping 20 feet below the Confederate fort. (Using a borrowed and obsolete theodolite, Pleasants had been able to triangulate the exact directions and distances for his tunnel from the parapets of the front trench lines, albeit under the demanding condition of having to expose himself fully to sniper fire in order to sight the transit and take readings for his trigonometric calculations. Strangely, none of the Confederate sharpshooters seemed to connect his activity with the rumors of the mine. And more strangely, he was never even scratched by the marksmen, possibly because he had had his own men, as a ruse, put their caps on their bayonets and stick them over the parapets to draw Rebel fire away from him.)[10]

On the following day, July 18, lateral shafts were started at the end of the tunnel underneath the Confederate redoubt, extending 37 feet to the left and 38 feet to the right. (The total distance of the completed project was 586.8 feet, with 18,000 cubic feet of earth excavated.) At six-thirty in the evening of Saturday, July 23, the entire project was complete. Henry Pleasants and his staff inspected the tunnel, and the colonel nodded his approval. The following morning, he reported to General Meade that all was ready and that the black powder now could be installed in the magazines that had been dug into the walls of the lateral galleries.[11]

In those right-angled caches was placed a total of 8,000 pounds of black powder in 320 black-painted wooden kegs. The gunpowder arrived at Petersburg by mule train from Fort Monroe at Hampton Roads on Chesapeake Bay early on the morning of Thursday, July 27. The men began putting it in place at once. But when it came time to attach the fuses, the miners discovered that the requisitioned material for them had not been sent, and they had to make do with splicing together short fuses that Pleasants had foraged.[12]

Meanwhile, the Confederates, some of whom thought that they could hear the dull, faint sounds of digging and movement in the earth below them, continued to sink a few more vertical shafts trying to find the mine, but those were halfhearted attempts, as the Rebel officers still insisted that the project could not be accomplished under any circumstances without exposed ventilation, that the rumors flying around from the Yankee lines were perpetrated for the sole purpose of unnerving them and their soldiers, and that their own jittery men were hearing things as a result.

★

During the time that all of the tunneling was going on, the IX Corps—because it held the position opposite from where the mine would explode—was ordered to prepare part of its force for the initial attack coordinated to take place immediately following the detonation. The 4th Division had seen no fighting of any consequence since its organization, and the black soldiers were spoiling for a chance at their former masters. Accordingly, Burnside had ordered them to begin training in the rear areas of the Federal front for the assault that would follow the explosion of the mine. Their fervor aside, the primary reason that they had been chosen was that the other three divisions had been under fire perpetually since crossing the Rapidan in May, and they were decimated and thoroughly worn out, while the black regiments were relatively fresh and unscathed. Another reason was that from their long stay behind the protection of the trench walls the men of the other divisions had grown increasingly gun-shy, and the IX Corps brass, quite correctly, questioned their ability to force a strong offensive.

The all-white officer corps of General Ferrero's division was ecstatic that they had been chosen to spearhead the advance. No one knew for sure just what that new offensive entailed, but because of the gossip going around the army, everybody had a pretty good guess.

When the black soldiers were told that they were to begin preparations for the coming assault, they were proud of, but entirely sobered by, their future role. Every one of them understood that sooner or later he would have to pay the military debt he now owed for his liberty, and for that reason, in part, the blacks' original misgivings were supressed, and their outlook on their role in the future battle gradually took on the enthusiasm of a religious crusade. They also felt strongly that a victory achieved by them would help dispel the deep prejudice held against their race by their white comrades in the Federal army.

As it had not yet been engaged in any significant combat, the 4th Division, recruited from all parts of the country and organized in Philadelphia during the previous winter, was large. The 1st Brigade, commanded by Colonel Joshua K. Siegfried, ironically the former commander of the 48th Pennsylvania, had about two thousand men in four regiments—the 27th, 30th, 39th, and 43rd United States Colored Troops—and the 2nd Brigade, under the leadership of Colonel Henry Goddard Thomas, counted close to twenty-three hundred soldiers on its returns in five regiments—the 19th, 23rd, 28th, 29th, and 31st United States Colored Troops. Each day during July, one of those black regiments was rotated to the rear to practice drills and special movements that would be required for the assault. The Negro troops rapidly perfected their maneuvers, the skill of which they diligently learned, becoming obsessed with their work, and referring to it as "studying." At night the ex-slaves, now wearing blue uniforms, sang around their hundreds of campfires with great pride a military song belonging to them and them alone: "We looks like men amarchin' on / We looks like men o' war!"[13]

★

All the arrangements for the action, which had been scheduled for the morning of July 30, were being accomplished with barely a hitch, when suddenly fate's hammer struck a decisive blow. On July 26, General Burnside went to army headquarters and submitted his final battle plans to Meade and Grant. The first problem Meade saw with those plans was the use of General Ferrero's colored troops. The blacks had never been tested in battle, and their reliability in combat was unknown. Besides, if anything went wrong, he insisted, the country would be up in arms, and the abolitionists would accuse him of needlessly sacrificing black soldiers. After all, he reasoned, they were now the main issue in all this bloody business, and they could not be used wantonly. Sam Grant also saw the political ramifications of a disaster involving blacks and seconded the judgment of the commander of the Army of the Potomac, over Burnside's strong objections that they were the most suitable men available in his command and had been specially trained for that very job. "If it should prove a failure," Meade later stated, "it would then be said, and very properly, that we were shoving those people ahead to get killed because we did not care anything about them, but that could not be said if we put white troops in front."[14]

The other exception taken to the plan was tactical. Burnside wanted the leading regiments of the first division arriving on the scene—the 4th, as he had planned—to fan out its troops left and right into the Confederate trenches, sweep through the ditches and capture them, and dig in hard in the confusion which he was sure would follow the explosion. Those men would then lay down a sustained covering fire, flank and forward, for the other regiments of the 4th Division, as well as the following divisions of the IX Corps, who would then rush on to capture Cemetery Hill near the eighteenth-century brick Episcopal Blanford Church, thirteen hundred yards to the northwest of where the blast would occur. Once the three white divisions of the corps all had arrived and the targeted rise was secured, the blacks would then proceed on to take the town. With the majority of Lee's army off on a wild goose chase after Hancock's infantrymen and Sheridan's cavalry, Burnside felt strongly that as soon as the hill, located in the easternmost outskirts of the city of Petersburg and just north of the waterworks, was taken, he and his men could virtually walk in unopposed and capture the city intact. (So confident was the IX Corps commander in the outcome of his plan, he had his baggage packed prior to the day of the attack and ready to move into Petersburg with his victorious troops.) Meade thought so, too, but he felt the operation would have more chance of success—and would be far less complicated—if the first division into the Confederate lines continued on to take Cemetery Hill at once, and the two following divisions fanned out as support for it, with a backup advance then being initiated by the 4th Division against the slope, reinforced if necessary by reserve elements of the XVIII, V, and the newly arrived X Corps of the Army of the James.

Those objections and subsequent changes took a while for Meade and Grant to formulate in detail, and the final meeting communicating them to Burnside did not take place until noon on July 29—the eleventh hour.[15]

General Meade, with General Grant's approval, instructed General Burnside orally that he was to "lose no time after passing through the crater [that would form as a result of the explosion] in seizing the crest beyond, known as Cemetery Hill," and then reiterated, "lose no time in making formations, but rush for the crest." Meade then issued the following written orders that same day to all the appropriate commanders of the Army of the Potomac:

1. As soon as dark, Major General Burnside, commanding Ninth Corps, will withdraw his two brigades under General [Julius] White, occupying the intrenchments between the [Jerusalem] plank and the Norfolk roads, and bring them to his front. Care will be taken not to interfere with the troops of the Eighteenth Corps moving into their position in rear of the Ninth Corps. General Burnside will form his troops for assaulting the enemy's works at daylight of the 30th, prepare his parapets and abatis for the passage of the columns, and have the pioneers equipped for work in opening passages for artillery, destroying the enemy's abatis, etc., and the intrenching tools distributed for effecting lodgments, etc.

2. Major General Warren, commanding Fifth Corps, will reduce the number of his troops holding the intrenchments of his front to the minimum, and concentrate all of his available force on his right and hold them prepared to support the assault of Major General Burnside. The preparations in respect to pioneers, intrenching tools, etc., enjoined upon the Ninth Corps, will also be made by the Fifth Corps.

3. As soon as it is dark Major General [E.O.C.] Ord, commanding Eighteenth Corps, will relieve his troops in the trenches by General Mott's division of the Second Corps, and form his corps in rear of the Ninth Corps, and be prepared to support the assault of Major General Burnside.

4. Every preparation will be made for moving forward the field artillery of each corps.

5. At dark Major General Hancock, commanding the Second Corps, will move from Deep Bottom to the rear of the intrenchments now held by the Eighteenth Corps, resume the command of Mott's division and be prepared at daylight to follow up the assaulting and supporting column, or for such other operations as may be found necessary.

6. Major General Sheridan, commanding Cavalry Corps will proceed at dark from the vicinity of Deep Bottom to Lee's Mill, and at daylight will move with his whole corps, including Wilson's division, against the enemy's troops, defending Petersburg on their right, by the roads leading from the southward and westward.

7. Major Duane, acting Chief Engineer, will have the pontoon trains parked at convenient points in the rear, prepared to move. He will see that supplies of sand bags, gabions, fascines, etc., are in depot, near the lines, ready for use. He will detail engineer officers for each corps.

8. At half past three in the morning of the 30th, Major General Burnside will spring his mine, and his assaulting columns will immediately move rapidly upon the breach, seize the crest in rear, and effect a lodgment there. He will be followed by Major General Ord, who will support him on the right, directing his movement to the crest indicated, and by Major General Warren, who will support him on the left. Upon the explosion of the mine the artillery of all kinds in battery will open upon those points of the enemy's works whose fire covers the ground over which our columns must move, care being taken to avoid impeding the progress of our troops. Special instructions respecting the direction of the fire will be issued through the Chief of Artillery.

9. Corps commanders will report to the Commanding General when their prepa-

rations are complete, and will advise him of every step in the progress of the operation and of everything important that occurs.

10. Promptitude, rapidity of execution and cordial cooperation are essential to success, and the Commanding General is confident that this indication of his expectations will insure the hearty efforts of the commanders and troops.

11. Headquarters during the operation will be at the headquarters of the Ninth Corps.

By command of

MAJOR GENERAL MEADE
[signed] S. Williams
Assistant Adjutant General[16]

At three o'clock that afternoon, following his meeting with the two top generals, Burnside called in the commanders of two of his three white divisions, Potter and Willcox, to explain the situation to them. General Ledlie was not invited to attend the conference simply because General Burnside was fed up with his ineptitude, but General Willcox was of the decided opinion that he should be briefed regardless, and at Willcox's suggestion, Burnside relented and called the commander of the 1st Division into the council. When the changes in plans were related to the three division commanders, Burnside asked which of them would volunteer his command to replace the 4th Division, and when none of his generals displayed any willingness to step forward—for the simple reason that all of their divisions were in terrible shape and in no condition to spearhead any such movement—he left his tent, returning momentarily holding three blades of grass in his hand. He told his commanders that he saw no reason to pick one division over the other to lead the assault, and that, therefore, he thought that the only fair thing to do under the circumstances was for them to draw straws, which they did. Willcox drew first, Potter second, and Ledlie third. General Ledlie drew the short straw, and the 1st Division, the 57th's—the most used-up of the three—was to have the distinction of making the initial drive.[17]

Burnside then had the following orders drawn up and issued to the IX Corps' commanders:

1. The mine will be exploded tomorrow morning at half past three, by Colonel Pleasants.

2. General Ledlie will, immediately upon the explosion of the mine, move his division forward as directed by verbal orders, and if possible, crown the crest at the point known as Cemetery Hill, occupying, if possible, the cemetery.

3. General Willcox will move his division forward as soon as possible after General Ledlie has passed through the first line of the enemy's works, bearing off to the left, so as to effectually protect the left flank of General Ledlie's column, and make a lodgment, if possible, on the Jerusalem plank road to the left of General Ledlie's division.

4. General Potter will move his division forward to the right of General Ledlie's division, and will as near as possible, protect the right flank of General Ledlie from any attack on that quarter, and establish a line on the crest of a ravine, which seems to run from the crest of Cemetery Hill nearly at right angles to the enemy's main line directly in our front.

5. General Ferrero will move his division immediately after General Willcox's until he reaches our present advanced line, where he will remain until the ground in his front is entirely cleared by the other three divisions, when he will move forward over the same ground that General Ledlie moved over, will pass through our line, and if possible move down and occupy the village to the right.[18]

Meade's orders, both oral and written, were direct and unquestionable, and Burnside's instructions, though salted with several "if possibles," were clear, if not strong.

After being thoroughly instructed orally by Burnside as to what was expected of him and the other division commanders, Ledlie returned to his headquarters and at four o'clock summoned his two brigade leaders, General William F. Bartlett and Colonel E. G. Marshall, formerly commander of the 14th New York Heavy Artillery, and some of their staff to a meeting regarding the impending action and a trip to the front near Fort Morton to look over the planned battlefield. At a little before dark, Marshall called in his assistant adjutant general, Captain Thomas W. Clarke, commander of Company A, 29th Regiment, Massachusetts Volunteer Infantry.

Captain Clarke was a thirty-one-year-old lawyer from Boston, and, with a lawyer's tenacity for detail, he later recalled the meeting held on that late summer afternoon:

The plan as given by General Ledlie to Bartlett and Marshall, and as given by Marshall to his battalion commanders, was to this effect, and it was on this plan that Marshall and Bartlett worked. The Second Brigade was to be formed in column of battalion front. [It made three lines of about four hundred men each.] On the explosion of the mine it was to move forward and occupy the enemy's works on the right of the crater, skirting its edge, but not going into it. The First Brigade was to follow with about the same front and occupy the works on the left of the crater, but not going into it. When the lodgment had been made, it was to be secured and connected to our lines by our engineer regiment, 35th Massachusetts. The Second Division was then to extend this lodgment still more to the right, the Third Division was to extend it to the left in the enemy's works by a front attack, and the colored division was then to pass through the crater and assault the hill in the rear. Marshall's distinct instructions were that the security of the lodgment was the prime duty of the First Division and the hill was a subordinate object; and General Ledlie's instructions, as heard, conveyed no other meaning to me, or, as will appear later, to General Bartlett or Adjutant Warren [Bartlett's adjutant].

The drill and habits of the First Division, accoustomed to line attacks and not to regimental column manoeuvres, were not adapted to the plan of formation designed for the colored division, with its proposed tactical conversions to right and left after the works were reached, but the ultimate effect of the manoeuvres was to be the same. The flanks were to be cleared before the attack on the hill. Marshall was explicit that his brigade was to confine its attention to seizing and holding as great a length of line on the right of the crater as possible, and that the work beyond [Cemetery Hill], to the enemy's rear, was to be done by other troops. His phrase about it was this: "When we have secured the lodgment, Ferrero will take the negroes through the crater, which we shall have left clear for them, and see what they can do beyond."[19]

Clearly Ledlie's instructions to his brigade commanders were in direct contradiction of those of Generals Meade and Burnside. Nevertheless, late in the evening of July 29, Bartlett and Marshall, in turn, gathered their regimental commanders and explained the secret plan as revealed by James Ledlie.

But the plan, of course, really was not very secret except for its details, as every front-line Union soldier in that part of the Federal trenches was by now well aware of what the 48th Pennsylvania had been up to, and the solution that they had devised to the ventilation problem was common knowledge in the ranks. The grapevine was stout in the Army of the Potomac—there had been little else to do lately but talk—and the gossipy enlisted soldiers seemed to know something about everything. The men were very much in tune with the endless buzz of chatter in the rifle pits, and they knew of Burnside's rift with Meade over the change in his plans—secrets were practically impossible to keep in that army, and they made the rounds at dizzying speeds. The Rebels learned many of them, too, and in the matter of the mine, which they still refused to believe existed, the Southerners had been ridiculing the men of the IX Corps, taunting them between the lines and yelling and joking between shots, "When you'all Yankee nigger lovers agoin' ta blow us'ns up?" and the Federals chided them back saying, " 'Fore you know it, Johnny, you'll be chasin' after your rights with your tail between your legs, clean through Rebeldom!" "Come on then, you damn Yanks!" the Rebels would answer.

The regimental commanders returned to their units after meeting with their brigade commanders and informed the other officers that they were to have their men ready to move at a moment's notice and not to tell them about the plan, but, as mentioned, the men knew almost as much as the officers did—sometimes more—and the officers knew that they knew.[20]

Except for the usual artillery duels at sundown, the night of the 29th of July was fairly quiet. The sky was clear, with a three-quarter waning moon rising in the east over the forest which skirted the nearly open area between the opposing forces, illuminating the stark landscape of the battlefield, and no one had any trouble seeing in any direction.[21]

Following the briefing with Bartlett, Major Prescott returned to the 57th's headquarters, located in a bombproof hut behind the regiment's trenches, and he and his four remaining officers sat around killing time before the attack. Albert Prescott was very despondent and depressed that evening, and he sat quietly alone, brooding about the fate of his wife and children, convinced that he would see them no more. Often he drew deep and melancholy sighs, and the other officers did their best to cheer him up, but it was no use; he was sunk in despair. "I wonder where we will all be at this time tomorrow night," he said to no one in particular, adding, "If it were not for thinking of my family, who are dependent on me, I could be as lighthearted as the rest of you." Lieutenant Barton tried to cheer up the major and the others with funny stories and jokes, and he got a laugh or two out of the only other remaining combat officers left in the regiment, Lieutenants Anderson, Reade, and Doty, but only just. Prescott, however, was not to be consoled.[22]

Captain Edson Dresser, who had formerly commanded Company D, had been detached some weeks earlier as acting ordnance officer for the 1st Division. He got wind of the change in the planned operation and late that evening dropped in at the 57th's headquarters and requested of Major Prescott that he be allowed to rejoin the regiment for the fight. Prescott gave his assent.[23]

No one slept much that night, neither the six officers nor the ninety-one enlisted men answering the combat roll call in the 57th that day. The officers talked nostalgically and forlornly about their once mighty Massachusetts regiment, and they could scarcely believe how it had been reduced to such a fragment in such a short time. There was barely anything left of its ranks, and they wagged their heads, frowning, knowing that shortly things could get much worse.[24]

At around ten o'clock that night, the boys were relieved by black troops of the XVIII Corps. The IX Corps men were directed by their commanders and sergeants to leave their trenches quietly and move to the rear. There, they lined up, filling their cartridge and cap boxes with ammunition, topping off their canteens from the wells, and stuffing their haversacks with three days' cooked rations. Following inspection, the 57th mustered with the 1st Brigade, which had assembled outside of the woods close to its base camp. After they had lain on the sandy ground for about an hour awaiting the order to move, that order finally came at about two o'clock the next morning, July 30. Falling in with other regiments of the division, the men were given their instructions, and they then moved silently and cautiously, keeping their tin cups, canteens, and bayonets from banging together, in a southerly direction, following elements of the 2nd Division along a rough and narrow army road cut through the piny woods, passing behind Taylor's chimney and the fourteen-gun battery in Union Fort Morton.[25]

Taylor's chimney was the sole remains of the home of William Byrd Taylor, which had been burned to the ground in the early stages of the war, and the tall red brick monolith, visible from long distances on the battlefield, provided a valuable geographic reference to the soldiers.[26]

Fort Morton, named for Major St. Clair Morton, who had been killed near its site during July 1864, was considered the strongest of the forts in the Federal lines at Petersburg. There, General Burnside made his headquarters in order to oversee the pending contest.[27]

The men were directed from behind the fort through the widest covered way, known as Willcox's, which zigzagged to the extreme forward earthworks of General Potter's 2nd Division's lines at a section of the Norfolk & Petersburg Railroad cut. The men of the 1st Division were totally unfamiliar with that particular stretch of Union trenches—the works had changed radically with all the Yankee construction since the area was carried in the assault way back in June—and the soldiers were entirely disoriented in them. Ordered to lie down and remain silent, the soldiers were positioned in breastworks on the far side of a small valley through which, in its lowest part in their rear, ran the foul and infested Poor Creek. Directly in front of them on a gently sloping incline was the Confederate fort at Elliott's Salient, and directly behind them was Fort Morton.[28]

The plan was for the mine to be detonated at three-thirty that morning, and shortly before then, the commanders assembled the men in their battle order to be ready to move out when the time came. The 2nd Brigade was in the van, and Colonel Marshall's outfit consisted of the Provisional 2nd Pennsylvania Heavy Artillery Regiment, a unit that had been stationed in the defenses of Washington until ordered to the front by Grant and had seen no action but for the June 17 assault; the 3rd Maryland Volunteer Infantry Battalion, about half a regiment, with tried and true veterans in its ranks; six companies of the new, but used-up, 179th New York Volunteer Infantry Regiment, another half of a regiment; and the 14th New York Heavy Artillery Regiment, an organization with a record similar to that of the 2nd Pennsylvania. The 14th Regiment was large, and recently it had been organized into two battalions of six companies each, with each battalion acting, in effect, as a separate regiment.

The 2nd Brigade was directed into three lines of battle, with the 2nd Pennsylvania in the first rank, the 3rd Maryland Regiment and 179th New York battalions in the second, and finally, the 14th New York in the third line.[29]

Following immediately behind the 2nd Brigade would be the almost all-Massachusetts 1st Brigade. General Bartlett assigned its right wing to Colonel J. P. Gould and the left to Colonel Stephen Weld. Just prior to Frank Bartlett's return to duty, the brigade, as previously mentioned, had been reorganized again, and it now was made up of the 21st, 29th, 35th, 56th, 57th, and 59th Massachusetts Volunteers along with the maverick, tough, veteran 100th Pennsylvania. The 100th Pennsylvania had returned recently from its reenlistment furlough with a number of new recruits, and it was by far the fullest regiment in the brigade, comprising some five hundred men. Bartlett's regiments had a total strength at that time, since bolstered by conscripts and returning soldiers in outfits other than the 100th Pennsylvania, of nearly eighteen hundred combat infantrymen.

Gould's right wing, taking the first line, consisted of, from left to right, the 29th Massachusetts Regiment, the 57th, commanded by Albert Prescott, and the 59th Massachusetts. Weld's left wing, placed temporarily in the 1st Brigade's second battle rank until it cleared the trenches, was composed of, from left to right, the 100th Pennsylvania, the 56th Massachusetts, and the 21st Massachusetts. The 35th Massachusetts was assigned duty as brigade pioneers to help clear away the abatis and any other impediments remaining in front of the Southern works after the explosion.

The 57th and the 29th Massachusetts were deployed in regimental lines beside each other immediately to the rear of the 14th New York. They were to lead off their own brigade, with the 59th Regiment changing position just to the right rear of the 57th. Those first four lines of the assaulting troops lay down in tight double ranks with file closers on their flanks in an area of formation a scant forty yards deep.[30]

After they were told their assigned places, the men in the other regiments of the 1st Brigade stood or lay down, packing themselves in tightly against the walls of the covered way while waiting behind the salient of assembly. That covered way was simply a deep trench dug at a right angle to the main-line fortifications. It was only a few feet wide, and it was used to provide safety for the passage of troops, ammunition, and other supplies from the rear to the front.[31]

The men stood by, tense and uneasy, as they waited for three-thirty, the proposed hour of the detonation, to arrive. Their morale was at rock bottom, and they cursed their orders to lead the assault. All along, around every flickering campfire, the rumor had been that the 4th Division was to lead the charge, and the white soldiers felt it deeply unfair that, once again, they were to be sacrificed for the blacks' emancipation while the Negro regiments would remain, once again, safely in the rear—or so the soldiers thought.[32]

In truth, however, the blacks were greatly disappointed and bitter that their orders had been changed. They were in good shape physically, with respectably filled regiments; they were well trained for the assault and eager to prove themselves, and their morale was high.[33]

Compounding the gloom and pessimism of the men of the 1st Brigade, they no longer had any confidence whatsoever in General Ledlie. He had thrown them to the wolves once too often, and they knew intuitively that today would be no exception.[34]

The men's rifles were loaded and capped at half-cock and their bayonets were fixed, as they fidgeted in the trenches. There was little talking, only some low murmuring and rustling from time to time which the officers promptly hushed—the success of the operation depended upon complete surprise. The night just then on that part of the front was very quiet, with almost no sounds but those of nature, when, at three-fifteen, a jumpy soldier accidentally fired his rifle and the unexpected shot sent a shock wave through the restive ranks, heightening the nerve-racking tension already saturating the soldiers. Order was restored swiftly, but the incident put the men more on edge.[35]

All the boys were well aware that they were in for something very different that day, and they were not fond of those kinds of surprises. Just when they thought they had gotten used to one way of doing things, the field and staff officers would dream up another experiment in killing them, and they were heartily sick and tired of the whole business of war and the butchering generals.

As they whiled away their time in the trenches during those early morning hours, the solemn infantrymen reflected more and more on the value of trying to blow up the Confederates, because of the gossip lately circulating among their ranks that the Army of the Potomac's top brass thought the mine dangerous. If something did go wrong, they reasoned, because they were so close to the site of the nearing explosion, they might be atomized right along with the Rebel fort.[36]

Watching the silhouetted figure of the commander of the 48th Pennsylvania against the night sky—the man responsible for carrying out the idea behind the whole affair—standing on the parapet resolutely checking his watch that morning, a good many of the officers and men in the 1st Division, with no rational basis save that rooted in their emotional stress, considered Colonel Pleasants rash and irresponsible, a man who would stop at nothing, including their needless slaughter, to bring attention to himself in Washington. They gave him and his regiment of miners credit for knowing how to dig the precious, warming anthracite out of the ground, but blowing Elliott's Salient to eternity was not quite the same thing as far as they were concerned. The men had been excited about exploding the Rebel stronghold when it was thought that others would go in first. Now the tables had turned on them, and because they, along with all of the officers and men in the Army of the Potomac, including Pleasants and his digger soldiers, had no idea what the effects of the detonation would be, the boys were not eager to be in the position that they were currently occupying.[37]

Licking their dry lips and restlessly shifting the weight of their bodies around as they impatiently withstood the suspense, apprehension, and anticipation of what they sensed to be their certain death, the soldiers believed that Armageddon was at hand. The Irish cursed their luck on the one hand, and on the other fervently crossed themselves and said their Hail Marys and Our Fathers, as a hedge, while their Protestant comrades silently said their own prayers.[38]

Three-thirty came and went, then four o'clock. Still nothing happened, as sweaty palms held pocket watches that anxious eyes strained to see with the aid of the barely lightening eastern sky. The minutes seemed hours, and the expectation of what was to come grew more and more nerve wrenching. The tension finally reached a level that some of them could no longer endure, and many of the men fell into a fitful sleep.[39]

Pressured by the coming of dawn that would preclude the element of surprise, and by his superiors to do something about the explosion's delay, at fifteen minutes after four the frustrated Pleasants agreed to allow a volunteer, Sergeant Harry Rees of his regiment, into the mine and locate and fix whatever it was that was vexing the operation. Accompanied by a lieutenant of the 48th, Jacob Douty, who offered to go along with him on his dangerous mission, Sergeant Rees, carrying a lantern to light his way, crept cautiously into the tunnel—situated on the right of the 1st Division's formation—until he found the trouble. The fuse that Colonel Pleasant's men had lit had failed at the first joint because of a faulty splice, and with Douty desperately hurrying in the necessary supplies, the cool-headed Rees cut the fuse above the burned section and repaired it quickly. After he lighted it again, the two soldiers sprinted for safety out of the shaft as the blue flame hissed its way along its charted course toward the deadly black gunpowder kegs.[40]

18

Bury Them If They Won't Move

A T 4:42, under a dawn sky that was light enough for them to see the
outlines of trees and the dim shape of the Southern fort opposite, the
Federal soldiers felt a low, rumbling tremor pass through the ground beneath
them, and then, looking off towards Elliott's Salient, they saw that the fort
and the earth surrounding it were rising, in apparent slow motion, out of the
Confederate lines—seeming to the men to take forever. But rapidly, the
upward-moving debris increased in speed as beneath the roiling shambles a
gigantic plume shaped like a magnificent waterspout of red and yellow fire
laced with dark splotches and streaks of dirt pushed its way into the twilight
heavens. Huge clumps of brown clay, cannon barrels, wheels, limbers, human
bodies, timber, and military equipment went soaring up through the air some
sixty or seventy feet, and one almost intact bronze twelve-pounder gun was
hurled across the sky, nearly landing in the Union lines.[1]

The men were transfixed at the phenomenal display of flame and smoke,
but most of the soldiers in the front ranks of the 1st Division—the 2nd
Brigade infantrymen—were terrified that the dirt and wreckage would rain
down on them and, panicking, they broke formation to take cover. There
proved to be little danger to the Yankee troops from the falling debris,
however, and the officers had them re-formed about ten minutes later, but
vital time was lost in the process.[2]

Very few of the Union soldiers actually were able to hear much of the
sound of the explosion, though, for at the first sign of detonation the Federal
artillery released a hammering salvo from 144 pieces of artillery—18 4½-inch
seige cannons, some 80 regular field guns, 18 10-inch mortars, and 28 5.8-inch
Coehorn mortars—into the Confederate works. The sudden barrage was
deafening, and many of the men reacted instinctively, clapping their hands
over their ears for protection against the din. Those massed batteries were
one of the largest single assemblies of artillery in the Civil War, and as the

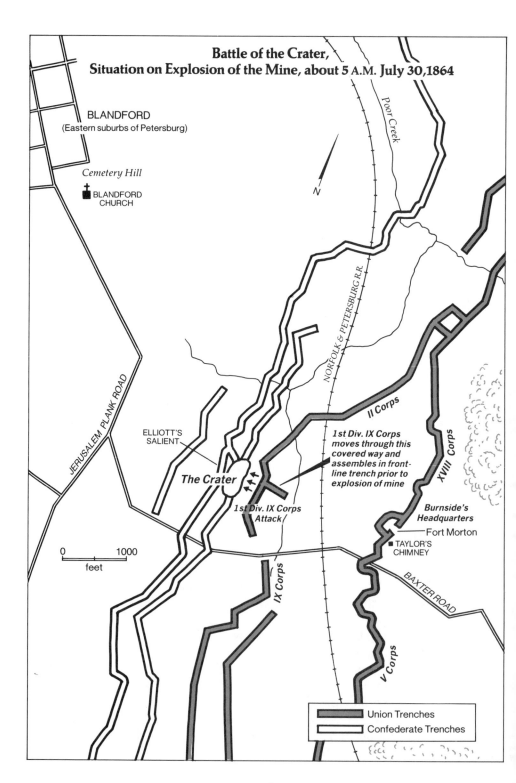

**Battle of the Crater,
Situation on Explosion of the Mine, about 5 A.M. July 30, 1864**

BLANDFORD
(Eastern suburbs of Petersburg)

Cemetery Hill

BLANDFORD
CHURCH

Poor Creek

N

NORFOLK & PETERSBURG R.R.

II Corps

JERUSALEM PLANK ROAD

ELLIOTT'S
SALIENT

The Crater

1st Div. IX Corps
Attack

1st Div. IX Corps
moves through this
covered way and
assembles in front-
line trench prior to
explosion of mine

XVIII Corps

*Burnside's
Headquarters*

Fort Morton

TAYLOR'S
CHIMNEY

0   1000
feet

IX Corps

BAXTER ROAD

V Corps

Union Trenches
Confederate Trenches

smoke from the guns drifted forward, it mixed with the dust from the explosion, causing the rising sun to appear blood red through orange haze.[3]

The men in the 1st Division of the IX Corps stood motionless and awestruck for several minutes after their lines were re-formed, overwhelmed at the sights and sounds in front of them and waiting for the order from the division commander to advance. But Mr. Ledlie evidently had other plans that morning, as he was nowhere to be found. He was, in fact, sitting on a cracker box in a bombproof some distance to the rear, drinking brandy—procured from Surgeon H. E. Smith of the 27th Michigan Infantry—with General Ferrero. But no one knew that at the time, and since he could not be found, General Bartlett, the division's ranking officer, assumed command.[4]

At a few minutes before five o'clock, Colonel Marshall gave the order to the 2nd Brigade to move forward, and the leading regiment, the 2nd Pennsylvania Heavy Artillery, tried to climb out, but the men immediately ran into a problem that no one had attended to. The trenches were eight feet deep in that part of the line, and the soldiers, loaded down with all their gear, could not get over the parapets. No one had thought to provide ladders for their egress. Nonplussed, they stood dumbly around until someone finally hit on the idea of sticking their bayonet points between the logs of the trench's front wall while other men held the opposite ends at knee and shoulder level. The triangular bayonet blades, used in this fashion and strong enough to hold a man's weight, provided makeshift ladders, and the soldiers began to scale the barricades and advance. Sandbags also were arranged quickly as steps, while the men who had made it to the top helped by pulling their comrades up onto the parapet. Still others climbed on the backs and shoulders of fellow soldiers to get over the edge of the pits. All of this scaling took time, and time was not a luxury the Army of the Potomac could afford that July morning. The troops behind the 2nd Pennsylvania moved too fast trying to follow, and everyone got tangled up for a while, and still more minutes were wasted separating the ranks.[5]

But that was only part of the trouble that day. When the 2nd Brigade finally got out of the earthworks, the foot soldiers saw that the Federal sappers had removed only a small section of the heavy collection of abatis, chevaux-de-frise, and the strong wire that held them together in front of their trenches, and, consequently, the brigade was unable to form battle lines. Instead, the soldiers—with their bayonet-fixed muskets at the right-shoulder-shift position in order not to accidentally stick the men in front of them—had to take off in column for the wrecked fort, the men gagging and coughing through the thick, acrid smoke and choking fumes and dust. Strict and explicit orders for the removal of nearly two hundred yards of the defensive material had been issued, but somewhere along the chain of command those orders had been disregarded. Now a full frontal assault was reduced to men double-quicking in columns three and four abreast toward the objective.[6] Nothing, it seemed, was going right for the attackers.

Immediately after the 2nd Brigade had cleared the trenches, Bartlett gave the command, "First Brigade, forward!" with Major Prescott adding to his regiment, "57th, Rise up! Forward, march! By the right flank; march! Over the parapet and swing up on your left!" The first regiments of the brigade, the 57th and the 29th Massachusetts, which had received similar orders, scrambled up over the top in the same way as had the units of the 2nd Brigade.[7]

The other regiments of the 1st Brigade had a more bewildering time clearing the works. As they had been crowded into the covered way in careless formation behind the leading units, they had to be sorted out first, then formed into regimental lines, and finally moved forward to scale the trench wall. All of this activity cost much of the division another ten minutes.[8]

When the 1st Brigade was at last marshaled on the periphery of the earthworks, Bartlett's men quickly moved forward behind Colonel Marshall's brigade towards the Rebel fort, which lay about thirty degrees to the right of the brigade's point of formation. The boys rapidly advanced, cheering loudly, with Bartlett trying to stay in the lead, battle flags streaming, and with a few drummers beating the roll. "General Bartlett commanded the Brigade," recalled George Barton, "he was perfectly splendid, and led us in the charge on foot. It was a gallant affair. . . ." The men lost no time crossing the cleared ground that sloped gently upwards for a little more than one hundred yards to Elliott's Salient. Protected by a heavy concentration of covering Union artillery shells flying just over their heads and by a ridge off to their left which warded off serious Confederate enfilading fire from that direction, the men's assault was virtually unopposed, and they faced only a weak and insignificant scattering of enemy rifle shots. The truth was that the Confederates who had not been killed or injured in the blast had run for their lives to their army's rear, frightened, dazed, and unsure of what might come next from the diabolical Yankee lines, and as the Union soldiers made for the destroyed Southern works, very few Rebels were left to oppose them.[9]

★

The explosion of the mine had created an irregular, elliptically shaped crater 30 feet deep, about 60 feet wide, and over 170 feet long. In front was a 12-foot crest that resulted from the explosion, and inside the steep banks were piles of loose, pulverized sand with great chunks of clay protruding from them. On either side of the crater was ground thoroughly unfavorable to charging troops. One officer described it as "involuted and complex, filled with pits, traverses, and bombproofs, forming a labyrinth as difficult of passage as the crater itself."[10]

From the first, when the 2nd Brigade arrived on the crater's edge after charging in unavoidable disorder up the final yards of the slope, everything started to fall apart for the Union soldiers. The blast had knocked down or covered up only a small section of abatis in front of the fort, and once again, the men, who could barely see for all the smoke and dust, had to thread their way through the Confederate defensive apparatus. But when they reached the lip of the crater, a strange thing happened. Whether it was caused by lack of proper leadership at the division, corps, or army level, by light resistance from the Confederates, or simply by the common soldiers' natural curiosity—or, more likely, by a combination of all three—most of the men just came to a stop. The 1st Brigade, which arrived on the heels of the 2nd, halted also—Bartlett's infantrymen equally entranced by the carnage—and almost the entire three-thousand-man 1st Division turned into a mob of sightseers. Some of the boys, in order to explore the devastation, slid down the vertical walls of the depression, marveling at the wreckage and enjoying themselves. The tensions and fears experienced during the wait in the trenches had evaporated for the most part.[11]

Meanwhile, desperate, frustrated officers were trying to rally the wandering, wide-eyed men and begin seizing the Rebel works in the vicinity. Those of the 2nd Brigade that could be assembled in the circuslike confusion and hazy atmosphere skirted the rim of the depression to the right and began to capture some of the Southern rifle pits near the ruined fort. Besides the front-line earthworks, three other trenches ran out from the north side of the crater, and the one closest to the Federal lines was occupied swiftly by elements of Lieutenant Colonel Gilbert P. Robinson's 179th New York and the 3rd Maryland. That ditch was a partial covered way, running about three hundred and fifty yards and dead-ending into a protective traverse. The leading troops of Robinson's regiment rushed in as far as the right-angled earthwork, took position behind it, and opened fire into a Southern flanking trench close by, which was filling up rapidly with Confederate soldiers who had come to their senses and were returning to the front lines to drive the Federals off.[12]

General Bartlett, on the other hand, had misunderstood his instructions, which had been to advance to the left of the pit and first secure as much of the Confederate works as possible in that direction. He had interpreted the orders to mean the Confederate left—exactly the opposite direction—and since the brigade commander, Ledlie, was not present to direct him properly, the thought that he had erred never crossed his mind, at least not at the time. He collected what he could of his men and followed the same course as the 2nd Brigade.[13]

The objective of Cemetery Hill lay at about twenty-five degrees to the right (northwest) of the crater and some thirteen hundred yards distant, and the opportunity to rush and capture it at that time was ripe, as the explosion had thoroughly confounded the Rebels in that part of their line. Most had retired quickly to the safety of the rear fearing a second detonation. Because Frank Bartlett—as well as Colonel Marshall—clearly understood his orders from General Ledlie to be that he was to capture and hold the Southern main line of works primarily, he felt all was proceeding according to plan, sightseeing notwithstanding. Actually the new brigadier general was in a cheery mood. Only a few of the Union troops were in the crater at that time— although it was continuing to fill up at an alarming rate with the awed soldiers—as Bartlett came hopping along with the help of an ivory-handled Malacca cane, smiling broadly at Colonel Marshall as he approached him.[14]

As the two commanders talked over the situation, some of the soldiers in the blown-up fort were busying themselves righting a twelve-pounder bronze Napoleon gun. Two other twelve-pounders were discovered undamaged in the left wing of the Confederate fort by some of the men of the 14th New York, and because that regiment had been trained originally as artillery, Major Charles H. Houghton, one of the battalion commanders, detailed a sergeant and several others to locate a magazine that he was convinced was nearby. It was found, and the heavy gunners hauled the two cannons back to a position that would allow them a clear field of fire on a Rebel piece on the left that was pelting the Union soldiers with grapeshot. The men of the 14th New York knocked the Confederate artillery out with one of the captured cannons and, as a result, forty-five prisoners were taken, who were sent to the Union lines immediately.[15]

At the same time, other Federals were digging out the Rebels buried in the dirt beneath the immense dust cloud that still hung over the massive hole. The Northerners were captivated by the destruction caused by the mine, and most of them continued in their role as tourists, ignoring their pleading officers.

All over the crater were overturned guns, broken gun carriages, destroyed military and fortification material, and half-buried Confederate soldiers— some with only their legs or arms sticking out of the ground. Other corpses appeared to have had every bone in their bodies broken by the concussion. One Southern boy was found, with both legs blown off, helplessly trying to crawl to safety, all the while leaving two wakes of blood behind him from his dragging stumps. An arm was found still holding a musket in its hand, the rope sling of which was intertwined through its lifeless fingers. A second lieutenant of John Pegram's battery was dug out, and in a few minutes was able to walk and talk. He told his Yankee captors that he had been asleep when the mine was exploded and had been awakened only when he felt himself being hurled high in the air atop the blast's plume. In all, 278 Rebels had been injured or killed when the mine was detonated.[16]

What with the confusion of their activities, the dust through which they could not see, and, most importantly, the absence of the division commander, Ledlie, the soldiers of the different regiments and brigades soon became hopelessly entangled with each other, and the officers could not separate out their commands.[17]

Because of the inert state of the first wave of the attack, the opportunity to move on to Cemetery Hill was being lost rapidly. Recognizing an excellent chance to fulfill what he thought to be his second objective and take the cemetery because of the feeble resistance being offered by the Confederates at that time, Bartlett tried desperately—but, as it turned out, futilely—to rally the 1st Brigade to push on the extra four thousand feet, capture the rise, and quite possibly end the war, but most of the men just milled around, perplexed and mesmerized by the events surrounding them.[18]

About 250 Confederate gunners from Pegram's four-gun battery were scattered around, and the Federals took most of them prisoner. The 57th Massachusetts soon occupied about 100 yards of trenches on the right of the hole, and the men had captured almost 50 prisoners and sent them to the rear. Other Rebels were seen scampering off to their rear lines as the soldiers took potshots at them.[19]

Bartlett finally got some of the 57th, 59th, and 29th Massachusetts into the covered way occupied by Robinson's troops, but the Massachusetts men only added to the pandemonium in the trench, and they eventually were pushed back into the crater, which continued to fill up with disorganized and disoriented men of the 1st Division.[20]

Bartlett and Marshall now ordered the men of both brigades whom they could rally to attack toward Cemetery Hill via another covered way that ran toward the hill on an oblique angle. The 57th, 59th, and 29th Massachusetts were to form a second line to that made up of elements of the 2nd Brigade— largely the 2nd Pennsylvania—in order to support those soldiers by keeping down flank and rear Confederate fire, which was thickening. The action was muddled totally, and Robinson and his men made almost no forward progress and accomplished nothing. The worst of the Rebel fire in those early moments of the fight was now coming from that direction (the Union right) and Colonel Robinson's men were sitting ducks in the face of the deadly fusillade.[21]

All of the chaos and commotion on the part of the 1st Division began in the first few minutes of the battle, and during those minutes ominous events were developing fast that would take advantage of that chaos and commotion. At about five-thirty that morning, the air began to clear of dust, and it could be seen readily that the crater was becoming clogged with puzzled and idling 1st Division men. They were not moving. Many of them felt that there was little to fear from the Confederates who, for the most part, were returning fire like slow-cooking popcorn. Neither the Federal soldiers nor their officers seemed to appreciate the urgency required of them at that early hour of the battle, and without their division commander to lead and direct the operation, they remained almost static.

A good deal of the problem that July 30, which extended into the other white divisions of the IX Corps as well, was the men's extremely low morale from their long stay in the front-line trenches in the worst part of the Federal lines. Because of the black 4th Division, they were never given a break by the incensed Rebels, who shot at them night and day without mercy. Their physical condition had also deteriorated from the terrific heat under the unrelenting Virginia sun and the constant construction of defenses under the ceaseless enemy gunfire. At that point in the siege of Petersburg, the 1st Division of the IX Corps was probably the worst possible choice of any division in the Army of the Potomac or the Army of the James for the assignment.

Soon after the arrival of Ledlie's command, the other two divisions of the IX Corps were on their way from the Union lines. Those divisions were supposed to fan out left and right, but, again owing to the small amount of abatis removed from in front of the Confederate defenses, many men of the 2nd and 3rd divisions had to funnel through that narrow opening that led directly into the crater. With Ledlie's men causing a total obstruction to the incoming troops' order of deployment—left and right—the new divisions were caught in the melee also, and the soldiers of the 1st Division were being pushed back against the depression's far walls as the influx of men increased.[22]

★

While all of that pandemonium was occurring in the Yankee ranks, the shaken Confederates gradually were remanning their lines. The shock of the explosion had worn off, and the Rebels, taking advantage of the confusion of the Northern soldiers, began pouring a murderous fire into them from small arms and field pieces loaded with grapeshot, canister, and any scrap that would fit down the muzzles. By then, the IX Corps was so packed into the crater and the neighboring trenches—men of the 1st Division especially— that only those at the very edges of the colossal hole could shoot back. The various brigade commanders desperately tried to re-form their troops outside the pit, but its sides rose so precipitously that any chance of more than a few of them getting out just then was prevented. The best that most of the Federals could do was put their backs to the vertical walls, dig in their heels for support, and try to return fire.[23]

Eventually several of the officers had a little success in leading some of the men out of the jumbled Union throng to form battle lines. But because everything was in such turmoil, and regiments and brigades had become so mixed together, those re-formed units were made up of soldiers from a variety of the regiments involved in the engagement at that time. However, after the Union officers got the men moving forward they immediately encountered a solid wall of advancing Rebels belonging to Brigadier General William Mahone's division of the Confederate Third Corps, composed of Colonel D. A. Weisiger's Virginia Brigade and Brigadier General Ambrose R. Wright's Georgia Brigade, and the Federals were blasted back by the screaming and yelling Southerners.[24]

Every attempt of the 1st Division to extricate itself from the hole was quashed by volleys of musket fire and blasts from cannon that tore its ranks to bloody shreds and sent soldiers flying for shelter and safety. The officers and men had no idea what was going on or what was expected of them—they could not have had; there was no one in control, no focal point. Some officers tried in vain to do what they thought necessary, but they seemed only to make matters worse, and one order usually contradicted another. Many screamed themselves hoarse in the din: "Halt and entrench, you men!" or "Forward, boys!" or "Give way to the right there!" And the frightened and confused enlisted men, not knowing just what to do, froze in their tracks and glanced from side to side in utter bewilderment at this proliferation of nonsensical instructions. One officer stated later, "I received so many orders from so many different commanders at that time that I did not know which to obey."[25]

For a short time there was some improvement in the situation when a small part of the 1st Division that had not been caught in the hole finally moved off to the left followed by some of Willcox's 3rd Division and managed to gain a foothold in some trenches south of the crater. At about that time, Robert Potter's 2nd Division moved off to the right in the direction of Cemetery Hill, capturing about two hundred yards of rifle pits, and in the only Federal action that came anywhere near success that black day, managed to get very close to reaching the cemetery at Blanford Church. However, Robert E. Lee directed the five-foot, one-hundred-twenty-five-pound Mahone to plow in the 2nd Division no matter the cost. His desperate Southerners, fighting for the very survival of their cause, mauled Potter's unsupported men, and the Federals were ordered to withdraw. The Rebels chased after them, sending the Yankees running for their lives back to the crater.[26]

★

At about six o'clock, the 4th Division was ordered to advance. Almost immediately it became entangled in the covered way back in the Union works, and its commander, Brigadier General Edward Ferrero, who still was indulging in a little early-morning courage with General Ledlie in the bombproof shelter, was quite unable to render his men service of any value. Not until seven-thirty that morning could the exasperated brigade commanders of the black troops get the division straightened out and on the move with orders to rush and capture the crest of Cemetery Hill. But the next disaster came with the 4th Division's advance.[27]

The enthusiastic black soldiers, anxious for their first taste of battle and spoiling for revenge, rushed forward by the flank, passing through the narrow opening in the Confederate abatis. Colonel Siegfried's 1st Brigade troops, followed by Thomas's 2nd Brigade, were shot up badly by enfilading fire as they climbed the slope leading to the fight. But the survivors moved along at the double-quick, and upon reaching the crater, their officers led part of them straight through the mass of white soldiers, while others moved off to the Union right. There they made a gallant charge around and through distraught white Union soldiers against the Confederate rifle pits where the 2nd Division had been routed earlier, capturing close to two hundred thoroughly humiliated Confederate prisoners and a stand of Rebel colors. The black soldiers also recaptured a stand of colors previously lost by one of the white Union regiments, an incident no less shameful to many of the Yankees.[28]

But the Negro troops' early glories were short-lived. Colonel Thomas's 2nd Brigade was shot to pieces by Rebel rifle fire so pernicious that barely a fragment of the brigade got away alive or without injury, and after suffering its staggering losses, the brigade was driven back in panic to the great hole. In addition, the Georgia and Virginia troops in Mahone's command were pushed up to it and fired volleys into the blacks with a venomous and unrequited fury. For a while, the black troops, reinforced by some white units, held their ground and then overwhelmed and forced the Confederates to give ground, even attacking a second line of Rebel earthworks. But there their luck ended, and they were beaten back by their implacable foes in Mahone's brigades who, though outnumbered, launched a successful charge against them. By eight-forty-five, Ferrero's men and their white comrades were in full retreat in a crazed disorder and, like lemmings diving senselessly to their death in the sea, jumped into the crater, forcing the soldiers already in it further up against the steep walls of the pit and touching off a terrific frenzy of shoving and pushing and cursing for space to fight. Stephen Weld, who was in the crater, remembered that the Rebels drove "the negroes head over heels onto us, trampling everyone down, and adding still more to the confusion." There they were trapped like fish in a barrel, and the Confederates on the rim just above them poured a barrage of musket and cannon fire into their exposed ranks.[29]

Though they faced the wrath of Lee's men, they were not safe from Federal soldiers either. A 1st Division officer wrote later, "It has been positively asserted that white men [Federal troops] bayoneted blacks who fell back into the crater. This was in order to preserve the whites from Confederate vengeance. Men boasted in my presence that blacks had thus been disposed of, particularly when the Confederates came back up."[30]

George Barton chronicled his impression of the affair:

. . . Yet hardly had we got possession of their works, when the 4th Div. of the 9th Corps (Colored) came up, and were ordered to charge upon the "Johnnies" Again, which they *did for a short* distance, then *broke & ran* like a *flock* of *sheep,* & black at that falling back upon our trenches they completely jamed us up into a heap so that there was no *room* to *fight.* The Rebs taking advantage of this state of affairs Charged upon *us* and our forces *skedaddled. Our men* [presumably the 57th Regiment] *fought like Tigers* Men could not have done any *better.* . . . This war must be *fought out* by *white men* & we might as well make up our minds to it first at last to say it.[31]

Almost all of the fifteen thousand men of the IX Corps were either in or around the crater by nine o'clock that morning when part of the XVIII Corps was sent in, adding to the madness. Two of its brigades won control of some trenches on the right, but their victory was unsupported, and they, like every other Northern unit, were smashed and routed back to the crater.[32]

There, desperate orders were received to re-form and charge the crest of Cemetery Hill from commanders so far in the rear and so out of touch with the liquid situation of the battle that their instructions were ludicrous. At that time Grant, Meade, and Burnside each thought that everything was going as planned, but all of them were so removed from the front that they had no real idea of what actually was happening there, and their contradictory and unrealistic instructions flew fast and furious. Though those generals did not know it then, no chance of victory existed any longer, and it remained only for the Federal soldiers to get back to the safety of their own lines in any way possible.[33]

Mahone's Confederates were now left, right, and center of the Union troops, forming for their annihilation, but when the Southerners made their charge, it was repelled violently. This did not deter the Rebels, however, and they continued battling the Federals without respite.[34]

★

In the 57th Massachusetts, Major Prescott had tried to re-form the remains of the regiment, which was in as much disarray as any other, and while he was yelling orders, his premonitions of the night before were realized, and he was shot dead. Captain Dresser, being senior in rank, took his place immediately and just as quickly was killed. Captain George Howe, formerly of Company E, who, like Dresser, had been detached and detailed safely on the 1st Brigade staff, but who somehow found himself in the fight that day, took command next. He was able to climb to the extreme western edge of the crater, where he waved his sword at the Rebels and tried to rally not only the 57th, but the whole 1st Brigade. He died instantly from a bullet straight through his heart.[35]

Lieutenants Barton and Anderson of the 57th had been among the first men wounded, and the regiment was losing its enlisted men at an alarming rate. Lieutenant Reade was missing and would turn up a prisoner of war. That left the men with only one officer in the entire regiment, the newly commissioned Lieutenant Doty. The whole officer corps of the 57th Massachusetts had been wiped out, save one very inexperienced young man.[36]

★

Eventually the ranking officers of the 1st Division were again able to rally some of their men, and for a while they managed to establish a temporary defense and push some of the Confederates back. But the Southerners swiftly regrouped, and after several countercharges they finally dug in permanently— many within ten feet of the Union soldiers in the pit.[37]

Back in the Federal lines, Grant and Meade realized at last that the battle could not be won, and that the best chance the North had had during the entire campaign for ending the war had been lost that morning due to the conduct of the 1st Division of the IX Army Corps. (Grant later remarked that it was the worst-commanded division in the whole Army of the Potomac.) At nine-forty-five Meade sent a dispatch to Burnside ordering him to get his men back to their own lines while there was yet a chance that they might be saved. But General Burnside, occluded from the reality of events and making decisions in the safety of Fort Morton based on secondhand reports from the front, erroneously thought that a possibility of victory still existed, and his troops were not recalled.[38]

The crater by then was a scene of unparalleled horror. In places, the panic-stricken soldiers were so tightly packed together that they could not move or even raise their arms to defend themselves. Scores of the dead and wounded could not fall to the ground, and their blood, brains, and bone fragments spattered the living men near them. The slain that were able to fall were often stomped beyond recognition by the shoes and boots of their terrorized comrades, and sometimes the injured were trampled to death. The close-range gunfire was gouging, and the shrapnel from the artillery crushing. Mortar shells exploded into lethal iron fragments, smashing the blue ranks to scrap, tearing off heads and arms and ripping bodies to bloody pulp. The incessant firing created a thunderous roar, but it could not quite overpower the grisly screaming of the men who were trapped, or the spitting, cursing, and furious yelling of their Confederate antagonists, who continued to destroy the Federals with unabated vengeance. Those Northerners that could move tried to hold off the enemy; others fought desperately to free themselves from the tangle in order to shoot back. Some just tried to find a place to hide.[39]

By this time many of the Confederates had run out of ammunition, and some of them began fixing their bayonets on their rifles and throwing them like spears, harpooning the Federals. Others hurled rocks, bottles, or anything dangerous they could find.[40]

Most of the men in the 57th, who were in a position to return fire, had run out of ammunition too, and they gathered cartridges from the dead and wounded, while others who were able to move threw back the bottles, stones, and debris at the Rebels. Because the Union and Confederate troops were so near to each other in some places, many on both sides were cut by broken glass, bruised by thrown rocks, or stabbed by bayonets. The close-range fighting was virulent and unmerciful, and blood that ran down in streams in the hard, brown clay formed pools in which the men slipped, and it got on everything.[41]

Still inflamed by the use of black troops against them, some Confederates stood on the edge of the crater and took deliberate aim at helpless black soldiers, shooting them down in cold blood. The Rebel cry of "Shoot the nigger, but don't kill the white man!" was heard many times that morning. Lieutenant Colonel John A. Bross, commanding the 29th United States Colored Troops, was able to mount the parapet of the crater at one point, and waving a flag, he called for his men to follow him. The blacks tried, but they were caved in.[42]

The Confederate government had passed a law by which Southerners could execute white Union officers commanding Negro troops, and those officers were not anxious to be taken prisoner. Men of any rank who were taken that day were treated far worse than usual for having fought with the blacks. The Southerners clearly were venting their rage.

★

As the sun rose higher in the sky—at about ten-thirty—the Federals began to suffer dreadfully from heat and thirst, their canteens long since having run dry. Most everyone was also either out of or low on ammunition. Soldiers were dispatched back to the Union trenches to fill the canteens and bring up cartridges, but the one hundred yards of ground in between that had been crossed so easily earlier that morning now was being raked by the Rebels with a deadly crossfire, and anyone attempting to pass over that strip of land did so at perilous risk. Not many of the canteen bearers or ammunition carriers—who carried their bullets in shelter tent halves—survived the round trip, and between them and others who did not make it, such as couriers, the wounded going to the rear, and slackers, the ground in the middle of the lines was littered with downed soldiers.[43]

The desperate Union men in the crater were whipped badly, and the dead and dying were piled everywhere—sometimes as many as eight deep. A number of the wounded tied rags to sticks and bayonets to fan themselves from the awful heat and battle smoke and to drive away the flies that had gathered by the thousands to make use of the newly torn flesh. The frustrated survivors, fighting frantically for their lives, occasionally turned a quick and anxious glance in the direction of their own lines, wondering why they were not being reinforced by the V and II Corps (Hancock's men had doubled back to the Union lines at Petersburg on a forced night march when they discovered the Rebels too well fortified at Deep Bottom to attack them). They felt they were being abandoned deliberately by the rest of the army, and some of them made their feelings clear, loudly cursing what in their eyes was an unbelievable desertion. Their own artillery was decreasing almost proportionally to the increase of the Confederate's big guns. Still the men fought on as well as they could, but at about noon, the Rebels that had been sent north of the James River to check Hancock were returning and adding their weight to the massacre. General Burnside realized at that point that the situation was hopeless and the day lost, and he ordered a retreat at 12:20 that afternoon.[44]

At about the same time, the men of Brigadier General J. C. C. Saunders's Alabama Brigade of Mahone's division, who had arrived to shore up the Confederate troops, crept close to the crater's edge and defiantly raised their caps and hats on their ramrods above their protected position. Some deceived Union troops, those who could, fired a volley, blasting the headgear to shreds, and before the startled Federals could reload, the Alabama men charged into the hole, and a furious hand-to-hand battle followed. Men bashed each other's brains out with rifle butts and stabbed one another to death with bayonets. Fist fights broke out, and the soldiers groveled among the dead and wounded in the blood and dust. But the exhausted and demoralized Union troops could take no more, and the battle could go on no longer. Hundreds of the surviving Yankees surrendered, and thousands more fled to the safety of their own lines.[45]

The retreat became a rout, with the men running at top speed through the thick battle smoke, ducking bullets and shells, and jumping over the dead and wounded. It was bedlam, and the chasing Confederates often fired at such close range that many of the men who were shot had powder burns on their bodies. The Rebel artillery concentrated its killing crossfire all along the line of withdrawal, and men fell at every step, yet all that time the Yankee cannons remained silent, giving no covering fire to their exposed comrades.

It was mass murder. Those who made it back quickly jumped into their trenches and breathed with relief at having run the gauntlet safely. They were exhausted, filthy, hungry, thirsty, and shamed, but they were glad to be alive.

During the action that day the 35th Massachusetts, still on duty as the 1st Division engineers, had been ordered to dig a covered way between the crater and the Federal lines as a route by which the men remaining in the crater could escape. The men of that regiment had made some progress, but soon wounded men trying to shelter themselves from the battle began filling up the trench, and they would not move. Finally, in frustration, the officers of the regiment told the 35th's soldiers, "Bury them if they won't move." There was little pity for anyone that black day.[46]

★

As the men started to withdraw, the left wing of the 57th Massachusetts containing the color guard was forced to surrender, and the regimental banners were captured by Lieutenant St. Julien Wilson, of Company C, 61st Virginia Volunteer Infantry Regiment of Mahone's division. That was the ultimate disgrace, and all the men of the regiment were depressed and humiliated at their loss.[47]

A little earlier in the fight, a shell had exploded near General Bartlett, knocking down a huge chunk of hard Virginia clay which killed the man next to him and fell on his artificial leg, crushing it to pieces. He had been sitting on a pile of timber nearby, and now he told his boys that the day was lost, that it was senseless to go on, and for them to get back to their own lines in any way that they could, while they could. As for him, he had no choice but to surrender to General Mahone, which he soon did.[48]

Colonel Stephen Weld, who had led the 1st Brigade in past battles, also surrendered with Bartlett. He had taken refuge in a bombproof with another officer and a black soldier. The Rebels who soon captured them summarily executed the black. They then took Weld's sword and hat, saying, "Come out of that hat, you Yank!" and, after cursing him soundly for being on Southern soil, sent him to the rear of their lines. As he was walking to the rear, he was following one of Ferrero's men, when three Confederates rushed up and coolly shot the unarmed black dead. Of the battle, Stephen Weld said, "It was altogether the most miserable and meanest experience I ever had in my life. You could not fight, you could not give an order, you could not get anything done."[49]

★

When the men were rounded up and the roll was called later that day, the 57th was discovered to be all but wiped out. Six out of the regiment's 7 officers were either killed, wounded, or missing, and 45 of its 91 enlisted men suffered the same fate. Lieutenant Albert Doty now commanded a force of 46 badly used-up soldiers. Of the 98 officers and enlisted men who had gone into battle with the regiment that day, there were 4 killed, 4 mortally wounded, 4 missing in action and presumed killed, 16 wounded, and 25 taken prisoner of war, two of whom were among the wounded—a loss of 52 percent. All of the companies were now counted in the single digits except K, which mustered 12 men. In contrast, Companies B and E could claim only 2 combat soldiers each available for the line.[50]

Private Thomas Mara of Company A, from Kilkenny, Ireland, had just been wounded while on duty in the trenches on July 2, but he was a fighter who had been in every battle with the 57th since crossing the Rapidan, and he was not about to shirk his regiment simply because he had been injured. Into the crater went Thomas Mara, only to receive a more serious wound. Sent to the U.S. Army general hospital in Brattleboro, Vermont, he evidently, as did many of his brave comrades, found the medical facility unbearable, and he deserted while on furlough in August, never to be heard from again.[51]

Another soldier cut from the same cloth as Thomas Mara was Private William Roper, also of Company A. Roper, too, had been wounded—at North Anna River—but like Mara, he had elected to stay with the regiment. Having fought in all the engagements since the Wilderness, he took his wound at the crater, as well. However, he would return to duty.[52]

Sergeant George Parks went into battle suffering from chronic diarrhea. Company A lost another man when he was captured and sent to prison in Danville, Virginia.[53]

Private Charles Francis Paddock of Company B, from Holden, Massachusetts, at age fifteen was one of the youngest members of the 57th Regiment. Since May 6, he had participated in nearly every fight. During the action that July 30, Paddock took three gunshot wounds in the same leg and was captured. Miraculously, he would survive his ordeal and be discharged later on a Surgeons Certificate of Disability.[54]

A sergeant in Company C, James Powers from New Haven, Connecticut, aroused "capital interest" from army surgeons with his wound. He was shot in the chest, the Minié ball fracturing his fifth and sixth ribs, carrying away part of his sternum, and then exiting into his left arm, smashing the humerus. Dr. White gave him chloroform and ether at the 1st Division field hospital and amputated his arm. Because the sternum had been shot away, a gaping hole that apparently could not be closed was left in the living soldier's chest, "so that," as surgeon George M. McGillis reported, "an observer looks upon the heart invested with pericardium, and distinguishes plainly diastole and systole of the auricles. . . . The wound is a human vivisection." With such a wound no one could be expected to survive for long, and the young man died on August 16.[55]

His officers called Augustus Champney, from Hoosic, New York, a "Noble Boy." The young private in Company G had been wounded at Spotsylvania, but had returned to the regiment and fought at Cold Harbor and in the Petersburg assault. However, his old wound had not healed sufficiently, and after being captured at the crater, he died from its effects seven days later.[56]

Private Michael Cadigan, of Company G, was severely wounded by a bullet that passed through his right arm and fractured his fifth and sixth ribs. Transported to Washington on a steamer, he had the limb amputated by Dr. A. F. Sheldon on August 4, but Cadigan died two days later anyway. The surgeons performed an autopsy and found the Minié ball that caused his mortal wound. It was lying in the boy's stomach.[57]

Private Alfred Howe, a member of Company K, was shot severely in the left forearm. His comrades managed to carry him to a Federal field hospital, where the doctors bandaged his wound and sent him to City Point. There Dr. George W. Snow, surgeon of the 35th Massachusetts, amputated his mangled left radius later that day, and Howe was placed on the steamer *De Molay* bound for Lovell U.S. Army General Hospital in Portsmouth Grove, Rhode Island. But he never reached his destination. He bled to death en route.[58]

Francis M. Harrington, Company K's diarist, fought through the whole battle that July 30 safely, but when Frank Bartlett warned the men to get out while they could, Harrington had remained behind to aid his helpless general and was captured with him.[59]

George Barton's wound was not serious. He had been clipped by a piece of shrapnel and would return to duty in a few weeks.[60]

The 57th Massachusetts had been heavily engaged in the battle, being one of the first regiments to enter the crater, and the men had earned the reputation among the other outfits that day as members of the most unlucky regiment in the brigade.[61]

★

Almost four thousand union soldiers had been lost in that battle, and more than five hundred dead soldiers had been left in the crater. The whole operation had been a disastrous and demoralizing defeat for the Army of the Potomac. Ledlie's 1st Division was singled out by the rest of the army's soldiers as having been the cause, and the men in it were abused and scorned without pity. A perfect opportunity to win the war had been theirs for the taking, and they had made a mess of it, and now the war would continue for who knew how long, claimed the soldiers in the other outfits.[62]

The loss of their colors and the debasing attitude of the other troops, plus their frightful losses, was almost more than the survivors of the 57th could stand, and they defended themselves vigorously. Not one of them had shirked or run away. They had done their duty as well as they could. They had faced death obediently, and they would have charged the crest of Cemetery Hill in the first place if they had been given proper orders. But the coward Ledlie had skulked in a safe bombproof shelter so far behind the lines that he never once witnessed any of the battle, and he was full of John Barleycorn.[63] Some of them must have felt so degraded that they wept in frustration and rage. All were furious with their tormenters, asking why they had not come to help them, and they could hardly help but take note that as they made their way back from the carnage, there was no covering fire from their own artillery to protect them.

★

Soon after the battle General Meade ordered, with Grant's approval, a court of inquiry to look into the reasons for the day's disaster. General Burnside, General Ledlie, and General Ferrero were all censured and relieved of their commands as a result of the court's findings. Burnside and Ledlie later resigned, and Ferrero was transferred to other duties.[64]

Although the black 4th Division had done remarkably well at first, it was given severe abuse throughout the white regiments for its complete rout, and no one, it seemed, stopped to consider that their division commander also had not been with them. The white divisions of the IX Corps, including the maligned 1st, heaped disdain on them, and all the pent-up prejudice flew. It was an injustice, but there were few men in the 1st Division with justice for anybody else on their minds just then, with the exception of wanting to string their division commander up to the nearest stout tree branch.

As the men lay in their works that night, the battleground displayed the usual horrors. The pickets kept up an all-night fire, and the wounded moaned, screamed, and pleaded for help and water and merciful death, but once more, no one had any intention of leaving the safety of his trench for any reason. The wailing never let up, and the Federals tried to arrange a burial truce with the Confederates the next day, but they would not have any of it. The Northerners repeatedly made the same request over the next two broiling hot days while the wounded died in droves from thirst and lack of medical attention—some going mad from having no water. The Union soldiers were enraged at the inhuman barbarity of the Rebels until, on the third day, Tuesday, August 2, a truce was agreed upon from five to nine o'clock in the morning, and burial parties met under a white flag near the crater.

The 35th Massachusetts and one of the black regiments from the 4th Division were assigned as burial detachments, and the scenes that the men encountered on the battlefield were worse than they ever could imagine. Three days of intense heat had bloated and blackened the cadavers so that the men could only distinguish between black and white soldiers by their hair.

Some had bloated from gases to the point of bursting and viscera popped out of ripped abdomens, and others were simply mutilated and torn apart from the hideous small arms and cannon fire. Still others had been trampled to masses of unrecognizable flesh by their stampeding comrades. The smell and the flies were unbearable, and maggots crawled back and forth in wounds, mouths, eyes, or any opening available, infesting the corpses. Some of the men searched the putrid dead for identification, then wrapped them in blankets, and pinned their names to their shrouds if they could be identified. Others dug shallow trench graves and covered the victims as fast as they could, transferring their names to wooden markers. Several hundred men were interred that morning by soldiers who would not get the stench out of their nostrils for three or four days. And of the many wounded left on the ground after the battle, only four or five remained alive through their terrible ordeal.[65]

The only body recovered by the 57th was that of Captain Howe. Most of those taken prisoner would die later from starvation and disease in the Rebel prison camps at Danville, Virginia, and Andersonville, Georgia.[66]

★

Who should have shouldered the blame for the disaster of July 30, 1864? That question has been debated since the day of the battle, with the consensus agreeing that the 1st Division of the IX Corps was at fault to a great extent because the men of that unit were poor soldiers—some historians calling them the worst soldiers in the Army of the Potomac. Their records, however, do not support such conclusions. The old regiments, such as the 29th and 35th Massachusetts, the 100th Pennsylvania, and the 3rd Maryland had all fought well during their long careers. The new veteran regiments, like the 57th, had proved themselves since the Wilderness. The heavy artillery outfits, which probably should not have spearheaded the attack (an event over which they had no control), nevertheless fought as well as could have been expected.

General Meade's decision to use worn-out divisions that had been under the worst and most demoralizing fire in the Petersburg lines because of the 4th Division being in their corps seems to have been anything but prudent. But worn-out and demoralized soldiers are not synonomous with bad soldiers. They simply were not in any condition at that time for the job that they were asked to perform. General Burnside's luck-of-the-draw choice of the 1st Division to lead the way is almost beyond belief. He himself had not wanted his incompetent 1st Division commander present at the final briefing, and only relented when pressured by General Willcox. Knowing full well from past experience General Ledlie's lack of military ability, that he should have allowed himself to be persuaded by a junior officer to go against his own sensibilities says little for Burnside's resolve. But to have actually given Ledlie the responsibility for such a critical undertaking was unforgivably bad judgment. And Burnside certainly must have been aware of the physical and mental condition of the men in the 1st Division.

General Meade's orders to Burnside were clear and direct. General Burnside's orders to Ledlie and the other division commanders were also clear, but they were not direct. The "if possibles" allowed too much latitude in decision making on the part of the division commanders. General Ledlie's orders to his brigade commanders, Bartlett and Marshall, flatly contradicted those of Meade and Burnside. General Bartlett's misinterpretation of Ledlie's orders concerning the direction in which he should have led his men is difficult to understand from a Harvard graduate and a well-seasoned field-grade officer.

Supervision was the key to the failure. While it is a fact that Ledlie (who through the years has been the whipping boy, along with his men, for the disaster—and rightly so for the part he played) was not on the field to direct his troops, it is also clear that Burnside was not there either to direct Ledlie and his other division commanders. And the same holds true for Meade and Grant. Meade was Burnside's boss as Grant was Meade's.

There were the little things that were related directly to that lack of supervision, as well. Among them, the mine exploded more than an hour late because nobody had seen to it that Colonel Pleasants had received the proper fuse; no ladders had been placed in the Union trenches for the soldiers to climb out on; the abatis had not been removed in front of the IX Corps' lines, and the troops could not form properly, nor had adequate steps been taken to clear the same from in front of Elliott's Salient during the initial charge; troops piling into the rear of the 2nd Pennsylvania in the overcrowded staging area only added to the confusion already being caused by the residue of the explosion; regimental commanders in some cases were inexperienced—for example, the 57th's Major Prescott—and neither Bartlett nor Marshall was able to maintain the cohesion of their brigades.

There is little doubt that had the 1st Division rushed Cemetery Hill right away, the outcome would have been quite different for the Union, but General Bartlett claimed, and rightly so, that his orders from Ledlie were not to take the hill, but to fortify the Rebel trenches. He tried to do what he had been told to do. When the general finally realized that he could move on to the crest, his men were so scattered that they could not be rallied.

Because Bartlett had not gone ahead, when the 2nd and 3rd Divisions arrived they became entangled with the 1st, considerably aggravating an already serious situation.

The 4th Division's attack was late. When the blacks did charge, their general, Ferrero, was with Ledlie, drunk, and the Negro troops, too, suffered from lack of top command.

The elements from the XVIII corps simply made matters worse. They should not have been dispatched, but the V Corps, on the left of the IX Corps' lines, should have been—not into the crater, but into that section of the Rebel trenches south of the crater, thus relieving Confederate pressure from that quarter.

That Meade suspended support from other infantry corps at nine-forty-five after the battle was determined to be unwinnable for the North is understandable, but why he called off Federal artillery supporting fire as the Southerners increased the use of their heavy guns is almost incomprehensible.

There are other factors that could be added to the list, but it is obvious that the failure that day rests primarily with the commanders—army, corps, division, and, to a much lesser extent, brigade and regiment—and not with the average fighting man, white or black. When the heavy combat started, the vast majority of the men fought as hard as they knew how under the circumstances.[67]

★

The battle of the Crater was an affair so confusing that many contemporary accounts differ wildly in regard to its details. In a sense, it was a fight very much like that fought in the Wilderness, where often an overview is all that can be pieced together because of the bedlam brought on by the conditions inherent to the engagement. (Parts of the crater, for example, were so packed with troops that they could not move, while in other areas of the huge hole there was room to maneuver and return fire.) Irrespective of those conditions, however, certain facts, well documented, cannot be ignored.

19

Thirty Men

O N JULY 31, Lieutenant Barton, after reflecting on the events of the preceding day, wrote his mother and family from the 1st Division, IX Corps, field hospital at Petersburg concerning his feelings about the battle of the Crater: "We *accomplished Nothing* in the end. Although we drove the Johnnies from their works and held them for a time. . . .

"The Rebs now hold *all* the ground that we took in the morning. Genl Bartlett is a *Prisoner too bad* is it not?

"A 'flag of truce' was sent out this A M to exchange *wounded prisoners* with the Johnnies and they drove *it back*. All on account of the 'darkies' "

And on August 3, he added, "I trust the Colored troops did not win many laurels in this last Charge in fact the entire failure of the undertaking is laid upon their shoulders."[1]

While Barton's opinion of the 4th Division's performance in the Crater cannot be taken as correct in light of the facts, his attitude towards Ferrero's men was typical of the majority of Federal soldiers of the 1st Division who were engaged in the battle. The blacks, unjustly, were made scapegoats.

★

Meanwhile, the small remaining band of combat soldiers of the 57th Massachusetts continued their tedious routine in the trenches. Every day was a repeat of the previous one as the men stood picket duty, built and strengthened earthworks, dodged bullets and shells, and performed other fatigue duties equally dangerous and monotonous. And every day was another of endless boredom, sickness, wounds, death, and, above all for most of the boys, depressive loneliness. The filth and stagnation of the trenches grew worse, and the weather was cruel. The men thought the war and the misery it had wrought would never end.

With almost all of their comrades gone, would they be spared? Would they see home again? Those nagging questions were asked over and over. Some, however, took the attitude that fate was out of their hands, and that they would do what they had to do from day to day and not concern themselves with the consequences. It was useless to worry about what they could not control, they said. But others, a more pragmatic few, looked on their emaciated 57th Regiment and knew that the law of averages was catching up with them, and they knew that death or wounds most likely would be waiting for them in the next fight. But the majority of the tiny group tried to remain hopeful. On the outside they were hard, brown, sinewy veteran soldiers, but inside—deep in the dark places inside—they still were sensitive men who wanted their families, their homes, and peace. It was well known in the Army of the Potomac that the disease of "nostalgia" claimed many soldiers.

From July 31 until August 14, the regiment remained in its trenches across from the crater getting but very little rest. One day was spent on the picket line and the next on fatigue duty in the rear, and this routine never faltered. The Confederate harrassment was without letup, and during that time the 57th had one man killed, one man mortally wounded, and four wounded by sharpshooters and bombardment.[2]

Private Wesley Goddard, of Company F, a pensioned veteran of the 25th Massachusetts Volunteer Infantry, was critically injured on August 9 by the explosion of a shell from a Rebel mortar battery while he was on duty in the breastworks. Goddard, who had fought in every one of the regiment's battles, died from his shrapnel wounds on August 18.[3]

Like Goddard, Private William O. Hastings, of Company E, had participated in all of the 57th's engagements without serious harm. But on August 5, while on duty in the trenches, he was killed by a Rebel bullet.[4]

Those 6 losses reduced the regiment to 41 men present for duty, but 4 men who had been on convalescent leave returned, and by August 18, Lieutenant Albert Doty counted 45 soldiers in his command.[5]

One of the returning soldiers was Company C's Gustavus Holden, who had been convalescing at Carver U.S. Army General Hospital in Washington from the wound he had received at the Wilderness. He returned for duty on August 1, but during his absence he had not been idle. As he related, "My wound being healed, I joined a provisional battalion forming a part of the forces which drove [Confederate] Gen. [Jubal Anderson] Early back when he attempted to take Washington July 11 and 12, 1864." (That raid was made in an attempt to compel Grant into sending troops from Petersburg to the capital in order to relieve the pressure against Lee. The VI Corps was detached from the front lines and hurriedly sent north to defend Washington. However, nothing out of the ordinary occurred at Petersburg and Early did little more than scare "Abe Lincoln like hell!")[6]

★

The men drew clothing and equipment on August 6, and the Commonwealth of Massachusetts issued the regiment a new national flag and color staff on August 15, the 57th receiving it several days later. Even though the replacement could not dispel the regret associated with the lost banners and the shame of their capture, at least the soldiers had something symbolic to follow now, and the flag probably raised their morale a bit.[7]

★

The 1st Division of the IX Corps was in a shambles, and the generals thought that a temporary reorganization was necessary, so soon after the mine explosion, the 57th was assigned to a newly formed provisional 3rd Brigade (this assignment would last only a few days, after which the regiment would resume its place in the 1st Brigade). General Ledlie went home, later to resign in disgrace from the army on January 16, 1865. John Anderson noted, "His removal from command was a heavy loss to the enemy." Brigadier General Julius White assumed Ledlie's position on August 6, and Lieutenant Colonel Joseph H. Barnes of the 29th Massachusetts took charge of the brigade as a result of the capture of General Bartlett and Colonel Weld. Colonel Barnes was very popular with the 57th's soldiers, and they welcomed his choice as their new brigade leader. He was a veteran officer of many years of combat experience, and his understanding of military matters lent the men confidence.

On August 13, General Burnside left the Army of the Potomac on a leave of absence to his home in Rhode Island—he would never be recalled to duty. The boys were overjoyed at the departure of their nemesis Ledlie, but their corps commander was a different matter. They felt he had been cast as a whipping boy for the Crater disaster, that he was being used by Grant and Meade to cover their own poor judgments in the battle. The men genuinely liked Ambrose E. Burnside, and most of them were unhappy to see him depart. Two days after he left the IX Corps, he was succeeded in command by Major General John G. Parke, his former aide, who would remain with the men until the end.[8]

★

Lieutenant General U. S. Grant's strategy of pounding Lee's lines into atoms was not working. The Confederates were too well entrenched, and nothing that the Federal chief could do with his mighty Army of the Potomac, it seemed, could dislodge them—at least nothing in the conventional siege-warfare approach of the time. So Sam Grant came up with a new idea. What if, he reasoned, with his superior number of troops, he continued his lines to the left, gradually encircling Petersburg, and, therefore, Lee and his army, causing the Rebels to stretch their defenses so thin to counter him that they would become more vulnerable to a concentrated attack at any given point? At the same time, it would be possible to bottle up still another railroad, the Weldon & Petersburg, and further cut Lee's supply lines. Perhaps the Rebel commander could be starved into surrender. The more Grant thought about it, and the more he discussed the notion with his staff and George Gordon Meade, the more feasible the plan sounded. And there was something else that added to that feasibility.

At that time General Hancock's II Corps was again on the the offensive north of the James River at Deep Bottom, and intelligence obtained from Confederate prisoners indicated that Lee had withdrawn at least two and possibly three more brigades from the Petersburg defenses on August 14 to move north of the river and reinforce his troops, who were trying to keep Hancock at bay. That was good news to Grant, and he intended to exploit the consequently weak Southern lines at Petersburg.[9]

General Warren was summoned to the army's headquarters at City Point, and his bosses, Grant and Meade, explained the idea to him. Gouverneur Kemble Warren's V Corps was stationed on the left of the Union lines, and the aim was for it to march about three miles west and capture the area around Globe Tavern and destroy a large section of the adjacent Weldon Railroad. When he had accomplished that, Warren was to swing north, following the route of the Halifax road—which parallelled the railroad tracks—and march as far as he could towards Petersburg, taking all the ground possible.[10]

At eleven o'clock on the night of August 14, the 1st Brigade (to which the 57th had been reassigned recently, with Colonel Barnes still in command) of the 1st Division and other elements of the IX Corps were ordered to vacate their lines opposite the Crater and move four miles to the left, to Hancock Station on the U.S. Military Railroad close to where it intersected with the Jerusalem Plank road. As the men were leaving quietly, the XVIII Corps moved up and took over their position. For the first time in two months the entire brigade was out of the dangerous forward areas, and the soldiers felt relieved. After a short halt in the woods along the line of march, the regiments of the brigade stretched themselves out at daybreak and occupied the old trenches of the V Corps with the purpose of relieving the troops of that unit for a forced reconnaissance on the Weldon Railroad.[11]

The 57th, along with the rest of the 1st Brigade, was assigned to picket duty on the skirmish line right away. A drenching rain was falling that dark and muddy night, and as the men took up station in front of the trenches they found themselves in an open area completely exposed to Rebel skirmishers and sharpshooters and with no defensive works. In their old position they had had holes that gave them some protection, but here there was nothing.

The situation was frightening until they accustomed themselves to the fact that the distance was so great between the opposing siege lines that they were perfectly safe. Using the cover of darkness in the downpour, they went to work, out of the well-learned habit of self-preservation, quickly digging and building until they had enough earthworks and shelters to protect themselves. That night most of the soldiers had their first good, uninterrupted sleep in eight weeks. But there were some who could not sleep because the night was so quiet, and those men were anxious and spooked by the stillness surrounding them. The IX Corps remained in that position for the next three days.[12]

★

Early on the morning of August 18, the V Corps moved out toward the Weldon Railroad, and Warren's men began to engage the enemy before noon. Grant had learned the day before, as a result of the further interrogation of Confederate prisoners, that Major General William Mahone's division and one brigade of Major General Bushrod Johnson's Army of Northern Virginia, had been sent north of the James to bolster the Southern efforts against Hancock, and that news made Grant a happy man indeed. In a telegram to Meade that night, the lieutenant general relayed, "This leaves the [Confederate] force at Petersburg reduced to what it was when the mine was sprung [on July 30]. Warren may find an opportunity to do more than expected." Clearly the commanding general of all the United States armies was optimistic.[13]

On August 19, the IX Corps was ordered to move further to the west, its left, to connect with and support the V Corps, which had been fighting for possession of the Weldon Railroad most of the previous day. At three o'clock that morning, the 57th was awakened by the beating of the long roll of reveille, and the men got themselves up for the march to Globe Tavern, or "The Yellow House," as the soldiers called it, several miles away. At that hour, troops of the XVIII Corps were beginning to arrive to take over the trenches occupied by General Willcox's 3rd Division, and Willcox had his men on the road by 3:30 A.M.[14]

Brigadier General Gershom Mott, meanwhile, had arrived with some of his division of II Corps men, and he began to relieve White's division of the IX Corps. But it took until two o'clock that afternoon to bring up enough of Colonel John Pulford's brigade of Mott's division to allow White to pull out completely. Finally General White assembled the 1st Division near the Jones house three hundred yards northwest of Hancock Station, and after drawing ammunition and three days' rations, the men stood around in a drizzling rain and deep mud waiting for the order to march.[15]

With the division's artillery left behind to protect Pulford's brigade, White's infantrymen finally got under way at three o'clock, with the 1st

Brigade in the lead. As the worn-out 57th Regiment started off in the ranks, the few survivors passed by their division commander and their surgeon, Dr. Whitman White, who was now in charge of the 1st Division hospital three miles in the rear. Dr. White had come to the front to visit his regiment the previous night and to check on the health and well-being of his remaining men. He had found the lines quiet and the men relaxing in their trenches. It had been a balmy evening, with the Massachusetts soldiers enjoying the pleasant weather.[16]

Dr. White thought himself a compassionate man and a friend of every soldier in the regiment, and as his worn-out men passed where he and General White were standing that wet and hot August afternoon on their way to battle, Private Uriah Bassett of Company A broke ranks and went to speak to the doctor. "Doctor," pleaded Bassett, "I have no musket. May I go to the rear?" Dr. White, who was also a major in the regiment, answered, "Go with us, my boy, we will take care of you."[17]

Private Bassett, who had been wounded in the Wilderness and who had just returned to the regiment for duty on August 12, fell in, and the 57th trudged on with the division down the Jerusalem Plank road, and then swung west and continued on over two miles of muddy, secondary country lanes in Prince George County through the piny forests of Petersburg. The rain came down in sheets, and the going was hard, and the division did not reach the Aiken house, located a mile northeast of Globe Tavern, until five o'clock that afternoon. But Lieutenant Doty and his bedraggled little group of forty-four men kept up like the veterans that they had become, and no one straggled.[18]

Except for the slippery, fouled roads, the stormy weather that slowed the men down to an agonizing pace, and occasional shots heard in the distance, the march was uneventful until the head of the column, Barnes's 1st Brigade, reached the vicinity of the right of the V Corps lines in clearings north of the Lanier house, four hundred yards west of Aiken's. Shortly after the 1st Division's arrival, suddenly and without warning, the 3rd Division of the IX Corps, which had arrived early that morning—bivouacking in the farm fields on the east side of Globe Tavern—and had been engaged during the day, was attacked on its right by Rebels firing furiously into Willcox's flank from the protection of the dense woods that skirted the cornfields to the north.[19]

Hearing the battle get under way in front of him, Julius White ordered the brigade commanders of the 1st Division to move their men in the direction of the fighting while he sent an aide galloping off to locate General Warren to ask where his division would serve the most good.[20]

With Dr. White riding beside General White and his staff, the soldiers moved forward at the double-quick and entered a cornfield in the right rear of Willcox's 3rd Division. No one in the 1st Division suspected the presence of Rebel troops in their immediate vicinity. Commanders and privates alike thought them all up ahead in the direction of the shooting, which was coming generally from the west. Then, from the woods on their right, just as unexpectedly as the attack on Willcox's troops had come, a Confederate volley ripped through the 1st Division's flank, held by the 1st Brigade. One of the first victims was unarmed Uriah Bassett, dead with a bullet hole square through the center of his forehead.[21]

The men quickly formed into battle lines amid the tall brown cornstalks, tore open paper cartridges, rammed Minié balls home, fixed bayonets, and kept on going forward through the fields and over fences toward the western woods, returning fire in volleys. Colonel Barnes's 1st Brigade in the lead fell in with its right flank on the rough north-south Johnson road near Lanier's. The boys formed line of battle in double ranks, with the 59th Massachusetts on the left, the 57th next to it, then the 100th Pennsylvania and the 21st, 35th, 56th, and 29th Massachusetts. The regiments kept good lines, performing complicated field maneuvers under the direction of General White, who was astride his horse out in front of the men waving his felt hat and shouting orders and encouragement. The soldiers were inspired by the general, and they cheered him and the Union loudly. After a short halt caused by a driving Confederate volley on the 1st Brigade's left and an orderly retreat of about fifty feet, the regiments turned forward and advanced once again toward the left and then front. They were isolated from the rest of the corps and the army—entirely on their own—but were making a parade-ground show of their situation.[22]

The Confederates, under the command of General A. P. Hill, were from Alfred Colquitt's brigade of Mahone's division—which had been rushed back from Deep Bottom to help stem the Yankee advance on the railroad—and what with their rattling barrages of musket fire and nerve-chilling, high-pitched Rebel yells, the Northerners were threatened with disaster, and for a time they were staggered. But the order was heard above the racket, "Fire, and give them hell!" and the men of the 1st Division knelt in the mud, and loading and firing as fast as they could, returned a killing wall of lead, knocking Colquitt's line of veteran Georgia foot soldiers to fragments. "Fire low, men, fire low!" were the only commands screamed by the officers as they themselves grabbed muddy Springfields and Enfields from the fallen and joined in the slaughter.[23]

Almost immediately the Federal artillery in the rear opened in support of the infantrymen, their deadly shells fired so low over the men's heads that the boys swore the missiles cut off the tops of the cornstalks as they slammed into the butternut lines. White's soldiers finally established a solid defense near the woods in an area formerly held by General John Hartranft's brigade of Willcox's 3rd Division. It had been a vile little battle lasting about half an hour in the smoky, rain-soaked fields, with the Southerners repeatedly

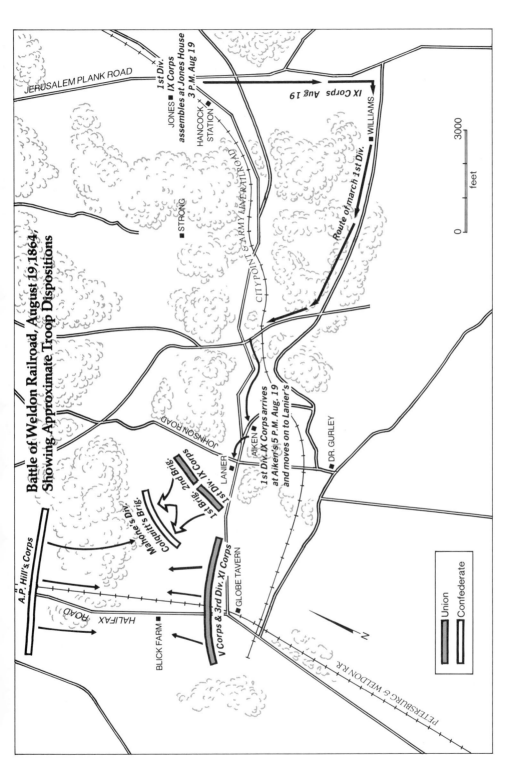

Battle of Weldon Railroad, August 19, 1864, Showing Approximate Troop Dispositions

JERUSALEM PLANK ROAD

1st Div.
IX Corps
assembles at Jones House
3 P.M. Aug 19

JONES ■
HANCOCK
STATION

IX Corps Aug 19

WILLIAMS ■

STRONG ■

CITY POINT & ARMY LINE RAILROAD

Route of march 1st Div.

0   3000   feet

JOHNSON ROAD

LANIER ■

AIKEN ■

1st Div. IX Corps arrives
at Aiken's 5 P.M. Aug 19
and moves on to Lanier's

DR. GURLEY ■

2nd Brig.
1st DIV. IX Corps
1st Brig.

Mahone's Div.
Colquitt's Brig.

A.P. Hill's Corps

HALIFAX ROAD

BLICK FARM ■

V Corps & 3rd Div. XI Corps
GLOBE TAVERN ■

N

PETERSBURG & WELDON RR

Union
Confederate

273

charging the Federal position, each time being thrown back wickedly. Lee's soldiers suffered heavy casualties, and the Confederates were driven in thoroughly on that part of the battlefield by the 1st Division of the IX Corps.[24]

John Anderson, in his original history of the regiment, told an interesting story about Sergeant Edward F. Potter, a member of Company K.

Among the many instances related around the campfires, one of surpassing bravery has been told us, which is vouched for on good authority [Anderson was absent wounded during the battle]. During the engagement known as the Weldon Railroad, while the 57th was under command of 1st Lieutenant Doty, it was posted in an exposed position and unsupported. 1st Serg. [actually only sergeant at that time] Edward F. Potter of Company K was posted as a marker on the left of the regiment, but before the line could be established a terrible assault was made by the enemy and the regiment driven back, but the sergeant remained at his post amidst a shower of leaden bullets. The right general guide was killed [that man could not have been a member of the 57th]. The general commanding the division [White] rode up and exclaimed to the regimental commander [Doty], "What in hell is that damned fool [Potter] doing out there? Who in [hell] is he?" To which [Doty] replied, "That, sir, is my left general guide, posted by your order, which he obeys." [White] then said, "Doesn't the darned fool know enough to come in?" The reply was: "That man always obeys orders and will stand there until shot, unless relieved by proper authority." "Well, relieve him mighty quick," said the general. The next morning an order came from the general for the sergeant to report to him in person. He reported as directed, but with many misgivings as to what it all meant, whether it foreboded good or evil for him. He finally stood trembling in [the] presence of the general, who proceeded to take the chevrons denoting the rank of sergeant from his arms, but in place of them he sent him back to the regiment wearing the straps of a commissioned officer, which he wore with honor until the regiment was mustered out of service.

That field commission, however, was not confirmed until January 3, 1865, and Potter remained an enlisted man until then. But on November 8, he was promoted to first sergeant.[25]

★

Dr. White, meanwhile, seeing the urgent need for a dressing station immediately upon the beginning of the fight, had gathered his staff and galloped to the rear. There they discovered, under a nearby hill, the Gurley house, which they immediately requisitioned for a field hospital.

Soon, the wounded were pouring into the house and yard, and pandemonium took charge as the doctors and hospital orderlies tried to keep up with their gruesome work. Men of the IX and V Corps and Confederate wounded alike were being brought into the dressing station, and the place soon took on the look of a butchery. Macabre piles of bloody amputated limbs began to accumulate in the yard. Screaming, moaning, dying, and bloody men clogged all the space around and in the building as assistant surgeons and hospital orderlies tried to give them whiskey and opium pills to counteract shock and quiet them. All night and into the next day the surgeons worked while the rains continued to fall, making everyone miserable. The roads in that part of the woods were practically nonexistent—little more than cow paths—and bringing up ambulances to move men to proper medical facilities was almost impossible on those narrow, mired lanes, so many of the wounded died as a result of not being able to be transported to the better-equipped field hospitals in the rear.[26]

Dr. White later expressed his remorse for young Bassett's unnecessary death and his own mistaken judgment. "The worn-out little private who had asked to go to the rear when we started, lay dead with a bullet hole through his forehead. When I saw his lifeless form, as he lay between the rows of corn, I reproached myself for not allowing him to go to the rear," he said.[27]

On the battlefield, the dead and wounded were scattered over the muddy ground and among the cornstalks—scores of which had been chopped down by the thousands and thousands of bullets and shells that went clipping through them—and the blood from those soldiers diluted in the rainwater, turning it pink in little pools.

Darkness came soon after the men had fired their last shots, and under orders from General White, who suspected a renewal of the battle in the morning, the division moved off to its left into the pines and oaks, which dripped on the exhausted soldiers all during the dismal night as they tried to sleep on beds hastily fashioned from cornstalks. But it was not only nature that made the night uncomfortable, as the sleepless soldiers kept one eye open and one ear cocked in the direction of the Rebels, ready for any eventuality.[28]

The V Corps very well might have caved in had it not been for the arrival of the IX Corps—the shamed corps of the Army of the Potomac—and the men knew it. That night they began to feel a little of their old pride again as they lay in the woods, wretched and wet. This had been the first time since the disgrace of the Crater that most of them had seen combat, and they were proud that they had won the day from some of the same troops that had ruined them at Elliott's Salient. The boys had reached the cornfield just in time to help check an attack by the enemy on the V Corps' flank. They had gotten some revenge, and it made them feel good. All night the Confederate wounded moaned and cried out, but aside from that inconvenience the hours passed uneventfully.[29]

In the end, the Federals not only prevailed but gained significant ground for the Army of the Potomac in the battle for the Weldon Railroad on August 19, although they suffered heavy casualties. The V Corps' drive up the Halifax road into Petersburg had failed, however. It was forced back to its position of August 18 at Globe Tavern, but despite repeated attacks from the Southerners, the IX and V Corps lines were held. A. P. Hill's corps had been staved off, but his men captured almost twenty-seven hundred Union prisoners of war during the fight.[30]

★

Early the next day, August 20, after waiting a few hours for a renewed attack which never materialized, at least not in its area, White's division established picket lines, and all the rest of the morning was spent retrieving the hundreds of corpses from the forest and burying them—some of the men looted trophies from the dead before putting the bodies into the ground—and taking the wounded to the hospitals. The Federals, in surveying the field that day, found 60 injured Confederates and 516 Southern rifles. Several Rebels had deserted to the Union lines, as well.[31]

After the battlefield had been mopped up pretty well, White's division was drawn back to the east side of the clearing, where new earthworks were constructed connecting to the right of Hartranft's brigade of the 3rd Division and the left of Potter's 2nd Division. General Parke's IX Corps' lines now extended northeastward towards Petersburg, and by August 21, they were complete, with the men entrenched well and connected to other sections of the Federal works.

The IX Corps was now posted between the V Corps on the left at Weldon Railroad and elements of the II Corps on the right near the Jerusalem Plank road, and Parke's lines stretched in an arc, bulging to the east, for almost three miles. Willcox's 3rd Division was to the right of the V Corps two miles southeast of the main Confederate trench line. Along the Jerusalem Plank road, the nearest that the men got to the Rebel works was a mile, so the IX Corps' soldiers, except for the few days preceding the Battle of Weldon Railroad were in a more comfortable position than they had been for some time. Before, most of their trenches had been separated from the Confederate fortifications by about one hundred yards. Nevertheless, the close vigils on the skirmish lines were maintained, and the men dug in hard and built solid breastworks. They expected an attack by Lee at any time to attempt to recover his railroad, and on August 21, the attack came on the Federal left. But the Yankees were positioned too solidly, and the repeated Southern assaults gained the Rebels nothing except heavy loss of life. The Union ranks were culled well also, but they could not be broken. The 1st Division of the IX Corps, which was not engaged on August 21, then numbered fewer than one thousand combat soldiers.[32]

★

The 57th was reduced severely once again in the Weldon Railroad action. One man had been killed, 2 mortally wounded, and 6 wounded. Four others were missing and presumed dead and 3 more taken prisoners of war, including one of the wounded. Companies B and D had been destroyed totally, and Company A could muster only one combat soldier, Sergeant John O'Donnell, from County Waterford, Ireland. The 57th Massachusetts Volunteers now mustered on the line only 29 enlisted men, of which almost half were non-commissioned officers, and Lieutenant Doty—barely the strength of one-third of a company. It was smashed to bits. But most of those men left were the toughest in the regiment, and 10 of them—10 out of the original 916 men who left Worcester—somehow would see it through to the end, fighting in every battle and skirmish, and marching on every march with the 57th from first to last.[33]

But at least one in their ranks had had enough. Private Oscar Phelps, of Company G, one of the thirty unwounded survivors, deserted the day after the fight, August 20. Phelps had been in most of the 57th's battles and hardly could be called a coward. In fact, the young private was to return later, only to be taken prisoner of war the following year.[34]

★

Not only was the 57th a near-total wreck now, but the whole IX Corps was not in much better shape, and it was ordered consolidated and reorganized by General Parke on September 13, under General Orders No. 39. General White had taken sick leave on August 28, and under the general order he was formally relieved of his duties as commander of the 1st Division, General Willcox taking his place. The 4th Division became the 3rd Division. "The following changes in the corps are hereby announced," read the orders. "The 3rd Division, Brig. General O. B. Willcox commanding, will be known as the 1st Division. The 4th Division, Brig. General Edward Ferrero commanding, will be known as the 3rd Division." However, a circular order was issued two days later, on September 15, allowing the men to retain their original color corps badges and flags (for example, the old 3rd Division men, who had worn a light blue badge, would not have to change them to the red of the 1st Division). Robert Potter still retained command of the 2nd Division. A new 3rd Brigade of the 1st Division was organized also, and it was made up of what was left of the 57th, along with the 29th and 59th Massachusetts, the 3rd Maryland, the 100th Pennsylvania, and the 14th New York Heavy Artillery.[35]

All of those outfits had lost heavily, and the brigade barely came to a regiment's strength of one thousand soldiers. They were hard men, and their battle flags were shot to shreds, some being little more than rags attached to their staffs. The soldiers' uniforms, from regiment to regiment, were hardly uniform, and they wore whatever was available. Many of the forage caps had given way to black felt slouch hats—the 56th Massachusetts, now in another brigade, wore them exclusively—that were more comfortable and practical.

Some of the enterprising men had managed to wrangle a pair of cavalry boots from some unsuspecting trooper, and blanket rolls over the shoulder had replaced some of their knapsacks. The majority of the soldiers in the ranks could not have cared less about military regulations at that stage of their army experience; comfort, practicality, and self-preservation were the order of the day.

For the next few weeks the front in the area around the 57th remained quiet except for some minor sniping and picket firing. The men tried to rest as much as possible, but there was not much time for that with the constant building of fortifications. On August 25, the regiment moved to the left about one-half mile to Blick's Station on the Weldon Railroad, seven hundred yards west of Globe Tavern, and remained there until September 29.[36] As soon as they arrived at their new location, the men went to work constructing strong defensive breastworks. Some dug the pits, while others chopped down big, solid pines to shore up the soil. Still others stood guard over their comrades. It was hot, wearisome work, but the men kept at it constantly; their survival depended on good defenses.

During the regiment's stay at Blick's Station, some of the officers and men, who had been recuperating from wounds or sickness, returned to duty. And on September 2, Lieutenant Hitchcock and 20 of the original 28 enlisted men who had been detached serving on the IX Corps' cattle guard also returned to duty. (The other 8 were absent sick. During its duty as cattle guard, the detail had seen no combat of any kind.) When the 57th was ready to move out at the end of September, it had present 93 officers and enlisted men for combat duty.[37]

On August 31, the regiment had been mustered for pay, and even then the ranks were beginning to swell with returning soldiers. Company C, for example, had 3 men remaining after the battle of Weldon Railroad, but when the paymaster, Major Wheeler, showed up to settle accounts, 14 privates and 3 noncommissioned officers signed Company C's payroll vouchers.[38]

Corporal Henry Perry, of Company K, who had been promoted to his rank for bravery during the June 17 assault, took over the duties of regimental postmaster on August 30, when Corporal Lowell was detailed as clerk for Company C. Perry had just missed out on the battle at Weldon Railroad because of a slight wound he had taken on August 14 while the regiment was pulling out of its trenches across from the Crater.[39]

On September 3, Julius Tucker returned to the 57th with the rank of lieutenant colonel, to which he had been promoted after the June 17 assault. Tucker was not fully recovered, and some remarked that he should still be convalescing, but the lieutenant colonel answered that he was well enough to be with his regiment, and he felt that his duty was there and not at home in bed. He praised the frazzled Lieutenant Doty for his conduct and asked many questions as to what had happened to the regiment. The colonel scarcely could believe that only those few were all that remained. Doty briefed him as well as he could.[40]

On September 14, Napoleon Bonaparte McLaughlen was mustered into the United States service as colonel of the 57th. The men had been waiting for him for a long time, and when he arrived the battle-wise veteran volunteers sized him up quickly for what he was: ambitious, cool, strict, and regular army, and they wanted no part of him. They had given enough, and they had no intention of giving any more to finance a brigadier's star on the shoulder of someone whom they did not know or like.[41]

Even so, McLaughlen inventoried his new regiment right away and was appalled at what he found. On the day of his arrival, he wrote a desperate letter to William Schouler, adjutant general for the Commonwealth of Massachusetts:

General,
I have the honor to require for my regiment—57th Mass. Infty.—three hundred and seventy seven recruits. I have but one hundred and thirty four for duty—the balance being absent sick or wounded.
I find six hundred and sixty nine borne on the "muster roll." Consequently my command is but one hundred and thirty four men. It is very desirable to increase my command as soon as possible. If you will send me five hundred men I will make good use of them.
I presume that out of the five hundred and thirty five absent I will never see three.[42]

Although he claimed 134 men for duty, many of those were still detached on various assignments—ambulance corps, clerks, hospital duty, quartermaster and commissary departments, and so on.[43]

Receiving no satisfaction from his request, he wrote to the adjutant general again in exasperation on October 15, "For God sake send me some recruits if possible." But five hundred new soldiers for the 57th was wishful thinking, and, with the exception of six recruits—almost an insult to McLaughlen's request—the regiment would continue to the end with only whatever it could muster in the field at any given time.[44]

Much to the satisfaction of the men of the 57th, McLaughlen very soon discerned that he was senior to Lieutenant Colonel Barnes. Barnes was relieved and sent back to the 29th Massachusetts, and McLaughlen took command of the brigade. Tucker was left in charge of the 57th, although the new brigade commander maintained a close watch on the regiment as he was still its official leader.[45]

★

In general, the month of September was quiet for the regiment and for most of the army. The men of the 57th took time to rest. They drew new uniforms and equipment on September 27 and managed to keep themselves much cleaner in their relatively peaceful works at Blick's Station. There was the usual picket duty, but because they were so far away from the Rebel trenches, there was not as much activity on the skirmish line as they were used to. George Barton had returned to the regiment on September 11, his wound healed, and he reported home, "We are not troubled at all with any of those 'shells' that I dislike so much. . . ."[46] The only real excitement occurred when Confederate General Wade Hampton, leading the late General J. E. B. Stuart's cavalry troopers, went on a raid around the Federal rear and captured two thousand steers and three hundred prisoners on September 17, at the Army of the Potomac's cattle corrals near Coggin's Point and Harrison's Landing on the James River. The soldiers on both sides enjoyed Hampton's audacity, and the raid was the subject of countless stories and jokes.

Lieutenant Barton recorded two good descriptions of the 57th's activity during the month of September. On September 16, he wrote his mother from Blick's Station (actually a farm close to the tracks of the Weldon Railroad):

It is a lovely night, *full moon* the Pickets make just enough noise to keep us from feeling *lonesome*—& going to sleep too early. I have been on Picket & "fatigue" duty *every day* since I reported for duty. Today I have worked building an "Abbattis" in front of our lines. Yesterday was detailed to take charge of a working party to make a Corderroy [corduroy] road. Our works at this place are very strong with two lines of "Abbattis" in front making them almost & *we think impregnable.* At least we are anxious to have them tried, but it has not been *our luck* to fight *behind* our *own* works. We must never *Charge* upon theirs. It will prove a sad day for the "Johnnies" if they ever attempt to charge upon this line of works. The Chaplain [Dashiell] has just treated us to a pail of lemonade. . . ."

And on September 27, addressing his letter to the whole family, he wrote,

Our Division has just been relieved from duty in the *front lines* by a portion of the 5th Corps. We are now in camp in *the woods* & very Comfortably situated. Cant tell how long we shall remain so. Today our *entire regiment* officers & all were detailed to work on a *large "fort"* [probably Fort Blaisdell], which will mount 27 guns. This fort protects our *rear* & covers the *"Jerusalem Plank Road"* it is a very strong work & when finished could never be taken by the "Johnnies" without paying us *our price* for it and we should set it *very* high.[47]

Much of the talk around the campfires during that time was about the upcoming presidential election in November between Abraham Lincoln, the incumbent Republican, and his challenger, the former commander of the

Army of the Potomac, Major General George Brinton McClellan, a Democrat running on an immediate-end-to-the-war platform. The majority of the army upheld Lincoln, particularly the old veterans who had been in the war from the early days, and they were not inclined to support their former commander, McClellan, with his party's political views. After all, the Democrats wanted to make concessions to Jefferson Davis, and the old campaigners did not think it right that they had been fighting and suffering and seeing their comrades killed and maimed for the past three and a half years only to see McClellan siding with people who wanted to give it all up. And, for the most part, the new veterans, such as those in the 57th, who had sacrificed as much as anyone, agreed. Lincoln won in November with a great boost from the soldiers' votes.

★

So the days of early autumn of 1864 passed by, and the routine and boredom of life in the foul trenches continued. But the men hoped for one last, decisive battle that year which would end the war and get them home for Christmas.

20

This Damnable Place for a Dog

S PRING AND SUMMER in South Georgia were torrid in 1864, and for the men of the 57th Massachusetts and the thousands of other Union soldiers imprisoned there, Andersonville Prison was a nightmare of hell incarnate. Within the stockade, not one tree had been left standing under which a man might find some shady relief. The only shelters available in which to find refuge from the merciless sun were wretched shanties that the prisoners slapped together from torn blankets and rags thrown over crude stick and brush frames. These shanties, called "shebangs" by the inmates and packed tightly one against the other, were laid out in a haphazard fashion with no thought given to order; open space was nearly nonexistent and the men constantly crowded in upon one another. The condition of the camp was one of unparalleled filth, and disease was rampant. A branch of Sweetwater Creek flowed east to west in a hollow on the camp's south end, and in this creek the captured soldiers were expected to find their drinking water and to wash. In addition, the stream was to be used as a latrine. The creek, however, passed through the area used by the prison guards for their bivouac before it entered the stockade, and because the Confederate sentries also used it for their own latrine purposes, the water that flowed through the camp was putrid and unfit for drinking or bathing—it was literally an open sewer. Nevertheless, Sweetwater Creek was the only source of water initially, and the men had no choice but to drink from it, and, if they wanted to wash, they were compelled to bathe in it as well. (As time went on, though, the prisoners would dig wells, and a spring—"Providence Spring"—would appear rather mysteriously that August, and the water problem would be alleviated somewhat.)[1]

At the North Gate, hundreds of new arrivals poured daily into the already overcrowded compound, while from the South Gate vast numbers of corpses were carried to the dead house each day only to be laid shoulder to shoulder

Southwest view of the stockade prison in Andersonville, Georgia, August 17, 1864;
note the dead line, prisoners' "shebangs," and
Confederate guard tower *(top right).*
(USAMHI, Carlisle Barracks, Pa.)

with their comrades in shallow trench graves that were filled in hastily and unceremoniously with red Georgia clay. A camp hospital had been set up by the Southerners, but it was woefully lacking in medical supplies and adequate personnel. As a consequence, thousands of afflicted men who otherwise might have survived died from the lack of proper medical attention. But men died constantly within the stockade from disease, too, as well as from exposure, starvation, and being shot by Confederate guards, and some even died at the hands of their own comrades. A hundred or so corpses a day would be thrown on wagons like cordwood to make the short trip to the cemetery about three hundred yards northwest of the prison pen.[2]

Food, and the lack of it, was one of the primary causes of the suffering, disease, and death at Andersonville. The men were supposed to be issued the same ration their guards received, but that was hardly the case. William Peabody wrote in his diary of being given "Mush, Corn Bread, ham, ½ ration." Those rations were of abysmally poor quality and provided precious few of the nutrients needed to sustain human life. Prisoners who survived a long term of incarceration at Andersonville arrived back in the Federal lines skin and bones, and many, if not all, suffered from the effects of prison for the rest of their lives.[3]

Daily life for the prisoners was one of endless tedium and misery in Andersonville. The only required routine of the day was for the soldiers to assemble in detachments of 270 men each at seven o'clock every morning for roll call and disbursement of rations. Unless he was detailed for other duties, such as burial, wood gathering, or such other work, a man had nothing to do but to pass the time as best he could and protect himself from the elements. Little mail was allowed in or out, and the only news of events beyond the stockade walls usually came when new prisoners were brought in. Insanity was hardly unknown at Andersonville.[4]

Because it was all but impossible to wash in Sweetwater Creek, the prisoners were foul almost beyond imagination. They were covered with lice and bitten endlessly by chiggers, gnats, and mosquitoes, their faces and hands were blackened from the pitch smoke of the mean little cooking fires they made, their hair and beards were matted and caked with dirt, and their clothes hung in rags, some men being entirely naked. No clothing of any kind was issued to Federal soldiers by the Confederate States government at that prison. And with all that filth, the slightest scratch or sore could take a man's life as gangrene set in. Open wounds were rarely survivable.[5]

This chapter is not intended to undertake a detailed study of Andersonville Prison. Excellent accounts of that camp have been written by others, and one more examination would be redundant. Rather, this chapter will focus on the daily life endured by the prisoners through the eyewitness accounts of the two men from the 57th Regiment who chronicled their stay in that vile place. While every one of the roughly forty-five thousand men who were incarcerated there during the prison's existence surely had his own unique experiences and troubles, it is equally certain that all of them shared a great deal in common. William Peabody's daily writings in his diary address much that was singular about himself, but at the same time they offer a day-to-day, first-person glimpse of existence there that was shared by all. Austin Gould's overview account of the prison adds an appropriate counterpoint and balance to Peabody's commentary.

★

Private William T. Peabody appears to have begun his stay at Andersonville in a hopeful frame of mind. Of his first night in the stockade that May 29, 1864, he wrote the following morning that it was "Beautiful to contemplate; sleep on the ground and nothing to cover him[self] with but the canopy of Heaven and the ground for a bed." At that time, he estimated that there were eighteen thousand men with him in confinement.

The weather for May 31 was "fine, no rain"; however, he complained of having "to sit in the shade [i.e., in a shebang] in the middle of the day it is so hot." But the heat and the lack of proper nutrition apparently were already beginning to tell on him. He had gone down to the foul creek to wash his socks and towel, and that small chore had made him "very tired."

The days for William Peabody and his fellow prisoners, he wrote, were "spent in cooking, catching lice and hanging around; it is mighty hard work. . . ." And he complained on June 2 and 3 that he was "not feeling very well . . . [in] the prisoners hell . . . feet very much swollen and my big toe is very sory [sorry]." It had also begun to rain on June 3, and the following day thunderstorms continued all day. Certainly those showers must have been welcome to the men, not only for their cooling effect, but also for a chance to collect some fresh water in their tin drinking cups. Peabody and many other prisoners probably would have taken the opportunity to wash a bit in the rain. "All I do is keep clean," he noted that day but added that he had "no soap or anything else."

Nevertheless, his attitude seemed to remain positive through early June and he remarked that his "courage is good" and that he was "bound to come out all right and be at home soon as possible." Physically he was not in as good a condition. His feet remained "very much swollen," and he had "nothing to wear upon them." But his principal concern evidently was for his family, and he was distraught because he was certain that his wife, Hannah, had no idea what had become of him after the battle of the Wilderness. He tried, however, as no doubt did most prisoners early in their stay at Andersonville, to put his situation in perspective by keeping a sense of humor. In the second week of the month, he wrote that he was "still here in this place of confinement enjoying life hugely cooking and [doing] other business to keep us alive until we get into our lines where a fellow can live. Devil take this place."

Gossip and false rumors that they soon would be repatriated were rife among the soldiers incarcerated at the prison, and William Peabody and the other Federals, at first, seemed to clutch desperately for any such tales. Given the intolerable conditions in which they had to exist, it is quite understandable for men to be so gullible and naive—they had nothing else on which to pin any hope of surviving except a firm belief that their government would not abandon them, and that their exchange was imminent. "2 Catholic priests have been into this place today," he wrote on June 9, "and they say that we shall soon be out of this place and I think so too. Can't do it too quick for our health. I feel the best I have today," no doubt from this intelligence, even though his feet continued to be "very much swollen."

Two days later, when no more news of release was in the air, he still had, at least, "some hopes of getting out of this poor hole." But, in reality, Peabody was beginning to slip psychologically, and his physical health was deteriorating rapidly. "I am not very well today, it is hot in this place. Oh, I don't like a prisoner's life at all," he anguished. "God spare my life to get out of the Southern States—I don't like them at all."

Over the next few days, he kept a running commentary that is worth repeating in its entirety because he was beginning to show the incredible emotional stress experienced by his stay at Andersonville. From the stories left by men from other Union regiments who were there, it is certain that Peabody's feelings were hardly unique.

Still here in this damnable place for a dog. Hannah, should I get home, which I intend to do, I have a story to tell you that you will hardly credit. I have seen the Southern Confederacy to my sorrow still there are better times coming and I will be with you soon too and I think I can enjoy life better. Friends will be dearer to me than ever before and my family too. May God keep them from all harm safe until we all meet again to part not until Death shall part us. Hannah, pray God this prove true to you and me and our friends. I keep thinking do you know where I am; if you do but know my situation you would weep day and night. I have not written [he was not allowed to] for I don't wish you to know I am a prisoner. Hannah, I am very sick for me, with the dysentery. I am very poor, courage good and I think we shall soon be in our lines and then I will have a furlough & come home & see you & the rest of the family. It will be the best time you & I ever saw in our lives. May God keep you free from all harm, Hannah.

His wishful thinking about being released continued on through mid-June when he wrote, in a hopeful vein, "I think July will find us out of this place—at least I hope so." And the literal starvation to which he was being subjected was causing him to dream of sumptuous meals at home—a near-universal dream among the inmates. "How I wish I could get to your [Hannah's] table—couldn't I eat some! I reckon so, good," he wrote. He also suffered very much from homesickness and worried constantly about his wife and children: "Oh, little Abby [the youngest of his four daughters, four years old at that time], I wish to see you very much and all of you, you may bet on that."

On a rainy and nasty June 18, some measure of the reality of his predicament appears to have surfaced when he admitted there really were "no signs of leaving this poor place." But he had not given up hope and reasoned that the Confederate authorities "can't always keep us: There is a little prospect of leaving soon. . . ."[6] And his swollen feet continued to plague him.

★

Dr. Austin K. Gould was faring not much better than his comrade. He relates more of his ordeal at Andersonville.

This Damnable Place for a Dog

When I entered the prison, May 29, the number of prisoners was about nine thousand, which was gradually increased to thirty-two thousand, in the fore part of July. Their condition was enough to make one sick, on first entering the place, but it was nothing in comparison with what I experienced afterwards. To see my fellow prisoners suffering for the want of food and clothing as I did; to see them stretching out their bony hands for the mearest morsel to eat; to hear their piteous inquiries, "shall we ever go home;" to see how they died, poor fellows, wasting away, little by little, exposed to the scorching rays of a Georgia sun; this was enough to break the hardest heart.[7]

★

William Peabody began a downhill plunge in the last weeks of June. And in his helpless frustration and anguish his mind was grappling more and more in pathetic desperation for any form of salvation, however delusional, any fancy that showed a glimmer of promise to his worsening physical and mental state for delivering him from his hell. His diary is woven with fantasy, wishful thinking, religious fervor and other spiritual crutches, and, occasionally, reality.

One rumor that was circulating on rainy June 19, according to Peabody, was that "Secretary Stanton [Federal secretary of war] says we shall be out of this place this month; may it prove true soon—I think it must be so." But over the next two days he wrote in despair, "Hannah, I am still a prisoner in the pen. Oh what living for a human being. I shall appreciate good living after this; I would give any amount to be at your table. 200 died last night; it rains too much for the poor fellows—nothing to protect them from the rain and sun. Some of them are old Bell Islanders; they must all die." Belle Island, in the James River near Richmond, was used as a Confederate prison also. Those Belle Islanders were transferred to Andersonville so that it would be more difficult for Union forces to liberate them. They were the first inmates at the Georgia prison.

"Another man shot yesterday, got over the dead line." The dead line was a rail fence set up about nineteen feet inside the stockade wall running parallel to it in an unbroken line around the entire interior. Any prisoner would be shot instantly by the Confederate guards for so much as letting his hand cross it. "I shall have a story to tell when I get home. Grant has ordered the surrender of Richmond & it will be taken this time too. Our regiment is all bust up." This information, presumably, was learned from other prisoners of the 57th, or those from regiments brigaded with it, who were captured later.

For the rest of June, the routine of Peabody's incarceration remained unchanged. He continued to fantasize about being released at any time, and he fretted constantly about his family. He could not bear his surroundings and wrote, "I have learned a lesson I shall never forget in this life if I live forever and I never will find fault with anything again." The weather remained stifling, and he and his fellow prisoners suffered from it dreadfully: "I am very weak and lie in the tent [shebang] most of the time it is so hot. My seat [of his pants] is worn out; when will I sit in a chair!" William Peabody summed up his daily activities on June 27 and 28, writing, "For exercise I have washed two towels myself and hunted lice—found 6 old settlers; they are plenty. I do that most of the time. . . . Going through the usual routine of business—cooking . . . drawing rations and sitting in the shade for it is very hot—and such grub, our hogs feed better in the North."[8]

The stockade at Andersonville was expanded on the south end another twenty-six-and-a-half acres in June to accommodate the tremendous numbers of Union prisoners who were being sent there.[9] Peabody and his companions were among those who found new quarters in the new section, and he mentioned, "July 2 Today moved in to the new stockade got a new tent for six [where he came by that tent is a mystery, as the Confederates did not issue any]. Had a hot time moving, came very near being sunstruck. Very weak in the knees and my feet are [still] very much swollen but I think they are getting better."

On the 3rd, he wrote, "Second day in the new S[tockade]. There has been some 16 shot for getting over the dead line and fights occur very often in this place; cross and crabbed as they [the prisoners] can be and live. Oh, it is a perfect Hell here, if there ever was one on earth it is here." And his observations on the Fourth of July were, "Raining very hard but the camp fires are burning for supper. This is a hard 4th I tell you, I never expect or wish to [see one like it] again; this is horrible to see. . . ."

A bitter Peabody, now pretty much resigned to no early release, noted on July 6, "Hannah, there is not money enough in the United States to hire me to stop in the army. It is disgusting to see them [his fellow inmates]. I would give anything to be out of this and think I will too this Fall, say Sept. if possible." Continuing his thoughts on July 8, he noted, "I do not feel very well, my knees and ankles trouble me. It is very hot; nights are pleasant. Nothing of importance occurred today but cooking out of doors with pitch pine. Hair full of smoke, faces all black; I don't like the style. God deliver us from this place soon."

A new form of hope appeared in the camp on July 10, and, Peabody, desperate for relief from his sufferings, began a relationship with the occult. "Hannah, the spiritualist Mr. Richardson is here. I will write down what he says. This is the month to be paroled he says but we shan't know until we start from here about it. I shall write these things to you if they prove true. We have sittings to pass the time."[10] How pervasive spiritualism became in the camp is unknown, but, given the situation confronted by those imprisoned in Andersonville, it is not surprising that it existed. The prisoners reached for hope in any direction.

At the end of June, six Union prisoners who were the ringleaders of about three hundred other Federal toughs were arrested by the Confederate authorities at the camp and turned over to their Federal comrades for trial. Those men had preyed on the weaknesses of their comrades, killing and robbing them in order to insure their own survival. They were condemned by their fellow prisoners and hung, with the cooperation of the camp commandant, Henry Wirz. (Another prisoner belonging to the 57th, Private Herbert O. Smith, of Company K, was one of their victims, although he was killed in August by members of the gang's remnants.) The six condemned men were John Sarsfield, 144th New York, William Collins, 88th Pennsylvania, Charles Curtis, 5th Rhode Island Artillery, Patrick Delaney, 83rd Pennsylvania, A. Mun, U.S. Navy, and W. R. Rickson, U.S. Navy. Some experts, however, believe these to be assumed names.[11] Peabody mentioned the events of July 11, when the six were executed. "Today at 5 o'clock P.M. 5 [actually six] men have been hung in this pen for murder and robbery since they have been in this place; buried them in their tents. Justice is done them. I did not see them hung, I have no taste for that style, they are tough."

Continuing to mix some reality with his delusional thinking, his diary entry for July 12 states, "Report says that the 15th is the day to begin to pack but I don't believe them [the Rebels], they lie like the devil—they ought to be hung." And also mixing his Christianity with his newfound spiritualism, he mentioned two days later that he "Went to a prayermeeting Tuesday night, very good."

By mid-July, Peabody's physical condition was getting worse, and along with his swollen feet, and sore knees and legs, he reported that "I have a very sore throat today and a severe headache but I must do my best." And his homesickness and regret for joining the army continued to manifest itself: "Would to God I was with you, I would stay there too, and the children— how I would love to see them. I Shant always stay in this damnable hole, Hannah, good will come out of it."[12]

★

"Another feature of this place," wrote the 57th's Dr. Gould about Andersonville prison,

was the "damnable stocks." I never suffered in them, but have often seen my fellows tortured in them. The pain was excruciating in the extreme. The men were put into a hellish machine that would stretch them all muscles and cords would bear, and with their faces turned up to the scorching sun, they were left from twenty-four to forty-eight hours. This was the most barbarous act of all, and this to men already completely emaciated by their sickness. I have seen men taken from the "stocks" only to expire in a few minutes. All this was done by authority of the officers in charge.

Some of the prisoners thought they might escape if they got out, but the blood-hounds were too much for them. A pack was kept for the purpose of hunting all such, and very savage they were too, so that few escaped them who ever tried.

There were many other wicked cruelties practiced upon the prisoners, but I have not time to dwell on them.[13]

★

Meanwhile, William T. Peabody drifted in and out of reality until, at last, hallucinations and fantasy became his only escape from his horror. He also vented his rage at the president, a feeling probably shared by many other prisoners. On July 16, he wrote, "Gould is sifting corn meal and it is hotter than thunder here. If the government don't get us out they may go to the Devil with Abraham Lincoln and his vote. I will never vote for him again. . . ."

And turning more and more toward his religion, he wrote a plea in his diary to his wife a couple of days later: "I hope, Hannah you and the children will never see what I am suffering at the present time. How I would like to be with you and the children today to attend church. Hannah, pray for me, neglect none of the duties of religion on any account, do your duty to God for He is just and good and He will overrule all things for the best. Put your trust in Him entirely. Hannah, if I ever return to you I shall return a different man, I hope a better [man]; perhaps I shall fail, I hope not." And he followed up this plea a few days later by pledging, "Hannah, if God spares my life I shall devote the rest of my days to the Christian religion. Hannah, I have commenced reading the New Testament; I intend to read it through and practice its precepts." He added on July 22, "I have read several chapters today in the Testament. There are not many books here and not many to read the Bible. It is a great place for swearing and all kinds of wickedness. Oh, how I wish I were out of this and I hope to be soon."

His despair increased and his courage faded further at the end of July, when he wrote bitterly, "Oh, I am sick, poor and lame and tired of this place even most unto Death. I never ought to have left Home for this place; it is not the place for me. . . ." His only solace at that time was his religious faith, and in another passage to his wife, Peabody implored,

Hannah, if I never see you again please bring the children up in the Christian faith and erect the family altar and always keep the fire burning under the Sacrifice, for it is our only *Hope* in the hour of Death, and Hannah would it not be pleasant to have one unbroken family in the Kingdom of Heaven. Hannah I never thought so much of the Christian religion as I do since I came into this wicked place. I hope to be able to tell you someday in Sept. 1864 more about it. I think I shall see you then. I hope to regain my health and I think I shall with the blessing of God our Heavenly Father.

The end of July found him writing of his conditions, his wants, and his hopes.

How I would like to see all the family and friends. Yes I would like a letter from you all. Over three months I have not heard a word from any of you and cannot write to you. Soon I hope to be able to write and not only write but visit you to stay. This is about the last of July and not out yet I think the prospect is good for this month [August] and I hope soon to be where I can recruit [recuperate] for I am very poor and weak, never so poor, but I have made up my mind to live through this, come home and enjoy life better than I have. I can love you and the family more and be a better husband and father and I hope a better man. My prayer to God is I may be a true Christian, that is what we ought to live for in this world. Time passes very fast for this place; all days are alike in this place. I would like to attend church again. Hannah, I often dream of you and Ham & Eggs but don't get a chance to eat with you. Last night I dreamt of coming home. Uncle John M Ruth, Mrs. Wright and two or three other women were present and any quantity of ham & eggs—I could not eat any for I was in the bull pen [prison]: I didn't think much of that you better believe.

From about August 2, Peabody seems to have gone over the brink of sanity. He fantasized that his tent mate, Austin Gould, was somehow making daily trips to his hometown in Massachusetts to check on the condition of his family:

Yesterday I sent Gould up to Westminster & saw you and the family—you were going to make doughnuts. All there but Frank [his second son, aged nine years], could not find him; guess that he is at school. The girls, Sa[rah] was cutting up her capers and Henrietta too and Ab[bie].

A week later, he wrote of his situation,

Reports are thick but no truth in them. The Southerners are the most deceitful fellows I ever saw—lie, they can't tell the truth any how it is not in them; for that I hope they will get their deserts and they are getting the worst of it this time and no mistake. Grant and Sherman are just giving it to them. Prisoners still coming in but not very fast. they shoot a man if he gets over the dead line here—they have averaged one a day since we came here, they have no mercy on us; they will get their payment with interest. Mr. Gould has been to see you [Hannah] today and you were preparing for doughnuts and the family were all well. Ab[bie] has been sick and Sarah but they are both better now; he goes to see you about every day. I would like to know if they [probably referring to the spiritualists] can tell correct; if so it is a great thing for us for it is the only way we have for news from home. Mr. Gould goes to Westminster about every day to see you and the children. You were all well and enough to eat—that is more than we can say or do. I am very weak but I am bound to put it through.

It is quite likely that Dr. Gould was a willing participant in these fantasies and that he encouraged Peabody's delusions. It may have been the only way that Gould felt it was possible to keep his friend from giving up hope. That numerous other prisoners suffered from hallucinations in their forlorn conditions would hardly be surprising.

Peabody also continued his sittings with spiritual mediums. He wrote down his thoughts about those sittings, but often without dates. However, they probably occurred at about this time.

Hannah I have just had a spirit communication from you, and it is between the hours of two and three, by a gentleman; I don't know him but he says you are all well but you are troubled about me, don't know where I am but missing, and the family are well and you are sewing and the children are out at play. The furniture he described it to my satisfaction,—that is good. Now remember, he says I shall come home all right.

And:

8 o'clock Sunday Night—Hannah I have heard from you tonight and I wish for the test, and the first chance I have I shall write you and see the truth of the case. It was a spiritual sitting, Spirit Doc Bromfield of Philadelphia, the medium Oliver Fairbanks lives at Patterson N.[ew] Jersey. I wished to have him see how the family were and he described you and Ellen better than I could. Ellen was bothering the children and you told her you would think she would get tired. Sarah has been unwell but is better and the rest were well, and for a test he told a dream of yours—it was not the only one either. It was this: you dreamt I was in a battle with the cannon roaring and the guns. I was afraid but I came out all right. Another was that you had received a letter and the envelope was yellow, stamped on the left hand of the letter P.S. the initials of your name were upon it and it contained bad news. There was a young man there about 20 years old, was Henry at home?—it was his description and there were several persons as company. I wish you to write the facts of the case. He stated that I had a very pleasant family, Hannah, and had great sport with them. You know that is so and I hope to again soon.

And once again:

Had a sitting today and the spirit says that we shall soon be out of this; Gould says by the 15th of this month. . . . [Evidently, from the following, Peabody is considering going into business as a medium himself.] Is it best for us to go into business as we have talked. If we do shall we be successful? Where shall we locate?

Shall we be in it soon after we are liberated from this prison? Can we make a good living? Will it be pleasant for our families? Will both parties be honest? Are we both well adapted for that business? Will the business be pleasant for us? What amount of capital will it take? Is my throat anything that will trouble me? [Apparently he had a chronic throat problem.] If I attend the sittings is it possible for me to make a good medium?

Clearly, the man was fast losing his mind.

In mid-August, he wrote,

Hannah I have spent another day in this cursed place of misery. I wish you could see it, Fancy cannot describe the misery of this place. I cannot but just get up the hill with a pail of water; I am very poor but feel as well as I expect to under the circumstances. . . . My grub is very poor for my stomach. I hope to get from this place soon and that truly.

And a few days later he noted,

Today is another for the Bull pen and it is rather poor country I will just tell you. Beans, rice, unsifted bread, bacon, beef alternately, it is devilish poor living for a man to fat on; your food is what I want and I hope soon to get some of your victuals I could fat right up. If I don't make a little I shall starve for the want of food it is so poor, but God is with me and will be to the end of time. . . . Henrietta [his daughter], you fat rascal you, how I wish I could get hold of you, I would shake you until you gave me something to eat.

He was starving to death.

Aug 22 God spare my life if possible until the end of this which I hope will be soon. Hannah, this will be the end of my soldiering. I shall return home soon, I hope, to remain with you. I am bound to put it through.

There are no further entries until September 1, 1864. The last entry almost certainly was written by Dr. Austin K. Gould: "Sept 1 *Wm. T. Peabody died last night.*"[14]

★

Dr. Gould was paroled and exchanged from Confederate captivity on December 15, 1864. He was one of the few men of the 57th to live through the horrors of Andersonville prison,[15] and shortly after the war he wrote his short narrative concerning his imprisonment.

We were taken from this place [Andersonville] to the city of Charleston, September 14th, where we were kept under fire of our batteries for three weeks, but fared

much better than elsewhere, being fed and cared for by the "Sisters of Charity."
From there we were taken to another most damnable prison pen—a second Andersonville, called Florence [South Carolina].

Here the same usages, the same fare and treatment [as at Andersonville] were dealt out to us, but there was one new phase presented to us, and that was, the compulsory movement to make our men enlist in their service. This was done by extra starvation, in some cases depriving us of food for three days at a time.

I was finally released December 15, having been in prison seven months and two days.

And he remembered that an old comrade, "Wm. T. Peabody, was captured with me, and remained with me until he died, Sept. 1st, 1864, poor fellow, literally starved to death, no disease about him, but reduced to a living skeleton. . . ."[16]

★

Private Francis M. Harrington, the young diarist from Company K, was captured at the Crater on July 30, 1864. In sharp contrast to Peabody, Harrington almost never wrote emotionally of his prison experience, and his entries are very matter of fact. He was sent to the Confederate prison in Danville, Virginia, and although life in that place was hard and deadly for the prisoners, Danville could not compare to Andersonville for sheer horror. In the first place, the men confined in Danville were housed in several buildings. On the morning of August 2, Harrington and his contingent of prisoners arrived at Danville, and he noted that they "were put into good brick buildings." (He was held in "Prison No. 3," but there were at least six buildings in which the Federal soldiers were confined. Also in the compound was a general hospital.) That being the case, there was considerably less danger for the men from exposure to the elements, and only on one occasion in October did Francis Harrington mention that he was cold: "rather of a shivering crowd in here today," adding with his usual positive outlook, ". . . but we must make the best of it till we see better times."

Secondly, at least according to Harrington's journal, the men appear to have been fed somewhat better. Not untypically, Francis Harrington was a soldier very concerned with his rations, and in his diary he frequently described what he had eaten on a particular day. When he first arrived, he wrote that the men had "plenty of Corn Bread and bacon & Rice soup" and the following day "corn bread and bacon plenty." The diet at Danville evidently consisted of various soups such as pea and rice, corn bread, wheat bread, fresh beef, corned beef, bacon, and tea and coffee. While the quality of the food probably was lamentable, Harrington never once complained about his fare. Only while he was in the hospital during his last days as a prisoner, in

February of 1865, did he mention that there was beginning to be a shortage of food.

On February 13, 1865, Francis Harrington celebrated his twenty-first birthday at Danville Prison. And he was paroled and exchanged on February 22.[17]

John Anderson wrote about Harrington's and another private's experiences as prisoners of war:

Of the [57th's] enlisted men who were captured, very few survived the sufferings and privations of prison life. A very touching incident is related of two who were taken prisoners at the crater and confined in the Confederate prison at Danville, Va. Sergt. George [H.] Parks of Company A was sick when he went into the engagement [his first and only]. After having been captured, and thus deprived of proper medical attendance, his condition became worse. A Confederate prison was not conducive to the good health of even the strongest constitution, but to a man going there sick, the chances of ever getting out alive were very poor. He lingered day after day, clinging to the fond hope that possibly he might be exchanged and his life saved. Anxiously and patiently he waited and eagerly caught at every rumor of exchange as "a drowning man clasps at a straw," but it was only repeated disappointment. His condition grew worse from day to day. Finally a list of names came for exchange, and every man listened with breathless interest as it was read. How anxiously did poor Parks listen in hopes of hearing his own name, but the list was completed, the paper folded and his name was not called. Turning sadly away, it seemed as if the last ray of hope had disappeared and he was to be left to a lingering death. Those whose names had been called were happy in anticipation of getting into "God's country" once more (wherever our flag floated was called by prisoners "God's country"), of seeing friends and home and of getting away from suffering and starvation. A comrade, Francis M. Harrington by name, private of Company K, Fifty-seventh, who was captured at the same time with Parks, was made happy by hearing his own name called from the list for exchange, but witnessing Parks' bitter disappointment and knowing that it was sure death for him to remain longer in prison, with heroic self-sacrifice, stepped aside and gave way to Parks, and the latter was exchanged in his place [on August 30, 1864]. He never lived to reach that home he so longed for, but died [from chronic diarrhea] Sept. 19, 1864, soon after reaching [the Federal parole camp at] Annapolis, Md. Prison life had killed him. Harrington remained in prison for sometime longer, and when finally exchanged was completely broken in health.

Another comrade, J. Brainard Hall, writing to the *Worcester Gazette* upon the occasion of Harrington's death in 1915, described him as "a premature old man," as a result of his incarceration. That Private Harrington truly was "completely broken in health" and "a premature old man" is highly debatable. A photograph of him taken shortly after the war shows him smiling and looking fit. And although he never married, he was very active in veterans' organizations after the war, as well as president of the 57th's regimental association from 1880 until 1882, and he was also the town clerk and postmaster of Northboro, Massachusetts. He lived with his sister Ada for the rest of his life until he died at seventy-one.[18]

★

Every one of the 57th's men who spent time in a Confederate prisoner of war camp suffered beyond comprehension. That so many of them died in prison, or shortly after release, attests to that. Perhaps some inkling of the misery to which they were subjected can be gleaned from the stories of the three men presented here. While it is certainly true that death, surgery, debilitating wounds, disease, hunger, homesickness, and lengthy and painful hospital stays were frightening, no horror in the Civil War quite equaled a prolonged stay in a military prison.

21

Hard Seasons

T HE FEDERAL ARMY had been through some terrible campaigning since crossing the Rapidan River in May, and, through battle and disease, it had lost a great many of its best and most experienced officers and enlisted men. That, coupled with the softening of the troops from living in the routine of trench life and the expiration of a number of the veteran regiments' enlistments of service, was having a deleterious effect on the Army of the Potomac. The commanders complained that the combat efficiency of the soldiers was debilitated, and in many instances those officers were justified in their assessments. The replacement troops that were coming in to swell the Union ranks were, on the whole, men conscripted in the summer drafts of 1864, substitutes, and high-bounty men—many of whom had to be brought into the regiments at the point of a loaded gun.

Some of those bounty soldiers had been paid eight hundred dollars or more to join the army, and the authorities did all in their power to see that they did not skip. The late bounty men, substitutes, and draftees were often worthless good-for-nothings who would not fight unless they were prodded into battle with a bayonet—and many were. The veterans despised them. Many of them were thieves and robbers, murderers, rapists, and degenerates, and because of them, discipline was once again being enforced strongly throughout the army.[1] Veterans who once had been considered trustworthy now were far too often lumped by the commanders into categories that they strongly and rightfully resented. Perhaps this was one reason why the 57th and the rest of the 3rd Brigade of the IX Corps' 1st Division had been blessed, finally, with the ramrod disciplinarian Mr. McLaughlen.

The firing on the lines remained light at the end of September, and most major construction was about finished—at least in the 57th's section of the works. But, regardless of the seeming change of mood on the lines, the men were cautious, and they kept their rifles in good shape and loaded at all times.

★

On September 28, with a great commotion and shouted orders to deceive the Confederates, the 1st and 2nd Divisions of the IX Corps were massed with the V Corps near the Gurley house and supplied for a new advance. The object was the capture of the South Side Railroad, Lee's vital rail link running west of the city of Petersburg through Lynchburg as well as branching off into North Carolina, and the subsequent forcing of the Confederate leader to extend his dangerously thin lines even further. The men were anxious to get the war finished and realize their dream of being home before the long winter—maybe even in time for Christmas. They fully understood the importance of shutting down another of the Army of Northern Virginia's supply routes, and in the clear, cool autumn weather, they were ready to get to work.[2]

On the morning of September 30, the men of the IX and V Corps, accompanied by a cavalry escort of Brigadier General David M. Gregg's troopers, moved off to the left approximately two miles west of the Weldon Railroad. The first part of their objective was to gain possession of the intersection of two battered wagon roads. Those were the Poplar Spring and Squirrel Level roads, which converged around Peebles's farm. Once that crossroads was secured as a staging area, the men could move further west to the Boydton Plank road, take it, and continue north about four miles and attempt to capture and disrupt the South Side Railroad.[3]

With the V Corps in the lead, the columns marched through the fiery, tangled autumn woods on the Vaughn road around the Arthur Swamp, and then over the Poplar Spring road until they came to the meadows and fields of Peebles's farm. There the forward elements of Warren's V Corps found Confederate Major General Bushrod R. Johnson's division of infantry and Major General Wade Hampton's cavalrymen waiting for them. The Rebels were dug in strongly on a ridge of hills northwest of the farm. Brigadier General Charles Griffin formed his division of the V Corps into battle lines, and, over six hundred yards of open ground, the cheering Union soldiers charged the Confederates in their works, dislodged them, and drove the Southerners back a half-mile to stronger trenches in their rear. The 57th's men, observing the assault from the safety of their reserve position, thought Griffin's charge gallant.[4]

The IX Corps was ordered up on the line right away and it quickly moved to support Warren's corps, moving through the Pegram farm, a mile to the northwest, towards the Boydton Plank road. The 2nd Division stepped off in front of the 1st in battle formation, drums rolling, and Potter's men formed their lines on the left of the V Corps. Suddenly its 2nd Brigade moved forward to attack, but the Confederates pounded the Yankee soldiers back in a bloody firefight, causing the line to snap between the two Federal corps and spreading panic through the Union troops.[5]

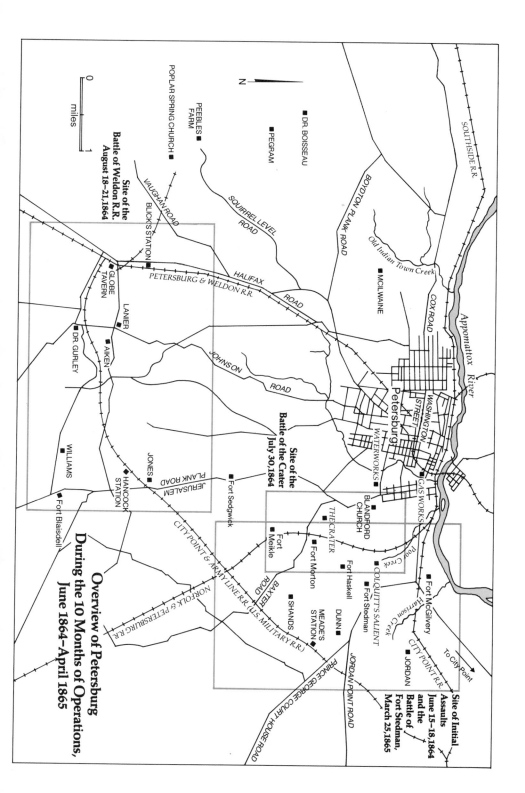

Overview of Petersburg
During the 10 Months of Operations,
June 1864–April 1865

N

0 ... 1
miles

POPLAR SPRING CHURCH
PEEBLES FARM
PEGRAM
DR. BOISSEAU

Site of the
Battle of Weldon R.R.
August 18–21, 1864

VAUGHAN ROAD
BLICKS STATION
SQUIRREL LEVEL ROAD
BOYDTON PLANK ROAD
Old Indian Town Creek
MCILWAINE
COX ROAD
SOUTHSIDE R.R.
Appomattox River

GLOBE TAVERN
LANIER
PETERSBURG & WELDON R.R.
HALIFAX ROAD

DR. GURLEY
AIKEN
JOHNSON ROAD

WILLIAMS
JONES
HANCOCK STATION
JERUSALEM PLANK ROAD

Fort Blaisdell
Fort Sedgwick

Site of the
Battle of the Crater
July 30, 1864

Petersburg
WASHINGTON STREET
WATERWORKS
GAS WORKS
BLANDFORD CHURCH
THE CRATER
Fort Meikle
Fort Morton
Fort Haskell
Fort Stedman
COLQUITT'S SALIENT
Poor Creek
Harrison Creek
Fort McGilvery
CITY POINT & ARMY LINE R.R. (U.S. MILITARY R.R.)
NORFOLK & PETERSBURG R.R.
BAXTER ROAD
SHANDS
DUNN
MEADE'S STATION
PRINCE GEORGE COURT HOUSE ROAD
JORDAN POINT ROAD
JORDAN
CITY POINT R.R.
To City Point

Site of Initial
Assaults
June 15–18, 1864
and the
Battle of
Fort Stedman,
March 25, 1865

The 1st Division, in reserve in a ravine between Dr. Boisseau's deserted house and a sorghum field, responded at once, rushing forward with a yell and a cheer to plug the gap between the two halves of the line, aiding General Potter to restore his division's formation. While Willcox was helping Potter reestablish order, the V Corps shifted its position to the left and checked the Confederates. It was a vigorous fight, and the division's regiments made a stubborn stand, the men gathering in groups around their colors. The soldiers held their ground, and the action did not end until it was too dark to see any longer. The exhausted men of the IX Corps, softened by their long interval in the trenches, slumped into the captured rifle pits—which the Southerners had dug hastily on the ridge at Peebles's farm—for a brief rest before continuing to fortify the Rebel works and shuffle around into new positions. The fight on September 30, 1864, was called the battle of Poplar Grove Church.[6]

George Barton was one of the four officers in 57th who was with the regiment, commanded that day by Lieutenant Colonel Tucker—the other officers were Major Doherty and Lieutenant Hitchcock—and Barton described the action in a letter to his mother.

> "at work on brestworks" Va
> Oct 3d 1864

Dear Mother

Knowing that my last letter must have made you feel *rather anxious* I hasten to inform you that I am *still* O.K. As good luck would have it the order to *Charge* was *Counter Manded.* [He is referring to an order given subsequent to the battle, on October 2.] Lucky for the 57th for Many of us would have *bitten* the *dust.* We have *hard* work and plenty of it for the last four days but our boys are *veterans* and behaved *Magnificently.* The 31st [sic] of Sept we lay under a very *heavy fire* and were prepared to *Charge.* The 57th when the order to *advance* was given did so in *gallant* style & led the entire *brigade* & kept so until the order to halt & *lay down.* We lost on that day only one man killed Lyman Broad of Holden I think there were some others *wounded* in My Command alone two Companies K & C, 20 men, Making the Company, 3 were wounded. *Cups* shot through, Knapsacks *bored* through & through with many other Narrow escapes. A bullet cut my Sword *Knot* into so that my scabbard dropped off [He must have meant the straps that held the scabbard to his belt, as the sword knot was attached to the basket of the sword handle itself.] I went back about ten rods under a heavy fire to pick it up. you know it wouldn't do to lose my *toad striker.*

We have been working all night throwing up brestworks. it is now about six oclock A.M. There is no telling what will turn up next suffice it to say we are very *Much nearer Petersburg* today than we were three days ago

The night of the 31st [probably September 30 or October 1] was a hard one for us all Rained All Night we were kept Counter Marching all night. The next day on Picket I had Charge of the "Picket Line". Everything looks Cheering & the boys felt well, but are anxious to be *paid.* . . . I must go to work goodbye love to all from your Soldier boy Geo. E. Barton[7]

When Private Gustavus Holden, of Company C, recounted the events after the war, he remembered, "During the battle of Preble's [sic] Farm Sept 30, 1864, I had the top of my canteen cut off by one bullet, another passed through my cartridge box, while still another struck the brass plate on my belt." Holden, it will be remembered, was the young soldier who, while recuperating from his Wilderness wound, had helped to man the Washington defenses during General Early's raid in July.[8]

As George Barton mentioned, the only man killed that day was Private Lyman Broad. Broad had been born in Sterling, Massachusetts, and he lived in the old, historic town of Concord when he enlisted in Company A at age twenty-eight. Because he was a teamster in civilian life he had been detached to the ambulance corps on April 27, and the battle of Poplar Grove Church was his first and only time in combat. After the war, one of the men—very likely Private Thomas Gerry, a member of the same company and also from Sterling, who was one of three other men present at the battle from Company A—described Lyman Broad's conduct that day:

His comrades recall how one of their comrades was frightfully wounded when struck by a solid shot which almost severed a limb. The poor fellow was bleeding to death. Lyman Broad volunteered to go out on the battlefield in the face of almost certain death to bring in his wounded comrade. He said that he had neither wife nor child to care for and that he would volunteer. He went out on the field, picked up the wounded man and brought him into camp amidst the rain of bullets. He came in so promptly that all watching felt that he had escaped unscathed. Broad laid down his burden saying "I may have saved his life, but I have lost my own." He was vitally injured [shot through the bowels] and died soon after.[9]

The man whom Broad had saved was Private John F. Wellman, of Company H. The battle had been his first, as well. Young Wellman was taken to the 1st Division, IX Corps, field hospital where Dr. White amputated his left arm by the flap method the following day, October 1. He survived the ordeal and was discharged on May 4, 1865.[10]

Wellman's brother, George, was also wounded that day, but he would return to duty only to be wounded again in the 57th's last battle.[11]

The regiment had gone into the engagement with 4 officers and 89 enlisted men and the roll call that night showed one killed and eight wounded, about a 10-percent loss. The 57th could have fielded at least one other private, Smith J. Lee of Company K, but he was reported to have "shirked the battle."[12]

The Federals had lost two thousand men during the battle of Poplar Grove Church, and of that number over half had been taken prisoner of war. Johnson and Hampton had stopped the Union advance to the South Side

Railroad, but at the expense of extending the overstretched Rebel lines several miles further.[13]

The IX Corps lines connected to the left of those of the V Corps, and the boys remained in that position until October 2, staying busy reinforcing their earthworks and dodging enemy fire. Along with the II Corps, the IX Corps made a reconnaissance in force toward the Boydtown Plank road on the 2nd, but found the Rebels too well entrenched for an assault. The generals called off the action, and the soldiers returned to their trenches.[14]

By military telegraph, Major General John Parke, commanding the IX Corps, reported a summary of the day's events to Chief of Staff Humphreys at ten-fifteen that night:

This morning General Mott's division moved out on the Squirrel Level road, and after taking position on the left of the Ninth Corps the whole left of our line, which had been repaired during the night previous, was advanced, and with it the left of the Fifth Corps. The movement resulted in our reoccupying the Pegram house and extending our left to the westward from that point. The only opposition met was a skirmish [line] of the enemy until our extreme left, Mott's division, came upon a battery in position. By my direction, General Mott deployed a brigade to develop the position and force of the enemy. It was found they had four guns in position, supported by infantry. This was accompanied by a slight loss on our part. The detailed report of losses has not yet been received. In the advance of General Mott in the morning he found line of the enemy's rifle pits extending off to the westward of Peebles's as far as the cross-roads at J. Smith's, where the enemy had a strong redoubt surrounded by heavy slashing. In the afternoon we again retired, our left taking up the line from Pegram's, south of the Squirrel Level road.[15]

★

For five more tedious days the men worked on their rifle pits just north of Peebles's farm. "We have 600 men at work day and night," telegraphed General Parke to army headquarters on October 3.[16] But although the soldiers were kept busy, their morale was sinking. Winter was not far off, and they were getting the notion that there would be no end to the war that season. The draftees, substitutes, and bounty men were showing up in the ranks with more frequency, as every day veteran soldiers were taken out for one reason or another. Those new men were worse than all the parasites combined that plagued the army, and they severely depressed the old campaigners.

Two of the 57th's men had further reason for being downhearted, and in a letter to Mr. H. K. Oliver, an official of the Commonwealth of Massachusetts, Lieutenant Hitchcock expressed their concern on October 7:

Sir

Will you please inform me what course must be pursued by soldiers who have not received their "state pay", in order to procure it? Sergt Theodore L. Kelly [actually Kelley] and Priv. Samuel H. Holyoke of K Co. 57th Regt Mass Vols. elected to receive the monthly pay "from the state" They have never received this pay and their friends are now unable to procure it and receive no satisfactory reason for the refusal. The above mentioned men have never been paid by the U.S. Gov—and consequently are in great need of the money. The families of these men receive "state aid" regularly. Kelly and Holyoke are with the Regt on duty.

Very Respectfully Your Ob Serv
Alfred O Hitchcock
Lt 57th Mass Vols[17]

The disposition of those men's cases is not known, but almost certainly they were paid at some later time.

★

On October 8, the 1st Division was ordered to make another reconnaissance in force. The 57th was commanded by Major Doherty, who had returned in September from convalescent leave for the hand wound that he had received in the June 17 assault. Lieutenant Colonel Tucker was just not well enough to lead the regiment, so the intrepid major took over. Before seven that morning the 57th, with the rest of the division, left camp in "light marching order," traveling on an old woods road which passed the Clement house, a thousand yards south of Peebles's. The men were traveling in a direction to the left of Pegram's farm towards Hatcher's Run, a small, brown creek that flowed southeasterly into the Staunton River. Arriving at the picket line near the junction of the Vaughn and Squirrel Level roads, Doherty deployed the 57th as skirmishers covering the 3rd Brigade and in line with the 1st Brigade's skirmishers. The regiment contained barely enough soldiers to form that forward position.[18]

After advancing over some cleared ground for about a half-mile, the men could see a small number of Confederate cavalry vedettes stationed at the edge of the woods in front of them just to the rear of a few deserted Rebel trenches. The 57th continued moving forward and drove the cavalry pickets through the timber and across a glade into a forest beyond. But in their enthusiasm, the boys got themselves detached from their place on the right of the 1st Division's line because the other two brigades—the 1st and 2nd—of the division had changed position, having obliqued to the left. The 57th was in trouble. The men knew it, and the Rebels knew it.[19]

Their exposed left flank invited retaliation, and the Southerners wasted no time taking advantage of the regiment's predicament. Doherty saw them

303

coming, charging the open flank, and above the rattle he yelled for a change of position. The regiment responded immediately. The enemy fire raked the left of the line as the men, in good order, wheeled around to face it. They volleyed back, but the little group was overwhelmed. The killing Rebel fire broke the formation, and the Massachusetts soldiers fell back on the run three hundred yards to a new location, one wing of the regiment occupying a farmhouse and some outbuildings and the other lying at the edge of the woods. There they remained until nightfall fighting off their attackers. With darkness as cover, the men quietly and quickly withdrew and returned to their camp, and the second battle of Poplar Grove Church—or as some preferred to call it, the battle of Squirrel Level road—was concluded. One of Company F's men, Irish-born Private John Sullivan, had "1 gun & equipment complete lost by [him] during the skirmish," but Lieutenant Hitchcock was quick to point out in the company journal that there was "no blame on him."[20]

Once more, the 57th's short line had been culled. The regiment had left camp that morning with 90 officers and enlisted men, and the casualties suffered were 2 killed and 12 wounded. Because of the men who had returned from the cattle guard, Company F was the strongest company, with 23 effectives, but Company D could not field a single soldier that day and Companies B and I mustered but one man each when the battle was over. The two men killed, Private George Jamieson from New York City and Private George W. Shaw from Stephentown, New York, both members of Company I, had gone into battle that day for only the second time. Jamieson was a recruit who had just joined the regiment and Shaw had been absent until September for unknown reasons.[21]

★

The 57th's men were issued clothing on October 10, and because of the changing seasons, that time they drew lined sack coats and greatcoats, as well as new woolen blankets.[22] The awful Petersburg heat was about finished, but the winter of 1864 and '65 was to prove no joy in the trenches, by any means.

On the 13th, the boys were mustered for pay, and on the 14th the regiment was required to witness an execution. The condemned was a private in the 2nd Maryland Infantry named Merlin who was convicted of attempting to desert to the enemy. "The division was formed," a soldier remembered, "in an open field on three sides of a square, in the center of which the doomed man was seated, blindfolded, on a coffin placed at the side of an open grave." The provost guard firing squad came up quietly, one of the men's rifles loaded with a blank. The prisoner was reported to have been as calm as the surrounding troops, and while the warrant of execution was being read, he calmly reached down and picked up a straw. At the drop of a handkerchief, they shot and killed him.

304

Executions were quite common in the Army of the Potomac during the last part of 1864, and the troops were required to witness them in the hope that they would set an example for those men who contemplated desertion or any other crime. Only a few Massachusetts soldiers were executed during the Civil War. All were shot for desertion except Private Thomas R. Dawson of Company I, 20th Massachusetts Volunteer Infantry, who was hanged for rape on April 14, 1864. No soldiers in the 57th were executed, but two were sentenced to be shot for desertion. However, those judgments were commuted by President Lincoln.[23]

Also during October, all of the companies began to be issued a limited quantity of the Spencer repeating rifles. On October 19, Company F received eight of those weapons and Company E drew seven. (Quantities for the other companies are unknown.) In consequence, the regiment's firepower was increased dramatically, and the quick-firing breechloaders made up for a great deal of lost manpower on the line.[24]

★

For the rest of the month the men worked long hours every day strengthening their works. They were several miles from the South Side Railroad, and different outfits in the IX and V Corps reconnoitered daily towards it, always looking for a weak spot in the Southern defenses. Sam Grant had decided that the time had come to stop fooling around and cut both the railroad and the Boydton Plank road—another important Confederate overland supply route—before winter set in, and on October 27, early in the morning, the II, V, and IX Corps, with several light batteries and General David Gregg's Cavalry Division as a screen—forty-three thousand soldiers in all—were ordered to move out and capture the two targets.[25]

The action had been in the planning stages for some time, and in compliance with orders issued from army headquarters, General Parke directed the following to his IX Corps on October 24:

Division commanders will be prepared to carry out the following instructions in the event of a movement being ordered:

1. Troops remaining to garrison [the] line of works and picket the front from Fort Fisher to Fort Cummings [the extreme left of the Northern lines; the regiments assigned that task were from the 2nd Division of the corps] will be supplied with six days' rations and [the] amount of ammunition previously prescribed (200 rounds per man).

2. The troops, except those selected to remain for purpose above indicated, will be massed at convenient points for movement out of view of the enemy.

3. The troops that march will have three days' full rations in haversack and three days bread and small rations in knapsack, sixty rounds of ammunition on the person, and forty rounds per man in wagons. Three days' beef will be driven.

4. Half the ambulances, one hospital and one medicine wagon to a brigade, and the intrenching tools will be taken.

5. No baggage or headquarters wagons will be taken, but instead such pack animals as may be absolutely necessary to carry the rations, tents and baggage of officers, and forage for officers' horses.

6. All other trains and wagons than those above specified will be sent within the intrenchments covering City Point.

7. Clerks, orderlies, and every other man on detached, special, extra, or daily duty will be armed and sent to the ranks, unless his services are absolutely necessary out of his regiment on the duties named.

By command of Major-General Parke.[26]

And the next day specific orders were issued to all corps commanders for the action to be taken on Thursday, October 27, for the battle which would be known as Burgess Mill. The IX Corps received the following:

4. Major-General Parke, commanding Ninth Corps, will move at such hour of the morning of the 27th as will enable him to attack the right of the enemy's infantry, between Hatcher's Run and their new works at Hawk's [house] and Dabney's [house, about five hundred yards to the northeast of Hatcher's Run], at the dawn of day. It is probable that the enemy's line of intrenchment's is incomplete at that point, and the commanding general expects, by a secret and sudden movement, to surprise them and carry their half-formed works. General Parke will therefore move and attack vigorously at the time named, not later than 5:30, and, if successful, will follow up the enemy closely, turning toward the right. Should he not break the enemy's line, General Parke will remain confronting them until the operations on the left draw off the enemy.[27]

The IX Corps was occupying a position on the left of the Union lines, and the II Corps was to move around it in the rear to take the lead. Gregg's cavalry would move even further left to cover Hancock's men. Hoping to surprise and rout the Confederates entrenched near Hatcher's Run, the IX Corps would move quickly along the Squirrel Level road with the 1st Division in the advance. The intelligence reports suggested that those trenches were not complete or well manned, and the generals wanted to take advantage of the situation to capture more forward ground. The V Corps would follow the IX Corps as support.[28]

George Barton was looking forward to the fight, as were most of the soldiers, and he wrote his mother on October 25, "We are ordered to be ready to *March* at a *Moments Notice* 3 days rations in haversacks and 3 more in Knapsack. It means a *forward* movement and I trust with no *back steps.*" And while he had been on the picket line the night before, he noted that he could "hear *bands* of the 'Johnnies' playing the Bonnie Blue flag & c.," and that "one Johnnie *came in* & gave himself up. he said there were plenty more of

306

his comrades who would like to 'get in' if possible that they were heartily sick of fighting & hope we should soon have pease."[29]

★

Reveille was early, and the men awoke to a dark and rainy morning. With no time to cook breakfast or even boil coffee, the regiment was formed up with the corps, and the soldiers moved out stumbling and bumbling along in the pitch-black predawn hours. In no time they were soaking wet, miserable, and hungry. There was a fall chill in the Virginia air, and the cold added terribly to the men's discomfort. They passed over a narrow, muddy crossroads and proceeded through dense, dripping woods littered with fallen trees that had to be cleared, which slowed the march to a crawl.[30]

Under the morning's dismal gray skies, the men soon discovered the Rebel picket lines in front of them. The IX and V Corps formed battle lines, with the 57th one of the regiments on the skirmish line, and drove the butternuts off, but Confederate Major General Cadmus M. Wilcox's main works were stronger than anticipated, and any attack, it was soon discovered, merely would push the Southerners back to reserve positions equally strong. In addition, the countryside was heavily treed, and construction material, therefore, was available readily to Wilcox's men for building even stronger positions of defense. The expedition had reached a point north of Hatcher's Run about six miles below the South Side Railroad, but the commanders, Parke and Warren, could not seem to synchronize their troops that day, and they decided that to go on would result in heavy casualties. The Federal generals canceled the movement. Nevertheless, persistent and brisk skirmish fire was kept up by both sides all day. Hancock's II Corps had taken the brunt of the Confederate attacks over near the Boydton Plank road, but the IX and V Corps suffered little damage. The 57th lost one man wounded, and he accidentally, on the skirmish line—Private William Worthy, of Company G.[31]

The men stayed the night in their makeshift works sleeping with their accoutrements on, while one-third of their comrades at a time took turns keeping watch. In the morning, they withdrew to their former positions at Peebles's farm, and Lieutenant Barton, for one, was not happy with the turn of events, writing his mother on November 1,

This is my first opportunity [to write] since our last "raid" or as we call it "fizzle". We certainly expected to have a "shenanigan" and were fully prepared for it but Genl Grant did not see fit to risk a *general engagement* so we *fell back* in *good order* that is the 9th Corps, Our Brigade Covered the retreat and a portion of our regiment were on the *"skirmish line"* which line was commanded by our *Major Doherty.* I do not think it shall *remain quiet* for any great "length of space" but we get used to almost anything in this country—Our lines are quite near to the enemy at this point we can hear their bands playing every Night, such things as "the Bonnie Blue Flag" & c. We can also hear their "yells" to which our boys reply with *vim*. We are *hard* at *work drilling* as *"skirmishers"*, and Making out Pay Rolls. . . . Those "Johnnies" are *yelling* just now like so many *demons* while *our bands* are playing *Patriotic airs*. . . . Well Mother My Candle is going *out* and I am going to bed I retire at 9 oclock P.M.[32]

And one of Company K's soldiers, Sergeant Theodore Kelley, summed up in his company's journal the regiment's unspectacular movements that day: "broke camp before dawn and started on a reconnaissance on the South Side RR advanced 5 miles and laid in line of battle overnight the regiment was under fire but lost no men [at least not from enemy fire] Returned to camp on the afternoon of the 28th."[33]

★

With the completion of the exercise at Hatcher's Run, battle operations for the 57th were ended for the year. On October 30, the adjutant general for the Commonwealth of Massachusetts, William Schouler, visited the 1st Brigade's camp to inspect the men and to report his findings to Governor Andrew upon his return. Colonel McLaughlen, never one to miss an opportunity to impress his superiors—and especially a state envoy with Schouler's influence—turned out his weary men for a full-dress parade. The boys brushed their uniforms, shined their steel and brass, blackened their leather, and marched before the visiting dignitary and his staff. They were thoroughly put out by what they considered such nonsense, but they did their best to act respectful, and Schouler reported that the men were in "generally good health and spirits."[34]

The 57th was rewarded for its stoicism at parade the following day. The paymaster made a visit, and those of the regiment present were paid up to date. Now the men truly were in good spirits. That was the first money many had seen in months, and they must have been mighty pleased. Some, no doubt, sent a portion of their pay home, but most probably headed straight for the sutler's tent behind the lines where they could buy molasses cookies and other treats—and not a few under-the-counter bottles. Card games were sure to have sprung up and dice tossed, and there would have been winners and losers in camp that night, and hangovers the following morning.[35]

Hard, cold rain started on November 2 and lasted through the next day.[36] The winter weather was beginning in earnest, and the boys huddled in their shelter tents and around their campfires, collars of their caped greatcoats turned up around their red ears. Those on the picket line suffered even more as they lay in their shallow rifle pits, soaking up the cold water that puddled in the holes.

★

The wearing of the IX Corps badge had become lax in the 3rd Brigade of the 1st Division and, now that hostilities were letting up on the front and the men were settling down for the winter, Colonel McLaughlen turned his attention to seeing that the emblem was worn by everyone in his command. On November 9, he issued the following "Circular" order:

1. Regimental commanders will make immediate requisitions for corps badges on the assistant quartermaster of the brigade in such numbers as may be necessary to furnish each man of their commands with two badges. One of these badges will be carefully kept that a new and clean one may always be ready for reviews and contingencies. Each officer and soldier will wear the prescribed shield in red cloth on the center of the top of the cap which will be the prescribed head dress for reviews, parades and occasions of ceremony for all enlisted men. This badge will be worn on all occasions of duty. By command of Colonel N. B. McLaughlen.[37]

★

Private George Monroe of Company G had been mustered in with his company at Camp Wool, but, feigning illness, he was sent to Boston before the regiment left for Virginia. He was finally sent to the front, and his officers reported that he had "skulked at Gallops Island [Boston Harbor], Mass. from April 19, 1864 until Nov. 10, 1864."[38] There can be little doubt of the treatment he had to have received from his battle-toughened comrades in the ranks when he showed up in camp. They must have handled him without mercy.

★

The regiment had another clothing issue on November 15, and the men drew everything from caps to shoes.[39] The quartermaster's department of the Army of the Potomac took excellent care of its soldiers while they were at Petersburg. Not so fortunate were their ragged opponents across the way, who suffered from a lack of everything.

★

The 29th and 31st Regiments of U.S. Colored Troops were withdrawn from the IX Corps on November 18, and transferred to the Army of the James at Bermuda Hundred, and on the 26th of the month General Ferrero removed most of the rest of the 3rd Division to the same place. With the departure of the blacks, life in the IX Corps became less dangerous. When the Rebels learned that the former slaves were gone, they became more tolerant of the corps and pretty much abandoned their merciless harassment of the men. Trading between the pickets that had gone on for so long in other corps then began between the Confederates and the IX Corps' soldiers, and the men felt a great relief with the relaxation of tensions. Many of them, in total agreement with Southern opinon, were glad to see the Negro troops gone at last. A few differed with their comrades, though, pointing out that the blacks had performed better than expected, but those dissenters were in the small minority.[40]

★

A now-mysterious event happened in the regiment on November 22. Assistant Surgeon Heath was court-martialed and dishonorably discharged as of that day. No records of why he was cashiered have been uncovered, but in his original history of the regiment, John Anderson had nothing but praise for the doctor. Charles Heath certainly had not been disloyal or cowardly.[41] Perhaps he had too much fondness for the medicinal whiskey supply.

★

George Barton gives us a glimpse of life in camp on the "Cold Morning" of the day before Thanksgiving.

Dear Mother
Col Tucker goes home this afternoon on a 15 day "leave" and very kindly offered to take my things home that I wish to send. I thought a letter would be as pleasant as *anything* though my hands are just about froze. Still I will just say that I am withstanding the cold weather wet with snow and all kinds of weather I remain well and in *good spirits* working anxiously for my turn to go home [on leave]. . . . I am now detailed on "Court Martial" at Division Hd. Quarters. . . . All ready think I shall miss the mince pies tomorrow Thanksgiving. . . . boxes arrive almost *every day* for the regiment by express *Adams*. . . .[42]

★

The men remained in their trenches around Pegram's farm until November 29, when, as Sergeant Kelley noted, they "broke camp and changed our position to the right relieved 2nd Corps." The IX Corps had been ordered to return to the position in the Petersburg lines that it had occupied originally after the June 17 assault. The move was made in compliance with Special Orders No. 322 from the Army of the Potomac's headquarters at City Point on November 28. The 57th took up station by 3:40 on the morning of November 30 around the Friend house, located five hundred yards northeast of Harrison's Creek and three hundred yards east of the Petersburg & City Point Railroad tracks. The men were almost a mile in rear of the front lines and were being held in reserve.[43]

Lieutenant Barton explained the regiment's situation on November 30:

We took upon line of march yesterday for this point. Our *division* occupies nearly the same position as in "July" The 57th strange to say does not go into the *trenches*. We are held in reserve to support a battery which is posted in a square fort mounting 4 guns [probably Battery No. 5 in the original Dimmock Line]. We are liable to be moved it does not seem possible that the 57 Mass can hold so soft a "posich" as we have at present for any great length of period. of course we pray for the best and at all events keep our powder dry as Circumstances will allow. . . . Thanksgiving passed off in good style Some of the officers received turkeys. . . . We expect our division to hold the right as far as the Appomattox [River]. . . .[44]

George Barton's intuition was right; the regiment did not stay at the Friend house long, and within a few days it was posted back at the front performing the normal routines of that duty. After returning to the familiar area, the men were directed to construct winter quarters, and they set to work building their log huts with "hearty good will." The soldiers drew axes and saws from the brigade quartermaster, and from the abundant forests in the rear, they chopped and cut rough pine logs and hauled them back to their area in army wagons. On each side of the company streets that had been laid out by the officers, the men traced simple lines in the dirt as guides for their walls. Four to six men were to occupy each shack, and all contributed to its raising. While some were occupied cutting and transporting the timber, the others notched and set the logs horizontally, assembling the walls and then chinking them with the Virginia clay they dug from the ground. Doorways were cut and canvas flaps hung from them to protect against the chilly, wet wind. Fireplaces were built of alternate layers of mud and sticks, lined with stone, and topped with old commissary barrels for chimneys, and a supply of firewood was laid in.

Rough poles were erected for rafters, and scraps of foraged canvas, tents, and rubber blankets were thrown over them. Some of the more industrious dug their floors down to have more headroom. All the floors were covered with pieces of boards and boxes. Double-decked bunks were made combining green branches, barrel staves, and hardtack crates. Crude tables and chairs were fashioned from whatever the ingenious men could find, and photographs of friends and loved ones and woodcut pictures from the illustrated newspapers were pasted and pinned to the walls. Evergreen branches were woven into elaborate arbors which graced many doorways, and, all in all, the little huts were homey and comfortable, cheery and artistic. The men were delighted with their handiwork at first. Inside they would keep dry and warm around the little fires, and they enjoyed the fresh pine aroma given off by the pitch.

To the men of the 57th—as well as their comrades and their adversaries—who had suffered so much living in the elements for so long, some without even a three-by-five-foot shelter tent half, those tiny dwellings seemed palatial, and the boys thought their first night's sleep under such magnificent cover wonderful. The only drawback was that they had to build the officers' quarters, and they had to build them first.[45]

The 57th's winter camp was located just to the rear of the Federal trenches across from Colquitt's Salient, near Fort Stedman on the eastern part of the Union's far right. The men were but a few hundred yards from the Southern works. The implied promise of rest that the winter quarters seemed to suggest was broken almost immediately when the boys were told that their trenches had to be guarded day and night, and that duty in the forward picket lines was to be maintained. It was the same old story; three or four men in each of the picket post's rifle pits at twenty-four-hour intervals, except now, instead of baking in the hot Southern sun, they froze in the bitter Virginia winter. They lay in snowstorms and freezing rain in the rock-hard, icy pits, their fingers and toes numbed and blue. They brought rubber and woolen blankets and shelter tents with them when they went on duty, but those items did not help much.[46]

Winter was, however, quite a bit safer on the picket line. Both sides were so cold and miserable that neither was inclined to provoke the other. The attitude was one of laissez-faire. The lassitude that resulted from the rough weather preempted much serious gunfire, and the Federals and Rebels just tried to survive the elements on their picket tours. Soon the 57th's men found themselves talking to the Confederates across the lines, and that led to open meetings for trade. The bartering took place in the area between the works.

As soon as the officers were out of earshot, the enlisted soldiers of both sides crossed from their picket lines to meet and exchange goods. The Confederates were half starved, and it was evident to the regiment's men that the Southern commissary department must be empty. All of those soldiers mainly wanted food, and they willingly traded tobacco and Southern newspapers for anything that the Federals would give them to eat. They were interested, too, in the Northern view of the news, and they tried to get Yankee newspapers when they could. Each side thoroughly digested the contents of those journals, with the educated often reading aloud to the illiterate. Sometimes fires were built in the no-man's-land, and, every so often, a game of cards was played around the flames while the common soldiers from the North and South discussed the events of the war from their individual perspectives. The men of the 57th looked on their enemies with a mixture of disgust, compassion, and pity—but most often with disgust. When they compared themselves to the Confederate soldiers, they counted their blessings.

The United States government had spared no expense in caring for its troops, and they were relatively well clothed and fed, all agreed. But looking at the Rebels, the Union soldiers saw emaciated, filthy men, low in morale and dressed in rags. Some were barefoot in the bitter temperatures, some only had scraps of cloth to tie around their feet. All were hungry, often starving. Scraggly beards covered their dirty, caved-in faces, smiles were filled with decayed and missing teeth, and long, matted hair stuck out wildly from beneath torn hats and caps. Now and then, one of the enterprising Federals would see some interesting Confederate item that he wanted as a souvenir, and one whole piece of moldy hardtack could be a powerful bargaining chip in the trade.[47]

Desertions into the Union lines were commonplace—the IX Corps usually reported two or three daily. Many of the Southern soldiers could take no more of the hunger, and the promise of food in the Union lines was just too tempting. The winter saw them come over in droves from one end of the thirty-five-mile-long line to the other. The Northern troops had little genuine sympathy for the Rebels, and they often poked fun at them when they had the opportunity. New Englanders especially were prone to finding them unlettered, ignorant, illiterate, and generally stupid and provincial. They mocked their speech and grammar and felt themselves far superior in education and intellect. Perhaps a lot of them were, but many were not, and about the only real difference for the majority was in accent and dialect. The Irish who often joined in those opinions certainly had little room to maneuver, but that mattered little; it was fun to provoke the Confederates, and when a Southern letter was captured, there was no end to the hilarity as it was read aloud among the Federals.

From their travels and experiences in the war, the men of the 57th—as did most Northern soldiers—thought the South a century behind times. The Rebels, they said, could neither tell time nor judge distance. They found Southern prisoners of war sickly, sallow, and gaunt. They simply could not understand how men in that condition had resisted the Federal armies so desperately and for so long. The Confederates easily reinforced the Yankees' opinions of their own inept commanders. Occasionally the men would run into a Southern woman, and they saved their greatest disdain for them. "Ugly," "skinny," "saucy," "coarse," "tobacco-chewing," "unkempt," "unclean," "slovenly," "disgusting," and "vulgar" were all words used to describe them at one time or another by the Federals.[48]

Although the firing was light on the picket lines at that point in the siege, the forward rifle pits could be dangerous yet. The last man to be wounded in the 57th during the year 1864 was Private Cornelius J. Daily, of Company G. The Irish-born farmer also had been wounded in the Wilderness and had reported back just recently for duty with the regiment. He would see no more battles, but he would return in time to be mustered out with the regiment after the war ended.[49]

★

General Grant sent General Warren and the V Corps on a raid and reconnaissance against the Weldon Railroad during the second week of December. General Parke was ordered to detach several of the IX Corps' regiments to follow him and act as support if needed, and on December 9, under Special Orders No. 115, from General Willcox's 1st Division headquarters, the 57th was assigned to a provisional brigade which was commanded by Colonel Gilbert P. Robinson of the 3rd Maryland Volunteer Infantry. That brigade was to assist the V Corps. The other regiments included in the organization were the 3rd Maryland, 109th New York, 37th Wisconsin, and 60th Ohio. The 1st Division regiments were to be under the overall command of General Robert Potter, who would lead them to the Nottaway River. At 5:57 on the evening of December 10, General Potter sent a dispatch to army headquarters stating that his troops were then under way to the Jones house, where he would mass the men and await further orders.[50]

The night was freezing, and all along the twenty-mile route of the forced march the men were plagued by snow, sleet, and rain, which caused much suffering in the ranks. The soldiers reached Hawkinsville at 4:00 A.M. on the morning of the 11th, and Potter was told later in the day that his services would not be necessary. The exhausted infantrymen bivouacked that night, and at 2:00 in the afternoon of December 13, the regiments were forced-marched back to their lines—marching at one stretch eighteen miles without a halt. Upon its return, the provisional brigade was disbanded and the men returned to their original positions and units. The thought of their warm huts must have been on their minds almost exclusively as the 57th's men made the return journey. Sergeant Kelley noted in Company K's journal that the regiment "returned to camp after a cold & very severe march." And, as usual, Lieutenant George Barton had some comment to his mother in a letter dated December 15 regarding the excursion: "The 57th in Company with the 3d Maryland of our Brig. and also regiments of other Brigades started off on a *little expedish* of about 20 miles toward 'stoney creek' to look up the 5th Corps, which we had not heard from for some time. We marched this 20 miles in about '12 hours only' and *such* a *march* and *such* *weather* I never wish to experience again *'Rain and mud'*—"[51]

When the 57th's men returned to duty in their sector of the lines, they found that Colonel McLaughlen had issued General Orders No. 6 on December 11, which read in part, "The troops, both officers and men, in the trenches will stand to arms, with equipments on, at 5 A.M., and remain in line until half an hour after daylight. The same trench guards heretofore established by General Orders No. 5, from these headquarters, current series, will be continued and will remain constantly awake in the trenches. Two sentinels will be posted on the regimental fronts, and will keep constantly on the lookout for the enemy and prevent the destruction of the palisades, abatis, and revetments of the works."[52]

★

Certainly one of the most colorful characters in the 57th Massachusetts Volunteers was Company F's forty-year-old Sergeant Edward Hanrahan from Limerick, Ireland. He seems to have embodied all the clichés that characterized Irish Civil War soldiers. Sergeant Hanrahan fought in every battle and marched on every march with the regiment and was mustered out with the unit after the war. He was one of only ten men who could claim that record. But if he was a tough and fearless campaigner, he was a tough drinker and a fearless talker, as well. It seems that the sergeant got pretty well lubricated on December 17, and proceeded to voice his opinion of officers in clear, if basic, English. That did not sit well with the officers in question, and he was arrested, confined, and tried by general court-martial. Found guilty of "drunkeness and using insulting and abusive language," Hanrahan was broken to the ranks and held in the guardhouse until the end of January 1865. That, however, was not the last of the former sergeant's adventures.[53]

★

New uniforms, long underwear, flannel shirts, caps, shoes, and, at long last, mittens were issued to the regiment on December 18.[54] How welcome those mittens must have been when the men had to stand picket during that cold winter.

★

Christmas came and went for the 57th with little fanfare for the enlisted men, but the officers seem to have had it a bit better. George Barton wrote on Christmas day that *"dinner* has just been brought in by my cook a 'Christmas' dinner 'Oysters' and *fried 'Indian corn pudding.'* " The 57th had at least one black servant, a former slave named Donnohoe, and it is quite possible that he was responsible for the newly commissioned captain's tasty repast.[55]

★

It appears that the wearing of the IX Corps' badge by the men was still a problem. From 1st Division headquarters on December 28, General Willcox issued General Orders No. 66, which directed,

> In compliance with General Orders No. 49, Headquarters 9th Army Corps, the hat badge of this division will be worn by troops of the command as follows: By enlisted men on top, and by officers on the left side of the hat or cap to which it will be securely sewed. The latter are at liberty to wear the complete badge with cannon and anchor. Whenever badges are lost or torn off they must be immediately replaced. Provost marshals will arrest as stragglers all troops of this command found without badges and return them to their command under guard. Brigade commanders and heads of division staff departments will be held responsible for the execution of this order.

Four of the regiment's men were arrested and confined for that infraction two days later.[56]

★

As 1864 came to a close, the routine and filth of winter camp life was beginning to catch up with the 57th. The huts that smelled so sweetly when new were becoming lice infested and smoke blackened. They smelled of soldier smells—sweat, dirt, body odors, and rotting garbage. The shacks were poorly ventilated, and the result was a stale and sickly environment, always smoky from the poorly flued chimneys. Disease spread easily in such an atmosphere, and new cases of dysentery, typhoid, typhus, and acute and chronic diarrhea, as well as lesser ailments, were reported daily. Colds, bronchial infections, and fevers were common results of picket duty, and communicable disease spread rapidly in the foul huts.[57]

The men stayed in their shanties as much as possible to avoid the elements. Unless they had duty, the only reason to venture out was for roll call, firewood, rations, or a trip to the sinks, and that constant, close contact in their closed environments augmented and enhanced the chances of spreading infection. Daily, the officers and first sergeants sent sick men to Dr. White, who in turn shipped them to the hospitals at City Point for treatment or discharge. Others went to the medical facilities around Washington and some of the more chronic cases were shipped home to U.S. Army general hospitals in Massachusetts.[58]

While the afflicted were being sent into hospitals every day, soldiers who had been on convalescent and sick leave were returning to take their places. To some, it seemed like a constant changeover as old comrades rejoined the regiment to replace those leaving in the ambulances and on the steamers. The personnel situation in the 57th, as in other regiments, was extremely fluid, and no one knew from one day to the next who would answer the roll.[59]

22

To Have This Business Closed Up

THE MONTHS OF January and February 1865 were stormy and cold in the Petersburg trenches, and the 57th Regiment suffered from the weather, as did all of the army. The same tedious routines were followed every twenty-four hours, and the men grew more weary of their situation with each passing day. They hoped for an early spring and a quick end to the Confederacy. While they performed their daily chores and duties without comment in front of their officers, in the privacy of their quarters they were not in the least afraid to speak their minds regarding their circumstances. And they did so freely.

The IX Corps remained on duty in the earthworks on the right of the Army of the Potomac, with the 1st Division on the corps' right. Willcox's soldiers were opposite Confederate General John Gordon's men, and both sides were strongly dug in.[1]

During the early winter months, as evidenced by the company morning reports, the traffic of men coming and going within the regiment increased dramatically. Fifteen- and twenty-day leaves of absence were granted liberally, and nearly everyone in the 57th got a chance to travel home. Being out of the trenches and completely removed from the war was a huge morale boost while the leave lasted, but the return to the drudgery, cold, and danger of the front when their time at home was up sank the men even further into the depths of heartache. However, there were probably a few men who were happy to get back to the army after they saw firsthand the problems faced by their families. In many cases the latter were close to destitution. For some, facing Rebel bullets may have been easier by far than listening to a nagging wife and complaining children. The army was a way to distance a soldier from the realities of the tribulations that spilled over onto the home front as a result of the war. Inflation was very high in the latter part of the Rebellion, and families often could not make ends meet on their small state allocation and the pitiful wage of a private soldier.[2] In any case, whether he was at the front or at home, the average soldier's lot was not a pleasant one.

During the winter months a number of men who had been wounded in earlier battles, absent sick, or on detached duty also were dribbling into the ranks. But sometimes, as in the case of Private Wesley Haywood, of Company K, they were not fit and should not have been sent back to duty by the surgeons. Haywood had been severely wounded in the back and thigh during the retreat at the battle of North Anna River, and since then he had been convalescing in an army hospital. On January 5 the doctors returned him to the regiment, but he was found unable to perform combat duties soon afterward when "his old wound rec'd. May 24 broke out." As a consequence, he was sent to the 1st Division field hospital, where he was treated and then assigned to Dr. White for duty there.[3]

Others returned from being sick, and like Haywood, were not physically capable of front-line duty. One such was Corporal Martin Farrell of Company F. He had been detached to Lieutenant Hitchcock's cattle guard detail at the time of the Wilderness battle, but he soon developed what the doctors of his day called "varicose veins" in his right leg. The disease actually was septic thrombophlebitis, however, and Farrell suffered intensely from its effects. Just before entering the hospital on August 30, his condition had worsened to such a degree that Hitchcock allowed him to ride a horse. When Dr. White examined Corporal Farrell, he recommended him for a discharge, but White was overruled by the surgeons at City Point, and the soldier was sent to a succession of hospitals and finally returned to duty on December 31. However, his leg still pained him greatly, and the company journals and morning reports show him on and off the sick list regularly until the regiment was mustered out of service. After the war, his condition plagued him until he could no longer walk or work, and the government had to pension him for his debility. Martin Farrell died from heart failure as a result of his illness.[4]

Sergeant John Clark of Company D was an ambitious man who had never been in combat, and on January 17, he took advantage of an opportunity to gain a pair of shoulder straps by applying for and accepting a position as a first lieutenant in the 8th United States Colored Troops Heavy Artillery.[5] Men who could never advance to commissioned rank in a white regiment during the Civil War often took the same course of action as Clark. It was well known that becoming an officer in a black regiment was relatively easy, because most whites wanted no part of the extreme hazards of those jobs. It will be remembered that the Confederates did not look kindly on the Negro regiments or their white commanders.

Some men were lost from the effects of the winter. Company F's Private Herbert Beckwith died from diphtheria in his hut in the 57th's camp at the front on January 18. He was probably one of those soldiers who refused to go to the hospital without a bullet wound. Like Corporal Farrell, Beckwith, too, had served on the cattle guard.[6]

Men were gained also in other than the conventional ways. On the march to the Rapidan River, Private Charles Barton (no relation to George), of Company G, had deserted at Rappahannock Station on May 4. But unlike most of his cronies who eluded capture, he was finally captured in Dauphin, Pennsylvania, on November 9. Barton was court-martialed in Alexandria, Virginia, on January 19 and returned to the regiment for duty on February 6. He would soon be taken prisoner of war.[7]

And Private Gusta Beltreau was gained in the same manner. The young French Canadian from Montreal had deserted from an army hospital while recovering from wounds received at the Wilderness. He was arrested in Worcester in the fall and found guilty by court-martial of being absent without leave—a much lighter verdict than desertion. He, too, was returned to the 57th, only to be wounded again in the regiment's last battle.[8]

William Cleveland was arrested in Hartford, Connecticut, and also found guilty of absence without leave. The private, a member of Company G, had deserted following the battle of North Anna River after fighting in all the regiment's battles until that time. He was sent back to the 57th on March 12, but his officers evidently held no animosity toward him, deeming him a "Good Soldier."[9]

But there were far more serious cases of desertion decided by the military tribunals in the winter of 1865. One of the most grave was that of Private Alexander McClellan, of Company E. McClellan, an Irish-born laborer, had deserted from Camp Wool, but he was arrested in Tolland, Connecticut, on December 29. Returned to the regiment, he was confined until his court-martial on March 8, when he was found guilty of desertion and sentenced to be shot. However, that sentence was commuted later to the loss of all pay, a dishonorable discharge, and three years in prison at hard labor.[10]

And some, like musician Cyrus Hadley, from Company G, who deserted from a hospital, were not missed at all. According to his officers, Hadley was "worthless."[11]

★

On the other hand, Confederates were being induced by the Federals to desert their army and come into the Union lines during that winter, and to enhance that inducement General Grant offered a deal to all who would surrender peacefully. First Lieutenant Thomas Sturgis, who was mustered into the 57th's Company I on January 27, 1865, and immediately assigned to duty as an assistant aide-de-camp to the recently breveted Brigadier General N. B. McLaughlen at 3rd Brigade headquarters, remembered Grant's plan years later. In 1911 he wrote that Grant "had printed a large number of leaflets in which the rebel soldiers were told that if when deserting to our lines, they brought in their guns, they would be paid a fair value for them and upon reaching City Point would be transported without charge to New York or any seaboard city in the North. Accompanying these leaflets were orders to distribute them among our pickets with instructions to get the papers into the hands of the rebel pickets by any convenient means." When General McLaughlen, an "officer of the old school and thorough soldier," received those orders from the lieutenant general commanding, he was furious, and told Lieutenant Sturgis, "Lieutenant, by God, sir, that is the first time in my life, from sergeant major to brigadier, that I was ever ordered to let an enemy approach my post with a gun in his hand!"[12] McLaughlen was correct in his judgment that the order was dangerous, and Grant's directive was to backfire on the Federal forces—particularly McLaughlen's command, and more particularly on the brigadier himself—very soon, costing many lives.

Lieutenant Colonel Napoleon Bonaparte McLaughlen had two promotions confirmed on March 13. In two separate commissions, he was made a full colonel by brevet, and brigadier general by brevet. He was a happy man—he had his star. More to the men's liking, however, was Lieutenant Doty's promotion to Captain of Company I on March 10.[13]

★

Nothing of consequence happened at Petersburg through early February, until Ulysses S. Grant received reports that the Rebels were moving huge supplies into their lines, first on trains that were coming up to Hicksford, Virginia, forty miles south of the lines, and then on wagons that traveled through the Meherrin River valley to the Boydton Plank road. From there the caravans passed through Dinwiddie Court House and on to Lee's men at Petersburg. The Weldon Railroad ran through Hicksford, with that section of its line that extended back to North Carolina still in Rebel hands, and the track was responsible for getting the supplies to the Confederate railhead. So Grant ordered another attack on the Weldon. He issued orders accordingly, hoping to destroy that supply system.

The 2nd Cavalry Division and the V and II Corps were instructed to accomplish the commanding general's objectives. General Hartranft's 3rd Division of the IX Corps, which was being held in reserve behind the corps' lines on the Federal right, was ordered to go along with the expedition as support. In addition, Colonel Gilbert P. Robinson of the 3rd Maryland was ordered to form the Provisional Brigade once more and accompany Hartranft. The regiments that made up the Provisional Brigade were the same as those that marched on December 11, including the 57th.

In intense cold the regiment fell in as ordered and the IX Corps' column followed Warren's V Corps in the direction of the Weldon Railroad yet again. The 57th was held in reserve from February 5 through 10, though, and saw no action and lost no men. The II and V Corps did most of the fighting, finally extending the Federal entrenchments further west, and once again forcing Robert E. Lee to stretch his beleaguered lines almost to the breaking point.

Nothing was accomplished by the participation of the 57th as reserves except the suffering of the men from the freezing weather. By evening on February 10, the regiment was back in its camp, and it remained there, seeing no action other than picket duty, until after March 24, 1865.[14]

Captain George Barton gave an idea of how things were in the 57th's area at that time in a letter to his mother dated March 2:

Well here I am again hard at work [he had just returned from furlough] No more *sleigh rides* and *late hours*. Was on duty yesterday as Brigade Officer of the Day Was obliged to visit the entire Picket line of our Brigade last *night*. The walking was decidedly *Moist* And Muddy knee deep in some places, ditches to jump over and into, first on your head and then on your knees. Taking everything into Consideration was rather a *tough* ministration, but all these little items form a part of *three* years service.

There is Nothing New to offer in the Shape of "Movements" of this Army "all quiet" with the exception of "sharpshooting" and "Artilery practice." Desertions from the enemy have been quite frequent of late. Wish they would all "come in" for my part I am anxious to have this business Closed up before another Summer Campaign opens.[15]

As March drew to an end, the weather was warming, and the bitterness of winter was almost gone. The roads were drying; spring birds were beginning to arrive, and their songs were heard more often. Green was showing, and even a few buds could be seen on some of the trees. The battle-wise veterans knew very well what that meant, and the men began to be more vigilant on the picket lines. It was only a matter of time until the war was over, and they wanted to live to see home again. After all that they had endured, to be killed or maimed now would be a shame, so they kept a sharp eye to the west on the Confederate trenches. The 57th, along with the 3rd Brigade, was still in its original position, close to the point of the regiment's initial assaults of June 17. They were opposite Colquitt's Salient, guarding Fort Stedman in the Federal lines.[16]

23

One Last Desperate Effort

WITH HIS LINES now thirty-seven miles long, his army depleted and unable to defend those lines in strengh, his soldiers worn out and woefully undersupplied, his commanders unable to get replacement troops from a South whose resources of manpower were dried up, and his foe stronger than ever and ready to force a conclusion to the war with the advent of spring, General Robert Edward Lee was convinced that he and his Army of Northern Virginia must abandon Petersburg as soon as they could. The only way possible to maintain the impetus of the broken Confederacy, Lee was certain, was for him to get his remaining troops to North Carolina and link up with the Southern forces of General Joseph E. Johnston. In order to accomplish such a withdrawal, Lee needed to create a diversion—anything to throw the Army of the Potomac off balance. Grant's attention would have to be focused elsewhere. For that purpose Lee selected Major General John Brown Gordon, instructing Gordon to find a weak spot in the Federal lines and engineer a plan to exploit that spot. With a vigorous drive, General Gordon set to work right away, and after a week's deliberation presented his ideas and conclusions to the Confederate commander. A night attack was the plan, Fort Stedman the target.

"The decision as to the most vulnerable point for attack," wrote Gordon forty years later, "involved two additional questions of vital importance. The first was: From what point on my own intrenchments could my assaulting column rush forth on its desperate night sally, with the least probability of arousing the sleeping foe? The second was: How many intervening ditches were there, and of what width and depth, over which my men were to leap or into which they might fall in the perilous passage?" The first question was answered easily. The opposing lines near Fort Stedman were only 150 yards apart and the picket lines but 50, and Gordon thought that a quick, sudden night attack over such a short distance could be carried with relative ease. The second question was more involved, as the ground over which the assault was to be made had to be looked over carefully; but when it was, it was considered to be mostly clear of obstructions and generally level.

General Gordon proposed to General Lee that he, Gordon, would hand-pick fifty reliable and robust men who would lead the attack armed only with stout and very sharp axes. Those fifty axemen were to slash away quickly the strong and well-secured Federal abatis in front of the fort so that the next elements of Rebel troops could penetrate the Union lines. Those next elements—following closely on the sappers' heels—were to be composed of three groups of one hundred infantrymen each, led by trusted officers who were each to assume the name of one of the ranking Federal officers known by Gordon to be commanding Yankee troops around the fort. The purpose of that subterfuge was to enable the three groups—after Fort Stedman was secured swiftly—to continue on and capture three redoubt forts thought to be in the rear of Stedman. If challenged by the Federals, the Confederate officer would use his assumed name to impress authority on the Union soldiers. In the dark, the color of the Rebel uniforms would be next to impossible to determine, and Gordon felt certain that his ruse would work. When the three supposed redoubts were in Rebel hands, Southern troops following could continue down the partially sunken wagon road that led from the rear of Fort Stedman to Meade's Station on the City Point & Army Line Railroad about a half-mile to the east. There they could destroy the IX Corps' supply base, as well as seize much-needed food and equipment.

Immediately behind the three advance elements would be Gordon's three divisions of regular foot soldiers—some ten thousand men reinforced by troops from Hill's and Anderson's corps—who were to fan out right and left and take the Yankee lines. That done, a Southern cavalry division commanded by W. H. F. Lee was to gallop to the Northern rear, cut all telegraph lines, and disrupt the Petersburg & City Point Railroad tracks, over which trains also carried provisions to Grant's troops on the right of his lines. After thinking over Gordon's proposition carefully, Lee approved, and agreed to find Gordon three men from among his Virginia regiments who were from the Petersburg area, knew the terrain, and could serve as guides for the initial three-group assaulting force. Gordon began his preparations at once.[1]

★

On March 24, the IX Corps lines "extended from the Appomattox River on the right, with pickets stretching some three miles down the river, to Fort Howard on the left, a distance of about seven miles." The 1st Division held the right of the line, with the 2nd on the left, and General John Hartranft's 3rd Division was kept in reserve on a commanding rise about a mile in the rear from Fort Friend on the north to Fort Prescott on the south—roughly

Interior of Fort Stedman at Petersburg. *(USAMHI, Carlisle Barracks, Pa.)*

four miles. The 1st Division was posted with the 2nd Brigade, under Lieutenant Colonel Ralph Ely of the 8th Michigan Volunteer Infantry, on the right from the Appomattox to about Union Battery No. 9; the 3rd Brigade under General McLaughlen ran from the left of the 2nd Brigade to Fort Haskell, about two thousand yards; and the 1st Brigade, commanded at that time by Colonel Samuel Harriman, extended the IX Corps lines from Fort Haskell to Fort Meikle. The 1st Division covered nearly three miles of the IX Corps' territory.[2]

In the 3rd Brigade's line were sequentially numbered batteries running from right to left beginning with Battery No. 9 to the left of Fort McGilvery and ending with Battery No. 12 to the right of Fort Haskell. Those batteries were protected by strong earth embankments open on either side and bastioned forts along the line located at strategic points. About three-quarters of a mile in a straight line to the left of Fort McGilvery was Fort Stedman, which previously had made up a portion of the Confederate defensive works that were captured during its initial assault at Petersburg on June 17. Fort

Stedman, which "could hardly be called a bastioned work," had been repaired hastily by the Union troops and was garrisoned then by eight companies of the 14th New York Heavy Artillery Regiment under Major George M. Randall. The left and center sections of the 19th New York Light Artillery Battery were stationed there also, their four light twelve-pounders loaded with canister. Although well manned, the fort itself was in poor shape; its walls had settled somewhat from the severe weather during the winter months and very little attention had been paid to their repair. Inside were makeshift bombproof quarters covered with logs and earth, which had been quickly dug out by the soldiers.[3]

Outside the fort, the ground was broken up entirely with mazes of trenches, batteries, redoubts, covered ways, and all nature of excavation. The area was not as conducive to an attacking party as General Gordon thought it was.

As noted earlier, the distance between Fort Stedman and the Rebel lines was scarcely one-hundred and fifty yards, and skirmishing and sharpshooting were kept up all day so that maintenance, repairs, and additions to the fort could be performed only rarely and only at night. Fort Stedman had been laid out roughly in a square, and it covered about half of a sparsely wooded acre on Hare House Hill close to where the Union trenches crossed Prince George Court House road.[4]

The fort was not far from the Petersburg & City Point Railroad, and the ground in Stedman's front was relatively flat and open. Fort Stedman was connected to the Union lines by irregular infantry trenches and covered ways—a typical Petersburg labyrinth. The fort extended a short distance forward of the main Federal trenches so that, in the event of an attack against those lines, the artillery within Stedman could lay down a front or flank fire on the enemy. With the cooperation of the forts on either side, a butchering crossfire could be established easily on the Southerners if they assaulted the Union works in any form of a frontal movement. In addition, the entire area forward of the fortifications had been planted with sharpened abatis to discourage a Confederate charge. Those pointed logs were driven into the ground solidly at roughly a thirty-degree angle of elevation. They were about six inches apart and tied together strongly with telegraph wire.[5]

Just to the right of Fort Stedman was Union Battery No. 10, occupied by one section—two three-inch ordnance rifles—of the 14th Massachusetts Light Artillery Battery, and just behind it, to the right and rear of the fort and the battery, on ground which rose sharply near the fort, the 57th made its camp to provide infantry support to the gunners. The regiment had relieved the 59th Massachusetts recently, which had been posted there. Sergeant Theodore Kelley, of Company K, noted on March 12, that the boys had "relieved the 59th Mass. Vols. in the trenches moved to the right 8 P.M."

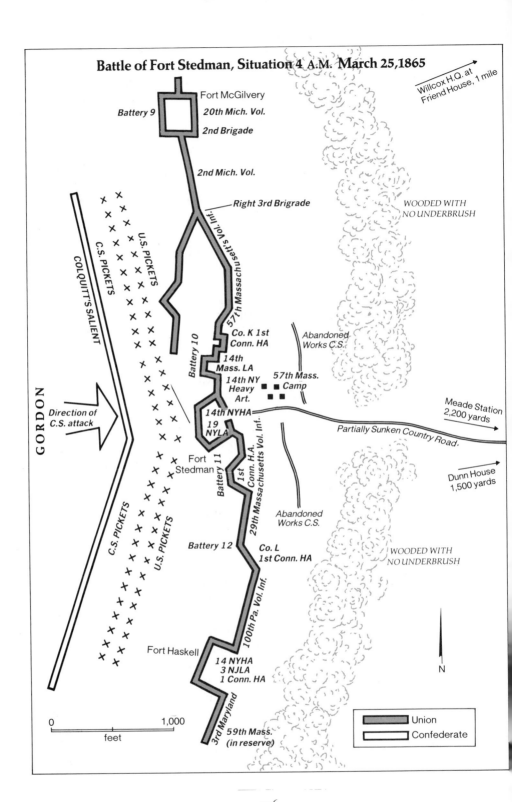

Battle of Fort Stedman, Situation 4 A.M. March 25, 1865

Willcox H.Q. at Friend House, 1 mile

Battery 9

Fort McGilvery
20th Mich. Vol.
2nd Brigade

2nd Mich. Vol.

Right 3rd Brigade

WOODED WITH NO UNDERBRUSH

57th Massachusett's Vol. Inf.

U.S. PICKETS

C.S. PICKETS

COLQUITT'S SALIENT

Battery 10

Co. K 1st Conn. HA

14th Mass. LA

14th NY Heavy Art.

Abandoned Works C.S.

57th Mass. Camp

Meade Station 2,200 yards

GORDON

Direction of C.S. attack

14th NYHA

19 NYLA

Partially Sunken Country Road.

Dunn House 1,500 yards

Fort Stedman

Battery 11

1st Conn. H.A.

29th Massachusetts Vol. Inf.

Abandoned Works C.S.

WOODED WITH NO UNDERBRUSH

C.S. PICKETS

U.S. PICKETS

Battery 12

Co. L 1st Conn. HA

100th Pa. Vol. Inf.

N

Fort Haskell

14 NYHA
3 NJLA
1 Conn. HA

3rd Maryland

59th Mass. (in reserve)

0   1,000
feet

Union
Confederate

A little farther to the right was a battery that contained four eight-inch mortars and three Coehorn mortars manned by a detachment of Company K, 1st Connecticut Heavy Artillery Regiment, and which was being supported in part by the 57th also. Because of the sloping terrain near the fort, the men were exposed to Rebel sharpshooters frequently, and, in their rat's maze of trenches and bombproof shelters, they moved about carefully.[6]

To the left of Fort Stedman was Battery No. 11, made up of light field guns and Coehorns supported by the 29th Massachusetts, and to its left and to the right of Fort Haskell was Battery No. 12, armed with two eight-inch mortars and four Coehorns served by the gunners of Company L, 1st Connecticut Heavy Artillery. The 100th Pennsylvania Volunteer Infantry was in the trenches from there to Fort Haskell. Fort Haskell was occupied by the rest of the 14th New York Heavy Artillery, the 3rd New Jersey Light Artillery Battery, and additional elements of the 1st Connecticut. Contingents of the 3rd Maryland and 100th Pennsylvania infantry regiments were in the trenches on the left. Just to the left of the fort was Battery No. 13. Near that battery the 59th Massachusetts Volunteers was being held in reserve. (The artillerymen were under the command of Colonel John C. Tidball, commander of the the IX Corps' Artillery Brigade.) That was the order of the lines of the 3rd Brigade, 1st Division, IX Corps, on the night of March 24.[7]

★

Earlier in the year General McLaughlen had proposed a Federal plan to attack Colquitt's Salient, and while the plan was under consideration McLaughlen had been training a large number of his troops as axmen, who were to be the advance soldiers sent in to cut away the Southern abatis. Those men came from each of the brigade's regiments, and the general kept them busy every day chopping wood in the forests behind his lines for fuel and repairs to the works, while at the same time mastering the use of the axes and keeping fit. Once a week, wagons would haul in the timber. But Lee was to beat McLaughlen to the punch—the Federal general's plan was still being mulled over by the Army of the Potomac's top brass as John Gordon got ready to launch his raid.[8]

The closeness of the lines made the men edgy, and McLaughlen issued standing orders that everyone was to be under arms one half-hour before daybreak. Staff officers were detailed to check the regiments to make certain that that order was enforced, and, consequently, inspections were made at midnight and just before dawn.[9]

The enlisted men were kept ready enough, but the long days of inactivity and boredom had taken their toll on the officers, who in many cases had nothing to do but pass their time swilling whiskey. McLaughlen was a teetotaler, and soon he had had enough of his drunken officer corps. He prohibited the sale of alchohol by the sutlers, but the officers circumvented that by getting their ration of commissary whiskey supplemented by friendly surgeons and intimidated hospital orderlies. The enlisted men were well aware of their superiors' propensity to drink themselves into a stupor ever since the battle at the North Anna River, when they had been led to slaughter by their besotted commander, and it was generally believed among the men in the ranks that whiskey had played a large part in their defeats and humiliations.[10]

★

The night of March 24 was black and quiet. Napoleon Bonaparte McLaughlen had ordered complete silence in his brigade, and after tattoo, started by the brigade band at headquarters and then picked up by the musicians in the lines, hardly a sound could be heard except those of the forest. No one was expecting an attack, but McLaughlen thought it wise to be cautious.[11]

Twenty-eight-year-old First Lieutenant Henry Joslyn of the 29th Massachusetts was captain of a section of the 3rd Brigade picket that dark night, and along his lines, except for the cold night breeze, things were equally quiet, and his men were pleasantly relaxed, yet alert. But just before four o'clock—two hours before sunrise the next morning, March 25—the pickets heard the footsteps of men moving easily toward them, and up and down the Union outposts musket hammers clicked back to full cock as rifle butts were brought up to shoulders. The Rebels approached and were challenged by the anxious Yankee sentinels. The Southerners claimed that they wanted to take advantage of Grant's surrender offer, but because there were so many, Lieutenant Joslyn was apprehensive and unnerved. He immediately dispatched a runner back to brigade headquarters with a message that an unusually large number of deserters was coming over with their weapons. What should he do, he queried his superiors?[12]

At about the time that Joslyn's messenger arrived at McLaughlen's headquarters, light musket fire had broken out along the picket line in front of Fort Stedman. The general got out of bed immediately and ordered all staff and orderly horses saddled at once, and he sent their riders galloping along the lines with instructions for each regiment of the brigade to get under arms without delay.[13]

Meanwhile, however, the Confederates—who wore strips of white cloth tied around their chests so that they could be identified by their comrades—had wasted no time, and they overpowered Joslyn and his men quickly, capturing a half-mile of the Federal picket line. (In the confusion Lieutenant Joslyn escaped.) The Rebel sappers moved out immediately and chopped up the obstructions in front of Fort Stedman, and the three hundred handpicked Southern fighters moved forward rapidly in three columns into the Federal works. The northernmost column broke through at Battery No. 10 and rolled up the 57th's trench guard and the artillery, shooting some men and taking many prisoners of war. The 14th Massachusetts Battery's gunners managed to get only two shots off before they were taken, the Confederates moving about their prisoners with cries of "Halt!" "Surrender!" "Down with your arms!" and "Strip off your belts!" Two of the 57th's soldiers escaped to the right and ran through the trenches to the section of works held by the 2nd Michigan Volunteer Infantry, "telling that their regiment was all captured, and that the Rebels were coming in our rear." Captain John C. Broughton, commanding the Michigan outfit, "ordered them to be arrested, and stopped their talking," which if left unchecked could panic his men as well as those of other nearby units.[14]

After smashing through Battery No. 10, Gordon's men sprinted around to the Federal left and took Fort Stedman from the rear, capturing many of the 14th New York Heavy Artillery's men, who were taken almost completely by surprise. Nearly simultaneously, the other two Confederate columns attacked, the center force hitting the trenches and batteries to the fort's left, and the other assaulting Fort Haskell. Ten thousand butternuts followed the advance party occupying Fort Stedman and fanned out to the left and right, filling the Union trenches. All of that activity had taken but a few minutes— the initial assault had been made with lightning speed.[15]

McLaughlen, hearing the disturbance in the fort, dashed in through the sally port to investigate personally. Not knowing that the Confederates had captured part of the works and unable to see in the pitch black, he asked some men what was going on. They asked him who he was. "Brigadier General McLaughlen," he replied. He was told promptly that he was now a prisoner of the Confederate States of America and was hustled off to the Rebel lines.[16]

The original three hundred Confederates wasted no time in the forts and works, but kept going, with some of their comrades following, their object to capture the three redoubts Gordon supposed to be in the Union rear. The problem was, however, that those forts did not exist. Frustrated and confused in their search—all three columns had lost their guides, as well—the Rebels later returned to Stedman, piling in and throwing the rest of the Southern force into some confusion.[17]

★

Because the works were muddy and wet, the 57th's men not on trench guard duty stayed out of them at all times, and that night had been no exception. When the attack had begun, most of the regiment's men had been sleeping soundly in their tents, winter quarters having been abandoned a while ago. But the shouting of orders, unusual musketry on the picket line, and the discharge of the 14th Massachusetts's field pieces, all of which seemed to happen at once, awoke them immediately. At almost the same instant Sergeant George Adams, of Company G, who had been on the picket line and escaped through one of the covered ways that led back to the trenches, came running into the camp sounding the alarm. The boys turned out immediately and formed their line. It was just after four o'clock.[18]

Lieutenant Colonel Tucker was detached on staff duty as Officer of the Day for the division at General Willcox's headquarters near the Friend house, so, once again, Major Doherty was in command. He deployed companies G and K as the regimental skirmishers, and when the 57th's men—wearing their greatcoats—moved forward from their camp in the pitch-black, foggy, and frosty morning to plug the gap in Battery No. 10, more of the men, on the regiment's right, were taken prisoners of war as the Southerners swarmed through the hole.[19]

The 57th, with support neither on the left nor right, was driven back through its camp—located one hundred yards northeast of Fort Stedman just above the old wagon road—under a compelling fire, men falling at each step. The Confederates, confident of success, stopped to loot the regiment's tents, even though Colonel Tidball, commander of the IX Corps Artillery Brigade, had trained some of his guns on the camp from his reserve batteries emplaced in the rear on a hill at the Dunn house, and was tearing the bivouac to shreds with case shot and shrapnel.[20]

Sergeant Major Charles H. Pinkham, a young man of nineteen from Grafton, Massachusetts, had been bunking with Captain Doty until the captain had gone home on leave of absence. Recently, he had taken up residence with Lieutenant Hitchcock, and in their tent the regimental colors were stored. In a letter to John Anderson written in 1895, Pinkham told his story:

As we were falling back, [Major Doherty] said to me, "Sergeant-Major, where in hell are the colors?" I replied that the color sergeant who was on furlough had left them in my tent. He then ordered me to return and get them. I went, in obedience to his orders, although it looked like a forlorn hope, but the colors must be saved at any cost. Having lost one stand of colors in the crater, we could poorly afford to lose another here. As I returned, the enemy was in possession of our camp, but, under cover of darkness, I gained the tent, seized the colors, and you may be sure I did not wait to hold conversation with them, but for the time being was a professional "sprinter." I ran the gauntlet and, save being half frightened to death by the bullets whizzing around my ears, reached the regiment in safety and turned the colors over to Sergeant Chase of Company H.

Twenty-two-year-old Charles S. Chase, also from Grafton, was actually the company's first sergeant as well as the acting regimental color sergeant during the battle.[21]

Meanwhile, Tidball's artillerymen continued to rake the 57th's camp in order to clear the Rebels. The gunners succeeded, at the expense of demolishing almost everything that the men owned.

★

After Battery No. 10 had been seized and the 57th routed, the Confederates turned the captured guns of the 14th Massachusetts Battery on Fort Stedman from the flank in order to drive out any remaining defenders. A portion of the 14th New York still hung on and gave the Southerners stiff and stubborn resistance, but those few were no match for the overwhelming numbers attacking them, and soon most of the New Yorkers were taken prisoner. A handful escaped, running for their lives through a covered way that connected to Fort Haskell. Fort Stedman was then in Confederate control.[22]

Next to fall was Battery No. 11 on the left of the fort. The men of the 29th Massachusetts fought gallantly and savagely, like the hard veterans that they were, but at first they could not stop the desperate soldiers of Lee's army, who knew that this was just about their last chance. Driven to a killing frenzy, they pushed the 29th back. But the Bay Staters rallied, made a stand, and finally drove the attackers off, taking many prisoners.[23]

The left flank of the Rebel troops continued its relentless drive to the Federal right, meanwhile, clearing the Union trenches. After the 57th had retreated, the Southerners pushed on into the 2nd Brigade of the 1st Division and plowed into the 2nd Michigan, who were thrown into some confusion at first, but rallied soon at Battery No. 9, standing firm and fighting off the invaders. Later, at twenty to seven that morning, the Michigan soldiers reoccupied their position.[24]

Moving further to the Union right with the temporary withdrawal of the 2nd Michigan, the Confederates had tried to forge ahead and capture the Coehorn mortars in Battery 9, but by then the whole Federal line was alerted to the attack, and the gunners in Fort McGilvery hoisted their field pieces over the parapets of that earthwork, trained their guns to the south, and cannonaded the front ranks of the charging Southerners to shreds with grapeshot and canister. The fire was awesome and destructive, and it held Gordon's troops in check on that part of the battlefield.[25]

While the artillerymen were busy stemming that charge, Colonel Ely's 2nd Brigade formed battle ranks at right angles to the trenches and, facing the Rebels to the south, the Federals poured on a heavy small-arms fire. With artillery support from Fort McGilvery and Batteries 5 and 9, the Confederate attack was repulsed completely and the Southerners pushed back to Fort Stedman by the cheering Union infantrymen. But the slaughter was awful, and the ground around Battery No. 9 was covered with broken, bloody dead and wounded.[26]

Meanwhile, the 3rd Brigade had formed in a similar fashion, perpendicular to the trenches, but it was at Fort Haskell in the opposite direction and so faced north, and it was gaining results similar to those of the 1st Brigade. Batteries 11 and 12 were recaptured before seven-thirty by the 29th and 59th Massachusetts, with the help of the 3rd Maryland, some of the 14th New York, and a few Pennsylvanians.[27]

While those actions were in progress, what was left of the 57th's men had found themselves in serious trouble. The Rebels had driven the boys relentlessly eastward towards Prince George Court House road, and they were being butchered. The killing was like the Wilderness all over again. The regiment retired to a line of abandoned works, but it was far outgunned by the desperate men in butternut, and the Confederates ripped into its flanks with murderous rifle fire, driving the Massachusetts veterans back to another series of deserted trenches.

Once more they were flanked, and once more they retired, but with less confusion, leaving many dead and wounded nevertheless.

After a third successful flanking movement by the Southerners, the 57th finally entrenched in a fourth line of abandoned works near the Federal batteries at the Dunn house. There on that crest, south of the sunken wagon road, the men made a final stand. They held their pursuers, but at a fearsome cost. The Confederates battled furiously to reach the Federal rear and gain possession of some detached batteries and access to the supply depot at Meade's Station, but the stubborn resistance of the regiment helped to keep them at bay. At just about that time, General John Hartranft brought up the 200th Pennsylvania Volunteers of his 3rd Division to the threatened position occupied by Colonel Tidball's batteries at the Dunn house. It was then about six o'clock.[28]

The commander of the Pennsylvanians, Lieutenant Colonel W. H. H. McCall, ordered the 57th, "a small body" of which "had rallied just in front of the 200th and were feebly replying to the enemy," to regain its bivouac, and he deployed the men as skirmishers in front of his regiment. "The Fifty-seventh Massachusetts . . . advanced . . . and by a succession [three] of brilliant skirmish charges recovered the slope on which their camp had stood and the crest above it overlooking Fort Stedman."[29]

Hartranft's division was made up of new, large, almost full-strength Pennsylvania infantry regiments recruited during the previous Christmas season, and he then began to concentrate them on the elevated ground in the rear of Fort Stedman. With the aid of Tidball's artillery and the tenacity of the worn-down 1st Division regiments, the Rebels were essentially checkmated. The Confederate objective of supplies and captured guns was smashed, and Lee's hope of a concentration of Federal forces on the Union right to fight

Gordon and allow the Army of Northern Virginia to depart Petersburg without hindrance was lost.

General Hartranft maintained the momentum, lining up his huge regiments in battle ranks along with Willcox's tattered remnants on his flanks—forming a mile-and-a-half semicircle containing thousands of soldiers—and at seven forty-five that morning, with the 211th Pennsylvania leading, the blue lines of infantrymen advanced down the slope to the rear of the beseiged Fort Stedman. A massive cordon was formed partially around the fort from north to south, with the Federal batteries holding a murderous crossfire over the intervening ground between Stedman and Colquitt's Salient, precluding retreat. It was the Crater all over again, noted the boys later with great satisfaction, but with the shoe on the other foot. During the action, the 57th Massachusetts held a position not far from its original one, but to the right of Battery No. 10.

The Union troops attacked the fort mercilessly on all three sides while the artillery's crossfire made any attempt to escape back to the Confederate works perilous at best. The Rebels had little choice but to maintain a defensive position in and around the fort.

Hartranft continued to move his line to recapture the fort. The 57th proceeded to take up station in front of the 3rd Division, forming part of the skirmish line. As the Federals advanced, the Confederates in position outside and on the open ground to the rear of Fort Stedman resisted vehemently at first, pouring volley after volley into the oncoming Union soldiers. But the Federal formations were irresistible, and the Southerners quickly sought shelter—in and around the fort—from their withering fire. Bodies began to pile up as the bullets whacked, whistled, and hummed through the cold spring morning air amid choking, gray smoke so thick that the men had the familiar problem of not being able to see very well.

With every foot of ground being resisted violently by the Confederates in Stedman, still the Union soldiers went forward until they reached the fort, storming its sally port and parapets.[30]

The fighting increased in ferocity and devastation. The 57th, being in the skirmish line, was one of the first regiments to enter the lion's den, and the two sides fought savagely, shooting, bayoneting, clubbing, and punching each other. The battle turned into a wild frenzy of bloodthirsty vengeance. In the turmoil Sergeant Major Pinkham dove for a Confederate battle flag that had gone down with its dead color sergeant and captured it for the regiment—its first and only trophy of colors. Astonishingly, the boys later discovered that it had belonged to the 57th North Carolina Volunteer Infantry, and some looked on it as a sign from Providence of vindication for the taking of their original colors at the Crater. Others called it poetic justice. Pinkham was later promoted to second lieutenant and received the medal of honor for his action—the only man in the 57th besides Sergeant Karpeles to gain that distinction.[31]

Color Sergeant Chase, in the lead with the regimental banner, was shot almost immediately, and the former regimental sergeant major, First Lieutenant Albert Murdock, who had been severely wounded at the Wilderness, seized the 57th's flag, and while holding the colors aloft and cheering the men on, he was cut down mortally wounded. His body caught in the folds of the flag, and he bled all over it in his death throes.[32]

By eight o'clock that morning, it was clear to the attackers that they were badly beaten, and the fighting tapered off, with 1,949 Confederates surrendering. Some of Gordon's men had managed to get through the artillery crossfire to the safety of their own lines, but most were killed, wounded, or captured. For the Rebel leaders, the battle had been a disastrous failure, but for the individual Confederate soldier, capture meant food and an end to the war that most of them realized they could not win now anyway.[33]

George Barton remembered the day in a letter to his mother.

. . . The "Johnnies" Charged upon our brigade about three oclock this A.M. took one of our forts—which they were not able to hold. Things looked very blue for a while, but at last we drove them *out* of the fort with our Artilery and gallant Infantry thank *God*, the Victory is *ours*, and the "Johns" paid very dear for their "Attempt." We [the IX Corps] took about 2500 [sic] prisoners 9 stands of Colors and now hold our *original* line. Our regiment lost *very heavily as usual.* I came out without a *scratch.* . . . I will not give any more details at present I am too full for *utterance* it does seem to me as if our poor Regiment was doomed. We are still in fighting trim and ready at any moment for another *"turn."* . . .

(In this letter, Barton showed that even he, an officer, was not above looting the dead. "I enclose a badge of rank 'Captains,'" he wrote in a postscript, "belonging or *did* belong to Capt E J Nickerson A.[ssistant] A.[djutant] Genl Ransome [sic] Rebel Brigade he was shot in our Camp I cut it from his *coat collar* The envelope is also Confederate."[34])

The remaining men of the 57th Massachusetts returned to their ruined camp after the fight, and they found that all not destroyed by cannon fire had been looted. They had lost everything that they owned except the clothes on their backs. The camp was a shambles, and so was the regiment. Two hundred and thirteen officers and enlisted men were known to have gone into the fight, and 93 had been killed, wounded, captured, or were listed as missing—nearly half the men mustered for battle that day. The rolls showed 120 officers and enlisted men left for combat duty.[35]

Major Doherty—"the brave Doherty," as some were fond of calling him—had been out in front of the regiment, as always the "raging lion in battle," yelling for his men to follow him with his unusually loud voice, when he was shot down. Lieutenant Hitchcock was nearby, and seeing that the major's wound probably was fatal, he and Sergeant William Oakes picked him up and quickly carried him to the rear. They found Doherty's tent and took him inside and laid him down on his cot. Hitchcock made a further examination, and confirmed his battlefield diagnosis.

"We can only make him comfortable, Oakes," the lieutenant said to the sergeant, and they loosened his coat which he kept fastidiously buttoned in battle to enhance his military bearing and which was also peppered with bullet holes from near misses in many fights—the result of a life up to then almost charmed. They then removed his sword belt and tried to make him as comfortable as they knew how.

Later in the day the major was taken to the division field hospital suffering terrible pain, and Reverend Dashiell "pressed upon him the gracious offer of salvation through Christ," to which Doherty replied that he "could not insult the savior by offering him the dregs of my life." With his final words of "God bless you, Chaplain," he closed his eyes and quietly slipped away.

Doherty had been "an erratic sort of man" according to Captain Anderson, "brusque in appearance, emphatic in speech, warm, true, brave." This was not the opinion of all of the enlisted men, some of whom saw him more as a wild, reckless type, not in the least bothered about taking chances with their lives.

One story about him that the men did enjoy, however, was of an incident that had occurred on the road as the regiment was departing the Wilderness battlefield. Doctor White approached him—Doherty was captain of Company G at the time—and told him that one of his men, Private George H. Wilcox, had died.

"Are you quite sure of what you say, Doctor?" he asked White.

"Certainly, quite sure," answered the doctor.

"Are you sure it was Wilcox?"

"Certainly. Captain Doherty, don't you suppose I know Wilcox often as he has been up to sick call in the morning?"

"Well, doctor," replied Doherty, "it's alright if you say so," and turning around to the company, he said, "Wilcox, turn in your gun and equipment to the first sergeant, go back to the hospital, and crawl into that grave. What the hell do you think that I'm made of that you, a dead man, dare to march around in the ranks of this company? Don't you hear the doctor say that you are officially dead? Get out of here!"

The company was hysterical with laughter as Wilcox obediently stepped out of line, and the red-faced doctor probably wished he could disappear.[36]

Color Corporal Frederick S. Cheney of Company C, from Middlebridge,

New York, had been one of eleven of the regiment's men who had fought in every battle. He had never been wounded in all that time, but his luck did not hold at Fort Stedman, and he was killed in the fight.[37]

Born in County Roscommon, Ireland, Private Patrick Flynn (the other of the regiment's two Patrick Flynns), of Company D, was a brave soldier. He took his first wound, in the foot, at Spotsylvania on May 12, his second, by a shell fragment in the left arm, at Poplar Grove Church on September 30, and his third that day at Fort Stedman. He also was captured as a prisoner of war.[38]

Another Irishman, First Sergeant George Adams, of Company G, from County Lough, received a commendation for his part in the battle that day. Incredibly, Sergeant Adams had taken his fifteenth wound.[39]

A "Good and Faithful Soldier" was how Corporal Charles Hamlin, from Springfield, Massachusetts, was known to his officers. He, too, was a member of Company G, and like Corporal Cheney, he had fought in every battle since the 57th had entered service. That day, Hamlin was captured, but was to be released shortly and would be mustered out with the regiment. He would be numbered among the ten men who had participated in all the regiment's engagements and survived.[40]

Company G's Corporal John Smith, from England, had a record identical to that of Charles Hamlin. He too was captured and later paroled, but was discharged in July for disability. His company commanders described him as a "Splendid soldier."[41]

Fifty-two of the 57th's men had been taken prisoner of war during the battle. They were marched into Petersburg along with other Federal captives, stripped of personal possessions, and held in warehouses out of artillery range until later in the day, when they boarded passenger and freight cars that took them to Richmond. There they arrived at about five o'clock the next morning. At Libby prison in the Confederate capital, the enlisted men and officers were separated and then jailed. But their imprisonment would be brief, and on Sunday, April 2, they would be paroled.[42]

★

Later on the day of the battle, while the cold wind blew and snow and rain fell alternately, the Confederates asked for a truce to bury their dead and bring in their wounded. The Union officers quickly granted their request, and between two and four that afternoon the fort was once again swarming with butternut uniforms, but this time the Rebels were peaceful. As they worked, their Federal counterparts joined in digging graves and helping their own wounded, a few of whom had not as yet been attended to, while the officers from both sides socialized with each other. As soon as the work was finished, the Southerners bid the Northerners chivalrous and warm good-byes, which were returned in kind—as if both sides had just finished a fraternal outing—and returned to their lines, took up station, and prepared to continue the bloodletting.[43]

An event happened during the battle that few of the men realized for some time. Abraham Lincoln had been meeting with General Grant at City Point discussing war matters when he heard the commotion on the right of the Federal lines and asked to be driven to the front. From the crest of the hill near the Dunn house batteries, where the 57th had been fighting just a short time earlier, he watched the final Union charge. The president termed the battle "a little rumpus." The regiment had had its second presidential review.[44]

★

The day after the engagement, the drummer boys beat reveille early, and the exhausted men of the 57th Regiment were ordered to go on high alert in the main line of works at Battery No. 11. They loaded their rifles and filled their cartridge and cap boxes, and after a hasty breakfast in the dark, the soldiers made their way into the filthy, damp trenches, tripping and stumbling over the trash of battle littering the ditches. They were wary and apprehensive, and after the events of the previous day they knew that the Rebels were desperate and willing to gamble anything, and so they peered into the blackness silently and vigilantly.

Even though they were aware instinctively that the war was in its last stages, no one was going to convince them that the Confederates did not have plenty of fight left. Beyond doubt, the battle of Fort Stedman had proved that. The Southerners recently had laced the ground in front of Colquitt's Salient with a type of land mine known to the men as torpedoes, and not a soul was anxious to venture out into that no man's land and be blown to pieces by one of those "infernal machines."[45]

On March 27, Sam Grant issued orders for a Federal movement to the left, the object being to turn Lee's right and, at the same time, capture the South Side Railroad. Grant also felt that to counter the Federal threat Lee would weaken his lines on the Confederate left to reinforce his right, and that the way would then be clear for a general assault on those Confederate defenses. The strike on Lee's right was to be undertaken by the Union cavalry under Major General Philip Sheridan, the V Corps, and about half of the Army of the James, the whole supported by the II Corps. Army headquarters dispatched orders for most of the IX Corps to move to the left of the Union lines and man the positions on the right of the VI Corps. An attack on the entire Confederate front was planned. On March 29, the march began in heavy rains, and the IX Corps took up its new station. It had not really moved very far, but all of the corps's baggage was sent to the depots at City Point.

While the movements were made to the left, the 57th and part of the 3rd Brigade remained in its position at Battery No. 11 to the south of Fort Stedman, putting up with constant Rebel skirmish fire and artillery bombardment.[46]

At about 10:30 that night, the Southerners sent signal rockets aloft, and then opened fire all along the 1st Division's front. Confederate artillerymen poured shot and shell into the IX Corps' 1st Brigade at Fort Morton and the 3rd Brigade at Fort Stedman. At the same time infantry volleys opened on the 57th from the Southern lines, and the Confederates advanced in the dark, rainy night and dug in in the picket line's rifle pits on the left of the 3rd Brigade's front, near the Norfolk & Petersburg Railroad bridge. The 57th's pickets resisted strongly, but were overwhelmed and driven back into the main lines. From there the boys made a strong stand, returning a deadly fire that forced the Rebels to retire to their lines. As soon as the ground was clear, the regiment restored its pickets. The Confederate artillery ceased fire at about 11:30 P.M., and the full attack that the men thought was coming never materialized. That action had been only a reconnaissance. Lee's soldiers were probing the strength of the Union lines in that section to determine whether they could break through for another try on the Federal supply depots. They were desperate for food. The 57th lost four wounded, and the men remarked that between the small arms and artillery, it had been the heaviest concentration of fire on that part of the line that they had seen.[47]

Captain Barton gave his assessment of the night of March 29, and the proposed attack by the IX Corps on March 31:

We had a *terrible Artilery duel* here the other night, 29th inst The air was *literally* filled with *Mortar shells.* four men wounded in the 57th by said *"Messengers of love".* Last night [March 30] we were under arms all night, had received orders to be ready to make a *Charge* upon the lines of the "Johnnies" in front [of] Fort "Steadman" The 57th 59th and 29th Mass Vols were to be the *assaulting party. A forlorn hope* indeed, with only about 200 men in the entire three regiments. it looked decidedly *blue* and *bloody.* A hard *rain* set in and the *Charge* was deferred. it will probably be made *tomorrow morning.* I have turned over all my *valuables, Money, watch,* and good *Clothes* to my *cook* [Private] William Lee in case *anything should happen* to me they can be sent home by him *I am* in *Command* of the *veteran 57th* they will do all that *men can* do, we must leave the rest to *God.* The "Johns" are *very strongly entrenched* in our *"front"* with *three* lines of "Abbattis" *for obstruction.* These must be *Cut away* by *Axemen,* detailed from different regiments in the Brigade. Under cover of our *skirmishers* They will have to advance in the face of a *"living fire"* from the enemy. if they *succeed* in this the *three above named* Regiments *slected* from the *entire Brigade* Must *"go in"* and effect a *lodgement* in their works. *What a prospect* for a *young* Man in the very *prime* of life—I am in great hopes that something will "turn up" to prevent our being obliged to undertake so *"doubtful"* an "affair" to say the least. My only hope is that the *enemy* will charge *upon our* lines.[48]

Heavy mortar fire had punctuated every day and night since the battle of Fort Stedman, and the men spent much of their time dodging the deadly missiles. In the 57th's part of the line the Confederate artillerymen had a breechloading English Whitworth rifled field gun, and the boys were terrified when its shells came swishing and whirring in fast and low. Those shells were impossible to duck, and it was only because the men kept down in the trenches that no one was taken out by them. One of the shells passed straight through Captain Albert Cook's tent, smashing its contents to slivers, but the captain, fortunately, was not in at the time.[49]

The Union commanders were alarmed that another surprise attack like the one at Fort Stedman would occur, and they generated orders to keep the men on an extremely sharp lookout. The soldiers also were directed to turn out and stand under arms an hour before sunset each evening and an hour before sunrise each morning, and the trench guard was doubled. The soldiers got almost no rest, and the eerie nights conjured hallucinations to the burning eyes of the stuporous men. The strain and tensions since the battle of Fort Stedman had worn their nerves thin, and they jumped at the slightest provocation. Anxiety coupled with sleeplessness and the fighting of the last ten months had frazzled them, and they became irritated at the most trivial incidents.[50]

While the men were in the lines, the orders that George Barton wrote about came down from headquarters for the 57th, along with the 29th and 59th Massachusetts, to charge Colquitt's Salient. Division, brigade, and regimental officers were instructed to have those regiments, as well as others in different brigades, prepared for field operations, and to be ready to move at a moment's notice. When they got the word, the 57th's men were incredulous. To make such a charge was nothing short of suicidal, and all knew it. They dreaded the thought of making another assault over open ground only to be slaughtered further.

Three lines of abatis in front of the Confederate lines had to be removed so that the attackers could reach the enemy trenches, and First Lieutenant James H. Marshall—a native of New Albany, Indiana, then in command of Company F—and forty men from various regiments volunteered to cut them away. Clearing that much abatis would take time, and these axmen would be in close range of Rebel marksmen. They were not given much of a chance of survival. Those volunteers certainly were not representative of the ordinary soldier, who thought the whole scheme insane. The time for the axmen to move out was set for three o'clock on the morning of March 31, and they took up position on the night of the 30th in front of the infantry regiments waiting for the order to move out. The foot soldiers were to follow at four.

The assault was to take place along the entire line of the IX and VI Corps. The 2nd and 3rd Divisions of the IX Corps were in rear of Fort Sedgewick, and part of the 1st Division, at Fort Stedman, was to make a feint at the enemy in front of the fort and, if they found the position weak, to carry out a full-scale attack.

The early morning of March 31 was black with heavy rains, and the men lingered in their water-filled trenches all night preparing for the assault to begin. The waiting seemed to go on forever, and they grew tired and nervous from the tedious delay. The suspense was painful. There was heavy artillery fire along the whole line that night, and because their signal to begin the advance was supposed to be the firing of two field guns at 1st Division headquarters, they wondered if they would be able to hear them, and they strained their ears in the direction of their command post.

The men of the 57th believed their chance of surviving the foolhardy and forlorn charge proposed for them slim, and they prepared for the worst. Many of them gave their personal belongings to Reverend Dashiell or to other noncombatants with instructions to send them home if they did not return. Tense and nervous, the soldiers lay in their sopping, swampy ditches hoping the hour of attack would never come, and when, early that morning, word came down countermanding the battle orders, tremendous relief surged through the lines.

By a miracle, some believed, army headquarters had realized its folly. But, in reality, Confederate troop strength had been determined to be too great— that part of the Confederate line had not been pulled out to reinforce the Rebel right after all—and the Federal soldiers had been spared. The dirty faces came alive with the white smiles of happy men, and bodies relaxed. A "circular" order had been received from 1st Division headquarters just after 4:00 A.M. that stated, "It will not be necessary to keep the men in ranks after daylight. The order in regard to keeping them with their commands in camp must be strictly observed," and the soldiers were allowed to return to their tents for much-needed rest.

Soon after dawn some of the men heard one of the Southerners yell over to them, "Well, Yank, why didn't y'all come over and cut away the abatis last night?" No one could say how the Rebels could have known about the aborted attack, until they learned later that a Union soldier had deserted to the Confederate lines and told them of the planned assault.[51]

★

At about ten o'clock on the night of April 1, almost all of the guns in the Federal artillery opened fire along the entire Union line from the James River to the South Side Railroad. Confederate artillerymen responded immediately, and the men in the trenches were treated to the most magnificent display of bursting shells and twirling, twinkling fuses that they had ever witnessed. The entire sky was ablaze as far as they could see, and the roar and boom of the guns was deafening while shock waves from the detonations reverberated through the ground. As the soldiers gazed up at that incredible event with the stars blinking in counterpoint in the background, they could not know that the siege of Petersburg was coming to an end.

Early the following morning, April 2, Grant ordered an assault by the Army of the Potomac against the Confederate defenses after he learned from Confederate deserters that Lee had pulled most of his troops out, and the 1st Division pickets pushed forward in front of Fort Stedman with the artillery in the fort coming to life in support. The charges along the line by the IX Corps were successful, and the men captured the Southern works in front of them after some last, desperate fighting by the Rebel defenders.

After the 57th had driven in the Confederate pickets, they were pulled out of line and held in reserve at Fort Stedman. They could hear the furious battle down to their left, and they watched the long blue lines of shouting and cheering men in their vicinity as the Federal soldiers made their last charge at Petersburg.[52]

24

The Ladies They Will All Turn Out

J UST AFTER MIDNIGHT the next morning, April 3, 1865, the 57th Massachusetts Veteran Volunteer Infantry Regiment sustained its last casualty at
the front. Corporal Alonzo Mason, of Company K, was wounded on the
picket line. But the injury was not serious, and after his recuperation he
returned to the regiment for duty later that spring. He was, his officers said,
a "Good Soldier."[1]

Around 2:00 A.M., the Rebel pickets were withdrawn from the Petersburg
works. The Confederate lines were silent, and when the Federal skirmishers
advanced to investigate at four o'clock, they met no resistance. Before long
the Union soldiers realized that the Southern trenches were empty. The
Army of Northern Virginia had evacuated Petersburg, but the Northerners
scarcely could believe what they saw. Except for a few bodies dead in the
muddy rifle pits and earthworks and piles of trash and left-behind army
equipment scattered about, Lee's fortifications were deserted, and the Union
troops wandered around staring at the debris and picking up trophies and
souvenirs. After ten months of unrelenting gunfire between the lines, at last
a man could stand in the open without fear. That realization was difficult to
accept for those men so accustomed to living constantly in danger and under
shelter.[2]

Soon after the situation was reported to Grant and Meade, most of the
Army of the Potomac moved out in pursuit of Lee and his soldiers, who had
slid off to the southwest. General Willcox was ordered to take his 1st Division
of the IX Corps and occupy the city of Petersburg with all haste. General
Parke, with the 2nd and 3rd Divisions of the corps, joined the rest of the
Federal forces in the chase after the Rebel army.[3]

Willcox's orders were to garrison and secure the city and the railroads,
and to protect the lives and property of the citizens. The 3rd Brigade set off
on the two-mile march to Petersburg at five o'clock that morning to help

Above, Confederate soldier killed by the IX Corps, April 2, 1865; *below*, Confederate dead in Fort Mahone at Petersburg; the IX Corps charged here, April 2, 1865. *(Minnesota Historical Society, Minneapolis)*

Above, Disemboweled and shoeless Confederate killed at Petersburg, April 2, 1865;
below, Confederate artilleryman killed during the IX Corps' assault, April 2, 1865.
(Chicago Historical Society)

accomplish those objectives. The 2nd Brigade had preceded the 3rd some-time earlier. As the soldiers passed through the abandoned Confederate works around Colquitt's Salient, the boys discovered that the Southerners had begun to dig a crude mine shaft toward Fort Stedman—the lesson of the Crater had not been lost on Lee's soldiers. But it was nowhere near completed, and the men were amused at the Rebels' primitive engineering skills—in their opinion, that is.[4]

For some time now, Captain Albert Cook, the 57th's senior remaining officer still in the field after the battle of Fort Stedman, had been detailed on brigade staff duty, and since March 26, Captain George Barton had commanded the regiment. He was still in command that morning. Colonel James Blintiff of the 38th Wisconsin Volunteer Infantry had relieved Colonel Gilbert P. Robinson of the 3rd Maryland—who had taken over when General McLaughlen was made a prisoner of war—as commander of the 3rd Brigade at nine o'clock on the night of April 2, and he, too, was yet in command of the brigade that day.[5]

It was a beautiful spring Monday as the long blue column of the 3rd Brigade followed the 2nd into the city from the east and the rising April sun glinted off of the many shouldered muskets with fixed bayonets. The excited men marched in their best order with tightly closed ranks while their officers strutted in the lead. "You Cant imagine how proud I was to be able to lead the 57th into 'Petersburg,' " wrote George Barton to his mother several days later, "I would not have missed the occasion for anything." And he added later, "Glory to God and his brave boys! We've entered the City." The march into the fallen city was the high-water mark of the men's military careers—and for most, the high-water mark of their lives—and they were in perfect bliss that morning. All regimental, brigade, and division banners, colorful and tattered, were aloft and fluttering in the soft breeze, and the brass bands played "We'll Rally 'Round the Flag, Boys," with great élan while the soldiers raised their voices in resonant and powerful song.[6]

Colonel Ralph Ely, in command of the 2nd Brigade, the leading elements of which had arrived during the early morning hours before dawn, accepted the formal surrender of Petersburg from the city officials, and then, at 4:28 A.M., the 1st Michigan Sharpshooters raised the national colors onto the flagpole of Petersburg's columned courthouse while the 2nd Michigan raised theirs on the custom house simultaneously. Their comrades cheered and a band struck up stirring, martial airs.[7]

The 3rd Maryland Infantry led the 3rd Brigade on the march into Petersburg that morning, arriving at six o'clock, and as the battle-worn, tiny 57th Massachusetts followed with Captain Barton in the lead, the boys behaved like tourists, looking around and pointing fingers at interesting sights in the battered and ravaged city that they had fought so long and hard to conquer.

345

Headquarters for the 3rd Brigade was set up at the Roger Pryor house, and some of the men volunteered to help that gentleman box up the books in his library for safekeeping.

Most of the prominent citizens, fearing for their lives, had fled the city along with the Southern army, but those of the poorer classes had remained behind. There were some desolate old men on the streets, but the women stayed indoors, and the soldiers caught fleeting glimpses of them from time to time as the ladies, with frightened, hollow eyes, peered back at them through curtained and partially shuttered windows.

Petersburg's children were curious to see the victors, and they peeped shyly around the corners of buildings, staring open-mouthed and wide-eyed at the notorious Yankees. As the columns marched by, the men joked with the dirty-faced, skinny little boys and girls, making faces and smiling at them.

Several hundred unarmed Confederate soldiers who had taken refuge in the cellars of Petersburg homes had been rounded up and were idling around under the careful watch of the division's provost detail. The forlorn Rebels were filthy, tattered, and emaciated, but they talked easily with their guards and accepted food eagerly and gratefully. Hostility had vanished from most of those men—the fire had gone out at last.

But the most visible group were the blacks. Hundreds of them were in the streets, dancing, frolicking, and shouting at the Union soldiers that the year of jubilee had come and expressing their joy at the arrival of the Yankees, come to set them free. They crowded around the men, and all they seemed to want was to ride on the railroad cars. The trains fascinated them, and they begged the soldiers to let them on.

In his original regimental history, Captain Anderson wrote of the blacks in Petersburg that day:

> Little did these poor, ignorant people realize the long, tiresome journey that was to lead them through the dark shadows of persecution and political intrigue, before they would be able to appreciate the great blessings of freedom and the responsible duties of citizenship, which were to be given them. They gave no thought as to what they were to do in the future. To them it was the one supreme moment when they lived entirely in the present, drawing nothing from the past and demanding nothing of the future. They were free to go where they pleased; their first great desire being to ride on the [railroad] cars.

While still some distance from Petersburg, the marching men had seen two huge columns of black smoke rising high into the air above the center of the city, and upon entering the town, the soldiers discovered that the fleeing Confederates had set fire to a large tobacco warehouse, assorted other buildings, and the railroad station in order to keep them from Federal hands.

The boys went to work immediately dousing the flames, but they focused their efforts on the warehouse because most had been out of tobacco for some time. They went about their work diligently, stuffing their haversacks full of the brown leaves at every opportunity. The men passed buckets of water and gagged on thick black and gray smoke, and in a short while the fires were under control. A small detachment of black troops had accompanied the division into the city, and the white soldiers left most of the hard work to them.

Except for liberating the supply of tobacco and smashing a sign to smithereens that had the Confederate colors painted on it, the Federal soldiers behaved reasonably well. There was no pillaging to speak of, and the citizens of Petersburg were not harassed. Guards were posted to protect private property, and soon heavy, covered army transport wagons laden with food lumbered along the city's cobblestone streets, and hungry Southern civilians lined up eagerly as the Federals distributed it among them. Burial parties had been organized right away, and the corpses found in the area were interred quickly. The wounded and injured were cared for at field dressing stations hastily set up in the city's buildings. Heavily armed patrols were stationed at strategic points in Petersburg, and two hours after the 1st Division had entered the town, order and discipline were established and strictly enforced. The people soon realized that they had little to fear from the Union soldiers, and the streets and alleys began to fill with more and more residents, cautious, but curious and hungry.[8]

★

The 57th did not remain in Petersburg for long. The men returned to camp at Fort Stedman to gather their few belongings, and the regiment then headed north with the brigade at ten that morning. After crossing the Appomattox River, the soldiers marched for two miles along the Richmond Turnpike toward Old Town Creek until they came to Violet Bank, where the 3rd Brigade's headquarters was established in a fine old plantation house. There were two pianos in the home, and some of the officers who were able played operas on them while the enlisted men speedily pitched the tents and then were detailed to guard the roads to Richmond that ran through Chesterfield County. Great, long lines of ragged, starving Confederate prisoners who had surrendered or had been flushed from the woods and other hiding places were marched into the area. Most of those beaten men were glad that their war was over, and, as their comrades in Petersburg had done, they mingled freely and pleasantly with their former enemies, who shared their rations with them generously. Generally, animosity was absent with the soldiers of the two great armies, and they called each other "Yank" and "Johnnie Reb" with sincere admiration. They shook hands, told stories, asked questions, and

IX Corps wagon train leaving Petersburg for the west on Washington Street, about April 10, 1865. *(Library of Congress, Washington, D.C.)*

remembered battles, and their camaraderie was respectful and genuine. Most all felt relieved—particularly the enlisted Confederate soldiers—and everyone knew that he would be going home soon. For the Federals, it was a great day to be alive, and for the first time in nearly a year the men not on the picket line slept soundly and securely that night.[9]

Early the following morning, April 4, the 3rd Brigade received orders to change position, and the men got under way at noon and recrossed the Appomattox. Continuing through Petersburg on Washington Street, they headed southwest along that thoroughfare until it became the Cox road. Marching another half-mile, the brigade's soldiers arrived near the McIlwaine house, close to Indian Town Creek, where they made camp in an old line of Confederate works on the western extremes of the Petersburg battlefield. The brigade stretched from the Appomattox River south to the Boydton Plank road, and when the men looked around them, they could see the former Federal positions just as the Rebels had seen them all those desperate months, and the Union soldiers reminisced and pointed to the places across the lines where the Army of the Potomac had been for so long. They were curious, too, and they explored the Confederate works intently, seeking treasures.[10]

Pickets were sent out, more as a matter of course than of need. With the possible exception of Confederate guerillas, there was no enemy there anymore, and as the men gathered around their campfires that night with the flames flickering delicate shadows on their sun-browned faces, the battlefield was deathly quiet, even ghostly in the blackness. Cold chills undoubtedly ran up a few backs, and some men must have shivered in the warm night air. In all the time that they had been at Petersburg, never a day had passed without ceaseless, killing gunfire on the line, and the silence now was macabre and frightening and difficult to get used to. Many of the men were silent themselves that night, and inwardly they reflected on their dead comrades as they sat on that grim but now hauntingly peaceful ground. They thought of home, now so close, and they drifted off into half-sleep with wispy half-dreams of the day when they would board the steamers and trains that would take them there.

★

At noon the next day, the 57th moved with the brigade about eight miles west through the green Petersburg fields and forests along the Cox road to Sutherland Post Office and relieved the pickets of the IX Corps' 3rd Division, who had been guarding the South Side Railroad and the Cox road, which ran nearly parallel to it on the south. The 3rd Brigade, "at five minutes past midnight, April 6, again started on the Cox road, relieving the pickets of the Third Division [IX Corps] from Poole's house below Ford's [Station], to a mile beyond Beasley's [house]." The entire 1st Division, each brigade taking up about nine miles of track, was now guarding the railroad from Sutherland Post Office to Wilson's Station eighteen miles to the west. There and further to the west, Willcox's men linked with Hartranft's 3rd Division now on station, and all roads crossing the South Side's tracks were picketed heavily.[11]

April 8 found the 57th Regiment near Ford's Station camped all along its section of the railroad in detachments, keeping a sharp eye out for Rebel marauders. The South Side Railroad was now Grant's logistical link with City Point, and if the trains were interrupted, the Army of the Potomac, hot on the heels of Lee and his army near Appomattox Court House, would be endangered. The situation was still volatile west of Petersburg, and the men were vigilant.[12]

★

Sunday, April 9, 1865, was a glorious day in Virginia. The sun shone warmly, and sweet, fragrant breezes drifted gently through the air. The trees and grass were fresh green, and birds chirped merrily. Awakened life teemed all about the landscape. Early that morning the 3rd Brigade had extended its lines to one mile beyond Wilson's Station, and the men were enjoying spring's soft rebirth.[13]

The 57th's officers had appropriated a nearby church at Hebron for their comfort that April 9. They all boarded there, and the pulpit became regimental headquarters. Every pew had a spittoon and they were soon overflowing, but when the regiment pulled out on April 12, the commanders left the little building in good shape. One of the 57th's scribes, however—probably George Barton—left a message for posterity in the church's register. He wrote, "Rededicated to his Yankee omnipotence, Abraham Lincoln, and his invincible 'Captain of the Host' U.S. Grant, and consecrated to the use of the armies of the U.S. who are shelterless. April 9, 1865."[14]

Captain Barton left a picture of what times were like for the regiment during that period in a letter to his mother.

> Camp 57th Mass Vol Infantry
> "Hebron Church" Near South Side RR Va
> "Sunday Eve" April 9, 1865

Dear Mother

Our Brigade is at present doing heavy "Picket" duty on the South Side RR and as you may suppose, we consider it a very "soft job" Much pleasanter than before Petersburg. We are about 25 miles south of Petersburg in a beautiful tract of country. I need not tell you that we fully appreciate the *change* in our position

The 57th "Hd Qrs" are in the above mentioned Church My own private quarters are in the pulpit where I have a very nice *lounge*, spitoon & c.

Every pew in the Church has several spitoons attached to it showing very clearly that "Members" used the "weed" *quite* freely. I have had the "Church" thoroughly "cleaned out" and everything put in order, so that should the "erring Members" care [to] return to their Alligience they will have a place of Worship.

At this very moment a young man brought in an accordian and we are having some very good Music both sacred and otherwise It seems delightful to be once more among Comparatively pleasant scenery.

There are quite a number of nice families in this vicinity and I take occasion to call upon them frequently. I find them all glad that the war is "right near ended." [The news of Lee's surrender at Appomattox Court House had not as yet reached the regiment.]

How long we shall remain here I am unable to say but trust until we are "recruited" [i.e., until more of the men return to the ranks from hospitals, etc.] somewhat. Have no doubt but that the Ninth Corps will be in at the "death"—hope so, at least. About ten thousand Rebel prisoners passed here today. They do so every day. [The 1st Division's provost guard responsible for those prisoners was the 17th Michigan Engineer Regiment.] The end is Near. One more regular "Waterloo" and the so called "Confederacy" is "gone up" so far we shall never hear from it again The impression here is that Lee will Make a stand at Lynchburg if he can only form a junction with Johnson [Johnston] he will probably turn upon Sherman and give him battle. in any Case the result will be in our favor by the grace of God and our *brave* boys. The Army never was in better "fighting trim", So "Johnnie" must look out for us, for we are not liable to "turn back". . . .

I picked up a horse in Petersburg and have had the pleasure of using him since. Very *Convenient* My health is good as *usual* for which I have to thank "Lee" who rations me principally upon "fried pudding" and potatoes. . . .[15]

General Robert E. Lee surrendered the Army of Northern Virginia—only about twenty-eight thousand men then—to Lieutenant General Ulysses S.

Grant in the McLean house at Appomattox Court House, Virginia, on the afternoon of April 9, 1865. The 57th learned the news on April 10, and that "night was one of general jollification, the memory of which will long linger with the many and varied experiences of the Fifty-seventh Massachusetts."[16]

Federal staff officers busied themselves from dawn to dusk over the next several days administering oaths of allegiance to the United States to the Rebels. After taking the oath, the former enemies were paroled and released to go home. Before the formal surrender at Appomattox, Confederate stragglers and detachments had been coming into the Union lines daily from the forests to surrender and accept their paroles, but many others just threw away their rifles and journeyed back to their little farms and families with no formalities. The Southern officers kept track of those surrendering by making out rolls of the men present, and after those rolls were signed and verified by the Union officers, the former Confederate commanders were paroled also, with the provision that they could keep their personal sidearms.[17]

The majority of Lee's soldiers were happy to put the hardships and miseries of the war behind them, and just a handful expressed resentment. The Federals simply ignored most of the diehards—they had had enough, too. John Singleton Mosby and his guerrillas—men who could not be ignored—were among those who were not willing to give up, and they continued their harassment and bushwhacking until April 21. The 57th's men feared him for his ruthless tactics and despised him for the atrocities he had committed upon the wounded after the battle of the Wilderness. Officers warned the pickets to be especially watchful for his presence. The thickly wooded countryside made it relatively easy for him to slip in and out of the Union lines at night, but the regiment went unhampered and suffered no loss from him or his cutthroat raiders.[18]

★

On April 13, the 57th moved to Wilson's Station on the South Side Railroad. There it remained guarding the tracks and countryside until April 20.[19]

★

During the morning of April 15, Army of the Potomac headquarters received the news by telegraph of the assassination of President Lincoln at Ford's Theater in Washington the previous evening. Major General George Gordon Meade issued General Orders No. 15 to his command on April 16, which read in part, "The major-general commanding [Meade] announces to the army that official intelligence has been received of the death, by assassination, of the President of the United States. The President died at 7.22 on the morning of the 15th instant."[20]

The men of the 57th—like all Northern troops—were stunned at that terrible report, which they could hardly credit at first. But the shock soon gave way to outrage as they accepted the truth, and a few wanted to take their fury out on the now defenseless Southerners. Wrote John Anderson,

> Had any of the Confederates expressed pleasure in it [the assassination] they would, most probably, have been made to suffer. The Confederate prisoners expressed a general regret and indignation towards the brutal assassins, and were anxious to disavow any responsibility in the horrible affair. If there were any who did not feel so they were wise enough to give no expression to it. The Confederate soldier who fought under Lee did all he could in manly battle, and when that battle ended he was the last one to resort to such dastardly means as assassination.[21]

George Barton summed up the soldiers' mood to his mother: "You Cannot possibly imagine the sorrow and honest indignation that pervades the Army at the *brutal assassination* of our Noble President. It is well for the Rebel Army that they have surrendered for should we meet them now [in battle] the *slaughter* would be *fearful* anyway very little mercy would be shown to any."[22]

The men were quiet around the fires on the night that the news of the tragedy had been received—their joy at peace shaken—and there were few dry eyes. No one could guess what might happen as a result of Lincoln's violent murder, and speculation ran the gamut in their imaginations.

★

Precipitated by the president's assassination, General Orders No. 99 from General Meade reached General Parke on April 19, for the IX Corps to proceed to Washington with all haste to help guard the city and maintain order. The IX Corps was to be relieved from guard duty on the railroad by the V Corps. Parke, in turn, issued General Orders No. 88 on April 20. Paragraph No. 1 of that order read, "The First and Third Divisions of this corps on being relieved by troops of the Fifth Corps will, without delay, and without waiting for further orders, take up their line of march for City Point, and endeavor to reach that place as soon as possible. All preliminary arrangements will be made at once."[23]

The corps began its march to City Point the following morning at daylight, and with its departure it severed its connection with the Army of the Potomac. The trek was a happy occasion for the men of the 57th Massachusetts and the rest of the corps as all knew now that they were on the first leg of the road home. They felt wonderful as they passed through the verdant Virginia countryside that bright spring morning, and not even the hard march could dampen the spirits of most of those tough veterans. About one hundred of the 57th's men were in the ranks that day, but two of Company F's men soon found the forced march more than they could handle. Private

Patrick Brennan and Private John Lawless, both from Ireland, fell out from the exhausting pace, not rejoining their company until April 25 in Washington.[24]

City Point was bustling with activity as the corps arrived later that Tuesday afternoon. Supply trains rolled with their great engines pouring black smoke and white steam into the blue skies, teamsters whipped and cursed reluctant mule teams, and the wharves were lined with all sorts of off-loading ships and boats. The war might be over, but the massive Federal armies remaining in the field still needed supplies, and the great quartermaster general, Montgomery C. Meigs, was not about to let the soldiers do without. Activity, confusion, and noise prevailed, and soldiers milled about everywhere. Belied by the apparent chaos, however, were order and organization, for the Army of the Potomac veterans who worked as supply and transportation clerks and administrators had learned their jobs well during their trying service, and the IX Corps was loaded on transport ships quickly and efficiently by their direction. The 2nd Brigade embarked first, and the 3rd Brigade, still commanded by James Blintiff, boarded the steamer *Fannie* later. She sailed that night. (The 1st Brigade departed the following day.)[25] The trip down the James River and up the Potomac to the capital was pleasant and relaxing, and the men lounged around the decks and hung over the transport's rails enjoying the countryside quietly slipping by.

Upon arrival in Washington the next morning, the 3rd Brigade, as well as the rest of the 1st Division, was reviewed by General Willcox, and, after bivouacking for six days at Towle's farm in Alexandria, Willcox's command was sent to Tennallytown, five and a half miles northwest of the center of Washington and four miles southwest of Silver Spring, Maryland, where the men camped near the Delaney house on the evening of April 27, to take up station as guards for the surrounding area and the Chain Bridge over the Potomac River. The soldiers cordoned off that section of Washington, and no one was allowed through without written authority.[26]

For the next three months, the 57th would remain in that area. The men pitched their tents on the slope of a green and shaded hillside. The setting was almost idyllic, and after what they had suffered in the trenches at Petersburg, they were grateful for their pleasant surroundings. Aside from their assigned duties, normal camp routine and drill resumed. The activities of keeping the area clean, supplied, and guarded were peformed without complaint, but drill was another matter. To those hardened combat veterans, dress parades—the men were issued the formal nine-button frock coats again that they had not worn since Camp Wool—seemed entirely frivolous and unnecessary, and served only the whims of the officers. The activity was loathed and performed without enthusiasm.[27]

One benefit the camp did provide, however, and which was welcomed

Survivors of Company I, 57th Massachusetts Veteran Volunteers. This reversed-image photograph was taken near Tennallytown in July 1865. *From left to right, front row:* Sergeant George Ober, Corporal Henry Gallup, Corporal Newton B. Pepoon, Corporal Ensign Simmons, Private Charles Sidell; *back row:* Private John Snow, Private John McGlinley, Private William McGuire, Private George White. (Note the full-dress uniforms that the men were required to wear after the war.) (*USAMHI, Carlisle Barracks, Pa.*)

universally, was the opportunity to wash and shave daily. Drawing new uniforms increased morale, too. With their tanned faces, new clothes, and lean, hard bodies, they looked liked the real soldiers that they had become. Wrote Captain Barton on May 5,

We are quietly Camping in a beautiful tract of Country, *drilling* four hours a day both battallion and brigade. We are obliged to put on all the "style" that "Regulations" demand. . . . We are kept *very close* here few passes are granted Officers or men to visit Washington. All sorts of rumors are afloat in regard to our *future.* suffice it to say it can never be as dark as the past, thank God. We have our regular routine of duties plenty of Company business squaring up acc'ts & c. have just finished making out Pay Rolls for two Companies "C" and "E". No small job I assure you. I am left in Command of the Regiment most of the time Col. Tucker being on Special duty. . . .[28]

While the regiment was at camp, some men returned who had been on convalescent leave or detached duty, and the ranks grew a little stronger. In a letter written on April 24, George Barton comments to his mother about those returning soldiers and adds a few other thoughts, as well:

We have received quite an addition to our Reg't Consisting of Hospital "bummers" & "dead beats" Sometimes Called "Professional beats." Men who have been "coufing" [coughing] away their time as "detailed in Hospital" for the past year shirking every fight that was possible how some of them can look their comrades in the face without *blushing* appears strange very strange to me

It was just about a year ago that the "57th" left Alexandria to join the "A of P" [Army of the Potomac] Many sad changes have occured since that time. instead of a full regiment as then, a mere *fragment* of our gallant band remains, so that with all our rejoicing and triumphs we Cannot help but feel a regret that they Could not have been spared to share with us in this glorius prospect of an "honorable peace."

. . . it seems to me that you will receive no more "battle letters" from the 57th I feel as though I had "fought the last fight" it may not be so, but I do *hope* so. I never was very *blood* thirsty, except "under orders."[29]

With respect to Captain Barton's observations about "Hospital bummers" and "dead beats," not all of the returning men could be lumped into that category. The records of some of them indicate that they truly were incapacitated for long periods of time. Such a blanket judgment is not warranted. However, there is not the slightest doubt—also based on individual records—that many of those soldiers were exactly what George Barton claimed them to be.[30]

While on the march to Tennallytown on April 27, Company F's quintessential Irishman, Edward Hanrahan, had been arrested and placed under guard. The sergeant—he had been reappointed to his former rank of late—

apparently had been up to his old tricks and took a "wee drop" too much, which undoubtedly had lubricated his vocal chords only too well. Undeterred by his sentries, the tough combat veteran of every one of the 57th's battles managed to slip away, but he was arrested again on May 3, confined and, once more, broken to the ranks. However, Lieutenant Colonel Tucker evidently had had enough of Hanrahan's antics, and on May 6, Julius Tucker had the new private shipped off and detailed as a teamster assigned to the 3rd Brigade Quartermaster's Department until the regiment was mustered out of service.[31] The colonel must have thought dealing with army mules an appropriate duty for him.

But Edward Hanrahan was far from the only man in the regiment who was tired of rules and regulations and pomp and circumstance. The young corporal who had won his chevrons for bravery at Spotsylvania a year earlier and who had fought faithfully in almost all of the regiment's engagements, Newton B. Pepoon, of Company I, also was reduced to the ranks for "insolence and unsoldierly conduct" on May 4. The former corporal was confined for two weeks, and, apparently contrite, he was given another chance and he sewed his two stripes back on his sleeves on July 1.[32]

Sergeant Michael Lovejoy, of Company C, from Cork, Ireland, was another of the ten men who had fought safely in every battle in which the 57th had been engaged. And of those ten, he was one of five who never had been wounded or taken prisoner of war—without question a fearless soldier. But the Southern rebellion was crushed, and the mindlessness of the unnecessary postwar discipline and ceremony he could not abide. On May 10, he simply decided to go home—and went.[33]

★

Provost duty in Washington was not difficult, but Lincoln's assassination had put everyone—soldier and civilian alike—on edge, and although the 57th encountered no incidents worthy of note, the men at first performed their work as sentries diligently and strictly. On April 1, 1865, the provost marshal-general's office had issued rules and regulations governing the duties of the provost guards and patrols in and around the city of Washington. The sentries assigned to those tasks were to patrol the streets three times a day, checking especially those places known to be frequented by soldiers, such as bars, theaters, and other places of amusement. Another sort of establishment was to be inspected at intervals, as well, and paragraph number seven of the orders gives an interesting glimpse into a different, less well-known side of army life in 1865 Washington. "All brothels and bawdy-houses will be visited as frequently as possible during the evening," read the paragraph, "and if found disorderly the inmates will be ordered to report at the Central Guard

House on the following morning, to be convicted by the testimony of the officer having command of the patrol." Clearly, the soldiers of the Civil War differed little from soldiers of all time, despite the fact that Victorian propagandists would have us believe otherwise. During the Rebellion, more than seventy-three thousand cases of syphilis and just under ninety-six thousand cases of gonorrhea were treated by the army doctors.[34] That the men of the 57th stationed in Washington indulged in activities with the city's "fallen flowers" is highly probable, although no cases of venereal disease in the regiment have as yet been uncovered. But that in no way precludes the possibility that there were some. The statement "absent sick" next to a soldier's name on the morning reports was a large umbrella.

One of the 57th's men who did see the inside of the guardhouse while in Washington was Company H's Private George Wakeman, an actor from Worcester with an undistinguished record of service. He was arrested and confined in the "Central Guard House for having committed a theft" on June 5, but he was not held long, and because of a wound sustained at Fort Stedman, Wakeman was given an early discharge for disability.[35]

A difficult time for the Federal guards came with the trial of the Lincoln conspirators. The Northern populace screamed for swift justice—that is, vengeance—to be meted out to the accused, and strong opinions were expressed throughout the Union. When the military judges reached their verdict on June 30 that four of the indicted—including a woman, Mary Surratt, who owned the boardinghouse where the plot had been engineered—were to be hanged, the soldiers were warned to be especially alert, as no one was certain that a rescue attempt might not be made in behalf of the condemned. The men did not relax until the executions had taken place on July 7 at the Old Penitentiary in the city. Justice had been served, all agreed that day, but many felt queasy about the hanging of a woman.

★

General McLaughlen had been released from Libby Prison in Richmond by the Confederates on April 2, and under General Orders No. 21, dated May 10, 1865, he was assigned by Genral Willcox to oversee the IX Corps' 1st Division's camp on the Tennallytown road. Willcox would remain in command of the division, but only in an administrative capacity dealing with the unit's paperwork from his office in Washington.[36]

★

Under General Orders No. 239, issued from the Adjutant General's Office on May 18, the Army of the Potomac and Major General William Tecumseh Sherman's Western armies—the armies of the Ohio, Tennessee, and Cumberland, newly arrived from the deep South—were ordered gathered in Washington for a grand review by government dignitaries, military officials, and the public. It was to be a spectacular event which would afford a final look at the great Federal forces that had squashed the Confederacy and preserved the Union. A large wooden reviewing stand was erected on Pennsylvania Avenue for the luminaries and decorated with bunting and the national colors. The wide avenue also was hung with the Federal banners, and all along the thoroughfare trees were green with spring leaves.

The IX Corps had been chosen to be the first infantry to pass in review, and the night before the event, its troops had been marched into the city, and the soldiers had bivouacked east of the Capitol. As the men assembled at six o'clock on the morning of May 23, crowds thronged the streets to take in the enormous blue ranks. The 57th had drawn new arms and equipment on May 16, and the men were in good shape for the extravaganza. The day of the great pageant, a Tuesday, was warm and sunny, and the ladies brought parasols to protect themselves from the heat. Children played in the street and ran through the crowds, as parents vainly tried to control them. Everyone was excited and cheerful.

The IX Corps started off with General Parke at its head riding his sorrel horse with a garland of laurel around its neck. Other mounted officers rode alongside and in his rear, and the corps' guidons floated gently in the soft spring air. The order of march was arranged numerically, and the 1st Division, led by General Willcox, followed the corps' commander. Two hours after the parade started, the 3rd Brigade, headed by General McLaughlen, stepped off down the avenue with the IX Corps. Out in front of the brigade was a detachment of pioneers followed by a symbolic mule with a pair of baskets full of entrenching tools draped across its back. Behind the sappers the brigade band and drum corps quickened the air with its most lively patriotic tunes. The crowds cheered wildly, men waving their hats and ladies their handkerchiefs. The atmosphere was electric with joy and the spectacle was thrilling—the greatest assemblage of soldiers and equipment the nation had ever known.

The 3rd Maryland marched next, followed by the 50th New York. Then came the few remaining boys of the 57th under Lieutenant Colonel Tucker, with the 59th Massachusetts and 100th Pennsylvania in the rear, "all 'bully boys,' marching square to the front, in ranks well dressed, pieces carried on a level, an easy springing step and elbows touching lightly." The brightly polished steel rifle barrels with fixed bayonets reflected brilliantly in the May sun, and the regimental color bearers held their ragged flags high on staffs decorated with flowers, for all to see and admire the names and dates of the battles—recently embroidered on the banners in gold thread—in which the regiments had been blooded. The soldiers marched from the Capitol to the

White House, and as they passed the reviewing stand, they got a good look at their new president, Andrew Johnson.

For two days the massive celebration continued, the Army of the Potomac's seventy-five thousand men passing the first day, and the Western armies' veterans all the next. The cheering, excitment, and festivity never stopped, and no one seemed to tire of watching the seemingly endless blue columns pass by. The people were fascinated by it all—the zouaves in their colorful, flashy dress, the dashing cavalry squadrons, the clattering horse artillery, the brass army bands, the strutting foot soldiers keeping a smart step to the drummer boys' rattling cadences, and all the pomp that the armies could muster. It was a time that no one, soldier or civilian, could ever forget. George Barton wrote to his mother that he "did not March with the Regiment but had the unspeakable pleasure of being a spectator," and that "The Review was a perfect success."[37]

★

Not long after the Grand Review, the complicted task of dissolving the enormous Federal armies began. The regiments that had the shortest period remaining on their enlistments were the first to be mustered out and sent home. Those with the longest times left, such as the 57th, which had enlisted for three years, were held over. The situation in Mexico was unstable with the French emperor, Napoleon III, in control of that government through his agents and military forces, and some United States officials were in favor of enforcing the Monroe Doctrine and sending the veterans south of the border to throw out the French and restore the Mexicans to power. The men in the ranks were having none of it, however. They felt their duty was done, and they were impatient to go home. They had volunteered to subdue the Confederacy and restore the Union, and that was all they had bargained for. They wanted no part of a fight with Mexico or anyone else. They had given enough, suffered enough, and they had done all that they were willing to do. Nevertheless, the army did not see things quite their way, and their service was not ended. The 57th, like many other regiments, had to wait until the American politicians decided on a course of action.[38] (The United States took no overt action against the French in Mexico. The Mexicans finally rebelled, and France's representative in their country, Maximilian, archduke of Austria and so-called emperor of Mexico, was executed by a firing squad in June of 1867.)

On June 6, Brigadier General William Francis Bartlett, paroled and exchanged from Confederate captivity sometime earlier, was ordered to return to duty under Special Orders No. 283 from army headquarters. On June 19, under Special Orders No. 47 from IX Corps headquarters, the general took command of the 1st Division of the IX Corps, relieving General

General William F. Bartlett and staff at the 1st Division, IX Corps,
headquarters camp near Tennallytown after the war, July 1865.
(USAMHI, Carlisle Barracks, Pa.)

McLaughlen, who returned as head of the 3rd Brigade. Bartlett "at once instituted a more thorough course of drill and discipline, which, in anticipation of an early discharge, had become lax." Bartlett later wrote:

> My Division lies up the road from Tenallytown—three brigades, well situated for water slope and air. . . . I found the command in rather a slack state of discipline, no attention paid to guard duty or drill. It is natural to feel, now that the war for which they enlisted is over, that there is no further need of discipline, and that the strict performance of guard-duty any longer is needless. (I only name guard-duty as one of the points by which you judge of a regiment's "breeding and efficiency".) In this they are rather encouraged by a certain class of officers . . . and this feeling of uncertainty about getting mustered out is prejudicial to discipline. I had all the regimental and brigade commanders here the other night, and gave them a lecture of an hour and a half. You would have smiled to see me laying down the law, surrounded by about twenty of these old birds.

Later he added, "These troops are restless and dissatisfied about getting mustered out, it is almost impossible to get men and officers to do their duty properly. . . . I have roughed more officers, and reduced more non-coms. to the ranks, these last two or three weeks, than in any other *year* of service."

After the Grand Review the 57th's men had lost all interest in things military, and they refused to take their jobs as soldiers seriously anymore. They felt that they had fulfilled the oaths of their enlistments, and they had no desire whatever to "play soldier." They wanted to go home. Their duties at Tennallytown were not arduous, and the men enjoyed many good times in the surrounding countryside, but they could endure military restraint no longer as they saw no purpose in it. The boys no longer thought themselves bound by the Articles of War—the country was out of peril—and the ignoring of orders, regulations, and strict discipline continued. The officers could do little to change the situation. Many of them agreed with the enlisted men's attitudes, often reflecting them themselves and generally overlooking their subordinates' infractions. Bartlett, even though much respected by the men, could change nothing either, and his poor health, caused by his wounds and augmented by his stay in a Confederate military prison, forced him to take a leave of absence and go home for good on July 14. And the men carried on acting pretty much as they pleased.[39]

In Company F, Captain Hitchcock—he had been mustered to that rank, on May 19—had been ordered on May 26 to the staff of Major General Nelson A. Miles at Fort Monroe on the Virginia peninsula. Jefferson Davis, the former president of the Confederacy, had been captured not long before, and he was being held in confinement there pending decisions about his future by the United States government.[40]

Also on May 26, the 59th Massachusetts was ordered to consolidate its remaining numbers with those of the 57th. The actual consolidation was to take place June 1, but was delayed until June 13. The number "57" was retained as the regiment's official designation, and that was a severe blow to the 59th's soldiers' pride. The men of that regiment had fought as valiantly as any, and they felt that the consolidation compromised their honor and achievements, not to mention robbing them of their unit identity. The 57th's men were not pleased with the change either. They preferred to remain homogenous and felt the transferred soldiers outsiders. The blending of the two regiments was successful in theory only, and each group kept to itself unless under orders. Officers and noncommissioned officers from each regiment rendered superfluous by the merger were mustered out of service and sent home. That increased the friction, and the men of both organizations were rebellious to any authority they did not recognize as their own. Later, when regimental reunions were sponsored by the men of the 57th, almost no former members of the 59th Regiment attended the gatherings.[41] A history of the 59th Regiment was never written either. Apparently those soldiers never recovered from the humiliation of the consolidation.

How the men were chosen for early discharge as supernumeraries has not been determined. There were no fewer than fourteen members of the 57th so chosen, however, all of whom were of at least noncommissioned rank. One such was Sergeant Calvin Bigelow of Company F. Bigelow had built up an impeccable service record, and he was one of the fraternity of ten who had fought in every fight and marched on every march with the regiment. Never had he been wounded, been taken prisoner of war, been absent sick, attempted desertion, or been arrested—one of only four of the ten who could lay claim to that distinction. Prior to his enlistment in the 57th Regiment, the twenty-one-year-old native of Fitchburg had fought without injury in the Port Hudson, Louisiana, campaign with the 53rd Massachusetts in 1863. Truly, Sergeant Bigelow could be called one of the regiment's outstanding soldiers.[42]

★

By Special Orders No. 56, the 57th was transferred for a time to the 1st Provisional Brigade at Camp Fry in Washington on July 1. That brigade was commanded by Brigadier General DeWitt. The nature of the regiment's duties at that posting are unknown, but a surviving letter indicates strongly that the boys were thoroughly tired of the army and its excessive and needless formalities. And this attitude prevailed right to the top of the regiment's command. On July 12, General Dewitt wrote to the acting assistant adjutant general of the army the following memorandum:

> The within order is a copy of one received this afternoon by the commanding officer [Lieutenant Colonel Tucker] of the 57th Reg't Mass Vols.
> A previous order was issued [by army command] to the commanding officer of said regiment to have his regiment turned out for inspection this morning which he declined to obey by authority from these headquarters based upon instructions received through Garrison Headquarters from Major General Parke then in command of the Department of Washington [evidently Parke thought things were getting out of hand, too].
> An official copy of the above decision of General Parke was forwarded by the officer of the 57th Reg't Mass Vols this day to the commanding officer of the 3rd Brigade 1st Division 9th A.C. as a reason for his [Tucker's] refusal to turn out his regiment for inspection.
> The accompanying order has been received and issued since.
> I have the honor to report the above fact for the consideration of higher authority and to state that unless otherwise ordered the 57th Reg't Mass Vols will *not* be turned out for inspection in compliance with the within order.[43]

Clearly, just about everyone had had enough of the army's needless red tape and senseless protocol. The veterans of the 57th were not professional soldiers, and they just wanted to be done with the military service of the United States as quickly as possible.

★

During the month of July the 57th's men watched enviously as regiment after regiment was mustered out and sent home daily. They knew their time for departure could not be far off, but the days seemed to drag on, and the men ached more and more for the moment that they, too, could leave. It was almost torture to watch the smiling faces of others getting ready to board trains for home. In yet another letter to his mother, written July 6, Captain Barton told of the happenings at that time: "the brave heroes of our Army are being sent *home* by thousands everyday. it does my soul good to see it and wish for the sake of the 'Boys' of My Regt that they could go to. They *deserve* to be sent home they have *well earned* an honorable *discharge* and *should have it Now.*" One of his boys, William Darling, an eighteen-year-old musician in Company A, who could see no point in staying any longer, simply packed up and headed home on June 30. He was the last deserter of the regiment, but he returned for the final disbandment of the 57th in Massachusetts and was honorably discharged with the others, his transgression forgiven.[44]

General Orlando B. Willcox issued his last order to the 1st Division of the IX Corps on July 27. It was the only division left in the corps—all the others were now mustered out—and that Thursday would mark its concluding assembly. After the men had formed ranks, the general gave them their final commands, wished all of the officers and enlisted men well, and thanked them for a job well done and for their terrible sacrifices. "There have been," he said, "various regiments which have left the bones of their dead to whiten on battlefields in seven different states. Your families and fellow citizens will welcome you in peace and victory. You will carry about you in civil life a sense of your own worth, and self respect will characterize those who have done and deserved so well of their country." He bid farewell, and the 1st Division and the IX Corps were no more.[45]

★

On July 30, 1865, the 57th received the long-awaited order to return to Massachusetts. The men were excited, and many barely could believe it was true. It took no great will power to line up for their final ceremony near the Delaney house in Tennallytown that would discharge them from United States service. The 57th Massachusetts Veteran Volunteers were officially mustered out under Special Orders No. 178 from the War Department, dated July 24, 1865. The mustering-out officer was Captain Sylvester Keyser, assistant commissary of muster, of the 2nd Michigan Infantry. Only 13 officers, the chaplain, and 239 enlisted men of the original 57th Regiment were present that hot and humid July day—just under 25 percent of the men who had left Worcester in April of 1864. Of the men there that final day, 208 had seen at least some combat service.[46]

When the grand totals were computed and the descriptive rolls completed, the record would show the appalling losses sustained by the 57th Massachusetts during its brief service. The regiment had lost 213 men killed or mortally wounded, 49 who died while prisoners of war, and 62 more who succumbed to disease, for a total of 324 men, or just over 31 percent of its original number. Three-hundred and seventy more had been wounded (including men who were wounded more than once), and 137 had been taken prisoners of war. Twenty-three had been rejected as unfit for duty at Camp Wool, 88 were surviving prisoners of war, and 158 additional men had deserted, some of whom were eventually returned to duty. In all, 963 men out of 1,038 enlistments and commissions were lost permanently or temporarily—some more than once—for reasons other than detached duty, sick leaves, or furloughs during the regiment's service, a total of 92.8 percent.

The number of killed and mortally wounded as given here is at odds with the official figures. John Anderson claimed a loss in killed and mortally wounded of 202, 19.2 percent of the regiment's original number based on his inaccurate count of a 1,052-man total membership. However, there were but 1,038 men ever borne on the 57th's muster rolls, and with 213 killed or mortally wounded, including the missing and presumed killed, the percentage of loss was actually 20.5 percent.

Captain Anderson related,

In the history of regimental losses of all the [Federal] regiments in the service during the whole period of the war, carefully compiled by Col. William F. Fox, U.S. Volunteers, from official records in the War Department, we find that the 2d Wisconsin Infantry heads the list with the heaviest loss of any regiment on the Federal side in killed or mortally wounded, being 238 out of 1,203 men enrolled or 19.7 [percent]. The second regiment in the list is the 1st Maine Heavy Artillery, with a loss of 423 killed or mortally wounded, out of a total number enrolled of 2,202, being 19.2 per cent.

The Fifty-seventh Massachusetts is credited with the third position, having lost 201 killed or mortally wounded, out of a total number enrolled of 1,052, being 19.1 per cent.

Because of an error that Anderson found, he upped the total to 202, or 19.2 percent, thereby giving the 57th the same status as that of the 1st Maine. By pointing out that the 2nd Wisconsin and the 1st Maine were in service for a considerably longer period than the 57th Massachusetts, he concluded that the 57th had a higher number of losses in killed and mortally wounded for the shortest period of enlistment than any other Federal regiment in the Civil War. However, the 57th actually sustained a loss of 20.5 percent, which, at first glance, seems to put it ahead of every other Union regiment regardless of time of service. But to draw that conclusion would be risky at best. If the

57th's figures were wrong, then there is a reasonable chance that the tallies of other regiments could be as well, and, so, until all original regimental records are analyzed again and numbers counted, no resolution of which regiment exceeded all others in the percentage of killed and wounded can be reached accurately. The numbers presented in this work are taken directly from the original descriptive lists, morning reports, and company order books, as well as other primary sources.[47]

★

The great adventure was over. The last regimental muster rolls had been made out and final pay and installments on bounties added up. The men would receive their money in Massachusetts. The boys packed their gear, shouldered their rifles, and marched casually to the depot in Washington to board a train that would return them home. Their traveling companions on the journey would be the men of the 29th Massachusetts, mustered out the day before. As the 57th's ranks contained the veterans of the 59th and the 29th's the transferred men of the 35th Massachusetts—who had joined late in the war and were not mustered out when that regiment was disbanded because the recruits had volunteered for three years—General McLaughlen, in charge of the trip home, actually was escorting elements of four regiments that had all at one time or another fought side by side.[48]

As the train slowly pulled out of the station, the men opened the windows of their passenger cars, sat back, and celebrated their official return to civilian status. The weather was uncomfortable, but nothing could dampen their spirits. A few had brought bottles, and they proceeded to pour the liquid contents down their throats freely, getting happier with each swallow. Certainly, some of the men must have felt opposing emotional tugs. They were happy, to be sure, to leave behind the killing and gore of the battlefield and the endless boredom of army life when the killing and gore had stopped. On the other hand, the conspicuous absence of their comrades not riding on the train that day—and who would never ride on any train again—must have been terribly painful to most of those otherwise hard-boiled veterans. Then, too, there surely were deep thoughts about their futures and their families. To have seen bewilderment in some of their eyes that Sunday would not have been surprising.

The train rolled through Baltimore, crossed the Delaware River, and continued on through Pennsylvania and Philadelphia, where the once mighty regiment had been so well treated on its way to the slaughter. There, as they watched that city pass by their windows, nostalgia no doubt overcame many of them.

When the train arrived in Jersey City the men were met by a delegation of the New England Association, and after speeches and welcomes, the former soldiers were invited to parade through the streets of New York City. They—the 57th and 29th Massachusetts regiments—were the last Civil War troops to do so as nondisbanded units. Chaplain Dashiell reported, "The sons of Massachusetts thronged the barracks at the battery and, as the [57th] regiment marched up Broadway with its tattered flags and scarred veterans, they received an ovation from the crowd which thronged the streets, which will never be forgotten." The men proceeded to the New England rooms, and upon arriving they were given an artillery salute and cheered by crowds waving American flags.

Their next stop was Union Square, where the enlisted men fell out and were feasted by the citizens of New York. The more privileged officers were entertained at the Union League Club. The men then marched back down Broadway and were reviewed at the Astor House by Major General Joseph Hooker and his staff. Finally, the boys returned to the battery, where they found another sumptuous dinner of tantalizing delicacies waiting for them. The food was wolfed down by those men who had eaten little but salt meat and hardtack for so long.

After the meal, a representative of the Sons of Massachusetts, Mr. I. C. Carter, welcomed the veterans on their return from victory. They showed respect and listened politely to his platitudes—the same sort of tired words that had sent them off to war the previous year. General McLaughlen answered for the regiments in a like manner. Their former corps commander, General Burnside, made an appearance, and the boys greeted him affectionately and enthusiastically. They had never blamed him for their misfortune in the Crater, and their good feelings for him were sincere.[49]

On August 2, the men boarded a steamer of the Providence Line in New York Harbor, and, after following the same course, in reverse, that they had taken more than a year before through Long Island Sound and up the Thames River, they landed at the piers in Norwich, Connecticut. A train of the Connecticut Shore Railroad was waiting to take them to Camp Meigs in Readville, Massachusetts, located ten miles west of Boston on the Boston & Providence Railroad near the Neponset River, where they arrived the next morning and took up temporary residence in the old wooden barracks of that training camp. Although officially discharged from the army, the men had to wait for the paymaster to get around to them before departing for home.[50]

After turning in their equipment to the quartermaster for the Commonwealth of Massachusetts, there was little to do. Life at Camp Meigs was free of military activity, and the boys lounged around, wrote letters home, and visited the towns near the camp. Many of the local citizens came out to see the regiment, and those visitors often brought food for the men. Several local dignitaries also came to the camp and made self-serving, pretentious, and boring speeches welcoming the discharged soldiers home. And, too, many—

particularly the young men who had not been old enough to join the army—came just to gawk at the battle-worn veterans. Articles very flattering to the regiment appeared in the New England and New York City newspapers, and the men read them with a great deal of pride and amusement. Some of them who had been furloughed on convalescent leave made their way to the camp to join their comrades for a final meeting. The days passed quietly and without event, but the men did not like the waiting—more "red tape," they felt.

On Wednesday, August 9, 1865, a clear day with temperatures in the mid-seventies, the army paymaster finally arrived at the camp, and the men lined up one last time. After their pay and bounties were disbursed, the officers said their good-byes, and everyone shook hands. They were happy and sad as they broke up and parted ways—some forever.[51] The 57th Regiment of Massachusetts Veteran Volunteer Infantry now existed only in memory and history.

Epilogue

A S WE BEGAN WITH THE RAISING of the Fitchburg Company, it seems appropriate that the story of the 57th Regiment of Massachusetts Veteran Volunteers end with those men, as they surely were representative of the whole regiment.

After traveling to Worcester, 38 men of the Fitchburg Company boarded a train of the Fitchburg & Worcester Railroad that August afternoon for the short trip home. That was nearly all that remained of the number who had left the town a year and a half before. Nine of the small returning group had been wounded, six had been taken prisoners of war, and many of the rest of them had suffered illnesses that would endure for the remaining years of their lives. Company F had been the most fortunate company in the regiment in a sense. It was coming home with 36.5 percent of its original membership, a significantly higher percentage than any other company. Part of the reason for that was that 21 of those men had served on the cattle guard, thereby missing the 57th's most serious battles. Some of the veterans on the train that day had seen much combat service, while five had never fired a gun in anger. The Irish immigrants had been lucky—14 of them were in the group. Their survival rate had been almost twice that of the native-born Americans, of whom there were 18 returning. Five Canadians and one German accounted for the balance of the tiny band. Of course there were other survivors—men who had been discharged early for wounds or sickness. And there were soldiers like Captain Hitchcock, who would come home later, and Sergeant Bigelow, who had received an early discharge.[1]

As the train neared the south side of Fitchburg, the conductor had it stopped just outside of the Patch, and the men got off and climbed down the banks of the Nashua River for a final wash before arriving at the depot.[2] The reception given the former soldiers when they finally detrained at the station was subdued. The local newspaper, the *Fitchburg Sentinel*, does not even mention it. Company F of the 57th Regiment was the last group of Civil War soldiers to return to the town, and by the time the men arrived, the civilian population probably had had its fill of gala receptions. Certainly, there must have been some minor formal welcome, but nothing on the scale given previously returned units. After leaving the station with families, friends, and loved ones, all ties with United States Army life were severed forever.

But their friendships would endure until the end of their days. They had experienced scenes and events that none could ever describe fully. Those who had never seen the battlefield or the effects of war could not possibly understand what they had been through. The civilian ideas of glorious war held at the time had changed very little since the days of 1861, and the men who had seen the reality of the killing grounds never would change those illusions. The gulf between truth and fiction would remain, and even today we barely can imagine what it must have been like for the soldiers who fought the Civil War.

★

Veterans of the 57th Massachusetts at a reunion with Confederate General William Mahone in the Crater on the Petersburg Battlefield, May 3, 1887. *(USAMHI, Carlisle Barracks, Pa.)*

Epilogue

So, the old campaigners formed regimental associations. The 57th had its own, and it existed until 1929, when most of the members had died. Lieutenant George Priest, the regimental quartermaster, wrote to General Bartlett right after the war about the possibility of forming such an association. Frank Bartlett replied from his home in Pittsfield, Massachusetts, on August 12, 1866.

> My dear Priest,
> A communication dated Boston Aug 5th relating to the formation of an association of the officers of the 57th Reg't has reached me.
> I think the plan of keeping up some friendly relation, having some common bond, with the men who have shared the same dangers & privations in the field, a good one.
> I should be glad to know that the officers who had been associated in the 57th, who had been true to it [this obviously is a dig at Hollister and Cushing] in the hour of peril and doubt, as well as in the hour of triumph; who had felt a common pride in its reputation, a common grief in its losses, were still drawn together by some common bond under some common name.
> But I would take the liberty of suggesting that the association be not confined to officers alone, but be open to every soldier of the command who had shown himself worthy of the name, and done his part in maintaining the honor of his regiment and his flag.
> Some of our people who have been at home these last five years, forget too quickly the debt that they owe to the *private soldiers* of our army. Let *us* who *know* the perils & privations they have passed, who have seen their daring and endurance, omit no opportunity for showing our recognition and appreciation of their good deeds.
> Though I may not be able to take any active part in the organization, it would always have my sympathy and best wishes.[3]

From the tone of Bartlett's letter, he seems to be rebuking Priest—who never saw combat—and others of his arrogant, elitist officer ilk, and well the general should have done so. For by far, it was the common enlisted man who suffered most in the Civil War, and Frank Bartlett rightly recognized that fact. But it is interesting that he, himself, felt that he would be unable to participate in the association. Though he understood and sympathized with his soldiers, he obviously remained the patrician to the last.

Many veterans joined the Grand Army of the Republic, as well. The G.A.R. initiated posts all over the country and served the needs of its dwindling fraternity until well after the start of the twentieth century. It was a powerful institution in its time.

★

As for the Irish, they fared somewhat better after the war, but the prejudices held against them from prewar days did not change a great deal for some years. However, as generations passed and the Irish prospered, the animosity against them declined and was passed on to a succession of other ethnic groups. Fitchburg was not unusual with respect to the sentiments of many of its non-Irish and non-Catholic residents. In one Massachusetts historical society in which research was conducted for this book, it was alleged on good authority that the Irish were blackballed from joining the local chapter of the G.A.R. in that town. No members of any other ethnic group belonging to the 57th, so far as can be determined, were so poorly thought of socially as were the Irish.

★

It is not within the scope of this work to follow the lives and careers of the men of the 57th after the war beyond a cursory glance. John W. Kimball, late colonel of the 15th and 53rd Massachusetts Volunteers, was asked soon after the war to assess the character of the returned soldiers then living in Fitchburg. It may be assumed safely that Kimball's candid report could have applied to most any man of the regiment—or any other regiment—regardless of his town or state of residence.

> Fitchburg Dec 25 1865
> Brig Genl Wm Schouler
> Adjt Genl M.V.M.

General

At the request of the Chairman of the Selectmen I have the honor to reply to yours of the 9th inst.

I have made careful enquiries of persons most likely to know the facts relative to your enquiries and I am unable to learn that there has been one single commitment for crime of a returned soldier who went into the U.S. service from this town.

There have been a few arrests for drunkenness but the number has been surprisingly small, less I think than one per cent, no more certainly and less I think than would have been the case had they remained at home.

In regards to the general habits of the returned Soldiers it gives me pleasure to say, which I can with truth and candor, that they are certainly no worse than before the war, and, in many cases an improvement is manifest, and in my opinion out of the same number of men, yes, of these same men themselves, there would have been as many or more dissipated, idle, and dissolute had there been no war.

It is a remarkable fact that out of so many young men who have been in the service from this town (being nearly one thousand [all regiments]) that so very few have returned with their characters tarnished or their moral habits degraded. To my mind it is the strongest evidence possible that they entered the service from the purest motives of patriotism and love of Country.[4]

Notes

ABOUT THE NOTES

In order to avoid excessive clutter, information that is widely available about the battles and campaigns in which the 57th Regiment participated is not referenced in the notes. This information has been well documented by historians and students of military affairs, and is readily available for those who wish to study further the 1864–65 Virginia campaigns. The reader is directed to the bibliography to find the titles of the books used in my research. Only primary source data and that which is unusual or not commonly found are referenced in the notes.

I have had personal experience for many years with original and reproduction Civil War firearms, equipment, and uniforms in all types of weather, both as a member of the North-South Skirmish Association, shooting live ammunition at targets with black-powder, muzzleloading Civil War weapons, and as a reenactor performing "living history." I have also hunted with muzzleloading firearms, and I know what a musket ball sounds like and what it does when it hits flesh. Consequently, I have annotated passages on which I feel qualified to comment as "personal experience" or "personal knowledge."

EPIGRAPH

1. "A Night Attack of the Cavalry," verse 4, a poem recited by Brevet Major Sidney De Kay, USV, during a meeting of the New York Commandery, April 4, 1888, in Wilson and Coan, eds., *Personal Recollections*, p. 171. Although a cavalry poem, its sentiments accurately and poignantly reflect those of any branch of the combat service during the Civil War.

CHAPTER 1 / CAMP JOHN E. WOOL

1. Anderson, *History of the 57th Regiment*, p. 4, hereinafter cited as Anderson; *Massachusetts Spy*, Sept. 24, 1862; Faust, ed., *Historical Times Illustrated Encyclopedia*, p. 842, hereinafter cited as Faust; "Map of the City of Worcester," published by Henry J. Rowland, 1862, Worcester Historical Museum; Wiley, *Life of Billy Yank*, p. 24.

2. Walcott, *21st Regiment*, p. 1, hereinafter cited as Walcott; Commonwealth of Massachusetts, *Massachusetts Soldiers, Sailors, and Marines*, vol. 3, p. 1, hereinafter cited as *MSSM*; Lincoln, *Life with the 34th Massachusetts*, p. 13, hereinafter cited as Lincoln; Committee of the Regimental Association, *History of the 36th Regiment*, pp. 2–3, hereinafter cited as *36th MVI*; Johns, *Life with the 49th Massachusetts*, p. 65, hereinafter cited as Johns; *MSSM*, vol. 4, pp. 470, 546.

3. Palfrey, *Memoir of Bartlett*, passim, hereinafter cited as Palfrey; *MSSM*, vol. 2, pp. 492, 568, and vol. 3, p. 470.

4. *MSSM*, vol. 4, pp. 470, 472.

5. Anderson, p. 1; *MSSM*, vol. 4, p. 817; Bowen, *Massachusetts in the War*, p. 679.

6. Anderson, p. 4.

7. Kirkpatrick, *City and the River*, p. 177 and passim, hereinafter cited as Kirkpatrick.

8. Ibid., pp. 178, 244.

9. Ibid., pp. 239, 244, 248. For further commentary on Yankee attitudes toward the Irish in Massachusetts in the mid-nineteenth century, see Handlin, *Boston's Immigrants*, pp. 159, 185, 198–99, 204, and passim, hereinafter cited as Handlin.

10. Kirkpatrick, p. 178. Also useful in determining the different types of employment are the 57th Regiment's descriptive rolls on file in the National Archives. These rolls, together with regimental and company order and letter books, morning reports, etc., are located in Record Group 94 at the archives, and much of this material will be found in the back of this work in the rosters. Hereinafter any records in Record Group 94 will be cited as RG 94.

11. RG 94.

12. Kirkpatrick, pp. xii, 244, 274.

13. Ibid., p. 285. See also Willis, *Fitchburg in the War*, pp. 106–112, hereinafter cited as Willis.

14. RG 94; Willis, p. 91.

15. *Worcester Evening Transcript*, Dec. 10, 1863; Willis, pp. 91–92; diary of Francis Moore Harrington, Company K, 57th Regiment, hereinafter cited as Harrington diary; diary of William T. Peabody, Company F, 57th Regiment, hereinafter cited as Peabody diary. (The bounty was actually paid later; see chapter 2.)

16. Willis, p. 92.

17. *Fitchburg Sentinel*, Jan. 8, 1864.

18. Willis, p. 91; *MSSM*, Vol. I, p. 708, and vol. 2, p. 145; Kirkpatrick, pp. 159, 235.

19. RG 94. Text of enlistment paper taken from the original of R. Wesley Williams, Company I, 57th Regiment, on file with the Military Records Depot, Massachusetts Adjutant General's Office, Natick, Massachusetts. Most of the 57th Regiment's soldiers' enlistment papers are located there, and they are all of identical form. Hereinafter the Military Records Depot will be cited as MRD.

20. Peabody diary.

21. Willis, p. 91. Jabez Fisher kept a handwritten, unpublished account of weather conditions in Fitchburg and, therefore, central Massachusetts. This journal is in the possession of the Fitchburg Historical Society. Kirkpatrick, pp. 179–80; RG 94; Anderson's roster, passim; the Peabody diary; and the Harrington diary all mention or allude to furloughs given commonly at Camp Wool.

22. *Massachusetts Spy*, Sept. 24, 1862; *Fitchburg Sentinel*, March 11, 1864; Johns, p. 65; Anderson, p. 7; Tarbox, *Missionary Patriots*, pp. 292, 293, hereinafter cited as Tarbox.

23. Johns, p. 65; other buildings cited as follows: cookhouses, RG 94 and Peabody diary; hospital and commissary, *Fitchburg Sentinel*, March 4 and March 25, 1864, respectively; guardhouse and transient barracks, RG 94 and Peabody diary.

24. *Fitchburg Sentinel*, March 11, 1864; Anderson, p. 7. Straw for bedding is mentioned in Regimental General Orders No. 7 of Feb. 13, 1864, RG 94. Hereinafter Regimental General Orders will be cited as RGO. All Regimental General Orders in their entirety will be found in appendix 6. Hygiene, RGOs, passim.

25. RGO No. 10, para. 2, March 16, 1864; RGO No. 6, para. 3, Feb. 12, 1864.

26. RGO No. 10, para. 1, March 16, 1864; RGO No. 1, para. 8, Jan. 25, 1864; RGO No. 3, para. 1, Jan. 27, 1864; RGO No. 7, Feb. 13, 1864.

27. RGO No. 6, para. 2, Feb. 12, 1864.

28. RGO No. 8, paras. 1 and 2, Feb. 15, 1864.

29. RGO No. 1, para. 4, Jan. 25, 1864.

30. Order of muster and letters of request for muster-in, RG 94.

31. Typical muster-in described in Wiley, *Life of Billy Yank*, p. 25.

32. RG 94.

33. Ibid.

34. Ibid.

35. Ibid. See also, for a discussion of education and literacy, Handlin, p. 142, and quartermaster's invoices, on which the men had to sign their names or make their marks to draw new clothing and equipment, contained in the Barton Family Civil War Letters (Lieutenant George E. Barton, Company C, 57th Regiment), American Antiquarian Society, hereinafter cited as Barton letters. Letters and diaries of the vast majority of Civil War soldiers, on both sides, reflect the basic moral values of that era and a simplistic concept of the war that they were fighting. All but a few, Yankees and Confederates alike, believed wholeheartedly that they were waging a war for a righteous cause and that God would see that cause triumph. Letters, diaries, and writings of this nature are found easily throughout the enormous amount of Civil War literature extant.

36. *MSSM*, vol. 4, pp. 762, 815, and vol. 5, pp. 1, 48, and passim; RG 94.

37. Anderson, pp. 4, 6–8; RG 94.

38. *MSSM*, vol. 4, p. 817.

39. Photographs extant of the regiment's men show the standard military uniform and equipment being used; Katcher, *Army of the Potomac*, p. 9, hereinafter cited as Katcher.

40. Gibbs, *U.S. Pattern Book*, p. 4, hereinafter cited as Gibbs; Anderson mentions the frequency of women in camp, (p. 6); William Peabody had his wife with him at Camp Wool (Peabody diary); RG 94 for tailors.

41. Tarbox, p. 292.

42. Gibbs, introduction and passim; personal experience.

43. Katcher, pp. 6, 10–11; Peabody diary; RGO No. 1, para. 3, Jan. 25, 1864.

44. Katcher, p. 10; personal knowledge; RGO No. 4, Feb. 3, 1864.

45. Personal knowledge.

46. *Fitchburg Sentinel*, March 11, 1864; *Massachusetts Spy*, March 9, 1864; photographs of men of the 57th; RGO No. 9, para. 1, March 4, 1864.

47. Anderson, p. 7; RG 94.

48. RGO No. 6, para. 1, Feb. 12, 1864.

CHAPTER 2 / FORMING THE LINE

1. RGO No. 9, para. 2, March 4, 1864; RGO No. 10, March 16, 1864.

2. RGO No. 1, para. 4, Jan. 25, 1864.

3. RGO No. 10, para. 1, March 16, 1864; Anderson, p. 7.

4. Peabody diary; *Fitchburg Sentinel*, March 25, 1864.

5. Anderson, p. 6; examples of such collations given in Marvin, *History of Worcester*, p. 240, hereinafter cited as Marvin; *Massachusetts Spy*, April 18, 1864; and Boeger, "Hardtack and Burned Beans," pp. 75–76, hereinafter cited as Boeger.

6. Peabody diary.

7. Anderson, p. 8; RGO No. 1, para. 2, Jan. 25, 1864; typical daily training camp life also detailed in Wiley, *Life of Billy Yank*, p. 45.

8. Wiley, *Life of Billy Yank*, p. 46; Anderson, pp. 8, 420–21; *MSSM*, vol. 4, p. 817; RGO No. 3, para. 2, Jan. 27, 1864; RGO No. 11, para. 4, March 17, 1864; RG 94.

9. RG 94; *Fitchburg Sentinel*, March 25, 1864.

10. Anderson, p. 8; RG 94; RGO No. 9, para. 2, March 4, 1864; *Fitchburg Sentinel*, March 11, 1864.

11. Anderson, p. 8; RG 94; RGO No. 8, para. 3, Feb. 15, 1864.

12. Anderson, p. 8; RGO No. 11, para. 3, March 17, 1864; RGO No. 1, para. 7, Jan. 25, 1864; Faust, p. 118; *MSSM*, passim.

13. Wiley, *Life of Billy Yank*, p. 49; Bartlett performing drill on one leg described in Johns, p. 58. He certainly would have put on the same performance for the 57th.

14. Anderson, pp. 8–9; bad weather cited in Tarbox, pp. 290, 293, 294; Palfrey, p. 99; *Massachusetts Spy*, March 9, 1864.

15. Wiley, *Life of Billy Yank*, p. 46; Anderson, p. 8.

16. RGO No. 1, para. 7, Jan. 25, 1864; *Fitchburg Sentinel*, March 25, 1864; RGO No. 11, para. 2, March 17, 1864. As late as July 27, 1864, Bartlett was still complaining of his regiment and its brigade performing drill poorly (Palfrey, p. 116).

17. RGO No. 10, para. 3, March 16, 1864.

18. Anderson, p. 10; *Fitchburg Sentinel*, March 25, 1864.

19. *Fitchburg Sentinel*, April 1, 1864; Tarbox, p. 242.

20. RGO No. 3, para. 1, Jan. 27, 1864; *MSSM*, vol. 4, p. 817; typical drill described in Wiley, *Life of Billy Yank*, p. 48.

21. Wiley, *Life of Billy Yank*, p. 48.

22. *MSSM*, vol. 4, p. 817.

23. RG 94; MRD.

24. MRD.

25. Anderson, p. 9; RG 94.

26. RGO No. 1, para. 3, Jan. 25, 1864; RG 94.

27. RG 94; Peabody diary; Lonn, *Desertion During the Civil War*, pp. 127–142 passim, 146, hereinafter cited as Lonn. Lonn cited nine reasons why soldiers deserted in the Civil War. From these, coupled with the data found in RG 94 on the 57th, the three distinct, but overlapping, patterns of desertion in the 57th Regiment are deduced, all of which are discussed in the text.

28. Catton, *Stillness at Appomattox*, p. 32; Lonn, p. 140; for bounty paid on April 16, 1864, see Harrington and Peabody diaries, and RG 94.

29. *Massachusetts Spy*, April 20, 1864; Harrington and Peabody diaries.

30. Lonn, pp. 139, 141–42; RG 94.

31. RG 94.

32. MRD; for example, see letter from the 57th's Regimental Quartermaster Sergeant James A. Robbins to Adjutant General William Schouler, April 18, 1864.

33. Lonn, pp. 134, 220; U.S. War Department, *War of the Rebellion: Official Records*, ser. 3, vol. 1, p. 655, hereinafter cited as OR.

34. Lonn, p. 139; MRD, letter from Lieutenant Charles Hollis, Company C, 57th Regiment, to Adjutant General William Schouler, April 13, 1864. This is the letter concerning Place and is but one of many on file concerning similar problems of other soldiers of the 57th.

35. RG 94.

36. Anderson, pp. 411–12; fees paid for deserters mentioned often in RG 94.

37. RG 94.

38. Anderson, p. 9.

39. Higgenson, *Massachusetts in the Army and Navy*, for quotation, hereinafter cited as Higgenson.

40. Peabody diary; RG 94.

41. Tarbox, p. 292; RG 94.

42. See Handlin, p. 215, for further discussion. During the course of my research, a curator of a Massachusetts historical society with excellent credentials, who wishes to remain anonymous, told me that she knew from stories handed down in her own family that the local G.A.R. post in her town had blackballed former soldiers of Irish descent. Other G.A.R. posts, however, are known to have had many Irish soldiers as members.

43. RG 94.

44. Anderson, p. 142.

Notes

45. RG 94; RGO No. 3, para. 3, Jan. 27, 1864; RGO No. 5, Feb. 6, 1864.
46. RGO No. 12, March 24, 1864; RG 94; Anderson, p. 7; *MSSM*, Vol. 3, p. 397.
47. *Fitchburg Sentinel*, March 4, 1864.
48. MSSM, vol. 2, p. 620.
49. Marvin, pp. 233–36, passim.
50. Marvin, ibid., Walcott, p. 308.
51. Anderson, p. 10; RG 94, in which the date cited in Anderson is contradicted.
52. Tarbox, pp. 293–94.
53. *Fitchburg Sentinel*, April 1, 1864; RG 94.
54. Anderson, p. 10; *Massachusetts Spy*, April 18, 1864.
55. *Massachusetts Spy*, April 18, 1864.
56. Tarbox, p. 294; Marvin, p. 240; Anderson, p. 14; *Massachusetts Spy*, April 18, 1864.
57. Marvin, p. 240.
58. Anderson, pp. 11, 14; Palfrey, pp. 96, 97; Peabody diary.
59. Marvin, p. 240.
60. *Massachusetts Spy*, April 20, 1864; Johns, p. 59; Palfrey, p. 96.

CHAPTER 3 / THE GIRL I LEFT BEHIND ME

1. Anderson, p. 14; Harrington diary; Peabody diary.
2. *Massachusetts Spy*, April 20, 1864.
3. Anderson, p. 14. John Anderson also remembered that "the efficient quartermaster had supplied the necessary camp equipage for field service and each soldier had the following articles issued to him, which he was required to carry on his person, viz.:—1 greatcoat, 1 fatigue coat [i.e. a standard four-button infantry blouse], 2 pairs flannel drawers, 2 flannel shirts, 2 pairs stockings, 1 pair shoes, 1 blanket, 1 knapsack, 1 tin cup, 1 knife and fork, 1 spoon, 1 tin plate, 1 rubber blanket, 1 haversack, 1 canteen." In addition, each soldier wore his dress uniform and leather equipment and carried his rifle, and most all the men had personal items.
4. Anderson, p. 15; *Massachusetts Spy*, April 20, 1864.
5. Twenty-two men had been rejected that morning as unfit for service and placed in the custody of First Lieutenant John Cook, of Company E, to be taken to the U.S. Army general hospital in Readville, Massachusetts, for in-depth medical examination. There were also a number of soldiers who were left behind in Camp Wool's hospital as too sick to travel. All of the former were discharged from the service, but most of the latter eventually made their way to the front. RG 94; *Massachusetts Spy*, April 20, 1864.
6. RG 94; Barton letters; Weld, *War Diary and Letters*, p. 260, hereinafter cited as Weld.
7. RG 94.
8. *Massachusetts Spy*, April 20, 1864; Gramm, *Gramm's Standard American Atlas*, hereinafter cited as Gramm; Harrington diary.
9. RG 94.
10. The descriptions of the facilities in Norwich were written based on photographs in Farnham, *Quickest Route*, between pp. 52 and 53, and between 84 and 85; RG 94.
11. The *City of Norwich* was built in New York City in 1862 and was owned by the Norwich & New York Transportation Co. from 1862 to 1894. She served as a barge in New Jersey in 1895 and 1896. She was 627 tons, was 200 feet long, had a beam of 36 feet, and drew 12 feet. From the dimensions given, 916 men would have been very tightly packed. (Source: Mystic Seaport Museum.)
12. Harrington diary.
13. Gramm.
14. Ibid.; Harrington diary.
15. Harrington diary; Peabody diary; Barton letters.
16. Harrington diary; RG 94.

17. Harrington diary; Gramm.

18. RG 94; Barton letters; Anderson, pp. 15–17.

19. Good descriptions of Cooper's are given in Lincoln, p. 24, and Putnam, *Story of Company A*, p. 33, hereinafter cited as Putnam; Harrington diary; Anderson, p. 17.

20. Gramm; Putnam, p. 34.

21. Putnam, p. 34; Lincoln, p. 24.

22. Harrington diary; Anderson, p. 17; Committee of the Regimental Association, *History of the 35th Regiment*, p. 14, hereinafter cited as *35th MVI*; Peabody diary.

23. Gramm; Harrington diary; Walcott, p. 9.

24. Peabody diary; returns for the IX Corps, April 1864, list its strength as 27,487 present and absent (OR, ser. I, vol. 33, p. 1045; as this number was fluid, with men coming and going for different reasons, the figure 25,000 is used in this work); Woodbury, *Burnside and the IX Army Corps*, p. 367, hereinafter cited as Woodbury; Harrington diary; Anderson, p. 17. From various descriptions the camp occupied by the 57th was located on a sandy plain two miles due west of the center of Annapolis opposite the Parole Camp, known as College Green Barracks, on an inlet of Chesapeake Bay at the present site of Parole, Maryland. For example, see *35th MVI*, p. 217, and Weld, p. 261. Both the 35th Regiment and Weld's 56th Regiment were brigaded with the 57th, and they were all camped near one another.

25. Harrington diary.

26. Faust, p. 521; *36th MVI*, p. 136; Weld, p. 275.

27. *35th MVI*, pp. 218, 220; Osborne, *The 29th Regiment*, pp. 291–92, hereinafter cited as Osborne.

28. *35th MVI*, p. 219; Weld, p. 272; see also Leech, *Reveille in Washington*, p. 351, hereinafter cited as Leech.

29. *35th MVI*, pp. 218, 219; for discussion of poor discipline in Annapolis, see Weld, pp. 267, 269.

30. Anderson, p. 106; *MSSM*, vol. 1, p. 4, and vol. 3, p. 617; Chandler was not mustered into the 40th Regiment, but was considered a veteran of it (see Anderson, p. 420).

31. Anderson, p. 18.

32. Harrington diary; Peabody diary. Peabody often wrote his diary entries as if he was writing them to his wife, Hannah.

33. *Battles and Leaders of the Civil War*, vol. 4, p. 181, hereinafter cited as *Battles and Leaders;* Walcott, p. 310; Woodbury, p. 368, cites 6,000 men in 4th Division; IX Corps returns for April 1864, OR, ser. 1, vol. 33, p. 1045.

34. *Battles and Leaders*, p. 181.

35. Ibid.; see Catton, *Stillness at Appomattox*, pp. 32–39 passim, for a discussion of how the veterans of the Army of the Potomac viewed the troops raised in late 1863 and 1864.

36. Weld, pp. 264–65.

37. Anderson, p. 18; Weld, p. 279; Harrington diary.

38. Marvin, p. 276; personal knowledge; see also Wiley, *Life of Billy Yank*, pp. 62–63.

39. Harrington diary; Peabody diary.

40. Weld, pp. 272, 277; Woodbury, p. 367; *36th MVI*, p. 136.

41. Harrington diary; Anderson, p. 18.

42. Ibid.

43. Anderson, p. 18; Wiley, *Life of Billy Yank*, pp. 64–65; Putnam, p. 28.

44. Anderson, pp. 18–19.

45. Harrington diary; Peabody diary. The precise time that Civil War marches began and ended are extremely difficult to verify. Soldiers who were on the same march will often differ considerably as to the hour that a march started and finished. There are several reasons why. A corps like the IX Corps, with twenty-five thousand men in its ranks and thousands of horse-drawn vehicles, was an immense body that stretched for miles along its routes of march. Naturally, every regiment had to wait for another to pass before it could join the column, hence the disparity in starting times. Similarly, the head of the column would have arrived at a destination long in advance of the rear. Even in a small brigade of, say, one or two thousand men, the same holds true on a smaller scale.

When Civil War–era roads are considered, which were primitive, narrow, and frequently clogged with slow-moving vehicular traffic, the problem of timing intensifies—part of a regiment, for example, might be cut off from the rest as the result of a traffic jam, and two men in the same unit might give different finishing times. Watches in the Civil War were of the pocket variety, and they had to be wound with a key. They were not nearly as accurate as a modern quartz watch, and even if they had been, there was no universal co-ordinated time in those days. A time reference from which to set a watch, such as another soldier's watch or a clock tower, was shaky at best. Because of the above reasons, I have, when possible, used the time given by a member of the 57th Regiment as being the actual time the regiment began or ended its march. If that time was not available, I next chose time given in order of its brigade, division, and corps. (The same holds true for the starting and ending times of battles and other significant events.)

46. *35th MVI*, p. 220; *36th MVI*, p. 140; Anderson, p. 19.

47. Anderson, p. 19.

48. *36th MVI*, p. 140; Weld, p. 280; Anderson, p. 19.

49. Weld, p. 280; Anderson, p. 19; Peabody diary; *35th MVI*, p. 220; Harrington diary.

50. Peabody diary.

51. *35th MVI*, p. 220; Barton letters.

52. Anderson, p. 19.

53. Weld, p. 280; Harrington diary; Anderson, p. 19.

54. Weld, p. 280.

55. Barton letters; Weld, p. 280.

56. *35th MVI*, p. 220.

57. Ibid.

58. Harrington diary; Anderson, p. 20; Peabody diary.

59. Weld, p. 280; Anderson, p. 20; Peabody diary.

60. All the following sources were used to write a description of the review: Leech, p. 351; Anderson, p. 20; Osborne, p. 291; Harrington diary; *35th MVI*, p. 221; Woodbury, pp. 368–69; Barton letters; *36th MVI*, p. 140; Sandburg, *Abraham Lincoln*, p. 442.

61. Weld, p. 280; Harrington diary; Peabody diary.

CHAPTER 4 / STORM ACROSS THE RAPIDAN

1. Anderson, p. 20; Woodbury, p. 369; *36th MVI*, pp. 141–42.

2. *35th MVI*, pp. 221, 223; *36th MVI*, p. 141. Officially the 56th Massachusetts had no band (see *MSSM*, vol. 4, pp. 762–814 passim). However, the regiment's officers pooled their money and hired twenty men who were mustered in as privates. Their only job was to play music, and they were paid twenty dollars per month each. They were led by Principal Musician William J. Martland, who was paid one hundred dollars per month, and Stephen Weld claimed that they were so well known that they had played at Lincoln's Gettysburg address on November 19, 1863 (see Weld, pp. 257, 326). The 57th, likewise, had no band officially (see *MSSM*, vol. 4, pp. 815–74 passim). It is known that the regiment did have a drum corps, though (see Marvin, pp. 233–34). However, the *Fitchburg Sentinel* did state in its April 1, 1864, issue that "the [57th] regiment is to have a band immediately, the men enlisted for that purpose having reported at camp on Monday." Other than that one reference, nothing further is known of any musicians attached to the unit, except for the company drummers and fifers, and RG 94 makes no mention of any band.

3. Weld, p. 281.

4. Faust, p. 828; *Battles and Leaders*, p. 181; Woodbury, p. 369.

5. Barton letters.

6. Ibid.

7. Peabody diary.

8. RG 94.

9. Harrington diary; Anderson, p. 20; Peabody diary.

10. Weld, p. 281.

11. For a discussion of Grant, see Catton, *Stillness at Appomattox*, pp. 45–57 passim; see also Catton, *Grant Takes Command*, p. 155; Palfrey, p. 99; Haley, *Rebel Yell and the Yankee Hurrah*, p. 148, hereinafter cited as Haley.

12. Weld, p. 281; Anderson, p. 20; *35th MVI*, p. 222; Harrington diary.

13. Anderson, p. 20; Barton letters.

14. Weld, p. 281; Anderson, p. 20; *MSSM*, vol. 4, p. 817; RG 94; Peabody diary; Harrington diary.

15. Weld, p. 281; Peabody diary; Anderson, p. 20; Harrington diary.

16. RG 94.

17. Weld, p. 281; Harrington diary; Anderson, p. 21; soldiers' right to grumble noted in *35th MVI*, p. 63.

18. Marvin, p. 276; Weld, p. 281.

19. Anderson, p. 21; Peabody diary; Harrington diary; *MSSM*, passim.

20. Peabody diary; RG 94.

21. Harrington diary; Weld, p. 281; Catton, *Grant Takes Command*, p. 153; Foote, *Civil War*, vol. 3, pp. 136–37, hereinafter cited as Foote.

22. Anderson, pp. 61–62; Catton, *Stillness*, pp. 73–74; *35th MVI*, p. 223.

23. For a discussion of Union soldiers' feelings about Mosby, see Linderman, *Embattled Courage*, p. 197, hereinafter cited as Linderman; *36th MVI*, p. 145; Harrington diary; Weld, pp. 281–82.

24. Weld, p. 282; Harrington diary.

25. RG 94.

26. Peabody diary; RG 94; Leech, p. 351.

27. Harrington diary; Anderson, p. 21; Peabody diary; Barton letters.

28. Harrington diary; Anderson p. 21; Faust, p. 470.

29. Haley, p. 140; Catton, *Stillness*, pp. 55, 64; Lord, *Civil War Sutlers*, p. 71, hereinafter cited as Lord; Foote, p. 144; Frassanito, *Grant and Lee*, p. 35, hereinafter cited as Frassanito; *35th MVI*, p. 223.

30. Harrington diary; Anderson, p. 21; Catton, *Stillness*, pp. 65, 66.

31. Harrington diary; Peabody diary.

32. Anderson, p. 22; Harrington diary.

33. Harrington diary; Peabody diary.

34. Barton letters; RG 94.

35. RG 94.

36. Ibid.; Kirkpatrick, p. 284.

37. RG 94.

38. Harrington diary; *35th MVI*, pp. 223–24.

39. The emotions and feelings of battle are discussed further on.

40. RG 94.

41. Haley, p. 142.

42. *MSSM*, passim.

43. Weld, p. 284; Palfrey, p. 99; Anderson, p. 69; Harrington diary.

44. Anderson, p. 34; *35th MVI*, p. 224.

45. Palfrey, pp. 55, 99.

46. Anderson, p. 34.

47. Ibid.; Weld, p. 285; *36th MVI*, p. 149. The historical base maps and troop movement maps that were drawn by historians of the National Park Service, cited in the sources section in the back of this work, have been used frequently to locate the movements of the 57th Regiment, as well as the pertinent movements of other forces, Union and Confederate. They were helpful also in locating buildings, roads, landmarks, trenches, fields, forests, streams, etc., and hereinafter are cited as TMM (for troop movement maps). The reader is directed to them for further study.

48. Anderson, p. 35.

49. Ibid.; *36th MVI*, p. 150. The conditions of battle and the feelings of Civil War soldiers before, during, and after a battle have been documented to some extent, and the reader is directed to three works in particular that I believe are excellent studies of those traumatic events and emotions; Linderman; Wiley, *Life of Billy Yank;* and Keegan and Holmes, *Soldiers,* hereinafter cited as Keegan. These books served as my principal, but not only, sources for describing the chaos and horrors of battle and the psychology of soldiers in battle. The following is an example of one Civil War soldier's account of his feelings before combat and his analysis of them. "A mortal fear came over me, and a deathly sickness. It seemed as if I had taken all the emetics and purgatives. . . . I felt I *could* not go. I was unmanned; amid all, my mind was preternaturally active, bringing up homes, friends, things past and things to come. . . . 'Bullet fever' [had gripped me]. . . . It was almost impossible to swallow hard bread and salt beef. . . . To feel fear is natural; to yield to fear is cowardice. . . . [It is a] sinking, and sickening, and trembling [fear] which . . . unmans more than mortal disease. . . . It is *will* that counts in the composition of the brave" (Johns pp. 227–28, 238). See also Johns, pp. 238–39, for further discussion, and *36th MVI*, p. 147, Putnam, pp. 223–24, and *35th MVI*, pp. 56, 97, as three more of many partial examples extant.

50. RG 94.

51. Weld, p. 285.

52. Anderson, p. 35; *36th MVI*, p. 150.

CHAPTER 5 / HELLFIRE . . .

1. *36th MVI*, p. 150; Anderson, pp. 35, 39; Weld, p. 285; TMM.

2. TMM.

3. Anderson, p. 59; TMM.

4. RG 94; Anderson, p. 48; Harrington diary.

5. RG 94.

6. For an example of prebattle talk, see Wiley, *Life of Billy Yank*, p. 67; Palfrey, p. 99.

7. Anderson, p. 49.

8. RG 94. Of the 548 effectives in the 57th, only 106 enlisted veteran soldiers and fourteen veteran officers—just under 22 percent combined—were in the ranks that day, and with curious precision, they accounted for just under 23 percent of the regiment's casualties on May 6, 1864. Besides Company F's cattle guard, Company K's baggage wagon train guard, the sick, and the shirkers, company and staff cooks were exempted from battle, as well as musicians, medical personnel and assistants, commissary and quartermaster people, and some company clerks, orderlies, hostlers, and men assigned as brigade headquarters guards. Also, during the march to the front, other soldiers of the regiment had been detailed to the ambulance corps and the pioneer battalions (what today would be designated engineers). TMM; Anderson, p. 39.

9. Catton, *Stillness at Appomattox*, pp. 102, 104.

10. Anderson, pp. 36, 39.

11. TMM; *35th MVI*, p. 226; OR, ser. 1, vol. 36, pt. 1, p. 441.

12. *35th MVI*, p. 226; Weld, p. 286; Cullen, *Battle of the Wilderness*, battle map, p. 12, hereinafter cited as Cullen.

13. OR, ser. 1, vol. 36, pt. 1, p. 438; Anderson, p. 36; Cullen, battle map, p. 12; *Battles and Leaders*, p. 183.

14. Weld, p. 286.

15. Palfrey, p. 100; Anderson, pp. 39, 68.

16. TMM; Cullen, battle map, p. 12; *Battles and Leaders*, p. 183.

17. Anderson, pp. 36, 37, 39.

18. Ibid., p. 68.

19. Barton letters. (This had to have been a secondhand story as George Barton was not in the battle.)

20. Personal knowledge; also see *35th MVI*, p. 325, for example.

21. Anderson, p. 68; RG 94.

22. Anderson, pp. 37–41 passim.

23. See, for example, *35th MVI*, p. 49.

24. Palfrey, pp. 99–100; Anderson, pp. 38–39; RG 94.

25. Anderson, pp. 52–53.

26. Ibid, p. 447.

27. Ibid., pp. 55–56.

28. Personal narrative, Winchendon Historical Society; RG 94.

29. Sterling Historical Society; RG 94.

30. Anderson, p. 425; RG 94.

31. *MSSM*, vol. 4, p. 481; Barnes, *Medical and Surgical Records*, p. 882, hereinafter cited as Barnes; RG 94.

32. Anderson, pp. 60–61.

33. *Fitchburg Sentinel*, May 20, 1864.

34. RG 94.

35. Ibid.

36. Ibid.

37. Ibid.; *Massachusetts Spy*, May 30, 1864; Barnes, p. 272.

38. RG 94.

39. Harrington diary.

40. Weld, pp. 286, 287–88.

41. RG 94.

42. Stearns, *Three Years with Company K*, p. 261, hereinafter cited as Stearns.

43. Anderson, p. 69; Stearns, p. 261.

44. Anderson, p. 69; TMM.

45. Anderson, pp. 39–40. Harrington diary; RG 94.

CHAPTER 6 / . . . AND THE FIRES OF HELL

1. Harrington diary; RG 94; Willis, p. 107.

2. Harrington diary.

3. Anderson, p. 45.

4. TMM; Weld, p. 287.

5. Anderson, p. 46.

6. Ibid., p. 45.

7. Ibid., pp. 44–46.

8. RG 94.

9. Anderson, p. 67; RG 94; Walcott, p. 315.

10. Palfrey, p. 100.

11. Barton letters.

12. Weld, pp. 287–88, 291.

13. Anderson, p. 46.

14. Ibid.

15. Harrington diary.

16. *36th MVI*, pp. 156, 158.

17. Stearns, p. 261.

Notes

CHAPTER 7 / MY SOUL TO KEEP

1. Anderson, p. 73; Weld, p. 289; Harrington diary.

2. Barton letters; *MSSM*, vol. 4, pp. 546–48; RG 94.

3. Anderson, p. 58.

4. Ibid., pp. 58–59.

5. Kirkpatrick, p. 287.

6. Anderson, p. 73.

7. Ibid., pp. 73–74; RG 94.

8. National Library of Medicine, *Medicine of the Civil War*, passim, hereinafter cited as Library of Medicine; Barnes, passim; for a good discussion of Civil War medicine, see Wiley, *Life of Billy Yank*, pp. 124–51, passim.

9. Anderson, p. 61.

10. Ibid., pp. 58, 59; *MSSM*, vol. 5, p. 50; RG 94.

11. Anderson, pp. 397–98; *MSSM*, vol. 4, p. 627; RG 94.

12. RG 94; *MSSM*, vol. 2, p. 194, and vol. 4, p. 572.

13. Peabody diary; RG 94.

14. RG 94.

15. Harrington diary; Anderson, p. 73.

16. Anderson, p. 74; *35th MVI*, p. 227.

17. RG 94.

18. Anderson, p. 74.

19. Anderson, p. 77; Harrington diary; Woodbury, pp. 376–77; Weld, p. 289; TMM.

20. Weld, p. 289; Harrington diary; TMM.

21. TMM; Harrington diary; Tarbox, p. 307.

22. Harrington diary; Anderson, p. 79; TMM; RG 94.

23. Anderson, p. 79; TMM.

24. Weld, p. 290; Walcott, p. 320; Faust, pp. 192–93.

25. Harrington diary.

26. OR, ser. 1, vol. 36, pt. 1, p. 909. The position of the IX Corps on the night of May 11, 1864, is something of a mystery. Some historians cite evidence that the entire corps moved back over the Ny River to the south side late in the afternoon on that day. This may or may not have been the case with much of the corps, but it seems certain that at least the 1st Brigade of the 1st Division remained north of the river, as indicated in the text. The troop movement map by Ralph Happel of the National Park Service—which is used here—for May 11 and 12, 1864, shows Weld's brigade in place as explained in the narrative. Mr. Happel's notes for the map do not survive, but after discussing this issue with Bob Krick of the National Park Service and chief historian at the Fredericksburg Spotsylvania National Military Park, I believe that Mr. Happel's map is reliable and correct in this instance. For that reason, as well as for other evidence of no move back to the south side of the river on the 11th—and lack of evidence of such a move—contained in the regimental histories, diaries, etc., used here as sources, the 1st Brigade is placed as it is in this work. (It should be noted also that the Happel map shows the entire IX Corps north of the Ny until the morning of May 12, when it shows it recrossing the river for the battle on that day. But, as that is of little importance to the story of the 57th Regiment on the night of May 11, I leave that information for others to ponder.)

27. Harrington diary.

28. Anderson, pp. 80–81; Harrington diary; Woodbury, pp. 384–85.

29. Weld, p. 291; TMM.

30. Besides other works cited in the bibliography, sources for details directly or indirectly relating to the 57th Massachusetts and the conditions surrounding it in relation to this battle were: Wood-

bury, pp. 383–86; Walcott, p. 321; Anderson, pp. 82–83; Harrington diary; *36th MVI*, p. 164; Haley, pp. 154–55; Weld, pp. 291–92; TMM.

31. Anderson, p. 84.
32. Ibid., pp. 84–85; Harrington diary.
33. Anderson, p. 85.
34. Ibid., pp. 85–86.

CHAPTER 8 / MOTHER, MAY YOU NEVER SEE
THE SIGHTS I HAVE SEEN

1. RG 94.
2. Ibid.; *MSSM*, vol. 4, p. 159; Ballou, *History of Milford*, p. 167, hereinafter cited as Ballou.
3. RG 94.
4. Ibid.
5. Ibid.
6. Ibid.
7. Ibid.
8. Ibid.
9. Ibid.
10. Ibid.
11. Ibid.
12. RG 94.
13. RG 94.
14. Ibid.; Anderson, p. 412.
15. Harrington diary; TMM; *35th MVI*, p. 231.
16. Anderson, p. 88.
17. Harrington diary.
18. Weld, p. 292; Faust, p. 428.
19. Anderson, pp. 88–89.
20. MRD; RG 94.
21. *35th MVI*, pp. 231–32.
22. RG 94; Harrington diary.
23. Weld, p. 294; *35th MVI*, p. 232; TMM; *Battles and Leaders*, p. 183.
24. Weld, p. 294; *35th MVI*, p. 232; TMM; Harrington diary; Marvin, p. 227.
25. *35th MVI*, p. 232.
26. Anderson, p. 91; RG 94.
27. *35th MVI*, pp. 233–34; RG 94.
28. *35th MVI*, p. 234.
29. Harrington diary.
30. *35th MVI*, pp. 234–35.
31. Barton letters.

CHAPTER 9 / TO GO TO YOUR CUPBOARD, HANNAH

1. RG 94.
2. The information used for prisoner of war exchanges and descriptions of Andersonville was taken from National Park Service sources at Andersonville National Historic Site in Andersonville, Georgia, and from Futch, *History of Andersonville Prison*, passim, hereinafter cited as Futch. See also Faust, pp. 603–4, for prisoner of war exchanges.

3. RG 94.
4. Peabody diary.
5. Willis, pp. 193–94.

CHAPTER 10 / THE BRAVE AMONGST THE BRAVEST

1. Harrington diary; TMM.
2. TMM.
3. RG 94; Barton letters.
4. RG 94; Barnes, p. 626.
5. Barnes, p. 534.
6. RG 94.
7. Ibid.
8. Ibid.
9. Anderson, p. 96.
10. *35th MVI*, p. 236; Weld, p. 295; Harrington diary; for examples of exhausted soldiers sleeping while marching, see *35th MVI*, pp. 26, 184.
11. *35th MVI*, p. 236.
12. Woodbury, p. 389; *35th MVI*, p. 236; Harrington diary; Weld, p. 295.
13. *35th MVI*, p. 236; Weld, p. 295; Harrington diary; *36th MVI*, p. 178.
14. *35th MVI*, p. 237.
15. Ibid.; Harrington diary; Walcott, p. 326.
16. *35th MVI*, p. 237; Harrington diary; Woodbury, p. 390; Weld, p. 295.
17. *35th MVI*, p. 237; Harrington diary.
18. Anderson, p. 98; Harrington diary; Weld, p. 297; *35th MVI*, p. 238.
19. Anderson, p. 105; *Worcester Evening Gazette*, June 17, 1925.
20. Ibid., p. 98.
21. Weld, p. 297; Anderson, pp. 98, 100–101; *35th MVI*, p. 239.
22. Anderson, pp. 99–100; Weld, p. 297.
23. Anderson, pp. 100, 106.
24. Ibid., p. 100.
25. Ibid., p. 101.
26. Ibid.
27. Ibid.; *35th MVI*, p. 239; Weld, p. 297.
28. Anderson, p. 101.
29. Ibid, pp. 101–2.
30. Ibid., p. 102; Weld, p. 297.
31. Weld, p. 297.
32. Ibid.; Anderson, p. 102; *35th MVI*, pp. 239–40.
33. Weld, p. 297.
34. Anderson, p. 102; *Worcester Evening Gazette*, June 17, 1865.
35. *35th MVI*, p. 240; Anderson, p. 103.
36. Anderson, p. 103.
37. Ibid., p. 102; Weld, pp. 296–97.
38. Weld, p. 297.
39. Anderson, p. 103.
40. Ibid., p. 102; Harrington diary; Barton letters.
41. Harrington diary; RG 94.

42. RG 94.
43. Anderson, p. 464; RG 94.
44. Anderson, p. 105.
45. RG 94; Barnes, p. 952; Barton letters.
46. Anderson, p. 104.
47. Ibid., pp. 106–7.
48. Ibid., p. 106.
49. Ibid., pp. 109–10.
50. Ibid., p. 110; *MSSM*, vol. 1, p. 704, and vol. 3, p. 402; RG 94; MRD, see letter from Shaftoe to Schouler, dated July 8, 1864.

CHAPTER 11 / SHELTER WITHOUT FIRE

1. Anderson, p. 110; RG 94.
2. Harrington diary.
3. Anderson, p. 111; Weld, p. 298; Harrington diary.
4. Anderson, p. 111.
5. Weld, p. 298.
6. Anderson, p. 111.
7. Harrington diary.
8. Weld, p. 298.
9. *36th MVI*, pp. 183, 184; Weld, p. 299; Harrington diary; Woodbury, p. 395.
10. Anderson, p. 111.
11. Ibid.; Harrington diary; *36th MVI*, pp. 184–85; Woodbury, p. 395; Walcott, pp. 328–29.
12. Anderson, p. 113; Woodbury, p. 395; Harrington diary; *36th MVI*, p. 186.
13. Harrington diary.
14. TMM; Weld, pp. 299–300; Harrington diary.
15. TMM; *35th MVI*, p. 240; Harrington diary; Tarbox, p. 311.
16. TMM; Harrington diary; RG 94.
17. RG 94.
18. TMM; Weld, p. 301; Harrington diary.
19. TMM; Harrington diary; *36th MVI*, p. 188; Woodbury, p. 396; Tarbox, p. 311.
20. Weld, pp. 302, 306; *36th MVI*, p. 191; Tarbox, p. 310.
21. TMM; Woodbury, p. 397.
22. Anderson, p. 115; RG 94.
23. TMM; Anderson, p. 117.
24. TMM; RG 94.
25. TMM; Anderson, p. 117.
26. Anderson, p. 117.
27. Harrington diary; TMM; Anderson, p. 122.
28. Anderson, pp. 122–23; TMM.
29. Anderson, p. 123; RG 94.
30. Anderson, pp. 121–22.
31. Ibid., pp. 120–23; Tarbox, p. 311; RG 94.
32. Anderson, p. 122; Tarbox, p. 313.
33. RG 94.
34. Ibid.
35. Ibid.

36. Ibid.; MRD; Barnes, p. 173.

37. Anderson, p. 124; *36th MVI*, p. 193; Harrington diary.

38. TMM; Harrington diary.

39. Ibid.

40. Ibid.

41. Anderson, p. 124; TMM.

42. TMM; Weld, p. 307.

43. Anderson, p. 124; TMM; Harrington diary.

44. Anderson, p. 124.

45. Ibid., pp. 124–25; Woodbury, p. 401.

46. Weld, p. 307; Anderson, p. 129; TMM.

47. Ibid.

48. Harrington diary.

49. Ibid.; MRD; Tarbox, p. 311.

50. Barton letters; Harrington diary.

51. RG 94.

52. Harrington diary; Woodbury, p. 407; Anderson, p. 130; TMM; Weld, p. 309; Walcott, p. 334; *36th MVI*, p. 199; OR, ser. I, vol. 40, pt. 1, pp. 521–22.

CHAPTER 12 / THE COCKADE CITY

1. Harrington diary; OR, ser. 1, vol. 40, pt. 1, pp. 521–22; Weld, p. 309; *35th MVI*, p. 251; Walcott, p. 334.

2. Harrington diary; OR, ser. 1, vol. 40, pt. 1, pp. 521–22.

3. Harrington diary; *35th MVI*, p. 252; *36th MVI*, p. 200.

4. *36th MVI*, p. 200; Weld, p. 309; Harrington diary.

5. OR, ser. 1, vol. 40, pt. 1, pp. 522.

6. Harrington diary; *36th MVI*, p. 200.

7. Anderson, p. 130.

8. Ibid.

9. Harrington diary; OR, ser. 1, vol. 40, pt. 1, pp. 521–22, and pt. 2, p. 68-69; Weld, p. 310.

10. Barton letters.

11. Frassanito, pp. 205, 207; Anderson, p. 131.

12. OR, ser. 1, vol. 40, pt. 2, p. 66; *35th MVI*, p. 252; Walcott, p. 335.

13. Porter, *Campaigning With Grant*, pp. 199–200, hereinafter cited as Porter.

14. Anderson, p. 131; OR, ser. 1, vol. 40, pt. 1, p. 532.

15. Pleasants and Straley, *Inferno At Petersburg*, pp. 5–6, hereinafter cited as Pleasants; additional data from the Petersburg Information Center and Petersburg Siege Museum, Petersburg, Virginia.

16. Anderson, pp. 131, 136; Woodbury, p. 408.

17. *35th MVI*, p. 254; Walcott, p. 335; *36th MVI*, p. 202.

18. OR, ser. 1, vol. 40, pt. 1, pp. 522, 532.

19. Ibid., pp. 522, 532; Frassanito, p. 213.

20. Anderson, p. 136.

21. OR, ser. 1, vol. 40, pt. 1, pp. 532–33; Anderson, pp. 136–37; Woodbury, pp. 409–10; Walcott, pp. 335–36.

22. Woodbury, p. 410; Anderson, p. 137; OR, ser. 1, vol. 40, pt. 1, p. 522.

23. Weld, p. 311; OR, ser. 1, vol. 40, pt. 1, pp. 532.

24. TMM; OR, ser. 1, vol. 40, pt. 1, pp. 522, 532; Barton letters; Weld, p. 311.

25. TMM; OR, ser. 1, vol. 40, pt. 1, pp. 532–33; Weld, p. 311.
26. OR, ser. 1, vol. 40, pt. 1, pp. 532–33.
27. Ibid.; Weld, pp. 311–12.
28. OR, ser. 1, vol. 40, pt. 1, pp. 532–33.

CHAPTER 13 / YOU LEG IT LIKE THE DEVIL

1. Weld, p. 312.
2. Ibid., p. 311; Anderson, p. 137; Barton letters.
3. Barton letters.
4. Ibid.; Anderson, pp. 137–38.
5. Anderson, p. 138; RG 94.
6. Weld, pp. 311–12; Anderson, p. 140.
7. Anderson, pp. 138, 148; Weld, p. 311; Barton letters; OR, ser. 1, vol. 40, pt. 1, p. 533.
8. Anderson, p. 138; OR, ser. 1, vol. 40, pt. 1, p. 523.
9. Faust, p. 316; *Battles and Leaders*, p. 183.
10. Anderson, pp. 138–39; RG 94; Barton letters; Marvin, pp. 502–3.
11. Anderson, p. 139; Weld, p. 312; Barton letters; OR, ser. 1, vol. 40, pt. 1, pp. 533, 537; Walcott, p. 336.
12. Weld, p. 312.
13. Anderson, pp. 145–48; Tarbox, pp. 317–23, 325, 330, 332–33, 337–39; RG 94.
14. RG 94; *MSSM*, vol. 3, p. 260; Anderson, p. 142.
15. Anderson, pp. 144–45; RG 94.
16. Anderson, p. 145; Barton letters; RG 94.
17. Ibid.; Marvin, pp. 502–3; RG 94.
18. RG 94.
19. Ibid.; Ballou, p. 128.
20. RG 94.
21. Ibid.; *MSSM*, vol. 4, p. 848; Barnes, p. 468.
22. RG 94.
23. Ibid.; Barnes, pp. 787–88.
24. RG 94.
25. Ibid.
26. Anderson, p. 139; Woodbury, p. 411.
27. Barton letters.
28. Anderson, p. 140; Weld, p. 313.
29. Bearss, *Meade's Assault Fails*, p. 2.
30. Ibid., p. 6; Anderson, pp. 140–41; Weld, p. 313.
31. Bearss, *Meade's Assault Fails*, pp. 7, 12.
32. Ibid., p. 6; Anderson, p. 141; Weld, p. 313; Woodbury, p. 412.
33. Anderson, p. 141; Bearss, *Meade's Assault Fails*, p. 26; Woodbury, pp. 411–12.
34. RG 94; Anderson, pp. 141–43.
35. Tarbox, pp. 318–21.

CHAPTER 14 / BLACK INTERLUDE

1. Harrington diary.
2. Ibid.

3. Ibid.; Weld, p. 316; Barton letters.

4. Ibid.; Anderson, pp. 152–53; RG 94.

5. *35th MVI*, pp. 256–57; Anderson, pp. 150–51, 153; Weld, pp. 331–32; TMM; Walcott, p. 341; *36th MVI*, pp. 226–27.

6. Pleasants, pp. 46, 65; *35th MVI*, p. 257.

7. *36th MVI*, pp. 220, 227; Weld, pp. 321, 323; Harrington diary.

8. Harrington diary; Anderson, p. 150; *36th MVI*, p. 226; Walcott, p. 341; Weld, p. 343.

9. *35th MVI*, pp. 258, 265; Harrington diary.

10. Weld, pp. 331–33; Anderson, pp. 150–51.

11. Harrington diary.

12. Ibid.; Barton letters.

13. Barton letters; RG 94.

14. Weld, p. 319; Harrington diary.

15. Harrington diary; Weld, p. 323.

16. Weld, p. 326, photo opposite p. 324; *35th MVI*, pp. 257–58.

17. Weld, pp. 341, 343; Anderson, pp. 150–51.

18. Anderson, p. 150; RG 94; Barnes, passim; Harrington diary; Barton letters; TMM.

19. Barton letters.

20. Harrington diary.

21. Weld, p. 335; Barton letters.

22. Barton letters.

23. Anderson, p. 152; *36th MVI*, p. 226; Walcott, p. 341.

24. Harrington diary.

25. Ibid.; Barton letters.

26. Barton letters; RG 94.

27. RG 94.

28. Ibid.

CHAPTER 15 / TO JUST ENDURE

1. Barton letters; Anderson, pp. 153, 157; RG 94; see Weld, p. 320, for example of sunstroke at Petersburg; *36th MVI*, pp. 226–27.

2. Weld, p. 243; Anderson, p. 158; *36th MVI*, p. 247.

3. Anderson, p. 158; Wiley, *Life of Billy Yank*, pp. 224–46 passim; Weld, p. 330; Boeger, passim; RG 94.

4. Williss, *Historical Base Maps*, passim, hereinafter cited as Williss; RG 94.

5. Lord, passim; RG 94; see Williss for historical base map of City Point; Barton letters; Harrington diary.

6. Wiley, *Life of Billy Yank*, pp. 157–60.

7. Ibid., pp. 153–57, 169–71.

8. Ibid., pp. 192–223 passim; RG 94; *35th MVI*, pp. 305–6; *36th MVI*, pp. 269–70.

9. RG 94.

10. Monaghan, *Civil War Slang*, passim; Wiley, *Life of Billy Yank*, passim.

11. RG 94.

CHAPTER 16 / A CONTINUAL RATTLE OF MUSKETRY

1. RG 94; MRD.

2. Ibid.

3. RG 94.

4. RG 94; MRD.

5. RG 94.

6. Ibid.

7. Ibid.; *MSSM*, vol. 4, pp. 491, 861.

8. RG 94.

9. Harrington diary; Barton letters.

10. Weld, p. 342; Harrington diary.

11. Ibid.

12. Anderson, pp. 155–56; Barton letters; RG 94; *MSSM*, vol. 4, p. 566.

13. Weld, pp. 342–43; *36th MVI*, pp. 228–31.

14. RG 94; Anderson, p. 157; *MSSM*, vol. 4, p. 866.

15. Lonn, pp. 175–77; Sturgis, "Prisoners of War," hereinafter cited as Sturgis; Wiley, *Life of Billy Yank*, p. 342; Faust, p. 780.

16. Phillips, *Civil War Corps Badges*, pp. iv–v, 2, 47–49, hereinafter cited as Phillips.

17. Ibid.

18. Higgenson, p. 988; RG 94; MRD; Anderson, pp. 162, 233, 419.

19. Anderson, pp. 156–57, 425; RG 94; Harrington diary; Barnes, p. 89.

20. Barton letters.

21. Anderson, pp. 157, 422–23; RG 94; Barnes, p. 626.

22. *35th MVI*, p. 264; Anderson, pp. 139, 160; Palfrey, pp. 106, 110.

23. RG 94.

24. Palfrey, pp. 112, 114; Anderson, p. 162.

25. Anderson, pp. 159–60; Harrington diary; Barton letters; RG 94; *MSSM*, vol. 4, p. 864.

26. Barton letters; RG 94.

27. RG 94; Weld, p. 346; *36th MVI*, p. 231.

28. Harrington diary; Anderson, p. 162; Weld, pp. 347–48.

29. Ibid.; Palfrey, p. 116.

30. RG 94; Anderson, p. 163.

31. Ibid.; *MSSM*, vol. 4, p. 864.

32. Anderson, p. 136.

33. Harrington diary.

CHAPTER 17 / RUMORS

1. *35th MVI*, pp. 264–65; Weld, p. 349; Pleasants, pp. 52, 74; U.S. Congress, *Committee on the Conduct of the War*, pp. 47, 54, hereinafter cited as Committee on Conduct; *36th MVI*, p. 227; Walcott, p. 341; Anderson, pp. 165, 168.

2. Committee on Conduct, pp. 49–50, 86, 123 (the three Confederate divisions remaining behind were those of Mahone, Johnson, and Hoke); Anderson, p. 165; Pleasants, p. 93.

3. Committee on Conduct, p. 123.

4. TMM; Anderson, p. 168; *Battles and Leaders*, p. 183; Harrington diary; Barton letters; Pleasants, p. 141.

5. *Battles and Leaders*, p. 181; Pleasants, p. 12; Committee on Conduct, p. 11.

6. Pleasants, pp. 48–49; Committee on Conduct, p. 11.

7. Committee on Conduct, pp. 2, 11.

8. Ibid., p. 2; Pleasants, pp. 59, 60, 66.

9. Committee on Conduct, pp. 131–32; Pleasants, p. 69.

10. Committee on Conduct, pp. 2–3, 132; Pleasants, p. 72.

11. Committee on Conduct, p. 2; Pleasants, pp. 77, 88.

12. Committee on Conduct, p. 132; Pleasants, p. 97.

13. Committee on Conduct, pp. 4, 120 (Burnside's personal feeling about black troops was that they were good soldiers overall, but he felt that they were inferior in intelligence to white soldiers and, therefore, not their equals; see p. 23); Pleasants, pp. 105–7; Woodbury, pp. 428–29, 430.

14. Committee on Conduct, pp. 3–5; Woodbury, p. 419.

15. Committee on Conduct, pp. 4, 5–6 (Meade claimed that he never interfered with Burnside's tactical plan—see p. 43—which, of course, was not true); Anderson, pp. 169–70; Woodbury, pp. 431–32.

16. Anderson, pp. 171–72; Woodbury, pp. 433–34.

17. Committee on Conduct, pp. 5, 124; Pleasants, pp. 112, 113; Anderson, p. 174.

18. Anderson, pp. 174–75; Woodbury, pp. 434–35.

19. Anderson, pp. 203–5.

20. Harrington diary; Anderson, p. 175.

21. Pleasants, pp. 115, 116; *35th MVI*, p. 266.

22. Anderson, pp. 175–76; Committee on Conduct, p. 18.

23. Ibid.

24. RG 94.

25. Weld, p. 351; TMM; Palfrey, pp. 118–19; Walcott, p. 345; *35th MVI*, p. 266; Woodbury, p. 435; Anderson, p. 176; *Battles and Leaders*, p. 561.

26. Petersburg National Battlefield Park.

27. Ibid.; Pleasants, p. 131.

28. *35th MVI*, p. 266; TMM; Anderson, p. 176; Pleasants, p. 46.

29. *Battles and Leaders*, p. 561; OR, ser. 1, vol. 40, pt. 1, p. 535.

30. OR, ser. 1, vol. 40, pt. 1, p. 535; Weld, p. 352.

31. Anderson, p. 176; *Battles and Leaders*, p. 561; Weld, p. 353; Pleasants, p. 119.

32. Weld, p. 353.

33. Woodbury, p. 430.

34. Weld, p. 353.

35. Pleasants, pp. 119–20, 121–22.

36. Ibid., pp. 120–21; Committee on Conduct, p. 90.

37. Pleasants, p. 121.

38. Ibid.

39. Anderson, p. 176.

40. Committee on Conduct, p. 6; *Battles and Leaders*, p. 551.

CHAPTER 18 / BURY THEM IF THEY WON'T MOVE

1. Committee on Conduct, p. 6; Anderson, pp. 176–77, 206; *Battles and Leaders*, pp. 551, 561; Woodbury, p. 437. Note to the reader: The battle of the Crater was fought in a very confined space, and the 57th Massachusetts was involved in the fight from beginning to end. For those reasons, more detail is presented in this chapter than usual. The men of the regiment who participated on that July 30, 1864, must have been influenced by almost everything that happened on the field. It should be understood, however, that while much detail is included, it is impossible and impractical to touch on every event of the battle for the purpose of a regimental history.

2. Anderson, p. 177; *Battles and Leaders*, pp. 551, 561; Committee on Conduct, p. 92.

3. Committee on Conduct, p. 199; *35th MVI*, p. 268.

4. Anderson, p. 177; Committee on Conduct, pp. 206, 222, see also p. 165. Burnside claimed that Ledlie was sick (see also pp. 207, 222). Ledlie claimed he could not go forward with his troops because he had been hit by a bullet and that he needed "stimulants" for "malaria."

5. *Battles and Leaders,* pp. 561–62; Pleasants, p. 126; Anderson, pp. 206–7; Weld, p. 355.

6. Weld, p. 354; Committee on Conduct, pp. 96–97; Pleasants, p. 126; *Battles and Leaders,* p. 551. Burnside claimed he did not remove the abatis because the Confederates would have been alerted that something was about to happen (Committee on Conduct, p. 10); Grant claimed the removal of the abatis would have gone unnoticed (ibid., p. 124); and Warren thought that it could have been removed in a half-hour, that to do so was absolutely necessary for success, and that even if the Rebels had noticed it, that would simply have meant more of them blown up anyway (ibid., p. 96).

7. Anderson, pp. 177, 206.

8. Ibid., p. 207.

9. Ibid., pp. 178, 207; Barton letters; Pleasants, p. 126; Committee on Conduct, p. 224.

10. *Battles and Leaders,* p. 551, also see diagram of the crater, p. 549; Committee on Conduct, pp. 20, 104.

11. Committee on Conduct, pp. 99, 104, 105; Weld, p. 353; Pleasants, p. 129.

12. Ibid.; Anderson, p. 207.

13. Anderson, p. 208.

14. Ibid.; TMM; Committee on Conduct, p. 92.

15. *Battles and Leaders,* p. 562.

16. Weld, p. 353; Anderson, pp. 117, 207; Pleasants, p. 128; *Battles and Leaders,* p. 551.

17. Committee on Conduct, p. 218.

18. Ibid., p. 134; Anderson, p. 178.

19. Anderson, pp. 177–78.

20. Ibid., p. 208.

21. Ibid., p. 210.

22. Anderson, pp. 178, 180.

23. Ibid., pp. 180, 181, 215; *Battles and Leaders,* p. 553.

24. Ibid., p. 187; *Battles and Leaders,* p. 183.

25. Anderson, p. 179; Committee on Conduct, p. 221. Grant blamed the problem of the 1st Division crowding into the crater squarely on Ledlie's shoulders (see p. 125).

26. *Battles and Leaders,* pp. 554–55.

27. Ibid., p. 564; Cornish, *Sable Arm,* p. 275, hereinafter cited as Cornish.

28. Committee on Conduct, pp. 21, 105, 122; Cornish, pp. 273, 275; *Battles and Leaders,* p. 567.

29. *Battles and Leaders,* pp. 566–67; Cornish, p. 275; Weld, pp. 353–54.

30. Cornish, p. 276.

31. Barton letters.

32. Anderson, pp. 180–81.

33. Committee on Conduct, passim, for the many various orders issued that day. Later, during the court of inquiry held to determine the causes of the outcome of the battle, Grant blamed the entire chain of command, including himself, for not personally seeing that orders were carried out (p. 124). But he seems to have been the only general officer who accepted that blame; see, for example, Meade's self-serving excuses, pp. 84–85 and 89, and others, passim.

34. Ibid., p. 21.

35. Anderson, p. 181.

36. Barton letters; RG 94.

37. Palfrey, p. 119. Bartlett wrote that in places the opposing side's flags were within seven feet of each other.

38. Committee on Conduct, pp. 21, 124.

39. Ibid., p. 112; Weld, p. 356; Anderson, pp. 178, 181–82.

40. Palfrey, p. 119.

41. *Battles and Leaders,* p. 562.

42. Ibid., p. 565; Weld, p. 356; see also, for example, Catton, *Stillness at Appomattox,* p. 300.

43. *Battles and Leaders*, pp. 558, 562; *36th MVI*, p. 238; Committee on Conduct, p. 21; *35th MVI*, p. 272; Anderson, p. 183.

44. Pleasants, p. 146; *35th MVI*, p. 279; Anderson, p. 182; Committee on Conduct, p. 21. As a result of the apparent failure of the IX Corps to reach its objective, Meade suspended all supporting activities from other corps of the Federal armies at 9:45 that morning (Committee on Conduct, p. 7).

45. *Battles and Leaders*, p. 558; Pleasants, p. 145.

46. *35th MVI*, p. 270.

47. Anderson, p. 184.

48. Ibid., p. 183; Harrington diary; Palfrey, p. 119.

49. Weld, pp. 356–57.

50. RG 94.

51. Ibid.

52. Ibid.

53. Ibid.

54. Ibid.; personal narrative, Gale Free Library.

55. RG 94; Barnes, pp. 535, 720.

56. RG 94.

57. Ibid.; Barnes, p. 585.

58. RG 94; Barnes, p. 952.

59. Harrington diary.

60. Barton letters.

61. *35th MVI*, p. 281.

62. OR, ser. 1, vol. 40, pt. 1, p. 246; see, for example, Catton, *Stillness at Appomattox*, p. 302.

63. Anderson, pp. 184–85, 198.

64. Ibid., pp. 196–97, for example of the court of inquiry's findings; Faust, pp. 97, 256, 428.

65. *35th MVI*, p. 280.

66. Anderson, p. 188; RG 94.

67. My interpretation of why the Federal assault of July 30 failed is admittedly brief and general. There simply is not room in this work to expand further. To write the entire story of the battle of the Crater properly would require a book of its own. However, to understand more fully the intricacies and complexities of this battle, the reader is directed to the report of the Committee on Conduct cited above, which he or she should read with great caution. This report covers the events of that day in minute detail from the perspective of some of the officers involved. (To give but one example, the reason Warren's V Corps was not sent in on the left is examined at length. To me, however, the reasons given are not persuasive.)

CHAPTER 19 / THIRTY MEN

1. Barton letters.

2. Anderson, pp. 229–30; RG 94.

3. RG 94.

4. Ibid.

5. Ibid.

6. Ibid.; personal narrative, Gale Free Library.

7. Barton letters; MRD, ordnance records.

8. Anderson, pp. 229–30; Woodbury, pp. 464–65.

9. Porter, pp. 276–78; Bearss, *Battle of the Weldon Railroad*, pp. 1–4.

10. Bearss, *Weldon Railroad*, pp. 1–2; TMM.

11. Bearss, *Weldon Railroad*, p. 1; TMM; Anderson, p. 230; *35th MVI*, p. 283.

12. Anderson, p. 230; *35th MVI*, p. 283; *36th MVI*, p. 245.
13. Bearss, *Weldon Railroad*, p. 4.
14. Ibid., p. 25; Anderson, p. 234; *35th MVI*, p. 285.
15. Bearss, *Weldon Railroad*, pp. 25–26; TMM.
16. Bearss, *Weldon Railroad*, p. 26; Anderson, p. 234.
17. Anderson, pp. 234–35.
18. RG 94; *36th MVI*, p. 248; TMM; Bearss, *Weldon Railroad*, p. 26.
19. TMM; Bearss, *Weldon Railroad*, pps. 25, 38–39; *Battles and Leaders*, pp. 568–69.
20. Bearss, *Weldon Railroad*, p. 26.
21. Ibid., p. 39; Anderson, p. 235; *35th MVI*, p. 285.
22. Bearss, *Weldon Railroad*, p. 39, ch. 2 notes, p. ix; Anderson, p. 235; *35th MVI*, p. 284.
23. *35th MVI*, pp. 285–86; Bearss, *Weldon Railroad*, p. 40.
24. *35th MVI*, pp. 285–86; Bearss, *Weldon Railroad*, pp. 40–41.
25. Anderson, pp. 407–8; RG 94.
26. Anderson, pp. 235–36; RG 94; Library of Medicine; TMM.
27. Anderson, p. 235.
28. Bearss, *Weldon Railroad*, pp. 41–42; *35th MVI*, pp. 286–87.
29. *35th MVI*, p. 287; Walcott, pp. 353–54.
30. Bearss, *Weldon Railroad*, pp. 42–46.
31. Ibid., p. 41; *35th MVI*, p. 287.
32. Bearss, *Weldon Railroad*, p. 52; *35th MVI*, pp. 287–88; TMM; Walcott, p. 354.
33. RG 94.
34. Ibid.
35. Phillips, p. 48; Woodbury, pp. 466–67; Anderson, p. 233.
36. TMM; Anderson, p. 233; RG 94.
37. RG 94.
38. Ibid.; Barton letters.
39. RG 94.
40. Ibid.; Anderson, p. 233; Barton letters.
41. Anderson, p. 233; RG 94.
42. RG 94.
43. Ibid.
44. Ibid.
45. Anderson, p. 233.
46. Barton letters; TMM.
47. Barton letters.

CHAPTER 20 / THIS DAMNABLE PLACE FOR A DOG

1. Futch, pp. 2, 17–19, 31, 45, 62; Andersonville National Historic Site, Andersonville, Georgia, hereinafter cited as ANHS.
2. Futch, pp. 18, 30, 98–112; ANHS.
3. Futch, pp. 18–19, 21, 32–35; ANHS.
4. Futch, pp. 21, 46, 58, 59; ANHS; Peabody diary.
5. Futch, pp. 23, 31–32; ANHS; Peabody diary.
6. Peabody diary.
7. Willis, pp. 194–95.
8. Peabody diary; ANHS.

9. Futch, pp. 30–31.

10. Peabody diary.

11. Futch, pp. 63–74; ANHS.

12. Peabody diary.

13. Willis, pp. 194–95.

14. Peabody diary.

15. RG 94.

16. Willis, pp. 194–95.

17. Harrington diary.

18. Anderson, pp. 191–92, 364–65; *Worcester Gazette*, Aug. 2, 1915.

CHAPTER 21 / HARD SEASONS

1. Woodbury, p. 469; *35th MVI*, p. 305; Lonn, p. 146. See Anderson, p. 239, for the 57th's feelings on this subject. Although the 57th was a bounty regiment raised late in the war, by the fall of 1864 the bounty jumpers in its ranks had deserted long ago, and the core of those men left on the line was made up of no-nonsense combat soldiers (see RG 94).

2. Anderson, p. 237; *36th MVI*, p. 235; TMM; Walcott, p. 356.

3. Anderson, p. 237; TMM.

4. Anderson, p. 238; TMM.

5. Ibid.

6. Ibid.; *36th MVI*, p. 261.

7. Barton letters.

8. Personal narrative, Gale Free Library.

9. RG 94; personal narrative, Sterling Historical Society.

10. RG 94; Barnes, p. 971.

11. RG 94.

12. Ibid.

13. Anderson, p. 238.

14. Ibid., pp. 238–39; Barton letters.

15. OR, ser. 1, vol. 42, pt. 3, p. 45.

16. Ibid., p. 63.

17. MRD, see letter from A. O. Hitchcock to H. K. Oliver, Oct. 7, 1864.

18. Anderson, p. 239; OR, ser. 1, vol. 42, pt. 3, p. 141; TMM; RG 94.

19. Anderson, p. 240.

20. Ibid.; RG 94.

21. RG 94.

22. Barton letters.

23. Ibid.; *36th MVI*, pp. 269–70; *35th MVI*, pp. 305–6; Lonn, pp. 181–82; *MSSM*, vol. 2, p. 570; RG 94.

24. RG 94.

25. Anderson, p. 241.

26. OR, ser. 1, vol. 42, pt. 3, p. 329.

27. Ibid., pp. 340–41.

28. Ibid.; Anderson, pp. 241–42; TMM.

29. Barton letters.

30. Anderson, p. 242.

31. Ibid., pp. 242–43; TMM; RG 94; OR, ser. 1, vol. 42, pt. 3, pp. 404–6.

32. OR, ser. 1, vol. 42, pt. 3, p. 389; Anderson, p. 243; Barton letters.

33. RG 94.

34. Schouler, *History of Massachusetts*, vol. 1, pp. 602–3, hereinafter cited as Schouler.

35. Ibid., p. 603; Barton letters; *36th MVI*, p. 254, which mentions that sutlers began to appear just behind the lines on that part of the Petersburg battlefield during September 1864. It also tells us that the weather was generally cool and delightful, and that the men were in little danger and were glad to be out of the front-line trenches. In addition, there was much leisure time, and the soldiers washed and mended their clothes, got rid of vermin, cleaned their weapons and polished their brass, and got haircuts.

36. Schouler, p. 605.

37. Phillips, p. 48.

38. RG 94.

39. Barton letters.

40. OR, ser. 1, vol. 42, pt. 3, pp. 651, 706–7, 715; *35th MVI*, p. 303. For a general discussion of how blacks were viewed by Northern white troops, see Wiley, *Life of Billy Yank*, pp. 109–23 passim.

41. RG 94; *MSSM*, vol. 4, p. 817; Anderson, pp. 396–97.

42. Barton letters.

43. RG 94; OR, ser. 1, vol. 42, pt. 3, p. 729; TMM.

44. Barton letters; TMM.

45. RG 94; Anderson, p. 243.

46. RG 94; Anderson, pp. 243–44.

47. Anderson, pp. 244–45.

48. OR, ser. 1, vol. 42, pt. 3, passim. For a general discussion of how Northern soldiers viewed the South and Southerners, see Wiley, *Life of Billy Yank*, pp. 96–108, passim.

49. RG 94.

50. OR, ser. 1, vol. 42, pt. 3, pp. 918, 935–36; RG 94; TMM.

51. RG 94; *35th MVI*, p. 314; Marvin, p. 281.

52. OR, ser. 1, vol. 42, pt. 3, p. 967.

53. RG 94.

54. Barton letters.

55. Ibid.; Barnes, p. 321.

56. Phillips, p. 48; RG 94.

57. RG 94.

58. Ibid.

59. Ibid.

CHAPTER 22 / TO HAVE THIS BUSINESS CLOSED UP

1. RG 94; MRD; Anderson, p. 247.

2. RG 94.

3. RG 94.

4. Ibid.; *Fitchburg Sentinel*, Dec. 13, 1902.

5. RG 94.

6. Ibid.

7. Ibid.

8. Ibid.

9. Ibid.

10. Ibid.

11. Ibid.

Notes

12. Ibid.; Sturgis.
13. *MSSM*, vol. 4, p. 817; RG 94.
14. Anderson, pp. 248–49; RG 94.
15. Barton letters.
16. TMM.

CHAPTER 23 / ONE LAST DESPERATE EFFORT

1. Gordon, *Reminiscences of the Civil War*, pp. 396–405 passim, hereinafter cited as Gordon. Note to the reader: Like the battle of the Crater, the battle of Fort Stedman was fought in a fairly confined area, and the 57th participated in it from beginning to end. For those reasons again, this battle is dealt with in some detail, as the men of the regiment would have been involved with and influenced by most of the events of the action. However, it was not nearly as confusing as the Crater, although it was no orderly affair either.
2. OR, ser. 1, vol. 46, pt. 1, p. 316; TMM.
3. TMM; Anderson, pp. 252–53; Woodbury, p. 476.
4. TMM; Anderson, p. 253; Woodbury, p. 476.
5. TMM; Anderson, p. 253; Gordon, p. 402; *Battles and Leaders*, p. 584.
6. TMM; OR, ser. 1, vol. 46, pt. 1, pp. 316, 355–56; *Battles and Leaders*, p. 585; Anderson, pp. 253, 266; RG 94.
7. TMM; OR, ser. 1, vol. 46, pt. 1, p. 356; *Battles and Leaders*, p. 579; Osborne, p. 326; Anderson, pp. 266–67.
8. Anderson, p. 267.
9. Ibid.
10. Ibid.; RG 94.
11. OR, ser. 1, vol. 46, pt. 3, p. 99; Anderson, pp. 267–68, 278; *Battles and Leaders*, p. 580.
12. *MSSM*, vol. 3, p. 281; Anderson, p. 268; *Worcester Evening Gazette*, June 18, 1911.
13. Anderson, p. 269.
14. Gordon, pp. 406, 410; Anderson, p. 254; OR, ser. 1, vol. 46, pt. 1, pp. 328, 356; RG 94; *Worcester Evening Gazette*, June 18, 1911.
15. Anderson, p. 255; OR, ser. 1, vol. 46, pt. 1, p. 317; Gordon, p. 410; *Battles and Leaders*, p. 584.
16. OR, ser. 1, vol. 46, pt. 1, pp. 331–32; Anderson, p. 270.
17. Gordon, p. 411.
18. Anderson, p. 275; RG 94.
19. Anderson, pp. 254, 275; OR, ser. 1, vol. 46, pt. 1, p. 339; Sturgis; RG 94.
20. Anderson, pp. 254, 264, 275; TMM; OR, ser. 1, vol. 46, pt. 1, pp. 359, 361.
21. RG 94; Anderson, pp. 275–76.
22. OR, ser. 1, vol. 46, pt. 1, p. 317.
23. Ibid., pp. 317, 338.
24. Ibid., pp. 317–18, 328; Anderson, p. 255.
25. OR, ser. 1, vol. 46, pt. 1, pp. 318, 356.
26. Ibid., p. 318.
27. Ibid.
28. Ibid., pp. 339, 357; Anderson, pp. 255–56; TMM; RG 94; *Battles and Leaders*, pp. 585–86.
29. *Battles and Leaders*, p. 586; OR, ser. 1, vol. 46, pt. 1, pp. 333, 339.
30. *Battles and Leaders*, pp. 586–88; OR, ser. 1, vol. 46, pt. 1, pp. 317–18, 324, 345–48; Anderson, pp. 256–57, 271–73.
31. Anderson, pp. 256–57, 276; *MSSM*, vol. 4, p. 861.
32. RG 94; Anderson, p. 261.

33. OR, ser. 1, vol. 46, pt. 3, p. 149, and pt. 1, p. 318; Gordon, pp. 411–13.
34. Barton letters.
35. Anderson, p. 264; RG 94.
36. Anderson, pp. 258–61.
37. RG 94.
38. Ibid.
39. Ibid.; OR, ser. 1, vol. 46, pt. 1, p. 340.
40. RG 94.
41. Ibid.
42. Ibid.; Sturgis; Anderson, pp. 279–80.
43. Anderson, pp. 264–65; OR, ser. 1, vol. 46, pt. 3, pp. 153, 154, 156, 157, 159.
44. Porter, p. 406; OR, ser. 1, vol. 46, pt. 3, p. 109.
45. Anderson, p. 299.
46. Ibid., pp. 276, 299–300, 302; OR, ser. 1, vol. 46, pt. 3, pp. 198–99.
47. Anderson, pp. 302–3; RG 94.
48. Barton letters.
49. Anderson, p. 303.
50. Ibid.; OR, ser. 1, vol. 46, pt. 3, pp. 233, 265.
51. Anderson, pp. 276, 304–5.
52. Ibid., pp. 276, 307–9.

CHAPTER 24 / THE LADIES THEY WILL ALL TURN OUT

1. RG 94.
2. Anderson, p. 309; OR, ser. 1, vol. 46, pt. 1, pp. 1018–19.
3. OR, ser. 1, vol. 46, pt. 1, pp. 604, 1047, 1051, and pt. 3, pp. 514, 523.
4. Ibid., pt. 3, p. 526; Anderson, pp. 309–10.
5. OR, ser. 1, vol. 46, pt. 1, p. 1051; Anderson, pp. 310, 311; Barton letters; RG 94.
6. Anderson, pp. 310, 313; Barton letters.
7. OR, ser. 1, vol. 46, pt. 1, pp. 1047–48.
8. Ibid., p. 1040; Barton letters; Anderson, pp. 310–13; Osborne, p. 335.
9. Anderson, pp. 311–12; OR, ser. 1, vol. 46, pt. 1, p. 1051; Osborne, p. 335.
10. OR, ser. 1, vol. 46, pt. 1, p. 1051; TMM; Anderson, p. 313.
11. OR, ser. 1, vol. 46, pt. 1, p. 1051; TMM.
12. Anderson, p. 314; RG 94.
13. OR, ser. 1, vol. 46, pt. 3, p. 652.
14. Anderson, p. 314.
15. Barton letters.
16. Anderson, p. 314.
17. Ibid., pp. 314–16.
18. Ibid., p. 315; OR, ser. 1, vol. 46, pt. 3, p. 675.
19. RG 94.
20. OR, ser. 1, vol. 46, pt. 3, p. 789.
21. Anderson, pp. 322–23; see also Woodbury, p. 487. For Confederate generals' reactions to the assassination, see OR, ser. 1, vol. 46, pt. 3, p. 787.
22. Barton letters.
23. OR, ser. 1, vol. 46, pt. 3, pp. 833, 864.
24. Anderson, p. 323; RG 94.

25. OR, ser. 1, vol. 46, pt. 3, p. 876; RG 94.

26. RG 94; Anderson, p. 323.

27. RG 94; Anderson, pp. 329, 331–32; Barton letters.

28. Barton letters.

29. Ibid.

30. RG 94.

31. Ibid.

32. Ibid.

33. Ibid.

34. OR, ser. 1, vol. 46, pt. 3, p. 1097; Library of Medicine.

35. RG 94.

36. Ibid.; OR, ser. 1, vol. 46, pt. 3, pp. 1130–31.

37. RG 94; OR, ser. 1, vol. 46, pt. 3, pp. 1171, 1181–82, 1188–89; Leech, pp. 454–56; Anderson, pp. 329–30; RG 94; Barton letters.

38. Anderson, pp. 330–31.

39. Ibid., p. 331; OR, ser. 1, vol. 46, pt. 3, pp. 1258, 1284; RG 94; Palfrey, pp. 150–51, 152, 155.

40. Anderson, p. 331; RG 94.

41. Ibid.

42. RG 94; *MSSM*, vol. 4, p. 626.

43. RG 94.

44. Ibid.; Barton letters.

45. Anderson, p. 332; OR, ser. 1, vol. 46, pt. 3, p. 1315.

46. Ibid.; RG 94.

47. RG 94; Anderson, pp. 334–37. Note to the reader: Other sources include those listed in the introduction to the rosters in the back of this work.

48. RG 94; Osborne, p. 337; *MSSM*, vol. 3, pp. 647–708 passim.

49. Anderson, pp. 332–33; Osborne, p. 337.

50. Anderson, p. 343; Osborne, pp. 337–38; RG 94; Eldridge, *Description of Camp Meigs.*

51. RG 94; Osborne, p. 339; Anderson, pp. 333–34; Fisher.

EPILOGUE

1. RG 94.

2. Kirkpatrick, p. 290.

3. Bartlett letter to Priest, August 12, 1866, Houghton Reading Room, Harvard.

4. MRD.

Abbreviations in the Rosters and Appendixes

ACM   Assistant Commissary of Muster
AGO   Adjutant General's Office
AWOL   absent without leave
Battln.   battalion
Cal.   caliber
Comp   complexion
CR   company records
CMR   court-martial records
Des.   deserted
DD   detached duty
DIA   deserted in action
Dis.   disability
Disch.   discharged
F&S   field and staff officers
FHS   Fitchburg Historical Society, Fitchburg, Mass.
FMH   diary of Francis M. Harrington
GAR   Grand Army of the Republic
GEB   letters of George E. Barton
GO   general orders
GPR   Gilbert P. Robinson, colonel, 3rd Maryland Infantry
Grd.   guard
HOM   Ballou, *History of Milford*
JA   John Anderson, captain, 57th MVI
JMT   Julius M. Tucker, lieutenant colonel, 57th MVI
KIA   killed in action
MIA   missing in action
MRD   Military Records Depot, Natick, Mass.
MSSM   Commonwealth of Massachusetts, *Massachusetts Soldiers, Sailors, and Marines*
MVI   Massachusetts Volunteer Infantry

Abbreviations in the Rosters and Indexes

MWIA*.	mortally wounded in action
Occup	occupation
OMR	official medical records
OR	official records
PMO	present for muster-out
Post 10	Post 10, Brinley Hall, Worcester, Mass.
POW	prisoner of war
Reg.	US regular infantry
Res.	residence
RGO	regimental general orders
RSO	regimental special orders
SFO	special field orders
SO	special orders
TO	transfer orders
USA	United States Army
USAMHI	United States Army Military History Institute, Carlisle Barracks, Pa.
USCT	United States Colored Troops
USV	United States Volunteers
VRC	Veteran Reserve Corps
WIA	wounded in action
WTP	diary of William T. Peabody

*MWIA is used to denote any death resulting from wounds received in action that occurred during the regiment's service.

Member of 57th Massachusetts Volunteers—recently identified as Corporal John Midgley of Company B—taken while regiment was at Camp Wool.   *(Mark Savolis)*

Rosters

INTRODUCTION TO THE ROSTERS

The company rosters and descriptive lists presented here have been prepared from the following documents and sources: original descriptive lists of the regiment, morning reports, assorted regimental orders and papers (RG 94, National Archives, Washington, D.C.); individual military and pension files (National Archives, Washington, DC); rosters and information contained in Anderson, *History of the 57th Regiment;* Commonwealth of Massachusetts, *Massachusetts Soldiers, Sailors, and Marines; Record of Massachusetts Volunteers;* Willis, *Fitchburg in the War of the Rebellion;* Higgenson, *Massachusetts in the Army and Navy;* Ballou, *History of Milford;* other primary source material on file with the Adjutant General's Office, Military Records Division, Commonwealth of Massachusetts, Natick, Massachusetts, including casualty lists, medical and surgical reports, descriptive lists, personal and official letters, and other pertinent papers; GAR records; personal narratives and personal diaries; various libraries, historical societies, newspapers, and private sources; the National Park Service at Andersonville National Historic Site, Andersonville, Ga.; letters and papers of Captain George E. Barton, American Antiquarian Society, Worcester, Mass.; and other sources.

All enlistments were for three years except as noted, and all places of enlistment were in Massachusetts.

Most of the remarks in quotations appear on original descriptive lists made out by company officers or noncommissioned officers. Other annotations in quotation marks derive from different sources, and the initials of the person or document responsible for the statement appear after the quote—e.g., JA refers to remarks made by Captain John Anderson, author of the original regimental history. (See the list of abbreviations.)

As evidenced by the handwriting in the original descriptive rolls, more than one man prepared these lists or added comments to them. The veracity of the quoted remarks appears suspect in several cases, in that these statements some-times are refuted by other evidence, and the comments may reflect the prejudices of that writer. As these records were written by different individuals, each com-pany varies somewhat in the content and style of information available. When coupled with other sources concerning individuals, the skeletal rosters become quite fleshed out in many cases, and often fascinating.

These rosters do not include the names of the men of the 59th Massachusetts Volunteer Infantry who were transferred to and consolidated with the 57th on June 1, 1865, because those men played no significant role with the regiment. Although the 59th MVI was brigaded with the 57th, the men of the 59th were in no way involved in the wartime ranks of the 57th Regiment, with the possible exception of becoming intermingled during a battle or socializing while off duty. An animosity for the 57th developed among the men of the 59th Massachusetts with the consolidation, as they resented the loss of their unit identity deeply. They reasoned—and rightly so—that they had as good a combat record as anybody, and to lose their regimental designation was humiliating. The story of the 59th Regiment deserves its own place.

Also not included in the roster are unassigned recruits, of which there were two, Benjamin F. Clark, a deserter, and Barnabas Sears, a rejected recruit, neither of whom ever joined the regiment. First Lieutenant Edwin Kimball, who was supposed to have been an officer of Company K, but who declined his commis-sion and never joined the regiment, is also not included. Company F, however, does contain the name of another recruit, Lorenzo Blodgett, who also never joined the regiment. His name is included because his story is interesting, and causes one to wonder about the actual circumstances behind his woeful tale.

To anyone familiar with the statistics set down in the original history of the 57th, it will become apparent immediately that the figures given in this book differ in many cases with those of Captain John Anderson. The captain, by his own admission, did not have access to the records available today. He seems to have been fairly accurate regarding the numbers of men engaged in particular battles, but his casualty figures were often incorrect. He also claims an original membership in the regiment of 1,052 soldiers; however, nothing else substanti-ates that number, including his own roster. In fact, 1,038 men were mustered into the 57th during its service.

Several towns and cities appear in the descriptions of the men that do not appear on modern maps. They have either ceased to be, have had a name change, or have been assimilated into larger metropolitan areas.

Residence in a particular town is separated from the town from which the individual is credited. The various towns and cities strove with a fervor to fill the required quotas for soldiers imposed on them by the Federal government, and every man who enlisted in a certain town or city was credited to the quota of that place.

The rank that follows the name of each soldier indicates the highest official rank achieved by him while a member of the 57th, regardless of whether he was later reduced or raised in rank. For example, if a man's record indicates that he was breveted major after the war, but was a captain while with his company, he appears as a captain on the roster.

Every effort has been made to ensure the accuracy of the following rosters and statistical breakdowns, but a certain margin of error is probably unavoidable. However, it is hoped that any inaccuracies are of no major importance. The responsibility is mine for any such misstatements.

Bounties authorized to be paid to the regiment's soldiers were $300 from the United States government and $325 from the Commonwealth of Massachusetts. In some cases, additional monies were paid by individual cities and towns as enlistment incentives. The town of Fitchburg, for example, paid an extra $100 to each of its recruits. Payments began to be made to some of the men on April 16, 1864.

The regiment was mustered out of service under Special Orders 178, Adjutant General's Office, War Department, Washington, D.C., dated July 24, 1865, by order of the secretary of war, Edwin M. Stanton. The place of muster-out was known as "Delaney house"; however, a search of period records has failed to disclose the location or function of the building. In all probability, it was a private residence close to or on the regiment's campground in Tennallytown, D.C.

FIELD AND STAFF ROSTER AND DESCRIPTIVE LIST

Commissioned Officers

Bartlett, William Francis "Frank," colonel. Res: Boston, MA. Credit: probably Boston, MA. Born: Haverhill, MA, June 6, 1840. Age: 23. Married. Height: unknown. Comp: light. Eyes: blue. Hair: brown. Occup: student. Graduate of Harvard College. Commissioned colonel, Aug. 17, 1863; mustered colonel, April 9, 1864. First commanding officer of the regiment. Wounded in the head in action at the Wilderness, May 6, 1864. Absent wounded until July 23, 1864, when he returned to command the 1st Brigade, 1st Division, IX Corps. Discharged the US service to accept appointment as brigadier general of US Volunteers, June 27, 1864, to date from July 20, 1864. Taken prisoner of war in action at the Petersburg Crater, July 30, 1864. Paroled and exchanged from Libby Prison in Richmond, VA, Sept. 30, 1864. Absent sick until placed in command of the 1st Division, IX Corps, in Tennallytown, DC, June 19, 1865. Promoted brevet major general of US Volunteers, to date from March 13, 1865, under GO 148, AGO, War Dept., dated Oct. 14, 1865, and GO 65, AGO, War Dept., dated June 22, 1867, for "gallant and meritorious services during the war" (JA). Had previous service as captain of Co. I in the 20th MVI. Commissioned captain, July 10, 1861; mustered captain, Aug. 8, 1861. Participated with that regiment at Ball's Bluff, Oct. 21, 1861, and was severely wounded in the leg in action at Yorktown during the Peninsula campaign, April 24, 1864 (leg surgically amputated). Absent wounded until discharged the US service, Nov. 12, 1862, to

Colonel William F. Bartlett. *(USAMHI)*

commanding officer as the result of Bartlett's wounding, May 6, 1864. In action at Spotsylvania Court House, May 10, 12, and 18, 1864, and was mortally wounded in action at North Anna River, May 24, 1864. Died in Confederate hands later that day. Had previous service as 1st lieutenant of Co. A, 1st MVI, from May 25, 1861, until mustered out to accept a commission as captain in the 34th MVI, Aug. 6, 1862. Participated with the 1st MVI in the 1st Bull Run campaign in July 1861, and the Peninsula campaign in 1862. Mustered captain of Co. F, 34th MVI, Sept. 26, 1862. Participated with that regiment on duty in the defenses of Washington, DC, in 1862–63, and in operations in Virginia in 1863. Resigned and discharged the US service, March 17, 1864, under SO 120, AGO, War Dept., to accept a commission in the 57th. "His whole military career was

accept a commission as colonel of the 49th MVI, under SO 341, AGO, War Dept. Mustered colonel, Nov. 19, 1862. Participated with that regiment in the Port Hudson, LA, campaign in 1863, and was wounded twice there on May 27, 1863. Mustered out, Sept. 1, 1863, to accept colonelcy of the 57th. Resided in Pittsfield, MA, after the war, and died there, Dec. 17, 1876, age 36. "The personal character of General Bartlett was noble and pure. His life was one of exalted honor and romantic heroism, and in his death there was something grandly sublime and sadly beautiful" (JA).

Chandler, Charles Lyon, lieutenant colonel. Res. and credit: Brookline, MA. Born: Brookline, MA. Age: 24. Height: unknown. Comp: light. Eyes: blue. Hair: brown. Occup: civil engineer. Commissioned lieutenant colonel, April 20, 1864; mustered lieutenant colonel, April 26, 1864. Second commanding officer of the regiment. In action at the Wilderness, May 6, 1864, and

Lieutenant Colonel Charles L. Chandler. *(Courtesy of Henry Deeks)*

marked by a fine sense of honor and loyal devotion to duty. Rarely has any man of his age acquitted himself so nobly, winning praise from his superiors and the love and respect of all who knew him" (JA).

Tucker, Julius M., lieutenant colonel. Res. and/or credit: Worcester, MA. Born: Massachusetts. Age: 23. Height: unknown. Comp: light. Eyes: brown. Hair: brown. Occup: clerk and machinist. Commissioned 1st lieutenant of Co. H, Jan. 1, 1864, but not mustered. Commissioned captain of Co. H, Jan. 6, 1864; mustered captain of Co. H, Jan. 11, 1864. Third commanding officer of the regiment. In action at the Wilderness, May 6, 1864, Spotsylvania Court House, May 10, 12, and 18, 1864, and North Anna River, May 24, 1864. Commanding officer as a result of Chandler's death, May 24, 1864. In action at Cold Harbor, June 3, 1864. Commissioned major, June 14, 1864, but not mustered. Commissioned lieutenant colonel,

Lieutenant Colonel Julius M. Tucker.
(USAMHI)

June 15, 1864. Shot through the face and severely wounded in action during the Petersburg assault, June 17, 1864. Absent wounded until Sept. 3, 1864, when he returned as commanding officer. Mustered lieutenant colonel, Sept. 2, 1864. On furlough in Massachusetts from Nov. 23 until Dec. 7, 1864. With the regiment in operations during the fall and winter of 1864–65. 1st Division, IX Corps, Officer of the Day during Fort Stedman, March 25, 1865, and not in action in that battle. On furlough after Fort Stedman for an unknown period ending no later than May 1, 1865. Mustered out with the regiment at Delaney house, Washington, DC, July 30, 1865, and discharged in Readville, MA, Aug. 9, 1865. Had previous service as a private in Co. A, 25th MVI, from Sept. 16, 1861, until discharged to accept a commission in the 36th MVI, Sept. 6, 1862. Participated with the 25th MVI in the North Carolina campaign in 1863. Commissioned 2nd lieutenant of Co. E, 36th MVI, Aug. 8, 1862. Date of muster unknown. Resigned and discharged for disability, July 29, 1863. Participated with that regiment at Fredericksburg in Dec. 1862, and on duty in Tennessee and Mississippi in 1863. Colonel of US Volunteers by brevet, to date from March 13, 1865, under GO 65, AGO, War Dept., June 22, 1865, for "gallant and meritorious services" (JA). Resided in Boston, MA, after the war and served as inspector in the Boston Customs House. Died from a severe cold contracted while inspecting steamship cargo in East Boston, June 22, 1866, age 26.

Prescott, Albert, major. Fourth commanding officer of the regiment as the result of Tucker being wounded, June 17, 1864. (See Co. I descriptive list.)

McLaughlen, Napoleon Bonaparte, colonel. Res: Vermont. Credit: probably Boston, MA. Born: Vermont, Dec. 8, 1823. Age: 42. Height: unknown. Comp: light.

Brigadier General N. B. McLaughlen.
(USAMHI)

Eyes: brown. Hair: brown. Occup: soldier. Commissioned colonel, July 21, 1864; mustered colonel, Sept. 14, 1864, to date from Dec. 17, 1862. Technically the fifth and last commanding officer of the regiment, but took command of the 3rd Brigade, 1st Division, IX Corps, upon joining the regiment at Petersburg in early Sept. 1864, and never in actual command of the 57th, until after the war ended when he assumed command for muster-out. In action at Poplar Grove Church, Sept. 30 and Oct. 8, 1864, and appointed brigadier general of US Volunteers for "gallant and distinguished service" there. With the brigade (regiment) in other operations during the fall and winter of 1864–65, and taken prisoner of war in action at Fort Stedman, March 25, 1865. Paroled and exchanged from Libby Prison in Richmond, VA, April 2, 1865. Returned to the brigade for duty from the Camp of Parole in Annapolis, MD, in April, 1865. Mustered out, Aug. 10, 1865. Colonel and brigadier general, USA, by brevet, to date from March 13,

1865, under GO 65, AGO, War Dept., dated June 22, 1867, for "gallant and meritorious services during the assault on Fort Stedman, VA," and "gallant and meritorious services in the field during the war" (JA). Had previous service as private, corporal, and sergeant in Co. F, 2nd United States Regular Dragoons and General Mounted Service, from May 27, 1850, until April 28, 1859. Commissioned 2nd lieutenant in the 1st United States Regular Cavalry, from March 27, 1861, until commissioned 1st lieutenant in the 4th US Regular Cavalry, May 3, 1861. Commissioned captain in the 4th US Regular Cavalry, from July 17, 1862, until commissioned colonel of the 1st MVI, from Oct. 1, 1862, until mustered out, May 28, 1864. Participated with that regiment in the 1st Bull Run campaign in July 1861, the Peninsula campaign in 1862, 2nd Bull Run campaign in Aug. 1862, Fredericksburg campaign in Dec. 1862, Chancellorsville campaign in May 1863, and the Gettysburg campaign in July 1863. Breveted major, USA, to date from May 3, 1863, by order of the AGO, War Dept., for "gallant and meritorious services in battle of Chancellorsville, VA" (JA), and lieutenant colonel, USA, to date from July 2, 1863, by order of the AGO, War Dept., for "gallant and meritorious services in the battle of Gettysburg, PA" (JA). Commissioned major in the 10th United States Regular Cavalry, May 17, 1876. Retired from active service, June 26, 1882. Resided in Middletown, NY, after retirement and died there, Jan. 27, 1887, age 63. "An officer of wide experience, brave and cool in action, firm in discipline, efficient in command and and ambitious to win the glittering star. . . ." (JA).

Doty, Albert, 1st lieutenant. Sixth commanding officer of the regiment as a result of Prescott's death, from July 30, 1864, until Sept. 3, 1864. (See Co. K descriptive list.)

Doherty, James, major. Seventh commanding officer of the regiment during the battle of Fort Stedman, March 25, 1865. (See Co. G descriptive list.)

Barton, George Edward, captain. Eighth commanding officer of the regiment after Doherty's death, from March 26, 1865, until late April, 1865. Also acting regimental adjutant at Camp Wool. (See Co. C descriptive list.)

Hollister, Edward P., lieutenant colonel. Res. and/or credit: Pittsfield, MA. Born: Massachusetts. Age: 27. Married. No description available. Occup: clerk. Commissioned lieutenant colonel, Dec. 21, 1863; mustered lieutenant colonel, Feb. 13, 1864. Resigned at the request of his wife and discharged the US service, April 16, 1864. Had previous service as captain of Co. A, 31st MVI, from Nov. 20, 1861, until discharged to accept a commission in the 57th, Feb. 1, 1864. On duty in Louisiana with the 31st MVI in 1862–63. Also had previous service as a private in the 7th New York Volunteer Militia from April 26, 1861, until mustered out, June 3, 1861. Resided in Buffalo, NY, after the war.

Cushing, James W., major. Res. and/or credit: Roxbury, MA. Born: Massachusetts. Age: 38. No description available. Occup: merchant. Commissioned major, Jan. 27, 1864; mustered major, March 2, 1864. In action at the Wilderness, May 6, 1864, and wounded on an unknown date later that month. Resigned and discharged the US service, May 26, 1864. Had previous service as 1st lieutenant and quartermaster of the 31st MVI from Feb. 20, 1862, until discharged to accept a commission in the 57th, Feb. 2, 1864. On duty with the 31st MVI in Louisiana in 1862–63, but saw no action with that regiment.

Priest, George E., 1st lieutenant and quartermaster. Res. and credit: Watertown,

Lieutenant George E. Priest, quartermaster. *(John Anderson)*

MA. Born: Watertown, MA. Age: 21. Height: unknown. Comp: light. Eyes: blue. Hair: brown. Occup: student. Commissioned 1st lieutenant, Nov. 5, 1863; mustered 1st lieutenant, Nov. 7, 1863. Appointed regimental quartermaster by order of Col. William F. Bartlett. Never in combat. Acting 3rd Brigade, 1st Division, IX Corps, quartermaster on Gen. McLaughlen's staff from Oct. 1864 until July 30, 1865. Mustered out with the regiment at Delaney house, Washington, DC, July 30, 1865, and discharged in Readville, MA, Aug. 9, 1865, expiration of service. Had previous service as a private and 1st lieutenant in Co. C, 53rd MVI, from Oct. 24, 1862, until mustered out, Sept. 2, 1863. Participated in the Port Hudson, LA, campaign with that regiment in 1863. President of the 57th's regimental association in 1877. Served on the committee to aid in writing the 57th's original history. Resided in Watertown, MA, after the war and served as treasurer of the Watertown Savings Bank and chairman of the Board of Trustees of the Watertown Public Library.

White, Whitman V., major and surgeon. Res. and/or credit: Stockbridge, MA. Born: New York. Age: 28. No description available. Occup: surgeon. Commissioned and mustered major, Dec. 5, 1863. Served as regimental surgeon throughout the entire service of the regiment. Mustered out with the regiment at Delaney house, Washington, DC, July 30, 1865, and discharged in Readville, MA, Aug. 9, 1865. Had previous service as major and surgeon in the 47th New York Volunteer Infantry (specifics unknown). Resided in New York City after the war.

Carpenter, Charles O., 1st lieutenant and assistant surgeon. Res. and/or credit: Holyoke, MA. Born: Massachusetts. Age: 26. No description available. Occup: surgeon. Commissioned 1st lieutenant, May 6, 1864; mustered 1st lieutenant, May 13, 1864. Served on the regimental medical staff until resigned and discharged for disability, Jan. 30, 1865. Had previous service as an assistant surgeon in the US Navy from July 30, 1861, until resigned, May 27, 1863. Served on the USS *Ottawa* in the South Atlantic Squadron. Resided in Holyoke, MA, after the war.

Gavin, Michael F., 1st lieutenant and assistant surgeon. Res. and/or credit: Boston, MA. Born: Massachusetts. Age: 23. No description available. Occup: surgeon. Commissioned 1st lieutenant, May 5, 1865; mustered 1st lieutenant, May 8, 1865. Served on the regimental medical staff until mustered out at Delaney house, Washington, DC, July 30, 1865, and discharged in Readville, MA, Aug. 9, 1865, expiration of service.

Heath, Charles E., 1st lieutenant and assistant surgeon. Res. and/or credit: Monterey, MA. Born: Massachusetts. Age: 32. No description available. Occup: surgeon. Commissioned 1st lieutenant, Jan. 13,

1864; mustered 1st lieutenant, Jan. 14, 1864. Served on the regimental medical staff until court-martialed and dishonorably discharged the US service (reason unknown), to date from Nov. 22, 1864, by order of the AGO, War Dept., dated Jan. 28, 1865. Resided in Lee, MA, after the war and died there, Oct. 5, 1887, age 55. "None who ever wore the uniform possessed a greater love for the old flag, or abiding loyalty to the country, than he. His manner was unassuming, with a generous heart, as sensitive and tender as that of a child" (JA).

Dashiell, Alfred H., chaplain. Res. and/or credit: Stockbridge, MA. Born: Massachusetts. Age: 40. Height: unknown. Comp: light. Eyes: blue. Hair: mixed. Occup: clergyman. Appointed April 14, 1864. Served as regimental chaplain throughout the regiment's service. Mustered out at Delaney house, Washington, DC, July 30, 1865, and discharged in Readville, MA, Aug. 9, 1865, expiration of service. Resided in Lakewood, NJ, after the war. Conferred DD by Rutherford College in North Carolina, June 15, 1891.

Reverend Alfred Dashiell, chaplain.
(John Anderson)

Noncommissioned Staff

Murdock, Albert M., sergeant major, Jan. 11 until May 6, 1864. (See Co. H descriptive list.)

Doty, Albert, sergeant major, May 8 until July 14, 1864. (See Co. K descriptive list.)

Pinkham, Charles H., sergeant major, Jan. 1 until June 12, 1865. (See Co. H descriptive list.)

Robbins, James A., quartermaster sergeant. Res. and credit: Watertown, MA. Born: Watertown, MA. Age: 22. Height: 5'10". Comp: dark. Eyes: brown. Hair: brown. Occup: clerk. Enlisted in Watertown by Lt. Edwin I. Coe, Feb. 1, 1864; mustered Feb. 18, 1864. Promoted quartermaster sergeant and transferred to noncommissioned officers' staff, Feb. 19, 1864, under RSO 10, by order of Lt. Col. Edward P. Hollister. Never in combat. Served in the quartermaster's dept. as assistant to Lt. Priest throughout the regiment's service. Mustered out with the regiment at Delaney house, Washington, DC, July 30, 1865, and discharged in Readville, MA, Aug. 9, 1865, expiration of service. Had previous service as a private in Co. E, 44th MVI, from Aug. 29, 1862, until mustered out, June 18, 1863. Participated in the North Carolina campaign with that regiment in 1862–63. Resided in Chicago, IL, after the war.

Lawry, David F., commissary sergeant. Res: Boston, MA. Credit: Worcester, MA. Born: Anson, ME. Age: 26. Height: 5'4½". Comp: light. Eyes: blue. Hair: dark. Occup: student. Enlisted in Co. H in Worcester by Capt. Julius M. Tucker, Dec. 1, 1863; mustered Jan. 11, 1864. Promoted commissary sergeant and transferred to the noncommissioned officers staff, Jan. 11, 1864, by order of Col. William F. Bartlett. Never in combat. Served in the commissary dept. throughout the regiment's service. On furlough in Massachusetts from about Jan. 13 until Jan. 28, 1865. Discharged the US service in Tennallytown, DC, June 13, 1865, to date June 1, 1865, as a supernumerary because of the consolidation of the 59th MVI with the 57th, under SO 254, par. 43, AGO, War Dept. Had previous service as a private in Co. I, 21st MVI, from Aug. 26, 1861, until discharged for disability in Washington, DC, Jan. 16, 1863. Participated with that regiment in the North Carolina campaign in 1862, and possibly at 2nd Bull Run, Aug. 30, 1862, Chantilly, Sept. 1, 1862, Antietam, Sept. 17, 1862, and Fredericksburg, Dec. 13, 1862. Died in East Hampton, CT, in 1873, age 36.

Prout, Henry G., hospital steward; Res. and/or credit: Great Barrington, MA. Born: Fairfax, VA (one of the four Southern-born men in the regiment). Age: 18. Height: 5'7". Comp: light. Eyes: blue. Hair: brown. Occup: student. Enlisted in Co. D in Great Barrington by Lt. Charles W. Kniffin, Dec. 28, 1863; mustered Jan. 25, 1864. Appointed hospital steward and transferred to the noncommissioned staff, Feb. 2, 1864, under RSO 10, to date from Jan. 25, 1864, by order of Lt. Col. Edward P. Hollister. Never in combat. Served as hospital steward until mustered out with the regiment at Delaney house, Washington, DC, July 30, 1865, and discharged in Readville, MA, Aug. 9, 1865, expiration of service.

Scott, Jesse S., principal musician, Jan. 7, 1865, until June 13, 1865. (See Co. B descriptive list.)

ROSTER AND DESCRIPTIVE LIST OF COMPANY A

Company A was the first company of the regiment to be mustered into United States service, and it was mustered by 2nd Lt. Daniel Madden, 6th United States Regular Cavalry. Those men mustered after Jan. 4, 1864, were mustered by both Madden and 1st Lt. Robert P. McKibben, 4th United States Regular Infantry. It was mustered out by Capt. Sylvester Keyser, 2nd Michigan Volunteer Infantry, ACM, 1st Division, IX Corps.

1. **Aldrich, William A.**, private. Res. and credit: Upton, MA. Born: Upton, MA. Age: 20. Height: 5′8″. Comp: light. Eyes: gray. Hair: light. Occup: bootmaker. Enlisted in Upton by A. S. Wood, Dec. 5, 1863; mustered Jan. 4, 1864. Never in major combat. Wounded, but not in a major battle, on an unknown date in May 1864. Absent wounded until discharged the US service for disability from an army general hospital in Washington, DC, Feb. 13, 1865, by order of Maj. Gen. Christopher C. Auger, commanding the Dept. of Washington, DC. Had previous service as a private in Co. C, 21st MVI, from Aug. 23, 1861, until discharged for disability, May 8, 1862. Possibly participated in the North Carolina campaign with that regiment in 1862. Resided in Westboro, MA, after the war.

2. **Alexander, Isaac**, private. Res. and/or credit: Ware, MA. Born: Scotland. Age: 26. Height: 5′11¾″. Comp: light. Eyes: blue. Hair: brown. Occup: shoemaker. Enlisted in Ware by H. P. Brainard, Nov. 21, 1863; mustered Jan. 4, 1864. Deserted from Camp Wool, Feb. 1, 1864. Never returned. Had previous service as a private in Co. E, 2nd MVI, from May 25, 1861, until discharged for disability, Oct. 9, 1862. Participated in the Shenandoah Valley campaign with that regiment in 1862. Taken prisoner of war at Harpers Ferry, VA, Aug. 1861. Exchanged and wounded in action near Winchester, VA, May 24 or 25, 1862.

3. **Allen, Albert S.**, corporal. Res. and/or credit: Worcester, MA. Born: Sturbridge, MA. Age: 36. Height: 5′8½″. Comp: light. Eyes: blue. Hair: light. Occup: musician. Enlisted in Worcester by Capt. John Sanderson, Dec. 5, 1863; mustered Jan. 4, 1864. Promoted corporal, March 1, 1864. Never in combat. Detached and detailed to "Camp Distribution" (*sic* in OR) on or before May 6, 1864, until discharged the US service for disability, June 24, 1865, by order of the War Dept. Died in 1895, age 67.

4. **Ballou, Hiram K.**, private. Res: Sutton, MA. Credit: Worcester, MA. Born: Burrsville, RI. Age: 38. Height: 5′5″. Comp: dark. Eyes: dark. Hair: black. Occup: farmer. Enlisted in Worcester by Capt. John Sanderson, Dec. 14, 1863; mustered Jan. 4, 1864. Wounded in action at the Wilderness, May 6, 1864. Absent wounded in an army general hospital until transferred to the 118th Co., 2nd Battln., VRC, Jan. 19, 1865, by order of the provost marshal general. Discharged the US service, Nov. 20, 1865, by order of the War Dept., expiration of service. Had previous service as a private in Co. I, 51st MVI, from Aug. 19, 1862, until mustered out, July 27, 1863. Participated in the North Carolina campaign with that regiment in 1862–63.

5. **Barrett, Thomas**, private. Res. and credit: Fitchburg, MA. Born: Ireland. Age: 21. Height: 5′5″. Comp: dark. Eyes: gray. Hair: brown. Occup: painter. Enlisted in Fitchburg by William H. Vose, Dec. 16, 1863; mustered Jan. 4, 1864. Never in combat. Absent sick or on detached duty from on or before May 6, 1864, until after March 25, 1865. Mustered out with the regiment at Delaney house, Washington, DC, July 30, 1865, and discharged in Readville, MA, Aug. 9, 1865, expiration of service.

6. **Bartlett, Ebenezer A.**, private. Res: Shrewsbury, MA. Credit: Worcester, MA. Born: Hancock, NH. Age: 46. Height: 6′2″. Comp: light. Eyes: gray. Hair: dark. Occup:

bootmaker. Enlisted in Worcester by Capt. John Sanderson, Nov. 30, 1863; mustered Jan. 4, 1864. Never in combat. Absent sick in an army general hospital from on or before May 6, 1864, until discharged the US service for disability, Aug. 10, 1865, by order of the War Dept. Died April 4, 1894, age 76.

7. **Bassett, Uriah B.,** private. Res: Holden, MA. Credit: Worcester, MA. Born: Holden, MA. Age: 18. Height: 5'6". Comp: light. Eyes: blue. Hair: auburn. Occup: laborer. Enlisted in Worcester by Capt. John Sanderson, Dec. 30, 1863; mustered Jan. 4, 1864. Sick in the hospital in Camp Wool from Feb. 15, 1864, until before April 18, 1864. Wounded in action at the Wilderness, May 6, 1864. Absent wounded in an army general hospital until Aug. 12, 1864. Killed in action by a bullet through his head at Weldon Railroad, Aug. 19, 1864. (He had lost his rifle prior to this battle, and had requested permission to remain in the rear. He was refused and was one of the first killed in that fight.)

8. **Bedreau, Alexander,** private. Res. and/or credit: Brookfield, MA. Born: province of Quebec, Canada. Age: 24. Height: 5'7". Comp: fair. Eyes: hazel. Hair: brown. Occup: bootmaker. Enlisted in Brookfield by H. L. Miller, Dec. 10, 1863; mustered Jan. 4, 1864. In action at the Wilderness, May 6, 1864, and Spotsylvania Court House, May 10, 1864; wounded in action there, May 12, 1864. Absent wounded in an army general hospital until Aug. 12, 1864. Wounded in action again at Weldon Railroad, Aug. 19, 1864. Absent wounded in an army general hospital until an unknown date between Oct. 8, 1864, and March 25, 1865. In action and taken prisoner of war at Fort Stedman, March 25, 1865. Paroled and exchanged from Libby Prison in Richmond, VA, March 30, 1865. Never returned to the regiment, and was discharged the US service for disability from the Camp of Parole in Annapolis, MD, June 5, 1865, under SO 77, par. 6, AGO, War Dept., dated April 28, 1865.

9. **Beltreau, Gusta,** private. Res: Shrewsbury, MA. Credit: Worcester, MA. Born: Montreal, Quebec, Canada. Age: 18. Height: 5'3½". Comp: dark. Eyes: hazel. Hair: dark. Occup: shoemaker. Enlisted in Worcester by Capt. John Sanderson, Dec. 4, 1863; mustered Jan. 4, 1864. Wounded in action at the Wilderness, May 6, 1864. Absent wounded in an army general hospital until deserted from that hospital on an unknown date in 1864. Arrested for desertion in Worcester, MA, on an unknown date in the fall of 1864. "Tried by general court martial and found guilty of being absent without leave. Sentenced by a G.O. from the Headquarters of the Military Governor in Alexandria, VA, dated Jan. 26, 1865, to lose all pay and allowances then due and to forfit $10.00 per month of his monthly pay for the space of three months" (CR). Returned to the regiment for duty on or before March 24, 1865, and wounded in action again at Fort Stedman, March 25, 1865. Absent wounded in an army general hospital until discharged the US service for disability from wounds, July 7, 1865, by order of the War Dept.

10. **Birmingham, Patrick,** private. Res. and/or credit: Milford, MA. Born: County Galway, Ireland, Dec. 20, 1836. Age: 27. Height: 5'9½". Comp: light. Eyes: blue. Hair: light. Occup: bootmaker. Enlisted in Milford by Leonard Hunt, Dec. 30, 1863; mustered Jan. 4, 1864. Wounded in action at the Wilderness, May 6, 1864. Absent wounded in an army general hospital until after March 25, 1865. Mustered out with the regiment at Delaney house, Washington, DC, July 30, 1865, and discharged in Readville, MA, Aug. 9, 1865, expiration of service.

11. **Bowman, Samuel M.,** 1st lieutenant. Res. and/or credit: Clinton, MA. Born: probably Clinton, MA. Age: 28. Single. No description available. Occup: machinist. Commissioned 1st lieutenant, Dec. 26, 1863; mustered 1st lieutenant, Jan. 4, 1864. Absent sick in an army general hospital in Washington, DC, from on or before May 6 until May 28, 1864. In action at Cold Harbor, June 3, 1864, and the Petersburg assaults, June 17 and 18, 1864. Mortally wounded in the thigh and leg by a Confederate mortar shell while on duty in the trenches at Petersburg, July 24, 1864. Died later that day. Remains embalmed and

Lieutenant Samuel Bowman. *(USAMHI)*

shipped to Clinton, MA, where he was buried, Aug. 5, 1864. Had previous service as a sergeant in Co. A, 51st MVI, from Aug. 16, 1862, until mustered out, July 27, 1863. Participated in the North Carolina campaign with that regiment in 1862–63. "He was considered an excellent and trustworthy officer, one who was greatly respected as a comrade and friend" (JA).

12. **Broad, Lyman,** private. Res: Concord, MA. Born and credit: Sterling, MA. Age: 28. Single. Height: 6'1". Comp: dark. Eyes: brown. Hair: black. Occup: teamster. Enlisted in Sterling by J. S. Butterick, Dec. 26, 1863; mustered Jan. 4, 1864. Detached and detailed on the 1st Division, IX Corps, ambulance wagon train from April 27 until Sept. 1864. Never in combat until mortally wounded by being shot through the bowels in action at Poplar Grove Church, Sept. 30, 1864, while trying to rescue a wounded comrade. Died later that day.

13. **Bryan, John B.,** private. Res. and/or credit: Auburn, MA. Born: Plymouth, England. Age: 23. Height: 5'7". Comp: light.

Eyes: gray. Hair: black. Occup: operative. Enlisted in Auburn by John Warren, Dec. 8, 1863; mustered Jan. 4, 1863. Deserted from Camp Wool, Feb. 1, 1864. Never returned.

14. **Callahan, Robert,** private. Res. and/or credit: Milford, MA. Born: County Kerry, Ireland. Age: 22. Height: 5'8". Comp: fair. Eyes: brown. Hair: sandy. Occup: laborer. Enlisted in Milford by Leonard Hunt, Dec. 9, 1863; mustered Jan. 4, 1864. In action at the Wilderness, May 6, 1864, and Spotsylvania Court House, May 10 and 12, 1864. Absent sick in the rear at Spotsylvania on May 18, 1864; left there when the regiment started the march to the North Anna River, and taken prisoner of war. Incarcerated in the Confederate prison camp in Andersonville, GA, May 29, 1864, where he died from chronic bronchitis, July 18, 1864. Buried in grave, Sec. J, No. 3158, at Andersonville. His death was reported to the regiment March 23, 1865.

15. **Cater, Silas N.,** private. Res: Shrewsbury, MA. Credit: Ware, MA. Born: Sudbury, MA. Age: 18. Height: 5'4½". Comp: light. Eyes: dark. Hair: dark. Occup: bootmaker. Enlisted in Ware by Capt. John Sanderson, Nov. 30, 1863; mustered Jan. 4, 1864. Killed in action at the Wilderness, May 6, 1864.

16. **Clanguin, Auguste,** private. Res. and/or credit: Cheshire, MA. Born: France. Age: 39. Height: 5'3". Comp: florid. Eyes: gray. Hair: dark. Occup: laborer. Enlisted in Cheshire by G. W. Fisher, Dec. 10, 1863; mustered Jan. 4, 1864. In action at the Wilderness, May 6, 1864, and Spotsylvania Court House, May 10, 1864; wounded in action there, May 12, 1864. Absent wounded in an army general hospital until between Oct. 8, 1864, and March 25, 1865. Taken prisoner of war at Fort Stedman, March 25, 1865. Paroled and exchanged from Libby Prison in Richmond, VA, March 29, 1865. Returned to the regiment for duty from the Camp of Parole in Annapolis, MD, on or about May 11, 1865. Mustered out with the regiment at Delaney house, Washington, DC, July 30, 1865, and discharged in Readville, MA, Aug. 9, 1865, expiration of service.

17. **Coderre, Louis C. E.,** private. Res: unknown. Credit: Ashburnham, MA. Born: St.

Hugues, Quebec, Canada. Age: 21. Height: 5'1½". Comp: light. Eyes: black. Hair: black. Occup: farmer. Enlisted in Ashburnham by I. D. Ward, Dec. 2, 1863; mustered Jan. 4, 1864. Deserted from Camp Wool, April 17, 1864. Never returned. Bounty jumper.

18. **Coe, Edwin I.**, 2nd lieutenant. Res. and/or credit: Worcester, MA. Born: Medway, MA. Age: 19. Height: unknown. Comp: fair. Eyes: dark. Hair: dark. Occup: clerk. Commissioned 2nd lieutenant, Dec. 26, 1863; mustered 2nd lieutenant, Jan. 4, 1864. Appointed acting commissary of recruits at Camp Wool, Jan. 10, 1864, under RSO 12, postdated Feb. 20, 1864, by order of Lt. Col. Edward P. Hollister. Relieved of that duty, March 10, 1864, under RSO 20, by order of Col. William F. Bartlett. Reported to the company for duty, March 11, 1864. Again appointed acting commissary of recruits at Camp Wool under RSO 27, March 16, 1864, to relieve Lt. John Cook, by order of Col. William F. Bartlett. Relieved of that duty by Lt. Cook, March 21, 1864, under RSO 29, by order of Col. William F. Bartlett. Also appointed acting regimental adjutant during his service with the regiment. In action at the Wilderness, May 6, 1864, and Spotsylvania Court House, May 10, 1864; slightly wounded in the head in action there, May 12, 1864. In action again at North Anna River, May 24, 1864, and shot through the head and killed in action during the Petersburg assault, June 17, 1864. (He predicted his own death and told some of his fellow officers that he would be killed by a bullet that would hit him in the same place he had been hit previously at Spotsylvania—he was correct.) Buried on the Petersburg battlefield by his brother, and later disinterred and reburied in the national cemetery there. Had previous service as a corporal in Co. F, 51st MVI, from Sept. 8, 1862, until mustered out, July 27, 1863. Participated in the North Carolina campaign with that regiment in 1862–63. "He was a young man of excellent character, fond of military service, zealous and ambitious in the faithful performance of duty, loved and esteemed by all who knew him" (JA).

19. **Cook, Silas W.**, private. Res. and/or credit: Warren, MA. Born: Hadley, MA. Age: 29. Height: 5'6". Comp: light. Eyes: blue. Hair: light. Occup: farmer. Enlisted in Warren by town selectmen, Dec. 19, 1864; mustered Jan. 4, 1864. In action at the Wilderness, May 6, 1864, Spotsylvania Court House, May 10, 12, and 18, 1864, North Anna River, May 24, 1864, and Cold Harbor, June 3, 1864; mortally wounded in the leg in action during the Petersburg assault, June 17, 1864. Died from wounds in an army general hospital, June 27, 1864. With the regiment on all marches and in all skirmishes and battles until wounded.

20. **Cooley, John J.**, sergeant. Res. and credit: Milford, MA. Born: County Galway, Ireland, June 23, 1837. Age: 27. Height: 5'10". Comp: dark. Eyes: brown. Hair: dark. Occup: boot treer. Enlisted in Milford by Lt. John Reade, Dec. 1, 1864; mustered Jan. 4, 1864. Promoted sergeant, March 1, 1864. In action at the Wilderness, May 6, 1864, Spotsylvania Court House, May 10, 12, and 18, 1864, North Anna River, May 24, 1864, and Cold Harbor, June 3, 1864; killed in action during the Petersburg assault, June 17, 1864. With the regiment on all marches and in all skirmishes and battles until killed. Buried on the battlefield. Had previous service as captain of Co. K, in the all-Irish 28th MVI, from Dec. 3, 1861, until resigned and discharged in Hilton Head, SC, to date April 4, 1862. On duty in South Carolina with that regiment in 1862. "A good soldier, a gallant man, and a genial comrade" (JA).

21. **Copeland, John**, private. Res. and credit: Westboro, MA. Born: Queen's County, Ireland. Age: 23. Height: 5'5". Comp: light. Eyes: gray. Hair: light. Occup: farmer. Enlisted in Westboro by Lt. John Reade, March 31, 1864; mustered April 6, 1864. Wounded and taken prisoner of war in action at the Wilderness, May 6, 1864. Incarcerated in the Confederate prison camp in Andersonville, GA, where he died from disease, Oct. 19, 1864. Buried in grave, Sec. H, No. 11,174, at Andersonville. Had previous service as a private in Co. K, 13th MVI, from July 16, 1861, until discharged for disability in Alexandria, VA, Jan. 7, 1863. Taken prisoner of war at 2nd Bull Run, Aug. 30, 1862, while serving with that regiment. Paroled and exchanged on an unknown date.

Lieutenant Edwin Coe. *(USAMHI)*

22. **Darling, William H.**, musician. Res: Clinton, MA. Credit: Worcester, MA. Born: Princeton, MA. Age: 18. Height: 5'4½". Comp: dark. Eyes: dark. Hair: dark. Occup: laborer. Enlisted in Worcester by Capt. John Sanderson, Dec. 14, 1863; mustered Jan. 4, 1864. Company drummer or fifer. Probably also served as a hospital orderly, stretcher bearer and/or nurse. Deserted from the regiment's camp near Tennallytown, DC, June 30, 1865. Surrendered voluntarily to the company commander in Readville, MA, Aug. 3, 1865. Mustered out and discharged the US service, to date Aug. 8, 1865, by order of the War Dept., expiration of service.

23. **Davis, John**, private. Res. and/or credit: Worcester, MA. Born: Ottawa, Ontario, Canada. Age: 21. Height: 5'6". Comp: dark. Eyes: blue. Hair: light. Occup: laborer. Enlisted in Worcester by Capt. John Sanderson, Dec. 2, 1863; mustered Jan. 4, 1864. Severely wounded in the right arm in action at the Wilderness, May 6, 1864. Taken to the 1st Division, IX Corps, Field Hospital where his arm was amputated by the flap method, May 12, 1864, by Dr. Whitman V. White. Absent wounded until discharged and pensioned from the US service on a Surgeons Certificate of Disability from wounds from Central Park US Army General Hospital in New York City, May 16, 1864, by order of Maj. Gen. John A. Dix, War Dept. Resided in Worcester, MA, after the war.

24. **Delaney, Michael**, private. Res. and credit: Fitchburg, MA. Born: Ireland. Age: 25. Height: 5'3½". Comp: light. Eyes: gray. Hair: red. Occup: painter. Enlisted in Fitchburg by William H. Vose, Nov. 30, 1863; mustered Jan. 4, 1864. Deserted from Camp Wool, Feb. 18, 1864. Never returned.

25. **Delaney, Patrick**, private. Res. and/or credit: Milford, MA. Born: County Galway, Ireland. Age: 45. Height: 5'6½". Comp: light. Eyes: blue. Hair: brown. Occup: bootmaker. Enlisted in Milford by J. Sumner, Dec. 8, 1863; mustered Jan. 4, 1864. In action at the Wilderness, May 6, 1864, Spotsylvania Court House, May 10, 12, and 18, 1864, North Anna River, May 24, 1864, Cold Har-

bor, June 3, 1864, Petersburg assaults, June 17 and 18, 1864, and Petersburg Crater, July 30, 1864; wounded while on duty in the trenches at Petersburg, Aug. 9, 1864. With the regiment on all marches and in all skirmishes and battles until wounded. Absent wounded in an army general hospital until between Oct. 8, 1864, and March 24, 1865. In action and taken prisoner of war at Fort Stedman, March 25, 1865. Paroled and exchanged from Libby Prison in Richmond, VA, March 29, 1865. Returned to the regiment for duty from the Camp of Parole in Annapolis, MD, on or about May 11, 1865. Mustered out with the regiment at Delaney house, Washington, DC, July 30, 1865, and discharged in Readville, MA, Aug. 9, 1865, expiration of service.

26. **Dillon, Patrick**, private. Res. and credit: Milford, MA. Born: County Galway, Ireland. Age: 45. Height: 5'5". Comp: fair. Eyes: gray. Hair: blond. Occup: bootmaker. Enlisted in Milford by Leonard Hunt, Dec. 28, 1863; mustered Jan. 4, 1864. In action at the Wilderness, May 6, 1864, and Spotsylvania Court House, May 10, 1864; wounded in action there, May 12, 1864. Absent wounded in an army general hospital where he died from his wounds, Aug. 25, 1864. Had previous service as a private in Co. K, of the all-Irish 28th MVI, from Oct. 23, 1861, until discharged for disability from "Convalescent Camp, VA" *(MSSM)* Feb. 4, 1863. Possibly participated with that regiment at James Island, SC, June 16, 1862, 2nd Bull Run, Aug. 29, 1862, Chantilly, Sept. 1, 1862, South Mountain, Sept. 14, 1862, Antietam, Sept. 17, 1862, and Fredericksburg, Dec. 13, 1862.

27. **Doherty, Patrick**, private. Res: Milford, MA. Credit: Worcester, MA. Born: Ireland. Age: 18. Height: 5'3½". Comp: dark. Eyes: dark. Hair: dark. Occup: bootmaker. Enlisted and mustered in Worcester for one year by Capt. Stone, Aug. 26, 1864. In action at Poplar Grove Church, Sept. 30, 1864 and Oct. 8, 1864, and other operations of the regiment during the fall and winter of 1864–65. In action and taken prisoner of war at Fort Stedman, March 25, 1865. Paroled and exchanged from Libby Prison in Richmond, VA, March 29, 1865. Returned to the regiment for duty

from the Camp of Parole in Annapolis, MD, on or about May 11, 1865. Discharged the US service in Tennallytown, DC, June 16, 1865, in compliance with a GO from the War Dept. discharging men with a one-year enlistment by order of Secretary of War Edwin M. Stanton.

28. **Dolan, William H.,** private. Res. and/or credit: Sterling, MA. Born: Ireland. Age: 21. Height: 5'6". Comp: light. Eyes: gray. Hair: brown. Occup: farmer and tanner. Enlisted in Sterling by J. S. Butterick, Dec. 22, 1863; mustered Jan. 4, 1864. Never in combat. Absent sick or on detached duty from on or before May 6, 1864, until after March 25, 1865. Mustered out with the regiment at Delaney house, Washington, DC, July 30, 1865, and discharged in Readville, MA, Aug. 9, 1865, expiration of service. Resided in North Leominster, MA, after the war.

29. **Doyle, Owen,** private. Res. and/or credit: Milford, MA. Born: County Galway, Ireland. Age: 34. Height: 5'6½". Comp: light. Eyes: blue. Hair: light. Occup: bootmaker. Enlisted in Milford by Louis Fay, Dec. 7, 1863; mustered Jan. 4, 1864. In action at the Wilderness, May 6, 1864, and Spotsylvania Court House, May 10, 1864; wounded in action there in the left hand, losing one finger, May 12, 1864. Absent wounded until discharged the US service on a Surgeons Certificate of Disability (loss of use of left hand) from Chester US Army General Hospital, Chester, PA, May 13, 1865, by order of Maj. Gen. John A. Dix, War Dept.

30. **Druitt, William,** sergeant. Res: Southbridge, MA. Credit: Worcester, MA. Born: London, England. Age: 25. Height: 5'10½". Comp: dark. Eyes: brown. Hair: black. Occup: clerk. Enlisted in Worcester by Lt. John Reade, March 29, 1864; promoted sergeant, April 1, 1864; mustered April 6, 1864. In action at the Wilderness, May 6, 1864, and Spotsylvania Court House, May 10, 12, and 18, 1864, and wounded in action at North Anna River, May 24, 1864. Absent wounded in an army general hospital until after March 25, 1865. Mustered out with the regiment at Delaney house, Washington, DC, July 30,

1865, and discharged in Readville, MA, Aug. 9, 1865, expiration of service.

31. **Dudley, Charles F.,** private. Res. and credit: Pittsfield, MA. Born: Pittsfield, MA. Age: 26. Height: 5'8". Comp: light. Eyes: blue. Hair: dark brown. Occup: blacksmith. Enlisted in Pittsfield by John C. West, Dec. 8, 1863; mustered Jan. 4, 1864. Never in major combat. Accidentally wounded on an unknown date while on picket duty in May 1864. Absent wounded in an army general hospital until discharged the US service for disability, June 12, 1865, by order of the War Dept. Had previous service as a private in Co. C, 49th MVI, from Sept. 11, 1862, until mustered out, Sept. 1, 1863. Participated in the Port Hudson, LA, campaign with that regiment in 1863. Also had previous service as a private in Co. D, 10th MVI, from June 14, 1861, until discharged on a Surgeons Certificate of Disability, Aug. 13, 1862. Possibly participated in the Peninsula campaign with that regiment in 1862. Resided in Pittsfield, MA, after the war.

32. **Dudley, Lyman,** private. Res: Pittsfield, MA. Credit: Springfield, MA. Born: Pittsfield, MA. Age: 21. Height: 5'7". Comp: light. Eyes: blue. Hair: brown. Occup: blacksmith. Enlisted and mustered in Springfield for one year by Capt. Morehouse, Aug. 18, 1864. Never in combat. Absent sick or on detached duty until discharged the US service in Tennallytown, DC, in compliance with a GO from the War Dept., discharging men with a one-year enlistment by order of Secretary of War Edwin M. Stanton. Resided in Pittsfield, MA, after the war.

33. **Ellard, John,** private. Res. and credit: Milford, MA. Born: County Cork, Ireland, June 24, 1838. Age: 25. Height: 5'8½". Comp: dark. Eyes: blue. Hair: dark. Occup: bootmaker. Enlisted in Milford by Lt. John Reade, Dec. 1, 1863; mustered Jan. 4, 1864. In action at the Wilderness, May 6, 1864. Absent sick or on detached duty from on or before May 10, 1864, until after March 25, 1865. Deserted from the regimental camp near Tennallytown, DC, June 2, 1865. Never returned.

34. **Flamsburg, Stephen,** private. Res. and/or credit: Worcester, MA. Born: Ottawa, Ontario, Canada. Age: 21. Height: 5′8½″. Comp: dark. Eyes: dark. Hair: dark. Occup: laborer. Enlisted in Worcester by Capt. John Sanderson, Dec. 2, 1863; mustered Jan. 4, 1864. In action at the Wilderness, May 6, 1864, and wounded, but not in a major battle, on an unknown date later that month. Absent wounded until deserted from the army general hospital in Brattleboro, VT, Sept. 13, 1864. Never returned.

35. **Flynn, Daniel,** private. Res. and/or credit: Milford, MA. Born: County Cork, Ireland. Age: 24. Height: 5′10″. Comp: dark. Eyes: dark. Hair: dark. Occup: bootmaker. Enlisted in Milford by Leonard Hunt, Dec. 30, 1863; mustered Jan. 4, 1864. In action at the Wilderness, May 6, 1864, Spotsylvania Court House, May 10, 12, and 18, 1864, North Anna River, May 24, 1864, and Cold Harbor, June 3, 1864; killed in action in the Petersburg assault, June 17, 1864. With the regiment on all marches and in all skirmishes and battles until killed.

36. **Flynn, Patrick,** private. Res. and/or credit: Milford, MA. Born: County Limerick, Ireland. Age: 26. Height: 5′8¼″. Comp: dark. Eyes: gray. Hair: dark. Occup: farmer. Enlisted in Milford by Leonard Hunt, Dec. 26, 1863; mustered Jan. 4, 1864. Sick in the hospital in Camp Wool from Feb. 7 until Feb. 11, 1864. In action at the Wilderness, May 6, 1864, Spotsylvania Court House, May 10, 12, and 18, 1864, and North Anna River, May 24, 1864; wounded in action at Cold Harbor, June 3, 1864. With the regiment on all marches and in all skirmishes and battles until wounded. Absent wounded until deserted from Fort Schuyler US Army General Hospital in New York Harbor, NY, Sept. 5, 1864. Evidently surrendered under President Abraham Lincoln's amnesty proclamation, as he is listed as mustered out but absent, at Delaney house, Washington, DC, July 30, 1865, expiration of service.

37. **Foster, Albert C.,** private. Res: Rutland, MA. Credit: Worcester, MA. Born: Worcester, MA. Age: 18. Height: 5′8″. Comp: light. Eyes: hazel. Hair: sandy. Occup: bootmaker. Enlisted in Worcester by Capt. John Sanderson, Dec. 24, 1863; mustered Jan. 4, 1864. Never in combat. Absent sick or on detached duty from on or before May 6, 1864, until after March 25, 1865. Mustered out with the regiment at Delaney house, Washington, DC, July 30, 1865, and discharged in Readville, MA, Aug. 9, 1865, expiration of service. Resided in Omaha, NE, after the war.

38. **Foster, George W.,** private. Res: Rutland, MA. Credit: Worcester, MA. Born: Rutland, MA. Age: 20. Height: 5′6½″. Comp: light. Eyes: gray. Hair: brown. Occup: shoemaker. Enlisted in Worcester by Capt. John Sanderson, Dec. 29, 1863; mustered Jan. 4, 1864. Detached and detailed to the 1st Division, IX Corps, Ambulance Corps from April 27 until late June or July, 1864. Wounded in action at the Petersburg Crater, July 30, 1864. Absent wounded in an army general hospital until after March 25, 1865. Mustered out with the regiment at Delaney house, Washington, DC, July 30, 1865, and discharged in Readville, MA, Aug. 9, 1865, expiration of service. Resided in Warren, MA, after the war.

39. **Fregeau, John,** private. Res: unknown. Credit: Ashburnham, MA. Born: St. Césaire, Quebec, Canada. Age: 22. Height: 5′6¾″. Comp: dark. Eyes: black. Hair: dark. Occup: farmer. Enlisted in Ashburnham by I. D. Ward, Dec. 2, 1863; mustered Jan. 4, 1864. Wounded in the right leg in action at the Wilderness, May 6, 1864. Leg surgically amputated by the circular method, May 25, 1864, by Dr. E. Bently, USV. Died from "exhaustion from his wounds" (OMR) in an army general hospital in Alexandria, VA, May 30, 1864.

40. **Gahagen, John,** private. Res. and/or credit: Milford, MA. Born: County Galway, Ireland. Age: 44. Height: 5′8″. Comp: fair. Eyes: blue. Hair: sandy. Occup: bootmaker. Enlisted in Milford by Leonard Hunt, Dec. 19, 1863; mustered Jan. 4, 1864. In action at the Wilderness, May 6, 1864, Spotsylvania Court House, May 10, 12, and 18, 1864, and North Anna River, May 24, 1864; taken prisoner of war at Cold Harbor, June 2, 1864.

Incarcerated in the Confederate prison in Millen, GA, where he died from disease, Oct. 1, 1864. On all marches and in all skirmishes and battles until taken prisoner.

41. **Gendron, John**, private. Res: Shrewsbury, MA. Credit: Worcester, MA. Born: Ste. Anne de Beaupré, Quebec, Canada. Age: 18. Height: 5′8½″. Comp: dark. Eyes: gray. Hair: dark. Occup: laborer. Enlisted in Worcester by Capt. John Sanderson, Dec. 9, 1864; mustered Jan. 4, 1864. Never in combat. Absent sick in an army general hospital (and then in Depot Field Hospital at City Point, Petersburg), from on or before May 6, 1864, until discharged the US service for disability, July 26, 1864, by order of Maj. Gen. John A. Dix, War Dept. Also had service in Co. K, 24th Regiment, VRC, using the name John B. Welcome, credit: New Hampshire.

42. **Gerry, Thomas L.**, private. Res. and credit: Sterling, MA. Born: Sterling, MA. Age: 41. Height: 5′3″. Comp: light. Eyes: gray. Hair: light. Occup: wheelwright. Enlisted in Sterling by A. J. Lussell, Dec. 15, 1863; mustered Jan. 4, 1864. Absent sick or detailed on detached duty from on or before May 6, 1864, until late Aug. or Sept. 1864. In action for the first time at Poplar Grove Church, Sept. 30 and Oct. 8, 1864, in operations of the regiment during the fall and winter of 1864–65, and at Fort Stedman, March 25, 1865. Absent sick in Carver US Army General Hospital in Washington, DC, from May 15, 1865, until discharged the US service for disability, July 18, 1865, to date July 6, 1865, under SO 77, par. 6, AGO, War Dept. Resided in Sterling, MA, after the war, and died there in 1919, age 96.

43. **Gillin, Michael**, private. Res. and/or credit: Worcester, MA. Born: Galway, Ireland. Age: 33. Height: 5′9½″. Comp: light. Eyes: gray. Hair: gray. Occup: tailor. Enlisted in Worcester by Capt. John Sanderson, Dec. 20, 1863; mustered Jan. 4, 1864. Killed in action at the Wilderness, May 6, 1864.

44. **Gleason, Charles F.**, private. Res: Shrewsbury, MA. Credit: Worcester, MA. Born: Worcester, MA. Age: 29. Height: 5′7″. Comp: light. Eyes: dark. Hair: dark. Occup:

bootmaker. Enlisted in Worcester by Capt. John Sanderson, Nov. 30, 1863; mustered Jan. 4, 1864. Never in combat. Absent sick from on or before May 6, 1864, and died from disease in an army general hospital in Philadelphia, PA, July 24, 1864.

45. **Glouster, Thomas**, private. Res. and/or credit: Worcester, MA. Born: London, England. Age: 19. Height: 5′5″. Comp: light. Eyes: blue. Hair: light. Occup: painter. Enlisted in Worcester by Capt. John Sanderson, Nov. 28, 1863; mustered Jan. 4, 1864. Detached and detailed as an orderly at regimental headquarters in Camp Wool, Feb. 9, 1864, under RSO 5, by order of Col. William F. Bartlett. Relieved of that duty April 10, 1864, under RSO 33, by order of Col. William F. Bartlett. Never in combat. Absent sick in an army general hospital from on or before May 6, 1864, until furloughed from the hospital, Aug. 4, 1864. Listed as a deserter, Aug. 22, 1864. Never returned.

46. **Goette, Peter**, private. Res: Shrewsbury, MA. Credit: Worcester, MA. Born: St. Johns, Newfoundland, Canada. Age: 18. Height: 5′7″. Comp: dark. Eyes: black. Hair: dark. Occup: currier. Enlisted in Worcester by Capt. John Sanderson, Dec. 1, 1863; mustered Jan. 4, 1864. Sick in the hospital in Camp Wool from Jan. 26 until Jan. 30, 1864. In action at the Wilderness, May 6, 1864, and wounded, but not in a major battle, on an unknown date later that month. Absent wounded until he deserted from an army general hospital Sept. 14, 1864. Never returned.

47. **Griffin, John**, private. Res. and/or credit: Milford, MA. Born: County Galway, Ireland. Age: 37. Height: 5′5″. Comp: fair. Eyes: brown. Hair: dark. Occup: bootmaker. Enlisted in Milford by Leonard Hunt, Dec. 25, 1863; mustered Jan. 4, 1864. Never in combat. Absent sick from on or before May 6, 1864, in Camp Meigs US Army General Hospital in Readville, MA, and discharged the US service for disability from Gallup's Island, Boston, MA, Oct. 15, 1864, by order of Maj. Gen. John A. Dix, War Dept. Resided in Milford, MA, after the war, and died there, Jan. 3, 1885. Buried in St. Mary's Catholic Cemetery in Milford.

48. **Heveron, Patrick**, private. Res: Lanesboro, MA. Credit: Pittsfield, MA. Born: Ireland. Age: 26. Height: 5'5". Comp: florid. Eyes: gray. Hair: brown. Occup: laborer. Enlisted in Pittsfield by Capt. Julius M. Tucker, Jan. 28, 1864; mustered April 6, 1864. In action at the Wilderness, May 6, 1864, and Spotsylvania Court House, May 10 and 12, 1864; wounded (probably while on picket duty or by a sniper) there, May 14, 1864. Died from wounds at an army general hospital in Washington, DC, June 1, 1864.

49. **Heyton, Anthony**, private. Res. and/or credit: Sterling, MA. Born: Leeds, Yorkshire, England. Age: 26. Height: 5'2". Comp: light. Eyes: gray. Hair: light. Occup: painter. Enlisted in Sterling by J. S. Butterick, Dec. 19, 1863; mustered Jan. 4, 1864. Wounded in action in the right hand, with the loss of several fingers, at the Wilderness, May 6, 1864. Absent wounded in an army field hospital in Fredericksburg, VA, for two weeks and then moved to Mt. Pleasant US Army General Hospital in Washington, DC until transferred to Co. I, 24th Regiment, VRC, Feb. 15, 1865. Discharged the US service for disability from wounds, Aug. 3, 1865, under SO 116, AGO, War Dept., predated June 17, 1865. Resided in East Princeton, MA, after the war.

50. **Higgins, Timothy**, private. Res. and/or credit: Clinton, MA. Born: Ireland. Age: 32. Height: 5'4". Comp: light. Eyes: gray. Hair: light. Occup: weaver. Enlisted in Clinton by E. Brimhall, Dec. 26, 1863; mustered Jan. 4, 1864. In action at the Wilderness, May 6, 1864, and Spotsylvania Court House, May 10, 1864; wounded in action there, May 12, 1864. Absent wounded in an army general hospital until transferred to the 76th Co., 2nd Battln., VRC, Oct. 22, 1864. Discharged the US service for disability from wounds, Feb. 25, 1865, by order of the War Dept. Had previous service as a private in Co. B, 34th MVI, from July 27, 1862, until discharged for disability, Jan. 16, 1863. On duty in the Washington, DC, defenses with that regiment. Resided in Boylston, MA, after the war.

51. **Howarth, James**, private. Res: Grafton, MA. Credit: Worcester, MA. Born: Lancashire, England. Age: 32. Height: 5'2½". Comp: dark. Eyes: gray. Hair: dark. Occup: bootmaker. Enlisted in Worcester by J. McClellan, Dec. 9, 1863; mustered Jan. 4, 1864. Wounded in action at the Wilderness, May 6, 1864. Absent wounded until discharged the US service for disability from wounds from Depot Field Hospital at City Point, Petersburg, Jan. 17, 1865, by order of Maj. Gen. John G. Parke, commanding IX Corps. Had previous service as a private in Co. K, 15th MVI, from July 12, 1861, until discharged for disability, Dec. 15, 1862. Possibly participated at Ball's Bluff, Oct. 21, 1861, in the Peninsula campaign, 1862, and at Antietam, Sept. 17, 1862. Resided in Webster, MA, after the war.

52. **Hull, Lavelle F.**, private. Res. and/or credit: Westfield, MA. Born: Writham, NY. Age: 27. Height: 5'2". Comp: dark. Eyes: gray. Hair: dark. Occup: painter. Enlisted in Westfield by Capt. Charles Hollis, Dec. 12, 1863; mustered Jan. 4, 1864. Sick in the hospital in Camp Wool from Jan. 30, 1864, until Feb. 2, 1864. In action at the Wilderness, May 6, 1864, Spotsylvania Court House, May 10, 12, and 18, 1864, North Anna River, May 24, 1864, Cold Harbor, June 3, 1864, and Petersburg assaults, June 17 and 18, 1864; taken prisoner of war at the Petersburg Crater, July 30, 1864. Incarcerated in the Confederate prison camp in Danville, VA, where he died from starvation, Nov. 30, 1864. With the regiment on all marches and in all skirmishes and battles until captured. Had previous service as a corporal in Co. E, 27th MVI, from Sept. 21, 1861, until discharged, Sept. 16, 1862, for disability from wounds received near New Bern, NC, March 14, 1862. Participated in the North Carolina campaign with that regiment in 1862.

53. **Jordan, John**, private. Res. and/or credit: Milford, MA. Born: County Cork, Ireland. Age: 24. Height: 5'5½". Comp: dark. Eyes: brown. Hair: dark. Occup: bootmaker. Enlisted in Milford by Leonard Hunt, Dec. 28, 1863; mustered Jan. 4, 1864. In action at the Wilderness, May 6, 1864, and Spotsylvania Court House, May 10, 1864; wounded in the leg near his ankle in action there, May 12, 1864. Absent wounded until discharged the

US service for disability from an army general hospital, June 14, 1865, by order of the War Dept. Resided in Boston, MA, after the war.

54. **Joslin, Philamon C.,** private. Res. and/or credit: Worcester, MA. Born: St. Charles, Quebec, Canada. Age: 38. Height: 5′3½″. Comp: florid. Eyes: hazel. Hair: brown. Occup: armorer. Enlisted in Worcester by Capt. John Sanderson, Dec. 13, 1863; mustered Jan. 4, 1864. Sick in the hospital in Camp Wool from Jan. 31 until Feb. 8, 1864. Never in combat. Absent sick from on or before May 6, 1864, until discharged the US service for disability from Camp Meigs US Army General Hospital in Readville, MA, Oct. 15, 1864, by order of Maj. Gen. John A. Dix, War Dept.

55. **Kelly, Thomas,** private. Res. and/or credit: Westfield, MA. Born: Wicklow, Ireland. Age: 40. Height: 5′7″. Comp: dark. Eyes: blue. Hair: dark. Occup: laborer. Enlisted in Westfield by L. C. Gillette, Dec. 18, 1863; mustered Jan. 4, 1864. Killed in action at the Wilderness, May 6, 1864.

56. **Landon, Daniel,** private. Res. and/or credit: Adams, MA. Born: Canada. Age: 22. Height: 5′10½″. Comp: light. Eyes: hazel. Hair: auburn. Occup: laborer. Enlisted in Adams by S. Johnson, Dec. 28, 1863; mustered Jan. 4, 1864. In action at the Wilderness, May 6, 1864, and wounded in action at Spotsylvania Court House, May 10, 1864. Absent wounded in an army general hospital until between Oct. 8 and Dec. 11, 1864. Reported deserted while on furlough, Dec. 31, 1864, but returned to the regiment after March 25, 1865, possibly under President Lincoln's proclamation of amnesty. Mustered out with the regiment at Delaney house, Washington, DC, July 30, 1865, and discharged in Readville, MA, Aug. 9, 1865, expiration of service.

57. **Lawson, George,** private. Res. and/or credit: Worcester, MA. Born: Lancashire, England. Age: 29. Height: 5′6″. Comp: light. Eyes: blue. Hair: light. Occup: armorer. Enlisted in Worcester by Capt. John Sanderson, Dec. 19, 1863; mustered Jan. 4, 1864. Slightly wounded in action at the Wilderness, May 6, 1864. Absent wounded until he deserted from an army general hospital on an unknown date in May 1864. Never returned.

58. **Lee, William,** private. Res. and/or credit: Worcester, MA. Born: Cork, Ireland. Age: 36. Height: 5′8½″. Comp: dark. Eyes: dark. Hair: dark. Occup: boot fitter. Enlisted in Worcester by Capt. John Sanderson, Dec. 30, 1863; mustered Jan. 4, 1864. Appointed company cook on or before May 6, 1864, and, therefore, exempted from combat service. Mustered out with the regiment at Delaney house, Washington, DC, July 30, 1865, and discharged in Readville, MA, Aug. 9, 1865, expiration of service. Had previous service as a private in Co. I, 50th MVI, from Aug. 13, 1862, until mustered out, Aug. 24, 1863. Participated in the Port Hudson, LA, campaign with that regiment in 1863.

59. **Locke, Francis,** private. Res. and/or credit: Worcester, MA. Born: Leeds, Yorkshire, England. Age: 21. Height: 5′5½″. Comp: light. Eyes: gray. Hair: brown. Occup: operative. Enlisted in Worcester by Capt. John Sanderson, Dec. 15, 1863; mustered Jan. 4, 1864. Deserted from Camp Wool, Feb. 7, 1864. Never returned.

60. **McDonald, Daniel,** corporal. Res. and/or credit: Milford, MA. Born: Prince Edward Island, Canada. Age: 28. Height: 5′9″. Comp: dark. Eyes: brown. Hair: dark. Occup: bootmaker. Enlisted in Milford by Leonard Hunt, Dec. 7, 1863; mustered Jan. 4, 1864. Promoted corporal, March 1, 1864. Killed in action at the Wilderness, May 6, 1864.

61. **Maghnie, Daniel,** private. Res. and/or credit: Worcester, MA. Born: Waterford, Ireland. Age: 34. Height: 5′9¾″. Comp: dark. Eyes: black. Hair: dark. Occup: laborer. Enlisted in Worcester by Capt. John Sanderson, Dec. 5, 1863; mustered Jan. 5, 1864. In action at the Wilderness, May 6, 1864, and Spotsylvania Court House, May 10, 1864; killed in action there, May 12, 1864.

62. **Maher, Martin,** private. Res: Oxford, MA. Credit: Webster, MA. Born: Tem-

plemore, County Tipperary, Ireland. Age: 38. Height: 5'5". Comp: fair. Eyes: gray. Hair: brown. Occup: shoemaker. Enlisted in Webster by L. B. Corbin, Nov. 30, 1863; mustered Jan. 4, 1864. In action at the Wilderness, May 6, 1864, Spotsylvania Court House, May 10, 12, and 18, 1864, and North Anna River, May 24, 1864; wounded in action at Cold Harbor, June 3, 1864. Absent wounded in an army general hospital until after March 25, 1865. With the regiment on all marches and in all skirmishes and battles until wounded. Mustered out with the regiment at Delaney house, Washington, DC, July 30, 1865, and discharged in Readville, MA, Aug. 9, 1865, expiration of service. Had previous service as a private in Co. G, 51st MVI, from Aug. 25, 1862, until mustered out, July 27, 1863. Participated in the North Carolina campaign with that regiment in 1862–63.

63. **Mara, Thomas**, private. Res. and/or credit: Worcester, MA. Born: Kilkenny, Ireland. Age: 28. Height: 5'7". Comp: light. Eyes: blue. Hair: light. Occup: laborer. Enlisted in Worcester by Capt. John Sanderson, Dec. 5, 1863; mustered Jan. 4, 1864. In action at the Wilderness, May 6, 1864, Spotsylvania Court House, May 10, 12, and 18, 1864, North Anna River, May 24, 1864, Cold Harbor, June 3, 1864, and Petersburg assaults, June 17 and 18, 1864. Slightly wounded on picket duty at Petersburg, July 2, 1864. Wound dressed and returned to the regiment for duty. Wounded again in action at the Petersburg Crater, July 30, 1864. With the regiment on all marches and in all skirmishes and battles until wounded for the second time. Absent wounded in the army general hospital in Brattleboro, VT, until given a furlough from that hospital, Aug. 25, 1864. Never returned and listed as a deserter as of Oct. 12, 1864.

64. **Martin, William G.**, private. Res. and/or credit: Milford, MA. Born: County Waterford, Ireland, June 20, 1840. Age: 23. Height: 5'5½". Comp: light. Eyes: gray. Hair: brown. Occup: bootmaker. Enlisted in Milford by J. C. Field, March 11, 1864; mustered April 6, 1864. In action at the Wilderness, May 6, 1864, and Spotsylvania Court House, May 10,

1864, where he was wounded in action on the skirmish line "by two balls through left hand, piece of shell in right side, and by a ball in right side of breast, all during same day" *(HOM)*, May 12, 1864. Absent wounded in an army general hospital until discharged the US service for disability from wounds, July 24, 1864, by order of the War Dept. Had previous service as a private in Co. D, 1st Massachusetts Volunteer Cavalry, from Aug. 1, 1862, until discharged, Jan. 22, 1864, from an army general hospital in Washington, DC, for disability from wounds received at Aldie, VA, June 17, 1863. Participated with that regiment in the North Carolina campaign in 1862 and on duty with the Army of the Potomac in 1863. In action at Fredericksburg, Dec. 13, 1863.

65. **Maynard, George W.**, private. Res. and credit: Sterling, MA. Born: Sterling, MA. Age: 17. Height: 5'2". Comp: light. Eyes: light. Hair: light. Occup: tanner. Enlisted in Sterling by J. S. Butterick, Dec. 21, 1863; mustered Jan. 4, 1864. Missing in action at the Wilderness, May 6, 1864. Never accounted for and presumed killed.

66. **Maynard, William**, private. Res. and credit: Sterling, MA. Born: Sudbury, MA. Age: 19. Height: 5'4". Comp: dark. Eyes: gray. Hair: brown. Occup: shoemaker. Enlisted in Sterling by J. S. Butterick, Dec. 26, 1863; mustered Jan. 4, 1864. Missing in action at the Wilderness, May 6, 1864. Never accounted for and presumed killed.

67. **Mills, John S.**, corporal. Res: Rutland, MA. Credit: Worcester, MA. Born: Providence, RI. Age: 22. Height: 5'4". Comp: light. Eyes: black. Hair: brown. Occup: bootmaker. Enlisted in Worcester by Capt. John Sanderson, Dec. 24, 1863; mustered Jan. 4, 1864. Promoted corporal, March 1, 1864. In action at the Wilderness, May 6, 1864, and Spotsylvania Court House, May 10, 1864; wounded in the side in action there by shrapnel from an exploding shell, May 12, 1864. Absent wounded in an army general hospital until between Oct. 8, 1864, and March 24, 1865. Severely wounded in the arm by a Minié ball in action again at Fort Stedman,

March 25, 1865. Died from wounds in an army general hospital in Annapolis, MD, April 15, 1865.

68. **Mooher, William**, private. Res. and/or credit: Milford, MA. Born: County Limerick, Ireland. Age: 25. Height: 5'4½". Comp: fair. Eyes: hazel. Hair: light. Occup: farmer. En- listed in Milford by Leonard Hunt, Dec. 26, 1863; mustered Jan. 4, 1864. In action at the Wilderness, May 6, 1864, and Spotsylvania Court House, May 10, 12, and 18, 1864, and taken prisoner of war at North Anna River, May 24, 1864. Paroled and exchanged from an unknown Confederate prison, Nov. 19, 1864. Probably received extra pay for having been a prisoner. Never returned to the regi- ment. Discharged the US service for dis- ability, Jan. 20, 1865, by order of the War Dept.

69. **Morris, Michael**, private. Res. and/or credit: Worcester, MA. Born: County Ty- rone, Ireland. Age: 20. Height: 5'4". Comp: light. Eyes: blue. Hair: light. Occup: laborer. Enlisted in Worcester by Capt. John Sander- son, Dec. 5, 1863; mustered Jan. 4, 1864. In action at the Wilderness, May 6, 1864, and Spotsylvania Court House, May 10, 12, and 18, 1864; taken prisoner of war at North Anna River, May 24, 1864. Incarcerated in the Confederate prison camp in Andersonville, GA, where he died from chronic diarrhea, Oct. 10, 1864. Buried as an "unknown" at Andersonville.

70. **Murphy, Cornelius**, private. Res. and/or credit: Milford, MA. Born: County Cork, Ire- land. Age: 18. Height: 5'4". Comp: dark. Eyes: brown. Hair: dark. Occup: bootmaker. Enlisted in Milford by Lt. John Reade, Dec. 18, 1863; mustered Jan. 4, 1864. In action at the Wilderness, May 6, 1864, Spotsylvania Court House, May 10, 12, and 18, 1864, North Anna River, May 24, 1864, and Cold Harbor, June 3, 1864; killed in action in the Petersburg assault, June 17, 1864. With the regiment on all marches and in all skirmishes and battles until killed.

71. **Murphy, Patrick**, private. Res. and/or credit: Milford, MA. Born: County Galway,

Ireland, Jan. 6, 1830. Age: 33. Height: 5'8". Comp: dark. Eyes: blue. Hair: dark. Occup: bootmaker. Enlisted in Milford by Lt. John Reade, Dec. 1, 1863; mustered Jan. 4, 1864. Sick in the hospital in Camp Wool from before Jan. 26 until Feb. 8, 1864. Killed in action at the Wilderness, May 6, 1864.

72. **Nelson, Dexter C.**, 1st sergeant. Res. and/or credit: Worcester, MA. Born: Shrews- bury, MA. Age: 19. Height: 5'7½". Comp: light. Eyes: blue. Hair: brown. Occup: clerk. Enlisted in Worcester by Capt. John Sander- son, Nov. 20, 1863; mustered Jan. 4, 1864. Promoted sergeant, March 1, 1864. In action at the Wilderness, May 6, 1864, Spotsylvania Court House, May 10, 12, and 18, 1864, and North Anna River, May 24, 1864. Promoted 1st sergeant, June 1, 1864, to replace 1st Sgt. Willson, killed at the Wilderness. In action at Cold Harbor, June 3, 1864, Petersburg as- saults, June 17 and 18, 1864, and Petersburg Crater, July 30, 1864. Absent sick in an army general hospital from on or before Aug. 19, 1864, until after March 25, 1865. Discharged the US service in Tennallytown, DC, June 16, 1865, to date June 1, 1865, as a supernumer- ary because of the consolidation of the 59th MVI with the 57th, under SO 254, par. 43, AGO, War Dept., dated May 26, 1865. Had previous service as a private in Co. K, 13th MVI, from July 16, 1861, until discharged for disability in Alexandria, VA, July 21, 1862. On duty in Virginia with that regiment in 1861–62. Resided in the Soldiers Home in Chelsea, MA, after the war.

73. **Neville, William**, private. Res. and/or credit: Milford, MA. Born: County Water- ford, Ireland. Age: 44. Height: 5'5½". Comp: fair. Eyes: blue. Hair: light. Occup: boot- maker. Enlisted in Milford by Leonard Hunt, Dec. 7, 1863; mustered Jan. 4, 1864. In action at the Wilderness, May 6, 1864, Spotsylvania Court House, May 10, 12, and 18, 1864, North Anna River, May 24, 1864, Cold Har- bor, June 3, 1864, Petersburg assaults, June 17 and 18, 1864, and Petersburg Crater, July 30, 1864; severely wounded in the left hip while on duty in the trenches at Petersburg, Aug. 9, 1864. Absent wounded in an army general hospital until April 25, 1865. Mustered out

with the regiment at Delaney house, Washington, DC, July 30, 1865, and discharged in Readville, MA, Aug. 9, 1865, expiration of service. With the regiment on all marches and in all skirmishes and battles until wounded.

74. **O'Clair, Peter,** private. Res. and/or credit: Pittsfield, MA. Born: Canada. Age: 22. Height: 5'8½". Comp: dark. Eyes: black. Hair: black. Occup: blacksmith. Enlisted in Pittsfield by John C. West, March 28, 1864; mustered April 6, 1864. In action at the Wilderness, May 6, 1864, Spotsylvania Court House, May 10, 12, and 18, 1864, North Anna River, May 24, 1864, and Cold Harbor, June 3, 1864; wounded in action in the Petersburg assault, June 17, 1864. With the regiment on all marches and in all skirmishes and battles until wounded. Absent wounded in Turner's Lane US Army General Hospital in Philadelphia, PA, until he deserted from there, Sept. 8, 1864. Never returned.

75. **O'Conner, Daniel,** private. Res: Winchendon, MA. Credit: Worcester, MA. Born: Cork, Ireland. Age: 27. Height: 5'3". Comp: light. Eyes: gray. Hair: brown. Occup: laborer. Enlisted in Worcester by Capt. John Sanderson, Dec. 21, 1863; mustered Jan. 4, 1864. In action at the Wilderness, May 6, 1864, and Spotsylvania Court House, May 10, 1864; killed in action there, May 12, 1864.

76. **O'Conners, David,** private. Res: Worcester, MA. Credit: Milford, MA. Born: County Wexford, Ireland, Feb. 12, 1833. Age: 31. Height: 5'6½". Comp: dark. Eyes: gray. Hair: dark. Occup: bootmaker. Enlisted in Milford by Leonard Hunt, Dec. 9, 1863; mustered Jan. 4, 1864. In action at the Wilderness, May 6, 1864, and Spotsylvania Court House, May 10, 1864; killed in action there, May 12, 1864.

77. **O'Donnell, John,** 1st sergeant. Res. and/or credit: Milford, MA. Born: County Waterford, Ireland, Feb. 10, 1843. Age: 20. Height: 5'10½". Comp: dark. Eyes: dark. Hair: dark. Occup: bootmaker. Enlisted in Milford by Lt. John Reade, Dec. 1, 1863; mustered Jan. 4, 1864. Promoted corporal, March 1, 1864. In action at the Wilderness, May 6, 1864, and Spotsylvania Court House, May 10, 1864;

slightly wounded in action there "by ball in right arm above elbow" *(HOM)*, May 12, 1864, but remained with the regiment. In action again at Spotsylvania, May 18, 1864, and North Anna River, May 24, 1864. Promoted sergeant, June 1, 1864, to replace Sgt. Nelson, promoted to 1st sergeant. In action again at Cold Harbor, June 3, 1864, Petersburg assaults, June 17 and 18, 1864, Petersburg Crater, July 30, 1864, Weldon Railroad, Aug. 19, 1864, Poplar Grove Church, Sept. 30 and Oct. 8, 1864, and Fort Stedman, March 25, 1865. One of the 11 men with the regiment on all marches and in all skirmishes and battles throughout its entire combat service, and one of the 30 men left of the regiment after Weldon Railroad, Aug. 19, 1864. Cited twice for bravery at Fort Stedman, March 25, 1865: "Sergeant John O'Donnell, Company A, . . . general good conduct" (GPR), and "Sergeant John O'Donnell, Company A, rallying and encouraging his men; had participated in every engagement with his company and regiment since its entry into service" (JMT). Promoted 1st sergeant, about June 16, 1865, to replace 1st Sgt. Nelson, mustered out. Mustered out with the regiment at Delaney house, Washington, DC, July 30, 1865, and discharged in Readville, MA, Aug. 9, 1865, expiration of service. Resided in the Soldiers Home in Chelsea, MA, after the war.

78. **Parks, George H.,** sergeant. Res. and credit: Winchendon, MA. Born: Winchendon, MA. Age: 19. Height: 5'9½". Comp: light. Eyes: blue. Hair: brown. Occup: clerk. Enlisted in Winchendon by B. Ellis, Dec. 22, 1863; mustered Jan. 4, 1864. Promoted corporal on an unknown date after muster-in. Absent on furlough from before Jan. 26, 1864, until Feb. 11, 1864. Promoted sergeant, March 1, 1864. Absent sick in an army general hospital from on or before May 6 until on or before July 29, 1864, when he was present sick with the regiment. Went into action sick at the Petersburg Crater, July 30, 1864; taken prisoner of war during that battle. Incarcerated in the Confederate prison camp in Danville, VA, until paroled and exchanged for sickness, Aug. 30, 1864. Died from chronic diarrhea in the army general hospital in the Camp of Parole in Annapolis, MD, Sept. 19,

1864. Had previous service as a private in Co. H, 53rd MVI, from Sept. 3, 1862 until discharged for disability in New Orleans, LA, May 22, 1863. On duty in Louisiana with that regiment in 1862–63.

79. **Parks, William**, private. Res. and/or credit: Milford, MA. Born: County Leitrim, Ireland, March, 1837. Age: 27. Height: 5'10". Comp: fair. Eyes: brown. Hair: light. Occup: jailer. Enlisted in Milford by Leonard Hunt, Dec. 30, 1863; mustered Jan. 4, 1864. Deserted from Camp Wool, Jan. 5, 1864. Arrested July 6, 1864, and returned to the regiment, July 21, 1864. Tried by general court-martial for desertion, found guilty, and sentenced (probably to loss of pay and allowances). Returned to the regiment between Oct. 8, 1864, and March 25, 1865. In action at Fort Stedman, March 25, 1865. Mustered out with the regiment at Delaney house, Washington, DC, July 30, 1865, and discharged in Readville, MA, Aug. 9, 1865, expiration of service. Had previous service as a private in Co. I, 27th MVI, from Oct. 10, 1861, until discharged for disability in New Bern, NC, Oct. 6, 1862. Saw no action with that regiment.

80. **Paul, Charles**, private. Res: Holden, MA. Credit: Worcester, MA. Born: Montreal, Quebec, Canada. Age: 44. Height: 6'0". Comp: dark. Eyes: black. Hair: dark. Occup: farmer. Enlisted in Worcester by Capt. John Sanderson, Dec. 12, 1863; mustered Jan. 4, 1864. Never in combat. Absent sick in an army general hospital from on or before May 6, 1864, until transferred to the 14th Co., 2nd Battln., VRC, for disability on an unknown date in June or July, 1864. Discharged the US service for disability, July 26, 1864, by order of Maj. Gen. John A. Dix, War Dept., to date Sept. 16, 1865.

81. **Petty, Adam**, private. Res. and/or credit: Worcester, MA. Born: Sheffield, Yorkshire, England. Age: 29. Height: 5'4". Comp: light. Eyes: blue. Hair: light. Occup: armorer. Enlisted in Worcester by Capt. John Sanderson, Dec. 19, 1863; mustered Jan. 4, 1864. In action at the Wilderness, May 6, 1864, Spotsylvania Court House, May 10, 12, and 18, 1864,

North Anna River, May 24, 1864, Cold Harbor, June 3, 1864, and Petersburg assaults, June 17 and 18, 1864; wounded in action at the Petersburg Crater, July 30, 1864. With the regiment on all marches and in all skirmishes and battles until wounded. Absent wounded until he deserted from Camp Meigs US Army General Hospital in Readville, MA, Dec. 14, 1864. Evidently surrendered to the authorities, probably under President Lincoln's proclamation of amnesty, as he was listed as mustered out but absent at Delaney house, Washington, DC, July 30, 1865, expiration of service.

82. **Porter, Adolphus**, private. Res. and credit: Worcester, MA. Born: Worcester, MA. Age: 21; Height: 5'8". Comp: dark. Eyes: dark. Hair: dark. Occup: bootmaker. Enlisted in Worcester by Capt. John Sanderson, Dec. 2, 1863; mustered Jan. 4, 1864. In action at the Wilderness, May 6, 1864, Spotsylvania Court House, May 10, 12, and 18, 1864, North Anna River, May 24, 1864, and Cold Harbor, June 3, 1864; wounded in the leg in action during the Petersburg assault, June 17, 1864. With the regiment on all marches and in all skirmishes and battles until wounded. Absent wounded until discharged the US service for disability from wounds, from Dale US Army General Hospital in Worcester, MA, April 11, 1865, to date April 1, 1865, by order of Maj. Gen. John G. Parke, commanding IX Corps. Had previous service as a private in Co. G, 27th MVI, from Sept. 15, 1861, until discharged, Feb. 22, 1863, for disability from wounds received near New Bern, NC, March 14, 1862. Participated in the North Carolina campaign with that regiment in 1862. Resided in South Framingham, MA, and died there in 1910, age 68.

83. **Porter, Alfred C.**, private. Res: Shrewsbury, MA. Credit: Worcester, MA. Born: Worcester, MA. Age: 18. Height: 5'6". Comp: dark. Eyes: dark. Hair: dark. Occup: bootmaker. Enlisted in Worcester by Capt. John Sanderson, Nov. 28, 1863; mustered Jan. 4, 1864. Sick in the hospital in Camp Wool from Jan. 26 until 30, 1864. In action at the Wilderness, May 6, 1864, Spotsylvania Court House, May 10, 12, and 18, 1864, North

Anna River, May 24, 1864, and Cold Harbor, June 3, 1864; wounded in the foot in action during the Petersburg assault, June 17, 1864. With the regiment on all marches and in all skirmishes and battles until wounded. Absent wounded in Dale US Army General Hospital in Worcester, MA, where he died from chronic diarrhea, April 22, 1865.

84. **Ray, Asa M.**, private. Res: Oxford, MA. Credit: Webster, MA. Born: Sutton, MA. Age: 37. Height: 5′6″. Comp: light. Eyes: blue. Hair: brown. Occup: shoemaker. Enlisted in Webster by L. B. Corbin, Dec. 7, 1863; mustered Jan. 4, 1864. Wounded in action at the Wilderness, May 6, 1864. Absent wounded in an army general hospital until after March 25, 1865. Mustered out with the regiment at Delaney house, Washington, DC, July 30, 1865, and discharged in Readville, MA, Aug. 9, 1865, expiration of service.

85. **Rice, William H.**, private. Res: Wolfboro, NH. Credit: Worcester, MA. Born: Wolfboro, NH. Age: 22. Height: 5′7½″. Comp: light. Eyes: blue. Hair: sandy. Occup: machinist. Enlisted in Co. B in Worcester by D. Waldo Lincoln, Jan. 2, 1864; mustered Jan. 11, 1864. Transferred to Co. A, Feb. 22, 1864, under RSO 13 by order of Col. William F. Bartlett, and joined the company on Feb. 23, 1864. Never in combat. Became sick about April 20, 1864, while the regiment was on the march to the front and was sent ahead to an army general hospital in Alexandria, VA, where he was discharged the US service for disability, April 24, 1864, by order of Maj. Gen. John A. Dix, War Dept. Had previous service as a private in Co. B, 13th MVI, from May 31, 1861, until discharged for disability from an army general hospital in Washington, DC, Jan. 13, 1863. Possibly participated with that regiment at 2nd Bull Run, Aug. 30, 1862, Antietam, Sept. 17, 1862, and Fredericksburg, Dec. 13, 1862. Resided in Worcester, MA, after the war.

86. **Richell, Louis**, private. Res: Brookfield, MA. Credit: Worcester, MA. Born: Trois Rivières, Quebec, Canada. Age: 28. Height: 5′4½″. Comp: light. Eyes: blue. Hair: light.

Occup: currier. Enlisted in Worcester by Capt. John Sanderson, Nov. 30, 1863; mustered Jan. 4, 1864. Missing in action at the Wilderness May 6, 1864. Never accounted for and presumed killed.

87. **Rivod, Moses**, private. Res: Grafton, MA. Credit: Worcester, MA. Born: Montgomery, NY. Age: 18. Height: 5′4″. Comp: dark. Eyes: black. Hair: black. Occup: card stripper. Enlisted in Worcester by Lt. Edwin I. Coe, Dec. 26, 1863; mustered Jan. 4, 1864. In action at the Wilderness, May 6, 1864, and Spotsylvania Court House, May 10, 1864; killed in action there, May 12, 1864.

88. **Roper, William J.**, private. Res. and credit: Sterling, MA. Born: Sterling, MA. Age: 18. Height: 5′6″. Comp: dark. Eyes: gray. Hair: dark. Occup: farmer. Enlisted in Sterling by J. S. Butterick, Dec. 28, 1863; mustered Jan. 4, 1864. In action at the Wilderness, May 6, 1864, and Spotsylvania Court House, May 10, 12, and 18, 1864; slightly wounded in action at North Anna River, May 24, 1864, but remained with the regiment. In action again at Cold Harbor, June 3, 1864, and Petersburg assaults, June 17 and 18, 1864; wounded in action again at the Petersburg Crater, July 30, 1864. Absent wounded in an army general hospital until between Oct. 8, 1864, and March 25, 1865. In action again and taken prisoner of war at Fort Stedman, March 25, 1865. Paroled and exchanged from Libby Prison in Richmond, VA, March 29, 1865, and returned to the regiment for duty from the Camp of Parole in Annapolis, MD, on or about May 11, 1865. Mustered out with the regiment at Delaney house, Washington, DC, July 30, 1865, and discharged in Readville, MA, Aug. 9, 1865, expiration of service. With the regiment on most marches and in most skirmishes and battles.

89. **Rugg, Charles H.**, private. Res and/or credit: Worcester, MA. Born: Winchendon, MA. Age: 21. Height: 5′5″. Comp: florid. Eyes: blue. Hair: light. Occup: car driver. Enlisted in Worcester by Capt. John Sanderson, Dec. 8, 1863; mustered Jan. 4, 1864. Severely wounded in the leg in action and taken prisoner of war at the Wilderness, May 6, 1864.

Incarcerated in the Confederate prison in Gordonsville, VA, where his leg was amputated. Died from wounds (probably infection), June 12, 1864. Had previous service as a private in Co. I, 15th MVI, from Aug. 3, 1861, until discharged for disability, Aug. 25, 1861. Saw no action with that regiment.

90. **Sanderson, John W.**, captain. Res. and or credit: Westboro, MA. Born: Massachusetts. Age: 32. Height: unknown. Comp: light. Eyes: blue. Hair: light brown. Occup: wireworker. Commissioned 1st lieutenant, Oct. 21, 1863; mustered 1st lieutenant, Nov. 3, 1863. Commissioned captain, Dec. 26, 1863; mustered captain, Jan. 4, 1864. Senior captain of the regiment. In action at the Wilderness, May 6, 1864, and Spotsylvania Court House, May 10, 1864; severely wounded in action there, May 12, 1864. Absent wounded until resigned and discharged the US service for disability from wounds from an army general hospital in Alexandria, VA, Nov. 10, 1864, under SO 393, AGO, War Dept. Had previous service as 1st lieutenant of Co. A, 51st MVI, from Sept. 25, 1862, until mustered out, July 27, 1863. Participated in the North Carolina campaign with that regiment in 1862–63. Also had previous service as 1st lieutenant of Co. C, 13th MVI, from June 29,

Captain John Sanderson. *(USAMHI)*

1861, until discharged for disability, July 22, 1861. Participated in no significant actions with that regiment. Resided in Colfax, IA, after the war, and died there Jan. 13, 1884, age 52. "He was a man of high personal character, untiring energy and an excellent officer, well trained in the duties pertaining to his position, and one who took a great pride in his profession" (JA).

91. **Sawtelle, Henry A.**, private. Res. and credit: Shrewsbury, MA. Born: Shrewsbury, MA. Age: 19. Height: 5′4″. Comp: dark. Eyes: black. Hair: brown. Occup: farmer. Enlisted in Shrewsbury by E. O. Green, Dec. 4, 1863; mustered Jan. 4, 1864. Wounded in action at the Wilderness, May 6, 1864. Died from his wounds at an army general hospital in Annapolis, MD, June 14, 1864. (Note: Someone wrote in under his name on the descriptive rolls the possibly derisive comment, "In action at Anapolis [*sic*], June, 64.")

92. **Seaver, Roswell R.**, private. Res: Holden, MA. Credit: Worcester, MA. Born: Holden, MA, Aug. 13, 1845. Age: 18. Height: 5′5½″. Comp: dark. Eyes: hazel. Hair: brown. Occup: farmer. Enlisted in Worcester by Lt. Edwin I. Coe, Jan. 2, 1864; mustered Jan. 4, 1864. Missing in action at the Wilderness, May 6, 1864, but returned to the regiment for duty between June 17 and July 13, 1864. Discharged for disability (probably at Petersburg), July 13, 1864, by order of Maj. Gen. John A. Dix, War Dept. Had subsequent service as a private in Co. C, 25th MVI, from Jan. 11, 1865, until mustered out, July 13, 1865. Participated at Wise's Forks, NC, March 8, 1865, with that regiment.

93. **Shaughnessey, Michael**, private. Res. and/or credit: Milford, MA. Born: Galway, Ireland. Age: 25. Height: 5′5″. Comp: dark. Eyes: dark. Hair: light. Occup: bootmaker. Enlisted in Milford by Leonard Hunt, Dec. 8, 1863; mustered Jan. 6, 1864. Killed in action at the Wilderness, May 6, 1864.

94. **Smith, Alfred**, corporal. Res. and/or credit: Worcester, MA. Born: Manchester, England. Age: 21. Height: 5′6″. Comp: florid. Eyes: black. Hair: brown. Enlisted in Worces-

ter by Lt. Edwin I. Coe, Dec. 31, 1864; mustered Jan. 4, 1864. Promoted corporal, March 1, 1864. Deserted near the Rapidan River while on the march to the Wilderness, May 4, 1864. Arrested in Worcester, MA, on an unknown date in the summer of 1864 and charged with desertion from the field. Tried before a general court-martial and found guilty. Sentenced by a SO from the Headquarters of the Military Governor in Alexandria, VA, dated Sept. 20, 1864, to lose all pay and allowances then due, and to forfeit $10 per month of his monthly pay for 15 months. Also reduced to the ranks, Sept. 20, 1864. In action at Fort Stedman, March 25, 1865, and wounded by shrapnel from the explosion of a Confederate mortar shell while on duty in the trenches there, March 27, 1865. Absent wounded in an army general hospital until no later than July 30, 1865. Mustered out with the regiment at Delaney house, Washington, DC, July 30, 1865, and discharged in Readville, MA, Aug. 9, 1865, expiration of service. Had previous service as a private in Co. C, 21st MVI, from Aug. 23, 1861, until discharged for disability, May 7, 1862. Possibly participated in the North Carolina campaign with that regiment in 1862.

95. **Smith, Eli**, private. Res: Ware, MA. Credit: Worcester, MA. Born: Montreal, Quebec, Canada. Age: 26. Height: 5'2¾". Comp: florid. Eyes: black. Hair: black. Occup: shoemaker. Enlisted in Worcester by H. P. Brainard, Nov. 21, 1863; mustered Jan. 4, 1864. Deserted from Camp Wool, Jan. 20, 1864. Arrested on an unknown date in the summer of 1864. Court-martialed for desertion, found guilty, and dishonorably discharged the US service in Sept. 1864, in New York City, by order of Maj. Gen. John A. Dix, War Dept. "Bounty jumper" (JA).

96. **Sweetser, Joseph E.**, private. Res. and/or credit: Barre, MA. Born: Warwick, MA. Age: 18. Height: 5'3¼". Comp: light. Eyes: blue. Hair: dark. Occup: mechanic. Enlisted in Barre by D. Rice, Dec. 29, 1863; mustered Jan. 4, 1864. Absent sick or on detached duty from on or before May 6, 1864, until between July 30 and Aug. 19, 1864. Wounded in action and taken prisoner of war at Weldon Railroad, Aug. 19, 1864. Incarcerated in the Confederate prison camp in Salisbury, NC, where he died from his wounds, Oct. 30, 1864. Had previous service as a private in Co. H, 53rd MVI, from Nov. 25, 1862, until mustered out, Sept. 2, 1863. Participated in the Port Hudson, LA, campaign with that regiment in 1863.

97. **Tappan, Francis**, private. Res. and/or credit: Worcester, MA. Born: Harlem, New York City. Age: 28. Height: 5'7½". Comp: dark. Eyes: dark. Hair: dark. Occup: harness maker. Enlisted in Worcester by Capt. John Sanderson, Nov. 24, 1863; mustered Jan. 4, 1864. "Deserted from the cars at Philadelphia, April 20, 1864" (CR). Arrested on an unknown date, probably in 1865. Court-martialed for desertion, found guilty, and dishonorably discharged the US service, June 27, 1865, by order of the War Dept.

98. **Taylor, George A.**, private. Res: South Franklin, MA. Born and credit: Attleboro, MA. Age: 18. Height: 5'2". Comp: dark. Eyes: blue. Hair: dark. Occup: farmer. Enlisted and mustered for one year in Attleboro by Capt. Stone, Aug. 10, 1864. Never in combat. Absent sick or on detached duty until after March 25, 1865. Discharged the US service in Tennallytown, DC, June 16, 1865, in compliance with a GO from the War Dept. discharging men with a one-year enlistment by order of Secretary of War Edwin M. Stanton.

99. **Teague, John**, private. Res. and/or credit: Worcester, MA. Born: County Monaghan, Ireland. Age: 26. Height: 5'9½". Comp: sandy. Eyes: blue. Hair: auburn. Occup: roller. Enlisted in Worcester by J. M. Standly, Dec. 11, 1863; mustered Jan. 4, 1864. In action at the Wilderness, May 6, 1864, and Spotsylvania Court House, May 10, 1864; wounded in action there, May 12, 1864. Absent wounded in an army general hospital until discharged the US service for disability from wounds, June 14, 1865, by order of the War Dept. Died July 1, 1881, age 43.

100. **Trussell, Augustus J.**, 1st sergeant. Res. and credit: Sterling, MA. Born: Belfast, ME.

Age: 25. Height: 5'6". Comp: dark. Eyes: brown. Hair: black. Occup: carpenter and teacher. Enlisted in Sterling by J. S. Butterick, Dec. 11, 1863; mustered Jan. 4, 1864. Promoted 1st sergeant, March 1, 1864. Reduced to duty sergeant, April 7, 1864, W. H. Willson promoted to 1st sergeant, under RSO 35, by order of Col. William F. Bartlett. Reduced to the ranks, May 1, 1865, H. A. Willson promoted sergeant. Never in combat; very likely a shirker. Wounded in the left leg while in the rear at Cold Harbor, June 3, 1863; "not known how done" (CR). Discharged the US service for disability from wounds, June 27, 1865, by order of the War Dept. Had previous service as a private in Co. D, 1st Massachusetts Volunteer Cavalry, from Sept. 16, 1861, until discharged for disability in Readville, MA, Nov. 15, 1861. Saw no action with that regiment. Also had previous service as a private in Co. K, 53rd MVI, from Sept. 6, 1862, until mustered out, Sept. 2, 1863. Participated in the Port Hudson, LA, campaign with that regiment in 1863. Died in 1883, age 44. "REGULAR DEAD BEAT" (CR).

101. **Tully, John,** private. Res: Oxford, MA. Credit: Webster, MA. Born: Ireland. Age: 39. Height: 5'5". Comp: fair. Eyes: hazel. Hair: black. Occup: farmer. Enlisted in Webster by L. B. Corbin, Dec. 12, 1863; mustered Jan. 4, 1864. Wounded in action at the Wilderness, May 6, 1864. Absent wounded in Sickel US Army General Hospital in Alexandria, VA, and died there, May 18, 1865, "from exhaustion from gunshot wound" (CR).

102. **Vaughn, Bartholomew,** private. Res. and/or credit: Milford, MA. Born: County Limerick, Ireland. Age: 41. Height: 5'5". Comp: fair. Eyes: blue. Hair: dark. Occup: bootmaker. Enlisted in Milford by Leonard Hunt, Dec. 15, 1863; mustered Jan. 4, 1864. In action at the Wilderness, May 6, 1864, and Spotsylvania Court House, May 10, 1864; wounded in action there, May 12, 1864. Absent wounded in Emory US Army General Hospital in Washington, DC, until given a furlough from there in late Oct. or early Nov., 1864. Never returned and listed as a deserter, Nov. 30, 1864. Surrendered to the authorities, probably under President Lincoln's proclama-

tion of amnesty, as he is listed as mustered out but absent at Delaney house, Washington, DC, July 30, 1865, expiration of service.

103. **Walker, William R.,** corporal. Res: Douglas, MA. Credit: Worcester, MA. Born: Douglas, MA. Age: 22. Height: 5'5". Comp: light. Eyes: dark. Hair: brown. Occup: jeweler. Enlisted in Worcester by Capt. John Sanderson, Dec. 27, 1863; mustered Jan. 4, 1864. Promoted corporal, March 1, 1864. In action at the Wilderness, May 6, 1864, and Spotsylvania Court House, May 10, 1864; wounded in action there, May 12, 1864. Absent wounded until discharged the US service for disability from wounds from Depot Field Hospital at City Point, Petersburg, March 17, 1865, to date March 1, 1865, by order of Maj. Gen. John G. Parke, commanding IX Corps. Had previous service as a private in Co. A, 43rd New York Volunteer Infantry (specifics unknown).

104. **Walsh, James,** private. Res. and/or credit: Milford, MA. Born: County Kilkenney, Ireland, March 8, 1824. Age: 39. Height: 5'7". Comp: light. Eyes: brown. Hair: dark. Occup: butcher. Enlisted in Milford by Leonard Hunt, Dec. 11, 1863; mustered Jan. 4, 1864. In action at the Wilderness, May 6, 1864; Spotsylvania Court House, May 10, 1864; wounded in action there, May 12, 1864. Absent wounded in an army general hospital until between Oct. 8, 1864, and March 25, 1865. Wounded in action again at Fort Stedman, March 25, 1865. "Case 727.—Private J. Walsh, Co. A, 57th Massachusetts, aged 39 years, was wounded at Fort Stedman, March 25, 1865, by a musket ball, which fractured the left leg in the upper third, perforating the tibia transversely and completely destroying the upper part of the fibula. Surgeon M. K. Hogan, U.S.V., reported the wounded man's admission to the field hospital of the 1st Division, Ninth Corps, where the leg was amputated below the knee by Surgeon W. C. Shurlock, 51st Pennsylvania. Assistant Surgeon S. Adams, U.S.A., who contributed the amputated bones [to the U.S. Army Medical Dept.] . . . reported that the patient nearly died during the operation from the effects of chloroform, having become pulseless and his

respiration having ceased. One week after the reception of the injury the patient was sent to City Point, and afterwards he passed through various hospitals . . ." (OMR) until discharged and pensioned from the US service on a Surgeons Certificate of Disability from wounds from an army general hospital, Sept. 12, 1865, by order of the War Dept. "In a subsequent statement furnished by B. F. Palmer, of Philadelphia, for an artificial leg, the amputation was described as having been performed by the flap method. In his application for commutation, dated 1870, the pensioner described the condition of the stump as sound and free from pain, and its length as one inch and three-fourths from the patella. The pensioner was paid March 4, 1875. He is reported as having died since that date" (OMR).

105. **Warren, Albert E.**, private. Res: Upton, MA. Credit: Worcester, MA. Born: Montpelier, VT. Age: 18. Height: 5′3″. Comp: light. Eyes: hazel. Hair: dark. Occup: bootmaker. Enlisted in Worcester by Capt. John Sanderson, Nov. 29, 1863; mustered Jan. 4, 1864. Deserted near the Rapidan River while on the march to the Wilderness, May 4, 1864. Never returned. "Bounty jumper" (JA).

106. **Warren, Hosea**, private. Res: Milford, MA. Born: Montpelier, VT. Age: 41. Comp: fair. Eyes: blue. Hair: light. Occup: bootmaker. Enlisted in Milford by Leonard Hunt, Dec. 18, 1863; mustered Jan. 4, 1864. Absent sick or on detached duty from on or before May 6 until between May 18 and May 24, 1864. In action at North Anna River, May 24, 1864, Cold Harbor, June 3, 1864, and Petersburg assaults, June 17 and 18, 1864; taken prisoner of war in action at the Petersburg Crater, July 30, 1864. Incarcerated in the Confederate prison in Danville, VA, where he died from disease, Oct. 1, 1864.

107. **White, William S.**, private. Res: Cornish, NH. Credit: Ashburnham, MA. Born: Cornish, NH. Age: 24. Married to Mary Emery, a volunteer nurse serving in Dale US Army General Hospital in Worcester, MA. Height: 5′8½″. Comp: fair. Eyes: hazel. Hair: dark. Occup: farmer. Enlisted in Ashburnham

by A. A. Walker, Dec. 29, 1863; mustered Jan. 4, 1864. In action and taken prisoner of war at the Wilderness, May 6, 1864. Paroled and exchanged on an unknown date. "Reported in the August rolls as a deserter, since discovered to have been a prisoner of war" (CR). Probably received extra pay for having been a prisoner of war. Discharged the US service for disability (probably from the army general hospital in the Camp of Parole in Annapolis, MD), July 20, 1865, by order of the War Dept. Had previous service as a private in Co. G, 5th New Hampshire Volunteer Infantry, from Sept. 2, 1861, until discharged for disability from Fortress Monroe, VA, March 26, 1863. Record of service with that regiment unknown. Resided in East Jaffrey, NH, and Gardner, MA, after the war. Died in Gardner, MA, in 1925, age 85, and buried in Greenbower cemetery there with his wife and two sons.

108. **Willson, Hugh A.**, sergeant. Res: Shrewsbury, MA. Credit: Worcester, MA. Born: Banbury, Oxfordshire, England. Age: 18. Height: 5′5″. Comp: light. Eyes: blue. Hair: dark. Occup: currier. Enlisted in Worcester by Capt. John Sanderson, Nov. 30, 1863; mustered Jan. 4, 1864. In action at the Wilderness, May 6, 1864, Spotsylvania Court House, May 10, 12, and 18, 1864, North Anna River, May 24, 1864, Cold Harbor, June 3, 1864, and Petersburg assaults, June 17 and 18, 1864; taken prisoner of war at the Petersburg Crater, July 30, 1864. Incarcerated in the Confederate prison in Danville, VA, until paroled and exchanged, Nov. 26, 1864. Probably received extra pay for having been a prisoner. Returned to the regiment for duty on or before Jan. 4, 1865. Promoted corporal, Jan. 4, 1865, to date from Jan. 1, 1865. With the regiment in operations during the winter of 1865, and in action at Fort Stedman, March 25, 1865. Promoted sergeant, May 1, 1865, under RSO 42, by order of Lt. Col. Julius M. Tucker. Mustered out with the regiment at Delaney house, Washington, DC, July 30, 1865, and discharged in Readville, MA, Aug. 9, 1865, expiration of service. With the regiment on most marches and in most skirmishes and battles. Resided in Great Bend, Barton County, KS, after the war.

109. **Willson, William H.**, 1st sergeant. Res: Shrewsbury, MA. Credit: Worcester, MA. Born: Banbury, Oxfordshire, England. Age: 20. Height: 5'7". Comp: light. Eyes: blue. Hair: brown. Occup: clerk. Enlisted in Worcester by Capt. John Sanderson, Nov. 20, 1863; mustered Jan. 4, 1864. Promoted 1st sergeant, April 7, 1864, to date March 1, 1864, when 1st Sgt. Trussell was reduced to duty sergeant, under RSO 35, by order of Col. William F. Bartlett, "and will be respected and obeyed accordingly" (RSO). Killed in action at the Wilderness, May 6, 1864. Had previous service as a private in Co. K, 13th MVI, from July 16, 1861 until discharged, Dec. 29, 1862, for disability from wounds received at 2nd Bull Run, Aug. 30, 1862.

ROSTER AND DESCRIPTIVE LIST OF COMPANY B

Company B, known as the "Andover Company," was the second company to be mustered into United States service, and it was mustered by 2nd Lt. Daniel Madden, 6th United States Regular Cavalry. Those men mustered after Jan. 4, 1864, were mustered by both Madden and 1st Lt. Robert P. McKibben, 4th United States Regular Infantry. It was mustered out by Capt. Sylvester Keyser, 2nd Michigan Volunteer Infantry, ACM, 1st Division, IX Corps.

1. **Adams, Daniel V.**, private. Res. and/or credit: Oxford, MA. Born: Leicester, MA. Age: 18. Height: 5'6". Comp: light. Eyes: blue. Hair: light. Occup: shoemaker. Enlisted in Oxford by L. B. Corbin, Nov. 28, 1863; mustered Jan. 4, 1864. In action at the Wilderness, May 6, 1864, Spotsylvania Court House, May 10, 12, and 18, 1864, North Anna River, May 24, 1864, and Cold Harbor, June 3, 1864; wounded in the chest in action during the Petersburg assault, June 17, 1864. With the regiment on all marches and in all skirmishes and battles until wounded. Absent wounded in an army general hospital until after June 1, 1865. Mustered out with the regiment at Delaney house, Washington, DC, July 30, 1865, and discharged in Readville, MA, Aug. 9, 1865, expiration of service. Resided in Oxford, MA, after the war.

2. **Adams, Loring J.**, private. Res. and/or credit: Oxford, MA. Born: Leicester, MA. Age: 20. Height: 5'8". Comp: dark. Eyes: hazel. Hair: black. Occup: shoemaker. Enlisted in Oxford by L. B. Corbin, Nov. 28, 1863; mustered Jan. 4, 1864. Never in combat. Absent sick from on or before May 6, 1864, until discharged the US service on a Surgeons Certificate of Disability from an army general hospital in Philadelphia, PA, Nov. 26, 1864, by order of the War Dept. Resided in Oxford, MA, after the war.

3. **Austin, Caleb S.**, private. Res. and/or credit: Northboro, MA. Born: Stowe, MA. Age: 38. Height: 5'5½". Comp: fair. Eyes: blue. Hair: brown. Occup: laborer. Enlisted in Northboro by W. C. Bush, Dec. 17, 1863; mustered Jan. 4, 1864. Absent sick or on detached duty from on or before May 6, 1864, until between Oct. 8 and Dec. 2, 1864. Listed in the company journal as absent without leave as a straggler, Dec. 2, 1864, but returned to the regiment, Dec. 3, 1864. With the regiment in operations during the winter of 1864–65, and wounded in action and taken prisoner of war at Fort Stedman, March 25, 1865. Paroled and exchanged from Libby Prison in Richmond, VA, about March 30, 1865. Never returned to the regiment, and was discharged the US service for disability from wounds, May 24, 1865, from the army general hospital in the Camp of Parole in Annapolis, MD, under GO 77, par. 6, AGO, War Dept. Resided in Wilkinsonville, MA, after the war.

4. **Ballou, George S.**, private. Res: Westboro, MA. Credit: Worcester, MA. Born: Saratoga, NY. Age: 25. Height: 5'8½". Comp: dark.

Eyes: gray. Hair: dark. Occup: bootmaker. Enlisted in Worcester by Lt. E. Dexter Cheney, Jan. 9, 1864; mustered Jan. 11, 1864. Never in combat. Absent sick in an army general hospital from on or before May 6, 1864, until discharged the US service for disability, Aug. 8, 1865, by order of the War Dept. Died before 1896, but date not known.

5. **Bates, William,** private. Res. and/or credit: North Brookfield, MA. Born: Charlton, MA. Age: 37. Height: 5′9″. Comp: dark. Eyes: black. Hair: brown. Occup: shoemaker. Enlisted in North Brookfield by Aaron Smith, Dec. 19, 1863; mustered Jan. 4, 1864. Wounded in action and taken prisoner of war at the Wilderness, May 6, 1864. Died from his wounds in the Confederate hospital in Gordonsville, VA, June 6, 1864.

6. **Bemis, Adelbert W.,** private. Res. and/or credit: Northboro, MA. Born: Southboro, MA. Age: 20. Height: 5′7⅜″. Comp: light. Eyes: blue. Hair: brown. Occup: laborer. Enlisted in Northboro by W. C. Bush, Dec. 17, 1863; mustered Jan. 4, 1864. In action at the Wilderness, May 6, 1864, and Spotsylvania Court House, May 10, 1864; taken prisoner of war in action there, May 12, 1864. Incarcerated in the Confederate prison camp in Andersonville, GA, May 29, 1864, where he died from scurvy, Sept. 11, 1864. Buried in grave, Sec. H, No. 8442, at Andersonville.

7. **Bemis, Ezra C.,** corporal. Res. and/or credit: Northboro, MA. Born: Southboro, MA. Age: 38. Height: 5′9″. Comp: dark. Eyes: brown. Hair: brown. Occup: shoemaker. Enlisted in Northboro by W. C. Bush, Dec. 17, 1863; mustered Jan. 4, 1864. Promoted corporal, Jan. 4, 1864. Absent sick in an army general hospital from on or before May 6 until Nov. 21, 1864. Issued a Springfield rifle, cartridge box, and bayonet by 1st Sgt. Paine of Co. E, Nov. 29, 1864. Reduced to the ranks by RSO from Lt. Col. Julius M. Tucker for an unknown reason, Dec. 19, 1864. With the regiment in operations during the winter of 1864–65, and in action at Fort Stedman, March 25, 1865. Detached and detailed to the 3rd Brigade, 1st Division, IX Corps, Quartermaster's Dept., in May or June 1865 until muster-out. Mustered out with the regiment at Delaney house, Washington, DC, July 30, 1865, and discharged in Readville, MA, Aug. 9, 1865, expiration of service. Had previous service as a private in Co. H, 29th MVI, from Dec. 23, 1861, until discharged for disability, Nov. 25, 1862. Observed the battle between the USS *Monitor* and CSS *Virginia (Merrimac)* fought in Hampton Roads, VA, March 9, 1862. Participated in the Peninsula campaign with that regiment in 1862, and possibly engaged at Antietam, Sept. 17, 1862. Died in 1874, age 49.

8. **Black, Henry E.,** private. Res: Holden, MA. Credit: Worcester, MA. Born: Holden, MA. Age: 18. Height: 5′9″. Comp: light. Eyes: blue. Hair: dark. Occup: farmer. Enlisted in Worcester by Capt. Joseph W. Gird, Dec. 7, 1863; mustered Jan. 4, 1864. In action at the Wilderness, May 6, 1864, and Spotsylvania Court House, May 10, 1864; wounded in the head in action there, May 12, 1864. Absent wounded in the 2nd Division, IX Corps, Hospital in Alexandria, VA, where he died, Feb. 22, 1865, of an "inflamed brain" (CR). Company received word of his death on March 2, 1865.

9. **Bradley, John,** private. Res. and/or credit: Milford, MA. Born: County Donegal, Ireland, Dec. 25, 1823. Age: 40. Height: 5′9¾″. Comp: fair. Eyes: gray. Hair: light. Occup: bootmaker. Enlisted in Milford by Leonard Hunt, Jan. 4, 1864; mustered Jan. 11, 1864. Furloughed home because of illness from March 10 until March 20, 1864, but furlough extended on March 20 to March 28, 1864, for the same reason. In action at the Wilderness, May 6, 1864, Spotsylvania Court House, May 10, 12, and 18, 1864, North Anna River, May 24, 1864, and Cold Harbor, June 3, 1864; wounded by Minié balls in the right hip, right side, and chest in action in the Petersburg assault, June 17, 1864. With the regiment on all marches and in all skirmishes and battles until wounded. Absent wounded in an army general hospital in Annapolis, MD, until May 27, 1865. Mustered out with the regiment at Delaney house, Washington, DC, July 30,

1865, and discharged in Readville, MA, Aug. 9, 1865, expiration of service. Died Dec. 23, 1871, age 47.

10. **Brewer, Warren E.**, private. Res. and/or credit: Worcester, MA. Born: Templeton, MA. Age: 18. Height: 5'5". Comp: light. Eyes: gray. Hair: light. Occup: machinist. Enlisted in Worcester by Lt. E. Dexter Cheney, Dec. 5, 1863; mustered Jan. 4, 1864. Wounded in action at the Wilderness, May 6, 1864. Absent wounded in an army general hospital until between Oct. 8 and Oct. 31, 1864. With the regiment in all operations during the fall and winter of 1864–65 from at least Oct. 31, 1864, and wounded again in action at Fort Stedman, March 25, 1865. Absent wounded in an army general hospital in Washington, DC, until discharged the US service for disability from wounds, June 14, 1865, under GO 77, par. 6, AGO, War Dept. Died in 1871, age 26.

11. **Brigdale, James**, private. Res. and/or credit: Milford, MA. Born: County Clare, Ireland, Dec. 25, 1819. Age: 45. Height: 5'5". Comp: dark. Eyes: dark. Hair: dark. Occup: bootmaker. Enlisted in Milford by Lt. John Reade, Dec. 2, 1863; mustered Jan. 4, 1864. Did not leave Camp Wool with the regiment, but sent to Camp Meigs in Readville, MA, April 18, 1864, under the supervision of Lt. John Cook, for a medical examination. Found unfit for duty by a "board of inspectors." Rejected recruit and discharged the US service in Worcester, MA, June 29, 1864, by order of Maj. Gen. John A. Dix, War Dept. Had previous service as a private in Co. K, in the all-Irish 28th MVI from Dec. 13, 1861, until discharged for disability in Falmouth, VA, April 20, 1863. Participated in operations in South Carolina with that regiment in 1862, 2nd Bull Run, Aug. 29, 1862, Chantilly, Sept. 1, 1862, South Mountain, Sept. 14, 1862, Antietam, Sept. 17, 1862, and Fredericksburg, Dec. 13, 1862.

12. **Brigham, Albert**, private. Res. and credit: Westboro, MA. Born: Westboro, MA. Age: 18. Height: 5'8". Comp: dark. Eyes: black. Hair: brown. Occup: farmer. Enlisted in Westboro by W. W. Fay, Dec. 1, 1863; mus-

tered Jan. 4, 1864. In action at the Wilderness, May 6, 1864, and Spotsylvania Court House, May 10, 1864; wounded in action there, May 12, 1864. Absent wounded in Emory US Army General Hospital in Washington, DC, until discharged the US service for disability from wounds, June 10, 1865, under SO 77, par. 6, AGO, War Dept. Died July 10, 1887, age 42.

13. **Brigham, Calvin L.**, private. Res. and credit: Westboro, MA. Born: Westboro, MA. Age: 19. Height: 5'9". Comp: fair. Eyes: gray. Hair: brown. Occup: farmer. Enlisted in Westboro by W. W. Fay, Dec. 1, 1863; mustered Jan. 4, 1864. In action at the Wilderness, May 6, 1864, Spotsylvania Court House, May 10, 12, and 18, 1864, North Anna River, May 24, 1864, and Cold Harbor, June 3, 1864; wounded in action in the Petersburg assault, June 17, 1864. With the regiment on all marches and in all skirmishes and battles until wounded. Absent wounded in an army general hospital until discharged the US service for disability from wounds, June 26, 1865, by order of the War Dept. Resided in Clinton, MA, after the war.

14. **Brigham, Charles L.**, private. Res. and/or credit: North Brookfield, MA. Born: Canada. Age: 36. Height: 5'7". Comp: light. Eyes: brown. Hair: brown. Occup: shoemaker. Enlisted in North Brookfield by Aaron Smith, Dec. 14, 1863; mustered Jan. 4, 1864. Detached and detailed on recruiting service in Springfield, MA, under Capt. Lewis A. Tifft from Feb. 13, 1864, until returned to the regiment for duty, April 5, 1864, under RSO 7, dated Feb. 12, 1864, by order of Col. William F. Bartlett. In action at the Wilderness, May 6, 1864, Spotsylvania Court House, May 10, 12, and 18, 1864, North Anna River, May 24, 1864, and Cold Harbor, June 3, 1864; mortally wounded through the genitals in action during the Petersburg assault, June 17, 1864. Died from wounds in the 1st Division, IX Corps, Field Hospital, June 22, 1864. With the regiment on all marches and in all skirmishes and battles until wounded.

15. **Bryant, Amasa**, private. Res. and/or credit: Northampton, MA. Born: England.

Age: 22. Height: 5'5½". Comp: light. Eyes: blue. Hair: brown. Occup: mechanic. Enlisted in Northampton by H. K. Starkweather, Dec. 16, 1863. Wounded in action at the Wilderness, May 6, 1864. Absent wounded in an army general hospital until returned to the regiment for duty between Oct. 8 and Nov. 19, 1864. Absent sick in the 1st Division, IX Corps, Field Hospital from Nov. 20 until Nov. 23, 1864. After turning over his rifle and complete equipment to Sgt. Horace Pike of Co. G, he was sent to the 1st Division, IX Corps, Field Hospital again from Dec. 10, 1864, until Jan. 2, 1865. With the regiment in operations during the winter of 1865, and in action at Fort Stedman, March 25, 1865. Wounded again by shrapnel from the explosion of a Confederate mortar shell while on duty in the trenches at Petersburg, March 29, 1865. Remained with the regiment until sent to the 1st Division, IX Corps, Field Hospital, April 5, 1865. Mustered out, as absent wounded, at Delaney house, Washington, DC, July 30, 1865, and discharged from an army general hospital, Aug. 23, 1865, expiration of service. Had previous service as a private in Co. E, 6th Vermont Volunteer Infantry (specifics unknown).

16. **Buckley, Jeremiah "Jerry,"** private. Res. and/or credit: Worcester, MA. Born: County Kerry, Ireland. Age: 32. Height: 5'2½". Comp: dark. Eyes: gray. Hair: dark. Occup: laborer. Enlisted in Worcester by Lt. E. Dexter Cheney, Jan. 2, 1864; mustered Jan. 4, 1864. Never in combat. Absent on detached duty from on or before May 6, 1864, until absent sick in the 1st Division, IX Corps, Field Hospital at Petersburg, Nov. 26, 1864. Transferred to an army general hospital in Baltimore, MD, on an unknown date, where he died from disease, Feb. 8, 1865. Company received notice of his death, Feb. 20, 1865.

17. **Bullard, Francis "Frank" W.,** private. Res: Westboro, MA. Credit: Worcester, MA. Born: Westboro, MA. Age: 18. Height: 5'2". Comp: light. Eyes: hazel. Hair: dark. Occup: farmer. Enlisted in Worcester by Capt. Joseph W. Gird, Nov. 19, 1863; mustered Jan. 4, 1864. Severely wounded in the left leg in action at the Wilderness, May 6, 1864. Left

leg surgically amputated by the flap method in the 1st Division, IX Corps, Field Hospital, May 7, 1864, by a captured Confederate surgeon, and reamputated higher up, May 8, 1864, following complications. Absent wounded in Camp Meigs US Army General Hospital in Readville, MA, until discharged and pensioned from the US service on a Surgeons Certificate of Disability for wounds, Nov. 23, 1865, by order of the War Dept. Resided in Westboro, MA, after the war and was the postmaster there for many years. President of the 57th's regimental association in 1886.

18. **Burke, Thomas,** private. Res. and/or credit: Worcester, MA. Born: County Kerry, Ireland. Age: 21. Height: 5'7". Comp: light. Eyes: blue. Hair: brown. Occup: molder. Enlisted in Worcester by J. M. Stridly, Dec. 22, 1863; mustered Jan. 11, 1864. In action at the Wilderness, May 6, 1864, and Spotsylvania Court House, May 10, 12, and 18, 1864; mortally wounded in action at North Anna River, May 24, 1864. Died from wounds, June 4, 1864.

19. **Callahan, Jeremiah,** private. Res. and/or credit: Northbridge, MA. Born: Ireland. Age: 30. Height: 5'7¾". Comp: dark. Eyes: brown. Hair: brown. Occup: laborer. Enlisted in Northbridge by L. F. Smith, Jan. 1, 1864; mustered Jan. 11, 1864. In action at the Wilderness, May 6, 1864, Spotsylvania Court House, May 10, 12, and 18, 1864, and North Anna River, May 24, 1864; taken prisoner of war at Cold Harbor, June 2, 1864. Incarcerated in the Confederate prison camp in Andersonville, GA, where he died from diarrhea and scurvy, Aug. 29, 1864. Buried in grave, Sec. E, No. 7230, at Andersonville. With the regiment on all marches and in all skirmishes and battles until captured.

20. **Chapin, David N.,** corporal. Res: Westboro, MA. Credit: Worcester, MA. Born: Westboro, MA. Age: 25. Height: 5'10". Comp: light. Eyes: hazel. Hair: dark. Occup: shoemaker. Enlisted in Worcester by Lt. E. Dexter Cheney, Jan. 2, 1864; mustered Jan. 4, 1864. Promoted corporal, Jan. 4, 1864. Never in combat. Absent sick from on or before May 6, 1864, until discharged the US service for

disability from an army general hospital in Washington, DC, July 7, 1864, by order of Maj. Gen. Christopher C. Auger, commanding the Dept. of Washington, DC. Had previous service as an enlisted man in the US Marine Corps from June 13, 1861, until discharged for disability from the Marine Corps barracks in Boston, MA, March 16, 1863. Served at the Marine Corps barracks in Brooklyn, NY, and on the USS *Potomac.* Resided in Westboro, MA, after the war and died there, Nov. 5, 1879, age 40. "He was a brave soldier, one who was faithful to his country during the dark days of the war, true to his friends and a devoted Christian" (JA). (Note: Part of this statement appears to be inconsistent with the facts.)

21. **Cheney, Eben Dexter,** 1st lieutenant. Res. and/or credit: Worcester, MA. Born: Massachusetts. Age: 21. No description available. Occup: clerk. Commissioned 2nd lieutenant, Dec. 31, 1863; mustered 2nd lieutenant, Jan. 4, 1864. Commissioned 1st lieutenant, Jan. 19, 1864; mustered 1st lieutenant, Jan. 20, 1864. In action at the Wilderness, May 6, 1864, Spotsylvania Court House, May 10, 12, and 18, 1864, North Anna River, May 24, 1864, Cold Harbor, June 3, 1864, and Petersburg assaults, June 17 and 18, 1864; shot through the head and killed by a Confederate sharpshooter while on duty in the trenches at Petersburg, July 19, 1864. Remains embalmed and sent home. Buried in Worcester, MA, July 28, 1864. With the regiment on all marches and in all skirmishes and battles until killed. Had previous service as a sergeant in Co. F, 51st MVI, from Sept. 8, 1862, until mustered out, July 27, 1863. Participated in the North Carolina campaign with that regiment in 1862–63. "Of high personal character and greatly esteemed, of a quiet, thoughtful disposition and one who always acted from conscientious motives without regard to whether they were in popular favor or not; strictly temperate, kind and considerate of others, a zealous officer, and loyal in his devotion to friends" (JA).

22. **Childs, James M.,** 2nd lieutenant. Res. and/or credit: Worcester, MA. Born: Rutland, MA. Age: 36. Height: 5'9". Comp: dark.

Eyes: blue. Hair: dark. Occup: tradesman. Enlisted in Worcester by Capt. Joseph W. Gird, Dec. 22, 1863; mustered Jan. 4, 1864. Promoted 1st sergeant, Jan. 4, 1864. Detached and detailed on recruiting service from Feb. 7, 1864, until before April 9, 1864, by RSO 16, postdated Feb. 29, 1864, from Col. William F. Bartlett. Commissioned 2nd lieutenant, April 9, 1864, but not mustered. Attached temporarily to Co. K. Missing in action at the Wilderness, May 6, 1864. Never accounted for and presumed killed. Had previous service as a private in Co. F, 51st MVI, from Sept. 8, 1862, until mustered out, July 27, 1863. Participated in the North Carolina campaign with that regiment in 1862–63. "He was of a quiet, retiring disposition, painstaking in all matters . . ." (JA).

23. **Clark, Robert,** private. Res. and/or credit: Worcester, MA. Born: Sturbridge, MA. Age: 17. Height: 5'4½". Comp: dark. Eyes: gray. Hair: dark. Occup: laborer. Enlisted from the reform school in Westboro by Lt. E. Dexter Cheney, Dec. 29, 1863; mustered Jan. 11, 1864. Deserted from Camp Wool, Feb. 3, 1864. Arrested, returned, and confined in the guardhouse in Camp Wool, Feb. 22, 1864. Escaped from the guardhouse during the evening of Feb. 27, 1864, and deserted again. Arrested, returned to the regiment, March 1, 1864, and confined in the guardhouse again. Escaped from the guardhouse and deserted yet again, March 6, 1864. Arrested and returned to the regiment for the third time, March 8, 1864, and confined in the guardhouse until March 27, 1864, when ordered released under guard by Dr. Whitman V. White. Deserted for the fourth time from Camp Wool, April 1, 1864. Arrested and returned to the regiment about April 7, 1864. Sick with typhoid fever and ordered to be released from the guardhouse and sent to the hospital at Camp Wool by Dr. White. Released from the hospital and returned to duty no later than April 18, 1864. Did not desert again. In action at the Wilderness, May 6, 1864, and Spotsylvania Court House, May 10, 1864; slightly wounded through the shoulder blade there, May 12, 1864. Absent wounded in an army general hospital until returned to the regiment for duty, Nov. 24, 1864. Sent

sick to the 1st Division, IX Corps, Field Hospital, Dec. 10, 1864, "and he did not turn in his gun" (CR). Returned to the regiment for duty, Dec. 27, 1864. Absent sick in the 1st Division, IX Corps, Field Hospital again, from Jan. 4 until Jan. 30, 1865. With the regiment in operations during the winter of 1865, and in action at Fort Stedman, March 25, 1865. Detached and detailed for duty (probably as a guard) at the quartermaster's dept. in Alexandria, VA, May 31, 1865, until muster-out. Mustered out with the regiment at Delaney house, Washington, DC, July 30, 1865, and discharged in Readville, MA, Aug. 9, 1865, expiration of service. Resided in Tolland, CT, after the war.

24. **Clark, William H.**, private. Res. and/or credit: Sutton, MA. Born: Grafton, MA. Age: 19. Height: 5′6″. Comp: dark. Eyes: gray. Hair: brown. Occup: bootmaker. Enlisted in Sutton by Capt. Joseph W. Gird, Nov. 23, 1864; mustered Jan. 4, 1864. Wounded in action at the Wilderness, May 6, 1864. Absent wounded in an army general hospital in Washington, DC, until discharged the US service on a Surgeons Certificate of Disability for wounds, Dec. 29, 1864, by order of the War Dept. Had previous service as a private in Co. I, 51st MVI, from Aug. 19, 1862, until mustered out, July 27, 1863. Participated in the North Carolina campaign with that regiment in 1862–63. Died Jan. 2, 1890, age 45.

25. **Crowe, Patrick**, corporal. Res: Westboro, MA. Credit: Worcester, MA. Born: County Clare, Ireland. Age: 23. Height: 5′8½″. Comp: dark. Eyes: hazel. Hair: black. Occup: farmer. Enlisted in Worcester by Capt. Joseph W. Gird, Dec. 29, 1864; mustered Jan. 4, 1864. Promoted corporal, Jan. 4, 1864. Wounded in action at the Wilderness, May 6, 1864. Absent wounded in an army general hospital until Feb. 20, 1865. In action at Fort Stedman, March 25, 1865. Absent sick in the 1st Division, IX Corps, Field Hospital from April 7 until April 22, 1865. Listed in the company journal as "present sick," April 26 until May 14, 1865, when he is listed as "present for duty." Mustered out with the regiment at Delaney house, Washington, DC, July 30, 1865, and discharged in Readville,

MA, Aug. 9, 1865, expiration of service. Had previous service as an enlisted man in the US Marine Corps from July 29, 1861, until discharged for disability from the Marine Corps barracks in Brooklyn, NY, Dec. 3, 1862. Served on the USS *Congress* and the USS *Powhatan*. Possibly aboard the *Congress* when the CSS *Virginia* ran her aground in Hampton Roads, VA, March 8, 1862.

26. **Culver, Charles E.**, private. Res. and/or credit: Otis, MA. Born: Naugatuck, CT. Age: 22. Height: 5′3″. Comp: dark. Eyes: blue. Hair: dark. Occup: farmer. Enlisted in Otis by A. Crittenden, Dec. 23, 1863; mustered Jan. 4, 1864. In action at the Wilderness, May 6, 1864, Spotsylvania Court House, May 10, 12, and 18, 1864; North Anna River, May 24, 1864, Cold Harbor, June 3, 1864, Petersburg assaults, June 17 and 18, 1864, and Petersburg Crater, July 30, 1864; missing in action at Weldon Railroad, Aug. 19, 1864. With the regiment on all marches and in all skirmishes and battles until missing. Absent missing until April 16, 1865. (His whereabouts during those eight months are unknown. He is not listed as a prisoner of war, a deserter, on detached duty, or sick. The entry in the company journal for April 16 simply states "Private Charles Culver from missing in action to present for duty.") Detached and detailed at the quartermaster's dept. (probably as a guard) in Alexandria, VA, from May 31, 1865, until muster-out. Mustered out with the regiment at Delaney house, Washington, DC, July 30, 1865, and discharged in Readville, MA, Aug. 9, 1865, expiration of service. Resided in Naugatuck, CT, after the war.

27. **Dayton, Benjamin F.**, corporal. Res: Auburn, MA. Credit: Worcester, MA. Born: Norton, MA. Age: 18. Height: 5′7½″. Comp: dark. Eyes: gray. Hair: dark. Occup: shoemaker. Enlisted in Worcester by Lt. E. Dexter Cheney, Jan. 5, 1864; mustered Jan. 11, 1864. Promoted corporal, to date from Jan. 4, 1864. In action at the Wilderness, May 6, 1864, and Spotsylvania Court House, May 10, 1864; wounded in the left leg in action there, May 12, 1864. Left leg surgically amputated by the circular method, May 27, 1864, by Dr. O. A. Judson, USV, and reamputated higher

up in Aug. 1864, following complications. Absent wounded until discharged and pensioned from the US service on a Surgeons Certificate of Disability for wounds from an army general hospital in Boston, MA, Dec. 27, 1864, by order of Maj. Gen. John A. Dix, War Dept.

28. **Dolan, John**, private. Res. and/or credit: Westboro, MA. Born: Roxbury, MA. Age: 18. Height: 5'4½". Comp: light. Eyes: brown. Hair: dark. Occup: chair seater. Enlisted in Westboro by E. Bullard, Dec. 22, 1863; mustered Jan. 4, 1864. Absent sick or on detached duty from on or before May 6, 1864, until after Oct. 8, 1864. Listed in the company journal as "present in confinement" from Dec. 30, 1864, until an unknown date and for an unknown reason. With the regiment in operations during the winter of 1865, and in action at Fort Stedman, March 25, 1865. Detailed on daily duty (probably as an orderly or guard) from May 28, 1865, until muster-out. Mustered out with the regiment at Delaney house, Washington, DC, July 30, 1865, and discharged in Readville, MA, Aug. 9, 1865, expiration of service. Resided in Worcester, MA, after the war.

29. **Donahue, John**, private. Res. and/or credit: Worcester, MA. Born: Ireland. Age: 30. Height: 5'2". Comp: light. Eyes: gray. Hair: light. Occup: tailor. Enlisted in Worcester by Capt. Joseph W. Gird, Nov. 30, 1863; mustered Jan. 4, 1864. Never in combat. Absent sick in Mount Pleasant US Army General Hospital in Washington, DC, from on or before May 6, 1864, until discharged the US service for disability, June 13, 1865, under GO 77, par. 6, AGO, War Dept. Died March 15, 1867, age 34.

30. **Flagg, Henry C.**, 1st sergeant. Res: Westboro, MA. Credit: Worcester, MA. Born: Westboro, MA. Age: 21. Height: 5'7½". Comp: dark. Eyes: gray. Hair: brown. Occup: shoemaker. Enlisted in Worcester by Capt. Joseph W. Gird, Nov. 30, 1863; mustered Jan. 4, 1864. Promoted sergeant, Jan. 4, 1864. Promoted 1st sergeant on an unknown date, but probably in May 1864 to replace 1st St. Souther, missing at the Wilderness, May 6, 1864. In action at the Wilderness, May 6,

1864, Spotsylvania Court House, May 10, 12, and 18, 1864, North Anna River, May 24, 1864, Cold Harbor, June 3, 1864, Petersburg assaults, June 17 and 18, 1864, and Petersburg Crater, July 30, 1864; wounded in action at Weldon Railroad, Aug. 19, 1864. With the regiment on all marches and in all skirmishes and battles until wounded. Absent wounded in an army general hospital until Jan. 3, 1865. Detached and detailed to the 1st Division, IX Corps, Ambulance Corps, Feb. 15, 1865, by SO 30, IX Corps Headquarters, from Maj. Gen. John G. Parke, commanding IX Corps, dated Feb. 13, 1865, and remained on this duty until mustered out. Discharged the US service in Tennallytown, DC, June 13, 1865, to date June 1, 1865, as a supernumerary because of the consolidation of the 59th MVI with the 57th, under SO 254, par. 43, AGO, War Dept., dated May 26, 1865. Had previous service in Co. G, 6th New Hampshire Volunteer Infantry (specifics unknown). Resided in Lindley, MO, after the war.

31. **Fleming, Michael**, private. Res. and/or credit: Worcester, MA. Born: County Kerry, Ireland. Age: 18. Height: 5'9". Comp: light. Eyes: gray. Hair: brown. Occup: machinist. Enlisted in Worcester by Capt. Joseph W. Gird, Dec. 21, 1863; mustered Jan. 4, 1864. Wounded in action at the Wilderness, May 6, 1864. Absent wounded in the Army general hospital in West Philadelphia, PA, until he deserted from there, July 24, 1864. Evidently surrendered, probably under President Lincoln's proclamation of amnesty, as he is listed as mustered out but absent wounded at Delaney house, Washington, DC, July 30, 1865, expiration of service. Resided in Worcester, MA, after the war.

32. **Forbes, Willis A.**, sergeant. Res: Westboro, MA. Credit: Boston, MA. Born: Westboro, MA. Age: 18. Height: 5'10". Comp: light. Eyes: blue. Hair: brown. Occup: clerk. Enlisted in Boston by C. F. Mills, Nov. 28, 1863; mustered Jan. 4, 1864. Promoted corporal, Jan. 4, 1864. In action at the Wilderness, May 6, 1864, Spotsylvania Court House, May 10, 12, and 18, 1864, and North Anna River, May 24, 1864. Promoted sergeant, June 1, 1864. In action at Cold Harbor, June 3, 1864,

and the Petersburg assaults, June 17 and 18, 1864. Absent sick in an army general hospital from before July 30, 1864, until Jan. 19, 1865. In action at Fort Stedman, March 25, 1865. Reduced to the ranks for an unknown reason, June 26, 1865. Promoted sergeant again on an unknown date in July 1865. Mustered out with the regiment at Delaney house, Washington, DC, July 30, 1865, and discharged in Readville, MA, Aug. 9, 1865, expiration of service. Died in 1895, age 50.

33. **Freeman, James B.**, sergeant. Res. and/or credit: Worcester, MA. Born: Pleasant River, Nova Scotia, Canada. Age: 30. Height: 5′5½″. Comp: light. Eyes: brown. Hair: light. Occup: bootmaker. Enlisted in Worcester by Capt. Joseph W. Gird, Dec. 11, 1863; mustered Jan. 4, 1864; Promoted sergeant, Jan. 4, 1864, to date from Jan. 1, 1864. Acting 1st sergeant from Jan. 26 until Jan. 29, 1864. Missing in action at the Wilderness, May 6, 1864. Never accounted for and presumed killed. Had previous service as a private in Co. F, 15th MVI, from July 12, 1861, until discharged for disability, July 21, 1862. Probably participated with that regiment at Ball's Bluff, Oct. 21, 1861, and in the Peninsula campaign in 1862.

34. **Fuller, J. Henry**, corporal. Res. and/or credit: Worcester, MA. Born: Warwick, MA. Age: 21. Height: 5′4½″. Comp: light. Eyes: blue. Hair: dark. Occup: machinist. Enlisted in Worcester by Capt. Joseph W. Gird, Dec. 21, 1863; mustered Jan. 4, 1864. Promoted corporal, Jan. 4, 1864. Missing in action at the Wilderness, May 6, 1864. Never accounted for and presumed killed. Had previous service as a private in Co. D, 15th MVI, from July 12, 1861, until discharged for disability in Boston, MA, Jan. 22, 1863. Taken prisoner of war at Ball's Bluff, Oct. 21, 1861. Paroled in 1862.

35. **Gelray, Joseph W.**, captain. Res. and/or credit: Lowell, MA. Born: England. Age: 27. No description available. Occup: weaver. Commissioned captain, July 25, 1864; mustered captain, to date Oct. 19, 1864. Never in action with the 57th. In command of the company from Oct. 12, 1864, but not present, until discharged the US service, Dec. 1, 1864,

to accept a promotion as major in the 4th Massachusetts Volunteer Heavy Artillery, under SO 397, AGO, War Dept., dated Nov. 14, 1864. Had previous service as 1st lieutenant in Co. A, 2nd MVI, from May 25, 1861, until discharged to accept a commission in the 57th, July 24, 1864. Participated with the 2nd MVI in the Shenandoah Valley campaign in 1862 and Cedar Mountain, August 9, 1862; wounded in action at Antietam, Sept. 17, 1862; participated in the Chancellorsville campaign in May 1863, and wounded in action again at Gettysburg, July 3, 1863 (enlisted as a private, promoted corporal May 25, 1861, sergeant, date unknown, 2nd lieutenant, Dec. 25, 1862, 1st lieutenant, Nov. 1, 1863). Had subsequent service as major on the staff of the 4th Massachusetts Volunteer Heavy Artillery from Dec. 7, 1864 (date mustered major; commission to date Nov. 14, 1864) until discharged, June 17, 1865. On duty in the defenses of Washington, DC, with that regiment in 1865. Also had subsequent service as captain in the 45th United States Regular Infantry from July 28, 1866, until retired from active service, Dec. 15, 1870, because of the loss of his right arm from wounds received in action. Appointed brevet lieutenant colonel, US Army, "for gallant and meritorious services in the battle of Gettysburg," to date from March 2, 1867, under GO 89, AGO, War Dept., Sept. 26, 1867.

36. **Gerry, Albert S.**, private. Res. and/or credit: Millbury, MA. Born: Grafton, MA. Age: 27. Height: 5′7″. Comp: dark. Eyes: blue. Hair: dark. Occup: gunsmith. Enlisted in Millbury by C. D. Morse, Dec. 29, 1863; mustered Jan. 4, 1864. In action at the Wilderness, May 6, 1864, Spotsylvania Court House, May 10, 12, and 18, 1864, North Anna River, May 24, 1864, and Cold Harbor, June 3, 1864; wounded in the face in action during the Petersburg assault, June, 17, 1864. With the regiment on all marches and in all skirmishes and battles until wounded. Absent wounded in an army general hospital until Jan. 6, 1865. Detached and detailed (probably as a guard) at the 3rd Brigade, 1st Division, IX Corps, Quartermaster's Dept., March 17, 1865, under RSO 30, dated March 15, 1865, by order of Lt. Col. Julius M. Tucker, until

muster-out. Mustered out with the regiment at Delaney house, Washington, DC, July 30, 1865, and discharged in Readville, MA, Aug. 9, 1865, expiration of service. Resided in the Soldiers Home in Togus, ME, after the war.

37. **Gird, Joseph W.**, captain. Res: Fitchburg, MA. Credit: Worcester, MA. Born: Jackson, LA (one of the four Southern-born soldiers in the regiment). Age: 24. Married. Height: unknown. Comp: light. Eyes: blue. Hair: brown. Occup: law student and assistant editor of the *Fitchburg Reveille.* Commissioned 1st lieutenant, Nov. 3, 1863; mustered 1st lieutenant, Nov. 4, 1863. Commissioned captain, Dec. 31, 1863; mustered captain, Jan. 4, 1864. Placed under arrest in Camp Wool for one day, Feb, 6, 1864, for an unknown reason. Shot through the head and killed in action at the Wilderness, May 6, 1864. Had previous service as a private in Co. F, 25th MVI, from Oct. 4, 1861, until discharged to accept a commission Aug. 26, 1862. Participated in the North Carolina campaign with that regiment in 1862. Also had service as 1st lieutenant and adjutant on the staff of the 36th MVI to date from Aug. 11, 1862, until resigned and discharged as a member of Co. H, May 19, 1863. Participated with that regiment at Fredericksburg, Dec. 13, 1862, and on duty in Kentucky in 1863.

Captain Joseph W. Gird.
(John Anderson)

38. **Goodnow, Hiram M.**, private. Res. and/or credit: Hubbardston, MA. Born: New Braintree, MA Age: 21. Height: 5'8". Comp: light. Eyes: blue. Hair: light. Occup: farmer. Enlisted in Hubbardston by J. F. Woodward, Dec. 10, 1863; mustered Jan. 4, 1864. Did not leave Camp Wool with the regiment, but was sent to Camp Meigs in Readville, MA, April 18, 1864, under the supervision of Lt. John Cook for a medical examination. Found unfit for duty by a "board of inspectors." Rejected recruit and discharged the US service in Worcester, MA, June 29, 1864, by order of Maj. Gen. John A. Dix, War Dept. Had previous service as a private in Co. G, 31st MVI, from Dec. 28, 1861, until discharged for disability, July 17, 1862. Possibly participated on guard and provost duty in New Orleans, LA, with that regiment in 1862.

39. **Graves, Charles B.**, private. Res. and/or credit: Sutton, MA. Born: Hopkington, MA. Age: 31. Height: 5'5". Comp: dark. Eyes: gray. Hair: dark. Occup: farmer. Enlisted in Sutton by J. A. Dodge, Jan. 4, 1864; mustered Jan. 11, 1864. Absent sick in an army general hospital from on or before May 6, 1864, until between Oct. 8, 1864, and March 25, 1865. Mortally wounded in action at Fort Stedman, March 25, 1865. Died from wounds in the 1st Division, IX Corps, Field Hospital at Petersburg, March 27, 1865. Had previous service as a private in Co. H, 31st MVI, from Jan. 25, 1862, until discharged for disability in Kenner, LA, Sept. 26, 1862. Participated on guard and provost duty in New Orleans, LA, with that regiment in 1862.

40. **Green, George S.**, 2nd lieutenant. Res. and/or credit: Springfield, MA. Born: probably Springfield, MA. Age: 30. No description available. Occup: bridge builder. Commissioned 2nd lieutenant to date March 4, 1864. Reported to the company for duty, April 14, 1864; mustered 2nd lieutenant, April 18, 1864. In action at the Wilderness, May 6, 1864, and Spotsylvania Court House, May 10 12, and 18, 1864. Whereabouts unknown at North Anna River, May 24, 1864. Wounded in action again at Cold Harbor, June 3, 1864. Absent wounded until resigned and discharged the US service for disability from

wounds from an army general hospital in Annapolis, MD, Oct. 5, 1864, by order of the War Dept. Had previous service as 1st sergeant of Co. F, 10th MVI, from May 31, 1861, until discharged to accept a commission in the 57th, March 8, 1864. Participated with the 10th MVI in the Peninsula campaign in 1862, Fredericksburg, Dec. 13, 1862, Chancellorsville campaign, May, 1863, Gettysburg, July 1, 2, and 3, 1863, Rappahannock Station, Nov. 7, 1863, and the Mine Run campaign, Nov.–Dec., 1863. Breveted major of USV to date March 13, 1865, under GO 67, AGO, War Dept., dated July 16, 1867. Resided in Aurora, IL, after the war.

41. **Green, Myron D.,** private. Res: Westboro, MA. Credit: Worcester, MA. Born: Westboro, MA. Age: 18. Height: 5'4". Comp: dark. Eyes: gray. Hair: brown. Occup: farmer. Enlisted in Worcester by Capt. Joseph W. Gird, Nov. 30, 1863; mustered Jan. 4, 1864. In action at the Wilderness, May 6, 1864, Spotsylvania Court House, May 10, 12, and 18, 1864, North Anna River, May 24, 1864, Cold Harbor, June 3, 1864, and Petersburg assaults, June 17 and 18, 1864; wounded while on duty in the trenches at Petersburg, June 27, 1864. With the regiment on all marches and in all skirmishes and battles until wounded. Absent wounded until discharged the US service for disability from wounds from Mount Pleasant US Army General Hospital in Washington, DC, May 11, 1865, under GO 77, AGO, War Dept. Resided in Golden Gate, CA, after the war.

42. **Hall, Josiah Brainard,** corporal. Res: Holland, MA. Credit: Worcester, MA. Born: Wallingford, CT. Age: 21. Married: Abbie A. Samson. Height: 5'6½". Comp: dark. Eyes: hazel. Hair: dark. Occup: clerk. Enlisted in Worcester by Lt. E. Dexter Cheney, Dec. 30, 1863; mustered Jan. 4, 1864. Promoted corporal, Jan. 4, 1864. Severely wounded in action at the Wilderness, May 6, 1864 (shot through the body while stationed on the left of the regiment's line). Taken to a field hospital in Fredericksburg, VA, treated, and placed in the Southern Methodist Episcopal Church to await transportation to a general hospital. Transported from there on an unknown date

Private J. Brainard Hall (postwar photo). *(Post 10)*

in May 1864 to Camp Meigs US Army General Hospital in Readville, MA, and remained there until transferred to Co. A, 14th Regiment, VRC, Sept. 23, 1864. Discharged the US service as a sergeant of the VRC for disability from wounds, Jan. 21, 1865, by order of the War Dept. Resided in Worcester, MA, after the war and was employed as the court reporter for the *Worcester Gazette* during the 1880s. Aided on the committee to write the original regimental history, published in 1896 by Capt. John Anderson. Died in 1934, age 92, and buried in the New Cemetery in Ashburnham, MA, beside his wife.

43. **Hart, John A.,** private. Res: Westboro, MA. Credit: Worcester, MA. Born: Boston, MA. Age: 19. Height: 5'4". Comp: dark. Eyes: brown. Hair: light. Occup: baker. Enlisted in Worcester by Capt. Joseph W. Gird, Nov. 30, 1863; mustered Jan. 4, 1864. Detached and detailed on recruiting service with Capt. Lewis A. Tifft in Springfield, MA, Feb. 13, 1864, under RSO 7, dated Feb. 12, 1864, by order of Col. William F. Bartlett. Returned to the regiment for duty before April 18, 1864. Severely wounded in action at the Wilderness. Died from his wounds at an army

general hospital in Washington, DC, May 26, 1864.

44. **Hayden, Henry C.**, private. Res: Oxford, MA. Credit: Worcester, MA. Born: Maine. Age: 18. Height: 5'7". Comp: light. Eyes: brown. Hair: light. Occup: shoemaker. Enlisted in Worcester by Capt. John W. Sanderson, Nov. 21, 1863; mustered Jan. 4, 1864. In action at the Wilderness, May 6, 1864, Spotsylvania Court House, May 10, 12, and 18, 1864, North Anna River, May 24, 1864, and Cold Harbor, June 3, 1864; severely wounded in the side in action during the Petersburg assault, June 17, 1864. Died from his wounds in an army general hospital in Annapolis, MD, July 4, 1864. With the regiment on all marches and in all skirmishes and battles until wounded.

45. **Heintzleman, John W. C.**, private. Res: Auburn, MA. Credit: Worcester, MA. Born: Rotterdam, Holland. Age: 39. Height: 5'6½". Comp: dark. Eyes: hazel. Hair: dark. Occup: seaman. Enlisted in Worcester by Lt. E. Dexter Cheney, Jan. 2, 1864; mustered Jan. 4, 1864. Wounded in action and taken prisoner of war at the Wilderness, May 6, 1864. Paroled and exchanged from Lynchburg, VA, Confederate prison on an unknown date (probably in Oct. or Nov. 1864) and returned to the regiment for duty from the Camp of Parole in Annapolis, MD, Nov. 30, 1864. Absent sick in Depot Field Hospital at City Point, Petersburg, from early Dec. 1864 until discharged the US service on a Surgeons Certificate of Disability, Dec. 23, 1864, by order of the War Dept.

46. **Hill, Franklin,** private. Res: Barre, MA. Credit: Worcester, MA. Born: Clairmont, NH. Age: 20. Height: 5'6". Comp: sandy. Eyes: gray. Hair: light. Occup: farmer. Enlisted in Worcester by Capt. John W. Sanderson, Dec. 8, 1863; mustered Jan. 4, 1864. Deserted from Camp Wool, Jan. 4, 1864. Never returned. Had previous service as a private in Co. K, 32nd MVI, from July 28, 1862, until discharged for disability, Dec. 7, 1863. Possibly participated with that regiment at Fredericksburg, Dec. 13, 1862, in the Chancellorsville campaign in May, 1863, at Gettys-

burg, July 1, 2, and 3, 1863, and in the Mine Run campaign, Nov.–Dec., 1863. Also had subsequent service as a private in Co. I, 19th MVI, from Jan. 26, 1865, until deserted, March 31, 1865. Listed as an "escaped prisoner, Jan. 30, 1865" (CR: the meaning of this journal entry is unclear, but may indicate that he was discovered, returned to the 57th, placed under arrest for desertion, and deserted again on Jan. 30, 1865). On duty with the 19th MVI in Fort Emory at Petersburg while with that regiment.

47. **Holland, James H.**, private. Res: Westboro, MA. Credit: Boston, MA. Born: Boston, MA. Age: 18. Height: 5'6". Comp: light. Eyes: blue. Hair: auburn. Occup: clerk. Enlisted in Boston by W. W. Fay, Nov. 30, 1863; mustered Jan. 4, 1864. Never in combat. Absent sick in Kent US Army General Hospital in New Haven, CT, from May 2, 1864, until discharged the US service for disability, Aug. 2, 1865, by order of the War Dept. Died Feb. 11, 1875, age 30, from the effects of disease incurred while in the service.

48. **Hood, George F.**, private. Res. and/or credit: Worcester, MA. Born: Hollis, NH. Age: 18. Height: 5'9". Comp: dark. Eyes: dark. Hair: dark. Occup: farmer. Enlisted in Worcester by Lt. E. Dexter Cheney, Dec. 8, 1863; mustered Jan. 4, 1864. In action at the Wilderness, May 6, 1864, Spotsylvania Court House, May 10, 12, and 18, 1864, North Anna River, May 24, 1864, and Cold Harbor, June 3, 1864; severely wounded in action in the Petersburg assault, June 17, 1864. Died from his wounds in an army general hospital in Annapolis, MD, July 2, 1864. With the regiment on all marches and in all skirmishes and battles until wounded.

49. **Hooley, Daniel,** private. Res. and/or credit: Worcester, MA. Born: Kilkerian Bay, County Galway, Ireland. Age: 35. Height: 5'9½". Comp: sandy. Eyes: gray. Hair: dark. Occup: laborer. Enlisted in Worcester by Lt. E. Dexter Cheney, Dec. 5, 1863; mustered Jan. 4, 1864. In action at the Wilderness, May 6, 1864, Spotsylvania Court House, May 10, 12, and 18, 1864, North Anna River, May 24, 1864, Cold Harbor, June 3, 1864, and Peters-

burg assaults, June 17 and 18, 1864; severely wounded while on duty in the trenches at Petersburg, July 12, 1864. Died from wounds in the army general hospital on David's Island in New York Harbor, NY, Aug. 10, 1864. With the regiment on all marches and in all skirmishes and battles until wounded.

50. **Hubbard, George R.**, private. Res: Paxton, MA. Credit: Worcester, MA. Born: Paxton, MA. Age: 41. Height: 5'10¼". Comp: florid. Eyes: blue. Hair: sandy. Occup: bootmaker. Enlisted in Co. D in Worcester by D. Waldo Lincoln, Jan. 5, 1864; mustered Jan. 25, 1864. Transferred to Co. B, Feb. 25, 1864, by RSO 14 from Lt. Col. Edward P. Hollister, dated Feb. 22, 1864. Known by the nickname of "Query." Furloughed home because of illness from March 3 until March 14, 1864, but furlough extended on March 14 until March 20, 1864, for the same reason. In action at the Wilderness, May 6, 1864, Spotsylvania Court House, May 10, 12, and 18, 1864, North Anna River, May 24, 1864, Cold Harbor, June 3, 1864, and Petersburg assaults, June 17 and 18, 1864; mortally wounded by a Confederate sharpshooter while on duty in the trenches at Petersburg, July 24, 1864. Died from wounds in the 1st Division, IX Corps, Field Hospital at Petersburg, July 27, 1864. With the regiment on all marches and in all skirmishes and battles until wounded.

51. **Inman, George J.**, private. Res. and/or credit: Worcester, MA. Born: Smithfield, RI. Age: 18. Height: 5'5". Comp: light. Eyes: blue. Hair: dark. Occup: machinist. Enlisted in Worcester by Lt. E. Dexter Cheney, Jan. 5, 1864; mustered Jan. 11, 1864. Never in combat. Did not leave Camp Wool with the regiment, but sent to Camp Meigs in Readville, MA, April 18, 1864, under the supervision of Lt. John Cook for a medical examination. Found unfit for duty by a "board of inspectors." Remained in the hospital in Camp Meigs until discharged the US service for disability, May 27, 1865, by order of the War Dept.

52. **Joan, Antonio**, private. Res: Westboro, MA. Credit: Worcester, MA. Born: Sicily, Italy. Age: 18. Height: 5'3". Comp: dark.

Eyes: brown. Hair: black. Occup: blacksmith. Enlisted in Worcester by Capt. Joseph W. Gird, Nov. 30, 1863; mustered Jan. 4, 1864. In action at the Wilderness, May 6, 1864, and Spotsylvania Court House, May 10 and 12, 1864; wounded in action there, May 18, 1864. Absent wounded in an army general hospital until an unknown date between Oct. 8 and Oct. 31, 1864. Absent sick in the 1st Division, IX Corps, Field Hospital from Jan. 6 until Jan. 29, 1865. In action at Fort Stedman, march 25, 1865. Supposed to have been promoted sergeant, but company records do not substantiate that. Mustered out with the regiment at Delaney house, Washington, DC, July 30, 1865, and discharged in Readville, MA, Aug. 9, 1865, expiration of service. Resided in Medfield, MA, after the war. Died after 1925, date unknown.

53. **Keily, Martin**, private. Res. and/or credit: Worcester, MA. Born: County Waterford, Ireland. Age: 32. Height: 5'10". Comp: dark. Eyes: gray. Hair: dark. Occup: blacksmith. Enlisted in Worcester by Lt. E. Dexter Cheney, Jan. 5, 1864; mustered Jan. 11, 1864. In action at the Wilderness, May 6, 1864, Spotsylvania Court House, May 10, 12, and 18, 1864, North Anna River, May 24, 1864, Cold Harbor, June 3, 1864, and Petersburg assaults, June 17 and 18, 1864; taken prisoner of war in action at the Petersburg Crater, July 30, 1864. With the regiment on all marches and in all skirmishes and battles until captured. Incarcerated in the Confederate prison in Danville, VA, where he died from disease, Jan. 6, 1865.

54. **King, Simeon E.**, private. Res. and credit: Sutton, MA. Born: Sutton, MA. Age: 19. Height: 5'2½". Comp: light. Eyes: gray. Hair: light. Occup: teacher. Enlisted in Sutton by J. A. Dodge, Jan. 2, 1864; mustered Jan. 4, 1864. Detached and detailed as a clerk at the office of Col. J. W. Kimball (15th MVI and 53rd MVI) in Worcester, MA, Jan. 19, 1864, under RSO 16, by order of Lt. Col. Edward P. Hollister, postdated Feb. 29, 1864. Returned to the regiment for duty, April 12, 1864. Never in combat. Detached and detailed as a clerk at 1st Division, IX Corps, Headquarters from on or before May 6, 1864,

until after June 1, 1865. Mustered out with the regiment at Delaney house, Washington, DC, July 30, 1865, and discharged in Readville, MA, Aug. 9, 1865, expiration of service. Resided in West Millbury, MA, after the war.

55. Kirkup, Charles A., private. Res. and/or credit: Westboro, MA. Born: Newton, MA. Age: 18. Height: 5'4". Comp: light. Eyes: black. Hair: brown. Occup: bootmaker. Enlisted in Westboro by E. Bullard, Nov. 30, 1863; mustered Jan. 11, 1864. Wounded in action at the Wilderness, May 6, 1864. Absent wounded in Armory Square US Army General Hospital in Washington, DC, until transferred to the 17th Co., 2nd Battln., VRC, Jan. 25, 1865. Discharged the US service on a Surgeons Certificate of Disability for wounds, Aug. 10, 1865, by order of the War Dept.

56. Langdon, Milo T., private. Res. and/or credit: Otis, MA. Born: Westhampton, MA. Age: 39. Height: 5'11". Comp: sandy. Eyes: blue. Hair: sandy. Occup: farmer. Enlisted in Otis by A. Crittenden, Dec 10, 1863; mustered Jan. 4, 1864. In action at the Wilderness, May 6, 1864, and one of the 34 enlisted men who remained with the colors during that battle. In action at Spotsylvania Court House, May 10, 12, and 18, 1864. Absent sick in an army general hospital from between May 18 and May 24, 1864, until transferred to Co. E, 24th Regiment, VRC, Oct. 6, 1864. Discharged the US service for disability, Nov. 27, 1864, by order of the War Dept.

57. Leary, John, private. Res. and/or credit: Worcester, MA. Born: County Kerry, Ireland. Age: 34. Height: 5'9". Comp: dark. Eyes: gray. Hair: light. Occup: machinist. Enlisted in Worcester by Lt. E. Dexter Cheney, Dec. 22, 1863; mustered Jan. 4, 1864. In action at the Wilderness, May 6, 1864, Spotsylvania Court House, May 10, 12, and 18, 1864, North Anna River, May 24, 1864, and Cold Harbor, June 3, 1864; severely wounded in the chest in action during the Petersburg assault, June 17, 1864. Died from his wounds in an army general hospital, July 5, 1864. With the regiment on all marches and in all skirmishes and battles until wounded.

58. Leonard, Benjamin L., private. Res. and/or credit: Rutland, MA. Born: Hubbardston, MA. Age: 30. Height: 5'6". Comp: dark. Eyes: dark. Hair: black. Occup: bootmaker. Enlisted in Rutland by H. Wilson, Jan. 2, 1864; mustered Jan. 11, 1864. In action at the Wilderness, May 6, 1864, and wounded, but not in a major battle, on an unknown date later that month. Absent wounded in an army general hospital until between Aug. 19 and Sept. 30, 1864. In action at Poplar Grove Church, Sept. 30, 1864, and wounded again in action there, Oct. 8, 1864. Absent wounded in an army general hospital until Jan. 15, 1865. Detailed on daily duty as company cook, Feb. 16, 1865, under RSO 15, by order of Lt. Col. Julius M. Tucker, dated, Feb. 15, 1865. Missing in action at Fort Stedman, March 25, 1865. Returned to the regiment for duty, March 28, 1865 (whereabouts while missing unknown). Mustered out with the regiment at Delaney house, Washington, DC, July 30, 1865, and discharged in Readville, MA, Aug. 9, 1865, expiration of service. Resided at the Soldiers Home in Chelsea, MA, after the war, and died there, Jan. 17, 1896, age 62.

59. Lines, Dennis, private. Res. and/or credit: Milford, MA. Born: County Galway, Ireland. Age: 45. Height: 5'8". Comp: light. Eyes: blue. Hair: light. Occup: laborer. Enlisted in Milford by Leonard Hunt, Dec. 4, 1863; mustered Jan. 4, 1864. Never in combat. Absent sick in Cuyler US Army General Hospital in Germantown, PA, from on or before May 6, 1864, until discharged the US service for disability in Philadelphia, PA, June 28, 1865, under GO 77, par. 6, AGO, War Dept.

60. Lowell, Edward, private. Res. and/or credit: Northboro, MA. Born: Massachusetts. Age: 18. No description available. Occup: laborer. Enlisted in Northboro (recruiter unknown), Dec. 14, 1863; mustered Jan. 4, 1864. In action at the Wilderness, May 6, 1864, and one of the 34 enlisted men who remained with the colors during that battle. In action at Spotsylvania Court House, May 10, 12, and 18, 1864. Absent sick in an army general hospital from between May 18 and May 24, 1864, until Nov. 7, 1864. With the regiment in operations during the winter of 1864–65, and in action again at Fort Stedman, March 25, 1865. Listed in the company journal as "present sick" on May 15 and 16, 1865. Also listed in the company journal as "present sick" from May 25, 1865, until an unknown date. Mustered out with the regiment at Delaney house, Washington, DC, July 30, 1865, and discharged in Readville, MA, Aug. 9, 1865, expiration of service. Died before 1896, but date not known.

61. **Lynch, Bernard**, private. Res: Northbridge, MA. Credit: Worcester, MA. Born: Baltimore, County Cork, Ireland. Age: 39. Height: 5'9". Comp: dark. Eyes: blue. Hair: sandy. Occup: laborer. Enlisted in Worcester by Lt. E. Dexter Cheney, Dec. 9, 1863; mustered Jan. 4, 1864. Deserted from Camp Wool, Jan. 30, 1864. Never returned.

62. **Lyons, Patrick**, private. Res. and/or credit: Worcester, MA. Born: Ireland. Age: 27. Height: 5'6". Comp: dark. Eyes: gray. Hair: dark. Occup: laborer. Enlisted in Worcester by Lt. E. Dexter Cheney, Dec. 24, 1864; mustered Jan. 4, 1864. Detached and detailed on duty with Capt. G. P. Ladd at the 1st Division, IX Corps, Quartermaster's Dept.. Never in combat. Mustered out with the regiment at Delaney house, Washington, DC, July 30, 1865, and discharged in Readville, MA, Aug. 9, 1865, expiration of service. Died March 1, 1892, age 55.

63. **McCarthy, Daniel**, sergeant. Res. and/or credit: Westboro, MA. Born: Boston, MA. Age: 22. Height: 5'7½". Comp: dark. Eyes: brown. Hair: dark. Occup: boatbuilder. Enlisted in Westboro by Capt. Henry C. Ward, March 16, 1864; mustered April 6, 1864. Joined the company, March 31, 1864. In action at the Wilderness, May 6, 1864, and Spotsylvania Court House, May 10, 1864; wounded in action there, May 12, 1864. Absent wounded in an army general hospital until between Oct. 8 and Oct. 31, 1864. Promoted corporal, Jan. 1, 1865. With the regiment in operations during the fall and winter of 1864–65, and in action at Fort Stedman, March 25, 1865. Promoted sergeant, May 13, 1865, to date from May 1, 1865, by RSO 42,

by order of Lt. Col. Julius M. Tucker, dated May 1, 1865. Mustered out with the regiment at Delaney house, Washington, DC, July 30, 1865, and discharged in Readville, MA, Aug. 9, 1865, expiration of service. Had previous service in Co. C, 36th New York Volunteer Infantry (specifics unknown). Also had previous service as a 2nd class fireman in the US Navy from Feb. 21, 1862, until discharged for disability, Dec. 20, 1862. Served on the USS *Cincinnati* and the USS *Clara Dolsen*. Also had previous service as a private in Co. C, 1st (Massachusetts) Provisional Guards, into which he was drafted, July 14, 1863, on Long Island, Boston, MA, until discharged, Dec. 8, 1863. Record of service with that unit unknown. Resided in the Soldiers Home in Togus, ME, after the war.

64. **McDonough, Patrick**, private. Res. and/or credit: Lee, MA. Born: Ireland. Age: 20. Height: 5'6". Comp: light. Eyes: gray. Hair: brown. Occup: laborer. Enlisted in Lee by Sylvester S. May, Dec. 12, 1863; mustered Jan. 4, 1864. Did not leave Camp Wool with the regiment, but sent to Camp Meigs in Readville, MA, April 18, 1864, under the supervision of Lt. John Cook for a medical examination. Found unfit for duty by a "board of inspectors." Rejected recruit and discharged the US service in Worcester, MA, June 29, 1864, by order of Maj. Gen. John A. Dix, War Dept. Spent time on Gallup's Island, Boston Harbor, MA, for an unknown reason (probably sick in the hospital) and an unknown period before discharge.

65. **Magner, William**, 1st sergeant. Res. and/or credit: Westboro, MA. Born: Boston, MA. Age: 19. Height: 5'7". Comp: light. Eyes: blue. Hair: light. Occup: farmer. Enlisted in Westboro by E. Bullard, Dec. 4, 1863; mustered Jan. 4, 1864. Promoted corporal, May 1, 1864. In action at the Wilderness, May 6, 1864, Spotsylvania Court House, May 10, 12, and 18, 1864, and North Anna River, May 24, 1864. Promoted sergeant, June 1, 1864. In action at Cold Harbor, June 3, 1864, and the Petersburg assaults, June 17 and 18, 1864. Absent sick in an army general hospital from between June 18 and July 30, 1864, until between Oct. 8, 1864, and Jan. 1, 1865. With

the regiment on all marches and in all skirmishes and battles until absent sick. Promoted 1st sergeant, Jan. 1, 1865. On furlough for illness from Jan. 29 until Feb. 14, 1865. In action at Fort Stedman, March 25, 1865, and cited twice for bravery in that battle: "First Sergeant William Magner, Company B, general bravery" (JMT and GPR). Absent sick from April 7 until April 22, 1865. Listed in the company journal, April 26, 1865, as "from present for duty to present sick" until May 20, 1865, when he is listed as "from present sick to present for duty." Mustered out with the regiment at Delaney house, Washington, DC, July 30, 1865, and discharged in Readville, MA, Aug. 9, 1865, expiration of service. Resided in Westboro, MA, after the war and was deputy sheriff there until killed in Chestnut Hill, MA, by a Boston-Worcester trolley car on an unknown date after 1887.

66. **Mahan, Patrick,** private. Res. and/or credit: Milford, MA. Born: Galway, Ireland. Age: 35. Height: 5'10½". Comp: dark. Eyes: blue. Hair: black. Occup: bootmaker. Enlisted in Milford by A. J. Summers, Dec. 28, 1863; mustered Jan. 4, 1864. Did not leave Camp Wool with the regiment, but sent to Camp Meigs in Readville, MA, April 18, 1864, under the supervision of Lt. John Cook for a medical examination. Found unfit for duty by a "board of inspectors." Rejected recruit and discharged the US service in Worcester, MA, June 29, 1864, by order of Maj. Gen. John A. Dix, War Dept.

67. **Marah, Michael,** private. Res. and/or credit: Worcester, MA. Born: County Kerry, Ireland. Age: 21. Height: 5'8½". Comp: light. Eyes: brown. Hair: brown. Occup: molder. Enlisted in Worcester by Capt. Joseph W. Gird, Dec. 28, 1863; mustered Jan. 4, 1864. Never in a major battle, but wounded on an unknown date in May 1864. Absent wounded in Mount Pleasant US Army General Hospital in Washington, DC, until discharged the US service for disability from wounds, May 11, 1865, under GO 77, par. 6, AGO, War Dept., dated May 3, 1865.

68. **May, John E.,** private. Res: Holden, MA. Born: Worcester, MA. Age: 18. Height: 5'2".

Comp: light. Eyes: blue. Hair: light. Occup: farmer. Enlisted in Holden by Lt. E. Dexter Cheney, Nov. 28, 1863; mustered Jan. 4, 1864. In action at the Wilderness, May 6, 1864; wounded, but not in a major battle, on an unknown date later that month. Absent wounded in an army general hospital until after June 1, 1865. Mustered out with the regiment at Delaney house, Washington, DC, July 30, 1865, and discharged in Readville, MA, Aug. 9, 1865, expiration of service. Resided in Lynn, MA, after the war.

69. **Midgley, John,** corporal. Res. and/or credit: Worcester, MA. Born: Rochdale, Manchester, England. Age: 34. Height: 5'8". Comp: dark. Eyes: gray. Hair: dark. Occup: bootmaker. Enlisted in Worcester by Lt. E. Dexter Cheney, Dec. 7, 1863; mustered Jan. 4, 1864. Promoted corporal, Jan. 4, 1864. Wounded in action and taken prisoner of war at the Wilderness, May 6, 1864. Paroled and exchanged from Lynchburg Confederate prison, Oct. 8, 1864. Probably received extra pay for having been a prisoner of war. Absent sick and wounded in Dale US Army General Hospital in Worcester, MA, until discharged the US service for disability from wounds, Oct. 30, 1865, by order of the War Dept. Resided in Cherry Valley, MA, after the war.

70. **Moore, Lewis,** private. Res. and/or credit: Worcester, MA. Born: Framingham, MA. Age: 44. Height: 5'10½". Comp: dark. Eyes: black. Hair: black. Occup: truckman. Enlisted in Worcester by Capt. Joseph W. Gird, Jan. 1, 1864; mustered Jan. 4, 1864. Killed in action at the Wilderness, May 6, 1864.

71. **Moore, William A.,** private. Res. and/or credit: Millbury, MA. Born: Pomfret, CT. Age: 18. Height: 5'7". Comp: dark. Eyes: black. Hair: black. Occup: woodcutter. Enlisted in Millbury by J. E. Waters, Jan. 5, 1864; mustered Jan. 11, 1864. Absent sick in an army general hospital from on or before May 6 until March 1, 1865. In action at Fort Stedman, March 25, 1865. Mustered out with the regiment at Delaney house, Washington, DC, July 30, 1865, and discharged in Readville, MA, Aug. 9, 1865, expiration of service. Died March 5, 1881, age 35.

72. **Murry, John,** private. Res. and/or credit: Worcester, MA. Born: Lowell, MA. Age: 18. Height: 5'5". Comp: light. Eyes: gray. Hair: light. Occup: mill hand. Enlisted in Worcester by Lt. E. Dexter Cheney, Dec. 7, 1863; mustered Jan. 4, 1864. In action at the Wilderness, May 6, 1864, and Spotsylvania Court House, May 10, 1864; and wounded in action there, May 12, 1864. Absent wounded in an army general hospital until between Oct. 8 and Oct. 31, 1864. Placed in confinement with the regiment, Dec. 30, 1864, for an unknown reason (probably disobedience of orders) and an unknown length of time. With the regiment in operations during the winter of 1865, and in action at Fort Stedman, March 25, 1865. Detached and detailed as a 1st Division, IX Corps, provost guard in June 1865. Mustered out with the regiment at Delaney house, Washington, DC, July 30, 1865, and discharged in Readville, MA, Aug. 9, 1865, expiration of service. Resided in Boston, MA, after the war.

73. **Nealy, Ephraim E.,** private. Res. and/or credit: Sutton, MA. Born: Grafton, NH. Age: 43. Height: 5'9½". Comp: dark. Eyes: blue. Hair: black. Occup: shoemaker. Enlisted in Co. D in Sutton by J. A. Dodge, Jan. 11, 1864; mustered Jan. 25, 1864. Transferred to Co. B, Feb. 22, 1864, under RSO 14, by order of Lt. Col. Edward P. Hollister, dated Feb. 22, 1864. Never in combat. Absent sick in Satterlee US Army General Hospital in Philadelphia, PA, from May 1, 1864, until discharged the US service for disability in West Philadelphia, PA, May 22, 1865, under GO 77, par. 6, AGO, War Dept., dated May 3, 1865. Resided in Shrewsbury, MA, after the war.

74. **Newton, Amos P. Jr.,** Private. Res. and credit: Oxford, MA. Born: Oxford, MA. Age: 20. Height: 5'11". Comp: light. Eyes: blue. Hair: brown. Occup: farmer. Enlisted in Co. D in Oxford by L. B. Corbin, Jan. 5, 1864; mustered Jan. 25, 1864. Transferred to Co. B, Feb. 25, 1864, under RSO 14, from Lt. Col. Edward P. Hollister, dated Feb. 22, 1864. In action at the Wilderness, May 6, 1864, and one of the 34 enlisted men who remained with the colors during that battle. In action at

Spotsylvania Court House, May 10, 12, and 18, 1864; killed in action at North Anna River, May 24, 1864.

75. **Newton, Charles H.,** private. Res. and/or credit: Worcester, MA. Born: Westboro, MA. Age: 18. Height: 5'5". Comp: light. Eyes: blue. Hair: light. Occup: farmer. Enlisted in Worcester by Lt. E. Dexter Cheney, Jan. 4, 1864; mustered Jan. 11, 1864. Absent sick in an army general hospital from on or before May 6, 1864 until between Aug. 19 and Sept. 23, 1864. In action at Poplar Grove Church, Sept. 30 and Oct. 8, 1864, in other operations of the regiment during the fall and winter of 1864–65, and at Fort Stedman, March 25, 1865. Mustered out with the regiment at Delaney house, Washington, DC, July 30, 1865, and discharged in Readville, MA, Aug. 9, 1865, expiration of service. Resided in Worcester, MA, after the war.

76. **O'Conner, James,** private. Res. and/or credit: Worcester, MA. Born: County Kerry, Ireland. Age: 42. Height: 5'5½". Comp: dark. Eyes: blue. Hair: brown. Occup: laborer. Enlisted in Worcester by Lt. E. Dexter Cheney, Dec. 29, 1863; mustered Jan. 4, 1864. Did not leave Camp Wool with the regiment, but sent to Camp Meigs in Readville, MA, April 18, 1864, under the supervision of Lt. John Cook for a medical examination. Found unfit for duty by a "board of inspectors." Rejected recruit and discharged the US service in Worcester, MA, June 29, 1864, by order of Maj. Gen. John A. Dix, War Dept.

77. **Paddock, Charles Francis,** private. Res: Holden, MA. Credit: Worcester, MA. Born: Holden, MA, Aug. 30, 1848. Age: 15 (one of the three youngest members of the regiment). Height: 5'5". Comp: light. Eyes: blue. Hair: light. Occup: farmer. Enlisted in Worcester by Lt. E. Dexter Cheney, Dec. 14, 1863; mustered Jan. 4, 1864. In action at the Wilderness, May 6, 1864, Spotsylvania Court House, May 10, 12, and 18, 1864, North Anna River, May 24, 1864, and Cold Harbor, June 3, 1864. Absent during the Petersburg assaults, June 17 and 18, 1864, for an unknown reason. Wounded three times in the leg in action and

Private Charles F. Paddock
(postwar photo). *(John Anderson)*

taken prisoner of war at the Petersburg Crater, July 30, 1864. Incarcerated in Poplar Grove at Petersburg until transferred to Libby Prison in Richmond, VA. Paroled and exchanged from there, Oct 9, 1864, and sent to the army general hospital in the Camp of Parole, Annapolis, MD. Transferred to Chestnut Hill US Army General Hospital in Philadelphia, PA, until discharged the US service on a Surgeons Certificate of Disability for wounds, May 30, 1865, by order of the War Dept. Probably received extra pay for having been a prisoner. Resided in Uxbridge, MA, after the war.

78. **Parmer, John T.**, corporal. Res. and/or credit: Northboro, MA. Born: Berlin, MA. Age: 18. Height: 5′7″. Comp: florid. Eyes: dark. Hair: red. Occup: farmer. Enlisted in Northboro by Capt. Joseph W. Gird, Dec. 16, 1863; mustered Jan. 4, 1864. Absent sick in an army general hospital from on or before May 6, 1864, until Dec. 15, 1864, when he was listed in the company journal as "returned to duty from the hospital." Promoted corporal, Dec. 19, 1864, to date from Dec. 17, 1864. With the regiment in operations during the winter of 1865, and in action at Fort Stedman, March 25, 1865. Mustered out with the regiment at Delaney house, Washington, DC, July 30, 1865, and discharged in Readville, MA, Aug. 9, 1865, expiration of service.

79. **Parsons, John A.**, private. Res. and/or credit: Otis, MA. Born: Bristol, CT. Age: 37. Height: 5′6⅛″. Comp: light. Eyes: blue. Hair: dark. Occup: farmer. Enlisted in Otis by A. Crittenden, Dec. 10, 1863; mustered Jan. 4, 1864. Did not leave Camp Wool with the regiment, but sent to Camp Meigs in Readville, MA, April 18, 1864, under the supervision of Lt. John Cook for a medical examination. Found unfit for duty by a "board of inspectors." Rejected recruit and discharged the US service in Worcester, MA, June 29, 1864, by order of Maj. Gen. John A. Dix, War Dept.

80. **Phillips, Antonio**, private. Res: Oxford, MA. Credit: Worcester, MA. Born: Leghorn (Livorno), Italy. Age: 44. Height: 5′6″. Comp: dark. Eyes: gray. Hair: brown. Occup: nurse. Enlisted in Worcester by Capt. Joseph W. Gird, Nov. 19, 1863; mustered Jan. 4, 1864. In action and taken prisoner of war at the Wilderness, May 6, 1864. Incarcerated in the Confederate prison camp in Andersonville, GA, May 29, 1864, where he died from starvation, Sept. 3, 1864. Had previous service as a private in Co. G, 51st MVI, from Aug. 25, 1862, until mustered out, July 27, 1863. Participated in the North Carolina campaign with that regiment in 1862–63. Also had previous service as a private in Co. I, 15th MVI, from May 20, 1861, until discharged for disability, May 12, 1862. Possibly participated with that regiment at Ball's Bluff, Oct. 21, 1861, and in the Peninsula campaign in 1862.

81. **Pierce, Royal F.**, private. Res. and/or credit: Worcester, MA. Born: Boylston, MA. Age: 44. Height: 5′7″. Comp: light. Eyes: blue. Hair: sandy. Occup: druggist. Enlisted in Worcester by Capt. Joseph W. Gird, Jan. 1, 1864; mustered Jan. 4, 1864. Detached and detailed to the 1st Division, IX Corps, Ambulance Corps (probably because of his professional experience), April 27, 1864. Never in combat. Mustered out with the regiment at

Delaney house, Washington, DC, July 30, 1865, and discharged in Readville, MA, Aug. 9, 1865, expiration of service. Had previous service as a private in Co. D, 51st MVI, from Aug. 28, 1862, until mustered out, July 27, 1863. Participated in the North Carolina campaign with that regiment in 1862–63. Died May 31, 1871, age 51.

82. **Randall, Charles T.**, private. Res: Uxbridge, MA. Credit: Worcester, MA. Born: Princeton, MA. Age: 24. Height: 5'5". Comp: light. Eyes: hazel. Hair: brown. Occup: mechanic. Enlisted in Worcester by Capt. Joseph W. Gird, Jan. 27, 1864; joined the company, March 31, 1864; mustered April 6, 1864. In action at the Wilderness, May 6, 1864, Spotsylvania Court House, May 10, 12, and 18, 1864, North Anna River, May 24, 1864, Cold Harbor, June 3, 1864, and Petersburg assaults, June 17 and 18, 1864; wounded in action at the Petersburg Crater, July 30, 1864. With the regiment on all marches and in all skirmishes and battles until wounded. Absent wounded in an army general hospital until transferred to Co. B, 11th Regiment, VRC, April 10, 1865, by order of the War Dept. Discharged the US service, Aug. 8, 1865, by order of the War Dept. expiration of service. Had previous service as a private in Co. E, 51st MVI, from Aug. 26, 1862, until mustered out, July 27, 1863. Participated in the North Carolina campaign with that regiment in 1862–63. Resided in Princeton, MA, after the war.

83. **Robbins, William**, private. Res. and/or credit: Oxford, MA. Born: Thomson, CT. Age: 36. Height: 5'7". Comp: light. Eyes: blue. Hair: brown. Occup: shoemaker. Enlisted in Oxford by L. B. Corbin, Jan. 4, 1864; mustered Jan. 11, 1864. Killed in action at the Wilderness, May 6, 1864.

84. **Roland, Louis**, private. Res. and/or credit: Worcester, MA. Born: Saxony, Germany. Age: 19. Height: 5'6". Comp: florid. Eyes: blue. Hair: brown. Occup: cigar maker. Enlisted in Worcester by D. Waldo Lincoln, Jan. 5, 1864; mustered Jan. 11, 1864. Deserted from Camp Wool, March 31, 1864. Never returned.

85. **Sawyer, Josiah**, private. Res: Oxford, MA. Credit: Worcester, MA. Born: Boston, MA. Age: 44. Height: 5'8". Comp: light. Eyes: blue. Hair: dark. Occup: farmer. Enlisted in Worcester by Capt. Joseph W. Gird, Dec. 28, 1863; mustered Jan. 4, 1864. Did not leave Camp Wool with the regiment, but sent to Camp Meigs in Readville, MA, April 18, 1864, under the supervision of Lt. John Cook for a medical examination. Found unfit for duty by a "board of inspectors." Rejected recruit and discharged the US service in Worcester, MA, June 29, 1864, by order of Jam. Gen. John A. Dix, War Dept. Died before 1896, but date not known.

86. **Sawyer, Warren W.**, private. Res. and/or credit: Worcester, MA. Born: North Island, VT. Age: 18. Height: 5'6". Comp: light. Eyes: gray. Hair: light. Occup: farmer. Enlisted in Worcester by Lt. E. Dexter Cheney, Dec. 11, 1863; mustered Jan. 4, 1864. Detached and detailed on recruiting service with Lt. Col. Luke Lyman in Northampton, MA, Feb. 13, 1864, under RSO 7, by order of Col. William F. Bartlett, dated Feb. 12, 1864. Returned to the regiment for duty, April 12, 1864. Wounded in action at the Wilderness, May 6, 1864. Absent wounded in an army general hospital until between Oct. 8 and Oct. 31, 1864. Absent sick in Depot Field Hospital at City Point, Petersburg, from Nov. 11, 1864, until discharged the US service on a Surgeons Certificate of Disability for wounds, Dec. 21, 1864, by order of the War Dept.

87. **Scott, Jesse S.**, principal musician. Res. and/or credit: Leicester, MA. Born: Paterson, NJ. Age: 22. Height: 5'8". Comp: dark. Eyes: gray. Hair: black. Occup: mechanic. Enlisted in Leicester by Silas Gleason, Dec. 5, 1863; mustered Jan. 4, 1864. Company drummer or fifer. Probably also served as a hospital orderly, nurse, and/or stretcher bearer. Promoted principal musician and transferred to the regimental noncommissioned staff, Jan. 7, 1865, to date from Jan. 1, 1865, under RSO 3, by order of Lt. Col. Julius M. Tucker, dated Jan. 1, 1865. Discharged the US service in Tennallytown, DC, June 13, 1865, to date June 1, 1865, as a supernumerary because of the con-

solidation of the 59th MVI with the 57th, under SO 254, par. 43, AGO, War Dept., dated May 26, 1865. Had previous service as a private in Co. B, 3rd Battalion of Rifles, Massachusetts Volunteer Militia, from May 19, 1861, until mustered out, Aug. 3, 1861. On duty at Fort McHenry with that battalion in 1861. Also had previous service as a musician in the regimental band of the 21st MVI from July 25, 1861, until mustered out at Cedar Run, VA, Aug. 17, 1862. On duty with that regiment in North Carolina in 1862. Resided in Leicester, MA, after the war, and died there, Sept. 28, 1892, age 51.

88. **Sheffield, John A.**, private. Res: Northbridge, MA. Credit: Worcester, MA. Born: Hopkinton, MA. Age: 24. Height: 5'11". Comp: light. Eyes: blue. Hair: Brown. Occup: shoemaker. Enlisted in Worcester by Capt. John W. Sanderson, Dec. 24, 1863; mustered Jan. 11, 1864. Did not leave Camp Wool with the regiment, but sent to Camp Meigs in Readville, MA, April 18, 1864, under the supervision of Lt. John Cook for a medical examination. Found unfit for duty by a "board of inspectors," and rejected as a recruit. Treated at the hospital at Camp Meigs until discharged the US service for disability, Aug. 10, 1865, by order of the War Dept.

89. **Simons, Daniel J.**, sergeant. Res. and/or credit: Wilbraham, MA. Born: Winchester, CT. Age: 27. Height: 5'8". Comp: light. Eyes: blue. Hair: light. Occup: farmer. Enlisted in Wilbraham by P. Cross, Dec. 8, 1863; mustered Jan. 4, 1864. Promoted sergeant, Jan. 4, 1864. Never in combat with the 57th. Absent sick from on or before May 6, 1864, until discharged the US service for disability in Alexandria, VA, May 9, 1864, by order of Maj. Gen. Christopher C. Auger, commanding the Dept. of Washington, DC. Had previous service in Co. E, 10th United States Regular Infantry (specifics unknown). Resided in Winsted, CT, after the war.

90. **Smith, Alpheus M.**, private. Res. and credit: Sutton, MA. Born: Sutton, MA. Age: 45. Height: 5'7½". Comp: dark. Eyes: gray.

Hair: brown. Occup: yeoman. Enlisted in Sutton by J. A. Dodge, Dec. 24, 1863; mustered Jan. 4, 1864. Did not leave Camp Wool with the regiment, but sent to Camp Meigs in Readville, MA, April 18, 1864, under the supervision of Lt. John Cook for a medical examination. Found unfit for duty by a "board of inspectors." Rejected recruit and discharged the US service from Gallup's Island, Boston Harbor, MA, July 16, 1864, by order of Maj. Gen. John A. Dix, War Dept. Had previous service as a private in Co. E, 42nd MVI, from Sept. 1, 1862, until mustered out Aug. 20, 1863. On duty in and around New Orleans, LA, with that regiment in 1862–63. Resided in North Leominster, MA, after the war.

91. **Smith, Edwin H.**, private. Res: Oxford, MA. Credit: Worcester, MA. Born: Lyndon, VT. Age: 36. Height: 5'9". Comp: light. Eyes: gray. Hair: light. Occup: farmer. Enlisted in Worcester by Lt. E. Dexter Cheney, Dec. 14, 1863; mustered Jan. 4, 1864. Wounded in action at the Wilderness, May 6, 1864. Absent wounded in an army general hospital until transferred to Co. B, 14th Regiment, VRC, April 1, 1865. Discharged the US service, Aug. 2, 1865, by order of the War Dept. Died before 1896, but date not known.

92. **Smith, Eugene,** musician. Res. and/or credit: Oxford, MA. Born: Uxbridge, MA. Age: 19. Height: 5'8". Comp: dark. Eyes: black. Hair: black. Occup: shoemaker. Enlisted in Oxford by L. B. Corbin, Nov. 28, 1863; mustered Jan. 4, 1864. Company drummer or fifer. Probably also served as a hospital orderly, nurse, and/or stretcher bearer. Absent sick in an army general hospital from before Oct. 31, 1864, until Feb. 20, 1865. Mustered out with the regiment at Delaney house, Washington, DC, July 30, 1865, and discharged in Readville, MA, Aug. 9, 1865, expiration of service. Had previous service as a private in Co. K, 51st MVI, from Sept. 12, 1862, until mustered out, July 27, 1863. Participated in the North Carolina campaign with that regiment in 1862–63. Died in 1893, age 49.

First Sergeant Samuel Souther.
(John Anderson)

93. **Souther, Samuel,** 1st sergeant. Res. and credit: Worcester, MA. Born: Fryburg, ME. Age: 44. Height: 5'11⅞". Comp: light. Eyes: gray. Hair: brown. Occup: Congregationalist clergyman. Enlisted in Worcester by Capt. Joseph W. Gird, Nov. 25, 1863; mustered Jan. 4, 1864. Promoted 1st sergeant, Jan. 4, 1864. Missing in action at the Wilderness, May 6, 1864. Never accounted for and presumed killed. Graduate of Dartmouth College and Bangor (Maine) Theological Seminary; "a man of high personal character and a devoted Christian, of strong religious convictions which he consistently maintained, and never allowed anything to interfere with his religious duties. He was a noble, honorable, true-hearted man" (JA).

94. **Squires, Truman,** private. Res. and/or credit: Pelham, MA. Born: Shutesbury, MA. Age: 18. Height: 5'8½". Comp: light. Eyes: blue. Hair: brown. Occup: laborer. Enlisted in Pelham by J. Jones, Dec. 21, 1863; mustered Jan. 4, 1864. Deserted from Camp Wool on the morning of April 16, 1864, but returned the same day at 4 PM. In action at the Wilderness, May 6, 1864, and Spotsylvania Court House, May 10 and 12, 1864; killed while on duty there, May 17, 1864 (probably by a Confederate sharpshooter).

95. **Sullivan, Jerry,** private. Res: Marlboro, MA. Credit: Milford, MA. Born: Bantry, County Cork, Ireland. Age: 34. Height: 5'5". Comp: dark. Eyes: dark. Hair: black. Occup: laborer. Enlisted in Milford by L. C. Gillette, Dec. 22, 1863; mustered Jan. 4, 1864. In action at the Wilderness, May 6, 1864, Spotsylvania Court House, May 10, 12, and 18, 1864, North Anna River, May 24, 1864, Cold Harbor, June 3, 1864, and Petersburg assaults, June 17 and 18, 1864; missing in action at the Petersburg Crater, July 30, 1864. Never accounted for and presumed killed. With the regiment on all marches and in all skirmishes and battles until missing.

96. **Sullivan, Timothy G.,** private. Res: Westboro, MA. Credit: Boston, MA. Born: Westboro, MA. Age: 18. Height: 5'6". Comp: light. Eyes: gray. Hair: brown. Occup: miller. Enlisted in Boston by W. W. Fay, Dec. 2, 1863; mustered Jan. 4, 1864. Wounded in action at the Wilderness, May 6, 1864. Absent wounded in Lincoln US Army General Hospital in Washington, DC, until discharged the US service for disability from wounds, May 11, 1865, under GO 77, par. 6, AGO, War Dept., dated May 3, 1865. Resided in Worcester, MA. after the war.

Private Timothy Sullivan
(postwar photo). *(Post 10)*

97. **Swan, James S.**, private. Res. and/or credit: Worcester, MA. Born: Paisely, Strathclyde, Scotland. Age: 44. Height: 5'8". Comp: light. Eyes: blue. Hair: light. Occup: laborer. Enlisted in Worcester by Lt. E. Dexter Cheney, Dec. 15, 1863; mustered Jan. 4, 1864. Deserted from Camp Wool, Feb. 24, 1864. Never returned.

98. **Terrill, Edward**, private. Res: Grafton, MA. Credit: Worcester, MA. Born: New York. Age: 44. Height: 5'6". Comp: light. Eyes: hazel. Hair: gray. Enlisted in Worcester by Capt. John W. Sanderson, Dec. 10, 1863; mustered Jan. 4, 1864. In action at the Wilderness, May 6, 1864, Spotsylvania Court House, May 10, 12, and 18, 1864, North Anna River, May 24, 1864, Cold Harbor, June 3, 1864, and Petersburg assaults, June 17 and 18, 1864; missing in action at the Petersburg Crater, July 30, 1864. With the regiment on all marches and in all skirmishes and battles until missing. Never accounted for and presumed killed.

99. **Thurston, George**, private. Res: Holden, MA. Credit: Worcester, MA. Born: Holden, MA. Age: 20. Height: 5'10". Comp: light. Eyes: blue. Hair: dark. Occup: farmer. Enlisted in Worcester by Capt. Joseph W. Gird, Dec. 7, 1863; mustered Jan. 4, 1864. Severely wounded in action at the Wilderness, May 6, 1864. Died from wounds in an army general hospital in Washington, DC, June 3, 1864.

100. **Tobey, John G.**, private. Res. and/or credit: Worcester, MA. Born: Eliot, ME. Age: 29. Height: 5'3". Comp: light. Eyes: gray. Hair: light. Occup: telegraph operator. Enlisted in Worcester by Capt. Joseph W. Gird, Dec. 3, 1863; mustered Jan. 4, 1864. Detached from the regiment, March 3, 1864, by the following order: "The following enlisted [man, John G. Tobey,] will be furloughed, without pay or emoluments, until further orders to enable [him] to enter the service of the U.S. Military Telegraph Corps. [He] will be borne on [his] compan[y's] rolls as on furlough," under SO 93, par. 35, AGO, War Dept., dated Feb. 26, 1864, by order of Assistant Adjutant General W. A. Nichols. However, this plan was changed; Tobey never

left with the regiment for the front and was discharged the US service to accept an appointment in the US Navy, June 27, 1864, by SO 220, AGO, War Dept. Was acting assistant navy paymaster, to date from June 22, 1864, until mustered out, April 19, 1866. Served on the USS *Chocura*. Resided in Boston, MA, after the war.

101. **Wallace, Patrick**, private. Res. and/or credit: Milford, MA. Born: County Tyrone, Ireland. Age: 42. Height: 5'6". Comp: dark. Eyes: hazel. Hair: black. Occup: bootmaker. Enlisted in Milford by Leonard Hunt, Jan. 4, 1864; mustered Jan. 11, 1864. In action at the Wilderness, May 6, 1864, and taken prisoner of war, but not in battle, on an unknown date later that month. Incarcerated in the Confederate prison camp in Andersonville, GA, May 29, 1864, where he died from scurvy, July 15, 1864. Company learned of his death, May 13, 1865.

102. **Ward, Peter**, private. Res. and/or credit: Worcester, MA. Born: Ireland. Age: 25. Height: 6'1". Comp: light. Eyes: gray. Hair: brown. Occup: farmer. Enlisted in Worcester by Capt. Joseph W. Gird, Dec. 24, 1863; mustered Jan. 4, 1864. Deserted from Camp Wool, March 30, 1864, but returned later that same day. Wounded in action at the Wilderness, May 6, 1864. Absent wounded in an army general hospital until he deserted while on furlough, Sept. 1, 1864. Evidently surrendered, probably under President Lincoln's proclamation of amnesty, as he is listed as mustered out but absent wounded at Delaney house, Washington, DC, July 30, 1865.

103. **Warren, Harris C.**, private. Res: Westboro, MA. Credit: Worcester, MA. Born: Marlboro, MA. Age: 18. Height: 5'10½". Comp: dark. Eyes: brown. Hair: dark. Occup: farmer. Enlisted in Worcester by Capt. Joseph W. Gird, Nov. 30, 1863; mustered Jan. 4, 1864. Absent sick or on detached duty from on or before May 6, 1864 until between Aug. 19 and Sept. 30, 1864. In action at Poplar Grove Church, Sept. 30, 1864; wounded in action there, Oct. 8, 1864. Absent wounded in an army general hospital until Feb. 11, 1865. In action and taken prisoner of war at

Fort Stedman, March 25, 1865. Paroled and exchanged from Libby Prison, Richmond, VA, March 29, 1865. Discharged the US service for disability from the Camp of Parole in Annapolis, MD, May 24, 1865, under GO 77, par. 6, AGO, War Dept., dated May 3, 1865. Resided in Westboro, MA, after the war.

104. **Waters, Hugh,** private. Res. and/or credit: Worcester, MA. Born: Ireland. Age: 29. Height: 5′7½″. Comp: light. Eyes: gray. Hair: brown. Occup: laborer. Enlisted in Worcester by Capt. Joseph W. Gird, Dec. 26, 1863; mustered Jan. 4, 1864. Did not leave Camp Wool with the regiment, but sent to Camp Meigs in Readville, MA, April 18, 1864, under the supervision of Lt. John Cook for a medical examination. Found unfit for duty by a "board of inspectors." Rejected recruit and discharged the US service in Worcester, MA, June 29, 1864, by order of

Maj. Gen. John A. Dix, War Dept. Died Aug. 6, 1884, age 50.

105. **Witherby, Harlen F.,** sergeant. Res: Westboro, MA; Credit: Boston, MA. Born: Grafton, MA. Age: 18. Height: 5′4″. Comp: light. Eyes: blue. Hair: brown. Occup: shoemaker. Enlisted in Boston by W. W. Fay, Dec. 2, 1863; mustered Jan. 4, 1864. Never in combat. Absent sick or on detached duty from on or before May 6 until after March 25, 1865. Promoted corporal, May 17, 1865, to date May 1, 1865, under RSO 42, by order of Lt. Col. Julius M. Tucker, dated May 1, 1865. Promoted sergeant, July 1, 1865. Mustered out with the regiment at Delaney house, Washington, DC, July 30, 1865, and discharged in Readville, MA, Aug. 9, 1865, expiration of service. Resided in Grove City, PA, after the war.

ROSTER AND DESCRIPTIVE LIST OF COMPANY C

Company C, known as the "Lynn Company" because its captain, Charles D. Hollis, came from that city, was the sixth company to be mustered into United States service, and it was mustered in by 1st Lt. Robert P. McKibben, 4th United States Regular Infantry, under SO 167 from the AGO, Boston, MA. Those men in the company mustered after Feb. 18, 1864, were mustered in by 2nd Lt. Daniel Madden, 6th United States Regular Cavalry. It was mustered out by Capt. Sylvester Keyser, 2nd Michigan Volunteer Infantry, ACM, 1st Division, IX Corps. This company is particularly interesting because a number of quartermaster and ordnance reports have survived, which not only document who received what uniforms and equipment and when, but reveal who was with the company during certain periods of the fall and winter of 1864–65 at Petersburg. They also clearly show how well the company, the rest of the regiment, and, by inference, the Army of the Potomac were cared for during the siege, since it can be assumed safely that the 57th was typical of other Federal regiments during that period. These papers are also especially noteworthy because the men had to sign for their issues, or make their marks, so their literacy—or lack of literacy—can be partly determined.

1. **Ackley, James,** private. Res: Leicester, MA. Credit: Worcester, MA. Born: Cambridge, Nova Scotia, Canada. Age: 32. Height: 5′5″. Comp: light. Eyes: gray. Hair: brown. Occup: blacksmith. Enlisted in Worcester by Silas Gleason, Feb. 8, 1864; mustered Feb. 18,

1864. Slightly wounded in action at the Wilderness, May 6, 1864. Treated at the 1st Division, IX Corps, Field Hospital on the battlefield, and returned to the regiment for duty. In action at Spotsylvania Court House, May 10, 1864, and wounded again in action there,

May 12, 1864. Absent wounded in an army general hospital until between Aug. 19 and Sept. 23, 1864. Issued one pair of shoes, Sept. 23, 1864. In action at Poplar Grove Church, Sept. 30 and Oct. 8, 1864. Issued one sack coat (unlined), one greatcoat, and one rubber blanket, Oct. 10, 1864. Mustered for pay, Oct 13, 1864. Issued two pairs of drawers and two pairs of socks, Nov. 15, 1864. Issued one pair of shoes, Jan. 27, 1864. Issued a new .58 cal. Springfield rifle and new leather equipment, Feb. 3, 1865. Was barely able to sign his name, and usually just made his mark. Detached and detailed as a pioneer at 3rd Brigade, 1st Division, IX Corps, Headquarters in early Feb. 1865 until muster-out. Did not participate at Fort Stedman, March 25, 1865. Mustered out with the regiment at Delaney house, Washington, DC, July 30, 1865, and discharged in Readville, MA, Aug. 9, 1865, expiration of service. Had previous service as an ordinary seaman in the US Navy from July 8, 1861, until mustered out, Aug. 5, 1863. Served on the receiving ships *Ohio* and *North Carolina,* and the USS *Pensacola.* Died in 1893, age 61.

2. **Allman, Samuel,** corporal. Res. and/or credit: Greenfield, MA. Born: Broxton, GA (one of the four Southern-born soldiers to serve with the regiment). Age: 23. Height: 5′10″. Comp: light. Eyes: blue. Hair: brown. Occup: farmer. Enlisted in Greenfield by C. Stearns, Jan. 23, 1864 (recruited by a recruiting broker who cheated Allman out of his state bounty of $325, telling him that that was the charge for his services); mustered Feb. 18, 1864. Promoted corporal, Feb. 18, 1864. In action at the Wilderness, May 6, 1864, Spotsylvania Court House, May 10, 12, and 18, 1864, North Anna River, May 24, 1864, Cold Harbor, June 3, 1864, and Petersburg assaults, June 17 and 18, 1864; severely wounded in the face and left arm by shrapnel from an exploding Confederate mortar shell while on duty in the trenches at Petersburg, July 20, 1864, which "nearly tore his left arm off. it was a hard looking wound" (GEB). With the regiment on all marches and in all skirmishes and battles until wounded. Absent wounded in Dale US Army General Hospital in Worcester, MA, until discharged the US ser-

vice for disability from wounds, March 13, 1865, by order of Maj. Gen. John A. Dix, War Dept.

3. **Barton, George Edward,** captain. Res. and credit: Worcester, MA. Born: Worcester, MA. Age: 22. Height: approx. 5′7″. Comp: light. Eyes: blue. Hair: brown. Occup: clerk. Commissioned 2nd lieutenant, Jan. 6, 1864; mustered 2nd lieutenant, Jan. 11, 1864. Acting adjutant of the regiment at Camp Wool and in the field until April 26, 1864. Commissioned 1st lieutenant, April 9, 1864. Transferred to Co. C, April 19, 1864, and joined the company that same day while the regiment was on the march to the front. Detached and detailed as commander of the 1st Division, IX Corps, ambulance wagon train, April 26, 1864. Mustered 1st lieutenant, June 21, 1864. Returned to the regiment for duty June 15, 1864. In action in the Petersburg assaults, June 17 and 18, 1864; very slightly wounded by the explosion of a Confederate mortar shell while on duty in the trenches at Petersburg, July 24, 1864. Slightly wounded in action at the Petersburg Crater, July 30, 1864. Absent wounded in the 1st Division, IX Corps, Field Hospital until transferred to Seminary US Army General Hospital, Aug. 3, 1864. Transferred to the officers' wards in the army general hospital in Annapolis, MD, from Aug. 7 until Aug. 25, 1864. Transported from Point Lookout, MD, and returned to the regiment for duty during the night of Sept. 10, 1864. Commissioned captain, Sept. 20, 1864. In action at Poplar Grove Church, Sept. 30 and Oct. 8, 1864. Mustered captain, Oct 20, 1864, to date Oct. 24, 1864. With the regiment in most operations during the fall and winter of 1864–65. Received a 20-day furlough from Jan. 31 until Feb. 19, 1865, under SO 30, by order of Maj. Gen. John G. Parke, commanding IX Corps. In action at Fort Stedman, March 25, 1865. In command of the regiment from March 26, 1865, until an unknown date in late April, 1865. Resigned and discharged the US service for expiration of service, June 26, 1865, by order of the War Dept. Had previous service in the 51st MVI from Aug. 25, 1862, when he enlisted as a private in Co. C of that regiment, until mustered out, July 27, 1863. Promoted

sergeant major on the noncommissioned staff of the 51st MVI, Nov. 4, 1862. Participated in the North Carolina campaign with that regiment in 1862–63. President of the 57th's regimental association in 1872. Cousin of Clara Barton. Resided in Worcester, MA, after the war and died there, May 29, 1878, age 36. Buried in Rural Cemetery, Worcester, MA. "Captain Barton was a great favorite in the army and will long be remembered for his genial, sunny disposition; always happy himself, he had a faculty of imparting his cheerful disposition to others" (JA).

4. **Benois, Joseph,** private. Res: Hinsdale, MA. Credit: Pittsfield, MA. Born: province of Quebec, Canada. Age: 19. Height: 5′6″. Comp: light. Eyes: brown. Hair: dark. Occup: laborer. Enlisted in Pittsfield by Joseph Tucker, March 21, 1864; mustered April 6, 1864. In action at the Wilderness, May 6, 1864, Spotsylvania Court House, May 10, 12, and 18, 1864, North Anna River, May 24, 1864, Cold Harbor, June 3, 1864, Petersburg assaults, June 17 and 18, 1864, and Petersburg Crater, July 30, 1864; missing in action at Weldon Railroad, Aug. 19, 1864. Returned to the regiment for duty on an unknown date in early 1865. With the regiment on all marches and in all skirmishes and battles until missing. Whereabouts while missing unknown (there is no record of him having been a prisoner of war, sick, a deserter, on detached duty, or wounded in action in that battle). Wounded in action at Fort Stedman, March 25, 1865. Absent wounded in an army general hospital in Washington, DC, where he died from disease, Aug. 2, 1865.

5. **Bertrand, Joseph,** private. Res: Hinsdale, MA. Credit: Pittsfield, MA. Born: Sand Lake, NY. Age: 18. Height: 5′7″. Comp: light. Eyes: blue. Hair: brown. Occup: farmer. Enlisted in Pittsfield by John C. West, March 31, 1864; joined the company from the transient barracks, April 6, 1864; mustered April 6, 1864. In action at the Wilderness, May 6, 1864, and one of the 34 enlisted men who remained with the colors during that battle. In action again at Spotsylvania Court House, May 10, 1864, and severely wounded in action there, May 12, 1864. Absent wounded in an

Lieutenant George E. Barton.
(USAMHI)

army general hospital until mustered out, but absent wounded, at Delaney house, Washington, DC, July 30, 1865, expiration of service.

6. **Bertrand, Moses,** private. Res: Hinsdale, MA. Credit: Pittsfield, MA. Born: Montreal, Quebec, Canada. Age: 24. Height: 5′3″. Comp: light. Eyes: brown. Hair: dark. Occup: laborer. Enlisted in Pittsfield by W. F. Carson, March 29, 1864; mustered April 6, 1864. Absent sick or on detached duty from on or before May 6, 1864, until between Aug. 19 and Sept. 23, 1864. Issued one forage cap, one sack coat (unlined), one pair of shoes, two pairs of socks, and one rubber blanket, Sept. 23, 1864. In action at Poplar Grove Church, Sept. 30 and Oct. 8, 1864. Mustered for pay Oct. 13, 1864. Issued one sack coat (lined), one pair of trousers, one flannel shirt, one pair of drawers, one greatcoat, one wool blanket, and one rubber blanket, Oct. 15, 1864. Issued one flannel shirt, Nov. 15, 1864. Issued one pair of drawers, one pair of socks, and one pair of mittens, Dec. 18, 1864. Issued one pair of trousers, one knitted shirt, one pair of shoes, two pair of socks, and one rubber blanket, Jan. 27, 1865. Issued a new .58 cal. Springfield rifle and new leather equipment, Feb. 3, 1865. Issued one forage cap, two knitted shirts, and two pairs of drawers, Feb. 10, 1865. Issued one sack coat (unlined), one pair of trousers, one pair of drawers, one pair of socks, and one knitted shirt, April 30, 1865. Illiterate. With the regiment in operations in the fall and winter of 1864–65. In action at Fort Stedman, March 25, 1865. Mustered out with the regiment at Delaney house, Washington, DC, July 30, 1865, and discharged in Readville, MA, Aug. 9, 1865, expiration of service.

7. **Billings, George,** corporal. Res: Chicopee, MA. Credit: Springfield, MA. Born: South Royalston, MA. Age: 22. Height: 5′7½″. Comp: light. Eyes: gray. Hair: brown. Occup: fisherman and tinner. Enlisted in Springfield by Capt. Charles D. Hollis, Jan. 20, 1864; mustered Feb. 18, 1864. Promoted corporal, Feb. 18, 1864. Wounded in action at the Wilderness, May 6, 1864. Absent wounded in an army general hospital until transferred to the 1st Co., 2nd Battln., VRC, June 10, 1865. Discharged the US service for disability from

wounds, July 24, 1865, by order of the War Dept.

8. **Bird, Frank,** private. Res. and/or credit: Spencer, MA. Born: Canada. Age: 18. Height: 5′8″. Comp: light. Eyes: blue. Hair: light. Occup: bootmaker. Enlisted in Spencer by L. Hill, Feb. 2, 1864; mustered Feb. 18, 1864. Killed in action at the Wilderness, May 6, 1864.

9. **Blanchard, Louis,** private. Res. and/or credit: Spencer, MA. Born: province of Quebec, Canada. Age: 36. Height: 5′9″. Comp: dark. Eyes: blue. Hair: black. Occup: bootmaker. Enlisted in Spencer by L. Hill, March 24, 1864; mustered April 6, 1864. In action at the Wilderness, May 6, 1864, Spotsylvania Court House, May 10, 12, and 18, 1864, North Anna River, May 24, 1864, and Cold Harbor, June 3, 1864; taken prisoner of war in action during the Petersburg assault, June 17, 1864. With the regiment on all marches and in all skirmishes and battles until captured. Paroled and exchanged from an unknown Confederate prison, Nov. 25, 1864. Probably received extra pay for having been a prisoner of war. Discharged the US service for disability (probably from the US Army general hospital in the Camp of Parole in Annapolis, MD) "to date from Jan. 3, 1865, to complete his military record, under provisions of Act of Congress approved April 5, 1884" (JA). Resided in Worcester, MA, after the war and died there in 1910, age 82.

10. **Booter, Anson,** private. Res: Rouses Point, NY. Credit: Greenfield, MA. Born: province of Quebec, Canada. Age: 39. Height: 5′7¼″. Comp: dark. Eyes: hazel. Hair: black. Occup: laborer. Enlisted in Greenfield by P. S. Cushman, Feb. 5, 1864; mustered Feb. 18, 1864. Absent sick in an army general hospital from on or before May 6 until Oct. 18, 1864. Absent sick again in the 1st Division, IX Corps, Field Hospital at Petersburg from Nov. 30 until Dec. 4, 1864. Issued one pair of socks and two pairs of mittens, Dec. 18, 1864. Issued one pair of trousers, one pair of drawers, two pairs of socks, and one rubber blanket, Jan. 27, 1865. Issued a new .58 cal. Springfield rifle and leather

equipment, Feb. 3, 1865. Issued one pair of trousers, Feb. 10, 1865. Illiterate. Taken prisoner of war in action at Fort Stedman, March 25, 1865. Paroled and exchanged from Libby Prison in Richmond, VA, March 29, 1865. Returned to the regiment for duty from the Camp of Parole in Annapolis, MD, on or about May 11, 1865. Issued a new .58 cal. Springfield rifle and new leather equipment, May 16, 1865. Mustered out with the regiment at Delaney house, Washington, DC, July 30, 1865, and discharged in Readville, MA, Aug. 9, 1865, expiration of service.

11. **Brazeau, Antoine**, private. Res: Hinsdale, MA. Credit: Pittsfield, MA. Born: Montreal, Quebec, Canada. Age: 26. Height: 5'5". Comp: light. Eyes: gray. Hair: dark. Occup: laborer. Enlisted in Pittsfield by Joseph Tucker, March 27, 1864; mustered April 6, 1864. Absent sick in an army general hospital from on or before May 6, 1864, until between Aug. 19 and Sept. 23, 1864. Issued one pair of trousers, one pair of drawers, and one pair of shoes, Sept. 23, 1864. In action at Poplar Grove Church, Set. 30 and Oct. 8, 1864. Mustered for pay, Oct. 13, 1864. Issued one pair of socks and one greatcoat, Oct. 15, 1864. Issued two flannel shirts and two pairs of drawers, Nov. 15, 1864. Issued one forage cap, one pair of trousers, and one pair of mittens, Dec. 18, 1864. Issued two pairs of drawers and four pairs of socks, Jan. 27, 1865. Issued a new .58 cal. Springfield rifle and new leather equipment, Feb. 3, 1865. Issued one rubber blanket, March 6, 1865. Issued one forage cap, two pairs of drawers, one pair of socks, one knitted shirt, and one rubber blanket, April 30, 1865. Illiterate. With the regiment in operations during the fall and winter of 1864–65, and in action at Fort Stedman, March 25, 1865. Mustered out with the regiment at Delaney house, Washington, DC, July 30, 1865, and discharged in Readville, MA, Aug. 9, 1865, expiration of service.

12. **Brotgers, Lewis**, private. Res: Hatfield, MA. Credit: Pittsfield, MA. Born: Montreal, Quebec, Canada. Age: 26. Height: 5'5". Comp: light. Eyes: gray. Hair: dark. Occup: laborer. Enlisted in Pittsfield by Joseph Tucker, March 29, 1864; mustered April 6,

1864. In action at the Wilderness, May 6, 1864, and Spotsylvania Court House, May 10, 1864; killed in action there, May 12, 1864.

13. **Brown, William**, private. Res. and/or credit: Spencer, MA. Born: Worcester, MA. Age: 26. Height: 5'4". Comp: fair. Eyes: hazel. Hair: brown. Occup: wiredrawer. Enlisted in Spencer by L. Hill, Feb. 7, 1864; mustered Feb. 18, 1864. In action at the Wilderness, May 6, 1864, Spotsylvania Court House, May 10, 12, and 18, 1864, North Anna River, May 24, 1864, Cold Harbor, June 3, 1864, and Petersburg assaults, June 17 and 18, 1864; severely wounded while on picket duty at Petersburg, July 19, 1864. With the regiment on all marches and in all skirmishes and battles until wounded. Absent wounded in an army general hospital until transferred to the 19th Co., 2nd Battln., VRC, on an unknown date. Discharged the US service for disability from wounds while absent wounded, Oct. 12, 1865, by order of the War Dept.

14. **Bryant, Eleazer**, musician. Res. and/or credit: Springfield, MA. Born: Covington, MA. Age: 17. Comp: dark. Eyes: hazel. Hair: dark. Occup: mechanic. Enlisted in Springfield by Capt. Charles D. Hollis, Dec. 29, 1863; mustered Feb. 18, 1864. Company drummer. Probably also served as a hospital orderly, nurse, and/or stretcher bearer. Absent sick in an army general hospital from before Oct 1 until Oct. 18, 1864. Issued one pair of drawers, one pair of shoes, and one pair of socks, Nov. 15, 1864. Issued one knitted shirt, one pair of trousers, one pair of socks, and new drum heads and drum straps, Jan. 27, 1865. Issued two pairs of drawers, one pair of shoes, and one pair of socks, Feb. 10, 1865. Present during the battle at Fort Stedman, March 25, 1865 (whether he actively participated in it is not known, but because of the nature of that fight, he probably did). Issued one sack coat (unlined), one pair of trousers, two pairs of drawers, one pair of socks, and a new drum, April 30, 1865. Literate. Mustered out with the regiment at Delaney house, Washington, DC, July 30, 1865, and discharged in Readville, MA, Aug. 9, 1865, expiration of service. Resided in Springfield, MA,

after the war and died there after mid-1927, date unknown.

15. **Bugard, John,** private. Res: Rouses Point, NY. Credit: Northampton, MA. Born: province of Quebec, Canada. Age: 42. Height: 5'7". Comp: dark. Eyes: black. Hair: black. Occup: farmer. Enlisted in Northampton by Lt. Col. Luke Lyman, Feb. 9, 1864; mustered Feb. 18, 1864. Deserted from Camp Wool, March 20, 1864. Never returned.

16. **Bullis, Jabez,** private. Res: Cape Vincent, NY. Credit: Greenfield, MA. Born: Farmersville, Ontario, Canada. Age: 38. Height: 5'10". Eyes: blue. Hair: light. Occup: farmer. Enlisted in Greenfield by H. Bascom, Feb. 13, 1864; mustered Feb. 18, 1864. Detailed as company cook, and, therefore, usually exempted from hard combat. Absent sick in the 1st Division, IX Corps, Field Hospital at Petersburg from Oct. 15, 1864, until no later than Feb. 10, 1865. Issued one greatcoat and one wool blanket, Oct. 15, 1864. With the regiment during clothing issues on Feb. 10 and March 6, 1865, but drew no supplies. Issued a new .58 cal. Springfield rifle and leather equipment, March 22, 1865. Issued one sack coat (unlined), one pair of trousers, two pairs of drawers, two knitted shirts, and two pairs of socks, April 30, 1865. Illiterate. In action at Fort Stedman, March 25, 1865. Mustered out with the regiment at Delaney house, Washington, DC, July 30, 1865, and discharged in Readville, MA, July 30, 1865, expiration of service.

17. **Burno, Charles,** private. Res: Fairfax Center, VT. Credit: Northampton, MA. Born: Montreal, Quebec, Canada. Age: 28. Height: 5'5". Comp: dark. Eyes: dark. Hair: dark. Occup: blacksmith. Enlisted in Northampton by Lt. Col. Luke Lyman, Jan. 26, 1864; mustered Feb. 18, 1864. Found to be a deserter from the 1st West Virginia Cavalry Regiment, and turned over to the provost marshal at Fairfax Court House, VA, about April 25, 1864, to be returned to his regiment, but records indicate that he apparently escaped and deserted again. "Bounty jumper" (JA).

18. **Buschier, Peter,** private. Res: Easthampton, MA. Credit: Northampton, MA. Born: Montreal, Quebec, Canada. Age: 22. Height: 5'6½". Comp: dark. Eyes: blue. Hair: auburn. Enlisted in Northampton by Lt. Col. Luke Lyman, Jan. 26, 1864; mustered Feb. 18, 1864. In action at the Wilderness, May 6, 1864, and Spotsylvania Court House, May 10 and 12, 1864; wounded in action there, May 18, 1864. Absent wounded in an army general hospital until transferred to the 21st Co., 2nd Battln., VRC, March 10, 1865. Discharged the US service, Aug. 11, 1865, expiration of service, by order of the War Dept.

19. **Butler, William W.,** private. Res: Bangor, NY. Credit: Northampton, MA. Born: Malone, NY. Age: 44. Height: 5'11". Comp: light. Eyes: blue. Hair: auburn. Occup: farmer. Enlisted in Northampton by Lt. Col. Luke Lyman, Feb. 29, 1864; mustered Feb. 18, 1864. Never in combat. Absent sick in Dale US Army General Hospital in Worcester, MA, from on or before May 6, 1864, until discharged the US service for disability, Feb. 9, 1865, by order of Maj. Gen. John A. Dix, War Dept.

20. **Casey, John H.,** private. Res. and/or credit: Lee, MA. Born: Chester, MA. Age: 18. Height: 5'7". Comp: light. Eyes: gray. Hair:

Private John H. Casey (postwar photo). *(John Anderson)*

dark. Occup: laborer. Enlisted in Lee by Sylvester S. May, Feb. 10, 1864; mustered Feb. 18, 1864. Wounded in action and taken prisoner of war at the Wilderness, May 6, 1864. Paroled and exchanged from an unknown Confederate prison, Sept. 1, 1864. Probably received extra pay for having been a prisoner. Absent sick and wounded in the army general hospital at the Camp of Parole in Annapolis, MD, until discharged the US service for disability from wounds and sickness, Feb. 7, 1865, by order of the War Dept. Illiterate. Resided in Lee, MA, after the war.

21. **Cheney, Frederick S.**, color corporal. Res: Fitchburg, MA. Credit: Worcester, MA. Born: Middlebridge, NY. Age: 18. Height: 5'3½". Comp: light. Eyes: black. Hair: brown. Occup: machinist. Enlisted in Worcester by Lt. Alfred O. Hitchcock, Feb. 27, 1864; mustered Feb. 18, 1864. In action at the Wilderness, May 6, 1864, Spotsylvania Court House, May 10, 12, and 18, 1864, North Anna River, May 24, 1864, Cold Harbor, June 3, 1864, Petersburg assaults, June 17 and 18, 1864, Petersburg Crater, July 30, 1864, Weldon Railroad, Aug. 19, 1864, Poplar Grove Church, Sept. 30 and Oct. 8, 1864, and in operations of the regiment during the fall and winter of 1864–65. Mustered for pay, Aug. 31, 1864 and Oct. 13, 1864. Issued one wool blanket, Nov. 15, 1864. Promoted color corporal, Nov. 16, 1864, and detailed on the regimental color guard by order of Lt. Col. Julius M. Tucker. Issued one pair of trousers and one pair of shoes, Jan. 27, 1865. Issued a new .58 cal. Springfield rifle and new leather equipment, Feb. 3, 1865. Literate. Killed in action at Fort Stedman, March 25, 1865. Cited twice for bravery in that battle: "Corporal Frederick S. Cheney, Company C (killed), color corporal, general bravery" (JMT), and "general bravery . . . Corporal F. S. Cheney, Company C (killed)" (GPR). One of the 30 combat soldiers remaining of the regiment after Weldon Railroad, Aug. 19, 1864, and the only one of the 11 combat soldiers who served with the regiment on all marches and in all skirmishes and battles throughout its entire wartime service to be killed.

22. **Collins, James,** private. Res: Sutton, MA. Credit: Worcester, MA. Born: Smithfield, RI.

Age: 23. Height: 5'8". Comp: light. Eyes: blue. Hair: light. Occup: sailmaker. Enlisted in Worcester by J. A. Dodge, Feb. 1, 1864; mustered Feb. 18, 1864. Deserted from Camp Wool, March 22, 1864, but was arrested, returned, and confined in the guardhouse in Camp Wool, March 25, 1864. Escaped from the guardhouse and deserted again on the morning of April 2, 1864, but was arrested and returned that same afternoon. Confined in the guardhouse at Camp Wool until April 18, 1864. Never in combat. Absent sick in an army general hospital from on or before May 6, 1864, until he deserted while on furlough from that hospital, Dec. 31, 1864. Never returned.

23. **Conway, Edward,** private. Res. and/or credit: Worcester, MA. Born: County Antrim, Ireland. Age: 34. Height: 5'8¾". Comp: light. Eyes: blue. Hair: brown. Occup: mason. Enlisted in Worcester by Lt. Charles H. Royce, March 19, 1864; mustered April 6, 1864. Absent sick in an army general hospital from on or before May 6, 1864, until between Oct. 8 and Oct. 13, 1864. Mustered for pay, Oct. 13, 1864. Issued one flannel shirt and two pairs of socks, Oct. 15, 1864. Issued one pair of trousers, two pairs of drawers, and two pairs of socks, Jan. 27, 1865. Issued a new .58 cal. Springfield rifle and new leather equipment, Feb. 3, 1865. Issued one pair of socks, April 30, 1865. Literate. With the regiment in at least some operations during the fall and winter of 1864–65, and in action at Fort Stedman, March 25, 1865. Detached and detailed as a guard on the 3rd Brigade, 1st Division, IX Corps, wagon train on an unknown date after April 30, 1865. Mustered out with the regiment at Delaney house, Washington, DC, July 30, 1865, and discharged in Readville, MA, Aug. 9, 1865, expiration of service.

24. **Croshier, George J.,** private. Res: Chicopee, MA. Credit: Springfield, MA. Born: Chicopee Falls, MA. Age: 18. Height: 5'2". Comp: dark. Eyes: brown. Hair: dark. Occup: painter. Enlisted in Springfield by Thomas Jordan, March 29, 1864; mustered April 6, 1864. In action at the Wilderness, May 6, 1864, and Spotsylvania Court House, May 10, 1864; killed in action there, May 12, 1864.

25. **Daley, John,** private. Res: Shrewsbury, MA. Credit: Worcester, MA. Born: Ireland. Age: 35. Height: 5'6". Comp: florid. Eyes: gray. Hair: brown. Occup: laborer. Enlisted in Worcester by Capt. Henry C. Ward, March 21, 1864; mustered April 6, 1864. Wounded in the head in action at the Wilderness, May 6, 1864. "[Private] John Daley, Co. C, 57th Massachusetts Volunteers, aged 36 years, was wounded in the head at the battle of the Wilderness, Virginia, May 6, 1864, by a conoidal [Minié] musket ball. He was sent to Washington [from Fredericksburg, VA] on the 16th [of May], and was admitted into the Lincoln [U.S. Army General] Hospital, where no fracture was suspected. On July 18th he was sent north, and on August 25th was admitted to the [U.S. Army General] hospital at Readville, Massachusetts. On October 24th he was sent to the Dale [U.S. Army General Hospital, Worcester, [MA,] where it was ascertained that the frontal bone was fractured and depressed. Convulsions of an epileptiform character supervened, but the patient finally recovered, and was discharged [on a Surgeons Certificate of Disability for wounds], Jan. 16, 1865. He was pensioned, and on July 20, 1867, was reported by pension examiner Oramel Martin, to be completely and permantly disabled" (OMR). Resided in Shrewsbury, MA, after the war, and died there, Oct. 30, 1895, age 66.

26. **Day, Charles W.,** private. Res: Peru, NY. Credit: Pittsfield, MA. Born: Lockport, NY. Age: 36. Height: 5'10". Comp: light. Eyes: blue. Hair: dark. Occup: mechanic. Enlisted in Pittsfield by W. H. Carson, Feb. 12, 1864; mustered Feb. 18, 1864. Deserted from Camp Wool, Feb. 29, 1864. Never returned.

27. **Day, Henry,** private. Res. and/or credit: Palmer, MA. Born: Dublin, Ireland. Age: 21. Height: 5'7". Comp: light. Eyes: gray. Hair: dark. Occup: engineer. Enlisted in Palmer by P. W. Webster, Feb. 8, 1864; mustered Feb. 18, 1864. In action at the Wilderness, May 6, 1864, Spotsylvania Court House, May 10, 12, and 18, 1864, North Anna River, May 24, 1864, Cold Harbor, June 3, 1864, and Petersburg assaults, June 17 and 18, 1864; killed in action at the Petersburg Crater, July 30, 1864.

With the regiment on all marches and in all skirmishes and battles until killed.

28. **Day, William,** private. Res. and/or credit: Springfield, MA. Born: Indianapolis, IN. Age: 19. Height: 5'8". Comp: light. Eyes: blue. Hair: brown. Occup: soldier. Enlisted in Co. G in Springfield by Capt. Charles D. Hollis, March 7, 1864; mustered March 10, 1864. Transferred to Co. C, March 31, 1864, under RSO 31, by order of Col. William F. Bartlett, dated March 30, 1864. Deserted from Camp Wool shortly after transfer, but exact date unknown. Arrested and returned by the provost marshal, April 15, 1864, and confined in the guardhouse until April 18, 1864. Never received his state bounty. Killed in action at the Wilderness, May 6, 1864.

29. **Defose, Charles L.,** 2nd lieutenant. Res. and/or credit: Worcester, MA. Born: Spencer, MA. Age: 22. Height: 5'5". Comp: dark. Eyes: black. Hair: black. Occup: shoemaker. Enlisted in Worcester by Capt. Henry C. Ward, Feb. 6, 1864; mustered Feb. 18, 1864. Promoted sergeant, Feb. 18, 1864. Promoted 1st sergeant, April 22, 1864. In action at the Wilderness, May 6, 1864, and one of the 34 enlisted men who remained with the colors during that battle. In action at Spotsylvania Court House, May 10, 12, and 18, 1864, North Anna River, May 24, 1864, Cold Harbor, June 3, 1864, and Petersburg assaults, June 17 and 18, 1864; wounded while on duty in the trenches at Petersburg, July 20, 1864, "hit with a minnie the ball passing just under the skin back of his shoulder" (GEB). Absent wounded in an army general hospital until Oct. 22, 1864. Issued one wool blanket, Nov. 15, 1864. Issued one pair of trousers, one flannel shirt, and one pair of mittens, Dec. 18, 1864. Issued a new Springfield rifle and new leather equipment, March 22, 1865. Issued one pair of trousers, two knitted shirts, one pair of drawers, and one pair of socks, Feb. 10, 1865. With the regiment in operations during the fall and winter of 1864–65, and slightly wounded again in the flesh of the hip in action at Fort Stedman, March 25, 1865. Absent wounded in the 1st Division, IX Corps, Field Hospital at Petersburg until an unknown date before April 30, 1865. Issued a new .58 cal.

Springfield rifle and new leather equipment, May 16, 1865. Discharged the US service to accept a commission, on or about June 11, 1865. Commissioned 2nd lieutenant, June 12, 1865; mustered 2nd lieutenant, June 26, 1865. Mustered out with the regiment, as 2nd lieutenant of Co. B, at Delaney house, Washington, DC, July 30, 1865, and discharged in Readville, MA, Aug. 9, 1865, expiration of service. Had previous service as a private in Co. D, 15th MVI, from July 12, 1861, until discharged for disability, April 10, 1863. Participated with that regiment at Ball's Bluff, Oct. 21, 1861, in the Peninsula campaign in 1862, and at Antietam, Sept. 17, 1862, and Fredericksburg, Dec. 13, 1862. Resided in Worcester, MA, after the war and died there in 1910, age 68.

30. **Devignon, Joseph David**, private. Res: Saranac Lake, NY. Credit: Pittsfield, MA. Born: Province of Quebec, Canada. Age: 29. Height: 5′9″. Comp: light. Eyes: blue. Hair: brown. Occup: laborer. Enlisted in Pittsfield by W. H. Carson, Jan. 28, 1864; mustered Feb. 18, 1864. Never in combat. Absent sick in an army general hospital from on or before May 6, 1864, until discharged the US service for disability, Aug. 10, 1865, by order of the War Dept.

31. **Dietrick, Christopher**, private. Res. and/or credit: Springfield, MA. Born: Germany. Age: 30. Height: 5′7½″. Comp: dark. Eyes: hazel. Hair: dark. Occup: carpenter. Enlisted in Springfield by Capt. Charles D. Hollis, Jan. 25, 1864; mustered Feb. 18, 1864. Never in combat. Absent sick in an army general hospital from on or before May 6, 1864 until after April 30, 1865. Issued a new .58 cal. Springfield rifle and new leather equipment, May 24, 1865. Mustered out with the regiment at Delaney house, Washington, DC, July 30, 1865, and discharged in Readville, Ma. Aug. 9, 1865, expiration of service.

32. **Dorr, Adam**, private. Res. and/or credit: Springfield, MA. Born: Germany. Age: 34. Height: 5′9″. Comp: dark. Eyes: black. Hair: black. Occup: shoemaker. Enlisted in Springfield by Capt. Charles D. Hollis, Jan. 21, 1864; mustered Feb. 18, 1864. Detached and

detailed as a pioneer at 1st Brigade, 1st Division, IX Corps, Headquarters from on or about May 1, 1864 until between Aug. 19 and Sept. 24, 1864. Issued one pair of drawers, Sept. 23, 1864. In action at Poplar Grove Church, Sept. 30 and Oct. 8, 1864. Mustered for pay, Oct. 13, 1864. Issued one flannel shirt, two pairs of socks, and one greatcoat, Oct. 15, 1864. Issued one sack coat (lined), and one pair of drawers, Nov. 15, 1864. Issued one forage cap, one pair of trousers, and one pair of mittens, Dec. 18, 1864. Issued one pair of drawers and two pairs of socks, Jan. 27, 1864. Issued a new .58 cal. Springfield rifle and new leather equipment, Feb. 3, 1864. Scarcely literate, could barely write his name. With the regiment in operations during the fall and winter of 1864–65 and in action at Fort Stedman, March 25, 1865. Mustered out with the regiment at Delaney house, Washington, DC, July 30, 1865, and discharged in Readville, MA, Aug. 9, 1865, expiration of service.

33. **Ellis, Albert F.**, private. Res. and credit: Worcester, MA. Born: Worcester, MA. Age: 18. Height: 5′½″. Comp: dark. Eyes: gray. Hair: black. Occup: farmer. Enlisted in Worcester by D. Waldo Lincoln, March 19, 1864; joined the company from the transient barracks, April 6, 1864; mustered April 6, 1864. Wounded in action at the Wilderness, May 6, 1864. Hospitalized in the Methodist Episcopal Church in Fredericksburg, VA, until transferred to another church being used as a hospital in Alexandria, VA. Remained there until sent home to recuperate. Absent wounded at home in Worcester, MA, until mustered out, as absent wounded, at Delaney house, Washington, DC, July 30, 1865, expiration of service.

34. **Farris, Daniel P.**, private. Res.: Uxbridge, MA. Credit: Worcester, MA. Born: North Vassalboro, ME. Age: 44. Height: 5′11″. Comp: dark. Eyes: blue. Hair: black. Occup: farmer. Enlisted in Worcester by J. W. Lampson, Feb. 8, 1864; mustered Feb. 18, 1864. Absent sick in an army general hospital from on or before May 6, 1864 until between Oct. 8 and Oct. 13, 1864. Mustered for pay, Oct. 13, 1864. Issued one pair of socks, one great-

coat, and one wool blanket, Oct. 15, 1864. Issued another wool blanket and one pair of mittens, Dec. 18, 1864. Issued one forage cap, one pair of trousers, one knitted shirt, one pair of drawers, and two pairs of socks, Jan. 27, 1865. Issued a new .58 cal. Springfield rifle and new leather equipment, Feb. 3, 1865. Issued one pair of socks, Feb. 10, 1865. Issued one pair of shoes and one knitted shirt, March 6, 1865. Issued one pair of shoes, April 30, 1865. Illiterate. Absent sick in the 1st Division, IX Corps, Field Hospital at Petersburg from Oct. 27 until Dec. 2, 1864. With the regiment in operations during most of the fall and winter of 1864–65, and in action at Fort Stedman, March 25, 1865. Absent sick in an army general hospital from after April 30, 1865, until discharged the US service for disability, Aug. 15, 1865, by order of the War Dept.

35. **Finn, Nicholas**, private. Res. and/or credit: Westfield, MA. Born: Ballyglass, County Mayo, Ireland. Age: 34. Height: 5'6½". Comp: light. Eyes: blue. Hair: brown. Occup: laborer. Enlisted in Westfield by L. C. Gillette, Jan. 29, 1864; mustered Feb. 18, 1864. Killed in action at the Wilderness, May 6, 1864.

36. **Flaviel, Robert**, private. Res: Ware, MA. Credit: Northampton, MA. Born: Province of Quebec, Canada. Age: 19. Height: 5'8". Comp: light. Eyes: gray. Hair: light. Occup: cooper. Enlisted in Northampton by Lt. Col. Luke Lyman, Jan. 30, 1864; mustered Feb. 18, 1864. Deserted while on furlough from Camp Wool, March 16, 1864, "at 11 o'clock, [his] furlough having expired" (CR). Never returned.

37. **Fosgate, Oliver**, private. Res: Westboro, MA. Credit: Worcester, MA. Born: Winchester, NH. Age: 43. Height: 5'6". Comp: light. Eyes: blue. Hair: brown. Occup: shoemaker. Enlisted in Worcester by E. Bullard, Feb. 11, 1864; mustered Feb. 18, 1864. In action at the Wilderness, May 6, 1864, and Spotsylvania Court House, May 10, 1864; wounded in the right index finger in action there, May 12, 1864. Absent wounded and on June 16, 1864, he underwent an "amputation

at lower third of [right] forearm by the circular method" performed by "A[cting] A[ssistant] Surgeon M. M. Jarratt" for "Felon on right index finger; fissures of hand sloughing; haemorrh[age] from palomar arch" (OMR). Absent wounded in an army general hospital until transferred to the 57th Co., 2nd Battln., VRC, Jan. 17, 1865; "sound stump" (OMR). Discharged the US service for disability, Sept. 20, 1865, by order of the War Dept.

38. **Frink, Charles F.**, private. Res. and/or credit: Sheffield, MA. Born: Cromwell, CT. Age: 20. Height: 5'8". Comp: dark. Eyes: black. Hair: black. Occup: laborer. Enlisted in Sheffield by E. E. Callender, Feb. 8, 1864; mustered Feb. 18, 1864. Deserted from Camp Wool, Feb. 18, 1864. Never returned.

39. **Gallen, Patrick**, corporal. Res. and/or credit: Milford, MA. Born: County Leitrim, Ireland. Age: 30. Height: 5'3½". Comp: fair. Eyes: blue. Hair: light. Occup: bootmaker. Enlisted in Milford by Leonard Hunt, Feb. 9, 1864; mustered Feb. 18, 1864. Promoted corporal, Feb. 18, 1864. Wounded in the left hand "losing his forefinger" *(HOM)* in action at the Wilderness, May 6, 1864. Absent wounded in an army general hospital until Oct. 13, 1864. Mustered for pay, Oct. 13, 1864. Issued one flannel shirt, one pair of socks, and one rubber blanket, Nov. 15, 1864. Issued one pair of drawers, one pair of socks, and one pair of mittens, Dec. 18, 1864. Issued one knitted shirt, Jan. 27, 1865. Issued a new .58 cal. Springfield rifle and new leather equipment, Feb. 3, 1865. Issued one pair of trousers, Feb. 10, 1865. Issued one pair of shoes, March 6, 1864. With the regiment in operations during the fall and winter of 1864–65, and taken prisoner of war in action at Fort Stedman, March 25, 1865. Paroled and exchanged from Libby Prison in Richmond, VA, April 1, 1865. Returned to the regiment for duty from the Camp of Parole in Annapolis, MD, on or about May 11, 1865. Issued a new .58 cal. Springfield rifle and new leather equipment, May 16, 1865. Mustered out with the regiment at Delaney house, Washington, DC, July 30, 1865, and discharged in Readville, MA, Aug. 9, 1865, expiration of service. Had previous service as a private in Co. F,

19th MVI, from Aug. 28, 1861, until discharged for disability from "Convalescent Camp, VA" *(MSSM)*, April 13, 1863. Participated with that regiment in the Peninsula campaign in 1862, at Antietam, Sept. 17, 1862, and Fredericksburg, Dec. 11 and 13, 1862. Resided in Grafton, MA, after the war.

40. **Glazier, Danforth**, private. Res: Duane, NY. Credit: Northampton, MA. Born: Brookfield, VT. Age: 43. Height: 5′5″. Comp: light. Eyes: blue. Hair: brown. Occup: farmer. Enlisted in Northampton by Lt. Col. Luke Lyman, Feb. 13, 1864; mustered Feb. 18, 1864. In action at the Wilderness, May 6, 1864, Spotsylvania Court House, May 10, 12, and 18, 1864, North Anna River, May 24, 1864, and Cold Harbor, June 3, 1864. Died from disease at Cold Harbor, June 12, 1864. With the regiment on all marches and in all skirmishes and battles until deceased.

41. **Gokey, Joseph**, private. Res: Duane, NY. Credit: Northampton, MA. Born: Sciota, NY. Age: 23. Height: 5′6″. Comp: dark. Eyes: gray. Hair: dark. Occup: farmer. Enlisted in Northampton by Lt. Col. Luke Lyman, Feb. 9, 1864; mustered Feb. 18, 1864. Deserted in Philadelphia, PA, during the march to the front, April 19, 1864. Never returned. "Bounty jumper" (JA). Had previous service as a private in Co. D, 34th New York Volunteer Infantry (specifics unknown).

42. **Gray, James**, private. Res. and/or credit: Springfield, MA. Born: Ireland. Age: 29. Height: 5′7½″. Comp: light. Eyes: blue. Hair: light. Occup: boilermaker. Enlisted in Springfield by Lt. Henry B. Fiske, Feb. 15, 1864; mustered Feb. 18, 1864. Deserted in Philadelphia, PA, during the march to the front, April 19, 1864. Never returned. "Bounty jumper" (JA).

43. **Harley, Cornelius**, private. Res. and/or credit: Springfield, MA. Born: Canada. Age: 45. Height: 5′6″. Comp: dark. Eyes: blue. Hair: dark. Occup: armorer. Enlisted in Springfield by Capt. Charles D. Hollis, Jan. 30, 1864; mustered Feb. 18, 1864. Wounded in action at the Wilderness, May 6, 1864. Absent wounded in an army general hospital until between Aug. 19 and Sept. 23, 1864. Issued one sack coat (unlined), one pair of trousers, and one pair of shoes, Sept. 23, 1864. In action at Poplar Grove Church, Sept. 30 and Oct. 8, 1864. Mustered for pay, Oct. 13, 1864. Issued one flannel shirt, one greatcoat, and one wool blanket, Oct. 15, 1864. Issued one sack coat (lined), one pair of trousers, one pair of socks, and one pair of mittens, Dec. 18, 1864. Issued two knitted shirts and one pair of socks, Jan. 27, 1864. Issued a new .58 cal. Springfield rifle and new leather equipment, Feb. 3, 1865. Illiterate. Detached and detailed at 3rd Brigade, 1st Division, IX Corps, Headquarters as a pioneer from Oct. 28, 1864, until muster-out. In action at Fort Stedman, March 25, 1865. Mustered out with the regiment at Delaney house, Washington, DC, July 30, 1865, and discharged in Readville, MA, Aug. 9, 1865, expiration of service. Died in 1895, age 76.

44. **Hastings, Russell**, private. Res: Hinsdale, MA. Credit: Pittsfield, MA. Born: Champion, NY. Age: 34. Height: 5′11″. Comp: fair. Eyes: blue. Hair: brown. Occup: farmer. Enlisted in Pittsfield by W. H. Carson, Jan. 28, 1864; mustered Feb. 18, 1864. Never in combat. Absent sick in an army general hospital in Washington, DC, from on or before May 6, 1864, where he died from disease, July 28, 1864.

45. **Holden, Gustavus S.**, private. Res. and credit: Holden, MA. Born: Holden, MA, Feb. 26, 1846. Age: 18. Height: 5′8″. Comp: light. Eyes: blue. Hair: light. Occup: bootmaker. Enlisted in Holden by Capt. Julius M. Tucker, Feb. 12, 1864; mustered Feb. 18, 1864. Wounded in action at the Wilderness, May 6, 1864. Absent wounded in Carver US Army General Hospital in Washington, DC. When Confederate Gen. Jubal A. Early made a foray against Washington on July 11 and 12, 1864, Holden (his wound being sufficiently healed) joined a provisional brigade in the capital to help repulse the Southerners. Returned to the regiment for duty, Aug. 1, 1864. Issued one canteen and one haversack, Aug. 6, 1864. In action at Weldon Railroad, Aug. 19, 1864, and one of the 30 combat soldiers remaining of the regiment after that battle.

Mustered for pay, Aug. 31, 1864. In action at Poplar Grove Church, Sept. 30 and Oct. 8, 1864. Mustered for pay, Oct. 13, 1864. Issued one pair of trousers and one greatcoat, Oct. 15, 1864. Issued a new .58 cal. Springfield rifle and new leather equipment, Feb. 3, 1865. Literate. With the regiment in operations during the fall and winter of 1864–65. Taken prisoner of war in action at Fort Stedman, March 25, 1865. Paroled and exchanged from Libby Prison in Richmond, VA, March 31, 1865. Returned to the regiment for duty from the Camp of Parole in Annapolis, MD, on or about May 11, 1865. Issued a new .58 cal. Springfield rifle and new leather equipment, May 16, 1865. Mustered out with the regiment at Delaney house, Washington, DC, July 30, 1865, and discharged in Readville, MA, Aug. 9, 1865, expiration of service. Resided in Holden, MA, after the war and died there after 1911, exact date unknown.

46. **Holland, John B.**, corporal. Res: Holyoke, MA. Credit: Springfield, MA. Born: Ireland. Age: 29. Height: 5'7". Comp: dark. Eyes: gray. Hair: black. Occup: mechanic. Enlisted in Springfield by Capt. Charles D. Hollis, Jan. 29, 1864; mustered Feb. 18, 1864. Promoted corporal, Feb. 18, 1864. Detached and detailed on recruiting service in Springfield, MA, from Feb. 18, 1864 until March 5, 1864 under RSOs 16 and 17, by order of Lt. Col. Edward P. Hollister, dated Feb. 29 and March 5, 1864, respectively. Detached and detailed at 1st Brigade, 1st Division, IX Corps, Headquarters as a pioneer from on or about May 1, 1864, until between Aug. 19 and Sept. 23, 1864. Issued one sack coat (unlined) and one pair of drawers, Sept. 23, 1864. Literate. In action at Poplar Grove Church, Sept. 30 and Oct. 8, 1864. Absent sick in an army general hospital from between Oct. 8 and Oct. 13, 1864, until after May 24, 1865. Mustered out with the regiment at Delaney house, Washington, DC, July 30, 1865, and discharged in Readville, MA, Aug. 9, 1865, expiration of service.

47. **Hollis, Charles D.**, captain. Res. and credit: Lynn, MA. Born: Lynn, MA. Age: 39. Height: unknown. Comp: fair. Eyes: blue. Hair: brown. Occup: bootmaker. Commis-

Captain Charles Hollis in very old age. *(USAMHI)*

sioned 2nd lieutenant, Oct. 13, 1863; mustered 2nd lieutenant, Oct. 16, 1863. Commissioned 1st lieutenant, Feb. 11, 1864; mustered 1st lieutenant, Feb. 18, 1864. Commissioned captain, April 9, 1864; mustered Captain April 20, 1864. Severely wounded in the genitals in action at the Wilderness, May 6, 1864. Absent wounded until resigned and discharged the US service for disability from wounds, Oct. 13, 1864, under SO 345, AGO, War Dept. Had previous service as a sergeant in Co. K, 46th MVI, from Oct. 12, 1862, until mustered out, July 29, 1863. Participated in the North Carolina campaign with that regiment in 1862–63. President of the 57th's regimental association in 1869. Resided in Lynn, MA, after the war, and died there after 1902, but date not known.

48. **Houle, Joseph**, private. Res: North Adams, MA. Credit: Adams, MA. Born: Canada. Age: 19. Height: 5'8". Comp: light. Eyes: black. Hair: dark. Occup: shoemaker. Enlisted in Adams by S. Johnson, Feb. 13, 1864; mustered Feb. 18, 1864. Wounded in action at the Wilderness, May 6, 1864. Absent

wounded in an army general hospital until he deserted from there, July 23, 1864. Surrendered to authorities on an unknown date and desertion charge dropped by act of Congress. Discharge certificate issued, to date from July 23, 1864.

49. **Howard, Charles**, sergeant. Res. and/or credit: Greenfield, MA. Born: Boston, MA. Age: 23. Height: 5′8″. Comp: light. Eyes: blue. Hair: brown. Occup: clerk. Enlisted in Greenfield by H. Stevens, Feb. 2, 1864; mustered Feb. 18, 1864. Promoted sergeant, Feb. 18, 1864. Deserted from Camp Wool, April 1, 1864. Never returned.

50. **Hughes, John**, private. Res. and/or credit: Great Barrington, MA. Born: Ireland. Age: 42. Height: 5′8¾″. Comp: light. Eyes: brown. Hair: black. Occup: laborer. Enlisted in Great Barrington by John M. Seeley, Feb. 4, 1864; mustered Feb. 18, 1864. Wounded in action at the Wilderness, May 6, 1864. Absent wounded in an army general hospital until between April 30 and May 24, 1865. Issued a new .58 cal. Springfield rifle and new leather equipment, May 24, 1864. Mustered out with the regiment at Delaney house, Washington, DC, July 30, 1865, and discharged in Readville, MA, Aug. 9, 1865, expiration of service.

51. **Kellogg, Charles F.**, 1st sergeant. Res: Amherst, MA. Credit: Northampton, MA. Born: Amherst, MA. Age: 38. Height: 5′9″. Comp: light. Eyes: blue. Hair: dark. Occup: railroad overseer. Enlisted in Northampton by C. Ingram, Feb. 2, 1864; mustered Feb. 18, 1864. Promoted 1st sergeant, Feb. 18, 1864. Reduced to sergeant, April 22, 1864. Wounded in action at the Wilderness, May 6, 1864. Absent wounded in an army general hospital until discharged the US service for disability from wounds, July 20, 1865, by order of the War Dept., discharge to date, July 30, 1865. Had previous service as a sergeant in Co. H, 2nd MVI, from May 11, 1861, until discharged for disability, Feb. 14, 1863. Participated with that regiment in the Shenandoah Valley campaign in 1862, at Cedar Mountain, Aug. 9, 1862, and An-

tietam, Sept. 17, 1862. Resided in Springfield, MA, after the war.

52. **Kelly, Michael**, private. Res. and/or credit: Worcester, MA. Born: Ireland. Age: 18. Height: 5′½″. Comp: dark. Eyes: gray. Hair: black. Occup: chair maker. Enlisted in Worcester by Capt. Henry C. Ward, Feb. 2, 1864; mustered Feb. 18, 1864. Wounded in action at the Wilderness, May 6, 1864. Absent wounded in an army general hospital until between Aug. 19 and Sept. 23, 1864. Issued one pair of shoes and one rubber blanket, Sept. 23, 1864. In action at Poplar Grove Church, Sept. 30 and Oct. 8, 1864. Mustered for pay, Oct. 13, 1864. Issued one forage cap and one greatcoat, Oct. 15, 1864. Issued two flannel shirts and one rubber blanket, Nov. 15, 1864. Issued one pair of trousers and one pair of mittens, Dec. 18, 1864. Issued one sack coat (lined), one knitted shirt, one pair of drawers, one pair of shoes, and four pairs of socks, Jan. 27, 1865. Issued a new .58 cal. Springfield rifle and new leather equipment, Feb. 3, 1865. Issued one knitted shirt, Feb. 10, 1865. Issued one pair of trousers, March 6, 1865. With the regiment in operations during the fall and winter of 1864–65, and in action at Fort Stedman, March 25, 1865. Issued one sack coat (unlined), one pair of drawers, one pair of shoes, and one pair of socks, April 30, 1865. Illiterate. Mustered out with the regiment at Delaney house, Washington, DC, July 30, 1865, and discharged in Readville, MA, Aug. 9, 1865, expiration of service. Resided in Worcester, MA, after the war.

53. **King, Victor**, private. Res: Webster, MA. Credit: Worcester, MA. Born: Canada. Age: 26. Height: 5′9″. Comp: dark. Eyes: gray. Hair: dark. Occup: weaver. Enlisted in Worcester by N. Joslin, Feb. 11, 1864; mustered Feb. 18, 1864. Deserted from Camp Wool, March 28, 1864. Arrested, returned, and confined in the guardhouse in Camp Wool from April 14 until April 18, 1864. Did not leave Camp Wool with the regiment, but sent to Camp Meigs in Readville, MA, April 18, 1864, under the supervision of Lt. John Cook for a medical examination. Found unfit for duty by a "board of inspectors." Rejected recruit and discharged the US service in

Worcester, MA, July 27, 1864, by order of Maj. Gen. John A. Dix, War Dept.

54. Kinnerney, George, private. Res. and/or credit: Warren, MA. Born: Ireland. Age: 28. Height: 5'7". Comp: light. Eyes: blue. Hair: auburn. Occup: laborer. Enlisted in Warren by D. Russell, Feb. 2, 1864; mustered Feb. 18, 1864. Detached and detailed as a guard or driver with the 1st Division, IX Corps, ambulance wagon train, April 27, 1864 until muster-out. Never in combat. Mustered out with the regiment at Delaney house, Washington, DC, July 30, 1865, and discharged in Readville, MA, Aug. 9, 1865, expiration of service.

55. Knight, Charles A., private. Res: Duane, NY. Credit: Northampton, MA. Born: Malone, NY. Age: 25. Height: 5'6". Comp: dark. Eyes: black. Hair: black. Occup: farmer. Enlisted in Northampton by Lt. Col. Luke Lyman, Feb. 9, 1864; mustered Feb. 18, 1864. Wounded in action at the Wilderness, May 6, 1864. Absent wounded in an army general hospital until transferred to Co. A, 14th Regiment, VRC, Jan. 10, 1865. Discharged the US service, July 30, 1865, by order of the War Dept., expiration of service.

56. Knox, Charles F., sergeant. Res: West Springfield, MA. Credit: Springfield, MA. Born: Medina, OH. Age: 25. Height: 5'7". Comp: dark. Eyes: black. Hair: black. Occup: farmer. Enlisted in Springfield by Capt. Charles D. Hollis, Dec. 28, 1863; mustered Feb. 18, 1864. Promoted sergeant, Feb. 18, 1864. Detached and detailed on recruiting service with Capt. Lewis A. Tifft in Springfield, MA, from Feb. 18 until March 5, 1864, under RSOs 9 and 17, dated Feb. 18 and March 5, 1864 respectively, by order of Col. William F. Bartlett. Shot between the eyes and killed in action at the Wilderness, May 6, 1864. Had previous service as a corporal in Co. E, 46th MVI, from Aug. 20, 1862, until mustered out, July 29, 1863. Participated in the North Carolina campaign with that regiment in 1862–63.

57. Kyle, William, private. Res. and/or credit: Northampton, MA. Born: Montreal, Quebec, Canada. Age: 25. Height: 5'7". Comp: light. Eyes: blue. Hair: light. Occup:

painter. Enlisted in Northampton by Lt. Col. Luke Lyman, Jan. 26, 1864; mustered Feb. 18, 1864. Wounded in action at the Wilderness, May 6, 1864. Absent wounded in an army general hospital until Oct. 24, 1864. Issued one rubber blanket, Oct. 24, 1864. Issued one pair of drawers, one pair of shoes, and one pair of socks, Nov. 15, 1864. Issued one pair of trousers and one pair of mittens, Dec. 18, 1864. Issued one sack coat (lined), one pair of trousers, one pair of shoes, and one pair of socks, Jan. 27, 1865. Issued a new .58 cal. Springfield rifle and new leather equipment, Feb. 3, 1865. Issued one pair of trousers and one knitted shirt, Feb. 10, 1865. Issued one forage cap and one pair of socks, March 6, 1865. Literate. With the regiment in operations during the fall and winter of 1864–65, and taken prisoner of war in action at Fort Stedman, March 25, 1865. Paroled and exchanged from Libby Prison in Richmond, VA, March 29, 1865. Returned to the regiment for duty from the Camp of Parole in Annapolis, MD, on or about May 11, 1865. Issued a new .58 cal. Springfield rifle and leather equipment, May 24, 1865. Mustered out with the regiment at Delaney house, Washington, DC, July 30, 1865, and discharged in Readville, MA, Aug. 9, 1865, expiration of service.

58. Labombard, Peter, private. Res: Hinsdale, MA. Credit: Pittsfield, MA. Born: province of Quebec, Canada. Age: 34. Height: 5'7". Comp: light. Eyes: blue. Hair: brown. Occup: farmer. Enlisted in Pittsfield by Joseph Tucker, March 10, 1864; joined the company from the transient barracks, April 6, 1864; mustered April 6, 1864. Killed in action at the Wilderness, May 6, 1864.

59. Lappelle, Cassimere, private. Res. and/or credit: Spencer, MA. Born: province of Quebec, Canada. Age: 26. Height: 5'8". Comp: dark. Eyes: blue. Hair: brown. Occup: bootmaker. Enlisted in Spencer by L. Hill, March 22, 1864; mustered April 6, 1864. In action at the Wilderness, May 6, 1864, and one of the 34 enlisted men who remained with the colors during that battle. In action at Spotsylvania Court House, May 10, 1864, and wounded in action there, May 12, 1864. Absent wounded in an army general hospital until discharged the US service for disability from wounds, Feb. 6, 1865, by order of the War Dept.

60. **Lavonta, David,** private. Res. and/or credit: Spencer, MA. Born: province of Quebec, Canada. Age: 19. Height: 5'7". Comp: fair. Eyes: gray. Hair: black. Occup: bootmaker. Enlisted in Spencer by L. Hill, Feb. 2, 1864; mustered Feb. 18, 1864. Wounded in action at the Wilderness, May 6, 1864. Absent wounded in an army general hospital until between Oct. 8 and Oct. 13, 1864. Mustered for pay, Oct. 13, 1864. Issued one wool blanket, Oct. 15, 1864. Issued one forage cap, one flannel shirt, one pair of drawers, and three pairs of socks, Nov. 15, 1864. Issued one sack coat (lined) and one pair of mittens, Dec. 18, 1864. Issued one pair of trousers, two knitted shirts, one pair of drawers, and two pairs of socks, Jan. 27, 1865. Illiterate. Absent sick in an army general hospital from shortly after Jan. 27, 1865, until discharged the US service for disability, June 23, 1865, by order of the War Dept.

61. **Lee, William,** private. Res: Worcester, MA. Credit: Springfield, MA. Born: Ireland. Age: 33. Height: 5'4¾". Comp: light. Eyes: blue. Hair: red. Occup: teamster. Enlisted in Springfield by Capt. Lewis A. Tifft, Feb. 26, 1864; mustered Feb. 18, 1864. Detached and detailed as a teamster on the 1st Brigade, 1st Division, IX Corps, wagon train from about May 1, 1864, until early in 1865 (as of 3rd Brigade). Never in combat. Mustered for pay, Oct. 13, 1864. Issued one forage cap, Oct. 15, 1864. Issued one pair of trousers and one pair of shoes, Jan. 27, 1865. Illiterate. Absent sick in an army general hospital from late Jan. or early Feb., 1865, until before March 25, 1865. Detailed as cook to Capt. Barton upon his return from the hospital. Present during the battle of Fort Stedman, but not in action. Absent sick in an army general hospital from after March 31, 1865, until discharged the US service for disability, Aug. 10, 1865, by order of the War Dept. Resided in Worcester, MA, after the war.

62. **Leroy, Frank B.,** private. Res: Lancaster, MA. Credit: Worcester, MA. Born: Howell, MI. Age: 18. Height: 5'5". Comp: light. Eyes: blue. Hair: light. Occup: farmer. Enlisted in Worcester by Capt. Henry C. Ward, Feb. 17, 1864; mustered Feb. 18, 1864. Never in combat. Absent sick in an army general hospital from on or before May 6, 1864, until discharged the US service for disability, June 22, 1865, by order of the War Dept.

63. **Love, John,** private. Res. and/or credit: Spencer, MA. Born: Canada. Age: 35. Height: 5'8". Comp: dark. Eyes: black. Hair: black. Occup: bootmaker. Enlisted in Spencer by L. Hill, Feb. 3, 1864; mustered Feb. 18, 1864. Absent sick or on detached duty from on or before May 6, 1864, until between Aug. 19 and Sept. 23, 1864. Issued one pair of trousers and one pair of shoes, Sept. 23, 1864. Illiterate. In action at Poplar Grove Church, Sept. 30, 1864, and wounded in the head in action there, Oct. 8, 1864. "Love, John, Private, Co. C, 57th Massachusetts, aged 35 years. Petersburg, October 8th, 1864. Depressed fracture of left parietal near vertex by conoidal [Minié] ball. [admitted to 1st Division, IX] Corps [field hospital], Beverly [U.S. Army General Hospital, Beverly, NJ], and Satterlee [U.S. Army General Hospital, Washington, DC] hospitals. Removal of large fragments" (OMR). Absent wounded until discharged and pensioned from the US service from Satterlee Hospital for disability from wounds, May 24, 1865, by order of the War Dept. "July 10, 1868, disability rated total by Examiner Oramel Martin, M.D." (OMR). Resided in Spencer, MA, after the war.

64. **Lovejoy, Michael,** sergeant. Res. and/or credit: Sheffield, MA. Born: Cork, Ireland. Age: 27. Height: 5'10". Comp: light. Eyes: blue. Hair: brown. Occup: fireman. Enlisted in Sheffield by E. E. Callender, Feb. 2, 1864; mustered Feb. 18, 1864. Deserted from Camp Wool, March 22, 1864. Arrested, returned, and confined in the guardhouse in Camp Wool from March 25 until March 30, 1864. In action at the Wilderness, May 6, 1864, Spotsylvania Court House, May 10, 12, and 18, 1864, North Anna River, May 24, 1864, Cold Harbor, June 3, 1864, Petersburg assaults, June 17 and 18, 1864, and Petersburg Crater, July 30, 1864. Promoted sergeant, July 30, 1864. In action at Weldon Railroad, Aug. 19, 1864, and one of the 30 men remaining of

the regiment after that battle. Mustered for pay, Aug. 31 and Oct. 13, 1864. In action at Poplar Grove Church, Sept. 30 and Oct. 8, 1864. With the regiment in operations during the fall and winter of 1864–65. Issued one sack coat (lined), one pair of trousers, and two pairs of socks, Nov. 9, 1864. Issued one wool blanket and one pair of mittens, Dec. 18, 1864. Issued one pair of trousers, one knitted shirt, and one pair of drawers, Jan. 17, 1865. Issued a new .58 cal. Springfield rifle and new leather equipment, Feb. 3, 1865. Issued one pair of drawers, Feb. 10, 1865. Literate. In action at Fort Stedman, March 25, 1865. Deserted in Washington, May 10, 1865. Never returned to the regiment, but some arrangements evidently were made with the War Dept. on an unknown date because he was eventually given a discharge to date from May 10, 1865. One of the 11 men who served with the regiment on all marches and in all skirmishes and battles through its entire wartime service, and of the surviving 10, one of the 5 that was never wounded or taken prisoner of war.

65. **McKenney, Michael,** private. Res. and/or credit: Mendon, MA. Born: Ireland. Age: 40. Height: 5′3″. Comp: dark. Eyes: black. Hair: black. Occup: bootmaker. Enlisted in Mendon by A. H. Allen, Jan. 29, 1864; mustered Feb. 18, 1864. Never in combat. Absent sick in an army general hospital from on or before May 6, 1864, until discharged the US service for disability, Aug. 10, 1865, by order of the War Dept.

66. **Meatte, Jacob,** private. Res: Madrid, NY. Credit: Pittsfield, MA. Born: province of Ontario, Canada. Age: 44. Height: 5′10½″. Comp: light. Eyes: blue. Hair: brown. Occup: farmer. Enlisted in Pittsfield by W. H. Carson, Jan. 28, 1864; mustered Feb. 18, 1864. Wounded in action at the Wilderness, May 6, 1864. Absent wounded in an army general hospital until between Aug. 19 and Sept. 23, 1864. Issued one sack coat (unlined), one pair of trousers, and one pair of drawers, Sept. 23, 1864. In action at Poplar Grove Church, Sept. 30 and Oct. 8, 1864. Mustered for pay Oct. 13, 1864. Issued one sack coat (lined), one pair of drawers, one pair of socks, and one

greatcoat, Oct. 15, 1864. Absent sick in the 1st Division, IX Corps, Field Hospital at Petersburg from Oct. 26 until Oct. 31, 1864. Issued one pair of trousers, Jan. 27, 1865. Issued a new .58 cal. Springfield rifle and new leather equipment, Feb. 3, 1865. Issued one rubber blanket, March 6, 1865. Illiterate. With the regiment in operations during the fall and winter of 1864–65, and taken prisoner of war in action at Fort Stedman, March 25, 1865. Paroled and exchanged from Libby Prison in Richmond, VA, March 29, 1865. Returned to the regiment for duty from the Camp of Parole in Annapolis, MD, on or about May 11, 1865. Issued a new .58 cal. Springfield rifle and new leather equipment, May 16, 1865. Mustered out with the regiment at Delaney house, Washington, DC, July 30, 1865, and discharged in Readville, MA, Aug. 9, 1865, expiration of service.

67. **Miller, Joseph,** sergeant. Res: South Hadley, MA. Credit: Northampton, MA. Born: Ludlow, MA. Age: 27. Height: 5′10″. Comp: light. Eyes: blue. Hair: dark. Occup: clerk. Enlisted in Northampton by H. Smith, Jr., Feb. 2, 1864; mustered Feb. 18, 1864. Promoted sergeant, Feb. 18, 1864. Detached and detailed to relieve Sgt. Knox on recruiting service in Springfield, MA, with Capt. Lewis A. Tifft from March 5, 1864, until before April 18, 1864. In action at the Wilderness, May 6, 1864, and Spotsylvania Court House, May 10, 12, and 18, 1864; taken prisoner of war in action at North Anna River, May 24, 1864. Incarcerated in the Confederate prison camp in Andersonville, GA, where he died from disease, July 26, 1864. Had previous service as a private in Co. A, 46th MVI, from Sept. 19, 1862, until mustered out, July 29, 1863. Participated in the North Carolina campaign with that regiment in 1862–63.

68. **Monney, Peter,** private. Res. and/or credit: Pittsfield, MA. Born: Switzerland. Age: 44. Height: 5′10″. Comp: dark. Eyes: blue. Hair: brown. Occup: laborer. Enlisted in Pittsfield by J. Colburn, Jan. 3, 1864; mustered Feb. 18, 1864. In action at the Wilderness, May 6, 1864, and Spotsylvania Court House, May 10, 1864; killed in action there, May 12, 1864.

69. **Murphy, John,** private. Res. and/or credit: Milford, MA. Born: Watertown, MA, June 29, 1845. Age: 19. Height: 5′7″. Comp: fair. Eyes: gray. Hair: black. Occup: boot-maker. Enlisted in Milford by Leonard Hunt, Feb. 9, 1864; mustered Feb. 18, 1864. Slightly wounded in action at the Wilderness, May 6, 1864. Absent wounded in an army general hospital until between Aug. 19 and Sept. 23, 1864. Issued one pair of trousers, Sept. 23, 1864. In action at Poplar Grove Church, Sept. 30 and Oct. 8, 1864. Mustered for pay, Oct. 13, 1864. Issued one forage cap, one pair of shoes, and one greatcoat, Oct. 15, 1864. Issued one pair of trousers, one flannel shirt, and one pair of drawers, Nov. 15, 1864. Issued one flannel shirt, one pair of drawers, one pair of socks, and one pair of mittens, Dec. 18, 1864. Issued one sack coat (lined), one pair of trousers, one pair of drawers, and one pair of socks, Jan. 27, 1865. Issued a new .58 cal. Springfield rifle and new leather equipment, Feb. 3, 1865. Issued one pair of trousers, Feb. 10, 1865. Illiterate. With the regiment in operations during the fall and winter of 1864–65, and taken prisoner of war in action at Fort Stedman, March 25, 1865. Paroled and exchanged from Libby Prison in Richmond, VA, April 1, 1865. Returned to the regiment for duty on or about May 11, 1865. Issued a new .58 cal. Springfield rifle and new leather equipment, May 24, 1865. Mustered out with the regiment at Delaney house, Washington, DC, July 30, 1865, and discharged in Readville, MA, Aug. 9, 1865, expiration of service.

70. **Newton, John,** private. Res: Millbury, MA. Credit: Worcester, MA. Born: Waterford, Ireland. Age: 28. Height: 5′6¼″. Comp: dark. Eyes: blue. Hair: brown. Occup: laborer. Enlisted in Worcester by Lt. John Reade, March 25, 1864; joined the company from the transient barracks, April 6, 1864; mustered April 6, 1864. In action at the Wilderness, May 6, 1864, and Spotsylvania Court House, May 10 and 12, 1864; wounded in action there, May 18, 1864. Absent wounded in an army general hospital until between April 30 and May 24, 1865. Issued a new .58 cal. Springfield rifle and new leather equipment, May 24, 1865. Mustered out with the regiment at Delaney house, Washington, DC, July 30, 1865, and discharged in Readville, MA, Aug. 9, 1865, expiration of service.

71. **Neylon, John,** private. Res. and/or credit: Worcester, MA. Born: County Clare, Ireland. Age: 40. Height: 5′4″. Comp: dark. Eyes: gray. Hair: black. Occup: laborer. Enlisted in Worcester by Lt. John Reade, Feb. 5, 1864; mustered Feb. 18, 1864. In action at the Wilderness, May 6, 1864, and Spotsylvania Court House, May 10 and 12, 1864; wounded in action there, May 18, 1864. Absent wounded in an army general hospital until between Aug. 19 and Sept. 23, 1864. Issued one rubber blanket, Sept. 23, 1864. In action at Poplar Grove Church, Sept. 30 and Oct. 8, 1864. Mustered for pay, Oct. 13, 1864. Issued a new .58 cal. Springfield rifle and new leather equipment, March 22, 1865. With the regiment in operations during the fall and winter of 1864–65, and in action at Fort Stedman, March 25, 1865. Issued one forage cap, one pair of drawers, and one knitted shirt, April 30, 1865. Mustered out with the regiment at Delaney house, Washington, DC, July 30, 1865, and discharged in Readville, MA, Aug. 9, 1865, expiration of service. Died in 1891, age 71.

72. **Norway, James,** private. Res: Hinsdale, MA. Credit: Pittsfield, MA. Born: Farrisburg, NY. Age: 19. Height: 5′8″. Comp: light. Eyes: blue. Hair: dark. Occup: farmer. Enlisted in Pittsfield by W. H. Carson, Feb. 12, 1864; mustered Feb. 18, 1864. Wounded in action at the Wilderness, May 6, 1864. Absent wounded in an army general hospital until just prior to March 25, 1865. Wounded in action at Fort Stedman, March 25, 1865. Absent wounded until mustered out as absent wounded at Delaney house, Washington, DC, July 30, 1865, expiration of service.

73. **O'Donnell, Patrick,** private. Res: Milford, MA. Credit: Worcester, MA. Born: County Donegal, Ireland. Age: 35. Height: 5′7½″. Comp: dark. Eyes: gray. Hair: dark. Occup: bootmaker. Enlisted in Worcester by Lt. John Reade, Feb. 4, 1864; mustered Feb. 18, 1864. Deserted from Camp Wool, March 28, 1864, but returned the following day, March 29,

1864. Never in combat. Absent sick from on or before May 6, 1864, until discharged the US service for disability from Dale US Army General Hospital in Worcester, MA, Dec. 13, 1864, by order of the War Dept.

74. **Pell, William,** private. Res. and/or credit: Westfield, MA. Born: Gibbon, NY. Age: 30. Height: 6'½". Comp: light. Eyes: gray. Hair: brown. Occup: watchmaker. Enlisted in Westfield by L. C. Gillette, Jan. 28, 1864; mustered Feb. 18, 1864. Confined in the guardhouse in Camp Wool for "disobedience of orders" (CR), Feb. 18, 1864. Deserted from Camp Wool, March 19, 1864. Never returned.

75. **Picardet, George,** private. Res. and/or credit: Pittsfield, MA. Born: Euzet, France. Age: 32. Height: 5"10¼". Comp: light. Eyes: blue. Hair: dark. Occup: laborer. Enlisted in Pittsfield by John C. West, March 12, 1864; mustered April 6, 1864. Wounded in action at the Wilderness, May 6, 1864. Absent wounded in Fairfax Seminary US Army General Hospital in Fairfax, VA, until discharged the US service for disability from wounds, March 29, 1865, by order of the War Dept.

76. **Place, Alonzo H.,** corporal. Res: province of Quebec, Canada. Credit: Greenfield, MA. Born: province of Quebec, Canada. Age: 23. Height: 5'7". Comp: light. Eyes: blue. Hair: light. Occup: laborer. Enlisted in Greenfield by H. Stevens, Jan. 18, 1864; mustered Feb. 18, 1864. Recruited by a broker who, for his services, was paid $225 of Place's state bounty, leaving Place with only $100. Promoted corporal on an unknown date. Absent sick or on detached duty during the battle of the Wilderness, May 6, 1864. In action at Spotsylvania Court House, May 10, 12, and 18, 1864, North Anna River, May 24, 1864, Cold Harbor, June 3, 1864, and Petersburg assaults, June 17 and 18, 1864; shot through the leg and wounded while on duty in the trenches at Petersburg, June 27, 1864. With the regiment on all marches and in all skirmishes and battles, except the Wilderness, until wounded. Absent wounded in an army general hospital until discharged the US ser-

vice for disability from wounds, May 18, 1865, by order of the War Dept.

77. **Poisson, Simeon,** private. Res: Ware, MA. Credit: Northampton, MA. Born: province of Quebec, Canada. Age: 19. Height: 5'8½". Comp: florid. Eyes: gray. Hair: brown. Occup: farmer. Enlisted in Northampton by Lt. Col. Luke Lyman, Jan. 13, 1864; mustered Feb. 18, 1864. Deserted while on furlough from Camp Wool, March 16, 1864, "at 11 o'clock, [his] furlough having expired" (CR). Never returned.

78. **Powers, James G.,** private. Res. and/or credit: Chicopee, MA. Born: New Haven, CT. Age: 18. Height: 5'8". Comp: light. Eyes: black. Hair: brown. Occup: harness maker. Enlisted in Chicopee by O. Chapman, Jan. 26, 1864; mustered Feb. 18, 1864. Absent sick or on detached duty during the battle of the Wilderness, May 6, 1864. In action at Spotsylvania Court House, May 10, 12, and 18, 1864, North Anna River, May 24, 1864, Cold Harbor, June 3, 1864, and Petersburg assaults, June 17 and 18, 1864; severely wounded in the chest in action at the Petersburg Crater, July 30, 1864. "Sergeant [sic] James G. Powers, Co. C, 57th Massachusetts Volunteers, was wounded at Petersburg, Virginia, July 30, 1864, by a conoidal [Minié] ball, which fractured the fifth and sixth ribs, and carried away a portion of the sternum. He also received a fracture of the middle third of the humerus [of the left arm]. He was carried to the field hospital of the 1st division, Ninth Corps, where surgeon W. V. White, 57th Massachusetts Volunteers, administered chloroform and ether and amputated the left arm at the junction at the middle and upper thirds by circular operation. He died August 16, 1864. This case is supposed to be the one alluded to by Assistant Surgeon George M. McGill, U.S.A., medical inspector, in a letter to Surgeon T. A. McParlin, U.S.A. (then medical director of the Army of the Potomac), dated August 13, 1864, in which he says: 'Among the surgical cases there is one in hospital now of capital interest. The mesosternum has been broken in two by a ball which lacerated the soft parts over it. The

broken pieces of bone have been removed; the soft parts are gone (by sloughing and retraction after incision), so that an observer looks upon the heart invested with pericardium, and distinguishes plainly diastole and systole of the auricles; at the same time the apex impulse can be felt. The wound is a human vivisection.' The identification of this case was correct. Surgeon Horace Ludington, 100th Pennsylvania, contributed, May 31st, 1875, a full account of the case . . ." (OMR). With the regiment on all marches and in all skirmishes and battles, except the Wilderness, until wounded.

79. **Powers, Michael,** private. Res. and/or credit: Springfield, MA. Born: Ireland. Age: 40. Height: 5'6". Comp: dark. Eyes: black. Hair: dark. Occup: laborer. Enlisted in Springfield by Capt. Lewis A. Tifft, Feb. 2, 1864; mustered Feb. 18, 1864. In action at the Wilderness, May 6, 1864, Spotsylvania Court House, May 10, 12, and 18, 1864, North Anna River, May 24, 1864, Cold Harbor, June 3, 1864, and Petersburg assaults, June 17 and 18, 1864; taken prisoner of war in action at the Petersburg Crater, July 30, 1864. Incarcerated in the Confederate prison in Danville, VA, where he died from disease, Nov. 23, 1864. With the regiment on all marches and in all skirmishes and battles until captured.

80. **Prouty, William Henry,** corporal. Res. and/or credit: Springfield, MA. Born: Amherst, MA. Age: 23. Height: 5'9". Comp: light. Eyes: gray. Hair: red. Occup: mechanic. Enlisted in Springfield by Capt. Charles D. Hollis, Feb. 6, 1864; mustered Feb. 18, 1864. Promoted corporal on an unknown date. Deserted from Camp Wool April 12, 1864. Returned to the regiment for duty on an unknown date on or before Sept. 11, 1864 (circumstances of surrender or arrest unknown; no record of court-martial). Reduced to the ranks for desertion. Issued one sack coat (unlined), one forage cap, and one pair of shoes, Sept. 11, 1864. In action at Poplar Grove Church, Sept. 30, 1864, and slightly wounded in action there, Oct. 8, 1864. Wound dressed in the 1st Division, IX Corps,

Field Hospital at Petersburg and returned to the regiment for duty. Mustered for pay, Oct. 13, 1864. Issued one flannel shirt, one pair of drawers, one pair of shoes, one pair of socks, and one wool blanket, Oct. 15, 1864. Deserted from the regiment near Pegram's farm at Petersburg, Oct. 28, 1864. Returned to the regiment for duty, April 23, 1865, probably under President Lincoln's proclamation of amnesty. Issued one forage cap, one sack coat (unlined), one pair of trousers, one pair of drawers, one pair of shoes, and one wool blanket, April 30, 1865. Issued a new .58 cal. Springfield rifle and new leather equipment, May 11, 1865. Literate. Detached and detailed as a guard at 1st Division, IX Corps, Headquarters in late May or early June, 1865. Mustered out with the regiment at Delaney house, Washington, DC, July 30, 1865, and discharged in Readville, MA, Aug. 9, 1865, expiration of service. Had previous service as a private in Co. A, 10th MVI, from June 14, 1861, until discharged on a Surgeons Certificate of Disability, Sept. 21, 1863. Deserted from that regiment, May 31, 1862, but returned on an unknown date. Possibly participated with that regiment in the Peninsula campaign in 1862, at Chancellorsville, May 3, 1863, and at Gettysburg, July 1, 2, and 3, 1863.

81. **Rice, Emery L.,** private. Res. and/or credit: Northampton, MA. Born: Ashfield, MA. Age: 18. Height: 5'8". Comp: florid. Eyes: black. Hair: brown. Occup: farmer. Enlisted in Northampton by Lt. Col. Luke Lyman, Feb. 28, 1864; mustered Feb. 18, 1864. In action at the Wilderness, May 6, 1864, and Spotsylvania Court House, May 10, 1864; killed in action there, May 12, 1864.

82. **Rodier, Louis N.,** musician. Res. and credit: Springfield, MA. Born: Springfield, MA. Age: 15 (one of the three youngest members of the regiment). Comp: light. Eyes: blue. Hair: light. Occup: waiter. Enlisted in Co. G in Springfield by Lt. Henry B. Fiske, Feb. 21, 1864; mustered March 10, 1864. Transferred to Co. C, March 30, 1864, under RSO 31, by order of Col. William F. Bartlett, dated March 30, 1864. Company drummer.

Detached and detailed as an orderly at IX Corps Headquarters for most of the regiment's service from about April 27, 1864. Mustered for pay, Oct 13, 1864. Issued one greatcoat and one rubber blanket, Nov. 15, 1864. Literate. Mustered out with the regiment at Delaney house, Washington, DC, July 30, 1865, and discharged in Readville, MA, Aug. 9, 1865, expiration of service. Resided in Springfield, MA, after the war.

83. **Rowe, Merwin**, private. Res: Hinsdale, MA. Credit: Pittsfield, MA. Born: Montreal, Quebec, Canada. Age: 21. Height: 5'4¾". Comp: dark. Eyes: brown. Hair: brown. Occup: farmer. Enlisted in Pittsfield by W. H. Carson, March 29, 1864; mustered April 6, 1864. Absent sick or on detached duty from on or before May 6, 1864, until between June 18 and July 30, 1864. In action at the Petersburg Crater, July 30, 1864, and missing in action at Weldon Railroad, Aug. 19, 1865. (Whereabouts while missing unknown; no record of him being taken prisoner of war, absent sick, wounded, on detached duty, or deserted.) Not with the regiment after that battle until between March 25 and May 1, 1865. Issued one pair of trousers, one pair of shoes, and one knitted shirt, April 30, 1865. Issued a new .58 cal. Springfield rifle and new leather equipment, May 16, 1865. Literate. Mustered out with the regiment at Delaney house, Washington, DC, July 30, 1865, and discharged in Readville, MA, Aug. 9, 1865, expiration of service.

84. **Rowland, Joseph**, private. Res. and/or credit: Deerfield, MA. Born: Pittsburg, PA. Age: 18. Height: 5'10". Comp: light. Eyes: blue. Hair: light. Occup: mechanic. Enlisted in Deerfield by Charles Ames, Feb. 9, 1864; mustered Feb. 18, 1864. Killed in action at the Wilderness, May 6, 1864.

85. **Royce, Charles Howard**, 1st lieutenant. Res: Monticello, NY; Credit: unknown. Born: Monticello, NY, June 13, 1844. Age: 20. Height: unknown. Comp: dark. Eyes: brown. Hair: brown. Occup: student. Commissioned 2nd lieutenant, Jan. 28, 1864; mustered 2nd lieutenant, March 15, 1864. Assigned and re-

Lieutenant Charles H. Royce.
(Robert Sherwood)

ported for duty to Co. C, March 16, 1864, under RSO 25, by order of Col. William F. Bartlett, dated March 15, 1864. In action at the Wilderness, May 6, 1864, and one of the two officers who remained with the colors during that battle. In action at Spotsylvania Court House, May 10, 12, and 18, 1864, and wounded in the arm in action at North Anna River, May 24, 1864. Absent wounded in an army general hospital in Washington, DC, until June 23, 1864. Wounded in the left leg and foot (badly burned by gunpowder) from the explosion of a Confederate mortar shell while on duty in the trenches at Petersburg, July 24, 1864. Absent wounded in the Officers' Hospital in Annapolis, MD, until Nov. 2, 1864. On furlough from Nov. 3 until Nov. 14, 1864. Detached and detailed for duty at the Camp of Parole, Annapolis, MD, Nov. 28, 1864. Commissioned 1st lieutenant, Oct. 7, 1864, while absent wounded; mustered 1st lieutenant, Dec. 19, 1864. Detached and detailed as acting enrolling officer for the Draft Rendezvous at Hart Island, New York Harbor, Dec. 13, 1864, under SO 282 from Headquarters, Annapolis, MD, dated Dec. 6, 1864, until muster-out. Discharged the US service, May 26, 1865, as a supernumerary because of the consolidation of the 59th MVI with the 57th, under SO 254, AGO War Dept., dated May 26, 1865. Had previous service as a private in Co. G, 37th MVI, from Aug. 13, 1862, until discharged in Boston, MA, to accept a commission in the 57th, to date April 8, 1864. Participated with the 37th at Fredericksburg, Dec. 13, 1862, Chancellorsville, May 1863, and Gettysburg, July 3, 1863. Appointed brevet captain of US Volunteers "for gallant and meritorious services at the battle of North Anna River, VA, to date from March 13, 1865, and major, U.S. Volunteers by brevet, as of same date, for gallant and meritorious services before Petersburg, VA, under General Orders [91], War Department, Oct. 9, 1867" (JA). Resided in Monticello, NY, after the war and served as US consul in Prague, Czechoslovakia, from 1868 until 1873. Died July 19, 1903, age 59.

86. **Rutledge, Thomas**, private. Res. and/or credit: Milford, MA. Born: County Galway, Ireland. Age: 27. Height: 5'7". Comp: dark. Eyes: gray. Hair: dark. Occup: bootmaker. Enlisted in Milford by Leonard Hunt, Feb. 9, 1864; mustered Feb. 18, 1864. Severely wounded in action at the Wilderness, May 6, 1864. Died from his wounds in Emory US Army General Hospital in Washington, DC, June 9, 1864.

87. **Ryan, John**, private. Res. and/or credit: Milford, MA. Born: County Tipperary, Ireland. Age: 25. Height: 5'6". Comp: dark.

Eyes: brown. Hair: dark. Occup: bootmaker. Enlisted in Milford by Leonard Hunt, Feb. 9, 1864; mustered Feb. 18, 1864. Wounded in action at the Wilderness, May 6, 1864. Absent wounded in an army general hospital until after April 30, 1865. Issued a new .58 cal. Springfield rifle and new leather equipment, May 24, 1865. Mustered out with the regiment at Delaney house, Washington, DC, July 30, 1865, and discharged in Readville, MA, Aug. 9, 1865, expiration of service.

88. **Sanderson, Henry R.**, corporal. Res: Whately, MA. Credit: Northampton, MA. Born: Whately, MA. Age: 21. Height: 5'8½". Comp: light. Eyes: hazel. Hair: brown. Occup: farmer. Enlisted in Northampton by Lt. Col. Luke Lyman, Feb. 5, 1865; mustered Feb. 18, 1864. Promoted corporal, Feb. 18, 1864. In action at the Wilderness, May 6, 1864, Spotsylvania Court House, May 10, 12, and 18, 1864, and North Anna River, May 24, 1864; wounded on an unknown date in June 1864, but not in a major battle. With the regiment on all marches and in all skirmishes and battles until wounded. Absent wounded in an army general hospital until Dec. 1, 1864. Reduced to the ranks for "incompetency" (CR), Dec. 7, 1864, to date from Nov. 1, 1864. Sent to the 1st Division, IX Corps, Field Hospital at Petersburg, Dec. 8, 1864, and discharged the US service from Depot Field Hospital at City Point, Petersburg, for disability from wounds, Dec. 23, 1864, by order of the War Dept.

NOTE:

The physical descriptions of the remaining members of this company were not completed.

---

89. **Sandy, Gilbert**, private. Res: Easthampton, MA. Credit: unknown. Born: province of Quebec, Canada. Age: 19. No description available. Occup: farmer. Enlisted Jan. 26, 1864; mustered Feb. 18, 1864. Wounded in action at the Wilderness, May 6, 1864, and taken prisoner of war while en route to a field hospital in Fredericksburg, VA, May 8, 1865. Released and exchanged from an unknown Confederate prison, April 26, 1865. Probably received extra pay for having been a prisoner

of war. Discharged the US service for disability and expiration of service in Boston, MA, Aug. 7, 1865.

90. **Sansoucy, Edward**, private. Res: North Adams, MA. Credit: unknown. Born: province of Quebec, Canada. Age: 18. No description available. Occup: shoemaker. Enlisted Feb. 13, 1864; mustered Feb. 18, 1864. Wounded in action at the Wilderness, May 6, 1864, and taken prisoner of war while en route

to a field hospital in Fredericksburg, VA, May 8, 1864. Released and exchanged from an unknown Confederate prison, April 29, 1865. Probably received extra pay for having been a prisoner of war. Discharged the US service for disability and expiration of service in Boston, MA, Aug. 7, 1865.

91. **Shailor, Joseph N.**, private. Res: Hartford, CT. Credit: Springfield, MA. Born: Connecticut. Age: 45. No description available. Occup: mason. Enlisted in Springfield, Feb. 11, 1864; mustered Feb. 18, 1864. In action at the Wilderness, May 6, 1864, and one of the 34 enlisted men who remained with the colors during that battle. In action at Spotsylvania Court House, May 10, 12, and 18, 1864, North Anna River, May 24, 1864, Cold Harbor, June 3, 1864, and Petersburg assaults, June 17 and 18, 1864. Absent sick in an army general hospital from before July 30, 1864, until discharged the U.S. service for disability, June 10, 1865, under GO 77, par. 6, AGO, War Dept. With the regiment on all marches and in all skirmishes and battles until becoming sick.

92. **Shehan, Thomas**, private. Res. and/or credit: Greenfield, MA. Born: Ireland. Age: 22. No description available. Occup: laborer. Enlisted in Greenfield by the selectmen, Jan. 29, 1864; mustered Feb. 18, 1864. Recruited by a broker and cheated by that broker out of his entire state bounty of $325. Wounded in action at the Wilderness, May 6, 1864. Absent wounded in an army general hospital until between Oct. 8 and Oct. 13, 1864. Mustered for pay, Oct. 13, 1864. Issued one forage cap, one sack coat (unlined), one flannel shirt, one pair of drawers, and one pair of socks, Oct. 15, 1864. Issued one pair of trousers, one pair of drawers, and one pair of shoes, Nov. 15, 1864. Absent sick or on furlough for an unknown period sometime between Nov. 15, 1864, and Jan. 27, 1865. Issued one pair of shoes, Jan. 27, 1865. Issued a new .58 cal. Springfield rifle and new leather equipment, Feb. 3, 1865. Listed on the supply invoice for Feb. 10, 1865, but drew nothing. With the regiment in most operations during the fall and winter of 1864–65, and in action at Fort Stedman, March 25, 1865. Issued one forage

cap, one sack coat (unlined), one pair of trousers, one pair of shoes, one pair of socks, and one knitted shirt, April 30, 1865. Illiterate. Mustered out with the regiment at Delaney house, Washington, DC, July 30, 1865, and discharged in Readville, MA, Aug. 9, 1865, expiration of service.

93. **Sherwin, Waldo**, private. Res: Springfield, MA. Credit: unknown. Born: Massachusetts. Age: 22. No description available. Occup: mechanic. Enlisted Jan. 15, 1864; mustered Feb. 18, 1864. In action at the Wilderness, May 6, 1864, and Spotsylvania Court House, May 10 and 12, 1864; severely wounded in the right arm in action there by a Confederate sharpshooter, May 18, 1864. Absent wounded in an army general hospital in Washington, DC, where he died from his wounds, June 2, 1864.

94. **Syancyear, Joseph A.**, private. Res: Hinsdale, MA. Credit: unknown. Born: province of Quebec, Canada. Age: 33. No description available. Occup: laborer. Enlisted March 21, 1864; mustered April 6, 1864. Wounded in action at the Wilderness, May 6, 1864. Absent wounded in an army general hospital in Alexandria, VA, until discharged the US service for disability from wounds, Jan. 13, 1865, by order of the War Dept.

95. **Sykes, Edwin**, private. Res: Salem, MA. Credit: Lancaster, MA. Born: Massachusetts. Age: 29. No description available. Occup: currier. Enlisted in Lancaster, Feb. 6, 1864; mustered Feb. 18, 1864. Deserted from the IX Corps camp in Annapolis, MD, April 22, 1864, but arrested and returned between April 26 and May 6, 1864. Wounded in action at the Wilderness, May 6, 1864. Absent wounded until he deserted from an army general hospital in Philadelphia, PA, June 6, 1864. Never returned.

96. **Taylor, Peter**, private. Res: Plainfield, CT. Credit: unknown. Born: Connecticut. Age: 22. No description available. Occup: laborer. Enlisted Feb. 1, 1864; mustered Feb. 18, 1864. Did not leave Camp Wool with the regiment but sent to Camp Meigs in Read-

ville, MA, April 18, 1864, under the supervision of Lt. John Cook for a medical examination. Found unfit for duty by a "board of inspectors." Rejected recruit and discharged the US service in Worcester, MA, June 29, 1864, by order of Maj. Gen. John A. Dix, War Dept.

97. **Wait, Martin**, private. Res: Buckland, MA. Credit: unknown. Born: Massachusetts. Age: 29. No description available. Occup: farmer. Enlisted Feb. 5, 1864; mustered Feb. 18, 1864. In action at the Wilderness, May 6, 1864, Spotsylvania Court House, May 10, 12, and 18, 1864, North Anna River, May 24, 1864, and Cold Harbor, June 3, 1864; wounded in action in the Petersburg assault, June 17, 1864. With the regiment on all marches and in all skirmishes and battles until wounded. Absent wounded in an army general hospital in Alexandria, VA, until discharged the US service for disability from wounds, Dec. 29, 1864, by order of the War Dept. Had previous service as a private in the 16th New York Volunteer Infantry (specifics unknown).

98. **Walch, Patrick D.**, private. Res. and/or credit: Milford, MA. Born: Ireland. Age: 20. No description available. Occup: bootmaker. Enlisted in Milford Feb. 10, 1864; mustered Feb. 18, 1864. Absent sick in an army general hospital from on or before May 6, 1864, until between Oct. 8 and Oct. 13, 1864. Mustered for pay, Oct. 13, 1864. Issued one forage cap, one pair of trousers, and one flannel shirt, Oct. 15, 1864. Issued one wool blanket and one pair of mittens, Dec. 18, 1864. Issued one pair of shoes, Jan. 27, 1865. Issued a new .58 cal. Springfield rifle and new leather equipment, Feb. 3, 1865. Issued two pairs of drawers and one pair of trousers, Feb. 10, 1864. Literate. With the regiment in most operations during the fall and winter of 1864–65, and in action at Fort Stedman, March 25, 1865. Detached and detailed as a guard at 1st Division, IX Corps, Headquarters in late May or early June, 1865, until muster-out. Mustered out with the regiment at Delaney house, Washington, DC, July 30, 1865, and discharged in Readville, MA, Aug. 9, 1865, expiration of service.

99. **Walker, Gilbert L.**, private. Res: Adams, MA. Credit: unknown. Born: Massachusetts. Age: 18. No description available. Occup: operative. Enlisted Feb. 10, 1864; mustered Feb. 18, 1864. Absent sick in an Army general hospital from on or before May 6 until Nov. 26, 1864. Issued one sack coat (lined), two pairs of trousers, two knitted shirts, two pairs of drawers, one pair of shoes, and one pair of socks, Jan. 27, 1865. Issued a new .58 cal. Springfield rifle and new leather equipment, Feb. 3, 1865. Issued one pair of socks, Feb. 10, 1865. Illiterate. With the regiment in most operations during the fall and winter of 1864–65, and taken prisoner of war in action at Fort Stedman, March 25, 1865. Paroled and exchanged from Libby Prison in Richmond, VA, March 29, 1865. Returned to the regiment for duty from the Camp of Parole in Annapolis, MD, on or about May 11, 1865. Issued a new .58 cal. Springfield rifle and new leather equipment, May 16, 1865. Mustered out with the regiment at Delaney house, Washington, DC, July 30, 1865, and discharged in Readville, MA, Aug. 9, 1865, expiration of service. Resided in North Adams, Ma, after the war.

100. **Walker, John F.**, private. Res. and/or credit: Springfield, MA. Born: Massachusetts. Age: 22. No description available. Occup: carpenter. Enlisted in Springfield Feb. 15, 1864; mustered Feb. 18, 1864. Deserted from Camp Wool, Feb. 18, 1864. Never returned.

101. **Welton, Walter B.**, private. Res: Newtown, CT. Credit: Springfield, MA. Born: Connecticut. Age: 38. No description available. Occup: teacher. Enlisted in Springfield by Capt. Charles D. Hollis, Jan. 28, 1864; mustered Feb. 18, 1864. Never in combat. Absent sick in an army general hospital from on or before May 6, 1864, until discharged the US service for disability, June 1, 1865, by order of the War Dept. Died Dec. 15, 1891, age 65.

102. **White, George**, private. Res: Needham, MA. Credit: unknown. Born: Massachusetts. Age: 21. No description available. Occup: bootmaker. Enlisted Feb. 6, 1864; mustered Feb. 18, 1864. Deserted from Camp Wool, March 6, 1864. "Private George White de-

serted while on guard duty leaving his gun on his beat" (CR). Never returned.

103. **Wilcox, Charles H.,** private. Res: New Marlboro, MA. Credit: unknown. Born: Massachusetts. Age: 18. No description available. Occup: laborer. Enlisted March 15, 1864; mustered April 6, 1864. Never in combat. Absent sick in an army general hospital from on or before May 6, 1864, until between March 25 and April 30, 1865. Issued one forage cap, one sack coat (unlined), one pair of trousers, one pair of drawers, one pair of shoes, one pair of socks, one wool blanket, one rubber blanket, one knitted shirt, one knapsack, and one haversack, April 30, 1865. Issued a new .58 cal. Springfield rifle and new leather equipment, May 16, 1865. Mustered out with the regiment at Delaney house, Washington, DC, July 30, 1865, and discharged in Readville, MA, Aug. 9, 1865, expiration of service.

104. **Wilcox, Henry L.,** private. Res: Great Barrington, MA. Credit: unknown. Born: Massachusetts. Age: 42. No description available. Occup: carpenter. Enlisted Jan. 5, 1864; mustered Feb. 18, 1864. Never in combat. Absent sick in an army general hospital from on or before May 6, 1864, until discharged the US service for disability, Aug. 9, 1865, by order of the War Dept. Had previous service as 1st lieutenant of Co. A, 10th MVI, from June 21, 1861, until resigned and discharged, Oct. 7, 1861. Saw no combat service with that regiment.

105. **Willis, George L.,** private. Res: Bolton, MA. Credit: unknown. Born: Massachusetts. Age: 38. No description available. Occup: farmer. Enlisted Jan. 12, 1864; mustered Feb. 18, 1864. Absent sick in an army general hospital from on or before May 6, 1864, until between Dec. 18, 1864, and Jan. 27, 1865. Issued one rubber blanket, Jan. 27, 1865. Issued a new .58 cal. Springfield rifle and new leather equipment, Feb. 3, 1865. Issued one pair of drawers, March 6, 1865. Illiterate. With the regiment in most operations during the winter of 1865, and taken prisoner of war in action at Fort Stedman, March 25, 1865. Paroled and exchanged from Libby Prison in

Richmond, VA, March 29, 1865. Returned to the regiment for duty from the Camp of Parole in Annapolis, MD, on or about May 11, 1865. Issued a new .58 cal. Springfield rifle and new leather equipment, May 16, 1865. Mustered out with the regiment at Delaney house, Washington, DC, July 30, 1865, and discharged in Readville, MA, Aug. 9, 1865, expiration of service. Had previous service as a private in Co. I, 36th MVI, from Aug. 27, 1862, until discharged for disability from Camp Dennison, OH, Nov. 17, 1863. Participated with that regiment at Fredericksburg, Dec. 13, 1862, on duty in Kentucky in early 1863, at Vicksburg in June and July, 1863, and on duty in Tennessee during the remaining summer months and early fall of 1863.

106. **Wilson, Hynes,** private. Res: Duane, NY. Credit: Northampton, MA. Born: New York. Age: 24. No description available. Occup: farmer. Enlisted in Northampton by Lt. Col. Luke Lyman, Feb. 9, 1864; mustered Feb. 18, 1864. In action at the Wilderness, May 6, 1864, and one of the 34 enlisted men who remained with the colors during that battle. In action at Spotsylvania Court House, May 10, 12, and 18, 1864, North Anna River, May 24, 1864, Cold Harbor, June 3, 1864, and Petersburg assaults, June 17 and 18, 1864; taken prisoner of war in action at the Petersburg Crater, July 30, 1864. With the regiment on all marches and in all skirmishes and battles until captured. Incarcerated in the Confederate prison in Danville, VA, where he died from disease, Dec. 17, 1864.

107. **Winters, James,** private. Res: Sheffield, MA. Credit: unknown. Born: Massachusetts. Age: 21. No description available. Occup: laborer. Enlisted Feb. 12, 1864; mustered Feb. 18, 1864. Deserted while on furlough from Camp Wool, April 2, 1864. Never returned.

108. **Zimmerman, John,** private. Res: Greenfield, MA. Credit: unknown. Born: Germany. Age: 41. No description available. Occup: mechanic. Enlisted Feb. 10, 1864; mustered Feb. 18, 1864. Killed in action at the Wilderness, May 6, 1864.

Rosters

ROSTER AND DESCRIPTIVE LIST OF COMPANY D

Company D, known as the "Stockbridge Company" because its captain, Edson T. Dresser, came from that town, was the fifth company to be mustered into United States service, and 82 men were originally mustered in by 2nd Lt. Daniel Madden, 6th United States Regular Cavalry. Those men in the company mustered after Jan. 25, 1864, were mustered in by both Madden and 1st Lt. Robert McKibben, 4th United States Regular Infantry, depending on the date of muster. It was mustered out by Capt. Sylvester Keyser, 2nd Michigan Volunteer Infantry, ACM, 1st Division, IX Corps.

1. **Alcombright, Daniel H.**, private. Res. and credit: Williamstown, MA. Born: Williamstown, MA. Age: 25. Height: 6'1½". Comp: dark. Eyes: blue. Hair: black. Occup: laborer. Enlisted in Williamstown by H. T. Cole, Jan. 12, 1864; mustered Feb. 18, 1864. Deserted from Camp Wool on the morning of March 20, 1864. Never returned.

2. **Alcombright, George F.**, private. Res. and credit: Williamstown, MA. Born: Williamstown, MA. Age: 29. Height: 5'10". Comp: dark. Eyes: blue. Hair: black. Occup: laborer. Enlisted in Williamstown by H. T. Cole, Jan. 15, 1864; mustered Feb. 18, 1864. Deserted from Camp Wool on the morning of March 20, 1864. Never returned.

3. **Alexander, George W.**, private. Res: Monterey, MA. Credit: Sandisfield, MA. Born: New Marlboro, MA. Age: 44. Height: 5'9½". Comp: fair. Eyes: blue. Hair: brown. Occup: laborer. Enlisted in Sandisfield by L. Hotchkiss, Jan. 1, 1864; mustered Jan. 25, 1864. Never in combat. Court-martialed and dishonorably discharged the US service with loss of all pay and allowances (reason unknown, but possibly for shirking or criminal activity, he is nowhere listed as a deserter), June 29, 1864, by order of Maj. Gen. John A. Dix, War Dept. Had previous service as a private in Co. F, 49th MVI, from Sept. 16, 1862, until mustered out, Sept. 1, 1863. Participated with that regiment in the Port Hudson, LA, campaign in 1863.

4. **Allen, Albert**, private. Res: North Adams, MA. Credit: Pittsfield, MA. Born: England.

Age: 23. Height: 5'6". Comp: light. Eyes: blue. Hair: black. Occup: shoemaker. Enlisted in Pittsfield by John C. West, Dec. 2, 1863; mustered Feb. 18, 1864. Deserted from Camp Wool on the morning of March 12, 1864, but arrested, returned, and confined in the guardhouse in Camp Wool the next day, March 13, until March 17, 1864. In action at the Wilderness, May 6, 1864, Spotsylvania Court House, May 10, 12, and 18, 1864, North Anna River, May 24, 1864, Cold Harbor, June 3, 1864, and Petersburg assaults, June 17 and 18, 1864. Absent sick in Camp Meigs US Army General Hospital in Readville, MA, from July 14, 1864, until mustered out, but absent sick, at Delaney house, Washington, DC, July 30, 1865, expiration of service. With the regiment on all marches and in all skirmishes and battles until becoming ill.

5. **Allen, Harrison B.**, private. Res. and/or credit: Charlton, MA. Born: Worcester, MA. Age: 18. Height: 5'3". Comp: dark. Eyes: blue. Hair: light. Occup: student. Enlisted in Charlton by Capt. Julius M. Tucker, Dec. 19, 1863; mustered Jan. 25, 1864. Never in combat. Absent sick or on detached duty from on or before May 6, 1864, until between March 25 and June 16, 1865. Detached and detailed to the quartermaster's dept. in Alexandria, VA, from June 16 until July 27, 1865. Mustered out with the regiment at Delaney house, Washington, DC, July 30, 1865, and discharged in Readville, MA, Aug. 9, 1865, expiration of service. Died in Warwick, MA, 1930, age 85.

6. **Avery, Peter**, private. Res. and/or credit: Pittsfield, MA. Born: Canada. Age: 44.

Height: 5'4". Comp: light. Eyes: blue. Hair: brown. Occup: shoemaker. Enlisted in Pittsfield by John C. West, Feb. 10, 1864; mustered Feb. 18, 1864. In action at the Wilderness, May 6, 1864, Spotsylvania Court House, May 10, 12, and 18, 1864, North Anna River, May 24, 1864, and Cold Harbor, June 3, 1864; wounded in action and taken prisoner of war in the Petersburg assault, June 17, 1864. With the regiment on all marches and in all skirmishes and battles until wounded and captured. Paroled and exchanged from an unknown Confederate prison, Nov. 26, 1864. Probably received extra pay for having been a prisoner of war. Returned to the regiment for duty after March 25, 1865. Mustered out with the regiment at Delaney house, Washington, DC, July 30, 1865, and discharged in Readville, MA, Aug. 9, 1865, expiration of service. Had previous service as a private in Co. I, 49th MVI, from Oct. 28, 1862, until mustered out, Sept. 1, 1863. Participated with that regiment in the Port Hudson, LA, campaign in 1863.

7. **Bassett, Joseph,** private. Res. and/or credit: Pittsfield, MA. Born: Canada. Age: 28. Height: 5'10½". Comp: light. Eyes: hazel. Hair: brown. Occup: miller. Enlisted in Pittsfield by John C. West, Feb. 9, 1864; mustered Feb. 18, 1864. Deserted from Camp Wool on the morning of March 17, 1864. Never returned.

8. **Bates, Charles A.,** private. Res. and/or credit: Worcester, MA. Born: Clinton, MA. Age: 18. Height: 5'7½". Comp: dark. Eyes: black. Hair: black. Occup: teamster. Enlisted in Worcester by D. Waldo Lincoln, Feb. 4, 1864; mustered Feb. 18, 1864. In action at the Wilderness, May 6, 1864, and Spotsylvania Court House, May 10 and 12, 1864; wounded in action there, May 18, 1864. Absent wounded in an army general hospital until between June 17 and July 30, 1864. In action at the Petersburg Crater, July 30, 1864; severely wounded in the leg at Weldon Railroad, Aug. 19, 1864 (leg surgically amputated). Absent wounded in an army general hospital until discharged the US service for disability from wounds, March 10, 1865, by

order of the War Dept. Resided in Worcester, MA, after the war.

9. **Bills, Charles W.,** private. Res: Great Barrington, MA. Credit: New Marlboro, MA. Born: Lee, MA. Age: 18. Height: 5'6½". Comp: light. Eyes: blue. Hair: brown. Occup: farmer. Enlisted in New Marlboro by Aaron Smith, Jan. 12, 1864; mustered Jan. 25, 1864. Never in combat. Absent sick in an army general hospital from on or before May 6, 1864, until after March 25, 1865. Mustered out with the regiment at Delaney house, Washington, DC, July 30, 1865, and discharged in Readville, MA, Aug. 9, 1865, expiration of service.

10. **Bills, Henry,** private. Res: Great Barrington, MA. Credit: Sandisfield, MA. Born: Tyringham, MA. Age: 30. Height: 5'7½". Comp: light. Eyes: dark. Hair: brown. Occup: farmer. Enlisted in Sandisfield by L. Hotchkiss, Jan. 2, 1864; mustered Jan. 25, 1864. Absent for unknown reasons during the battle of the Wilderness, May 6, 1864. In action at Spotsylvania Court House, May 10, 12, and 18, 1864, North Anna River, May 24, 1864, and Cold Harbor, June 3, 1864; killed in action in the Petersburg assault, June 17, 1864. With the regiment on all marches and in all skirmishes and battles except the Wilderness until killed. Had previous service as a private in Co. A, 49th MVI, from Sept. 3, 1862, until mustered out, Sept. 1, 1863. Participated in the Port Hudson, LA, campaign with that regiment in 1863.

11. **Bills, Wilbur H.,** private. Res: Great Barrington, MA. Credit: Sandisfield, MA. Born: Great Barrington, MA. Age: 23. Height: 6'1". Comp: light. Eyes: hazel. Hair: brown. Occup: teamster. Enlisted in Sandisfield by L. Hotchkiss, Jan. 2, 1864; mustered Feb. 18, 1864. Never in combat. Absent sick in an army general hospital from on or before May 6, 1864, until after March 25, 1865. Mustered out with the regiment at Delaney house, Washington, DC, July 30, 1865, and discharged in Readville, MA, Aug. 9, 1865, expiration of service. Had previous service as a private in Co. C, 24th MVI, from Sept. 10,

1861, until discharged for disability in New Bern, NC, May 28, 1863. Participated with that regiment in the North Carolina campaign in 1862–63.

12. **Boyden, Franklin,** musician. Res. and/or credit: Worcester, MA. Born: Fall River, MA. Age: 18. Height: 5'4". Comp: light. Eyes: blue. Hair: dark. Occup: musician. Enlisted in Worcester by Capt. Julius M. Tucker, Dec. 24, 1863; mustered Jan. 25, 1864. Company fifer. "Fell out on the march to the Wilderness, [May 5, 1864]" (CR), and taken prisoner of war. Incarcerated in the Confederate prison camp in Andersonville, GA, May 29, 1864, where he died from disease, Dec. 17, 1864.

13. **Brayne, Jonathan J.,** private. Res. and/or credit: Egremont, MA. Born: England. Age: 21. Height: 5'9½". Comp: fair. Eyes: blue. Hair: brown. Occup: farmer. Enlisted in Egremont by S. Goodell, Jan. 14, 1864; mustered Jan. 25, 1864. Deserted from Camp Wool, Feb. 16, 1864. Never returned. Had previous service as a private in Co. E, 49th MVI, from Sept. 1, 1862, until mustered out, Sept. 1, 1863. Participated with that regiment in the Port Hudson, LA, campaign in 1863.

14. **Bryant, Lyman,** private. Res. and/or credit: Hinsdale, MA. Born: Elmira, NY. Age: 21. Height: 5'9". Comp: light. Eyes: blue. Hair: brown. Occup: farmer. Enlisted in Hinsdale by W. F. Carson, Feb. 4, 1864; mustered Feb. 18, 1864. In action at the Wilderness, May 6, 1864, and Spotsylvania Court House, May 10, 12, and 18, 1864; taken prisoner of war in action at North Anna River, May 24, 1864. Incarcerated in the Confederate prison camp in Andersonville, GA, where he died from disease and starvation, July 27, 1864.

15. **Burroughs, Nelson,** private. Res. and/or credit: Westboro, MA. Born: Canada. Age: 20. Height: 5'5". Comp: dark. Eyes: brown. Hair: brown. Occup: shoemaker. Enlisted in Westboro by W. Wilson, Jan. 25, 1864; mustered Feb. 18, 1864. Died in the hospital in Camp Wool from pneumonia, April 3, 1864. First death in the regiment.

16. **Bush, Stephen F.,** private. Res. and/or credit: Hinsdale, MA. Born: Massena, NY. Age: 18. Height: 5'8". Comp: light. Eyes: gray. Hair: brown. Occup: farmer. Enlisted in Hinsdale by W. F. Carson, Dec. 24, 1863; mustered Jan. 25, 1864. In action at the Wilderness, May 6, 1864, and Spotsylvania Court House, May 10 and 12, 1864; wounded in action there, May 18, 1864. Absent wounded in an army general hospital until transferred to the 8th Co., 2nd Battln., VRC, April 30, 1865. Discharged the US service, Aug. 9, 1865, by order of the War Dept., expiration of service.

17. **Card, Franklin W.,** sergeant. Res. and credit: Williamstown, MA. Born: Williamstown, MA. Age: 22. Height: 6'0". Comp: light. Eyes: blue. Hair: brown. Occup: laborer. Enlisted in Williamstown by H. T. Cole, Jan. 1, 1864; mustered Jan. 25, 1864. Deserted, April 18, 1864, while the regiment was beginning its journey to the front, but returned to the regiment in Jersey City the following day, April 19, 1864 (undoubtedly he was quickly arrested and shipped off under guard to have been able to catch up with the regiment so fast). Absent sick or on detached duty from on or before May 6, 1864, until between Aug. 19 and Sept. 30, 1864. Wounded in action at Poplar Grove Church, Sept. 30, 1864. Absent wounded in an army general hospital until before Jan. 1, 1865. Promoted sergeant, Jan. 1, 1865. With the regiment in operations during the winter of 1865, and in action at Fort Stedman, March 25, 1865. Furloughed about June 1, 1864, and dropped from the company rolls as a deserter when he had not returned by June 27, 1865. Reported to the regiment for duty July 7, 1865. Mustered out with the regiment at Delaney house, Washington, DC, July 30, 1865, and discharged in Readville, MA, Aug. 9, 1865, expiration of service. Had previous service as a private in Co. G, 49th MVI, from Sept. 19, 1862, until mustered out Sept. 1, 1863. Participated in the Port Hudson, LA, campaign with that regiment in 1863. Died in 1891, age 49.

18. **Carey, Lockwood,** private. Res: Great Barrington, MA. Credit: Sandisfield, MA.

Born: Great Barrington, MA. Age: 45. Height: 5'8". Comp: light. Eyes: gray. Hair: gray. Occup: laborer. Enlisted in Sandisfield by L. Hotchkiss, Jan. 8, 1864; mustered Jan. 25, 1864. Reported sick, April 16, 1864; "Recommended for discharge. Sent to Readville [MA], April 18, 1864" (CR), under the supervision of Lt. John Cook for a medical examination. Found unfit for duty by a "board of inspectors." Rejected recruit and discharged the US service in Worcester, MA, June 29, 1864, by order of Maj. Gen. John A. Dix, War Dept.

19. **Clark, John B.,** sergeant. Res: Pittsfield, MA. Credit: Springfield, MA. Born: Pittsfield, MA. Age: 21. Height: 5'9½". Comp: light. Eyes: blue. Hair: light. Occup: butcher. Enlisted in Springfield by Capt. Charles D. Hollis, Jan. 22, 1864; mustered Jan. 25, 1864. Promoted sergeant, Jan. 25, 1864. Never in combat with the 57th. Absent on detached duty (the nature of which is unknown, but given his civilian occupation, possibly in the commissary dept.) from on or before May 6, 1864, until discharged the US service, Jan. 17, 1865, to be mustered as 1st lieutenant in the 8th United States Regiment of Colored Troops, Heavy Artillery. Discharged the US service from that regiment, Feb. 10, 1866, expiration of service. Had previous service as a private in Co. A, 49th MVI, from Sept. 3, 1862, until mustered out, Sept. 1, 1863. Participated in the Port Hudson, LA, campaign with that regiment in 1863.

20. **Cobleigh, Henry Edward,** private. Res. and credit: Williamstown, MA. Born: Williamstown, MA. Age: 21. Height: 5'9". Comp: florid. Eyes: gray. Hair: brown. Occup: operative. Enlisted in Williamstown by H. T. Cole, Jan. 14, 1864; mustered Feb. 18, 1864. In action at the Wilderness, May 6, 1864, and Spotsylvania Court House, May 10 and 12, 1864; killed in action there, May 18, 1864. Had previous service as a private in Co. G, 49th MVI, from Sept. 19, 1862, until mustered out, Sept. 1, 1863. Participated in the Port Hudson, LA, campaign with that regiment in 1863.

21. **Cobleigh, James M.,** private. Res. and credit: Williamstown, MA. Born: Williamstown, MA. Age: 18. Height: 5'11". Comp: florid. Eyes: blue. Hair: brown. Occup: operative. Enlisted in Williamstown by H. T. Cole, Jan. 19, 1864; mustered Feb. 18, 1864. Absent sick or on detached duty during the battle of the Wilderness, May 6, 1864. In action at Spotsylvania Court House, May 10, 12, and 18, 1864, North Anna River, May 24, 1864, Cold Harbor, June 3, 1864, and Petersburg assaults, June 17 and 18, 1864; taken prisoner of war in action at the Petersburg Crater, July 30, 1864. With the regiment on all marches and in all skirmishes and battles, except the Wilderness, until captured. Died in an unknown Confederate prison on an unknown date, probably from disease.

22. **Collins, Henry Alonzo,** private. Res. and/or credit: Lee, MA. Born: Tyringham, MA. Age: 39. Height: 5'9½". Comp: light. Eyes: blue. Hair: brown. Occup: teamster. Enlisted in Lee by William S. Merrill, Jan. 4, 1864; mustered Jan. 25, 1864. Killed in action at the Wilderness, May 6, 1864. Had previous service as a private in Co. I, 49th MVI, from Sept. 20, 1862, until mustered out Sept. 1, 1863. Participated in the Port Hudson, LA, campaign with that regiment in 1863.

23. **Cowden, James,** private. Res: Oxford, MA. Credit: Millbury, MA. Born: Princeton, MA. Age: 22. Height: 5'7". Comp: dark. Eyes: black. Hair: black. Occup: farmer. Enlisted in Millbury by C. D. Morse, Jan. 11, 1864; mustered Jan. 25, 1864. Never in combat. Absent sick in an army general hospital from on or before May 6, 1864, until discharged the US service for disability, July 13, 1864, by order of the War Dept.

24. **Crosby, John,** sergeant. Res. and credit: Stockbridge, MA. Born: Stockbridge, MA. Age: 25. Height: 5'7". Comp: dark. Eyes: brown. Hair: black. Occup: farmer. Enlisted in Stockbridge by W. Merrill, Jan. 4, 1864; mustered Jan. 25, 1864. Promoted sergeant, Jan. 25, 1864. Mortally wounded in action at the Wilderness, May 6, 1864, and died from his wounds in a field hospital in Fredericks-

burg, VA, May 12, 1864. Had previous service as a private in Co. F, 49th MVI, from Sept. 16, 1862, until mustered out, Sept. 1, 1864. Participated in the Port Hudson, LA, campaign with that regiment in 1863.

25. **Curley, John,** private. Res. and/or credit: Mendon, MA. Born: Ireland. Age: 37. Height: 5′5″. Comp: light. Eyes: blue. Hair: dark. Occup: farmer. Enlisted in Mendon by A. H. Allen, Feb. 6, 1864; mustered Feb. 18, 1864. Wounded in action at the Wilderness, May 6, 1864. Absent wounded in Fairfax Seminary US Army General Hospital in Fairfax, VA, until discharged the US service for disability from wounds, June 6, 1865, by order of the War Dept.

26. **Curley, Thomas,** private. Res. and/or credit: Upton, MA. Born: Ireland. Age: 44. Height: 5′7″. Comp: light. Eyes: blue. Hair: brown. Occup: farmer. Enlisted in Upton by A. Moore, Jan. 26, 1864; mustered Feb. 18, 1864. In action at the Wilderness, May 6, 1864, and one of the 34 enlisted men who remained with the colors during that battle. In action at Spotsylvania Court House, May 10, 12, and 18, 1864; killed in action at North Anna River, May 24, 1864.

27. **Dawley, Delbert S.,** private. Res. and/or credit: Williamstown, MA. Born: Hancock, MA. Age: 22. Height: 5′9″. Comp: light. Eyes: gray. Hair: brown. Occup: laborer. Enlisted in Williamstown by H. T. Cole, Jan. 23, 1864; mustered Feb. 18, 1864. Never in combat. Absent sick in an army general hospital from on or before May 6, 1864, until discharged the US service for disability, June 19, 1865, by order of the War Dept.

28. **Dewey, Edward S.,** 1st lieutenant. Res. and or credit: Montague, MA. Born: Massachusetts. Age: 20. Height: unknown. Comp: light. Eyes: blue. Hair: brown. Occup: artist. Commissioned 2nd lieutenant, Oct 13, 1863; mustered 2nd lieutenant, to date Jan. 18, 1864. Commissioned 1st lieutenant, March 2, 1864. Appointed to Co. C, March 3, 1864. Mustered 1st lieutenant, March 16, 1864. Wounded in the leg in action at the Wilder-

Lieutenant Edward Dewey. *(USAMHI)*

ness, May 6, 1864. Absent wounded in an army general hospital until May 27, 1864. Returned to the regiment for duty, May 28, 1864. In action at Cold Harbor, June 3, 1864, and Petersburg assaults, June 17 and 18, 1864. Readmitted to the Officer's Hospital in Annapolis, MD, before July 30, 1864, and resigned and discharged the US service from there for disability from wounds, Sept. 20, 1864, by order of the War Dept. Had previous service as a corporal in Co. G, 10th MVI, from June 21, 1861 until discharged to accept a commission in the 57th, to date Jan. 17, 1864. Participated with the 10th MVI in the Peninsula Campaign in 1862, and at Fredericksburg, Dec. 13, 1862, Chancellorsville, May 3, 1863, and Gettysburg, July 1, 2, and 3, 1863, and in the Mine Run campaign, Nov. 26 through Dec. 2, 1863. Resided in Boston, MA, after the war. Married in 1910 and (at the age of 68) fathered a child in 1911.

29. **Donnelly, John,** sergeant. Res. and/or credit: Springfield, MA. Born: Ireland. Age: 30. Height: 5′8″. Comp: dark. Eyes: gray. Hair: dark. Occup: laborer. Enlisted in Springfield by an unknown selectman, Jan.

14, 1864; mustered Jan. 25, 1864. Deserted from Camp Wool, March 2, 1864, but voluntarily returned, March 5, 1864, and not confined in the guardhouse. In action at the Wilderness, May 6, 1864, Spotsylvania Court House, May 10, 12, and 18, 1864, and North Anna River, May 24, 1864. Promoted sergeant, June 1, 1864. In action at Cold Harbor, June 3, 1864, Petersburg assaults, June 17 & 18, 1864, and Petersburg Crater, July 30, 1864. Absent sick in Beverly US Army General Hospital in Beverly, NJ, from before Aug. 19, 1864, where he died from rheumatic fever, "contracted on duty" (CR), Sept. 30, 1864. With the regiment on all marches and in all skirmishes and battles until becoming ill.

30. **Dougall, Julius,** corporal. Res. and/or credit: Hinsdale, MA. Born: Massena, NY. Age: 18. Height: 5'8". Comp: light. Eyes: hazel. Hair: brown. Occup: farmer. Enlisted in Hinsdale by W. F. Carson, Jan. 18, 1864; mustered Jan. 25, 1864. In action at the Wilderness, May 6, 1864, and one of the 34 enlisted men who remained with the colors during that battle. In action at Spotsylvania Court House, May 10, 12, and 18, 1864; wounded in action at North Anna River, May 24, 1864. Absent wounded in an army general hospital until between Oct. 8, 1864, and March 25, 1865. In action at Fort Stedman, March 25, 1865. Promoted corporal, to date June 1, 1865. Detached and detailed at the quartermaster's dept. in Alexandria, VA, in May 1865 until muster-out. Mustered out with the regiment at Delaney house, Washington, DC, July 30, 1865, and discharged in Readville, MA, Aug. 9, 1865, expiration of service.

31. **Dresser, Edson T.,** captain. Res. and credit: Stockbridge, MA. Born: Stockbridge, MA. Age: 24. Height: unknown. Comp: light. Eyes: brown. Hair: dark brown. Occup: student at Williams College. Commissioned and mustered captain, Jan. 25, 1864. Detached and detailed as 1st Division, IX Corps, acting ordnance officer from about May 1, 1864 until July 29, 1864. Killed in action at the Petersburg Crater, July 30, 1864. Had previous service as 1st lieutenant of Co. F, 49th MVI, from Sept. 16, 1862, until mustered out, Sept.

Captain Edson Dresser. *(USAMHI)*

1, 1863. Participated in the Port Hudson, LA, campaign with that regiment in 1863. "No officer in the regiment was more respected and beloved . . ." (JA).

32. **Everett, Charles F.,** musician. Res. and/or credit: Worcester, MA. Born: Norton, MA. Age: 16. Height: 5'4½". Comp: light. Eyes: blue. Hair: light brown. Occup: student at Worcester High School. Enlisted in Worcester by Lieut. John Anderson, Jan. 14, 1864; mustered Jan. 25, 1864. Company drummer. Detailed as a clerk in the regimental quartermaster's dept. under Lt. George Priest at Camp Wool, Feb. 8, 1864, under RSO 4, by order of Col. William F. Bartlett, until April 2, 1864, when relieved of that duty under RSO 32, by order of Lt. Col. Edward P. Hollister, dated April 1, 1864. Voluntarily—and against orders—left his post in the rear with the wagons to fight at the Wilderness, May 6, 1864. Mortally wounded in the right hip in action there and died upon the battlefield. "A fair-haired, blue-eyed boy, with a face as soft and smooth as a girl's" (JA).

33. **Finkle, Martin E.,** private. Res. and credit: Sheffield, MA. Born: Sheffield, MA. Age: 22. Height: 5'8". Comp: light. Eyes: light. Hair: light. Occup: laborer. Enlisted in

Sheffield by W. Walker, Dec. 30, 1863; mustered Jan. 25, 1864. Wounded in action at the Wilderness, May 6, 1864. Absent wounded in an army general hospital until discharged the US service for disability from wounds, June 20, 1865, by order of Maj. Gen. John A. Dix, War Dept. Had previous service as a private in Co. I, 9th Connecticut Volunteer Infantry (specifics unknown).

34. **Flynn, Patrick**, private. Res. and/or credit: Milford, MA. Born: County Roscommon, Ireland. Age: 30. Height: 5'8". Comp: fair. Eyes: blue. Hair: light brown. Occup: bootmaker. Enlisted in Milford by Leonard Hunt, Jan. 15, 1864; mustered Jan. 25, 1864. Deserted from Camp Wool, Feb. 22, 1864, but voluntarily returned Feb. 29, 1864, and was not confined in the guardhouse. In action at the Wilderness, May 6, 1864, and Spotsylvania Court House, May 10, 1864; wounded in the foot in action there, May 12, 1864. Absent wounded in an army general hospital until between Aug. 19 and Sept. 30, 1864. Wounded again by a piece of shrapnel in the left shoulder in action at Poplar Grove Church, Sept. 30, 1864. Absent wounded in an army general hospital until between Oct. 8, 1864, and March 25, 1865. Wounded in action again and taken prisoner of war at Fort Stedman, March 25, 1865. Paroled and exchanged from Libby Prison in Richmond, VA, about March 30, 1865. Sent to Harewood US Army General Hospital in Washington, DC, from the Camp of Parole in Annapolis, MD, and discharged the US service from that hospital for disability from wounds, June 17, 1865, by order of the War Dept.

35. **Fullerton, Stewart M. G.**, private. Res. and/or credit: Egremont, MA. Born: Watertown, CT. Age: 29. Height: 6'1½". Comp: light. Eyes: blue. Hair: red. Occup: machinist. Enlisted in Egremont by A. Goodell, Dec. 28, 1863; mustered Jan. 25, 1864. Wounded and taken prisoner of war in action at the Wilderness, May 6, 1864. Died in Confederate hands, but place and date of death unknown. Had previous service as a private in Co. K, 49th MVI, from Oct. 14, 1862, until mustered out Sept. 1, 1863. Participated in the Port Hudson, LA, campaign with that regi-

ment in 1863, and wounded in action there, May 27, 1863.

36. **Gallipaux, Joseph**, corporal. Res. and credit: Pittsfield, MA. Born: Pittsfield, MA. Age: 22. Height: 5'3½". Comp: dark. Eyes: blue. Hair: black. Enlisted in Pittsfield by John C. West, Jan. 4, 1864; mustered Jan. 25, 1864. Absent on detached duty (nature unknown) from on or before May 6, 1864, until between Oct. 8, 1864, and March 1, 1865. Promoted corporal, March 1, 1865. In action at Fort Stedman, March 25, 1865. Mustered out with the regiment at Delaney house, Washington, DC, July 30, 1865, and discharged in Readville, MA Aug. 9, 1865, expiration of service. Had previous service as a private in Co. I, 49th MVI, from Sept. 20, 1862, until mustered out, Sept. 1, 1863. Participated in the Port Hudson, LA, campaign with that regiment in 1863.

37. **Gilmore, Patrick**, 2nd lieutenant. Res. and/or credit: West Springfield, MA. Born: Ireland. Age: 43. Height: 5'4½". Comp: light. Eyes: blue. Hair: brown. Occup: mechanic. Enlisted in West Springfield by an unknown selectman, Jan. 12, 1864; mustered Jan. 25, 1864. Promoted 1st sergeant when 1st Sgt. Swift was reduced, March 9, 1864; promotion to date, Jan. 25, 1864. Wounded in action at the Wilderness, May 6, 1864. Absent wounded in an army general hospital until June 26, 1865. Commissioned 2nd lieutenant, June 12, 1865, while absent wounded; mustered 2nd lieutenant, June 26, 1865. Mustered out with the regiment at Delaney house, Washington, DC, July 30, 1865, and discharged in Readville, MA, Aug. 9, 1865, expiration of service.

38. **Goodell, Myron**, sergeant. Res. and/or credit: Lanesboro, MA. Born: New Ashford, MA. Age: 21. Height: 5'3". Comp: light. Eyes: blue. Hair: brown. Occup: farmer. Enlisted in Lanesboro by L. Lee, Nov. 20, 1863; mustered Jan. 25, 1864. Absent on detached duty (nature unknown) from on or before May 6, 1864, until between Oct. 8, 1864, and March 1, 1865. Promoted sergeant, May 1, 1865, under RSO 42, by order of Lt. Col.

Julius M. Tucker. In action at Fort Stedman, March 25, 1865. Discharged the US service, June 13, 1865, to date June 1, 1865, as a supernumerary because of the consolidation of the 59th MVI with the 57th, under SO 254, par. 43, AGO, War Dept., dated May 26, 1865. Had previous service as a private in Co. B, 49th MVI, from Sept. 6, 1862, until mustered out, Sept. 1, 1863. Participated in the Port Hudson, LA, campaign with that regiment in 1863. Died in 1891, age 48.

39. **Gregory, Charles C.**, private. Res. and/or credit: Sandisfield, MA. Born: Dover, MA. Age: 39. Height: 5'6½". Comp: light. Eyes: blue. Hair: brown. Occup: farmer. Enlisted in Sandisfield by L. Hotchkiss, Jan. 13, 1864; mustered Feb. 18, 1864. Never in combat. Absent sick in an army general hospital from on or before May 6, 1864, until discharged the US service for disability, July 28, 1865, by order of the War Dept.

40. **Harvey, Charles**, private. Res: West Stockbridge, MA. Credit: North Stockbridge, MA. Born: Austerlitz, NY. Age: 20. Height: 5'9½". Comp: light. Eyes: blue. Hair: brown. Occup: laborer. Enlisted in North Stockbridge by Lt. Charles W. Kniffin, Jan. 4, 1864; mustered Feb. 18, 1864. Deserted from Camp Wool, Feb. 11, 1864, but arrested, returned, and confined in the guardhouse in Camp Wool, Feb. 21, 1864. Arresting officer paid $30 reward for his capture. In action at the Wilderness, May 6, 1864, and taken prisoner of war later that month, but not in a major battle. Paroled and exchanged from an unknown Confederate prison, Dec. 17, 1864. Probably received extra pay for having been a prisoner of war. Absent sick in an army general hospital (probably in the Camp of Parole in Annapolis, MD) until discharged the US service for disability, June 1, 1865, by order of the War Dept.

41. **Haskell, David Jr.**, private. Res. and/or credit: Otis, MA. Born: Tyringham, MA. Age: 27. Height: 5'10½". Comp: dark. Eyes: blue. Hair: brown. Occup: farmer. Enlisted in Otis by A. Crittenden, Dec. 28, 1863; mustered Jan. 25, 1864. Never in combat with the 57th. Absent sick in an army general hospital

from on or before May 6, 1864, until discharged the US service for disability, June 13, 1865, by order of the War Dept. Had previous service as a private in Co. F, 49th MVI, from Sept. 16, 1862, until mustered out, Sept. 1, 1863. Participated in the Port Hudson, LA, campaign with that regiment in 1863.

42. **Hawes, Edward A.**, private. Res: Leicester, MA. Born and credit: Worcester, MA. Age: 18. Height: 5'7". Comp: dark. Eyes: hazel. Hair: dark. Occup: farmer. Enlisted in Worcester by Capt. Julius M. Tucker, Jan. 1, 1864; mustered Jan. 25, 1864. Never in combat. Dishonorably discharged the US service with loss of all pay and allowances for an unknown reason, but likely cowardice or crime, June 29, 1864, by order of Maj. Gen. John A. Dix, War Dept.

43. **Henry, Thomas**, private. Res. and/or credit: Lenox, MA. Born: England. Age: 27. Height: 5'11". Comp: light. Eyes: gray. Hair: brown. Occup: clerk. Enlisted in Lenox by William Durning, Jan. 5, 1864; mustered Jan. 25, 1864. Deserted from Camp Wool, Jan. 26, 1864. Never returned.

44. **Hinton, John E.**, private. Res. and credit: Sheffield, MA. Born: Sheffield, MA. Age: 45. Height: 5'5½". Comp: light. Eyes: brown. Hair: brown. Occup: cook. Enlisted in Sheffield by E. E. Callender, Jan. 4, 1864; mustered Feb. 18, 1864. In action at the Wilderness, May 6, 1864, and Spotsylvania Court House, May 10, 12, and 18, 1864; taken prisoner of war in action at North Anna River, May 24, 1864. Paroled and exchanged from an unknown Confederate prison, Nov. 27, 1864. Probably received extra pay for having been a prisoner of war. Absent sick in an army general hospital in Washington, DC, until discharged the US service on a Surgeons Certificate of Disability, March 25, 1865, by order of Maj. Gen. Christopher C. Auger, commanding the Dept. of Washington, DC. Had previous service as a private in Co. E, 49th MVI, from Sept. 1, 1862, until mustered out, Sept. 1, 1863. Participated in the Port Hudson, LA, campaign with that regiment in 1863, and wounded in action there, May 27, 1863.

45. **Hodge, George H.**, corporal. Res. and/or credit: Pittsfield, MA. Born: Burlington, VT. Age: 23. Height: 5'7". Comp: light. Eyes: blue. Hair: brown. Occup: cabinetmaker. Enlisted in Pittsfield by John C. West, Jan. 5, 1864; mustered Jan. 25, 1864. Promoted corporal, Jan. 25, 1864. Detached and detailed on recruiting service with the superintendent of recruiting in Berkshire County, MA, Jan. 26, 1864, under RSO 16, by order of Lt. Col. Edward P. Hollister, postdated Feb. 29, 1864. Severely wounded in the right arm in action at the Wilderness, May 6, 1864. Conveyed to a field hospital in Fredericksburg, VA, and transferred from there to an army general hospital in Washington, DC, where on May 29, 1864, he underwent surgery: "Complete excision of right elbow joint, by A[cting] A[ssistant] Surgeon F. G. H. Bradford for comminution of condyles of humerus and heads of radius and ulna. Died June 4, 1864, from exhaustion" (OMR). Had previous service as a private in Co. C, 49th MVI, from Sept. 11, 1862, until mustered out, Sept. 1, 1863. Participated in the Port Hudson, LA, campaign with that regiment in 1863.

46. **Hodge, James**, private. Res. and credit: Adams, MA. Born: Adams, MA. Age: 18. Height: 5'7". Comp: light. Eyes: gray. Hair: brown. Occup: operative. Enlisted in Adams by S. Johnson, Jan. 9, 1864; mustered Jan. 25, 1864. Missing in action at the Wilderness, May 6, 1864. Never accounted for and presumed killed.

47. **Hudson, George N.**, private. Res. and/or credit: Worcester, MA. Born: Milford, MA. Age: 19. Height: 5'8½". Comp: dark. Eyes: black. Hair: black. Occup: farmer. Enlisted in Worcester by D. Waldo Lincoln, Jan. 5, 1864; mustered Jan. 25, 1864. Wounded in action at the Wilderness, May 6, 1864. Absent wounded in an army general hospital until between March 25 and June 1, 1865. Mustered out with the regiment at Delaney house, Washington, DC, July 30, 1865, and discharged in Readville, MA, Aug. 9, 1865, expiration of service. Had previous service as a private in Co. A, 51st MVI, from Aug. 30, 1862, until mustered out, July 27, 1863. Participated in the North Carolina campaign with that regiment in 1862–63. Resided in Westboro, MA, after the war.

48. **Hulet, Orrin**, private. Res. and credit: Lee, MA. Born: Lee, MA. Age: 41. Height: 5'7". Comp: dark. Eyes: gray. Hair: brown. Occup: teamster. Enlisted in Lee by Sylvester S. May, Jan. 2, 1864; mustered Jan. 25, 1864. Never in combat. Absent sick in an army general hospital from on or before May 6, 1864, until discharged the US service for disability, Nov. 15, 1864, by order of the War Dept. Had previous service as a private in Co. F, 49th MVI, from Nov. 4, 1862, until mustered out Sept. 1, 1863. Participated in the Port Hudson, LA, campaign with that regiment in 1863. Also had previous service as a private in Co. E, 27th MVI, from Sept. 20, 1861, until discharged for disability, Aug. 24, 1862. Participated in the North Carolina campaign with that regiment in 1862. Resided in Lee, MA, after the war.

49. **Jaquins, Egbert J.**, private. Res. and/or credit: Lee, MA. Born: Clinton, MA. Age: 29. Height: 5'8". Comp: light. Eyes: black. Hair: brown. Occup: laborer. Enlisted in Lee by Sylvester S. May, Jan. 2, 1864; mustered Jan. 25, 1864. Deserted from Camp Wool, March 29, 1864, but arrested, returned, and confined in the guardhouse in Camp Wool, April 8, 1864. In action at the Wilderness, May 6, 1864, and Spotsylvania Court House, May 10, 12, and 18, 1864; taken prisoner of war in action at North Anna River, May 24, 1864. Incarcerated in the Confederate prison camp in Andersonville, GA, where he died from disease, Aug. 15, 1864.

50. **Jenne, William L.**, private. Res. and credit: Lenox, MA. Born: Lenox, MA. Age: 22. Height: 5'6". Comp: light. Eyes: hazel. Hair: light. Occup: farmer. Enlisted in Co. I in Lenox by Joseph Tucker, Feb. 26, 1864; mustered March 10, 1864; transferred to Co. D, April 13, 1864, under RSO 37, by order of Col. William F. Bartlett, dated April 12, 1864. In action at the Wilderness, May 6, 1864, and Spotsylvania Court House, May 10, 1864; wounded in action there, May 12, 1864. Absent wounded in Satterlee US Army General Hospital in Philadelphia, PA, until dis-

charged the US service for disability from wounds, June 9, 1865, under GO 77, par. 6, AGO, War Dept., dated April 28, 1865. Had previous service as a private in Co. D, 10th MVI, from June 14, 1861, until discharged on a Surgeons Certificate of Disability, July 18, 1862. Possibly participated with that regiment in the Peninsula campaign in 1862. Resided in Lenox, MA, after the war.

51. **Jones, Charles**, private. Res. and credit: Stockbridge, MA. Born: Stockbridge, MA. Age: 41. Height: 5'9". Comp: light. Eyes: blue. Hair: dark. Occup: butcher. Enlisted in Co. I in Stockbridge by Henry M. Binnott, Feb. 24, 1864; mustered March 10, 1864; transferred to Co. D, April 14, 1864, under RSO 38, by order of Col. William F. Bartlett, dated April 12, 1864. Killed in action at the Wilderness, May 6, 1864.

52. **Jordan, Charles A.**, private. Res. and/or credit: Millbury, MA. Born: Northbridge, MA. Age: 26. Height: 5'5". Comp: sandy. Eyes: dark. Hair: sandy. Occup: farmer. Enlisted in Millbury by C. D. Morse, Jan. 4, 1864; mustered Jan. 25, 1864. Deserted from Camp Wool on the afternoon of April 16, 1864. Never returned. "Bounty jumper" (JA).

53. **Jordan, Erastus C.**, private. Res. and/or credit: Millbury, MA. Born: Foster, RI. Age: 44. Height: 5'9". Comp: dark. Eyes: gray. Hair: dark. Occup: farmer. Enlisted in Millbury by C. D. Morse, Jan. 11, 1864; mustered Jan. 25, 1864. Never in combat with the 57th. Absent sick in an army general hospital from on or before May 6, 1864, until discharged the US service for disability, July 13, 1864, by order of the War Dept. Had previous service as a private in Co. K, 21st MVI, from July 19, 1861, until discharged for disability, May 8, 1862. Possibly participated in the North Carolina campaign with that regiment in 1862. Died before 1896, but date not known.

54. **Kelly, Martin**, private. Res. and/or credit: Adams, MA. Born: Ireland. Age: 38. Height: 5'7½". Comp: dark. Eyes: blue. Hair: brown. Occup: laborer. Enlisted in Adams by S. Thurston, Dec. 31, 1863; mustered Jan. 25, 1864. Wounded in action at the Wilderness,

May 6, 1864. Absent wounded in Mower US Army General Hospital in Philadelphia, PA, until he deserted from there while on furlough, Oct. 22, 1864. Never returned.

55. **Kendall, Theodore B.**, corporal. Res. and/or credit: Springfield, MA. Born: Rochester, NY. Age: 20. Height: 5'7". Comp: light. Eyes: blue. Hair: dark. Occup: farmer. Enlisted in Springfield by Capt. Charles D. Hollis, Dec. 5, 1863; mustered Jan. 25, 1864. Promoted corporal, Jan. 25, 1864. Given a furlough from Camp Wool in mid-March, 1864, and reported in the company journal as deserted on the morning of March 29, 1864, when he did not return on time. Returned the next day, March 30, 1864, and "he reports having been sick or would have returned on time" (CR). Wounded in action at the Wilderness, May 6, 1864. Absent wounded in an army general hospital until transferred to the 7th Co., 2nd Battln., VRC, in March 1865, by TO dated Nov. 29, 1864. Discharged the US service for disability from wounds, June 7, 1865, by order of the War Dept. Had previous service as a private in Co. G, 8th Vermont Volunteer Infantry (specifics unknown).

56. **Kimball, Oliver S.**, private. Res. and/or credit: Adams, MA. Born: Petersburg, NY. Age: 30. Height: 5'9". Comp: light. Eyes: gray. Hair: brown. Occup: spinner. Enlisted in Adams by S. Johnson, March 21, 1864; joined the company from the transient barracks, April 3, 1864; mustered April 6, 1864; transferred to Co. K, April 7, 1864, but transferred back to Co. D, April 12, 1864, under RSO 37, by order of Col. William F. Bartlett. In action at the Wilderness, May 6, 1864, Spotsylvania Court House, May 10, 12, and 18, 1864, North Anna River, May 24, 1864, and Cold Harbor, June 3, 1864; mortally wounded in the stomach in action during the Petersburg assault, June 17, 1864. Died from wounds in an army general hospital in Washington, DC, June 25, 1864. With the regiment on all marches and in all skirmishes and battles until wounded.

57. **Kirby, Jacob**, private. Res. and/or credit: Great Barrington, MA. Born: Claverack, NY. Age: 42. Height: 5'7". Comp: light. Eyes:

brown. Hair: brown. Occup: mechanic. Enlisted in Great Barrington by John M. Seeley, Dec. 12, 1864; mustered Jan. 25, 1864. In action at the Wilderness, May 6, 1864, and Spotsylvania Court House, May 10, 12, and 18, 1864; wounded in action at North Anna River, May 24, 1864. Absent wounded in an army general hospital until discharged the US service for disability from wounds, Feb. 24, 1865, by order of the War Dept. Had previous service as a private in Co. A, 31st MVI, from Oct. 4, 1861, until discharged for disability from Fort Jackson, LA, Oct. 3, 1862. On duty with that regiment in Louisiana in 1862.

58. **Lamont, Daniel,** private. Res. and/or credit: West Stockbridge, MA. Born: Ireland. Age: 34. Height: 5'10". Comp: fair. Eyes: blue. Hair: black. Occup: laborer. Enlisted in West Stockbridge by Lt. Charles W. Kniffin, Jan. 2, 1864; mustered Jan. 25, 1864. Never in combat with the 57th. Absent sick in Haddington US Army General Hospital in Philadelphia, Pa. from on or before May 6, 1864, where he died from disease, Feb. 5, 1865. Had previous service as a private in Cos. I and F, 49th MVI, from Sept. 20, 1862, until mustered out, Sept. 1, 1863. Participated in the Port Hudson, LA, campaign with that regiment in 1863.

59. **Lareby, George F.,** corporal. Res. and credit: Williamstown, MA. Born: Williamstown, MA. Age: 19. Height: 5'6". Comp: light. Eyes: black. Hair: brown. Occup: laborer. Enlisted in Williamstown by H. T. Cole, Dec. 29, 1864; mustered Jan. 25, 1864. Absent on detached duty (nature unknown) from on or before May 6, 1864, until between Oct. 8, 1864, and March 1, 1865. Promoted corporal, March 1, 1865. In action at Fort Stedman, March 25, 1865. Mustered out with the regiment at Delaney house, Washington, DC, July 30, 1865, and discharged in Readville, MA, Aug. 9, 1865, expiration of service. Died before 1896, but date not known.

60. **Larkins, James,** private. Res. and/or credit: Lenox, MA. Born: England. Age: 25. Height: 5'10". Comp: dark. Eyes: dark. Hair: dark. Occup: fireman. Enlisted in Lenox by William Durning, Jan. 5, 1864; mustered Jan. 25, 1864. Deserted from Camp Wool, Jan. 26, 1864. Never returned.

61. **Lee, Charles F.,** 2nd lieutenant. Res: Pittsfield, MA. Credit: Templeton, MA. Born: Massachusetts. Age: 22. No description available. Occup: clerk. Commissioned 2nd lieutenant, Oct. 21, 1863; mustered 2nd lieutenant, Nov. 5, 1863. Assigned to Co. D, March 3, 1864. Never left with the regiment for the front. Applied for a discharge from the US service, May 11, 1864, from Pittsfield, MA, and received that discharge, May 17, 1864, supposedly for disability. Had previous service as a corporal in Co. A, 18th MVI, from Sept. 19, 1861, until discharged for disability from wounds, Oct. 20, 1862. Participated with that regiment in the Peninsula campaign in 1862, but never in action there; however, wounded in action at 2nd Bull Run, Aug. 30, 1862. Had subsequent service as 1st lieutenant of Co. H, 55th MVI, from Dec. 10, 1864, until mustered out, Aug. 29, 1865. On duty with that regiment in South Carolina in 1864-65. Breveted captain of US Volunteers, to date March 13, 1865, by GO, AGO, War Dept., dated Oct. 14, 1868.

62. **Lee, Saybrook,** private. Res. and/or credit: Lenox, MA. Born: Glenville, NY. Age: 39. Height: 5'5½". Comp: light. Eyes: brown. Hair: brown. Occup: druggist. Enlisted in Lenox by an unknown selectman, Jan. 28, 1864; mustered Feb. 18, 1864. Wounded in action and taken prisoner of war at the Wilderness, May 6, 1864. Died in Confederate hands, but place and date of death not known.

63. **Long, Thomas,** private. Res. and/or credit: Cummington, MA. Born: England. Age: 42. Height: 5'6". Comp: light. Eyes: blue. Hair: brown. Occup: farmer. Enlisted in Cummington by an unknown selectman, Jan. 13, 1864; mustered Jan. 25, 1864. Wounded in action at the Wilderness, May 6, 1864. Absent wounded in an army general hospital until transferred to the 119th Co., 2nd Battln., VRC, Jan. 19, 1865. Readmitted to an army general hospital in Annapolis, MD, on an unknown date and discharged the US

service from there for disability from wounds, June 28, 1865, by order of the War Dept.

64. McCurdy, Robert F., corporal. Res. and/or credit: Alford, MA. Born: Haverhill, MA. Age: 24. Height: 5'5½". Comp: light. Eyes: blue. Hair: dark. Occup: blacksmith. Enlisted in Alford by E. C. Licknor, Jan. 3, 1864; mustered Jan. 25, 1864. Promoted corporal, Jan. 25, 1864. Wounded in action at the Wilderness, May 6, 1864. Absent wounded in an army general hospital until discharged the US service for disability from wounds, June 26, 1865, by order of the War Dept. Had previous service as a private in Co. D, 49th MVI, from Sept. 8, 1862, until mustered out, Sept. 1, 1863. Participated in the Port Hudson, LA, campaign with that regiment in 1863. Resided in Great Barrington, MA, after the war.

65. McDonald, Alfred, private. Res. and/or credit: Lee, MA. Born: New York City. Age: 34. Height: 5'9". Comp: light. Eyes: blue. Hair: dark. Occup: cabinetmaker. Enlisted in Lee by W. Merrill, Jan. 4, 1864; mustered Jan. 25, 1864. Wounded in action at the Wilderness, May 6, 1864. Absent wounded in Carver US Army General Hospital in Washington, DC, until discharged the US service for disability from wounds, July 19, 1865, by order of the War Dept.

66. McMahon, Martin, musician. Res. and/or credit: Worcester, MA. Born: Ireland. Age: 18. No description available. Occup: machinist. Enlisted and mustered for one year in Worcester by an unknown army recruiter, Aug. 29, 1864. Company drummer or fifer. With the regiment at Poplar Grove Church, Sept. 30 and Oct. 8, 1864, but probably not in action. Probably also served as a hospital orderly, stretcher bearer, and/or nurse. With the regiment in operations during the fall and winter of 1864–65, and taken prisoner of war in action at Fort Stedman, March 25, 1865. Paroled and exchanged from Libby Prison in Richmond, VA, April 1, 1865. Returned to the regiment for duty from the Camp of Parole in Annapolis, MD, on or about May 11, 1865. Discharged the US service in Tennallytown, DC, June 16, 1865, in compliance with a GO from the War Dept., discharging men

with a one-year enlistment, by order of Secretary of War Edwin M. Stanton.

67. Maloney, Henry C., private. Res: Leicester, MA. Credit: Worcester, MA. Born: Leicester, MA. Age: 18. Height: 5'8". Comp: light. Eyes: blue. Hair: brown. Occup: student at the Military Academy of Leicester. Enlisted in Worcester by Lt. Edwin I. Coe, Jan. 16, 1864; mustered Jan. 25, 1864. Wounded in action at the Wilderness, May 6, 1864. Absent wounded in an army general hospital until transferred to Co. K, 22nd Regiment, VRC, Aug. 1, 1864, and stationed in Troy, NY. Died from disease caused by his wounds in the army general hospital in Albany, NY, Oct. 5, 1864. Remains sent home and buried in Pine Grove Cemetery in Leicester, MA.

68. Maloney, William, color sergeant. Res. and/or credit: Great Barrington, MA. Born: Ireland. Age: 28. Height: 5'5". Comp: light. Eyes: blue. Hair: brown. Occup: laborer. Enlisted in Great Barrington by an unknown selectman, Jan. 1, 1864; mustered Jan. 25, 18964. In action at the Wilderness, May 6, 1864, Spotsylvania Court House, May 10, 12, and 18, 1864, and North Anna River, May 24, 1864. Promoted corporal, June 1, 1864. In action at Cold Harbor, June 3, 1864, and Petersburg assaults, June 17 and 18, 1864. Promoted color sergeant on an unknown date (but after Color Sgt. Karpeles, Company E, was wounded, May 24, 1864). Taken prisoner of war in action at the Petersburg Crater, July 30, 1864. With the regiment on all marches and in all skirmishes and battles until captured. Incarcerated in the Confederate prison in Danville, VA, until paroled and exchanged, Oct. 17, 1864, and died en route to a Federal hospital, Oct. 19, 1864, aboard the military steamer *New York* near Fort Monroe, VA, from disease contracted while a prisoner.

69. Mambert, Peter J., private. Res. and/or credit: Marlboro, MA. Born: Livingston, NY. Age: 38. Height: 5'8". Comp: light. Eyes: blue. Hair: brown. Occup: laborer. Enlisted in Marlboro by an unknown selectman, Jan. 25, 1864; mustered Feb. 18, 1864. Deserted from Camp Wool, April 7, 1864, but voluntarily returned the next day, April 8, 1864, and not confined in the guardhouse. In action at the Wilderness, May 6, 1864, Spotsylvania Court House, May 10, 12, and 18, 1864, and North Anna River, May 24, 1864; wounded in action at Cold Harbor, June 3, 1864. With the regiment on all marches and in all skirmishes and battles until wounded. Absent wounded in an army general hospital until between Oct. 8, 1864, and March 25, 1865. Taken prisoner of war in action at Fort Stedman, March 25, 1865. Paroled and exchanged from Libby Prison in Richmond, VA, March 29, 1865. Discharged the US service for disability from the army general hospital in the Camp of Parole in Annapolis, MD, June 19, 1865, under GO 77, par. 6, AGO, War Dept., dated April 28, 1865.

70. **May, Henry S.**, sergeant. Res. and/or credit: Stockbridge, MA. Born: Hartford, CT. Age: 44. Height: 5'9". Comp: dark. Eyes: blue. Hair: mixed. Occup: blacksmith. Enlisted in Stockbridge by H. M. Burrell, Dec. 15, 1863; mustered Jan. 25, 1864. Promoted sergeant, Jan. 25, 1864. Under SO 200, from Adjutant General William Schouler at the Military Headquarters of the Commonwealth of Massachusetts in Boston, dated Feb. 17, 1864: "Henry S. May is authorized to recruit for the 57th Massachusetts Volunteer Infantry in Berkshire County under the direction of the municipal authorities of the several towns in which he may enlist men." In action at the Wilderness, May 6, 1864, and Spotsylvania Court House, May 10, 1864; killed in action there, May 12, 1864. Had previous service as a corporal in Co. F, 49th MVI, from Sept. 16, 1862, until mustered out, Sept. 1, 1863. Participated in the Port Hudson, LA, campaign with that regiment in 1863.

71. **Merrill, John H.**, private. Res. and/or credit: Lee, MA. Born: Sandisfield, MA. Age: 34. Height: 5'11". Comp: Light. Eyes: hazel. Hair: brown. Occup: teamster and farmer. Enlisted in Lee by Sylvester S. May, Jan. 30, 1864; mustered Feb. 18, 1864. Never in combat with the 57th. Absent sick from on or before May 6, 1864, until discharged the US service for disability from the army general hospital in Boston, MA, Oct. 15, 1864, by order of the War Dept. Had previous service

as a private in Co. A, 10th MVI, from June 21, 1861, until discharged for disability from wounds in Washington, DC, Jan. 26, 1863. Participated with that regiment in the Peninsula campaign in 1862, and wounded in action at Malvern Hill, July 1, 1862.

72. **Moore, Charles E.**, sergeant. Res. and credit: Lee, MA. Born: Lee, MA. Age: 24. Height: 5'5". Comp: light. Eyes: blue. Hair: light. Occup: farmer. Enlisted in Co. I in Lee by Joseph Tucker, Feb. 4, 1864; mustered March 10, 1864. Promoted corporal, March 10, 1864. Transferred to Co. D, April 13, 1864, under RSO 37, by order of Col. William F. Bartlett, dated April 12, 1864. Wounded in action at the Wilderness, May 6, 1864. Absent wounded in an army general hospital until transferred to Co. K, 9th Regiment, VRC, Oct. 17, 1864. Discharged the US service, July 15, 1865, by order of the War Dept., expiration of service. Had previous service in Co. C, 13th Connecticut Volunteer Infantry (specifics unknown). Died in 1892, age 52.

73. **Morgan, Ambrose E.**, private. Res. and/or credit: Washington, MA. Born: West Springfield, MA. Age: 20. Height: 5'9½". Comp: light. Eyes: blue. Hair: light. Occup: farmer. Enlisted in Washington by Charles Crosier, Dec. 15, 1863; mustered Jan. 25, 1864. In action at the Wilderness, May 6, 1864, and Spotsylvania Court House, May 10, 1864; killed in action there, May 12, 1864. Had previous service as a private in Co. I, 49th MVI, from Sept. 20, 1862, until mustered out, Sept. 1, 1863. Participated in the Port Hudson, LA, campaign with that regiment in 1863.

74. **Morrissey, Daniel**, private. Res. and/or credit: Lenox, MA. Born: Ireland. Age: 25. Height: 5'8". Comp: dark. Eyes: brown. Hair: dark. Occup: shoemaker. Enlisted in Lenox by William Durning, Jan. 5, 1864; mustered Jan. 25, 1864. Deserted from Camp Wool, Jan. 26, 1864. Never returned.

75. **Oaks, Ensign A.**, private. Res. and/or credit: Williamstown, MA. Born: Pittsford, NY. Age: 18. Height: 5'8½". Comp: light.

Eyes: blue. Hair: light. Occup: laborer. Enlisted in Williamstown by H. T. Cole, Jan. 19, 1864; mustered Feb. 18, 1864. Mortally wounded at the Wilderness, May 6, 1864. Died from wounds in a field hospital in Fredericksburg, VA, May 11, 1864.

76. **O'Keefe, Daniel**, private. Res. and/or credit: Milford, MA. Born: County Kerry, Ireland, Oct. 17, 1845. Age: 18. Height: 5'8". Comp: fair. Eyes: blue. Hair: light. Occup: harness maker. Enlisted in Milford by Leonard Hunt, Jan. 13, 1864; mustered Jan. 25, 1864. In action at the Wilderness, May 6, 1864, Spotsylvania Court House, May 10, 12, and 18, 1864, North Anna River, May 24, 1864, Cold Harbor, June 3, 1864, and Petersburg assaults, June 17 and 18, 1864; wounded by the explosion of a Confederate mortar shell while on duty in the trenches at Petersburg, July 14, 1864 (thumb amputated by shrapnel). With the regiment on all marches and in all skirmishes and battles until wounded. Absent wounded in Fairfax Seminary US Army General Hospital in Fairfax, VA, until discharged the US service for disability from wounds, Feb. 20, 1865, by order of the War Dept.

77. **O'Neil, John**, private. Res. and/or credit: Stockbridge, MA. Born: Ireland. Age: 43. Height: 5'7½". Comp: dark. Eyes: blue. Hair: black. Occup: farmer. Enlisted in Stockbridge by H. M. Burrell, Feb. 8, 1864; mustered Feb. 18, 1864. Mortally wounded in action at the Wilderness, May 6, 1864, and died from his wounds later that same day. Had previous service as a private in Co. F, 49th MVI, from Sept. 16, 1862, until mustered out Sept. 1, 1863. Participated in the Port Hudson, LA, campaign with that regiment in 1863, and wounded in action near Donaldsonville, LA, July 13, 1863.

78. **O'Sullivan, John**, private. Res. and/or credit: Becket, MA. Born: Ireland. Age: 43. Height: 5'10". Comp: light. Eyes: blue. Hair: brown. Occup: blacksmith. Enlisted in Becket by T. F. Snow, Dec. 24, 1863; mustered Jan. 25, 1864. "Arrested and returned to camp [Wool] as a deserter, Feb. 10, 1864. Expense $20" (CR); confined in the guardhouse in Camp Wool, Feb. 10 and 11, 1864. Wounded in action at the Wilderness, May 6, 1864. Absent wounded in an army general hospital until between Oct. 8, 1864, and March 25, 1865. In action and taken prisoner of war at Fort Stedman, March 25, 1865. Paroled and exchanged from Libby Prison in Richmond, VA, about April 1, 1865. Returned to the regiment for duty from the Camp of Parole in Annapolis, MD, on or about May 11, 1865. Detached and detailed as a blacksmith at the 1st Division, IX Corps, quartermaster's dept., June 25, 1865. Mustered out, but absent still on detached duty, at Delaney house, Washington, DC, July 30, 1865. Returned to the regiment for duty in Readville, MA, Aug. 5, 1865, and discharged with the regiment from there, Aug. 9, 1865, expiration of service. Had previous service as a private in Co. D, 10th MVI, from June 14, 1861, until discharged on a Surgeons Certificate of Disability, Jan. 24, 1863. Participated in the Peninsula campaign with that regiment in 1862.

79. **Parker, Warren C.**, corporal. Res. and/or credit: Worcester, MA. Born: Phillips, ME. Age: 19. Height: 5'6". Comp: dark. Eyes: gray. Hair: dark. Occup: mechanic. Enlisted in Worcester by Capt. Julius M. Tucker, Jan. 4, 1864; mustered Jan. 25, 1864. Promoted corporal on an unknown date. In action at the Wilderness, May 6, 1864, and wounded later that month, but not in a major battle. Absent wounded in an army general hospital until after March 25, 1865. Mustered out with the regiment at Delaney house, Washington, DC, July 30, 1865, and discharged in Readville, MA, Aug. 9, 1865, expiration of service.

80. **Parsons, George C.**, private. Res. and/or credit: Worcester, MA. Born: Massachusetts. Age: 39. No description available. Occup: bootmaker. Enlisted and mustered for one year in Co. K in Worcester by an unknown army recruiter, Sept. 1, 1864; transferred to Co. D on an unknown date. Never joined the regiment at the front. Detached and detailed in the quartermaster's dept. in Alexandria, VA, for the length of his service. Discharged the US service in Tennallytown, DC, June 16, 1865, in compliance with a GO from the War

Dept. discharging men with a one-year enlistment, by order of Secretary of War Edwin M. Stanton.

81. **Patterson, Henry,** private. Res: Sandisfield, MA. Credit: New Marlboro, MA. Born: Mansfield, NJ. Age: 44. Height: 5'11½". Comp: dark. Eyes: blue. Hair: mixed. Occup: farmer. Enlisted in New Marlboro by Aaron Smith, Jan. 7, 1864; mustered Jan. 25, 1864. In action at the Wilderness, May 6, 1864, Spotsylvania Court House, May 10, 12, and 18, 1864, North Anna River, May 24, 1864, Cold Harbor, June 3, 1864, and Petersburg assaults, June 17 and 18, 1864; died suddenly in the trenches at Petersburg, July 14, 1864. Cause of death unknown, but likely a stroke or heart attack. With the regiment on all marches and in all skirmishes and battles until deceased.

82. **Peacock, James,** 2nd lieutenant. Res. and/or credit: Worcester, MA. Married. Born: Blackburn, Lancashire, England. Age: 23. Height: 5'7". Comp: light. Eyes: gray. Hair: red. Occup: farmer. Enlisted in Co. B in Worcester by Capt. Joseph W. Gird, Nov. 20, 1863; mustered Jan. 4, 1864. Detached and detailed on recruiting service, Feb. 7, 1864, under RSO 16, by order of Lt. Col. Edward P. Hollister, postdated Feb. 29, 1864. Commissioned 2nd lieutenant, April 9, 1864; mustered 2nd lieutenant, April 18, 1864. Transferred to Co. D after April 14, 1864. Absent on detached duty from on or before May 6, 1864 until between Oct. 8, 1864, and March 25, 1865. Wounded in the stomach in action at Fort Stedman, March 25, 1865. Absent wounded in an army general hospital until May 26, 1865. On leave of absence in Massachusetts from May 26 until June 14, 1865. Discharged the US service for disability from wounds on or about June 25, 1865. Had previous service as a private in Co. D, 15th MVI, from July 12, 1861, until discharged for disability, Nov. 22, 1862. Participated with that regiment at Ball's Bluff, Oct. 21, 1861, in the Peninsula campaign in 1862, and possibly at Antietam, Sept. 17, 1862. Resided in Worcester, MA, after the war and died there after a long illness caused by his wound, Aug. 6, 1882, age 42.

83. **Pearl, William N.,** private. Res. and credit: Otis, MA. Born: Otis, MA. Age: 26. Height: 5'9½". Comp: sandy. Eyes: blue. Hair: brown. Occup: farmer. Enlisted in Otis by A. Crittenden, Dec. 26, 1863; mustered Jan. 25, 1864. Never in combat. Detached and detailed at the regimental commissary from late April, 1864, until absent sick in an army general hospital from an unknown date until he returned to duty at the commissary from June 21 until July 18, 1865. Mustered out with the regiment at Delaney house, Washington, DC, July 30, 1865, and discharged in Readville, MA, Aug. 9, 1865, expiration of service. Had previous service as a private in Co. F, 49th MVI, from Sept. 16, 1862, until mustered out, Sept. 1, 1863. Participated in the Port Hudson, LA, campaign with that regiment in 1863. Resided in Otis, MA, after the war.

84. **Platt, James,** private. Res. and/or credit: Millbury, MA. Born: England. Age: 44. Height: 5'2½". Comp: dark. Eyes: hazel. Hair: dark. Occup: gunsmith. Enlisted in Millbury by J. E. Waters, Jan. 5, 1864; mustered Jan. 25, 1864. Never in combat. Absent sick in an army general hospital from on or before May 6, 1864, until after March 25, 1865. Mustered out with the regiment at Delaney house, Washington, DC, July 30, 1865, and discharged in Readville, MA, Aug. 9, 1865, expiration of service. Died in November, 1889, age 69.

85. **Rathburn, Charles,** private. Res. and credit: Stockbridge, MA. Born: Stockbridge, MA. Age: 37. Height: 5'9". Comp: dark. Eyes: blue. Hair: dark. Occup: teamster. Enlisted in Co. I in Stockbridge by Sgt. Henry S. May, Feb. 25, 1864; mustered March 10, 1864; transferred (very likely at his own request to be with his brother) to Co. D, April 14, 1864, under RSO 38, by order of Col. William F. Bartlett, dated April 13, 1864. In action at the Wilderness, May 6, 1864, Spotsylvania Court House, May 10, 12, and 18, 1864, North Anna River, May 24, 1864, Cold Harbor, June 3, 1864, Petersburg assaults, June 17 and 18, 1864, and Petersburg Crater, July 30, 1864; taken prisoner of war at Weldon Railroad, Aug. 19, 1864. With the regi-

ment on all marches and in all skirmishes and battles until captured. Paroled and exchanged from an unknown Confederate prison, March 12, 1865. Furloughed home to Stockbridge, MA, from the Camp of Parole in Annapolis, MD, and died at home, April 2, 1865 (probably from the effects of disease contracted while a prisoner of war).

86. **Rathburn, William H.**, private. Res. and credit: Stockbridge, MA. Born: Stockbridge, MA. Age: 27. Height: 5'6½". Comp: light. Eyes: blue. Hair: light. Occup: carpenter. Enlisted in Stockbridge by H. M. Burrell, Jan. 2, 1864; mustered Jan. 25, 1864. In action at the Wilderness, May 6, 1864, Spotsylvania Court House, May 10, 1864; and wounded in action there May 12, 1864. Absent wounded in an army general hospital until between March 25 and June 14, 1865. Mustered out with the regiment at Delaney house, Washington, DC, July 30, 1865, and discharged in Readville, MA, Aug. 9, 1865, expiration of service.

87. **Reed, Edwin R.**, private. Res. and/or credit: New Marlboro, MA. Born: Stockholm, NY. Age: 23. Height: 5'5". Comp: dark. Eyes: blue. Hair: brown. Occup: farmer. Enlisted in New Marlboro by Aaron Smith, Jan. 2, 1864; mustered Jan. 25, 1864. In action at the Wilderness, May 6, 1864, and Spotsylvania Court House, May 10, 12, and 18, 1864; missing in action at North Anna River, May 24, 1864. Never accounted for and presumed killed. Had previous service as a private in Co. I, 92nd New York Volunteer Infantry (specifics unknown).

88. **Remick, Augustus**, private. Res. and/or credit: Grafton, MA. Born: Strong, ME. Age: 21. Height: 5'8". Comp: light. Eyes: gray. Hair: sandy. Occup: shoemaker. Enlisted in Grafton by Capt. Joseph W. Gird, Jan. 4, 1864; mustered Jan. 25, 1864. In action at the Wilderness, May 6, 1864, Spotsylvania Court House, May 10, 12, and 18, 1864, North Anna River, May 24, 1864, Cold Harbor, June 3, 1864, and Petersburg assaults, June 17 and 18, 1864; wounded while on duty in the trenches at Petersburg on July 20, 1864. With the regiment on all marches and in all skirmishes and battles until wounded. Absent

wounded in an army general hospital until discharged the US service for disability from wounds, Feb. 27, 1865, by order of the War Dept. Had previous service as a private in Co. I, 15th MVI, from Aug. 8, 1861, until discharged for disability from wounds, April 7, 1862. Wounded in action with that regiment at Ball's Bluff, Oct. 21, 1861.

89. **Scriber, Henry C.**, private. Res. and/or credit: New Marlboro, MA. Born: Catskill, NY. Age: 22. Height: 5'7". Comp: fair. Eyes: brown. Hair: brown. Occup: farmer. Enlisted in New Marlboro by Aaron Smith, Dec. 28, 1864; mustered Jan. 25, 1864. Deserted from Camp Wool, April 7, 1864, but returned the next day, April 8, 1864. Wounded in action at the Wilderness, May 6, 1864. Absent wounded in an army general hospital until dishonorably discharged the US service without pay or allowances for an unknown reason Oct. 15, 1864, by order of Maj. Gen. John A. Dix, War Dept.; however, records indicate that his discharge was later amended to discharged for disability to date, July 13, 1864. Had previous service as a private in Co. C, 61st New York Volunteer Infantry (specifics unknown).

90. **Sears, George H.**, private. Res. and/or credit: Adams, MA. Born: Barre, MA. Age: 19. Height: 5'7¼". Comp: light. Eyes: dark. Hair: brown. Occup: painter. Enlisted in Adams by S. Johnson, Jan. 6, 1864; mustered Jan. 25, 1864. In action at the Wilderness, May 6, 1864, and Spotsylvania Court House, May 10, 1864; wounded in action there, May 12, 1864. Absent wounded in an army general hospital until between Oct. 8, 1864, and March 25, 1865. Slightly wounded in action again at Fort Stedman, March 25, 1865. Absent wounded in Depot Field Hospital at City Point, Petersburg, until before June 14, 1865. Mustered out with the regiment at Delaney house, Washington, DC, July 30, 1865, and discharged in Readville, MA, Aug. 9, 1865, expiration of service. Had previous service as a private in Co. E, 37th MVI, from July 15, 1862, until discharged for disability from White Oak Church, VA, April 15, 1863. Participated with that regiment in the Fredericksburg campaign, Dec. 11 to 15, 1862, and in the "Mud March" in January 1863.

91. **Shea, John,** private. Res. and/or credit: Springfield, MA. Born: Ireland. Age: 22. Height: 5'9". Comp: dark. Eyes: blue. Hair: dark. Occup: laborer. Enlisted in Springfield by Capt. Charles D. Hollis, Jan. 15, 1864; mustered Jan. 25, 1864. In action at the Wilderness, May 6, 1864, Spotsylvania Court House, May 10, 12, and 18, 1864, North Anna River, May 24, 1864, Cold Harbor, June 3, 1864, Petersburg assaults, June 17 and 18, 1864, and Petersburg Crater, July 30, 1864; taken prisoner of war at Weldon Railroad, Aug. 19, 1864. With the regiment on all marches and in all skirmishes and battles until captured. Paroled and exchanged from an unknown Confederate prison, March 8, 1865. Probably received extra pay for having been a prisoner of war. Returned to the regiment for duty from the Camp of Parole in Annapolis, MD, between March 25 and June 14, 1865. Mustered out with the regiment at Delaney house, Washington, DC, July 30, 1865, and discharged in Readville, MA, Aug. 9, 1865, expiration of service.

92. **Soudant, Joseph,** private. Res. and credit: Great Barrington, MA. Born: Great Barrington, MA. Age: 18. Height: 5'5". Comp: light. Eyes: blue. Hair: brown. Occup: laborer. Enlisted in Great Barrington by John M. Seeley, Feb. 2, 1864; mustered Feb. 18, 1864. Never in combat. Absent sick or on detached duty from on or before May 6, 1864, until after March 25, 1865. Mustered out with the regiment at Delaney house, Washington, DC, July 30, 1865, and discharged in Readville, MA, Aug. 9, 1865, expiration of service.

93. **Spaulding, William A.,** private. Res. and/or credit: Lenox, MA. Born: Cleveland, OH. Age: 24. Height: 5'10". Comp: dark. Eyes: hazel. Hair: dark. Occup: sailor. Enlisted in Lenox by William Durning, Jan. 5, 1864; mustered Jan. 25, 1865. Deserted from Camp Wool, Jan. 26, 1864. Never returned.

94. **Steadman, James S.,** private. Res. and/or credit: Lee, MA. Born: Tyringham, MA. Age: 22. Height: 5'10". Comp: light. Eyes: blue. Hair: brown. Occup: farmer. Enlisted in Co. I in Lee by Sylvester S. May, Feb. 6, 1864; mustered March 10, 1864; transferred to Co. D, April 13, 1864, under RSO 37, by order of Col. William F. Bartlett, dated April 12, 1864. Killed in action at the Wilderness, May 6, 1864. Had previous service as a private in Co. F, 49th MVI, from Sept. 16, 1862, until mustered out, Sept. 1, 1863. Participated in the Port Hudson, LA, campaign with that regiment in 1863.

95. **Stephens, Rufus,** private. Res. and/or credit: Charlton, MA. Born: Charlton, MA. Age: 26. Height: 6'0". Comp: dark. Eyes: blue. Hair: dark. Occup: laborer. Enlisted in Charlton by R. Hathaway, Jan. 5, 1864; mustered Jan. 25, 1865. Detailed as company cook, and, therefore, exempted from hard combat. Mustered out with the regiment at Delaney house, Washington, DC, July 30, 1865, and discharged in Readville, MA, Aug. 9, 1865, expiration of service.

96. **Stover, Simeon,** private. Res: Monterey, MA. Credit: New Marlboro, MA. Born: Winchester, CT. Age: 44. Height: 5'8". Comp: fair. Eyes: blue. Hair: brown. Occup: mechanic. Enlisted in New Marlboro by Aaron Smith, Jan. 18, 1864; mustered Jan. 25, 1864. "Sent home sick, April 18, 1864, with application for discharge" *(MSSM)*.

97. **Sweetser, James E.,** sergeant. Res. and/or credit: Sterling, MA. Born: Slatersville, RI. Age: 33. Height: 5'2". Comp: light. Eyes: gray. Hair: brown. Occup: tailor. Enlisted in Sterling by J. S. Butterick, Jan. 5, 1864; mustered Feb. 18, 1864. Detached and detailed as a cook in the hospital in Camp Wool from Feb. 24 until April 18, 1864. In action at the Wilderness, May 6, 1864, Spotsylvania Court House, May 10, 12, and 18, 1864, North Anna River, May 24, 1864, and Cold Harbor, June 3, 1864. Promoted sergeant, to date June 1, 1864. In action in Petersburg assaults, June 17 and 18, 1864, and Petersburg Crater, July 30, 1864. Absent sick or on detached duty from between July 30 and Aug. 19, 1864, until after March 25, 1865. With the regiment on all marches and in all skirmishes and battles at least through the Petersburg Crater. Mustered out with the regiment at Delaney house, Washington, DC, July 30, 1865, and discharged in Readville, MA, Aug. 9, 1865, expiration of service. Had previous service as a private in Co. K, 53rd MVI, from Sept. 6,

1862, until mustered out, Sept. 2, 1863. Participated in the Port Hudson, LA, campaign with that regiment in 1863.

98. **Swift, Silas C.**, 1st sergeant. Res: Great Barrington, MA. Credit: West Stockbridge, MA. Born: Great Barrington, MA. Age: 24. Height: 5'7". Comp: light. Eyes: gray. Hair: sandy. Occup: clerk. Enlisted in West Stockbridge by Lt. Charles W. Kniffin, Dec. 13, 1863; mustered Jan. 25, 1864. Promoted 1st sergeant, Jan. 25, 1864. Reduced to duty sergeant, March 9, 1864 (Gilmore promoted 1st sergeant). Never in combat with the 57th. Absent sick in an army general hospital from on or before May 6, 1864, (and "reduced to the ranks for absence" [CR]) until transferred to and promoted corporal in the 117th Co., 2nd Battln., VRC, July 20, 1865. Discharged the US service, Oct. 10, 1865, by order of the War Dept., expiration of service. Had previous service in Co. E, 96th New York Volunteer Infantry (specifics unknown).

99. **Townsend, Almond C.**, private. Res: Great Barrington, MA. Credit: New Marlboro, MA. Born: Becket, MA. Age: 19. Height: 5'4". Comp: light. Eyes: hazel. Hair: brown. Occup: laborer. Enlisted in New Marlboro by Aaron Smith, Jan. 12, 1864; mustered Jan. 25, 1864. In action at the Wilderness, May 6, 1864, and Spotsylvania Court House, May 10, 1864; wounded in action there, May 12, 1864. Absent wounded in an army general hospital until transferred to Co. G, 9th Regiment, VRC, Feb. 10, 1865. Discharged the US service, July 15, 1865, by order of the War Dept. expiration of service.

100. **Tyler, Lester**, corporal. Res. and/or credit: Pittsfield, MA. Born: Canton, CT. Age: 44. Height: 5'7½". Comp: light. Eyes: blue. Hair: brown. Occup: laborer. Enlisted in Pittsfield by John C. West, Jan. 4, 1864; mustered Jan. 25, 1864. Promoted corporal, Jan. 25, 1864. Killed in action at the Wilderness, May 6, 1864. Had previous service in Co. K, 14th New York Volunteer Infantry (specifics unknown).

101. **Viner, Benjamin A.**, private. Res. and credit: Pittsfield, MA. Born: Pittsfield, MA.

Age: 28. Height: 5'8". Comp: light. Eyes: blue. Hair: light. Occup: painter. Enlisted in Pittsfield by John C. West, Dec. 14, 1863; mustered Jan. 25, 1864. Deserted from Camp Wool, Feb. 23, 1864, but returned, Feb. 28, 1864, and was confined in the guardhouse in Camp Wool, Feb. 28 and 29, 1864. In action at the Wilderness, May 6, 1864, Spotsylvania Court House, May 10, 12, and 18, 1864, North Anna River, May 24, 1864, Cold Harbor, June 3, 1864, and Petersburg assaults, June 17 and 18, 1864; wounded while on duty in the trenches at Petersburg, July 14, 1864. With the regiment on all marches and in all skirmishes and battles until wounded. Absent wounded in an army general hospital in Philadelphia, PA, until he deserted from there, Dec. 2, 1864. Never returned.

102. **Vinton, George E.**, private. Res. and/or credit: Charlton, MA. Born: Dudley, MA. Age: 32. Height: 5'6½". Comp: dark. Eyes: gray. Hair: dark. Occup: shoemaker. Enlisted in Charleton by R. Dodge, Jan. 5, 1864; mustered Jan. 25, 1864. In action at the Wilderness, May 6, 1864, and Spotsylvania Court House, May 10, 1864; wounded in action there, May 12, 1864. Absent wounded in an army general hospital until transferred to the 52nd Co., 2nd Battln., VRC, in Feb. 1865. Discharged the US service, July 7, 1865, by order of the War Dept., expiration of service.

103. **Vocell, James**, private. Res. and credit: Stockbridge, MA. Born: Stockbridge, MA. Age: 25. Height: 5'6". Comp: dark. Eyes: brown. Hair: black. Occup: molder. Enlisted in Stockbridge by H. M. Burrell, Dec. 18, 1863; mustered Jan. 25, 1864. Deserted from Camp Wool, April 16, 1864, but returned the next day, April 17, 1864, and was confined in the guardhouse in Camp Wool until April 18, 1864. Wounded in action at the Wilderness, May 6, 1864. Absent wounded in an army general hospital until discharged the US service for disability from wounds, May 5, 1865, by order of the War Dept. Had previous service as a private in Co. B, 7th MVI, from June 15, 1861, until discharged on a Surgeons Certificate of Disability, Nov. 17, 1862. Participated in the Peninsula campaign with that regiment in 1862.

104. **Walker, Ephraim**, private. Res. and/or credit: Williamstown, MA. Born: Bennington, VT. Age: 40. Height: 5'7". Comp: light. Eyes: blue. Hair: light. Occup: laborer. Enlisted in Williamstown by H. T. Cole, Jan. 2, 1864; mustered Jan. 25, 1864. Never in combat. Absent sick in an army general hospital from on or before May 6, 1864, until discharged the US service for disability, July 14, 1864, by order of the War Dept. Had previous service as a private in Co. D, 24th MVI, from Oct. 9, 1861, until discharged for disability from wounds in New Bern, NC, May 9, 1863. Participated in the North Carolina campaign with that regiment in 1862–63, and wounded in action at New Bern, March 14, 1862.

105. **Wallace, Robert**, private. Res. and/or credit: Milford, MA. Born: County Tyrone, Ireland, March 17, 1825. Age: 38. Height: 5'3½". Comp: fair. Eyes: blue. Hair: light. Occup: boot crimper. Enlisted in Milford by Leonard Hunt, Jan. 16, 1864; mustered Jan. 25, 1864. Mortally wounded at the Wilderness and left on the battlefield, May 6, 1864. Reported to have died on the field later that day.

106. **Ward, Wilbur F.**, corporal. Res: Adams, MA. Born: Blackhook, NY. Age: 18. Height: 5'6". Comp: light. Eyes: hazel. Hair: red. Occup: operative. Enlisted in Adams by S. Johnson, Dec. 25, 1863; mustered Jan. 25, 1864. Promoted corporal, Jan. 25, 1864. Wounded in action and taken prisoner of war at the Wilderness, May 6, 1864. Incarcerated in an unknown Confederate prison. Released or escaped and died from wounds and disease in New Orleans, LA, June 5, 1864. Had previous service as a private in Co. F, 13th Vermont Volunteer Infantry (specifics unknown).

107. **Welch, Maurice**, musician. Res. and/or credit: Oxford, MA. Born: Cork, Ireland. Age: 18. Height: 5'5¾". Comp: light. Eyes: hazel. Hair: brown. Occup: shoemaker. Enlisted in Oxford by L. B. Larkin, Dec. 25, 1863; mustered Jan. 25, 1864. Company drummer. Probably also served as a hospital orderly, stretcher bearer, and/or nurse. Mus-

tered out with the regiment at Delaney house, Washington, DC, July 30, 1865, and discharged in Readville, MA, Aug. 9, 1865, expiration of service. Died in 1891, age 46.

108. **Willett, Alfred**, private. Res. and/or credit: Millbury, MA. Born: Canada. Age: 18. Height: 5'5¾". Comp: dark. Eyes: black. Hair: dark. Occup: blacksmith. Enlisted in Millbury by C. D. Morse, Jan. 6, 1864; mustered Jan. 25, 1864. In action at the Wilderness, May 6, 1864. Company records report him having deserted during the march to Spotsylvania Court House, May 7, 1864, but other records report him as deserted from an army general hospital in Philadelphia, PA, Feb. 20, 1865 (possibly taken prisoner of war while straggling on that march, May 7, 1864, and assumed deserted, and then later deserted while absent sick in the Philadelphia hospital as an exchanged prisoner). Never returned.

109. **Williams, Benjamin F.**, corporal. Res. and/or credit: New Marlboro, MA. Born: Sanford, NY. Age: 18. Height: 5'4". Comp: fair. Eyes: black. Hair: light. Occup: laborer. Enlisted in New Marlboro by W. Walker, Feb. 8, 1864; mustered Feb. 18, 1864. In action at the Wilderness, May 6, 1864, Spotsylvania Court House, May 10, 12, and 18, 1864, and North Anna River, May 24, 1864. Promoted corporal, June 1, 1864. Wounded in action at Cold Harbor, June 3, 1864. With the regiment on all marches and in all skirmishes and battles until wounded. Absent wounded in an army general hospital until discharged the US service for disability from wounds, May 25, 1865, by order of the War Dept.

110. **Williams, Charles K.**, 1st sergeant. Res. and credit: New Marlboro, MA. Born: New Marlboro, MA. Age: 19. Height: 5'6". Comp: fair. Eyes: brown. Hair: brown. Occup: clerk. Enlisted in New Marlboro by J. Andrews, Jan. 18, 1864; mustered Feb. 18, 1864. Promoted corporal, Feb. 18, 1864. In action at the Wilderness, May 6, 1864, Spotsylvania Court House, May 10, 12, and 18, 1864, and North Anna River, May 24, 1864. Promoted sergeant, June 1, 1864. In action at Cold Harbor, June 3, 1864, Petersburg assaults, June 17 and

18, 1864, and Petersburg Crater, July 30, 1864. Absent sick or on detached duty from between July 30 and Aug. 19, 1864, until after March 25, 1865. On furlough from June 24 until June 27, 1865. Promoted 1st sergeant, July 7, 1865. Mustered out with the regiment at Delaney house, Washington, D.C., July 30, 1865, and discharged in Readville, MA, Aug. 9, 1865, expiration of service. Had previous service as a private in Co. E, 49th MVI, from Sept. 1, 1862, until mustered out Sept. 1,

1863. Participated in the Port Hudson, LA, campaign with that regiment in 1863.

111. **Williams, John,** private. Res: Lowell, MA. Credit: Springfield, MA. Born: Ireland. Age: 21. Height: 5′5½″. Comp: fair. Eyes: blue. Hair: light. Occup: barber. Enlisted in Springfield by an unknown selectman, Jan. 13, 1864; mustered Jan. 25, 1864. Deserted from Camp Wool, April 17, 1864. Never returned. "Bounty jumper" (JA).

ROSTER AND DESCRIPTIVE LIST OF COMPANY E

Company E was the fourth company to be mustered into United States service, and it was mustered in on Jan. 25, 1864, by 2nd Lt. Daniel Madden, 6th United States Regular Cavalry, under SO 88 from the AGO, Boston, MA. Those men in the company mustered after Jan. 25, 1864, were mustered in by both Madden and 1st Lt. Robert McKibben, 4th United States Regular Infantry, depending upon the date of muster. It was mustered out by Capt. Sylvester Keyser, ACM, 1st Division, IX Corps.

1. **Abbott, Charles,** sergeant. Res. and/or credit: Springfield, MA. Born: Charlestown, NH. Age: 25. Height: 5′7½″. Comp: light. Eyes: blue. Hair: auburn. Occup: clerk. Enlisted in Springfield by H. Alexander, Jr., Jan. 7, 1864; mustered Jan. 25, 1864. Promoted sergeant, Jan. 25, 1864. Reduced to the ranks for an unknown reason in Feb. 1864. Deserted in Jersey City, April 19, 1864, while the regiment was en route to the front. Never returned. "Bounty jumper" (JA).

2. **Alden, George M.,** private. Res: Wilbraham, MA. Credit: Palmer, MA. Born: Wilbraham, MA. Age: 20. Height: 5′7″. Comp: dark. Eyes: blue. Hair: light. Occup: machinist. Enlisted in Palmer by Capt. George H. Howe, Dec. 21, 1863; mustered Jan. 25, 1864. Killed in action at the Wilderness, May 6, 1864.

3. **Anderson, John,** 2nd lieutenant. Res. and/or credit: Holland, MA. Born: Monson, MA. Age: 23. Height: unknown. Comp: light. Eyes: blue. Hair: brown. Occup: unknown. Commissioned 2nd lieutenant, Feb. 1, 1864; mustered 2nd lieutenant, Feb. 10, 1864. In action at the Wilderness, May 6, 1864, Spotsylvania Court House, May 10, 12, and 18,

1864, North Anna River, May 24, 1864, Cold Harbor, June 3, 1864, and Petersburg assaults, June 17 and 18, 1864; wounded in action at the Petersburg Crater, July 30, 1864. With

Lieutenant John Anderson.
(Mark Savolis)

496

the regiment on all marches and in all skirmishes and battles until wounded. Absent wounded in the 1st Division, IX Corps, Field Hospital until transferred to Seminary US Army General Hospital in Washington, DC, Aug. 3, 1864. Resigned and discharged the US service for disability from wounds, Jan. 21, 1865, under SO 33, par. 18, AGO, War Dept. Had previous service as an enlisted man in Co. E, 1st Michigan Sharpshooters, from Jan. 5, 1863, until discharged to accept a commission in the 57th, Feb. 9, 1864 (combat specifics with that regiment unknown). Had subsequent service as 2nd lieutenant in the 20th Regiment, VRC from March 25, 1865, until mustered out, June 30, 1866. Appointed 1st lieutenant and captain of US Volunteers by brevet for "gallant and meritorious service in the battles before Petersburg, VA," July 16, 1867, under GO 67, AGO, War Dept., to date from March 13, 1865. Also had subsequent service as 2nd lieutenant in the 25th United States Regular Infantry from Aug. 10, 1867, until transferred to the 18th United States Regular Infantry, April 26, 1869. Commissioned 1st lieutenant, Oct. 17, 1878. Commissioned captain, June 21, 1890. Served in Montana fighting against Sitting Bull, and later on duty in Texas. Retired from active service, June 6, 1894, for disability from illness contracted while serving in Texas. Author of the 57th's original regimental history. President of the 57th's regimental association in 1896. Resided in Belchertown, MA, after retirement, until joining the army again on an unknown date (probably during the Spanish-American War). Commissioned major on an unknown date, and retired permanently April 23, 1904. Died after 1911, date unknown.

4. **Anthony, William H.**, private. Res. and/or credit: Leicester, MA. Born: Quincy, MA. Age: 18. Height: 5'4". Comp: light. Eyes: blue. Hair: light. Occup: farmer. Enlisted in Leicester by Silas Gleason, Jan. 7, 1864; mustered Jan. 25, 1864. In action at the Wilderness, May 6, 1864, and Spotsylvania Court House, May 10, 12, and 18, 1864; killed in action at North Anna River, May 24, 1864. "One brave young boy . . ." (JA).

5. **Arnold, Henry**, corporal. Res: Boston, MA. Credit: Worcester, MA. Born: Bavaria, Germany. Age: 29. Height: 5'5". Comp: dark. Eyes: dark. Hair: dark. Occup: tailor. Enlisted in Worcester by Lt. John Anderson, Jan. 15, 1864; mustered Jan. 25, 1864. Promoted corporal, Jan. 25, 1864. Never in combat. Absent sick in Mower US Army General Hospital in Philadelphia, PA, from on or before May 6, 1864, until he deserted while on furlough from there, Nov. 29, 1864. Never returned.

6. **Barrows, William R.**, private. Res. and/or credit: Belchertown, MA. Born: Mansfield, CT. Age: 44. Height: 5'6". Comp: dark. Eyes: blue. Hair: brown. Occup: farmer. Enlisted in Belchertown by Wright Bridgeman, Jan. 5, 1864; mustered Jan. 25, 1864. Deserted while on furlough from Camp Wool, Feb. 2, 1864, but was arrested, returned, and incarcerated in the guardhouse in Camp Wool from March 20 until at least March 23, 1864. Never left with the regiment for the front, and was discharged the US service for disability in Worcester, MA, April 25, 1865, by order of Maj. Gen. John James Peck, commanding the Dept. of Virginia and North Carolina. Died before 1896, but date not known.

7. **Benroy, Thomas**, private. Res. and/or credit: Northampton, MA. Born: Canada. Age: 26. Height: 5'4½". Comp: light. Eyes: blue. Hair: dark. Occup: farmer. Enlisted in Northampton by W. F. Orcutt, Jan. 5, 1864; mustered Jan. 25, 1864. Killed in action at the Wilderness, May 6, 1864.

8. **Blair, Franklin**, private. Res: Palmer, MA. Credit: Springfield, MA. Born: Enfield, MA. Age: 44. Height: unknown. Comp: fair. Eyes: blue. Hair: gray. Occup: farmer. Enlisted in Springfield by Capt. George H. Howe, Dec. 30, 1863; mustered Jan. 25, 1864. In action at the Wilderness, May 6, 1864, Spotsylvania Court House, May 10, 12, and 18, 1864, North Anna River, May 24, 1864, Cold Harbor, June 3, 1864, and Petersburg assaults, June 17 and 18, 1864. With the regiment on all marches and in all skirmishes and battles until June 29, 1864. Absent sick in an army general hospital from June 29 until Nov. 30, 1864. Discharged the US service for disability at Petersburg, Feb. 27, 1865, by order of the War Dept. Died before 1896, but date not known.

9. **Blauvelt, William H.**, private. Res. and/or credit: Springfield, MA. Born: New York City. Age: 18. Height: 5'3". Comp: light. Eyes: hazel. Hair: dark. Occup: mechanic. Enlisted in Springfield by Capt. Charles D. Hollis, Jan. 1, 1864; mustered Jan. 25, 1864. Sick in the hospital in Camp Wool from about Jan. 15, 1864, until furloughed home about Feb. 1, 1864. Reported as a deserter when he had not returned by Feb. 13, 1864. Returned to the regiment for duty on the morning of Feb. 27, 1864. Never in combat. Absent sick in Lincoln US Army General Hospital in Washington, DC, from on or before May 6, 1864, until discharged the US service for disability, June 21, 1865, under GO 77, par. 6, AGO, War Dept. Resided in Worcester, MA, after the war.

10. **Bradeau, Alfred**, private. Res: Leicester, MA. Credit: Worcester, MA. Born: province of Quebec, Canada. Age: 24. Height: 5'5". Comp: light. Eyes: gray. Hair: brown. Occup: laborer. Enlisted in Worcester by Lt. John Anderson, Jan. 22, 1864; mustered Jan. 25, 1864. Deserted while on furlough from Camp Wool, Feb. 8, 1864. Never returned.

11. **Breau, Peter**, private. Res: Buckland, MA. Credit: Greenfield, MA. Born: province of Quebec, Canada. Age: 18. Height: 5'4". Comp: dark. Eyes: black. Hair: black. Occup: laborer. Enlisted in Greenfield by E. B. Williams, Jan. 15, 1864; mustered Jan. 25, 1864. In action at the Wilderness, May 6, 1864, and Spotsylvania Court House, May 10, 1864; wounded in action there, May 12, 1864. Absent wounded in an army general hospital until transferred to the 46th Co., 2nd Battln., VRC, April 28, 1865. Discharged the US service, Sept. 7, 1865, by order of the War Dept., expiration of service.

12. **Brown, John**, private. Res. and/or credit: Whately, MA. Born: Conway, MA. Age: 43. Height: 6'0". Comp: light. Eyes: blue. Hair: brown. Occup: farmer. Enlisted in Whately by L. B. White, Dec. 25, 1863; mustered Jan. 25, 1864. Deserted while on furlough from Camp Wool, Feb. 24, 1864, but returned on Feb. 28, 1864. In action and taken prisoner of war at the Wilderness, May 6, 1864. Incarcer-

ated in the Confederate prison camp in Andersonville, Ga, May 29, 1864, where he died from dysentery, Oct. 12, 1864. Buried in grave, Sec. H, No. 10819, at Andersonville. Had previous service as a private in Co. H, 8th MVI, from Oct. 10, 1862, until mustered out, Aug. 7, 1863. Participated with that regiment in the North Carolina campaign in 1862–63.

13. **Brown, Seva**, private. Res. and credit: Palmer, MA. Born: Palmer, MA. Age: 33. Height: unknown. Comp: ruddy. Eyes: blue. Hair: brown. Occup: farmer. Enlisted in Palmer by Capt. George H. Howe, Dec. 7, 1863; mustered Jan. 25, 1865. Killed in action at the Wilderness, May 6, 1864.

14. **Bryant, Michael**, private. Res. and/or credit: Springfield, MA. Born: Ireland. Age: 30. Height: 5'4". Comp: light. Eyes: blue. Hair: brown. Occup: laborer. Enlisted in Springfield by Capt. Lewis A. Tifft, Dec. 30, 1863; mustered Jan. 25, 1864. Absent sick in an army general hospital from on or before May 6, 1864, until after March 25, 1865. Issued two pairs of socks, April 30, 1865. Illiterate. Mustered out with the regiment at Delaney house, Washington, DC, July 30, 1865, and discharged in Readville, MA, Aug. 9, 1865, expiration of service.

15. **Bryant, Nahum**, corporal. Res. and/or credit: Springfield, MA. Born: New York City. Age: 37. Height: 5'8". Comp: dark. Eyes: black. Hair: brown. Occup: armorer. Enlisted in Springfield by Capt. Charles D. Hollis, Jan. 1, 1864; mustered Jan. 25, 1864. Promoted corporal, April 20, 1864. Wounded in action at the Wilderness, May 6, 1864. Absent wounded in an army general hospital until transferred to the 112th Co., 2nd Battln., VRC, Sept. 30, 1864. Discharged the US service for disability from wounds, Aug. 22, 1865, by order of the War Dept. Resided in Springfield, MA, after the war.

16. **Burleigh, Asa D.**, private. Res: Worthington, MA. Credit: Millbury, MA. Born: Monson, MA. Age: 29. Height: 5'6". Comp: dark. Eyes: gray. Hair: dark. Occup: butcher. Enlisted in Millbury by C. D. Morse, Jan. 8, 1864; mustered Jan. 25, 1864. Wounded in

action at the Wilderness, May 6, 1864. Absent wounded in an army general hospital until transferred to Co. I, 10th Regiment, VRC, Dec. 27, 1864, to date from Sept. 30, 1864, by TO 26 AGO, War Dept., dated Oct. 17, 1864. Discharged the US service for disability from wounds, July 26, 1865, by order of the War Dept. Died in 1884 from the effects of his wounds, age 49. "He was a brave soldier . . . a genial companion and an upright man" (JA).

17. **Burr, Charles,** private. Res. and/or credit: Millbury, MA. Born: Chesterfield, MA. Age: 42. Height: 5'10½". Comp: dark. Eyes: hazel. Hair: black. Occup: farmer. Enlisted in Millbury by J. E. Waters, Jan. 2, 1864; mustered Jan. 25, 1864. Killed in action at the Wilderness, May 6, 1864.

18. **Cahill, John,** corporal. Res. and/or credit: Northampton, MA. Born: Hampden, MA. Age: 21. Height: 5'8½". Comp: light. Eyes: hazel. Hair: brown. Occup: machinist. Enlisted in Northampton by H. K. Starkweather, Jan. 4, 1864; mustered Jan. 25, 1864. Promoted corporal, Jan. 25, 1864. In action at the Wilderness, May 6, 1864, and Spotsylvania Court House, May 10, 1864; killed in action there, May 12, 1864.

19. **Carpenter, Andrew N.,** corporal. Res: Springfield, MA. Credit: Palmer, MA. Born: Augusta, ME. Age: 28. Height: 5'11½". Comp: fair. Eyes: blue. Hair: dark. Occup: tailor. Enlisted in Palmer by Capt. George H. Howe, Dec. 5, 1863; mustered Jan. 25, 1864. Promoted corporal, Jan. 25, 1864. Deserted from Camp Wool, April 16, 1864. Never returned. "Bounty jumper" (JA).

20. **Cheney, George W.,** private. Res: Northbridge, MA. Credit: Worcester, MA. Born: Sutton, MA. Age: 22. Height: 5'11". Comp: dark. Eyes: dark. Hair: dark. Occup: bootmaker. Enlisted in Worcester by Lt. John Anderson, Jan. 20, 1864; mustered Jan. 25, 1864. Wounded in action at the Wilderness, May 6, 1864. Absent wounded in an army general hospital until discharged the US service for disability from wounds, May 25, 1865, by order of the War Dept.

21. **Coburn, Joseph,** private. Res: Upton, MA. Credit: Worcester, MA. Born: Woodstock, VT. Age: 22. Height: 5'4". Comp: light. Eyes: gray. Hair: brown. Occup: shoemaker. Enlisted in Worcester by Arba Wood, Jan. 21, 1864; mustered Jan. 25, 1864. Deserted from Camp Wool, Feb. 18, 1864. Never returned.

22. **Collins, Edwin,** sergeant. Res. and/or credit: Springfield, MA. Born: Ireland. Age: 26. Height: 5'8". Comp: light. Eyes: blue. Hair: sandy. Occup: candy maker. Enlisted in Springfield by Capt. Lewis A. Tifft, Jan. 6, 1864; mustered Jan. 25, 1864. In action at the Wilderness, May 6, 1864, Spotsylvania Court House, May 10, 12, and 18, 1864, North Anna River, May 24, 1864, Cold Harbor, June 3, 1864, and Petersburg assaults, June 17 and 18, 1864. Promoted corporal, July 1, 1864. In action and taken prisoner of war at the Petersburg Crater, July 30, 1864. With the regiment on all marches and in all skirmishes and battles until captured. Incarcerated in the Confederate prison in Danville, VA, until paroled and exchanged, Feb. 22, 1865. Probably received extra pay for having been a prisoner of war. Absent sick in the army general hospital in the Camp of Parole in Annapolis, MD, until between Jan. 30 and March 25, 1865. In action at Fort Stedman, March 25, 1865. Issued one forage cap, April 30, 1865. Illiterate. Promoted sergeant on an unknown date, but probably to date May 1, 1865, under RSO 42, by order of Lt. Col. Julius M. Tucker. Mustered out with the regiment at Delaney house, Washington, DC, July 30, 1865, and discharged in Readville, MA, Aug. 9, 1865, expiration of service. Resided in Springfield, MA, after the war.

23. **Collins, Thomas,** private. Res. and/or credit: Leominster, MA. Born: Ireland. Age: 44. Height: 5'5". Comp: sandy. Eyes: light. Hair: blue/gray. Occup: laborer. Enlisted in Leominster by an unknown selectman, Jan. 12, 1864; mustered Jan. 25, 1864. Did not leave Camp Wool with the regiment, but sent to Camp Meigs in Readville, MA, April 18, 1864, under the supervision of Lt. John Cook for a medical examination. Found unfit for duty by a "board of inspectors." Rejected re-

cruit and discharged the US service in Worcester, MA, June 29, 1864, by order of Maj. Gen. John A. Dix, War Dept.

24. **Connelly, John,** private. Res. and/or credit: Conway, MA. Born: Ireland. Age: 41. Height: 5'9". Comp: dark. Eyes: hazel. Hair: gray. Occup: currier. Enlisted in Co. I in Conway by Lt. Col. Luke Lyman, March 26, 1864; mustered April 6, 1864; transferred to Co. E, April 13, 1864, under RSO 38, by order of Col. William F. Bartlett. In action at the Wilderness, May 6, 1864, and Spotsylvania Court House, May 10, 1864; taken prisoner of war in action there, May 12, 1864. Paroled and exchanged from an unknown Confederate prison, May 8, 1865. Probably received extra pay for having been a prisoner of war. Absent sick in an army general hospital (probably in the Camp of Parole in Annapolis, MD) until discharged the US service, Sept. 3, 1865, by order of the War Dept., expiration of service.

25. **Cook, John H.,** 1st lieutenant. Res. and/ or credit: Northampton, MA. Born: Massachusetts. Age: 22. Married. Height: unknown. Comp: light. Eyes: brown. Hair: dark brown. Occup: clerk. Commissioned 2nd lieutenant, Nov. 27, 1863; mustered 2nd lieutenant, Dec. 14, 1863. Commissioned 1st lieutenant, Feb. 10, 1864; mustered 1st lieutenant, March 1, 1864. Under RSO 29, by order of Col. William F. Bartlett, dated March 21, 1864: "1st Lieutenant John Cook of Co. E, having reported for duty, is hereby ordered to relieve Lieutenant Coe as commissary of recruits." Remained behind in Massachusetts when the regiment left Camp Wool, April 18, 1864, and supervised the transportation of the men from the regiment going to Readville, MA, for medical examinations. Also remained behind to procure the Spencer rifles for Co. K. Reported to the regiment for duty at Petersburg on or about June 17, 1864, and was assigned to command of Co. K in July 1864. Severely wounded in the left side on the picket line, July 22, 1864: "Case 274.—Lieutenant J. H. Cook, Co. E, 57th Massachusetts, aged 23 years, was wounded at Petersburg, July [22], 1864, by a conoidal [Minié] ball. He was admitted to the field hospital of

the 1st division, Ninth Corps, on the same day, and the case reported as 'gunshot penetrating wound of the left hypochondriac region.' He was furloughed on July 25th [from an army general hospital in Washington, DC], and on October 31st, was admitted to [the army general] hospital at Readville, Massachusetts, with 'gunshot wound of side' " (OMR). Detailed as commander of the military guard detachment at Dale US Army General Hospital in Worcester, MA, in late November 1864 until resigned and discharged the US service for disability from wounds, Jan. 6, 1865, under SO 469, par. 18, AGO, War Dept., dated Dec. 27, 1864. Had previous service as a private in Co. C, 10th MVI, from June 21, 1861, until discharged for disability at Harrison's Landing, VA, July 17, 1862. Participated in the Peninsula campaign with that regiment in 1862. In regard to the Petersburg wound: "Pension examiner S. L. Sprague, of Boston, May 2, 1866, stated that he examined Lieutenant Cook on February 2, 1865, and that 'a minie ball, entering the left side beneath the twelfth rib, was cut out from over the spine of the lowest lumbar vertebra. The ball passed through the abdomen, wounding the intestine. Faecal discharge is now constant at the wound. There is numbness of the hip and thigh at the right side; he can walk one-half a mile with a cane; he is debilitated, and has constant pain in the hip.' Pension examiner W. H. Page, of Boston, reported, January 26, 1866: 'Ball entered at edge of left lower rib, centre of left side, about four inches above the superior process of ilium, and came out on right side of spine, about one inch to right and on level with the top of crest of ilium. He alleges that there were faecal discharges from the posterior wound for about four weeks; when it healed, but has broken out twice since—the last time being last July; it is now entirely healed; has trouble in passing urine when he gets cold; the urine is very offensive, and he has more or less pain in the kidneys; cannot lift any heavy thing, nor walk any great distance, without having very severe pain in the back. The left leg is also enfeebled by the cutting off of some of the nerves; disability three-fourths and permanent.' Pension last paid to December 4, 1872" (OMR). Breveted captain and major of

Lieutenant John Cook.
(Mark Savolis)

US Volunteers for gallant and meritorious conduct in the campaign before Petersburg, VA, Oct. 9, 1867, under GO 91, AGO, War Dept., to date from March 13, 1865. Served in the Boston Customs House, Boston, MA, for 25 years after the war, and was auditor during the last three of those years. Was department inspector for the Massachusetts GAR and commander of Kinsley GAR Post 113. Served in the General Court of Massachusetts in 1875, '76, and '77. President of the 57th's regimental association in 1873, '74, '75, and '78. Resided in Roxbury, MA, after the war and died in his home there, Aug. 19, 1893, age 51.

26. **Corbett, John,** private. Res: Spencer, MA. Credit: Worcester, MA. Born: Ireland. Age: 42. Height: 5'4". Comp; florid. Eyes: gray. Hair: black. Occup: farmer. Enlisted in Worcester by Lt. John Anderson, Jan. 22, 1864; mustered Jan. 25, 1864. Killed in action at the Wilderness, May 6, 1864.

27. **Cudworth, Edwin H.,** private. Res. and credit: Oxford, MA. Born: Oxford, MA. Age: 20. Height: 5'4". Comp: light. Eyes: blue. Hair: brown. Occup: boot crimper. Enlisted in Oxford by L. B. Corbin, Jan. 15, 1864; mustered Jan. 25, 1864. Wounded in action at the Wilderness, May 6, 1864. Absent wounded in an army general hospital until Oct. 9, 1864. Absent sick in the 1st Division, IX Corps, Field Hospital at Petersburg from Nov. 22 until Dec. 1, 1864, from Dec. 13 until Dec. 24, 1864, and from Dec. 25, 1864, until Jan. 26, 1865. With the regiment in operations during the winter of 1865, and killed in action at Fort Stedman, March 25, 1865.

28. **Day, Samuel M.,** musician. Res: West Springfield, MA. Credit: Westfield, MA. Born: Springfield, MA. Age: 18. Height: 5'2". Comp: light. Eyes: gray. Hair: dark. Occup: whip maker. Enlisted in Westfield by Capt. Charles D. Hollis, Dec. 14, 1863; mustered Jan. 25, 1864. Company drummer. Probably also served as a nurse, stretcher bearer, and/or hospital orderly. Present at the battle of Fort Stedman, March 25, 1865. Issued two pairs of trousers, three pairs of socks, and one knit shirt, April 30, 1865. Literate. Mustered out with the regiment at Delaney house, Washington, DC, July 30, 1865, and discharged in Readville, MA, Aug. 9, 1865, expiration of service.

29. **Demarets, Alexander,** private. Res. and/ or credit: Springfield, MA. Born: province of Quebec, Canada. Age: 21. Height: 5'4". Comp: ruddy. Eyes: dark. Hair: dark. Occup: laborer. Enlisted in Springfield by Aaron Bogg, Jan. 15, 1864; mustered Jan. 25, 1864. In action at the Wilderness, May 6, 1864, and wounded later that month, but not in a major battle. Absent wounded in Dale US Army General Hospital in Worcester, MA, until discharged the US service for disability from wounds, May 2, 1865, by order of Maj. Gen. John A. Dix, War Dept. Also known as Oliver Demerett in his military records.

30. **Demers, Henry,** private. Res: Rouses Point, NY. Credit: Springfield, MA. Born: province of Quebec, Canada. Age: 22. Height: 5'6". Comp: dark. Eyes: blue. Hair: black. Occup: teamster. Enlisted in Springfield by Capt. Charles D. Hollis, Jan. 16, 1864; mustered Jan. 25, 1864. Deserted while on furlough from Camp Wool, Feb. 20, 1865. Never returned.

31. **Desautel, Henry George,** corporal. Res. and/or credit: Milford, MA. Born: Castleton, VT, Aug. 5, 1845. Age: 18. Height: 5'7". Comp: fair. Eyes: blue. Hair: light. Occup: bootmaker. Enlisted in Milford by Leonard Hunt, Jan. 5, 1864; mustered Jan. 25, 1864. In action at the Wilderness, May 6, 1864, and promoted corporal that day (undoubtedly for bravery during the battle). In action at Spotsylvania Court House, May 10, 12, and 18, 1864, North Anna River, May 24, 1864, and Cold Harbor, June 3, 1864; wounded in the arm in action during the Petersburg assault, June 17, 1864. With the regiment on all marches and in all skirmishes and battles until wounded. Absent wounded in an army general hospital until transferred to Co. G, 24th Regiment, VRC, Feb. 15, 1865, by order of the provost marshal general. Discharged the US service, July 27, 1865, by order of the War Dept., expiration of service.

32. **Dorman, Anson A.**, private. Res. and/or credit: Palmer, MA. Born: Belchertown, MA. Age: 34. Height: 5'9". Comp: dark. Eyes: blue. Hair: brown. Occup: farmer and teacher. Enlisted in Palmer by Capt. George H. Howe, Jan. 8, 1864; mustered Jan. 25, 1864. Never in combat. Detached and detailed as a driver on the 1st Division, IX Corps, ambulance wagon train from April 27, 1864, until after March 25, 1865. Mustered out with the regiment at Delaney house, Washington, DC, July 30, 1865, and discharged in Readville, MA, Aug. 9, 1865, expiration of service. Had previous service as a sergeant in Co. H, 46th MVI, from Aug. 23, 1862, until mustered out, July 29, 1863. Participated with that regiment in the North Carolina campaign in 1862–63. Resided in Belchertown, MA, after the war.

33. **Dorr, Daniel L.**, private. Res: Sutton, MA. Credit: Worcester, MA. Born: Douglas, MA. Age: 39. Height: 5'4". Comp: light. Eyes: gray. Hair: gray. Occup: shoemaker. Enlisted in Worcester by Capt. John Sanderson, Dec. 15, 1863; mustered Jan. 25, 1864. Did not leave Camp Wool with the regiment, but sent to Camp Meigs in Readville, MA, under the supervision of Lt. John Cook, April 18, 1864, for a medical examination. Found unfit for duty by a "board of inspectors." Rejected recruit and discharged the US service in Worcester, MA, June 29, 1864, by order of Maj. Gen. John A. Dix, War Dept. Had previous service as a private in Co. H, 31st MVI, from Dec. 25, 1861, until discharged for disability in Kenner, LA, Sept. 26, 1862. On duty with that regiment in Louisiana in 1862.

34. **Drake, Elizur C.**, private. Res: Monson, MA. Credit: Palmer, MA. Born: Windsor, CT. Age: 44. Height: 5'10". Comp: light. Eyes: gray. Hair: brown. Occup: farmer. Enlisted in Palmer by David G. Patten, Jan. 5, 1864; mustered Jan. 25, 1864. In action at the Wilderness, May 6, 1864, Spotsylvania Court House, May 10, 12, and 18, 1864; North Anna River, May 24, 1864, and Cold Harbor, June 3, 1864; taken prisoner of war in action during the Petersburg assault, June 17, 1864. With the regiment on all marches and in all skirmishes and battles until captured. Incarcerated in the Confederate prison camp in Andersonville, GA, where he died from chronic diarrhea, June 30, 1864. Buried in grave, Sec. J, No. 2676, at Andersonville.

35. **Duncan, Walter H.**, sergeant. Res. and/or credit: Palmer, MA. Born: Warren, MA. Age: 20. Height: 5'5". Comp: fair. Eyes: gray. Hair: brown. Occup: mechanic. Enlisted in Palmer by E. B. Gates, Dec. 21, 1863; mustered Jan. 25, 1864. Promoted corporal, Jan. 25, 1864. Absent on detached duty from on or before May 6, 1864, until between Aug. 19 and Sept. 1, 1864. Promoted sergeant, Sept. 1, 1864. In action at Poplar Grove Church, Sept. 30 and Oct. 8, 1864. Absent sick in an army general hospital from Oct. 26 until Dec. 23, 1864. "Present in arrest" (CR) from Dec. 30, 1864, until Jan. 3, 1865 (reason unknown, but probably unsoldierly conduct, e.g., disobedience of orders or drinking), and reduced to the ranks, Jan. 4, 1865, under RSO 1, par. 1, to date Jan. 1, 1865, by order of Lt. Col. Julius M. Tucker and returned to duty. With the regiment in operations during the winter of 1865, and wounded and taken prisoner of war in action at Fort Stedman, March 25, 1865. Paroled and exchanged from Libby Prison in Richmond, VA, March 31, 1865. Absent wounded in the army general hospital in the Camp of Parole in Annapolis, MD, until discharged the US service, Aug. 9, 1865, by order of the War Dept., expiration of service. Had previous service as a private in Co. H, 46th MVI, from Oct. 25, 1862, until mustered out, July 29, 1863. Participated in the North Carolina campaign with that regiment in 1862–63. Resided in Indian Orchard, MA, after the war and died there after mid-1927, date unknown.

36. **Elliott, George**, private. Res: Buckland, MA. Credit: Greenfield, MA. Born: Covington, NY. Age: 19. Height: 5'6½". Comp: light. Eyes: blue. Hair: light. Occup: farmer. Enlisted in Greenfield by E. B. Williams, Jan. 16, 1864; mustered Jan. 25, 1864. Never in combat. Absent sick from on or before May 6, 1864, until between March 25 and April 30, 1865. Issued one forage cap and one pair of shoes, April 30, 1865. Illiterate. Mustered out with the regiment at Delaney house,

Washington, DC, July 30, 1865, and discharged in Readville, MA, Aug. 9, 1865, expiration of service.

37. **Farrell, Thomas,** private. Res. and/or credit: Springfield, MA. Born: Ireland. Age: 45. Height: 5'8". Comp: light. Eyes: blue. Hair: light. Occup: laborer. Enlisted in Springfield by Capt. Lewis A. Tifft, Jan. 2, 1864; mustered Jan. 25, 1864. Killed in action at the Wilderness, May 6, 1864.

38. **Finn, Bartholomew,** private. Res: Greenfield, MA. Credit: Northampton, MA. Born: Ireland. Age: 22. Height: 6'0". Comp: dark. Eyes: hazel. Hair: black. Occup: machinist. Enlisted in Northampton by Reuben H. Bolden, Jan. 4, 1864; mustered Jan. 25, 1864. In action at the Wilderness, May 6, 1864, Spotsylvania Court House, May 10, 12, and 18, 1864, North Anna River, May 24, 1864, Cold Harbor, June 3, 1864, and Petersburg assaults, June 17 and 18, 1864; missing in action at the Petersburg Crater, July 30, 1864. Never accounted for and presumed killed. With the regiment on all marches and in all skirmishes and battles until missing.

39. **Foster, James R.,** private. Res. and/or credit: Palmer, MA. Born: Livingston, ME. Age: 29. Height: 5'11". Comp: fair. Eyes: blue. Hair: black. Occup: painter. Enlisted in Co. I in Palmer by E. B. Gates, Feb. 22, 1864; mustered March 10, 1864; transferred to Co. E, March 13, 1864, under RSO 24, dated March 12, 1864, by order of Col. William F. Bartlett. Never in combat. Absent sick or on detached duty from on or before May 6, 1864, until between Oct. 8, 1864, and March 2, 1865. Detached and detailed as a teamster at 3rd Brigade, 1st Division, IX Corps, Headquarters from March 1, 1865 until musterout. Present in the vicinity during the battle of Fort Stedman, March 25, 1865, but not known to have been in action. Mustered out with the regiment at Delaney house, Washington, DC, July 30, 1865, and discharged in Readville, MA, Aug. 9, 1865. Had previous service as a musician in Co. H, 46th MVI, from Aug. 16, 1862, until mustered out, July 29, 1863. Participated in the North Carolina campaign with that regiment in 1862–63. Died before 1896, but date not known.

40. **Fuller, Francis D.,** corporal. Res. and/or credit: Palmer, MA. Born: Belchertown, MA. Age: 26. Height: 5'5". Comp: light. Eyes: gray. Hair: brown. Occup: farmer. Enlisted in Palmer by P. W. Webster, Feb. 2, 1864; mustered Feb. 18, 1864. Promoted corporal, April 20, 1864. Wounded in action at the Wilderness, May 6, 1864. Absent wounded in an army general hospital until between March 25 and April 30, 1865. Issued one pair of trousers and one pair of shoes, April 30, 1865. Literate. Mustered out with the regiment at Delaney house, Washington, DC, July 30, 1865, and discharged in Readville, MA, Aug. 9, 1865, expiration of service. Had previous service as a private in Co. A, 24th MVI, from Sept. 9, 1861, until discharged for disability in New Bern, NC, Sept. 11, 1862. Participated in the North Carolina campaign with that regiment in 1862. Resided in the Soldiers Home in Togus, ME, after the war.

41. **Gokey, Benjamin Jr.,** private. Res. and/or credit: Palmer, MA. Born: Fairfax, VT. Age: 18. Height: 5'6". Comp: fair. Eyes: blue. Hair: light. Occup: farmer. Enlisted in Palmer by Capt. George H. Howe, Dec. 11, 1863; mustered Jan. 25, 1864. In action at the Wilderness, May 6, 1864, and Spotsylvania Court House, May 10 and 12, 1864; mortally wounded in action there, May 18, 1864. Died from wounds in the 1st Division, IX Corps, Field Hospital at Spotsylvania, May 19, 1864.

42. **Gosler, Oliver,** private. Res. and/or credit: Leicester, MA. Born: Canada. Age: 19. Height: 5'7". Comp: light. Eyes: black. Hair: black. Occup: laborer. Enlisted in Leicester by Silas Gleason, Feb. 13, 1864; mustered Feb. 18, 1864. In action at the Wilderness, May 6, 1864, and Spotsylvania Court House, May 10, 12, and 18, 1864. Deserted while in action at North Anna River, but captured by Confederates and taken prisoner of war. Incarcerated in the Confederate prison in Salisbury, NC, where he died from disease, Nov. 26, 1864.

43. **Gray, John,** private. Res: Hatfield, MA. Credit: Northampton, MA. Born: Canada. Age: 32. Height: 5'7". Comp: dark. Eyes: dark. Hair: dark. Occup: shoemaker. Enlisted in Northampton by William Dickinson, Jan. 16, 1864; mustered Jan. 25, 1864. Deserted

while on furlough from Camp Wool, Feb. 2, 1864. Never returned.

44. **Greeley, Jonas E.**, sergeant. Res. and credit: Royalston, MA. Born: Royalston, MA. Age: 22. Height: 5′6″. Comp: dark. Eyes: gray. Hair: black. Occup: mechanic. Enlisted in Royalston by William Clement, Dec. 30, 1863; mustered Jan. 25, 1864. Promoted sergeant, Jan. 25, 1864. Never in combat. Absent sick in an army general hospital from on or before May 6, 1864, until after March 25, 1865. Mustered out with the regiment at Delaney house, Washington, DC, July 30, 1865, and discharged in Readville, MA, Aug. 9, 1865, expiration of service. Had previous service as a private in Co. A, 21st MVI, from Aug. 12, 1861, until discharged for disability, Jan. 10, 1863. Possibly participated with that regiment in the North Carolina campaign in 1862 and at 2nd Bull Run, Aug. 30, 1862, Chantilly, Sept. 1, 1862, Antietam, Sept. 17, 1862, and Fredericksburg, Dec. 13, 1862. Resided in Worcester, MA, after the war and died there after 1911, date unknown.

45. **Halloran, James O.**, sergeant. Res. and/or credit: Northampton, MA. Born: Ireland. Age: 24. Height: 5′9½″. Comp: light. Eyes: gray. Hair: black. Occup: laborer. Enlisted in Northampton by H. K. Starkweather, Dec. 31, 1863; mustered Jan. 25, 1864. Promoted sergeant, Jan. 25, 1864. Deserted while on parade in the city of Worcester, MA, Feb. 22, 1864, but arrested, returned, confined in the guardhouse in Camp Wool, and reduced to the ranks, Feb. 24, 1864. In action at the Wilderness, May 6, 1864, and wounded later that month, but not in a major battle. Absent wounded in McDougall US Army General Hospital in Fort Schuyler, New York Harbor, NY, until discharged the US service for disability from wounds, Oct. 29, 1864, by order of Maj. Gen. John A. Dix, War Dept.

46. **Hammond, George M.**, private. Res: North Adams, MA. Credit: Adams, MA. Born: Schuylerville, NY. Age: 22. Height: 5′4½″. Comp: light. Eyes: gray. Hair: brown. Occup: blacksmith. Enlisted in Adams by S. Johnson, Feb. 13, 1864; mustered Feb. 18, 1864. Severely wounded in action at the Wilderness, May 6, 1864. Died from his wounds in an army general hospital in Washington, DC, June 27, 1864.

47. **Hastings, William O.**, private. Res: Ware, MA. Credit: Northampton, MA. Born: Barnard, VT. Age: 35. Height: 5′5½″. Comp: florid. Eyes: gray. Hair: light. Occup: painter. Enlisted in Northampton by Otis Lane, Dec. 4, 1863; mustered Jan. 25, 1864. In action at the Wilderness, May 6, 1864, and one of the 34 enlisted men who remained with the colors during that battle. In action at Spotsylvania Court House, May 10, 12, and 18, 1864, North Anna River, May 24, 1864, Cold Harbor, June 3, 1864, Petersburg assaults, June 17 and 18, 1864, and Petersburg Crater, July 30, 1864. Killed while on duty in the trenches at Petersburg, Aug. 5, 1864. With the regiment on all marches and in all skirmishes and battles until killed.

48. **Hathaway, Joshua**, corporal. Res. and/or credit: Huntington, MA. Born: Madison, NY. Age: 44. Height: 5′7″. Comp: light. Eyes: hazel. Hair: dark. Occup: blacksmith. Enlisted in Huntington by W. F. Orcutt, Jan. 11, 1864; mustered Jan. 25, 1864. Promoted corporal, Jan. 25, 1864. Killed in action at the Wilderness, May 6, 1864.

49. **Hazen, Ralph**, private. Res: Easthampton, MA. Credit: Northampton, MA. Born: Northboro, VT. Age: 40. Height: 5′9½″. Comp: dark. Eyes: gray. Hair: dark. Occup: carpenter. Enlisted in Northampton by Edwin S. James, Jan. 20, 1864; mustered Jan. 25, 1864. Deserted while on furlough from Camp Wool, March 1, 1864, but returned to the regiment before April 18, 1864. Never in a major battle, but wounded (possibly while on picket duty) on an unknown date. Absent wounded in Summit House US Army General Hospital in Philadelphia, PA, until discharged the US service for disability from wounds, June 12, 1865, under GO 77, par. 6, AGO, War Dept.

50. **Howe, George H.**, captain. Res. and credit: Monson, MA. Born: Monson, MA. Age: 23. Height: unknown. Comp: dark. Eyes: brown. Hair: dark brown. Occup: schoolteacher in Canada. Commissioned and mustered 2nd lieutenant, Nov. 2, 1863. Com-

Captain George Howe. *(USAMHI)*

missioned and mustered captain, Jan. 25, 1864. Detached and detailed on the 1st Brigade, 1st Division, IX Corps staff as acting inspector general on or about April 30, 1864. Never on permanent duty with the regiment again. Record of other combat service unknown until shot through the heart and killed in action at the Petersburg Crater, July 30, 1864. Remains recovered, embalmed in or around Depot Field Hospital at City Point, Petersburg, and sent home to Monson, MA, for burial. Had previous service as elected 1st lieutenant of Co. G, 46th MVI, from Sept. 9, 1862, until mustered out, July 29, 1863. Participated in the North Carolina campaign with that regiment in 1862–63. "He believed that duty came before everything else, and while he was always rigid in the strict compliance of orders, he was just as rigid in exacting it of others who were under him" (JA).

51. **Hughes, Thomas,** private. Res: Monson, MA. Credit: Palmer, MA. Born: Canada. Age: 35. Height: unknown. Comp: light. Eyes: blue. Hair: brown. Occup: farmer. Enlisted in Palmer by Capt. George H. Howe, Jan. 15, 1864; mustered Jan. 25, 1864. Slightly wounded in action at the Wilderness,

May 6, 1864. Absent wounded in an army general hospital until an unknown date in July 1864. In action and taken prisoner of war at the Petersburg Crater, July 30, 1864. Incarcerated in the Confederate prison in Danville, VA, until paroled and exchanged, Feb. 22, 1865. Probably received extra pay for having been a prisoner of war. Returned to the regiment for duty from the Camp of Parole in Annapolis, MD, between March 25 and April 30, 1865. Issued one forage cap, one pair of trousers, one pair of shoes, one pair of socks, and one knit shirt, April 30, 1865. Illiterate. Detached and detailed as a provost guard in Georgetown, DC, in May or June, 1865. Mustered out with the regiment at Delaney house, Washington, DC, July 30, 1865, and discharged in Readville, MA, Aug. 9, 1865, expiration of service. Drowned in Three Rivers, MA, before 1896, but date not known.

52. **Jackson, James,** private. Res. and credit: Palmer, MA. Born: Palmer, MA. Age: 18. Height: 5'6". Comp: fair. Eyes: dark. Hair: light. Occup: farmer. Enlisted in Palmer by Capt. George H. Howe, Dec. 8, 1863; mustered Jan. 25, 1864. Detached and detailed as a guard attached to 1st Division, IX Corps, Headquarters from on or about May 1, 1864, until after March 25, 1865. Never in combat. Mustered out with the regiment at Delaney house, Washington, DC, July 30, 1865, and discharged in Readville, MA, Aug. 9, 1865, expiration of service.

53. **Jones, Eben,** private. Res. and/or credit: Palmer, MA. Born: Utica, NY. Age: 44. Height: 5'7". Comp: dark. Eyes: hazel. Hair: light. Occup: farmer. Enlisted in Palmer by Capt. George H. Howe, Jan. 4, 1864; mustered Jan. 25, 1864. Did not leave Camp Wool with the regiment, but sent to Camp Meigs in Readville, MA, April 18, 1864, under the supervision of Lt. John Cook for a medical examination. Found unfit for duty by a "board of inspectors." Rejected recruit and discharged the US service in Worcester, MA, June 29, 1864, by order of Maj. Gen. John A. Dix, War Dept.

54. **Karpeles, Leopold,** color sergeant. Res. and/or credit: Springfield, MA. Born: Hungary, and the only known Jewish member of

the regiment. Age: 23. Height: 5'5". Comp: dark. Eyes: black. Hair: black. Occup: clerk. Enlisted in Co. I in Springfield by Lt. Henry B. Fisk, March 7, 1864; mustered March 10, 1864; transferred to Co. E, March 10, 1864, under RSO 38, by order of Col. William F. Bartlett. Promoted sergeant, April 14, 1864. In action at the Wilderness, May 6, 1864, and one of the 34 enlisted men who remained with the colors during that battle. Received the Medal of Honor, April 30, 1870, for his actions at the Wilderness: "While color bearer, rallied the retreating troops and induced them to check the enemy's advance" (OR). In action at Spotsylvania Court House, May 10, 12, and 18, 1864, and severely wounded in action at North Anna River, May 24, 1864. Absent wounded in an army general hospital until Oct. 10, 1864. Absent sick from wounds received at North Anna River in Mt. Pleasant US Army General Hospital in Washington, DC, from Dec. 13, 1864, until discharged the US service for disability from wounds, May 7, 1865, under GO 77, par. 6, AGO, War Dept. Had previous service as color corporal in Co. A, 46th MVI, from Aug. 15, 1862, until mustered out, July 29, 1863. Participated in the North Carolina campaign with that regiment in 1862–63. "Received testimonials from Colonel, Lieut.-Colonel and Major of 46th Mass. for soldierly bearing

Color Sergeant Leopold Karpeles (postwar photo). *(John Anderson)*

and conspicuous bravery while in that regt." (JA). Resided in Washington, DC, after the war.

55. **Kenfield, Henry M.,** private. Res. and credit: Belchertown, MA. Born: Belchertown, MA. Age: 30. Height: 5'5". Comp: dark. Eyes: dark. Hair: dark. Occup: farmer. Enlisted in Belchertown by Capt. George H. Howe, Dec. 2, 1863; mustered Jan. 25, 1864. Never in major combat. Wounded on an unknown date in May 1864, but not in a major battle. Absent wounded in an army general hospital until transferred to the 14th Co., 2nd Battln., VRC, June 17, 1865, by order of the provost marshal general. Discharged the US service, Nov. 23, 1865, by order of the War Dept., expiration of service. Had previous service as a private in Co. H, 46th MVI, from Aug. 22, 1862, until mustered out, July 29, 1863. Participated in the North Carolina campaign with that regiment in 1862–63. Also had previous service as a private in Co. F, 31st MVI, from Oct. 30, 1861, until discharged for disability in New Orleans, LA, July 7, 1862. On duty in New Orleans with that regiment in 1862.

56. **Kerrigan, Martin,** private. Res. and/or credit: Ware, MA. Born: Ireland. Age: 24. Height: 5'8". Comp: florid. Eyes: blue. Hair: black. Occup: farmer. Enlisted in Ware by Otis Lane, Jan. 25, 1864; mustered Feb. 18, 1864. Wounded in action at the Wilderness, May 6, 1864. Absent wounded in an army general hospital until transferred to Co. G, 14th Regiment, VRC, Oct. 7, 1864, by order of the provost marshal general. Discharged the US service, July 25, 1865, by order of the War Dept., expiration of service. Died before 1896, but date not known.

57. **La Baslieus, Joseph,** corporal. Res: Rouses Point, NY. Credit: Easthampton, MA. Born: province of Quebec, Canada. Age: 26. Height: 5'9". Comp: dark. Eyes: dark. Hair: dark. Occup: farmer. Enlisted in Easthampton by Edwin S. James, Jan. 1, 1864; mustered Jan. 25, 1864. Promoted corporal, March 1, 1864. Deserted while on furlough from Camp Wool, March 29, 1864. Never returned. "Rouses Point [NY] Canadian looking for bounty" (JA).

58. **Lapoint, Joseph,** private. Res: Easthampton, MA. Credit: Northampton, MA. Born: Sheldon Creek, VT. Age: 22. Height: 5'7". Comp: dark. Eyes: blue. Hair: dark. Occup: farmer. Enlisted in Northampton by Edwin S. James, Jan. 20, 1864; mustered Jan. 25, 1864. Never in combat. Absent sick or on detached duty from on or before May 6, 1864, until between March 25 and April 30, 1865. Issued one sack coat, one pair of trousers, one pair of drawers, one pair of shoes, four pairs of socks, and one knit shirt, April 30, 1865. Literate. Mustered out with the regiment at Delaney house, Washington, DC, July 30, 1865, and discharged in Readville, MA, Aug. 9, 1865, expiration of service.

59. **Laraby, Peter,** private. Res: Wendell, MA. Credit: Holyoke, MA. Born: Rutland, VT. Age: 19. Height: 5'5½". Comp: dark. Eyes: dark. Hair: dark. Occup: mechanic. Enlisted in Holyoke by Davis Goddard, Jan. 20, 1864; mustered Jan. 25, 1864. In action at the Wilderness, May 6, 1864, and Spotsylvania Court House, May 10, 1864. Absent sick in the rear from May 12, 1864, until transferred to Mower US Army General Hospital in Philadelphia, PA, on an unknown date. Deserted from that hospital, Jan. 6, 1865. Never returned.

60. **Loker, Loring,** private. Res: Princeton, MA. Credit: Worcester, MA. Born: Wayland, MA. Age: 45. Height: 5'8". Comp: dark. Eyes: blue. Hair: dark. Occup: farmer. Enlisted in Worcester by Capt. Julius M. Tucker, Jan. 5, 1864; mustered Jan. 25, 1864. Absent sick in an army general hospital from on or before May 6, 1864, until Jan. 2, 1865. Appointed company cook, Jan. 2, 1865. In action at Fort Stedman, March 25, 1865. Mustered out with the regiment at Delaney house, Washington, DC, July 30, 1865, and discharged in Readville, MA, Aug. 9, 1865, expiration of service.

61. **Longdo, Joseph Jr.,** corporal. Res: Wendell, MA. Credit: Orange, MA. Born: Burlington, VT. Age: 19. Height: 5'3". Comp: dark. Eyes: dark. Hair: dark. Occup: painter. Enlisted in Orange by J. K. Reynolds, Jan. 16, 1864; mustered Jan. 25, 1864. In action at the Wilderness, May 6, 1864, and appointed corporal that day (undoubtedly for bravery in action during that battle). In action at Spotsylvania Court House, May 10, 12, and 18, 1864, and mortally wounded in action at North Anna River, May 24, 1864. Died in an army general hospital in Washington, DC, May 31, 1864.

62. **McCarty, Michael,** private. Res. and/or credit: New Braintree, MA. Born: Ireland. Age: 35. Height: 5'6". Comp: light. Eyes: blue. Hair: brown. Occup: laborer. Enlisted in New Braintree by M. (?) Pollock, Jan. 1, 1864; mustered Jan. 25, 1864. In action at the Wilderness, May 6, 1864, and Spotsylvania Court House, May 10, 12, and 18, 1864; killed in action at North Anna River, May 24, 1864.

63. **McClellan, Alexander,** private. Res. and/or credit: Palmer, MA. Born: Ireland. Age: 30. Height: 5' 7". Comp: dark. Eyes: blue. Hair: brown. Occup: laborer. Enlisted in Palmer by Capt. George H. Howe, Jan. 9, 1864; mustered Jan. 25, 1864. Deserted from Camp Wool, April 5, 1864. Arrested in Tolland, CT, Dec. 29, 1864, by Special Agent Ezra Chapman, and held in the General Rendezvous Conscript Camp in New Haven, CT. Returned to the regiment at Petersburg, Jan. 19, 1865, under arrest and held in confinement with the regiment pending a court-martial. Court-martialed March 8, 1865 (Lt. Col. C. K. Pier, 38th Wisconsin Volunteer Infantry, president of the court), and sentenced to be shot for desertion under GO 39, but sentence commuted to loss of all pay, three years in prison at hard labor, and a dishonorable discharge. Returned to the regiment until sentence could be carried out. With the regiment at Fort Stedman, March 25, 1865, but not in action. Issued one forage cap, one sack coat, one pair of trousers, two pairs of drawers, one pair of shoes, two pairs of socks, and one knit shirt, April 30, 1865. Quite literate and had beautiful penmanship. Incarcerated by the provost marshal general after April 30, 1865, and dishonorably discharged the US service, Sept. 15, 1865, by order of the War Dept.

64. **McCoy, Alexander,** corporal. Res. and/or credit: Springfield, MA. Born: Ireland. Age:

32. Height: 5'8". Comp: light. Eyes: gray. Hair: auburn. Occup: carpenter. Enlisted in Springfield by Capt. Lewis A. Tifft, Jan. 5, 1864; mustered Jan. 25, 1864. Wounded in action at the Wilderness, May 6, 1864; promoted corporal that day (undoubtedly for bravery in the battle). Absent wounded in an army general hospital until Dec. 14, 1864. With the regiment in operations during the winter of 1864–65, and taken prisoner of war in action at Fort Stedman, March 25, 1865. Paroled and exchanged from Libby Prison in Richmond, VA, March 29, 1865. Returned to the regiment for duty from the Camp of Parole in Annapolis, MD, on or about May 11, 1865. Mustered out with the regiment at Delaney house, Washington, DC, July 30, 1865, and discharged in Readville, MA, Aug. 9, 1865, expiration of service.

65. **McCoy, Robert,** private. Res. and/or credit: Springfield, MA. Born: Ireland. Age: 25. Height: 5'9". Comp: light. Eyes: blue. Hair: light. Occup: farmer. Enlisted in Springfield by Capt. Lewis A. Tifft, Jan. 12, 1864; mustered Jan. 25, 1864. Killed in action at the Wilderness, May 6, 1864. Had previous service as a private in Co. D, 16th Connecticut Volunteer Infantry (specifics unknown).

66. **McNamara, John,** private. Res. and/or credit: Northampton, MA. Born: Ireland. Age: 42. Height: 5'7½". Comp: light. Eyes: blue. Hair: brown. Occup: tanner. Enlisted in Northampton by W. F. Orcutt, Jan. 13, 1864; mustered Jan. 25, 1864. Never in combat. Absent sick in an army general hospital from on or before May 6, 1864, until transferred to Co. E, 14th Regiment, VRC, Sept. 10, 1864, by order of the provost marshal general. Discharged the US service, July 31, 1865, by order of the War Dept., expiration of service.

67. **McNamee, Patrick,** private. Res. and/or credit: Easthampton, MA. Born: Ireland. Age: 32. Height: 5'5". Comp: sandy. Eyes: black. Hair: brown. Occup: farmer. Enlisted in Easthampton by Edwin S. James, Jan. 16, 1864; mustered Jan. 25, 1864. Wounded in action at the Wilderness, May 6, 1864. Absent wounded in McClellan US Army General Hospital in Philadelphia, PA, until trans-

ferred to Co. K, 11th Regiment, VRC, Jan. 21, 1865, by order of the provost marshal general. Discharged the US service, Aug. 8, 1865, by order of the War Dept., expiration of service. Resided in Easthampton, MA, after the war.

68. **Mahoney, James,** corporal. Res: Boston, MA. Credit: Winchendon, MA. Born: Ireland. Age: 33. Height: 5'9". Comp: sandy. Eyes: blue. Hair: brown. Occup: soldier. Enlisted in Winchendon by B. Ellis, Feb. 12, 1864; mustered Feb. 18, 1864. Promoted corporal, April 1, 1864. Deserted from Camp Wool, April 16, 1864. Never returned. Probably a bounty jumper.

69. **Manley, William H.,** private. Res. and/or credit: Springfield, MA. Born: Harrison County, KY. Age: 24. Height: 5'7". Comp: light. Eyes: gray. Hair: brown. Occup: armorer. Enlisted in Springfield by Capt. Charles D. Hollis, Jan. 4, 1864; mustered Jan. 25, 1864. Did not leave Camp wool with the regiment, but sent to camp Meigs in Readville, MA, April 18, 1864, under the supervision of Lt. John Cook for a medical examination. Found unfit for duty by a "board of inspectors." Rejected recruit and discharged the US service in Worcester, MA, June 29, 1864, by order of Maj. Gen. John A. Dix, War Dept. Had previous service as a private in Co. F, 13th Connecticut Volunteer Infantry (specifics unknown).

70. **Meehan, Thomas,** private. Res. and/or credit: Princeton, MA. Born: Ireland. Age: 33. Height: 5'5". Comp: sandy. Eyes: blue. Hair: brown. Occup: laborer. Enlisted in Princeton by Davis Goddard, Feb. 3, 1864; mustered Feb. 18, 1864. In action at the Wilderness, May 6, 1864, Spotsylvania Court House, May 10, 12, and 18, 1864, North Anna River, May 24, 1864, Cold Harbor, June 3, 1864, Petersburg assaults, June 17 and 18, 1864, Petersburg Crater, July 30, 1864, Weldon Railroad, Aug. 19, 1864, and Poplar Grove Church, Sept. 30 and Oct. 8, 1864. With the regiment on all marches and in all skirmishes and battles until Oct. 25, 1864, and one of the 30 combat soldiers remaining of the regiment after Weldon Railroad, Aug.

19, 1864. Absent sick in the 1st Division, IX Corps, Field Hospital at Petersburg, from Oct. 25 until Oct. 29, 1864. Absent sick in Mower US Army General Hospital in Philadelphia, PA, from Nov. 29, 1864, until discharged the US service for disability, June 28, 1865, under GO 77, par. 6, AGO, War Dept.

71. **Murdock, Charles F.**, 1st sergeant. Res. and/or credit: Palmer, MA. Born: Monson, MA. Age: 30. Height: 5'4½". Comp: fair. Eyes: blue. Hair: dark. Occup: merchant. Enlisted in Palmer by an unknown recruiter, but probably Capt. George H. Howe, Nov. 28, 1863; mustered Jan. 25, 1864. Promoted 1st sergeant, Jan. 25, 1864. Reduced to the ranks, March 12, 1864 (reason unknown, but likely incompetency or unsoldierly behavior). Absent sick or on detached duty from on or before May 6, 1864, until between Oct. 8, 1864, and March 25, 1865. In action at Fort Stedman, March 25, 1865. Detached and detailed at 3rd Brigade, 1st Division, IX Corps, Headquarters as a "safe guard" (OR), from after April 30, 1865, until muster-out. Mustered out with the regiment at Delaney house, Washington, DC, July 30, 1865, and discharged in Readville, MA, Aug. 9, 1865, expiration of service. Had previous service as a corporal in Co. H, 21st MVI, from Aug. 5, 1861, until discharged for disability from wounds, Feb. 11, 1863. Participated with that regiment in the North Carolina campaign in 1862, and 2nd Bull Run, Aug. 30, 1862; wounded in action at Chantilly, Sept. 1, 1862. Resided in Three Rivers, MA, after the war.

72. **Norcross, Otis C.**, private. Res: Upton, MA. Credit: Worcester, MA. Born: Upton, MA. Age: 27. Height: 5'5½". Comp: light. Eyes: blue. Hair: brown. Occup: nurse. Enlisted in Worcester by S. J. Wood, Jan. 21, 1864; mustered Jan. 25, 1864. Detached and detailed as a nurse on the regimental medical staff from on or before May 6, 1864, until absent sick in an army general hospital from an unknown date until reported from the company journal as returned from the hospital, Dec. 14, 1864. Issued one .58 cal. Springfield rifle and bayonet from Maj. Doherty, Dec. 20, 1864. Issued one cartridge box and strap, and one waist belt with cap pouch and bayonet

scabbard from Maj. Doherty, Dec. 22, 1864. Arrested and confined, Jan. 7 and 8, 1865, for an unknown reason (probably disobedience of orders). Arrested and confined again, Jan. 19 and 20, 1865, for an unknown reason (probably the same offense). With the regiment in operations during the winter of 1865, and taken prisoner of war in action at Fort Stedman, March 25, 1865. Paroled and exchanged from Libby Prison in Richmond, VA, March 29, 1865. Returned to the regiment for duty from the Camp of Parole in Annapolis, MD, on or about May 11, 1865. Mustered out with the regiment at Delaney house, Washington, DC, and discharged in Readville, MA, Aug. 9, 1865, expiration of service.

73. **O'Conner, Michael**, private. Res. and/or credit: Northampton, MA. Born: Ireland. Age: 44. Height: 5'7½". Comp: light. Eyes: blue. Hair: auburn. Occup: laborer. Enlisted in Northampton by H. K. Starkweather, Jan. 4, 1864; mustered Feb. 18, 1864. Killed in action at the Wilderness, May 6, 1864.

74. **O'Keif, Thomas**, private. Res. and/or credit: Northampton, MA. Born: Ireland. Age: 28. Height: 6'3". Comp: florid. Eyes: hazel. Hair: sandy. Occup: laborer. Enlisted in Northampton by H. K. Starkweather, Jan. 4, 1864. Mustered Feb. 18, 1864. Never in major combat. Wounded on an unknown date in May 1864, but not in a major battle. Absent wounded in an army general hospital until between March 25 and April 30, 1865. Issued one sack coat, one pair of trousers, and two pairs of drawers, April 30, 1865. Mustered out with the regiment at Delaney house, Washington, DC, July 30, 1865, and discharged in Readville, MA, Aug. 9, 1865, expiration of service.

75. **Paine, Horace H.**, 1st sergeant. Res: Belchertown, MA. Credit: Palmer, MA. Born: Belchertown, MA. Age: 30. Height: 5'9½". Comp: fair. Eyes: blue. Hair: brown. Occup: farmer. Enlisted in Palmer by Capt. George H. Howe, Dec. 9, 1864; mustered Jan. 25, 1864. Promoted sergeant, Jan. 25, 1864. Wounded in action at the Wilderness, May 6, 1864. Absent wounded in an army general hospital until Oct. 10, 1864. Acting 1st ser-

geant from Oct. 23, 1864, until Jan. 11, 1865. With the regiment in operations during the fall and winter of 1864–65. Promoted 1st sergeant to replace 1st Sgt. Marshall (see Co. F), Jan. 11, 1865, to date from Jan. 3, 1865, under RSO 6, dated Jan. 10, 1865, by order of Lt. Col. Julius M. Tucker. Recommended for a commission on or about March 20, 1865, but never appointed. Wounded twice in action at Fort Stedman, March 25, 1865. Absent wounded in an army general hospital until discharged the US service for disability from wounds, Aug. 7, 1865, by order of the War Dept. Resided in Palmer, MA, after the war.

76. **Parker, Charles H.**, private. Res: New Braintree, MA. Credit: Worcester, MA. Born: West Brookfield, MA. Age: 24. Height: 5′5″. Comp: fair. Eyes: blue. Hair: brown. Occup: bootmaker. Enlisted in Worcester by Lt. John Anderson, Jan. 19, 1864; mustered Jan. 25, 1864. Deserted while on furlough from Camp Wool, March 1, 1864, but was arrested, returned, and confined in the guardhouse in Camp Wool, from March 16 until no later than April 5, 1864. In action at the Wilderness, May 6, 1864, Spotsylvania Court House, May 10, 12, and 18, 1864, North Anna River, May 24, 1864, Cold Harbor, June 3, 1864, and Petersburg assaults, June 17 and 18, 1864. With the regiment on all marches and in all skirmishes and battles until about mid-July 1864. Absent sick in Camp Meigs US Army General Hospital in Readville, MA, from July 16, 1864, until discharged the US service for disability, May 18, 1865, by order of the War Dept. Had previous service as a private in Co. H, 25th MVI, from from Sept. 24, 1861, until discharged for disability in Annapolis, MD, Dec. 27, 1861. Saw no action with that regiment. Died in 1881, age 41.

77. **Pasco, Cephas B.**, private. Res. and/or credit: Palmer, MA. Born: Granby, MA. Age: 27. Height: 5′3″. Comp: light. Eyes: black. Hair: dark. Occup: porter. Enlisted in Palmer by Capt. George H. Howe, Dec. 2, 1863; mustered Jan. 25, 1864. Wounded in action at the Wilderness, May 6, 1864. Absent wounded in an army general hospital until Nov. 11, 1864. Reported to the regiment for duty, Dec. 2, 1864. Absent sick in the 1st Division, IX Corps, Field Hospital at Petersburg from Dec. 13, 1865, until between Jan. 30 and March 25, 1865. In action at Fort Stedman, March 25, 1865. Issued one sack coat, April 30, 1865. Illiterate. Mustered out with the regiment at Delaney house, Washington, DC, July 30, 1865, and discharged in Readville, MA, Aug. 9, 1865, expiration of service. Died in 1876, age 40.

78. **Pasco, George W.**, corporal. Res. and credit: Palmer, MA. Born: Palmer, MA. Age: 19. Height: 5′7½″. Comp: light. Eyes: dark. Hair: brown. Occup: spinner. Enlisted in Palmer by Capt. George H. Howe, Nov. 28, 1863; mustered Jan. 25, 1864. Promoted corporal, Jan. 25, 1864. Deserted from Camp Wool, March 21, 1864, but was arrested, returned, reduced to the ranks, and confined in the guardhouse in Camp Wool, March 26, 1864. Absent sick or on detached duty from on or before May 6, 1864 until between Aug. 19 and Sept. 30, 1864. In action at Poplar Grove Church, Sept. 30 and Oct. 8, 1864. Absent sick in an army general hospital from Oct. 21, 1864, until furloughed to his home in Palmer, MA, for convalescence, where he died from disease, Jan. 23, 1865. Had previous service as a private in Co. D, 15th MVI, from Dec. 9, 1861, until discharged for disability at Fort Wood, VA, Dec. 17, 1862. Participated with that regiment at Ball's Bluff, Oct. 21, 1861, in the Peninsula campaign in 1862, and possibly at Antietam, Sept. 17, 1862.

79. **Pike, Charles F.**, corporal. Res. and/or credit: Worcester, MA. Born: Rutland, MA. Age: 23. Height: 5′5″. Comp: light. Eyes: blue. Hair: light. Occup: machinist. Enlisted in Worcester by Lt. John Reade, Feb. 10, 1864; mustered Feb. 18, 1864. In action at the Wilderness, May 6, 1864, and one of the 34 enlisted men who remained with the colors during that battle. In action at Spotsylvania Court House, May 10 and 12, 1864. Promoted corporal, May 12, 1864 (undoubtedly for bravery during that battle). Wounded in action at Spotsylvania, May 18, 1864. Absent wounded in an army general hospital until transferred to the 4th Co., 2nd Battln., VRC, on an unknown date. Discharged the US ser-

vice, Sept. 6, 1865, by order of the War Dept., expiration of service. Had previous service as a private in Co. B, 30th MVI, from Oct. 15, 1861, until discharged for disability from Ship Island, MS, April 11, 1862. On duty in the Gulf of Mexico with that regiment in 1862.

80. **Ring, Benjamin,** private. Res. and/or credit: Worcester, MA. Born: Massachusetts. Age: 45. No description available. Occup: mechanic. Enlisted in Worcester by Lt. George E. Barton, Jan. 4, 1864; mustered Jan. 25, 1864. Did not leave Camp Wool with the regiment, but sent to Camp Meigs in Readville, MA, April 18, 1864, under the supervision of Lt. John Cook for a medical examination. Found unfit for duty by a "board of inspectors." Rejected recruit and discharged the US service in Worcester, MA, June 29, 1864, by order of Maj. Gen. John A. Dix, War Dept. Rejected recruit from the 34th MVI also.

81. **Russell, Loren,** private. Res. and/or credit: Springfield, MA. Born: Springfield, MA. Age: 24. Height: 5'6". Comp: dark. Eyes: gray. Hair: light. Occup: farmer. Enlisted in Springfield by Capt. Charles D. Hollis, Jan. 22, 1864; mustered Jan. 25, 1864. Did not leave Camp Wool with the regiment, but sent to Camp Meigs in Readville, MA, April 18, 1864, under the supervision of Lt. John Cook for a medical examination. Found unfit for duty by a "board of inspectors." Rejected recruit and discharged the US service in Worcester, MA, June 29, 1864, by order of Maj. Gen. John A. Dix, War Dept. Had previous service as an unassigned recruit in the 1st Massachusetts Volunteer Cavalry from Sept. 30, 1862, until discharged for disability, Dec. 15, 1862. Saw no action with that regiment.

82. **Ryan, James B.,** private. Res: West Springfield, MA. Credit: Springfield, MA. Born: Ireland. Age: 21. No description available. Occup: mechanic. Enlisted in Springfield by Aaron Bogg, Jan. 2, 1864; mustered Jan. 25, 1864. Did not leave Camp Wool with the regiment, but sent to Camp Meigs in Readville, MA, April 18, 1864, under the supervi-

sion of Lt. John Cook for a medical examination. Found unfit for duty by a "board of inspectors." Rejected recruit and discharged the US service in Worcester, MA, June 29, 1864, by order of Maj. Gen. John A. Dix, War Dept.

83. **St. Dennis, Alfred,** private. Res: Hogansburg, NY. Credit: Greenfield, MA. Born: Hogansburg, NY. Age: 20. Single. Height: 5'4". Comp: light. Eyes: gray. Hair: brown. Occup: farmer. Enlisted in Greenfield by E. B. Williams, Jan. 15, 1864; mustered Jan. 25, 1864. Absent sick in an army general hospital from May 6, 1864, until discharged the US service for disability in late June 1864. (Note: Incorrectly reported in *MSSM* as deserted on May 6, 1864.) Did not receive his state bounty, and in a letter written to Adjutant General William Schouler of Massachusetts on his behalf to obtain his money, the postmaster of Hogansburg, NY, Mr. A. Trelton, asks, "Will you please inform me if you have any knowledge of the matter, as the young man is poor and his health very bad, and his father is in indigent circumstances and he can illy afford to support him in his present [state]?" (MRD) Consequently, his $325 state bounty was quickly paid to him, on July 11, 1864. Resided in Hogansburg, NY, after the war.

84. **St. Onge, Charles,** private. Res: Springfield, MA. Credit: Greenfield, MA. Born: province of Quebec, Canada. Age: 22. Height: 5'5½". Comp: light. Eyes: blue. Hair: light. Occup: farmer. Enlisted in Greenfield by J. Cufts, Jan. 8, 1864; mustered Jan. 25, 1864. Deserted while the regiment was on the march to Rappahannock Station, VA, April 25, 1864. "Canadian bounty jumper" (JA).

85. **Shea, James,** private. Res: Greenfield, MA. Credit: Northampton, MA. Born: Ireland. Age: 21. No description available. Occup: armorer. Enlisted in Northampton by H. H. Belden, Jan. 4, 1864; mustered Jan. 25, 1864. Absent sick or on detached duty from on or before May 6, 1864, until between Aug. 19 and Sept. 30, 1864. In action at Poplar Grove Church, Sept. 30 and Oct. 8, 1864. Absent sick in Harewood US Army General

Hospital in Washington, DC, from Oct. 25, 1864, until discharged the US service for disability, June 14, 1865, by order of the War Dept.

86. **Short, John,** private. Res. and/or credit: Orange, MA. Born: Canada. Age: 24. Height: 5'3¾". Comp: dark. Eyes: black. Hair: black. Occup: painter. Enlisted in Orange by Davis Goddard, Jan. 18, 1864; mustered Jan. 25, 1864. In action at the Wilderness, May 6, 1864, Spotsylvania Court House, May 10, 12, and 18, 1864, North Anna River, May 24, 1864, Cold Harbor, June 3, 1864, and Petersburg assaults, June 17 and 18, 1864; mortally wounded while on duty in the trenches at Petersburg, July 25, 1864. Died from wounds in an army general hospital in Arlington, VA, July 28, 1864. With the regiment on all marches and in all skirmishes and battles until wounded.

87. **Smith, Samuel S.,** private. Res: Whately, MA. Credit: Greenfield, MA. Born: Massachusetts. Age: 40. No description available. Occup: carpenter. Enlisted in Greenfield by S. White, Jan. 12, 1864; mustered Jan. 25, 1864. Wounded in action at the Wilderness, May 6, 1864. Absent wounded in an army general hospital until after April 30, 1865. Mustered out with the regiment at Delaney house, Washington, DC, July 30, 1865, and discharged in Readville, MA, Aug. 9, 1865, expiration of service. Had previous service as a private in Co. D, 52nd MVI, from Oct. 20, 1862, until mustered out, Aug. 14, 1863. Participated in the Port Hudson, LA, campaign with that regiment in 1863, and wounded in action at Port Hudson, June 16, 1863.

88. **Sullivan, Cornelius,** private. Res: Rouses Point, NY. Credit: Worcester, MA. Born: Ireland. Age: 33. Height: 5'4¾". Comp: light. Eyes: blue. Hair: light. Enlisted in Worcester by Capt. Julius M. Tucker, Jan. 2, 1864; mustered Jan. 25, 1864. Deserted from Camp Wool, April 17, 1864. Never returned. "Rouses Point [NY] bounty jumper" (JA).

89. **Sullivan, James,** musician. Res. and/or credit: Worcester, MA. Born: Ireland. Age: 18. Height: unknown. Comp: light. Eyes:

Musician James Sullivan.
(John Anderson)

blue. Hair: brown. Occup: bootmaker. Enlisted in Worcester by Lt. E. Dexter Cheney, Dec. 15, 1863; mustered Jan. 25, 1864. Company drummer or fifer. Probably also served as a nurse, stretcher bearer, and/or hospital orderly. Taken prisoner of war in action at Fort Stedman, March 25, 1865. Paroled and exchanged from Libby Prison in Richmond, VA, March 29, 1865. Returned to the regiment for duty from the Camp of Parole in Annapolis, MD, on or about May 11, 1865. Mustered out with the regiment at Delaney house, Washington, DC, July 30, 1865, and discharged in Readville, MA, Aug. 9, 1865, expiration of service. Resided in Worcester, MA, after the war.

90. **Thompson, Asa,** private. Res. and credit: Palmer, MA. Born: Palmer, MA. Age: 34. Height: 5'8". Comp: dark. Eyes: blue. Hair: light. Occup: blacksmith. Enlisted in Palmer by Capt. George H. Howe, Nov. 21, 1863; mustered Jan. 25, 1864. In action at the Wilderness, May 6, 1864, and Spotsylvania Court House, May 10 and 12, 1864; wounded in action there, May 18, 1864. Absent wounded in Mt. Pleasant US Army General Hospital in Washington, DC, until discharged the US

service for disability from wounds, May 18, 1865, under GO 77, par. 6, AGO, War Dept. Died before 1896, but date not known.

91. **Timothy, Thomas**, private. Res. and/or credit: Northampton, MA. Born: Ireland. Age: 44. Height: 5'6". Comp: dark. Eyes: blue. Hair: dark. Occup: laborer. Enlisted in Northampton by H. K. Starkweather, Jan. 2, 1864; mustered Jan. 25, 1864. In action at the Wilderness, May 6, 1864, and wounded later that month, but not in a major battle. Absent wounded in an army general hospital until discharged the US service for disability from wounds, March 1, 1865, by order of the War Dept. Resided in Northampton, MA, after the war.

92. **Tolman, David H.**, private. Res: Winchendon, MA. Credit: Ware, MA. Born: Winchendon, MA, Nov. 17, 1834. Age: 29. Height: 5'8¼". Comp: dark. Eyes: gray. Hair: black. Occup: farmer. Enlisted in Ware by Otis Lane, Dec. 2, 1863; mustered Jan. 25, 1864. Wounded in the left thigh in action at the Wilderness, May 6, 1864, after firing just two shots. Carried off the field to the 1st Division, IX Corps, Field Hospital, and moved to the basement of the Methodist Church in Fredericksburg, VA, the following day. Sent to Willet's Point Field Hospital in Washington, DC, May 9, 1864, treated and furloughed home for 30 days. However, he remained at home ill until returning to Willet's Point hospital in Aug. 1864. Sent to Camp Meigs US Army General Hospital in Readville, MA, in Nov. 1864 for several days and transferred to Dale US Army General Hospital in Worcester, MA, until discharged the US service for disability from wounds, June 13, 1865, by order of Maj. Gen. John A. Dix, War Dept. Resided in Winchendon, MA, after the war, and died there, March 14, 1896, age 61.

93. **Turner, Charles M.**, private. Res. and/or credit: Springfield, MA. Born: Jonesdale, MA. Age: 19. Height: 5'11". Comp: dark. Eyes: gray. Hair: dark. Occup: machinist. Enlisted in Springfield by Capt. Charles D. Hollis, Jan. 1, 1864; mustered Jan. 25, 1864. Did not leave Camp Wool with the regiment, but sent to Camp Meigs in Readville, MA, April 18, 1864, under the supervision of Lt. John Cook for a medical examination. Found unfit for duty by a "board of inspectors." Rejected recruit and discharged the US service in Worcester, MA, June 29, 1864, by order of Maj. Gen. John A. Dix, War Dept. Had previous service as a private in Co. H, 8th MVI, from Sept. 21, 1862, until mustered out, Aug. 7, 1863. Participated in the North Carolina campaign with that regiment in 1862–63.

94. **Turner, Richard S.**, private. Res. and/or credit: Springfield, MA. Born: Utica, NY. Age: 40. Height: unknown. Comp: fair. Eyes: blue. Hair: dark. Occup: machinist. Enlisted in Springfield by Capt. Charles D. Hollis, Jan. 2, 1864; mustered Jan. 25, 1864. Discharged the US service from Camp Wool for disability, Feb. 12, 1864, by order of the War Dept. Did not receive his state bounty of $325 until after his mother had a private "Bounty and Pension Agency" in Utica, NY, write to Adjutant General William Schouler about it on June 18, 1864. He was paid later that month. Resided in Utica, NY, after the war.

95. **Welsh, Thomas W.**, corporal. Res: Leominster, MA. Credit: Worcester, MA. Born: Ireland. Age: 18. Height: 5'8". Comp: fair. Eyes: blue. Hair: light. Occup: currier. Enlisted in Worcester by Lt. John Anderson, Jan. 18, 1864; mustered Jan. 25, 1864. In action at the Wilderness, May 6, 1864, Spotsylvania Court House, May 10, 12, and 18, 1864, North Anna River, May 24, 1864, Cold Harbor, June 3, 1864, and Petersburg assaults, June 17 and 18, 1864. Promoted corporal, June 20, 1864. In action and taken prisoner of war at the Petersburg Crater, July 30, 1864. With the regiment on all marches and in all skirmishes and battles until captured. Incarcerated in the Confederate prison in Danville, VA, and died from pneumonia in the general hospital there, Oct. 24, 1864. (Ironically, he was reduced to the ranks after being captured.)

96. **Wetherbee, Warren S.**, private. Res: Longmeadow, MA. Credit: Springfield, MA. Born: Cummington, MA. Age: 30. Height:

unknown. Comp: light. Eyes: blue. Hair: light. Occup: carpenter. Enlisted in Springfield by Capt. Charles D. Hollis, Jan. 4, 1864; mustered Jan. 25, 1864. In action at the Wilderness, May 6, 1864, Spotsylvania Court House, May 10, 12, and 18, 1864, North Anna River, May 24, 1864, Cold Harbor, June 3, 1864, and Petersburg assaults, June 17 and 18, 1864. With the regiment on all marches and in all skirmishes and battles until June 25, 1864. Absent sick in an army general hospital from June 25, 1864, until he deserted while on furlough from that hospital, Dec. 31, 1864. Never returned.

97. **White, Lorenzo,** private. Res. and/or credit: Palmer, MA. Born: Barre, MA. Age: 23. Height: 5′6″. Comp: dark. Eyes: blue. Hair: black. Occup: farmer. Enlisted in Palmer by Capt. George H. Howe, Dec. 24, 1863; mustered Jan. 25, 1864. Deserted while on furlough from Camp Wool, March 22, 1864, but was arrested, returned, and confined in the guardhouse in Camp Wool, March 26, 1864. Killed in action at the Wilderness, May 6, 1864. Had previous service as a private in Co. H, 21st MVI, from Aug. 5, 1861, until discharged for disability in Washington, DC, Jan. 19, 1863. Possibly participated in the North Carolina campaign in 1862 and at 2nd Bull Run, Aug. 30, 1862, Chantilly, Sept. 1, 1862, and Antietam, Sept. 17, 1862.

98. **Winch, Joseph B.,** private. Res: Buckland, MA. Credit: Leicester, MA. Born: Massachusetts. Age: 24. No description available. Occup: farmer. Enlisted in Leicester by Lt. John Anderson, Jan. 5, 1864; mustered Jan. 25, 1864. Never in combat. Absent sick in Harewood US Army General Hospital in Washington, DC, from on or before May 6, 1864, until discharged the US service for disability, Aug. 15, 1865, by order of the War Dept. Resided in Leicester, MA, after the war.

99. **Young, Joseph,** private. Res. and/or credit: Orange, MA. Born: Canada. Age: 29. Height: 5′8″. Comp: light. Eyes: blue. Hair: brown. Occup: laborer. Enlisted in Orange by Davis Goddard, Jan. 5, 1864; mustered Jan. 25, 1864. Absent for unknown reasons during the battle of the Wilderness, May 6, 1864. Missing in action at Spotsylvania Court House, May 12, 1864. Whereabouts while missing unknown, and no regimental records list him as sick, a prisoner of war, on detached duty, or having deserted. Returned to the regiment on an unknown date. Court-martialed (reason unknown, but likely something to do with his behavior while missing in action): "Special Orders, No. 159. War Department, Adjutant General's Office, Washington, April 4, 1865. (Extract) 52. The sentence of the General Court Martial, 'To be dishonorably discharged the military service of the United States, and confined in such prison as the Secretary of War may direct, for the period of three years, and to forfeit all pay and allowance now due or may become due,' as promulgated in General Orders, No. 124, Headquarters, Military Governor, Alexandria, Virginia, February 9, 1865, in the case of Private Joseph Young, Company 'E,' 57th Massachusetts Volunteers, is approved, and Clinton Prison, New York, designated the place of confinement, to which place the prisoner will be sent under proper guard, without delay. The Quartermaster's Department will furnish the necessary transportation. By order of the Secretary of War: E. D. Townsend, Assistant Adjutant General." Dishonorable discharge to date Feb. 9, 1865.

ROSTER AND DESCRIPTIVE LIST OF COMPANY F

Company F, known as the "Fitchburg Company" because most of its members were either citizens of that town or credited to it, was the seventh company to be mustered into the United States service, and it was mustered on Jan. 18, 1864 under SO 167, from the AGO, Boston, MA, by 1st Lt. Robert P. McKibbin, 4th United States Regular Infantry, except for those men mustered after Feb. 18, 1864, who were mustered by 2nd Lt. Daniel Madden, 6th United States Regular

Cavalry. The company was mustered out by Capt. Sylvester Keyser, 2nd Michigan Volunteer Infantry, ACM, 1st Division, IX Corps. This company is especially interesting because the original descriptive lists give some insightful evaluations—presumably by one of the company's officers or noncommissioned officers—of the military character of some of the men. Where no such comment occurs, mediocrity in the soldier's military behavior may, in most cases, be assumed safely.

1. **Babbitt, Charles W.**, private. Res: Groton Junction, MA. Credit: Fitchburg, MA. Born: Orange, NY. Age: 30. Married: Polly B. Height: 5'10½". Comp: light. Eyes: blue. Hair: brown. Occup: shoe cutter. Enlisted in Fitchburg by William H. Vose, Jan. 5, 1864; mustered Feb. 18, 1864. Wounded in the right arm in action at the Wilderness, May 6, 1864. Treated at the IX Corps Field Hospital in Fredericksburg, VA. Transferred to an army general hospital in Washington, DC, and remained there until discharged the US service on a Surgeons Certificate of Disability from wounds, Jan. 27, 1865, by order of Maj. Gen. Christopher C. Auger, commanding the Dept. of Washington, DC. Died Sept. 10, 1886, age 52. "Good Soldier" (CR).

Private Charles W. Babbitt
(postwar photo). *(FHS)*

2. **Bachant, Joseph**, private. Res. and credit: Worcester, MA. Born: Worcester, MA. Age: 18. Height: 5'4". Comp: light. Eyes: dark. Hair: dark. Occup: gunsmith. Enlisted in Worcester by Lt. John Reade, Feb. 2, 1864; mustered Feb. 18, 1864. Detached and detailed as a guard for the IX Corps cattle herd, May 4, 1864. Returned to duty with the regiment, Sept. 2, 1864. In action at Poplar Grove Church, Sept. 30 and Oct. 8, 1864, in other operations of the regiment during the fall and winter of 1864–65, and in action at Fort Stedman, March 25, 1865. Detached and detailed as a provost guard at 3rd Brigade, 1st Division, IX Corps, Headquarters under SO 120, from 3rd Brigade, 1st Division, IX Corps, Headquarters, June 30, 1865. Mustered out with the regiment at Delaney house, Washington, DC, July 30, 1865, and discharged in Readville, MA, Aug. 9, 1865, expiration of service.

3. **Baker, John**, private. Res. and/or credit: Sutton, MA. Born: Philadelphia, PA. Age: 22. Height: 5'4¾". Comp: dark. Eyes: blue. Hair: dark. Occup: shoemaker. Enlisted in Sutton by J. A. Dodge, Feb. 15, 1864; mustered Feb. 18, 1864. Deserted from Camp Wool, April 5, 1864. Arrested, returned to the regiment, and confined in the guardhouse in Camp Wool, April 6 and 7, 1864. Deserted again while on guard duty in Camp Wool, April 16, 1864. Charged by the US government $23.28 for uniform and rifle stolen and $1.00 for canteen and haversack stolen. Never returned. "Bounty jumper" (JA).

4. **Barker, Charles**, 1st lieutenant. Res. and credit: Fitchburg, MA. Born: Fitchburg, MA. Age: 41. Height: 5'11½". Comp: dark. Eyes: blue. Hair: gray. Occup: carpenter. Commissioned 1st lieutenant in Worcester by Gov.

John Andrew, Feb. 11, 1864; mustered 1st lieutenant, Feb. 18, 1864. Severely wounded in the arm and thigh in action at the Wilderness, May 6, 1864. Commissioned captain, Nov. 11, 1864, but not mustered. Returned to the regiment and listed as "Present, sick" (CR), Dec. 17, 1864. Left the regiment Jan. 6, 1865, for discharge, to date Dec. 27, 1864. Resigned and discharged the US service for disability from wounds under SO 469, par. 18, AGO War Dept. Had previous service as a lieutenant in the Fitchburg Guards, a local militia unit. Commissioned and mustered 1st lieutenant in Company D, 21st MVI, July 19, 1861. Participated in the North Carolina campaign with that regiment in 1862. Resigned and discharged because of poor health, June 16, 1862. Resided in Leominster, MA, after the war.

5. **Barnard, Charles E.**, 2nd lieutenant. Res. and/or credit: Worcester, MA. Born: Auburn, MA. Age: 22. Height: 5'11". Comp: dark. Eyes: blue. Hair: light. Occup: fireman. Enlisted in Worcester by D. Waldo Lincoln, Jan. 11, 1864; mustered Feb. 18, 1864. Promoted sergeant, Feb. 18, 1864. Detached and detailed as a guard for the IX Corps cattle herd, May 3, 1864. Promoted 1st sergeant, June 1, 1864. Absent sick in an army general hospital from July 23 until Nov. 6, 1864. With the regiment in operations after that date and during the winter of 1865. Wounded in the left shoulder and neck in action at Fort Stedman, March 25, 1865. Absent wounded in an army general hospital until May 18, 1865. Commissioned 2nd lieutenant, June 12, 1865; mustered 2nd lieutenant, June 26, 1865. Mustered out with the regiment at Delaney house, Washington, DC, July 30, 1865, and discharged in Readville, MA, Aug. 9, 1865, expiration of service. Had previous service as a private in Company E, 15th MVI, from July 12, 1861, until discharged for disability from wounds (shot through the chest at Antietam, Sept. 17, 1862), Nov. 24, 1862. Also participated with that regiment in the Peninsula campaign in 1862. Resided in Worcester, MA, after the war and was a cripple and an invalid for the rest of his life. Died in Worcester, MA, June 18, 1887, from war wounds, age 45. "Brave, honorable, and conscientious in the faithful discharge of his duties, and was loved and respected by his comrades in arms" (JA).

6. **Barnes, Charles H.**, private. Res. and/or credit: Gardner, MA. Born: West Cambridge, MA. Age: 27. Height: 5'4". Comp: light. Eyes: blue. Hair: dark. Occup: carpenter. Enlisted in Gardner by S. W. Bancroft, Jan. 2, 1864; mustered Feb. 18, 1864. Sick in the rear with the baggage wagons during the battle of the Wilderness, May 6, 1864. Absent sick in an army general hospital from on or shortly after May 7, 1864, until discharged the US service for disability, July 7, 1865, by order of the War Dept. Resided in Furnace, MA, after the war. "Never been to the regiment since May 4, 1864. Never in battle" (CR).

7. **Barnes, Willard F.**, private. Res: Westminster, MA. Credit: Fitchburg, MA. Born: West Cambridge, MA. Age: 25. Height: 5'4¾". Comp: light. Eyes: blue. Hair: brown. Occup: farmer. Enlisted in Fitchburg by William H. Vose, Feb. 2, 1864; mustered Feb. 18, 1864. Detached and detailed as a guard for

Private Charles H. Barnes
(postwar photo). *(John Anderson)*

Private Willard F. Barnes
(postwar photo). *(John Anderson)*

the IX Corps cattle herd, May 4, 1864. Returned to the regiment for duty, Sept. 2, 1864. In action at Poplar Grove Church, Sept. 30 and Oct. 8, 1864, and in other operations of the regiment during the fall of 1864. Detached and detailed as a 3rd Brigade, 1st Division, IX Corps, teamster from Dec. 6, 1864, until after June 1, 1865. Mustered out with the regiment at Delaney house, Washington, DC, July 30, 1865, and discharged in Readville, MA, Aug. 9, 1865, expiration of service. Resided in Standish, ME, after the war.

8. **Bartlett, George A.**, private. Res. and/or credit: Fitchburg, MA. Born: Nelson, NH. Age: 18. Height: 5'6¾". Comp: dark. Eyes: black. Hair: black. Occup: chair maker. Enlisted in Fitchburg by William H. Vose, Jan. 2, 1864; mustered Feb. 18, 1864. Left behind sick in an army general hospital in Annapolis, MD, April 21, 1864, as the regiment was on the march to the front. Returned to the regiment for duty May 9, 1864. In action at Spotsylvania Court House, May 10 and 12, 1864, and wounded while on duty there, May 13, 1864 (probably by a Confederate sniper). Absent wounded in an army general hospital until Sept. 4, 1864. In action at Poplar Grove

Church, Sept. 30 and Oct. 8, 1864. Absent sick in an army general hospital from Oct. 26 until Dec. 8, 1864. With the regiment in other operations during the fall and winter of 1864–65, and in action at Fort Stedman, March 25, 1865. Mustered out with the regiment at Delaney house, Washington, DC, July 30, 1865, and discharged in Readville, MA, Aug. 9, 1865, expiration of service. Resided in Concord, MA, after the war. "Not fit and never should have been a soldier" (CR).

9. **Bartlett, James F.**, 1st sergeant. Res. and credit: Fitchburg, MA. Born: Nelson, NH. Age: 24. Married. Height: 5'5½". Comp: dark. Eyes: black. Hair: dark. Occup: farmer. Enlisted in Fitchburg by William H. Vose, Jan. 5, 1864; mustered Feb. 18, 1865. Promoted sergeant, Feb. 18, 1864. Wounded in the head and arm in action at the Wilderness, May 6, 1864. Absent wounded in Emory US Army General Hospital in Washington, DC, until Sept. 1, 1864. In action at Poplar Grove Church, Sept. 30 and Oct. 8, 1864. Acting 1st sergeant from Oct. 14 until Nov. 6, 1864. In other operations of the regiment during the fall and winter of 1864–65, and in action at Fort Stedman, March 25, 1865. Listed as "absent without leave" in the company journal, May 25, 1865, but returned to duty May 26, 1865. Promoted 1st sergeant, July 1, 1865 (1st Sgt. Barnard promoted to lieutenant). Mustered out with the regiment at Delaney house, Washington, DC, July 30, 1865, and discharged in Readville, MA, Aug. 9, 1865, expiration of service. Had previous service as a corporal in Company A, 53rd MVI, from Sept. 2, 1862, until mustered out, Sept. 2, 1863. Participated in the Port Hudson, LA, campaign with that regiment in 1863. Also had previous service as a private in Company A, 15th MVI, from July 12, 1861, until discharged for disability, April 25, 1862. Probably at Ball's Bluff with that regiment, Oct. 21, 1861, in the Shenandoah Valley, 1862, and in the Peninsula campaign in 1862. Resided in Fitchburg, MA, after the war. "Always prompt for duty" (CR).

10. **Beckwith, Herbert D.**, private. Res. and/or credit: Fitchburg, MA. Born: Stoddard, NH. Age: 21. Height: 5'7¾". Comp: dark.

Eyes: blue. Hair: dark. Occup: mechanic. Enlisted in Fitchburg by William H. Vose, Jan. 5, 1864; mustered Feb. 18, 1864. Detached and detailed as a guard for the IX Corps cattle herd, May 4, 1864. Returned to the regiment for duty, Sept. 2, 1864. In action at Poplar Grove Church, Sept. 30 and Oct. 8, 1864, and in some operations of the regiment in the fall and early winter of 1864–65. Died from diphtheria in camp at Petersburg, Jan. 18, 1865. "Military character very good" (CR).

11. **Benson, William G.**, private. Res. and credit: Fitchburg, MA. Born: England. Age: 34. Married. Height: 5′6½″. Comp: light. Eyes: gray. Hair: light. Occup: mechanic. Enlisted in Fitchburg by William H. Vose, Jan. 5, 1864; mustered Feb. 18, 1864. Detached and detailed as a guard for the IX Corps cattle herd, May 4, 1864. Absent sick in an army general hospital from Aug. 30, 1864, until discharged the US service for disability, June 7, 1865. Resided in Fitchburg, MA, after the war. "Never been to regiment since [May 4, 1864]. Never in battle. Never done any duty at the front" (CR).

12. **Bigelow, Calvin A.**, sergeant. Res: Bolton, MA. Born and credit: Fitchburg, MA. Age:

Sergeant Calvin Bigelow
(postwar photo). *(FHS)*

21. Height: 5′9″. Comp: dark. Eyes: blue. Hair: black. Occup: machinist. Enlisted in Fitchburg by William H. Vose, Feb. 1, 1864; mustered Feb. 18, 1864. Promoted corporal, Feb. 18, 1864. In action at the Wilderness, May 6, 1864, Spotsylvania Court House, May 10, 12, and 18, 1864, North Anna River, May 24, 1864, Cold Harbor, June 3, 1864, Petersburg assaults, June 17 and 18, 1864, Petersburg Crater, July 30, 1864, Weldon Railroad, August 19, 1864, Poplar Grove Church, Sept. 30 and Oct. 8, 1864, and Fort Stedman, March 25, 1865. One of the 11 men who served with the regiment on all marches and in all skirmishes and battles throughout its entire wartime service, and of those 11, one of the 10 survivors and one of the 4 who was never wounded, was never taken prisoner of war, never absent sick, and never deserted. Promoted sergeant, May 1, 1865, under RSO 42, by order of Lt. Col. Julius M. Tucker. Discharged the US service in Tennallytown, DC, June 13, 1865, discharge to date June 1, 1865, as a supernumerary because of the consolidation of the 59th MVI with the 57th, under SO 254, par. 43., AGO, War Dept., dated May 26, 1865. Had previous service as a private in Company B, 53rd MVI, from Oct. 18, 1862, until mustered out, Sept. 2, 1863. Participated in the Port Hudson, LA, campaign with that regiment in 1863. Resided in Fitchburg, MA, after the war and died there, Sept. 14, 1911, age 68. "When the regiment was reduced to thirty men, Corporal Bigelow constituted one of that number" (CR).

13. **Bishop, Anson J.**, private. Res. and/or credit: Gill, MA. Born: Vermont. Age: 19. Height: 5′6″. Comp: fair. Eyes: blue. Hair: brown. Occup: farmer. Enlisted in Co. C in Gill by S. C. Phillips, March 24, 1864; mustered April 6, 1864; transferred to Co. F before May 4, 1864. Detached and detailed as a guard for the IX Corps cattle herd, May 4, 1864. Returned to the regiment for duty, Sept. 2, 1864. In action at Poplar Grove Church, Sept. 30 and Oct. 8, 1864, and in other operations of the regiment during the fall and winter of 1864–65; taken prisoner of war in action at Fort Stedman, March 25, 1865. Paroled and exchanged from Libby

Prison in Richmond, VA, April 1, 1865, and returned to the regiment for duty from the Camp of Parole in Annapolis, MD, May 11, 1865. Mustered out with the regiment at Delaney house, Washington, DC, July 30, 1865, and discharged in Readville, MA, Aug. 9, 1865, expiration of service.

14. **Blodgett, Lorenzo,** Res. and credit: Fitchburg, MA. No description available. Enlisted in Fitchburg by William H. Vose, Jan. 5, 1864; never mustered. Never reported to Camp Wool and was discharged from any military duties following a letter sent to Adjutant General William Schouler of Massachusetts from A. R. Ordway, selectman of Fitchburg, explaining that Blodgett had "been so unfortunate as to cut off the first three fingers of his right hand" (MRD).

15. **Blood, Charles F.,** private. Res: Burlington, MA. Credit: Boston, MA. Born: Fitchburg, MA. Age: 21. Height: 5'6". Comp: fair. Eyes: blue. Hair: brown. Occup: mechanic. Enlisted and mustered in Boston for one year by Captain Howe, Feb. 13, 1865; joined the regiment at Petersburg as a recruit, March 18, 1865. In action at Fort Stedman, March 25, 1865. Mustered out with the regiment at Delaney house, Washington, DC, July 30, 1865, and discharged in Readville, MA, Aug. 9, 1865, expiration of service. Died Dec. 27, 1887, age 44.

16. **Bourdon, Augustus,** private. Res: Windsor, CT. Credit: Northampton, MA. Born: province of Quebec, Canada. Age: 18. Height: 5'5½". Comp: light. Eyes: black. Hair: light. Occup: farmer. Enlisted in Northampton by Lt. Col. Luke Lyman, March 18, 1864; mustered April 6, 1864. Wounded in action at the Wilderness, May 6, 1864. Absent wounded in an army general hospital until Oct. 7, 1864. In action at Poplar Grove Church, Oct. 8, 1864, in other operations of the regiment during the fall and winter of 1864–65, and Fort Stedman, March 25, 1865. Mustered out with the regiment at Delaney house, Washington, DC, July 30, 1865, and discharged in Readville, MA, Aug. 9, 1865, expiration of service. Resided in Boston, MA, after the war.

17. **Brackett, Levi Curtis,** captain. Res. and/or credit: Boston, MA. Born: Ireland. Age: 23. No description available. Occup: clerk. Commissioned captain, Nov. 5, 1864. Joined the regiment as of Co. B by promotion from 1st lieutenant in the all-Irish 28th MVI, Dec. 14, 1864; muster to date Dec. 14, 1864. Technically in command of Co. B from Jan. to June 1865; however, he was never actually with the 57th but detached and detailed as an aide-decamp on the 1st Division, IX Corps, staff, Dec. 15, 1864, under SO 61 from 1st Division, IX Corps, Headquarters. Appointed major of US Volunteers by brevet for conspicuous gallantry in assisting in the charge of the 3rd Division, IX Corps, at Fort Stedman, March 25, 1865, and other actions at Petersburg under GO 65, AGO, War Dept., June 22, 1867, to date April 2, 1865. Officially transferred as captain of Co. F from Co. B on an unknown date in 1865. Resigned and discharged the US service, Aug. 4, 1865, by order of the War Dept., expiration of service. Had previous service as sergeant major on the noncommissioned staff and then 1st lieutenant in the 28th MVI from Oct. 12, 1861, until resigned and discharged for promotion in the 57th, Nov. 19, 1864. Commissioned 2nd lieutenant in the 28th MVI, April 4, 1862, but not mustered. Commissioned and mustered 1st lieutenant in the 28th MVI, Sept. 24, 1862. Commissioned captain in the 28th MVI, May 12, 1863, but declined. Participated with that regiment at 2nd Bull Run, Aug. 29, 1862, Chantilly, Sept. 1, 1862, South Mountain, Sept. 14, 1862, Antietam, Sept. 17, 1862, Marye's Heights at Fredericksburg, Dec. 13, 1862, Chancellorsville, May 3, 1863, and Gettysburg, July 1, 2, and 3, 1863. Wounded in action at Fredericksburg, Dec. 13, 1862.

18. **Brennan, Patrick,** private. Res. and credit: Fitchburg, MA. Born: Ireland. Age: 42. Married. Height: 5'4¼". Comp: dark. Eyes: gray. Hair: dark. Occup: laborer. Enlisted in Fitchburg by William H. Vose, Jan. 5, 1864; mustered Feb. 18, 1864. Detached and detailed as a guard for the IX Corps cattle herd, May 4, 1864. Returned to the regiment for duty, Sept. 2, 1864. In action at Poplar Grove Church, Sept. 30 and Oct. 8, 1864, some

Private Patrick Brennan. *(FHS)*

other operations of the regiment during the fall and winter of 1864–65, and Fort Stedman, March 25, 1865. Absent sick at the 1st Division, IX Corps, Field Hospital, from Nov. 17, 1864, until an unknown date, but probably in early 1865. Fell out during the march on April 22, 1865, but returned to the regiment for duty, April 25, 1865. Detached and detailed to the quartermaster's dept. in May 1865 until muster-out. Mustered out with the regiment at Delaney house, Washington, DC, July 30, 1865, and discharged in Readville, MA, Aug. 9, 1865, expiration of service. Resided in Fitchburg, MA, after the war and died there, Feb. 21, 1890, age 68.

19. **Brigham, Ozro A.,** private. Res. and credit: Fitchburg, MA. Born: Roxbury, VT. Age: 39. Height: 5′7½″. Comp: fair. Eyes: blue. Hair: black. Occup: jobber. Enlisted in Fitchburg by William H. Vose, Jan. 5, 1864; mustered Feb. 18, 1864. Absent sick or on detached duty from on or before May 6, 1864 until between May 18 and May 24, 1864. In action at North Anna River, May 24, 1864, and Cold Harbor, June 3, 1864, and wounded in action in the Petersburg assault, June 17, 1864. Absent wounded in an army general hospital until Nov. 6, 1864. With the regiment in operations from that date through the winter of 1865, and killed in action at Fort Stedman, March 25, 1865. Drafted from

Fitchburg during the July 17, 1863 draft, but exempted for disability. "Good soldier" (CR).

20. **Brown, Robert,** private. Res. and/or credit: Fitchburg, MA. Born: Boston, MA. Age: 22. Height: 5′8¼″. Comp: light. Eyes: gray. Hair: brown. Occup: shoemaker. Enlisted in Fitchburg by William H. Vose, Jan. 1, 1864; mustered Feb. 18, 1864. Detached and detailed as a guard for the IX Corps cattle herd, May 4, 1864. Returned to the regiment for duty, Sept. 2, 1864. In action at Poplar Grove Church, Sept. 30 and Oct. 8, 1864. Absent sick in an army general hospital from Oct. 26 until Dec. 28, 1864. With the regiment in other operations during the winter of 1865, and in action at Fort Stedman, March 25, 1865. Mustered out with the regiment at Delaney house, Washington, DC, July 30, 1865, and discharged in Readville, MA, Aug. 9, 1865, expiration of service. Had previous service in the US Navy as a landsman from Sept. 15, 1862, until mustered out, Sept. 17, 1863. Served on the receiving ship *Ohio*, the USS *Saint Mary's,* and the *North Carolina.*

21. **Burke, John,** corporal. Res. and credit: Fitchburg, MA. Born: Ireland. Age: 36. Married. Height: 5′9½″. Comp: dark. Eyes: blue. Hair: brown. Occup: laborer. Enlisted in Fitchburg by William H. Vose, Feb. 2, 1864; mustered Feb. 18, 1864. Detached and detailed as a guard for the IX Corps cattle herd, May 4, 1864. Returned to the regiment for duty, Sept. 2, 1864. In action at Poplar Grove Church, Sept. 30 and Oct. 8, 1864. Absent sick in an army general hospital from Nov. 11 until Dec. 20, 1864. With the regiment in other operations during the winter of 1864–65, and in action at Fort Stedman, March 25, 1865. Promoted corporal, May 1, 1865, under RSO 42, by order of Lt. Col. Julius M. Tucker. On furlough from May 21 until June 10, 1865. Mustered out with the regiment at Delaney house, Washington, DC, July 30, 1865, and discharged in Readville, MA, Aug. 9, 1865, expiration of service. Resided in Fitchburg, MA, after the war.

22. **Carey, James,** private. Res. and credit: Fitchburg, MA. Born: Ireland. Age: 19. Height: 5′3¼″. Comp: light. Eyes: blue.

Hair: brown. Occup: laborer. Enlisted in Fitchburg by William H. Vose, Feb. 3, 1864; mustered Feb. 18, 1864. Deserted, April 14, 1864, from Camp Wool but was arrested, returned, and confined in the guardhouse in Camp Wool, April 15 to 17, 1864. Detached and detailed as a guard for the IX Corps cattle herd, May 4, 1864. Returned to the regiment for duty, Sept. 2, 1864. In action at Poplar Grove Church, Sept. 30 and Oct. 8, 1864, and in other operations of the regiment during the fall and winter of 1864–65; wounded in action at Fort Stedman, March 25, 1865. Absent wounded in Summit House US Army General Hospital in Philadelphia, PA, until discharged the US service for disability from wounds, June 26, 1865, under GO 77, par. 6, AGO, War Dept.

23. **Carey, Michael,** private. Res. and/or credit: Milford, MA. Born: County Galway, Ireland. Age: 25. Height: 5'9". Comp: light. Eyes: blue. Hair: fair. Occup: bootmaker. Enlisted in Milford by Lt. John Reade, Feb. 15, 1864; mustered Feb. 18, 1864. "Sunday Apl 3 [1864] Micel Cory ran guard to the city and was caught and put on guard Monday" (WTP). Detached and detailed as a guard for the IX Corps cattle herd, May 4, 1864. Returned to the regiment for duty, Sept. 2, 1864. Absent for unknown reasons during the battles at Poplar Grove Church, Sept. 30 and Oct. 8, 1864. Detailed as company cook, Feb. 18, 1865, under RSO 15, by order of Lt. Col. Julius M. Tucker, dated Feb. 15, 1865. In action at Fort Stedman, March 25, 1865. Mustered out with the regiment at Delaney house, Washington, DC, July 30, 1865, and discharged in Readville, MA, Aug. 9, 1865, expiration of service. Resided in Medway, MA, after the war.

24. **Casey, John,** private. Res. and credit: Fitchburg, MA. Born: Ireland. Age: 26. Married. Height: 5'6". Comp: dark. Eyes: gray. Hair: brown. Occup: laborer. Enlisted in Fitchburg by William H. Vose, Jan. 1, 1864; mustered Feb. 18, 1864. Detached and detailed as a guard for the IX Corps cattle herd, May 4, 1864. Returned to the regiment for duty, Sept. 2, 1864. In action at Poplar Grove Church, Sept. 30 and Oct. 8, 1864, in other

Private John Casey (postwar photo). *(FHS)*

operations of the regiment during the fall and winter of 1864–65, and taken prisoner of war in action at Fort Stedman, March 25, 1865. Paroled and exchanged from Libby Prison in Richmond, VA, April 1, 1865 and returned to the regiment for duty from the Camp of Parole in Annapolis, MD, May 11, 1865. Mustered out with the regiment at Delaney house, Washington, DC, July 30, 1865, and discharged in Readville, MA, Aug. 9, 1865, expiration of service. Resided in Fitchburg, MA, after the war and died there, Jan. 24, 1911, age 73.

25. **Changyon, Joseph,** private. Res. and credit: Fitchburg, MA. Born: province of Quebec, Canada. Age: 21. Height: 5'4¼". Comp: dark. Eyes: black. Hair: black. Occup: laborer. Enlisted in Fitchburg by William H. Vose, Jan. 28, 1864; mustered Feb. 18, 1864. Detached and detailed as a guard for the IX Corps cattle herd, May 4, 1864. Returned to the regiment for duty, Sept. 2, 1864. In action at Poplar Grove Church, Sept. 30 and Oct. 8, 1864, in other operations of the regiment during the fall and winter of 1864–65, and at Fort

Stedman, March 25, 1865. Mustered out with the regiment at Delaney house, Washington, DC, July 30, 1865, and discharged in Readville, MA, Aug. 9, 1865, expiration of service.

26. **Changyon, Levi,** private. Res. and credit: Fitchburg, MA. Born: province of Quebec, Canada. Age: 24. Height: 5'7". Comp: dark. Eyes: dark. Hair: black. Occup: farmer. Enlisted in Fitchburg by William H. Vose, Jan. 5, 1864; mustered Feb. 18, 1864. "Obtained a furlough to Fitchburg [from Camp Wool] and deserted" (CR), March 13, 1864. Never returned.

27. **Changyon, William,** private. Res. and credit: Fitchburg, MA. Born: province of Quebec, Canada. Age: 18. Height: 5'4¼". Comp: dark. Eyes: dark. Hair: dark. Occup: laborer. Enlisted in Fitchburg by William H. Vose, March 31, 1864; mustered April 6, 1864. Detached and detailed as a guard for the IX Corps cattle herd, May 4, 1864. Never in combat. Absent sick on furlough to Fitchburg from Aug. 27, 1864, until discharged the US service for disability, Nov. 14, 1864, by order of the War Dept.

28. **Clark, Caleb,** private. Res. and/or credit: Fitchburg, MA. Born: Clinton, NY. Age: 18. Height: 5'5½". Comp: dark. Eyes: dark. Hair: light. Occup: farmer. Enlisted in Fitchburg by William H. Vose, Jan. 5, 1864; mustered Feb. 18, 1864. Detached and detailed as a guard for the IX Corps cattle herd, May 4, 1864. Never in combat. Present sick in the rear from on or before May 6, 1864, until absent sick in an army general hospital from June 10, 1864. Obtained a furlough from that hospital and deserted, Nov. 9, 1864. Never returned.

29. **Classon, Henry,** private. Res. and credit: Fitchburg, MA. Born: Digby, Nova Scotia, Canada. Age: 38. Married. Height: 5'4". Comp: fair. Eyes: blue. Hair: dark. Occup: mechanic. Enlisted in Fitchburg by William H. Vose, Jan. 5, 1864; mustered Feb. 18, 1864. Detached and detailed as a guard for the IX Corps cattle herd, May 4, 1864. Returned to the regiment for duty, Sept. 2, 1864. In action at Poplar Grove Church, Sept. 30

Private Henry Classon (postwar photo). *(FHS)*

and Oct. 8, 1864, and in other operations of the regiment during the fall and winter of 1864–65. On furlough from March 15 until April 4, 1865. Mustered out with the regiment at Delaney house, Washington, DC, July 30, 1865, and discharged in Readville, MA, Aug. 9, 1865, expiration of service. Had been drafted in the July 17, 1863, draft in Fitchburg, but exempted for being over 35 years old and married. Resided in Fitchburg, MA, after the war and died there Jan. 6, 1901, age 75.

30. **Costello, Thomas T.,** private. Res. and credit: Fitchburg, MA. Born: Ireland. Age: 32. Married: Mary Kelley. Height: 5'8½". Comp: dark. Eyes: dark. Hair: dark. Occup: laborer. Enlisted in Fitchburg by William H. Vose, Jan. 5, 1864; mustered Feb. 18, 1864. Detached and detailed as a guard for the IX Corps cattle herd, May 4, 1864. Returned to the regiment for duty, Sept. 2, 1864. Absent for unknown reasons during the battles at Poplar Grove Church, Sept. 30 and Oct. 8, 1864. Present sick with the regiment from Feb. 20 until March 16, 1865. Absent sick in Depot Field Hospital at City Point, Petersburg, from March 16 until April 21, 1865.

Private Thomas Costello
(postwar photo). *(FHS)*

Mustered out with the regiment at Delaney house, Washington, DC, July 30, 1865, and discharged in Readville, MA, Aug. 9, 1865, expiration of service. Drafted in the July 17, 1863, draft in Fitchburg, but exempted for disability. Resided in Fitchburg, MA, after the war and died there Nov. 3, 1909, age 77. Buried in St. Bernard's Cemetery in Fitchburg, MA. "Never in battle" (CR).

31. **Coughlin, John**, private. Res. and credit: Fitchburg, MA. Born: Ireland. Age: 43. Married. Height: 5'4". Comp: light. Eyes: blue. Hair: light. Occup: laborer. Enlisted in Fitchburg by William H. Vose, Jan. 5, 1864; mustered Feb. 18, 1864. Detached and detailed as a guard for the IX Corps cattle herd, May 4, 1864. Returned to the regiment for duty, Sept. 2, 1864. In action at Poplar Grove Church, Sept. 30 and Oct. 8, 1864, and in other operations of the regiment during the fall and winter of 1864–65; taken prisoner of war in action at Fort Stedman, March 25, 1865. Paroled and exchanged from Libby Prison in Richmond, VA, April 1, 1865, and returned to the regiment for duty from the Camp of Parole in Annapolis, MD, May 11, 1865. Mustered out with the regiment at Delaney house, Washington, DC, July 30, 1865,

and discharged in Readville, MA, Aug. 9, 1865, expiration of service. Resided in Fitchburg, MA, after the war.

32. **Crawford, John S.**, private. Res. and/or credit: Sutton, MA. Born: Philadelphia, PA. Age: 22. Height: 5'6". Comp: light. Eyes: blue. Hair: light brown. Occup: brush maker. Enlisted in Sutton by J. A. Dodge, Feb. 15, 1864; mustered Feb. 18, 1864. Deserted while on guard duty in Camp Wool, April 17, 1864. Charged by the US government $23.28 for uniform and rifle stolen and $1.00 for canteen and haversack stolen. Never returned. "Bounty jumper" (JA).

33. **Daily, Charles**, private. Res. and credit: Fitchburg, MA. Born: Ireland. Married. Age: 33. Height: 5'2". Comp: dark. Eyes: dark. Hair: dark. Occup: laborer. Enlisted in Fitchburg by William H. Vose, Jan. 5, 1864; mustered Feb. 18, 1864. In action at the Wilderness, May 6, 1864, and one of the 34 enlisted men who remained with the colors during that battle. In action at Spotsylvania Court House, May 10, 12, and 18, 1864, North Anna River, May 24, 1864, Cold Harbor, June 3, 1864, Petersburg assaults, June 17 and 18, 1864, Petersburg Crater, July 30, 1864, and Weldon Railroad, Aug. 19, 1864. On all marches and in all battles and skirmishes until at least this date. Absent sick in an army general hospital from between Aug. 19 and Sept. 30, 1864, until March 11, 1865, when he is listed in the company journal as "present sick." Accidentally wounded in camp at the front at Petersburg, March 19, 1865, and absent wounded in an army general hospital in Alexandria, VA, from soon after that date until discharged the US service on a Surgeons Certificate of Disability for wounds, Aug. 7, 1865. One of the 30 combat soldiers left of the regiment after Weldon Railroad. Resided in Fitchburg, MA, after the war.

34. **Davis, Freeman**, corporal. Res: Bolton, MA. Credit: Leicester, MA. Born: New Market, NH. Age: 21. Single. Height: 5'5". Comp: dark. Eyes: black. Hair: black. Occup: shoemaker. Enlisted in Leicester by Silas Gleason, Feb. 10, 1864; mustered Feb. 18, 1864. Promoted corporal, Feb. 18, 1864.

Killed in action at the Wilderness, May 6, 1864. Had previous service as a private in Co. E, 15th MVI, from July 12, 1861, until discharged for disability, May 14, 1863. Probably engaged at Ball's Bluff, Oct. 21, 1861, in the Shenandoah Valley, 1862, and the Peninsula campaign in 1862, at Antietam, Sept. 17, 1862, and possibly at Chancellorsville, May 3, 1863.

35. **Davis, Oscar D.**, 1st sergeant. Res. and/or credit: Fitchburg, MA. Born: Brattleboro, VT. Age: 30. Height: 5'11½". Comp: dark. Eyes: blue. Hair: black. Occup: mechanic. Enlisted in Fitchburg by William H. Vose, Jan. 3, 1864; mustered Feb. 18, 1864. Promoted 1st sergeant, Feb. 18, 1864. Deserted on the march from Brandy Station, VA, to the Wilderness, May 4, 1864. Arrested by the provost marshal in Baltimore, MD, and sent back to the regiment for duty. Deserted again at White House Landing, VA, June 12, 1864. Charged by the US government $4.71 for two shelter tent halves, haversack, canteen, and cap bugle (infantry insignia) stolen and $24.88 for rifle, uniform, and equipment stolen. Never returned. "Never in battle . . . COWARD" (CR).

36. **Delaney, John**, private. Res. and credit: Fitchburg, MA. Born: Ireland. Age: 31. Height: 5'6". Comp: dark. Eyes: dark. Hair: black. Occup: laborer. Enlisted in Fitchburg by William H. Vose, Jan. 5, 1864; mustered Feb. 18, 1864. Detached and detailed as a guard for the IX Corps cattle herd, May 4, 1864. Returned to the regiment for duty, Sept. 2, 1864. Absent sick in an army general hospital from Sept. 11, 1864, until discharged the US service for disability, May 30, 1865, by order of the War Dept. Resided in Fitchburg, MA, after the war. "Never in battle" (CR).

37. **Derby, Edward M.**, corporal. Res. and credit: Fitchburg, MA. Born: Fairlee, VT. Age: 30. Height: 5'5". Comp: dark. Eyes: dark. Hair: dark. Occup: machinist. Enlisted in Fitchburg by William H. Vose, Jan. 5, 1864; mustered Feb. 18, 1864. Promoted corporal, Feb. 18, 1864. In action at the Wilderness, May 6, 1864, and one of the 34 enlisted men who remained with the colors during

that battle. In action at Spotsylvania Court House, May 10, 1864, and shot through the head and killed in action there, May 12, 1864. "Military character very good" (CR).

38. **Dolan, Timothy**, private. Res. and/or credit: Fitchburg, MA. Born: Ireland. Age: 26. Married. Height: 5'4¼". Comp: dark. Eyes: gray. Hair: dark. Occup: shoemaker. Enlisted in Fitchburg by William H. Vose, Jan. 4, 1864; mustered Feb. 18, 1864. Listed in the company journal as "absent without leave" from Camp Wool, April 3 and 4, 1864. Detached and detailed as a guard for the IX Corps cattle herd, May 4, 1864. Returned to the regiment for duty, Sept. 2, 1864. Absent for unknown reasons during the battles of Poplar Grove Church, Sept. 30 and Oct. 8, 1864. Absent sick in the 1st Division, IX Corps, Field Hospital at Petersburg from Feb. 22 until March 11, 1865. In action at Fort Stedman, March 25, 1865. Mustered out with the regiment at Delaney house, Washington, DC, July 30, 1865, and discharged in Readville, MA, Aug. 9, 1865, expiration of service. Resided in Clinton, MA, after the war.

39. **Dunn, William**, sergeant (acting). Res. and/or credit: Fitchburg, MA. Born: Gibraltar, Spain (so officially listed in his army records). Age: 23. Married. Height: 5'8". Comp: light. Eyes: blue. Hair: light. Occup: carpenter. Enlisted in Fitchburg by William H. Vose, Jan. 5, 1864; mustered Feb. 18, 1864. Promoted corporal, Feb. 18, 1864. Severely wounded in the arm in action at the Wilderness, May 6, 1864, as acting sergeant (arm probably surgically amputated). Discharged on a Surgeons Certificate of Disability for wounds from an army general hospital in Washington, DC, Nov. 30, 1864. Resided in Marlboro, MA, after the war.

40. **Edgecomb, George R.**, private. Res. and credit: Fitchburg, MA. Born: Bath, ME. Age: 35. Height: 5'3½". Comp: dark. Eyes: blue. Hair: black. Occup: grocer. Enlisted in Fitchburg by William H. Vose, Feb. 4, 1864; mustered Feb. 18, 1864. Detached and detailed at the 1st Brigade, 1st Division, IX Corps, Commissary Dept. (probably because of his civilian profession) under Capt. H. H. Davidson from

Private George Edgecomb. *(FHS)*

April 26 until Sept. 20, 1864, under SO 24, from 1st Brigade, 1st Division, IX Corps, Headquarters, postdated June 24, 1864. In action at Poplar Grove Church, Sept. 30 and Oct. 8, 1864. Absent sick in an army general hospital from Oct. 26, 1864, until furloughed home to Fitchburg, sick, Feb. 24, 1864. Returned to the regiment for duty from furlough, March 8, 1865. Taken prisoner of war in action at Fort Stedman, March 25, 1865. Paroled and exchanged from Libby Prison in Richmond, VA, April 1, 1865, and returned to the regiment for duty from the Camp of Parole in Annapolis, MD, May 7, 1865. Mustered out with the regiment at Delaney house, Washington, DC, July 30, 1865, and discharged in Readville, MA, Aug. 9, 1865, expiration of service. Had been drafted in the summer of 1863 draft in Fitchburg, but exempted for disability. Resided in Fitchburg, MA, after the war and died there May 2, 1873, age 44.

41. **Farnsworth, Joseph W.**, private. Res: Waltham, MA. Credit: Fitchburg, MA. Born: Massachusetts. Age: 19. Description not available. Occup: chair maker. Enlisted and mustered in Fitchburg by C. W. Jaquith, April 14, 1864. Reported to the regiment for

duty before April 18, 1864. In action at the Wilderness, May 6, 1864, Spotsylvania Court House, May 10, 12, and 18, 1864, North Anna River, May 24, 1864, and Cold Harbor, June 3, 1864; severely wounded in his left leg in action during the Petersburg assault, June 17, 1864. Taken to the 1st Division, IX Corps, Field Hospital where his left leg was surgically amputated by the flap method, May 18, 1864, by Dr. T. Fletcher Oakes, surgeon of the 56th MVI. Leg reamputated due to complications, March 23, 1865. Absent wounded in Dale US Army General Hospital in Worcester, MA, until discharged and pensioned from the US service on a Surgeons Certificate of Disability for wounds, June 2, 1865, by order of Maj. Gen. John A. Dix, War Dept. Had previous service as a private in Co. C, 3rd Rhode Island Volunteer Cavalry (specifics unknown). Resided in Waltham, MA, after the war and died there in 1924, age 79.

42. **Farnsworth, Rufus G.**, sergeant. Res. and credit: Fitchburg, MA. Born: Fitchburg, MA. Age: 23. Single. Height: 5'8½". Comp: dark. Eyes: blue. Hair: dark. Occup: mechanic. Enlisted in Fitchburg by William H. Vose, Jan. 5, 1864; mustered Feb. 18, 1864. Left behind sick in the hospital in Camp Wool when the regiment left for the front, April 18, 1864. Rejoined the regiment between June 3 and June 17, 1864. In action at the Petersburg assaults, June 17 and 18, 1864, and wounded in the knee in action at the Petersburg Crater, July 30, 1864. Absent wounded in an army general hospital until Jan. 7, 1865. Promoted sergeant, Feb. 28, 1865. Wounded in the left shoulder in action at Fort Stedman, March 25, 1865. Absent wounded in an army general hospital until discharged the US service for disability from wounds, June 28, 1865, by order of the War Dept. Had been drafted in the summer of 1863 draft in Fitchburg, but exempted for disability. Resided in Fitchburg, MA, after the war.

43. **Farrell, Martin**, corporal. Res. and credit: Fitchburg, MA. Born: Swifts Heath, County Kilkenny, Ireland, Dec. 17, 1820. Age 44. Married: Margaret Drinnan. Height: 5'6". Comp: dark. Eyes: gray. Hair: black. Occup: machinist. Enlisted in Fitchburg by William

Corporal Martin Farrell (postwar photo).
(FHS)

H. Vose, Jan. 5, 1864; mustered Feb. 18, 1864. Promoted corporal, May 1, 1864. Detached and detailed as a guard for the IX Corps cattle herd, May 4, 1864. Absent sick in Depot Field Hospital at City Point, Petersburg, with "varicose veins" (septic thrombophlebitis) in the right leg, from Aug. 31, 1864, until transferred to Douglas US Army General Hospital in Washington, DC, Sept. 8, 1864. Transferred, Nov. 4, 1864, and admitted, Nov. 7, 1864, to Camp Meigs US Army General Hospital in Readville, MA. Transferred and admitted to Dale US Army General Hospital in Worcester, MA, Nov. 26, 1864. Discharged from that hospital, Dec. 29, 1864, and returned to the regiment for duty, Dec. 31, 1864. Absent sick in the 1st Division, IX Corps, Field Hospital at Petersburg with the same complaint from after Dec. 31, 1864, until Feb. 22, 1865. Absent sick in the 1st Division, IX Corps, Field Hospital again with the same complaint from March 16 until April 22, 1865. Mustered out with the regiment at Delaney house, Washington, DC, July 30, 1865, and discharged in Readville, MA, Aug. 9, 1865, expiration of service. Had enlisted in Co. A, 36th MVI, in late July 1862. Sent to Camp Wool, Aug. 1, 1862, and rejected or exempted from that regiment for an unknown reason, Aug. 1862. Drafted in

the summer of 1863 draft in Fitchburg, but exempted for being over 35 years old and married. Resided in Fitchburg, MA, after the war and served as constable and tax collector. Died at his daughter's home in Manomet, MA, Dec. 12, 1902, of heart failure, age 82. Buried in St. Bernard's Cemetery in Fitchburg, MA. "Never in battle or done duty at the front . . . Always taken sick before a battle" (CR). Lt. Hitchcock, commanding the cattle guard, stated in a sworn affidavit, however: "Farrell had been able to do full duty up to this time [Aug. 31, 1864]. . . . His leg was so bad that he was allowed to ride a horse."

44. **Flagg, Edwin Albro,** private. Res. and credit: Fitchburg, MA. Born: Fitchburg, MA, Jan. 7, 1846. Age: 18. Height: 5'5". Comp: light. Eyes: gray. Hair: brown. Occup: cooper. Enlisted in Fitchburg by William H. Vose, Jan. 28, 1864; mustered Feb. 18, 1864. Wounded in the left hip in action at the Wilderness, May 6, 1864. Treated at a field hospital in Fredericksburg, VA, until transferred to Lovell US Army General Hospital in Portsmouth Grove, RI, on an unknown date in May 1864. Absent wounded until discharged the US service from that hospital on a Surgeons Certificate of Disability for wounds, May 25, 1865. Resided in Fitzwilliam, NH, after the war and died there in April 1896, from blood poisoning as a result of his wound, age 50.

45. **Frost, James M.,** private. Res. and/or credit: Washington, MA. Born: Monson, MA. Age: 18. Height: 5'8". Comp: dark. Eyes: blue. Hair: brown. Occup: farmer. Enlisted in Washington by Charles Grosier; mustered Feb. 18, 1864. Wounded in action at the Wilderness, May 6, 1864. Absent wounded in an army general hospital until discharged the US service for disability from wounds, July 3, 1865, by order of the War Dept.

46. **Fuller, Henry,** private. Res. and credit: Fitchburg, MA. Born: Nelson, NH. Age: 28. Height: 5'5¼". Comp: dark. Eyes: blue. Hair: dark. Occup: shoemaker. Enlisted in Fitchburg by William H. Vose, Jan. 5, 1864; mustered Feb. 18, 1864. Wounded in action at

the Wilderness, May 6, 1864. Absent wounded in an army general hospital until discharged the US service for disability from wounds, May 25, 1865, by order of the War Dept. Had been drafted in the July 17, 1863 draft in Fitchburg, but exempted for disability. Resided in Fitchburg, MA, after the war.

47. **Gardner, Horace O.**, private. Res. and/or credit: Hancock, MA. Born: Berlin, NY. Age: 19. Height: 5'5". Comp: light. Eyes: blue. Hair: light. Occup: farmer. Enlisted in Hancock by H. H. Whitman, March 14, 1864; mustered April 6, 1864. Detached and detailed as a guard for the IX Corps cattle herd, May 4, 1864. Returned to the regiment for duty, Sept. 2, 1864. In action at Poplar Grove Church, Sept. 30, 1864. Absent sick in an army general hospital from Oct. 7, 1864, until Feb. 10, 1865. In action at Fort Stedman, March 25, 1865. Mustered out with the regiment at Delaney house, Washington, DC, July 30, 1865, and discharged in Readville, MA, Aug. 9, 1865, expiration of service.

48. **Goddard, Wesley D.**, private. Res. and credit: Royalston, MA. Born: Royalston, MA. Age: 39. Height: 5'7". Comp: light. Eyes: blue. Hair: light. Occup: farmer. Enlisted in Royalston by William W. Clement, Feb. 8, 1864; mustered Feb 18, 1864. In action at the Wilderness, May 6, 1864, Spotsylvania Court House, May 10, 12, and 18, 1864, North Anna River, May 24, 1864, Cold Harbor, June 3, 1864, Petersburg assaults, June 17 and 18, 1864, and Petersburg Crater, July 30, 1864; mortally wounded by the explosion of a Confederate mortar shell while on duty in the trenches at Petersburg, Aug. 9, 1864. Died from wounds, Aug. 18, 1864. With the regiment on all marches and in all skirmishes and battles until wounded. Had previous service as a private in Co. I, 25th MVI, from Oct. 1, 1861, until discharged for disability in New Bern, NC, Aug. 4, 1862. Participated in the North Carolina campaign with that regiment in 1862. Received a pension for disability incurred while serving with that regiment.

49. **Gould, Austin K.**, private. Res. and/or credit: Fitchburg, MA. Born: Hadley, MA.

Private Austin K. Gould (postwar photo; note 57th Massachusetts Regimental Association badge, G.A.R. badge, and IX Corps pin). *(Post 10)*

Age: 38. Married. Height: 5'10½". Comp: dark. Eyes: blue. Hair: black. Occup: physician. Enlisted in Fitchburg by William H. Vose, Jan. 5, 1864; mustered Feb. 18, 1864. Detailed on hospital staff duty in Camp Wool until April 18, 1864. Detailed to field hospital service with the regiment, April 18, 1864. Detached with the 1st Division, IX Corps, ambulance wagon train, May, 3, 1864. In action at the Wilderness treating the wounded on the battlefield, May 6, 1864. Remained behind on the field with 50 wounded men when the Union lines retreated to the Brock road. Captured by and escaped from the Confederates twice. Captured a third time and incarcerated in the Confederate prison camp at Andersonville, GA, May 29, 1864. Transferred to Charleston, SC, on Sept. 14, 1864, and remained there until transferred to the Confederate prison in Florence, SC, about Oct. 5, 1864. Paroled and exchanged from that prison, Dec. 15, 1864. In prison for seven months and two days. Never rejoined the regiment. Received three months' extra pay for being a prisoner of war. Discharged the US service for disability from an army general hospital, June 17, 1865, by order of the War Dept. Had previous service as a private in Co. B, 53rd MVI, from Aug. 25, 1862, until mustered out, Sept. 2, 1863. In charge of one of the XIX Corps division hospitals at Baton Rouge, LA, while serving with that regiment in the Port Hudson, LA, campaign in 1863. Resided and was a practicing physician in Worcester, MA, after the war, and died there in his home on Sept. 8, 1893, age 67. Buried in Amherst, MA. "He was loved and respected by every Union soldier who was ever blest with a personal acquaintance with him" (JA, from his eulogy).

50. **Gove, Alfred E.**, private. Res. and/or credit: Milford, MA. Born: Augusta, ME, Nov. 25, 1844. Age: 19. Height: 5′2¾″. Comp: light. Eyes: blue. Hair: auburn. Occup: laborer. Enlisted in Milford by Leonard Hunt, Feb. 9, 1864; mustered Feb. 18, 1864. Assigned to work in the cookhouse in Camp Wool, April 4, 1864. Wounded in action at the Wilderness, May 6, 1864. Absent wounded in an army general hospital until Oct. 29, 1864. With the regiment in operations during the fall and winter of 1864–65. On furlough from Feb. 17 until March 11, 1865. Slightly wounded in action at Fort Stedman, March 25, 1865. Detailed as a nurse at the 1st Division, IX Corps, Field Hospital at Petersburg and Tennallytown, DC, for an unknown period after March 25, 1865. Mustered out with the regiment at Delaney house, Washington, DC, July 30, 1865, and discharged in Readville, MA, Aug. 9, 1865, expiration of service.

51. **Hall, Rodney**, musician. Res. and credit: Fitchburg, MA. Born: Fitchburg, MA. Age: 18. Height: 5′9½″. Comp: light. Eyes: gray. Hair: brown. Occup: peddler. Enlisted in Fitchburg by William H. Vose, Jan. 23, 1864; mustered Feb. 18, 1864. Company drummer.

Probably also served as a nurse, hospital orderly, and/or stretcher bearer. Present during the battle of Fort Stedman, March 25, 1865, but unknown what his participation was. Absent sick in an army general hospital from after March 25, 1865, until discharged the US service for disability, Aug. 10, 1865, by order of the War Dept. Resided in Fitchburg, MA, after the war and died there, before Oct. 1, 1866, from the effects of disease incurred while in the army.

52. **Hanrahan, Edward**, sergeant. Res: Bolton, MA. Credit: Millbury, MA. Born: Limerick, Ireland. Age: 40. Married. Height: 5′9½″. Comp: dark. Eyes: dark. Hair: dark. Occup: laborer. Enlisted in Millbury by Lt. John Reade, Feb. 2, 1864; mustered Feb. 18, 1864. In action at the Wilderness, May 6, 1864, Spotsylvania Court House, May 10, 12, and 18, 1864, North Anna River, May 24, 1864, Cold Harbor, June 3, 1864, Petersburg assaults, June 17 and 18, 1864, Petersburg Crater, July 30, 1864, Weldon Railroad, Aug. 19, 1864, Poplar Grove Church, Sept. 30 and Oct. 8, 1864, and Fort Stedman, March 25, 1865. One of the 11 men who served with the regiment on all marches and in all skirmishes and battles throughout its entire wartime service, and of those 11, one of the 3 who was never wounded or taken prisoner of war, and who served his entire enlistment from muster-in until the regiment's muster-out. He was also one of the 30 combat soldiers remaining of the regiment after Weldon Railroad, Aug. 19, 1864, and appears to have been one of the regiment's more colorful characters. Promoted acting sergeant on an unknown date in the fall of 1864. Placed under arrest and confined, Dec. 17, 1864, until tried by general court-martial under GO 2, dated Jan. 19, 1865, at 1st Division, IX Corps, Headquarters, Col. Gilbert P. Robinson, 3rd Maryland Volunteer Infantry, president of the court. Found guilty of "1. drunkenness, and 2. using insulting and abusive language" (CMR), under SO 122 from 1st Division, IX Corps, Headquarters, predated Dec. 19, 1864. Reduced to the ranks, and held in confinement (other punishment, if any, unknown). Released from arrest and returned to the regiment for duty, Jan. 31, 1865. Promoted ser-

geant again before April 27, 1865. Placed under arrest again, April 27, 1865, reason unknown, but probably for similar offenses or for disobedience of orders. Deserted from under guard while on a march near Tennallytown, DC, April 29, 1865. Returned to the regiment for duty in Tennallytown, DC, May 3, 1865, and reduced to the ranks again, and arrested and confined for desertion until detailed as a 3rd Brigade, 1st Division, IX Corps, teamster under Capt. G. P. Ladd at the 1st Division, IX Corps, Quartermaster's Dept. from May 6, 1865, until muster-out, by order of Lt. Col. Julius M. Tucker under RSO, as directed by SO 126 from 3rd Brigade, 1st Division, IX Corps, Headquarters. Mustered out with the regiment at Delaney house, Washington, DC, July 30, 1865, and discharged in Readville, MA, Aug. 9, 1865, expiration of service. Died in 1890, age 72.

53. **Harris, Michael,** private. Res. and/or credit: Longmeadow, MA. Born: Ireland. Age: 34. Married. Height: 5'3½". Comp: light. Eyes: hazel. Hair: brown. Occup: laborer. Enlisted in Longmeadow by S. F. Colton, Feb. 16, 1864; mustered Feb. 18, 1864. Deserted from Camp Wool, March 13, 1864. Arrested and returned to the regiment on the evening of March 16, 1864. Confined in the guardhouse in Camp Wool from March 17 until March 23, 1864. Mortally wounded in action at the Wilderness, May 6, 1864. Died from his wounds at a field hospital in Fredericksburg, VA, May 15, 1864. "Military character good" (CR).

54. **Hastings, John M.,** sergeant. Res. and/or credit: Fitchburg, MA. Born: Boston, MA. Age: 37. Height: 5'4¾". Comp: dark. Eyes: dark. Hair: dark. Occup: mechanic. Enlisted in Fitchburg by William H. Vose, Jan. 5, 1864; mustered Feb. 18, 1864. Promoted sergeant, Feb. 18, 1864. In action at the Wilderness, May 6, 1864, and Spotsylvania Court House, May 10 and 12, 1864; reported missing there, May 13, 1864. Never accounted for and presumed killed. Had previous service as a private in Co. A, 53rd MVI, from Aug. 23, 1862, until mustered out, Sept. 2, 1863. Participated in the Port Hudson, LA, campaign with that regiment in 1862.

55. **Hennessey, John,** private. Res. and credit: Fitchburg, MA. Born: Ireland. Age: 37. Married. Height: 6'0½". Comp: light. Eyes: blue. Hair: brown. Occup: laborer. Enlisted in Fitchburg by William H. Vose, Jan. 27, 1864; mustered Feb. 18, 1864. In action at the Wilderness, May 6, 1864, Spotsylvania Court House, May 10, 12, and 18, 1864, North Anna River, May 24, 1864, Cold Harbor, June 3, 1864, Petersburg assaults, June 17 and 18, 1864, Petersburg Crater, July 30, 1864, and Weldon Railroad, Aug. 19, 1864; wounded in action at Poplar Grove Church, Sept. 30, 1864. With the regiment on all marches and in all skirmishes and battles until wounded, and one of the 30 combat soldiers remaining of the regiment after Weldon Railroad, Aug. 19, 1864. Absent wounded in an army general hospital until about mid-Nov. 1864. Detailed to 3rd Brigade, 1st Division, IX Corps, Headquarters as a pioneer, Nov. 16, 1864, under SO 78, by order of Brig. Gen. Napoleon B. McLaughlen. Absent sick in the 1st Division, IX Corps, Field Hospital from Feb. 8 until Feb. 9, 1865. Assigned to daily duty, Feb. 23, 1865 (nature of duty unknown). Mustered out with the regiment at Delaney house, Washington, DC, July 30, 1865, and discharged in Readville, MA, Aug. 9, 1865, expiration of service. Died in 1889, age 64.

56. **Henry, George A.,** private. Res. and/or credit: Fitchburg, MA. Born: Boston, MA. Age: 21. Height: 5'5½". Comp: fair. Eyes: blue. Hair: brown. Occup: machinist. Enlisted in Fitchburg by William H. Vose, Feb. 1, 1864; mustered Feb. 18, 1864. In action at the Wilderness, May 6, 1864, and Spotsylvania Court House, May 10, 1864; wounded in action there, May 12, 1864. Absent wounded in an army general hospital until transferred to Co. K, 22nd Regiment, VRC, Sept 2, 1864, by order of the War Dept. Discharged the US service, Aug. 9, 1865, by order of the War Dept., expiration of service. Resided in Cambridgeport, MA, after the war and died there after 1911, date unknown.

57. **Hitchcock, Alfred O.,** captain. Res. and credit: Fitchburg, MA. Born: Ashby, MA. Age: 23. Height: 5'3½". Comp: dark. Eyes:

Captain Alfred O. Hitchcock
(in old age). *(USAMHI)*

solidation of the 59th MVI with the 57th, under SO 254, par. 43, AGO, War Dept. Rejoined the army and assigned as aide-de-camp to Maj. Gen. Nelson A. Miles. Was also provost marshal at the Military District of Fort Monroe, VA, where Jefferson Davis was confined, from May 26, 1865, until April, 1866. Mustered out by SO 178, War Dept., April 19, 1866. Appointed brevet major for gallant and meritorious services in the field by GO 65, War Dept., June 22, 1867, to date from March 13, 1865. Had previous service as a private in Co. A, 53rd MVI, from Dec. 13, 1862, until mustered out, Sept. 2, 1863. Wounded in the right eye in action at Port Hudson, LA, with that regiment, June 14, 1863, and sight in that eye was permanently lost. Graduated medical school after the war and was a practicing physician in Fitchburg, MA. Elected president of the 57th's regimental association at the 26th annual reunion of the regiment, June 17, 1892. Died in early 1917, age 76.

gray. Hair: brown. Occup: medical student. Commissioned 2nd lieutenant by Gov. John Andrew, Oct. 13, 1863; Mustered 2nd lieutenant in Boston, MA, by 1st Lt. Robert P. McKibben, 4th US Infantry, Oct. 17, 1863. Assigned as 2nd lieutenant of Co. F, March 10, 1864, under RSO 18, by order of Col. William F. Bartlett. Detailed at Rappahannock Station, VA, as commander of the guard detail detached with the IX Corps cattle herd, May 3, 1864. Returned to the regiment for duty, Sept. 2, 1864. In action at Poplar Grove Church, Sept. 30 and Oct. 8, 1864. Mustered out as 2nd lieutenant of Co. F, Oct. 23, 1864, and mustered in as 1st lieutenant of Co. D, Oct 24, 1864. Commissioned captain, Nov. 11, 1864. With the regiment in operations during the fall and winter of 1864–65. On leave of absence in Massachusetts from Feb. 10 until March 2, 1865. In action at Fort Stedman, March 25, 1865. Acting regimental adjutant, March 1865. Also in command of Co. G from March 27 until May 12, 1865, and Co. K from March 26 until May 10, 1865. Mustered captain, May 19, 1865. Resigned and discharged the US service in Tennallytown, DC, June 27, 1865, to date June 1, 1865, as a supernumerary because of the con-

58. **Keilty, Daniel,** private. Res. and credit: Fitchburg, MA. Born: County Mayo, Ireland. Age: 40. Married: Bridget. Height: 5'9¾". Comp: light. Eyes: blue. Hair: auburn. Occup: laborer. Enlisted in Fitchburg by William H. Vose, Jan. 23, 1864; mustered Feb. 18, 1864. Killed in action at the Wilderness, May 6, 1864. Remains sent home and buried in St. Bernard's Cemetery, Fitchburg, MA. Had been drafted in the summer draft of 1863 in Fitchburg, but exempted for being over 35 and married.

59. **Lawless, John,** private. Res. and credit: Fitchburg, MA. Born: Ireland. Age: 36. Married. Height: 5'8". Comp: dark. Eyes: black. Hair: black. Occup: laborer. Enlisted in Fitchburg by William H. Vose, Jan. 5, 1864; mustered Feb. 18, 1864. In action at the Wilderness, May 6, 1864, and Spotsylvania Court House, May 10, 1864; slightly wounded in the thigh there, May 12, 1864. Treated at a field hospital in Fredericksburg, VA. Transferred to a US army general hospital and absent wounded there until Aug. 21, 1864. In action at Poplar Grove Church, Sept. 30 and Oct 8, 1864. Absent sick in an army general hospital from Dec. 8, 1864, until March 1, 1865. With

the regiment in some operations during the fall and winter of 1864–65, and in action at Fort Stedman, March 25, 1865. Fell out on the march to City Point, VA, April 22, 1865, but returned to the regiment for duty in Alexandria, VA, April 25, 1865. Detached and detailed on daily duty as a pioneer at 3rd Brigade, 1st Division, IX Corps, Headquarters, from May 2, 1865, until muster-out. Mustered out with the regiment at Delaney house, Washington, DC, July 30, 1865, and discharged in Readville, MA, Aug. 9, 1865, expiration of service.

60. **Lawrence, Levi,** captain. Res. and credit: Fitchburg, MA. Born: Ashby, MA. Age: 38. Height: 5'8". Comp: dark. Eyes: black. Hair: black. Occup: carpenter. Commissioned captain by Gov. John Andrew, Feb. 11, 1864; mustered captain with the company in Camp Wool, Feb. 18, 1864. Wounded by buckshot in the neck in action at the Wilderness, May 6, 1864. Treated in a field hospital in Fredericksburg, VA, after narrowly escaping capture by Confederate guerillas. Absent wounded in an army general hospital until June 15, 1864. Wounded in the leg in action during the Petersburg assault, June 17, 1864, as acting major. Absent wounded in an army general hospital and at home until Sept. 10, 1864. Resigned and discharged the US service for disability from wounds at Petersburg, Sept. 19, 1864. Had previous service as 1st lieuten-

ant of Co. F, 25th MVI, from Oct. 12, 1861, until resigned and discharged in New Bern, NC, July 21, 1862. Participated in the North Carolina campaign with that regiment in 1862. Resided in Fitchburg, MA, after the war until 1876 when he moved to Ashby, MA. Drowned at sea in the wreck of the steamer *City of Columbus* of the Savannah Line, off Gays Head, MA, while on a voyage to Florida for health reasons, Jan. 18, 1884, age 58. "Of gentle disposition and sterling worth, cool and brave in the hour of danger, and thoroughly conscientious in the discharge of every duty" (JA).

61. **Luchay, Abraham,** private. Res. and/or credit: Spencer, MA. Born: Leicester, MA. Age: 21. Height: 5'6½". Comp: light. Eyes: blue. Hair: dark. Occup: wiredrawer. Enlisted in Spencer by Luther Hill, March 19, 1864; mustered April 6, 1864. Deserted from Camp Wool, April 5, 1864, but returned before April 18, 1864. Missing in action at the Wilderness, May 6, 1864. Never accounted for and presumed killed.

62. **McCarthy, Patrick,** private. Res. and credit: Fitchburg, MA. Born: Ireland. Age: 38. Married. Height: 5'9". Comp: light. Eyes: blue. Hair: brown. Occup: papermaker. Enlisted in Fitchburg by William H. Vose, Jan. 30, 1864; mustered Feb. 18, 1864. Absent sick or on detached duty from on or before May 6, 1864, until between May 12 and May 18, 1864. In action at Spotsylvania Court House, May 18, 1864, North Anna River, May 24, 1864, and Cold Harbor, June 3, 1864; severely wounded in action during the Petersburg assault, June 17, 1864. Died from his wounds in Harewood US Army General Hospital, Washington, DC, July 5, 1864. "Military character good" (CR).

63. **McDowell, John,** private. Res. and credit: Fitchburg, MA. Born: Ireland. Age: 20. Single. Height: 5'7". Comp: light. Eyes: blue. Hair: brown. Occup: laborer. Enlisted in Fitchburg by William H. Vose, Jan. 5, 1864; mustered Feb. 18, 1864. Wounded in action at the Wilderness, May 6, 1864. Absent wounded in an army general hospital until Aug. 7, 1864, and from Aug. 18, 1864, until

Captain Levi Lawrence. *(FHS)*

an unknown date in Sept. 1864. In action at Poplar Grove Church, Sept. 30 and Oct. 8, 1864, in other operations of the regiment during the fall and winter of 1864–65, and in action at Fort Stedman, March 25, 1865. Mustered out with the regiment at Delaney house, Washington, DC, July 30, 1865, and discharged in Readville, MA, Aug. 9, 1865, expiration of service. Resided in Fitchburg, MA, after the war.

64. **McGonn, Michael,** private. Res: Palmer, MA. Credit: Springfield, MA. Born: Ireland. Age: 39. Height: 5′3½″. Comp: light. Eyes: blue. Hair: light. Occup: weaver. Enlisted and mustered in Springfield by Capt. Morehouse, Aug. 8, 1864. Joined the regiment after Oct. 8, 1864. With the regiment in operations during the fall and winter of 1864–65, and taken prisoner of war in action at Fort Stedman, March 25, 1865. Paroled and exchanged from Libby Prison in Richmond, VA, April 1, 1865, and discharged the US service (probably for disability, as his enlistment was for three years) from the Camp of Parole in Annapolis, MD, June 27, 1865, to date June 15, 1865, under GO 77, par. 6, AGO, War Dept. Resided in Easthampton, MA, after the war.

65. **McIntire, Albion,** private. Res. and credit: Fitchburg, MA. Born: Fitchburg, MA. Age: 18. Height: 5′6½″. Comp: dark. Eyes: dark. Hair: brown. Occup: shoemaker. Enlisted in Fitchburg by William H. Vose, Jan. 16, 1864; mustered Feb. 18, 1864. Wounded in the head in action at the Wilderness, May 6, 1864. Treated in a field hospital in Fredericksburg, VA, until transferred to Mt. Pleasant US Army General Hospital in Washington, DC. Returned to the regiment for duty from the hospital, Sept. 9, 1864. Wounded again by the accidental discharge of a rifle in the trenches at Petersburg, Sept. 14, 1864. Absent wounded in an army general hospital until transferred to Co. B, 11th Regiment, VRC, May 6, 1865. Discharged the US service, Aug. 8, 1865, by order of the War Dept., expiration of service. Resided in Worcester, MA, after the war.

66. **McMaster, George C.,** private. Res. and/or credit: Sturbridge, MA. Born: Palmer, MA.

Age: 34. Height: 5′8″. Comp: sandy. Eyes: blue. Hair: sandy. Occup: mechanic. Enlisted in Sturbridge by E. L. Bates, March 21, 1864; mustered April 6, 1864. Taken prisoner of war in action at the Wilderness, May 6, 1864. Incarcerated in the Confederate prison camp in Andersonville, GA, May 29, 1864, where he died from disease, Sept. 29, 1864. Buried at Andersonville as an "unknown."

67. **McSherry, John,** private. Res. and/or credit: Shelburne, MA. Born: New Ireland, (province unknown) Canada. Age: 33. Height: 5′10½″. Comp: dark. Eyes: blue. Hair: brown. Occup: farmer. Enlisted in Shelburne by Pliny Fisk, March 25, 1864; mustered April 6, 1864. Detached and detailed as a guard for the IX Corps cattle herd, May 4, 1864. Returned to the regiment for duty, Sept. 2, 1864. Absent for unknown reasons during the battles of Poplar Grove Church, Sept. 30 and Oct. 8, 1864. Probably with the regiment in some operations during the fall and winter of 1864–65. Absent on furlough from Feb. 23 until March 17, 1865. In action at Fort Stedman, March 25, 1865. Detailed on daily duty as a cook at 1st Division, IX Corps, Headquarters from May 2, 1865, until muster-out. Mustered out with the regiment at Delaney house, Washington, DC, July 30, 1865, and discharged in Readville, MA, Aug. 9, 1865, expiration of service.

68. **Marshall, James H.,** 1st lieutenant. Res. and/or credit: Hancock, MA. Born: New Albany, IN. Age: 21. Height: 5′10″. Comp: light. Eyes: blue. Hair: black. Occup: teacher. Enlisted as a private in Co. I in Hancock by H. H. Whitman, Jan. 27, 1864; mustered March 10, 1864; transferred to Co. E, March 3, 1864, under RSO 34, by order of Col. William F. Bartlett. Promoted 1st sergeant, March 10, 1864. In action at the Wilderness, May 6, 1864, Spotsylvania Court House, May 10, 12, and 18, 1864, North Anna River, May 24, 1864, Cold Harbor, June 3, 1864, Petersburg assaults, June 17 and 18, 1864, Petersburg Crater, July 30, 1864, Weldon Railroad, Aug. 19, 1864, and Poplar Grove Church, Sept. 30, 1864. Promoted 1st lieutenant, Oct. 7, 1864. In action again at Poplar Grove Church, Oct. 8, 1864. Mustered 1st lieuten-

ant, to date Jan. 3, 1865. Transferred to and in command of Co. F as 1st lieutenant, Jan. 9, 1865. Absent on furlough from March 5 until April 1, 1865. With the regiment on all marches and in all skirmishes and battles except Fort Stedman, March 25, 1865, and one of the 30 combat soldiers remaining of the regiment after Weldon Railroad, Aug. 19, 1865. Breveted captain of US Volunteers for gallant and meritorious service in the battles before Richmond, VA, by GO 65, AGO, War Dept., June 22, 1867, to date from March 29, 1865. On leave of absence in Massachusetts from June 6 until June 21, 1865. Mustered out with the regiment at Delaney house, Washington, DC, July 30, 1865, and discharged in Readville, MA, Aug. 9, 1865, expiration of service. Resided in Washington, DC, after the war and served as private secretary to Sen. Henry Laurens Dawes of Massachusetts and as clerk for the Senate Committee on Indian Affairs. Died in Washington, DC, Dec. 10, 1892, age 49. "Serving through all the battles of the war [with the exception of Fort Stedman], he was conspicuous for his courage and gallantry" (JA).

69. **Maynard, John P.**, private. Res. and/or credit: Dudley, MA. Born: Worcester, MA. Age: 38. Height: 5'7". Comp: fair. Eyes: gray. Hair: dark. Occup: laborer. Enlisted in Dudley by J. E. Edwards, Feb. 11, 1864; mustered Feb. 18, 1864. Killed in action at the Wilderness, May 6, 1864.

70. **Miles, Michael**, private. Res. and credit: Fitchburg, MA. Born: Ireland. Age: 40. Height: 5'4¼". Comp: fair. Eyes: gray. Hair: dark. Occup: papermaker. Enlisted in Fitchburg by William H. Vose, Jan. 5, 1864; mustered April 6, 1864. Absent sick or on detached duty from on or before May 6, 1864, until between May 12 and May 18, 1864. In action at Spotsylvania Court House, May 18, 1864, North Anna River, May 24, 1864, Cold Harbor, June 3, 1864, and Petersburg assaults, June 17 and 18, 1864; taken prisoner of war in action at the Petersburg Crater, July 30, 1864. Incarcerated in Libby Prison in Richmond, VA, Oct. 14, 1864. Transferred to the Confederate prison in Danville, VA, and died from disease there while a prisoner of war, but date not known.

71. **Nickerson, Albert M.**, corporal. Res. and/or credit: Sheffield, MA. Born: Walpole, MA. Age 21. Height: 5'10". Comp: dark. Eyes: gray. Hair: brown. Occup: machinist. Enlisted in Sheffield by E. E. Callender, Feb. 16, 1864; mustered Feb. 18, 1864. Promoted corporal, Feb. 18, 1864. Deserted from Camp Wool, April 3, 1864, but was arrested and returned April 11, 1864. Reduced to the ranks, and confined in the guardhouse in Camp Wool until April 17, 1864. Absent on detached duty from on or before May 6, 1864, until absent sick in an army general hospital from Aug. 20, 1864, until Oct. 26, 1864. Promoted corporal again on an unknown date in the fall of 1864. Placed under arrest with the regiment from Dec. 30, 1864, until Jan. 3, 1865 (reason unknown, but probably disobedience of orders or drinking). With the regiment in most operations during the fall and winter of 1864–65, and severely wounded in the arm in action at Fort Stedman, March 25, 1865 (arm surgically amputated). Absent wounded in an army general hospital until discharged the US service for disability from wounds, June 28, 1865, by order of the War Dept. Had previous service as a private in Co. E, 3rd Massachusetts Volunteer Cavalry, from Sept. 8, 1862, until discharged for disability, Jan. 18, 1864. Probably participated in the Port Hudson, LA, campaign with that regiment in 1863.

72. **Norwood, George**, private. Res. and/or credit: Greenfield, MA. Born: Enfield, CT. Age: 39. Height: 5'6½". Comp: dark. Eyes: blue. Hair: brown. Occup: shoemaker. Enlisted and mustered in Greenfield by Capt. Merriam, Dec. 20, 1864; joined the regiment as a recruit, Jan. 7, 1865. With the regiment in operations during the winter of 1865 and in action at Fort Stedman, March 25, 1865. Mustered out with the regiment at Delaney house, Washington, DC, July 30, 1865, and discharged in Readville, MA, Aug. 9, 1865, expiration of service.

73. **Nourse, Stephen H.**, private. Res. and/or credit: Fitchburg, MA. Born: Bolton, MA. Age: 26. Married. Height: 5'5". Comp: dark. Eyes: dark. Hair: black. Occup: carpenter. Enlisted in Fitchburg by William H. Vose, Jan. 4, 1864; mustered Feb. 18, 1864. Never in

combat. Detached and detailed as a stretcher bearer in the 1st Division, IX Corps, Ambulance Corps from April 27 until July 3, 1864. Absent sick in an army general hospital from July 12, 1864, until after Oct. 8, 1864, again from Feb. 6, 1865, until April 24, 1865, and again from after June 1, 1865, until discharged the US service for disability from "insanity" (MRD), Sept. 12, 1865, discharge to date July 30, 1865, by order of the War Dept. Died May 16, 1890, age 52.

74. **O'Brien, Darby**, private. Res. and credit: Fitchburg, MA. Born: Ireland. Age: 21. Married. Height: 5′8½″. Comp: dark. Eyes: dark. Hair: dark. Occup: laborer. Enlisted in Fitchburg by William H. Vose, Jan. 5, 1864; mustered Feb. 18, 1864. In action at the Wilderness, May 6, 1864, Spotsylvania Court House, May 10, 12, and 18, 1864, North Anna River, May 24, 1864, and Cold Harbor, June 3, 1864; slightly wounded in action in the Petersburg assault, June 17, 1864. Absent wounded in the 1st Division, IX Corps, Field Hospital at Petersburg until before July 5, 1864. Killed on picket duty at Petersburg, July 5, 1864. With the regiment on all marches and in all skirmishes and battles until killed.

75. **O'Donnell, Michael II**, private. Res: Bolton, MA. Credit: Fitchburg, MA. Born: Ireland. Age: 30. Married. Height: 5′8¾″. Comp: dark. Eyes: blue. Hair: dark. Occup: laborer. Enlisted in Fitchburg by William H. Vose, Jan. 5, 1864; mustered Feb. 18, 1864. Severely wounded in the arm in action at the Wilderness, May 6, 1864. Treated at a field hospital (arm probably surgically amputated) and sent to Emory US Army General Hospital in Washington, DC. Transferred to Dale US Army General Hospital in Worcester, MA, on an unknown date. Absent wounded in that hospital until discharged the US service on a Surgeons Certificate of Disability for wounds, July 10, 1865, by order of the War Dept. Had previous service as a private in Co. C, of the all-Irish 28th MVI, from Dec. 21, 1861, until discharged, April 14, 1863, for disability from wounds received at Chantilly, VA, Sept. 1, 1862. Probably participated on duty in North Carolina in 1862, and at 2nd Bull Run, Aug. 29, 1862. Died May 15, 1879, age 45.

76. **Parks, Frederick W.**, private. Res. and/or credit: Fitchburg, MA. Born: Westminster, MA. Age: 19. Height: 5′7″. Comp: dark. Eyes: dark. Hair: dark. Occup: porter. Enlisted in Fitchburg by William H. Vose, Jan. 16, 1864; mustered Feb. 18, 1864. Absent sick or on detached duty from on or before May 6, 1864, until between May 12 and May 18, 1864. In action at Spotsylvania Court House, May 18, 1864, North Anna River, May 24, 1864, Cold Harbor, June 3, 1864, and Petersburg assaults, June 17 and 18, 1864. Absent sick in an army general hospital from June 26 until Sept. 1, 1864. Wounded in action near Poplar Grove Church, Sept. 30, 1864. Absent wounded in an army general hospital until Feb. 10, 1865. Killed in action at Fort Stedman, March 25, 1865.

77. **Partland, Patrick**, private. Res. and/or credit: Fitchburg, MA. Born: Ireland. Age: 31. Height: 5′6″. Comp: light. Eyes: blue. Hair: sandy. Occup: laborer. Enlisted in Fitchburg by William H. Vose, March 10, 1864; mustered April 6, 1864. Absent sick or on detached duty from on or before May 6, 1864 until between May 12 and May 18, 1864. In action at Spotsylvania Court House, May 18, 1864, North Anna River, May 24, 1864, Cold Harbor, June 3, 1864, and Petersburg assaults, June 17 and 18, 1864. Absent sick in an army general hospital from June 29 until Oct. 19, 1864. With the regiment in operations during the fall and winter of 1864–65, and wounded in action at Fort Stedman, March 25, 1865. Absent wounded in an army general hospital until discharged the US service for disability from wounds, July 13, 1865, by order of the War Dept. Resided in Boston, MA, after the war.

78. **Peabody, William T.**, private. Res: Westminster, MA. Credit: Fitchburg, MA. Born: Pepperell, MA, Feb. 21, 1819. Age: 44. Married: Hannah Howe. Height: 5′8½″. Comp: dark. Eyes: gray. Hair: dark. Occup: chair maker. Enlisted in Fitchburg by William H. Vose, Jan. 18, 1864; mustered Feb. 18, 1864. Company cook and in the rear with the baggage wagons during the battle of the the Wilderness, May 6, 1864, when he was taken prisoner of war behind the lines near Brandy Station, VA, May 8, 1864. Incarcerated in the

Confederate prison camp in Andersonville, GA, May 29, 1864, where he died from starvation and chronic diarrhea, Sept. 1, 1864. Buried in grave, Sec. H., No. 7556, at Andersonville.

79. **Ploof, Louis F.,** private. Res. and/or credit: Easthampton, MA. Born: Schuylerville, NY. Age: 18. Height: 5'4". Comp: dark. Eyes: dark. Hair: black. Occup: farmer. Enlisted in Easthampton by S. D. Lyman, Feb. 20, 1864; mustered Feb. 18, 1864. Obtained a furlough from Camp Wool to go to Canada and deserted while absent, March 29, 1864. Never returned. Had previous service as a private in Co. K, 16th New York Volunteer Infantry (specifics unknown).

80. **Pyne, Edmund,** private. Res. and/or credit: Westfield, MA. Born: Waterford, Ireland. Age: 26. Married. Height: 5'10". Comp: fair. Eyes: light blue. Hair: light brown. Occup: laborer. Enlisted in Westfield by L. C. Gilbert, Feb. 12, 1864; mustered Feb. 18, 1864. Wounded in the left arm in action at the Wilderness, May 6, 1864. Absent wounded in a field hospital in Fredericksburg, VA, until transferred to Emory US Army General Hospital in Washington, DC, May 17, 1864. Absent in that hospital until Aug. 13, 1864. Wounded again in action at Weldon Railroad, Aug. 19, 1864. Absent wounded in an army general hospital until Oct. 14, 1864. Taken prisoner of war in action at Fort Stedman, March 25, 1865. Paroled and exchanged from from Libby Prison in Richmond, VA, April 1, 1865, and returned to the regiment for duty from the Camp of Parole in Annapolis, MD, May 11, 1865. Mustered out with the regiment at Delaney house, Washington, DC, July 30, 1865, and discharged in Readville, MA, Aug. 9, 1865, expiration of service.

81. **Raymond, Oren T.,** private. Res: Westminster, MA. Born and credit: Fitchburg, MA. Age: 18. Height: 5'6". Comp: light. Eyes: gray. Hair: brown. Occup: farmer. Enlisted in Fitchburg by William H. Vose, Feb. 5, 1864; mustered Feb. 18, 1864. Killed in action at the Wilderness, May 6, 1864.

82. **Richards, James,** private. Res. and/or credit: Lee, MA. Born: Byngham, MA. Age: 18. Height: 5'7". Comp: dark. Eyes: gray. Hair: black. Occup: farmer. Enlisted in Lee by William S. Merrill, Feb. 10, 1864; mustered Feb. 18, 1864. Severely wounded and taken prisoner of war in action at the Wilderness, May 6, 1864. Died from wounds in a Confederate field hospital at Parker's Store, VA, June 1, 1864.

83. **Roche, Redmond,** private. Res. and/or credit: Dudley, MA. Born: Ireland. Age: 31. Married. Height: 5'8". Comp: fair. Eyes: hazel. Hair: brown. Occup: weaver. Enlisted in Dudley by J. E. Edwards, Feb. 1, 1864; mustered Feb. 18, 1864. Absent on detached duty from on or before May 6, 1864, until absent sick in an army general hospital from Aug. 21, 1864. Transferred to the 23rd Co., 2nd Battln., VRC from that hospital, April 27, 1865. Discharged the US service, Aug. 12, 1865, by order of the War Dept., expiration of service.

84. **Ryan, Charles,** private. Res: North Adams, MA. Credit: Adams, MA. Born: Canada. Age: 18. Single. Height: 5'5½". Comp: dark. Eyes: blue. Hair: brown. Occup: shoemaker. Enlisted in Adams by S. Johnson, Feb. 13, 1864; mustered Feb. 18, 1864. In action at the Wilderness, May 6, 1864, and Spotsylvania Court House, May 10, 1864; taken prisoner of war in action there, May 12, 1864. Paroled and exchanged from an unknown Confederate prison, Nov. 24, 1864. Absent sick in an army general hospital until April 1, 1865. Probably received extra pay for having been a prisoner. Detached and detailed on guard duty in Alexandria, VA, from May 6, 1865 until after June 1, 1865. Mustered out with the regiment at Delaney house, Washington, DC, July 30, 1865, and discharged in Readville, MA, Aug. 9, 1865, expiration of service.

85. **Ryan, Martin,** private. Res. and credit: Fitchburg, MA. Born: Ireland. Age: 29. Married. Height: 5'6½". Comp: light. Eyes: blue. Hair: sandy. Occup: laborer. Enlisted in Fitchburg by William H. Vose, Jan. 9, 1864;

mustered Feb. 18, 1864. Absent sick or on detached duty from on or before May 6, 1864, until between May 12 and May 18, 1864. In action at Spotsylvania Court House, May 18, 1864, North Anna River, May 24, 1864, and Cold Harbor, June 3, 1864; missing in action during the Petersburg assault, June 17, 1864. Never accounted for and presumed killed.

86. **Sabin, George Frederick,** sergeant. Res: Bolton, MA. Credit: Fitchburg, MA. Born: Fitzwilliam, NH. Age: 20. Height: 6'1". Comp: light. Eyes: gray. Hair: brown. Occup: clerk. Enlisted in Fitchburg by Lt. Hitchcock, Jan. 14, 1864; mustered Feb. 18, 1864. Promoted sergeant, Feb. 18, 1864. Left behind sick in an army general hospital in New York City during the march to the front, April 19, 1864. Returned to the regiment for duty, June 20, 1864. Wounded by gunshot through the calf of his leg as acting sergeant major in action at the Petersburg Crater, July 30, 1864. Absent wounded in an army general hospital until transferred to Co. B, 1st Battln., 19th Regiment, VRC, Feb. 28, 1865, by order of the provost marshal general. Discharged the US service, Aug. 3, 1865, by order of the War Dept., expiration of service. Had previous service as a private in Co. B, 53rd MVI, from Aug. 25, 1862, until mustered out, Sept. 2, 1863. Participated in the Port Hudson, LA, campaign with that regiment in 1863. Resided in Fitchburg, MA, after the war.

87. **Sawyer, Edgar F.,** private. Res. and/or credit: Fitchburg, MA. Born: Northboro, MA. Age: 26. Height: 5'5½". Comp: dark. Eyes: blue. Hair: dark. Occup: painter. Enlisted in Fitchburg by William H. Vose, Jan. 1, 1864; mustered Feb. 18, 1864. Detached and detailed as a guard for the IX Corps cattle herd, May 4, 1864. Absent sick in an army general hospital from Aug. 27, 1864, until Feb. 1, 1865. In action at Fort Stedman, March 25, 1865. Mustered out with the regiment at Delaney house, Washington, DC, July 30, 1865, and discharged in Readville, MA, Aug. 9, 1865, expiration of service. Died May 14, 1894, age 56.

88. **Sheehan, Redmond,** private. Res: Bolton, MA. Born and credit: Worcester, MA. Age:

21. Height: 5'6". Comp: light. Eyes: gray. Hair: dark. Occup: machinist. Enlisted in Worcester by Capt. Henry C. Ward, Feb. 1, 1864; mustered Feb. 18, 1864. Deserted on the march from Annapolis, MD, to Washington, DC, April 23, 1864. Never returned. Charged by the US government $2.89 for cap bugle (infantry insignia), shelter tent half stolen, and $27.28 for rifle, equipment, uniform, canteen, and haversack stolen. "Obtained bounty and deserted" (JA). Had previous service as a private in Co. I, 50th MVI, from Aug. 13, 1862, until mustered out, Aug. 24, 1863. Participated in the Port Hudson, LA, campaign with that regiment in 1863.

89. **Sherman, Edwin P.,** private. Res. and/or credit: Adams, MA. Born: Williamstown, MA. Age: 20. Height: 5'7". Comp: sandy. Eyes: blue. Hair: brown. Occup: shoemaker. Enlisted in Adams by S. Johnson, March 10, 1864; mustered April 6, 1864. Detached and detailed as a guard for the IX Corps cattle herd, May 4, 1864. Absent sick in an army general hospital from June 3, 1864, until April 27, 1865. Never in combat. Detached and detailed for guard duty in Alexandria, VA, from May 6, 1865, until after June 1, 1865; Mustered out with the regiment at Delaney house, Washington, DC, July 30, 1865, and discharged in Readville, MA, Aug. 9, 1865, expiration of service.

90. **Simmons, Wesley T.,** private. Res: Williamstown, MA. Credit: Washington, MA. Born: Hinsdale, MA. Age: 18. Height: 5'7". Comp: dark. Eyes: blue. Hair: brown. Occup: farmer. Enlisted in Washington, MA, by Charles Crosier, Feb. 8, 1864; mustered Feb. 18, 1864. Detached and detailed as a guard for the IX Corps cattle herd, May 4, 1864. Returned to the regiment for duty, Sept. 2, 1864. In action at Poplar Grove Church, Sept. 30 and Oct. 8, 1864, in other operations of the regiment during the fall and winter of 1864–65, and in action at Fort Stedman, March 25, 1865. Absent sick in the 1st Division, IX Corps, Field Hospital from April 7, 1864, until April 18, 1865. Mustered out with the regiment at Delaney house, Washington, DC, July 30, 1865, and discharged in Readville, MA, Aug. 9, 1865, expiration of service.

91. **Skye, William**, private. Res. and credit: Fitchburg, MA. Born: Canada. Age: 29. Married: Rhoda. Height: 5′1″. Comp: light. Eyes: blue. Hair: red. Occup: currier. Enlisted in Fitchburg by William H. Vose, Jan. 1, 1864; mustered Feb. 18, 1864. Received a flesh wound in his right leg in action at the Wilderness, May 6, 1864. Treated in a field hospital in Fredericksburg, VA, and transferred to Armory Square US Army General Hospital in Washington, DC, where he died from his wounds (almost certainly as the result of gangrene or blood poisoning), June 6, 1864.

92. **Southey, John**, sergeant. Res. and/or credit: Fitchburg, MA. Born: England. Age: 22. Single. Height: 5′8½″. Comp: dark. Eyes: gray. Hair: dark. Occup: farmer. Enlisted in Fitchburg by William H. Vose, Jan. 5, 1864; mustered Feb. 18, 1864. Promoted sergeant, Feb. 18, 1864. In action at the Wilderness, May 6, 1864, and one of the 34 enlisted men who remained with the colors during that battle. In action at Spotsylvania Court House, May 10, 12, and 18, 1864, North Anna River, May 24, 1864, and Cold Harbor, June 3, 1864; wounded in action in the Petersburg assault, June 17, 1864. With the regiment on all marches and in all skirmishes and battles until wounded. Absent wounded in an army general hospital until transferred to Co. G, 7th Regiment, VRC, on an unknown date. Promoted 1st sergeant in the VRC, date unknown. Discharged the US service, July 28, 1865, by order of the War Dept., expiration of service.

93. **Southwick, Francis S.**, corporal. Res: Bolton, MA. Credit: Leicester, MA. Born: Charlestown, MA. Age: 21. Height: 5′6″. Comp: light. Eyes: blue. Hair: brown. Occup: bootmaker. Enlisted in Leicester by Silas Gleason, Feb. 10, 1864; mustered Feb. 18, 1864. Promoted corporal, Feb. 18, 1864. Left behind sick in an army general hospital in Alexandria, VA, while the regiment was on the march to the front, April 27, 1864. Returned to the regiment for duty, Aug. 5, 1864, and sent sick to the 1st Division, IX Corps, Field Hospital the same day. Returned to the regiment for duty, Sept. 9, 1864. Absent sick in Hough US Army General Hospital in Alex-

andria, VA, from Sept. 28, 1864, until discharged the US service, June 27, 1865, under GO 77, par. 6, AGO, War Dept., dated June 10, 1865. Had previous service as a private in Co. C, 21st MVI, from Aug 13, 1861, until discharged, March 6, 1863, in Washington, DC, for disability from wounds received in action with that regiment at Antietam, Sept 17, 1862. "Never in Battle [with the 57th]. Never did any duty at the front" (CR).

94. **Sterner, Matthew**, private. Res. and/or credit: Easthampton, MA. Born: Franklin, NY. Age: 24. Height: 5′10½″. Comp: light. Eyes: gray. Hair: brown. Occup: farmer. Enlisted in Easthampton by S. D. Lyman, Jan. 26, 1864; mustered Feb 18, 1864. Never in combat. Left behind sick in the hospital in Camp Wool when the regiment departed for the front, April 18, 1864, and discharged the US service from an army general hospital in New York City, on a Surgeons Certificate of Disability, Aug. 25, 1864, by order of Maj. Gen. John A. Dix, War Dept.

95. **Stevens, Alden W.**, private. Res. and/or credit: Fitchburg, MA. Born: Wendall, MA. Age: 21. Height: 5′4½″. Comp: light. Eyes: gray. Hair: brown. Occup: clerk. Enlisted in Fitchburg by William H. Vose, Feb. 2, 1864; mustered Feb. 18, 1864. In action at the Wilderness, May 6, 1864, and Spotsylvania Court House, May 10, 1864; wounded in the right hand in action there, May 12, 1864. Treated at a field hospital in Fredericksburg, VA, and sent to an army general hospital until transferred to the 39th Co., 2nd Battln., VRC, Aug. 26, 1864. Discharged the US service, Aug. 23, 1865, by order of the War Dept., expiration of service. Resided at the Soldiers Home in Togus, ME, after the war.

96. **Stock, Henry**, private. Res. and/or credit: Hancock, MA. Born: Germany. Age: 22. Height: 5′10½″. Comp: light. Eyes: dark. Hair: black. Occup: farmer. Enlisted in Hancock by H. H. Whitman, March 25, 1864; mustered April 6, 1864. Detached and detailed as a guard for the IX Corps cattle herd, May 4, 1864. Returned to the regiment for duty Sept. 2, 1864. Absent sick in an army general hospital from Sept. 28, 1864, until

May 3, 1865. Never in combat. Detached and detailed on guard duty in Alexandria, VA, in June 1865 until muster-out. Mustered out with the regiment at Delaney house, Washington, DC, July 30, 1865, and discharged in Readville, MA, Aug. 9, 1865, expiration of service.

97. **Sullivan, John**, private. Res. and/or credit: Worcester, MA. Born: Ireland. Age: 29. Married. Height: 5'6". Comp: dark. Eyes: brown. Hair: dark. Occup: blacksmith. Enlisted in Worcester by Capt. Henry C. Ward, Jan. 29, 1864; mustered Feb. 18, 1864. Absent sick or on detached duty from on or before May 6, 1864, until between Aug. 19 and Sept. 30, 1864. In action at Poplar Grove Church, Sept. 30 and Oct. 8, 1864. "1 gun & equipment complete lost by John Sullivan during the skirmish—no blame on him" (company journal entry for Oct. 9, 1864, referring to the battle on Oct. 8). On furlough in Worcester, MA, from Jan. 29 until Feb. 18, 1865. With the regiment in operations during the fall and winter of 1864–65, and in action at Fort Stedman, March 25, 1865. Mustered out with the regiment at Delaney house, Washington, DC, July 30, 1865, and discharged in Readville, MA, Aug. 9, 1865, expiration of service. Died in 1894, age 59.

98. **Sweet, Daniel J.**, private. Res. and/or credit: Williamstown, MA. Born: unknown. Age: 18. No description available. Occup: laborer. Enlisted in Williamstown by a selectman, Jan. 25, 1864; mustered Feb. 18, 1864. Deserted from Camp Wool, April 11, 1864. Arrested on an unknown date in the summer of 1864. Court-martialed and very likely sentenced to be shot. Pardoned for desertion by order of President Lincoln and dishonorably discharged the US service in Washington, DC, Oct. 3, 1864, by order of the War Dept.

99. **Twiss, James P.**, private. Res. and/or credit: Longmeadow, MA. Born: Enfield, CT. Age: 31. Height: 5'10". Comp: dark. Eyes: brown. Hair: brown. Occup: farmer. Enlisted in Longmeadow by S. G. Cotten, Feb. 3, 1864; mustered Feb. 18, 1864. Never in combat. Detached and detailed as a guard for the IX Corps cattle herd, May 4, 1864. Absent

sick from an unknown date in Harewood US Army General Hospital in Washington, DC, where he died from typhoid fever, Aug. 2, 1864.

100. **Vickery, Charles W.**, sergeant. Res. and/or credit: Hancock, MA. Born: Nassau, NY. Age: 18. Height: 5'10½". Comp: light. Eyes: black. Hair: brown. Occup: farmer. Enlisted in Hancock by H. H. Whitman, March 25, 1864; mustered April 6, 1864. In action at the Wilderness, May 6, 1864, Spotsylvania Court House, May 10, 12, and 18, 1864, North Anna River, May 24, 1864, Cold Harbor, June 3, 1864, and Petersburg assaults, June 17 and 18, 1864. Absent sick in an army general hospital from June 26 until Dec. 8, 1864. With the regiment on all marches and in all skirmishes and battles until becoming ill. Promoted corporal, March 1, 1865. In action at Fort Stedman, March 25, 1865. Promoted sergeant, May 1, 1865, under RSO 42, by order of Lt. Col. Julius M. Tucker. Detached and detailed as a provost guard at 3rd Brigade, 1st Division, IX Corps, Headquarters in Tennallytown, DC, June 30, 1865, under 3rd Brigade SO 120, dated June 30, 1865, until muster-out. Mustered out with the regiment at Delaney house, Washington, DC, July 30, 1865, and discharged in Readville, MA, Aug. 9, 1865, expiration of service.

101. **Watts, George**, private. Res. and/or credit: Fitchburg, MA. Born: England. Age: 29. Single. Height: 5'5". Comp: dark. Eyes: gray. Hair: black. Occup: carpenter. Enlisted in Fitchburg by William H. Vose, Jan. 18, 1864; mustered Feb. 18, 1864. Absent sick from on or before May 6, 1864, and died from typhoid fever in Depot Field Hospital at City Point, Petersburg, July 22, 1864. "Military character good" (CR).

102. **Wetherbee, Warren S.**, musician. Res. and/or credit: Fitchburg, MA. Born: Rutland, MA. Age: 18. Height: 5'7¾". Comp: light. Eyes: gray. Hair: brown. Occup: machinist. Enlisted in Fitchburg by William H. Vose, Jan. 5, 1864; mustered Feb. 18, 1864. Company fifer. Probably served as a nurse, stretcher bearer, and/or hospital orderly. Absent sick in an army general hospital from

Dec. 15, 1864, until Feb. 10, 1865. Present at the battle of Fort Stedman, March 25, 1865, but the extent of his participation is not known. Mustered out with the regiment at Delaney house, Washington, DC, July 30, 1865, and discharged in Readville, MA, Aug. 9, 1865, expiration of service. Resided in Fitchburg, MA, after the war.

103. **Wilkins, Aaron,** corporal. Res. and credit: Fitchburg, MA. Born: England. Age: 42. Married. Height: 5'9". Comp: light. Eyes: blue. Hair: brown. Occup: machinist. Enlisted in Fitchburg by William H. Vose, Jan. 5, 1864; mustered Feb. 18, 1864. Promoted corporal, Feb. 18, 1864. Severely wounded in the right arm in action at the Wilderness, May 6, 1864. Absent wounded in an army general hospital until transferred to the 38th Co., 2nd Battln., VRC, March 4, 1864. Discharged the US service for disability from wounds, April 7, 1865, by order of the War

Dept. Had been drafted in the summer draft of 1863 in Fitchburg, but exempted for being over 35 years old and married. Resided in Fitchburg, MA, after the war, and died there, Aug. 5, 1887, age 65.

104. **Wilkins, Henry A.,** private. Res. and/or credit: Fitchburg, MA. Born: Pepperell, MA. Age: 18. Height: 5'7½". Comp: dark. Eyes: blue. Hair: black. Occup: baker. Enlisted in Fitchburg by William H. Vose, Jan. 5, 1865; mustered Feb. 18, 1864. Wounded in the left thigh and back in action at the Wilderness, May 6, 1864. Treated in a field hospital in Fredericksburg, VA, and sent to an army general hospital until transferred to Co. G, 10th Regiment, VRC, Oct. 4, 1864, by order of the provost marshal general. Discharged the US service, July 26, 1865, by order of the War Dept., expiration of service. Died before 1896, but date not known.

ROSTER AND DESCRIPTIVE LIST OF COMPANY G

Company G was the ninth company to be mustered into United States service and it was mustered on March 10, 1864, under SO 279, from the AGO, Boston, MA, by 1st Lt. Robert P. McKibben, 4th US Regular Infantry, except those men mustered after March 10, 1864, who were mustered by 2nd Lt. Daniel Madden, 6th United States Regular Cavalry. It was mustered out by Capt. Sylvester Keyser, 2nd Michigan Volunteer Infantry, ACM, 1st Division, IX Corps. This company's records, like those of Company F, also contain comments concerning many of its members' military behavior, which were written into the original descriptive lists in the spring of 1865. They offer an interesting glimpse into the character of many of Company G's soldiers, at least from the writer's often passionate perspective. As with Company F, a lack of annotation is also revealing.

1. **Adams, Charles O.,** private. Res. and/or credit: New Braintree, MA. Born: Spencer, MA. Age: 18. Height: 5'3". Comp: light. Eyes: blue. Hair: brown. Occup: operative. Enlisted in New Braintree by M. Pollard, Feb, 26, 1864; mustered March 10, 1864. Severely wounded in the upper right arm in action at the Wilderness, May 6, 1864. Taken to the 1st Division, IX Corps, Field Hospital where his right arm was surgically amputated by the flap method, May 8, 1864, by Surgeon D. W. Maull, 1st Delaware Volunteer Infan-

try. Discharged and pensioned from the US service on a Surgeons Certificate of Disability for wounds from Central Park US Army General Hospital in New York City, Jan. 14, 1865, by order of Maj. Gen. John A. Dix, War Dept. "Was a Brave and Faithful Soldier" (CR).

2. **Adams, George,** 1st lieutenant. Res. and/or credit: Boston, MA. Born: County Louth, Ireland. Age: 25. Height: 5'10". Comp: dark. Eyes: blue. Hair: dark. Occup: peddler. En-

listed in Boston by N. C. Nash, Feb. 26, 1864; mustered March 10, 1864. Promoted sergeant, March 30, 1864. Wounded twice in action at the Wilderness, May 6, 1864. Absent wounded in an Army general hospital until between Oct. 8 and Dec. 31, 1864. Promoted 1st sergeant, Dec. 31, 1864. Absent sick or wounded (possibly wounded on the picket line or in the trenches at Petersburg) in the 1st Division, IX Corps, Field Hospital at Petersburg from after Dec. 31, 1864, until Feb. 10, 1865. Wounded in action (may have received up to 13 wounds) at Fort Stedman, March 25, 1865, and cited twice for bravery: "First Sergeant George Adams, Company G, conspicuous bravery on skirmish line, receiving his fifteenth wound, continuing with regiment after being wounded" (JMT), and "First Sergeant George Adams, Company G, wounded for the fifteenth time" (GPR). Absent wounded in an army general hospital from March 25 until May 17, 1865. Commissioned 1st lieutenant, June 12, 1865; mustered 1st lieutenant, June 26, 1865. Mustered out with the regiment at Delaney house, Washington, DC, July 30, 1865, and discharged in Readville, MA Aug. 9, 1865, expiration of service. "Efficient, Brave, Faithful" (CR).

3. **Allen, Alfred M.**, corporal. Res. and credit: Worcester, MA. Born: Worcester, MA. Age: 19. Height: 5'4". Comp: light. Eyes: gray. Hair: light. Occup: candy maker. Enlisted in Worcester by Capt. Henry C. Ward, Feb. 15, 1864; mustered March 10, 1864. Confined in the guardhouse in Camp Wool for an unknown reason (probably disobedience of orders) from March 11 until March 15, 1864. Not in action at the Wilderness, May 6, 1864, but was present, and may have been detached as an orderly or knapsack guard. In action at Spotsylvania Court House, May 18, 1864, North Anna River, May 24, 1864, Cold Harbor, June 3, 1864, Petersburg assaults, June 17 and 18, 1864, Petersburg Crater, July 30, 1864, Weldon Railroad, Aug. 19, 1864, and Poplar Grove Church, Sept. 30, 1864; wounded in action near Poplar Grove Church, Oct. 8, 1864. With the regiment on all marches and in all skirmishes and battles between May 18 and Oct 8, 1864, and one of

the 30 combat soldiers remaining of the regiment after Weldon Railroad, Aug. 19, 1864. Absent wounded in an army general hospital until before Feb. 16, 1865. Promoted corporal, Feb. 16, 1865, under RSO 16, by order of Lt. Col. Julius M. Tucker. In action at Fort Stedman, March 25, 1865. Detached and detailed to the quartermaster's dept. in Washington, DC, from May 31, 1865, until musterout. Mustered out with the regiment at Delaney house, Washington, DC, July 30, 1865, and discharged in Readville, MA, Aug. 9, 1865, expiration of service. Had previous service as a private in Co. H, 177th New York Volunteer Infantry (specifics unknown).

4. **Barton, Charles H.**, private. Res: Hadley, MA. Credit: Northampton, MA. Born: Leverette, MA. Age: 37. Height: 5'9". Comp: dark. Eyes: hazel. Hair: brown. Occup: butcher. Enlisted in Northampton by J. S. Bill, Feb. 20, 1864; mustered April 6, 1864. Deserted at Rappahannock Station, VA, May 4, 1864. Arrested at Dauphin, PA, Nov. 9, 1864, and "tried by court martial at Alexandria, VA, Jan. 19, 1865. Sentenced to lose all pay and allowances due and $10.00 per month of his pay for eighteen months and to make good all the time lost by desertion" (CR). Also charged by the US government $3.42 for "camp and garrison" (CR) equipment stolen. Returned to the regiment for duty, Feb. 6, 1865. Taken prisoner of war in action at Fort Stedman, March 25, 1865. Paroled from Libby Prison, Richmond, VA, March 29, 1865, and exchanged, April 2, 1865. Returned to the regiment for duty from the Camp of Parole in Annapolis, MD, May 11, 1865. Mustered out with the regiment at Delaney house, Washington, DC, July 30, 1865, and discharged in Readville, MA, Aug. 9, 1865, expiration of service.

5. **Bovia, Lewis**, private. Res: West Brookfield, MA. Credit: Brookfield, MA. Born: Southboro, MA. Age: 18. Height: 5'6½". Comp: fair. Eyes: black. Hair: dark. Occup: laborer. Enlisted in Brookfield by H. Brown, Feb. 23, 1864; mustered March 10, 1864. Deserted from Camp Wool, April 5, 1864, but was arrested, returned, and confined in the guardhouse in Camp Wool, April 15 and 16,

1864. Never in combat. Absent sick in an army general hospital in Washington, DC, from on or before May 6, 1864, where he died from disease, July 20, 1865.

6. **Boulette, Fortuna,** private. Res. and/or credit: Spencer, MA. Born: province of Quebec, Canada. Age: 21. Height: 5′9″. Comp: fair. Eyes: blue. Hair: brown. Occup: bootmaker. Enlisted in Spencer by L. Hill, March 7, 1864; mustered March 10, 1864. Wounded in action and taken prisoner of war at the Wilderness, May 6, 1864. Paroled and exchanged from an unknown Confederate prison, March 5, 1865, and listed in the company journal as "returned to duty," May 22, 1865. However, he evidently was unfit for service and was discharged for disability from wounds on a Surgeons Certificate of Disability from Jarvis US Army General Hospital in Baltimore, MD, May 30, 1865. Probably received extra pay for having been a prisoner of war. Resided in Spencer, MA, for a time after the war.

7. **Bourne, William S.,** private. Res. and/or credit: Pittsfield, MA. Born: Wallingford, NY. Age: 18. Height: 5′5″. Comp: light. Eyes: blue. Hair: light. Occup: farmer. Enlisted in Pittsfield by Joseph Tucker, Feb. 12, 1864; mustered March 10, 1864. Killed in action at the Wilderness, May 6, 1864. "Good Soldier" (CR).

8. **Brown, Charles M.,** private. Res. and/or credit: Winchendon, MA. Born: Reading, VT. Age: 18. Height: 5′7½″. Comp: light. Eyes: blue. Hair: light. Occup: farmer. Enlisted in Winchendon by B. Ellis, Feb. 22, 1864; mustered March 10, 1864. Deserted near Germanna Ford on the march to the Wilderness, May 4, 1864. Charged by the US government $23.85 for rifle and equipment stolen and $3.42 for "camp and garrison" (CR) equipment stolen. Arrested and returned to the regiment several days later and was slightly wounded in action at Spotsylvania Court House about May 12, 1864. Treated at a field hospital in Fredericksburg, VA, and discharged to rejoin his company at the front. Killed by Confederate guerrillas while return-

ing to the regiment at Spotsylvania, May 14, 1864.

9. **Bullard, Charles M.,** private. Res. and/or credit: Worcester, MA. Born: Westboro, MA. Age: 42. Height: 5′11″. Comp: dark. Eyes: black. Hair: black. Occup: carpenter. Enlisted in Worcester by Capt. Henry C. Ward, Feb. 24, 1864; mustered March 10, 1864. Detached and detailed to the 1st Division, IX Corps, Ambulance Corps from April 27, 1864, until after June 20, 1865. Never in combat. Mustered out with the regiment at Delaney house, Washington, DC, July 30, 1865, and discharged in Readville, MA, Aug. 9, 1865, expiration of service. Resided in Worcester, MA, after the war.

10. **Cadigan, Michael,** private. Res. and/or credit: Worcester, MA. Born: Ireland. Age: 19. Height: 5′7½″. Comp: light. Eyes: gray. Hair: light. Occup: laborer. Enlisted in Co. K in Worcester by Col. John W. Kimball, March 22, 1864; mustered April 6, 1864; transferred to Co. G by his own request, April 14, 1864, under RSO 39, by order of Col. William F. Bartlett, and joined the company, April 16, 1864. In action at the Wilderness, May 6, 1864, Spotsylvania Court House, May 10, 12, and 18, 1864, North Anna River, May 24, 1864, Cold Harbor, June 3, 1864, and Petersburg assaults, June 17 and 18, 1864; severely wounded in the right shoulder in action at the Petersburg Crater, July 30, 1864. Transported by steamer to Washington, DC, where he underwent surgery, Aug. 4, 1864, for the "excision for the head and three inches of the shaft of humerus by Surgeon A. F. Sheldon, U.S.V." because of the "comminution of surgical neck of right humerus by a musket ball, which also fractured fifth and sixth ribs, and was found post-mortem in the abdomen" (OMR). Died from his wounds in an army general hospital in Washington, DC, Aug. 6, 1864. With the regiment on all marches and in all skirmishes and battles until wounded. "Good Soldier" (CR).

11. **Champney, Augustus,** private. Res. and/or credit: Adams, MA. Born: Hoosick, NY. Age: 18. Height: 5′4″. Comp: light. Eyes:

gray. Hair: light. Occup: molder. Enlisted in Adams by S. Johnson, March 7, 1864; mustered March 10, 1864. In action at the Wilderness, May 6, 1864, and Spotsylvania Court House, May 10, 1864; wounded in action there, May 12, 1864. Treated in a field hospital in Fredericksburg, VA, and returned to the regiment for duty between May 24 and June 3, 1864. In action at Cold Harbor, June 3, 1864, and Petersburg assaults, June 17 and 18, 1864; taken prisoner of war at the Petersburg Crater, July 30, 1864. Incarcerated in Libby Prison in Richmond, VA, where he died from his wounds, Aug. 6, 1864. "Noble Boy" (CR).

12. **Charlesworth, David**, private. Res. and/or credit: Holyoke, MA. Born: England. Age: 35. Height: 5'6½". Comp: light. Eyes: blue. Hair: light. Occup: spinner. Enlisted in Holyoke by Lt. Henry B. Fiske, March 4, 1864; mustered March 10, 1864. In action at the Wilderness, May 6, 1864, Spotsylvania Court House, May 10, 12, and 18, 1864, North Anna River, May 24, 1864, and Cold Harbor, June 3, 1864; wounded in action in the Petersburg assault, June 17, 1864. With the regiment on all marches and in all skirmishes and battles until wounded. Absent wounded in an army general hospital in Philadelphia, PA, until he deserted from there, Jan. 6, 1865. Returned to the regiment for duty after March 25, 1865 (circumstances of his return are unknown, but there are no records indicating that he was court-martialed or placed in confinement for desertion; he probably surrendered under President Lincoln's proclamation of amnesty). Absent sick again in an army general hospital from an unknown date in the spring of 1865 until discharged the US service for disability, July 12, 1865, by order of the War Dept. "Splendid Soldier" (CR).

13. **Cleveland, William E.**, private. Res. and credit: Westfield, MA. Born: Westfield, MA. Age: 23. Height: 5'6". Comp: dark. Eyes: gray. Hair: brown. Occup: tinsmith. Enlisted in Westfield by Lt. George S. Green, Feb. 27, 1864; mustered March 10, 1864. In action at the Wilderness, May 6, 1864, Spotsylvania Court House, May 10, 12, and 18, 1864, and North Anna River, May 24, 1864. Deserted

between May 24 and June 3, 1864. $36.00 was paid by the regiment for his arrest in Hartford, CT, on an unknown date, probably in Jan. 1865. "Tried by gen. court martial at Headquarters of Military Gov., Alexandria, VA, Feb. 6, 1865 and by SO 109 sentenced to lose all pay and allowances then due and to forfit $10.00 per month of his monthly pay for the period of two months and make good the time lost by absence without leave" (CR). Returned to the regiment for duty, March 12, 1865. In action and taken prisoner of war at Fort Stedman, March 25, 1865. Paroled March 29, 1865, and exchanged from Libby Prison, Richmond, VA, April 4, 1865. Discharged the US service for disability from the Camp of Parole in Annapolis, MD, June 2, 1865, under GO 77, par. 6, AGO, War Dept. "Good Soldier" (CR).

14. **Connell, Charles**, private. Res. and/or credit: Holyoke, MA. Born: Ireland. Age: 26. Height: 5'5½". Comp: light. Eyes: blue. Hair: dark. Occup: laborer. Enlisted in Holyoke by Lt. Henry B. Fiske, March 7, 1864; mustered March 10, 1864. In action at the Wilderness, May 6, 1864, Spotsylvania Court House, May 10, 12, and 18, 1864, North Anna River, May 24, 1864, Cold Harbor, June 3, 1864, and Petersburg assault, June 17, 1864; wounded in action at the Petersburg Crater, July 30, 1864. Absent wounded in an army general hospital until March 27, 1865. Returned to the 1st Division, IX Corps, Field Hospital at Petersburg the next day, March 28, 1865. Returned to the regiment for duty after June 20, 1865. With the regiment on all marches and in all skirmishes and battles until wounded. Mustered out with the regiment at Delaney house, Washington, DC, July 30, 1865, and discharged in Readville, MA, Aug. 9, 1865, expiration of service. "Brave Soldier" (CR).

15. **Conner, Humphrey**, private. Res: Holyoke, MA. Credit: Fitchburg, MA. Born: Ireland. Age: 24. Height: 5'6". Comp: light. Eyes: blue. Hair: light. Occup: laborer. Enlisted in Fitchburg by William H. Vose, Feb. 24, 1864; mustered March 10, 1864. Absent sick or on detached duty from on or before

May 6, 1864, until between May 24 and June 2, 1864. In action at Cold Harbor, June 3, 1864, and Petersburg assaults, June 17 and 18, 1864; wounded in action at the Petersburg Crater, July 30, 1864. Absent wounded in an army general hospital until between Oct. 8, 1864, and March 25, 1865. In action and taken prisoner of war at Fort Stedman, March 25, 1865. Paroled March 31, 1865, and exchanged from Libby Prison in Richmond, VA, April 2, 1865. Never returned to the regiment and discharged the US service for disability, June 29, 1865, by order of the War Dept. "Good Soldier" (CR).

16. **Cooley, Francis F.**, private. Res. and/or credit: Sutton, MA. Born: Springfield, MA. Age: 26. Height: 5'1". Comp: light. Eyes: blue. Hair: light. Occup: teamster. Enlisted in Sutton by Lt. Hitchcock, Feb. 13, 1864; mustered March 10, 1864. Wounded in action at the Wilderness, May 6, 1864. Absent wounded in an army general hospital until after June 20, 1865. Mustered out with the regiment at Delaney house, Washington, DC, July 30, 1865, and discharged in Readville, MA, Aug. 9, 1865, expiration of service. Resided in Belchertown, MA, after the war. "Good Soldier" (CR).

17. **Covell, Augustus L.**, private. Res. and/or credit: Gardner, MA. Born: Webster, MA. Age: 20. Height: 5'2¾". Comp: light. Eyes: blue. Hair: brown. Occup: chair maker. Enlisted in Gardner by S. W. Bancroft, Feb. 19, 1864; mustered March 10, 1864. Wounded in action and taken prisoner of war at the Wilderness, May 6, 1864. Paroled and exchanged from an unknown Confederate prison, Sept. 1, 1864, and died from wounds and disease in the army general hospital in the Camp of Parole in Annapolis, MD, Sept. 14, 1864. "Good Soldier" (CR).

18. **Covell, John B.**, private. Res. and/or credit: Gardner, MA. Born: Webster, MA. Age: 18. Height: 5'5". Comp: light. Eyes: blue. Hair: brown. Occup: chair maker. Enlisted in Gardner by S. W. Bancroft, Feb. 19, 1864; mustered March 10, 1864. Wounded in action and taken prisoner of war at the Wilderness, May 6, 1864. Paroled and exchanged

from an unknown Confederate prison, Sept. 1, 1864, and discharged the US service for disability from wounds from an army general hospital, March 30, 1865, by order of the War Dept. Resided in Cleveland, OH, after the war and died there in 1924, age 78. "Good Soldier" (CR).

19. **Curtis, David B.**, private. Res. and credit: Douglas, MA. Born: Douglas, MA. Age: 18. Height: 5'11". Comp: light. Eyes: blue. Hair: black. Occup: farmer. Enlisted in Douglas by A. Hall, Feb. 22, 1864; mustered March 10, 1864. Absent sick or on detached duty from on or before May 6, 1864, until between May 24 and June 2, 1864. In action at Cold Harbor, June 3, 1864, and Petersburg assaults, June 17 and 18, 1864; taken prisoner of war at the Petersburg Crater, July 30, 1864. Incarcerated in the Confederate prison in Danville, VA, until paroled and released Feb. 22, 1865. Reported in the company journal for March 1, 1865, as "gained from missing in action." Absent sick in an army general hospital until on or after July 30, 1865. Mustered out as absent sick at Delaney house, Washington, DC, July 30, 1865, expiration of service. "Good Soldier" (CR).

20. **Daily, Cornelius J.**, private. Res. and/or credit: Orange, MA. Born: Ireland. Age: 35. Height: 5'7". Comp: dark. Eyes: gray. Hair: dark. Occup: farmer. Enlisted in Orange by Davis Goddard, Feb. 27, 1864; mustered March 10, 1864. Wounded in action at the Wilderness, May 6, 1864. Absent wounded in an army general hospital until an unknown date, probably in Nov. or early Dec. 1864. Wounded again on picket duty at Petersburg, Dec. 7, 1864 (the last casualty in the regiment for the year 1864). Absent wounded in an army general hospital until after June 20, 1865. Mustered out with the regiment at Delaney house, Washington, DC, July 30, 1865, and discharged in Readville, MA, Aug. 9, 1865, expiration of service. Resided in Brushton, NY, after the war. "Good Soldier" (CR).

21. **Damon, George B.**, private. Res. and credit: Leominster, MA. Born: Leominster, MA. Age: 19. Height: 5'7". Comp: dark.

Eyes: blue. Hair: dark. Occup: laborer. Enlisted in Leominster by C. H. Meinard, Jan. 11, 1864; mustered March 10, 1864. Deserted from Camp Wool, March 18, 1864. Arrested and returned to the regiment on April 17 or 18, 1864. Deserted at Rappahannock Station, VA, on the march to the Wilderness, May 4, 1864. No record of having received his bounty. Charged by the US government $23.85 for rifle, equipment, and uniform stolen, and $3.42 for "camp and garrison" (CR) equipment stolen. Never returned. Had previous service as a private in Co. F, 1st New York Light Artillery, under the name George W. Clarke. Possibly a bounty jumper in that regiment. Also had previous service as a private in Co. C, 53rd MVI, from Sept. 14, 1862, until mustered out, Sept. 2, 1863. Participated in the Port Hudson, LA, campaign with that regiment in 1863. Also had previous service as a private in Co. A, 15th MVI, from July 12, 1861, until discharged for disability, April 25, 1862. Possibly participated at Ball's Bluff, Oct. 21, 1861. Resided in Leominster, MA, after the war. "VILLIAN: dyed in the wool" (CR).

22. **Danyon, Horace,** private. Res and/or credit: Pittsfield, MA. Born: Sheffield, Ontario, Canada. Age: 21. Height: 5'7". Comp: light. Eyes: blue. Hair: dark. Occup: laborer. Enlisted in Pittsfield by G. C. Herritz, Feb. 27, 1864; mustered March 10, 1864. Deserted from the IX Corps camp in Annapolis, MD, April 23, 1864. Charged by the US government $23.85 for rifle, uniform, and equipment stolen, and $3.42 for "camp and garrison" (CR) equipment stolen. $30.00 paid by the regiment for his arrest. Sent back to the regiment for duty on or before May 5, 1864. Wounded in action at the Wilderness, May 6, 1864. Died from his wounds in an army general hospital in Washington, DC, July 18, 1864.

23. **Davenport, Elisha C.,** private. Res: Holden, MA. Credit: Worcester, MA. Born: Holden, MA. Age: 21. Height: 5'7". Comp: light. Eyes: gray. Hair: light. Occup: baker. Enlisted in Worcester by H. Leland, Feb. 24, 1864; mustered March 10, 1864. Confined in the guardhouse for an unknown reason (prob-ably disobedience of orders) in Camp Wool from March 11 until March 15, 1864. Killed in action at the Wilderness, May 6, 1864.

24. **Doherty, James,** major. Res. and credit: Boston, MA. Born: possibly Ireland. Age: 36. Married. Height: unknown. Comp: light. Eyes: blue. Hair: light brown. Occup: mariner. Commissioned captain, March 17, 1864. mustered captain, March 27, 1864. Assigned to and took command of Co. G, March 23, 1864, under RSO 30, dated March 23, 1864, by order of Col. William F. Bartlett. In action at the Wilderness, May 6, 1864, Spotsylvania Court House, May 10, 12, and 18, 1864, North Anna River, May 24, 1864, and Cold Harbor, June 3, 1864; severely wounded in action in the hand by canister during the Petersburg assault, June 17, 1864. With the regiment on all marches and in all skirmishes and battles until wounded. Absent wounded in an army general hospital until between Aug. 19 and Sept. 30, 1864. Commissioned major while absent wounded, July 31, 1864, but never mustered. In action at Poplar Grove Church, Sept. 30, 1864. In action again and in command of the regiment at Poplar Grove

Major James Doherty. *(USAMHI)*

Church, Oct. 8, 1864. Absent on furlough from on or about Feb. 1 until Feb. 23, 1865. Absent again for an unknown reason, but not sick, from March 1 until March 3, 1865. With the regiment in operations during the fall and winter of 1864–65, and mortally wounded in action at Fort Stedman, March 25, 1865. Died from his wounds in the 1st Division, IX Corps, Field Hospital at Petersburg, March 26, 1864. Posthumously breveted lieutenant colonel of US Volunteers by recommendation of Lt. Col. Julius M. Tucker, to date from March 25, 1865, for gallantry at Fort Stedman, under GO 133, War Dept., dated Aug. 22, 1865. Had previous service in Co. I, 1st MVI, from May 24, 1861, until resigned and discharged, Jan. 27, 1864. Commissioned 2nd lieutenant, Sept. 9, 1862. Participated with that regiment in the Peninsula campaign, 1862, at 2nd Bull Run, Aug. 29, 1862, and Fredericksburg, Dec. 13, 1862; wounded in action at Chancellorsville, May 2, 1863. Participated again at Gettysburg, July 1, 2, and 3, 1863. "Rather brusque in appearance and often emphatic in speech, yet he had a heart as warm and true and brave as ever beat in a human breast. . . . always spoken of as the 'brave Doherty' . . . never knew fear. . . . Upon the battlefield he was like a raging lion . . . seemed to bear a charmed life. Military in bearing . . . an erratic sort of man. . . ." (JA).

25. **Donovan, Dennis**, private. Res. and credit: Fitchburg, MA. Born: Ireland. Age: 19. Height: 5'5". Comp: dark. Eyes: blue. Hair: light. Occup: laborer. Enlisted in Fitchburg by S. Thurston, March 7, 1864; mustered March 10, 1864. In action at the Wilderness, May 6, 1864, Spotsylvania Court House, May 10, 12, and 18, 1864, North Anna River, May 24, 1864, Cold Harbor, June 3, 1864, and Petersburg assault, June 17, 1864; wounded in action at the Petersburg Crater, July 30, 1864. With the regiment on all marches and in all skirmishes and battles until wounded. Absent wounded in an army general hospital until he deserted on furlough from there, Oct 22, 1864. Surrendered to the authorities on an unknown date, but never returned to the regiment. Mustered out as absent sick at Delaney house, Washington,

DC, July 30, 1865, expiration of service. Died in 1894, age 49. "Splendid Soldier" (CR).

26. **Drake, William M.**, private. Res. and credit: Westfield, MA. Born: Westfield, MA. Age: 20. Height: 5'5". Comp: light. Eyes: black. Hair: dark. Occup: carpenter. Enlisted in Westfield by L. C. Gilbert, Feb. 29, 1864; mustered March 10, 1864. Wounded in action at the Wilderness, May 6, 1864. Absent wounded in an army general hospital until discharged the US service for disability from wounds, June 17, 1865, under GO 77, par. 6, AGO, War Dept.

27. **Fales, Henry M.**, corporal. Res. and credit: Holden, MA. Born: Holden, MA. Age: 23. Height: 5'6". Comp: light. Eyes: light. Hair: light. Occup: butcher. Enlisted in Holden by Capt. Henry C. Ward, Feb. 25, 1864; mustered March 10, 1864. Promoted corporal, March 30, 1864. Killed in action at the Wilderness, May 6, 1864. Had previous service as a private in Co. B, 3rd Battalion of Rifles, Massachusetts Volunteer Militia (Holden Rifles), from April 19, 1861, until mustered out, Aug. 3, 1861. On duty with that unit at Fort McHenry. Also had previous service as a private in Co. B, 51st MVI, from Aug. 8, 1862, until mustered out, July 27, 1863. Participated in the North Carolina campaign with that regiment in 1862. "Good Soldier" (CR).

28. **Fiske, Henry B.**, 2nd lieutenant. Res. and/or credit: Springfield, MA. Born: unknown. Age: 30. No description available. Occup: inspector of ordnance. Commissioned 2nd lieutenant in Co. C, Feb. 11, 1864; mustered 2nd lieutenant, Feb. 18, 1864. Detailed as a recruiting officer for the regiment under Capt. Lewis A. Tifft in Springfield, Feb. 18, 1864, under RSO 16, postdated Feb. 29, 1864, by order of Lt. Col. Edward P. Hollister. Transferred to Co. G, March 16, 1864, under RSO 26, dated March 15, 1864, by order of Col. William F. Bartlett. Reported to the company for duty, March 17, 1864. In action at the Wilderness, May 6, 1864 and Spotsylvania Court House, May 10, 1864; wounded in the leg in action there, May 12, 1864. Absent wounded until resigned and dis-

charged the US service for disability from wounds, Sept. 5, 1864. Offered a commission as 1st lieutenant in the company, Oct. 7, 1864, but declined. Resided in Cleveland, OH, after the war.

29. **Fitzgerald, Garrett,** private. Res. and/or credit: Springfield, MA. Born: Ireland. Age: 21. Height: 5'8½". Comp: dark. Eyes: black. Hair: black. Occup: teamster. Enlisted in Springfield by Lt. George S. Green, March 22, 1864; joined the company from the transient barracks, March 26, 1864; mustered April 6, 1864. Wounded in action at the Wilderness, May 6, 1864. Absent wounded in an army general hospital until discharged the US service for disability from wounds, May 23, 1865, by order of the War Dept. Resided in Salem, MA, after the war.

30. **Flagg, William H.,** private. Res. and/or credit: Springfield, MA. Born: Burlington, VT. Age: 29. Height: 5'6". Comp: light. Eyes: gray. Hair: light. Occup: armorer. Enlisted in Springfield by Lt. Henry B. Fiske, Feb. 27, 1864; mustered March 10, 1864. Wounded in action at the Wilderness, May 6, 1864. Absent wounded until discharged the US service for disability from wounds from Dale US Army General Hospital in Worcester, MA, June 7, 1865, by order of the War Dept. Died Jan. 1, 1871, age 36.

31. **Flanagan, William,** private. Res. and credit: Springfield, MA. Born: Springfield, MA. Age: 19. Height: 5'5½". Comp: dark. Eyes: gray. Hair: dark. Occup: armorer. Enlisted in Springfield by Lt. Henry B. Fiske, March 3, 1864; mustered March 10, 1864. Killed in action at the Wilderness, May 6, 1864.

32. **Fleming, John,** corporal. Res. and/or credit: Worcester, MA. Born: County Kerry, Ireland. Age: 30. Height: 5'8½". Comp: fair. Eyes: blue. Hair: brown. Occup: carpenter. Enlisted in Worcester by Lt. John Reade, March 4, 1864; mustered March 10, 1864. Promoted corporal, March 30, 1864. Slightly wounded in the head in action at the Wilderness, May 6, 1864. Absent wounded in an army general hospital until discharged the US

service for disability from wounds, July 3, 1865, by order of the War Dept. Reduced to the ranks for an unknown reason, but probably absence, while absent wounded by Lt. Col. Julius M. Tucker, Oct. 31, 1864. "WORTHLESS" (CR).

33. **Fletcher, Lorenzo,** private. Res: Northboro, MA. Credit: Westboro, MA. Born: New Hampshire. Age: 19. Height: 5'7". Comp: light. Eyes: blue. Hair: light. Occup: farmer. Enlisted in Westboro by Capt. Henry C. Ward, Jan. 29, 1864; mustered March 10, 1864. Severely wounded in action at the Wilderness, May 6, 1864. Died from his wounds in an army general hospital in Washington, DC, May 19, 1864. "Good Soldier" (CR).

34. **Frelick, Charles W.,** private. Res. and/or credit: Worcester, MA. Born: Canajoharie, NY. Age: 19. Height: 5'9½". Comp: florid. Eyes: blue. Hair: brown. Occup: farmer. Enlisted in Worcester by E. M. Lincoln, March 2, 1864; mustered March 10, 1864. Wounded in action at the Wilderness, May 6, 1864. Died from his wounds in an army general hospital in Washington, DC, June 29, 1864.

35. **Gaskell, Hubbard,** private. No information available except that he was discharged the US service from Camp Wool on a Surgeon's Certificate of Disibility, April 6, 1864. This man appears on no other published rosters of the 57th Regiment.

36. **Gaskell, John N.,** private. Res. and/or credit: Douglas, MA. Born: Magetown, VT. Age: 37. Height: 5'3½". Comp: dark. Eyes: hazel. Hair: black. Occup: mechanic. Enlisted in Douglas by D. Hall, Feb. 25, 1864; mustered March 10, 1864. Absent sick or on detached duty from May 6, 1864, until between May 12 and May 18, 1864. In action at Spotsylvania Court House, May 18, 1864, and North Anna River, May 24, 1864; killed while the regiment was in reserve at Cold Harbor, June 1, 1864, probably by a Confederate sharpshooter. "Brave Soldier" (CR).

37. **Goff, Frederick E.,** private. Res. and/or credit: Westfield, MA. Born: Chicopee, MA. Age: 18. Height: 5'9½". Comp: fair. Eyes:

black. Hair: black. Occup: whip maker. Enlisted in Westfield by L. Gilbert, Feb. 27, 1864; mustered March 10, 1864. In action at the Wilderness, May 6, 1864, Spotsylvania Court House, May 10, 12, and 18, 1864, and North Anna River, May 24, 1864. Absent sick in an army general hospital from between May 24 and June 3, 1864, until after June 20, 1865. Mustered out with the regiment at Delaney house, Washington, DC, July 30, 1865, and discharged in Readville, MA, Aug. 9, 1865, expiration of service. Resided in Westfield, MA, after the war and died there, Aug. 10, 1895, age 49.

38. **Hadley, Cyrus,** musician. Res. and/or credit: Leominster, MA. Born: Woburn, MA. Age: 40. Height: 5′9½″. Comp: dark. Eyes: blue. Hair: dark. Occup: cordwainer. Enlisted in Leominster by C. H. Merriam, Feb. 24, 1864; mustered March 10, 1864. Probably company fifer. Deserted from Dale US Army General Hospital in Worcester, MA, while absent sick, Feb. 1, 1865. Never returned. "WORTHLESS" (CR).

39. **Ham, John,** private. Res. and/or credit: Boston, MA. Born: Albany, NY. Age: 21. Height: 5′4½″. Comp: light. Eyes: gray. Hair: brown. Occup: farmer. Enlisted in Boston by N. C. Nash, March 23, 1864; joined the company from the transient barracks, March 26, 1864; mustered April 6, 1864. Deserted from the IX Corps camp in Annapolis, MD, April 23, 1864. Charged by the US government $23.85 for rifle, uniform, and equipment stolen, and $3.42 for "camp and garrison" (CR) equipment stolen. Never returned. "bounty jumper" (JA), "THIEF" (CR).

40. **Hamlin, Charles,** corporal. Res. and credit: Springfield, MA. Born: Springfield, MA. Age: 21. Height: 5′9½″. Comp: dark. Eyes: black. Hair: dark. Occup: machinist. Enlisted in Springfield by Lt. Henry B. Fiske, Feb. 20, 1864; mustered March 10, 1864. In action at the Wilderness, May 6, 1864, Spotsylvania Court House, May 10, 12, and 18, 1864, North Anna River, May 24, 1864, Cold Harbor, June 3, 1864, Petersburg assaults, June 17 and 18, 1864, Petersburg Crater, July 30, 1864, Weldon Railroad, Aug. 19, 1864,

and Poplar Grove Church, Sept. 30 and Oct. 8, 1864; taken prisoner of war at Fort Stedman, March 25, 1865. Paroled from Libby Prison in Richmond, VA, March 29, 1865, and exchanged April 2, 1865. Returned to the regiment for duty from the Camp of Parole in Annapolis, MD, May 11, 1865. Promoted corporal, Feb. 16, 1865, under RSO 16, by order of Lt. Col. Julius M. Tucker. One of the 11 men who served with the regiment on all marches and in all skirmishes and battles throughout its entire wartime service, and one of the 30 combat soldiers remaining of the regiment after Weldon Railroad, Aug. 19, 1864. Mustered out with the regiment at Delaney house, Washington, DC, July 30, 1865, and discharged in Readville, MA, Aug. 9, 1865, expiration of service. Resided in Chicago, IL, after the war. "Good and Faithful Soldier" (CR).

41. **Hawkins, Luther C.,** private. Res. and/or credit: Dudley, MA. Born: Foster, RI. Age: 42. Height: 5′8″. Comp: light. Eyes: gray. Hair: dark. Occup: shoemaker. Enlisted in Dudley by Capt. Charles D. Hollis, March 3, 1864; mustered March 10, 1864. Wounded in action and taken prisoner of war at the Wilderness, May 6, 1864. Paroled and exchanged from an unknown Confederate prison on an unknown date. Discharged the US service for disability from an army general hospital, June 19, 1865, by order of the War Dept. Had previous service as a private in Co. E, 13th Connecticut Volunteer Infantry (specifics unknown). Died in 1875, age 53. "Good Soldier" (CR).

42. **Horton, Joseph,** private. Res. and/or credit: Chicopee, MA. Born: England. Age: 25. Height: 5′7½″. Comp: light. Eyes: blue. Hair: dark. Occup: silversmith. Enlisted in Chicopee by Lt. George S. Green, Feb. 27, 1864; mustered March 10, 1864. Absent sick or on detached duty from on or before May 6, 1864, until between May 12 and May 18, 1864. In action at Spotsylvania Court House, May 18, 1864, and mortally wounded in action at North Anna River, May 24, 1864. "Private J. Horton, G, 57th Massachusetts; ball lodged in first dorsal vertebra; May 31, haemorrhage from occipital; artery ligated in

wound by Surgeon R. B. Bontecou, U.S.V.; haemorrhage recurred; artery re-ligated June 2, 1864" (CMR). Died from his wounds in an army general hospital in Washington, DC, June 2, 1864. "Good Soldier" (CR).

43. **Hutchins, Henry E.**, sergeant. Res. and/or credit: Worcester, MA. Born: Winchester, NH. Age: 21. Height: 5′7″. Comp: light. Eyes: blue. Hair: light. Occup: clerk. Enlisted in Worcester by Capt. Henry C. Ward, March 2, 1864; mustered March 10, 1864. Promoted corporal, March 30, 1864. In action at the Wilderness, May 6, 1864, Spotsylvania Court House, May 10, 12, and 18, 1864, North Anna River, May 24, 1864, and Cold Harbor, June 3, 1864. Absent sick or on detached duty from between June 3 and June 17, 1864, until between Oct. 8, 1864, and Feb. 16, 1865. With the regiment on all marches and in all skirmishes and battles until absent. Promoted sergeant, Feb. 16, 1865, under RSO 16, by order of Lt. Col. Julius M. Tucker. Taken prisoner of war in action at Fort Stedman, March 25, 1865. Paroled from Libby Prison in Richmond, VA, March 29, 1865 and exchanged, April 2, 1865. Returned to the regiment for duty from the Camp of Parole in Annapolis, MD, May 11, 1865. Mustered out with the regiment at Delaney house, Washington, DC, July 30, 1865, and discharged in Readville, MA, Aug. 9, 1865, expiration of service. "Good Soldier" (CR).

44. **Jordan, Thomas J.**, sergeant. Res. and/or credit: Springfield, MA. Born: Eden, VT. Age: 24. Height: 5′9½″. Comp: dark. Eyes: blue. Hair: dark. Occup: lumberman. Enlisted in Springfield by Lt. Henry B. Fiske, Feb. 22, 1864; mustered March 10, 1864. Detailed on recruiting service with Lt. Henry B. Fiske in Springfield, March 11, 1864, under RSO 21, by order of Col. William F. Bartlett. Promoted sergeant, March 30, 1864. Wounded in action at the Wilderness, May 6, 1864. Absent wounded until discharged the US service for disability from wounds from Summit House US Army General Hospital in Philadelphia, PA, Jan. 25, 1865. Had previous service in Co. E, 14th New Hampshire Volunteer Infantry (specifics unknown). "Good Soldier" (CR).

45. **Laley, Frank**, private. Res. and/or credit: Hinsdale, MA. Born: Ireland. Age: 28. Height: 5′6″. Comp: dark. Eyes: gray. Hair: dark. Occup: laborer. Enlisted in Hinsdale by W. H. Carson, March 4, 1864; mustered March 10, 1864. Absent sick or on detached duty from on or before May 6, 1864, until between May 24 and June 3, 1864. In action at Cold Harbor, June 3, 1864. Absent for unknown reasons during the Petersburg assaults, June 17 and 18, 1864. Taken prisoner of war in action at the Petersburg Crater, July 30, 1864. Incarcerated in the Confederate prison in Danville, VA, until paroled and exchanged, Oct. 17, 1864. Probably received extra pay for having been a prisoner of war. Absent sick in an Army general hospital until discharged the US service for disability, June 1, 1865, by order of the War Dept.

46. **Lashua, Francis**, private. Res. and/or credit: Hinsdale, MA. Born: Canada. Age: 21. Height: 5′5″. Comp: light. Eyes: gray. Hair: light. Occup: farmer. Enlisted in Hinsdale by W. H. Carson, March 9, 1864; mustered March 10, 1864. Killed in action at the Wilderness, May 6, 1864.

47. **Lee, Dennis**, private. Res. and/or credit: Springfield, MA. Born: Conway, MA. Age: 44. Height: 5′8″. Comp: dark. Eyes: gray. Hair: dark. Occup: farmer. Enlisted in Springfield by Lt. Henry B. Fiske, March 7, 1864; mustered March 10, 1864. Absent sick or on detached duty from on or before May 6, 1864, until between July 30 and Aug. 19, 1864. Severely wounded in the left leg in action at Weldon Railroad, Aug. 19, 1864. Taken to the 1st Division, IX Corps, Field Hospital where his left leg was amputated by the circular method, Aug. 20, 1864, by Dr. T. Fletcher Oakes, 56th MVI. Died from his wounds from pyemia in an army general hospital in Washington, DC, Sept. 27, 1864. "Good Soldier" (CR).

48. **Leland, Abner A.**, private. Res. and/or credit: Douglas, MA. Born: Milford, MA. Age: 44. Height: 5′10″. Comp: light. Eyes: blue. Hair: light. Occup: farmer. Enlisted in Douglas by A. Hall, Feb. 22, 1864; mustered March 10, 1864. Absent sick or on detached

duty from on or before May 6, 1864, until between June 3 and June 17, 1864. In action at the Petersburg assaults, June 17 and 18, 1864. Killed almost instantly by a ricocheting Minié ball which penetrated his neck while on duty in the trenches at Petersburg, June 22, 1864. "Good Soldier" (CR).

49. **Leslie, James,** private. Res. and/or credit: Hinsdale, MA. Born: Ireland. Age: 23. Height: 5′6″. Comp: dark. Eyes: gray. Hair: dark. Occup: laborer. Enlisted in Hinsdale by W. H. Carson, March 4, 1864; mustered March 10, 1864. Absent sick or on detached duty from on or before May 6, 1864, until between Aug. 19 and Sept. 30, 1864. In action at Poplar Grove Church, Sept. 30 and Oct. 8, 1864, and in other operations of the regiment during the fall and winter of 1864–65. Killed in action at Fort Stedman, March 25, 1865.

50. **Lewis, Timothy,** private. Res. and/or credit: Fitchburg, MA. Born: Gill, MA. Age: 18. Height: 5′5″. Comp: light. Eyes: blue. Hair: dark. Occup: laborer. Enlisted in Fitchburg by S. Thurston, Feb. 29, 1864; mustered March 10, 1864. Wounded in action at the Wilderness, May 6, 1864. Absent wounded in an army general hospital until after June 20, 1865. Mustered out with the regiment at Delaney house, Washington, DC, July 30, 1865, and discharged in Readville, MA, Aug. 9, 1865, expiration of service. Resided in Westport, NH, after the war and died at the Soldiers' Home in Chelsea, MA, age 81. "Good Soldier" (CR).

51. **Lowe, James,** private. Res: Hinsdale, MA. Credit: Pittsfield, MA. Born: Dublin, Ireland. Age: 34. Height: 5′3½″. Comp: dark. Eyes: gray. Hair: dark. Occup: druggist. Enlisted in Pittsfield by Joseph Tucker, March 11, 1864; joined the company from the transient barracks, March 26, 1864; mustered April 6, 1864. Wounded in action at the Wilderness, May 6, 1864. Absent wounded in an army general hospital until Feb. 27, 1865. On furlough from March 2 until March 21, 1865. In action at Fort Stedman, March 25, 1865. Mustered out with the regiment at Delaney house, Washington, DC, July 30, 1865, and discharged in Readville, MA, Aug. 9, 1865,

expiration of service. "Brave, Faithful, Willing" (CR).

52. **Mallet, Masial,** private. Res. and/or credit: West Boylston, MA. Born: Canada. Age: 20. Height: 5′4″. Comp: dark. Eyes: blue. Hair: black. Occup: bootmaker. Enlisted in West Boylston by D. C. Murdock, Feb. 10, 1864; mustered March 10, 1864. Severely wounded in action at the Wilderness, May 6, 1864, and died from his wounds in an army general hospital in Washington, DC, May 20, 1864.

53. **Melvin, Michael,** private. Res. and/or credit: Northampton, MA. Born: Ireland. Age: 19. Height: 5′6″. Comp: light. Eyes: blue. Hair: light. Occup: laborer. Enlisted in Northampton by Lt. Col. Luke Lyman, Feb. 1, 1864; mustered March 10, 1864. Wounded in action at the Wilderness, May 6, 1864. Absent wounded in an army general hospital until an unknown date. Mustered out as absent wounded at Delaney house, Washington, DC, July 30, 1865, expiration of service.

54. **Monahan, Daniel,** corporal (acting). Res. and/or credit: Worcester, MA. Born: Ireland. Age: 25. Height: 5′10″. Comp: light. Eyes: blue. Hair: light. Occup: manufacturer. Enlisted in Worcester by Capt. Henry C. Ward, Feb. 22, 1864; mustered March 10, 1864. Confined in the guardhouse in Camp Wool for fighting, as acting corporal, March 15, 1864, but escaped and deserted that same day. Arrested and returned on March 21, 1864. Deserted from Camp Wool again that same day and was arrested and returned again on March 25, 1864. $33 paid for his arrest from desertion. Deserted again from Camp Wool, March 25, 1864. No record of him having received his bounty. Never returned.

55. **Monroe, George A.,** private. Res. and credit: Grafton, MA. Born: Grafton, MA. Age: 20. Height: 5′6″. Comp: light. Eyes: gray. Hair: light. Occup: farmer. Enlisted in Grafton by Capt. Henry C. Ward, Feb. 22, 1864; mustered March 10, 1864. Did not leave Camp Wool with the regiment for the front, and did not join it in the field until Nov. 10, 1864. With the regiment in operations during the late fall and winter of 1864–65,

and taken prisoner of war in action at Fort Stedman, March 25, 1865. Paroled from Libby Prison, Richmond, VA, March 29, 1865, and exchanged, April 2, 1865. Discharged the US service for disability from the Camp of Parole in Annapolis, MD, June 21, 1865, under GO 77, par. 6, AGO, War Dept. Had previous service as a private in Co. G, 15th MVI, from Dec. 11, 1861, until discharged for disability, Oct. 15, 1862. Possibly at Ball's Bluff, Oct. 21, 1861, and on the Peninsula campaign in 1862. "Skulked at Gallops Island, [Boston Harbor] Mass. from April 19, [1864] until Nov. 10, 1864" (CR).

56. **Morrissey, John**, private. Res. and/or credit: Uxbridge, MA. Born: County Clare, Ireland. Age: 25. Height: 5'7". Comp: light. Eyes: blue. Hair: dark. Occup: card grinder. Enlisted in Uxbridge by J. W. Capern, March 24, 1864; mustered April 6, 1864. Wounded in action at the Wilderness, May 6, 1864. Absent wounded until discharged the US service by order of President Andrew Johnson from an army general hospital in Philadelphia, PA, May 22, 1865. Died March 17, 1892, age 53.

57. **Moulton, Austin N.**, private. Res. and/or credit: Worcester, MA. Born: Munson, MA. Age: 41. Height: 6'2". Comp: light. Eyes: black. Hair: light. Occup: melter. Enlisted in Worcester by Capt. Henry C. Ward, Feb. 12, 1864; mustered March 10, 1864. Absent sick or on detached duty from on or before May 6, 1864, until between July 30 and Aug. 19, 1864. In action at Weldon Railroad, Aug. 19, 1864, and one of the 30 combat soldiers remaining of the regiment after that battle. Absent sick or on detached duty again from between Aug. 20 and Sept. 30, 1864, until between March 24 and May 31, 1865. Detached and detailed as a guard at the quartermaster's dept. in Washington, DC, from May 31, 1865, until muster-out. Mustered out with the regiment at Delaney house, Washington, DC, July 30, 1865, and discharged in Readville, MA, Aug. 9, 1865, expiration of service. Resided in Brimfield, MA, after the war. "Good Man, Poor Soldier" (CR).

58. **Mountain, Lewis**, private. Res. and/or credit: Douglas, MA. Born: province of Que-

bec, Canada. Age: 22. Height: 5'4". Comp: dark. Eyes: black. Hair: dark. Occup: mechanic. Enlisted in Douglas by A. Brown, Feb. 29, 1865; mustered March 10, 1865. Wounded in action at the Wilderness, May 6, 1864. Absent wounded in an army general hospital until between Aug. 19 and Sept. 30, 1864. In action at Poplar Grove Church, Sept. 30 and Oct. 8, 1864, and in other operations of the regiment during the fall and winter of 1864–65. Taken prisoner of war in action at Fort Stedman, March 25, 1865. Paroled from Libby Prison in Richmond, VA, March 30, 1865, and exchanged April 2, 1865. Returned to the regiment for duty from the Camp of Parole in Annapolis, MD, May 11, 1865. Mustered out with the regiment at Delaney house, Washington, DC, July 30, 1865, and discharged in Readville, MA, Aug. 9, 1865, expiration of service. Resided in Douglas, MA, after the war.

59. **Mulstead, Richard**, private. Res. and/or credit: Southboro, MA. Born: County Longford, Ireland. Age: 45. Height: 5'6". Comp: light. Eyes: blue. Hair: brown. Occup: laborer. Enlisted in Southboro by P. Fay, Feb. 16, 1864; mustered March 10, 1864. Absent sick or on detached duty from on or before May 6, 1864, until between May 18 and May 24, 1864. Killed in action at North Anna River, May 24, 1864. "Good Soldier" (CR).

60. **Pattison, James William**, corporal. Res. and/or credit: Worcester, MA. Born: Roxbury, MA. Age: 19. Height: 5'10". Comp: dark. Eyes: gray. Hair: black. Occup: artist. Enlisted in Worcester by Lt. Henry S. Hitchcock (of the 21st MVI and brother of Capt. Alfred O. Hitchcock of the 57th), March 14, 1864; escorted to the company by Lt. John Cook, March 25, 1864; mustered April 6, 1864. Promoted corporal, Feb. 16, 1865, under RSO 16, by order of Lt. Col. Julius M. Tucker. On furlough from about Jan. 29 until Feb. 17, 1865. Discharged the US service for an unknown reason, Aug. 8, 1865, by order of the War Dept. "Never in battle . . . RASCAL" (CR).

61. **Phelps, Oscar B.**, private. Res. and/or credit: Leominster, MA. Born: Lebanon, NH. Age: 23. Height: 5'5". Comp: light. Eyes:

gray. Hair: light. Occup: teamster. Enlisted in Leominster by Lt. Hitchcock, Feb. 25, 1864; mustered March 10, 1864. Wounded in action and taken prisoner of war at the Wilderness, May 6, 1864. Released or escaped on an unknown date and returned to the regiment for duty during the last week of May 1864. In action again at Cold Harbor, June 3, 1864, Petersburg assaults, June 17 and 18, 1864, and Weldon Railroad, Aug. 19, 1865 (not in action at the Petersburg Crater for an unknown reason). One of the 30 combat soldiers remaining of the regiment after Weldon Railroad. Deserted from the front at Petersburg, Aug. 20, 1864. Charged by the US government $23.85 for rifle, uniform, and equipment stolen, and $3.42 for "camp and garrison" (CR) equipment stolen. Returned to the regiment for duty between Oct. 8, 1864 and March 25, 1865 (no record of him having been court-martialed for desertion or held in confinement; probably surrendered under President Lincoln's proclamation of amnesty). Taken prisoner of war in action at Fort Stedman, March 25, 1865. Paroled from Libby Prison in Richmond, VA, March 29, 1865, and exchanged, April 2, 1865. Returned to the regiment for duty from the Camp of Parole in Annapolis, MD, May 11, 1865. Detached and detailed at 1st Division, IX Corps, Headquarters, probably as a guard or teamster, from May 30, 1865 until muster-out. Mustered out with the regiment at Delaney house, Washington, DC, July 30, 1865, and discharged in Readville, MA, Aug. 9, 1865, expiration of service.

62. **Pike, Horace S.,** sergeant. Res. and/or credit: Leicester, MA. Born: Stark, NH. Age: 18. Height: 5′11″. Comp: light. Eyes: gray. Hair: light. Occup: barber. Enlisted in Leicester by Capt. Henry C. Ward, Feb. 6, 1864; mustered March 10, 1864. Promoted sergeant, March 30, 1864. Absent sick or on detached duty from on or before May 6, 1864, until between May 12 and May 18, 1864. In action at Spotsylvania Court House, May 18, 1864, North Anna River, May 24, 1864, and Cold Harbor, June 3, 1864; wounded in action in the Petersburg assault, June 17, 1864. Absent wounded in an army general hospital until between Aug. 19 and Sept. 30, 1864. In

action at Poplar Grove Church, Sept. 30 and Oct. 8, 1864, and in other operations of the regiment during the fall and early winter of 1864–65 until wounded again on picket duty at Petersburg, Feb. 7, 1865. Treated at the 1st Division, IX Corp, Field Hospital until Feb. 21, 1864, when he was transferred to an army general hospital. Discharged the US service from Dale US Army General Hospital in Worcester, MA, June 21, 1865, under GO 254, par. 43, AGO, War Dept., as a supernumerary because of the consolidation of the 59th MVI with the 57th, to date from June 1, 1865. Had previous service as a private in Co. G, 51st MVI, from Aug. 25, 1862, until mustered out, July 27, 1863. Participated in the North Carolina campaign with that regiment in 1862–63. Resided in Worcester, MA, after the war. "Good Soldier" (CR).

63. **Putnam, Rufus E.,** private. Res. and/or credit: Pittsfield, MA. Born: Blanford, MA. Age: 18. Height: 5′5″. Comp: light. Eyes: blue. Hair: brown. Occup: mechanic. Enlisted in Pittsfield by Sgt. James M. Childs, Feb. 11, 1864; mustered March 10, 1864. Wounded in action at the Wilderness, May 6, 1864. Absent wounded in an army general hospital until transferred to Co. H, 9th Regiment, VRC, Aug. 3, 1864. Discharged the US service, July 21, 1865, expiration of service. "Accounts Settled" (CR).

64. **Ramsdell, Cyrus R.,** private. Res. and/or credit: Wilbraham, MA. Born: Palmer, MA. Age: 18. Height: 5′7″. Comp: light. Eyes: blue. Hair: light. Occup: farmer. Enlisted in Wilbraham by P. Cross, Feb. 23, 1864; mustered March 10, 1864. Wounded in action at the Wilderness, May 6, 1864. Absent wounded until discharged the US service on a Surgeons Certificate of Disability from wounds from Judiciary Square US Army General Hospital, Washington, DC, Oct. 17, 1864. "Left haversack at hospital" (CR).

65. **Reed, George E.,** private. Res. and/or credit: West Stockbridge, MA. Born: Carroan, NY. Age: 19. Height: 5′5″. Comp: light. Eyes: blue. Hair: brown. Occup: farmer. Enlisted in West Stockbridge by John M. Seeley, Feb. 24, 1864; mustered March 10, 1864.

Killed in action at the Wilderness, May 6, 1864.

66. **Richmond, Jason H.,** private. Res. and/or credit: Holyoke, MA. Born: Whitinsville, MA. Age: 19. Height: 5'6½". Comp: light. Eyes: blue. Hair: brown. Occup: mechanic. Enlisted in Holyoke by Lt. Henry B. Fiske, Feb. 15, 1864; mustered March 10, 1864. Never in combat. Probably absent sick in an army general hospital from on or before May 6, 1864, until after June 20, 1865. Mustered out with the regiment at Delaney house, Washington, DC, July 30, 1865, and discharged in Readville, MA, Aug. 9, 1865, expiration of service.

67. **Rosette, Victor,** corporal. Res. and/or credit: South Hadley, MA. Born: France. Age: 33. Height: 5'5". Comp: dark. Eyes: dark. Hair: black. Enlisted in South Hadley by Lt. Col. Luke Lyman, Feb. 26, 1864; mustered March 10, 1864. Promoted corporal, March 30, 1864. Severely wounded in the right leg in action at the Wilderness, May 6, 1864. Transported by steamer from Fredericksburg, VA, to Washington, DC, where he underwent surgery for the amputation of his right leg, May 9, 1864. Died from pyemia in an army general hospital in Washington, DC, June 1, 1864. "Good Soldier" (CR).

68. **Rumney, Edwin E.,** sergeant. Res. and/or credit: Springfield, MA. Born: Roxbury, VT. Age: 21. Height: 5'8". Comp: dark. Eyes: gray. Hair: dark. Occup: farmer. Enlisted in Springfield by Lt. Henry B. Fiske, Feb. 29, 1864; mustered March 10, 1864. Promoted corporal, March 30, 1864. In action at the Wilderness, May 6, 1864, and Spotsylvania Court House, May 10, 1864; wounded in action there, May 12, 1864. Absent wounded in an army general hospital until between Aug. 19 and Sept. 30, 1864. In action at Poplar Grove Church, Sept. 30 and Oct. 8, 1864, in other operations of the regiment during the fall and winter of 1864–65, and in action at Fort Stedman, March 25, 1865. Promoted sergeant, Feb. 16, 1865, under RSO 16, by order of Lt. Col. Julius M. Tucker. Mustered out with the regiment at Delaney house, Washington, DC, July 30, 1865, and dis-

charged in Readville, MA, Aug. 9, 1865, expiration of service. "Good Soldier" (CR).

69. **Sheehan, Timothy,** private. Res. and/or credit: Springfield, MA. Born: Ireland. Age: 24. Height: 5'8½". Comp: light. Eyes: hazel. Hair: dark. Occup: brass finisher. Enlisted in Springfield by Lt. George S. Green, March 19, 1864; joined the company from the transient barracks, March 26, 1864; mustered April 6, 1864. Wounded in action at the Wilderness, May 6, 1864. Absent wounded in an army general hospital until after June 20, 1865. Mustered out with the regiment at Delaney house, Washington, DC, July 30, 1865, and discharged in Readville, MA, Aug. 9, 1865, expiration of service.

70. **Smith, Frank,** private. Res. and/or credit: Springfield, MA. Born: New York City. Age: 19. Height: 5'11". Comp: light. Eyes: blue. Hair: light. Occup: brakeman. Enlisted in Springfield by Lt. George S. Green, Feb. 26, 1864; mustered March 10, 1864. Confined in the guardhouse in Camp Wool for an unknown reason from March 11 until March 15, 1864. Deserted from the IX Corps camp in Annapolis, MD, April 23, 1864. Charged by the US Government $23.85 for rifle, uniform, and equipment stolen and $3.42 for "camp and garrison" (CR) equipment stolen. $30 paid by the regiment for his arrest and return to the regiment for duty on or about May 5, 1864. In action at the Wilderness, May 6, 1864. Deserted again at the Wilderness during or after the battle, May 6, 1864. Charged again by the US government $23.85 for rifle, uniform, and equipment stolen. Never returned. "Bounty jumper" (JA).

71. **Smith, John,** corporal. Res: Windsor, CT. Credit: Northampton, MA. Born: England. Age: 20. Height: 5'8". Comp: dark. Eyes: hazel. Hair: brown. Occup: laborer. Enlisted in Co. K in Northampton by Lt. Col. Luke Lyman, March 23, 1864; mustered April 6, 1864; transferred to Co. G by his own request, April 14, 1864, under RSO 39, by order of Col. William F. Bartlett, and joined the company, April 16, 1864. In action at the Wilderness, May 6, 1864, Spotsylvania Court House, May 10, 12 and 18, 1864, North Anna River,

May 24, 1864, Cold Harbor, June 3, 1864, Petersburg assaults, June 17 and 18, 1864, Petersburg Crater, July 30, 1864, Weldon Railroad, Aug. 19, 1864, and Poplar Grove Church, Sept. 30 and Oct. 8, 1864. Slightly wounded in May 1864, but circumstances and exact date unknown. Promoted corporal, Feb. 16, 1865, under RSO 16, by order of Lt. Col. Julius M. Tucker. Taken prisoner of war in action at Fort Stedman, March 25, 1865. Paroled from Libby Prison in Richmond, VA, March 29, 1865, and exchanged, April 2, 1865. One of the 11 men who served with the regiment on all marches and in all skirmishes and battles throughout its entire wartime service, and one of the 30 combat soldiers remaining of the regiment after Weldon Railroad, Aug. 19, 1864. Discharged the US service for disability from the Camp of Parole in Annapolis, MD, July 20, 1865. "Splendid Soldier" (CR).

72. **Soulie, Frederick**, sergeant. Res. and/or credit: Northampton, MA. Born: France. Age: 31. Height: 5'2". Comp: light. Eyes: brown. Hair: dark. Occup: confectioner. Enlisted in Northampton by Lt. Col. Luke Lyman, March 18, 1864; joined the company from the transient barracks, March 26, 1864; mustered April 6, 1864. In action at the Wilderness, May 6, 1864, and Spotsylvania Court House, May 10 and 12, 1864; wounded in action there, May 18, 1864. Absent wounded in an army general hospital until between Aug. 19 and Sept. 1, 1864. Promoted corporal, Sept. 1, 1864, as the result of Corp. Tuttle having been killed in action, May 6, 1864. Absent for unknown reasons during the battles at Poplar Grove Church, Sept. 30 and Oct. 8, 1864. With the regiment in other operations during the fall and possibly early winter of 1864–65. Promoted sergeant, Dec. 6, 1864, as the result of Sgt. Trowbridge having been reduced to the ranks, Nov. 1, 1864. Transferred to Co. D, 19th Regiment, VRC, Jan. 28, 1865. Discharged the US service, July 31, 1865, expiration of service. "Splendid Soldier" (CR).

73. **Starr, Joseph J.**, corporal. Res. and/or credit: Westfield, MA. Born: Southwick, MA. Age: 34. Height: 5'9½". Comp: light. Eyes: gray. Hair: brown. Occup: machinist. Enlisted in Westfield by L. Gilbert, Feb. 25, 1864; mustered March 10, 1864. Promoted corporal, March 30, 1864. Absent sick or on detached duty from on or before May 6, 1864, until between May 12 and May 18, 1864. In action at Spotsylvania Court House, May 18, 1864, North Anna River, May 24, 1864, and Cold Harbor, June 3, 1864; killed in action in the Petersburg assault, June 17, 1864. "Good Soldier" (CR).

74. **Sullivan, Daniel**, corporal. Res: Fitchburg, MA. Credit: Worcester, MA. Born: Ireland. Age: 24. Height: 5'4½". Comp: dark. Eyes: gray. Hair: dark. Occup: farmer. Enlisted in Worcester by D. Waldo Lincoln, Feb. 29, 1864; mustered March 10, 1864. Promoted corporal, March 30, 1864. Wounded in action at the Wilderness, May 6, 1864. Absent wounded in an army general hospital until discharged the US service for disability, May 25, 1865, by order of the War Dept. Had been drafted in Fitchburg, July 17, 1863, but paid $300 for a substitute to take his place in the army. Perhaps feeling guilty, he finally enlisted in the 57th. At the battle of the Wilderness, he was left on the field wounded. The Confederates captured him, but because of the confusion during the fight, they forgot to bring him back to their lines, and he was able to save himself from probable death in a Southern prison. Resided in Fitchburg, MA, after the war. "Good Soldier" (CR).

75. **Sullivan, George**, musician. Res. and/or credit: Worcester, MA. Born: Boston, MA. Age: 19. Height: 5'4½". Comp: dark. Eyes: gray. Hair: dark. Occup: laborer. Enlisted in Worcester by Lt. John Reade, Feb. 18, 1864; mustered March 10, 1864. Confined in the guardhouse in Camp Wool for an unknown reason from March 11 until March 15, 1864. Deserted from Camp Wool, March 31, 1864, but voluntarily returned to the regiment, April 1, 1864. Company drummer or fifer. Probably also served as a nurse, stretcher bearer, and/or hospital orderly. Present with the regiment during the battle of Fort Stedman, March 25, 1864, but if he was in action is not known. Mustered out with the regiment at Delaney house, Washington, DC, July 30, 1865, and discharged in Readville, MA, Aug.

9, 1865, expiration of service. Resided in Worcester, MA, after the war.

76. **Taft, Alfred C.**, private. Res. and credit: Worcester, MA. Born: Worcester, MA. Age: 21. Height: 5′5½″. Comp: dark. Eyes: dark. Hair: dark. Occup: barkeeper. Enlisted in Worcester by Lt. John Reade, Feb. 3, 1864; mustered March 10, 1864. Deserted in Washington, DC, during the march to the front, April 25, 1864. Charged by the US government $23.85 for rifle, uniform, and equipment stolen, and $3.42 for "camp and garrison" equipment stolen. Enlisted in Co. B, 11th Connecticut Volunteer Infantry, using the name George E. Jennings, May 14, 1864. Deserted from that regiment at Petersburg, July 5, 1864. Surrendered to the provost marshal in Worcester, MA, as of Co. G, 57th MVI, March 28, 1865, under President Lincoln's proclamation of amnesty of Nov. 11, 1864. Returned to the regiment for duty in May 1865. Almost certainly a bounty jumper. Mustered out with the regiment at Delaney house, Washington, DC, July 30, 1865, and discharged in Readville, MA, Aug. 9, 1865, expiration of service. "THIEF" (CR).

77. **Thompson, Andrew C.**, private. Res: Pittsfield, MA. Credit: Springfield, MA. Born: West Lenox, MA. Age: 18. Height: 5′7″. Comp: light. Eyes: hazel. Hair: brown. Occup: farmer. Enlisted in Springfield by Lt. George S. Green, March 22, 1864; mustered April 6, 1864. Absent sick or on detached duty from on or before May 6, 1864, until between July 30 and Aug. 19, 1864. In action at Weldon Railroad, Aug. 19, 1864, and Poplar Grove Church, Sept. 30 and Oct. 8, 1864, and one of 30 combat soldiers remaining of the regiment after Weldon Railroad, Aug. 19, 1864. With the regiment in operations during the fall and winter of 1864–65, and in action at Fort Stedman, March 25, 1865. Mustered out with the regiment at Delaney house, Washington, DC, July 30, 1865, and discharged in Readville, MA, Aug. 9, 1865, expiration of service.

78. **Towner, John E.**, private. Res. and/or credit: Boston, MA. Born: Brandon, VT. Age: 22. Height: 5′7″. Comp: florid. Eyes: blue. Hair: auburn. Occup: clerk. Enlisted in Boston by N. C. Nash, March 31, 1864; joined the company from the transient barracks, April 5, 1864; mustered April 6, 1864. Deserted at Bladensburg, MD, during the march to the front, April 29, 1864. Charged by the US government $23.85 for rifle, uniform, and equipment stolen, and $3.42 for "camp and garrison" equipment stolen. Never returned. Had previous service as a private in Co. G, 1st Illinois Volunteer Infantry (specifics unknown). "Bounty jumper" (JA); "SCOUNDREL" (CR).

79. **Trowbridge, Charles A.**, sergeant. Res. and/or credit: Northboro, MA. Born: Westfield, MA. Age: 36. Height: 5′11″. Comp: light. Eyes: blue. Hair: light. Occup: comb maker. Enlisted in Northboro by A. Rice, Feb. 16, 1864; mustered March 10, 1864. Promoted sergeant, March 30, 1864. In action at the Wilderness, May 6, 1864, Spotsylvania Court House, May 10, 12, and 18, 1864, North Anna River, May 24, 1864, and Cold Harbor, June 3, 1864; wounded in action in the Petersburg assault, June 17, 1864. With the regiment on all marches and in all skirmishes and battles until wounded. Absent wounded in an army general hospital until Feb. 21, 1865. Reduced to the ranks while absent wounded by Lt. Col. Julius M. Tucker. Reinstated to the rank of sergeant upon his return to the regiment for duty by Tucker, Feb. 21, 1865. In action again at Fort Stedman, March 25, 1865. Listed March 30, 1865, in the company journal as missing in action, but returned March 31, 1865 (whereabouts while missing unknown). Detached and detailed as a guard at the quartermaster's dept. in Washington, DC, May 31, 1865. Discharged the US service in Tennallytown, DC, June 19, 1865, as a supernumerary because of the consolidation of the 59th MVI with the 57th, under GO 254, par. 43, AGO, War Dept., to date June 1, 1865. Had previous service as a private in Co. C, 15th MVI, from July 12, 1861, until discharged for disability at Bolivar, VA, Oct. 29, 1862. Probably participated at Ball's Bluff, Oct. 21, 1861, in the Peninsula campaign, 1862, and at Antietam, Sept. 17, 1862.

80. **Tuttle, John E.**, corporal. Res. and/or credit: Springfield, MA. Born: Wallkill, NY.

Age: 39. Height: 5'5". Comp: light. Eyes: gray. Hair: light. Occup: painter. Enlisted in Springfield by Lt. Henry B. Fiske, Feb. 27, 1864; mustered March 10, 1864. Promoted corporal, March 30, 1864. Killed in action at the Wilderness, May 6, 1864. (Note: The correct spelling of his name is supposed to have been Tuthill, but he signed his military papers as Tuttle.) "Good Soldier" (CR).

81. **Waite, Charles H.**, private. Res. and credit: Charlton, MA. Born: Charlton, MA. Age: 19. Height: 5'8½". Comp: light. Eyes: blue. Hair: light. Occup: farmer. Enlisted in Charlton by Capt. Henry C. Ward, Feb. 26, 1864; mustered March 10, 1864. Killed in action at the Wilderness, May 6, 1864.

82. **Welsh, Daniel**, corporal. Res. and/or credit: Springfield, MA. Born: Chicopee, MA. Age: 28. Height: 5'8". Comp: dark. Eyes: blue. Hair: light. Occup: machinist. Enlisted in Springfield by Lt. Henry B. Fiske, Feb. 1, 1864; mustered March 10, 1864. Deserted from Camp Wool, April 1, 1864, but returned to the regiment before April 18, 1864. In action at the Wilderness, May 6, 1864, Spotsylvania Court House, May 10, 12, and 18, 1864, North Anna River, May 24, 1864, Cold Harbor, June 3, 1864, Petersburg assaults, June 17 and 18, 1864, Petersburg Crater, July 30, 1864, Weldon Railroad, Aug. 19, 1864, and Poplar Grove Church, Sept. 30 and Oct. 8, 1864. Promoted corporal, Sept. 1, 1864, as a result of Cpl. Fales having been killed. On furlough from about Feb. 5 until Feb. 25, 1865. In action again at Fort Stedman, March 25, 1865. One of the 11 men who served with the regiment on all marches and in all skirmishes and battles during its entire wartime service, and of the 10 survivors, one of the three men never to be wounded, absent sick, or taken prisoner of war, and who served his entire enlistment from muster-in to the regiment's muster-out. Also one of the 30 combat soldiers remaining of the regiment after Weldon Railroad. Mustered out with the regiment at Delaney house, Washington, DC, July 30, 1865, and discharged in Readville, MA, Aug. 9, 1865, expiration of service. Resided for some time in Springfield, MA, after the war. "Good and Faithful Soldier" (CR).

83. **White, Albert**, private. Res. and/or credit: Grafton, MA. Born: St. Albans, VT. Age: 20. Height: 5'6". Comp: dark. Eyes: blue. Hair: dark. Occup: machinist. Enlisted in Grafton by Capt. Henry C. Ward, March 3, 1864; joined the company from the transient barracks, March 26, 1864; mustered April 6, 1864. Deserted from Camp Wool while on guard duty, April 17, 1864. Charged by US government $23.85 for rifle, uniform, and equipment stolen. Never returned. "Bounty jumper" (JA).

84. **White, Goss**, private. Res. and/or credit: Worcester, MA. Born: Lancashire, England. Age: 24. Height: 5'3". Comp: light. Eyes: gray. Hair: dark. Occup: spinner. Enlisted in Worcester by Capt. Henry C. Ward, Feb. 24, 1864; mustered March 10, 1864. In action at the Wilderness, May 6, 1864, Spotsylvania Court House, May 10, 12, and 18, 1864, North Anna River, May 24, 1864, Cold Harbor, June 3, 1864, and Petersburg assaults, June, 17 and 18, 1864. Absent sick or on detached duty from before July 30, 1864, until between Aug. 19 and Sept. 30, 1864. In action again at Poplar Grove Church, Sept. 30 and Oct. 8, 1864. Absent sick in an army general hospital from after Oct. 8, 1864, until discharged the US service for disability, June 16, 1865, under GO 77, par. 6, AGO, War Dept. With the regiment on most marches and in most skirmishes and battles until becoming sick. "Good Soldier" (CR).

85. **White, John**, private. Res. and/or credit: Brookline, MA. Born: New Haven, CT. Age: 22. Height: 5'4½". Comp: fair. Eyes: blue. Hair: black. Occup: farmer. Enlisted in Brookline by T. Parsons, March 19, 1864; joined the company from the transient barracks, March 26, 1864; mustered April 6, 1864. Deserted from the IX Corps camp in Annapolis, MD, April 23, 1864, but was arrested and returned to the regiment on or about May 5, 1864. In action and taken prisoner of war at the Wilderness, May 6, 1864. Paroled and exchanged from an unknown Confederate prison, March 29, 1865. Returned to the regiment for duty from the Camp of Parole in Annapolis, MD, May 19, 1865. Probably received extra pay for having been a prisoner of war. Mustered out with the regiment at De-

laney house, Washington, DC, July 30, 1865, and discharged in Readville, MA, Aug. 9, 1865, expiration of service. "THIEF AND PICK-POCKET" (CR).

86. **Whitney, George A.**, 1st sergeant. Res: Chicopee, MA. Credit: Worcester, MA. Born: Greenfield, MA. Age: 25. Height: 5'8". Comp: dark. Eyes: blue. Hair: light. Occup: engraver. Enlisted in Co. D in Worcester by Lt. Daniel Madden, Jan. 25, 1864; mustered Feb. 18, 1864. Promoted sergeant, Feb. 18, 1864. Detached and detailed on recruiting service in Chicopee, Feb. 18, 1864, under RSO 8, by order of Col. William F. Bartlett. Transferred to Co. G under RSO 28, March 17, 1864, and joined the company, March 18, 1864, as acting 1st sergeant; promoted 1st sergeant, March 30, 1864. Absent sick or on detached duty during the battle of the Wilderness, May 6, 1864. In action at Spotsylvania Court House, May 10, 12, and 18, 1864; injured in battle, but not wounded, at North Anna River, May 24, 1864. On furlough at home in Chicopee, MA, injured, until after July 5, 1864, when a letter was written in his behalf stating that he was at home recovering. Reduced to the ranks for an unknown reason, but probably absence, Aug. 31, 1864, by order of Lt. Col. Julius M. Tucker. Returned to the regiment for duty after Oct. 8, 1864. On furlough from about Feb. 2 until Feb. 22, 1865. In action at Fort Stedman, March 25, 1865. Mustered out, but absent for an unknown reason, at Delaney house, Washington, DC, July 30, 1865. "P.B." [pretty bad?] (CR).

87. **Wilcox, George H.**, private. Res. and credit: Adams, MA. Born: Adams, MA. Age: 18. Height: 5'8". Comp: light. Eyes: blue. Hair: brown. Occup: operative. Enlisted in Adams by S. Johnson, March 7, 1864; mustered March 10, 1864. In action at the Wilderness, May 6, 1864, Spotsylvania Court House, May 10, 12, and 18, 1864, North Anna River, May 24, 1864, Cold Harbor, June 3, 1864, and Petersburg assaults, June 17 and 18, 1864. Absent sick or on detached duty from between June 19 and July 30, 1865, until after June 20, 1865. With the regiment on all marches and in all skirmishes and battles until his absence. Mustered out with the regiment at Delaney house, Washington, DC, July 30,

1865, and discharged in Readville, MA, Aug. 9, 1865, expiration of service. "Good Soldier" (CR).

88. **Willard, James J.**, private. Res. and credit: Worcester, MA. Born: Worcester, MA. Age: 27. Height: 5'7". Comp: light. Eyes: gray. Hair: dark. Occup: machinist. Enlisted in Worcester by Capt. Henry C. Ward, Feb. 27, 1864; mustered March 10, 1864. Confined in the guardhouse in Camp Wool for an unknown reason from March 11 until March 15, 1864. Wounded in action and taken prisoner of war at the Wilderness, May 6, 1864. Incarcerated in the Confederate prison in Lynchburg, VA, where he died from his wounds, July 26, 1864. "Good Soldier" (CR).

89. **Wing, Joseph**, private. Res. and/or credit: Springfield, MA. Born: Canada. Age: 31. Height: 5'7". Comp: fair. Eyes: blue. Hair: brown. Occup: farmer. Enlisted in Springfield by Lt. George S. Green, March 23, 1864; joined the company from the transient barracks, March 16, 1864; mustered April 6, 1864. Deserted from the IX Corps camp in Annapolis, MD, April 23, 1864. Charged by the US government $23.85 for rifle, uniform, and equipment stolen, and $3.42 for "camp and garrison" (CR) equipment stolen. Never returned. Not paid his bounty and may have deserted for that reason.

90. **Worthy, William H.**, corporal. Res. and/or credit: Williamstown, MA. Born: Stuyvesant, NY. Age: 19. Height: 5'7". Comp: light. Eyes: blue. Hair: brown. Occup: laborer. Enlisted in Williamstown by H. T. Cole, Dec. 29, 1863. Mustered March 10, 1864. Wounded in action at the Wilderness, May 6, 1864. Absent wounded in an army general hospital until between Oct. 8 and Oct. 27, 1864. Wounded again, but accidentally, at Petersburg, Oct. 27, 1864. Absent wounded in an army general hospital until before March 16, 1865. Absent sick in the 1st Division, IX Corps, Field Hospital from March 16 until March 17, 1865. In action at Fort Stedman, March 25, 1865. Absent sick in the 1st Division, IX Corps, Field Hospital again from March 27, 1865, until no later than May 19, 1865. Promoted corporal, May 29, 1865, to

date May 1, 1865, under RSO 42, by order of Lt. Col. Julius M. Tucker. Mustered out with the regiment at Delaney house, Washington, DC, July 30, 1865, and discharged in Readvile, MA, Aug. 9, 1865, expiration of service. "Good Soldier" (CR).

ROSTER AND DESCRIPTIVE LIST OF COMPANY H

Company H was the third company of the regiment to be mustered into United States service, and it was mustered on Jan. 11, 1864, under SO 21, from the AGO, Boston, MA, by 1st Lt. Robert P. McKibben, 4th United States Regular Infantry. It was mustered out by Capt. Sylvester Keyser, 2nd Michigan Volunteer Infantry, ACM, 1st Division, IX Corps. Company H was the color company.

1. **Ainsworth, Otis D.**, private. Res. and/or credit: Worcester, MA. Born: Hanover, NH. Age: 22. Height: 5'10½". Comp: light. Eyes: blue. Hair: brown. Occup: clerk. Enlisted in Worcester by D. Waldo Lincoln, Jan. 8, 1864; mustered Jan. 11, 1864. Wounded in action at the Wilderness, May 6, 1864. Absent wounded until discharged the US service from Patterson Park US Army General Hospital for disability from wounds, May 18, 1865, in compliance with a telegram from the AGO, War Dept., dated May 4, 1865.

2. **Allen, Dwight D.**, 1st sergeant. Res. and/or credit: Worcester, MA. Born: Massachusetts. Age: 26. Height: unknown. Comp: dark. Eyes: black. Hair: dark. Occup: merchant. Enlisted in Worcester by Capt. Julius M. Tucker, Dec. 18, 1863; mustered Jan. 11, 1864. Promoted 1st sergeant, Jan. 11, 1864. In action at the Wilderness, May 6, 1864, Spotsylvania Court House, May 10, 12, and 18, 1864, North Anna River, May 24, 1864, Cold Harbor, June 3, 1864, and Petersburg assaults, June 17 and 18, 1864, and mortally wounded in action at the Petersburg Crater, July 30, 1864. Left on the field and died in Confederate hands that day. With the regiment on all marches and in all skirmishes and battles until mortally wounded. "Sergeant Allen was a brave soldier and one who was greatly beloved and respected by both officers and enlisted men. He is spoken of as 'genial, kind, and faithful in all his intercourse with the regiment' " (JA).

3. **Anderson, James G.**, private. Res. and/or credit: Leominster, MA. Born: Leominster, MA. Age: 18. Height: 5'3½". Comp: light. Eyes: blue. Hair: brown. Occup: laborer. Enlisted in Leominster by C. H. Merriam, Jan. 4, 1864; mustered Jan. 11, 1864. Absent sick or on detached duty from on or before May 6, 1864, until between June 17 and June 27, 1864. Wounded in the trenches at Petersburg, June 27, 1864. Absent wounded in an army general hospital until Jan. 1, 1865. With the regiment in operations during the winter of 1865, and in action at Fort Stedman, March 25, 1865. Mustered out with the regiment at Delaney house, Washington, DC, July 30, 1865, and discharged in Readville, MA, Aug. 9, 1865, expiration of service. Resided in Boston, MA, after the war.

4. **Arnold, Nathan S.**, private. Res. and credit: Sutton, MA. Born: Sutton, MA. Age: 26. Height: 5'9". Comp: light. Eyes: blue. Hair: light. Occup: stone worker. Enlisted in Sutton by J. A. Dodge, Jan. 5, 1864; mustered Jan. 11, 1864. Never in combat with the 57th. Absent sick from on or before May 6, 1864, until discharged the US service by order of Maj. Gen. John A. Dix, War Dept., for general disability at Petersburg, July 1, 1864. Had previous service as a private in Co. H, 15th MVI, from June 27, 1861, until discharged for disability, April 27, 1862. Possibly participated at Ball's Bluff with that regiment, Oct. 21, 1861.

5. **Binney, Joseph H.**, private. Res. and/or credit: Worcester, MA. Born: Boston, MA. Age: 18. Height: 5'4". Comp: light. Eyes: blue. Hair: light. Occup: clerk. Enlisted in Worcester by Capt. Julius M. Tucker, Jan. 1,

1864; mustered Jan. 11, 1864. Wounded in action at the Wilderness, May 6, 1864. Absent wounded in an army general hospital until after March 25, 1865. Detailed as a clerk at 3rd Brigade, 1st Division, IX Corps, Headquarters in April 1865. Absent sick in an army general hospital from an unknown date until discharged the US service for disability, Aug. 10, 1865, by order of the War Dept. Resided and was a practicing physician in Fullerton, Nance County, NE, after the war.

6. **Bond, Herbert W.**, sergeant. Res: Westboro, MA. Credit: Worcester, MA. Born: Massachusetts. Age: 18. Height: unknown. Comp: light. Eyes: blue. Hair: dark. Occup: shoemaker. Enlisted in Worcester by Capt. Julius M. Tucker, Dec. 14, 1863; mustered Jan. 11, 1864. Promoted sergeant, March 1, 1864. Killed in action at the Wilderness, May 6, 1864. Had previous service as a musician in Co. D, 15th MVI, from July 12, 1861, until discharged for disability, Aug. 12, 1861. Saw no action with that regiment.

7. **Bowen, Isaac**, private. Res: Paxton, MA. Credit: Worcester, MA. Born: Dorchester, MA. Age: 33. Height: 5'7½". Comp: light. Eyes: blue. Hair: light. Occup: farmer. Enlisted in Worcester by Capt. Julius M. Tucker, Jan. 1, 1864; mustered Jan. 11, 1864. In action at the Wilderness, May 6, 1864, and Spotsylvania Court House, May 10, 1864; wounded in action there, May 12, 1864. Absent wounded in an army general hospital until after March 25, 1865. Mustered out with the regiment at Delaney house, Washington, DC, July 30, 1865, and discharged in Readville, MA, Aug. 9, 1865, expiration of service.

8. **Bowen, Michael**, corporal. Res: New Braintree, MA. Credit: North Brookfield, MA. Born: Ireland. Age: 21. Height: 5'11". Comp: light. Eyes: blue. Hair: brown. Occup: shoemaker. Enlisted in North Brookfield by Aaron Smith, Dec. 11, 1863; mustered Jan. 11, 1864. Promoted corporal, March 1, 1864. In action at the Wilderness, May 6, 1864, and Spotsylvania Court House, May 10 and 12, 1864; wounded in the left foot in action there, May 18, 1864. Transported to Washington,

DC, where he underwent surgery for the amputation of his left foot "portion on calcis" (OMR) on May 28, 1864, by Acting Assistant Surgeon F. G. H. Bradford. Absent wounded until discharged and pensioned from the US service on a Surgeons Certificate of Disability from an army general hospital in Washington, DC, May 13, 1865, by order of Maj. Gen. Christopher C. Auger, commanding the Dept. of Washington, DC. Had previous service as a private in Co. F, 51st MVI, from Sept. 8, 1862, until mustered out, July 27, 1863. Participated in the North Carolina campaign with that regiment in 1862–63.

9. **Brown, George A.**, private. Res. and/or credit: Worcester, MA. Born: West Boylston, MA. Age: 18. Height: 5'7". Comp: light. Eyes: blue. Hair: light. Occup: mechanic. Enlisted in Worcester by Capt. Julius M. Tucker, Jan. 4, 1864; mustered Jan. 11, 1864. Wounded in action at the Wilderness, May 6, 1864. Absent wounded until discharged the US service for disability from wounds from an army general hospital in Philadelphia, PA, May 22, 1865, in compliance with a telegram, dated May 4, 1865, from the AGO, War Dept. Resided in Worcester, MA, after the war.

10. **Brown, John S.**, private. Res: Athol, MA. Credit: Worcester, MA. Born: Lowell, MA. Age: 32. Height: 5'4". Comp: dark. Eyes: blue. Hair: dark. Occup: farmer. Enlisted in Worcester by Capt. Julius M. Tucker, Jan. 6, 1864; mustered Jan. 11, 1864. Never in combat with the 57th. Absent sick in an army general hospital from on or before May 6, 1864, until discharged the US service for disability not caused by wounds, July 1, 1864, by order of Maj. Gen. John A. Dix, War Dept. Had previous service as a private in Co. I, 25th MVI, from Oct. 1, 1861, until discharged, Oct. 2, 1862, for wounds received at Roanoke Island, NC, on Feb. 8, 1862. Participated in the North Carolina campaign with that regiment in 1862. Resided in Athol, MA, after the war.

11. **Bullard, Ira**, color corporal. Res: Sutton, MA. Credit: Worcester, MA. Born: Holden, MA. Age: 26. Height: 5'9". Comp: light.

Color Corporal Ira Bullard.
(Mark Savolis)

12. **Burridge, George N.**, private. Res: Leominster, MA. Credit: Worcester, MA. Born: Lunenburg, MA. Age: 18. Height: 5'10". Comp: dark. Eyes: black. Hair: black. Occup: farmer. Enlisted in Worcester by Capt. Julius M. Tucker, Jan. 6, 1864; mustered Jan. 11, 1864. Never in combat. Absent sick or on detached duty from on or before May 6, 1864, until after March 25, 1865. Mustered out with the regiment at Delaney house, Washington, DC, July 30, 1865, and discharged in Readville, MA, Aug. 9, 1865, expiration of service.

13. **Caldwell, William M.**, private. Res: Fitchburg, MA. Credit: Worcester, MA. Born: Fitchburg, MA. Age: 22. Height: 5'7¾". Comp: dark. Eyes: hazel. Hair: black. Occup: clerk. Enlisted in Worcester by Capt. Julius M. Tucker, Dec. 31, 1863; mustered Jan. 11, 1864. Killed in action at the Wilderness, May 6, 1864. Had previous service as a private in Co. A, 53rd MVI, from Oct. 27, 1862, until mustered out, Sept. 2, 1863. Participated in the Port Hudson, LA, campaign with that regiment in 1863.

Eyes: blue. Hair: light. Occup: carpenter. Enlisted in Worcester by J. A. Dodge, Dec. 31, 1863; mustered Jan. 11, 1864. Promoted corporal, March 1, 1864. Member of the regimental color guard. In action at the Wilderness, May 6, 1864, and Spotsylvania Court House, May 10, 1864; slightly wounded in action there, May 12, 1864. In action, although wounded, at Spotsylvania, May 18, 1864, and severely wounded in the upper left forearm and slightly wounded in the leg in action at North Anna River, May 24, 1864. Taken to the 1st Division, IX Corps, Field Hospital where his left arm was amputated at the upper left radius, May 24, 1864. Died from his wounds in Mount Pleasant US Army General Hospital in Washington, DC, May 30, 1864. Had previous service as a private in Co. C, 51st MVI, from Aug. 20, 1862, until mustered out, July 27, 1863. Participated in the North Carolina campaign with that regiment in 1862–63. "Ira proved himself to be an excellent soldier, both cool and plucky in a fight and always faithful when on duty" (JMT).

14. **Chase, Charles S.**, 1st sergeant. Res. and/or credit: Worcester, MA. Born: Grafton, MA. Age: 22. Height: 5'10". Comp: light. Eyes: blue. Hair: light. Occup: mechanic. Enlisted in Worcester by Capt. Julius M. Tucker, Jan. 1, 1864; mustered Jan. 11, 1864. Promoted corporal, March 1, 1864. Wounded in action at the Wilderness, May 6, 1864. Absent wounded in an army general hospital until between Aug. 19 and Sept. 30, 1864. Promoted sergeant, Oct 1, 1864. In action at Poplar Grove Church, Sept. 30 and Oct. 8, 1864. With the regiment in other operations during the fall and winter of 1864–65. Promoted 1st sergeant, March 1, 1865. In action as acting color sergeant at Fort Stedman, March 25, 1865. Cited twice for bravery at that battle: "First Sergeant Charles S. Chase, Company H, general good conduct" (GPR), and "First Sergeant Charles S. Chase, Company H, acting color sergeant, general good conduct" (JMT). On furlough from July 7 until July 24, 1865. Mustered out with the regiment at Delaney house, Washington,

DC, July 30, 1865, and discharged in Readville, MA, Aug. 9, 1865, expiration of service. Had previous service as a private in Co. D, 51st MVI, from Sept. 30, 1862, until mustered out, July 27, 1863. Participated in the North Carolina campaign with that regiment in 1862–63.

15. **Clark, Horace Jr.**, musician. Res. and/or credit: Springfield, MA. Born: Dedham, MA. Age: 35. Height: 5′7½″. Comp: light. Eyes: blue. Hair: light. Occup: carriage painter. Enlisted in Co. D in Springfield by Capt. Lewis A. Tifft, Jan. 11, 1864; mustered Jan. 25, 1864; transferred to Co. H, Feb. 20, 1864, under RSO 11, dated Feb. 19, 1864, by order of Lt. Col. Edward P. Hollister. Served as company fifer. Died from heat prostration during the march from Washington, DC, to the front, April 29, 1864. First fatality of the regiment in the field.

16. **Conners, Thomas**, private. Res. and/or credit: Worcester, MA. Born: Ireland. Age: 30. Height: 5′9″. Comp: light. Eyes: blue. Hair: light. Occup: hostler. Enlisted in Worcester by Capt. Julius M. Tucker, Dec. 19, 1863; mustered Jan. 11, 1864. In action at the Wilderness, May 6, 1864, and Spotsylvania Court House, May 10, 12, and 18, 1864; wounded in action at North Anna River, May 24, 1864. Absent wounded in an army general hospital until discharged the US service for disability from wounds, July 27, 1865, by order of the War Dept. Died July 15, 1867, age 33.

17. **Connolly, William**, sergeant. Res. and/or credit: Worcester, MA. Born: Ireland. Age: 21. Height: 5′5½″. Comp: sandy. Eyes: blue. Hair: light. Occup: wiredrawer. Enlisted in Worcester by D. Waldo Lincoln, Jan. 5, 1864; mustered Jan. 11, 1864. Absent sick or on detached duty from on or before May 6, 1864, until between June 17 and July 1, 1864. Promoted corporal, July 1, 1864. In action and taken prisoner of war at the Petersburg Crater, July 30, 1864. Incarcerated in the Confederate prison in Danville, VA, until paroled and exchanged, Feb. 22, 1865, and returned to the regiment for duty from the

Camp of Parole in Annapolis, MD, no later than March 1, 1865. Probably received extra pay for having been a prisoner of war. Promoted sergeant, March 1, 1865. In action at Fort Stedman, March 25, 1865. Mustered out with the regiment at Delaney house, Washington, DC, July 30, 1865, and discharged in Readville, MA, Aug. 9, 1865, expiration of service. Resided in Worcester, MA, after the war. Had previous service in Co. F, 17th United States Regular Infantry (specifics unknown).

18. **Crowley, John W.**, private. Res: Westboro, MA. Credit: Holliston, MA. Born: Frederickton, New Brunswick, Canada. Age: 32. Height: 5′8″. Comp: dark. Eyes: blue. Hair: light brown. Occup: shoemaker. Enlisted in Co. I in Holliston by D. M. Cutler, Feb. 17, 1864; mustered March 10, 1864; transferred to Co. G, March 12, 1864, under RSO 42, by order of Col. William F. Bartlett. In action and taken prisoner of war at the Wilderness, May 6, 1864. Paroled and exchanged from an unknown Confederate prison, March 19, 1865. Probably received extra pay for having been a prisoner of war. Returned to the regiment for duty from the Camp of Parole in Annapolis, MD, after March 25, 1865. Mustered out with the regiment at Delaney house, Washington, DC, July 30, 1865, and discharged in Readville, MA, Aug. 9, 1865, expiration of service.

19. **Cummings, Joseph L.**, musician. Res. and/or credit: Spencer, MA. Born: Springfield, MA. Age: 38. Height: 5′7″. Comp: florid. Eyes: gray. Hair: brown. Occup: bootmaker. Enlisted in Spencer by L. Hill, Dec. 18, 1863. Mustered Jan. 11, 1864. Company drummer. Wounded in May 1864; exact date and circumstances unknown, but not in a major battle. Absent wounded in an army general hospital until before March 25, 1865. Taken prisoner of war at Fort Stedman, March 25, 1865. Paroled, probably March 29, 1865, and exchanged about April 2, 1865. Never returned to the regiment, and was discharged the US service for disability, Aug. 8, 1865, by order of the War Dept. Had previous service as a musician in Co. G, 15th MVI,

from July 30, 1861, until discharged for disability, Feb. 13, 1862. Probably present with that regiment at Ball's Bluff, Oct. 21, 1861.

20. **Doane, Amos L.**, private. Res. and/or credit: Worcester, MA. Born: Brookfield, MA. Age: 44. Height: 5'8". Comp: light. Eyes: hazel. Hair: black. Occup: mechanic. Enlisted in Worcester by Capt. Julius M. Tucker, Dec. 28, 1863; mustered Jan. 11, 1864. Never in combat. Absent sick in an army general hospital from on or before May 6, 1864, until discharged the US service for disability, June 9, 1865, by order of the War Dept. Resided in Worcester, MA, after the war.

21. **Ellick, Eli A.**, private. Res. and/or credit: Leominster, MA. Born: Fitchburg, MA. Age: 18. Height: 5'4½". Comp: light. Eyes: blue. Hair: brown. Occup: harness maker. Enlisted in Leominster by C. H. Merriam, Jan. 1, 1864; mustered Jan. 11, 1864. Absent sick or on detached duty from on or before May 6, 1864, until between May 12 and May 18, 1864. In action at Spotsylvania Court House, May 18, 1864, North Anna River, May 24, 1864, and Cold Harbor, June 3, 1864; killed in action in the Petersburg assault, June 17, 1864.

22. **Emerson, George W.**, private. Res. and credit: Millbury, MA. Born: Millbury, MA. Age: 23. Height: 5'3". Comp: dark. Eyes: black. Hair: black. Occup: molder. Enlisted in Millbury by J. E. Waters, Jan. 3, 1864; mustered Jan. 11, 1864. In action and taken prisoner of war at the Wilderness, May 6, 1864. Incarcerated in the Confederate prison camp in Andersonville, GA, where he died from chronic diarrhea and starvation, Aug. 27, 1864. Buried in grave, Sec. E, No. 6994, at Andersonville.

23. **Evans, Joshua**, private. Res. and credit: Oxford, MA. Born: Oxford, MA. Age: 30. Height: 5'5½". Comp: light. Eyes: blue. Hair: brown. Occup: shoemaker. Enlisted in Oxford by L. B. Corbin, Dec. 19, 1863; mustered Jan. 11, 1864. Never in combat with the 57th. Absent sick in an army general hospital from on or before May 6, 1864, until discharged the US service for disability from an army general hospital in Washington, DC, May 12, 1865, in compliance with a telegram from the AGO, War Dept., dated May 4, 1865. Had previous service as an unassigned recruit in the 25th MVI from July 31, 1862, until discharged for disability, Dec. 8, 1862.

24. **Ewing, Albert S.**, private. Res: Rochester, NY. Credit: Springfield, MA. Born: Pembroke, NY. Age: 26. Height: 5'8½". Comp: light. Eyes: blue. Hair: brown. Occup: clerk. Enlisted in Springfield by Capt. Charles D. Hollis, Dec. 29, 1863; mustered Jan. 11, 1864. Killed in action at the Wilderness, May 6, 1864.

25. **Fitts, Charles A.**, private. Res: Boston, MA. Credit: Worcester, MA. Born: Manchester, NH. Age: 18. Height: 5'4". Comp: light. Eyes: blue. Hair: brown. Occup: student. Enlisted in Worcester by Capt. Julius M. Tucker, Jan. 2, 1864; mustered Jan. 11, 1864. In action at the Wilderness, May 6, 1864, and Spotsylvania Court House, May 10, 1864; mortally wounded in both legs in action there, May 12, 1864. Treated in a field hospital in Fredericksburg, VA, and transported aboard the steamer *Columbus* to Washington, DC, where he died from his wounds in Armory Square US Army General Hospital, May 17, 1864.

26. **Fogerty, Edward J.**, private. Res. and/or credit: Worcester, MA. Born: Halifax, Nova Scotia, Canada. Age: 20. Height: 5'5". Comp: fair. Eyes: blue. Hair: brown. Occup: mechanic. Enlisted in Worcester by D. Waldo Lincoln, Jan. 5, 1864; mustered Jan. 11, 1864. Absent sick or on detached duty from on or before May 6 until before May 12, 1864. In action at Spotsylvania Court House, May 12 and 18, 1864, North Anna River, May 24, 1864, and Cold Harbor, June 3, 1864; wounded in action in the Petersburg assault, June 17, 1864. With the regiment on most marches and in most skirmishes and battles until wounded. Absent wounded in an army general hospital until between Oct. 8, 1864, and March 25, 1865. In action at Fort Stedman, March 25, 1865. Mustered out with the regiment at Delaney house, Washington,

DC, July 30, 1865, and discharged in Readville, MA, Aug. 9, 1865, expiration of service. Resided in Worcester, MA, after the war.

27. **Foster, Walter R.**, corporal. Res. and/or credit: Worcester, MA. Born: Hubbardston, MA. Age: 18. Height: 5'6". Comp: sandy. Eyes: blue. Hair: light. Occup: student. Enlisted in Worcester by D. Waldo Lincoln, Jan. 5, 1864; mustered Jan. 11, 1864. In action at the Wilderness, May 6, 1864, Spotsylvania Court House, May 10, 12, and 18, 1864, North Anna River, May 24, 1864, Cold Harbor, June 3, 1864, Petersburg assaults, June 17 and 18, 1864, Petersburg Crater, July 30, 1864, Weldon Railroad, Aug. 19, 1864, Poplar Grove Church, Sept. 30 and Oct. 8, 1864, and Fort Stedman, March 25, 1865. One of the 11 men who served with the regiment on all marches and in all skirmishes and battles throughout its entire wartime service, and of the 10 survivors, one of the 3 who were never wounded, absent sick, deserted, or taken prisoner. Of the 10, he served in the regiment longest, from Jan. 5, 1864, until the regiment was disbanded, Aug. 9, 1865. Also one of the 30 combat soldiers remaining of the regiment after Weldon Railroad, Aug. 19, 1864. Promoted corporal, Feb. 21, 1865. Mustered out with the regiment at Delaney house, Washington, DC, July 30, 1865, and discharged in Readville, MA, Aug. 9, 1865, expiration of service. Resided in Worcester, MA, after the war and was employed as a railroad ticket agent. Died in Worcester Oct. 23, 1879, age 33. "[He] was a quiet, unassuming man, but had a large, warm heart. . . . As a soldier he was brave, reliable and trustworthy" (JA).

28. **Fox, Patrick W.**, sergeant. Res: Athol Depot, MA. Credit: Athol, MA. Born: County Meath, Ireland. Age: 21. Height: 5'11". Comp: light. Eyes: gray. Hair: brown. Occup: carpenter. Enlisted in Athol by C. Kelton, Dec. 26, 1863; mustered Jan. 11, 1864. Promoted sergeant, April 1, 1864. Wounded in action at the Wilderness, May 6, 1864. Absent wounded in an army general hospital until transferred to the 58th Co., 2nd Battln., 10th Regiment, VRC, Aug. 20, 1864. Discharged the US service, Aug. 24, 1865, by order of the War Dept., expiration of service.

Had previous service as a corporal in Co. C, 21st MVI, from Aug. 7, 1861, until discharged for disability as a private, Feb. 14, 1863. Participated with that regiment in the North Carolina campaign in 1862, and at 2nd Bull Run, Aug. 30, 1862; wounded in action at Chantilly, Sept. 1, 1862.

29. **Gates, Daniel C.**, private. Res. and/or credit: Worcester, MA. Born: Lyndon, VT. Age: 45. Height: 5'10". Comp: light. Eyes: blue. Hair: brown. Occup: saloon keeper. Enlisted in Worcester by Capt. Julius M. Tucker, Dec. 18, 1863; mustered Jan. 11, 1864. Never in combat. Absent sick in an army general hospital from on or before May 6, 1864, until discharged the US service for disability, July 6, 1865, by order of the War Dept. Had previous service as a bandsman in the 25th MVI from Sept. 26, 1861, until mustered out, Aug. 30, 1862. Resided in Worcester, MA, after the war.

30. **Geer, Edward D.**, private. Res: Worcester, MA. Credit: Grafton, MA. Born: Worcester, MA. Age: 21. Height: 5'8". Comp: fair. Eyes: blue. Hair: dark. Occup: machinist. Enlisted in Co. D in Grafton by Lt. John Anderson, Jan. 16, 1864; mustered Jan. 25, 1864; transferred to Co. H, Feb. 20, 1864, under RSO 11, dated Feb. 19, 1864, by order of Lt. Col. Edward P. Hollister. Absent sick or on detached duty from on or before May 6, 1864, until between May 12 and May 18, 1864. In action at Spotsylvania Court House, May 18, 1864, North Anna River, May 24, 1864, Cold Harbor, June 3, 1864, and Petersburg assaults, June 17 and 18, 1864; wounded while on duty in the trenches at Petersburg, June 27, 1864. Absent wounded in Camp Meigs US Army General Hospital in Readville, MA, until on or about Nov. 1, 1864. Absent sick from the effects of his wounds again in an army general hospital from the early winter of 1864 until after March 25, 1865. Mustered out with the regiment at Delaney house, Washington, DC, July 30, 1865, and discharged in Readville, MA, Aug. 9, 1865, expiration of service.

31. **Gleason, Charles W.**, private. Res. and/or credit: Millbury, MA. Born: probably Ire-

land. Age: 23. Height: 5'7". Comp: dark. Eyes: hazel. Hair: dark. Occup: farmer. Enlisted in Millbury by J. E. Waters, Jan. 4, 1864; mustered Jan. 11, 1864. Discharged the US service in Camp Wool for physical disability in March 1864, by order of the War Dept.

32. **Goodwin, John L.**, 1st lieutenant. Res. and/or credit: Worcester, MA. Born: Massachusetts. Age: 22. Height: unknown. Comp: fair. Eyes: blue. Hair: light brown. Occup: machinist. Commissioned 1st lieutenant, Jan 6, 1864; mustered 1st lieutenant, Jan. 11, 1864. Wounded by a gunshot in the thigh in action at the Wilderness, May 6, 1864. Absent wounded in an army general hospital until July 20, 1864. Severely wounded in the right foot while on duty in the trenches at Petersburg, July 22, 1864. Taken to the 1st Division, IX Corps, Field Hospital where the second and third metatarsals of the right foot were amputated, July 22, 1864. Absent wounded in an army general hospital in Annapolis, MD, until resigned and discharged the US service on a Surgeons Certificate of Disability for wounds, Nov. 29, 1864, by order of the War Dept. Commissioned captain, July 31, 1864, but not mustered because he

Lieutenant John L. Goodwin.
(John Anderson)

was absent wounded. Had previous service as a private in Co. A, 25th MVI, from Sept. 14, 1861, until mustered out to accept a commission in the 57th, Jan. 5, 1864. Participated in the North Carolina campaign with the 25th in 1862–63. Resided in Worcester, MA, after the war and died there from disease (consumption) contracted while in the service, Nov. 22, 1867, age 25. Buried in Hope Cemetery, Worcester, MA.

33. **Grout, John E.**, private. Res. and credit: Spencer, MA. Born: Spencer, MA. Age: 32. Height: 6'2". Comp: light. Eyes: blue. Hair: black. Occup: farmer. Enlisted in Spencer by L. Hill, Dec. 19, 1863; mustered Jan. 11, 1864. Never in combat. Absent sick from on or before May 6, 1864, until discharged the US service for physical disability (not wounds) at Petersburg, July 1, 1864, by order of Maj. Gen. John A. Dix, War Dept. Died in 1875, age 43.

34. **Hair, Charles N.**, private. Res. and/or credit: Worcester, MA. Born: unknown. Age: 32. 5'11½". Comp: dark. Eyes: blue. Hair: dark. Occup: mechanic. Enlisted in Worcester by Capt. Julius M. Tucker, Jan. 5, 1864; mustered Jan. 11, 1864. Wounded in May 1864, but exact date and circumstances unknown; however, not in a major battle. Absent wounded in an army general hospital until furloughed home and discharged the US service in July 1864, to date Aug. 23, 1864, to accept a commission, Aug. 23, 1864 (see below). Had previous service as sergeant in Co. C, 51st MVI, from Aug. 20, 1862, until mustered out, July 27, 1863. Participated in the North Carolina campaign with that regiment in 1863. Had subsequent service as 1st lieutenant of Co. D, 4th Massachusetts Volunteer Heavy Artillery, from Aug. 12, 1864, until mustered out, June 17, 1865. Performed garrison duty in the defenses of Washington, DC, with that regiment in 1864–65. Died Oct. 19, 1890, age 58.

35. **Handly, John**, private. Res. and/or credit: Worcester, MA. Born: Massachusetts. Age: 18. Height: 5'6½". Comp: dark. Eyes: blue. Hair: brown. Occup: mechanic. Enlisted in Worcester by D. Waldo Lincoln, Jan. 5,

1864; mustered Jan. 11, 1864. Killed in action at the Wilderness, May 6, 1864.

36. **Holbrook, Phineas L.**, private. Res. and/or credit: Leicester, MA. Born: Worcester, MA. Age: 28. Height: 5′6″. Comp: light. Eyes: blue. Hair: brown. Occup: farmer. Enlisted in Leicester by Silas Gleason, Jan. 2, 1864; mustered Jan. 11, 1864. In action at the Wilderness, May 6, 1864, and Spotsylvania Court House, May 10, 12 and 18, 1864; wounded in action at North Anna River, May 24, 1864. Absent wounded in an army general hospital until discharged the US service for disability from wounds, July 20, 1865, by order of the War Dept. Resided in Cherry Valley, MA, after the war.

37. **Horton, James B.**, private. Res. and/or credit: Worcester, MA. Born: Killingly, CT. Age: 28. Height: 5′6″. Comp: light. Eyes: gray. Hair: light. Occup: machinist. Enlisted in Worcester by Capt. Julius M. Tucker, Jan. 4, 1864; mustered Jan. 11, 1864. Never in combat with the 57th. Absent sick or on detached duty from May 6, 1864, until detached and detailed as a stretcher bearer to the 1st Division, IX Corps, Ambulance Corps, from July 11, 1864, until after March 25, 1865. Mustered out with the regiment at Delaney house, Washington, DC, July 30, 1865, and discharged in Readville, MA, Aug. 9, 1865. Had previous service as a private in Co. K, 25th MVI, from Sept. 16, 1861, until discharged for disability in New Bern, NC, April 24, 1863. Participated in the North Carolina campaign with that regiment in 1862–63.

38. **Hoyt, Henry A. F.**, private. Res. and/or credit: Worcester, MA. Born: New York City. Age: 19. Height: 5′6″. Comp: light. Eyes: gray. Hair: light. Occup: conductor. Enlisted in Worcester by D. Waldo Lincoln, Jan. 5, 1864; mustered Jan. 11, 1864. Wounded in action at the Wilderness, May 6, 1864. Absent wounded in an army general hospital until discharged the US service for disability from wounds, April 8, 1865, by order of the War Dept. Resided in Philadelphia, PA, after the war, where he was chaplain-general of the Pennsylvania National Guard. Died after 1929, date unknown.

39. **Hutchins, Frederick P.**, private. Res. and/or credit: Worcester, MA. Born: Thompson, CT. Age: 43. Height: 5′5½″. Comp: dark. Eyes: gray. Hair: light. Occup: landlord. Enlisted in Worcester by Capt. Julius M. Tucker, Jan. 4, 1864; mustered Jan. 11, 1864. Absent sick or on detached duty from on or before May 6, 1864, until between Oct. 8, 1864, and March 25, 1865. Missing in action at Fort Stedman, March 25, 1865, but returned to the regiment for duty on an unknown date (whereabouts while missing unknown). On furlough from July 14 until July 29, 1865. Discharged the US service, Aug. 10, 1865, by order of the War Dept., expiration of service. Not known why he was not mustered out with the regiment. Resided in Putnam, CT, after the war.

40. **Johnson, James T.**, private. Res. and/or credit: Sutton, MA. Born: Northbridge, MA. Age: 19. Height: 5′8″. Comp: light. Eyes: black. Hair: auburn. Occup: shoemaker. Enlisted in Sutton by J. A. Dodge, Jan. 2, 1864; mustered Jan. 11, 1864. In action and taken prisoner of war at the Wilderness, May 6, 1864. Released or escaped on an unknown date, and died from chronic diarrhea (probably contracted while a prisoner of war) in Harewood US Army General Hospital, Washington, DC, June 16, 1864.

41. **Johnson, Joseph J.**, private. Res. and/or credit: Sutton, MA. Born: Northbridge, MA. Age: 18. Height: 5′8″. Comp: light. Eyes: gray. Hair: auburn. Occup: shoemaker. Enlisted in Sutton by J. A. Dodge, Jan. 2, 1864; mustered Jan. 11, 1864. In action at the Wilderness, May 6, 1864, and Spotsylvania Court House, May 10, 1864; killed in action there, May 12, 1864.

42. **Jordan, Martin L.**, private. Res: Leominster, MA. Credit: Worcester, MA. Born: West Brookfield, MA. Age: 18. Height: 5′11″. Comp: light. Eyes: blue. Hair: light. Occup: clerk. Enlisted in Worcester by Capt. Julius M. Tucker, Dec. 28, 1863; mustered Jan. 11, 1864. Never in combat. Absent sick from on or before May 6, 1864, and died from chronic diarrhea in an army general hospital in Washington, DC, May 31, 1864.

Private Martin L. Jordan (taken while regiment was at Camp Wool). *(Mark Savolis)*

43. **Kennay, William,** 1st lieutenant. Res. and/or credit: Boston, MA. Born: unknown. Age: 26. Description not available. Occup: cabinetmaker. Enlisted, Jan. 4, 1864. Commissioned 2nd lieutenant, April 9, 1864; mustered 2nd lieutenant, April 16, 1864. In action at the Wilderness, May 6, 1864, Spotsylvania Court House, May 10, 12 and 18, 1864, North Anna, River, May 24, 1864, Cold Harbor, June 3, 1864, and Petersburg assaults, June 17 and 18, 1864. Wounded in the thigh as acting adjutant while on duty in the trenches at Petersburg, July 20, 1864. With the regiment on all marches and in all skirmishes and battles until wounded. Commissioned 1st lieutenant, Oct. 7, 1864, but not mustered because he was absent wounded. Resigned and discharged the US service, Dec. 27, 1864, for disability from wounds under SO 469, War Dept., dated Oct. 8, 1864. Had previous service as a sergeant in Co. C, 13th MVI, from June 29, 1861, until discharged to accept a commission in the 57th, Jan. 1, 1864. Participated with the 13th at 2nd Bull Run, Aug. 30, 1862, South Mountain, Sept. 14, 1862, Antietem, Sept. 17, 1862, Fredericksburg, Dec. 13, 1862, and Chancellorsville, May 1 through 4, 1863; taken prisoner of war at Gettysburg, July 1, 1863. Paroled and exchanged in Aug. 1863.

44. **Ladaux, Isaac,** private. Res: Saundersville, MA. Credit: Worcester, MA. Born: Platford, province of Quebec, Canada. Age: 21. Height: 5'7". Comp: light. Eyes: blue. Hair: light. Occup: farmer. Enlisted in Worcester by Capt. Julius M. Tucker, Jan. 4, 1864; mustered Jan. 11, 1864. In action at the Wilderness, May 6, 1864, and Spotsylvania Court House, May 10, 1864; wounded in action there, May 12, 1864. Absent wounded in an army general hospital until after March 25, 1865. Detached and detailed as a pioneer at 3rd Brigade, 1st Division, IX Corps, Headquarters in May 1865. Mustered out with the regiment at Delaney house, Washington, DC, July 30, 1865, and discharged in Readville, MA, Aug. 9, 1865, expiration of service.

45. **Leonard, Charles H.,** private. Res. and/or credit: Rutland, MA. Born: Hubbardston, MA. Age: 22. Height: 5'10". Comp: dark. Eyes: dark. Hair: dark. Occup: farmer. Enlisted in Rutland by S. Stone, Jan. 9, 1864; mustered Jan. 11, 1864. Wounded in the head in action at the Wilderness, May 6, 1864. "Private Charles H. Leonard, Co. H, 57th Massachusetts Volunteers, aged 22 years, was wounded at the battle of the Wilderness, Virginia, May 6th, 1864, by a conoidal [Minié] ball, which fractured the left parietal bone at its eminence. He was conveyed to Washington, and entered Columbian [US Army General] Hospital on May 11th. The wound was in good condition, the bone being slightly fractured but not depressed, but the patient was nearly comatose and greatly prostrated. On May 15th, Acting Assistant Surgeon H. D. Vosburg removed portions of the left parietal bone with a trephine, and then took out a fragment of the inner table, which was lying loose on the dura mater. Stimulants and nourishment were freely administered, but the coma became gradually more complete, and the patient died on May 17th, 1864, from cerebritis" (OMR). Remains shipped to Rutland, MA, and buried in a cemetery there. "He was a good soldier, cheerful companion, a true patriot, and an unflinching hero" (*Massachusetts Spy*, May 30, 1864).

46. **Leonard, Daniel A.,** private. Res. and/or credit: Rutland, MA. Born: Hubbardston, MA. Age: 19. Height: 6'0". Comp: dark. Eyes: dark. Hair: black. Occup: farmer. Enlisted in Rutland by S. Stone, Jan. 9, 1864; mustered Jan. 11, 1864. In action at the Wilderness, May 6, 1864, Spotsylvania Court House, May 10, 12, and 18, 1864, North Anna River, May 24, 1864, Cold Harbor, June 3, 1864, and Petersburg assaults, June 17 and 18, 1864; taken prisoner of war at the Petersburg Crater, July 30, 1864. Incarcerated in the Confederate prison in Danville, VA, where he died from disease, Sept. 9, 1864. With the regiment on all marches and in all skirmishes and battles until captured.

47. **Lincoln, George T.,** private. Res: Warren, MA. Credit: Worcester, MA. Born: Warren, MA. Age: 23. Height: 5'7". Comp: light. Eyes: hazel. Hair: light. Occup: farmer. Enlisted in Worcester by Capt. Julius M. Tucker, Jan. 5, 1864; mustered Jan. 11, 1864.

Wounded in action at the Wilderness, May 6, 1864. Absent wounded in an army general hospital until discharged the US service for disability from wounds, Sept. 4, 1865, by order of the War Dept., discharge to date July 30, 1865.

48. **Little, John**, private. Res. and/or credit: Westboro, MA. Born: Haverhill, MA. Age: 21. Height: 5′4″. Comp: light. Eyes: gray. Hair: light. Occup: painter. Enlisted in Westboro by Capt. Julius M. Tucker, Dec. 13, 1863; mustered Jan. 11, 1864. Never in combat. Absent sick or on detached duty from on or before May 6, 1864, until after March 25, 1865. Mustered out with the regiment at Delaney house, Washignton, DC, July 30, 1865, and discharged in Readville, MA, Aug. 9, 1865, expiration of service.

49. **Loomis, Rodney D.**, private. Res: Brasher Falls, NY. Credit: Millbury, MA. Born: St. Albans, VT. Age: 31. Height: 5′5½″. Comp: light. Eyes: blue. Hair: dark. Occup: carpenter. Enlisted in Millbury by J. E. Waters, Jan. 5, 1864; mustered Jan. 11, 1864. In action at the Wilderness, May 6, 1864, and Spotsylvania Court House, May 10, 1864; severely wounded in the left leg in action there, May 12, 1864. Taken to the 1st Division, IX Corps, Field Hospital where his left leg was amputated by the circular method, May 13, 1864, by Assistant Surgeon S. Adams. Absent wounded in an army general hospital until discharged and pensioned from the US service on a Surgeons Certificate of Disability for wounds, Sept. 12, 1865, by order of the War Dept. Resided in Millbury, MA, after the war.

50. **Lovering, Samuel M.**, private. Res. and/or credit: Worcester, MA. Born: Townshend, VT. Age: 40. Height: 5′11½″. Comp: fair. Eyes: blue. Hair: gray. Occup: carpenter. Enlisted in Worcester by D. Waldo Lincoln, Jan. 5, 1864; mustered Jan. 11, 1864. Mortally wounded in action at the Wilderness, May 6, 1864. Died from his wounds at a field hospital in Fredericksburg, VA, May 14, 1864.

51. **Manville, Patrick H.**, private. Res. and/or credit: Leicester, MA. Born: Dundalk, County Louth, Ireland. Age: 18. Height: 5′3½″. Comp: light. Eyes: hazel. Hair: brown. Occup: mechanic. Enlisted in Leicester by Silas Gleason, Jan. 2, 1864; mustered Jan. 11, 1864. In action at the Wilderness, May 6, 1864, and Spotsylvania Court House, May 10, 12, and 18, 1864; killed in action at North Anna River, May 24, 1864.

52. **Marshall, James A.**, private. Res. and/or credit: Worcester, MA. Born: Fitchburg, MA. Age: 25. Height: 5′4½″. Comp: dark. Eyes: brown. Hair: dark. Occup: artist and photographer. Enlisted in Worcester by Capt. Julius M. Tucker, Dec. 23, 1863; mustered Jan. 11, 1864. Wounded in action at the Wilderness, May 6, 1864. Absent wounded in an army general hospital until between Oct. 8, 1864, and March 25, 1865. In action at Fort Stedman, March 25, 1865. Mustered out with the regiment at Delaney house, Washington, DC, July 30, 1865, and discharged in Readville, MA, Aug. 9, 1865, expiration of service. Had previous service as a private in Co. A, 36th MVI, from Aug. 15, 1862, until discharged for disability in Boston, MA, Dec. 8, 1862. Saw no action with that regiment. Resided in North Leominster, MA, after the war.

53. **Mathews, Eli**, private. Res. and/or credit: Worcester, MA. Born: Stafford, CT. Age: 34. Height: 5′7½″. Comp: light. Eyes: blue. Hair: light. Occup: wheelwright. Enlisted in Worcester by Capt. Julius M. Tucker, Dec. 26, 1863; mustered Jan. 11, 1864. Slightly wounded in action at the Wilderness, May 6, 1864. Absent wounded in an army general hospital until between Oct. 8, 1864, and March 25, 1865. In action at Fort Stedman, March 25, 1865. Detached and detailed at the 1st Division, IX Corps, Field Hospital at Petersburg as a nurse, April 12, 1865. Mustered out with the regiment at Delaney house, Washington, DC, July 30, 1865, and discharged in Readville, MA, Aug. 9, 1865, expiration of service.

54. **Merriam, Henry**, private. Res. and/or credit: Worcester, MA. Born: Stafford, CT. Age: 30. Height: 5′10½″. Comp: light. Eyes: black. Hair: dark. Occup: mechanic. Enlisted

Private Rodney Loomis (taken while regiment was at Camp Wool). *(John Anderson)*

in Worcester by Capt. Julius M. Tucker, Jan. 4, 1864; mustered Jan. 11, 1864. Never in combat. Present sick or absent on detached duty from on or before May 6, 1864, until listed on his descriptive roll as absent sick from an unknown date in June 1864 until discharged the US service from New York General Hospital for physical disability not caused by wounds, June 17, 1865, by order of the War Dept.

55. **Merriam, Horace,** private. Res: Palmer, MA. Credit: Worcester, MA. Born: Martinsburg, NY. Age: 21. Height: 5'11". Comp: light. Eyes: blue. Hair: light. Occup: mechanic. Enlisted in Worcester by Capt. Julius M. Tucker, Jan. 4, 1864; mustered Jan. 11, 1864. Never in combat. Absent sick in an army general hospital from on or before May 6, 1864, until discharged the US service on a Surgeons Certificate of Disability, Sept. 30, 1864. Resided in New Haven, CT, after the war.

56. **Mills, Isaac M.,** private. Res. and credit: Worcester, MA. Born: Worcester, MA. Age: 26. Height: 5'9". Comp: dark. Eyes: hazel. Hair: dark. Occup: machinist. Enlisted in Worcester by Capt. Julius M. Tucker, Jan. 5, 1864; mustered Jan. 11, 1864. In action at the Wilderness, May 6, 1864, and one of the 34 enlisted men who remained with the colors during that battle. In action at Spotsylvania Court House, May 10, 1864, and slightly wounded in action there, May 12, 1864. Absent wounded in an army general hospital until an unknown date in July 1864. Absent sick (probably from wounds received at Spotsylvania) in an army general hospital from before July 30, 1864, until discharged the US service for disability, Aug. 8, 1865, by order of the War Dept. Resided in Worcester, MA, after the war and died there Sept. 17, 1927, age 90.

57. **Murdock, Albert M.,** 1st lieutenant. Res: West Boylston, MA. Credit: Worcester, MA. Born: Arkansas (one of the four Southern-born soldiers in the regiment). Age: 18. Height: 5'8". Comp: dark. Eyes: black. Hair: dark. Occup: clerk. Enlisted in Worcester by Capt. Julius M. Tucker, Dec. 29, 1863; mus-

Sergeant Major Albert Murdock.
(Mark Savolis)

tered Jan. 11, 1864. Promoted sergeant major and transferred to the regimental noncommissioned staff, Jan. 11, 1864. Slightly wounded in the arm in action at the Wilderness, May 6, 1864. Absent wounded in an army general hospital until Jan. 3, 1865. Commissioned 1st lieutenant of Co. H, Oct. 7, 1864, while absent wounded; mustered 1st lieutenant, to date, Jan. 3, 1865. Killed in action at Fort Stedman, March 25, 1865. Remains shipped to West Boylston, MA, and buried in a cemetery there.

58. **Murray, Andrew,** private. Res: Barre, MA. Credit: Worcester, MA. Born: Barre, MA. Age: 21. Height: 5'8". Comp: dark. Eyes: black. Hair: black. Occup: butcher. Enlisted in Worcester by Capt. Julius M. Tucker, Jan. 4, 1864; mustered Jan. 11, 1864. Absent for unknown reasons during the battle of the Wilderness, May 6, 1864. In action at Spotsylvania Court House May 10, 12, and 18, 1864, North Anna River, May 24, 1864, Cold Harbor, June 3, 1864, and Petersburg assaults, June 17 and 18, 1864; missing in action at the Petersburg Crater, July 30, 1864. Never accounted for and presumed killed. With the regiment on all marches and in all skirmishes and battles, except the Wilderness, through July 30, 1864. (Requested in writing

a transfer to the US Navy from Brig. Gen. James B. Fry, provost marshal general, July 11, 1864. No reply ever received.)

59. **Paine, John A.**, private. Res: Sutton, MA. Credit: Worcester, MA. Born: Grafton, MA. Age: 38. Height: 5'5". Comp: light. Eyes: blue. Hair: light. Occup: bootmaker. Enlisted in Worcester by Capt. Julius M. Tucker, Jan. 5, 1864; mustered Jan. 11, 1864. In action at the Wilderness, May 6, 1864, and Spotsylvania Court House, May 10, 12, and 18, 1864; taken prisoner of war at North Anna River, May 24, 1864. Incarcerated in the Confederate prison camp in Andersonville, GA, where he died from scurvy, Sept. 16, 1864. Buried in a grave at Andersonville marked "unknown."

60. **Park, Henry L.**, corporal. Res. and/or credit: Worcester, MA. Born: Shrewsbury, MA. Age: 19. Height: 5'10½". Comp: light. Eyes: blue. Hair: dark. Occup: armorer. Enlisted in Worcester by Capt. Julius M. Tucker, Dec. 14, 1863; mustered Jan. 11, 1864. Promoted corporal, March 1, 1864. In action at the Wilderness, May 6, 1864, and Spotsylvania Court House, May 10, 12, and 18, 1864; killed in action at North Anna River, May 24, 1864.

61. **Park, William C.**, sergeant. Res. and/or credit: Worcester, MA. Born: Shrewsbury, MA. Age: 18. Height: unknown. Comp: light. Eyes: blue. Hair: dark. Occup: student. Enlisted in Worcester by Capt. Julius M. Tucker, Dec. 14, 1863; mustered Jan. 11, 1864. Promoted sergeant, March 1, 1864. Wounded in action at the Wilderness, May 6, 1864. Absent wounded in an army general hospital until between June 17 and July 11, 1864. Wounded in action again and taken prisoner of war at the Petersburg Crater, July 30, 1864. Incarcerated in the Confederate prison in Danville, VA, where he died from his wounds, Jan. 31, 1865. (Requested in writing a transfer to the US Navy from Brig. Gen. James B. Fry, provost marshal general, July 11, 1864. No reply ever received.)

62. **Parker, Marshall**, private. Res: West Boylston, MA. Credit: Worcester, MA. Born: Boxford, ME. Age: 27. Height: 5'11". Comp:

light. Eyes: blue. Hair: dark. Occup: blacksmith. Enlisted in Worcester by Capt. Julius M. Tucker, Jan. 1, 1864; mustered Jan. 11, 1864. In action at the Wilderness, May 6, 1864, and Spotsylvania Court House, May 10, 12, and 18, 1864; wounded in action at North Anna River, May 24, 1864. Absent wounded until discharged the US service for disability from wounds from Carver US Army General Hospital, Washington, DC, by order of the War Dept., Feb. 21, 1865.

63. **Patch, George E.**, corporal. Res. and credit: Worcester, MA. Born: Worcester, MA. Age: 26. Height: 5'6". Comp: light. Eyes: gray. Hair: light. Occup: farmer. Enlisted in Worcester by Capt. Julius M. Tucker, Jan. 4, 1864; mustered Jan. 11, 1864. Promoted corporal, March 1, 1864. In action at the Wilderness, May 6, 1864, Spotsylvania Court House, May 10, 12, and 18, 1864, North Anna River, May 24, 1864, and Cold Harbor, June 3, 1864; wounded on the march to Petersburg on June 16 or 17, 1864. Absent wounded in an army general hospital until transferred to Co. K, 10th Regiment, VRC, March 25, 1865. With the regiment on all marches and in all skirmishes and battles until wounded. Reduced to the ranks, Feb. 21, 1864, probably because he was absent wounded. Discharged the US service, Sept. 14, 1865, by order of the War Dept., expiration of service. Resided in Worcester, MA, after the war.

64. **Pinkham, Charles H.**, 2nd lieutenant. Res. and/or credit: Worcester, MA. Born: Grafton, MA. Age: 19. Height: 5'4". Comp: light. Eyes: blue. Hair: dark. Occup: clerk. Enlisted in Worcester by Capt. Julius M. Tucker, Dec. 27, 1863; mustered Jan. 11, 1864. Promoted corporal, March 1, 1864. Wounded in action at the Wilderness, May 6, 1864. Absent wounded in an army general hospital until between Aug. 19 and Sept. 1, 1864. Promoted sergeant, Sept. 1, 1864. In action at Poplar Grove Church, Sept 30 and Oct. 8, 1864, and in other operations of the regiment during the fall and winter of 1864–65. Promoted 1st sergeant, Nov. 1, 1864. Promoted sergeant major and transferred to the regimental noncommissioned staff, Jan. 1,

Second lieutenant Charles Pinkham
(postwar photo). *(USAMHI)*

1865. On leave of absence in Massachusetts from Jan. 19 until Feb. 7, 1865. In action at Fort Stedman, March 25, 1865, and won the Medal of Honor for saving the regiment's colors from capture: "Captured the flag of the 57th North Carolina Infantry (C.S.A.) and saved his own colors by tearing them from the staff while the enemy was in the camp" (JA). Cited twice for his actions on March 25, 1865: "Sergeant-Major C. H. Pinkham, captured battle-flag of 57th North Carolina and saved his own colors by seizing them from the staff while the enemy were in the camp" (GPR), and "Sergeant-Major Charles H. Pinkham, captured battle-flag of Fifty-Seventh North Carolina (rebel); saved colors of his regiment from capture, seizing them from a tent after the enemy had entered the regimental camp" (JMT). On leave of absence in Massachusetts from May 19 until June 7, 1865. Commissioned 2nd lieutenant, June 12, 1865, and transferred to Co. K; mustered 2nd lieutenant, June 26, 1865. Mustered out with the regiment at Delaney house, Washington, DC, July 30, 1865, and discharged in Readville, MA, Aug. 9, 1865, expiration of service.

Appointed 1st lieutenant and captain of US Volunteers by brevet to date from March 13, 1865, under GO 67, AGO, War Dept., dated July 16, 1867, for "gallant and meritorious services while in front of Petersburg in 1864, and more especially for gallantry on the 25th of March, 1865, he at that time, capturing the colors of the 57th North Carolina Volunteers of Gordon's rebel brigade" (OR). Resided in Worcester, MA, after the war. Treasurer of the 57th's regimental association, 1867. President of the 57th's regimental association, 1886, '87, and '88. Died after 1915, date unknown.

65. **Puffer, Jonathan,** private. Res: Holliston, MA. Credit: Worcester, MA. Born: Sudbury, MA. Age: 39. Height: 5'6". Comp: dark. Eyes: gray. Hair: dark. Occup: mechanic. Enlisted in Worcester by Capt. Julius M. Tucker, Jan. 4, 1864; mustered Jan. 11, 1864. In action and taken prisoner of war at the Wilderness, May 6, 1864. Paroled and exchanged from an unknown Confederate prison, Nov. 27, 1864. Never returned to the regiment and discharged the US service for disability, June 17, 1865, by order of the War Dept. Probably received extra pay for having been a prisoner of war. Had previous service as a private in Co. K, 43rd MVI, from Aug. 20, 1862, until mustered out, July 30, 1863. Participated in the North Carolina campaign with that regiment in 1862–63.

66. **Raymore, James H.,** private. Res. and/or credit: Worcester, MA. Born: Sterling, MA. Age: 45. Height: 5'6". Comp: dark. Eyes: black. Hair: dark. Occup: millwright. Enlisted in Worcester by Capt. Julius M. Tucker, Jan. 2, 1864; mustered Jan. 11, 1864. Detailed as company cook, Feb. 14, 1864, under RSO 13, by order of Col. William F. Bartlett. On leave of absence in Massachusetts from about Jan. 13 until about Jan. 28, 1865. Never in combat until taken prisoner of war at Fort Stedman, March 25, 1865. Paroled from Libby Prison, Richmond, VA, March 29, 1865, and exchanged, April 2, 1865. Returned to the regiment for duty from the Camp of Parole in Annapolis, MD, on or about May 11, 1865. On furlough from June 24 until July 7, 1865. Discharged the US service for disability, prob-

ably from an army general hospital, Aug. 10, 1865, by order of the War Dept. Died May 23, 1879, age 60.

67. **Reed, Thomas R.**, private. Res. and/or credit: Springfield, MA. Born: England. Age: 33. Height: 5'10½". Comp: light. Eyes: blue. Hair: dark. Occup: saddler. Enlisted in Co. D in Springfield by Capt. Charles D. Hollis, Dec. 23, 1863; mustered Jan. 25, 1864; transferred to Co. H, Feb. 20, 1864, under RSO 11, dated Feb. 19, 1864, by order of Col. William F. Bartlett. Absent sick or on detached duty from on or about May 6, 1864, until between Oct. 8, 1864, and March 25, 1865. In action at Fort Stedman, March 25, 1865. Detached and detailed as a clerk at 3rd Brigade, 1st Division, IX Corps, Headquarters, June 1, 1865. Mustered out with the regiment at Delaney house, Washington, DC, July 30, 1865, and discharged in Readville, MA, Aug. 9, 1865, expiration of service.

68. **Rice, William H.**, private. Res. and credit: Oxford, MA. Born: Oxford, MA. Age: 34. Height: 5'8½". Comp: light. Eyes: gray. Hair: brown. Occup: farmer. Enlisted in Oxford by L. B. Corbin, Dec. 23, 1863; mustered Jan. 11, 1864. In action at the Wilderness, May 6, 1864, Spotsylvania Court House, May 10, 12, and 18, 1864, North Anna River, May 24, 1864, Cold Harbor, June 3, 1864, and Petersburg assaults, June 17 and 18, 1864. Absent sick in an army general hospital from an unknown date in July 1864 until discharged the US service for disability, May 25, 1865, by order of the War Dept. On all marches and in all skirmishes and battles until the time of his illness. Resided in Worcester, MA, after the war.

69. **Richards, William E.**, sergeant. Res. and/or credit: Worcester, MA. Born: Massachusetts. Age: 19. Height: unknown. Comp: light. Eyes: blue. Hair: light. Occup: student. Enlisted in Worcester by Capt. Julius M. Tucker, Dec. 14, 1863; mustered Jan. 11, 1864. Promoted sergeant, March 1, 1864. Wounded on an unknown date in May 1864, but not in a major battle. Absent wounded in an army general hospital until between June 17 and July 20, 1864. Reduced to the ranks to

accept a position as a clerk in the 4th Division, IX Corps, with USCT, July 20, 1864. Died from chronic diarrhea in Dale US Army General Hospital in Worcester, MA, March 16, 1865. Had previous service as a private in Co. F, 51st MVI, from Sept. 8, 1862, until mustered out, July 27, 1863. Participated in the North Carolina campaign with that regiment in 1862–63.

70. **Richardson, Lewis**, private. Res. and/or credit: Leominster, MA. Born: Sterling, MA. Age: 18. Height: 5'4". Comp: dark. Eyes: hazel. Hair: brown. Occup: machinist. Enlisted in Leominster by C. H. Merriam, Jan. 5, 1864; mustered Jan. 11, 1864. Killed in action at the Wilderness, May 6, 1864.

71. **Ricker, Albert M.**, corporal. Res: Dover, NH. Credit: Worcester, MA. Born: Rochester, NH. Age: 21. Height: 5'6". Comp: light. Eyes: hazel. Hair: black. Occup: mechanic. Enlisted in Worcester by Capt. Julius M. Tucker, Jan. 4, 1864; mustered Jan. 11, 1864. Absent sick or on detached duty from on or before May 6, 1864, until between Oct. 8 and Nov. 1, 1864. Promoted corporal, Nov. 1, 1864. Reduced to the ranks for an unknown reason, Feb. 18, 1864. With the regiment in operations during the fall and winter of 1864–65, and in action at Fort Stedman, March 25, 1865. Mustered out with the regiment at Delaney house, Washington, DC, July 30, 1865 and discharged in Readville, MA, Aug. 9, 1865, expiration of service. Resided in Boston Highlands, Boston, MA, after the war.

72. **Robinson, George A.**, private. Res. and/or credit: Worcester, MA. Born: Newton, MA. Age: 18. Height: 5'7". Comp: dark. Eyes: black. Hair: dark. Occup: machinist. Enlisted in Worcester by Capt. Julius M. Tucker, Jan. 5, 1864; mustered Jan. 11, 1864. Absent sick or on detached duty from on or before May 6, 1864, until between May 12 and May 18, 1864. In action at Spotsylvania Court House, May 18, 1864, North Anna River, May 24, 1864, Cold Harbor, June 3, 1864, and Petersburg assaults, June 17 and 18, 1864; wounded while on duty in the trenches at Petersburg, June 30, 1864. Absent wounded in an army general hospital until

discharged the US service for disability from wounds, July 5, 1865, by order of the War Dept. Resided in Meriden, CT, and Belvidere, IL, after the war and died in Belvidere after mid-1927, date unknown.

73. **Rollins, Stephen H.,** private. Res. and/or credit: Spencer, MA. Born: Leicester, MA. Age: 19. Height: 5'4½". Comp: light. Eyes: blue. Hair: light. Occup: bootmaker. Enlisted in Spencer by L. Hill, Dec. 14, 1864; mustered Jan. 11, 1864. Never in combat with the 57th. Absent sick from on or before May 6, 1864, until discharged the US service for physical disability not caused by wounds on a Surgeons Certificate of Disability from an army general hospital in Washington, DC, Sept. 12, 1864, by order of the War Dept. Had subsequent service as a private in Co. L, 4th Massachusetts Volunteer Cavalry, from from Dec. 8, 1864, until discharged in Varina, VA, Jan. 19, 1865. Assigned to corps's headquarters duties at Petersburg with that regiment.

74. **Ryan, John,** private. Res. and/or credit: Worcester, MA. Born: County Tipperary, Ireland. Age: 18. Height: 5'7". Comp: dark. Eyes: brown. Hair: dark. Occup: bootmaker. Enlisted in Worcester by Capt. Julius M. Tucker, Dec. 23, 1863; mustered Jan. 11, 1864. In action at the Wilderness, May 6, 1864, Spotsylvania Court House, May 10, 12, and 18, 1864, North Anna River, May 24, 1864, Cold Harbor, June 3, 1864, and Petersburg assaults, June 17 and 18, 1864; taken prisoner of war at the Petersburg Crater, July 30, 1865. With the regiment on all marches and in all skirmishes and battles until captured. Incarcerated in the Confederate prison in Danville, VA until paroled and exchanged, Feb. 22, 1865. Probably received extra pay for having been a prisoner of war. Discharged the US service for disability not caused by wounds, June 29, 1865, by order of the War Dept. Died March 18, 1867, age 21. (Death likely caused as the result of his imprisonment during the war.)

75. **Savage, Henry G.,** private. Res. and credit: Worcester, MA. Born: Worcester, MA. Age: 18. Height: 5'6½". Comp: light.

Eyes: blue. Hair: light. Occup: clerk. Enlisted in Worcester by Capt. Julius M. Tucker, Jan. 4, 1864; mustered Jan. 11, 1864. Never in combat. Detached and detailed as a clerk at 1st Brigade, 1st Division, IX Corps, Headquarters from on or before May 6, 1864, until wounded by the accidental explosion of gunpowder at those headquarters at Petersburg on an unknown date in July 1864. Absent wounded in Camp Meigs US Army General Hospital in Readville, MA, until transferred to Co. I, 2nd Regiment, VRC, Feb. 14, 1865. Discharged the US service, July 22, 1865, by order of the War Dept., expiration of service. Resided in Chicago, IL, after the war.

76. **Shamboo, Christopher,** private. Res. and/or credit: Sutton, MA. Born: Vermont. Age: 18. Height: 5'6". Comp: light. Eyes: blue. Hair: auburn. Occup: wall layer. Enlisted in Sutton by J. A. Dodge, Jan. 2, 1864; mustered Jan. 11, 1864. In action at the Wilderness, May 6, 1864, and Spotsylvania Court House, May 10, 1864; wounded in action there, May 12, 1864. Absent wounded in an army general hospital until mustered out, but absent wounded, at Delaney house, Washington, DC, July 30, 1865, expiration of service.

77. **Shamboo, Edward,** private. Res: Sutton, MA. Credit: Grafton, MA. Born: province of Quebec, Canada. Age: 21. Height: 5'8". Comp: dark. Eyes: blue. Hair: light. Occup: shuttle maker. Enlisted in Grafton by J. S. Nelson, Jan. 1, 1864; mustered Jan. 11, 1864. Never in combat. Absent sick in an army general hospital from on or before May 6, 1864, until after March 25, 1865. Mustered out with the regiment at Delaney house, Washington, DC, July 30, 1865, and discharged in Readville, MA, Aug. 9, 1865, expiration of service. Resided in Wilkinsonville, MA, after the war.

78. **Sharp, Charles,** private. Res: Haverhill, MA. Credit: Worcester, MA. Born: Springfield, MA. Age: 25. Height: 5'6". Comp: dark. Eyes: gray. Hair: dark. Occup: mechanic. Enlisted in Worcester by D. Waldo Lincoln, Jan. 5, 1864; mustered Jan. 11, 1864. Severely wounded in action at the Wilderness, May 6, 1864. Absent wounded in an army general

hospital until transferred to the 38th Co., 2nd Battln., VRC, March 4, 1865. Discharged the US service, Aug. 11, 1865, by order of the War Dept., expiration of service.

79. **Short, Frank**, private. Res: Worcester, MA. Credit: Harvard, MA. Born: Ireland. Age: 24. Height: 5'8½". Comp: dark. Eyes: gray. Hair: dark. Occup: laborer. Enlisted in Harvard by Lt. John L. Goodwin, Jan. 8, 1864; mustered Jan. 11, 1864. Never in combat. Fell out on the march to the Wilderness, May 5, 1864. However, he was wounded in the Wilderness area, but not on the battle line (probably accidentally or by Confederate guerillas). Absent wounded in an army general hospital. Company records show him as missing since May 5, 1864, yet mustered out, but absent sick at Delaney house, Washington, DC, July 30, 1865, expiration of service.

80. **Shurn, Dennis**, private. Res. and/or credit: Millbury, MA. Born: Canada. Age: 18. Height: 5'8". Comp: light. Eyes: blue. Hair: dark. Occup: spinner. Enlisted in Millbury by C. D. Morse, Jan. 7, 1864; mustered Jan. 11, 1864. In action at the Wilderness, May 6, 1864, and Spotsylvania Court House, May 10, 1864; wounded in action there, May 12, 1864. Absent wounded until he deserted from an army general hospital while on a furlough to Canada, Dec. 25, 1864. Surrendered to authorities May 9, 1865, under President Lincoln's proclamation of amnesty. Discharged the US service (probably for disability), May 15, 1865, by order of the War Dept. Died in 1891, age 45.

81. **Smith, Eugene**, private. Res. and/or credit: Worcester, MA. Born: Bainbridge, NY. Age: 18. Height: 5'6". Comp: dark. Eyes: dark. Hair: dark. Occup: baker. Enlisted in Worcester by Capt. Julius M. Tucker, Jan. 4, 1864; mustered Jan. 11, 1864. Killed in action at the Wilderness, May 6, 1864.

82. **Spencer, David F.**, musician. Res: Thomaston, CT. Credit: Worcester, MA. Born: Pomfret, CT. Age: 30. Height: 5'6". Comp: light. Eyes: blue. Hair: light. Occup: machinist. Enlisted in Worcester by Capt. Julius M. Tucker, Dec. 21, 1863; mustered

Jan. 11, 1864. Company drummer. Probably also served as a nurse, stretcher bearer, and/or hospital orderly. Present with the regiment during the battle of Fort Stedman, but if he was in action is unknown. Mustered out with the regiment at Delaney house, Washington, DC, July 30, 1865, and discharged in Readville, MA, Aug. 9, 1865, expiration of service. Resided in Worcester, MA, after the war.

83. **Sprague, Amos Jr.**, private. Res. and/or credit: Worcester, MA. Born: New Bedford, MA. Age: 24. Height: 5'4". Comp: light. Eyes: gray. Hair: light. Occup: painter. Enlisted in Worcester by Capt. Julius M. Tucker, Jan. 5, 1864; mustered Jan. 11, 1864. Absent for unknown reasons during the battle of the Wilderness, May 6, 1864. In action at Spotsylvania Court House, May 10, 12, and 18, 1864, North Anna River, May 24, 1864, Cold Harbor, June 3, 1864, and Petersburg assaults, June 17 and 18, 1864; severely wounded in the upper right forearm (ulna) while on picket duty at Petersburg, June 26, 1864. Underwent surgery for the removal of a musket ball from his right arm at the 1st Division, IX Corps, Field Hospital, June 26, 1864, but no amputation was made. Absent wounded in an army general hospital until discharged and pensioned from the US service on a Surgeons Certificate of Disability for wounds ("no power in hand or forearm" [OMR]), July 22, 1865, by order of the War Dept. With the regiment on all marches in all skirmishes and battles, except the Wilderness, until being wounded. Had previous service as a corporal in Co. D, 51st MVI, from Aug. 28, 1862, until discharged for disability, Nov. 25, 1862. Saw no action with that regiment. Also had previous service as a private in Co. D, 15th MVI, from July 12, 1861, until discharged for disability, April 15, 1862. Possibly participated at Ball's Bluff, Oct 21, 1861. Died Jan. 20, 1890, age 50.

84. **Stetson, James M.**, private. Res: North Bridgewater, MA. Credit: Worcester, MA. Born: West Bridgewater, MA. Age: 21. Height: 5'10½". Comp: light. Eyes: black. Hair: black. Occup: tailor. Enlisted in Worcester by Capt. Julius M. Tucker, Jan. 2, 1864; mustered Jan. 11, 1864. In action at the

Wilderness, May 6, 1864, and Spotsylvania Court House, May 10, 1864; severely wounded in the right thigh in action there, May 12, 1864. Taken to the 1st Division, IX Corps, Field Hospital where he underwent surgery, May 13, 1864, for the amputation of his right leg to the lower third of the thigh by the anterior/posterior flap method. Transferred to an army general hospital in Washington, DC, where he died from pyemia, May 31, 1864.

85. **Stockwell, Warren H.**, private. Res. and/or credit: Millbury, MA. Born: Millbury, MA. Age: 18. Height: 5'8". Comp: sandy. Eyes: blue. Hair: light. Occup: farmer. Enlisted in Millbury by C. D. Morse, Jan. 8, 1864; mustered Jan. 11, 1864. Wounded in action at the Wilderness, May 6, 1864. Absent wounded in an army general hospital until between Oct. 8, 1864, and March 25, 1865. In action at Fort Stedman, March 25, 1865. Mustered out with the regiment at Delaney house, Washington, DC, July 30, 1865, and discharged in Readville, MA, Aug. 9, 1865, expiration of service.

86. **Streeter, Hiram**, private. Res. and/or credit: Leicester, MA. Born: Whitingham, VT. Age: 38. Height: 5'8". Comp: light. Eyes: blue. Hair: brown. Occup: farmer. Enlisted in Leicester by Silas Gleason, Dec. 31, 1863; mustered Jan. 11, 1864. In action at the Wilderness, May 6, 1864, and one of the 34 enlisted men who remained with the colors during that battle. In action at Spotsylvania Court House, May 10, 12, and 18, 1864, North Anna River, May 24, 1864, and Cold Harbor, June 3, 1864; killed in action during the Petersburg assault, June 17, 1864. With the regiment on all marches and in all skirmishes and battles until killed.

87. **Taft, Edward P.**, private. Res. and credit: Worcester, MA. Born: Worcester, MA. Age: 19. Height: 5'7". Comp: light. Eyes: blue. Hair: light. Occup: conductor. Enlisted in Worcester by D. Waldo Lincoln, Jan. 5, 1864; mustered Jan. 11, 1864. Absent sick or on detached duty from on or before May 6, 1864, until between Oct. 8, 1864, and March 25, 1865. Wounded in action at Fort Sted-

man, March 25, 1865. Absent wounded until discharged the US service for disability from wounds from an army general hospital in Washington, DC, May 24, 1865, under SO 77, par. 6, AGO, War Dept. Resided in Worcester, MA, after the war.

88. **Timon, Charles,** private. Res: Fitchburg, MA. Credit: Worcester, MA. Born: Fitchburg, MA. Age: 21. Height: 5'9". Comp: light. Eyes: blue. Hair: dark. Occup: clerk. Enlisted in Worcester by Capt. Julius M. Tucker, Jan. 4, 1864; mustered Jan. 11, 1864. Never in combat. Likely detached and detailed as a clerk at brigade, division, or corps headquarters from on or before May 6, 1864, until after March 25, 1865. Possibly present during the battle of Fort Stedman, March 25, 1865, but not in action. Mustered out with the regiment at Delaney house, Washington, DC, July 30, 1865, and discharged in Readville, MA, Aug. 9, 1865, expiration of service. Had previous service as a private in Co. I, 15th MVI, from Aug. 6, 1861, until discharged for disability near Yorktown, VA, April 12, 1862. Possibly participated at Ball's Bluff, Oct. 21, 1861, in the Shenandoah Valley, 1862, and in part of the Peninsula campaign, 1862. Resided in Brooklyn, NY, after the war and died there in 1886, age 43.

89. **Tourtellott, George W.**, sergeant. Res. and credit: Sutton, MA. Born: Sutton, MA. Age: 19. Height: 5'9". Comp: light. Eyes: blue. Hair: light. Occup: laborer. Enlisted in Sutton by J. A. Dodge, Dec. 31, 1863; mustered Jan. 11, 1864. Absent sick or on detached duty from on or before May 6, 1864, until between Oct. 8 and Nov. 11, 1864. Promoted corporal, Nov. 11, 1864. Promoted sergeant, Jan. 20, 1865. With the regiment in operations during the fall and winter of 1864–65, and in action at Fort Stedman, March 25, 1865. Mustered out with the regiment at Delaney house, Washington, DC, July 30, 1865, and discharged in Readville, MA, Aug. 9, 1865, expiration of service. Had previous service as a private in Co. C, 51st MVI, from Aug. 20, 1862, until mustered out July 27, 1863. Participated in the North Carolina campaign with that regiment in 1862–63. Resided in Kansas City, MO, after the war.

Sergeant G. W. Tourtellot
(postwar photo). *(John Anderson)*

90. **Tourtellott, Thomas J.**, private. Res. and/ or credit: Millbury, MA. Born: Sutton, MA. Age: 25. Height: 5'11". Comp: light. Eyes: blue. Hair: light. Occup: hostler. Enlisted in Millbury by C. D. Morse, Dec. 22, 1863; mustered Jan. 11, 1864. In action at the Wilderness, May 6, 1864, and Spotsylvania Court House, May 10, 12, and 18, 1864; wounded in action at North Anna River, May 24, 1864. Absent wounded in an army general hospital until between Oct. 8, 1864, and March 25, 1865. Severely wounded in the left leg in action at Fort Stedman, March 25, 1865. Underwent surgery for the amputation of his left leg by the circular method, May 28, 1865, by Surgeon W. O. McDonald, USV. Absent wounded in an army general hospital until discharged and pensioned from the US service on a Surgeons Certificate of Disability for wounds, Oct. 20, 1865, to date Aug. 3, 1865, by order of the War Dept. Had previous service as a private in Co. E, 42nd MVI, from Sept. 1, 1862, until mustered out, Aug. 20, 1863. Participated in operations in Louisiana with that regiment in 1863. Resided in Millbury, MA, after the war.

91. **Wakeman, George M.**, private. Res. and credit: Worcester, MA. Born: Worcester, MA. Age: 21. Height: 5'8". Comp: light. Eyes: blue. Hair: brown. Occup: actor. Enlisted in Worcester by Capt. Julius M. Tucker, Dec. 30, 1863; mustered Jan. 11, 1864. Absent sick or on detached duty from on or before May 6, 1864, until between Oct. 8, 1864, and March 25, 1865. Wounded in action at Fort Stedman, March 25, 1865. Absent wounded in Lincoln US Army General Hospital in Washington, DC, until June 5, 1865, when he was arrested and incarcerated in the "Central Guard House [Washington, DC] for having committed a theft" (CR), June 5, 1865. Discharged the US service for disability from wounds, July 12, 1865, by order of the War Dept.

92. **Walton, Edward Alonzo**, private. Res. and/or credit: Worcester, MA. Born: West Boylston, MA, Oct. 2, 1835. Age: 28. Married. Height: 5'11". Comp: dark. Eyes: gray. Hair: dark. Occup: machinist. Enlisted in Worcester by Capt. Julius M. Tucker, Jan. 4, 1864; mustered Jan. 11, 1864. In action at the Wilderness, May 6, 1864, and Spotsylvania Court House, May 10, 12, and 18, 1864; taken prisoner of war at North Anna River, May 24, 1864. Incarcerated in the Confederate prison camp in Andersonville, GA, where he died from chronic diarrhea, dysentery, and starvation, Aug. 10, 1864. Buried in grave No. 5191 at Andersonville.

93. **Webb, Joseph C.**, private. Res. and/or credit: Grafton, MA. Born: Smithfield, VT. Age: 32. Height: 5'6". Comp: light. Eyes: blue. Hair: brown. Occup: shuttle maker. Enlisted in Grafton by J. S. Nelson, Jan. 1, 1864; mustered Jan. 11, 1864. Never in combat. Absent sick from on or before May 6, 1864, and died from chronic diarrhea in an army general hospital in Philadelphia, PA, Aug. 18, 1864.

94. **Wellman, George H.**, private. Res: Palmer, MA. Credit: Worcester, MA. Born: Palmer, MA. Age: 19. Height: 5'11". Comp: light. Eyes: blue. Hair: light. Occup: machinist. Enlisted in Worcester by Capt. Julius M. Tucker, Jan. 4, 1864; mustered Jan. 11, 1864.

Absent sick or on detached duty from on or before May 6, 1864, until between June 17 and July 30, 1864. In action at Petersburg Crater, July 30, 1864, and Weldon Railroad, Aug. 19, 1864; one of the 30 combat soldiers remaining of the regiment after that battle. Wounded in action near Poplar Grove Church, Sept. 30, 1864. Absent wounded in an army general hospital until on or before March 25, 1865. Wounded in action again at Fort Stedman, March 25, 1865. Absent wounded in an army general hospital until discharged the US service for disability from wounds, Aug. 3, 1865, by order of the War Dept. Had previous service as a private in Co. H, 46th MVI, from Aug. 21, 1862, until mustered out, July 29, 1863. Participated in the North Carolina campaign with that regiment in 1862–63. Resided in New York City after the war and died there in 1880, age 35.

95. **Wellman, John F.**, private. Res: Palmer, MA. Credit: Worcester, MA. Born: Palmer, MA. Age: 18. Height: 5'8". Comp: light. Eyes: hazel. Hair: brown. Occup: farmer. Enlisted in Worcester by Capt. J. M. Tucker, Jan. 4, 1864; mustered Jan. 11, 1864. Absent sick or on detached duty from on or before May 6, 1864, until between Aug. 19 and Sept. 30, 1864. Severely wounded in the left forearm in action near Poplar Grove Church, Sept. 30, 1864. Taken to the 1st Division, IX Corps, Field Hospital where he underwent surgery, Oct. 1, 1864, for the amputation of the left forearm by the flap method. Absent wounded until discharged and pensioned from the US service on a Surgeons Certificate of Disability from Chester US Army General Hospital in Chester, PA, May 4, 1865, to date June 16, 1865. "Stump tender" (OMR). Died in 1876, age 30.

96. **Willard, George W.**, corporal. Res. and/or credit: Worcester, MA. Born: Charlton, MA. Age: 34. Height: 5'7½". Comp: light. Eyes: blue. Hair: light. Occup: carriage maker. Enlisted in Worcester by Capt. Julius M. Tucker, Dec. 15, 1863; mustered Jan. 11, 1864. Promoted corporal, March 1, 1864. In action at the Wilderness, May 6, 1864, and one of the the 34 enlisted men who remained

with the colors during that battle. In action at Spotsylvania Court House, May 10, 12, and 18, 1864, North Anna River, May 24, 1864, Cold Harbor, June 3, 1864, Petersburg assaults, June 17 and 18, 1864, and Petersburg Crater, July 30, 1864; severely wounded in action at Weldon Railroad, Aug. 19, 1864. Died from his wounds in De Camp US Army General Hospital, New York Harbor, NY, Sept. 17, 1864. With the regiment on all marches and in all skirmishes and battles until wounded.

97. **Williams, John S.**, private. Res: Union, CT. Credit: Worcester, MA. Born: Tolland, CT. Age: 23. Height: 5'8". Comp: dark. Eyes: blue. Hair: brown. Occup: carpenter. Enlisted in Worcester by D. Waldo Lincoln, Jan. 5, 1864; mustered Jan. 11, 1864. Wounded in action at the Wilderness, May 6, 1864. Absent wounded in an army general hospital until discharged the US service on a Surgeons Certificate of Disability, May 4, 1865, discharge to date July 30, 1865.

98. **Wilson, Charles H.**, corporal. Res: Worcester, MA. Credit: Harvard, MA. Born: Worcester, MA. Age: 18. Height: 5'6". Comp: sandy. Eyes: blue. Hair: sandy. Occup: machinist. Enlisted in Harvard by Lt. John L. Goodwin, Jan. 7, 1864; mustered Jan. 11, 1864. Wounded in action at the Wilderness, May 6, 1864. Absent wounded in an army general hospital until between Oct. 8, 1864, and Feb. 21, 1865. Promoted corporal, Feb. 21, 1865. Wounded in action again at Fort Stedman, March 25, 1865. Discharged the US service for disability from wounds from an army general hospital in Boston, MA, May 26, 1865, under GO 77, par. 6, AGO, War Dept.

99. **Wood, George H.**, private. Res. and/or credit: Worcester, MA. Born: Berlin, NH. Age: 24. Height: 5'4". Comp: dark. Eyes: blue. Hair: black. Occup: wireworker. Enlisted in Worcester by D. Waldo Lincoln, Jan. 5, 1864; mustered Jan. 11, 1864. Wounded in action at the Wilderness, May 6, 1864. Absent wounded until discharged the US service on a Surgeons Certificate of Dis-

ability from Mower US Army General Hospital in Philadelphia, PA, June 9, 1865. Resided in Worcester, MA, after the war.

100. **Woodcock, Isaac A.,** private. Res. and/or credit: Worcester, MA. Born: Springfield, MA. Age: 21. Height: 5'9½". Comp: dark. Eyes: black. Hair: black. Occup: blacksmith. Enlisted in Worcester by D. Waldo Lincoln, Jan. 5, 1864; mustered Jan. 11, 1864. Absent sick or on detached duty from on or before May 6, 1864, until between Oct. 8, 1864, and Feb. 1, 1865. Wounded while on duty in the trenches at Petersburg on an unknown date in Feb. 1865. Absent wounded in an army general hospital until discharged the US service for disability from wounds, June 9, 1865, under GO 77, par. 6, AGO, War Dept. Resided in Worcester, MA, after the war and died there in 1886, age 43.

101. **Young, Charles E.,** corporal. Res: New London, CT. Credit: Worcester, MA. Born: New London, CT. Age: 18. Height: 5'9". Comp: dark. Eyes: gray. Hair: dark. Occup: armorer. Enlisted in Worcester by Capt. Julius M. Tucker, Dec. 29, 1865; mustered Jan. 11, 1864. Promoted corporal, March 1, 1864. Killed in action at the Wilderness, May 6, 1864.

ROSTER AND DESCRIPTIVE LIST OF COMPANY I

Company I was the eighth company of the regiment to be mustered into United States service, and it was mustered March 10, 1864, under SO 279, from the AGO, Boston, MA, by 1st Lt. Robert P. McKibben, 4th United States Regular Infantry. Those men mustered on April 6, 1864, were mustered by 2nd Lt. Daniel Madden, 6th United States Regular Cavalry. The company was mustered out by Capt. Sylvester Keyser, 2nd Michigan Volunteer Infantry, ACM, 1st Division, IX Corps.

1. **Agnew, Henry,** private. Res. and/or credit: Harvard, MA. Born: Portland, ME. Age: 23. Height: 5'8". Comp: light. Eyes: light. Hair: light. Occup: machinist. Enlisted in Harvard by Caleb S. Gerry, March 25, 1864; mustered April 6, 1864. Deserted from Camp Wool, April 17, 1864. Never returned. "Bounty jumper" (JA).

2. **Anderson, John,** private. Res. and/or credit: Harvard, MA. Born: Portland, ME. Age: 19. Height: 5'4". Comp: light. Eyes: light. Hair: light. Occup: helper. Enlisted in Harvard by Caleb S. Gerry, March 25, 1864; mustered April 6, 1864; Deserted from Camp Wool, April 17, 1864. Never returned. Probably a bounty jumper.

3. **Barker, Daniel E.,** private. Res. and/or credit: Pittsfield, MA. Born: Sand Lake, NY. Age: 18. Height: 5'11". Comp: light. Eyes: blue. Hair: brown. Occup: farmer. Enlisted in Pittsfield by John C. West. March 19, 1864; mustered April 6, 1864. Before being killed in action at the Wilderness, May 6, 1864, one of the 34 enlisted men to remain with the colors during that battle.

4. **Beckwith, Joseph,** private. Res. and/or credit: Pittsfield, MA. Born: Stephenstown, NY. Age: 24. Height: 5'4". Comp: dark. Eyes: gray. Hair: brown. Occup: laborer. Enlisted in Pittsfield by John C. West, Feb. 27, 1864; mustered March 10, 1864. Absent sick or on detached duty from on or before May 6, 1864, until between May 18 and May 24, 1864. In action at North Anna River, May 24, 1865, Cold Harbor, June 3, 1864, Petersburg assaults, June 17 and 18, 1864, and Petersburg Crater, July 30, 1864; missing in action at Weldon Railroad, Aug. 19, 1864. Never accounted for and presumed killed.

5. **Bolton, Henry,** private. Res. and/or credit: Worcester, MA. Born: London, England. Age: 26. Height: 5'7". Comp: fair. Eyes: gray.

Hair: light. Occup: carpenter. Enlisted in Worcester by Capt. Albert Prescott, Feb. 25, 1864; mustered March 10, 1864. Deserted from Camp Wool on an unknown date in March 1864. Never returned. No record of him having received his bounty.

6. **Bonner, James H.**, private. Res. and/or credit: South Hadley, MA. Born: Burke, NY. Age: 22. Height: 5'9". Comp: florid. Eyes: gray. Hair: black. Occup: farmer. Enlisted in South Hadley by John S. Bell, Feb. 20, 1864; mustered March 10, 1864. In action at the Wilderness, May 6, 1864, Spotsylvania Court House, May 10, 12, and 18, 1864, North Anna River, May 24, 1864, and Cold Harbor, June 3, 1864; slightly wounded in action in the Petersburg assault, June 17, 1864. With the regiment on all marches and in all skirmishes and battles until wounded. Absent wounded until discharged the US service from Central Park US Army General Hospital in New York City, for disability from wounds, June 3, 1865, in compliance with a telegram from the AGO, War Dept., dated May 4, 1865.

7. **Bowe, George D.**, private. Res. and/or credit: Pittsfield, MA. Born: New Hartford, CT. Age: 18. Height: 5'4". Comp: light. Eyes: blue. Hair: dark brown. Occup: student. Enlisted in Pittsfield by John C. West, March 25, 1864; mustered April 6, 1864. Absent sick in an army general hospital from on or before May 6, 1864, until Feb. 22, 1865. In action at Fort Stedman, March 25, 1865. Mustered out with the regiment at Delaney house, Washington, DC, July 30, 1865, and discharged in Readville, MA, Aug. 9, 1865, expiration of service.

8. **Brennan, Luke,** private. Res. and/or credit: New Marlboro, MA. Born: Ireland. Age: 24. Height: 5'7". Comp: fair. Eyes: dark. Hair: brown. Occup: laborer. Enlisted in New Marlboro by Aaron Smith, Feb. 3, 1864; mustered March 10, 1864. Deserted from Camp Wool on an unknown date in March 1864. Never returned. No record of him having received his bounty. Had previous service as a private in Co. E, 49th MVI, from Sept. 1, 1862, until mustered out, Sept. 1, 1863. Participated in the Port Hudson, LA, campaign with that regiment in 1863.

9. **Brill, Albert E.**, private. Res. and/or credit: Southampton, MA. Born: Canada. Age: 20. Height: 5'8". Comp: light. Eyes: blue. Hair: dark. Occup: farmer. Enlisted in Southampton by Lt. Col. Luke Lyman, Feb. 23, 1864; mustered March 10, 1864. Wounded in action at the Wilderness, May 6, 1864. Absent wounded in an army general hospital until discharged the US service, Dec. 17, 1864, on a Surgeons Certificate of Disability for wounds by order of Maj. Gen. Christopher C. Auger, commanding the Dept. of Washington, DC.

10. **Brown, John,** private. Res. and/or credit: Springfield, MA. Born: Germany. Age: 29. Height: 5'5". Comp: dark. Eyes: blue. Hair: dark. Occup: farmer. Enlisted in Springfield by Lt. George S. Green, March 5, 1864; mustered April 6, 1864. Wounded in action at the Wilderness, May 6, 1864. Absent wounded until discharged the US service for disability from wounds from an army general hospital in Philadelphia, PA, May 20, 1865.

11. **Bullock, Amasa R.**, private. Res. and/or credit: Adams, MA. Born: Reidsboro, UT. Age: 19. Height: 5'8". Comp: dark. Eyes: black. Hair: dark. Occup: laborer. Enlisted in Adams by S. Johnson, March 2, 1864; mustered March 10, 1864. In action at the Wilderness, May 6, 1864, and Spotsylvania Court House, May 10, 12, and 18, 1864; missing in action at North Anna River, May 24, 1864. Never accounted for and presumed killed.

12. **Burrows, Peter A.**, private. Res. and/or credit: West Stockbridge, MA. Born: Oxford, NY. Age: 44. Height: 5'6". Comp: fair. Eyes: blue. Hair: brown. Occup: tailor. Enlisted in West Stockbridge by George W. Griffen, Feb. 13, 1864; mustered March 10, 1864. Severely wounded in the left leg and taken prisoner of war in action at the Wilderness, May 6, 1864. Underwent surgery for the amputation of his left leg by an unknown Confederate surgeon and died from "exhaustion" (OMR) in a Confederate field hospital at Parker's Store, VA, near the Wilderness bat-

tlefield, June 1, 1864. Very likely a deserter from the 30th New York Volunteer Infantry.

13. **Carroll, Edward,** private. Res. and/or credit: New Marlboro, MA. Born: Ireland. Age: 44. Height: 5'8". Comp: sandy. Eyes: blue. Hair: black. Occup: laborer. Enlisted in New Marlboro by Jemain Andred, Feb. 13, 1864; mustered March 10, 1864. In action at the Wilderness, May 6, 1864, and Spotsylvania Court House, May 10, 1864; wounded in action there, May 12, 1864. Absent wounded in an army general hospital until transferred to Co. H, 14th Regiment, VRC, Jan. 2, 1865. Discharged the US service, July 26, 1865, by order of the War Dept., expiration of service. Died before 1896, but date unknown.

14. **Chambers, James K.,** corporal. Res. credit: Hancock, MA. Born: Candor, NY. Age: 18. Height: 5'8". Comp: light. Eyes: light. Hair: light. Occup: farmer. Enlisted in Hancock by H. H. Whitman, Jan. 29, 1864; mustered March 10, 1864. Absent sick or on detached duty from on or before May 6, 1864, until between Oct. 8, 1864, and Jan. 1, 1865. Promoted corporal, Jan. 1, 1865. Absent sick in an army general hospital from after Jan. 1 until Jan. 24, 1864. With the regiment in at least some operations during the winter of 1865, and in action at Fort Stedman, March 25, 1865. Mustered out with regiment at Delaney house, Washington, DC, July 30, 1865, and discharged in Readville, MA, Aug. 9, 1865, expiration of service.

15. **Chapman, Ralph,** private. Res. and/or credit: Hancock, MA. Born: Stephenstown, NY. Age: 42. Height: 5'9". Comp: dark. Eyes: dark. Hair: black. Occup: farmer and blacksmith. Enlisted in Hancock by H. H. Whitman, Jan. 29, 1864; mustered March 10, 1864. Served as company cook, and therefore exempted from hard combat service. On daily duty under RSO 19, by order of Lt. Col. Julius M. Tucker, from Feb. 24 until March 15, 1865 (nature of duty unknown but probably cook). In action at Fort Stedman, March 25, 1865. On daily duty again, March 26, 1865, until an unknown date (nature of duty unknown but probably cook). Absent sick in an army general hospital from after March 26, 1865, until discharged the US service for disability, Aug. 8, 1865, by order of the War Dept.

16. **Church, Horace,** private. Res. and/or credit: Richmond, MA. Born: Washington, MA. Age: 18. Height: 5'5". Comp: light. Eyes: blue. Hair: brown. Occup: teamster. Enlisted in Richmond by Lewis C. Sherrill, Feb. 29, 1864; mustered March 10, 1864. Never in major combat, but wounded on an unknown date before Nov. 23, 1864 (probably accidentally or on picket duty). Deserted Nov. 23, 1864, probably from an army general hospital while absent wounded. Returned on an unknown date and under unknown circumstances. Mustered out, but absent, at Delaney house, Washington, DC, July 30, 1865, expiration of service.

17. **Clark, James,** private. Res. and/or credit: Millbury, MA. Born: Carlow, Ireland. Age: 25. Height: 5'8". Comp: light. Eyes: brown. Hair: sandy. Occup: farmer. Enlisted in Millbury by Lt. John Reade, March 31, 1864; mustered April 6, 1864. Deserted from Camp Wool, April 17, 1864. Never returned. Bounty jumper.

18. **Collins, Dennis,** private. Res. and credit: Washington, MA. Born: Washington, MA. Age: 19. Height: 5'9". Comp: light. Eyes: blue. Hair: brown. Occup: farmer. Enlisted in Washington by Charles Crosier, Feb. 25, 1865; mustered March 25, 1864. Severely wounded in action at the Wilderness, May 6, 1864. Absent wounded in an army general hospital until transferred to the 2nd Co., 2nd Battln., VRC, April 24, 1865. Deserted July 27, 1865. Never returned.

19. **Conway, Thomas,** private. Res. and/or credit: Springfield, MA. Born: Ireland. Age: 35. Height: 5'6". Comp: fair. Eyes: blue. Hair: light. Occup: farmer. Enlisted in Springfield by Capt. Lewis A. Tifft, Dec. 30, 1863; mustered March 10, 1864. In action at the Wilderness, May 6, 1864, and Spotsylvania Court House, May 10, 12, and 18, 1864; killed in action at North Anna River, May 24, 1864.

20. **Cook, Albert W.,** captain. Res. and/or credit: Milford, MA. Born: Shelburne Falls, MA, Sept. 18, 1843. Age: 21. Height: unknown. Comp: light. Eyes: blue. Hair: light. Occup: student. Commissioned 2nd lieutenant of Co. B, Jan. 7, 1864; mustered 2nd lieutenant, Feb. 1, 1864. Commissioned 1st lieutenant, March 4, 1864. Transferred to Co. I, March 12, 1864, under RSO 23, by order of Col. William F. Bartlett. Mustered 1st lieutenant, March 21, 1864. In action at the Wilderness, May 6, 1864, Spotsylvania Court House, May 10, 12, and 18, 1864, North Anna River, May 24, 1864, and Cold Harbor, June 3, 1864. Commissioned captain, June 15, 1864. Absent for unknown reasons from on or before June 17, 1864 until between Oct. 8 and Nov. 12, 1864. Mustered captain, Nov. 12, 1864. In command of Co. E from Nov. 30, 1864, until Jan. 30, 1865. With the regiment in operations during the fall and winter of 1864–65, and in action at Fort Stedman, March 25, 1865. In joint command of the regiment with Capt. George E. Barton from March 26 until April 3, 1865. Transferred to special duty, April 9, 1865, on the staff of 3rd Brigade, 1st Division, IX Corps, Headquar-

ters as provost marshal, by SO 99 from IX Corps Headquarters. Acting assistant adjutant-general of the 3rd Brigade, 1st Division, IX Corps, from an unknown date in May 1865 until transferred to Co. C, June 28, 1865. Mustered out, as captain of Co. C, with the regiment at Delaney house, Washington, DC, July 30, 1865, and discharged in Readville, MA, Aug. 9, 1865, expiration of service. Had previous service as 1st sergeant of Co. B, 25th MVI, from Sept. 6, 1861, until discharged to accept a commission in the 57th, Jan. 9, 1864. Participated in the North Carolina campaign with the 25th in 1862–63. Resided in Malden, MA, after the war.

21. **Crowe, John,** private. Res: Westboro, MA. Credit: Northboro, MA. Born: unknown. Age: 21. No description available. Occup: sailor. Enlisted in Co. B in Northboro by E. Bullard, March 30, 1864; mustered April 6, 1864; transferred to Co. I during the march to the front, April 21, 1864, under RSO 43, by order of Col. William F. Bartlett, April 26, 1864. Wounded in action at the Wilderness, May 6, 1864. Absent wounded in an army general hospital until between Oct. 8, 1864, and March 8, 1865. Arrested and placed in confinement for an unknown reason while on duty with the regiment at Petersburg, from March 8 until March 11, 1865. In action at Fort Stedman, March 25, 1865. Absent without leave on May 24, 1865. Detached on daily duty as a cattle drover from June 30, 1865, until muster-out. (Note: By the appearance of the handwriting in this entry in the company journal—e.g., "cattle drover" is capitalized and underscored—it seems that the officer making the entry was glad to be rid of Crowe and thought the duty appropriate for some unknown reason. Crowe appears to have been a disciplinary problem.) Mustered out with the regiment at Delaney house, Washington, DC, July 30, 1865, and discharged in Readville, MA, Aug. 9, 1865, expiration of service. Resided in Boonville, MO, after the war and died there, Aug. 1, 1879, age 36.

Captain Albert Cook. *(USAMHI)*

22. **Culliton, Pierce,** corporal. Res. and/or credit: Shelburne, MA. Born: Ireland. Age: 34. Height: 5'2". Comp: sandy. Eyes: blue.

Hair: sandy. Occup: tailor. Enlisted in Shelburne by Pliny Fisk, Feb. 26, 1864; mustered March 10, 1864. Promoted corporal, April 30, 1864. Wounded in action at the Wilderness, May 6, 1864. Absent wounded in an army general hospital and then in Depot Field Hospital at City Point, Petersburg, until discharged the US service on a Surgeons Certificate of Disability from wounds, Dec. 21, 1864, by order of Maj. Gen. John G. Parke, commanding IX Corps, discharge to date July 30, 1865.

23. **Culliton, Patrick,** private. Res. and/or credit: Sterling, MA. Born: Ireland. Age: 29. Height: 5′7″. Comp: light. Eyes: gray. Hair: light. Occup: farmer. Enlisted in Sterling by Ezra Sawyer, March 10, 1864; mustered April 6, 1864. Wounded in action at the Wilderness, May 6, 1864, and died from his wounds in Depot Field Hospital at City Point Petersburg, on an unknown date in Aug. 1864. (Note: His name also appears on some army records as Patrick Carlton.)

24. **Curtin, Timothy,** private. Res. and/or credit: New Marlboro, MA. Born: County Cork, Ireland. Age: 23. Height: 5′8″. Comp: fair. Eyes: blue. Hair: brown. Occup: laborer. Enlisted in New Marlboro by Jemain Andred, Feb. 12, 1864; mustered March 10, 1864. Wounded in action at the Wilderness, May 6, 1864. Absent wounded in an army general hospital until April 30, 1865. On furlough from May 16 until May 25, 1865. Mustered out, but absent (probably sick), at Delaney house, Washington, DC, July 30, 1865, expiration of service. Resided in Monterey, MA, after the war.

25. **Daniels, John G.,** private. Res. and/or credit: Chicopee, MA. Born: Chesterfield, NH. Age: 43. Height: 5′3″. Comp: dark. Eyes: blue. Hair: dark. Occup: machinist. Enlisted in Chicopee by Lt. George S. Green, Feb. 2, 1864; mustered March 10, 1864. Wounded in action at the Wilderness, May 6, 1864. Absent wounded in an army general hospital until transferred to the 14th Co., 2nd Battln., VRC, Sept. 1, 1864, by order of the provost marshal general. Discharged the US service, Sept. 1, 1865, expiration of service.

26. **Denio, Joseph,** private. Res. and/or credit: Gill, MA. Born: Chateaugay, NY. Age: 19. Height: 5′6″. Comp: dark. Eyes: hazel. Hair: dark. Occup: groom. Enlisted in Gill by Henry Bascom, Feb. 20, 1864; mustered March 10, 1864. Never in combat. Absent sick in an army general hospital from on or before May 6, 1864, until he deserted from that hospital, Nov. 30, 1864. Never returned.

27. **Dooley, Thomas,** private. Res. and/or credit: Middlefield, MA. Born: Ireland. Age: 19. Height: 5′4″. Comp: dark. Eyes: black. Hair: dark. Occup: laborer. Enlisted in Middlefield by Matthew Smith, Feb. 25, 1864; mustered March 10, 1864. Never in combat. Absent sick in an army general hospital from on or before May 6, 1864. Transferred to Depot Field Hospital at City Point, Petersburg, on an unknown date and died there from disease, July 26, 1864.

28. **Dwyer, Michael,** private. Res: Malden, MA. Credit: Worcester, MA. Born: New South Wales, Australia. Age: 21. Height: 5′11″. Comp: light. Eyes: blue. Hair: red. Occup: farmer. Enlisted in Worcester by Lt. Henry C. Ward, March 3, 1864; mustered March 10, 1864. In action at the Wilderness, May 6, 1864, Spotsylvania Court House, May 10, 12, and 18, 1864, North Anna River, May 24, 1864, Cold Harbor, June 3, 1864, and Petersburg assaults, June 17 and 18, 1864; wounded while on duty in the trenches at Petersburg, July 12, 1864. With the regiment on all marches and in all skirmishes and battles until wounded. Absent wounded in an army general hospital until between March 25, 1865, and May 7, 1865. Deserted at Petersburg, May 7, 1865, until he was arrested and placed in confinement at Petersburg from May 13 until May 15, 1865. Deserted at Petersburg again May 27, 1865, until he was arrested and placed in confinement again at Petersburg from May 28 until May 29, 1865. Detached and detailed on daily duty as a guard at the quartermaster's dept. in Washington, DC, May 31, 1865, until muster-out. Mustered out with the regiment at Delaney house, Washington, DC, July 30, 1865, and discharged in Readville, MA, Aug. 9, 1865,

expiration of service. Resided in Hill City, Pennington County, SD, after the war.

29. **Elkins, William G. II,** private. Res. and/ or credit: Southampton, MA. Born: Canada. Age: 21. Height: 6'0". Comp: light. Eyes: blue. Hair: brown. Occup: farmer. Enlisted in Southampton by Lt. Col. Luke Lyman, Feb. 25, 1864; mustered March 10, 1864. In action at the Wilderness, May 6, 1864, Spotsylvania Court House, May 10, 12, and 18, 1864, North Anna River, May 24, 1864, and Cold Harbor, June 3, 1864; severely wounded in the arm in action during the Petersburg assault, June 17, 1864. With the regiment on all marches and in all skirmishes and battles until wounded. Absent wounded in an army general hospital until transferred to the 5th Co., 2nd Battln., VRC, Sept. 23, 1864. Discharged the US service on a Surgeons Certificate of Disability from wounds, Dec. 14, 1864. Discharge to date July 30, 1865.

30. **Fortin, Joseph,** private. Res. and/or credit: Hinsdale, MA. Born: Cheneville, Quebec, Canada. Age: 19. Height: 5'5". Comp: dark. Eyes: black. Hair: black. Occup: laborer. Enlisted in Hinsdale by W. H. Carson, March 31, 1864; mustered April 6, 1864. Killed in action at the Wilderness, May 6, 1864.

31. **French, Albert V.,** private. Res. and/or credit: Ware, MA. Born: Barnard, VT. Age: 23. Height: 5'9". Comp: light. Eyes: black. Hair: brown. Occup: butcher. Enlisted in Ware by Otis Lane, Feb. 29, 1864; mustered March 10, 1864. Never in combat. Wounded on an unknown date, either accidentally or on picket duty, but not in a major battle. Absent wounded until discharged the US service for disability from wounds from an army general hospital in Washington, DC, June 2, 1865, under GO 77, par. 6, AGO, War Dept.

32. **Gallup, Henry C.,** corporal. Res. and credit: Dalton, MA. Born: Dalton, MA. Age: 24. Height: 5'8". Comp: light. Eyes: gray. Hair: sandy. Occup: papermaker. Enlisted in Dalton by D. C. Smith, Feb. 13, 1864; mustered March 10, 1864. Promoted corporal, March 10, 1864. Absent sick or on detached duty from on or before May 6, 1864, until between Oct. 8, 1864, and Jan. 1, 1865. With the regiment in operations during the winter of 1865 and in action at Fort Stedman, March 25, 1865. Present sick with the regiment from March 30 until April 5, 1865, when he is listed in the company journal as absent sick at 1st Division, IX Corps, Field Hospital. Returned to the regiment for duty, May 25, 1865. Mustered out with the regiment at Delaney house, Washington, DC, July 30, 1865, and discharged in Readville, MA, Aug. 9, 1865, expiration of service. Had previous service as a private in Co. C, 49th MVI, from Sept. 11, 1862, until mustered out Sept. 1, 1863. Participated in the Port Hudson, LA, campaign with that regiment in 1863. Resided in Dalton, MA, after the war.

33. **Gavin, George,** private. Res: Pittsfield, MA. Credit: Springfield, MA. Born: Housten, Scotland. Age: 33. Height: 5'6". Comp: light. Eyes: hazel. Hair: dark. Occup: baker. Enlisted and mustered by Capt. Morehouse in Springfield, Aug. 1, 1864. In action at Poplar Grove Church, Sept. 30, 1864, and wounded in action there, Oct. 8, 1864. Absent wounded in an army general hospital until April 22, 1865. On extra duty from after April 22 until July 2, 1865 (nature of duty unknown, but the assignment was probably for disciplinary reasons). Mustered out with the regiment at Delaney house, Washington, DC, July 30, 1865, and discharged in Readville, MA, Aug. 9, 1865, expiration of service.

34. **Gould, Harvey W.,** corporal. Res. and/or credit: North Brookfield, MA. Born: Waterford, NY. Age: 18. Height: 5'2". Comp: fair. Eyes: gray. Hair: brown. Occup: farmer. Enlisted in North Brookfield by Augustus Smith, March 26, 1864; mustered April 6, 1864. In action at the Wilderness, May 6, 1864, and promoted corporal that same day for "good conduct in action" (CR). One of the 34 enlisted men who remained with colors during that battle. In action at Spotsylvania Court House, May 10, 1864, and wounded in action there, May 12, 1864. Absent wounded until discharged the US service for disability from wounds from an army general hospital under instructions from the AGO, War Dept., May 22, 1865, by order of Secretary of War Edwin M. Stanton, dated May 3, 1865. Died before 1896, but date not known.

35. **Gover, John,** private. Res. and credit: Millbury, MA. Born: Millbury, MA. Age: 18. Height: 5′7″. Comp: dark. Eyes: black. Hair: dark. Occup: shoemaker. Enlisted in Millbury by C. D. Morse, Feb. 22, 1864; mustered March 10, 1864. In action at the Wilderness, May 6, 1864, and slightly wounded on an unknown date later that month, but not in a major battle. Absent wounded in an army general hospital until between June 17 and July 12, 1864. Wounded again while on duty in the trenches at Petersburg, July 12, 1864. Absent wounded until discharged the US service on a Surgeons Certificate of Disability from wounds, Jan. 21, 1865, from an army general hospital in Washington, DC, by order of Maj. Gen. Christopher C. Auger, commanding the Dept. of Washington, DC.

36. **Green, George A.,** private. Res. and/or credit: Ware, MA. Born: Norton, MA. Age: 43. Height: 5′10″. Comp: florid. Eyes: blue. Hair: brown. Occup: carpenter. Enlisted in Ware by Otis Lane, Feb. 17, 1864; mustered March 10, 1864. Never in combat. Absent sick from on or before May 6, 1864, until discharged the US service on a Surgeons Certificate of Disability for disease from Cliffburne US Army General Hospital in Washington, DC, April 7, 1865.

37. **Haley, Martin,** private. Res. and/or credit: Northampton, MA. Born: Germany. Age: 37. Height: 5′8″. Comp: fair. Eyes: hazel. Hair: brown. Occup: laborer. Enlisted in Northampton by Lt. Col. Luke Lyman, Feb. 22, 1864; mustered March 10, 1864. In action at the Wilderness, May 6, 1864, and Spotsylvania Court House, May 10, 1864; wounded in action there, May 12, 1864. Absent wounded in Chester US Army General Hospital in Chester, PA, until he deserted from that hospital, Sept. 26, 1864. Surrendered to the authorities and sent sick to Beverly US Army General Hospital in Beverly, NJ, where he died from chronic diarrhea, Oct. 16, 1864.

38. **Hardy, Elmer J.,** private. Res. and/or credit: Easthampton, MA. Born: Canada. Age: 20. Height: 5′9″. Comp: light. Eyes: blue. Hair: dark. Occup: farmer. Enlisted in Easthampton by Lt. Col. Luke Lyman, Feb.

26, 1864; mustered March 10, 1864. Mortally wounded in action at the Wilderness, May 6, 1864. Died from his wounds in the 1st Division, IX Corps, Field Hospital, May 7, 1864.

39. **Hardy, Marshal G.,** private. Res. and/or credit: Southampton, MA. Born: Canada. Age: 22. Height: 5′7″. Comp: light. Eyes: black. Hair: dark. Occup: farmer. Enlisted in Southampton by Lt. Col. Luke Lyman, Feb. 26, 1864; mustered March 10, 1864. Never in combat. Absent sick in an army general or field hospital from on or about May 6, 1864, until discharged the US service on an unknown date for disability by order of the War Dept., discharge to date July 8, 1864.

40. **Holmes, Loren S.,** musician. Res. or credit: Washington, MA. Born: Massachusetts. Age: 41. No description available. Occup: farmer. Enlisted in Co. D, March 30, 1864; joined the company from the transient barracks, April 6, 1864; mustered April 6, 1864; officially transferred to Co. I, April 12, 1864, under RSO 37, by order of Col. William F. Bartlett. Company fifer. Wounded on an unknown date in May 1864. Circumstances unknown, but if in a major battle, not part of the formal battle roster. Absent wounded in an army general hospital until on or before Jan. 2, 1865. With the regiment in operations during the winter of 1865, and in action and taken prisoner of war at Fort Stedman, March 25, 1865. Paroled and exchanged from Libby Prison, Richmond, VA, March 29, 1865. Returned to the regiment for duty from the Camp of Parole in Annapolis, MD, May 11, 1865. Mustered out with the regiment at Delaney house, Washington, DC, July 30, 1865, and discharged in Readville, MA, Aug. 9, 1865, expiration of service.

41. **Houlihan, John,** private. Res. and/or credit: Chicopee, MA. Born: County Limerick, Ireland. Age: 45. Height: 5′8″. Comp: sandy. Eyes: blue. Hair: brown. Occup: farmer. Enlisted in Chicopee by Sgt. George A. Whitney, Feb. 22, 1864; mustered March 10, 1864. Wounded and taken prisoner of war at the Wilderness, May 6, 1864. Paroled and exchanged from an unknown Confederate prison (very likely Andersonville), March 15, 1865. Died from chronic diarrhea in the army

general hospital in the Camp of Parole in Annapolis, MD, March 21, 1865. Had previous service as a private in Co. H, 52nd MVI, from Oct. 11, 1862, until mustered out Aug. 14, 1864. Participated in the Port Hudson, LA, campaign with that regiment in 1863.

42. **Howard, William F.**, sergeant. Res. and credit: Ware, MA. Born: Ware, MA. Age: 19. Height: 5'10". Comp: dark. Eyes: gray. Hair: brown. Occup: teamster. Enlisted in Ware by Otis Lane, Feb. 1, 1864; mustered March 10, 1864. Promoted sergeant, March 10, 1864. In action at the Wilderness, May 6, 1864, Spotsylvania Court House, May 10, 12, and 18, 1864, North Anna River, May 24, 1864, Cold Harbor, June 3, 1864, and Petersburg assaults, June 17 and 18, 1864; taken prisoner of war at the Petersburg Crater, July 30, 1864. With the regiment on all marches and in all skirmishes and battles until captured. Incarcerated in the Confederate prison in Danville, VA, where he died, Feb. 23, 1865, probably from disease, one day after the remaining prisoners from the 57th were paroled from that prison. Had previous service as a private in Co. K, 42nd MVI, from Sept. 10, 1862, until mustered out, Aug. 20, 1863. Detached and detailed to the 2nd Vermont Battery, Jan. 28, 1863, by SO, Dept. of the Gulf, but returned to his own regiment before muster-out.

43. **Hunt, Alvah A.**, private. Res. and/or credit: Pittsfield, MA. Born: Nassau, NY. Age: 20. Height: 5'6". Comp: light. Eyes: blue. Hair: light. Occup: teamster. Enlisted in Pittsfield by John C. West, March 19, 1864; mustered April 6, 1864. In action at the Wilderness, May 6, 1864, and Spotsylvania Court House, May 10, 1864; wounded in the right arm in action there, May 12, 1864. Absent wounded until discharged the US service for disability from wounds ("loss of use of right arm" [CR]) from an army general hospital in Philadelphia, PA, by order of Surgeon Hayes, May 6, 1865. Resided in Pittsfield, MA, after the war.

44. **Ide, Henry M.**, 1st lieutenant. Res. and/or credit: Worcester, MA. Born: Providence, RI. Age: 33. Height: 5'7½". Comp: light. Eyes: blue. Hair: light. Occup: machinist. Enlisted in Co. H in Worcester by Capt. Julius M. Tucker, Dec. 26, 1863;

mustered Jan. 11, 1864. Promoted sergeant in Co. H, March 1, 1864; transferred by RSO to Co. I, April 12, 1864, and promoted 1st sergeant April 12, 1864. In action at the Wilderness, May 6, 1864, Spotsylvania Court House, May 10, 12, and 18, 1864, North Anna River, May 24, 1864, and Cold Harbor, June 3, 1864; slightly wounded in the arm in action during the Petersburg assault, June 17, 1864. Absent wounded in an army general hospital until on or about Jan. 2, 1865. With the regiment on all marches and in all skirmishes and battles until wounded. Commissioned 1st lieutenant, Oct. 7, 1864, while absent wounded. Discharged the US service at Petersburg by order of Maj. Gen. John G. Parke, commanding IX Corps, to accept promotion, Jan. 2, 1865. Mustered 1st lieutenant, Jan. 3, 1865. On leave of absence in Massachusetts from Jan. 11 until Jan. 30, 1865. With the regiment in most operations during the winter of 1865 and in action at Fort Stedman, March 25, 1865. In command of the company from April 10 until June 13, 1865. Mustered out with the regiment, as 1st lieutenant of Co. A, at Delaney house, Washington, DC, July 30, 1865, and discharged in Readville, MA, Aug. 9, 1865, expiration of service. Had previous service as a sergeant in Co. B, 3rd Battalion of Rifles, Massachusetts Volunteer Militia, from May 19, 1861, until mustered out, Aug. 3, 1861. Also had previous service as a corporal in Co. A, 25th MVI, from Sept. 14, 1861, until discharged for disability in New Bern, NC, Jan. 10, 1863. Participated in the North Carolina campaign with that regiment in 1862–63. Died in 1881, age 50.

45. **Jamieson, George**, private. Res: West Stockbridge, MA. Credit: Springfield, MA. Born: New York City. Age: 33. Height: 5'4¾". Comp: dark. Eyes: blue. Hair: dark. Occup: blacksmith. Enlisted and mustered in Springfield by Capt. Morehouse, Aug. 1, 1864; joined the regiment at Petersburg as a recruit between Aug. 20 and Sept. 29, 1864. In action at Poplar Grove Church, Sept. 30, 1864, and killed in action there, Oct. 8, 1864.

46. **King, John**, private. Res. and/or credit: Hadley, MA. Born: Ireland. Age: 21. Height: 5'6". Comp: florid. Eyes: gray. Hair: brown.

Occup: laborer. Enlisted in Hadley by John S. Bill, Feb. 23, 1864; mustered March 10, 1864. Deserted from Camp Wool, March 18, 1864. Never returned. No record of him having received his bounty.

47. **Kinney, George W.**, private. Res. and/or credit: Uxbridge, MA. Born: Cumberland, RI. Age: 37. Height: 6'4". Comp: light. Eyes: blue. Hair: dark. Occup: bootmaker. Enlisted in Uxbridge by John W. Capron, Feb. 25, 1864; mustered March 10, 1864. Absent sick or on detached duty from on or before May 6, 1864, until between July 30 and Aug. 9, 1864. Wounded while on duty in the trenches at Petersburg, Aug. 9, 1864. Died from wounds in Beverly US Army General Hospital in Beverly, NJ, Sept. 29, 1864. Had previous service as a private in Co. D, 1st Rhode Island Detached Militia, from April 17, 1861, until mustered out, Aug. 2, 1861. Also had previous service as a private in Co. D, 30th MVI, from Oct. 24, 1861, until discharged for disability in New Orleans, LA, Jan. 6, 1863. On duty in Louisiana with that regiment in 1862.

48. **Lacount, Emerson B.**, musician. Res. and/or credit: Leicester, MA. Born: Rutland, MA. Age: 15 (one of the three youngest members of the regiment). Height: 5'5". Comp: light. Eyes: blue. Hair: light. Occup: student. Enlisted in Leicester by Samuel Smith, March 29, 1864; mustered April 6, 1864. Company drummer. Probably also served as a nurse, stretcher bearer and/or hospital orderly. Absent sick in an army general hospital from an unknown date until transferred to Co. G, 2nd Regiment, VRC, April 15, 1865, for disability from disease, by order of Secretary of War Edwin M. Stanton. Discharged the US service for disability by order of the War Dept., discharge to date July 21, 1865. Resided in Leicester, MA, after the war.

49. **Lally, Michael**, private. Res. and/or credit: Milford, MA. Born: Kings County, Ireland. Age: 21. Height: 5'9". Comp: fair. Eyes: blue. Hair: black. Occup: boot crimper. Enlisted in Milford by Leonard Hunt, Feb. 4, 1864; mustered March 10, 1864. In action at the Wilderness, May 6, 1864, and Spotsylvania Court House, May 10, 1864; wounded in action and taken prisoner of war there, May

12, 1864. Incarcerated in Libby Prison in Richmond, VA, for ten days and transferred to the Confederate prison camp in Andersonville, GA. Subsequently confined in the Confederate prison in Florence, SC, until paroled and exchanged from there, Dec. 14, 1864. Probably received extra pay for having been a prisoner. Rejoined the regiment briefly, Jan. 3, 1865. Absent sick in College Green Barracks US Army General Hospital in Annapolis, MD, from Jan. 4, 1865, until discharged the US service for disability, Jan. 21, 1865, by order of the War Dept. Resided in Westboro, MA, after the war. Died Feb. 8, 1914, age 71, and buried in St. Mary's Catholic Cemetery in Milford, MA.

50. **Legrave, Adolphus**, private. Res. and/or credit: Gill, MA. Born: Chateaugay, NY. Age: 18. Height: 5'3". Comp: dark. Eyes: gray. Hair: black. Occup: groom. Enlisted in Gill by Henry Bascom, Feb. 13, 1864; mustered March 10, 1864. In action at the Wilderness, May 6, 1864, and Spotsylvania Court House, May 10, 1864; wounded in action there, May 12, 1864. Absent wounded in an army general hospital until mustered out, but absent wounded, at Delaney house, Washington, DC, July 30, 1865, expiration of service.

51. **Loud, William Harrison**, private. Res: Savoy, MA. Credit: Lenox, MA. Born: Plumfield, MA. Age: 24. Height: 5'5". Comp: dark. Eyes: blue. Hair: brown. Occup: farmer. Enlisted in Lenox by Ambrose B. Perkins, Feb. 22, 1864; mustered March 10, 1864. Never in combat. Absent sick from on or before May 6, 1864, and died from disease in Moore US Army General Hospital in Philadelphia, PA, Aug. 1, 1864.

52. **McDaniel, William**, private. Res. and credit: Lanesboro, MA. Born: Lanesboro, MA. Age: 19. Height: 5'6". Comp: dark. Eyes: blue. Hair: dark. Occup: laborer. Enlisted in Lanesboro by S. T. Whipple, March 25, 1864; mustered April 6, 1864. In action at the Wilderness, May 6, 1864, Spotsylvania Court House, May 10, 12, and 18, 1864, North Anna River, May 24, 1864, Cold Harbor, June 3, 1864, and Petersburg assaults, June 17 and 18, 1864; wounded while on duty in the trenches at Petersburg, July 12, 1864.

With the regiment on all marches and in all skirmishes and battles until wounded. Absent wounded in an army general hospital until between Sept. 30 and Oct. 8, 1864. Wounded in action again at Poplar Grove Church, Oct. 8, 1864. Absent wounded until discharged the US service for disability from disease from Depot Field Hospital at City Point, Petersburg, Dec. 23, 1864, by order of Maj. Gen. John G. Parke, commanding IX Corps. Had previous service as a private in Co. I, 49th MVI, from Sept 20, 1862, until mustered out, Sept. 1, 1863. Participated in the Port Hudson, LA, campaign with that regiment in 1863. Resided in Lanesboro, MA, after the war.

53. **McFarland, Edwin D.**, 1st sergeant. Res. and/or credit: Worcester, MA. Born: Chicopee, MA. Age: 31. Height: 5'8". Comp: light. Eyes: blue. Hair: light. Occup: mechanic. Enlisted in Worcester by Capt. Albert Prescott, Feb. 29, 1864; mustered March 10, 1864. Promoted sergeant, March 10, 1864. In action at the Wilderness, May 6, 1864, Spotsylvania Court House, May 10, 12, and 18, 1864, North Anna River, May 24, 1864, Cold Harbor, June 3, 1864, and Petersburg assaults, June 17 and 18, 1864; wounded while on duty in the trenches at Petersburg (shot through

Sergeant Edwin D. McFarland
(postwar photo). *(Post 10)*

both wrists), July 20, 1864. With the regiment on all marches and in all skirmishes and battles until wounded, and one of the 34 enlisted men who remained with the colors at the Wilderness, May 6, 1864. Absent wounded in an army general hospital until between Oct. 8, 1864, and Jan. 1, 1865. Promoted 1st sergeant, Jan. 1, 1865. Absent sick from his previous wounds in an army general or field hospital from after Jan. 1, 1865, until transferred to Co. B, 1st Regiment, VRC, Feb. 17, 1865. Discharged the US service for disability from wounds, June 19, 1865, by order of the War Dept. Had previous service as a corporal in Co. F, 51st MVI, from Sept 8, 1862, until mustered out, July 27, 1863. Participated in the North Carolina campaign with that regiment in 1862–63. Resided in Worcester, MA, after the war. Elected president of the 57th's regimental association in 1890 and '91.

54. **McGlinley, John**, private. Res. and/or credit: Shelburne, MA. Born: Ireland. Age: 41. Height: 5'10". Comp: dark. Eyes: hazel. Hair: brown. Occup: farmer. Enlisted in Shelburne by Pliny Fisk, Feb. 26, 1864; mustered March 10, 1864. Never in combat. Absent sick in an army general hospital from on or before May 6, 1864, until May 22, 1865. Mustered out with the regiment at Delaney house, Washington, DC, July 30, 1865, and discharged in Readville, MA, Aug. 9, 1865, expiration of service.

55. **Maguire, William**, private. Res. and/or credit: Ware, MA. Born: Canada. Age: 19. Height: 6'1". Comp: light. Eyes: blue. Hair: brown. Occup: farmer. Enlisted in Ware by Lt. Col. Luke Lyman, Feb. 24, 1864; mustered March 10, 1864. In action at the Wilderness, May 6, 1864, and Spotsylvania Court House, May 10, 1864; wounded in action there, May 12, 1864. Absent wounded in an army general hospital until Feb. 15, 1865, when the company journal reports him as "present sick." In action and taken prisoner of war at Fort Stedman, March 25, 1865. Paroled and exchanged from Libby Prison, Richmond, VA, March 29, 1865. Returned to the regiment for duty from the Camp of Parole in Annapolis, MD, May 11, 1865. De-

tached and detailed on daily duty as a provost guard at 1st Division, IX Corps, Headquarters in Tennallytown, DC, from May 30, 1865, until after July 21, 1865. Mustered out with the regiment at Delaney house, Washington, DC, July 30, 1865, and discharged in Readville, MA, Aug. 9, 1865, expiration of service. Resided in Westboro, MA, after the war.

56. **Mayo, Frank,** private. Res. and/or credit: Fitchburg, MA. Born: Trois-Rivières, Quebec, Canada. Age: 28. Height: 5'11". Comp: dark. Eyes: black. Hair: black. Occup: laborer. Enlisted in Fitchburg by William H. Vose, Feb. 24, 1864; mustered March 10, 1864. Deserted from Camp Wool, March 16, 1864. Never returned. No record of him having received his bounty.

57. **Miller, Alfred B.,** private. Res. and/or credit: Wales, MA. Born: Sturbridge, MA. Age: 18. Height: 5'10". Comp: light. Eyes: hazel. Hair: light. Occup: farmer. Enlisted in Wales by Absolom Gardner, Feb. 22, 1864; mustered March 10, 1864. Absent sick in an army general hospital from on or before May 6, 1864, until Feb. 21, 1865. Wounded in action at Fort Stedman, March 25, 1865. Absent wounded until discharged the US service on a Surgeons Certificate of Disability from wounds from an army general hospital in Washington, DC, June 14, 1865, by order of the War Dept.

58. **Moore, William K.,** private. Res. and/or credit: Worcester, MA. Born: Barre, MA. Age: 22. Height: 5'3". Comp: fair. Eyes: dark. Hair: dark. Occup: bartender. Enlisted in Worcester by D. Waldo Lincoln, Feb. 20, 1864; mustered March 10, 1864. Absent sick or on detached duty from on or before May 6, 1864, until between Sept. 30 and Oct. 8, 1864. Wounded in action at Poplar Grove Church, Oct. 8, 1864. Died from his wounds in Beverly US Army General Hospital in Beverly, NJ, Nov. 22, 1864.

59. **Myers, Sylvester,** private. Res. and/or credit: Northampton, MA. Born: Germany. Age: 42. Height: 5'4". Comp: light. Eyes: gray. Hair: black. Occup: physician. Enlisted in Northampton by Lt. Col. Luke Lyman,

Feb. 22, 1864; mustered March 10, 1864. Wounded in action at the Wilderness, May 6, 1864. Absent wounded until discharged the US service on a Surgeons Certificate of Disability for wounds from an army general hospital in Washington, DC, Dec. 17, 1864, by order of Maj. Gen. Christopher C. Auger, commanding the Dept. of Washington, DC.

60. **Noble, Cyrus H.,** corporal. Res. and/or credit: Ware, MA. Born: Norfolk, NY. Age: 19. Height: 5'11". Comp: light. Eyes: blue. Hair: dark. Occup: farmer. Enlisted in Ware by Otis Lane, Feb. 9, 1864; mustered March 10, 1864. Promoted corporal, March 10, 1864. Never in combat. Absent sick in an army general hospital in Alexandria, VA, from on or before May 6 until Sept. 27, 1864. Whereabouts unknown during the battles of Poplar Grove Church, Sept. 30 and Oct. 8, 1864. Reduced to the ranks for "unsoldierly conduct" (CR: possibly for shirking those battles), on an unknown date in the fall of 1864. Absent sick in an army general hospital from before Jan. 1, 1865, until discharged the US service for disability, by order of the War Dept., discharge to date July 30, 1865.

61. **Ober, George K.,** sergeant. Res. and/or credit: Southampton, MA. Born: Chicopee, MA. Age: 21. Height: 5'9". Comp: light. Eyes: blue. Hair: brown. Occup: farmer. Enlisted in Southampton by Lyman G. Tiffany, Feb. 29, 1864; mustered March 10, 1864. Promoted corporal, March 10, 1864. In action at the Wilderness, May 6, 1864, and Spotsylvania Court House, May 10, 1864; wounded in action there, May 12, 1864. Absent wounded in an army general hospital until between Oct. 30, 1864, and March 25, 1865. In action at Fort Stedman, March 25, 1865. Acting 1st sergeant from March 26 until June 13, 1865. Promoted permanent sergeant, May 18, 1865, under RSO 42, by order of Lt. Col. Julius M. Tucker, to date from May 1, 1865. Mustered out with the regiment at Delaney house, Washington, DC, July 30, 1865, and discharged in Readville, MA, Aug. 9, 1865, expiration of service. Had previous service as a corporal in Co. I, 46th MVI, from Sept. 2, 1862, until mustered out, July 29, 1863. Participated in the North Carolina

campaign with that regiment in 1862–63. Resided in Bakersfield, Kern County, CA, after the war.

62. **Olds, William G.**, corporal. Res. and credit: West Stockbridge, MA. Born: West Stockbridge, MA. Age: 26. Height: 6′2″. Comp: fair. Eyes: blue. Hair: brown. Occup: laborer. Enlisted in West Stockbridge by Lt. Charles W. Kniffin, Feb. 19, 1864; mustered March 10, 1864. Promoted corporal, March 10, 1864. Mortally wounded in action at the Wilderness, May 6, 1864. Died from his wounds, May 8, 1864.

63. **Pepoon, Newton B.**, corporal. Res. and credit: Stockbridge, MA. Born: Stockbridge, MA. Age: 18. Height: 5′7″. Comp: light. Eyes: gray. Hair: light. Occup: blacksmith. Enlisted in Stockbridge by Sgt. Henry S. May, Feb. 25, 1864; mustered March 10, 1864. In action at the Wilderness, May 6, 1864, and Spotsylvania Court House, May 10, 1864; promoted corporal for "gallant conduct" (CR) there, May 12, 1864. In action at Spotsylvania Court House, May 18, 1864, North Anna River, May 24, 1864, Cold Harbor, June 3, 1864, Petersburg assaults, June 17 and 18, 1864, Petersburg Crater, July 30, 1864, and Weldon Railroad, Aug. 19, 1864, and one of the 30 combat soldiers remaining of the regiment after that battle. Absent sick in an army general hospital from between Aug. 19 and Sept. 30, 1864, until Jan. 23, 1865. With the regiment on all marches and in all skirmishes and battles until becoming sick. With the regiment in operations during the winter of 1865, and in action at Fort Stedman, March 25, 1865. Reduced to the ranks, May 4, 1865, for "insolence and unsoldierly conduct" (CR), and placed in confinement until May 17, 1865. Promoted corporal again, July 1, 1865. Mustered out with the regiment at Delaney house, Washington, DC, July 30, 1865, and discharged in Readville, MA, Aug. 9, 1865, expiration of service.

64. **Powers, Andrew**, corporal. Res. and/or credit: Adams, MA. Born: Ireland. Age: 21. Height: 5′10″. Comp: dark. Eyes: black. Hair: black. Occup: carpenter. Enlisted in Adams by S. Johnson, Feb. 24, 1864; mustered March 10, 1864. Promoted corporal, March 10, 1864. Reduced to the ranks for unsoldierly conduct before May 18, 1864. In action at the Wilderness, May 6, 1864, and Spotsylvania Court House, May 10 and 12, 1864; wounded in action there, May 18, 1864. Absent wounded until discharged the US service on a Surgeons Certificate of Disability for wounds from an army general hospital in Washington, DC, Nov. 28, 1864, by order of Maj. Gen. Christopher C. Auger, commanding the Dept. of Washington, DC. Resided in Passaic, NJ, after the war.

65. **Prescott, Albert**, major. Res: Charlestown, MA. Born: Massachusetts. Age: 34. Married. Height: unknown. Comp: light. Eyes: brown. Hair: dark brown. Occup: spar maker. Commissioned captain, March 2, 1864; mustered captain, March 10, 1864. In command of the 1st Division, IX Corps, baggage wagon train guard from Co. K during the battle of the Wilderness, May 6, 1864. In action at Spotsylvania Court House, May 10, 12, and 18, 1864, North Anna River, May 24, 1864, Cold Harbor, June 3, 1864, and Petersburg assaults, June 17 and 18, 1864; killed in action at the Petersburg Crater, July 30, 1864. Commissioned major, June 17, 1864. Mus-

Major Albert Prescott.
(John Anderson)

tered major, July 26, 1864. In command of the regiment from June 17, 1864, until killed, July 30, 1864. Had previous service as 1st sergeant of Co. K, 5th Massachusetts Volunteer Militia, from April 19, 1861, until mustered out, July 31, 1861. Also had previous service as 1st sergeant and captain of Co. B, 36th MVI, from July 30, 1862, until resigned and discharged, April 29, 1863. Participated in operations with the IX Corps, including Fredericksburg, with that regiment in 1862–63. "A man of genial disposition, generous hearted and a true friend. . . . His character as a soldier was upright and honorable" (JA).

66. **Reno, Louis,** private. Res. and/or credit: Hinsdale, MA. Born: Montreal, Quebec, Canada. Age: 19. Height: 5'6". Comp: dark. Eyes: hazel. Hair: dark. Occup: laborer. Enlisted in Hinsdale by W. H. Carson, March 30, 1864; mustered April 6, 1864. Wounded in action at the Wilderness, May 6, 1864. Absent wounded in the army general hospital in New Haven, CT, until he deserted from there, July 24, 1864. Apparently surrendered to authorities on an unknown date, probably under President Lincoln's proclamation of amnesty, as he listed as being discharged the US service, to date July 30, 1865.

67. **Richards, John H.,** private. Res. and/or credit: Richmond, MA. Born: Stockbridge, MA. Age: 20. Height: 5'7". Comp: light. Eyes: brown. Hair: brown. Occup: farmer. Enlisted in Co. K in Richmond by Lewis C. Sherrill, March 7, 1864; mustered April 6, 1864; transferred to Co. I by his own request, April 13, 1864, under RSO 38, by order of Col. William F. Bartlett, April 13, 1864. Missing in action at the Wilderness, May 6, 1864. Never accounted for and presumed killed.

68. **Ross, Edward,** private. Res. and/or credit: Granby, MA. Born: Burrville, RI. Age: 26. Height: 5'5". Comp: light. Eyes: hazel. Hair: brown. Occup: farmer. Enlisted in Granby by Lt. Col. Luke Lyman, April 5, 1864; mustered April 6, 1864. In action at the Wilderness, May 6, 1864, and Spotsylvania Court House, May 10, 1864; killed in action there, May 12, 1864.

69. **St. Antoine, Gilbert,** private. Res. and/or credit: Shelburne, MA. Born: province of Quebec, Canada. Age: 28. Height: 5'5". Comp: dark. Eyes: hazel. Hair: brown. Occup: farmer. Enlisted in Shelburne by Pliny Fisk, Feb. 26, 1864; mustered March 10, 1864. In action at the Wilderness, May 6, 1864, and one of the 34 enlisted men who remained with the colors during that battle. In action at Spotsylvania Court House, May 10 and 12, 1864, and killed in action there, May 18, 1864.

70. **Sancomb, David,** private. Res. and/or credit: Gill, MA. Born: Chateaugay, NY. Age: 18. Height: 5'6". Comp: dark. Eyes: gray. Hair: brown. Occup: clerk. Enlisted in Gill by Henry Bascomb, Feb. 13, 1864; mustered March 10, 1864. In action at the Wilderness, May 6, 1864, and Spotsylvania Court House, May 10, 12, and 18, 1864; killed in action at North Anna River, May 24, 1864.

71. **Schafer, George Jacob,** private. Res. and/or credit: Stockbridge, MA. Born: Germany. Age: 42. Height: 5'10". Comp: light. Eyes: gray. Hair: dark. Occup: manufacturer. Enlisted in Stockbridge by Sgt. Henry S. May, Feb. 24, 1864; mustered March 10, 1864. Never in combat. Absent sick from on or before May 6, 1864, until discharged the US service on a Surgeons Certificate of Disability for disease from an army general hospital in Alexandria, VA, May 23, 1865.

72. **Shaw, George W.,** private. Res. and/or credit: Great Barrington, MA. Born: Stephentown, NY. Age: 44. Height: 5'5". Comp: light. Eyes: blue. Hair: dark. Occup: tailor. Enlisted in Great Barrington by John M. Seeley, March 1, 1864; mustered April 6, 1864. Absent sick or on detached duty from on or before May 6, 1864, until between Aug. 19 and Sept. 30, 1864. In action at Poplar Grove Church, Sept. 30, 1864, and killed in action there, Oct. 8, 1864.

73. **Shelby, Michael,** private. Res. and credit: Great Barrington, MA. Born: Great Barrington, MA. Age: 18. Height: 5'6". Comp: light. Eyes: brown. Hair: brown. Occup: laborer. Enlisted in Great Barrington by John M. See-

ley, Feb. 19, 1864; mustered March 10, 1864. Killed in action at the Wilderness, May 6, 1864.

74. **Sidell, Charles**, private. Res. and/or credit: Northampton, MA. Born: Germany. Age: 32. Height: 5'7". Comp: sandy. Eyes: gray. Hair: brown. Occup: teamster. Enlisted in Northampton by Lt. Col. Luke Lyman, Feb. 22, 1864; mustered March 10, 1864. In action at the Wilderness, May 6, 1864, Spotsylvania Court House, May 10, 12, and 18, 1864, North Anna River, May 24, 1864, and Cold Harbor, June 3, 1864; wounded in the arm in action during the Petersburg assault, June 17, 1864. With the regiment on all marches and in all skirmishes and battles until wounded. Absent wounded in an army general hospital until between Oct. 8, 1864, and Jan. 29, 1865. On furlough from Jan. 29 until Feb. 12, 1865. In action at Fort Stedman, March 25, 1865. Mustered out with the regiment at Delaney house, Washington, DC, July 30, 1865, and discharged in Readville, MA, Aug. 9, 1865, expiration of service. Resided in Northampton, MA, after the war.

75. **Simmons, Ensign J.**, corporal. Res. and credit: Washington, MA. Born: Washington, MA. Age: 21. Height: 5'7". Comp: light. Eyes: gray. Hair: brown. Occup: farmer. Enlisted in Washington by Charles Crosier, Feb. 13, 1864; mustered March 10, 1864. Promoted corporal, March 10, 1864. In action at the Wilderness, May 6, 1864, and Spotsylvania Court House, May 10, 1864; wounded in action there, May 12, 1864. Absent wounded in an army general hospital until listed in the company journal as "present sick," Jan. 17, 1865. Listed as still "present sick" in the company journal, Feb. 15, 1865. In action at Fort Stedman, March 25, 1865. Reduced to the ranks for unsoldierly conduct, on an unknown date. Promoted corporal again, July 1, 1865. Mustered out with the regiment at Delaney house, Washington, DC, July 30, 1865, and discharged in Readville, MA, Aug. 9, 1865, expiration of service. Had previous service as a private in Co. B, 49th MVI, from Sept. 6, 1862, until mustered out, Sept. 1, 1863. Participated in the Port

Hudson, LA, campaign with that regiment in 1863. Resided in Windsor, MA, after the war.

76. **Snow, John**, private. Res. and/or credit. Millbury, MA. Born: Montreal, Quebec, Canada. Age: 31. Height: 5'5". Comp: dark. Eyes: black. Hair: black. Occup: shoemaker. Enlisted in Millbury by C. D. Morse, Feb. 19, 1864; mustered March 10, 1864. In action at the Wilderness, May 6, 1864, and Spotsylvania Court House, May 10, 1864; wounded in action there May 12, 1864. Absent wounded in an army general hospital until March 21, 1865, when he is listed in the company journal as "present sick." In action and taken prisoner of war at Fort Stedman, March 25, 1865. Paroled and exchanged from Libby Prison, Richmond, VA, March 29, 1865. Returned to the regiment for duty from the Camp of Parole in Annapolis, MD, May 11, 1865. Mustered out with the regiment at Delaney house, Washington, DC, July 30, 1865, and discharged in Readville, MA, Aug. 9, 1865, expiration of service. Resided in Worcester, MA, after the war.

77. **Stanley, Michael**, private. Res. and/or credit: Middlefield, MA. Born: Ireland. Age: 22. Height: 5'5". Comp: light. Eyes: blue. Hair: sandy. Enlisted in Middlefield by Matthew Smith, Feb. 25, 1864; mustered March 10, 1864. Killed in action at the Wilderness, May 6, 1864.

78. **Stevens, Romanzo**, private. Res. and credit: Richmond, MA. Born: Richmond, MA. Age: 21. Height: 5'8". Comp: light. Eyes: blue. Hair: light. Occup: farmer. Enlisted in Richmond by Lewis C. Sherrill, Feb. 29, 1864; mustered March 10, 1864. Absent sick or on detached duty from on or before May 6, 1864, until between Sept. 30 and Oct. 8, 1864. Wounded in action at Poplar Grove Church, Oct. 8, 1864. Absent wounded in an army general hospital until after March 25, 1865. Detached and detailed as a guard at the quartermaster's dept. in Washington, DC, from May 31, 1865, until muster-out. Mustered out with the regiment at Delaney house, Washington, DC, July 30, 1865, and dis-

Private Romanzo Stevens (in old age).
(USAMHI)

charged in Readville, MA, Aug. 9, 1865, expiration of service. Resided in West Stockbridge, MA, after the war.

·79. **Sturgis, Thomas,** 1st lieutenant. Res: New York City. Credit: unknown. Born: New York. Age: 18. No description available. Commissioned 1st lieutenant, Jan. 7, 1865; mustered 1st lieutenant, Jan. 27, 1865. Assigned to special duty as assistant aide-de-camp to Brig. Gen. Napoleon B. McLaughlen at 3rd Brigade, 1st Division, IX Corps, Headquarters. In action and taken prisoner of war at Fort Stedman, March 25, 1865. Paroled and exchanged from Libby Prison, Richmond, VA, April 1 or 2, 1865. Returned to 3rd Brigade, 1st Division, IX Corps, Headquarters for special duty from the Camp of Parole in Annapolis, MD, May 25, 1865. Resigned and discharged the US service, June 26, 1865. Had previous service as 1st lieutenant and adjutant in the 60th MVI from Aug. 1, 1864, until mustered out, Nov. 30, 1864. Resided in New York City after the war.

80. **Sullivan, Daniel,** private. Res. and/or credit: Worcester, MA. Born: Ireland. Age: 24. Height: 5'9". Comp: fair. Eyes: blue.

Hair: brown. Enlisted in Worcester by D. Waldo Lincoln, Feb. 29, 1864; mustered March 10, 1864. Wounded in action at the Wilderness, May 6, 1864. Absent wounded until he deserted from an army general hospital in Philadelphia, PA, July 13, 1864. Surrendered to authorities on an unknown date and discharged the US service, discharge to date, July 30, 1865. Resided in Fitchburg, MA, after the war.

81. **Thornton, Patrick,** private. Res. and/or credit: Pittsfield, MA. Born: Ireland. Age: 28. Height: 5'6". Comp: sandy. Eyes: blue. Hair: brown. Occup: farmer. Enlisted in Pittsfield by John C. West, Feb. 16, 1864; mustered March 10, 1864. In action at the Wilderness, May 6, 1864, and Spotsylvania Court House, May 10, 1864; wounded in action there, May 12, 1864. Died from his wounds in an army general hospital in Baltimore, MD, June 18, 1864.

82. **Tyler, Titus,** 1st sergeant. Res. and/or credit: Springfield, MA. Born: Haddam, CT. Age: 27. Height: 5'7". Comp: dark. Eyes: hazel. Hair: dark. Occup: laborer. Enlisted in Springfield by H. B. Fish, Feb. 20, 1864; mustered March 10, 1864. Promoted sergeant, March 10, 1864. Never in combat. Absent sick in an army general hospital from on or before May 6, 1864, until March 30, 1865. Reduced to the ranks while absent sick by order of Lt. Col. Julius M. Tucker, Feb. 4, 1865. Listed in the company journal for April 1, 1865, as "present sick." Absent sick in the 1st Division, IX Corps, Field Hospital at Petersburg from April 6 until April 24, 1865. Absent without leave May 5 and 6, 1865. Detached and detailed on daily duty (nature of duty unknown) until June 11, 1865. Promoted 1st sergeant, July 1, 1865. Mustered out with the regiment at Delaney house, Washington, DC, July 30, 1865, and discharged in Readville, MA, Aug. 9, 1865, expiration of service.

83. **Waters, John,** private. Res. and credit: Middlefield, MA. Born: Middlefield, MA. Age: 23. Height: 5'10". Comp: light. Eyes: blue. Hair: brown. Occup: laborer. Enlisted in Middlefield by Matthew C. Smith, Feb. 25,

1864; mustered March 10, 1864. In action at the Wilderness, May 6, 1864, Spotsylvania Court House, May 10, 12, and 18, 1864, North Anna River, May 24, 1864, and Cold Harbor, June 3, 1864; killed in action in the Petersburg assault, June 17, 1864. With the regiment on all marches and in all skirmishes and battles until killed.

84. **Webster, Silas D.**, private. Res. and/or credit: Richmond, MA. Born: Stockbridge, MA. Age: 21. Height: 5'8". Comp: light. Eyes: blue. Hair: brown. Occup: farmer. Enlisted in Richmond by Lewis C. Sherrill, Feb. 29, 1864; mustered March 10, 1864. Never in combat. Absent sick from on or before May 6, 1864, until discharged the US service on a Surgeons Certificate of Disability for disease from an army general hospital in Washington, DC, May 11, 1865, by order of Secretary of War Edwin M. Stanton, per a telegram from the AGO, War Dept., dated May 3, 1865.

85. **Wheeler, Otis E.**, private. Res. and/or credit: Windsor, MA. Born: Winchester, NH. Age: 22. Height: 5'6". Comp: florid. Eyes: blue. Hair: brown. Enlisted in Windsor by Lt. Col. Luke Lyman, March 15, 1864; mustered April 6, 1864. Severely wounded in action at the Wilderness, May 6, 1864. Died from his wounds, May 15, 1864 (place unknown, but likely Fredericksburg, VA).

86. **Wheeler, Warren W.**, private. Res. and credit: Holliston, MA. Born: Holliston, MA. Age: 37. Height: 5'10". Comp: dark. Eyes: blue. Hair: black. Enlisted in Holliston by Capt. Henry C. Ward, Feb. 16, 1864; mustered March 10, 1864. Absent sick or on detached duty from on or before May 6, 1864, until between Oct. 8, 1864, and Jan. 1, 1865. On furlough from Feb. 23 until March 15, 1865. With the regiment in most operations during the winter of 1865. Detached and detailed on daily duty as a guard at 1st Division, IX Corps, Headquarters from March 15 until March 25, 1865. In action and taken prisoner of war at Fort Stedman, March 25, 1865. Paroled and exchanged from Libby Prison, Richmond, VA, April 1, 1865. Returned to the regiment for duty from the Camp of Parole in Annapolis, MD, May 7, 1865. De-

tached and detailed on daily duty (probably as a guard) at 1st Division, IX Corps, Headquarters by SFO 14, May 31, 1865. Listed as absent without leave in the company journal, July 16, 1865, but returned between July 21 and July 30, 1865. Mustered out with the regiment at Delaney house, Washington, DC, July 30, 1865, and discharged in Readville, MA, Aug. 9, 1865, expiration of service. Had previous service as a private in Co. I, 23rd MVI, from Sept. 3, 1861, until discharged for disability at New Bern, NC, May 30, 1863. Participated in the North Carolina campaign with that regiment in 1862–63. Resided in West Medway, MA, after the war.

87. **White, George E.**, private. Res. and credit: Millbury, MA. Born: Millbury, MA. Age: 18. Height: 5'3". Comp: dark. Eyes: black. Hair: black. Occup: farmer. Enlisted in Millbury by C. D. Morse, Feb. 20, 1864; mustered March 10, 1864. Never in combat. Detailed as an orderly for Dr. Whitman V. White (no relation). Assisted in caring for the wounded in the 1st Division, IX Corps, Field Hospital on the various battlefields. Absent sick from typhus in the 1st Division, IX Corps, Field Hospital at Petersburg from an unknown date in Aug. 1864 until Jan. 2, 1865.

Private George White (postwar photo). *(John Anderson)*

Detailed on daily duty, again with Dr. White, as a nurse from Jan. 2 until Feb. 15, 1865. Detailed on extra duty (probably with Dr. White) from an unknown date until July 3, 1865. Mustered out with the regiment at Delaney house, Washington, DC, July 30, 1865, and discharged in Readville, MA, Aug. 9, 1865, expiration of service. Resided in Chicago, IL, after the war and operated a hardwood lumber company there. Director of Chicago National Bank. Alderman for the City of Chicago and state senator in the Illinois legislature. Member of the 54th US Congress from Illinois. Died May 17, 1935, age 89.

88. **White, Joseph,** corporal. Res. and/or credit: West Boylston, MA. Born: Canada. Age: 21. Height: 5'7". Comp: dark. Eyes: black. Hair: black. Occup: blacksmith. Enlisted in West Boylston by D. C. Murdock, Feb. 25, 1864; mustered March 10, 1864. Promoted corporal, March 10, 1865. In action at the Wilderness, May 6, 1864, and Spotsylvania Court House, May 10 and 12, 1864; killed in action there, May 18, 1864.

89. **Whiton, Henry,** corporal. Res. and/or credit: Ware, MA. Born: Rocky Hill, CT. Age: 19. Height: 5'2". Comp: light. Eyes: blue. Hair: brown. Occup: clerk. Enlisted in Ware by Otis Lane, Feb. 24, 1864; mustered March 10, 1864. Promoted corporal, March 10, 1864. In action at the Wilderness, May 6, 1864, and Spotsylvania Court House, May 10, 1864; severely wounded in action there, May 12, 1864. Absent wounded in an army general hospital until transferred to the 143rd Co., 2nd Battln., VRC, to date from Sept. 30, 1864, by order of Secretary of War Edwin M. Stanton, under SO 26, AGO, War Dept., Oct. 17, 1864. Discharged the US service for disability from wounds, Aug. 31, 1866, as corporal of 17th Co., 2nd Battln., VRC.

90. **Wilcox, George W.,** private. Res. and credit: Great Barrington, MA. Born: Great Barrington, MA. Age: 24. Height: 5'7". Comp: light. Eyes: blue. Hair: black. Occup: farmer. Enlisted in Great Barrington by John M. Seeley, Feb. 15, 1864; mustered March 10, 1864. Severely wounded in the forearm in action at the Wilderness, May 6, 1864. Trans-ported to Washington by steamer from Fredericksburg, VA, where he underwent surgery, May 23, 1864, for removal of damaged bones in the forearm. Died from his wounds in an army general hospital in Washington, DC, June 11, 1864. Had previous service as a private in Co. I, 49th MVI, from Sept. 20, 1862, until mustered out Sept. 1, 1863. Participated in the Port Hudson, LA, campaign with that regiment in 1863.

91. **Williams, R. Wesley,** 1st sergeant. Res. and/or credit: Lee, MA. Born: Unadilla, NY. Age: 21. Height: 5'7". Comp: dark. Eyes: dark. Hair: black. Occup: agent. Enlisted in Lee by Sylvester S. May, Feb. 13, 1864; mustered March 10, 1864; Promoted sergeant, March 10, 1864. In action at the Wilderness, May 6, 1864, Spotsylvania Court House, May 10, 12, and 18, 1864, North Anna River, May 24, 1864, Cold Harbor, June 3, 1864, Petersburg assaults, June 17 and 18, 1864, Petersburg Crater, July 30, 1864, Weldon Railroad, Aug. 19, 1864, and Poplar Grove Church, Sept. 30 and Oct. 8, 1864. Acting 1st sergeant from on or before Jan. 1, 1865, until promoted 1st sergeant, March 1, 1865, as the result of 1st Sgt. McFarland having been transferred to the VRC. Severely wounded in action at Fort Stedman, March 25, 1865. Right leg shattered by a musket ball and surgically amputated in the 1st Division, IX Corps, Field Hospital. Absent wounded until discharged and pensioned from the US service on a Surgeons Certificate of Disability for wounds from an army general hospital in Tennallytown, DC, by order of Secretary of War Edwin M. Stanton, under GO 77, par. 6, AGO, War Dept. Also discharged as a supernumerary because of the consolidation of the 59th MVI with the 57th under SO 254, par. 43, AGO, War Dept., dated May 26, 1865. Released from an army general hospital in Boston, MA, Oct. 30, 1865. Cited twice for bravery at Fort Stedman: "Sergeant Wesley R. Williams [sic], Company I (wounded), general bravery" (GPR and JMT). One of the 11 men who served with the regiment on all marches and in all skirmishes and battles throughout its entire wartime service, and of the 11, one of the 10 who survived. Also one of the 30 combat soldiers remaining of the

regiment after Weldon Railroad, Aug. 19, 1865. Resided in Mt. Vernon, Skagit County, WA, after the war.

92. **Woodville, William,** private. Res. and credit: Springfield, MA. Born: Springfield, MA. Age: 27. Height: 5'8". Comp: light. Eyes: blue. Hair: brown. Occup: wheelwright. Enlisted in Springfield by Lt. George S. Green, March 9, 1864; mustered March 10, 1864. Wounded in action at the Wilderness, May 6, 1864. Absent wounded in an army general hospital until between Oct. 8, 1864, and Jan. 1, 1865. Detached and detailed to the Pioneer Corps at 3rd Brigade, 1st Division, IX Corps, Headquarters, Feb. 19, 1865, until muster-out. Mustered out with the regiment at Delaney house, Washington, DC, July 30, 1865, and discharged in Readville, MA, Aug. 9, 1865, expiration of service.

93. **Wright, Charles,** private. Res. and/or credit: Adams, MA. Born: Ireland. Age: 40. Height: 5'7". Comp: light. Eyes: brown. Hair: black. Occup: laborer. Enlisted in Adams by Joseph Tucker, Feb. 17, 1864; mustered March 10, 1864. In action at the Wilderness, May 6, 1864, Spotsylvania Court House, May 10, 12, and 18, 1864, North Anna River, May 24, 1864, Cold Harbor, June 3, 1864, and Petersburg assaults, June 17 and 18, 1864; wounded in action at the Petersburg Crater, July 30, 1864. With the regiment on all marches and in all skirmishes and battles until wounded. Absent wounded until discharged the US service for disability from Dale US Army General Hospital in Worcester, MA, May 30, 1865, by order of Maj. Gen. John A.

Dix, War Dept. Had previous service as a private in Co. H, 49th MVI, from Sept. 22, 1862, until mustered out, Sept. 1, 1863. Participated in the Port Hudson, LA, campaign with that regiment in 1863.

94. **Writer, Orion E.,** private. Res. and/or credit: Hadley, MA. Born: Canada. Age: 20. Height: 5'6". Comp: light. Eyes: blue. Hair: light. Occup: farmer. Enlisted in Hadley by Lt. Col. Luke Lyman, Feb. 25, 1864; mustered March 10, 1864. Wounded in action at the Wilderness, May 6, 1864. Absent wounded until he deserted from an army general hospital in Washington, DC, Nov. 26, 1864. Returned to the regiment for duty under President Lincoln's proclamation of amnesty, April 29, 1865. Absent sick in the 1st Division, IX Corp, Field Hospital, from June 15 until June 22, 1865, and again from June 23, 1865, until on or before July 30, 1865. Mustered out with the regiment at Delaney house, Washington, DC, July 30, 1865, and discharged in Readville, MA, Aug. 9, 1865, expiration of service.

95. **Young, Daniel W.,** private. Res. and/or credit: Dalton, MA. Born: Washington, MA. Age: 20. Height: 5'6". Comp: light. Eyes: blue. Hair: brown. Occup: teamster. Enlisted in Dalton by D. C. Smith, Feb. 13, 1864; mustered March 10, 1864. Wounded on an unknown date, but not in a major battle. Absent wounded from an unknown date in 1864 until discharged the US service for disability from wounds, May 29, 1865, from an army general hospital in Washington, DC, under GO 77, par. 6, AGO, War Dept.

ROSTER AND DESCRIPTIVE LIST OF COMPANY K

Company K, the "Sharpshooter Company," was the tenth and last company of the regiment to be mustered into United States service, and it was mustered on April 6, 1864, under SO 415, from the AGO, Boston, MA, by 2nd Lt. Daniel Madden, 6th United States Regular Cavalry. It was mustered out by Capt. Sylvester Keyser, 2nd Michigan Volunteer Infantry, ACM, 1st Division, IX Corps. The records of Company K, like those of Companies F and G, are replete with comments concerning the military character of its members. This unit, however, contains few negative remarks, and in the cases where no evaluation is given, poor or fair performance of the individual may be assumed.

1. **Adams, John,** private. Res. and/or credit: Oakham, MA. Born: Oakham, MA. Age: 36. Height: 5′10″. Comp: dark. Eyes: black. Hair: black. Occup: farmer. Enlisted in Oakham by M. Haskell, March 21, 1864; mustered April 6, 1864. Detached and detailed as a guard for the 1st Division, IX Corps, baggage and supply wagon train during the battle of the Wilderness, May 6, 1864. In action at Spotsylvania Court House, May 10, 12, and 18, 1864, North Anna River, May 24, 1864, Cold Harbor, June 3, 1864, Petersburg assaults, June 17 and 18, 1864, Petersburg Crater, July 30, 1864, Weldon Railroad, Aug. 19, 1864, and Poplar Grove Church, Sept. 30, 1864; slightly wounded in action there, Oct. 8, 1864. With the regiment on all marches and in all skirmishes and battles except the Wilderness through Oct. 8, 1864, until wounded, and one of the 30 combat soldiers remaining in the regiment after Weldon Railroad, Aug. 19, 1864. Detached and detailed on daily duty as a clerk at the 3rd Brigade, 1st Division, IX Corps, Commissary Dept. from Dec. 5, 1864, until at least June 1, 1865. Mustered out with the regiment at Delaney house, Washington, DC, July 30, 1865, and discharged in Readville, MA, Aug. 9, 1865, expiration of service. Had previous service as a private in Co. G, 44th MVI, from Aug. 29, 1862, until mustered out, June 18, 1863. Participated in the North Carolina campaign with that regiment in 1862–63. "Good Soldier" (CR).

2. **Allcott, Frank,** private. Res: Newton, MA. Credit: Boston, MA. Born: Marshall, MI. Age: 18. Height: 5′10″. Comp: light. Eyes: blue. Hair: light. Occup: clerk. Enlisted in Boston by W. W. Clapp, March 11, 1864; mustered April 6, 1864. Sick on the march to the Rapidan River, May 4, 1864, and present sick in the rear until June 8, 1864, when he was sent to the hospital. Absent sick in an army general hospital until Jan. 1, 1865. With the regiment in operations during the winter of 1865 and slightly wounded in action and taken prisoner of war at Fort Stedman, March 25, 1865. Paroled and exchanged from Libby Prison, Richmond, VA, March 31, 1865. Returned to the regiment for duty from the Camp of Parole in Annapolis, MD, on or about May 11, 1865. Transferred to Co. H

after June 1, 1865. Absent sick in an army general hospital from after June 1, 1865, until discharged the US service for disability, June 19, 1865, by order of the War Dept.

3. **Allen, Henry,** private. Res: Ludlow, MA. Credit: Springfield, MA. Born: Hartford, CT. Age: 18. Height: 5′4″. Comp: dark. Eyes: brown. Hair: brown. Occup: laborer. Enlisted in Springfield by Lt. George S. Green, March 30, 1864; mustered April 6, 1864. Deserted during the morning of April 22, 1864, as the regiment began its march from Annapolis, MD. Surrendered to the authorities under President Lincoln's proclamation of amnesty. Never returned to the regiment, and never in combat. Mustered out, but absent, at Delaney house, Washington, DC, July 30, 1865, expiration of service.

4. **Andrews, William,** private. Res: Millbury, MA. Credit: Boston, MA. Born: Hingham, MA. Age: 21. Height: 5′7″. Enlisted in Boston by Lt. John Reade, March 24, 1864; mustered April 6, 1864. Detached and detailed as a guard for the 1st Division, IX Corps, baggage and supply wagon train during the battle of the Wilderness, May 6, 1864. In action at Spotsylvania Court House, May 10, 1864, and accidentally wounded in the hand by his own rifle just before the battle began there again, May 12, 1864. Absent wounded in an army general hospital until he deserted while on furlough from that hospital, Aug. 10, 1864. Surrendered to the authorities under President Lincoln's proclamation of amnesty. Never returned to the regiment. Discharged the US service while absent wounded, to date July 30, 1865.

5. **Armstrong, James,** private. Res: Charlton, MA. Credit: Boston, MA. Born: Philadelphia, PA. Age: 30. Height: 5′9″. Comp: light. Eyes: blue. Hair: light. Occup: painter. Enlisted in Boston by Lt. Wells, April 1, 1864; mustered April 6, 1864. Deserted from Camp Wool, April 17, 1864. Never returned. Bounty jumper.

6. **Barnes, Joseph W.,** sergeant. Res: Marlboro, MA. Credit: Boston, MA. Born: Marlboro, MA. Age: 25. Height: 5′10½″. Comp:

light. Eyes: hazel. Hair: brown. Occup: student. Enlisted in Boston by W. W. Clapp, March 26, 1864; mustered April 6, 1864. Promoted sergeant, April 6, 1864. Detached and detailed as a guard for the 1st Division, IX Corps, baggage and supply wagon train during the battle of the Wilderness, May 6, 1864. In action at Spotsylvania Court House, May 10, 12, and 18, 1864, and wounded in the leg in action at North Anna River, May 24, 1864. Absent wounded in Lincoln US Army General Hospital in Washington, DC, until discharged the US service for disability. Reduced to the ranks, May 28, 1865, by RSO 42 from Lt. Col. Julius M. Tucker, to date May 1, 1865, for accepting a position on a detail at Lincoln Hospital on Dec. 17, 1864 (and, thereby, remaining safe from combat duty). Discharged the US service by order of the War Dept., while absent wounded, Aug. 8, 1865. Had previous service as a private in Co. I, 5th MVI, from Aug. 20, 1862, until mustered out July 2, 1863. Participated in the North Carolina campaign with that regiment in 1862–63. Resided in Marlboro, MA, after the war and died there in 1910, age 71.

7. **Bemis, Amasa B.**, private. Res. and credit: Chester, MA. Born: Chester, MA. Age: 35. Height: 6'0". Comp: dark. Eyes: gray. Hair: dark. Occup: blacksmith. Enlisted in Chester by Sgt. Charles W. Knox, Feb. 29, 1864; mustered April 6, 1864. Detailed as company cook, April 6, 1864, until absent sick in an army general hospital from July 5 until Sept. 10, 1864. In action for the first time at Poplar Grove Church, Sept. 30 and Oct. 8, 1864. With the regiment in operations during the fall and winter of 1864–65 and in action at Fort Stedman, March 25, 1865. Mustered out with the regiment at Delaney house, Washington, DC, July 30, 1865, and discharged in Readville, MA, Aug. 9, 1865, expiration of service. Resided in Springfield, MA, after the war and died there in 1883, age 54.

8. **Benton, George W.**, private. Res. and/or credit: Springfield, MA. Born: Stewardston, NH. Age: 43. Height: 5'7". Comp: dark. Eyes: brown. Hair: dark. Occup: farmer. Enlisted in Springfield by Sgt. Daniel F. Pinder (23rd MVI), March 29, 1864; mustered April

6, 1864. Detached and detailed as a guard for the 1st Division, IX Corps, baggage and supply wagon train during the battle of the Wilderness, May 6, 1864. In action at Spotsylvania Court House, May 10, 1864, and mortally wounded in action there, May 12, 1864. Died from his wounds in an army general hospital in Washington, DC, May 29, 1864. "Good Soldier" (CR).

9. **Bigelow, Theodore S.**, private. Res. and/or credit: Boston, MA. Born: Medford, MA. Age: 37. Height: 5'9". Comp: fair. Eyes: blue. Hair: brown. Occup: clerk. Enlisted in Boston by D. Davis, March 29, 1864; mustered April 6, 1864. Left behind sick in an army general hospital in Washington, DC, as the regiment passed through there on the march to the front, April 26, 1864. Detailed to serve in that hospital (probably as a nurse) until discharged the US service for disability, June 5, 1865, by order of Secretary of War Edwin M. Stanton under GO 77, par. 6, AGO, War Dept., dated June 27, 1865, discharge to date June 10, 1865.

10. **Boyce, Daniel**, private. Res: Southbridge, MA. Credit: Worcester, MA. Born: Ireland. Age: 32. Height: 5'6". Comp: sandy. Eyes: gray. Hair: sandy. Occup: cabinetmaker. Enlisted in Worcester by Lt. John Reade, March 31, 1864; mustered April 6, 1864. Deserted from Camp Wool, April 17, 1864. Never returned. Bounty jumper.

11. **Brigham, George H.**, sergeant. Res. and credit: Marlboro, MA. Born: Marlboro, MA. Age: 18. Height: 5'8½". Comp: dark. Eyes: gray. Hair: dark. Occup: shoemaker. Enlisted in Marlboro by F. H. Morse, March 26, 1864; mustered April 6, 1864. Detached and detailed as a guard for the 1st Division, IX Corps, baggage and supply wagon train during the battle of the Wilderness, May 6, 1864. In action at Spotsylvania Court House, May 10, 12, and 18, 1864. Detached and detailed as a guard at 1st Brigade, 1st Division, IX Corps, Headquarters during the battle of North Anna River, May 24, 1864. In action at Cold Harbor, June 3, 1864, Petersburg assaults, June 17 and 18, 1864, Petersburg Crater, June 30, 1864, and Weldon Railroad, Aug. 19,

1864. Promoted corporal after Aug. 19, 1864, to replace Cpl. Spear, to date from April 6, 1864. Detached and detailed as a guard at 3rd Brigade, 1st Division, IX Corps, Headquarters from Aug. 31, 1864, until before Sept. 30, 1864. In action at Poplar Grove Church, Sept. 30 and Oct. 8, 1864, in operations during the fall and winter of 1865, and in action at Fort Stedman, March 25, 1865. Acting 1st sergeant from March 26 until April 9, 1865. With the regiment on all marches and in all battles except the Wilderness and North Anna River, and one of the 30 combat soldiers remaining of the regiment after Weldon Railroad, Aug. 19, 1864. Promoted sergeant, May 28, 1865, to replace Sgt. Barnes, under RSO 42, by order of Lt. Col. Julius M. Tucker, to date May 1, 1865. Mustered out with the regiment at Delaney house, Washington, DC, July 30, 1865, and discharged in Readville, MA, Aug. 9, 1865, expiration of service. Had previous service as a landsman in the US Navy from Aug. 5, 1862, until mustered out, Sept. 12, 1863. Served on the receiving ship *Ohio* and the USS *Ino*. Resided in Marlboro, MA, after the war and died there after mid-1927, date unknown. "Brave Soldier" (CR).

12. **Brooks, James P.**, sergeant. Res. and/or credit: Boston, MA. Born: Newmarket, NH. Age: 26. Height: 5'8½". Comp: fair. Eyes: hazel. Hair: chestnut. Occup: molder. Enlisted in Boston by G. W. Messenger, March 10, 1864; mustered April 6, 1864. Appointed acting corporal, April 6, 1864. Detached and detailed as a guard for the 1st Division, IX Corps, baggage and supply wagon train during the battle of the Wilderness, May 6, 1864. Promoted sergeant, May 12, 1864. In action at Spotsylvania Court House, May 10 and 12, 1864, and wounded in the left leg in action there, May 18, 1864. Underwent surgery for the amputation of his left leg by the anterior/posterior flap method, June 5, 1864, by Dr. C. Page, USA. Died from typhoid fever in an army field hospital (probably Depot) at Petersburg, July 14, 1864. Had previous service as a sergeant in Co. I, 10th MVI, from June 21, 1861, until transferred on an unknown date to the Massachusetts Recruiting Service. No further record with that organization. Also had service as a private in Co. C, 6th New Hampshire Volunteer Infantry (specifics unknown). "Good Soldier" (CR).

13. **Bushnell, Levi B.**, private. Res: Hinsdale, MA. Credit: Pittsfield, MA. Born: South Hero, VT. Age: 36. Height: 5'10". Comp: fair. Eyes: blue. Hair: brown. Occup: axe maker. Enlisted in Pittsfield by Sgt. James M. Childs, March 10, 1864; mustered April 6, 1864. Deserted from the IX Corps camp in Annapolis, MD, April 22, 1864. "Bounty jumper" (JA).

14. **Byam, Salathial A.**, private. Res. and/or credit: Boston, MA. Born: Carlisle, MA. Age: 38. Height: 5'5". Comp: light. Eyes: blue. Hair: black. Occup: watchman. Enlisted in Boston by W. W. Clapp, March 28, 1864; mustered April 6, 1864. Detached and detailed as a guard for the 1st Division, IX Corps, baggage and supply wagon train during the battle of the Wilderness, May 6, 1864. In action at Spotsylvania Court House, May 10, 1864, and slightly wounded in action there, May 12, 1864. Absent wounded in the 1st Division, IX Corps, Field Hospital until May 30, 1864. In action at Cold Harbor, June 3, 1864, and killed in action during the Petersburg assault, June 17, 1864. "Good Soldier" (CR).

15. **Carleton, Hubbard**, private. Res. and/or credit: Shelburne, MA. Born: Lanesbury, VT. Age: 34. Height: 5'5". Comp: dark. Eyes: blue. Hair: brown. Occup: farmer. Enlisted in Shelburne by G. L. Foster, March 24, 1864; mustered April 6, 1864. Detached and detailed as a guard for the 1st Division, IX Corps, baggage and supply wagon train during the battle of the Wilderness, May 6, 1864. In action at Spotsylvania Court House, May 10, 12, and 18, 1864, and North Anna River, May 24, 1864. Died from exhaustion and diarrhea on the march to Cold Harbor, June 1, 1864. "Good Soldier" (CR).

16. **Chapman, Henry C.**, private. Res. and credit: Hancock, MA. Born: Hancock, MA. Age: 21. Height: 5'7". Comp: light. Eyes: blue. Hair: brown. Occup: farmer. Enlisted in Hancock for one year by H. H. Whitemore, Sept. 10, 1864; mustered Sept. 15, 1864. As-

signed to the company as a recruit, Oct. 15, 1864, under RSO 5, by order of Lt. Col. Julius M. Tucker. Detached and detailed on daily duty at the quartermaster's dept. (probably at City Point, Petersburg) until Dec. 1, 1864. With the regiment in operations during the late fall and winter of 1864–65, and in action at Fort Stedman, March 25, 1865. Discharged the US service in Tennallytown, DC, June 16, 1865, in compliance with a GO from the AGO, War Dept., discharging men with a one-year enlistment by order of Secretary of War Edwin M. Stanton.

17. **Daniels, Charles L.**, private. Res. and/or credit: Pittsfield, MA. Born: Stephentown, NY. Age: 19. Height: 5'7½". Comp: light. Eyes: blue. Hair: dark. Occup: farmer. Enlisted in Pittsfield by John C. West, March 25, 1864; mustered April 6, 1864. Detached and detailed as a guard for the 1st Division, IX Corps, baggage and supply wagon train during the battle of the Wilderness, May 6, 1864. In action at Spotsylvania Court House, May 10, 12, and 18, 1864, North Anna River, May 24, 1864, Cold Harbor, June 3, 1864, and Petersburg assaults, June 17 and 18, 1864. Severely wounded in the right leg while on duty in the trenches at Petersburg on the morning of July 20, 1864. Taken to the 1st Division, IX Corps, Field hospital where his right leg was amputated by "Chopart's" (OMR) method, July 20, 1864, by Dr. H. Ludington, 100th Pennsylvania Volunteer Infantry. Sent to Depot Field Hospital at City Point, Petersburg, where he died from typhoid fever, July 29, 1864. With the regiment on all marches and in all skirmishes and battles, except the Wilderness, until wounded. "Good Soldier" (CR).

18. **Daniels, Lowell B.**, private. Res. and/or credit: Pittsfield, MA. Born: Troy, NY. Age: 18. Height: 5'8". Comp: dark. Eyes: brown. Hair: brown. Occup: farmer. Enlisted in Pittsfield by John C. West, March 25, 1864; mustered April 6, 1864. Detached and detailed as a guard for the 1st Division, IX Corps, baggage and supply wagon train during the battle of the Wilderness, May 6, 1864. In action at Spotsylvania Court House, May 10 and 12, 1864, and mortally wounded in action there, May 18, 1864. Died in the 1st Division, IX Corps, Field Hospital later that day. "Brave Soldier" (CR).

19. **Doolittle, William H.**, private. Res: Windsor, MA. Credit: Northampton, MA. Born: Windsor, MA. Age: 22. Height: 5'10½". Comp: florid. Eyes: black. Hair: black. Occup: farmer. Enlisted in Northampton by Lt. Col. Luke Lyman, March 15, 1864; mustered April 6, 1864. Detached and detailed as a guard for the 1st Division, IX Corps, baggage and supply wagon train during the battle of the Wilderness, May 6, 1864. In action at Spotsylvania Court House, May 10, 12, and 18, 1864, North Anna River, May 24, 1864, and Cold Harbor, June 3, 1864. Absent for an unknown reason (but likely sick in the rear) during the Petersburg assaults, June 17 and 18, 1864. Absent sick in an army general hospital from July 10, 1864, until Feb. 21, 1865. In action at Fort Stedman, March 25, 1865. Wounded by shrapnel from the explosion of a Confederate mortar shell while on picket duty at Petersburg, March 27, 1865. Absent wounded in the 1st Division, IX Corps, Field Hospital until transferred to an army general hospital in Boston, MA, April 7, 1865. Absent wounded in that hospital until discharged the US service for disability from wounds, May 3, 1865, by order of Maj. Gen. John A. Dix, War Dept., discharge to date May 3, 1865. Resided in Northfield, MA, after the war.

20. **Doty, Albert**, captain. Res. and credit: Hancock, MA. Born: Hancock, MA. Age: 23. Height: 5'8". Comp: light. Eyes: light. Hair: brown. Occup: carpenter. Enlisted in Co. I in Hancock by H. H. Whitman, Jan. 27, 1864; mustered March 10, 1864; transferred to Co. K, April 13, 1864, under RSO 38, par. 2, by order of Col. William F. Bartlett. Promoted 1st sergeant, to date from April 6, 1864. Detached and detailed as a guard for the 1st Division, IX Corps, baggage and supply wagon train during the battle of the Wilderness, May 6, 1864. Detailed as acting regimental sergeant major on the noncommissioned staff, May 8, 1864, because of Sgt. Maj. Murdock having been wounded. In action at Spotsylvania Court House, May 10, 12, and 18, 1864, North Anna River, May 24, 1864, and Cold Harbor, June 3, 1864, slightly

Captain Albert Doty. *(USAMHI)*

wounded in action during the Petersburg assault, June 17, 1864. Commissioned 1st lieutenant, July 14, 1864. Slightly wounded by the explosion of a mortar shell while on duty in the trenches at Petersburg, July 24, 1864. Discharged the US service, July 28, 1864, at Petersburg by order of Maj. Gen. Ambrose Burnside, commanding IX Corps, to accept his commission. Mustered 1st lieutenant, July 28, 1864. In action at the Petersburg Crater, July 30, 1864. After this battle he was the only commissioned officer remaining on combat duty with the regiment until Sept. 1864. In command of the regiment from July 31 until Sept. 1, 1864. In action at Weldon Railroad, Aug. 19, 1864, and one of the 30 combat soldiers remaining of the regiment after that battle. Appointed regimental adjutant, Sept. 14, 1864, under RSO 1, by order of Lt. Col. Julius M. Tucker. With the regiment in operations during the fall and winter of 1864-65. Promoted captain of US Volunteers by brevet under GO 15, War Dept., Feb. 6, 1865, to date from Aug. 18, 1864, for "gallant services in the operations on the Weldon Railroad, VA." On furlough at the time of the battle of Fort Stedman, March 25, 1865. Mustered out with the regiment at Delaney house, Washington, DC, July 30, 1865, and discharged in Readville, MA, Aug. 9, 1865, expiration of service. With the regiment on most marches

and in most battles and skirmishes. Had previous service as adjutant of a New York infantry regiment (specifics unknown). Died in 1874, age 33. "He was conspicuous for gallantry and was regardless of personal safety, even to the extent of recklessness" (JA); "Brave Soldier" (CR).

21. **Dow, Albert W.**, private. Res. and/or credit: Springfield, MA. Born: Pepperell, MA. Age: 29. Height: 5'6½". Comp: light. Eyes: blue. Hair: sandy. Occup: bookkeeper. Enlisted in Springfield by Lt. John Reade, March 15, 1864; mustered April 6, 1864. Missing in action at the Wilderness, May 6, 1864. Never accounted for and presumed killed. "Good Soldier" (CR).

22. **Dunbar, Thomas F.**, private. Res: Southboro, MA. Credit: Worcester, MA. Born: Westerly, RI. Age: 37. Height: 5'6". Comp: sandy. Eyes: gray. Hair: dark. Enlisted in Worcester by Lt. John Reade, March 31, 1864; mustered April 6, 1864. Left behind sick in an army general hospital in Washington, DC, when the regiment passed through there on the way to the front, April 26, 1864. Never rejoined the regiment, and was discharged the US service for disability from Gallup's Island, Boston Harbor, MA, July 18, 1864, by order of Maj. Gen. John A. Dix, War Dept. "Good Soldier" (CR).

23. **Eaton, John Jr.**, private. Res. and/or credit: Marlboro, MA. Born: Gardner, MA. Age: 34. Height: 5'10". Comp: dark. Eyes: hazel. Hair: dark. Occup: carpenter. Enlisted in Marlboro by F. H. Morse, March 29, 1864; mustered April 6, 1864. Detached and detailed as a guard for the 1st Division, IX Corps, baggage and supply wagon train during the battle of the Wilderness, May 6, 1864. In action at Spotsylvania Court House, May 10, 12, and 18, 1864. Sent sick with chronic diarrhea via Port Royal, VA, to Lincoln US Army General Hospital in Washington, DC, May 25, 1864, where he died, May 30, 1864, from typhoid fever and chronic diarrhea.

24. **Ewell, Frederic H.**, sergeant. Res. and credit: Marshfield, MA. Born: Marshfield, MA. Age: 21. Height: 5'11". Comp: light. Eyes: blue. Hair: brown. Occup: shoemaker.

Enlisted in Co. G in Marshfield by L. Hatch, Feb. 22, 1864; mustered March 10, 1864; transferred by his own request to Co. K, April 11, 1864, under RSO 36, by order of Col. William F. Bartlett. Detached and detailed as a guard for the 1st Division, IX Corps, baggage and supply wagon train during the battle of the Wilderness, May 6, 1864. In action at Spotsylvania Court House, May 10, 12, and 18, 1864, and North Anna River, May 24, 1864. Absent sick in an army general hospital from June 1 until Aug. 30, 1864. Promoted corporal, Sept. 1, 1864. Absent sick again in an army general hospital from Sept. 3, 1864, until Jan. 28, 1865. In action at Fort Stedman, March 25, 1865. Promoted sergeant, May 28, 1865, under RSO 42, to date May 1, 1865, by order of Lt. Col. Julius M. Tucker. Mustered out with the regiment at Delaney house, Washington, DC, July 30, 1865, and discharged in Readville, MA, Aug. 9, 1865, expiration of service. Resided in Marshfield, MA, after the war. "Good Soldier" (CR).

25. **Ewell, Isaiah A.**, private. Res. and credit: Marshfield, MA. Born: Marshfield, MA. Age: 19. Height: 6′2″. Comp: light. Eyes: blue. Hair: brown. Occup: farmer. Enlisted in Co. G in Marshfield by L. Hatch, Feb. 19, 1864; mustered March 10, 1864; transferred by his own request to Co. K, April 11, 1864, under RSO 36, by order of Col. William F. Bartlett. Detached and detailed as a guard for the 1st Division, IX Corps, baggage and supply wagon train during the battle of the Wilderness, May 6, 1864. In action at Spotsylvania Court House, May 10, 12, and 18, 1864, and North Anna River, May 24, 1864. Absent sick in an army general hospital from June 1 until Oct. 2, 1864. In action at Poplar Grove Church, Oct. 8, 1864. Absent sick from Dec. 10, 1864, until discharged the US service for disability from the 1st Division, IX Corps, Field Hospital at Petersburg by order of Maj. Gen. John G. Parke, commanding IX Corps, Dec. 28, 1864. Resided in Marshfield, MA, after the war and died there after 1911, date unknown.

26. **Ewell, Melvin**, private. Res. and credit: Marshfield, MA. Born: Marshfield, MA. Age: 26. Height: 5′10½″. Comp: dark. Eyes: blue.

Hair: brown. Occup: shoemaker. Enlisted in Co. G in Marshfield by L. Hatch, Feb. 16, 1864; mustered March 10, 1864; transferred by his own request to Co. K, April 11, 1864, under RSO 36, by order of Col. William F. Bartlett. Absent sick in an army general hospital from May 4, 1864, until transferred to the 23rd Co., 2nd. Battln., VRC, April 27, 1865. Discharged the US service, Aug. 12, 1865, by order of the War Dept., expiration of service. Died in 1891, age 53.

27. **Exley, Edwin W.**, private. Res. and/or credit: Marlboro, MA. Born: Lowell, MA. Age: 18. Height: 5′7″. Comp: light. Eyes: gray. Hair: light. Occup: shoemaker. Enlisted in Marlboro by F. H. Morse, March 26, 1864; mustered April 6, 1864. Detached and detailed as a guard for the 1st Division, IX Corps, baggage and supply wagon train during the battle of the Wilderness, May 6, 1864. In action at Spotsylvania Court House, May 10, 12, and 18, 1864, North Anna River, May 24, 1864, Cold Harbor, June 3, 1864, and Petersburg assaults, June 17 and 18, 1864. Absent sick in an army general hospital from June 30 until Sept. 3, 1864. In action at Poplar Grove Church, Sept. 30 and Oct. 8, 1864, in operations of the regiment during the fall and winter of 1864–65, and in action at Fort Stedman, March 25, 1865. Mustered out with the regiment at Delaney house, Washington, DC, July 30, 1865, and discharged in Readville, MA, Aug. 9, 1865, expiration of service. "Brave Soldier" (CR).

28. **Fairfield, John H.**, private. Res. and/or credit: Windsor, MA. Born: Charlestown, MA. Age: 40. Height: 5′8½″. Comp: light. Eyes: blue. Hair: auburn. Occup: farmer. Enlisted in Windsor by C. Baldwin, Feb. 29, 1864; mustered Feb. 29, 1864. Did not join the regiment until June 2, 1864 (probably absent sick). In action during the Petersburg assaults only, June 17 and 18, 1864. Detached and detailed as a pioneer at IX Corps Headquarters, July 4, 1864, until mustered out with the regiment at Delaney house, Washington, DC, July 30, 1865, and discharged in Readville, MA, Aug. 9, 1865, expiration of service. Had previous service as a private in Co. K, 49th MVI, from Oct. 14, 1862, until mus-

tered out, Sept. 1, 1863. Participated in the Port Hudson, LA, campaign with that regiment in 1863.

29. **Fitts, Lyman B.**, private. Res. and/or credit: Marshfield, MA. Born: Hanover, MA. Age: 26. Height: 5'7". Comp: dark. Eyes: blue. Hair: black. Occup: shoemaker. Enlisted in Co. G in Marshfield by L. Hatch, Feb. 16, 1864; mustered March 10, 1864; transferred by his own request to Co. K, April 11, 1864, under RSO 36, by order of Col. William F. Bartlett. Detached and detailed as a guard for the 1st Division, IX Corps, baggage and supply wagon train during the battle of the Wilderness, May 6, 1864. In action at Spotsylvania Court House, May 10, 12, and 18, 1864, North Anna River, May 24, 1864, Cold Harbor, June 3, 1864, and Petersburg assaults, June 17 and 18, 1864. Detailed as company cook, July 6, 1864, and therefore exempted from hard combat service. Absent sick in an army general hospital from Nov. 22 until Dec. 28, 1864. In action at Fort Stedman, March 25, 1865. Mustered out with the regiment at Delaney house, Washington, DC, July 30, 1865, and discharged in Readville, MA, Aug. 9, 1865, expiration of service.

30. **Gildea, Charles M.**, private. Res: Newton, MA. Credit: Boston, MA. Born: St. Catherines, Ontario, Canada. Age: 18. Height: 5'9". Comp: light. Eyes: hazel. Hair: brown. Occup: fireman. Enlisted in Boston by W. W. Clapp, March 11, 1864; mustered April 6, 1864. Detached and detailed as a guard for the 1st Division, IX Corps, baggage and supply wagon train during the battle of the Wilderness, May 6, 1864. In action at Spotsylvania Court House, May 10, 12, and 18, 1864, and North Anna River, May 24, 1864. Absent sick in an army general hospital from June 1, 1864, until May 4, 1865, when he returned to the regiment for duty in Georgetown, DC. Mustered out with the regiment at Delaney house, Washington, DC, July 30, 1865, and discharged in Readville, MA, Aug. 9, 1865, expiration of service.

31. **Gill, Henry L.**, private. Res: Holyoke, MA. Credit: Springfield, MA. Born: Canada. Age: 26. Height: 5'5½". Comp: dark. Eyes:

black. Hair: dark. Occup: blacksmith. Enlisted in Springfield by H. D. Foster, March 10, 1864; mustered April 6, 1864. In action at the Wilderness, May 6, 1864, and Spotsylvania Court House, May 10, 12, and 18, 1864; slightly wounded in the hand in action at North Anna River, May 24, 1864. Sent to an army general hospital in Washington, DC, via Port Royal, VA. Absent wounded in that hospital until transferred to Co. I, 2nd Regiment, VRC, on an unknown date. Discharged the US service, July 22, 1865, by order of the War Dept., expiration of service.

32. **Gouch, Edwin J.**, private. Res: Northampton, MA. Credit: Greenfield, MA. Born: Westampton, MA. Age: 44. Height: 5'7". Comp: light. Eyes: blue. Hair: gray. Occup: carpenter. Enlisted and mustered in Greenfield by Capt. Penicema, Sept. 1, 1864; assigned to the company as a recruit at Petersburg, Oct. 17, 1864, under RSO 5, by order of Lt. Col. Julius M. Tucker. Absent sick in an army general hospital from Dec. 7, 1864, until Feb. 26, 1864. In action at Fort Stedman, March 25, 1865. Absent sick in an army general hospital from after May 30, 1865, until discharged the US service for disability, Aug. 8, 1865, by order of the War Dept., dated Aug. 8, 1865. Had previous service as a private in Co. K, 27th MVI, from Aug. 18, 1862, until discharged for disability in New Bern, NC, March 25, 1863. Participated in the North Carolina campaign with that regiment in 1862–63.

33. **Goulding, Henry C.**, corporal. Res. and/or credit: Northboro, MA. Born: West Boylston, MA. Age: 34. Height: 5'8". Comp: light. Eyes: gray. Hair: brown. Occup: engineer. Enlisted in Northboro by A. Rice, March 19, 1864; mustered April 6, 1864. Promoted corporal, April 6, 1864. Detailed to take charge of the regimental pioneer detachment. Never in combat. Detached, detailed, and transferred to Nashville, TN, as an engineer, July 22, 1864, by order of the War Dept. Mustered out, while still absent on detached service, at Delaney house, Washington, DC, July 30, 1865, by SO 393, War Dept., dated July 24, 1865. Resided in Chicago, IL, after the war.

34. **Gregory, Henry A.**, private. Res. and/or credit: Chicopee, MA. Born: Boston, MA. Age: 34. Height: 5'7½". Comp: dark. Eyes: hazel. Hair: dark. Occup: mechanic. Enlisted in Chicopee by Otis Chapman, March 22, 1864; mustered April 6, 1864. Detached and detailed as a guard for the 1st Division, IX Corps, baggage and supply wagon train during the battle of the Wilderness, May 6, 1864. In action at Spotsylvania Court House, May 10, 12, and 18, 1864, and slightly wounded in action at North Anna River, May 24, 1864. Remained with the regiment until June 1, 1864, when he was sent to the hospital. Absent wounded until discharged the US service on a Surgeons Certificate of Disability for wounds from an army general hospital in Washington, DC, Nov. 27, 1864, by order of Maj. Gen. Christopher C. Auger, commanding the Dept. of Washington, DC.

35. **Harrington, Francis Moore**, private. Res: Boylston, MA. Credit: Northboro, MA. Born: Boston, MA, Feb. 13, 1845. Age: 20. Height: 5'3". Comp: light. Eyes: gray. Hair: brown. Occup: student. Enlisted in Northboro by A. Rice, March 19, 1864; mustered April 6, 1864. Fell out on the march to the Rapidan River, May 4, 1864, but returned May 6, 1864, in time to take part in the action at the Wilderness that day, and was one of the 34 enlisted men who remained with the colors during that battle. In action at Spotsylvania Court House, May 10, 12, and 18, 1864. Detached and detailed as a guard at 1st Brigade, 1st Division, IX Corps, Headquarters from the evening of May 18, 1864, until after the battle of North Anna River, May 24, 1864. In action at Cold Harbor, June 3, 1864. Detailed as acting company clerk, June 8, 1864. Detailed to care for Pvt. Elijah Hayward, who was sick, on the march to Petersburg, June 15, 1864. Returned to the regiment, June 18, 1864. Carried Spencer rifle, serial number 23978. Taken prisoner of war at the Petersburg Crater, July 30, 1865. With the regiment on all marches and in all skirmishes and battles except North Anna River and the Petersburg assault of June 17, 1864, until captured. Incarcerated in the Confederate prison in Danville, VA, until paroled and exchanged, Feb. 22, 1865. Probably received extra pay for having been a prisoner of war. Discharged the US service, July 20, 1865, by order of the War Dept., probably from the Camp of Parole in Annapolis, MD, and probably on a Surgeons Certificate of Disability. Had previous service as a private in Co. K, 53rd MVI, from Sept. 6, 1862, until mustered out Sept. 2, 1863. Participated in the Port Hudson, LA, campaign with that regiment in 1863. Resided in Northboro, MA, after the war and died there in July 1915, age 70. "Good Soldier" (CR).

Private Francis M. Harrington
(postwar photo). *(Muriel Ryan)*

36. **Hart, David A.**, private. Res. and credit: Adams, MA. Born: Adams, MA. Age: 19. Height: 5'8½". Comp: light. Eyes: blue. Hair: brown. Occup: carpenter. Enlisted in Adams by Sgt. James M. Childs, March 24, 1864; mustered April 6, 1864. Detached and detailed as a guard for the 1st Division, IX Corps, baggage and supply wagon train during the battle of the Wilderness, May 6, 1864. In action at Spotsylvania Court House, May 10, 12, and 18, 1864, North Anna River, May 24, 1864, and Cold Harbor, June 3, 1864. Sent sick to Mower US Army General Hospital in Chestnut Hill, Philadelphia, PA, June 12, 1864, where he died from disease, July 13, 1864.

37. **Hayward, Elijah B.**, private. Res. and/or credit: Chicopee, MA. Born: Burke, VT. Age: 42. Height: 5'9". Comp: light. Eyes: blue.

Hair: brown. Occup: carpenter. Enlisted in Chicopee by Lt. George S. Green, March 17, 1864; mustered April 6, 1864. Detached and detailed as a guard for the 1st Division, IX Corps, baggage and supply wagon train during the battle of the Wilderness, May 6, 1864. In action at Spotsylvania Court House, May 10, 12, and 18, 1864, North Anna River, May 24, 1864, and Cold Harbor, June 3, 1864. Sick on the march to Petersburg, June 15, 1864, and admitted to the 1st Division, IX Corps, Field Hospital. Rejoined the regiment in late June 1864. Absent sick again from July 6, 1864, until discharged the US service for disability from Camp Meigs US Army General Hospital in Readville, MA, Feb. 28, 1865, by order of Maj. Gen. John A. Dix, War Dept., discharge to date May 18, 1865. With the regiment on all marches and in all skirmishes and battles, except the Wilderness and the Petersburg assault, until becoming sick.

38. **Haywood, Wesley F.**, private. Res. and/or credit: Chicopee, MA. Born: Burke, VT. Age: 19. Height: 5'7". Comp: light. Eyes: blue. Hair: light. Occup: farmer. Enlisted in Chicopee by Lt. George S. Green, March 18, 1864; mustered April 6, 1864. Detached and detailed as a guard for the 1st Division, IX Corps, baggage and supply wagon train during the battle of the Wilderness, May 6, 1864. In action at Spotsylvania Court House, May 10, 12, and 18, 1864, and severely wounded in the back and thigh in action at North Anna River, May 24, 1864. Absent wounded in an army general hospital until Jan. 5, 1865, when he returned to the regiment for duty. Soon found unfit for front line duty when "his old wound rec'd. May 24 broke out" (CR) and detached and detailed (probably as an orderly or nurse) at the 1st Division, IX Corps, Field Hospital at Petersburg and Tennallytown, DC, from March 16, 1865, until muster-out. Mustered out with the regiment at Delaney house, Washington, DC, July 30, 1865, and discharged in Readville, MA, Aug. 9, 1865, expiration of service.

39. **Heath, Guilford P.**, private. Res. and/or credit: Northboro, MA. Born: Barre, VT. Age: 21. Height: 5'9½". Comp: light. Eyes: blue. Hair: light. Occup: farmer. Enlisted in Northboro by A. Rice, March 19, 1864; mustered April 6, 1864. Detached and detailed as a guard for the 1st Division, IX Corps, baggage and supply wagon train during the battle of the Wilderness, May 6, 1864. In action at Spotsylvania Court House, May 10, 12, and 18, 1864, North Anna River, May 24, 1864, Cold Harbor, June 3, 1864, and Petersburg assaults, June 17 and 18, 1864. Absent sick in the 1st Division, IX Corps, Field Hospital and Depot Field Hospital at City Point, Petersburg, from June 26, 1864, until between July 30 and Aug. 19, 1864. Wounded in action at Weldon Railroad, Aug. 19, 1864. Absent wounded in an army general hospital until Nov. 25, 1864. With the regiment in operations during the late fall and winter of 1864–65, and in action at Fort Stedman, March 25, 1864. With the regiment on most marches and in most skirmishes and battles. Mustered out with the regiment at Delaney house, Washington, DC, July 30, 1865, and discharged in Readville, MA, Aug. 9, 1865, expiration of service. Had previous service as a private in Co. D, 51st MVI, from Aug. 28, 1862, until mustered out, July 27, 1863. Participated in the North Carolina campaign with that regiment in 1862–63. Resided in Northboro, MA, after the war and died there after 1911, date unknown.

40. **Hill, Joseph W.**, corporal. Res. and credit: Marlboro, MA. Born: Marlboro, MA. Age: 26. Height: 5'7½". Comp: dark. Eyes: hazel. Hair: black. Occup: carpenter. Enlisted in Marlboro by F. H. Morse, March 23, 1864; mustered April 6, 1864. Detached and detailed as a guard for the 1st Division, IX Corps, baggage and supply wagon train during the battle of the Wilderness, May 6, 1864. In action at Spotsylvania Court House, May 10, 12, and 18, 1864, and North Anna River, May 24, 1864. Absent sick in an army general hospital from June 1 until June 25, 1864, and again from after June 25 until July 20, 1864. In action at the Petersburg Crater, July 30, 1864. Absent sick again in an army general hospital from Aug. 10, 1864, until Jan. 5, 1865. With the regiment in operations during the winter of 1865, and in action at Fort Stedman, March 25, 1865. Promoted corporal, May 28, 1865, under RSO 42, to date from May 1, 1865, by order of Lt. Col. Julius M. Tucker. Mustered out with the regiment at

Corporal Joseph W. Hill
(postwar photo). *(John Anderson)*

Delaney house, Washington, DC, July 30, 1865, and discharged in Readville, MA, Aug. 9, 1865, expiration of service. Resided in Charlestown, MA, after the war. "Good Soldier" (CR).

41. **Holyoke, Eugene J.**, private. Res: Marlboro, MA. Credit: Boston, MA. Born: Marlboro, MA. Age: 22. Height: 5'8". Comp: light. Eyes: blue. Hair: brown. Occup: farmer. Enlisted in Boston by G. S. Quincy, March 23, 1864; mustered April 6, 1864. In action at the Wilderness, May 6, 1864, and Spotsylvania Court House, May 10, 12, and 18, 1864. Detached and detailed as a guard at 1st Brigade, 1st Division, IX Corps, Headquarters from the evening of May 18, 1864, until after the battle of Cold Harbor, June 3, 1864. Wounded in the thigh in action in the Petersburg assault, June 17, 1864. With the regiment on all marches and in all skirmishes and battles, except North Anna River and Cold Harbor, until wounded. Absent wounded until discharged and pensioned from the US service on a Surgeons Certificate of Disability for wounds, May 27, 1865, from Chester US Army General Hospital in Chester, PA, by order of Maj. Gen. John A. Dix, War Dept. Had previous service as a private in Co. I, 13th MVI, from July 16, 1861, until discharged for disability in Washington, DC,

Nov. 17, 1862. Possibly participated with that regiment at 2nd Bull Run, Aug. 30, 1862, and Anteitam, Sept. 17, 1862. Died before 1896, but date not known. "Good Soldier" (CR).

42. **Holyoke, Samuel H.**, private. Res: Westboro, MA. Born and credit: Marlboro, MA. Age: 39. Married. Height: 5'9". Comp: dark. Eyes: blue. Hair: dark. Occup: shoemaker. Enlisted and mustered in Marlboro by Lt. John Reade, March 31, 1864. Did not join the regiment at the front until May 30, 1864 (probably absent sick). In action at Cold Harbor, June 3, 1864, and Petersburg assaults, June 17 and 18, 1864. Absent sick in an army general hospital from after June 17 until Sept. 28, 1864. In action at Poplar Grove Church, Sept 30 and Oct. 8, 1864. Had received no pay from enlistment through Oct. 7, 1864, and his family was existing on state aid from the Commonwealth of Massachusetts. Absent sick in the 1st Division, IX Corps, Field Hospital from Dec. 20, 1864, until Jan. 1, 1865. With the regiment in operations during the winter of 1865, and in action and taken prisoner of war at Fort Stedman, March 25, 1865. Paroled from Libby Prison in Richmond, VA, March 30, 1865, and noted in the company journal as exchanged April 26, 1865. Returned to the regiment for duty from the Camp of Parole in Annapolis, MD, May 11, 1865. Mustered out with the regiment at Delaney house, Washington, DC, July 30, 1865, and discharged in Readville, MA, Aug. 9, 1865, expiration of service. Died before 1896, but date not known.

43. **Hopkins, Sterling A.**, sergeant. Res. and/or credit: Boston, MA. Born: Ellsworth, ME. Age: 36. Height: 5'9". Comp: dark. Eyes: blue. Hair: black. Occup: miner. Enlisted in Boston by James Nigner, Feb. 22, 1864; mustered April 6, 1864. Promoted sergeant, April 6, 1864. Mortally wounded at the Wilderness, May 6, 1864, and died from his wounds later that day. "Good Soldier" (CR).

44. **Howe, Alfred W.**, private. Res: Marlboro, MA. Credit: Worcester, MA. Born: Marlboro, MA. Age: 19. Height: 5'7". Comp: dark. Eyes: blue. Hair: dark. Occup: shoemaker. Enlisted in Worcester by Lt. John

Reade, March 31, 1864; mustered April 6, 1864. Detached and detailed as a guard for the 1st Division, IX Corps, baggage and supply wagon train during the battle of the Wilderness, May 6, 1864. In action at Spotsylvania Court House, May 10, 12, and 18, 1864, North Anna River, May 24, 1864, Cold Harbor, June 3, 1864, and Petersburg assaults, June 17 and 18, 1864; severely wounded in the left forearm in action at the Petersburg Crater, July 30, 1864. "Carried to field hospital, wound dressed, and sent to City Point" (CR), where he underwent surgery for the amputation of his right forearm, July 30, 1864, "two and a half, left radius" (OMR), by Dr. George W. Snow, 35th MVI. "Put on a boat," the steamer *De Molay,* bound for Lovell US Army General Hospital in Portsmouth Grove, RI. "Bled to death" (CR); "Died Aug. 8, 1864, haemorrhage" (OMR). With the regiment on all marches and in all skirmishes and battles, except the Wilderness, until wounded. "Good Soldier" (CR).

45. **Howe, Sanborn O.,** private. Res: Marlboro, MA. Credit: Worcester, MA. Born: Summerville, ME. Age: 18. Height: 5′6½″. Comp: dark. Eyes: black. Hair: dark. Occup: shoemaker. Enlisted in Worcester by Lt. John Reade, March 31, 1864; mustered April 6, 1864. Detached and detailed as a guard for the 1st Division, IX Corps, baggage and supply wagon train during the battle of the Wilderness, May 6, 1864. In action at Spotsylvania Court House, May 10, 12, and 18, 1864, North Anna River, May 24, 1864, and Cold Harbor, June 3, 1864; slightly wounded in the hand in action in the Petersburg assault, June 17, 1864. Absent wounded in an army general hospital until Sept. 7, 1864. In action at Poplar Grove Church, Sept 30 and Oct. 8, 1864. With the regiment in operations during the fall and winter of 1864–65, and severely wounded in the left ankle in action at Fort Stedman, March 25, 1865. Transported from the 1st Division, IX Corps, Field Hospital to Washington, DC, where he underwent surgery for the amputation of his lower leg (probably because of gangrene) by the circular method, June 8, 1865, by Dr. D. W. Bliss. With the regiment on most marches and in most skirmishes and battles. Discharged and

pensioned from the US service on a Surgeons Certificate of Disability for wounds from an army general hospital in Washington, DC, Aug. 4, 1865, by order of the War Dept., discharge to date July 30, 1865. Resided in Hudson, MA, after the war. "Brave Soldier" (CR).

46. **Kelley, Theodore L.,** 1st sergeant. Res. and credit: Boston, MA. Born: Boston, MA. Age: 30. Married. Height: 5′7½″. Comp: light. Eyes: gray. Hair: brown. Occup: stucco worker. Enlisted in Boston by W. W. Clapp, March 30, 1864; mustered April 6, 1864. Promoted corporal, April 6, 1864. Detached and detailed as a guard for the 1st Division, IX Corps, baggage and supply wagon train during the battle of the Wilderness, May 6, 1864. In action at Spotsylvania Court House, May 10, 12, and 18, 1864. North Anna River, May 24, 1864, Cold Harbor, June 3, 1864, Petersburg assaults, June 17 and 18, 1864, Petersburg Crater, July 30, 1864, Weldon Railroad, Aug. 19, 1864, and Poplar Grove Church, Sept. 30 and Oct. 8, 1864. "Been with the regiment throughout the entire campaign up to present date, Jan. 24, 1865" (CR). One of the 30 combat soldiers remaining of the regiment after Weldon Railroad, Aug. 19, 1864. Received no pay from enlistment through Oct. 7, 1864, and his family was living on state aid from the Commonwealth of Massachusetts. Promoted sergeant, Aug. 31, 1864, to date from May 7, 1864. With the regiment in operations during the fall and winter of 1864–65, but on furlough by order of Maj. Gen. John G. Parke, commanding IX Corps, from March 19 until April 10, 1865, so was not in the battle of Fort Stedman, March 25, 1865. Acting 1st sergeant from April 10 until May 10, 1865. Absent with leave in Massachusetts from May 11 until June 11, 1865. Promoted 1st sergeant June 12, 1865. Mustered out with the regiment at Delaney house, Washington, DC, July 30, 1865, and discharged in Readville, MA, Aug. 9, 1865, expiration of service. Had previous service as a corporal in Co. I, 45th MVI, from Sept. 17, 1862, until mustered out, July 7, 1863. Participated in the North Carolina campaign with that regiment in 1862–63. Resided in South Boston, MA, after the war. "Brave Soldier" (CR).

47. **Lee, Smith J.**, private. Res. and/or credit: Grafton, MA. Born: Uxbridge, MA. Age: 20. Height: 5'3". Comp: dark. Eyes: gray. Hair: brown. Occup: shoemaker. Enlisted and mustered in Grafton by J. S. Nelson, April 8, 1864. Did not join the regiment at the front until May 30, 1864 (probably absent sick). In action at Cold Harbor, June 3, 1864, and Petersburg assaults, June 17 and 18, 1864. Absent sick in an army general hospital from July 10 until Sept. 28, 1864. "Shirked the battle of Poplar Grove Church, but on hand [in the battle], Oct. 8, 1864" (CR). With the regiment in operations during the winter of 1865, and severely wounded in action at Fort Stedman, March 25, 1865. Absent wounded in the 1st Division, IX Corps, Field Hospital until sent to an army general hospital, March 29, 1865. Never returned to the regiment and discharged the US service for disability from wounds, Sept. 16, 1865, by order of the War Dept. Resided in Marlboro, MA, after the war and died there after 1929, date unknown. "Good Soldier" (CR).

48. **Lewis, Charles A.**, private. Res: Roxbury, MA. Credit: Boston, MA. Born: Yarmouth, ME. Age: 18. Height: 6'0". Comp: light. Eyes: blue. Hair: brown. Occup: carpenter. Enlisted in Boston by W. W. Clapp, March 30, 1864; mustered April 6, 1864. Detached and detailed as a guard for the 1st Division, IX Corps, baggage and supply wagon train during the battle of the Wilderness, May 6, 1864. In action at Spotsylvania Court House, May 10, 12, and 18, 1864, and North Anna River, May 24, 1864. Detached and detailed at the 1st Brigade, 1st Division, IX Corps, Commissary Dept. until July 1, 1864. Severely wounded in the left arm in action at the Petersburg Crater, July 30, 1864. Taken to the 1st Division, IX Corps, Field Hospital, where his left arm was amputated by the flap method, July 30, 1864, by Dr. T. Fletcher Oakes, 56th MVI. Transferred to Washington, DC, by steamer. Absent wounded until discharged and pensioned from the US service on a Surgeons Certificate of Disability for wounds, Feb. 25, 1865, to date Feb. 17, 1865, from an army general hospital in Washington, DC, by order of Maj. Gen. Christopher C. Auger, commanding the Dept. of Washington, DC. "Brave Soldier" (CR).

49. **Lowd, Charles Q.**, sergeant. Res. and/or credit: Westboro, MA. Born: Boston, MA. Age: 21. Height: 6'2". Comp: light. Eyes: hazel. Hair: dark. Occup: farmer. Enlisted and mustered in Westboro by E. Barnard, March 23, 1864. Did not join the regiment at the front until May 30, 1864 (probably absent sick). In action at Cold Harbor, June 3, 1864, and Petersburg assaults, June 17 and 18, 1864. Promoted sergeant, July 14, 1864, to fill the vacancy as the result of Sgt. Brooks having died from wounds, July 14, 1864. Absent sick in an army general hospital from July 21 until Sept. 14, 1864. Detailed as a clerk at regimental headquarters during the battle of Poplar Grove Church, Sept. 30, 1864, but in action there, Oct. 8, 1864. Detached and detailed as a clerk at the 1st Division, IX Corps, Ordnance Office, from Nov. 11, 1864, until muster-out. Reduced to the ranks for accepting this assignment. Mustered out with the regiment at Delaney house, Washington, DC, July 30, 1865, and discharged in Readville, MA, Aug. 9, 1865, expiration of service. Had previous service as a private in Co. E, 51st MVI, from Aug. 26, 1862, until discharged for disability in New Bern, NC, Jan. 16, 1863. Participated in the North Carolina campaign with that regiment in 1862–63. Resided in Northboro, MA, after the war.

50. **Lowell, Frank H.**, corporal. Res. and/or credit: Marlboro, MA. Born: Portland, ME. Age: 20. Height: 5'8½". Comp: light. Eyes: blue. Hair: brown. Occup: shoemaker. Enlisted in Marlboro by F. H. Morse, March 23, 1864; mustered April 6, 1864. In action at the Wilderness, May 6, 1864, and one of the 34 enlisted men who remained with the colors during that battle. In action at Spotsylvania Court House, May 10 and 12, 1864, and slightly wounded in the shoulder in action there, May 18, 1864. Wound dressed, he remained with the regiment. Continued in action at North Anna River, May 24, 1864, Cold Harbor, June 3, 1864, and Petersburg assaults, June 17 and 18, 1864. Present sick during the battle of the Petersburg Crater, July 30, 1864, but not in action. Appointed regimental postmaster by Lt. Col. Charles L. Chandler, May 20, 1864, and remained in that position until Aug. 1, 1864. Absent sick in the 1st Division, IX Corps, Field Hospital

at Petersburg from Aug. 1 until Sept. 10, 1864 (had a furlough during this period, but dates unknown). In action at Poplar Grove Church, Sept. 30, 1864, and wounded in action there, Oct. 8, 1864. Absent wounded in an army general hospital until on or before Jan. 20, 1865. Promoted corporal, Jan. 20, 1865, to date from Jan. 1, 1865, under RSO 16, by order of Lt. Col. Julius M. Tucker and Capt. Henry C. Ward when Cpl. Page was reduced to the ranks. In action and taken prisoner of war at Fort Stedman, March 25, 1865. Paroled and exchanged from Libby Prison in Richmond, VA, April 1, 1865. Returned to the regiment for duty from the Camp of Parole in Annapolis, MD, May 11, 1865. Mustered out with the regiment at Delaney house, Washington, DC, July 30, 1865, and discharged in Readville, MA, Aug. 9, 1865, expiration of service. With the regiment on most marches and in most skirmishes and battles. Had previous service as a private in Co. I, 5th MVI, from Aug. 20, 1862, until mustered out July 2, 1863. Participated in the North Carolina campaign with that regiment in 1862–63. Resided in Bangor, ME, after the war. "Brave Soldier" (CR).

51. **Mahan, Dallas P.**, private. Res. and credit: Marlboro, MA. Born: Marlboro, MA. Age: 19. Height: 5'6½". Comp: dark. Eyes: gray. Hair: black. Occup: shoemaker. Enlisted in Marlboro by F. H. Morse, March 23, 1864; mustered April 6, 1864. In action at the Wilderness, May 6, 1864, and Spotsylvania Court House, May 10, 12, and 18, 1864. Detached and detailed as a guard at 1st Brigade, 1st Division, IX Corps, Headquarters during the battle of North Anna River, May 24, 1864. In action at Cold Harbor, June 3, 1864, and Petersburg assaults, June 17 and 18, 1864. Detached and detailed as a guard at 1st Brigade, 1st Division, IX Corps, Headquarters during the battles of the Petersburg Crater, July 30, 1864, and Weldon Railroad, Aug. 19, 1864. Absent sick in an army general hospital from Aug. 25, 1864, until Jan. 4, 1865. With the regiment in operations during the winter of 1865, and in action at Fort Stedman, March 25, 1865. With the regiment on most marches and in most skirmishes and battles. Mustered out with the regiment at Delaney house, Washington, DC, July 30, 1865, and discharged in Readville, MA, Aug. 9, 1865, expiration of service. Resided in Worcester, MA, after the war. "Good Soldier" (CR).

52. **Marsh, Jeremiah William**, private. Res. and/or credit: Westboro, MA. Born: Exeter, NH. Age: 32. Married. Height: 6'1½". Comp: dark. Eyes: hazel. Hair: brown. Occup: carpenter. Enlisted in Westboro by E. Bullard, March 31, 1864; mustered April 6, 1864. Mortally wounded in action at the Wilderness, May 6, 1864, and died on the battlefield from his wounds later that day. "Good Soldier" (CR).

53. **Mason, Alonzo R.**, corporal. Res. and/or credit: Springfield, MA. Born: Sturbridge, MA. Age: 40. Height: 5'7". Comp: light. Eyes: hazel. Hair: brown. Occup: mechanic. Enlisted in Springfield by Capt. Lewis A. Tifft, March 30, 1864; mustered April 6, 1864. Promoted corporal on an unknown date. Detached and detailed as a guard for the 1st Division, IX Corps, baggage and supply wagon train during the battle of the Wilderness, May 6, 1864. In action at Spotsylvania Court House, May 10, 12, and 18, 1864, and North Anna River, May 24, 1864. Absent sick in an army general hospital from June 1 until Sept. 10, 1864. In action at Poplar Grove Church, Sept. 30 and Oct. 8, 1864. Reduced to the ranks and appointed company cook under RSO 15, by order of Lt. Col. Julius M. Tucker, Feb. 15, 1865. With the regiment in operations during the fall and winter of 1864–65, and missing in action at Fort Stedman from March 25 until March 28, 1865 (whereabouts during that time unknown). Slightly wounded while on picket duty, April 3, 1865 (the last man in the regiment to be shot during the war). Absent wounded in the 1st Division, IX Corps, Field Hospital from April 3, 1865, until transferred to an army general hospital, April 7, 1864. Returned to the regiment for duty after May 30, 1865. Mustered out with the regiment at Delaney house, Washington, DC, July 30, 1865, and discharged in Readville, MA, Aug. 9, 1865, expiration of service. "Good Soldier" (CR).

54. **Maynard, Isaac G.**, private. Res. and credit: Marlboro, MA. Born: Marlboro, MA. Age: 42. Height: 5'8½". Comp: light. Eyes:

blue. Hair: dark. Occup: carpenter. Enlisted in Marlboro by F. H. Morse, March 29, 1864; mustered April 6, 1864. In action at the Wilderness, May 6, 1864, Spotsylvania Court House, May 10, 12, and 18, 1864, North Anna River, May 24, 1864, and Cold Harbor, June 3, 1864. Absent in the rear (probably sick) during the Petersburg assaults, June 17 and 18, 1864. Absent sick from July 9, 1864, until discharged the US service on a Surgeons Certificate of Disability (nature of disability unknown) from Fairfax Seminary US Army General Hospital in Alexandria, VA, May 30, 1865, by order of Maj. Gen. Christopher C. Auger, commanding the Dept. of Washington, DC. Died Aug. 8, 1893, age 75.

55. **Miller, Andrew J.**, private. Res. and/or credit: Boston, MA. Born: Ryegate, VT. Age: 22. Height: 5'5½". Comp: light. Eyes: blue. Hair: brown. Occup: farmer. Enlisted in Boston by W. W. Clapp, March 31, 1864; mustered April 6, 1864. Detached and detailed as a guard for the 1st Division, IX Corps, baggage and supply wagon train during the battle of the Wilderness, May 6, 1864. In action at Spotsylvania Court House, May 10, 12, and 18, 1864, North Anna River, May 24, 1864, Cold Harbor, June 3, 1864, and Petersburg assaults, June 17 and 18, 1864. Absent sick in an army general hospital from July 2 until Sept. 20, 1864. In action at Poplar Grove Church, Sept. 30 and Oct. 8, 1864. Absent sick in an army general hospital from Dec. 17, 1864, until discharged the US service for disability, Aug. 10, 1865, by order of the War Dept. With the regiment on most marches and in most skirmishes and battles until becoming sick. Had previous service in Co. F, 15th Vermont Volunteer Infantry (specifics unknown). "Good Soldier" (CR).

56. **Miller, John A. Jr.**, private. Res. and/or credit: Boston, MA. Born: Newbury, VT. Age: 18. Height: 5'7". Comp: light. Eyes: blue. Hair: light. Occup: farmer. Enlisted in Boston by W. W. Clapp, March 31, 1864; mustered April 6, 1864. Detached and detailed as a guard for the 1st Division, IX Corps, baggage and supply wagon train during the battle of the Wilderness, May 6, 1864. In action at Spotsylvania Court House, May 10,

12, and 18, 1864, North Anna River, May 24, 1864, Cold Harbor, June 3, 1864, Petersburg assaults, June 17 and 18, 1864, and Petersburg Crater, July 30, 1864. Absent sick in an army general hospital from Aug. 9, 1864, until Feb. 21, 1865. In action at Fort Stedman, March 25, 1865. With the regiment on most marches and in most skirmishes and battles. Mustered out with the regiment at Delaney house, Washington, DC. Discharged in Readville, MA, Aug. 9, 1865. "Good Soldier" (CR).

57. **Miller, Wallace T.**, private. Res: Abington, Credit: Boston, MA. Born: Westboro, MA. Age: 22. Height: 5'8½". Comp: light. Eyes: blue. Hair: brown. Occup: shoemaker. Enlisted in Co. G in Boston by W. W. Clapp, March 8, 1864; mustered April 6, 1864. Absent without leave from Camp Wool from March 25, 1864, until before April 11, 1864. Transferred to Co. K by his own request under RSO 36, by order of Col. William F. Bartlett, April 11, 1864. Never in combat. Left behind sick in an army general hospital in Washington, DC, when the regiment passed through there on the march to the front, April 26, 1864. Transferred to Lovell US Army General Hospital in Portsmouth Grove, RI, on an unknown date, and discharged the US service from there on a Surgeons Certificate of Disability, Jan. 1, 1865, by order of Maj. Gen. John A. Dix, War Dept. Became a minister after the war and resided in Springfield, MA.

58. **Mitchell, Charles**, private. Res. and/or credit: Springfield, MA. Born: Holden, MA. Age: 21. Height: 5'8½". Comp: fair. Eyes: blue. Hair: dark. Occup: blacksmith. Enlisted in Springfield by Lt. George S. Green, March 26, 1864; mustered April 6, 1864. Detached and detailed as a guard for the 1st Division, IX Corps, baggage and supply wagon train during the battle of the Wilderness, May 6, 1864. In action at Spotsylvania Court House, May 10, 12, and 18, 1864, and slightly wounded in action at North Anna River, May 24, 1864. Remained with the regiment until sent to an army general hospital wounded, June 1, 1864. Never returned to the regiment and deserted while on furlough from that hospital, Nov. 20,

1864. Apparently surrendered to authorities, probably under President Lincoln's proclamation of amnesty, as he is listed as mustered out but absent sick at Delaney house, Washington, DC, July 30, 1865.

59. **Mitchell, John F.**, private. Res. and/or credit: Grafton, MA. Born: Brookfield, MA. Age: 18. Height: 5'6". Comp: light. Eyes: blue. Hair: light. Occup: shoemaker. Enlisted in Grafton by J. S. Nelson, March 25, 1864; mustered April 6, 1864. Never in combat. Left behind sick in an army general hospital in Washington, DC, when the regiment passed through there on the march to the front, April 26, 1864. Remained in the hospital until transferred to Co. E, 24th Regiment, VRC, Sept. 29, 1864. Discharged the US service, July 24, 1865, by order of the War Dept., expiration of service. Resided in North Grafton, MA, after the war and died there after 1911, date unknown.

60. **Morse, Charles S.**, private. Res: Readville, ME. Credit: Boston, MA. Born: Readville, ME. Age: 35. Height: 5'10½". Comp: light. Eyes: blue. Hair: brown. Occup: artist. Enlisted and mustered in Boston by W. W. Clapp, March 21, 1864. Did not join the regiment at the front until May 30, 1864 (probably absent sick). In action and taken prisoner of war at Cold Harbor, June 2, 1864. Incarcerated in the Confederate prison in Florence, SC, where he died from disease, Nov. 13, 1864. Had previous service as a private in the 3rd Maine Battery of Light Artillery (specifics unknown).

61. **Needham, James W.**, private. Res. and credit: New Braintree, MA. Born: New Braintree, MA. Age: 24. Height: 5'7". Comp: light. Eyes: gray. Hair: light. Occup: farmer. Enlisted in Co. G in New Braintree by M. Pollard, Feb. 19, 1864; mustered March 10, 1864; transferred to Co. K by his own request, April 11, 1864, under RSO 36, by order of Col. William F. Bartlett. Detached and detailed as a guard for the 1st Division, IX Corps, baggage and supply wagon train during the battle of the Wilderness, May 6, 1864. In action at Spotsylvania Court House, May 10, 12, and 18, 1864, and North Anna River, May

24, 1864. Detailed as a cook for Capt. Albert Prescott, in command of the company at that time, June 1, 1864. Detached and detailed as hostler for Prescott, June 30, 1864, after he was promoted major and took command of the regiment. In action at Weldon Railroad, Aug. 19, 1864, and one of the 30 combat soldiers remaining of the regiment after that battle. In action at Poplar Grove Church, Sept. 30 and Oct. 8, 1864. Detached and detailed as an orderly at 3rd Brigade, 1st Division, IX Corps, Headquarters by SO 99, from Nov. 11, 1864, until Feb. 19, 1865, when he received a 20-day furlough. When he had not returned to the regiment by March 18, 1865—7 days overdue—he was declared a deserter by Brig. Gen. Napoleon B. McLaughlen. On March 21, 1865, he returned to duty, but there is no evidence that he was punished for being overdue. In action at Fort Stedman, March 25, 1865. Mustered out with the regiment at Delaney house, Washington, DC, July 30, 1865, and discharged in Readville, MA, Aug. 9, 1865, expiration of service. Had previous service as a private in Co. H, 46th MVI, from Oct. 12, 1862, until mustered out, July 29, 1863. Participated in the North Carolina campaign with that regiment in 1862–63. Resided in New Braintree, MA, after the war.

62. **Nolan, Morris H.**, private. Res. and/or credit: Marlboro, MA. Born: Boston, MA. Age: 27. Height: 5'5". Comp: light. Eyes: blue. Hair: brown. Occup: clerk. Enlisted in Marlboro by W. Wilson, March 28, 1864; mustered April 6, 1864. Never in a major battle with the 57th. Left behind sick and unable to travel at an army general hospital in Washington, DC, when the regiment passed through there on the march to the front, April 26, 1864. Joined the regiment for duty, May 22, 1864, and was detached and detailed that same day as a cook at IX Corps Headquarters. Returned to the regiment and detailed as a cook at regimental headquarters, Sept 4, 1864. With the regiment in operations during the fall and winter of 1864–65, but not in combat. Severely wounded in the back and side while on duty in the trenches at Petersburg, March 16, 1865. Absent wounded in the 1st Division, IX Corps, Field Hospital at

Petersburg until sent to Fairfax Seminary US Army General Hospital in Alexandria, VA, April 7, 1865. Remained at that hospital until discharged the US service on a Surgeons Certificate of Disability for wounds, June 12, 1865, by order of Maj. Gen. Christopher C. Auger, commanding the Dept. of Washington, DC. Had previous service as a landsman in the US Navy from Sept. 11, 1861, until mustered out, Dec. 30, 1862. Served on the receiving ship *Ohio*, the USS *Vandalia*, and the USS *North Carolina*. Resided in San Diego, CA, after the war.

63. Oakes, William F., sergeant. Res: Bernardston, MA. Credit: Springfield, MA. Born: Bernardston, MA. Age: 21. Height: 5'5". Comp: dark. Eyes: brown. Hair: dark. Enlisted in Springfield by Lt. Henry B. Fiske, March 12, 1864; mustered April 6, 1864. Fell out on the march to the Rapidan River, May 4, 1864, but rejoined the regiment, May 6, in time to take part in the action at the Wilderness that day. In action at Spotsylvania Court House, May 10, 12, and 18, 1864, and North Anna River, May 24, 1864. Promoted corporal, May 25, 1864, probably for bravery in the battle of the North Anna. In action again at Cold Harbor, June 3, 1864, and Petersburg assaults, June 17 and 18, 1864. Appointed acting sergeant, June 18, 1864, again probably for bravery in the assault on Petersburg. In action again at the Petersburg Crater, July 30, 1864. Appointed acting regimental sergeant major, July 30, 1864, again probably for bravery in action. In action again at Weldon Railroad, Aug. 19, 1864, and one of the 30 combat soldiers remaining of the regiment after that battle. Promoted permanent sergeant, Aug. 31, 1864, to date from April 6, 1864. In action again at Poplar Grove Church, Sept. 30 and Oct. 8, 1864. With the regiment in operations during the fall and winter of 1864–65. On furlough from Jan. 23 until Feb. 11, 1865. Appointed acting 2nd lieutenant on an unknown date in 1865. In action again and taken prisoner of war at Fort Stedman, March 25, 1865. Paroled and exchanged from Libby Prison in Richmond, VA, March 30, 1865. Cited twice for bravery during the battle of Fort Stedman: "Sergeant William F. Oakes, Company K (acting officer), for saving Captain Doherty when wounded . . ." (GPR), and

"Sergeant William F. Oakes, Company K (missing in action and acting lieutenant), for gallantry while in command of portion of skirmish line; carried Captain Doherty to rear; resisted attempt of enemy to kill him (Doherty) after being taken prisoner" (JMT). Discharged the US service from the Camp of Parole in Annapolis, MD (probably for disability), June 2, 1865, under GO 77, par. 6, AGO, War Dept., dated April 28, 1865: "With regiment throughout entire campaign" (CR) except for furlough and time after Fort Stedman. One of the 11 combat soldiers who served with the regiment on every march and in every skirmish and battle during its entire wartime service, and of the 11, one of the 10 survivors. Had previous service as a corporal in Co. A, 52nd MVI, from Sept. 9, 1862, until mustered out, Aug. 14, 1863. Participated in the Port Hudson, LA, campaign with that regiment in 1863. Resided in Fitchburg, MA, after the war. "Good Soldier" (CR).

64. Ordway, William D., private. Res. and/or credit: Marlboro, MA. Born: Concord, NH. Age: 21. Height: 5'5". Comp: dark. Eyes: hazel. Hair: black. Enlisted in Marlboro by W. Wilson, March 24, 1864; mustered April 6, 1864. Detached and detailed as a guard for the 1st Division, IX Corps, baggage and supply wagon train during the battle of the Wilderness, May 6, 1864. In action at Spotsylvania Court House, May 10, 12, and 18, 1864, and North Anna River, May 24, 1864. Absent sick from May 25, 1864, until discharged the US service for disability from Lincoln US Army General Hospital in Washington, DC, May 22, 1865, by GO 77, par. 6, AGO, War Dept., dated April 28, 1865, discharge to date May 3, 1865. Resided in Hudson, MA, after the war.

65. Page, Robert A., corporal. Res: Springfield, MA. Credit: Boston, MA. Born: Hardwick, VT. Age: 28. Height: 5'5½". Comp: light. Eyes: blue. Hair: light. Occup: barber. Enlisted in Boston by W. W. Clapp, March 21, 1864; mustered April 6, 1864. Promoted corporal before June 1, 1864. Detached and detailed as a guard for the 1st Division, IX Corps, baggage and supply wagon train during the battle of the Wilderness, May 6, 1864. In action at Spotsylvania Court House, May 10, 12, and 18, 1864, and North Anna River, May 24, 1864. Absent sick in an army general hospital from June 1, 1864, until discharged the US service for disability and expiration of service, Aug. 10, 1865, by order of the War Dept. Reduced to the ranks (probably for absence) while absent sick, Jan. 1, 1865, under RSO 16, by order of Lt. Col. Julius M. Tucker. Had previous service as a corporal in Co A, 46th MVI, from Sept. 12, 1862, until mustered out, July 29, 1863. Participated in the North Carolina campaign with that regiment in 1862–63.

66. **Parker, Carlos S.**, corporal. Res. and/or credit: Springfield, MA. Born: Glover, VT. Age: 26. Height: 5'8½". Comp: light. Eyes: blue. Hair: light. Occup: carpenter. Enlisted in Co. G in Springfield by Lt. Henry B. Fiske, Feb. 3, 1864; mustered March 10, 1864. Confined in the guardhouse in Camp Wool for fighting, from March 15 until March 17, 1864. Transferred to Co. K, April 14, 1864, under RSO 39, by order of Col. William F. Bartlett. Promoted corporal, April 14, 1864, to date from April 6, 1864. Detached and detailed as a guard for the 1st Division, IX Corps, baggage and supply wagon train during the battle of the Wilderness, May 6, 1864. In action at Spotsylvania Court House, May 10, 12, and 18, 1864, North Anna River, May 24, 1864, Cold Harbor, June 3, 1864, and Petersburg assaults, June 17 and 18, 1864. Absent sick in the 1st Division, IX Corps, Field Hospital from June 20 until June 25, 1864. Absent sick from "fainting fits" (FMH) in an army general hospital again from June 26 until Sept. 17, 1864. Wounded in action at Poplar Grove Church, Sept. 30, 1864. Absent wounded in an army general hospital until discharged the US service, June 12, 1865, to date June 1, 1865, as a supernumerary because of the consolidation of the 59th MVI with the 57th, under SO 254, par. 43, AGO, War Dept., dated May 26, 1865. Had previous service in Co. G, 3rd Vermont Volunteer Infantry (specifics unknown).

67. **Perry, Henry H.**, corporal. Res: Marlboro, MA. Credit: Boston, MA. Born: Granger, NY. Age: 19. Height: 5'9". Comp: fair. Eyes: gray. Hair: light. Occup: shoemaker. Enlisted

in Boston by G. S. Quincy, March 24, 1864; mustered April 6, 1864. In action at the Wilderness, May 6, 1864, and Spotsylvania Court House, May 10, 12, and 18, 1864. Detached and detailed as a guard at 1st Brigade, 1st Division, IX Corps, Headquarters during the battles of North Anna River, May 24, 1864, and Cold Harbor, June 3, 1864. In action again in the Petersburg assaults, June 17 and 18, 1864. Promoted corporal, June 17, 1864 (probably for bravery in action during the assault on Petersburg), to date from April 6, 1864. In action again at the Petersburg Crater, July 30, 1864, and slightly wounded while on duty in the trenches at Petersburg, Aug. 14, 1864. Absent wounded in the 1st Division, IX Corps, Field Hospital at Petersburg until Aug. 30, 1864. Appointed regimental postmaster, Aug. 30, 1864, to replace Cpl. Lowell, who was detailed as a clerk for Company C that day. Carried Spencer rifle, serial number 23816. Absent detailed in the rear during the battles of Poplar Grove Church, Sept. 30 and Oct. 8, 1864. On furlough from Jan. 20 until Feb. 13, 1865 (charged with being five days absent without leave, but not punished). With the regiment in operations during the fall and winter of 1864–65, and severely wounded in the leg in action at Fort Stedman, March 25, 1865 (leg surgically amputated). Died from his wounds in the 3rd Division, IX Corps, Hospital in Alexandria, VA, April 9, 1865 (officially the last day of the war in the east; the last man in the regiment to die during the war). With the regiment on most marches and in most skirmishes and battles. Had previous service as a sergeant in Co. I, 5th MVI, from Sept. 16, 1862, until mustered out, July 2, 1863. Participated in the North Carolina campaign with that regiment in 1862–63. "Brave Soldier" (CR).

68. **Phelps, Stephen H.**, private. Res: Marlboro, MA. Credit: Boston, MA. Born: Marlboro, MA. Age: 19. Height: 5'7½". Comp: light. Eyes: blue. Hair: light. Occup: mechanic. Enlisted in Boston by W. F. Brigham, March 28, 1864; mustered April 6, 1864. In action at the Wilderness, May 6, 1864, Spotsylvania Court House, May 10, 12, and 18, 1864, North Anna River, May 24, 1864, Cold Harbor, June 3, 1864, and Petersburg assaults, June 17 and 18, 1864; taken prisoner of war

at the Petersburg Crater, July 30, 1864. Died on or about Aug. 26, 1864, from starvation, exposure, and disease in the Confederate prison in Danville, VA. With the regiment on all marches and in all skirmishes and battles until captured. "Good Soldier" (CR).

69. **Pickett, George T.**, corporal. Res. and/or credit: Boston, MA. Born: Cambridge, MA. Age: 30. Height: 5'6½". Comp: light. Eyes: blue. Hair: light. Occup: mason. Enlisted in Boston by W. W. Clapp, March 30, 1864; mustered April 6, 1864. Detached and detailed as a guard for the 1st Division, IX Corps, baggage and supply wagon train during the battle of the Wilderness, May 6, 1864. In action at Spotsylvania Court House, May 10, 12, and 18, 1864, and North Anna River, May 24, 1864. Promoted corporal, May 26, 1864, to date from, April 6, 1864. Absent sick in an army general hospital from June 1 until July 31, 1864. In action again at Weldon Railroad, Aug. 19, 1864, Poplar Grove Church, Sept. 30 and Oct. 8, 1864, in operations during the fall and winter of 1864–65, and taken prisoner of war at Fort Stedman, March 25, 1865. Paroled and exchanged from Libby Prison, March 29, 1865. Returned to the regiment for duty from the Camp of Parole in Annapolis, MD, May 11, 1865. Discharged the US service, June 12, 1865, to date June 1, 1865, as a supernumerary because of the consolidation of the 59th MVI with the 57th, under SO 254, par. 43, AGO, War Dept., dated May 26, 1865. With the regiment on most marches and in most skirmishes and battles, and one of the 30 combat soldiers remaining of the regiment after Weldon Railroad, Aug. 19, 1864. Resided in Boston, MA, after the war. "Good Soldier" (CR).

70. **Pike, William**, private. Res: Gill, MA. Credit: Greenfield, MA. Born: Everett, MA. Age: 39. Height: 5'10". Comp: dark. Eyes: hazel. Hair: brown. Occup: farmer. Enlisted in Greenfield by S. C. Phillips, March 4, 1864; mustered April 6, 1864. In action at the Wilderness, May 6, 1864. Detailed company cook, May 10, 1864, and therefore exempted from hard combat service. Absent sick in an army general hospital from June 26, 1864, until Jan. 5, 1865. Detailed as company cook

again, March 24, 1865. Missing in action at Fort Stedman, March 25, 1865, but returned to the regiment, March 28 (whereabouts unknown during that time). Mustered out with the regiment at Delaney house, Washington, DC, July 30, 1865, and discharged in Readville, MA, Aug. 9, 1865, expiration of service. Had previous service as a private in Co. I, 4th Vermont Volunteer Infantry (specifics unknown). "Good Soldier" (CR).

71. **Pond, Erastus W.**, private. Res. and/or credit: Marlboro, MA. Born: Franklin, MA. Age: 22. Height: 5'6". Comp: dark. Eyes: gray. Hair: black. Occup: shoemaker. Enlisted in Marlboro by F. H. Morse, March 30, 1864; mustered April 6, 1864. Detached and detailed as a guard for the 1st Division, IX Corps, baggage and supply wagon train during the battle of the Wilderness, May 6, 1864. In action at Spotsylvania Court House, May 10 and 12, 1864, and shirked the battle there, May 18, 1864. Detached and detailed as a hostler at 1st Brigade, 1st Division, IX Corp, Headquarters from May 20, 1864 until Nov. 11, 1864, when he was detailed as an orderly at the same headquarters (now 3rd Brigade) by SO 99. Remained on this duty until mustered out with the regiment at Delaney house, Washington, DC, July 30, 1865, and discharged in Readville, MA, Aug. 9, 1865, expiration of service.

72. **Potter, Edward F.**, 1st lieutenant. Res. and credit: Greenfield, MA. Born: Greenfield, MA. Age: 21. Height: 5'11". Comp: dark. Eyes: hazel. Hair: black. Occup: farmer. Enlisted in Greenfield by M. Stevens, March 9, 1864; mustered April 6, 1864. Promoted corporal, April 6, 1864. Left behind sick in an army general hospital in Alexandria, VA, when the regiment passed through there on the march to the front, April 26, 1864. Returned to the regiment for duty, June 25, 1864. Promoted sergeant, July 18, 1864. In action at Petersburg Crater, July 30, 1865, Weldon Railroad, Aug. 19, 1864, and Poplar Grove Church, Sept. 30 and Oct. 8, 1864. Promoted 1st sergeant, Nov. 8, 1864, when 1st Sgt. Shaftoe was reduced to duty sergeant, by order of Lt. Col. Julius M. Tucker. Discharged the US service at Petersburg to ac-

cept a commission, Jan. 3, 1865, by order of Maj. Gen. John G. Parke, commanding IX Corps. Commissioned and mustered 1st lieutenant of Co. B, Jan. 3, 1865, commission to date Oct. 7, 1864. Carried Spencer rifle, serial number 23677, which he turned in to the company, Jan. 5, 1865, after being commissioned. With the regiment in operations during the fall and winter of 1864–65, and slightly wounded in action at Fort Stedman, March 25, 1865. Absent wounded in an army general hospital until an unknown date. One of the 30 combat soldiers remaining of the regiment after Weldon Railroad, Aug. 19, 1864. Mustered out with the regiment at Delaney house, Washington, DC, July 30, 1865, and discharged in Readville, MA, Aug. 9, 1865, expiration of service. Had previous service as a private in Co. G, 10th MVI, from June 21, 1861, until discharged for disability, Jan. 14, 1863. Participated with that regiment in the Peninsula campaign in 1862. Resided in West Gardner, MA, after the war and was postmaster there. "Brave Soldier" (CR).

73. **Pratt, Edwin,** corporal. Res: Marlboro, MA. Credit: Boston, MA. Born: Framingham, MA. Age: 18. Height: 5'5". Comp: light. Eyes: hazel. Hair: brown. Occup: shoemaker. Enlisted in Boston by W. W. Clapp, March 28, 1864; mustered April 6, 1864. Detached and detailed as a guard for the 1st Division, IX Corps, baggage and supply wagon train during the battle of the Wilderness, May 6, 1864. In action at Spotsylvania Court House, May 10, 12, and 18, 1864, North Anna River, May 24, 1864, Cold Harbor, June 3, 1864, and Petersburg assaults, June 17 and 18, 1864. Absent sick in an army general hospital from June 20 until Aug. 27, 1864. In action again at Poplar Grove Church, Sept. 30 and Oct. 8, 1864. Slightly wounded there on Sept. 30, 1864. With the regiment in operations during the fall and winter of 1864–65, and in action again at Fort Stedman, March 25, 1865. Detached and detailed at the 1st Division, IX Corps, Quartermaster's Dept. from April 30, 1865, until muster-out. Promoted corporal when Cpl. Brigham was promoted sergeant, May 28, 1865, under RSO 42, to date May 1, 1865, by order of Lt. Col. Julius M. Tucker. Mustered

out with the regiment at Delaney house, Washington, DC, July 30, 1865, and discharged in Readville, MA, Aug. 9, 1865, expiration of service. With the regiment on most marches and in most skirmishes and battles. "Good Soldier" (CR).

74. **Prentiss, William Jr.,** private. Res: Acworth, NH. Credit: Holyoke, MA. Born: Acworth, NH. Age: 20. Height: 5'7". Comp: light. Eyes: hazel. Hair: dark. Occup: machinist. Enlisted and mustered in Holyoke by Lt. George S. Green, March 24, 1864. Did not join the regiment at the front until May 30, 1864 (probably absent sick). In action at Cold Harbor, June 3, 1864, and mortally wounded in action in the Petersburg assault, June 17, 1864. Died from his wounds, June 18, 1864. "Good Soldier" (CR).

75. **Rawson, Lester W.,** private. Res: Great Barrington, MA. Credit: Barrington, MA. Born: New Marlboro, MA. Age: 28. Height: 5'9". Comp: light. Eyes: blue. Hair: brown. Occup: tinsmith. Enlisted in Barrington by J. W. Sally, March 5, 1864; mustered April 6, 1864. Detached and detailed as a guard for the 1st Division, IX Corps, baggage and supply wagon train during the battle of the Wilderness, May 6, 1864. In action at Spotsylvania Court House, May 10, 12, and 18, 1864, North Anna River, May 24, 1864, and Cold Harbor, June 3, 1864; killed in action "by a musket ball in the head" (CR) in the Petersburg assault, June 17, 1864. With the regiment on all marches and in most skirmishes and battles until killed. "Good Soldier" (CR).

76. **Reade, John,** 2nd lieutenant. Res. and/or credit: Milford, MA. Born: County Kilkenny, Ireland, Dec. 1, 1824. Age: 39. Height 5'8". Comp: light. Eyes: blue. Hair: light. Occup: trader. Enlisted as a private in Co. A in Milford by Leonard Hunt, Dec. 30, 1863; mustered Jan. 4, 1864. Discharged the US service at Camp Wool to accept a commission, April 4, 1864, under SO 123, AGO, War Dept., dated March 21, 1864. Commissioned 2nd lieutenant, to date March 2, 1864; mustered 2nd lieutenant into Co. K, April 6, 1864. Detached and detailed as second in command of the guard for the 1st Division, IX Corps, bag-

gage and supply wagon train during the battle of the Wilderness, May 6, 1864. In action at Spotsylvania Court House, May 10, 12, and 18, 1864, North Anna River, May 24, 1864, Cold Harbor, June 3, 1864, and Petersburg assaults, June 17 and 18, 1864; taken prisoner of war at the Petersburg Crater, July 30, 1864. With the regiment on all marches and in all skirmishes and battles, except the Wilderness, until captured; ". . . confined successively at Danville, Colombia, Charlotte, and Goldsboro" (HOM). Paroled March 16, 1865, and exchanged March 25, 1865, from an unknown Confederate prison, but very likely Goldsboro Prison in Goldsboro, NC. Resigned and discharged the US service for disability from the Camp of Parole in Annapolis, MD, May 17, 1865, by SO 235, under GO 82 of May 6, 1865, from the AGO, War Dept. Breveted 1st lieutenant and captain of US Volunteers, to date from March 13, 1865, for "faithful services during the campaigns of 1864 and 1865," by GO 45, AGO, War Dept., April 24, 1869. Had previous service as 1st lieutenant of Co. I, 48th MVI, from Nov. 13, 1862, until resigned and discharged, March 7, 1863. Participated in the Port Hudson, LA, campaign with that regiment in 1863. Resided in Charlestown, MA, after the war. Served in the General Court of Massachusetts in 1879, '80, and '81. Member of the Massachusetts State Senate, 1891 and '92.

77. **Rice, Edwin C.**, private. Res. and credit: Marlboro, MA. Born: Marlboro, MA. Age: 18. Height: 5'5". Comp: fair. Eyes: blue. Hair: brown. Occup: shoemaker. Enlisted in Marlboro by F. H. Morse, March 23, 1864; mustered April 6, 1864. Detached and detailed as a guard for the 1st Division, IX Corps, baggage and supply wagon train during the battle of the Wilderness, May 6, 1864. In action at Spotsylvania Court House, May 10 and 12, 1864, and slightly wounded in action there, May 18, 1864. Remained with the regiment and in action again at North Anna River, May 24, 1864, and Cold Harbor, June 3, 1864. In the rear during the Petersburg assaults, June 17 and 18, 1864. Shot through the temple and instantly killed, by a Confederate sharpshooter, while on picket duty at Petersburg on the morning of June 22, 1864.

Body carried to the rear and buried on the battlefield. Had been a rejected recruit from the 9th Massachusetts Battery of Light Artillery, Jan. 7, 1864. "Good Soldier" (CR).

78. **Rice, Lucien B.**, private. Res: Marlboro, MA. Credit: Worcester, MA. Born: Marlboro, MA. Age: 18. Height: 5'5". Comp: fair. Eyes: light. Hair: brown. Occup: shoemaker. Enlisted in Worcester by Lt. John Reade, March 31, 1864; mustered April 6, 1864. Detached and detailed as a guard for the 1st Division, IX Corps, baggage wagon train during the battle of the Wilderness, May 6, 1864. In action at Spotsylvania Court House, May 10, 12, and 18, 1864, North Anna River, May 24, 1864, and Cold Harbor, June 3, 1864. Absent in the rear during the Petersburg assaults, June 17 and 18, 1864. Absent sick in an army general hospital from July 10 until Dec. 5, 1864. Returned to the hospital sick again from Dec. 15, 1864, until Jan. 7, 1865. With the regiment in operations during the winter of 1865, and in action at Fort Stedman, March 25, 1865. Mustered out with the regiment at Delaney house, Washington, DC, July 30, 1865, and discharged in Readville, MA, Aug. 9, 1865, expiration of service. Resided in Pittsfield, MA, after the war. "Good Soldier" (CR). (Note: It appears likely that the Rices were twin brothers, the only twins in the regiment.)

79. **Richardson, Gustavus**, private. Res. and/or credit: Northboro, MA. Born: Bolton, MA. Age: 18. Height: 5'8". Comp: light. Eyes: brown. Hair: brown. Occup: farmer. Enlisted in Northboro by A. Rice, March 19, 1864; mustered April 6, 1864. Detached and detailed as a guard for the 1st Division, IX Corps, baggage and supply wagon train during the battle of the Wilderness, May 6, 1864. In action at Spotsylvania Court House, May 10, 12, and 18, 1864. Absent (reason unknown) during the battle of North Anna River, May 24, 1864. In action again at Cold Harbor, June 3, 1864, and in the Petersburg assaults, June 17 and 18, 1864. Absent sick from "fainting fits" (FMH) in an army general hospital in Philadelphia, PA, from June 26, 1864, and died from disease there, July 25, 1864. With the regiment on most marches and in

most skirmishes and battles until becoming sick. "Good Soldier" (CR).

80. **Ripley, Willard,** private. Res: Southbridge, MA. Credit: Worcester, MA. Born: Halifax, Nova Scotia, Canada. Age: 31. Height: 5′11½″. Comp: light. Eyes: blue. Hair: brown. Occup: carpenter. Enlisted in Worcester by Lt. John Reade, March 31, 1864; mustered April 6, 1864. Deserted from Camp Wool, April 17, 1864. Never returned. Bounty jumper.

81. **Rogers, John B.,** corporal. Res: Newton, MA. Credit: Boston, MA. Born: Newton, MA. Age: 30. Height: 5′6″. Comp: light. Eyes: blue. Hair: brown. Occup: woodcarver. Enlisted in Boston by W. W. Clapp, March 24, 1864; mustered April 6, 1864. Promoted corporal, April 6, 1864. Detached and detailed as a guard for the 1st Division, IX Corps, baggage and supply wagon train during the battle of the Wilderness, May 6, 1864. In action at Spotsylvania Court House, May 10, 12, and 18, 1864, North Anna River, May 24, 1864, and Cold Harbor, June 3, 1864; severely wounded in the left hand in action during the Petersburg assault, June 17, 1864. "Case 1703.—Corporal J. B. Rogers, Co. K, 57th Massachusetts, aged 30 years, was wounded at Petersburg, June 17, 1864, and admitted to the field hospital of the 1st division, Ninth Corps" (OMR), where he underwent the partial amputation of the left hand, June 17, 1864. "Surgeon M. K. Hogan, U.S.V., noted: 'Wound of left hand by minie ball; amputation of second finger, and removal of last two fingers with excision of last two metacarpal bones.' On June 24th, the patient entered Emory [U.S. Army General] Hospital at Washington, where the arm was amputated on July 19th. Acting Assistant Surgeon E. B. Harris forwarded the pathological specimen, consisting of 'the lower extremities of the bones of the forearm, the scaphoid, semilunar, cuneiform, trapezium, trapezoid, and the first two metacarpals, showing the bones entering the articulation to be carious.' The remainder of the bones of the hand had been removed on the field. The following description of the case was transmitted with the specimen: 'From the effects of disease of the soft parts

it was found best to remove the limb at the middle third of the arm. Death resulted on the morning of July 26, 1864.' The stump of the amputated limb was also contributed to the [U.S. Army Medical] Museum (Cat. Surg. Sect., 1866, p. 136, Spec. 2894 . . . is the upper half of the humerus, showing the effects of osteitis.) by Dr. Harris, who described the post-mortem appearance as follows: 'No union of flaps save a slight degree of granulation at the bottom of the wound; soft parts around bone remaining healthy, with appearance of general inactivity of the muscular tissues; the medullary substance of a dark grumous character and showing evidence of disease.' " (OMR). With the regiment on all marches and in all skirmishes and battles, except the Wilderness, until wounded. Had previous service as a private in Co. E, 32nd MVI, from Dec. 2, 1861, until discharged for disability, Nov. 1, 1862. Saw no action with that regiment. "Good Soldier" (CR).

82. **Sabourin, Charles,** private. Res: Montreal, Quebec, Canada. Credit: Hinsdale, MA. Born: Montreal, Quebec, Canada. Age: 19. Height: 5′4″. Comp: dark. Eyes: gray. Hair: dark. Occup: teamster. Enlisted and mustered in Hinsdale by W. H. Carson, March 31, 1864. Did not join the regiment at the front until May 30, 1864 (probably absent sick). In action at Cold Harbor, June 3, 1864. Absent in the rear during the Petersburg assaults, June 17 and 18, 1864. In action again at the Petersburg Crater, July 30, 1864. Absent sick in the 1st Division, IX Corps, Field Hospital from Aug. 1, 1864, until sent to Beverly US Army General Hospital in Beverly, NJ, on an unknown date. Transferred from Beverly Hospital to White Hall US Army General Hospital in Philadelphia, PA, Oct. 7, 1864. No further record of service, except that the company journal lists him as discharged the US service in Readville, MA, when the regiment was disbanded, Aug. 9, 1865. (Note: From a letter written in his behalf by Lt. John Cook at Petersburg, July 9, 1864: ". . . has never received his bounty (state) on account of his being a minor. I have never received his muster roll and cannot find out from him what town he enlisted from so as to [undecipherable, probably endorse] the Selectmen's

certificate that he has no parents living in the state." Evidently Sabourin had trouble with the English language, as he was almost certainly a French Canadian, or had difficulties with New England geography, or both.)

83. **Sargent, Henry,** private. Res. and/or credit: Northboro, MA. Born: Lancaster, MA. Age: 28. Height: 5'9". Comp: light. Eyes: blue. Hair: light. Occup: brakeman. Enlisted in Northboro by A. Rice, March 19, 1864; mustered April 6, 1864. Detached and detailed to the regimental pioneer corps at Camp Wool by order of Col. William F. Bartlett before April 18, 1864. Never in combat. Acting pioneer until Aug. 10, 1864. Absent sick in an army general hospital from Aug. 10, 1864, until discharged the US service for disability, June 21, 1865, by order of the War Dept. Resided in Northboro, MA, after the war.

84. **Sargent, Simon B.,** private. Res. and/or credit: Worcester, MA. Born: Springfield, MA. Age: 35. Height: 5'4½". Comp: florid. Eyes: blue. Hair: brown. Occup: shoemaker. Enlisted in Co. D in Worcester by D. Waldo Lincoln, March 21, 1864; mustered April 6, 1864; transferred to Co. K, April 14, 1864, under RSO 39, by order of Col. William F. Bartlett. Left behind sick in an army general hospital in Washington, DC, when the regiment passed through there on the march to the front, April 26, 1864. Absent sick until Feb. 20, 1865. In action at Fort Stedman, March 25, 1865. Absent sick in an army general hospital from after May 30, 1865, until discharged the US service for disability, Aug. 8, 1865, by order of the War Dept. Resided in Worcester, MA, after the war.

85. **Schneider, Edward M.,** private. Res: Andover, MA. Credit: Boston, MA. Born: Bronza, Turkey. Age: 17. Single. Height: 5'6". Comp: dark. Eyes: gray. Hair: black. Occup: student at Phillips Andover Academy. Enlisted in Boston by G. W. Messenger, March 8, 1864; mustered April 6, 1864. Detached and detailed as a guard for the 1st Division, IX Corps, baggage and supply wagon train during the battle of the Wilderness, May 6, 1864. In action at Spotsylvania

Private Edward M. Schneider.
(Increase Tarbox)

Court House, May 10, 12, and 18, 1864, and slightly wounded in the foot in action at North Anna River, May 24, 1864. Treated in a field hospital and returned to the regiment for duty. In action again at Cold Harbor, June 3, 1864, and shot five times and mortally wounded in action in the Petersburg assault, June 17, 1864. Died in the 1st Division, IX Corps, Field Hospital at Petersburg, June 19, 1864, and buried on the battlefield. With the regiment on most marches and in most skirmishes and battles until wounded. "Brave Soldier" (CR).

86. **Shaftoe, William,** 1st sergeant. Res: West Springfield, MA. Credit: Springfield, MA. Born: Paterson, NJ. Age: 41. Married. Height: 5'9". Comp: dark. Eyes: blue. Hair: dark. Occup: weaver. Enlisted in Springfield by Capt. Lewis A. Tifft, Feb. 26, 1864; mustered April 6, 1864. Promoted sergeant, April 6, 1864. Detached and detailed as a guard for the 1st Division, IX Corps, baggage and supply wagon train during the battle of the Wilderness, May 6, 1864. In action at Spotsylvania Court House, May 10, 12, and 18, 1864,

First Sergeant William Shaftoe
(postwar photo). *(John Anderson)*

and North Anna River, May 24, 1864; wounded in the head while on duty at Cold Harbor during the evening of June 2, 1864. "Sergeant William Shaftoe, Co. K, 57th Massachusetts Volunteers, aged 41 years was wounded at the battle of Cold Harbor, Virginia, June 2nd, 1864, by a fragment of shell which struck over the right eye, causing a slight depression. He was admitted to hospital 1st Division, Ninth Corps; on June 6th sent to Mount Pleasant [US Army General] Hospital, Washington, D.C., and on June 19th to Mower [US Army General] Hospital, Philadelphia, whence he was returned to duty September 5, 1864" (OMR). Furloughed wounded to his home in West Springfield, MA, during July 1864. Reported to the regiment for duty, Sept. 10, 1864. Promoted 1st sergeant to date from July 1, 1864. In action at Poplar Grove Church, Sept. 30 and Oct. 8, 1864. Reduced to duty sergeant, Nov. 8, 1864, by order of Lt. Col. Julius M. Tucker. Absent sick in the 1st Division, IX Corps, Field Hospital from Dec. 12 until Dec. 16, 1864. Promoted 1st sergeant again, Jan. 3, 1865, when 1st Sgt. Potter was mustered 1st lieutenant. In action and taken prisoner of war at Fort Stedman, March 25, 1865.

Paroled and exchanged from Libby Prison in Richmond, VA, March 29, 1865. Returned to the regiment for duty from the Camp of Parole in Annapolis, MD, May 11, 1865. Resumed duties as 1st sergeant from May 11, 1865, until discharged the US service in Tennallytown, DC, June 12, 1865, to date June 1, 1865, as a supernumerary because of the consolidation of the 59th MVI with the 57th, under SO 254, par. 43, AGO, War Dept., dated May 26, 1865. Had previous service as a sergeant in Co. B, 10th MVI, from June 21, 1861, until discharged for disability, Aug. 12, 1861. Saw no action with that regiment. Also had previous service as 1st sergeant of Co. A, 31st MVI, from Oct. 3, 1861, until discharged for disability, July 28, 1862. On duty with that regiment in New Orleans, LA in 1862. Resided in Fall River, MA, after the war. "Good Soldier" (CR). "Pension Examiner P. L. Stickney, of Chicopee, Massachusetts, reports, February 13th, 1869, that this man was on the Pension List, and that his disabilities had so much increased since his discharge that he was incapable of enduring labor. He had lost his hearing in his right ear, and he suffered from headache, giddiness, and fainting fits, and that his disability was undoubtedly permanent" (OMR).

87. **Sinclair, Henry C.**, private. Res. and/or credit: Shelburne, MA. Born: Whilton, NY. Age: 30. Height: 5′7″. Comp: light. Eyes: blue. Hair: brown. Occup: farmer. Enlisted in Shelburne by S. S. Foster, March 31, 1864; mustered April 6, 1864. Deserted in Philadelphia, PA April 19, 1864, while the regiment was on the march to the front. "Bounty jumper" (JA).

88. **Smith, Herbert O.**, private. Res: Westboro, MA. Credit: Northboro, MA. Born: Leicester, MA. Age: 26. Height: 5′11″. Comp: light. Eyes: gray. Hair: brown. Occup: farmer. Enlisted in Northboro by E. Bullard, March 31, 1864; mustered April 6, 1864. Slightly wounded in action at the Wilderness, May 6, 1864. In action at Spotsylvania Court House, May 10, 12, and 18, 1864, and taken prisoner of war at North Anna River, May 24, 1864. Incarcerated in the Confederate prison camp in Andersonville, GA, until killed there,

Aug. 29, 1864, by "the Raiders" (CR). (Note: "The Raiders" were a group of Union prisoners of war in Andersonville who survived by preying brutally on weaker inmates for anything of value. Six of them were later hanged for their exploits in the prison.) "Good Soldier" (CR).

89. **Smith, Vernon,** private. Res. and credit: Boston, MA. Born: Boston, MA. Age: 25. Height: 5'5½". Comp: light. Eyes: gray. Hair: dark. Occup: seaman. Enlisted and mustered in Boston by W. W. Clapp, April 11, 1864. Did not join the regiment at the front until May 30, 1864 (probably absent sick). In action and taken prisoner of war at Cold Harbor, June 3, 1864. Incarcerated in the Confederate prison camp in Andersonville, GA, where he died from disease, March 9, 1865. (One of the few prisoners remaining in the prison at that time, and one of the last to die there.) "Good Soldier" (CR).

90. **Spear, Benjamin A. Jr.,** corporal. Res. and credit: Boston, MA. Born: Boston, MA. Age: 25. Height: 5'9½". Comp: light. Eyes: hazel. Hair: brown. Occup: clerk. Enlisted in Boston by G. B. Farnsworth, March 16, 1864; mustered April 6, 1864. Promoted corporal, April 6, 1864. "Fell out on the march from the Rapidan River to the Wilderness [May 4, 1864]. Not seen again until sent from the hospital to the regiment, July 20, 1864. Reduced to the ranks by order of the commanding officer [Maj. Prescott]" (CR). In action and taken prisoner of war at the Petersburg Crater, July 30, 1864. Incarcerated in the Confederate prison in Danville, VA, until paroled and exchanged, March 16, 1865. Discharged the US service for disability, June 2, 1864 (probably from the Camp of Parole in Annapolis, MD) by GO 77, par. 6, AGO, War Dept., dated April 28, 1865. Probably received extra pay for having been a prisoner of war. Had previous service as a private in Co. I, 1st MVI, from Dec. 2, 1861, until discharged on a Surgeons Certificate of Disability, Jan. 26, 1863. Participated in the Peninsula campaign and in the 2nd Bull Run campaign with that regiment in 1862.

91. **Stevens, Fred W.,** private. Res. and credit: Marlboro, MA. Born: Marlboro, MA.

Age: 18. Height: 5'7½". Comp: light. Eyes: gray. Hair: light. Occup: shoemaker. Enlisted in Marlboro by F. H. Morse, March 26, 1864; mustered April 6, 1864. Detached and detailed as a guard for the 1st Division, IX Corps, baggage and supply wagon train during the battle of the Wilderness, May 6, 1864. In action at Spotsylvania Court House, May 10, 12, and 18, 1864. Absent in the rear during the battles of North Anna River, May 24, 1864, and Cold Harbor, June 3, 1864, and the Petersburg assaults, June 17 and 18, 1864, "cause: 'SORE FEET'" (CR). In action again at the Petersburg Crater, July 30, 1864. Absent sick from Aug. 15, 1864, until discharged on a Surgeons Certificate of Disability, June 6, 1865, from Dale US Army General Hospital in Worcester, MA, by order of Maj. Gen. John A. Dix, War Dept.

92. **Stickney, Lafayette,** private. Res. and/or credit: Marlboro, MA. Born: Methuen, MA. Age: 19. Height: 5'6½". Comp: dark. Eyes: gray. Hair: brown. Occup: shoemaker. Enlisted in Marlboro by W. W. Clapp, March 30, 1864; mustered April 6, 1864. Detached and detailed as a guard for the 1st Division, IX Corps, baggage and supply wagon train during the battle of the Wilderness, May 6, 1864. In action at Spotsylvania Court House, May 10, 12, and 18, 1864, and North Anna River, May 24, 1864. Sent sick to an army general hospital from Cold Harbor, June 2, 1864, and remained there until Dec. 14, 1864. With the regiment in operations during the winter of 1864–65. Slightly wounded in action in the hand at Fort Stedman, March 25, 1865. Absent wounded until discharged the US service for disability, June 22, 1865, from White Hall US Army General Hospital in Philadelphia, PA, by GO 77, par. 6, AGO, War Dept., dated April 28, 1865. Resided in Marlboro, MA, after the war and died there after 1925, date unknown. "Good Soldier" (CR).

93. **Stowe, George H.,** private. Res. and credit: Marlboro, MA. Born: Marlboro, MA. Age: 19. Height: 5'4". Comp: dark. Eyes: hazel. Hair: dark. Occup: shoemaker. Enlisted in Marlboro by F. H. Morse, March 26, 1864; mustered April 6, 1864. Detached and detailed as a guard for the 1st Division, IX Corps, baggage and supply train during the

battle of the Wilderness, May 6, 1864. In action at Spotsylvania Court House, May 10 and 12, 1864, and mortally wounded in action there, May 18, 1864. Died in the 1st Division, IX Corps, Field Hospital later that day. "Brave Soldier" (CR).

94. **Strong, Franklin F.**, private. Res. and/or credit: Marlboro, MA. Born: Marblehead, MA. Age: 18. Height: 5'6½". Comp: dark. Eyes: black. Hair: dark. Occup: shoemaker. Enlisted in Marlboro by C. W. Robinson, March 30, 1864; mustered April 6, 1864. Detached and detailed as a guard for the 1st Division, IX Corps, baggage and supply wagon train during the battle of the Wilderness, May 6, 1864. In action at Spotsylvania Court House, May 10, 12 and 18, 1864, North Anna River, May 24, 1864, Cold Harbor, June 3, 1864, Petersburg assaults, June 17 and 18, 1864, Petersburg Crater, July 30, 1864, Weldon Railroad, Aug. 19, 1864, and Poplar Grove Church, Sept. 30 and Oct. 8, 1864, and in operations during the fall and winter of 1864–65. On furlough by order of Maj. Gen. John G. Parke, commanding IX Corps, from Feb. 17 until March 11, 1865 (listed in the company journal as two days absent without leave). Slightly wounded on the knee while on picket duty at Petersburg, March 20, 1865. Wound bandaged, he remained with the regiment. In action again at Fort Stedman, March 25, 1865. Mustered out with the regiment at Delaney house, Washington, DC, July 30, 1865, and discharged in Readville, MA, Aug. 9, 1865, expiration of service. "With the regiment the entire campaign up to present date, April 2, 1865" (CR). Except for the battle of Wilderness, served with the regiment on all marches and in all skirmishes and battles, and was one of the 30 combat soldiers remaining of the regiment after Weldon Railroad, Aug. 19, 1864. Resided in Marlboro, MA, after the war. "Brave Soldier" (CR).

95. **Walcott, Thomas W.**, private. Res: Marlboro, MA. Credit: Boston, MA. Born: Walton, MA. Age: 25. Height: 5'6½". Comp: light. Eyes: gray. Hair: brown. Occup: shoemaker. Enlisted in Boston by W. W. Clapp, March 29, 1864; mustered April 6, 1864. Detached and detailed as a guard for the 1st Division, IX Corps, baggage and supply wagon train during the battle of the Wilderness, May 6, 1864. In action at Spotsylvania Court House, May 10, 12, and 18, 1864, North Anna River, May 24, 1864, Cold Harbor, June 3, 1864, and Petersburg assaults, June 17 and 18, 1864. Absent sick from "fainting fits" (FMH) in the 1st Division, IX Corps, Field Hospital from June 26, 1864, until before July 18, 1864, and in an army general hospital from July 18 until Sept. 12, 1864. In action again at Poplar Grove Church, Sept. 30 and Oct. 8, 1864. Absent sick in the 1st Division, IX Corps, Field Hospital at Petersburg from Nov. 11 until Dec. 4, 1864. With the regiment in operations during the fall and winter of 1864–65, and in action at Fort Stedman, March 25, 1865. With the regiment on most marches and in most skirmishes and battles. Mustered out with the regiment at Delaney house, Washington, DC, July 30, 1865, and discharged in Readville, MA, Aug. 9, 1865, expiration of service. Resided in Marlboro, MA, after the war. "Good Soldier" (CR).

96. **Ward, Henry C.**, captain. Res. and/or credit: Worcester, MA. Born: Massachusetts. Age: 20. Height: unknown. Comp: light. Eyes: blue. Hair: light. Occup: mechanic. Commissioned 1st lieutenant, March 9, 1864; mustered 1st lieutenant of Co. G, March 26,

Captain Henry C. Ward. *(USAMHI)*

1864. In action at the Wilderness, May 6, 1864, and Spotsylvania Court House, May 10, 1864; slightly wounded in the arm in action there, May 12, 1864. Absent wounded in an army general hospital until May 28, 1864. In action at Cold Harbor, June 3, 1864, and wounded in the leg in action again in the Petersburg assault, June 17, 1864. Absent wounded in an army general hospital until Oct. 15, 1864. Also in command of Co. E from Oct. 23 until Nov. 18, 1864. Commissioned captain, July 31, 1864, while absent wounded; mustered captain of Co. K, Oct. 24, 1864, at Pegram's farm, Petersburg. Also in command of Co. G from Feb. 1 until March 24, 1865. With the regiment in operations during the fall and winter of 1864–65, and taken prisoner of war in action while 3rd Brigade, 1st Division, IX Corps, Officer of the Day at Fort Stedman, March 25, 1864. Paroled from Libby Prison in Richmond, VA, April 2, 1865, and exchanged April 26, 1865, by GO 75, War Dept. Returned to the regiment for duty from the Camp of Parole in Annapolis, MD, May 11, 1865. Also in command of Co. G again from May 13 until May 30, 1865. One of the two officers who remained with the colors during the battle of the Wilderness, May 6, 1864. Mustered out with the regiment at Delaney house, Washington, DC, July 30, 1865, and discharged in Readville, MA, Aug. 9, 1865, expiration of service. Had previous service as regimental sergeant major and 2nd lieutenant of Co. D, 15th MVI, from July 21, 1861, until resigned and discharged, to date Sept. 4, 1863. Participated at Ball's Bluff, Oct. 21, 1861, and in the Peninsula campaign, 1862; wounded in action at Antietam, Sept. 17, 1862. Also participated at Fredericksburg, Dec. 13, 1862, the Chancellorsville campaign, May, 1863, and the Gettysburg campaign, July 1863. Had subsequent service in the regular army as a 1st lieutenant in the 11th US Infantry from Feb. 23, 1866, until transferred to the 16th US Infantry, April 14, 1869. Regimental quartermaster from March 1, 1875, until Feb. 8, 1880. Breveted captain of US Volunteers, to date from March 2, 1867, for gallant and meritorious services during the Civil War and in action at Fort Stedman, March 25, 1865, by GO 33, War Dept., April 9, 1869. Military ad-

viser on the staff of the governor of Tennessee in Nashville from 1892 until after 1896. Retired as a brigadier general in 1907 and died Nov. 16, 1925, in Wellesly Hills, MA, age 82.

97. **West, Milo,** private. Res: Windsor, MA. Credit: Northampton, MA. Born: Derby, VT. Age: 21. Height: 6'0". Comp: light. Eyes: blue. Hair: brown. Occup: carpenter. Enlisted in Northampton by the town selectmen, March 14, 1864; mustered April 6, 1864. Detached and detailed as a guard for the 1st Division, IX Corps, baggage and supply wagon train during the battle of the Wilderness, May 6, 1864. In action at Spotsylvania Court House, May 10, 12 and 18, 1864, North Anna River, May 24, 1864, Cold Harbor, June 3, 1864, and Petersburg assaults, June 17 and 18, 1864. Wounded in the thigh while on duty in the trenches at Petersburg, July 22, 1864. Died from his wounds in an army general hospital in Washington, DC, Aug. 4, 1864. With the regiment on all marches and in all skirmishes and battles, except the Wilderness, until wounded. "Good Soldier" (CR).

98. **Wheeler, Albert C.,** private. Res: Windsor, MA. Credit: Northampton, MA. Born: Northfield, MA. Age: 21. Height: 5'10". Comp: dark. Eyes: black. Hair: black. Occup: stonecutter. Enlisted in Northampton by Lt. Col. Luke Lyman, March 15, 1864; mustered April 6, 1864. Wounded in action at the Wilderness, May 6, 1864. Absent wounded until discharged the US service on a Surgeons Certificate of Disability for wounds from Chester US Army General Hospital in Chester, PA, April 14, 1865, by order of Maj. Gen. John A. Dix, War Dept. "Good Soldier" (CR).

99. **Whipple, William H.,** private. Res: Boylston, MA. Credit: Northboro, MA. Born: Sommerville, MA. Age: 18. Height: 6'1". Comp: dark. Eyes: gray. Hair: brown. Occup: farmer. Enlisted in Northboro by A. Rice, March 19, 1864; mustered April 6, 1864. Detached and detailed as a guard for the 1st Division, IX Corps, baggage and supply wagon train during the battle of the Wilderness, May 6, 1864. In action at Spotsylvania Court House, May 10, 12 and 18, 1864,

Private W. H. Whipple (postwar photo).
(John Anderson)

North Anna River, May 24, 1864, Cold Harbor, June 3, 1864, and Petersburg assaults, June 17 and 18, 1864. Absent sick from July 18, 1864, until discharged the US service for disability from an army general hospital in Washington, DC, May 29, 1865, under GO 77, par. 6, AGO, War Dept., dated April 28, 1865, by order of Maj. Gen. Christopher C. Auger, commanding the Dept. of Washington, DC. With the regiment on all marches and in all skirmishes and battles, except the Wilderness, until becoming sick. Elected president of the regimental association in 1893 and reelected in 1894. Resided in Sommerville, MA, after the war and died there in 1910, age 64.

100. **Williams, Daniel,** private. Res. and/or credit: Adams, MA. Born: Glouster, MA. Age: 26. Height: 5'11". Comp: dark. Eyes: black. Hair: black. Occup: mechanic. Enlisted in Adams by Sgt. James M. Childs, March 28, 1864; mustered April 6, 1864. Deserted from Camp Wool, April 17, 1864. Never returned. "Bounty jumper" (JA).

101. **Woodruff, John,** private. Res: Southampton, MA. Credit: Northampton, MA. Born: Connecticut. Age: 36. Height: 5'11". Comp: light. Eyes: blue. Hair: brown. Occup: engineer. Enlisted in Northampton by Lt. Col. Luke Lyman, March 9, 1864; mustered April 6, 1864. Never in combat. Detailed as hostler for the regimental quartermaster, Lt. George E. Priest. Accidentally shot in the leg at City Point, Petersburg, July 4, 1864 (leg surgically amputated). Discharged and pensioned from the US service on a Surgeons Certificate of Disability for wounds from Dale US Army General Hospital in Worcester, MA, June 27, 1865, by order of Maj. Gen. John A. Dix, War Dept. "Good Soldier" (CR).

Appendixes

APPENDIX 1: BATTLE STATISTICS

TABLE 1. THE WILDERNESS

	Engaged	KIA	MWIA	WIA	MIA	POW	WIA & POW	DIA	Total Lost	%	Remaining
Co. A	72	7	3	9	3	2	2	0	26	36.1	46
Co. B	64	3	2	12	4	1	3	0	25	39.1	39
Co. C	61	7	1	23	0	0	3	0	34	55.7	27
Co. D	65	4	6	15	1	1	3	0	30	46.2	35
Co. E	52	10	1	13	0	1	0	0	25	48.1	27
Co. F	42	4	2	15	1	2	1	0	25	59.5	17
Co. G	58	8	5	18	0	1	6	1	39	67.2	19
Co. H	60	7	2	17	0	4	0	0	30	50.0	30
Co. I	56	4	5	12	0	0	2	0	23	41.1	33
Co. K	15	0	2	1	1	0	0	0	4	26.6	11
F&S	3	0	0	1	0	0	0	0	1	33.3	2
Totals	548	54	29	136	10	12	20	1	262	47.8	286

Note: This count of the number of men engaged in the battle differs from the official figures by three. The total number of casualties including prisoners of war, however, differs markedly from the official record of 251. A loss of 262 is substantiated by the evidence from all available records. Similar discrepancies appear in most of the following tables.

TABLE 2. SPOTSYLVANIA (MAY 12, 1864)

	Engaged	KIA	MWIA	WIA	POW	MIA & POW	Total Lost	%	Remaining
Co. A	41	3	1	14	0	0	18	43.9	23
Co. B	36	0	1	5	1	0	7	19.4	29
Co. C	30	4	0	3	0	0	7	23.3	23
Co. D	35	2	0	6	0	0	8	22.8	27
Co. E	24	1	0	1	1	1[a]	4	16.6	20
Co. F	17	0	0	3	1	0	4	23.5	13
Co. G	19	0	0	3	0	0	3	15.7	16
Co. H	32	1	1	8	0	0	10	31.2	22
Co. I	33	1	1	10	0	1	13	39.3	20
Co. K	65	0	1	3	0	0	4	6.1	61
F&S	1	0	0	0	0	0	0	0	1
Totals	333	12	5	56	3	2	78	21.4	255

Note: The official loss was 71, including prisoners of war.
[a]Not taken prisoner of war.

Appendixes

TABLE 3. NORTH ANNA RIVER

	Engaged	KIA	MWIA	WIA	MIA	POW	Total Lost	%	Remaining
Co. A	23	0	0	2	0	2	4	17.3	19
Co. B	24	1	1	0	0	0	2	8.3	22
Co. C	18	0	0	1	0	1	2	11.1	16
Co. D	24	1	0	1	1	3	6	25.0	18
Co. E	17	2	1	1	0	1	5	29.4	12
Co. F	16	0	0	0	0	0	0	0	16
Co. G	22	1	1	0	0	0	2	9.1	20
Co. H	26	2	1	3	0	2	8	30.7	18
Co. I	18	1	0	0	1	0	2	11.1	16
Co. K	48	0	0	5	0	1	6	12.5	42
F&S	1	1	0	0	0	0	1	100.0	0
Totals	237	9	4	13	2	10	38	16.0	199

Note: The official loss was 36, including prisoners of war.

TABLE 4. PETERSBURG ASSAULT (JUNE 17, 1864)

	Engaged	KIA	MWIA	WIA	MIA	POW	WIA & POW	Total Lost	%	Remaining
Co. A	18	4	1	3	0	0	0	8	44.4	10
Co. B	20	0	3	5	0	0	0	8	40.0	12
Co. C	15	0	0	1	0	1	0	2	13.3	13
Co. D	16	1	1	0	0	0	1	3	18.7	13
Co. E	13	0	0	1	0	1	0	2	15.3	11
Co. F	18	0	1	4	1	0	0	6	33.3	12
Co. G	18	1	0	4	0	0	0	5	27.7	13
Co. H	14	2	0	1	0	0	0	3	21.4	11
Co. I	14	1	0	4	0	0	0	5	35.7	9
Co. K	37	2	2	5	0	0	0	9	24.3	28
F&S	1	0	0	1	0	0	0	1	100.0	0
Totals	184	11	8	29	1	2	1	52	28.3	132

Note: The official number of men engaged was 186. However, two men cited on the original battle roster, Harrington and Hayward of Co. K, were not there. The official loss was 44, including prisoners of war.

TABLE 5. THE CRATER

	Engaged	KIA	MWIA	WIA	MIA	POW	WIA & POW	Total Lost	%	Remaining
Co. A	13	0	0	4	0	4	0	8	61.5	5
Co. B	7	0	0	1	2	1	1	5	71.4	2
Co. C	10	1	1	1	0	3	0	6	60.0	4
Co. D	9	1	0	0	0	2	0	3	33.3	6
Co. E	8	1	0	1	1	3	0	6	75.0	2
Co. F	9	0	0	2	0	1	0	3	33.3	6
Co. G	11	0	1	3	0	3	0	7	63.6	4
Co. H	8	0	1	0	1	2	1	5	62.5	3
Co. I	5	0	0	1	0	1	0	2	40.0	3
Co. K	17	0	1	1	0	3	0	5	29.4	12
F&S	1	1	0	0	0	0	0	1	100.0	0
Totals	98	4	4	14	4	23	2	51	52.0	47

Note: All figures tally with the official statistics.

Appendixes

TABLE 6. WELDON RAILROAD

	Engaged	KIA	MWIA	WIA	MIA	POW	WIA & POW	Total Lost	%	Remaining
Co. A	4	1	0	1	0	0	1	3	75.0	1
Co. B	2	0	0	1	1	0	0	2	100.0	0
Co. C	5	0	0	0	2	0	0	2	40.0	3
Co. D	3	0	0	1	0	2	0	3	100.0	0
Co. E	2	0	0	0	0	0	0	0	0	2
Co. F	5	0	0	1	0	0	0	1	20.0	4
Co. G	8	0	1	0	0	0	0	1	12.5	7
Co. H	3	0	1	0	0	0	0	1	33.3	2
Co. I	3	0	0	0	1	0	0	1	33.3	2
Co. K	10	0	0	1	0	0	0	1	10.0	9
Totals	45	1	2	5	4	2	1	15	33.3	30

Note: No field or staff were in action.

TABLE 7. POPLAR GROVE CHURCH (SEPT. 30, 1864)

	Engaged	KIA	MWIA	WIA	MIA	POW	Total Lost	%	Remaining
Co. A	4	1	0	0	0	0	1	25.0	3
Co. B	3	0	0	0	0	0	0	0	3
Co. C	16	0	0	0	0	0	0	0	16
Co. D	2	0	0	2	0	0	2	100.0	0
Co. E	4	0	0	0	0	0	0	0	4
Co. F	25	0	0	2	0	0	2	8.0	23
Co. G	10	0	0	0	0	0	0	0	10
Co. H	5	0	0	2	0	0	2	40.0	3
Co. I	4	0	0	0	0	0	0	0	4
Co. K	19	0	0	2	0	0	2	10.5	17
F&S	1	0	0	0	0	0	0	0	1
Totals	93	1	0	8	0	0	9	9.8	84

Note: The official loss was 8.

TABLE 8. POPLAR GROVE CHURCH (OCT. 8, 1864)

	Engaged	KIA	MWIA	WIA	MIA	POW	Total Lost	%	Remaining
Co. A	3	0	0	0	0	0	0	0	3
Co. B	3	0	0	2	0	0	2	66.6	1
Co. C	16	0	0	2	0	0	2	12.5	14
Co. D	0	0	0	0	0	0	0	0	0
Co. E	4	0	0	0	0	0	0	0	4
Co. F	23	0	0	0	0	0	0	0	23
Co. G	9	0	0	1	0	0	1	11.1	8
Co. H	3	0	0	0	0	0	0	0	3
Co. I	7	2	0	4	0	0	6	85.7	1
Co. K	21	0	0	3	0	0	3	14.2	18
F&S	1	0	0	0	0	0	0	0	1
Totals	90	2	0	12	0	0	14	15.6	76

Note: All figures tally with the official statistics.

TABLE 9. FORT STEDMAN

	Engaged	KIA	MWIA	WIA	MIA	POW	WIA & POW	Total Lost	%	Remaining
Co. A	13	0	0	3	0	5	0	8	61.5	5
Co. B	19	0	1	1	1	1	1	5	26.3	14
Co. C	26	1	0	3	0	8	0	12	46.2	14
Co. D	11	0	0	1	0	3	1	5	45.5	6
Co. E	10	1	0	1	0	3	1	6	60.0	4
Co. F	40	2	0	6	0	6	0	14	35.0	26
Co. G	21	1	1	1	1	9	0	13	61.9	8
Co. H	22	1	0	5	1	2	0	9	40.9	13
Co. I	18	0	0	2	0	5	0	7	38.8	11
Co. K	32	0	1	4	2	6	1	14	43.8	18
F&S	0	0	0	0	0	0	0	0	0	0
Totals	212	6	3	27	5	48	4	93	43.9	119

Notes: (1) The total number of men engaged with the regiment is given officially as 217, which is 5 more than shown here. The discrepancy may be explained, however, by the fact that several of the regiment's men were on daily duty as teamsters, guards, and orderlies at 3rd Brigade Headquarters, 5 of whom may have joined the battle. There were also musicians who may have participated. (2) The official loss was 89, including prisoners of war.

APPENDIX 2: THE THIRTY COMBAT SOLDIERS REMAINING AFTER WELDON RAILROAD

Co. A

1. Sgt. John O'Donnell

Co. C

2. Pvt. Frederick S. Cheney
3. Pvt. Gustavus Holden
4. Sgt. Michael Lovejoy

Co. E

5. Pvt. Thomas Meehan
6. Sgt. James H. Marshall

Co. F

7. Cpl. Calvin A. Bigelow
8. Pvt. Charles Daily
9. Sgt. Edward Hanrahan
10. Pvt. John Hennessey

Co. G

11. Pvt. Alfred M. Allen
12. Pvt. Charles Hamlin
13. Pvt. Austin N. Moulton
14. Pvt. Oscar B. Phelps

15. Pvt. John Smith
16. Pvt. Andrew C. Thompson
17. Pvt. Daniel Welsh

Co. H

18. Pvt. Walter R. Foster
19. Pvt. George Wellman

Co. I

20. Cpl. Newton B. Pepoon
21. Sgt. R. Wesley Williams

Co. K

22. Pvt. John Adams
23. Pvt. George H. Brigham
24. 1st Lt. Albert Doty
25. Cpl. Theodore L. Kelley
26. Pvt. James W. Needham
27. Sgt. William F. Oakes
28. Cpl. George T. Pickett
29. Sgt. Edward F. Potter
30. Pvt. Franklin F. Strong

APPENDIX 3: MEN IN EVERY BATTLE OF THE REGIMENT

1. 1st Sgt. John O'Donnell, Co. A, WIA, Dec. 1, 1863, to Aug. 9, 1865

2. Color Cpl. Frederick S. Cheney, Co. C, KIA, Feb. 27, 1864, to Mar. 25, 1865

3. Sgt. Michael Lovejoy, Co. C, Des., Feb. 2, 1864, to May 10, 1865

4. Sgt. Calvin Bigelow, Co. F, Feb. 1, 1864, to June 13, 1865

5. Pvt. Edward Hanrahan, Co. F, Feb. 2, 1864, to Aug. 9, 1865

6. Cpl. Charles Hamlin, Co. G, POW, Feb. 20, 1864, to Aug. 9, 1865

7. Cpl. John Smith, Co. G, WIA, POW, DD, Mar. 23, 1863, to July 20, 1865

8. Cpl. Daniel Welsh, Co. G, Feb. 1, 1864, to Aug. 9, 1865

9. Cpl. Walter R. Foster, Co. H, Jan. 5, 1864, to Aug. 9, 1865

10. 1st Sgt. R. Wesley Williams, Co. I, WIA, Feb. 13, 1864, to June 13, 1865

11. Sgt. William F. Oakes, Co. K, POW, Mar. 12, 1864, to June 2, 1865

Note: Dates are from enlistment to discharge, death, or desertion.

APPENDIX 4: DEMOGRAPHICS OF NATIVITY

						Companies							
	A	*B*	*C*	*D*	*E*	*F*	*G*	*H*	*I*	*K*	*F&S*	*Total*	*%*
Massachusetts	30	54	28	56	38	37	37	63	28	64	11	446	43.0
Maine	1	3	1	2	2	2	0	1	2	5	1	20	1.9
New Hampshire	3	3	1	0	1	6	4	4	2	5	0	29	2.8
Vermont	2	2	1	2	8	4	7	6	1	10	1	44	4.2
Connecticut	0	6	5	4	2	2	1	7	3	2	0	32	3.1
Rhode Island	2	1	1	2	0	0	1	0	3	1	0	11	1.1
New York	3	2	11	15	8	6	8	4	16	4	1	78	7.5
New Jersey	0	1	0	1	0	0	0	0	0	1	0	3	0.3
Pennsylvania	0	0	1	0	0	2	0	0	0	1	0	4	0.4
Ohio	0	0	1	1	0	0	0	0	0	0	0	2	0.2
Indiana	0	0	1	0	0	1	0	0	0	0	0	2	0.2
Michigan	0	0	1	0	0	0	0	0	0	1	0	2	0.2
Utah	0	0	0	0	0	0	0	0	1	0	0	1	0.1
Kentucky	0	0	0	0	1	0	0	0	0	0	0	1	0.1
Virginia	0	0	0	0	0	0	0	0	0	0	1	1	0.1
Georgia	0	0	1	0	0	0	0	0	0	0	0	1	0.1
Arkansas	0	0	0	0	0	0	0	1	0	0	0	1	0.1
Louisiana	0	1	0	0	0	0	0	0	0	0	0	1	0.1
Canada	15	2	29	4	12	8	6	5	12	4	0	97	9.4
Ireland	40	22	21	17	25	28	17	8	17	2	0	197	18.0
England	11	3	0	7	0	4	4	0	1	0	0	30	2.9
Scotland	1	1	0	0	0	0	0	0	1	0	0	3	0.3
Holland	0	1	0	0	0	0	0	0	0	0	0	1	0.1
France	1	0	1	0	0	0	2	0	0	0	0	4	0.4
Switzerland	0	0	1	0	0	0	0	0	0	0	0	1	0.1
Germany	0	1	3	0	1	1	0	0	5	0	0	11	1.1
Gibraltar	0	0	0	0	0	1	0	0	0	0	0	1	0.1
Italy	0	2	0	0	0	0	0	0	0	0	0	2	0.2
Hungary	0	0	0	0	1	0	0	0	0	0	0	1	0.1
Turkey	0	0	0	0	0	0	0	0	0	1	0	1	0.1
Australia	0	0	0	0	0	0	0	0	1	0	0	1	0.1
unknown	0	0	0	0	0	2	3	2	1	0	0	8	0.8

APPENDIX 5: COMPANY STATISTICAL SUMMARIES

	Co. A	Co. B	Co. C	Co. D	Co. E	Co. F	Co. G	Co. H	Co. I	Co. K	F&S	Total
Enlisted	109	105	108	111	99	104	90	101	95	101	15	1038
Veterans	29	26	15	48	22	18	9	25	16	27	10	245
% veterans	*26.6*	*24.8*	*13.9*	*43.2*	*22.2*	*17.3*	*10.0*	*24.8*	*16.8*	*26.7*	*66.6*	*23.6*
Left camp	99	86	95	96	79	92	86	100	85	88	10	916
Cattle guard	0	0	0	0	0	29	0	0	0	0	0	29
Train guard	0	0	0	0	0	0	0	0	1	56	0	57
No. of men in Action												
Wilderness	70	64	61	65	52	42	58	60	56	15	3	548
Spotsylvania 5/12	41	36	30	35	24	17	19	32	33	65	1	333
North Anna River	23	24	18	24	17	16	22	26	18	48	1	237
Petersburg assault	18	20	15	16	13	18	18	14	14	37	1	184
Petersburg Crater	13	7	10	9	8	9	11	8	5	17	1	98
Weldon Railroad	4	2	5	3	2	5	8	3	3	10	0	45
Poplar Grove 9/30	4	3	16	2	4	25	10	5	4	19	1	93
Poplar Grove 10/8	3	3	16	0	4	23	9	3	7	21	1	90
Fort Stedman	13	19	26	11	10	40	21	22	18	32	0	212
KIA/MWIA	29	24	16	19	20	16	26	22	24	16	1	213
% KIA/MWIA	*26.6*	*22.9*	*14.8*	*17.1*	*20.2*	*15.4*	*28.8*	*21.8*	*25.3*	*15.8*	*6.6*	*20.5*
WIA	42	34	43	34	27	31	35	48	42	32	2	370
% WIA	*38.5*	*32.4*	*39.8*	*30.6*	*27.3*	*29.8*	*38.8*	*47.5*	*44.2*	*31.7*	*13.3*	*35.6*
Died from disease	8	6	6	11	5	5	1	9	4	7	0	62
% died from disease	*7.3*	*5.7*	*5.5*	*9.9*	*5.1*	*4.8*	*0.1*	*8.9*	*4.2*	*6.9*	*0*	*6.0*
POW	17	11	15	18	11	12	17	12	9	14	1	137
Deserted	23	8	21	23	23	12	20	1	17	10	0	158
% deserted	*21.1*	*7.6*	*19.4*	*20.7*	*23.2*	*11.5*	*22.2*	*0.9*	*17.9*	*9.9*	*0*	*15.2*
Discharged for disability	25	35	29	29	30	25	22	39	23	30	2	289
VRC	5	5	5	8	9	8	2	4	6	3	0	55
PMO	18	24	31	21	18	38	25	22	21	28	7	253
% PMO	*16.5*	*22.9*	*28.7*	*18.9*	*18.2*	*36.5*	*27.7*	*21.8*	*22.1*	*27.7*	*46.6*	*24.4*

APPENDIX 6: TABLE OF ORGANIZATION (infantry)
May to September, 1864

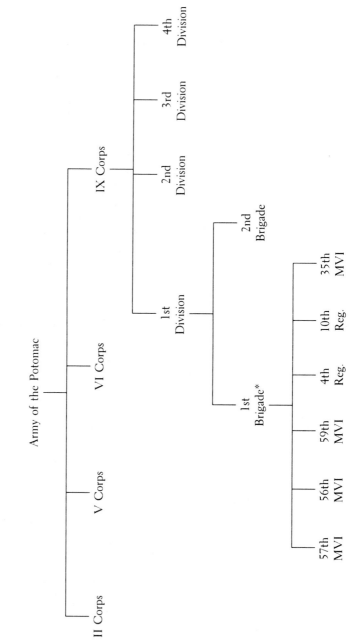

*The organization of the brigade was fluid, and this represents only a sample of its actual regimental structure. For exact formations on a given date, see text.

APPENDIX 7: REGIMENTAL GENERAL ORDERS

The general orders below—all that are known to have survived from the regiment—have been copied with the spelling and punctuation of the original manuscripts. Evidently neither adjutant cared much for periods or commas.

G.O. No. 1 Jan 25, 1864 HQ 57th MVI Camp Wool

1. No officer will leave camp without the approval of the officer in command.

2. There must always be at least one officer with each company.

3. No enlisted man shall leave camp except upon a written pass signed by the commanding officer of his company and approved by the officer in command of the camp, and there shall not be more than eight men absent at a time from any company. Any man found beyond the lines of the camp without such a pass will be arrested and held as deserters. All passes must be presented for approval before 10 o'clock A.M.

4. The men will use the sink intended for their use, and anyone committing any nuisance in or around the barracks or campground will be dealt with accordingly. Fuel must be squarely piled in two piles on one side of the cookhouses, and the sawing and splitting done between these piles.

5. Each captain will see that the roll of his company is called as often as once every three hours during the day, and at least one officer must be with each company at every roll call.

6. Each captain will draw and issue to his men the numbers and letters of the regiment and company and will see that each man of his company wears the same on his cap.

7. Each captain will see that his company is drilled in the "school of the soldier" (squad drills) one hour and a half every morning and in the "school of the company" two hours every afternoon.

8. Commanders of companies will be held responsible for the appearance of their company barracks and cookhouses and the vicinity. Particular personal attention will be given to this order, as the health and comfort of the men depend very much on the cleanliness of the camp.

9. Commanders of the companies will not send their men to these headquarters. All business with the men must be done through the company officers.

It is expected that all orders will be cheerfully and promptly complied with and that each officer will use every effort that this camp may gain and retain a reputation for its cleanliness and good discipline.

By order of
E. P. Hollister
Lt. Col. Comdg.

Geo E. Barton
Lt. & acting Adjt of Post

Appendixes

Gen'l Orders No. 3 Hd Quarters 57th Mass Reg Vet Vols Camp Wool Jan 27, 1864

1. Captains will inspect their companies every Sunday at 9:30 A.M. No soldier will be excused from Sunday inspection except the guard, the sick, and the necessary attendants in the hospital.

2. Commanders of companies are hereby notified that they will not excuse any man from the regular drills, the surgeon being the only officer having that authority.

3. The men will be instructed as to the respect due to the officers, the manner of saluting, etc.

By order of   Geo E. Barton
E. P. Hollister   Lt. and acting Adjutant
Lt. Col. Comdg.

Gen'l Orders No. 4 Head Quarters 57th Mass Reg Vet Vol Camp Wool Feb. 3, 1864

Commanders of companies will see that none other than the uniform prescribed by the Army Regulations is worn by their non-commissioned officers and privates and that the blouse and not the frock coat is worn by their men while in camp.

By order of   Geo E. Barton
E. P. Hollister   Lt. & acting Adjutant
Lt. Col. Comdg.

Gen'l Orders No. 5 Head Quarters 57th Mass Reg Vet Vols. Camp Wool Feb. 6, 1864

No gambling of any description will be allowed in this camp. Commanders of companies will see that this order is strictly enforced.

By order of   Geo. E Barton
E. P. Hollister   Lt. & acting Adjutant
Lt. Col. Comdg.

Gen'l Orders No. 6 Hd. Qtrs 57th Mass Vet Vols. Camp Wool Feb. 12, 1864

1. Commanders of companies will cause all pistols in possession of their men to be disposed of immediately or given into their charge. Enlisted men are not allowed to carry any arms except the one provided by the government. Any pistol found in possession of any enlisted man except a first sergent after *one week* from this date *will be* confiscated.

2. Lines will be placed on the west side of the company barracks six feet from the ground, on which all the blankets of the company will be hung every pleasant day to air from 10 AM to 12 M. Companies will do their washing of *clothes* on Mondays and Tuesdays and will use those lines for drying them. The sentry opposite the barracks will be instructed by the officer of the guard to watch these clothes and be responsible for their safety.

3. Captains of companies are again cautioned about having the clothing of their men folded neatly and placed at the head of their respective bunks.

By order of   Geo. E. Barton,
Wm F. Bartlett   Lt. & acting
Col. Comdg.   Adjutant

Gen Orders No. 7 Head Quarters 57th Regt Vet Vols Camp Wool Feb. 13, 1864

Commanding officers of companies will make the regular Sunday morning inspections most minute and thorough tomorrow. Particular attention will be paid to the personal cleanliness of the men, the condition of their underclothing, etc. They will see that each man has two shirts, two pair of drawers and stockings. In the inspection of their barracks they will see that no straw is left in any of the bunks. Each officer is in a degree responsible for the health and comfort of his men and he should make every exertion to secure it for them.

By order of   Geo E. Barton
Wm F Bartlett   Lieut. and Acting
Col. Comdg.   Adjutant

Gen. Orders No. 8 Head Quarters 57th Reg Vet Vols Camp Wool Feb. 15, 1864

1. Commanders of companies will proceed to divide their men into squads as prescribed by Army Regulations each under the charge of a sergeant who looks out for the personal cleanliness and appearance of his men, sees that they wash regularly and thoroughly both person and underclothing. See XII article, paragraphs 90 to 101 inclusive.

2. Recruits sent to camp for any company will be placed in charge of Lieut. Coe who will keep them in his barrack two or three days, or until they have their hair and beards cut and trimed and been thoroughly clensed when he will deliver them to the commanding officer of the company to which they have been assigned, taking his receipt for the same.

3. The officer of the day will read to each relief of the guard, once during the day, article XXXII, revised Army Regulations on the subject of guards, and duties of sentinels.

By order of   Geo. E Barton
Wm F Bartlett   Lt. Acting Adjutant
Col. Comdg.

Appendixes

Gen'l Orders No. 9 Head Qrs. 57th Regt. Vet. Vols Camp Wool March 4, 1864

1. Captains of companies will have the men of their commands numbered alphabetically, so that each man will know his number, which will be marked on all articles belonging to him including gun and equipments.

2. Captains of companies will have their barracks whitewashed on the inside, also the cookhouses. They will purchase the lime necessary and a brush out of the company fund. The white washing must be *finished* before the Sunday morning inspection.

by order of	Geo E Barton
Wm. F Bartlett	Lt. & A.A.
Col. Comdg.	

Gen'l Orders No. 10 Hd Qrts. 57th Vet Vols. Camp Wool Mar. 16, 1864

1. The number of cooks allowed to the company is two which may not in any case be exceeded. Two men will be detailed for the police of the company quarters daily and one corporal who will be responsible for the appearance of the same. The sergeant who has charge of the cookhouse will be responsible for the drawing of rations and will not be excused from drill. Rations will be issued by the Quartermaster at 8 o'clock A.M.

2. The arrangements of the bunks will be as follows. The heads of the bunks will all be the same way. The rubber blanket will be spread the glazed side up over the bottom of the bunk or bedsack. The woolen blanket, dress coat and overcoat will be folded compactly and separately and laid at the head of the bunk outside of the rubber blanket. The gun and equipments of each man will be hung beside his bunk. Officers and non-commissioned officers in inspecting bunks will see that no clothing or articles of any sort are placed *under* the bedsack.

3. Non-commissioned officers will be drilled and examined in their duties not only in the manual of arms in the ranks but in quarters and on guard one hour each evening by the comdg. officers of the company. Officers and non-commissioned officers in drilling the men will follow the rules and observe the directions prescribed by the "tactics" with the modification of the comdg. officer of the Regt and will *use no other method.*

4. Commanding officers of companies will see that their men are shaved as heretofore directed, leaving only the mustache and "imperial".

By order of	Geo E Barton
Wm F Bartlett	Lt. & A.A.
Col. Comdg.	

Appendixes

Gen Orders No. 11 Head Quarters 57th Regt. Vet Vols Camp Wool March 17, 1864

1. Officers obtaining leave of absence from these Hd. Qrs. will report to the adjutant the time at which their leaves begin and terminate and will report to him *in person* immediately on their return.

2. Every commanding officer of a company will institute an "awkward squad". Men who are backward in drill, slow to learn, careless or inattentive to orders, will be placed in this squad and drilled carefully by a good non-commissioned officer in addition to the regular drill hours of the company.

3. In the morning drill, the companies will be divided into squads and drilled by the officers and non-commissioned officers at open ranks under the immediate supervision of the captain.

4. Captains of companies will *not excuse any man* from any drill except by the recommendation of the surgeon. Men coming off guard are excused from drill until afternoon.

By order of   Geo. E Barton
Wm. F. Bartlett   Lt. & A.A.
Col. Comdg.

Gen.' Order No. 12 Head Quarters 57 Regt Vet. Vols. Camp Wool March 24, 1864

In accordance with an order of the War Dept (directing that in the place of a regimental court martial, a field officer shall be appointed to hear & try such cases as would naturally be brought before such court and decide on the punishment) Major J. W. Cushing 57 Vet Vols. is hereby appointed for that purpose, with authority to summon such witnesses as he may deem necessary to insure justice to the prisoner. The sentences are to have the same limit as those prescribed by Army Regs for Regt Courts Martial.

By order of   Geo. E Barton
Wm F Bartlett   Lt & A.A.
Col. Comdg.

Gen Orders No. 13 Head Qrs. 57th Regt Vet Vols. Camp Wool April 7, 1864

Hereafter all company officers will report to the adjutant at Hd Qrs. at reveille immediately after roll call. He will report to the commanding officer the name of any officer failing to report.

By order of   Geo. E. Barton
Wm F Bartlett   Lt. & A.A.
Col. Comdg.

PETERSBURG

General Orders No. 1 Head Quarters 57th Mass. Infty. January 19, 1865

I. Hereafter company morning reports will be left at the adjutants office by 1st Sergt. or acting 1st Sergts of companies before 7½ o'clock AM.

II. Before being forwarded to the adjutants office, the reports will be carefully examined by Co. commanders and by them properly signed their official title.

III. All changes in the aggregates Present and Present and Absent will be concicly noted on the page for remarks.

IV. 1st Sergts or acting 1st Sergts of companies will report to the adjts office for their report books at the time of their sounding 1st Sergts call—viz—one o'clock P.M.

By command of   A. Doty
J M Tucker   Bvt Capt. and Adjt
Lieut Col Comdg 57th Mass

General Orders No. 2 Head Quarters 57th Mass Infty. February 2, 1865

I. Hereafter the following "roll calls" will be observed by companies of this command viz
Reveille—5 o'clock A.M.
Retreat—5 o'clock P.M.
Tatoo—8 o'clock " "

II. Each "roll call" will be attended by commandants of companies *in person* who will report (immediately after each roll call) to the adjutant at Regt Head Quarters the names of all unauthorized absentees

By command of
J M Tucker   Bvt Capt and Adjt
Lieut Col. Comdg.   Albert Doty

APPENDIX 8: MEDICAL ADVICE

The following is the text of a pamphlet distributed to the 57th Regiment's soldiers before they left Camp Wool. The copy from which this transcription has been made was given to Pvt. Francis M. Harrington of Company K by Cpl. Henry Goulding of the same company. The leaflet is printed on yellow stock, is 16 pages long, and measures 2⅜ by 3½ inches.

Appendixes

[Front Cover]

TAKE CARE OF YOUR HEALTH

Advice to Soldiers

by

W. W. HALL, M.D.

Published by the

American Tract Society

28 Cornhill, Boston

1. In any ordinary campaign, sickness disables or destroys three times as many as the sword.

2. On a march, from April to November, the entire clothing should be a colored flannel shirt, with a loosely-buttoned collar, cotton drawers, woolen pantaloons, shoes and stockings, and a light-colored felt hat, with broad brim to protect the eyes and face from the glare of the sun and from the rain, and a substantial but not heavy coat when off duty.

3. Sunstroke is most effectually prevented by wearing a silk handkerchief in the crown of the hat.

4. Colored blankets are best, and if lined with brown drilling, the warmth and durability are doubled, while the protection against dampness from lying on the ground is almost complete.

5. Never lie or sit down on the bare earth for a moment; rather use your hat—a handkerchief, even, is a great protection. The warmer you are, the greater need for this precaution, as a damp vapor is immediately generated, to be absorbed by the clothing, and to cool you off too rapidly.

6. While marching, or on other active duty, the more thirsty you are, the more essential is it to the safety of life itself, to rinse out the mouth two or three times, and *then* take a swallow of water a time, with short intervals. A brave French General, on a forced march, fell dead on the instant by drinking largely of cold water, when snow was on the ground.

7. Abundant sleep is essential to bodily efficiency, and to that alertness of mind which is all-important in an engagement; and few things more certainly and more effectually prevent sound sleep than eating heartily after sundown, especially after a heavy march or desperate battle.

8. Nothing is more certain to secure endurance and capability of long-continued effort, than the avoidance of everything as a drink except cold water, not excluding coffee at breakfast. Drink as little as possible of even cold water.

9. After any sort of exhausting effort, a cup of coffee, hot or cold, is an admirable sustainer of the strength, until Nature begins to recover herself.

10. Never eat heartily just before a great undertaking, because the nervous power is irresistibly drawn to the stomach to manage the food eaten, thus draining off that supply which the brain and muscles so much need.

11. If persons will drink brandy, it is incomparably safer to do so *after* an effort than before, for it can give only a transient strength, lasting but a few minutes; but as it can never be known how long any given effort is to be kept in continuance, and if longer than the few minutes, the body becomes more feeble than it would have been without stimulus, it is clear that the use *before* an effort is always hazardous, and is always unwise.

12. Never go to sleep, especially after a great effort, even in hot weather, without some covering over you.

13. Under all circumstances, rather than lie down on the bare ground, lie in the hollow of two logs placed together, or across several smaller pieces of wood laid side by side; or sit on your hat, leaning against a tree. A nap of ten or fifteen minutes in that position will refresh you more than an hour on the bare earth, with the additional advantage of perfect safety.

14. A *cut* is less dangerous than a bullet-wound, and heals more rapidly.

15. If from any wound the blood spurts out in jets instead of a steady stream, you will die in a few minutes unless it is remedied, because an artery has been divided, and that takes the blood direct from the fountain of life. To stop this instantly, tie a handkerchief or other cloth very loosely BETWEEN the wound and the heart; put a stick, bayonet, or ramrod *between* the skin and the handkerchief, and twist it around until the bleeding ceases, and keep it thus until the surgeon arrives.

16. If the blood flows in a slow, regular stream, a vein has been pierced, and the handkerchief must be on the other side of the wound from the heart; that is *below* the wound.

17. A bullet through the abdomen (belly or stomach) is more certainly fatal than if aimed at the head or heart; for in the latter cases the ball is often glanced off by the bone, or follows round it under the skin; but when it enters the stomach or bowels, from any direction, death is inevitable under all conceivable circumstances, but is scarcely ever instantaneous. Generally the person lives a day or two with perfect clearness of intellect, often *not* suffering greatly. The practical bearing of this statement in reference to the great future is clear.

18. Let the whole beard grow, but not longer than some three inches. This strengthens and thickens its growth, and thus makes a more perfect protection for the lungs against dust, and of the throat against winds and cold in the winter, while in the summer a greater perspiration of the skin is induced, with an increase of evaporation; hence, greater coolness of the parts on the outside, while the throat is less feverish, thirsty, and dry.

19. Avoid fats and fat meats in summer and in all warm days.

20. Whenever possible, take a plunge into any lake or running stream every morning, as soon as you get up; if none at hand, endeavor to wash the body all over as soon as you leave your bed, for personal cleanliness acts like a charm against all diseases, always either warding them off altogether, or greatly mitigating their severity and shortening their duration.

21. Keep the hair of the head closely cut, say within an inch and a half of the scalp in every part, repeated on the first of each month, and wash the whole scalp plentifully in cold water every morning.

22. Wear woolen stockings and moderately loose shoes, keeping the toe and finger-nails always cut close.

23. It is more important to wash the feet well every night; because it aids to keep the skin and nails soft, and to prevent chafing, blistering, and corns, all of which greatly interfere with a soldier's duty.

24. The most universally safe position, after all stunnings, hurts, and wounds, is that of being placed on the back, the head being elevated three or four inches only; aiding, more than any one thing you can do, to equalize and restore the proper circulation of the blood.

25. The more weary you are after a march or other work, the more easily will you take cold, if you remain still after it is over, unless, the moment you cease motion, you throw a coat or blanket over your shoulders. This precaution should be taken in the warmest weather, especially if there is even a slight air stirring.

26. The greatest physical kindness you can show a severely wounded comrade is first to place him on his back, and then run with all your might for some water to drink; not a second ought to be lost. If no vessel is at hand, take your hat; if no hat, off with your shirt, wring it out once, tie the arms in a knot, as also the lower end, thus making a bag, open at the neck only. A fleet person can convey a bucketful half a mile in this way. I've seen a dying man clutch at a single drop of water from the finger's end with the voraciousness of a famished tiger.

27. If wet to the skin by rain or by swimming rivers, keep in motion until the clothes are dried, and no harm will result.

28. Whenever it is possible, do, by all means, when you have to use water for cooking or drinking from ponds or sluggish streams, boil it well, and when cool, shake it, or stir it, so that the oxygen of the air shall get to it, which greatly improves it for drinking. This boiling arrests the process of fermentation which arises from the presence of organic and inorganic impurities, thus tending to prevent cholera and all bowel diseases. If there is no time for boiling, at least strain it through a cloth, even if you have to use a shirt or trouser-leg.

29. Twelve men are hit in battle, dressed in red, where there are only five dressed in a bluish gray—a difference of more than two to one; green, seven; brown, six.

30. Water can be made almost ice cool even in the hottest weather, by closely enveloping a filled canteen, or other vessel, with woolen cloth kept plentifully wetted and exposed.

31. While on a march, lie down the moment you halt for a rest; every minute spent in that position refreshes more than five minutes standing or loitering about.

Appendixes

32. A daily evacuation of the bowels is indispensable to bodily health, vigor, and endurance; this is promoted, in many cases, by stirring a tablespoonful of corn (Indian) meal in a glass of water, and drinking it on rising in the morning.

33. *Loose bowels*, namely, acting more than once a day, with a feeling of debility afterward, is the first step toward cholera; the best remedy is instant and perfect quietude of body, eating nothing but boiled rice with or without boiled milk; in more decided cases, a woolen flannel, with two thicknesses in front, should be bound tightly around the abdomen, especially if marching is a necessity.*

34. To have "been to the wars" is a life-long honor, increasing with advancing years, while to have died in defense of your country will be the boast and glory of your children's children.

[Back Cover]

Behold the fear of the Lord, that is wisdom, and to depart from evil is understanding.
—JOB 28:28

The eyes of the Lord run to and fro throughout the whole earth, to show himself strong in behalf of them whose heart is perfect toward him. —2 CHRON. 16:9

Godliness is profitable unto all things, having promise of the life that now is, and of that which is to come. —1 TIM. 4:8

For we must all appear before the judgement seat of Christ; that every one may receive the things done in his body, according to that he hath done, whether it be good or bad.
—2 COR. 5:10

*The following remedy for complaints of the bowels is said to have been extensively used in the Russian war. Ed. Take 2 ounces laudanum, 2 ounces spirits of camphor, 2 drams tincture Cayenne pepper, 1 ounce tincture ginger, 2 ounces essence peppermint, 2 ounces Hoffman's anodyne. Mix well, and take one teaspoonful in a little warm water, after each operation of the bowels, or oftener if the case is violent.

Bibliography

Adjutant General, Commonwealth of Massachusetts. *Record of Massachusetts Volunteers*, vol. 1. Boston: Wright, Potter, 1896.

Anderson, Captain John, U.S.A. *History of the 57th Regiment of Massachusetts Volunteers.* Boston: E. B. Stilling, 1896.

Angle, Paul M. *A Pictorial History of the Civil War Years.* New York: Doubleday, 1967.

Ballou, Adin. *History of Milford.* N. p., 1880.

Barnes, Joseph K., Surgeon General, U.S.A. *Volume II of Parts 2 & 3 of the Medical and Surgical Records of the Rebellion Being the Second Surgical Volume.* 2nd issue. Washington, D.C.: Government Printing Office, 1875.

Barton, Michael. *Goodmen: The Character of Civil War Soldiers.* University Park: Pennsylvania State University Press, 1981.

Battles and Leaders of the Civil War. vol. 4, *The Way to Appomattox.* New York: Thomas Yoseloff, 1956.

Bearss, Edwin C. *Battle of the Weldon Railroad.* Denver: United States Department of the Interior, National Park Service, n.d.

————. *Meade's June 18 Assault on Petersburg Fails and the Investment Begins.* Denver: United States Department of the Interior, National Park Service, 1964.

Boeger, Palmer H. "Hardtack and Burned Beans." *Civil War History,* vol. 4, no. 1, March 1958.

Bowen, James L. *Massachusetts in the War, 1861–1865.* Springfield, Mass.: n.p., 1883.

Bowman, John S. *The Civil War Almanac.* New York: World Almanac Publications, 1983.

Bright, Thomas R. "Yankees in Arms: The Civil War As a Personal Experience." *Civil War History,* vol. 19, no. 3, Sept. 1973.

Cain, Marvin R. *"A 'Face of Battle' Needed: An Assessment of Motives and Men in Civil War Historiography." Civil War History,* vol. 28, no. 1, March 1982.

Catton, Bruce. *Grant Takes Command.* Boston: Little, Brown, 1968.

————. *Never Call Retreat.* New York: Doubleday, 1965.

————. *Reflections on the Civil War.* Edited by John Leekly. New York: Doubleday, 1981.

Bibliography

————. *A Stillness at Appomattox.* New York: Doubleday, 1953.

Commager, Henry Steele. *The Blue and Gray.* Indianapolis: Bobbs-Merrill, 1950.

Committee of the Regimental Association. *History of the 35th Regiment, Massachusetts Volunteers, 1862–1865.* Boston: Mills, Knight, 1884.

————. *History of the 36th Regiment, Massachusetts Volunteers.* Boston: Rockwell & Churchill, 1884.

Commonwealth of Massachusetts. *Massachusetts Commandery of the Military Order of the Loyal Legion of the United States.* Official Records. N.p., n.d.

————. *Massachusetts Soldiers, Sailors, and Marines in the Civil War.* Official Records (various volumes). Norwood, Mass.: Norwood Press, 1932.

Cornish, Dudley Taylor. *The Sable Arm: Black Troops in the Union Army, 1861–1865.* Lawrence: University Press of Kansas, 1987.

Cudworth, Warren H. *The 1st Massachusetts Regiment.* Boston: Walker, Fuller, 1866.

Cullen, Joseph P. *Battle of the Wilderness.* Harrisburg, Pa.: Historical Times, 1971.

————. *Battle of Spotsylvania.* Harrisburg, Pa.: Historical Times, 1971.

————. *Detour on the Road to Richmond.* Harrisburg, Pa.: Historical Times, 1965.

————. *A Report on the Physical History of the Crater.* Petersburg, Va.: Petersburg National Military Park, 1975.

————. *The Siege of Petersburg.* Harrisburg, Pa.: Historical Times, 1970.

Davis, William C., and Frassanito, William. *Touched by Fire: A Photographic Portrait of the Civil War.* Boston: National Historical Society, Little, Brown, 1985.

Dornbush, C. E. *Regimental Publications and Personal Narratives of the Civil War.* Vol. 1, part 3, "New England States." New York: New York Public Library, 1961.

Dyer, Frederick H. *A Compendium of the War of the Rebellion.* Vol. 3. New York: n.p. 1959.

Eldridge, D. *Description of Camp Meigs, Readville, Massachusetts, 1861–1865.* Unpublished ms., Military Records Depot, Mass. Adjutant General's Office, Natick, Mass.

Espirito, Brigadier General Vincent J., chief ed. *The West Point Atlas of American Wars.* Vol. 1, 1689–1900. New York: Praeger, 1959.

Farnham, Elmer F. *The Quickest Route: The History of the Norwich and Worcester Railroad.* Chester, Conn.: Pequot, 1973.

Faust, Patricia L., ed. *Historical Times Illustrated Encyclopedia of the Civil War.* New York: Harper & Row, 1986.

Fisher, Jabez. "Weather and Farm Reports" (handwritten journal of weather reports in Worcester County during the Civil War). Fitchburg Historical Society, Fitchburg, Mass.

Foote, Shelby. *The Civil War: A Narrative.* Vol. 3. New York: Random House, 1947.

Frassanito, William A. *Grant and Lee: The Virginia Campaigns.* New York: Scribner's, 1983.

Futch, Ovid L. *History of Andersonville Prison.* Gainesville: University of Florida Press, 1968.

Gardner, Alexander. *Gardner's Photographic Sketch Book of the Civil War,* New York: Dover, 1959.

Gibbs, Patricia T. *U.S. Pattern Book: Patterns for U.S. Fatigue Uniform, 1861–1865.* Fredericksburg, Va.: Historians Unlimited, 1980.

Bibliography

Gordon, General John B., C.S.A. *Reminiscences of the Civil War.* New York: Scribner's, 1903.

Gramm, George F. *Gramm's Standard American Atlas of the United States.* Chicago: n.p. 1884.

Grand Army of the Republic, Edwin V. Sumner Post #19, Department of Massachusetts. *Personal War Sketches.* Vols. 1, 2, and 3 (handwritten). Fitchburg Historical Society, Fitchburg, Mass., 1890.

Haley, Private John W., 17th Regiment, Maine Volunteer Infantry. *The Rebel Yell and the Yankee Hurrah.* Edited by Ruth M. Silliker. Camden, Maine: Down East Books, 1985.

Hall, W. W., M.D. *Take Care of Your Health: Advice to Soldiers.* Boston: American Tract Society, 1864.

Handlin, Oscar. *Boston's Immigrants.* Cambridge, Mass.: Harvard University Press, 1941.

Higgenson, Thomas Wentworth, State Military and Naval Historian. *Massachusetts in the Army and Navy During the War of 1861–1865.* Official Records, Commonwealth of Massachusetts. Boston: Wright, Potter, 1896.

Jaynes, Gregory. *The Killing Ground,* Alexandria, Va.: Time-Life Books, 1986.

Jacob, Stanley W., M.D., F.A.C.S., and Francome, Clarice A. *Structure and Function in Man.* 3d ed. Philadelphia: W. B. Saunders, 1974.

Johns, Private Henry T. *Life with the 49th Massachusetts Volunteers.* Washington: Ramsey & Bisbee, 1890.

Katcher, Phillip R. N. *Army of the Potomac.* London: Osprey, 1975.

Keegan, John, and Holmes, Richard. *Soldiers: A History of Men in Battle.* New York: Viking Penguin, 1986.

Kimball, Edward P. *Brinley Hall Album and Post Ten Sketchbook.* Worcester, Mass.: F. F. Blanchard, 1896.

Klein, Maury. *Life in Civil War America.* Harrisburg, Pa: Historical Times, Eastern Acorn, 1984.

Kirkpatrick, Doris. *The City and the River.* Vol. 1, Fitchburg, Mass.: Fitchburg Historical Society, 1971.

Leech, Margaret. *Reveille in Washington.* New York: Harper & Row, 1941.

Lincoln, William S. *Life with the 34th Massachusetts Infantry in the War of the Rebellion.* Worcester, Mass.: Noyes, Snow, 1879.

Linderman, Gerald F. *Embattled Courage: The Experience of Combat in the American Civil War.* New York: Free Press, 1987.

Lonn, Ella. *Desertion During the Civil War.* American Historical Association, 1928.

Lord, Francis A. *Civil War Sutlers and Their Wares.* New York: Thomas Yoseloff, 1969.

Lykes, Richard Wayne. *Campaign for Petersburg.* Washington: United States Department of the Interior, National Park Service, 1985.

McDonald, John. *Great Battles of the Civil War.* New York: Macmillan, 1988.

Marvin, A. P. *History of Worcester in the War of the Rebellion.* Cleveland: Arthur H. Clark, 1870.

Melcher, Holman S. *Cut Off in the Wilderness.* Harrisburg, Pa.: Historical Times, 1969.

Monaghan, Jay. "Civil War Slang and Humor." *Civil War History,* vol. 3, no. 2, June 1957.

Bibliography

National Historical Society. *The Image of War: 1861–1865*. Vol. 5, *The South Besieged*. New York: Doubleday, 1983.

―――. *The Image of War: 1861–1865*. Vol. 6, *The End of an Era*. New York: Doubleday, 1984.

National Library of Medicine. *Medicine of the Civil War* (pamphlet). N.p., n.d.

National Park Service. *The Battle of Hatchers Run*. Washington, D.C.: United States Department of the Interior, n.d.

Nevins, Allan. *The War for the Union*. Vol. 4. New York: Scribner's, 1971.

Osborne, William H. *The 29th Regiment, Massachusetts Volunteer Infantry*. Boston: Albert J. Wright, 1887.

Palfrey, Winthrop Francis. *Memoir of William Francis Bartlett*. Boston: Houghton, Osgood, 1878.

Pearce, C. F. *Co. C. 51st Regt. Mass. Vol. Militia 1862–1863*. Worcester, Mass.: n.p., 1886.

Phillips, Stanley S. *Civil War Corps Badges and Other Related Awards, Badges, Medals of the Period*. Lanham, Md.: privately published, 1982.

Pleasants, Henry, Jr., and Straley, George H. *Inferno at Petersburg*. Philadelphia: Chilton, 1961.

Porter, Horace. *Campaigning with Grant*. New York: Century, 1897.

Putnam, Samuel H. *The Story of Company A, 25th Massachusetts Volunteers in the War of the Rebellion*. Worcester, Mass.: Putnam, Davis, 1886.

Sandburg, Carl. *Abraham Lincoln*. Vol. 2, *The War Years (1861–1864)*. New York: Harcourt, Brace, 1939.

Schouler, William, Adjutant General for the Commonwealth of Massachusetts. *History of Massachusetts in the Civil War*. Vols. 1 and 2. Boston: Official Records, 1871.

Smith, Gene. *Lee and Grant*. New York: McGraw-Hill, 1984.

Spears, John Pearl. *Old Landmarks and Historic Spots of Worcester, Massachusetts*. 1st ed. Worcester: Commonwealth Press, 1931.

Stearns, Sergeant Austin K., 13th Regiment, Massachusetts Volunteer Infantry. *Three Years with Company K*. Edited by Arthur A. Kent. Rutherford, N.J.: Farleigh Dickinson University Press, 1976.

Sturgis, Lieutenant Thomas. *Prisoners of War: Personal Recollections of the Rebellion*. Address before the New York Commandery of the Loyal Legion, 4th Series, New York, 1897.

Symonds, Craig L. *A Battlefield Atlas of the Civil War*. Baltimore: Nautical and Aviation Publishing Company of America, 1983.

Tarbox, Increase N. *Missionary Patriots: Memoirs of James H. Schneider and Edward M. Schneider*. Boston: Massachusetts Sabbath School Society, 1867.

United States Congress. *Committee on the Conduct of the War on the Attack on Petersburg on the 30th Day of July, 1864*. 38th Congress, 2nd session. Washington: Government Printing Office, 1865.

United States War Department. *War of the Rebellion: A Compilation of the Official Records of the Union and Confederate Armies*. Various volumes. Washington: Government Printing Office, 1902.

Walcott, Charles F. *The 21st Regiment, Massachusetts Volunteers, 1861–1865*. New York: Houghton, Mifflin, 1882.

Bibliography

Weld, Stephen M. *War Diary and Letters of Stephen Minot Weld, 1861–1865.* 2nd ed. Boston: Massachusetts Historical Society, 1979.

Wiley, Bell I. *The Life of Billy Yank.* Baton Rouge: Louisiana State University Press, 1986.

————. *The Common Soldier in the Civil War.* Harrisburg: Eastern Acorn, n.d.

Willis, Henry A. *Fitchburg in the War of the Rebellion.* Stephen A. Shepley, 1866.

Williss, G. Frank. *Historical Base Maps: Appomattox Manor–City Point, Petersburg National Battlefield.* Denver: United States Department of the Interior, National Park Service, 1982.

Wilson, James Grant, and Coan, Titus Munson, M.D., eds. *Personal Recollections of the War of the Rebellion, Addresses Delivered Before the New York Commandery of the Loyal Legion of the United States 1883–1891.* New York: New York Commandery of the Loyal Legion of the United States, 1891.

Woodbury, Augustus. *Burnside and the IX Army Corps.* Providence: n.p., 1867.

SOURCES

American Antiquarian Society, Worcester, Massachusetts, Barbara Trippel Simmons, curator of manuscripts (regimental supply documents, general information, and Civil War letter collection of 1st Lieutenant George E. Barton, Co. C, 57th MVI).

Ashburnham Historical Society, Ashburnham, Massachusetts, J. F. Von Deck (primary source material on several members of the 57th MVI).

Athol Public Library, Athol, Massachusetts, Jean Fuller (newspaper articles from the *Athol Transcript* relating to the 57th MVI).

Atlanta Public Library, Atlanta, Georgia (general information).

Bartow County Public Library, Cartersville, Georgia (general information and interlibrary loans).

Clinton Historical Society, Clinton, Massachusetts, Terrance Ingano (information on several men from Clinton in the 57th MVI).

Commonwealth of Massachusetts, Military Division, Military Records, bldg. no. 2, Natick, Massachusetts, James E. Fahey, archivist (personal and official regimental correspondence, muster-in rolls, muster-out rolls, descriptive rolls, casualty lists, enlistment papers, medical and surgical reports, general official information).

Department of the Army, U.S. Army Military Historical Institute, Carlisle Barracks, Pennsylvania (regimental records and photographs).

Emory University Library, Decatur, Georgia (regimental histories, records, general information).

Fitchburg Historical Society, Fitchburg, Massachusetts, Eleanora F. West, curator (unpublished, handwritten personal war sketches [GAR] of men from Fitchburg in the 57th MVI, weather records, local newspapers, genealogical information, information on the town of Fitchburg, general information).

Fitchburg Sentinel, January 8, March 4, March 11, March 25, April 1, and May 20, 1864 (local and war news).

Gale Free Library, Holden, Massachusetts, Landy C. Johnson, reference department (unpublished, handwritten personal war sketches [GAR] of men from Holden in the 57th MVI).

Bibliography

Georgia State Archives, Atlanta, Georgia (pension records).

Houghton Reading Room, Harvard University, Cambridge, Massachusetts, James J. Lewis, curator (correspondence of General William F. Bartlett).

Maud Burris Public Library, Decatur, Georgia, Steve Hurd, head librarian (general information and interlibrary loans).

Massachusetts Spy (Worcester), September 17 and September 24, 1862, and March 9, April 18, and April 20, 1864 (events concerning Camp Wool and 57th MVI).

Milford Historical Museum, Milford, Massachusetts, Marilyn Lovell, historian (information regarding men from Milford in the 57th MVI).

Mystic Seaport Museum, Mystic, Connecticut, Philip L. Budlong, registrar (information about the troopship *City of Norwich*).

National Archives, Washington, D.C. (personal military records, personal pension records, regimental morning reports, order books, descriptive lists, miscellaneous regimental papers).

National Archives, Atlanta Branch, Atlanta, Georgia (census information).

National Park Service, United States Department of the Interior, Andersonville National Historic Site, Andersonville, Georgia (records of some of the men who were incarcerated in that prison; also the war diary of William T. Peabody, Co. F, 57th MVI, in conjunction with Mrs. Raymond H. Allard of Dunnellon, Florida).

National Park Service, United States Department of the Interior, Chancellorsville and Spotsylvania National Military Park, Fredericksburg, Virginia (troop movement maps for the Wilderness and Spotsylvania battles, general information).

National Park Service, United States Department of the Interior, Denver Service Center, Denver, Colorado (troop movement maps for the assault on Petersburg, the battles of Cold Harbor, the Crater, Weldon Railroad, Hatchers Run, Fort Stedman, and Peeble's Farm, and plan of City Point).

National Park Service, United States Department of the Interior, Petersburg National Military Park, Petersburg, Virginia (troop movement maps for the battle of the Crater, general information).

National Park Service, United States Department of the Interior, Richmond National Military Park, Richmond, Virginia (general information, battle of Cold Harbor).

National Union Catalog Manuscript Collections, number 75–1895 (information on location of war letters of Captain George E. Barton, Co. C, 57th MVI).

Northboro Historical Society, Northboro, Massachusetts, Fran Doherty, curator (diary of Private Francis M. Harrington, Co. K, 57th MVI; medical pamphlet of 1864).

Petersburg Siege Museum, Petersburg, Virginia (general information on the siege of Petersburg).

Petersburg Welcome Center, Petersburg, Virginia (general information on the siege of Petersburg).

St. Bernard's Parish Church Records, Fitchburg, Massachusetts, Alice Mainguy, secretary (parish records on several members of the 57th MVI).

Sterling Historical Society, Sterling, Massachusetts, Ruth Hopfman, curator (primary source material on several members of the 57th MVI from Sterling).

Winchendon Historical Society, Winchendon, Massachusetts, Lois S. Greenwood, curator (handwritten, unpublished personal war sketches [GAR] of men from Winchendon in the 57th MVI).

Worcester Evening Gazette, June 17, 1925, and June 18, 1911.

Bibliography

Worcester Evening Transcript, December 10 and December 17, 1863 (events concerning Camp Wool and 57th MVI).

Worcester Historical Museum, Worcester, Massachusetts, Mark Savolis, curator of manuscripts (information about Worcester during the Civil War, Camp Wool, carte-de-visite photographs, railroad and steamship lines, etc.).

Note: Private sources are cited in the acknowledgments.

Index

Detailed biographical information about the men of the 57th may be found in the rosters.

Index

Index

Index

veterans: at Annapolis, 40–41; chosen as noncommissioned officers, 12; and the journey to the front, 45, 46, 48, 50, 52, 53, 54; and the Rapidan River march, 59, 60–61; resentment by, 297; in the Second Army Corps, 70; and the tossing away of equipment, 45; volunteer units of, 2; at the Wilderness, 65, 66, 73, 76, 85. *See also name of specific outfit*

Virginia, 61st Volunteer Regiment, 259

Virginia Central Railroad, 148, 230

Vose, William H., 6, 7

Wadsworth, James S., 76

Wakeman, George, 357

Walker, E. A., 32

Ward, Henry, 82, 185

Warren, Albert, 65

Warren, Gouverneur Kemble, 64, 269, 307. *See also* Fifth Army Corps

Warren, Hosea, 65

Warrenton Junction, 54, 59

Washington, D.C., 48–49, 267, 355–62

Water, 191, 205–6, 257–58, 262, 282

Webb, Alexander S., 73

Weisiger, D. A., 253

Weld, Stephen Minot, Jr: as commander of the 1st Brigade, 89, 116, 175; and the North Anna River battle, 139–40, 141; at Petersburg, 176, 177, 179, 186, 241–42, 254, 259; and the Spotsylvania Court House battle, 109, 116; surrender of, 259; at the Wilderness, 89; wounding of, 140

Weldon & Petersburg Railroad, 170, 194, 269, 270–76, 298, 314–15, 320–21

Wellman, George, 301

Wellman, John F., 301

Western Armies, 357–58, 359

White, John, 65

White, Julius, 236, 268, 271, 272, 274, 275, 277

White, Whitman V. [doctor]: after the battle of the crater, 271; at Camp Wool, 12, 18, 26–27; and Clark's desertion, 26–27; and the Fort Stedman battle, 335; at Fort Stedman, 316, 318; joke on, 335–36; and the journey to the front, 46, 52; at Petersburg, 180, 223, 260; and the Poplar Grove Church battles, 301; and the Spotsylvania Court House battle, 110–11, 114; and the Weldon Railroad battle, 274–75; at the Wilderness, 81–82, 97

White House Landing, 59, 157, 161, 162, 167

Whitney, George, 54

Wilcox, Cadmus M., 307

Wilcox, George H., 335

Wilderness: after the battle of the, 84–92; and the ambulance train to Fredericksburg, 93, 95–96, 97, 98; Army of the Potomac arrives at the, 62, 64; battles of the, 64–84, 114; casualties at the, 76, 77–80, 86, 87–88; death at the, 66, 75–76, 85–86, 89–90; field hospitals at the, 96, 98; headquarters at the, 68; prisoners of war at the, 70, 72, 81, 82, 88, 99–100; wounded at the, 68, 69, 72, 75–76, 77–80, 81–82, 84, 85, 86, 87–88, 89–90, 93, 95–99

Wilderness Church, 91, 93

Wilkins, Aaron, 79

Wilkins, Henry, 79, 81

Willcox, Orlando Bolivar: as commander of the 1st Division, 277, 357; and the Confederate withdrawal from Petersburg, 342; gives his last order, 363; and the grand review, 358; and the journey to the front, 50–51; at Petersburg, 237, 238, 263–64; in Washington, 353. *See also* Ninth Army Corps, 3rd Division

Williams, Alpheus, 3–4

Williams, S., 237

Wilson, St. Julien, 259

Wilson, Thomas, 206

Wilson's Station, 349, 351

Wirz, Henry, 128, 289

Wisconsin troops, 314, 364

women, 13, 17, 96, 313, 346

Woodruff, John, 218

Worcester State Guards, 32

Worthy, William, 307

wounded: and the ambulance train to Fredericksburg, 93, 95–96, 97, 98, 121; and the Cold Harbor battle, 151, 154, 155–56, 157, 158–59; and the Colquitt's Salient charge, 338; Confederate, 97, 110, 274, 275; and the Fort Stedman battle, 331, 335–36; at Fredericksburg, 93, 95–99, 121, 130; and the North Anna River battle, 142, 143; at Petersburg, 174, 178–83, 184–86, 200, 201, 210, 216, 217–18, 219, 224, 226–27, 228, 256–57, 259–61, 262–63; and the Poplar Grove Church battles, 300, 301, 304; return to Fitchburg, 368; and the Spotsylvania Court House battle, 103, 104, 110–11, 112–13, 115, 116–17, 118, 120, 130–31; total number of 57th Regiment, 364–65; and the Union occupation of Petersburg, 347; and the Weldon Railroad battle, 274–75, 276–77; at the Wilderness, 68, 69, 72, 75–76, 77–80, 81–82, 84, 85, 86, 87–88, 89–90, 93, 95–99; women caring for the, 96

Wright, Ambrose R., 253

665